Human Geography

Culture, Society, and Space

Seventh Edition

Human Geography

Culture, Society, and Space

Seventh Edition

H. J. de Blij
Distinguished Professor of Geography,
Michigan State University

Alexander B. Murphy
Rippey Chair in Liberal Arts and Sciences and Professor of Geography,
University of Oregon

WILEY
John Wiley & Sons, Inc.

Acquisitons Editor: Ryan Flahive
Editorial Assistant: Denise Powell
Marketing Manager: Kevin Malloy
Associate Production Manager: Kelly Tavares
Cover and Text Designer: Dawn L. Stanley
Photo Editor: Jennifer MacMillan
Illustration Editor: Sigmund Malinowski
Front Cover Photo: Jochen D. Wijnands / FPG International
Back Cover Photo: H.J. de Blij

This book was set in 10/12 ITC Garamond Light by UG / GGS Information Services, Inc. and printed and bound by Von Hoffman Press. The cover was printed by Phoenix Color Corp.

This book is printed on acid-free paper. ∞

The paper in this book was manufactured by a mill whose forest management programs include sustained yield harvesting of its timberlands. Sustained yield harvesting principles ensure that the number of trees cut each year does not exceed the amount of new growth.

Library of Congress Cataloging-in-Publication Data

de Blij, Harm J.
Human geography : culture, society, and space.—7th ed. / H.J. de Blij, Alexander B. Murphy.
p. cm.
Includes bibliographical references and index.
ISBN 0-471-44107-4 (pbk. : alk. paper)
1. Human geography. I. Murphy, Alexander B., 1954- II. title.

GF41. D4 2003
304.2—dc21 2002066396

10 9 8 7 6 5 4 3 2 1

Preface

If recent events tell us anything, it is that we cannot possibly confront the challenges of the twenty-first century without understanding the geography of our planet. Fault lines among cultures have produced new and pernicious forms of violence; groups competing for control over the same piece of the Earth's surface have created local havoc while altering the terrain of international relations; the movement of people and ideas from one place to another has led to unprecedented cultural exchange, while fostering deep resentments; and human activity continues to remake the very environment in which we live. Each of these developments is rooted in the geographic patterns and processes that define the contemporary world. Helping students develop a basic understanding of those patterns and process is the fundamental aim of **Human Geography: Culture, Society, and Space**.

One of the challenges that geography still faces is the tendency to view it simply as a discipline concerned with place names and product lists. The ability to identify key places and regions on a map is important, of course, but that is simply a beginning. For those seeking to understand where we have come from and where we are going, what is critical is to develop an awareness of how the world is organized and how peoples and places affect each other. Matters such as these go to the very heart of geography—a discipline concerned with analyzing the nature and implications of particular physical and human patterns on the Earth's surface, the networks and interactions that link peoples and places, and the changing character of the environments and landscapes within which life is situated.

Most disciplines focus on a particular phenomenon and try to understand its character and significance. Geography, by contrast, is an integrative field—seeking to understand how things (including people) are distributed, how they relate to one another on the surface of the Earth, and why these distributions and relationships matter. Through its spatial perspective, geography offers a way of understanding patterns and connections that are of profound importance in shaping the world in which we live. Because maps provide a powerful means of conveying the insights of geography, they have long been a key part of the geographer's tool kit. And that tool kit is expanding as our ability to present and analyze geographic information increases with the growing sophistication of remote sensing technologies and Geographic Information Systems (GIS). Using these tools in intelligent ways, however, requires a strong grounding in the types of geographic ideas and concepts introduced in **Human Geography**.

Geography is divided into two main branches—physical (natural) geography and human geography; as the title implies, this book is designed for an introductory college course in the latter of these two. But ultimately physical and human geography are linked. When physical geographers analyze the natural processes shaping coastlines, their conclusions also tell us about these areas as places of human habitation and impact. When human geographers study cities, they often do so with reference to the physical landscape on which the urban area lies, and the role this physical stage has played in the city's evolution. Because of this overlap, we seek to emphasize the connections between physical and human geography. Accordingly, we urge readers to see this as an introduction to an important branch—but not all—of geography.

THE SEVENTH EDITION

This is the seventh edition of a book that appeared more than twenty-five years ago. Since that time the book has become a standard work for introductory courses in human geography. As we set to work on this edition, we saw the need for a more fundamental reworking of the text to take into account some of the momentous developments unfolding around us: the diverse impacts of globalization, the changing relationships between the physical and human environment, the evolving geopolitical picture, and the accelerating process of urbanization. We also wanted to address the needs of students taking advantage of the new Advanced Placement Human Geography program.

Given our desire to produce a useful, timely book, this edition incorporates a number of key changes. These include:

- An entirely new section on globalization that includes new chapters on the impacts of an increasingly interconnected world on cities in particular (chapter 28) and on culture in general (chapter 29).

- Considerable new material on the physical environment and its connection to society—including an entirely chapter situating humanity within a long-term view of the Earth's environmental history (chapter 33). [Some readers may want to look at this chapter up front, as it provides a broad context into which much that follows can be situated.]
- Extensive reworking of material on political, ethnic, and religious themes in response to the changing global geopolitical scene.
- Substantial modification of sections on population and rural areas to reflect rapidly changing demographic and economic circumstances.
- The replacement of fully half of the photographs in the book by new photos taken by one of us as we traveled, observed, and studied the evolving geographical landscape over the past few years.

Many of these new features lie well into the book, so users of the Sixth Edition should not be deceived if the opening pages look relatively familiar. Our goal has been to produce a volume that effectively reflects the complicated, fast-changing world in which we live. The alterations we have made are not simply the product of arm-chair analysis; over the past few years one or the other us has been in every major geographic realm except Antarctica, and we have used the opportunity to record, study, and analyze many of the most important geographic developments of our time. The photographs in this book are a testament to that endeavor. Unlike any other book of its sort, every photograph in this book except one (the collapsing World Trade Center in New York City on September 11, 2001) was taken by one of us. At times these may not look like professional photographs, but there is nothing "canned" about them. They reflect our determination to observe first-hand the things about which we write.

Organization

The book contains 11 parts and 35 short chapters. This structure gives instructors the flexibility either to break major topics into smaller units—or the parts can be treated as one long chapter that can be assigned as a whole. Each part addresses a major subject-matter focus of human geography, such as population, language, religion, economics, politics, globalization, and the environment. Given the introductory character of the book, much of the discussion focuses on the global and regional scales—but local examples are used throughout. The concept of scale itself is introduced in Part 1, and subsequent parts contain boxes showing how processes operating at the global and regional scales play out at the local scale, and vice versa. Geographers use the tools of spatial analysis not just to say something about the present, but to offer insights into where we are headed. Hence, each part also contains a "Looking Ahead" box that draws on elements of the current geographic scene to suggest the changes we may be confronting later in the twenty-first century.

Pedagogical Structure

Since students are our audience, we have asked for their opinions in shaping this edition. This feedback has resulted in the new, open design for the Seventh Edition. As part of this student-oriented plan, students will be presented with many opportunities to apply geographic perspectives and methods to the problems and issues they face in this fast-changing world.

• ***At Issue*** — Every part opens with a key contemporary issue, such as who should inhibit world population growth or if a global system should be established to regulate industrial pollution, raised at the beginning, discussed in various contexts during the chapter sequence, and reconsidered at the conclusion. This guides readers toward an awareness of the utility of the geographic perspective in addressing some of our world's major challenges.

• ***Key Points*** — The most important concepts to be covered in the chapter are listed on the opening page of each chapter. These can serve the student as a preview organizer and as a review after completing the chapter.

• ***Headings and Subheadings*** — The hierarchy of headings and subheadings has been strengthened to help readers discern and grasp the main geographical concepts and their relationships.

• ***From the Field Notes*** — All photographs in this book were taken by the authors and are accompanied by the notes they wrote in the field. This unique feature has drawn praise from our readers, because of its ability to convey a geographer's particular vision. Because of their popularity, we have chosen to open each chapter with the "From the Field Notes" feature.

• ***Sense of Scale*** — To illustrate the crucial role that the concept of scale plays in geographic analysis, each part includes a special 'Sense of Scale' feature, such as Euroregions in southwestern Poland, social and economic change and the Los Angeles riots, Nike and economic globalization.

• ***Focus On*** — special boxes highlight topics that provide background (such as theories of migration) or illustrate geographic concepts (such as acculturation and transculturation).

• ***Key Terms & Concepts*** — As a helpful review, the main terms and concepts discussed in the chapter are listed at the end. These terms are also defined in the Glossary at the end of the book.

• ***Applying Geographic Knowledge*** — To encourage students to think as geographers do, every chapter ends with two or more questions that require some spatial analysis.

• ***Selected Bibliographies*** — As with all sciences, geographic knowledge is established by research. The Selected Bibliography, including important work of geographers past and present, has been reorganized and moved forward from the back of the book to follow the appropriate parts and is thoroughly updated in this edition.

• ***Demographic Table*** — A new World Population Data Table (Resource B) reflects the global situation as of 2002.

Maps and Photos

Maps are among the most important tools of geographers and this text has long been known for accurate and up-to-date maps. All cartography has been restylized and updated to enhance clarity and effectiveness of the maps. New maps have been prepared. ***Human Geography*** also retains its signature photography, providing a distinct and unusual perpective. Looking at the world through a geographer's eyes is part of a geographic education.

SUPPLEMENTS

The ***Study Companion with GeoDiscoveries CD-Rom*** is packaged at no extra cost with every textbook. The printed Study Companion, written by A. Steele Becker and Jacqueline Becker, helps student prepare for exams with a combination of true/false, multiple choice, and conceptual questions. The *GeoDiscoveries CD-Rom* offers a rich electronic medium for exploring the core concepts of human geography and the tools that geographers use to answer geographic questions. *GeoDiscoveries* offers unique present/interact/assess modules that help students visualize spatial relationships and think critically about human geography. Move beyond the textbook with interactive exercises, animations, videos, and a virtual globe.

The ***Virtual Field Guide Website*** gives students first-hand experience with the geographic principles discussed in the main text by presenting them with a framework to apply their knowledge at the local and global scales. Through a range of hands-on exercises, this website promotes interactive learning, demonstrates linkages between global and local issues, and exposes students to contemporary trends in geographic research.

• ***Microsoft Encarta Virtual Globe, and Activity Guide*** — Instructors and students will be able to explore the globe thematically and regionally using a variety of resources, including a wide range of maps and map styles, videos, sounds, animations, up-to-date statistics, and links to Web sites that provide an amazing range of resources for every country. The ***Activity Guide*** links the content of the CD directly to every chapter of de Blij and Murphy's ***Human Geography*** text. Our offer of ***Encarta Virtual Globe*** is tied to an exclusive agreement between Microsoft and John Wiley & Sons, which allows us to offer the product at a deeply discounted price when shrink-wrapped with our textbooks.

• ***Kuby, Gober and Harner's Human Geography in Action*** — Used as a supplement or a stand-alone text, this workbook integrates the most fundamental concepts of human geography with interactive, hands-on applications located on a dual-platform CD-ROM in the back of the book. Students can manipulate data, create maps, and explore the implications of these concepts using this first-hand data. Guidance for using *Human Geography in Action* in conjunction *Human Geography* by de Blij and Murphy is offered on the *Human Geography in Action* web site at <www.wiley.com/college/kuby>.

For the Instructor

• ***Transparencies and Slides*** — 100 full-color maps, illustrations, and tables from the text are included in each of these presentation packages. The Seventh Edition cartography and illustration program uses a richer color palette than the Sixth Edition. The effect this has on transparencies and slides, when combined with enhanced labeling of the type, is a set of strong, clear images when projected in the classroom.

• ***H.J. de Blij's Worldview Geography CD-ROM (Dual-Platform)*** — This rich collection of multimedia resources allows professors to design presentations and on-line projects. The resources include: 15 videos, animations that bring geographic themes to life; over 350 unique photographs with detailed field notes and captions; 65 detailed maps with a unique thematic layering feature. Although *Worldview Geography* is organized regionally, it is an effective resource of media for a thematic approach.

• ***Geography On-Location with H.J. de Blij Video Series*** — Each video in this three-video set comprises fifty minutes of original, current footage taken during the author's travels. The tapes cover a range of themes. Although *Worldview Geography* is organized regionally, it too is an effective resource of media for a thematic approach. The book's main Web site, under "Instructor's Resources," catalogs each of the *Series'* many video segments from a systematic perspective.

• ***Web Site*** — The book's main Web site features a secure Instructor's Resources section. Organized by book part, it includes an *Instructor's Manual, Test Bank* and detailed descriptions of the various media and supplements (Overheads, Slides, Encarta Virtual Globe CD, Virtual Field Guide & Web Site, Worldview Geography CD, Geography On-Location Videos) that support the part.

ACKNOWLEDGMENTS

In preparing the Seventh Edition of **Human Geography** we have benefited form the advice and assistance of numerous colleagues. Some told us of their experiences using the Sixth Edition; others helped us formulate the revision plan now reflected in our Table of Contents; still others responded to the survey we distributed to solicit views on the revision plan; and yet others reviewed the manuscript of this new edition as it was going into production. The list that follows acknowledges this support, but it cannot begin to measure our gratitude for all they contributed:

Ian Ackroyd-Kelly	*East Stroudsburg University*
James Ashley	*University of Toledo*
Sarah W. Bednarz	*Texas A&M University*
Sari Bennett	*University of Maryland, Baltimore County*
J. Best	*Frostburg State University*
Brian Blouet	*College of William & Mary*
Margaret F. Boorstein	*C. W. Post College of Long Island University*
Evan Denney	*University of Montana*
Sr. James Dyer	*Mount St. Mary's College*
Adrian X. Esparza	*University of Arizona*
Stephen Frenkel	*University of Washington, Seattle*
Lay James Gibson	*University of Arizona*
Abe Goldman	*University of Florida*
Alyson Greiner	*Oklahoma State University*
Jeffrey A. Gritzner	*University of Montana*
Qian Guo	*Northern Michigan University*
Peter R. Hoffmann	*Loyola Marymount University*
Peter Hugill	*Texas A&M University*
Tarek A. Joseph	*Central Michigan University*
Artimus Keiffer	
Les King	*McMaster University*
Ann Legreid	*Central Missouri State University*
Jess A. Le Vine	*Brookdale Community College*
David Lyons	*University of Minnesota, Duluth*
Ian MacLachlan	*University of Lethbridge*
Wayne McKim	*Towson University*
Glenn Miller	*Bridgewater State College*
Katharyne Mitchell	*University of Washington, Seattle*
John M. Morris	*University of Texas, San Antonio*
Garth A. Myers	*University of Kansas*
Darrell Norris	*SUNY Geneseo*
Walter Peace	*McMaster University*
Jeffrey Richetto	*University of Alabama*
James Saku	*Frostburg State University*
Joseph E. Schwartzberg	*University of Minnesota*
Gary W. Shannon	*University of Kentucky*
Betty Shimshak	*Towson University*
Andrew Sluyter	*Pennsylvania State University*
Herschel Stern	*Mira Costa College*
Neva Duncan Tabb	*University of South Florida*
James A. Tyner	*University of Southern California*
George W. White	*Frostburg State University*
Donald Zeigler	*Old Dominion University*
Robert C. Ziegenfus	*Kutztown University*

In addition, we are grateful to Minna Pavulans, Hunter Shobe, Rob Kerr, and Roberto Serralles, graduate students at the University of Oregon, for valuable research and technical assistance during the preparation of this edition. Also, Mary Milo and Kimberly Stalker, both in the front office of the Department of Geography, University of Oregon, contributed much through their assistance with various organizational, typing, and mailing tasks. Finally, we would like to express our most sincere appreciation to the staff of John Wiley & Sons, who contributed much to this project. Ryan Flahive, Geography Editor, and his assistant, Denise Powell, were cheerful and determined supporters of the project. Leslie Taggart, Development Editor, provided useful input on features of the manuscript and helped to move the project along; Kelly Tavares, Senior Production Editor, was a marvelous coordinator of the entire production process. In addition, we are grateful for the significant contributions of Sigmund Malinowski, Illustration Editor, and Jennifer MacMillan, Photo Editor. We are also appreciative of the efforts of several other individuals who helped to see the project through: Betty Pesagno, copyeditor; Dawn Stanley, designer; and Kevin Molloy, Marketing Manager.

Our greatest thanks of all go to our wives, Bonnie de Blij and Susan Gary, who through their support, understanding, and patience contributed more than we can ever express.

H.J. de Blij
East Lansing, Michigan

Alexander B. Murphy
Eugene, Oregon

About the Authors

H.J. de Blij

Harm de Blij received his early schooling in Europe, his college education in Africa, and his higher degrees in the United States (Ph.D. Northwestern, 1959). He has published more than 30 books and over 100 articles, and has received five honorary degrees. Several of his books have been translated into foreign languages.

Dr. de Blij is Distinguished Professor of Geography at Michigan State University. He has held the George Landegger Chair in Georgetown University's School of Foreign Service and the John Deaver Drinko Chair of Geography at Marshall University, and has also taught at the Colorado School of Mines and the University of Miami. He was the Geography Editor on ABC-TV's "Good Morning America" program for seven years and later served as Geography Analyst for NBC News. He was for more than 20 years a member of the National Geographic Society's Committee for Research and Exploration and was the founding editor of its scholarly journal, *National Geographic Research*. He is an honorary lifetime member of the Society.

Prof. de Blij is a soccer fan, an avid wine collector, and an amateur violinist. His web site is at www.deblij.com. The photograph above was taken on a field trip in Hanoi, Vietnam in April, 2002.

Alexander B. Murphy

Alec Murphy grew up in the western United States, but he spent several of his early years in Europe and Japan. He went to college at Yale University, studied law at the Columbia University School of Law, practiced law for a short time in Chicago, and then pursued a doctoral degree in geography (Ph.D. University of Chicago, 1987). After graduating, Dr. Murphy joined the faculty of the University of Oregon, where he is now Professor of Geography and holder of the James F. and Shirley K. Rippey Chair in Liberal Arts and Sciences. Professor Murphy is a widely published scholar in the fields of political, cultural, and environmental geography, with a regional emphasis on Europe. His work has been supported by the National Science Foundation, the National Endowment for the Humanities, and the Fulbright-Hays foreign fellowship program.

Professor Murphy was elected Vice-President of the Association of American Geographers in 2002; the Vice-President stands unopposed for the Presidency after one year. He is also Vice-President of the American Geographical Society and one of the editors of *Progress in Human Geography* and *Eurasian Geography and Economics*. His interests include hiking, skiing, camping, music—and of course exploring the diverse places that make up our planet.

To

Richard and George Murphy,

who help light up the world
and offer hope for the future

Contents

Part Nine
FROM DEINDUSTRIALIZATION TO GLOBALIZATION, *407*

Part Ten
SOCIAL GEOGRAPHIES OF THE MODERN WORLD, *453*

Part Eleven
THE CHANGING ENVIRONMENTAL CONTEXT, *511*

Resources

Part One

GEOGRAPHY, CULTURE, AND ENVIRONMENT

At Issue

The past decade has seen extraordinary, rapid changes in political, social, and environmental arrangements. The Cold War order has come to an end, ethnic conflicts have intensified in many places, and we increasingly read about the myriad ways in which humans are altering the environment. In the midst of these developments, policy-makers and scholars are scrambling to find new ways of making sense of the world—and a growing number of them are looking to geographical concepts and tools in the process. They are seeking insight into how things are organized and relate to one another on the surface of the Earth; they are using geographic information systems (GISs) to study the relationship among spatial data; and they are asking questions about the importance of "location," "place," and "region" in human affairs. *Why is geography so much a part of the effort to come to terms with our rapidly changing world? What does it mean to think geographically? Can geography offer insights into the diversity of changes unfolding around us?*

Green and gold in the skyline of a city with a high-tech hinterland: San Francisco.

Part Outline

Chapter 1

Geography and Human Geography

From the field notes

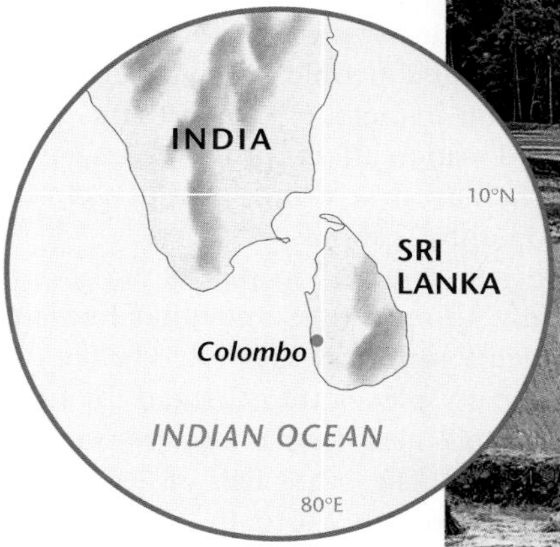

"Along the road north from Colombo, capital of Sri Lanka, on the way to Kandy, every square foot of level land, natural or (terraced) artificial, seems to be devoted to the cultivation of rice. The rich, well-watered soil yields bountiful crops, but farming methods remain labor-intensive. I stopped here to watch about 20 workers unwrap the bundles of shoots and plant them in the muddy paddy. Standing in the waterlogged soil, bent over almost without letup, they filled the paddy with amazing dexterity and speed; soon they moved to the waiting field in the foreground, where the bundles were already waiting. It is a scene repeated countless times in much of tropical Asia, where a majority of the population remains rural and where survival depends directly on what the paddies can produce."

KEY POINTS

◆ **Geography offers fundamental insights into the world in which we live through its concern with the spatial organization and character of the Earth's surface.**

◆ **Physical and human geography are two great branches of the discipline, but environmental geography is emerging as a link between the two.**

◆ **Geography's spatial perspective promotes a focus on location, interaction between humans and the environment, regions, place, movement, and landscape.**

◆ **The use of maps and Geographic Information Systems reflects the centrality of a spatial perspective to geography.**

◆ **Maps are used to portray the distinctive character of places; their relationship to environmental issues; the movements of people, goods, and ideas; and regions of various types.**

◆ **People's perceptions of places and regions are influenced by their individual mental maps as well as by printed maps.**

Geography is at the very heart of the human experience. For many people, place of birth is one of the most powerful determinants of a lifetime's experiences. Even in the modern era of migration and travel, global interaction, and mass communication, the vast majority of people do not move far beyond their places of birth, and even those who do are influenced by where they were born. The first language you learn, the first foods you eat, the first religion of which you become aware, the first clothing with which you become comfortable—all these, and much else, are associated with your birthplace.

Yet this is only the beginning. How and where you move through life, the people you meet, and what you are able to see and acquire are all tied to geography—for each of these is fundamentally influenced by the character of the places you encounter and by the human and environmental patterns that make up our world. We now live in an age of increasing globalization. Peoples and economies throughout the world are interconnected as never before. Nevertheless, our world still encompasses a jigsaw of countries, a collage of religions, a Babel of thousands of languages, a hodgepodge of settlement types, an assortment of innumerable customs and modes of livelihood. Each of these is constantly in flux, and they each influence the others in important ways. Moreover, they come together in different ways around the globe to create a world of endlessly diverse places. Understanding and explaining this diversity is the mission of ***human geography***.

Geography sometimes is referred to as the "study of place," but it is much more than that. Knowing where countries and important places are located is useful, but it is only a beginning, a bit like knowing some introductory vocabulary when you start studying a foreign language. Knowing why places and people are where they are; what their location means in the past, present, and future, and how their location affects other places—understanding matters such as these brings us much closer to knowing what geography is about.

Note that we just referred to places and people. This book is mainly about places and their human inhabitants. It also deals with how the world has become organized, and in many places transformed, by human activity. But make no mistake: there is more to geography than human geography. The other half of geography is termed ***physical geography***. Actually, a more precise name for this subdiscipline might be natural geography because it deals not only with mountains, glaciers, coastlines, and climates but also with soils, plants, and animals. As we will see, it is often difficult to discuss human geography without also referring to the physical stage on which the human drama is being played out. Indeed, so many contemporary issues occur at the intersection of human and physical geography that ***environmental geography*** is emerging as a third basic subdivision of geography. However, in this book our focus will be on human geography. Although it represents only part of the discipline, human geography encompasses several subfields (Fig. 1-1). Each of these has an environmental component that connects it to the domains of physical and environmental geography.◆

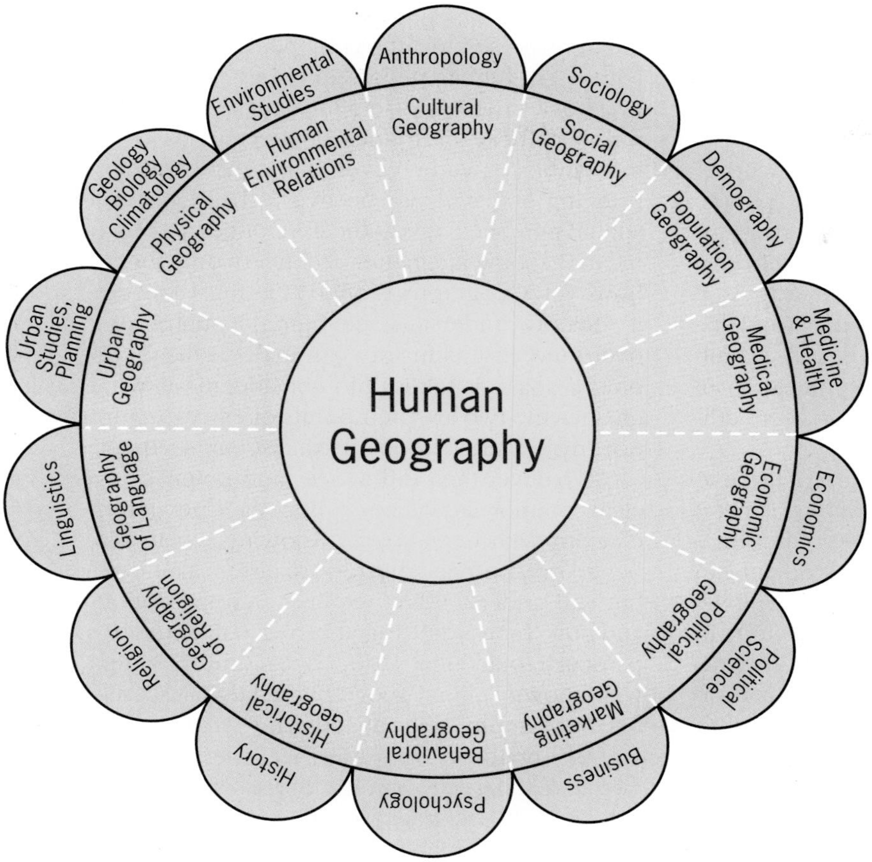

Figure 1-1 Fields of Human Geography. A schematic diagram showing the relationships among the fields of human geography and related fields outside the discipline. Geography brings a spatial perspective to questions raised in adjacent fields—situating different areas of inquiry within a spatial and environmental context. *Source:* From authors' sketch.

◆ THE COMMON BOND: A SPATIAL PERSPECTIVE

If geography deals with so many aspects of our world, ranging from people and places to coastlines and climates, what do the various facets of this wide-ranging discipline have in common? The answer lies in a term that often is used most effectively as an adjective: ***spatial.*** Whether they are human geographers or physical geographers, virtually all geographers are interested in the way places and things are laid out, organized, and arranged on the surface of the Earth. Sometimes a particular spatial arrangement of human activities or conditions leads geographers to raise questions as to how this arrangement has come about, what processes create and sustain particular ***patterns***, and what relationships exist between different places and things. In such instances, the spatial pattern already is evident, and the search is on for an explanation. But in other cases the spatial arrangement may not be evident at all and must be discovered before it can lead to answers. As we will see in our discussions of medical geography, for example, the mapping of the ***distribution*** of people afflicted by certain illnesses led researchers directly to the sources of the illnesses and thus to remedies for them.

Medical geography is just one part of human geography in which spatial analysis has practical application. Yet another interest of geographers is the impact of particular spatial patterns on some process or idea. Political geographers, for example, are interested in how the division of the world into discrete countries influences everything from concepts of nationality—"I am a German, Russian, Pole"—to how environmental issues are understood and addressed.

Like their human geographer counterparts, physical geographers are also concerned with the spatial organization of the planet. Early in the twentieth century a climatologist, Alfred Wegener, became convinced after extended observation that the jigsaw-like fit of the continental landmasses on opposite sides of the North and South Atlantic oceans could not be a matter of chance. He marshaled a vast array of geographical and geological evidence, most of it spatial in nature, and on the basis of this evidence he proposed a hypothesis of continental drift. His theory was that the continental landmasses were once united as a giant supercontinent that later broke apart. Wegener's geographic hypothesis, based on the spatial layout of the physical world he knew so well, set the direction for the geological research that was to lead (a half century later) to the discovery of plate tectonics and crustal spreading, the mechanism that drives the continents apart.

Human and physical geographers thus share this ***spatial perspective***, this way of looking at the world's—and the Earth's—layout. So the language of geography is not only the language of places and people but also a whole vocabulary of spatial terms, many of which will become familiar (though occasionally from a new viewpoint) as we proceed. We have already used some of these terms: location is one, and pattern and distribution are others. In due course we will become familiar with others, making geographic communication in the pages that follow not only easier but also more efficient and accurate.

The important point here is that we cannot hope to understand the complexity and diversity of our planet if we do not think geographically. No amount of information about the workings of the Russian government can provide insight into the future of the Russian state if we do not understand the distribution of ethnic groups in and around Russia and their differing ideas about territory and place. And no amount of analysis of data on trade among the countries in Pacific Asia can provide a sense of the economic challenges facing the region if we do not consider the patterns of advantage and disadvantage within individual countries. In short, geography is indispensable to an appreciation of who we are, where we came from, and where we are going.

◆ THE NATURE AND IMPORTANCE OF GEOGRAPHIC INQUIRY

What does it mean to look at the world from a geographic perspective? Much more than many people seem to think. Those with little understanding of geography sometimes treat it as an exercise in place-name memorization. If you know where things are on a map, you are said to be geographically literate. Yet no one would claim that someone has a deep knowledge of history just because they know the dates of major events. Instead, to understand history is to appreciate how events, circumstances, and ideas came together at particular times to produce certain outcomes. And a knowledge of how things have developed over time is thought to be critical to understanding who we are and where we are going.

If a concern with understanding change over time is of critical importance, wouldn't it make sense that understanding change across space would be of importance as well? This was the view of the great German philosopher, Immanuel Kant, who argued that we need disciplines focused not only on particular phenomena (economics, sociology, etc.), but on the perspectives of time (history) and space (geography) as well. Following this view, history and geography can be understood as disciplines that have intellectual cores defined not so much by subject matter as by perspective. Returning to Figure 1-1, human geography can be seen as a meeting point of a variety of disciplines not because it covers the turf of all those disciplines, but because it offers insights into subject matter covered by those disciplines by bringing a spatial perspective to bear. Just because a spatial perspective is at the core of geography does not mean that time is a matter of concern only for historians, however. Geography is often at its most powerful when it seeks to understand changing spatial arrangements over time, just as history can make sense of the world only if space is taken into consideration. What distinguishes the two are their points of entry or emphases—not any definable boundary that separates them.

Whatever their differences and points of overlap, a clear commonality between history and geography is their concern with explanation. Knowing when things happened may be a first step toward historical understanding, but real understanding requires an appreciation of why and how things came together at certain times to produce particular outcomes. Adopting a similar approach, the well-known cultural geographer Marvin Mikesell has defined geography in shorthand as the "why of where." Why and how do things come together in certain places to produce particular outcomes? Why are some things found in certain places but not in others? To what extent do things in one place influence those in other places? Questions such as these are at the core of geographic inquiry—and they are of critical importance in any effort to make sense of our world. They help explain why geography has become a core intellectual concern in major universities around the world. They also reveal why efforts are being mounted to enhance geography's role in education and research in the United States.

During the 1980s, when concern about geographic illiteracy in the United States was growing, several organizations began campaigns to reintroduce geography into school curricula. Leading these campaigns was the Geography Education National Implementation Project (GENIP)—an initiative of the four major U.S. geographical organizations. The National Geographic Society published the results of their work in a document entitled ***Maps, the Landscape, and Fundamental Themes in Geography*** (1986), which introduced "Five Themes" of geography. Several million copies of the publication were disseminated to schools throughout the United States, and the "Five Themes" became, for many students, an introduction to the perspectives of geography.

Geography's Themes and Perspectives

It is worth considering the themes proposed by the GENIP initiative, for they provide insight into what lies behind geography's spatial emphasis. The first theme, ***location***, highlights how the geographical position of people and things on the Earth's surface affects what happens and why. A concern with location underlies almost all geographical work, for location helps to establish the context within which events and processes are situated. Some geographers seek to develop elaborate (usually quantitative) models describing the locational properties of particular phenomena—and even predicting where things are likely to occur. Such undertakings have fostered an interest in ***location theory***, an element of contemporary human geography that seeks answers to a wide range of questions—some of them theoretical, others highly practical: Why are villages, towns, and cities spaced the way they are? Given a market of a certain size and wealth, where in the surrounding countryside should particular products be grown or raised? What would be the best location for a new shopping center or medical facility, given existing settlement patterns, road networks, and the like?

A spatial perspective invites consideration of the relationship among phenomena in individual places—including the relationship between humans and the natural world. Thus, the second of the "Five Themes" identified by GENIP concerns ***human–environment interactions***. How do different culture groups understand, use, and transform their environments? And how does environment influence human activity? Many years ago, some geographers were tempted to generalize about the impacts of the natural environment (mainly climate) on the technological development of societies—concluding that the natural environment played the most important role in determining whether and how human societies progressed. As we will see, this led to assumptions about predictable advantages and disadvantages of different environments, which were both highly controversial and misused by demagogues. The result is that most geographers turned away from work on the role of environment in human affairs. Yet societies and cultures are situated in physical-environmental contexts that necessarily influence important aspects of what they do—a point that is increasingly recognized in the wake of more general concerns about human–environment interactions. Armed with new, nondeterministic perspectives, geographers are now making fundamental contributions to an understanding of the interrelationships between humans and the environments in which they live and work.

The third highlighted theme of geography is that of the ***region***. Phenomena are not evenly distributed on the surface of the Earth. Instead, features tend to be concentrated in particular areas, which we often think of as regions. And throughout history, humans have divided up the surface of the Earth into regions in their struggles to organize political, economic, and social activity. The character and location of regions is thus a critical element of the Earth's geography—not simply reflecting particular geographic concentrations, but influencing how they change over time.

From the field notes

"On the main street of Dalian, Northeast China, I watched this artist create an image full of symbolism: the computer in the land (and the hand) of the Manchus. This was no mass-produced billboard. He had painted these images on large sheets of paper, had pasted these up, and was now adding the finishing touches. I pointed to the computer and asked if he knew how to use it. He shook his head, grabbed a paint brush, and pointed it to himself. But his work symbolized the importance of understanding the diffusion of ideas from one place to another in our ever-more interconnected world."

Geographers have long sought to develop insightful descriptions of different regions of the Earth. More recently, efforts to develop formal approaches to the delimitation and analysis of regions led to the development of ***regional science***—an undertaking that involves the application of modern quantitative spatial-analytic techniques to regional questions. In whatever form it exists and whatever it is called, regional study will survive as one of the central traditions of geography. James Michener once wrote that whenever he started writing a new book, he first prepared himself by turning to books written by regional geographers about the area where the action was to occur. Geography's regional dimension is, indeed, one of its permanent traditions.

In addition to the foregoing traditional themes, the National Geographic Society's publication identified two others. The fourth theme is represented by the seemingly simple word ***place***. All places on the surface of the Earth have distinguishing human and physical characteristics, and one of the purposes of geography is to study the special character and meaning of places. Indeed, human understanding of the Earth's diversity is often rooted in place, so a focus on this concept is critical to bringing human experience into the geographic picture. The fifth theme, ***movement***, refers to the mobility of people, goods, and ideas across the surface of the planet. Interactions of many kinds shape the human geography of the world, and understanding these is an important aspect of the global spatial order.

Although not specifically highlighted by GENIP as one of the core themes of geography, one other concept figured in the committee's work and is widely seen as a core element of geography: ***landscape***. Geographers use the term ***landscape*** to refer to the material character of a place—the complex of natural features, human structures, and other tangible objects that give a place a particular form. Human geographers look to landscape both to obtain clues into the processes that create individual places and to understand how the form of a place shapes the ideas and interactions of those who inhabit it. A concern with landscape is fundamental to a spatial perspective because landscapes are the product of particular spatial convergences. The landscape of the Mississippi delta reflects the convergence of different cultural, social, economic, and political influences in a particular place, as well as the interaction of those influences with the natural environment. As such, the landscape can be read as a text offering insights into the forces and processes that have shaped human occupance of the portion of the planet where the Mississippi River flows into the Gulf of Mexico.

Taken as a set, the "Five Themes" plus the concept of landscape provide a sense of what is entailed when one adopts a spatial perspective—and these themes have been promoted to good advantage in efforts to build geography in American education. Geography's importance is not limited to the educational arena, however; it also has an important role to play in academic research and policy making. This was highlighted in a recent report of the National Research Council entitled ***Rediscovering Geography: New Relevance for Science and Society***. The report focuses on the integrative character of geography's perspective through its identification of three spatial themes that cut across the human, environmental, and physical parts of the discipline: integration in place, interdependencies between places, and interdependencies among scales (Fig. 1-2).

The concept of ***integration in place*** concerns how and why people or things found in the same place on the surface of the Earth influence each other and shape the character of places. Why are areas of high population density so often areas with good arable land? How does the configuration of the street pattern in a particular suburb affect the location of retail establishments? How do the distinctive social, cultural, political, and environmental characteristics of a town or region shape its character as a place? Questions such as these are all tied to the quest to understand integration in place.

Geography's interest in ***interdependencies between places*** reflects its focus on the nature and significance of the patterns and networks that tie places together. How did migration out of southeastern Europe in the 1990s affect the relationship of parts of Western Europe to the Balkans? What impact is the Internet having on the ability of people in one place to influence those living in another? How has the European integration project altered the relationships among peoples located on either side of international boundaries? These questions are illustrative of a concern with interdependencies between places.

An emphasis on the nature and significance of ***interdependencies among scales*** is tied to geography's spatial perspective. It is impossible to understand the character of most places or spatial patterns without considering the role of arrangements and processes operating at different scales. For example, the location and character of an immigrant neighborhood within a city is not just the

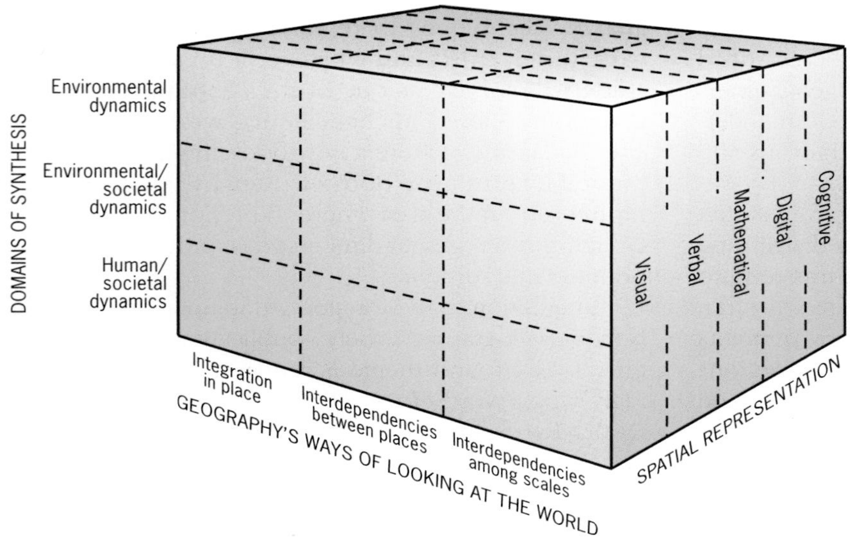

Figure 1-2 Matrix of Geographic Perspectives. Geography's ways of looking at the world—through its focus on place and scale (horizontal axis)—cuts across its three domains of synthesis: human-societal dynamics, environmental dynamics, and environmental-societal dynamics (vertical axis). Spatial representation, the third dimension of the matrix, underpins and sometimes drives research in geography. *Source:* National Research Council, *Rediscovering Geography: New Relevance for Science and Society*. Washington, D.C.: National Academy Press, 1997.

A SENSE OF SCALE

Geography and Scale

Geographers examine places and patterns at a variety of scales, from local to regional to global. Indeed, geography's concern with space puts scale at the center of its agenda. After all, the very process of examining and mapping a phenomenon involves making choices about scale. The things one might say about the distribution of French speakers will change depending on whether one looks at that distribution throughout the world, in Europe, in France, or in a Paris neighborhood. And geographers' sensitivity to scale leads them always to question what is revealed and what is hidden when a generalization is made about a people or a place at a particular scale.

The geographer's concern with scale goes beyond an interest in the scale of individual phenomena to a concern with how processes operating at different scales influence one another. If one is to understand the conflict between the Tutsi and the Hutu people in Rwanda, for example, one cannot look solely at this small African country. That conflict is influenced by developments at a variety of different scales, including patterns of migration and interaction in Central Africa, the economic and political relations between Rwanda and parts of Europe, and the variable impacts of globalization—economic, political, and cultural. The extent to which phenomena at one scale are influenced by those at other scales is so great that some scholars talk about a "local-global continuum."

It is impossible for a single text to cover all the complexities of the local-global continuum. We have therefore chosen to focus on the global and regional scales, both because this book is designed as an introductory survey of the field and because an understanding of developments at larger scales is critical to an appreciation of what is happening at smaller scales. Nevertheless, it is important to understand that influences flow not just from top to bottom, but in the other direction as well, and we talk about some of these in the book. It is also important to recognize that the tools of inquiry that we employ in this book can be employed at smaller scales as well: population can be mapped and analyzed in a neighborhood, cultural landscapes can be studied in a village, and the environmental impacts of agriculture can be studied in a watershed. To help highlight this point, the Sense of Scale boxes scattered through the text highlight local manifestations of larger-scale phenomena and show how developments at one scale influence those at another scale.

product of local social, political, and environmental circumstances. It likely also reflects regional/state policies, interstate migration patterns, economic and environmental forces operating at the global scale, and much more. The scale issue is so key to geography that it deserves special emphasis in an introductory text that must necessarily be selective about the scale at which most material will be presented (see "Sense of Scale: Geography and Scale").

The third dimension in Figure 1-2—shown on the right-hand side of the diagram—depicts the tools geographers use in their efforts to understand and explain facets of the world's spatial organization. As we will see, visual representations such as the map are key, but geographers also use descriptions (the verbal "line"), mathematical representations and calculations, digital displays and manipulations, and tools designed to understand how people think about space and environment (the cognitive "line").

Geography's Importance

The National Research Council's interest in the current status of geography reflects growing recognition of the insights to be gained from a focus on the spatial organization and material character of the Earth's surface. Can we really hope to develop sensible trade policies if we do not understand changing patterns of economic interaction among peoples? How can we prepare individuals for intelligent participation in a democratic society without providing them with an understanding of the impacts of changing political boundaries on citizenship and governance? What progress can we make in researching biodiversity loss if we do not understand the pressures on tropical rainforests resulting from different patterns of human activity? Geography's importance is revealed in the obvious answers that each of these questions elicits.

Against this backdrop, it will not surprise you to know that geographers (although often too few of them!) are employed by universities, research institutes, laboratories, public agencies, and private businesses to work on issues of contemporary relevance and concern. For example, geographers study where medical facilities should be located to benefit the largest number of people, they research why states are fighting over particular territories, they investigate why some areas are becoming richer while others are becoming poorer, and they develop land-use maps designed to minimize the negative environmental impacts of development. Their work often looks backwards as well so that we can better understand how the world got to be the way that it is.

Geography also can be forward looking. What do changing demographic trends in different regions suggest about the population issues countries will be facing in the middle of the twenty-first century? What does the growing use of English portend for the linguistic diversity of the planet? What are the likely implications of the acceleration of rural-to-urban migration for the character of human settlement in the decades to come? Each of these is a geographic question that helps crystallize the issues that will shape our world in the years and decades to come. We will focus on such matters in a series of "Looking Ahead" boxes at the end of each part of this book. The goal is to see how human geography can shed light on the world that is coming into being.

◆ USING THE SPATIAL PERSPECTIVE

There is no better way to demonstrate the insights gained through spatial analysis than through the use of ***maps***. Maps are an incredibly powerful geographic tool, and mapmaking is as old as geography itself. (For details on cartography, see Resource A at the end of this book.) Maps are used to wage war, to make political propaganda, to solve medical problems, to locate shopping centers, to bring relief to refugees, to warn of natural hazards—in short, for countless purposes.

We have already seen that the theme of location is fundamental to geography. Maps tell us where places are located in relation to other places. However, there is more to this statement than first meets the eye. True, maps provide the locations of places in terms of the Earth's latitude-longitude grid, but it really means very little to know that Chicago lies at 41 degrees, 53 minutes North Latitude and 87 degrees, 38 minutes West Longitude. Those data identify Chicago's ***absolute location***—its location in relation to a neutral, agreed-upon frame of reference. They become interesting when compared to other absolute locations, but for our purposes they are not useful for much else. By checking a map, we can determine that Chicago lies approximately at the same latitude as Madrid, Spain, and Beijing, China, and (this may surprise you) at the same longitude as the Galapagos Islands in the Pacific Ocean. So the coordinates of absolute location are useful mainly in determining exact distances and directions.

The ***relative location*** of a place is a very different matter. This is its location relative to other human and physical features on the landscape. Where does Chicago lie in relation to Lake Michigan, its important waterway; to Milwaukee, its not-too-distant neighbor; to the mineral resources and farmlands of the Midwest; or to the road and railroad networks? All of these could be represented on maps. Note that a vast system of roads and railroads converges on Chicago from all parts of the surrounding region (Fig. 1-3). This means that the city's interconnections with the region around it are exceptionally efficient. Whether you wanted to distribute something from Chicago to the four states that lie within 60 miles (100 kilometers) of it, or reach the Chicago market from someplace in the region, surface communications are readily available. What the map does not show is Chicago's role as a hub of airline transportation. As urban geographers (those who study the spatial organization and landscapes of cities) say, Chicago has great centrality. Centrality is a function of location, relative to other

From the field notes

"As I walked into the control room of Tokyo's earthquake emergency response center, I was dazzled by the technology that surrounded me. Rows of the latest, most sophisticated computers faced toward large screens where digital maps of the Tokyo metropolitan area were displayed. A quick run through a few simulations showed me that the system was based on an elaborate GIS. The impacts of a disaster hitting one part of the city could be traced and analyzed through the manipulation of spatial information on everything from transportation networks to population concentrations. Geography is no luxury here; it is a matter of life and death."

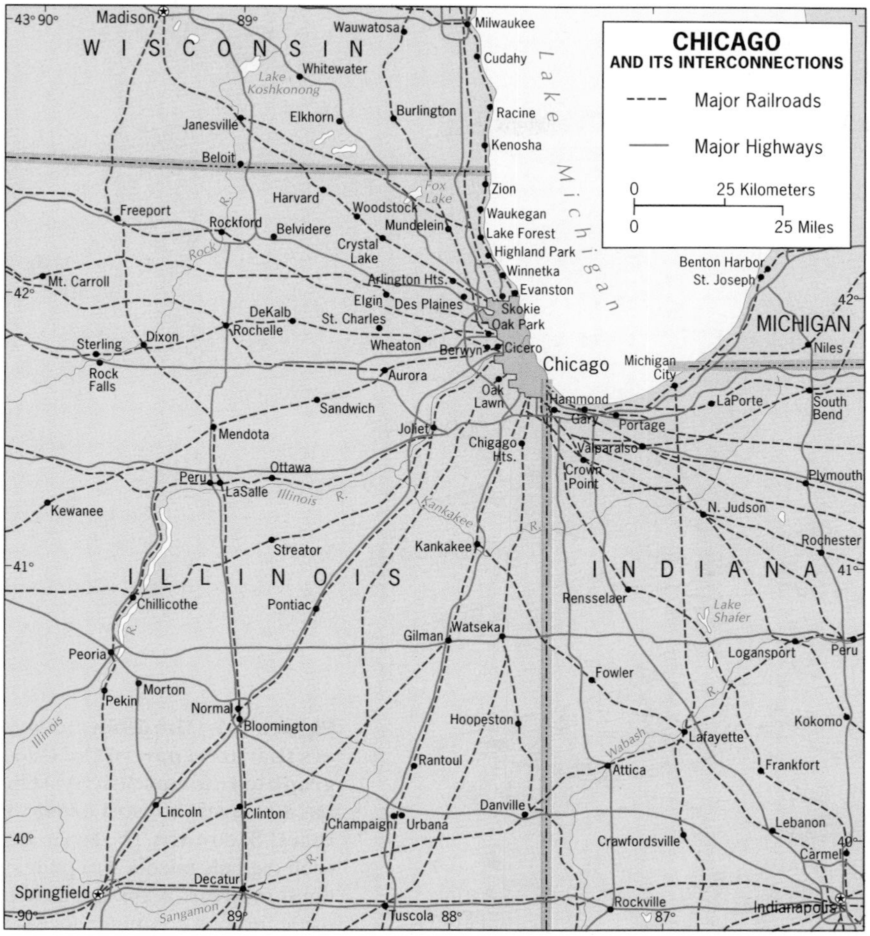

Figure 1-3 Chicago and Its Interconnections. Notice how surface communication lines converge on Chicago—reflecting and shaping its dominance in the region.

urban places, resources, productive farmlands, and efficient transport linkages.

Whereas the absolute location of a place does not change, its relative location is subject to constant modification. From its beginning, Chicago was an important city in the interior of North America, but its relative location changed markedly in 1959 when the St. Lawrence Seaway was opened and the city acquired a direct maritime connection to the North Atlantic Ocean. Although the seaway closes in the winter when ice blocks navigation, Chicago can be reached by oceangoing vessels throughout the rest of the year. As an inland port, its relative location has changed substantially. Ships that could once get no closer than the eastern ports of North America now dock in sight of Chicago's downtown skyline.

An especially dramatic change in relative location has affected an entire country, Japan, during the past century. As late as the mid-nineteenth century, Japan was relatively isolated from the developing global economy. When the Japanese decided to embark on the road to industrialization, they chose Britain as their model (which is why they still drive on the left side of the road). However, Japan was half a world removed from Europe, the center of the industrial world at the time. Then during the twentieth century, the United States became the world's most important industrial power, and now Japan lay directly across the Pacific from the newly dominant American market. Today, Japan's relative location is changing again as China, right across the East China Sea, becomes a growing trading partner and Russia beckons from across the Sea of Japan. In relative location Japan thus has gone from remote isolation to global hub—but its absolute location has never changed!

◆ THE ROLE OF MAPS IN HUMAN GEOGRAPHY

One of the ways geographers can gain a better understanding of places and issues is by comparing spatial data. Frequently, these comparisons make use of ***geographic information systems*** (GISs), a powerful new tool that allows geographers to combine layers of spatial data in a computerized environment, creating maps in which patterns and processes are superimposed. GISs

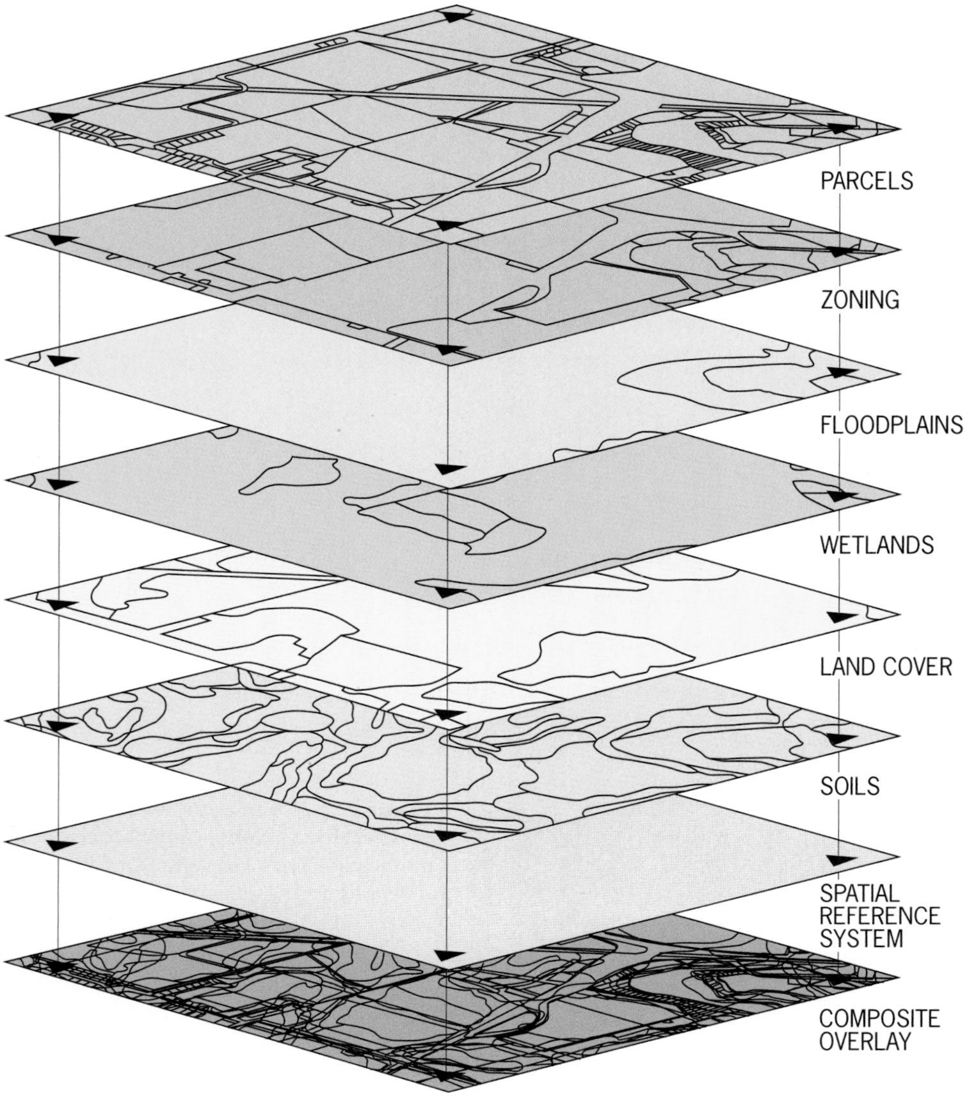

Figure 1-4 The different layers that are a part of the Geographic Information System used to evaluate soil erosion in a U.S. county. The layers are each digitally encoded as points, lines, or areas. Assessments are made through computer analysis of the different layers and their relationships to one another. *Source:* N. Chrisman, *Exploring Geographic Information Systems*, 2nd ed. New York: John Wiley & Sons, 2002, p. 6.

are used not only to display data in the form of maps, but also to analyze those data—in the process creating new insights into geographic patterns and relationships (see Fig. 1-4).

Maps and Places

Maps demonstrate a vital rule of geography: that places on the Earth have their own distinctive properties which, taken together, give each place its own character. No place is exactly like another, and a map is the best way to demonstrate this. Geographers study both the physical and human properties of places. The Earth's surface, its elevation and relief, slopes and drainage, soils, natural vegetation, and atmospheric conditions (climate and weather) form the physical setting. The uses to which people put this setting—in the form of settlement layout, population patterns, transport networks, land use, and other activity—create the human imprint. Together, these physical and human features constitute the overall geographic character of a particular place.

Geographers therefore have a special interest in the quality of places. Whether it's a fishing village on China's coast or a bustling Arab town, geographers want to know how the people have implanted their traditions on that locale, why they have done so, what sustains them now, and how they interact with the outside world. It is impossible, of course, to study all these aspects at once, so geographers tend to specialize in certain features of places. Some study the street layout and architecture of a town; others concentrate on the transport systems that serve it; still others focus on the business and industry that sustain the local economy. In the process, a kind of geographic overview of the place emerges. If you were to become a professional geographer and found yourself assigned to study, say, the growth of suburbs around Santiago, the capital of Chile, you would first read what geographers (and others) have already written about that city. With the many specialized maps they have prepared, you would be well informed before you ever set foot in the field.

Maps and Environmental Issues

Throughout this book the theme of human interaction with the environment emerges time and again. Human geography, whether economic, political, urban, or cultural, cannot be studied without reference to the environment in which the action takes place. In the course of our journey, we will look at maps of "acid rain" distribution, deforestation, river basins, ice ages, and other aspects of the natural environment. Some of these maps will raise as many questions as they answer. For example, if Bangladesh faces certain disaster from cyclones that can kill hundreds of thousands, why do people continue to inhabit low-lying ground in the most dangerous areas? Is the southward spread of the Sahara in West Africa a natural phenomenon, or are human groups and their livestock responsible for this devastating process? If the Amazonian rainforest in Brazil and adjacent countries continues to be destroyed at present rates, what will happen to rainfall patterns there?

In Part One we will take a closer look at past and present global environments, but it is useful now to consider a map of one vital ingredient of our Earthly existence: water. Figure 1-5 is a map of the mean annual precipitation around the world. Note the prevalence of dry conditions over much of the globe, from inner Asia to western Africa to central Australia. As the Earth's human population grows, the demands on this limited supply of water also increase. Drought-caused famines have struck many vulnerable areas, including the northeastern corner of South America, the southern margins of the Sahara in Africa, and south-central Asia. Often such death-dealing droughts cause people to seek relief elsewhere, creating migration streams that cause further dislocation in neighboring zones. For example, thousands of people and their livestock, fleeing from the last drought in West Africa, migrated southward into the moister savanna lands of coastal countries. Their cattle trampled crops and destroyed harvests, and the result was armed conflict between the local farmers and the migrants.

Water shortages are not confined to desert-edge grazing lands in remote corners of the world. Water rationing became a fact of life in California in the early 1990s, yet people continue to move not only into California but also into other water-deficient areas of the American Southwest. As Figure 1-5 suggests, the prospects for water supply in a burgeoning world are worrisome. Expensive desalinization plants, using ocean water, modeled after those on the Arabian shore of the Persian Gulf, are making their appearance in California. But their capacity is a drop in the proverbial bucket.

The map of world precipitation also emphasizes the importance of the Atlantic Ocean. Note that except for South Asia and Southeast Asia, the moistest areas of the world lie clustered against Atlantic shores, from water-warmed Western Europe to Amazonian South America and from the southeastern United States to West and Equatorial Africa. These regions owe most of their annual water supply to the Atlantic Ocean, whose slowly circulating waters bring warmth and moisture to areas from Britain to Brazil. Even the peaks of the Andes Mountains in western South America, and the densely populated highlands of eastern Africa, get most of their snow and rain not from the neighboring Pacific and Indian oceans but from the faraway Atlantic. Here again we see that a map can tell far more than mere distribution.

Field observation can provide many insights into the Earth's changing environment, but to understand the scale and rate of environmental change it is often necessary to monitor the Earth's surface from a distance using modern technology. ***Remote sensing*** is thus an important geographic technique. Remote sensing data collected by satellites and aircraft (airplanes, balloons, etc.) reveal both physical changes, such as the extent of flooding in the Mississippi River Valley, and changes that are more directly due to human activity, such as deforestation in the Brazilian Amazon resulting from agricultural activities. More recently, the establishment of a satellite-based global positioning system (GPS) has allowed us to locate things on the surface of the Earth with extraordinary accuracy. Not only does this permit locational data to be collected more quickly and easily in the field, but GPS units also have more mundane uses, such as helping lost campers find their way out of the woods.

Maps and Human Mobility

It is one thing to map static features, such as existing patterns and distributions or the locations of cities and towns, but it is quite another to represent movement on the map. Yet movement is a central theme of geography. Whether it is the movement of goods from factories to markets, the flow of oil from Middle Eastern wells to American consumers, or the migration of people from one region to another, movement must be recorded on maps and interpreted.

To indicate movement, cartographers use many symbols. For example, you can represent the number of travelers on key highways or major airline routes using arrows of varying width; the widths of the arrows reveal

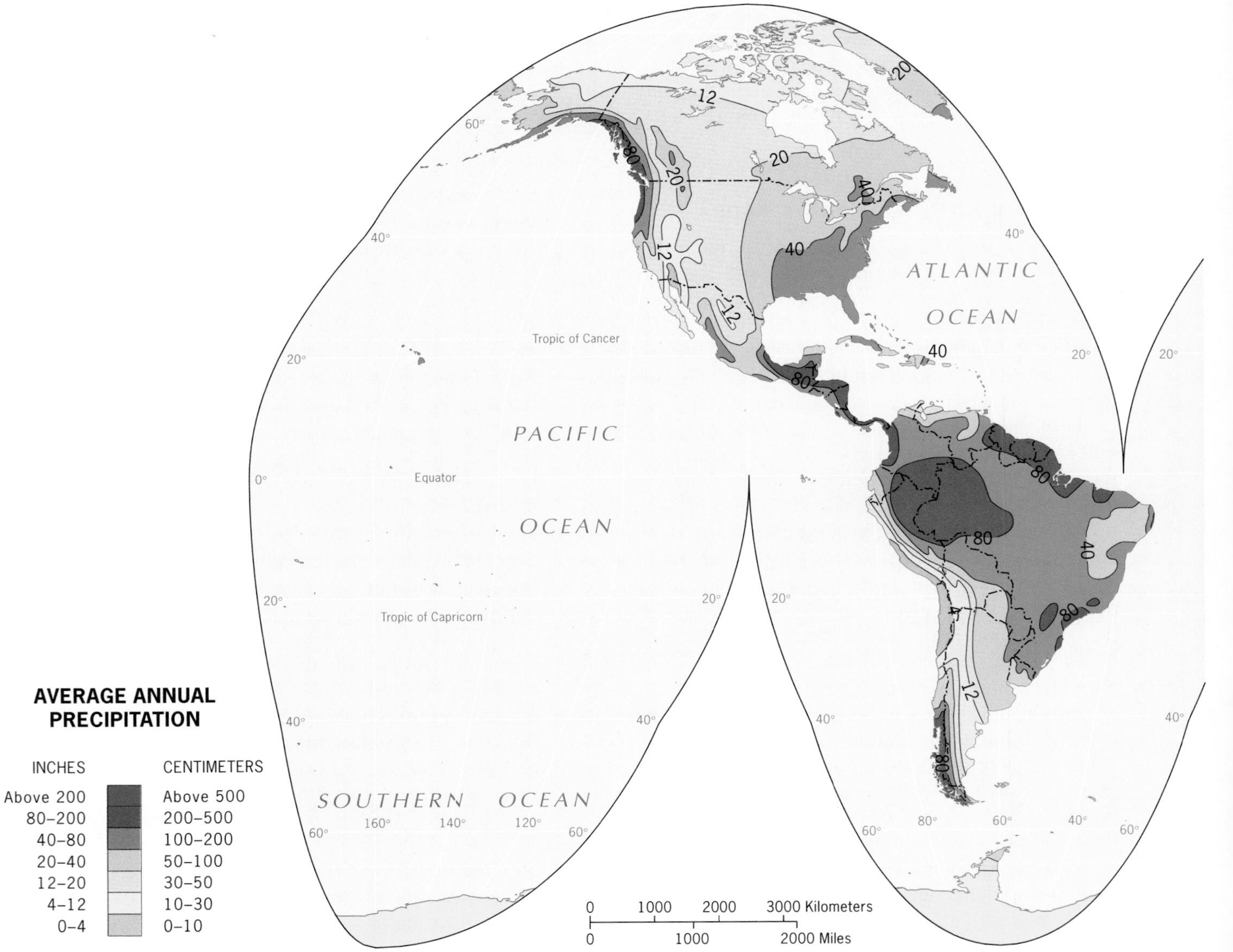

Figure 1-5 Average Annual Precipitation of the World. A generalized map of the mean annual precipitation received around the world. Note that this map projection (see Resource A) is interrupted in the oceans, allowing for maximum clarity of detail on the landmasses.

the comparative quantities of traffic (Fig. 1-6). Such maps show at a glance the intensity of movement along certain routes, and more careful examination reveals the actual numbers or volumes involved.

But there are times when it is not so much the actual volume but the direction of movement that matters most. Where money flows, for example, can be just as important as how much money is moving out of a particular place. More often it is the movement of ideas, notions, and innovations that matters, but such movement cannot be quantified. The geographic term for this is ***diffusion***, the spread of ideas or knowledge from their origins to areas where they are adopted. Much as we would like to, we cannot always measure such diffusion quantitatively, but we can trace its direction. So some maps representing this process have arrows that reflect direction only, not volume.

Maps showing movement of various kinds are among the most interesting in geography. In the chapter on medical geography, you will find a series of maps with arrows showing the routes of invasion of cholera, a dreaded illness of the nineteenth century, which occasionally reappears today. At its height over 100 years ago, no one knew what caused cholera; hundreds of thousands of people died of it. But others were somehow spared. As it turned out, a map was the key to dis-

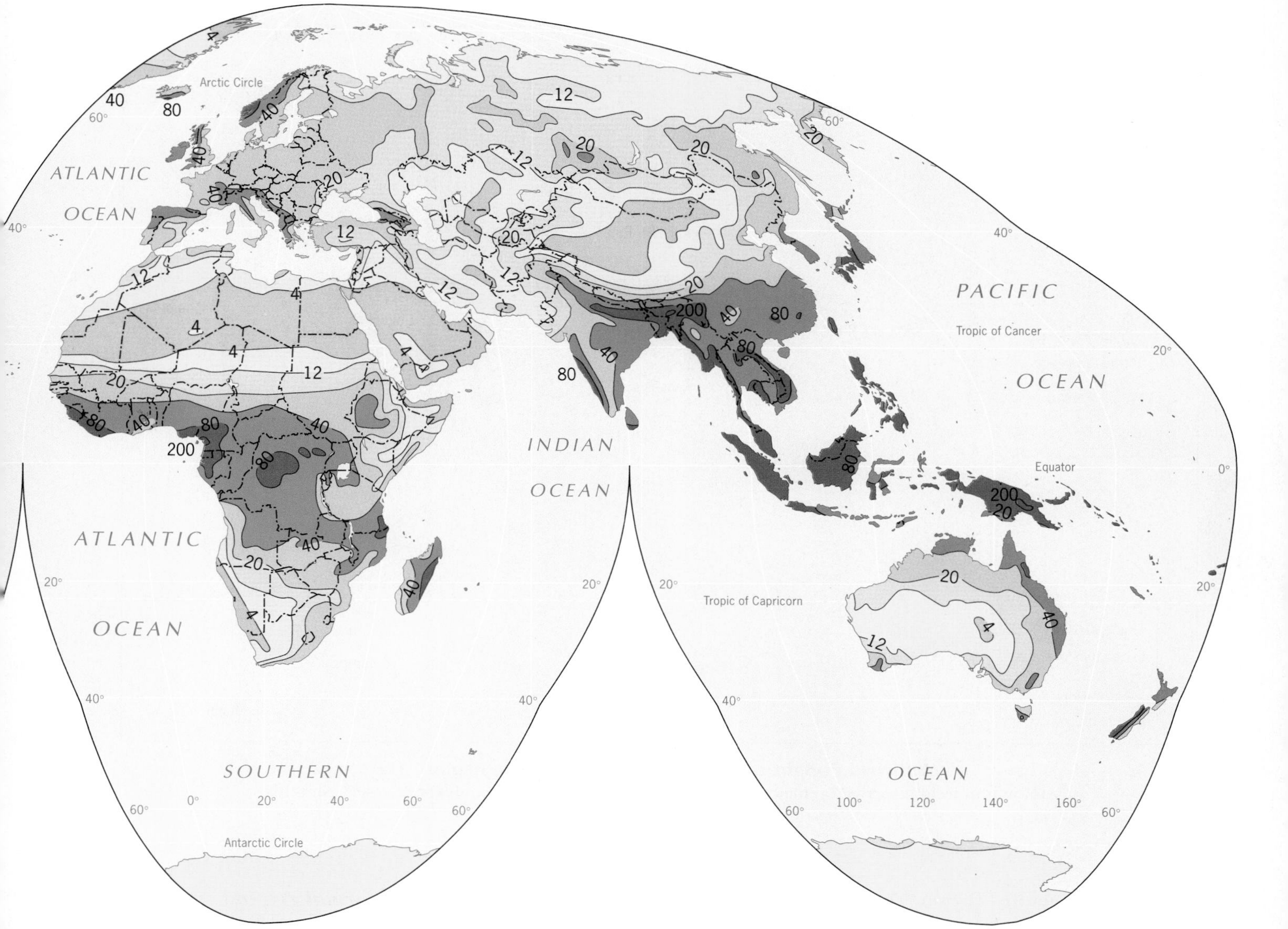

covering the answer, and a medical geographer solved the problem. Today, similar efforts are being made to combat AIDS, another dreaded disease affecting millions. And again medical geographers are using maps to help.

Regions on the Map

Throughout this book we will use regions, and the regional concept, to clarify what is being discussed. Actually, we use some form of the regional idea all the time, even in everyday conversation. When you plan a vacation in "the Rockies," or a hiking trip in New England, or a cruise in the Caribbean, you are using regional notions to convey what you have in mind. Regions, used this way, serve as informal frames of reference.

In geography, the regional concept is, of course, more specific. To refer to "the Rockies" as a perceived region summarizes what is prominent about this region: steep slopes, dramatic mountain scenery, snowcapped peaks, and ski slopes. But as a geographer you might be asked to define and delimit a Rocky Mountains region. Exactly where are the boundaries of "the Rockies"? In some places, the answer is easily found as the mountains rise suddenly from the adjacent Great Plains (another region). Elsewhere, however, the mountainous terrain rises gradually; the plains become hilly, and the slopes become steeper. Where, and on what basis, do you draw the regional boundary?

To identify and delimit regions, we must establish criteria for them. Imagine that, as an exercise in physical geography, you were asked to delimit the Amazon River

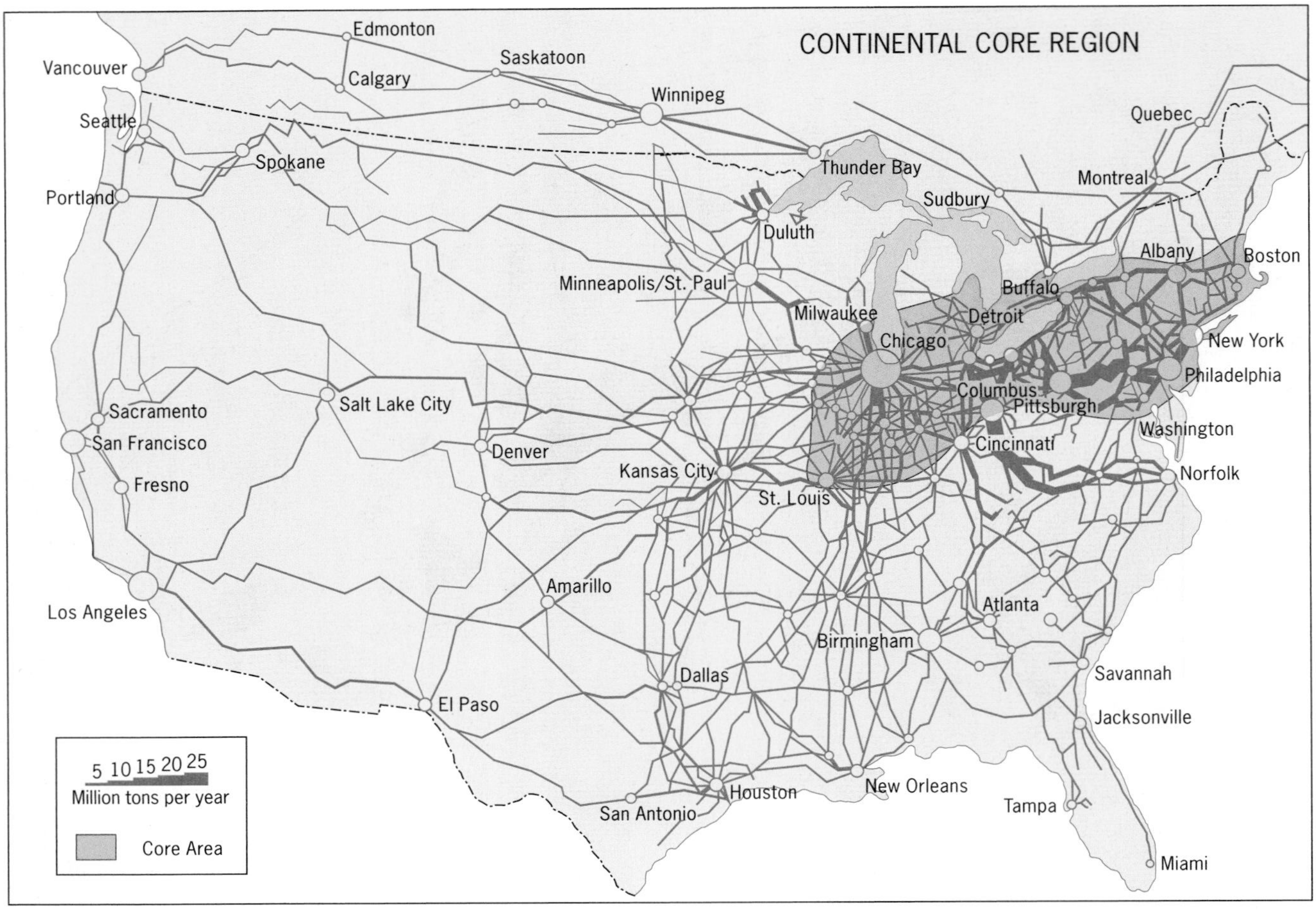

Figure 1-6 Railroad Freight in the U.S. Continental Core Region. The comparative amount of freight carried on major North American railroads can be quickly assessed from this map.

Basin as a geographic region. There would be various ways to do this: you might use vegetation distribution, soil properties, slope angles, or drainage patterns. When you presented your results, you would first state the basis on which you had mapped the region and then produce the resulting map. On a small scale, the map might resemble Figure 1-7, which uses drainage lines to define the Amazon Basin on the basis of the rivers and tributaries that ultimately drain into this great South American river.

Thus we know that all regions have certain characteristics. These include ***area***—that is, they all have some defined spatial extent; location, in that all regions lie somewhere on the Earth's surface; and limits or ***boundaries***, which are sometimes evident on the ground and sometimes not, and are often based on specifically chosen criteria.

Regions are not all of the same type. Some are marked by visible uniformity, for example, a desert basin marked by severe aridity, sandy surface, and steep surrounding mountain slopes. Geographers refer to such a homogeneous region as a ***formal region***. Formal regions can also be defined by cultural (as opposed to physical) criteria. A region within which French is spoken by, say, 90 percent or more of the population, is also

Figure 1-7 Amazon Basin. The Amazon Basin as a region defined by the main tributaries and topography.

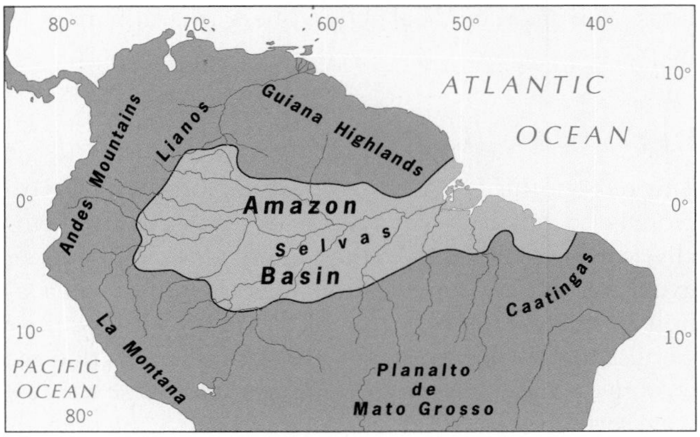

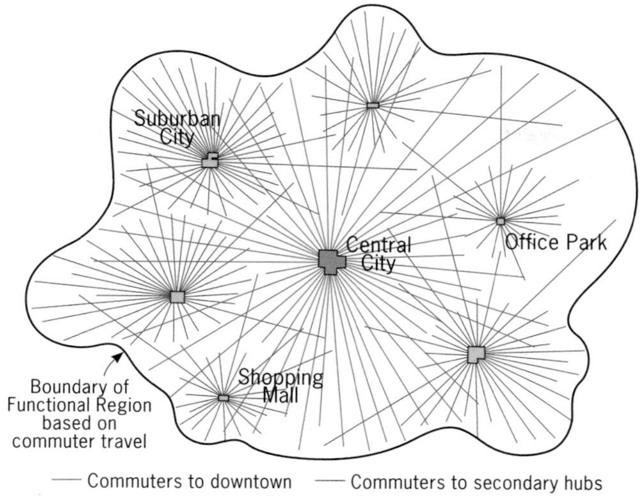

Figure 1-8 Commuter Travel Patterns. Commuter travel patterns in an urban area. The lines show the catchment areas of various places in an urbanized area. *Source:* From authors' sketch.

a formal region. A ***functional region***, on the other hand, is the product of interactions, of movement of various kinds. A city, for example, has a surrounding region within which workers commute, either to the downtown area or to subsidiary centers such as office parks and shopping malls (Fig. 1-8). That entire urban area, defined by people moving toward and within it, is a functional region. Thus a functional region is a spatial system; its boundaries are defined by the limits of that system. Finally, regions may be primarily in the minds of people. These ***perceptual regions*** are not just curiosities. How people think about regions has influenced everything from daily activity patterns to large-scale international conflict. Regions can be seen in a vertical order or ***hierarchy***. The French-speaking region to which we referred earlier can be thought of as a region within a larger region, namely, Western Europe. Western Europe, in turn, is a region of the European geographic realm. Regions often form a hierarchy based on size and importance.

Regions, therefore, are ways of organizing humans geographically. They are a form of spatial classification, a means of handling large amounts of information so that it makes sense. Thus the regional concept is an indispensable aid in our journey through human geography.

Maps in the Mind

Whether we like it or not, we see and study things from a particular viewpoint, which is shaped by our cultural environment. No matter how hard we try to be objective, a view of the world and its problems (geographic and otherwise) from the United States is not the same as the view from Tanzania or China. Certainly, a map of mountain ranges or known oil reserves might look the same whether it was drawn in China or America, but when we study more subjective things—culture and tradition, politics, or economic development—we may have quite a different outlook. Take, for example, a standard picture of a major city in another country, such as Mexico City, Mexico, or Nairobi, Kenya. Such a picture is likely to show the modern, high-rise buildings of the "downtown" area, the heart of the city. However, the fact is that the great majority of the people of Mexico City and Nairobi (and dozens of other large cities) live in modest, often inadequate dwellings in vast, sprawling housing tracts that surround the urban core. For many of these people, the skyscrapers of the central city are irrelevant, and city life is a battle for survival in quite a different environment. Shouldn't a "typical" picture of Mexico City or Nairobi show that image rather than the downtown area?

It is important to realize that our study of the human world contains some cultural bias, no matter how hard we try to see alternative viewpoints. As you get to know geographers, you will find that they tend to be drawn to the field partly because of their interest in, and respect for, other societies and cultures. That, however, does not make us immune to bias or insensitivity. After all, human geography deals with population growth and control, race and religion, economic development, and political institutions, all of which can be touchy subjects.

Mental Maps Imagine that you are attending a seminar discussion on the political geography of Southern Africa, but there is no wall map to which you can refer. What is your frame of reference? Obviously, it is the countries of the region: South Africa, Namibia, Swaziland, Lesotho, Botswana, Zimbabwe, and their neighbors. As you speak, you will use the map that is in your mind, your ***mental map*** of that part of the world. That mental map has developed over years of looking at wall maps, atlas maps, maps in books, magazines, and newspapers.

Mental maps are a fundamental part of our general knowledge; we use them constantly. If someone were to call you to suggest that you go to the theater, a mental map would come to mind: the hallway, the front door, the walk to your car, the lane to choose in order to be prepared for the left turn you must make, where you would prefer to park, and so forth. If your mental map is vague, you will need a city map to find your way. However, if the issue is more serious than a trip to the theater, and a large number of people are poorly informed, vague mental maps can lead to major policy mistakes.

Environmental Perception Mental maps (also called cognitive maps) are derived from visual observation of the real world (your city or town, college campus, shopping center) and from the scrutiny and study of printed

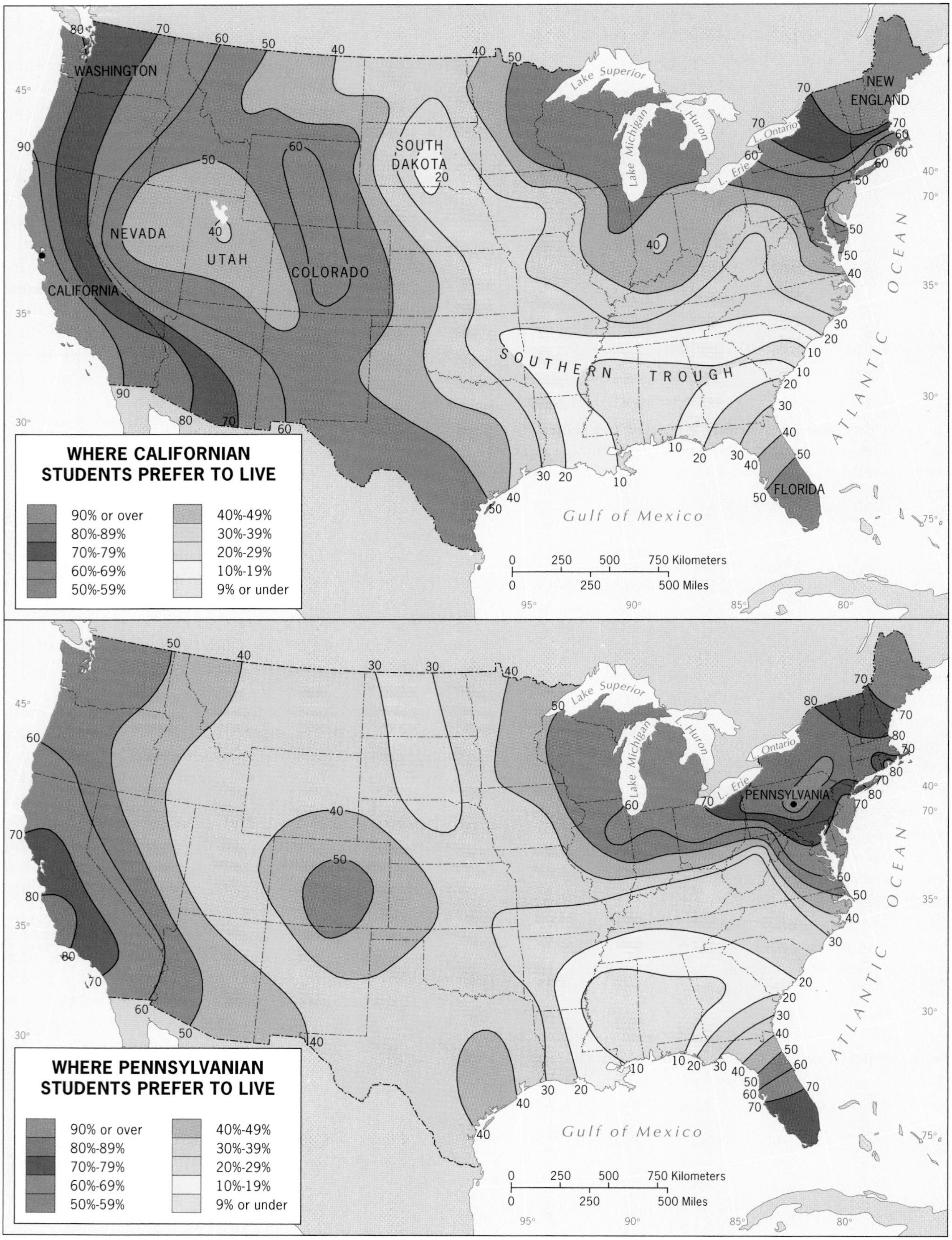

Figure 1-9 Different Living Preferences. Where Californians and Pennsylvanians would prefer to live based on questionnaires completed by college students. *Source:* P. R. Gould and R. White, *Mental Maps*. Harmondsworth: Penguin Books, 1986, pp. 55 and 58. Redrawn by permission of the publisher.

maps. Sights are supplemented by sounds and smells, and the total impression is ***environmental perception***. This is the impression that generates our mental map.

Since geographers are interested in both the physical world and the human organization of it, environmental perception is a popular geographic topic. We have perceptions of places we know by personal experience, but we also carry images of places we have never visited. What shapes these perceptions? To what extent are they accurate or distorted? In a fascinating book titled ***Mental Maps*** (1982), geographers Peter Gould and Rodney White begin by asking the following question: If you could move to any place of your choice, without any of the usual financial and other obstacles, where would you like to live? (For their respondents' answers, see Fig. 1-9.) Perhaps you would select a location that you perceive as attractive but have never personally experienced. However, the actual environment may turn out to be quite different from your perception of it.

A crucial part of our perception of a place lies in its layout, that is, its spatial arrangement and organization. To know the location of a country (whether it is Laos or Afghanistan or Bolivia) is only a beginning. From maps we can gain impressions of topography and relief, climate and weather, the quality of roads, the layout of villages and towns, and countless other conditions—without ever having been there. The map is thus our window on the world.

See Resource A, Maps, at the end of the book for guidelines on how to read and use maps.

◆ KEY TERMS ◆

absolute location
area
boundary
diffusion
distribution
environmental geography
environmental perception
formal region
functional region
geographic information systems
hierarchy
human–environment interactions
human geography
landscape
location (absolute, relative)
location theory
map
mental map
movement
pattern
perceptual region
physical (natural) geography
place
regional science
regions (formal, functional)
relative location
remote sensing
spatial perspective

◆ APPLYING GEOGRAPHIC KNOWLEDGE ◆

1. Imagine yourself living and working in a small town in a rural area of the Midwest. Your family owns and operates a small department store located at the busiest intersection in town, where the through road crosses the main shopping street. Now the State Highway Department is building a four-lane highway that will bypass your town about six miles away. How will this change your store's relative location? How will it affect your market? What might you and other shop owners do to counter the impact of the new highway?

2. The editor of a city newspaper has appointed you to her staff, and your first job as a geographer is to draw a map of the region within which the paper sells, that is, its market. Describe how you will go about this: what will be the criteria on which this functional region is based? When you have finished your map, the region turns out to be quite asymmetrical; the paper sells as far as 100 miles north of the city but only 60 miles to the south. What might explain this variable "reach" of the newspaper?

Chapter 2

Cultures, Environments, and Regions

From the field notes

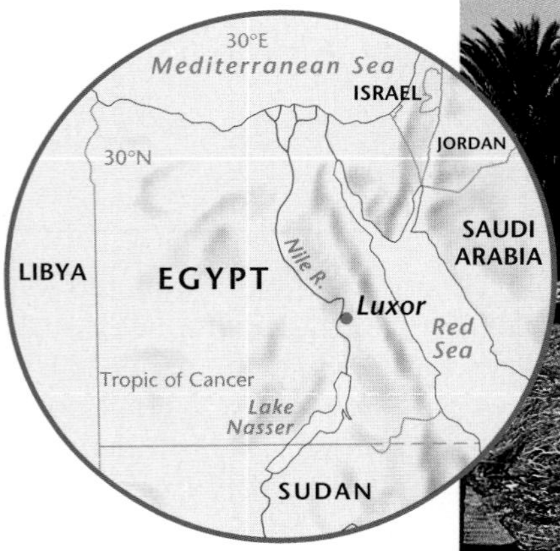

"Crossing the Nile at Luxor, I made my way along the west bank of the river heading toward the Valley of the Kings. The narrow strip of fertile land I traversed was a world apart from the arid landscape that lay just a few miles farther to the west. Passing through a series of tiny towns, I was struck by the visible interplay between culture and environment. The modest houses were surrounded by reminders of the agricultural life of their inhabitants—farm tools, animals, and storage containers. Mosques dotted the landscape, and trees had been planted strategically to provide a modicum of shade and a buffer between road and field. Here, people's lives are inextricably intertwined with the environment, and the landscapes they create reflect both their culture and the environment in which it is situated."

KEY POINTS

- **The concept of culture lies at the heart of human geography, for culture mediates all human decisions and actions.**
- **Cultural geography focuses on where cultural ideas and practices developed, how and where they diffused, and how they affect landscape, human perception, and human-environment relations.**
- **Cultural hearths are the sources of civilizations; ideas, innovations, and ideologies radiate outward from them.**
- **Cultural diffusion can take the form of expansion diffusion or relocation diffusion.**
- **Perceptual regions depend on an individual's cultural context and the mental maps he or she uses to make sense of the world.**
- **The doctrine of environmental determinism, which holds that human behavior is limited or controlled by the environment, has been a subject of intense debate, and broad generalizations about the impact of environment on humans have been discredited.**

Human geography, as we saw in Chapter 1, is a major component of the discipline of geography. It is unified by its spatial perspective and by its focus on the concrete character of human impact on the Earth's surface. How are the products of human activity arranged on the Earth? What forces and factors influenced their location and distribution? Do different societies organize their space in different ways, and if so, what can be learned from the patterns we observe? How do humans shape the landscape—and with what result? ◆

◆ CULTURE AND HUMAN GEOGRAPHY

At the heart of the wide-ranging subdiscipline of human geography lies the concept of ***culture***, for location decisions, patterns, and landscapes are fundamentally influenced by cultural attitudes and practices. Like the regional concept discussed in the previous chapter, the concept of culture appears to be deceptively simple, but in fact it is complex and challenging. You can prove this just by looking up the word "culture" in several dictionaries and introductory anthropology texts and noting how widely their definitions vary. Our uses of the word also vary. When we speak of a "cultured" individual, we tend to mean someone with refined tastes in music and the arts, a highly educated, well-read person who knows and appreciates the "best" attributes of society. As a scientific term, however, culture refers not only to the music, literature, and arts of a society but also to all the other features of its way of life: prevailing modes of dress; routine living habits; food preferences; the architecture of houses and public buildings; the layout of fields and farms; and systems of education, government, and law. Thus culture is an all-encompassing term that identifies not only the whole tangible lifestyle of peoples, but also their prevailing values and beliefs.

The concept of culture is closely identified with the discipline of anthropology, and over the course of more than a century anthropologists have defined it in many different ways. Some have stressed the contributions of humans to the environment (e.g., M. J. Herskovitz), whereas others have emphasized learned behaviors and ways of thinking (e.g., M. Harris). Several decades ago the noted anthropologist E. Adamson Hoebel defined culture as:

> The integrated system of learned behavior patterns which are characteristic of the members of a society and which are not the result of biological inheritance . . . culture is not genetically predetermined; it is noninstinctive . . . [culture] is wholly the result of social invention and is transmitted and maintained solely through communication and learning.

Hoebel's emphasis on communication and learning anticipated the current view that culture is a system of meaning, not just a set of acts, customs, or material products. Clifford Geertz advances this view in his classic work, ***The Interpretation of Cultures*** (1973); much recent work in human geography has been influenced by it. Hence, human geographers are interested not just in the different patterns and landscapes associated with different culture groups, but in the ways in which cultural understandings affect both the creation and significance of those patterns and landscapes.

The concept of culture is so broad ranging that cultural geography is sometimes considered to be synonymous with human geography. More often, however, it is considered to be a subset of human geography because many questions about population, economy, and politics can be posed without emphasizing their cultural dimensions. Does this mean that cultural geography is limited to the study of particular elements of culture (language, religion, etc.)? Few contemporary cultural geographers would see it that way. Instead, they would argue that cultural geography looks at the ways culture is implicated in the full spectrum of topics addressed in human geography. As such, cultural geography can be seen as a perspective on human geography as much as a component thereof. And this, in turn, exposes the limitations of viewing the discipline strictly along the lines suggested by Figure 1-1. There is much blurring among and between the various components of the discipline, and certain topics (particularly culture, politics, and economics) cut across the entire field.

Components of Culture

Culture is so complex that it is useful to identify some of its interconnected parts. Certain of these parts tie in directly with geography's emphasis on space. A ***culture region*** (the area within which a particular culture system prevails) is marked by all the attributes of a culture, including modes of dress, building styles, farms and fields, and other material manifestations. Cultural geographers identify a single attribute of a culture as a ***culture trait***. For example, the wearing of a turban can be a culture trait of certain Muslim societies; for centuries, it was obligatory for Muslim men to wear this headgear. Although it is no longer required everywhere, the turban continues to be a distinctive trait of many Muslim cultures. The use of simple tools also constitutes a culture trait, and eating with certain utensils (knife and fork or chopsticks) is a culture trait.

Culture traits are not necessarily confined to a single culture. More than one culture may exhibit a particular culture trait, but each will consist of a discrete combination of traits. Such a combination is referred to as a ***culture complex***. In many cultures, the herding of cattle is a trait. However, cattle are regarded and used in different ways by different cultures. The Maasai of East Africa follow their herds along seasonal migration paths, consuming blood and milk as important ingredients of a unique diet. Cattle occupy a central place in Maasai existence; they are the essence of survival, security, and prestige. Although the Maasai culture complex is only one of many cattle-keeping complexes, no other culture complex exhibits exactly the same combination of traits. In Europe, cattle are milked and dairy products, such as butter, yogurt, and cheese, are consumed as part of a diet very different from that of the Maasai.

Thus culture complexes have traits in common, and so it is possible to group certain complexes together as ***culture systems***. Ethnicity, language, religion, and other cultural elements enter into the definition of a culture system; for example, much of China may be so designated. China's culture system consists of a number of quite distinct culture complexes, united by strong cultural bonds. Northern Chinese people may eat wheat and those in the south may eat rice as their staple, and the Chinese language as spoken in the north may not be quite the same as that spoken in the south, but history, philosophy, environmental adaptation and modification, and numerous cultural traditions and attitudes give coherence to the Chinese culture system.

On the map, a culture region can represent an entire culture system. West Africa, Polynesia, and Central America are sometimes designated as culture regions of sorts, each consisting of a combination of culture complexes of considerable diversity but still substantial uniformity. Many geographers, however, prefer to describe regions such as Han China, West Africa, and Polynesia as ***geographic regions*** rather than as culture regions because their definition is based not only on cultural properties but on locational and environmental circumstances as well.

An assemblage of culture (or geographic) regions forms a ***culture realm***, the most highly generalized regionalization of culture and geography. Together, the culture regions of West, East, Equatorial, and Southern Africa can be thought of as collectively constituting the Subsaharan African culture realm. Once again, there are good reasons for calling these ***geographic realms*** of the human world: the criteria on which they are based, though dominated by cultural characteristics, extend beyond culture.

Cultural Geographies Past and Present

The colonization and Europeanization of much of the world have obliterated a great deal of the cultural geography of earlier times. Very little is left of the map we might have constructed of indigenous North American culture regions (Fig. 2-1); similarly, a historical map of aboriginal Australian cultures would differ radically from the contemporary version. At the same time, maps of indigenous or "traditional" culture complexes do not show the regional patterns resulting from the European colonization and its associated migrations. Thus, when viewing any map showing culture regions or geographic realms, it is important to be sensitive to what is being depicted—and when.

The importance of the latter point becomes clear if you compare Figure 2-1 with Figure 2-2. Figure 2-2 is a

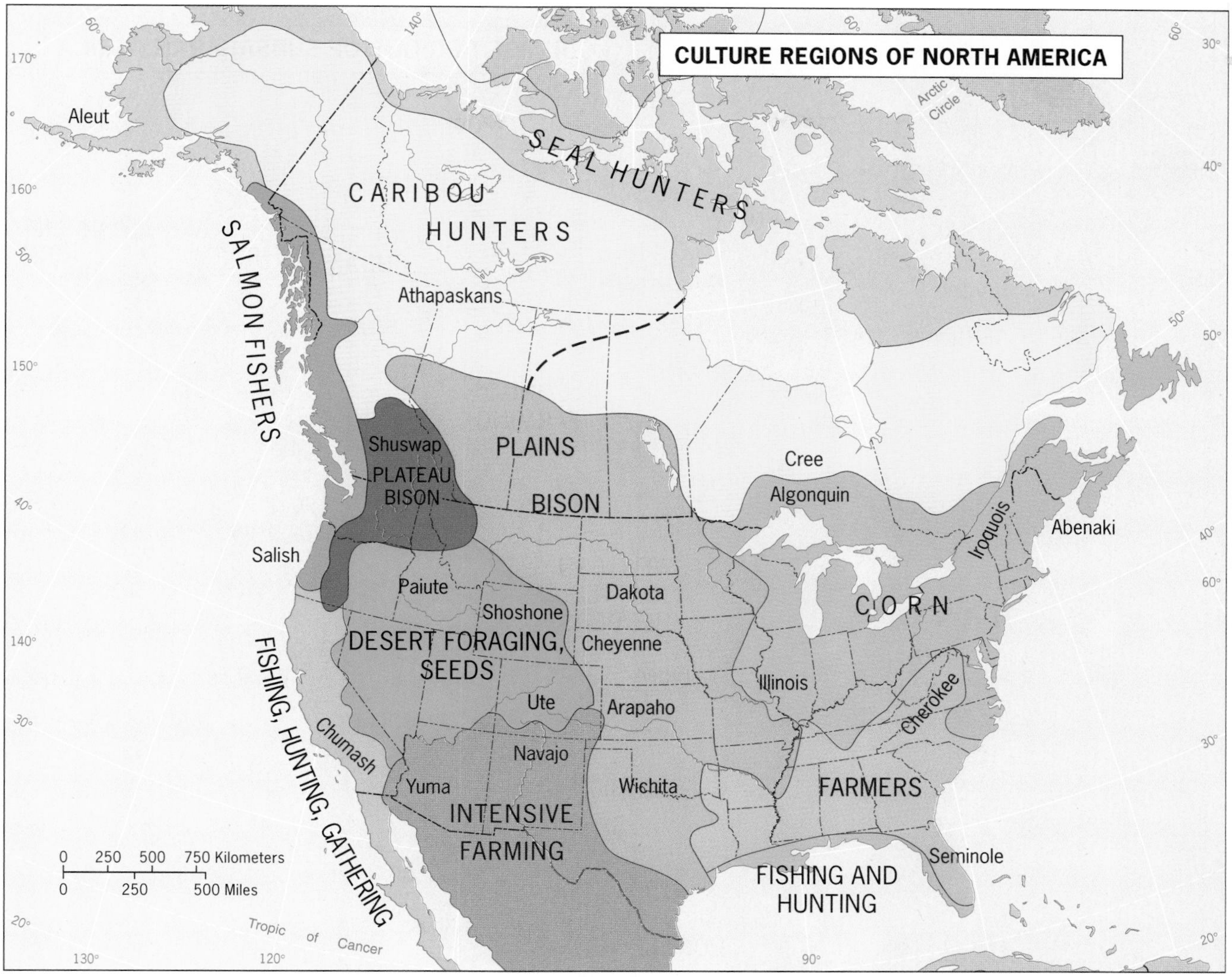

Figure 2-1 Culture Regions of North America. One approach to the regionalization of indigenous American cultures. Modern boundary lines are included for spatial references.

recent attempt to divide up Subsaharan Africa into different culture regions. This attempt to depict "modern" culture regions and geographic realms does not reflect the historical patterns shown in Figure 2-1; instead it seeks to represent dominant present-day realities—at least as seen by one commentator. Yet elements of the historic pattern still exist—and even influence present patterns. The reality is that the world is made up of a constantly changing, often overlapping mix of traditional and modern culture regions.

◆ KEY TOPICS IN CULTURAL GEOGRAPHY

The field of cultural geography is wide-ranging and comprehensive. To understand the various ways in which geographers look at culture, it is useful to focus on five traditionally prominent areas of study and research.

1. ***Cultural Landscape.*** The imprint of cultures on the land creates distinct and characteristic cultural landscapes.
2. ***Culture Hearths.*** Several sources, crucibles, of cultural growth and achievement developed in Eurasia, Africa, and America.
3. ***Cultural Diffusion.*** From their sources, cultural innovations and ideas spread to other areas. The process of cultural diffusion continues to this day.
4. ***Cultural Perception.*** Culture groups have varying ideas and attitudes about space, place, and territory.
5. ***Cultural Environments.*** This area deals with the role of culture in human understanding, use, and alteration of the environment.

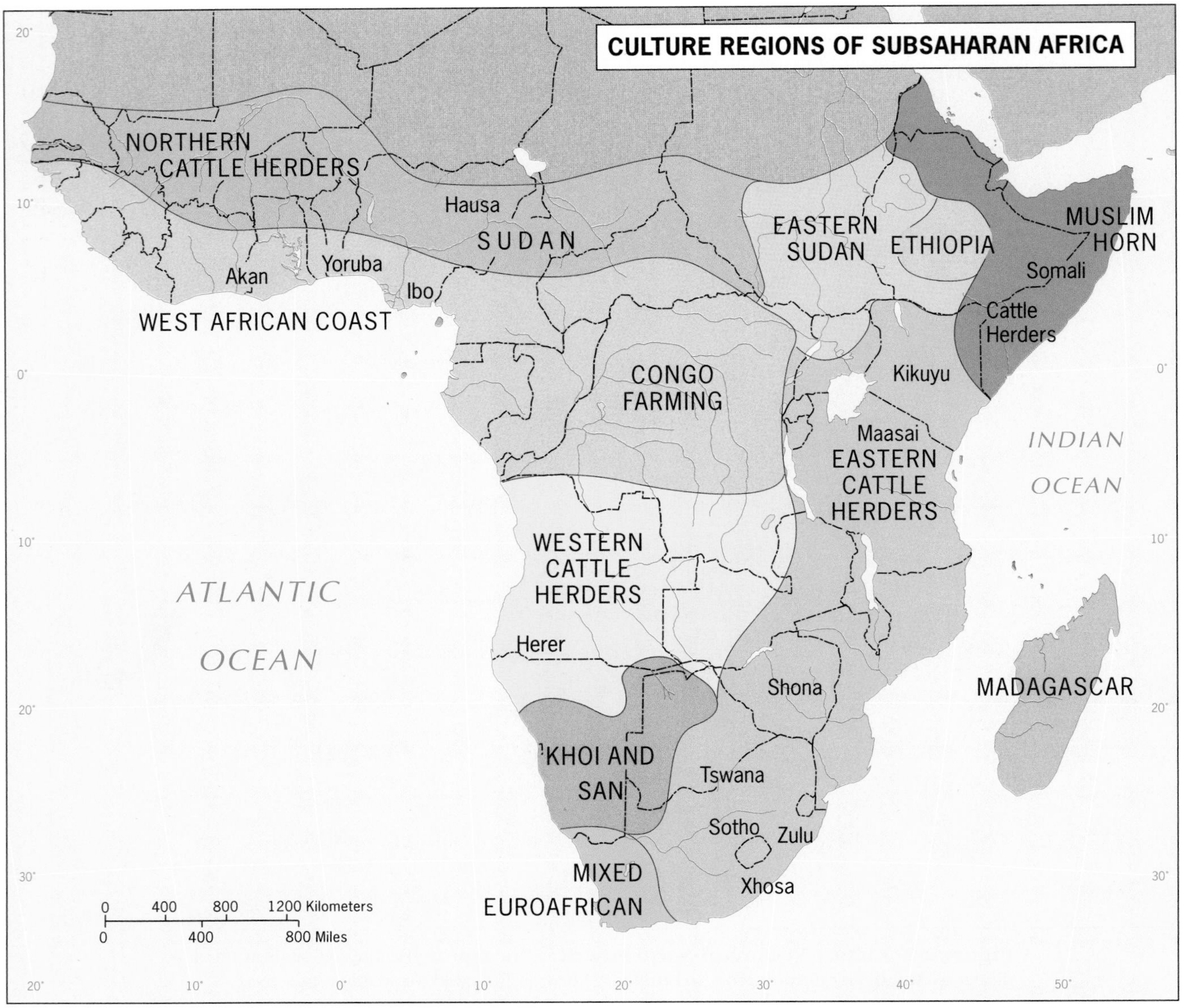

Figure 2-2 Culture Regions of Subsaharan Africa. Generalized regionalization of indigenous cultures in mainland Africa south of the Sahara.

In the remainder of this chapter, we focus on these areas in more detail.

The Cultural Landscape

The cultures that occupy or influence an area leave their imprint on the landscape. Often, a single scene, a photograph or picture, can reveal the cultural milieu in which it was made. The architecture, the mode of dress of the people, the means of transportation, and perhaps the goods being carried—all reveal a distinctive cultural environment.

The people of any particular culture transform their living space by building structures on it, creating lines of contact and communication, tilling the land, and channeling the water. There are a few exceptions: nomadic peoples may leave a minimum of permanent evidence on the land, and some peoples living in desert margins (such as the few remaining San clans) and in tropical forest zones (Pygmy groups) do not greatly alter their natural environment. However, most of the time there is change: asphalt roads, irrigation canals, terraced hillslopes.

This composite of artificial features is the ***cultural landscape***, a term that came into general use in geography in the 1920s. The geographer whose name is still most closely identified with this concept is University of California at Berkeley Professor Carl Sauer. In 1927 Sauer wrote an article entitled "Recent Developments in Cultural Geography," in which he argued that cultural landscapes are comprised of the "forms superimposed on the physical landscape" by human activity. However, when human activities change the physical or natural landscape, the physical landscape itself can take on cultural properties. For example, a dam built in the upper course of a river can affect the whole character of the river downstream, even hundreds of miles away. It can alter the strength of the river's flow and the rate of deposition of sediments in a delta. As such, perhaps the best definition of cultural landscape is the broadest: that the cultural landscape includes all identifiably human-induced changes in the natural landscape, changes that involve the surface as well as the biosphere.

The concept of cultural landscape takes on a practical aspect when an area has been inhabited—and transformed—by a succession of culture groups, each of which leaves a lasting imprint. As successive occupiers arrive, they bring their own technological and cultural traditions—and transform the landscape accordingly. Yet successive occupiers can also be influenced by what they find when they arrive—and leave some of it in place. In 1929, Derwent Wittlesey proposed the term ***sequent occupance*** to refer to such cultural succession and its lasting imprint.

The Tanzanian city of Dar es Salaam provides an interesting urban example of this process. Its site was first chosen for settlement by Arabs from Zanzibar who sought a mainland retreat. Next it was selected by the German colonizers as a capital for their East African domain, and it was given a German layout and architectural imprint. After World War I, when the Germans were ousted, a British administration took over and the city began yet another period of transformation. A large Asian population created a zone of three- and four-story apartment houses, which look as if they had been transplanted from Bombay. Then, in the early 1960s, Dar es Salaam became the capital of newly independent Tanzania. Thus, the city experienced four stages of cultural dominance in less than one century, and each stage of the sequence remains imprinted in the cultural landscape.

The cultural landscape, then, can be seen as a kind of text offering clues into the cultural practices and priorities of its various occupiers. Some cases do not offer the relatively distinct phases of occupance that characterize the Dar es Salaam example, however, and cultural influences from outside often complicate the picture. Hence, rather than emphasizing distinct phases of settlement, geographers now tend to think more in terms of processes of cultural intermixing in particular places—and the transitions over time they produce. Nonetheless, it is still useful to think about dominant influences at particular times as emphasized in the sequent occupance concept, for these often have the most visible impact on an area.

The concrete properties of a cultural landscape can be observed and recorded with relative ease. Take, for example, the urban "townscape" (a prominent element of the overall cultural landscape), and compare a major U.S. city with, say, a leading Japanese city. Visual representations would quickly reveal the differences, of course, but so would maps of the two urban places. The U.S. central city, with its rectangular layout of the central business district (CBD) and its far-flung, sprawling suburbs, contrasts sharply with the clustered, space-conserving Japanese city (Fig. 2-3). Again, the subdivision and ownership of American farmland, represented on a map, looks unmistakably different from that of a traditional African rural area, with its irregular, often tiny patches of land surrounding a village. These things help to shape the personality of a region.

Still, the whole of a cultural landscape can never be represented on a map. A cultural landscape consists of buildings and roads and fields and more, but it also has an intangible quality, an "atmosphere," which is often so easy to perceive and yet so difficult to define. The smells and sights and sounds of a traditional African market are unmistakable, but try to record those qualities on maps or in some other way for comparative study! A challenge for anyone interested in place is to appreciate its less tangible characteristics that give it personality—its visual appearance, its noises and odors, and even its pace of life.

From the field notes

"The Atlantic-coast city of Bergen, Norway, displayed the Norse cultural landscape more comprehensively, it seemed, than any other Norwegian city, including Oslo. The high-relief site of Bergen creates great vistas, but also long shadows: windows are large to let in maximum light. Red-tiled roofs are pitched steeply to enhance runoff and inhibit snow accumulation; streets are narrow and houses clustered, conserving warmth."

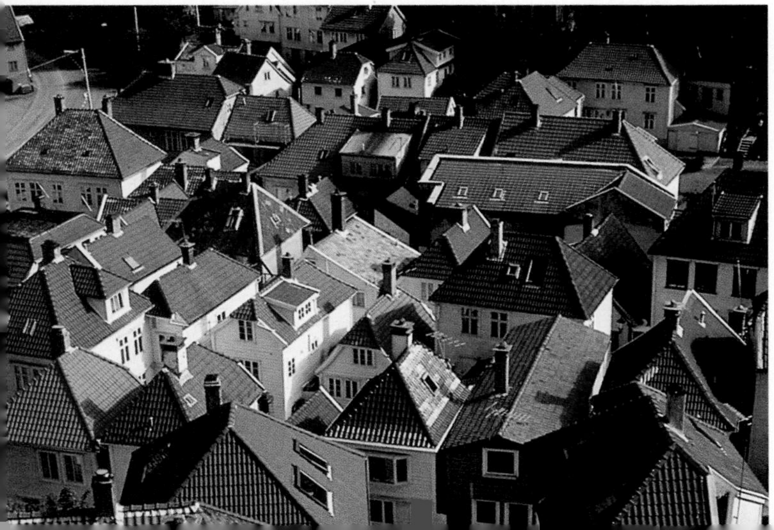

Culture Hearths

For as long as human communities have existed on Earth, there have been places where people have thrived, where invention and effort have resulted in an increase in

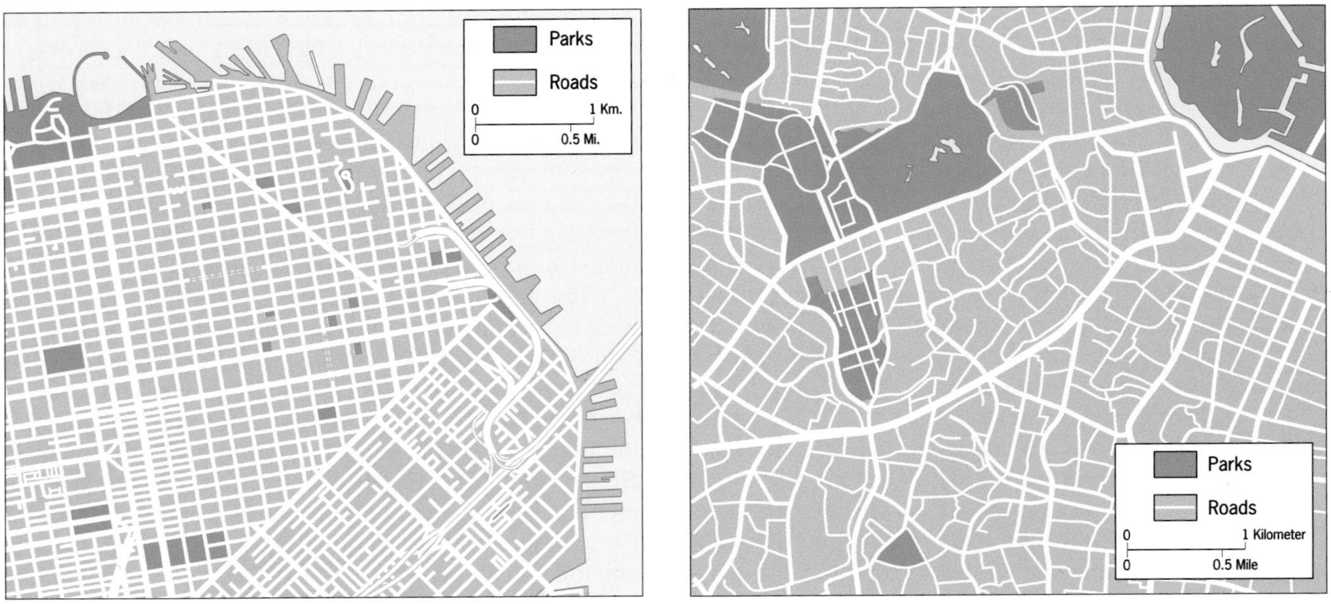

SAN FRANCISCO

TOKYO

Figure 2-3 San Francisco and Tokyo Maps. Both San Francisco and Tokyo are laid out on a comparatively high-relief urban topography, but their street patterns differ markedly. As a result, moving around in these two cities is quite different.

numbers, growing strength, comparative stability, and technological development. Conversely, there have been areas where this has not occurred. The areas where success and progress prevailed were the places where the first large clusters of human population developed, both because of sustained natural increase and because other people were attracted to those places. The increasing numbers of people led to the development of new ways to exploit locally available resources and gain power over resources located farther away. Progress was made in farming techniques and, consequently, in crop yields. Settlements could expand. Societies grew more complex, and there were people who could afford to spend time not merely in subsistence activities, but in such pursuits as politics and the arts. The circulation of goods and ideas intensified. Traditions developed, along with ways of life that set an example for people in other places, far and near. These areas were humanity's early ***culture hearths***—the sources of civilization, outward from which radiated the ideas, innovations, and ideologies that would change the world beyond.

Culture hearths should be viewed in the context of time as well as space. Long before human communities began to depend on cultivated crops or domesticated animals, culture hearths developed in response to the discovery and development of a tool or weapon that made subsistence easier or more efficient. Fishing techniques improved, and waterside communities prospered and grew. Thus the Inuit people, with their early and inventive adaptation to their frigid, watery environment, developed a culture hearth, just as the ancient Mesopotamians did. The nomadic Maasai and their remarkable cattle-based culture still inhabit the region in which they developed their culture hearth.

Some culture hearths, therefore, remain comparatively isolated and self-contained, whereas others have an impact far beyond their bounds. When the innovation of agriculture was added to the culture complexes that already existed in the zone of the Fertile Crescent, it soon diffused to areas where it was not yet practiced and affected other culture complexes far and wide. In the culture hearth itself, the practice of cultivation led to the evolution of an infinitely more elaborate civilization, where one innovation followed another.

Thus it is appropriate to distinguish between culture hearths, thousands of which have evolved across the Earth from the Inuit Arctic to Maori New Zealand, and the source areas of ***civilizations***. These latter also began as culture hearths, but their growth and development had a wider, sometimes global impact. Early culture hearths (Fig. 2-4) developed in Southwest Asia and North Africa, South and Southeast Asia, and East Asia in the valleys and basins of the great river systems. The Middle and South American culture hearths evolved thousands of years later, not in river valleys but in highlands. The West African culture hearth emerged later still, strongly influenced by innovations made by the peoples of the Nile Valley and Southwest Asia.

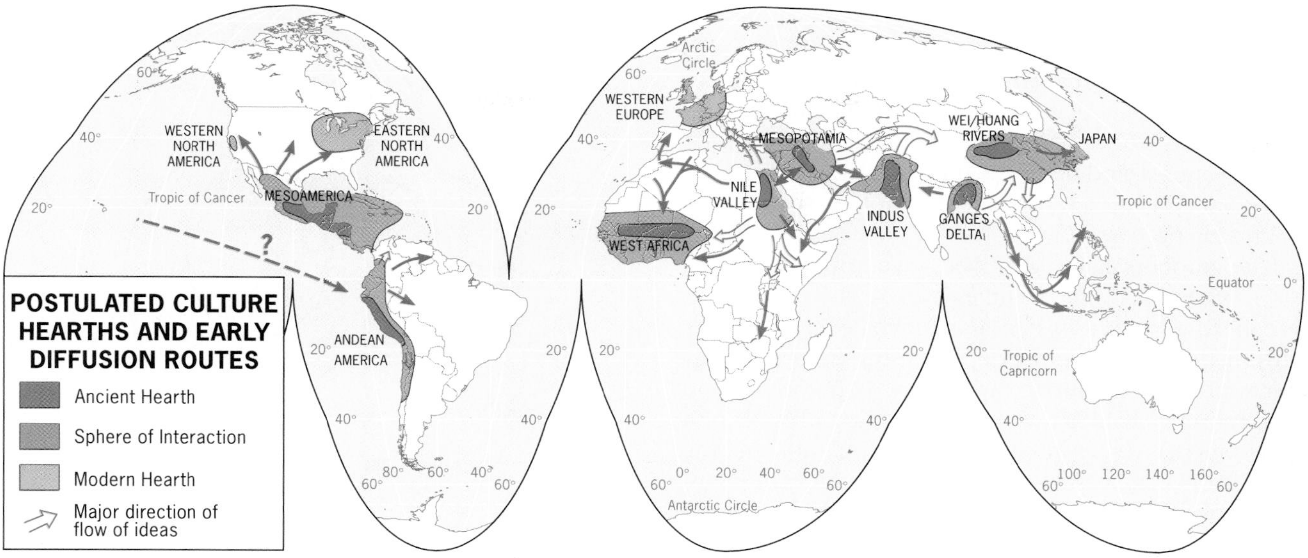

Figure 2-4 Postulated Culture Hearths and Early Diffusion Routes. Ancient and modern culture hearths. The ancient hearths and their diffusion routes are speculative; today's industrial and technological culture hearths are superimposed. *Source:* From authors' sketch.

It is important to note that all the ancient culture hearths shown in Figure 2-4 achieved breakthroughs in agriculture. Irrigation techniques, crop domestication, planting, seeding and weeding methods, harvesting, storage, and distribution systems all progressed, and individual cultures achieved remarkable adaptations in order to maximize the opportunities offered by their environment.

Shifts in Culture Hearths The locations and nature of the cultural innovations of recent centuries are very different. With the onset of the Industrial Revolution, the world was transformed by the spread of innovations from new hearths, new sources of invention and diffusion. The ancient agricultural and urban revolutions were followed, millennia later, by equally consequential industrial and technological revolutions that created totally new cultural landscapes. These revolutions were (and are) centered in Europe, North America, and East Asia (Fig. 2-4). And one of the great—and not entirely answered—geographic questions is why there, as opposed to somewhere else.

Think of the ways in which our daily lives have been changed by the inventions made in these hearths of innovation and how effective modern dissemination systems are. Also note that in the nineteenth century, Western Europe was the dominant industrial hearth—a position that was taken over by the United States during the twentieth century. More recently Japan emerged as a major industrial hearth, and despite current economic difficulties other East Asian industrial-technological giants have sprung up as well. Will the next century witness yet another shift?

Cultural Diffusion

The ancient culture hearths were focal points of innovation and invention; they were sources of ideas and stimuli. From these source areas, newly invented techniques, tools, instruments, and ideas about ways of doing things radiated outward, carried by caravans and armies, merchant mariners, teachers, and clergy. Some of the innovations that eventually reached distant peoples were quickly adopted and often modified or refined; others fell on barren ground.

The process of dissemination, the spread of an idea or innovation from its source area to other cultures, is known as ***cultural diffusion***. Today the great majority of the world's cultures are the products of innumerable ideas and innovations that have arrived in an endless, centuries-long stream. Often it is possible to isolate and trace the origin, route, and timing of the adoption of a particular innovation. The phenomenon of ***diffusion*** is therefore an essential part of the study of cultural geography.

The appearance of a particular technique or device in widely separated areas does not necessarily prove that diffusion occurred. Various cultures in parts of Asia, Africa, and the Americas developed methods of irrigation, learned to domesticate animals and plants, and reached other achievements through ***independent invention***. Moreover, a major invention did not guarantee rapid diffusion and adoption everywhere. The wheel, surely a momentous invention, was not adopted in Egypt until 20 centuries after its introduction in nearby Mesopotamia.

Diffusion occurs through the movement of people, goods, or ideas. Carl Sauer focused attention on this process in ***Agricultural Origins and Dispersals*** (1952), which was published at about the same time that the pioneering diffusion research by the Swedish geographer Torsten Hägerstrand began to appear in print. This fascinating research attracted many geographers to the study of diffusion processes.

Geographers have identified several different processes whereby diffusion takes place. The differences have to do with various conditions: whatever it is that is diffusing through a population, the distribution and character of that population, the distances involved, and much more. Consider two examples: the diffusion of a disease such as Asian "flu" through a population and the diffusion of fax machines. The first case involves involuntary exposure and the second voluntary adoption. Both, however, are manifestations of diffusion processes.

Expansion Diffusion Geographers classify diffusion processes into two broad categories: expansion diffusion and relocation diffusion. In the case of ***expansion diffusion***, an innovation or idea develops in a source area and remains strong there while also spreading outward. Later, for example, we will study the spread of Islam from its hearth on the Arabian Peninsula to Egypt and North Africa, through Southwest Asia, and into West Africa. This is a case of expansion diffusion. If we were to draw a series of maps of the Islamic faithful at 50-year intervals beginning in A.D. 620, the area of adoption of the Muslim religion would be larger in every successive period. Expansion diffusion thus is a very appropriate term (Fig. 2-5).

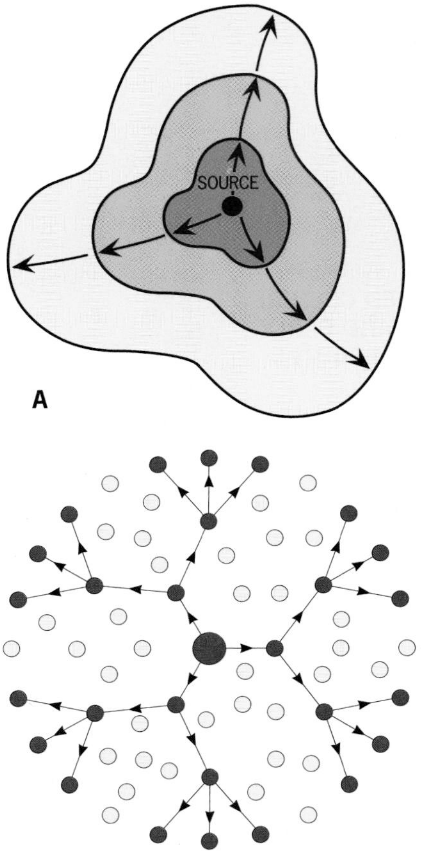

A

B

Figure 2-5 Types of Diffusion. Schematic representation of spatial flows associated with expansion diffusion (A) and hierarchical diffusion (B).

Expansion diffusion takes several forms. The spread of Islam is an example of ***contagious diffusion***, a form of expansion diffusion in which nearly all adjacent individuals are affected. A disease can spread in this way, infecting almost everyone in a population (although not everyone may show symptoms of the disease).

However, an idea (or a disease, for that matter) may not always spread throughout a fixed population. For example, the spread of AIDS in the United States has not affected everyone in the population. Instead, it has affected particularly vulnerable groups, leapfrogging over wide areas and appearing on maps as clusters in distantly separated cities. This represents another kind of expansion diffusion, ***hierarchical diffusion***, in which the main channel of diffusion is some segment of those who are susceptible to (or adopting) what is being diffused. In the case of the diffusion of AIDS, the hierarchy is the urban structure in the United States; the sizes of cities, towns, and villages are reflected in the clusters of infected people.

Hierarchical diffusion is also illustrated by the spread of the use of fax machines. Here the hierarchy is determined by the equipment's affordability and the potential users' perception of need. Again, the pattern is likely to show an urban-based order. But not all innovations are adopted in cities and towns. The diffusion pattern for an improved piece of farm machinery will be quite different.

A third form of expansion diffusion is ***stimulus diffusion***. Not all ideas can be readily and directly adopted by a receiving population; some are simply too vague, too unattainable, too different, or too impractical for immediate adoption. But this does not mean that such ideas have no impact at all. They may indirectly promote local experimentation and eventual changes in ways of doing things. For example, the diffusion of mass-produced food items in the late twentieth century—pushed by multinational retailers—led to the introduction of the hamburger to India. Yet the Hindu prohibition on the consumption of beef presented a cultural obstacle to the adoption of this food item. However, retailers began selling burgers made of vegetable products—an adaptation that was stimulated by the diffusion of the hamburger but that took on a new form in the cultural context to which it diffused.

Relocation Diffusion As noted earlier, expansion diffusion takes place through populations that are stable and fixed. It is the innovation, the idea, or the disease that does the moving. ***Relocation diffusion***, in contrast, involves the actual movement of individuals who have already adopted the idea or innovation, and who carry it to a new, perhaps distant, locale, where they proceed to disseminate it.

When cultures make contact through relocation diffusion, one culture often comes to dominate another. In the process, the less dominant culture adopts elements of the cultural practices and ideas of the dominant culture. This process is known as ***acculturation***. In extreme cases, the adoption of cultural elements from the dominant culture can be so complete that the two cultures become indistinguishable. This is known as ***assimilation***. Yet acculturation, and even assimilation, are not necessarily one-way streets; dominant cultures often adopt aspects of the latter's culture even as their own culture has a disproportionate influence.

After Spanish invaders overthrew the Aztec kingdom, Spanish culture began to prevail: towns were transformed, a new religious order was introduced, and new crops were planted. Acculturation proceeded, but most people maintained significant elements of their own culture, so assimilation did not occur. But the peoples of Latin America were not the only ones affected by this encounter. Spanish culture also absorbed Aztec influences. Aztec motifs pervaded Spanish architecture, Aztec crops were transplanted to Iberia, and Spaniards began to wear clothing that reflected Aztec influences.

Relocation diffusion has usually produced the type of cultural contact where one culture has dominated another. Occasionally there is contact between culture complexes that are more nearly equal in numbers, strength, and complexity. In such cases, a genuine exchange follows, in which both cultures function as sources and adopters. This process is referred to as ***transculturation***.

A particular form of relocation diffusion is known as ***migrant diffusion***. There are times when an innovation originates somewhere and enjoys strong, but brief, adoption there. By the time it reaches distant places, it has already lost its strength at the place where it started. The diffusion map thus would show a continuous outward shift to new adopters, but there would be no stable core area. Some diseases, such as milder influenza pandemics, display this process as well. By the time these reach North America and Europe, they already have faded away in China, so that the diffusion pattern is one of migrant, rather than contagious, diffusion.

These are some of the leading processes of diffusion and the factors involved. However, there are also forces that can work against diffusion and the adoption of new ideas and innovations. One of these is distance; another is time. The farther it is from its source, the less likely an innovation is to be adopted, and the "innovation waves" become weaker. Similarly, the acceptance of an innovation becomes less likely the longer it takes to reach its potential adopters. In combination, time and distance cause ***time-distance decay*** in the diffusion process.

Cultural barriers can also work against diffusion. Certain innovations, ideas, or practices are not acceptable or adoptable in particular cultures because of prevailing attitudes or even taboos. Prohibitions against alcoholic beverages, as well as certain forms of meat, fish, and other foods, have restricted their consumption. Cultural barriers against other practices, such as the use of contraceptives, also have inhibited diffusion processes. Cultural barriers can pose powerful obstacles to the spread of ideas as well as artifacts.

Cultural Perception

Although architecture—even simple dwellings in remote forests or mountains—dominates the cultural landscape, other aspects of daily life also contribute to the character of places. One of those aspects is the pace of life as it is lived in a given area. During the 1960s, when thousands of students from African countries came to study in the United States, a geography professor conducted a survey of their perceptions of this country. Among the top five impressions was a variation of the following: "People and things move so fast here! Everyone seems to be running from one appointment to the next!"

The pace of life is not something that can be easily mapped, but it is an important aspect of place. Courtesy is another. A similar survey in Britain produced many references to the British habit of "queueing," or lining up neatly to await one's turn boarding a bus or paying a bill. Again, while tradition does not have the permanence of an architectural style, it is nonetheless part of the cultural character of places. Such intangible elements help define the personality of a region. They also can contribute to cultural conflict. Violation of such traditions by outsiders can even lead to strife.

Perceptual Regions How is the cultural landscape perceived? In Chapter 1, we noted that people of all cultures have spatial memories, or mental maps, that influence their perception. Thus, from the viewpoint of the United States, many countries appear to be technologically unsophisticated and poor. But from the perspective of those countries, U.S. society may seem overdeveloped and wasteful. So it is with culture and the cultural landscape. Our perceptions of our own community and culture may differ quite sharply from those of people in other cultures. ***Perceptual regions*** are intellectual constructs designed to help us understand the nature and distribution of phenomena in human geography. Geographers do not agree entirely on their properties, but they do concur that we all have impressions and images of various regions and cultures. These perceptions are based on our accumulated knowledge about such regions and cultures. The natural environment, too, is part of this inventory. Think of Swiss culture, and the image of a single Alpine environment may come to mind, even though, in fact, Swiss culture is divided into several distinct regions by language, religion, and tradition, and the majority of Swiss citizens today do not live in such environments.

Although we can easily explain in general terms how we perceive a culture region, it is much more difficult to put our impressions on a map. For example, consider the ***Mid-Atlantic Region***. Weather forecasters refer to the "Mid-Atlantic area" or the "Mid-Atlantic States" as they divide their maps into manageable pieces. But where is this Mid-Atlantic Region? If Maryland and Delaware are part of it, then eastern Pennsylvania is, too. But where across Pennsylvania lies the boundary of this partly cultural, partly physical region, and on what basis can it be drawn? There is no single best answer (Fig. 2-6).

Again, we all have a mental map of the South as a culture region of the United States. But if you drive southward from, say, Pittsburgh or Detroit, you will not pass a specific place where you enter this perceptual region. You will note features in the cultural landscape that you perceive to be associated with the South, and at some stage of the trip they will begin to dominate the area to such a degree that you will say, "I am really in the South now." This may result from a combination of features of the region's material as well as nonmaterial culture: the form of houses and their porches, items on a roadside restaurant menu (grits, for example), a local radio station's music, the sound of accents that you perceive to be Southern, a succession of Baptist churches in a town along the way. These combined impressions become part of your overall perception of the South as a region.

Figure 2-6 Mid-Atlantic Folk-Culture Region. One delimitation of a Mid-Atlantic culture region. *Source:* H. Glassie, *Pattern in the Material Folk Culture of the Eastern United States*. Philadelphia: University of Pennsylvania Press, 1968, p. 39.

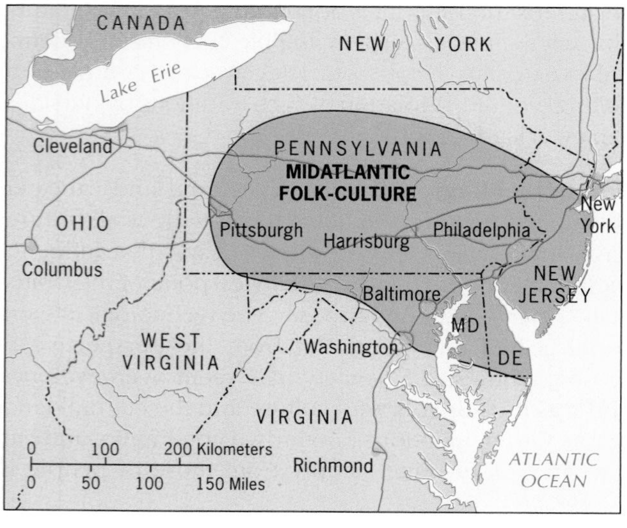

Perceptual regions can be studied at a variety of levels. The 12 world geographic realms that form the basis of many courses in world regional geography are perceptual units at the smallest of scales; at the opposite, largest end of the scale would be a tiny region defined by one of the remaining communities of Amish people in the United States. Quite possibly, our perceptions are weakest and least accurate at each end of the scale: at the small scale because so much information must be synthesized that images become distorted, and at the large scale because most diminutive cultures within cultures are not well-defined parts of our general spatial knowledge. An interesting example of regional definition at an intermediate scale is found in an article by Terry Jordan entitled "Perceptual Regions in Texas" (1978). Like all of us, Texans use regional-cultural names for various parts of their state, and in this article Jordan identifies where names such as Panhandle, Gulf Coast, Permian Basin, and Metroplex actually apply (Fig. 2-7).

Perceptual Regions in the United States The cultural geographer Wilbur Zelinsky tackled the enormous, complex task of defining and delimiting the perceptual regions of the United States and southern Canada. In an article entitled "North America's Vernacular Regions" (1980), he identified 12 major perceptual regions on a series of maps. Figure 2-8 summarizes these regions. Of necessity, it shows overlaps between certain units. For example, the more general term "the West" obviously incorporates more specific regions, such as the Pacific Region and part of the Northwest.

The problem of defining and delimiting perceptual regions can be approached in several ways. One is to conduct interviews in which people residing within as well as outside a region are asked to respond to questions about their home and cultural environment. Zelinsky used a different technique; he analyzed the telephone directories of 276 metropolitan areas in the United States and Canada, noting the frequencies with which businesses and other enterprises use regional or locational terms (such as "Southern Printing Company") in their listings. The resulting maps show a close similarity between these perceptual regions and culture regions identified by geographers.

Regional Identity Culture regions also represent an emotional commitment. Among the perceptual regions shown in Figure 2-8, one, the South, is unlike any of the others. Even today, five generations after the Civil War,

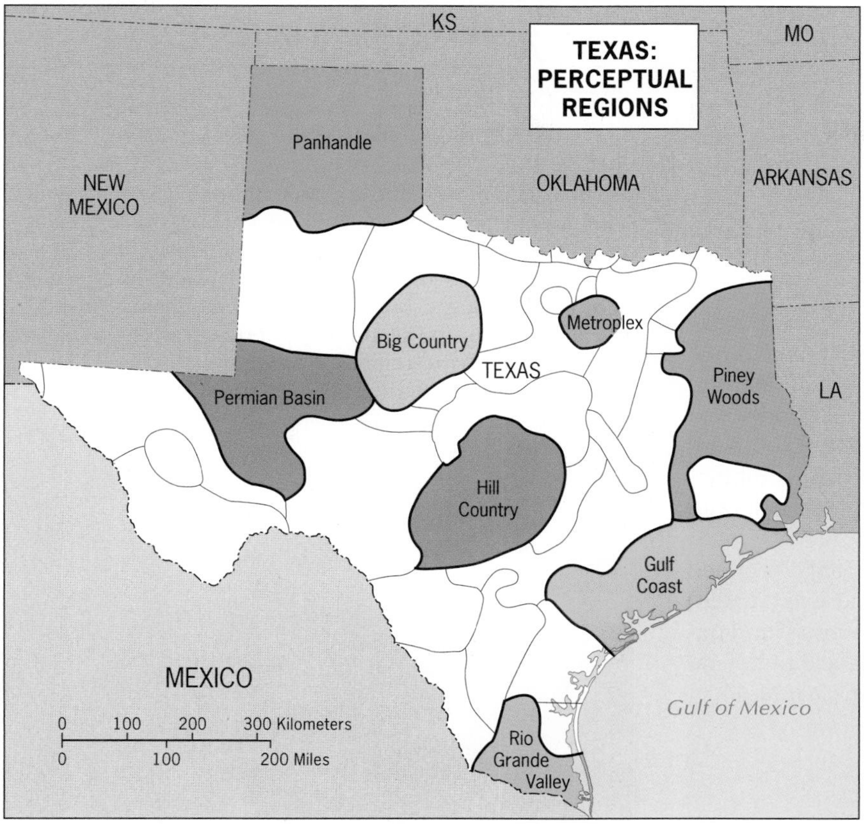

Figure 2-7 Perceptual Regions of Texas. Prominent perceptual regions in Texas. *Source:* T. G. Jordan, "Perceptual Regions in Texas." *Geographical Review* 68, 1978, p. 295.

the Confederate flag still evokes regional sentiments; the "Bible belt" still has some meaning; and the South's unique position among American regions is entrenched in songs and dialects. Certainly a "New South" has emerged over the past several decades, forged by Hispanic immigration, urbanization, Sunbelt movements, and other processes. But the South—especially the rural South—continues to carry imprints of a material culture long past. Its legacy of nonmaterial culture is equally strong, preserved in language, religion, music, food preferences, and other traditions and customs.

Such cultural attributes give a certain social atmosphere to the region, an atmosphere that is appreciated by many of its residents and is sometimes advertised as

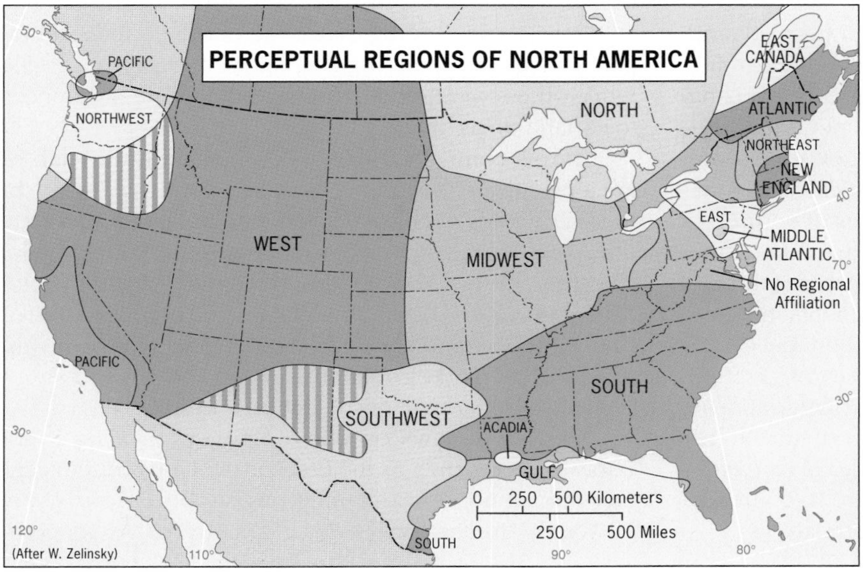

Figure 2-8 Perceptual Regions of North America *Source:* W. Zelinsky, "North America's Vernacular Regions," *Annals of the AAG*, 1980, p. 14.

an attraction for potential visitors. "Experience the South's warmth, courtesy, and pace of life," said one such commercial, which portrayed a sun-drenched seaside landscape, a bowing host, and a couple strolling along a palm-lined path. Such images may or may not represent the perceptions of most inhabitants of the region, but few Southerners would object to publicity of this kind.

The South has its vigorous supporters and defenders, and occasionally a politician uses its embattled history to arouse racial antagonism. But today the South is so multifaceted, so diverse, so vigorous, and so interconnected with the rest of the United States that its regional identity is much more complicated than traditional images suggest. This serves as an important reminder that perceptual regions are not static. Images of the South are rapidly changing, and no identifiable group, or combination of groups, clings to the idea that the region should secede from the United States.

Elsewhere, however, discrete and strongly defined culture regions have become political (and even actual) battlegrounds. Emotional attachments to territory and tradition can run so strong that they supersede feelings of national (state) identity, an issue we take up in Chapter 16.

Cultural Environments

The relationships between human societies and the natural environment are complex. Environment affects society in countless ways, some of which are reflected by the different types of houses people build, the diverse crops they grow, and the kinds of livestock they can maintain. Societies modify their natural environments in ways that range from slight to severe. In this book we will frequently encounter evidence of human impact on natural environments. Public art and monumental architecture are parts of the cultural landscape, but so are pollution-belching smokestacks, contaminant-oozing landfills, and sludge-clogged streams.

But there is another question involving society and environment. Human cultures exist in a long-term accommodation with their physical environments, seizing opportunities presented by those environments and suffering from the limitations and extremes they sometimes impose. No culture, no matter how sophisticated technologically, can completely escape the forces of nature, as can be seen in the annual list of tornado casualties in the United States. But some cultures have overcome the apparent limitations of their natural environments more effectively than others. How can this be explained?

In the 1940s, the geographer Harlan Barrows argued that this is a central question for geographers, and he proposed the term ***cultural ecology*** to identify the arena in which the necessary research would take place. Actually, the whole issue of nature and culture had already taken center stage, albeit under a different heading.

From the field notes

"Looking down on Florence from above, what stands out are the symbols of church and state. And what symbols they are! The magnificent dome of the Cathedral was designed by one of the giants of the Italian Renaissance, Brunelleschi, whereas the Palazzo Vechio (the Old Palace) was clearly meant to reflect both the authority of local governmental leaders and the greatness to which they aspired. Here is a landscape created by and for humans. It evokes much more than the aesthetic preferences of the Italians. It provides a dramatic reminder of where power and money were concentrated in the evolving city."

Environmental Determinism Efforts to explain the achievements of certain cultures under particular environmental regimes had been going on for decades before Barrows tried to focus the debate. In fact, the fundamental questions were raised centuries earlier. The ancient Greeks, finding that some of the peoples subjugated by their expanding Empire were relatively docile while others were rebellious, attributed such differences to variations in climate.

In this connection, let us look again at the map of ancient culture hearths (Fig. 2-4). Note that many of these crucibles of cultural achievement lie in apparently unfavorable climatic zones such as deserts. Nonetheless, 23 centuries ago, Aristotle described the peoples of cold, distant Europe as being "full of spirit . . . but incapable of ruling others" and those of Asia (by which he meant modern-day Turkey) as "intelligent and inventive . . . [but] always in a state of subjection and slavery."

Aristotle's views on this topic were nothing if not durable. As recently as the first half of the twentieth century, similar notions still had strong support. Here is how Ellsworth Huntington (1876–1947), an early-twentieth-century geographer, stated this idea in ***Principles of Human Geography***, published in 1940:

> The well-known contrast between the energetic people of the most progressive parts of the temperate zone and the inert inhabitants of the tropics and even of intermediate regions, such as Persia, is largely due to climate . . . the people of the cyclonic regions rank so far above those of the other parts of the world that they are the natural leaders.

The doctrine expressed by these statements is referred to as environmentalism or, more precisely, ***environmental determinism***. It holds that human behavior, individually and collectively, is strongly affected by—even controlled or determined by—the physical environment. It suggests that climate is the critical factor. Yet what constitutes an "ideal" climate lies in the eyes of the beholder. For Aristotle, it seems to have been the climate of Greece. Through the eyes of more recent commentators from Western Europe and North America, the climates most suited to progress and productiveness in culture, politics, and technology are (you guessed it) those of Western Europe and the northeastern United States.

For a time, some geographers attempted to explain the distribution of centers of culture in terms of the "dictating environment." Quite soon, however, some geographers doubted whether these sweeping generalizations were valid. They recognized exceptions to the environmentalists' postulations (e.g., the Maya civilization in Mesoamerica arose under tropical conditions) and argued that humanity was capable of much more than merely adapting to the natural environment. As for the supposed "efficiency" produced by the climate of Western Europe, this idea ignored the fact that for millennia the most highly developed civilizations were found outside of Western Europe (North Africa, Southeast Asia, East Asia, etc.). Surely it was best not to base "laws" of environmental determinism on inadequate data in the face of apparently contradictory evidence.

Such arguments helped guide the search for answers to questions about the relationships between human society and the natural environment in different directions, but for several decades some geographers still held to the environmentalist position. In this connection it is interesting to read S. F. Markham's ***Climate and the Energy of Nations*** (1947). Markham thought that he could detect in the migration of the center of power in the Mediterranean (from Egypt to Greece to Rome and onward) the changing climates of that part of Europe during several thousand years of glacial retreat. Markham saw the northward movement of isotherms—lines connecting points of equal temperature values—as a key factor in the shifting centers of power in the Ancient World.

Geographers grew increasingly cautious about such speculative notions, however, and they began asking new questions about societal-environmental relationships. If generalizations were to be made, they felt they ought to arise from detailed, carefully designed research. Everyone agrees that the natural environment affects human activity in some ways, but people are the decision makers and the modifiers—not the slaves of environmental forces. And the decisions people make about their environment are influenced by culture.

Reactions to environmentalism produced counterarguments. An approach known as ***possibilism*** emerged—espoused by geographers who argued that the natural environment merely serves to limit the range of choices available to a culture. The choices that a society makes depend on its members' requirements and the technology available to them. The doctrine of possibilism became increasingly accepted, and environmental determinism became increasingly discredited—at least within geography. For those who have thought less carefully about the human–environment dynamic, environmentalism continues to hold an allure, leading to some highly questionable generalizations about the impact of the environment on humans.

Even possibilism has its limitations, for it encourages a line of inquiry that starts with the physical environment and asks what it allows. Yet human cultures have frequently pushed the boundaries of what was once thought to be environmentally possible by virtue of their own ideas and ingenuity. Moreover, in the interconnected, technologically dependent world we live in today, it is possible to do many things that are seemingly at odds with the local environment. Hence, research today tends to focus on how and why humans have altered the environment, and the sustainability of their practices. And in the process the perspectives of cultural ecology have been supplemented by those of ***political ecology***—an area of inquiry fundamentally concerned with the environmental consequences of dominant political-economic arrangements and understandings.

The fundamental point is that human societies are sufficiently diverse and the human will is too powerful to be the mere objects of nature's designs. We cannot escape the environmental contexts in which we are situated—nor should we try if the environmental degradation that has followed such efforts is any guide. Indeed, the effort to avoid any semblance of determinism has perhaps overly discouraged consideration of the impact of the environment on humans. What is clear, however, is that any inquiry that does not give credence to the extraordinary power of the intertwined domains of culture, politics, and economy in human–environment relations embarks on a path that has consistently been shown to be simplistic, if not fundamentally wrong.

◆ KEY TERMS ◆

acculturation
assimilation
civilization
contagious diffusion
cultural diffusion
cultural landscape
culture
culture complex
culture hearth
culture realm
culture region
culture system
culture trait
diffusion
environmental determinism
expansion diffusion
geographic realm
geographic region
hierarchical diffusion
independent invention
migrant diffusion
perceptual region
political ecology
possibilism
relocation diffusion
sequent occupance
stimulus diffusion
transculturation

◆ APPLYING GEOGRAPHIC KNOWLEDGE ◆

1. During a certain week some years ago, several people in a village near a large East Asian city got the flu. Within days, hundreds of people in the city came down with it. In the surrounding countryside, numerous villagers in an ever-widening area became ill. Meanwhile, this Asian flu appeared in such cities as San Francisco, New York, London, and Moscow. What processes spreading this malady were at work in China and worldwide, and how do they differ? If you were unable to be immunized, how would you use your knowledge of geography to best protect yourself?

2. Ask a classmate to join you in a geographic experiment involving perceptual regions. The idea is to confirm, through a simple test, how regional perceptions can vary. First, agree on a U.S. or Canadian region to be defined; this should not be the region in which either of you resides. Next, take a blank outline map of North America (or at a larger scale, the United States or Canada), and separately draw a boundary that, in your view, delimits the region in question (such as the U.S. South or the Canadian West). Now compare your maps and, most importantly, explain why you defined the region as you did. What underlies your differing perceptions?

Chapter 3

The Earth as Humanity's Home

From the field notes

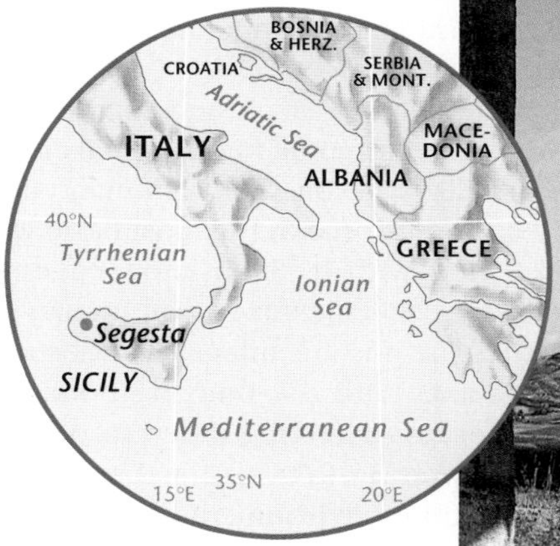

"Sicily held a special place in both the Greek and the Roman Empires because of its strategic location and agricultural potential. Yet the physical environment must have been an allure as well. How else can one explain the decision by the Greeks to build some of their most majestic temples on this island—including the Temple of Segesta? Set amid the rolling hills of southwestern Sicily, the temple almost seems to grow out of the physical landscape. Gazing through its massive columns to the vista beyond, I feel as if I can sense a synergy between the human and physical worlds, for what makes both the temple and the surrounding hills truly extraordinary is their mutual presence."

KEY POINTS

◆ **Environmental change is humanity's constant companion and is a key to understanding the geography of culture.**

◆ **Plant and animal domestication transformed human communities' ways of life and led to the first clustering of significant numbers of people in villages.**

◆ **State formation and urbanization transformed the world, beginning in the Fertile Crescent more than six millennia ago.**

◆ **The Earth is presently in the grip of a series of ice ages, but humanity is benefiting from a warm spell that has lasted about 12,000 years and has witnessed the formation of complex civilizations.**

◆ **Global terrain varies from flat plains to high and rugged mountains; the varying terrain forms are still reflected in the distribution of human population.**

◆ **Global climates range from humid equatorial to cold polar; humanity's technological capabilities notwithstanding, climate continues to influence global population patterns.**

The study of human geography is a search for answers to some of the most fascinating questions about humanity, behavior, and environment. What factors helped to fuel and sustain conflicts between ethnic groups? How did food supply catch up with population growth when the threat of mass starvation seemed inescapable? Why are socioeconomic differences so great from place to place—and why are they so intractable? Such questions range from the global to the local, from national cultures to village life.

Questions such as these raise a myriad of political, economic, and social issues, but each of them is also tied in some fundamental way to the environment. Concerns over access to water are of great importance in the conflict between the Palestinians and the Israelis. The impact of biotechnology on hunger has been so great because new hybrid, high-yielding seed varieties are suited to environments in places like India with large concentrations of people. In countries as diverse as Poland and Indonesia, regions of environmental devastation are also regions of acute poverty. All of these examples show that critical issues in human geography require some understanding of the physical-environmental context in which humans live. The better we know the physical geography of our planet, the better we are able to understand its human patterns and processes.

To provide a foundation for such understanding, in Chapter 3 our aim is to define some fundamental characteristics of the physical stage on which human action takes place and to consider some of the most basic ways humans have interacted with it. Such knowledge will help us appreciate the challenges faced by human cultures now and in the past, the advantages and obstacles experienced by migrants, and the unifying bonds—as well as the divisive forces—affecting different peoples. We will return in Chapter 33 to a matter that must be kept in mind here: natural environments are not static but change over time. Only in recent years have scientists become fully aware of the dimensions of this change. In the process, our understanding of the emergence of humanity and the patterns of civilization has been altered. ◆

◆ THE CHANGING EARTH

From the surface of the Moon, our Earth, as seen by the first lunar astronauts, was a pearl of bright colors in a black sky. Great swirls of white clouds partly veiled blue oceans and brown-gray continents. Emerald-green patches of land drew the eye to the oases of life on Earth. The glistening white snows of the polar regions really did look like ice caps. It was a lesson in geography that no ordinary Earthling had ever had.

The photographs taken on that lunar mission have become commonplace. Again and again we see the Earth from space—in books and journals, in advertising, and on television and film. But what about the geography lesson? How well do we remember just how small our Earth really is, how thin that layer of clouds, how tiny those specks of life-giving green? Over 6 billion people depend on the air, water, and land of this small planet. The term ***spaceship earth*** came into use to signify the finiteness of these and other resources. However, the real meaning of this notion did not seem to strike home. The triumph of technology that sent the astronauts to the Moon was not followed by a victory on Earth. Weapons of mass destruction were manufactured in growing quantities, resource exploitation intensified, and air, water, and soil absorbed increasing amounts of pollutants, raising fears for the planet's environmental future.

From the Moon, the astronauts saw the Earth at a single instant in its 4.6-billion-year history. They saw an Earth on which the blue of the oceans was the dominant color because approximately 70 percent of the planet's surface is water. They saw landmasses colored gray and brown because more than 70 percent of the land surface is desert, steppe, rock, or otherwise sparsely vegetated. The swirls of clouds seemed thin because the atmosphere that envelops our planet is so shallow. The Earth was described as an oasis of life, but, as in any oasis, the environment is fragile and subject to damage and destruction.

What the astronauts could not see in that moment of revelation was the changeable nature of the Earth's environments. If they had stood on the Moon's surface just 20,000 years earlier (not long ago, given the age of our planet), they would have seen larger ice caps, huge ice sheets in North America and Eurasia, lower sea levels, and very different continental outlines. If they had been there 20 million years ago, the continents themselves would have been in locations quite different from those of today.

So what the astronauts saw was a still frame in a moving picture: the Earth at a moment in time. They saw an Earth with small ice caps and large oceans, continents with flooded margins, and an Earth warmer than it has been for much of the past 2 million years. During these past 2 million years, and for some time previously, the Earth has been in an ice age, referred to by physical geographers as the ***Late Cenozoic Ice Age***. During this ice age, the global temperature fell and rebounded repeatedly, causing the polar ice caps to expand and retract. During periods of glacial advance, ice sheets pushed relentlessly into lower latitudes, scouring the rocky surface and carrying millions of tons of debris as they expanded. In highlands, great glaciers filled the valleys, and the whole landscape was practically buried under ice and snow. These were frigid times, and the Earth's livable space was much reduced. Animals and plants migrated to warmer latitudes, but many, deprived of suitable environments, died out. Others managed to adjust and even thrive, and as a result the biological map changed continuously.

The environmental variations during the ice age strongly influenced humanity's emergence and dispersal across the planet. For example, current evidence indicates that humans, originating in Africa, reached Australia as long as 50,000 to 60,000 years ago. The major migration into North America, across the Bering Strait and via Alaska, occurred only about 13,000 years ago—not only a longer but also an environmentally much more difficult route, even in warmer times.

Holocene Humanity

Scientists refer to the most recent 12,000 years of Earth history as the ***Holocene epoch***, the warm phase that followed the latest advance of the ice. Just 20,000 years ago, when the Earth was frigid, sheets of ice (***glaciers***) covered almost all of Canada and much of the interior United States, reaching as far south as the Ohio River.

Although this Holocene epoch may not merit designation as a distinct geologic phase, since it may turn out to be just another warm spell between advances of the ice, it does deserve recognition because of its cultural-geographical characteristics. Compared to other geological epochs, which lasted millions of years, the Holocene began only about 12,000 years ago. Within that short time, however, humanity did what it had not done during previous ***interglaciations***. In the wake of the retreating ice and in the comfort of a warming planet, a tremendous drama began: plants and animals were domesticated, agriculture developed, and surpluses were stored for future use; villages grew larger, towns and cities emerged, and political organization became increasingly complex; inventions multiplied, and tools became more efficient. Certain communities thrived and expanded, sometimes at the expense of others. Religious ideas spread over increasingly large domains. The spiral leading toward states and empires, colonial realms, and global power struggles had begun.

Another spiral also began: that of population growth. No one knows how many people were living on Earth at the beginning of the Holocene epoch. Perhaps there were 4 million, possibly as many as 8 million. During the Holocene epoch, however, human population growth began—slowly at first, then ever faster—giving rise to a modern population that is many orders of magnitude larger than it was 10,000 years ago. Modern humanity is indeed the product of the Holocene.

During the Holocene the Earth changed as never before, not because of geologic forces (10,000 years is not long in geologic time) but because of the imprint of humanity. As we will see, that imprint has become stronger over time. Especially during the past two centuries, the Earth has been transformed by the expansion of the human population and the impact of human activities. Many of the changes occurred through human effort to make their world more habitable. Hillslopes were carefully terraced and made productive; wild, flood-prone rivers were controlled and their floodplains converted into fertile farmlands; land was reclaimed from the sea and made livable. However, the impacts of human-induced environmental change, especially during the twentieth century, have unfolded at an unprecedented rate, leading to ever more serious environmental problems. Soil erosion is more severe than ever. Rivers, lakes, and even parts of the oceans are polluted. Gases of many kinds are spewed into the atmosphere. Raw materials such as fuels and ores are used up at an ever faster rate. Our need to dispose of wastes (many of them hazardous or poisonous) has led to the contamination of drinking water and the fouling of the air we breathe. And as humanity and its activities expand, nature recedes. Many species of animals and plants are becoming extinct, and we may never know what role some of them might have played in sciences such as medicine and plant physiology.

◆ ORGANIZING HUMANITY

After numerous advances and recessions of Late Cenozoic Ice, the Holocene warm phase began in much the same way as preceding periods. Humans of the ***Paleolithic*** period (the earliest and longest stage of the ***Stone Age***, marking the period when simple stone tools were made and fire was used) lived in scattered groups and depended on hunting and gathering for their survival. As had happened before, the retreat of the ice expanded the amount of available living space and widened the range of environments open to the moving bands. There was plenty of wildlife to be hunted, fish to be caught, and edible plants and fruits to be gathered. There is evidence that goods (such as cured animal skins for clothing, flint, and obsidian weapons and tools) were traded. Nevertheless, a map of the human population of 12,000 years ago would show mostly small, isolated groups of people numbering perhaps 20 to 60 members, their cultures diverging as a result of contrasting ecological settings.

Although survival was the principal objective of those hunting-and-gathering communities, there was time for other things. From the cave-wall paintings of European Paleolithic groups, we have learned how and what they hunted, what kinds of weapons they used, and other aspects of their culture. In addition to art, there were local developments in language, religion, and customs (such as burial of the dead). Recent research shows that hunting (sometimes accompanied by burning of grassland or forest to drive herds toward the hunters) often went far beyond what the community needed, destroying many forest animals and altering the vegetation of plains. Something akin to the destruction of the present Amazon rainforest occurred as more numerous and efficient hunters exterminated entire species of animals in northern America, Eurasia, and Africa.

When the ***global warming*** began that drove back the glaciers that covered much of North America 18,000 years ago, there was little to foreshadow the momentous events soon to come. Humans still were living in small numbers from hunting and gathering; their control of fire had begun to have major impact on regional ecologies, but ecological change still was caused mainly by natural forces. Anthropologists report that some hunter-gatherer groups probably had started using plants in new ways. The notion that useful or sacred plants could be protected by pulling weeds away from them added a new dimension to food production. But since a patch of food-producing plants could not move with a migrating band, the idea of plant care is likely to have taken hold around stable, long-term settlements assured of a dependable supply of food from other sources.

Domestication of Plants

Simply caring for plants that yield desired products is not the same as ***plant domestication*** and organized, planned farming, but it was an important step in that direction. Human groups lived in widely diverse environments, and they learned to exploit them in diverse ways. The domestication of root crops, plants that grow as tubers in the tropics (such as manioc or cassava, yams, and sweet potatoes), is not the same as the sowing of seed for fields of barley or wheat under more temperate environments. So the domestication of plants took different paths in different places at different times—but this was a process unique to the Holocene; it was to transform patterns of human livelihood.

Where did plant domestication begin? Cultural geographer Carl Sauer, who spent a lifetime studying cultural origins and diffusion, suggested that southeastern Asia may have been the scene, more than 14,000 years ago, of the first domestication of tropical plants (Fig. 3-1). There, he believed, the combination of human settlements, forest margins, and freshwater streams may have given rise to the earliest planned cultivation of root crops (i.e., crops that are reproduced by cultivating either the roots or cuttings from the plants). A similar but later development may have taken place in northwestern South America.

The planned cultivation of seed plants (plants that are reproduced by cultivating seeds) is a more complex process, involving seed selection, sowing, watering, and well-timed harvesting. Again, the practice seems to have developed in more than one area and at different times. Some scholars believe that the first domestication of seed plants may have occurred in the Nile River Valley in North Africa, but the majority view is that this crucial development took place in a region of southwestern Asia, through which flow the two major rivers of present-day Iraq: the Tigris and the Euphrates. This marked the beginning of what has been called the First ***Agricultural Revolution***, and the area where it occurred is known as the ***Fertile Crescent***. The grain crops, wheat and barley, grew in the warming Southwest Asian climate. When rainfall diminished as the interglaciation wore on, the river-inundated plains of Mesopotamia provided alter-

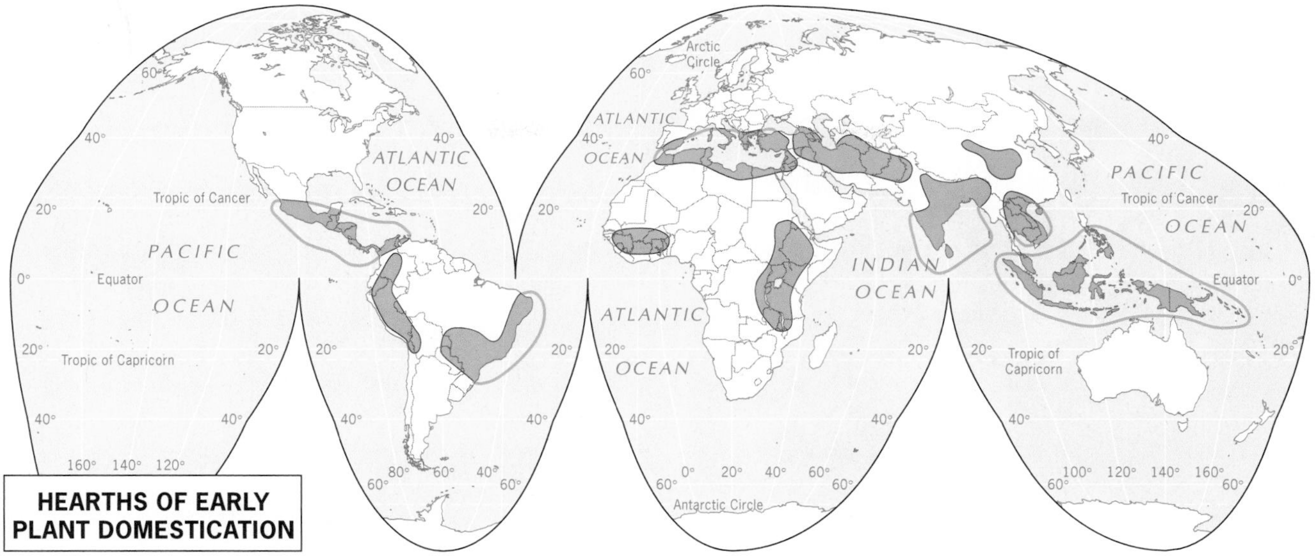

Figure 3-1 Hearths of Early Plant Domestication. Areas of earliest plant domestication, as postulated by C. O. Sauer. *Source:* J. E. Spencer & W. L. Thomas, Introducing Cultural Geography. New York: Wiley, 1973, p. 67.

nate, irrigable fields for farming (Fig. 3-2). Food surpluses could now be stored for long-term distribution and use.

Domestication of Animals

The domestication of animals appears to have taken place during the same period, also in different ways and different areas and times. As with the growing of root crops, the notion of ***animal domestication*** must have emerged quite naturally. Hungry animals foraged through garbage near human settlements; orphaned young probably were adopted as pets; some wild animals were docile and easily penned up. Goats were domesticated in the Zagros Mountains as long as 10,000 years ago; sheep some 9500 years ago in Anatolia (Turkey); pigs and cattle shortly thereafter. The advantages of animal domestication—their use as beasts of burden, as a source of meat, and as providers of milk—stimulated the rapid diffusion of this idea throughout the inhabited world and gave the sedentary farmers of southwestern Asia and elsewhere a new measure of security. Again, an idea that was probably not totally new to the Holocene took on revolutionary form in the present epoch.

Early Settlements and Networks

The domestication of plants and animals allowed humans to live in stable, permanent settlements for the first time in human history. About 10,000 years ago, a network of farm villages appeared across the area between the Mediterranean Sea, the Persian Gulf, the Caspian Sea, and the Black Sea. These villages were not large by modern standards, but they contained hundreds of

From the field notes

"Our ideas about early civilizations are so often shaped by the great monuments and tombs that are left behind. Yet here in Deir el-Medina (Egypt) I gain a glimpse into the ordinary lives that lie behind the more visible symbols of the Ancient world. These are the remains of the stone and mud-brick houses occupied by those who helped to build the great temples of Ancient Egypt's civilization. A society cannot support the occupational specialization implied by the existence of such "worker's villages" if it is not prosperous and well organized. Egypt had obviously achieved that position when Deir el-Medina was built—over 3500 years ago."

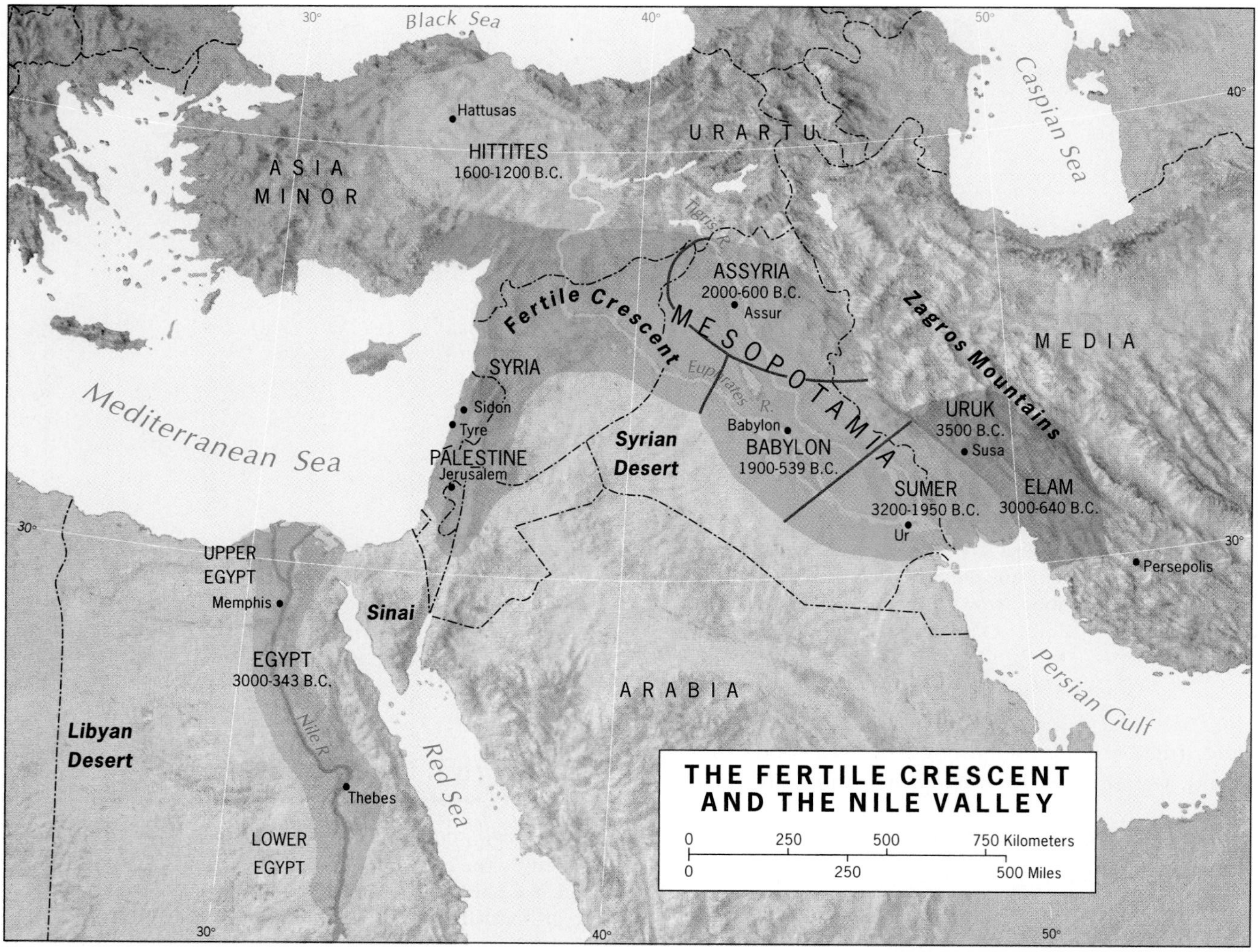

Figure 3-2 The Fertile Crescent. The Fertile Crescent and ancient states (in different colors) of Mesopotamia and adjacent areas, and of the Nile Valley. Modern political boundaries are shown for reference.

inhabitants rather than the dozens that were typical of nomadic hunter-gatherer settlements.

The implications of this transformation were far-reaching. Some of the people in the farm villages were nonfarmers who performed other work, including not only activities directly related to farming (toolmaking, bagging, transport) but also teaching, administration, and policing. Thus a set of social strata or layers, termed ***social stratification***, developed. People found themselves on different rungs on a social ladder. At the top were those with prestige, influence, and power (the elite). Below them were the lower classes engaged in production and provision.

Conflict and competition also arose. Some villages had more productive lands; others were less fortunate. Stronger villages took control over weaker ones, and some became regional centers. The transition from village to city was under way.

Just what stimulated the rise of cities in Southwest Asia is not yet certain. It may have been a combination of circumstances: prospering regional centers, strong militias, the strength of numbers, and the rise of larger scale, well-organized religious orders. Possibly the role of irrigation was crucial because towns that controlled irrigation works could deny their competitors access to water. Perhaps some villages grew stronger and larger because technological inventions enhanced their productivity and power. Some geographers believe that the rise of certain cities (and the decline of other places) was related to continuing climatic change. For example, when the region's rainfall declined, the Fertile Crescent's towns located on the slopes, far from controllable river water, were at a disadvantage relative to those towns in the river basins. Whatever the cause(s), urbanization had begun and would eventually affect all of humanity everywhere on the Earth.

Although there is little doubt that the development of sedentary and irrigated agriculture and the rise of villages and towns initially occurred in Southwest Asia, we should remember that the dispersal of humans into other regions had already taken place. During the period from about 10,000 to 5000 years ago, important advances were being made in those regions as well as in the Fertile Crescent. In Africa, the Nile River Valley was a ribbon of agriculture. Rice-farming villages arose in Southeast Asia. And in China, momentous developments were occurring in the basins of the Chang (Yangtzi) and the Yellow (Huang) rivers, where rice and millet farmers supplied villages in networks not unlike those of Southwest Asia. On the North China Plain, the Shang Dynasty emerged, with its capital at Anyang and its core area in the confluence of the Huang and Wei rivers (Fig. 3-3). Whether these were independent innovations or the consequence of the diffusion of ideas from Southwest Asia remains an open question.

Early Cities and States

Even after the development of the first villages, it would not yet have been possible to draw a map of the next stage of regional organization: the state. There were networks of farm settlements and established trade routes; fields and pastures marked the countryside; and some villages were growing larger. But political states, with capitals and boundaries and military forces, had not yet developed.

This next stage of human organization was not long in coming. The cities of the Fertile Crescent in particular became centers of political power, economic strength, and religious dominance. Indeed, Babylon was one of the largest and most powerful cities of antiquity—controlling a significant domain in Mesopotamia. Situated on the Euphrates River in present-day Iraq, Babylon endured for nearly 2000 years (from 4100 B.P.) as a walled, fortified center endowed with temples, towers, palaces, river docks, and a stone bridge. Rising above the townscape was the tallest structure in Mesopotamia at the time: the ***Ziggurat***, or tower of the great temple. With a base of 90 m (300 ft), and rising in seven levels more than 90 m above the plain, this magnificent tower was a symbol of power that could be seen for miles around. Outside the town's fortified walls lay irrigated fields and an artificial, terraced hill built and planted over an elaborate vaulted foundation. When the Greeks under Alexander the Great conquered Babylon in 331 B.C., they called

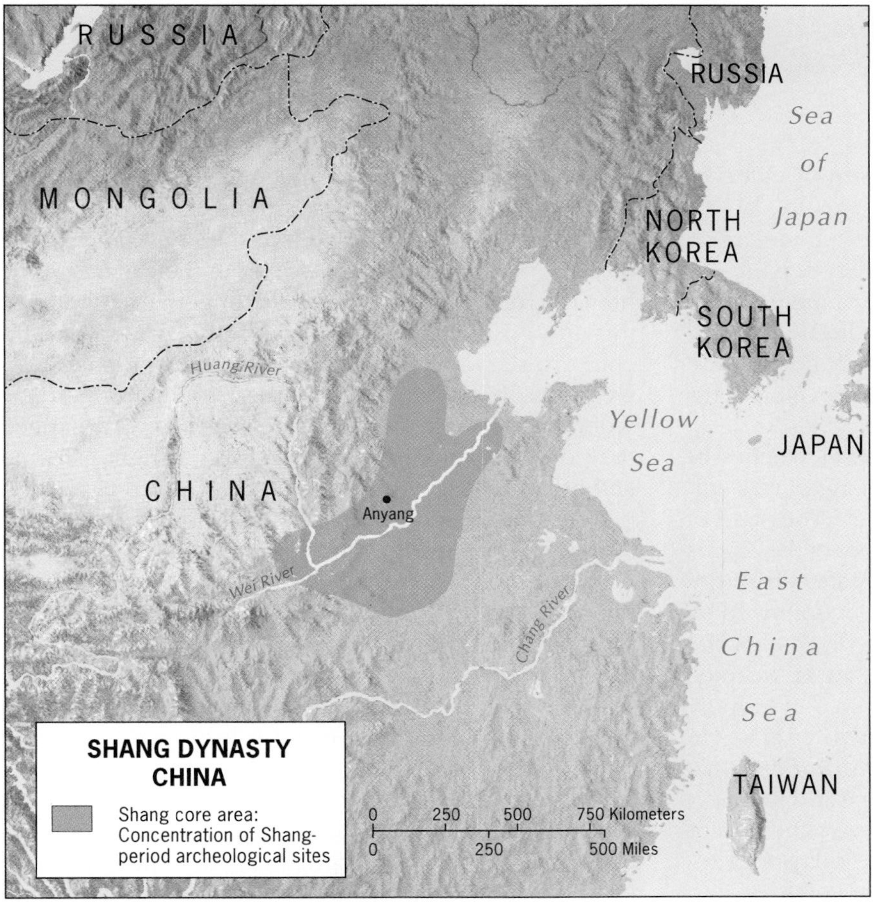

Figure 3-3 Shang Dynasty in China. The geographical origins of what may be the world's oldest continuous civilization.

From the field notes

"When the Ancient Romans built their empire in North Africa, they could visit the Giza pyramids (on the outskirts of present-day Cairo) and gaze upon monuments that, for them, were older than the Ancient Roman ruins are for us. When one stops to reflect that the first of the Giza pyramids rose from the Saharan sands more than 2500 years before Julius Caesar led the Roman armies into battle, one gains some perspective on just how old the Egyptian civilization really is. Yes, the development of cities and states has happened only in the most recent period of humanity's time on earth, but the story still has deep roots in human history."

these "Hanging Gardens" one of the Seven Wonders of the World.

Although scholars are not in complete agreement on the subject, clearly a relationship exists between the rise of powerful cities such as Babylon and the emergence of large and durable states. We will discuss the character of ancient cities in Part Seven, but it is worth noting here that momentous political and geographic developments followed the emergence of large cities.

The Sumerian state arose in the lower reaches of Mesopotamia at about the same time that Egypt was unified politically for the first time (Fig. 3-2). The state of Uruk developed on the southwestern slopes of the Zagros Mountains in what is now Iran. These states arose between 6000 and 5000 years ago, soon to be followed by Babylon (north of Sumer) and Assyria (a state in the Tigris Valley). Later the Hittites forged a state in Anatolia, but by then Southwest Asia no longer had a monopoly over the development of states. Large states had arisen in the Indus Valley (in present-day Pakistan) and China, and the stage was set for the rise of Greece and Rome.

As we know, not only urban life but also the idea of the state spread throughout the world. Today, as a result, the planet's living space is compartmentalized into over 200 states, dependencies, and other bounded territories. From a comparatively small number of migrating hunter-gatherer groups that represented the most complex spatial-organizational system on Earth just 12,000 years ago, we have reached a point where theirs is now the simplest form, represented by a few surviving hunter-gatherer groups like the San of Botswana's Kalahari Desert.

◆ IMPRINTS OF HUMAN ORGANIZATION

Time and again over the past million years, ***deglaciation*** was followed by sustained interglaciation, and during the warm interglaciations our hominid ancestors spread far and wide. They left their imprint on the landscape: they burned forests, killed wildlife, built encampments, inhabited caves, and in some instances buried their dead. Their bone and stone tools are found at fossil sites, sometimes in large quantities. But until about 12,000 years ago, when the present interglaciation began, our ancestors had left only the slightest imprint on the Earth as a whole.

Why Is the Holocene Different?

The Holocene began with little indication that this interglaciation would be different. Perhaps this was so because for the first time humans living in more or less stable communities had to adapt to changing environments in particular settings. People were living, for example, in the tundras and grasslands of northern Europe, following migratory herds and killing animals for meat whenever they needed it. But the warming climate caused the tundras and grasslands to shift to the north, and forests of pine, oak, and birch developed in their place. Some human groups moved northward, but others adapted to this new environment in which hunting was more difficult. Those who stayed behind learned to make new weapons that were better suited to hunting in the woods. Their fossil teeth indicate that they also changed their diets. They collected wild grains, caught fish, and gathered mollusks. Importantly, they began to fashion better stone axes and were able to cut down trees. Now they could build log houses and hollow out trees to make canoes. Their settlements took on the look of permanence.

Even then, however, toward the end of the Mesolithic, there was no indication of what lay ahead. Had the Holocene interglaciation come to a close, there would have been little to differentiate it from previous warm phases. Human communities remained small, and most still were migratory.

Human populations also remained very small. Because the data can be interpreted in different ways, there is no consensus on this subject. But around the beginning of the Neolithic, some 10,000 years ago, when animal and plant domestication commenced, the total human population was almost certainly below 6 million. Although they had spread far and wide, humans occupied but a tiny fraction of the Earth's surface.

And yet the world has been transformed during the Holocene epoch. Several theories have been proposed to explain why the transformation occurred this time. After all, humans had been confronted by environmental change during previous interglaciations as well, and nothing comparable had happened. In truth, there still is no satisfactory answer. Some historical geographers suggest that this enormous change was the result of comparatively rapid population growth in the Middle East, which pushed people into less hospitable regions where their knowledge of agriculture helped them to adapt. Adaptation led to the domestication of animals and plants, and this set in motion the First Agricultural Revolution. It is true that population differences stand out when we try to identify ways in which the early Holocene differed from the previous interglaciation. ***Homo sapiens*** was not nearly as numerous, nor as widely dispersed, during the previous warm phase.

In other areas population numbers were substantial, and yet no revolutionary changes occurred there. The special combination of conditions that was to propel the world into its modern age seems to have existed in only a few places.

How Did Holocene Humanity Transform the Earth?

Let us consider the human imprint on the Earth during the Holocene. We will look at several major areas, although of course we could mention many others.

Farming The First Agricultural Revolution has been followed by two more, one organizational and the other (still in progress) the product of biotechnology. Entire regions of the Earth have been plowed, terraced, fenced, and covered with crops; huge herds of livestock graze on fields from Tierra del Fuego to Finland. No human activity transforms as much of the Earth's surface as farming does.

Administration The world has been compartmentalized into more than 200 countries and other entities, heirs to the state idea that first arose about 5500 years ago. The imprint of the modern state is complex and includes its capital city, its provincial or other subsidiary capitals, its heartland or core area, and its boundaries—the last often marked by walls, fences, or posts.

Urbanization In a matter of centuries, urban dwellers, rather than villagers, have become the majority of the world population. The earliest cities, established less than 6000 years ago, had successors (such as Babylon, Damascus, and Athens) that anchored growing civilizations, but until the twentieth century they were relatively rare. Today many cities house more people than entire nations. Nothing symbolizes Holocene humanity as much as the great cities of the present day.

Capitalism Societies have long engaged in the exchange of goods and services. In late medieval Europe, however, the foundations were laid for a competitive economic system in which goods and services were assigned a monetary value and in which those with the greatest wealth in land, goods, and money (capital) could exert the greatest influence over the exchange process. The resulting concentrations of wealth and investment fueled the rise of a global system of production and exchange that, together with industrialization (see the next subsection), promoted an enormous expansion in production and consumption with significant environmental impacts. Other economic systems have fostered significant environmental change as well (e.g., communism as practiced in the former Soviet Union and China), but taking a broad historical and geographical view, capitalism's impact is of particular note because of its long history and global reach.

Industrialization Even in the context of the Holocene, industrialization as we know it is a late development. Industries existed 6000 years ago, and they spread throughout the world. "Preindustrial" India and Japan had major complexes of workshops that produced goods ranging from textiles to ceramics. The Industrial Revolution occurred little more than two centuries ago; but it transformed manufacturing and vastly expanded the demand for natural resources. From the great industrial complexes to the slag heaps at the mines, the impact of industrialization is etched in the landscape.

Transportation and Communication Another symbol of humanity's imprint is the global network of transportation and communication routes and lines crisscrossing the Earth's surface. Railroads, highways, ports, pipelines, airfields, power lines, and other signs of the transportation age bear witness to modern civilization; not even a new glaciation could erase all of this evidence.

Population Cutting across all of the preceding developments is the almost unimaginable expansion of the human population during the Holocene, especially in recent centuries. Every month, more people are added to the world population than existed on the entire planet at the beginning of the Holocene. From 6 million the population has grown to 6 billion, a thousandfold increase, most of which has taken place in less than two centuries. In Part Two we begin our geographic look at the modern world by turning our attention to population.

◆ THE CONTEMPORARY PHYSICAL FRAMEWORK

To understand both how humans live in the environment and how they are transforming it, some basic familiarity with the world's contemporary physical geographic organization is needed. Two important maps presented in the following section provide critical insights into the habitable space of our planet.

Land and Space

It is hardly necessary to remind ourselves that only about 30 percent of the Earth's surface consists of land, but Figure 3-4 emphasizes how little of this 30 percent is capable of sustaining dense human populations. Much of the land surface of the Earth is mountainous and rugged. Certainly, mountains can sustain people in sizable clusters (the Inca Empire was a mountain-based state in the Andes of South America), but generally mountains do not support populations comparable to those found in river basins and plains, where accessibility, circulation, and the growing of crops are easier. In Part Two, where we focus on present population patterns, distribution, and density, Figure 4-1, when compared with Figure 3-4, reveals the sparseness of population in the mountainous regions of the world.

High plateaus also tend to support sparse populations. It is no coincidence that the entire continent of Africa, much of which consists of plateau, sustains

Figure 3-4 Global Terrain. Despite centuries of technological progress, the influence of terrain as an element of the overall natural environment still is reflected in world population distribution. Mountains and high plateaus do not generally support large or dense population clusters.

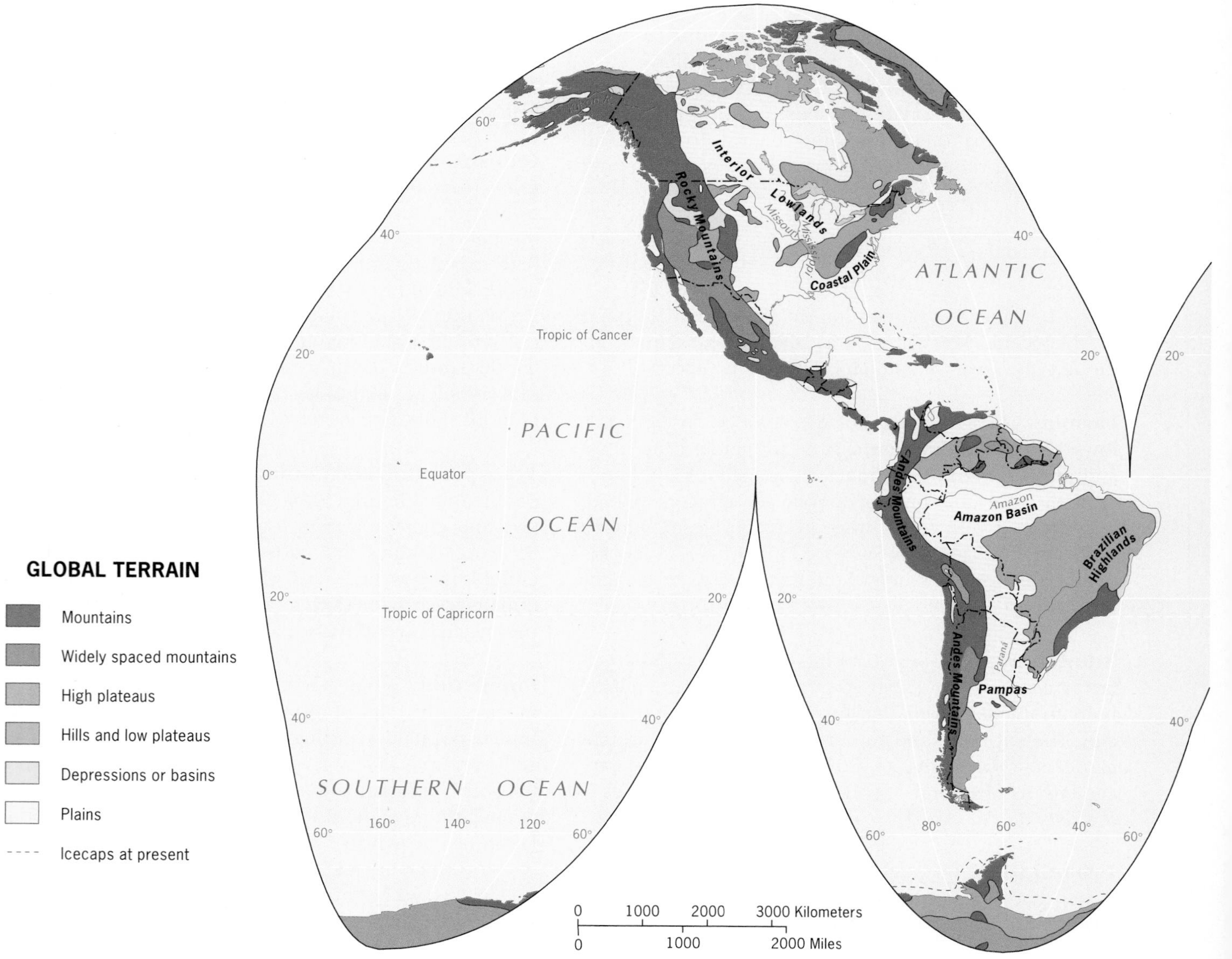

fewer people than the single country of India. The elevation of high plateaus like that of Tibet makes living conditions difficult. Severe erosion can create problems similar to those presented by mountainous terrain. Again, the high-plateau regions stand out as low-population areas.

Land and Climate

In combination, all the elements of weather, the sweep of the Sun's energy, the rotation of the Earth, the circulation of the oceans, the movement of weather systems, and the rush of air in jet stream produce a pattern of climates that is represented in Figure 3-5. We owe this remarkable map to the work of Wladimir Köppen (1846–1940), who devised a scheme for classifying the world's climates on the basis of temperature and precipitation.

Köppen's map displays the present distribution of ***climatic regions*** across the planet. The legend looks complicated, but it really is not; here is one of those maps worth spending some time on. For our purposes, it is enough to get a sense of the distribution of the major types of climate. The letter categories in the legend give a clear indication of the conditions they represent.

The (A) climates are hot or very warm and generally humid. The "no dry season" (Af) regions are *equatorial rainforest* regions. The "short dry season" (Am) climate is known as the *monsoon climate*. And if you can envisage an African savanna, you know what the (Aw, *savanna*) designation means.

Once you realize that the yellow and light brown colors on the map represent dry climates (BW, *desert* and BS, *steppe*), it becomes clear how much of the

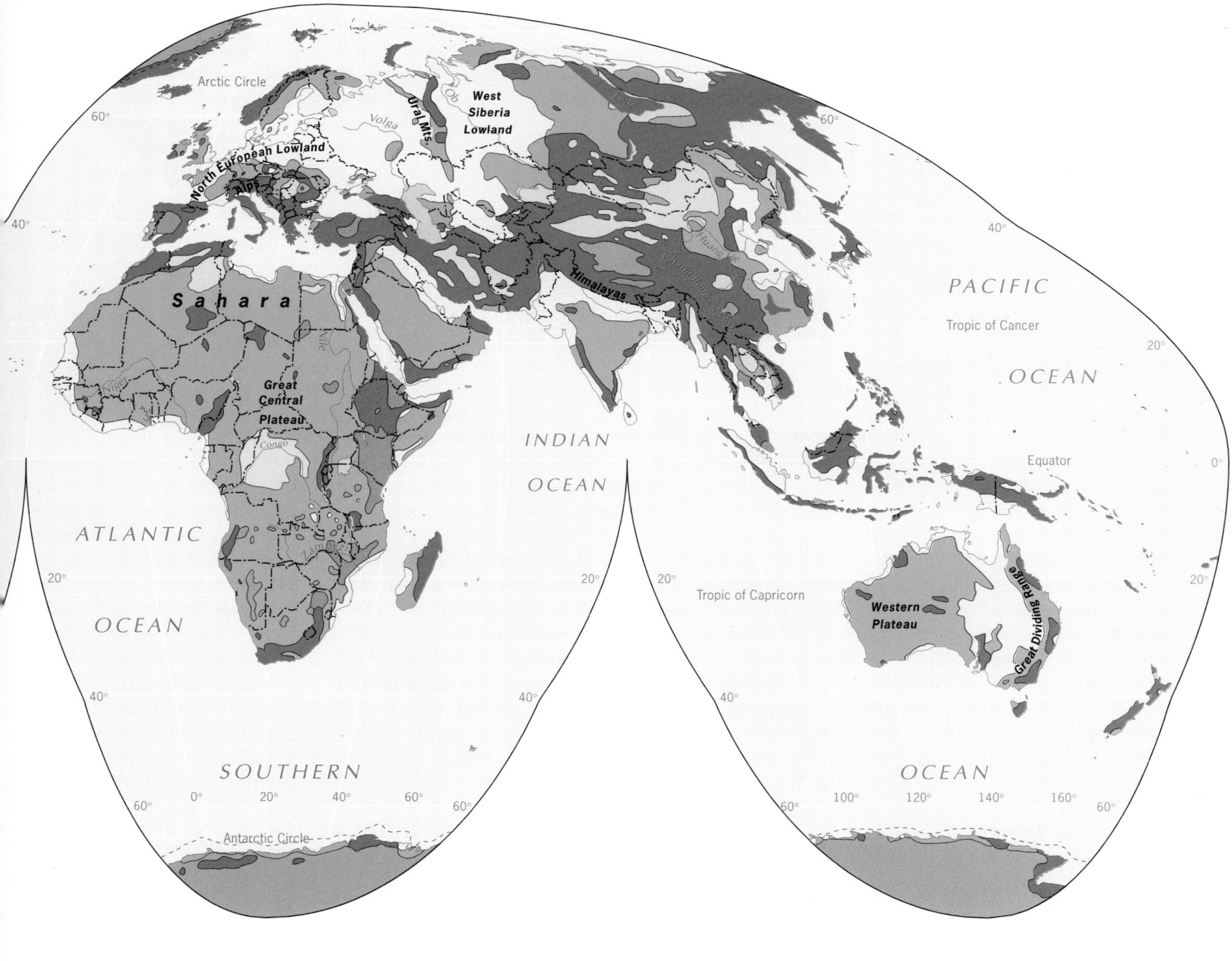

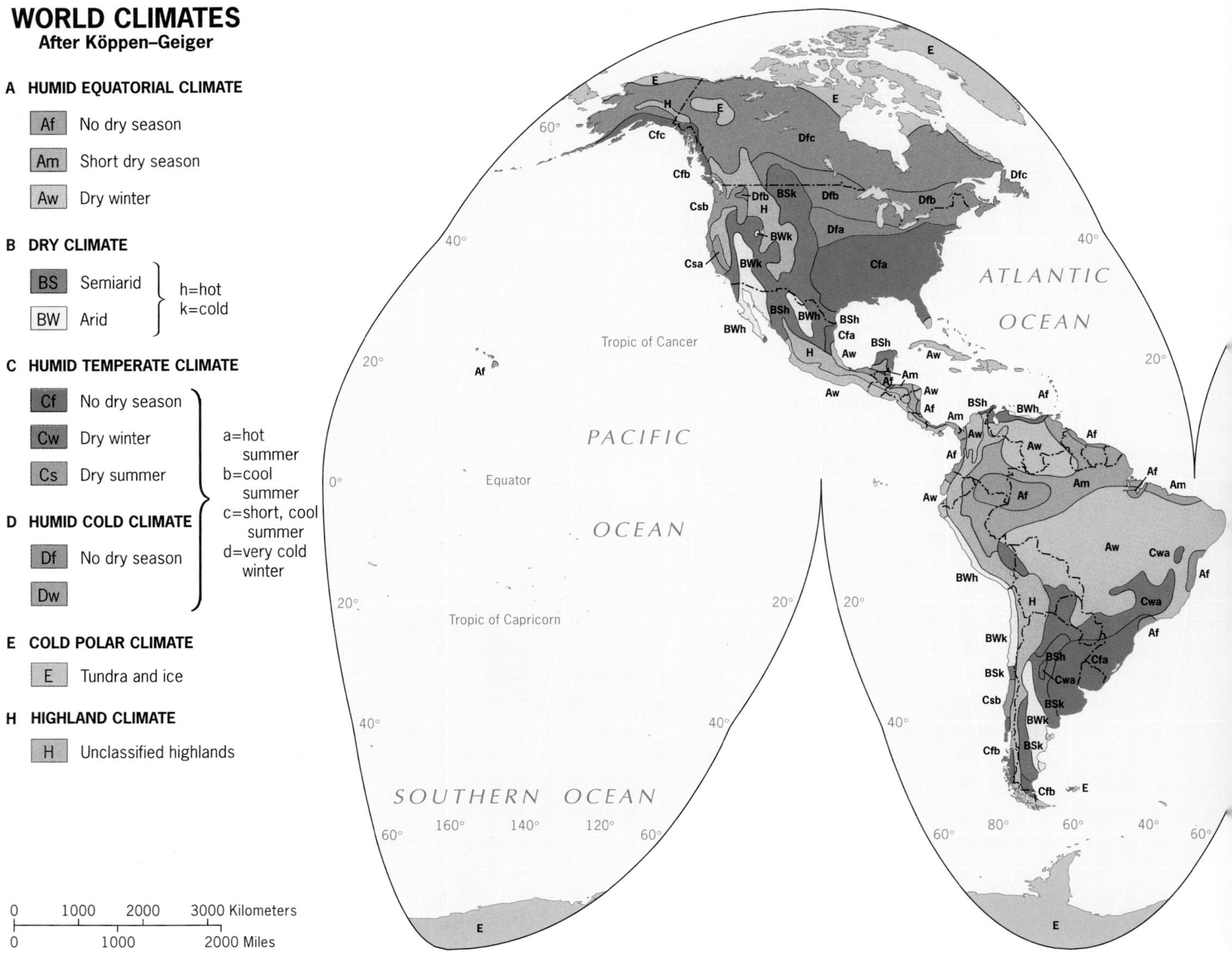

Figure 3-5 World Climates. The Köppen map of world climates as modified by R.Geiger. These, of course, are macroclimatic regions; microclimates are set within these but cannot be shown at this scale.

world is always in need of water. As we will see later, some very large population clusters have developed in these water-deficient regions, especially at lower (and warmer) latitudes. The world faces a long-term water crisis, and the Köppen map helps explain why.

The (C) climates also have familiar names. The (Cf) climate, represented by dark green, prevails over the southeastern United States. If you know the local weather in Atlanta or Nashville or Jacksonville, you understand why this climate is often called "humid temperate." It is moist, and it does not get as cold as it does in Canada or as warm (continuously, anyway) as in the Amazon Basin. If you have experienced this kind of climate, the map gives you a good idea of what it's like in much of eastern China, southeastern Australia, and a large part of southeastern South America.

The "dry summer" (C) climates are known as *Mediterranean* climates (the small s in Cs means that summers are dry). This mild climate occurs not only around the Mediterranean Sea, and thus in the famous wine countries of France, Italy, and Spain, but also in California, Chile, South Africa's Cape, and southern parts of Australia. So you know what kind of weather to expect in Rome, San Francisco, Santiago, Cape Town, and Adelaide.

Farther toward the poles, the planet gets rather cold. Note that the (D) climates dominate in the United States' upper Midwest and Canada, but it gets even colder in

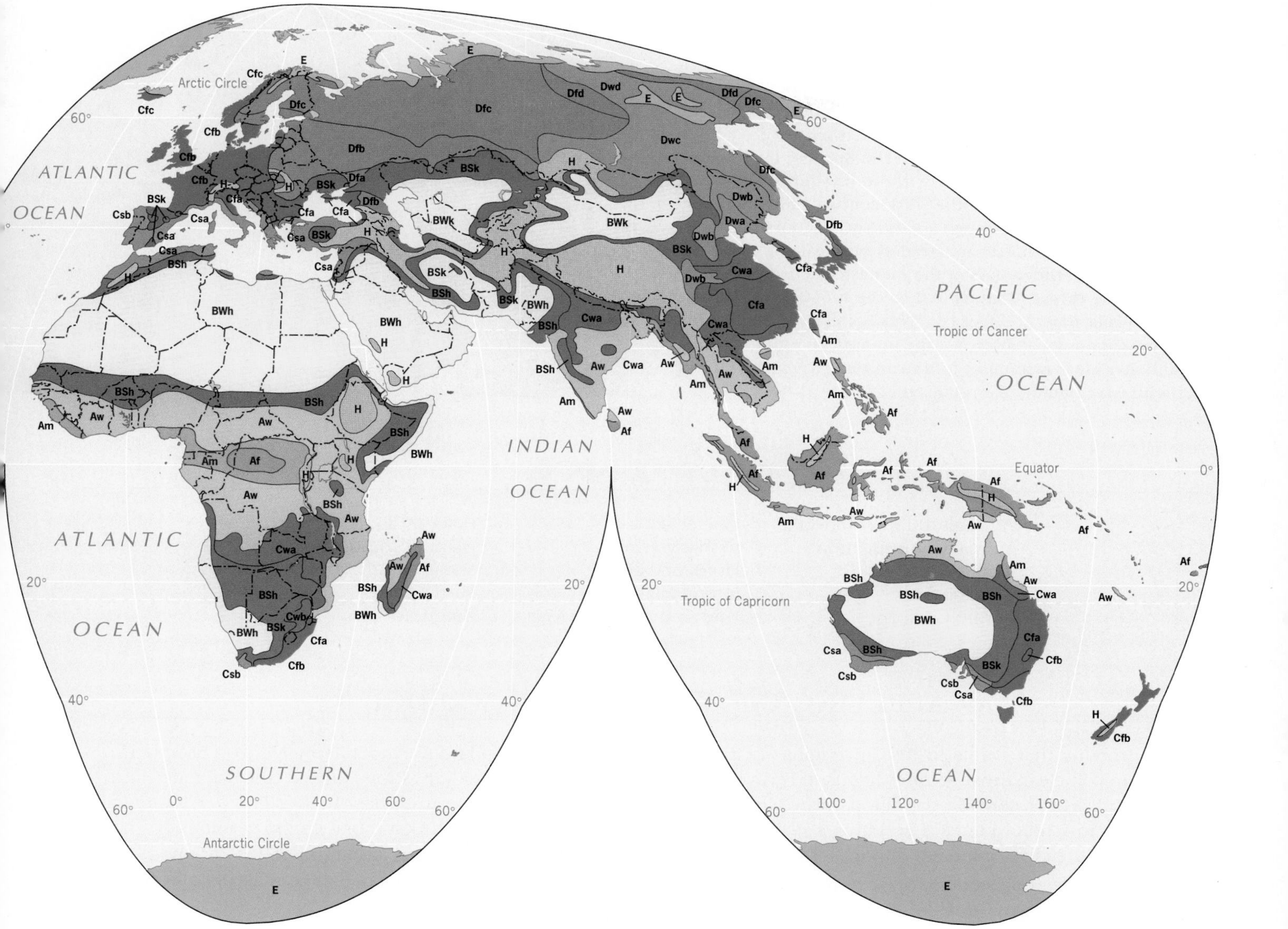

Siberia. The "milder" (Da) climates (here the key is the small a, which denotes a warm summer) have a very limited extent in Eurasia. Winters are very cold in all the (D) climates and downright frigid (and long) in the (Dfb) and (Dfc) regions. The latter merge into the *polar* climates, where tundra and ice prevail.

The climate map, like the landscape map, reflects the limited habitable areas of the Earth. Vast portions of the planet's landmasses are extremely arid or frigid or excessively hot and humid and therefore cannot sustain large populations that depend directly on the land for their sustenance. And despite technological advances, hundreds of millions of people still live off the land.

Figure 3-5 is a still photo of a changing pattern. When pre-Holocene conditions prevailed, the habitable zone of the Earth was much narrower, and polar (E) climates reached as far south as the central Great Plains and the Alpine slopes of southern Europe. Today the Earth is much warmer, but it will not remain warm forever. Eventually the Köppen map will look quite different.

The two world maps presented here provide a good portrait of the physical stage on which the events described in the rest of this book take place. For example, we will discuss places like Nigeria (Africa's most populous country) and Quebec (the Canadian province where separatism is a popular sentiment). From these maps we can deduce basic aspects of the terrain, the climate, and the precipitation in those places, and thus obtain some notion of what their environments are like. Such information can be useful in understanding much that follows in this book.

From the field notes

"After driving for hours though the open expanses of the southern Sinai peninsula, I come to a little oasis in the form of the Christian Monastery of St. Catherine. Erected on what was believed to be the site of the Burning Bush where God revealed himself to Moses, the monastery has been a presence in the Sinai since the sixth-century. Relying on periodic flows of water through a *wadi* (watercourse), as well as what could be made and traded with surrounding nomadic peoples, the monks of the monastery eked out an existence. The threat of attack led to the building of massive granite walls 40 to 200 feet tall. This is clearly a challenging site for human occupance, yet the monastery's longstanding vitality is a clear testament to human tenacity in the face of difficult environmental circumstances."

◆ KEY TERMS ◆

Agricultural Revolution	glacier	Paleolithic
animal domestication	global warming	plant domestication
climatic regions	Holocene epoch	social stratification
deglaciation	interglaciation	Stone Age
Fertile Crescent	Late Cenozoic Ice Age	Ziggurat

◆ APPLYING GEOGRAPHIC KNOWLEDGE ◆

1. A company that wants to test an engine for an all-terrain vehicle in those settings has asked you to write a report on the climatic conditions prevailing in the world's low-relief plains. Use Figures 3-4 and 3-5 to establish the environmental setting.
2. You have been offered the opportunity to lead a tour group consisting of travelers from North America to New Zealand and Australia. How will you use Figure 3-5 to answer questions about the climate and weather in those countries? If your guests resided in Vancouver, British Columbia, where would they find a familiar environment "downunder?" in Phoenix, Arizona? Jacksonville, Florida? San Francisco, California?

Part One

GEOGRAPHY, CULTURE, AND THE ENVIRONMENT

At Issue: Revisited

Why is geography so much a part of the effort to come to terms with our rapidly changing world? What does it mean to think geographically? Can geography offer insights into the diversity of changes unfolding around us? The developments of the past decade have shown that we live in a world of constant change—a world that defies easy generalization. Differences from place to place matter, and no one map can capture the dynamism of our situation. At the same time, the practice of separating the study of physical and human phenomena seems increasingly problematic. Small wonder, then, that geography is being looked to for ideas and approaches. As one geographer put it, place matters—as does the relationship among phenomena in place and space. The concepts and tools of geography are thus an indispensable part of our effort to come to terms with the world around us.

◆ SELECTED REFERENCES ◆

Part One Geography, Culture, and the Environment

Abler, R., et al., eds. *Human Geography in a Shrinking World*. North Scituate, Mass.: Duxbury Press, 1975.

Allen, J., & Massey, D., eds. *Geographical Worlds*. Oxford, U.K.: Oxford University Press, 1995.

Amedeo, D., & Golledge, R. *An Introduction to Scientific Reasoning in Geography*. New York: John Wiley & Sons, 1975.

Bailey, R., ed. *The True State of the Planet*. New York: The Free Press, 1995.

Brown, L. A. *Innovation Diffusion: A New Perspective*. New York: Methuen, 1981.

Buttimer, A. *Geography and the Human Spirit*. Baltimore: Johns Hopkins University Press, 1993.

Campbell, B. G. & Loy, J. D., eds. *Humankind Emerging*. 8th rev. ed. Boston: Longman, 2000.

Campbell, J. *Map Use and Analysis*. Dubuque, Iowa: Wm. C. Brown, 1991.

Chrisman, N. R. *Exploring Geographic Information Systems*. New York: John Wiley & Sons, 2002.

Cloke, Paul, Crang, P., & Goodwin, M. *Introducing Human Geographies*. New York: Oxford, 1999.

Cox, C. B., & Moore, P. D. *Biogeography: An Ecological and Evolutionary Approach*. 6th ed. Oxford, U.K.: Blackwell Scientific Publications, 2000.

Crang, M. *Cultural Geography*. New York: Routledge, 1998.

de Blij, H. J., & Muller, P. O. *Geography: Realms, Regions and Concepts*. 10th rev. ed. New York: John Wiley & Sons, 2002.

Dent, B. *Principles of Thematic Map Design*. Reading, Mass.: Addison-Wesley, 1984.

Ember, C. R., & Ember, M. E. *Cultural Anthropology*. 6th rev. ed. Englewood Cliffs, N.J.: Prentice-Hall, 1990.

Espenshade, E. B., Jr., ed. *Goode's World Atlas*. 20th rev. ed. Chicago: Rand McNally, 2000.

Gaile, G. L., & Willmott, C. J., eds. *Geography in America*. Columbus, Ohio: Merrill, 1989.

Geertz, C. *The Interpretation of Cultures*. New York: Basic Books, 1973.

Gibbons, A. "First Hominid Finds from Ethiopia in a Decade." *Science*, 22 March 1991, p. 1428.

Gold, J. *An Introduction to Behavioral Geography*. New York: Oxford University Press, 1980.

Gould, P. *The Geographer at Work*. London: Routledge & Kegan Paul, 1985.

Gould, P., & White, R. *Mental Maps*. 2nd rev. ed. Boston: Allen & Unwin, 1992.

Graedel, T. E., & Crutzen, P. J. *Atmosphere, Climate and Change*. New York: Scientific American Library, 1995.

Gregory, D. *Ideology, Science and Human Geography*. London: Hutchinson, 1978.

Gregory, D., & Walford, R., eds. *Horizons in Human Geography*. Totowa, N.J.: Barnes & Noble Books, 1989.

Grove, J. M. *The Little Ice Age*. London: Methuen, 1988.

Harris, C. D., ed. *A Geographical Bibliography for American Libraries*. Washington, D.C.: Association of American Geographers and the National Geographic Society, 1985.

Hartshorne, R. *The Nature of Geography*. Washington, D.C.: Association of American Geographers, 1939.

Hartshorne, R. *Perspective on the Nature of Geography*. Chicago: Rand McNally, 1959.

Holz, R., ed. *The Surveillant Science: Remote Sensing of the Environment*, 2nd rev. ed. New York: John Wiley & Sons, 1985.

Houghton, J. T., Ding, Y., Griggs, D.J., Noguer, M., van der Linden P. J. & Xiaosu, D., eds. *Climate Change 2001: The Scientific Basis Contribution of Working Group I to the Third Assessment Report of the Intergovernmental Panel on Climate Change (IPCC)*. Cambridge: Cambridge University Press, UK, 2001, p. 944.

Huntington, E., and Cushing, S.W., *Principles of Human Geography*, 5th ed. New York: John Wiley & Sons, 1940.

Jackson, P. *Maps of Meaning*. London: Unwin Hyman, 1989.

James, P. E., & Jones, C. F., eds. *American Geography: Inventory and Prospect*. Syracuse, N.Y.: Syracuse University Press, 1954.

James, P. E., & Martin, G. *All Possible Worlds: A History of Geographical Ideas*, 3rd rev. ed. New York: John Wiley & Sons, 1993.

Johnston, R. J. *Geography and Geographers: Anglo-American Human Geography since 1945*. 5th ed. London; New York: Arnold, 1997.

Johnston, R. J. *On Human Geography*. Oxford, New York: Blackwell, 1986.

Johnston, R. J., et al., eds.; Smith, D. M., consultant editor. *The Dictionary of Human Geography*. 4th ed. Oxford, U.K.: Malden, Mass. Blackwell Publishers, 2000.

Johnston, R. J., Taylor, P., & Watts, M. J. *Geographies of Global Change: Remapping the World in the Late Twentieth Century*. Cambridge: Blackwell, 1995.

Levenson, T. *Ice Time: Climate, Science and Life on Earth*. New York: Harper & Row, 1989.

Lewis, M. W., & Wigen, K. E. *The Myth of Continents: A Critique of Metageography*. Berkeley: University of California Press, 1997.

Markham, S. F. *Climate and the Energy of Nations*. London and New York: Oxford University Press, 1947.

Massey, D., & Allen, J., eds. *Geography Matters! A Reader*. New York: Cambridge University Press, 1985.

Michener, J. "The Mature Social Studies Teacher." *Social Education*, November 1970, pp. 760–766.

Monmonier, M. S. *Computer-Assisted Cartography: Principles and Prospects*. Englewood Cliffs, N.J.: Prentice-Hall, 1982.

Monmonier, M. S. *How to Lie with Maps*. Chicago: University of Chicago Press, 1990.

Monmonier, M. S. *Mapping It Out: Expository Cartography for the Humanities and Social Sciences.* Chicago: University of Chicago Press, 1993.

Monmonier, M. S. *Maps with the News.* Chicago: University of Chicago Press, 1989.

National Geographic Society, *Maps, the Landscape, and Fundamental Themes in Geography.* Washington, D.C., 1986.

National Geographic Society. *Historical Atlas of the United States.* Washington, D.C.: National Geographic Society, 1988.

National Research Council. *Rediscovering Geography: New Relevance for Science and Society.* Washington, D.C.: National Academy Press, 1997.

Pattison, W. "The Four Traditions of Geography." *Journal of Geography* 63 (1964): 211–216.

Peet, R. *Modern Geographical Thought.* Oxford: Malden, Mass.: Blackwell Publishers, 1998.

Pielou, E. C. *After the Ice Age: The Return of Life to Glaciated North America.* Chicago: University of Chicago Press, 1991.

Rand McNally & Co. *The New International Atlas.* 25th anniversary ed. Chicago: Rand McNally, 1999.

Roberts, N. *The Holocene: An Environmental History.* New York: Basil Blackwell, 1989.

Robinson, A. H., et al. *Elements of Cartography.* 6th rev. ed. New York: John Wiley & Sons, 1995.

Sauer, Carl. "Recent Developments in Cultural Geography." In *Recent Developments in the Social Sciences,* Elwood, C. A., Wissler, C., and Gault, R. H., eds. Philadelphia: J. B. Lippincott, 1927, pp. 154–212.

Schneider, S. H. *Laboratory Earth: The Planetary Gamble We Can't Afford to Lose.* New York: Basic Books, 1997.

Sheffield, C. *Man on Earth: How Civilization and Technology Changed the Face of the World—A Survey from Space.* New York: Macmillan, 1983.

Simons, E. L. "Human Origin." *Science,* 22 September 1989, pp. 133–135.

Strahler, A. N., & Strahler, A. H. *Modern Physical Geography.* 4th rev. ed. New York: John Wiley & Sons, 1992.

Thomas, W., ed. *Man's Role in Changing the Face of the Earth.* Chicago: University of Chicago Press, 1956.

Tufte, E. R. *Envisioning Information.* Cheshire, Conn.: Graphics Press, 1990.

Weaver, K. "The Search for Our Ancestors." *National Geographic,* November 1985, pp 560–623.

Wegener, A. *The Origin of Continents and Oceans.* Trans. J. Biram, New York: Dover, 1966.

Wenke, R. J. *Patterns in Prehistory: Humankind's First Three Million Years.* 4th rev. ed. New York: Oxford University Press, 1999.

Williams, M.A.J., et al. *Quaternary Environments.* London: Edward Arnold, 1993.

Wood, D., with J. Fels. *The Power of Maps.* New York: Guilford Press, 1992.

Part Two

POPULATION PATTERNS AND PROCESSES

At Issue

The world's growing human population has passed the 6-billion mark, four times the number just one century ago. The rate of overall growth is declining, but the actual increase continues at about 80 million per year. Reducing this annual increment is an objective advocated vigorously by the wealthier, low-growth, Western countries. Improved living standards, they argue, can be achieved only by controlling population growth. Some poorer countries, notably China, have adopted policies designed to reduce their population growth rates. But a world population conference held by the United Nations in 1994 revealed some deep disagreements among the participants. Many Islamic countries argued that population control of the kind advocated by Western nations violated Muslim precepts. (They found support in the Vatican, also represented at the conference.) Other countries maintained that the high rate of consumption in the rich Western countries constitutes a larger problem than rapid population growth in poorer regions. In a lifetime, an American will consume 30 times as much of the world's food and other resources as, say, a Bangladeshi does. *So how serious a problem is population growth? Should lowering the world's population growth rate be a global objective at all?*

A warning from the authorities in Chengdu, China.

Part Outline

Chapter 4

Fundamentals of Population: Location, Distribution, and Density

From the field notes

"No matter where you are, the Indonesian island of Jawa (Java) leaves no doubt that this is one of the most densely populated places on Earth. The back roads I traveled seemed to be lined with houses for endless miles, the houses clustering into villages and towns every few minutes. Here in Jakarta, the national capital, the crush of people reminds you that this is the world's fourth-most populous country. During much of the day, traffic is so congested that it crawls along, so that pedestrians simply mix with road vehicles. It is all a sign of a burgeoning economy, but what happens when the economy falters? Will food supply always suffice, as it does today?"

KEY POINTS

◆ **The world's population is currently growing by about 80 million per year; the bulk of this growth is occurring in the world's poorer countries.**

◆ **The distribution of population describes the locations on the Earth's surface where individuals or groups live. By contrast, population density is a measure of the number of people per unit area.**

◆ **At a global scale, there continues to be a remarkably strong correlation between areas of high population density and areas with significant expanses of arable land.**

◆ **Population data often are unreliable because of the high cost and organizational challenges of census taking.**

◆ **The world's three largest population concentrations all lie on the Eurasian landmass, and the smallest of the three is the most highly developed and urbanized.**

◆ **By itself, population density tells us little about the capacity of individual countries to support their inhabitants. This is because density does not take into account global economic position or access to technology.**

Historical geographers of the future will undoubtedly look back upon the twentieth century as the century of the human "population explosion." After tens of thousands of years (perhaps as long as 90,000 years) of growth, the Earth's human population at the beginning of the twentieth century stood at about 1.5 billion. By the end of that century, it exceeded 6 billion. During the 1960s and 1970s, the rate of population growth increased so fast that disaster seemed to lie ahead in the form of mass famines and global social dislocation. Since then, technological advances have expanded food production even faster than the population has grown, and the global population's growth rate has begun to slow. But, as we will see, the problems resulting from the population explosion still prevail. Hundreds of millions of people, mostly children, remain malnourished. Many countries, mostly in the poorer parts of the world, continue to have population increases with which they cannot cope.

The study of population is termed ***demography*** (from the ancient Greek words ***demos***, meaning populace or people, and ***graphe***, meaning to describe). The focus of the field of ***population geography*** is on the spatial aspects of demography. Demographic problems and issues vary not only from region to region and country to country, but also *within* countries. Our spatial inquiry leads to some penetrating insights into demographic predicaments. ◆

◆ KEY ISSUES IN POPULATION GEOGRAPHY

In Part Two we address several fundamental issues in population geography, and others arise later in this book. First, we should acquaint ourselves with the present ***distribution*** of population at several levels of scale. We may know the total current population of a country, but ***where*** in that country are the people concentrated? Figure 4-1 reveals that about 90 percent of the people in the world's most populous country, China, live in the easternmost one-third of its territory—creating vast interior frontiers of sparsely peopled, minority-inhabited borderland. The map suggests why China's leaders have encouraged Han Chinese to move westward. Historic factors created the present distribution of population, but modern times often demand change.

Problems associated with ***population growth*** remain paramount in population geography. The Earth's environments and natural resources are strained by the needs of the mushrooming population, which farms and erodes its soils, fishes and depletes its oceans, mines and consumes its minerals and fuels, and cuts and destroys its forests. But, as we will see, historically population growth has not been a linear process. Regional populations have grown and declined as a result of epidemics and famines; only after the onset of the Industrial Revolution has growth been the dominant trend.

Today, however, the populations of certain countries are again declining, not for reasons of health or food, but through other causes. Some scholars suggest that population shrinkage, which has its own set of associated problems, will become a major issue during the present century. They argue that population ***change***, not only population ***growth***, will challenge the world of the twenty-first century.

Another issue we address is ***migration***. Waves of human migration have changed—and continue to modify—the demographic map of the world. The movement of millions of people across international borders, mostly in search of jobs and a better life but sometimes to escape war or natural disaster, continues. Indeed, immigration into certain countries adds more to the total population than natural population increase in those countries; governments try to stem the tide of migrants by closing borders or refusing domicile to those who do manage to enter. Related to the process of migration is the dislocation of millions of people who become ***refugees***, a topic we examine in some detail.

Virtually all governments have ***population policies*** that promote national objectives, ranging from control over immigration to internal relocation. These policy responses to demographic changes often have ethnic as well as spatial overtones, favoring a particular (usually dominant) sector of the national population or promoting a country's heartland, its core area, and its inhabitants over outlying areas. Other policies target growth rates and involve mass sterilization or support for family planning. As we will see, such policies sometimes have unintended consequences.

Later in this book we examine other issues relating to population geography, including ***food supply*** and the possibility that world population growth will again overtake total production; ***health*** and well-being, about as unevenly distributed across the globe as any social condition; and the ***status of women***, often hidden by statistics that report averages for entire populations without revealing sharp contrasts between males and females in terms of education, income, nourishment, infant and child mortality, freedom of movement, and many other indices.

◆ ELEMENTS OF POPULATION GEOGRAPHY

How can a geographic approach to issues such as those just described improve our understanding of them? To begin with, we should consider some of the spatial aspects of the human world. Not only does less than 30 percent of the Earth's surface consist of solid ground, but of that living space, only a fraction (at most, around one-third) is arable—that is, able to produce crops and livestock. Vast stretches of land are desert, frigid, mountainous, or otherwise agriculturally unproductive, or of such low productivity that only very small human populations can subsist there.

Population and Space

From the very beginning, humanity has been unevenly distributed over the land, and the contrasts between crowded countrysides and bustling cities on the one hand and empty reaches on the other have only intensified—especially during the twentieth century. Even countries with huge populations, such as China and India, have large areas where people are absent or

Reliability of Population Data

When the United States conducted its 1990 population ***census*** and the results began to be published, there was an uproar from several quarters. Mayors of major cities insisted that the census had undercounted their populations. This would put them at a financial disadvantage during coming years because federal aid is based on ***population data***. Governors complained that undependable population data could affect the number of congressional seats allotted to their seats. Independent observers found that the census had been carried out well but that as many as 2 million people may not have been counted.

If a prosperous country such as the United States has problems conducting an accurate census, imagine the difficulties that must be overcome in less well-off countries. The cost, organization, and reporting of a census go beyond what many countries can afford or handle.

World population data are collected by several agencies. The United Nations records official statistics that have been assembled and reported by national governments. The U.S. Census Bureau also gathers global population data. The World Bank and the Population Reference Bureau are among other organizations that conduct research and report on the population of the world and of individual countries.

The population data published by these and other organizations frequently are inconsistent. If you examine various statistical tables in detail, inconsistencies will inevitably emerge. Growth rates and other vital statistics, data on food availability, health conditions, and incomes are at times informed estimates rather than hard facts. Thus, while the figures used in this book are based on careful assessments, they are still subject to error.

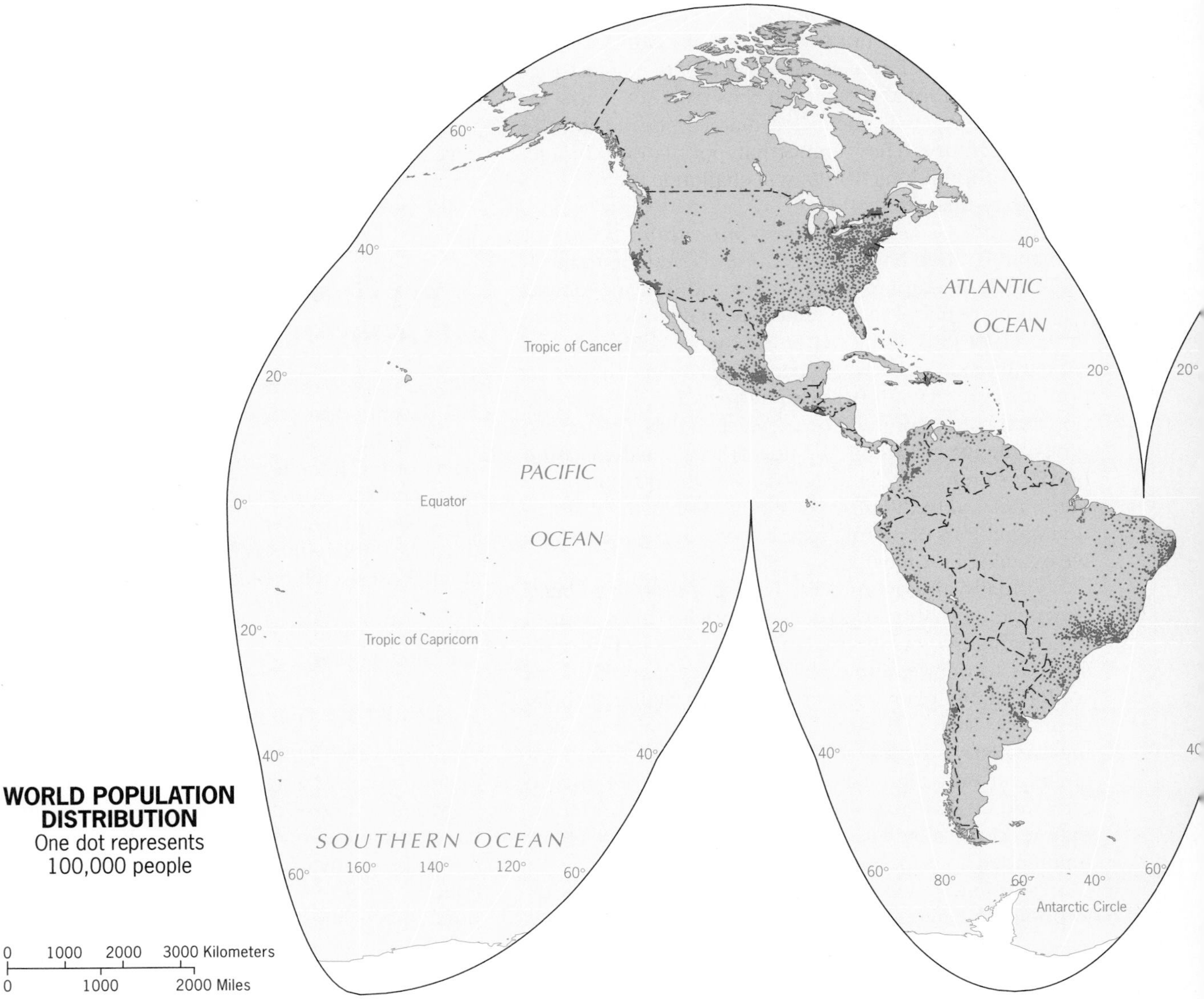

Figure 4-1 World Population Distribution.

sparsely distributed. The peoples of China and India still depend quite heavily on the food their farmers can produce, so the clustering of the population in those countries continues to reflect the availability and fertility of farmland. China's interior deserts, cold, windswept plateaus, and snowcapped mountains remain as empty as they have always been, except for small settlements in areas where minerals or fuels are mined.

In countries with more technologically advanced economies, people tend to leave the land and to cluster in cities and towns. Mushrooming urbanization, in which rural, farm-based societies are transformed into urban, trade-based ones, is a dominant theme of contemporary human geography. To be sure, cities are also growing in such countries as India and China, but the percentage of those countries' population that is urbanized remains far below that of, say, the United States or Western Europe. (For comparisons among these and other countries, consult Resource B, page R-10, where demographic data for all the world's principal countries are provided.)

Population Distribution and Density

To represent contrasts of the kind just discussed on maps, population geographers use measures of population ***distribution*** and ***density***.

The distribution of population describes the locations on the Earth's surface where individuals or groups (depending on the scale) live. It is represented most efficiently by a so-called ***dot map***. At the largest scale—for example, part of a rural county in the United States—such a map can actually show the location of every indi-

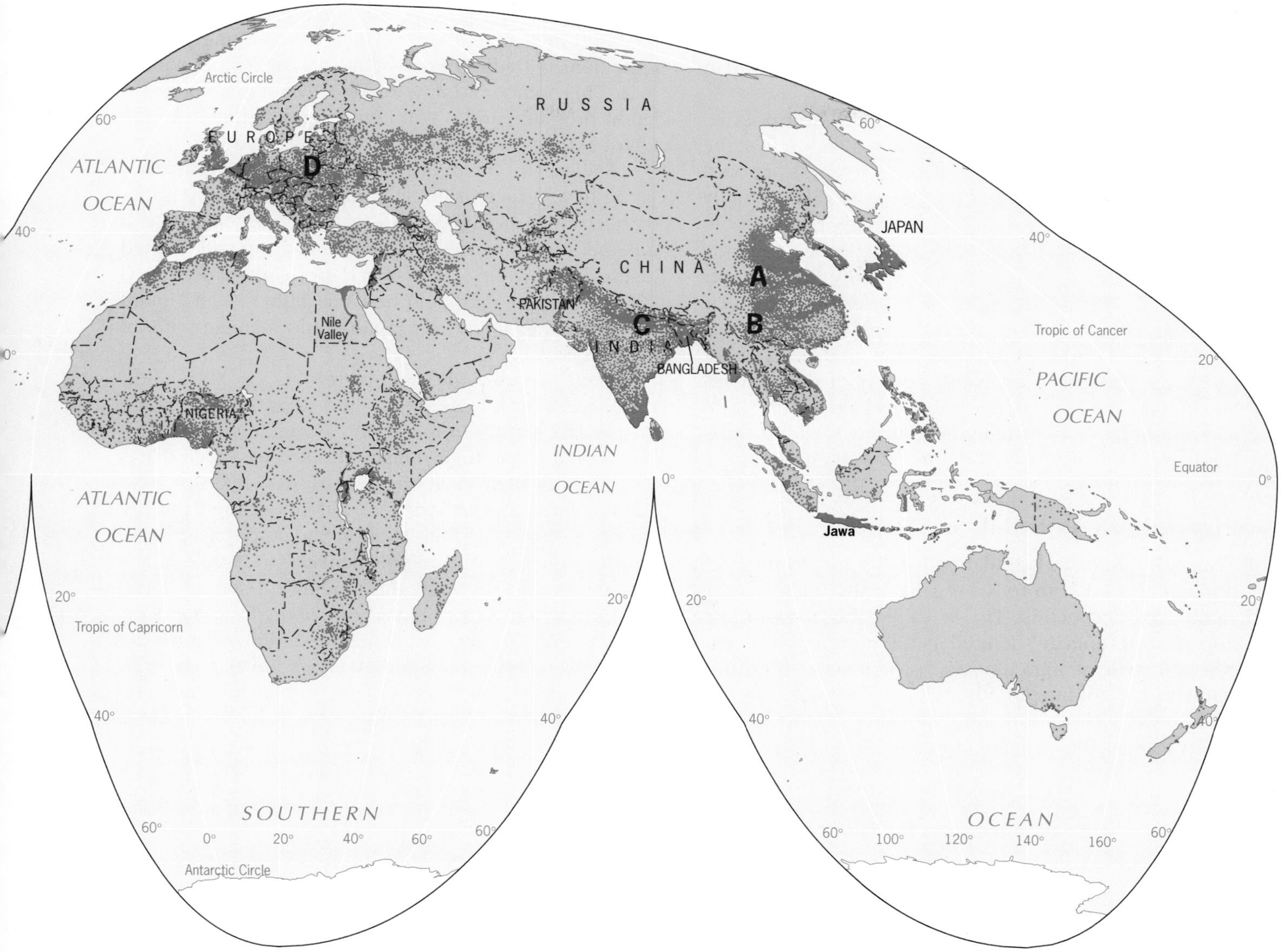

vidual, with each dot representing one person. At a medium scale—say an entire country such as France—one dot would represent a cluster of perhaps 5000 people, and the map would reveal where the population is concentrated and where the number of people in an area would not add up to 5000. At the smallest scale, a world map of ***population density*** would use a single dot to represent as many as 100,000 people.

Maps of population distribution have many uses. Famine-relief campaigns, for example, use them in their efforts to deliver supplies to remote areas more efficiently. Closer to home, electoral redistricting maps cannot be drawn without data on where voters live. For such purposes, too, distribution maps are needed.

Population density is another matter. Here the measure is of the number of people per unit area, such as a square kilometer or square mile. The data in Resource B (page R-10) provide the area, total population, and density per square mile for every country (but see the box, "Reliability of Population Data").

Note, however, that no country has an evenly distributed population, so that the average derived by dividing the national area by the total number of people may not have much practical meaning. The United States, for example, with a territory of 3,717,425 square miles or 9,629,167 square kilometers (including the surfaces of lakes and ponds and coastal waters up to three nautical miles from shore) had a population of 285.4 million in 2002. This yields an average population density for the United States of just under 77 per square mile (29.6 per square kilometer). This figure is the country's ***arithmetic population density***, and in a very general way it emphasizes the contrasts between the United States and such nations as Bangladesh (2644 per square mile), the Netherlands (1224), and Japan (875).

But no country has an evenly distributed population, and arithmetic population figures do not reflect the emptiness of most of Alaska and the sparseness of population in much of the West. In other cases it is actually quite misleading. Take the example of Egypt which, with a population of 71.1 million in 2002, has a seemingly moderate arithmetic population density of 185 per square mile. Egypt's territory of 284,300 square miles, however, is mostly desert, and the vast majority of the population is crowded into the valley and delta of the Nile River. It is estimated that 98 percent of all Egyptians live on just 3 percent of the country's land, so the arithmetic population density figure is pretty well meaningless here.

Physiologic Population Density

A superior index of population density relates the total population of a country or region to the area of cultivated land it contains. This is called the ***physiologic population density***, defined as the number of people per unit area of agriculturally productive land. Take again the case of Egypt. Although millions of people live in its great cities (Cairo and Alexandria) and smaller urban centers, the irrigated farmland is densely peopled as well. When the entire population is divided in Egypt's confined ***arable*** (farmable) land, the resulting physiologic density figure for the year 2002 is 9245 per square mile. This number is far more reflective of Egypt's population pressure, and it continues to rise rapidly despite Egypt's efforts to expand its irrigated farmlands.

The case of Japan is also instructive. Not only does Japan have a high arithmetic population density (more than 11 times as high as that of the United States), but Japan is a mountainous, high-relief country with limited arable land. Japan's physiologic population density is 7950, which is almost 20 times as high as the United States. Neither Egypt nor Japan could manage without food imports.

Table 4-1 provides complete data on both arithmetic and physiologic population densities, and some of the data stand out markedly. Mountainous Switzerland's high physiologic density should be expected: it is 10 times as high as its arithmetic density. But note Ukraine, with its vast farmlands: its physiologic density is only 1.7 times as high as its arithmetic density. Also compare the high physiologic densities in Middle America (see Puerto Rico!) to the moderate data for South America, where Argentina has one of the lowest indices in the world. Furthermore, note that India's physiologic density is the lowest in South Asia despite its huge population (and is less than twice as high as its arithmetic density), whereas China's physiologic density in 2002 was almost 10 times higher.

Table 4-1 Population Densities for Selected Countries, 2001

Country	2001 Population in millions	Area thousands sq mi/km	Arithmetic Density sq mi/km	Physiologic Density sq mi/km	% Arable Land
Argentina	37.5	1056.6 mi–2736.6 km	35/mi 15/km	394/mi 152/km	9
Bangladesh	133.5	51.7 mi–133.9 km	2582/mi 997/km	3541/mi 1362/km	73
China	1273.3	3600.9 mi–9326.4 km	354/mi 137/km	3521/mi 1365/km	10
Colombia	43.1	401 mi–1038.7 km	107/mi 41/km	2694/mi 1036/km	4
Egypt	69.8	384.3 mi–995.4 km	182/mi 70/km	9064/mi 3508/km	2
India	1033	1147.9 mi–2973.1 km	900/mi 347/km	1607/mi 620/km	56
Japan	127.1	144.6 mi–374.7 km	879/mi 339/km	7944/mi 3085/km	11
Netherlands	16	13.1 mi–33.9 km	1221/mi 472/km	4849/mi 1882/km	25
Nigeria	126.6	351.7 mi–910.8 km	360/mi 139/km	1090/mi 421/km	33
Puerto Rico	3.9	3.5 mi–9.0 km	1114/mi 433/km	3900/mi 975/km	4
Switzerland	7.2	15.4 mi–40.0 km	468/mi 180/km	4800/mi 1800/km	10
Ukraine	49.1	233.0 mi–603.7 km	211/mi 81/km	363/mi 140/km	58
United States	284.5	3536.3 mi–9159.0 km	80/mi 31/km	423/mi 163/km	19

Sources: Calculated from World Population Datasheet, 2001, published by the Population Reference Bureau, Inc., and from the World Factbook, 2001, published by the United States' Central Intelligence Agency.

Note that the population data in this table may not correspond precisely to statistics from other sources. (See box, "Reliability of Population Data.")

◆ MAJOR POPULATION CONCENTRATIONS

Figures 4-1 and 4-2 show patterns of distribution and density in the world population. Figure 4-1 displays distribution using the dot method, whereas Figure 4-2 illustrates density via the isopleth method. Both maps confirm that the world's three largest ***population concentrations*** are all found on the same landmass: Eurasia. They also remind us that the overwhelming majority of the world's population inhabits the Northern Hemisphere.

From the field notes

"This dirt road along the shore of Bombay Harbor provided some useful insights into Mumbai's diversity, and I followed it as far as I could. The apartment buildings in the background house the fortunate in this teeming city, but make no mistake: the dwellings in the left foreground, with their jute (burlap) covers and palm-frond roofs, are superior to those of millions living in this city's outskirt shantytowns. Fishermen and their families live here (the man sitting on the left is working on his nets, see the boat across the road), and this is no poverty-stricken district. The flags ahead alert the traveler to the small Hindu shrine to their right. A dog sleeps in the road; she is thin, but no one will disturb her. As I kept walking I wondered what the white box to the right of the road might be. It turned out to be a refrigerator truck that would carry the next morning's catch to nearby markets."

The three Eurasian concentrations are in East Asia, South Asia, and Europe. Each is associated with a major civilization: China, India, and Western Europe. The fourth-ranking concentration, North America, is centered in the United States and represents still another important civilization. In this section we explore some of the significant differences among these leading population clusters.

East Asia

Although the distribution map (Fig. 4-1) requires no color contrasts, Figure 4-2 depicts population density through shading: the darker the color, the larger the number of people per unit area. The most extensive area of dark shading lies in ***East Asia***, primarily in China but also in Korea and Japan. About one-quarter of the world's population is concentrated here—nearly 1.3 billion people in China alone.

The East Asian population cluster adjoins the Pacific Ocean from Korea to Vietnam; the number of people per unit area tends to decline from this coastal zone toward the interior. Also visible are several ribbon-like extensions of dense population (Fig. 4-2 A and B). These extensions represent populations that are clustered in the basins and lowlands of China's major rivers. This serves to remind us that the great majority of people in East Asia are farmers, not city dwellers. True, China has large cities, such as Shanghai and Beijing. However, the total population of these and other cities is far outnumbered by the farmers, who produce crops of wheat and rice to feed not only themselves but also those in the cities and towns.

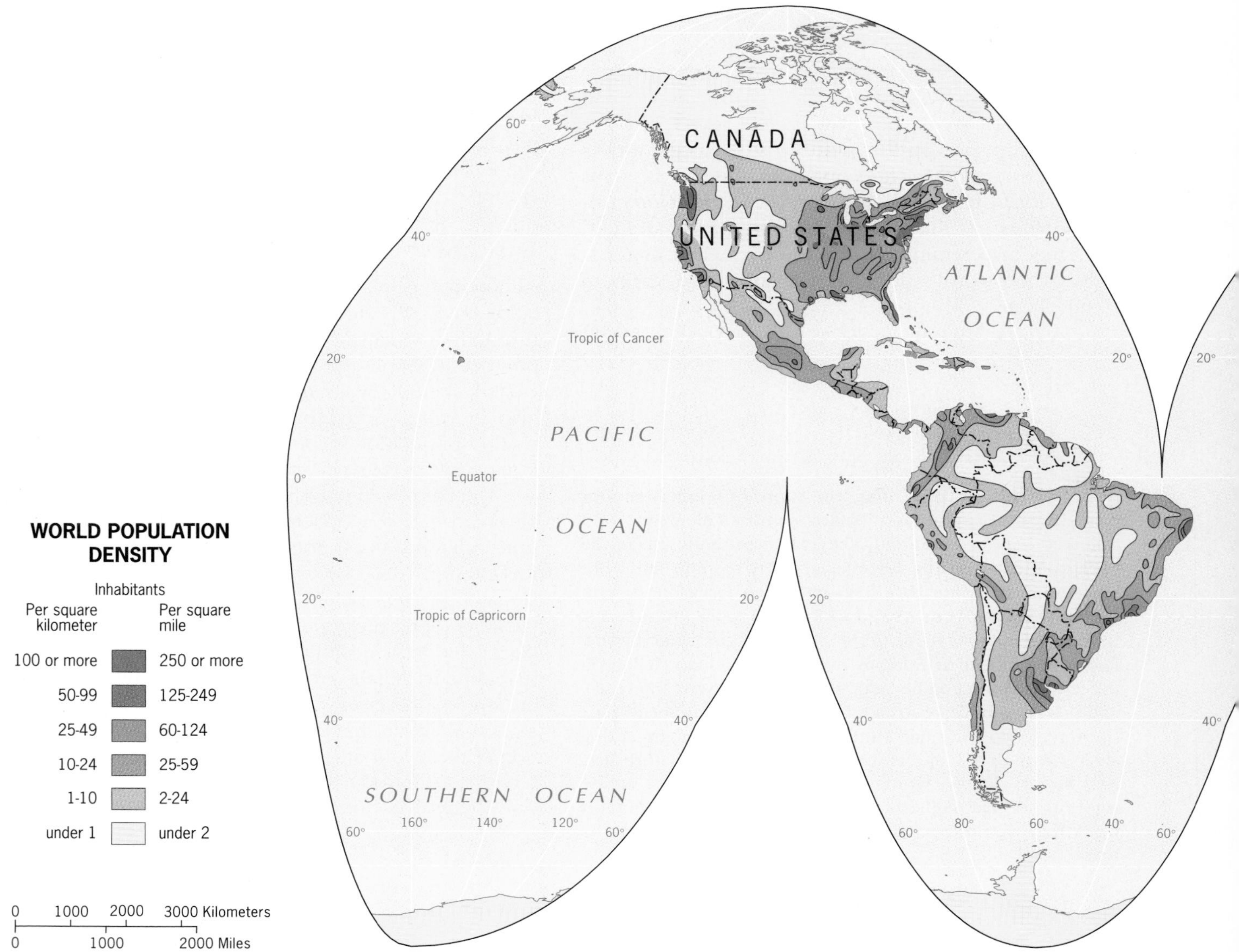

Figure 4-2 World Population Density.

South Asia

The second major population concentration also lies in Asia and is similar in many ways to that of East Asia. At the heart of this cluster lies India, but the concentration also extends into Pakistan and Bangladesh and onto the island of Sri Lanka. Again, note the riverine and coastal orientation of the most densely inhabited zones and the finger-like extension of dense population on the plain of the Ganges River in northern India (Fig. 4-2 C). This is one of the greatest concentrations of people on the Earth.

There are about 1.5 billion people in the South Asia population cluster. Our map shows how sharply this region is marked off by physical barriers: the Himalaya Mountains to the north and the desert west of the Indus River Valley in Pakistan. This is a confined region with a rapidly growing population. The capacity of the region to support this population has, by almost any estimate, already been exceeded. As in East Asia, the overwhelming majority of the people here are farmers, but in South Asia the pressure on the land is even greater. In Bangladesh, nearly 133 million people, almost all of them farmers, are crowded into an area about the size of Iowa. Over large parts of Bangladesh the rural population density is between 3000 and 5000 people per square mile. By comparison, in 2002 the population of Iowa was about 3 million people, and less than 40 percent lived on the land rather than in cities and towns. The rural population density was under 30 people per square mile.

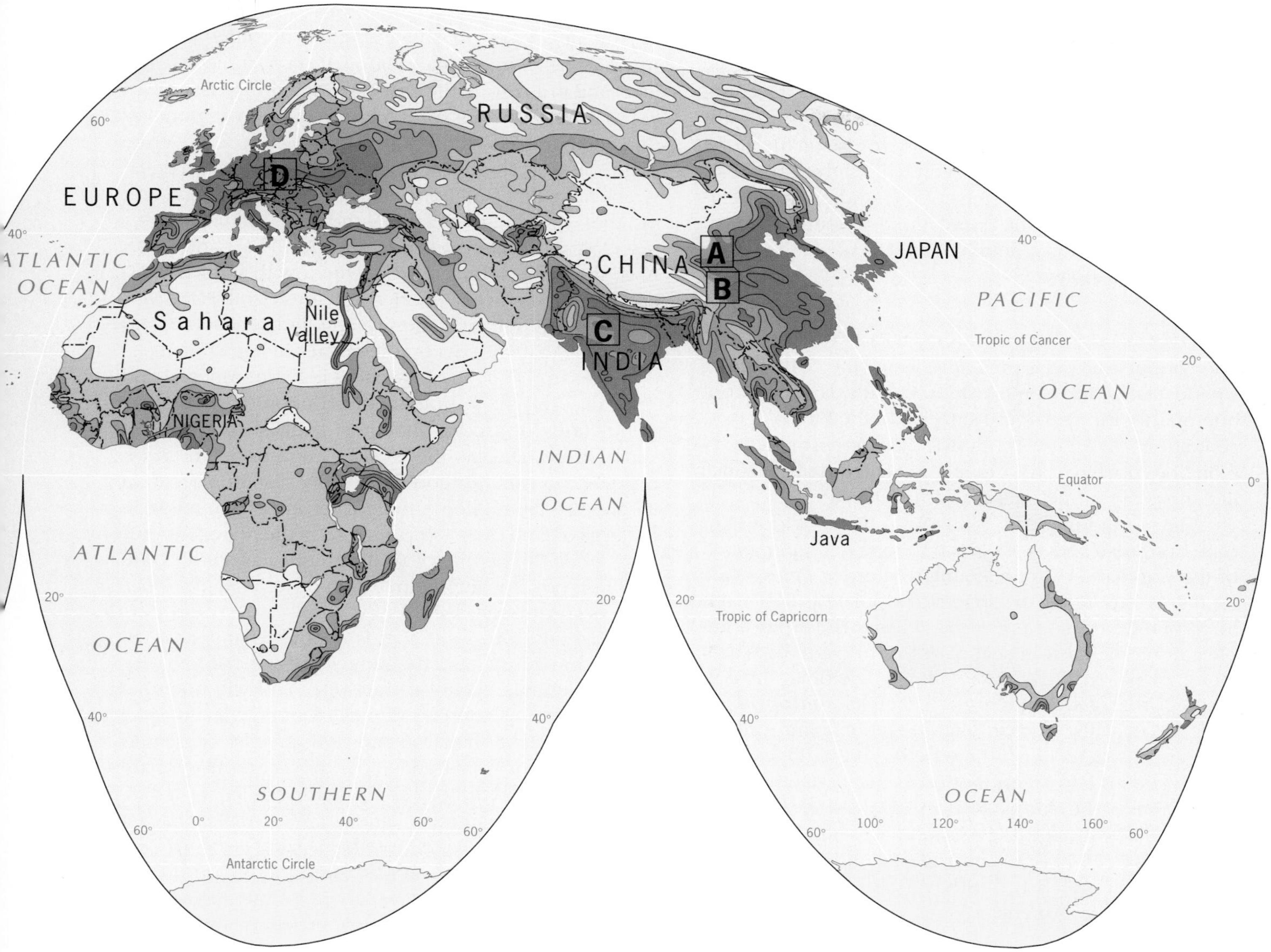

Europe

Further inspection of Figures 4-1 and 4-2 reveals that the third-ranking population cluster also lies in Eurasia—at the opposite end from China. An axis of dense population extends from the British Isles into Russia and includes large parts of Germany, Poland, Ukraine, and Belarus. It also includes the Netherlands and Belgium, parts of France, and northern Italy. This European cluster contains about 700 million inhabitants, which puts it in a class with the South Asia concentration—but there the similarity ends. A comparison of the population and physical maps indicates that in Europe terrain and environment are not as closely related to population distribution as they are in East and South Asia. For example, note that lengthy extension marked D in Figure 4-2, which protrudes far into Russia. Unlike the Asian extensions, which reflect fertile river valleys, the European extension reflects the orientation of Europe's coal-fields. If you look more closely at the physical map, you will note that comparatively dense population occurs even in mountainous, rugged country, such as the boundary zone between Poland and its neighbors to the south. A much greater correspondence exists between coastal and river lowlands and high population density in Asia than in Europe generally.

Another contrast can be seen in the number of Europeans who live in cities and towns. The European population cluster includes numerous cities and towns, many of which developed as a result of the Industrial Revolution. In Germany, 85 percent of the people live in such urban places; in the United Kingdom, over 90 percent; and in France, 74 percent. With so many people concentrated in the cities, the rural countryside is more open and sparsely populated than in East and South Asia, where about 30 percent of the people reside in cities and towns.

The three major population concentrations we have discussed—East Asia, South Asia, and Europe—account for over 4 billion of the total world population of approximately 6 billion people. Nowhere else on the globe is there a population cluster even half as great as any of these. Look at the dimensions of the landmasses in Figure 7-1 and note that the populations of South America, Africa, and Australia combined barely exceed the population of India alone.

North America

The population cluster comprising the east-central United States and southeastern Canada is only about one-quarter the size of the smallest of the Eurasian concentrations. As Figure 4-2 shows, the North American region does not have large, contiguous high-density zones like those of Europe or East and South Asia.

The North American population cluster outdoes Europe in some respects. As in the European region, much of the population is concentrated in major cities while rural areas are relatively sparsely populated. The major focus of the North America cluster lies in the urban complex along the eastern seaboard from Boston to Washington, which includes New York, Philadelphia, and Baltimore. Urban geographers use the term ***megalopolis*** to refer to such huge urban agglomerations, and predict that it is only a matter of time before these agglomerations coalesce into an enormous megacity. Other major focal points of the North American population cluster are Chicago, Detroit, and Cleveland, and with some interruptions, San Francisco, Los Angeles, and San Diego. If you study Figure 7-1 carefully, you will note other prominent North American cities standing out as small areas of high-density population; they include Pittsburgh, St. Louis, Minneapolis-St. Paul, and Seattle.

Other Regions

Further examination of Figures 4-1 and 4-2 reveals substantial population clusters in Southeast Asia. These are actually discrete clusters rather than a contiguous population concentration. The largest of them is the Indonesian island of Jawa (Java), with more than 120 million inhabitants. Elsewhere in the region populations cluster in the lowlands of major rivers, such as the Mekong. Neither these river valleys nor the rural surroundings of the cities have population concentrations comparable to those of either China or India, and under normal circumstances Southeast Asia is able to export rice to its hungrier neighbors. Over many decades of strife, however, the region has been disrupted to such a degree that its productive potential has not been attained.

South America, Africa, and Australia do not have population concentrations comparable to those we have considered so far. Subsaharan Africa's nearly 650 million inhabitants cluster in above-average densities in West Africa (where Nigeria has a population of some 130 million) and in a zone in the east extending from Ethiopia to South Africa. Only in North Africa is there an agglomeration comparable to those found on the crowded riverine plains of Asia. This cluster is in the Nile Valley and delta, which has over 66 million residents. Note that the pattern of the Nile agglomeration—not the dimensions—resembles the pattern seen in Asia. As in East and South Asia, the Nile Valley and delta teem with farmers who cultivate every foot of the rich and fertile soil. However, the lowlands of the Ganges, Chang Jiang (Yangtzi), and Huang He (Yellow) rivers contain far more inhabitants.

The large light-shaded spaces in South America and Australia, and the peripheral distribution of the modest populations of these continents, suggest that there is some space here for the world's huge population. Indeed, South America could probably sustain more than its present 360 million people if reforms were made in patterns of land ownership and use in the region. At present, while the people of South America as a whole are well fed, poverty and malnutrition occur in some areas, such as northeast Brazil.

This raises an issue that is central to any study of population density and the capacity of a country to support its people: level of technology. You will note that Japan, a small island country, has a population of over 127 million. Its population density is at least as great as that of parts of China and India, but its farmlands are quite limited, not only by its small size but, as we noted, also by its mountainous character. What makes such a large population in Japan possible is Japan's technological prowess, industrial capacity, and money-producing exports. Japan imports raw materials from all over the world, converts them into finished products, and exports those products to most parts of the globe. With the income brought in by these exports, Japan can buy the food that it cannot produce at home. Thus it is not enough to say that a country cannot support more than a specific number of people. We should qualify this statement by observing that ***under present economic, political, and technological conditions*** it can or cannot support a given population, depending on its status in the world market. So, while Australia could not find a place for tens of millions of Chinese farmers, if tens of millions of Japanese came to Australia with their skills, technologies, factories, and international connections, Australia would be quite capable of accommodating them—and many more.

Having examined the distribution and general density of global and regional populations, we now come to the crucial issue: population growth—its history, dimensions, and spatial expression. The next chapter links the maps of distribution and density with the dynamics of demographic change.

◆ KEY TERMS ◆

arithmetic population density
census
demography
density
distribution
megalopolis
physiologic population density
population concentration
population data
population density
population geography

◆ APPLYING GEOGRAPHIC KNOWLEDGE ◆

1. If the arithmetic density measure is of so little practical use, why do you suppose it is listed in virtually every database published by population-monitoring agencies? Which State in the United States has the lowest arithmetic density, and how meaningful is that statistic? When it comes to physiologic density, this measure is much more relevant, in practical terms, for some countries than for others. Compare the Netherlands and Bangladesh in this context.

2. Some of the world's largest cities, such as Mumbai (Bombay), Shanghai, and Cairo, lie in countries that rank among the world's least urbanized societies. Explain this apparent contradiction.

3. An international food-relief agency has asked you to prepare a report to help make food distribution in a certain area, threatened by famine, more efficient. Will you use maps of population distribution (dot maps) or population density (isopleth maps) to support your case? What role will scale play in your presentation?

Chapter 5

Processes and Cycles of Population Change

From the field notes

"China, 1981. In town after town, we were the first Westerners people had seen, and they followed us in droves, curious, friendly, yet reticent. Here, in a town on the outskirts of Anyang, we had hoped to find archeological items from the Shang dynasty in a long-shuttered museum. The news of our visit had spread and a crowd was waiting. As with all the others, what struck me was the predominance of youngsters. In the rural villages and towns, the population seemed to practically *consist* of children. No wonder the new leadership in Beijing was trying to devise ways to reduce family size throughout the country. (No archaeological treasures remained. Destroyed during the Cultural Revolution, we were told)."

KEY POINTS

◆ **The population explosion of the past 200 years has increased the world's population from under 1 billion to over 6 billion.**

◆ **Although hundreds of millions of people remain inadequately nourished, the threat of global hunger has receded—perhaps temporarily.**

◆ **Rapid population growth varies over time and space. Europe's rapid growth occurred during the nineteenth century; Africa's great increases occurred during the second half of the twentieth century.**

◆ **Total fertility rates are falling almost everywhere on Earth, and in some countries they are declining dramatically.**

◆ **Keys to the reduction of population growth rates include providing greater access to education for women and securing their rights in society.**

◆ **The demographic transition model suggests that the world's population will stabilize in the twenty-first century, but the model may not be universally applicable.**

During the twentieth century not a single country, colony, or dependency escaped the population explosion. No state had fewer people in the year 2000 than it did in 1900, and in many the population did not just grow, it multiplied. It took from the dawn of history to the year 1820 for the Earth's population to reach 1 billion, and the 2-billion mark was not reached until more than a century later, in 1930. But by the 1970s, it took just *12 years* for world population to add 1 billion, and in 1999 the total reached 6 billion. Even if the global rate of population growth slows down in the decades ahead, there still may be 10 billion human inhabitants on this planet by the middle of the century. ◆

◆ WORLDWIDE POPULATION TRENDS

In 2002, about 137 million babies were born worldwide, and approximately 56 million people died. This means that we are adding about 80 million inhabitants to the global population every year. Most of this increase is occurring in regions that are least able to support the new arrivals, and of those who die, many millions are young children who succumb to disease or malnutrition. Girls are at far greater risk than boys in the poorer countries of the world.

Some indicators suggest that the worst may be over, that the explosive population growth of the twentieth century will be followed by a marked and accelerating slowdown during the twenty-first. And indeed, as Figure 5-1 shows, a number of countries' populations have not only stopped growing but are actually declining, notably in Europe. The table in Resource B confirms that Italy, Sweden, Hungary, and Ukraine—among a total of 14 European states—exhibit "negative population growth," a rate of natural increase that is below 0.0 percent. Indeed, Europe as a geographic realm is not growing any longer, and only immigration keeps population growth going.

Russia's population, too, is declining, and quite rapidly, and as we will note in more detail later, Japan's population is set to begin a long, initially slow, then accelerating decline. But none of this stops the still-rapid global rate of natural increase. That is because the total populations of the stabilizing and declining countries are dwarfed by the huge numbers in countries where growth rates are still high, such as India, Indonesia, Bangladesh, Pakistan, and Nigeria.

As a result, world population continues to grow by nearly 1 billion per decade. In 1990 the U.S. Census Bureau reported that the overall growth rate of the world's population had declined from approximately 2.1 percent per year during the 1965–1969 period to 1.6 percent during 1985–1989. But when the growth rate was 2.1 percent, the world's population was approaching 4 billion, resulting in 80 million additional inhabitants each year. By the time the rate was down to 1.6 percent per year

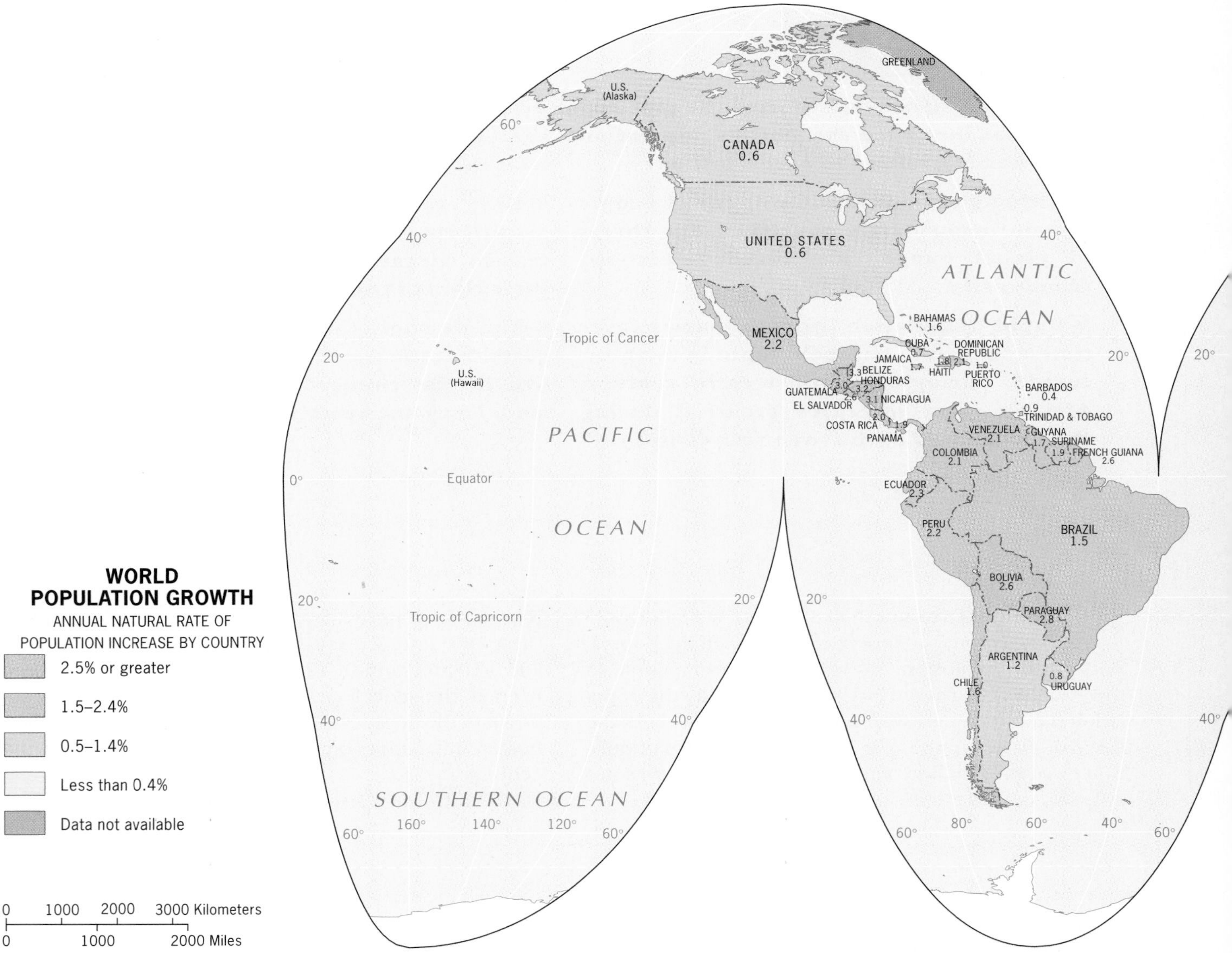

Figure 5-1 World Population Growth. Annual natural rate of population increase by country, 2002. *Based on data from several sources.*

(possibly a low estimate), the population base was already 5 billion. Calculate it for yourself: a 1.6-percent increase, on a base of 5.0 billion, ***still*** produces over 80 million additional people.

Now we are in the new century, and the global growth rate (see the top of the table in Resource B) is down to 1.4 percent, perhaps slightly lower. But today the world's population is well over 6 billion, yielding an increase that still exceeds 80 million annually. The rate of increase will have to come down well below 1.0 percent to make a real difference.

The world map of population growth rates (Fig. 5-1), displayed by country, confirms the wide range of natural increases in different geographic realms. These variations have existed as long as records have been kept: countries and regions go through stages of expansion and decline at varying times. In the mid-twentieth century, the population of the former Soviet Union was growing vigorously. Thirty years ago, India's population was growing at nearly 3.0 percent, more than most African countries; then India's growth rate fell below that of Subsaharan Africa. Today, Africa's rate of natural increase still is higher than India's (2.6 percent to 1.8 percent), but now Subsaharan Africa faces the impact of the AIDS epidemic, which is killing millions, orphaning children, reducing life expectancies, and curtailing growth rates.

The map also reveals the continuing high growth rates in Muslim countries of North Africa and Southwest Asia. Saudi Arabia has one of the highest growth rates in

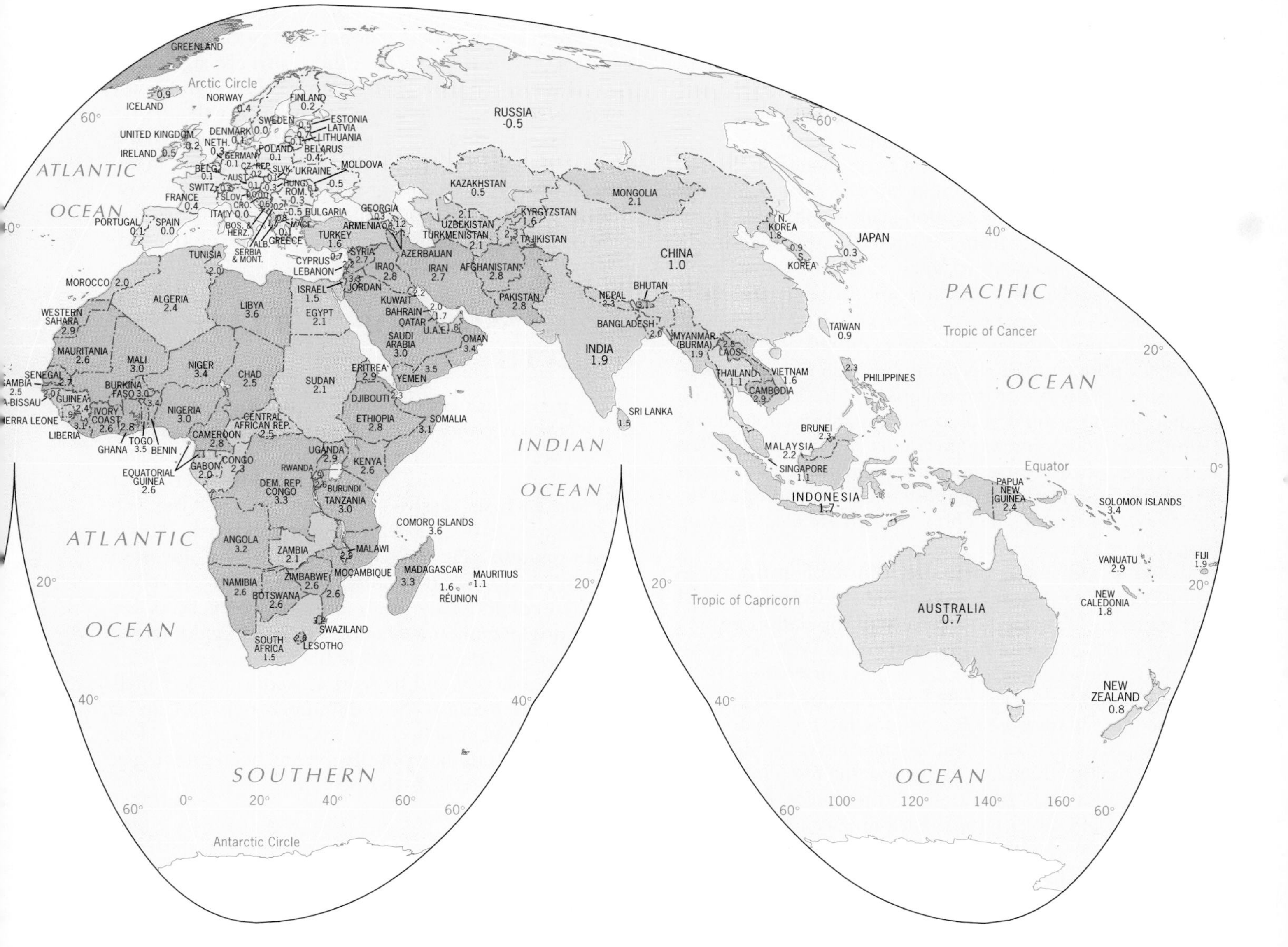

the world, but some smaller countries in this realm are increasing even faster. For some time during the second half of the twentieth century, countries in this realm saw their growth rates increase even as those in most of the rest of the world were declining. But more recently several of the fast-growing populations, for example, those of Iran and Morocco, have shown significant declines. Demographers often point to the correlation between high growth rates and the low standing of women: where cultural traditions restrict educational and professional opportunities for women and men dominate as a matter of custom, rates of natural increase tend to be high.

No geographic realm is more important in the population picture than South Asia, with nearly 1.4 billion people, including the country that appears destined to overtake China as the world's most populous, India. Only one country in this realm has a rate of increase lower than the world average: Sri Lanka. But Sri Lanka's total population is only 20 million, whereas the fast-growing countries, Pakistan and Bangladesh, have a combined population approaching 300 million. India, as the map shows, is still growing well above the world average. The situation in East Asia, the world's most populous realm, is more encouraging. China's official rate of natural growth has fallen well below 1.0 percent, Japan's population is stable and will soon begin to decline, and the Koreas average below the global mean. Southeast Asia's growth rates remain higher, but this realm's total population is much lower than either East or South Asia and key countries, such as Indonesia, Thailand, and Vietnam, have declining growth rates.

Significant reductions in natural population growth rates are also occurring in South America, where those rates were alarmingly high just a generation ago. The realm as a whole is still growing at 1.7 percent, but Brazil's population, for example, has declined from 2.9 percent in the mid-1960s to 1.5 percent today. And the populations of the southern cone (Argentine, Chile, and Uruguay) are growing at rates well below the world average.

As Figure 5-1 shows, the slowest-growing countries—including those with declining rates of natural population increase—lie in the economically wealthier areas of the world extending from the United States and Canada across Europe, Russia, and Japan. In the Southern Hemisphere, Australia, New Zealand, and Uruguay are in this category. As we have noted, not all countries with low or negative population growth are economically well off. Russia's population is declining because of social dislocation in the wake of the collapse of the Soviet Union: deteriorating health conditions, rampant alcoholism and drug use, and economic problems combine to shorten life expectancies (especially among males) and to lower birth rates. Similar problems afflict Ukraine and Kazakhstan, two of Russia's neighbors which are also showing slow or negative growth.

No single factor, therefore, can explain the variations shown on Figure 5-1. Economic prosperity as well as social dislocation reduce natural population growth rates. Economic well-being, associated with urbanization, higher levels of education, later marriage, family planning, and other factors, lowers population growth. In the table in Resource B, compare the indices for natural population increase and the percentage of the population that is urbanized; in general, the higher the population's level of urbanization, the lower its natural increase. Cultural traditions also influence rates of population growth: religion, for example, has a powerful impact not only in Islamic countries but also in Christian societies (note the Roman Catholic Philippines' growth rate) and in Hindu-dominated communities.

It is important to note that the information provided in Figure 5-1 is based on national (that is, countrywide) statistics. As we will discover, there also are significant demographic variations ***within*** countries. In India, for example, some States record population growth rates far above the national average; these States lie mostly in the east and northeast of the country. But other States, in the west and southwest, are growing much more slowly. Our map, therefore, is a small-scale, global overview, a mere introduction to the complexities of the global geography of population.

◆ DIMENSIONS OF POPULATION GROWTH

As the figures just quoted indicate, the human population has not expanded in a linear manner, in which increases occur in uniform amount during a series of equal time periods. If you have \$100 and add \$10 to it the first year and each successive year, your \$100 will become \$200 after 10 years, \$300 after 20 years, and so on. This is ***linear growth*** (Fig. 5-2A). However, if you invested your initial \$100 at an interest rate of 10 percent, compounded continuously, each increase would be based on the original amount plus previously added interest. After 10 years, your \$100 would have increased to \$259; after 20 years, it would have increased to \$673. This is ***exponential growth***. The difference between linear and exponential growth is obvious, and it is equally clear that the world's human population has been growing at exponential rates (Fig. 5-2B).

Doubling Time

Another way of looking at exponential growth is to compare a population's rate of growth to its ***doubling time***. Every rate of growth has a doubling time; for ex-

Figure 5-2 Population Growth. (A) linear; (B) exponential; (C) doubling time.

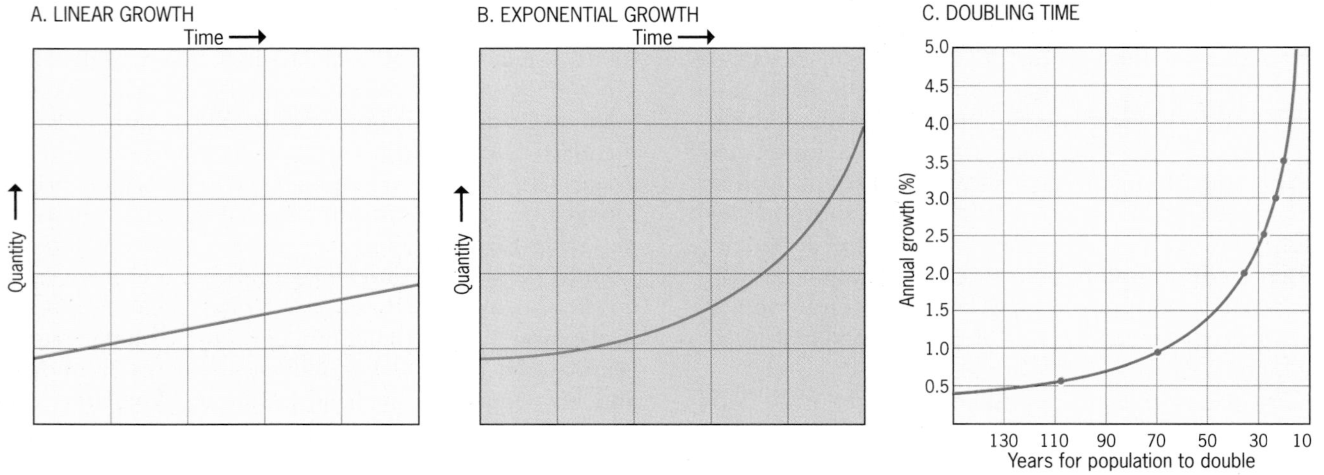

ample, your $100 invested at 10 percent took about 7 years to double to $200, and then another 7 years to become $400, and then another 7 years to become $800. When the growth rate is 10 percent, therefore, the doubling time is around 7 years. During the middle of this century, when the world's population was increasing at an average rate of 2 percent, its doubling time was 35 years (Fig. 5-2C). During the mid-1980s, when the rate declined to 1.8 percent, the doubling slowed to 39 years. Today, world population is doubling in 51 years, and the continuing slowdown is one of the bright spots in the problematic demographic picture.

The table in Resource B records the 2002 doubling time for the populations of all the countries of the world. Start by looking at the regional situation: no figure is given for Europe because Europe's population is not growing (by natural means) at all. North America is doubling in 124 years, and East Asia in 87, still far slower than the global average. But South Asia in 2002 was still doubling in 36 years (Pakistan in only 25!), much faster than the world average and indicative of the changing population map. Muslim-dominated North Africa and Southwest Asia, too, continues to double in 35 years despite the economic gains made in some of this realm's countries. When you compare countries' doubling times to their economic well-being (for example, per capita GNP), you can observe the burden fast-growing societies must carry.

Lessons from the Population Explosion

It is estimated that 2000 years ago the world's population was about 250 million. More than 16 centuries passed before this total had doubled to 500 million, the estimated population in 1650. Just 170 years later, in 1820, the population had doubled again, to 1 billion (Fig. 5-3). And barely more than a century after this, in 1930, it reached 2 billion. Now the doubling time was down to 100 years and dropping fast; the ***population explosion*** was in full gear. Only 45 years elapsed during the next doubling, to 4 billion (1975). In that decade the rate of growth was approximately 2 percent per year, and the doubling time (Fig. 5-2C) had declined to 35 years. The history of humanity thus is one of growing numbers and ever-higher rates of increase.

Figure 5-3 Population Growth, 1650 to (estimated) 2050. The dashed line indicates a possible scenario for the next 50 years.

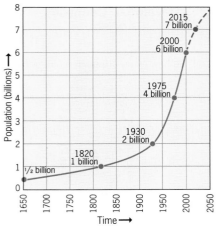

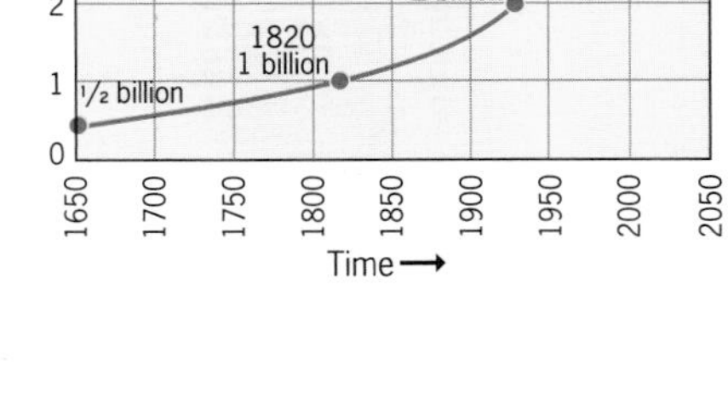

◆ EARLY WARNINGS

Concern over population growth arose even before the full impact of the population explosion was felt. As long ago as 1798, a British economist named Thomas Malthus published ***An Essay on the Principle of Population as It Affects the Future Improvement of Society***. In this work he sounded the alarm: the world's population was increasing faster than the food supplies needed to sustain it. Recognizing the nature of exponential growth, Malthus pointed out that population increases at what he called a geometric rate. The means of subsistence, in contrast, grow at an arithmetic (linear) rate. From 1803 to 1826, Malthus issued revised editions of his essay and responded vigorously to a barrage of criticism. He suggested that population growth in Britain might be checked by hunger within 50 years after the first appearance of his warning.

Malthus could not have foreseen the impacts of colonization and migration, and he would not have believed that the United Kingdom could sustain between 50 and 60 million people, as it does today. Nor was he correct about the linear increase of food production. It, too, has grown exponentially as the acreage under cultivation has expanded, improved strains of seed have been developed, and more fertilizers have been used. Those who continue to share Malthus' concerns (even if they do not agree with every detail of his argument) are sometimes called neo-Malthusians and they continue to be alarmed. They point out that human suffering is now occurring on a scale unimagined even by Malthus, and they argue that it is not enough simply to assert that this is an inevitable stage in the history of the world's population. Despite predictions that the population will stabilize later in the twenty-first century, they believe that the problem must be addressed now.

Once one moves below the global scale, it becomes increasingly difficult to apply Malthus' ideas. Some commentators speak of a "Malthusian crisis" occurring in particular regions or countries, by which they mean that population growth is outstripping food supplies. But at the time that Malthus was writing, he could treat Britain as a more or less closed system and confine his analysis to the population trends and resources of the British Isles. Few places in the world come close to being closed systems anymore. Switzerland and Japan are countries with large numbers of people living in areas with relatively few natural resources and limited agricultural land. Yet there is little hunger or suffering in those countries because of the strength of their political and economic institutions and their global economic position.

Hence, analysis of population growth at the regional scale requires a level of geographic understanding that is often missing. It requires seeing regions not as isolated places but as places whose nature and character are shaped both by their internal characteristics and by their external geographical relationships.

◆ POPULATION STRUCTURE

Maps showing the regional distribution and density of populations tell us about the numbers of people in countries or regions, but they cannot reveal two other aspects of those populations: the numbers of men and women and their ages. These aspects are important because a populous country in which half the population is very young has very different problems than a country in which a large proportion of the population is elderly. When geographers study populations, therefore, they are concerned not only with spatial distribution but also with ***population structure***.

Population Composition

The ***composition*** or *structure* of a population is its makeup in terms of age, sex, and other properties such as marital status and education. The key indicators are age and sex, represented visually by the ***age-sex pyramid***. The pyramid displays the percentages of each age group in the total population (normally five-year groups) by a horizontal bar whose length represents its share. Males in the group are to the left of the center line, females to the right.

An age-sex pyramid can instantly convey the demographic situation in a country. In the so-called developing countries, where birth and death rates generally remain high, the pyramid looks like a Christmas tree, with wide branches at the base and short ones near the top (Fig. 5-4). The youngest age groups have the largest share of the population; in the composite pyramid shown here, the three groups up to age 14 account for more than 30 percent of it. Older people, in the three highest age groups, represent only about 4 percent of the total. Slight variations of this pyramidal shape mark the population structure of such countries as Pakistan, Yemen, Guatemala, The Congo, and Laos. From age group 15 to 19 upward, each group is smaller than the one below it.

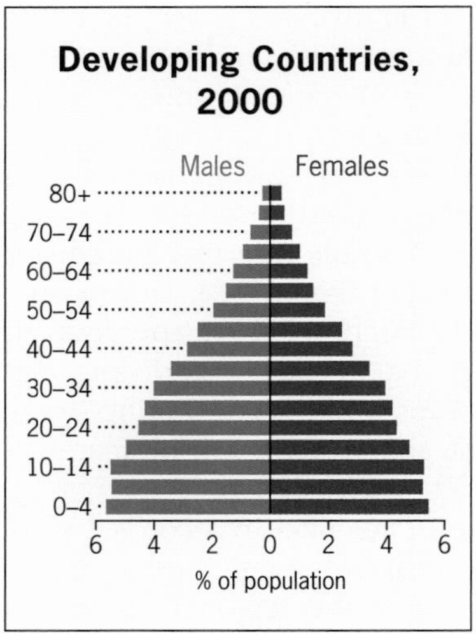

Figure 5-4 Age-Sex Pyramids for Countries with High Rates of Natural Population Increase. *Source:* U.S. Bureau of the Census, 2001.

With economic development, however, the shape of the pyramid changes. Families become smaller, children fewer. A composite population pyramid for the economically more advanced countries looks like a slightly lopsided vase, with the largest components of the population ***not*** at the bottom, but in the middle. And that middle-age bulge is moving upward, reflecting the ***aging*** of the population (Fig. 5-5). In the "developed" world, this is where the population explosion is now happening, and its social and economic consequences will be significant (see Looking Ahead Box).

Figure 5-5 Age-Sex Pyramids for Countries with Low Growth Rates. *Source:* U.S. Bureau of the Census, 2001.

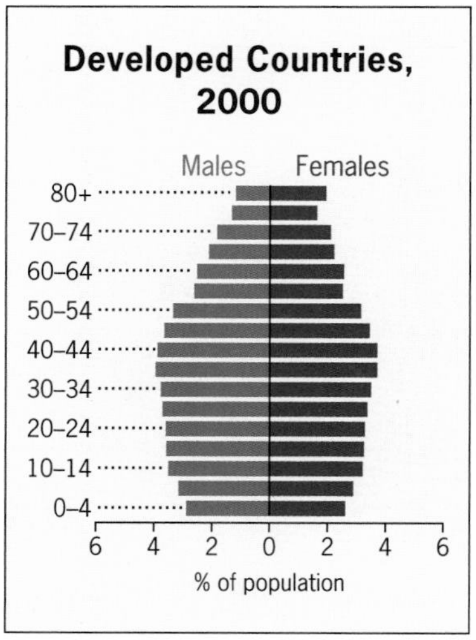

Looking Ahead

An Aging Population

Projections by the American Association for the Advancement of Science suggest that while the world's total population between 2000 and 2050 may grow about 40 percent, the number of people over 60 will increase by more than 230 percent. This means that the pyramid in Figure 5-5 will eventually become top-heavy, looking like a thick-stemmed mushroom with a cap representing the aged.

The pyramid representing the economically richer countries may look attractive to population geographers because it signals reduced population growth and even stabilizing populations, but aging societies will face a set of serious challenges. By 2030, people in Germany over 65 may well account for close to half the adult population, as compared with one-fifth now. Many other European countries are on a similar trajectory, and even developing countries such as Brazil and China will likely experience a substantial aging of the population as growth rates slow.

These changed demographics will require substantial social adjustments. Older people retire and eventually suffer health problems, so they need pensions and medical care. The younger workers in the population must provide the tax revenues to enable the state to pay for these services—but the number of younger workers will decline sharply. One response to this will be a rise in the age at which retirement benefits begin. But the only alternative that can really address the problem is immigration: influxes of younger workers to do the work locals are unable (or unwilling) to do. This has been the alternative followed by the United States in recent decades, and it has helped sustain the economic boom of the 1980s and 1990s. Yet immigration can create its own set of social problems, as has already happened in Germany with its large Turkish and Kurdish immigration, in France with its Algerian-Muslim influx, and in the United States with the arrival of Latinos.

There are important consequences to an aging and declining population as well. Significant economic sectors in many countries are geared toward the production of goods and materials for young people. Increasingly, however, the mass market will be more elevated in age, which in turn will require dramatic shifts in what is produced. Businesses producing such youth-oriented items as sportswear and video games will either have to find new foreign markets or face declining sales. And this is only one small part of a larger picture of adjustment that will be required as economies geared toward ever-increasing production face the new demographic reality.

Over the next half century, Japan will be an interesting test case. Japan's population will begin declining in 2007, and some projections indicate that the Japanese population will shrink as it ages, from over 127 million in 2007 to perhaps 70 million in 2050. Japan has long had one of the world's leading economies, but the population's aging will make it increasingly difficult to sustain this position—unless the Japanese allow foreign workers to immigrate. But as we will see in Chapter 7, this has been strongly resisted as a matter of tradition.

◆ DEMOGRAPHIC CYCLES

The study of population is called ***demography***, and its spatial component is population geography. We now turn to the demographic factors that underlie the patterns shown in Figure 5-1. So far we have viewed global population growth. But while some countries and regions are growing faster than the world average, others are growing much more slowly. And some countries actually have declining populations, that is, "negative" population growth.

A population goes through stages of growth each of which forms part of its demographic cycle. Populations in different parts of the world, and sometimes even in different parts of the same country, are at different stages in their demographic cycles—and these differences can have serious economic and political consequences.

Natural Increase

The rate of ***natural increase*** of a population is the difference between the number of births and the number of deaths during a specific period. These two measures, the birth rate and the death rate, are commonly expressed in terms of the number of individuals per thousand. In statistical tables these are reported as the ***crude birth rate (CBR)***—the number of live births per year per thousand people in the population—and the ***crude death rate (CDR)***—the number of deaths per thousand.

The Birth Rate

As Figure 5-6 shows, birth rates vary widely around the world. In 2002, South Asia, Subsaharan Africa, and North Africa and Southwest Asia continued to record the highest birth rates by region, although India has dropped from the highest category. Many countries in Africa still have birth rates over 40 per thousand, and a few have reached or exceeded 50. But deteriorating health conditions are causing death rates in Africa to rise, reducing rates of natural increase.

The lowest birth rates are in Europe, where most countries have CBRs below 15. Other areas with low birth rates are North America, Australia, New Zealand,

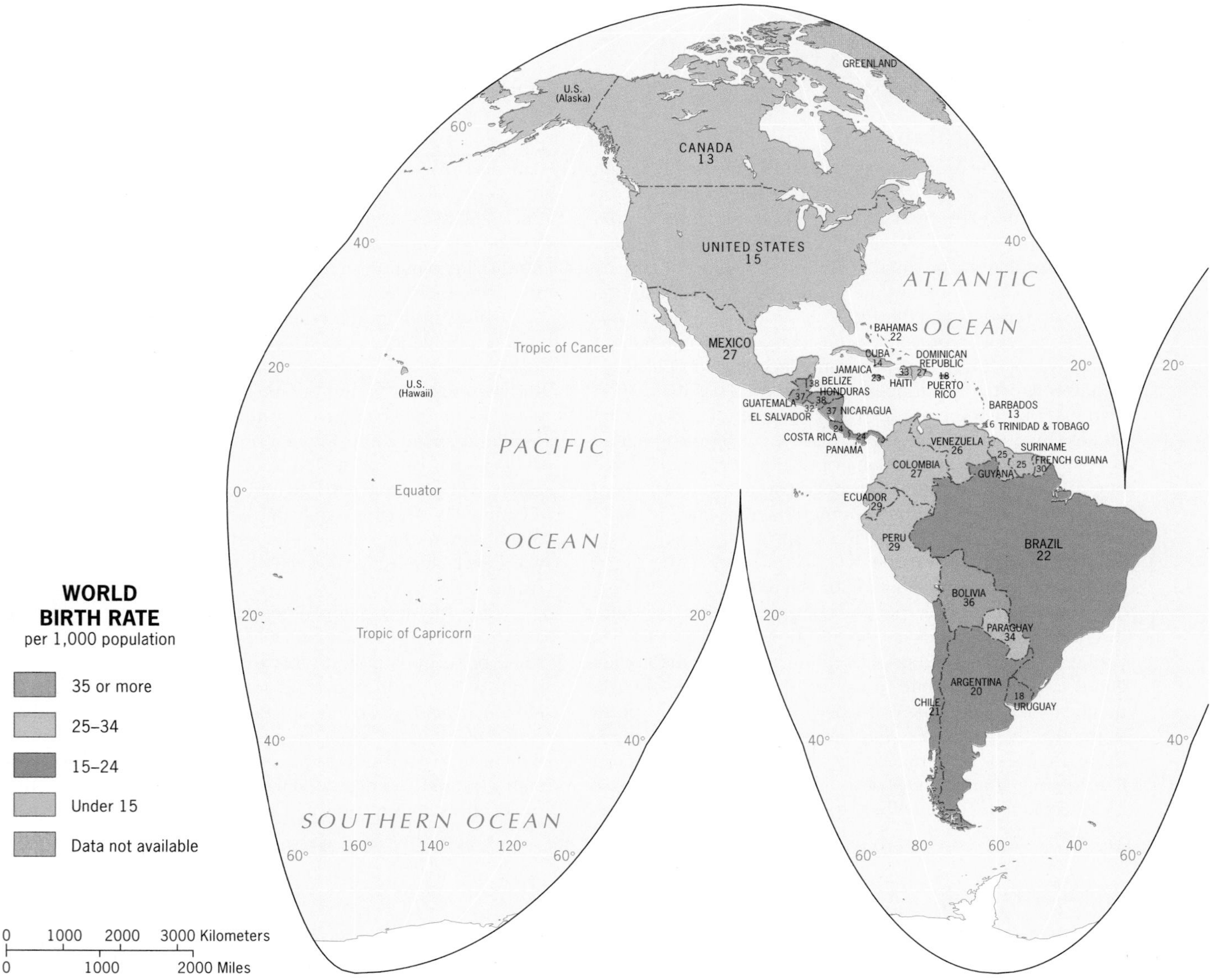

Figure 5-6 World Birth Rate. World birth rates by country. *Source:* Based on data from several sources.

Japan, and China. It is clear that low birth rates are associated with modernization—industrialization and urbanization—except in the case of China. Just one generation ago China still had high birth rates. Although it is not yet an industrialized, urbanized nation, China achieved its present low birth rate by imposing stringent population controls.

Looking more closely at Figure 5-6, we can see that a number of countries that are somewhere between poor and prosperous, such as Argentina, Colombia, and Thailand, also have intermediate (or transitional) birth rates. This would suggest that birth rates are related to the country's level of economic development. Again this generalization does not hold in the case of China. Economic development is crucial, but other factors, including cultural traditions, affect the patterns shown on Figure 5-6.

The Total Fertility Rate

Another measure of the reproductive status of a population is the ***total fertility rate (TFR)***. This is a measure of the number of children born to women of childbearing age. The TFR is usually reported as the number of children per woman, and it is a revealing statistic. For example, at the height of Kenya's population explosion in the 1980s, the number of children per woman of childbearing age was 8.1, among the highest ever recorded.

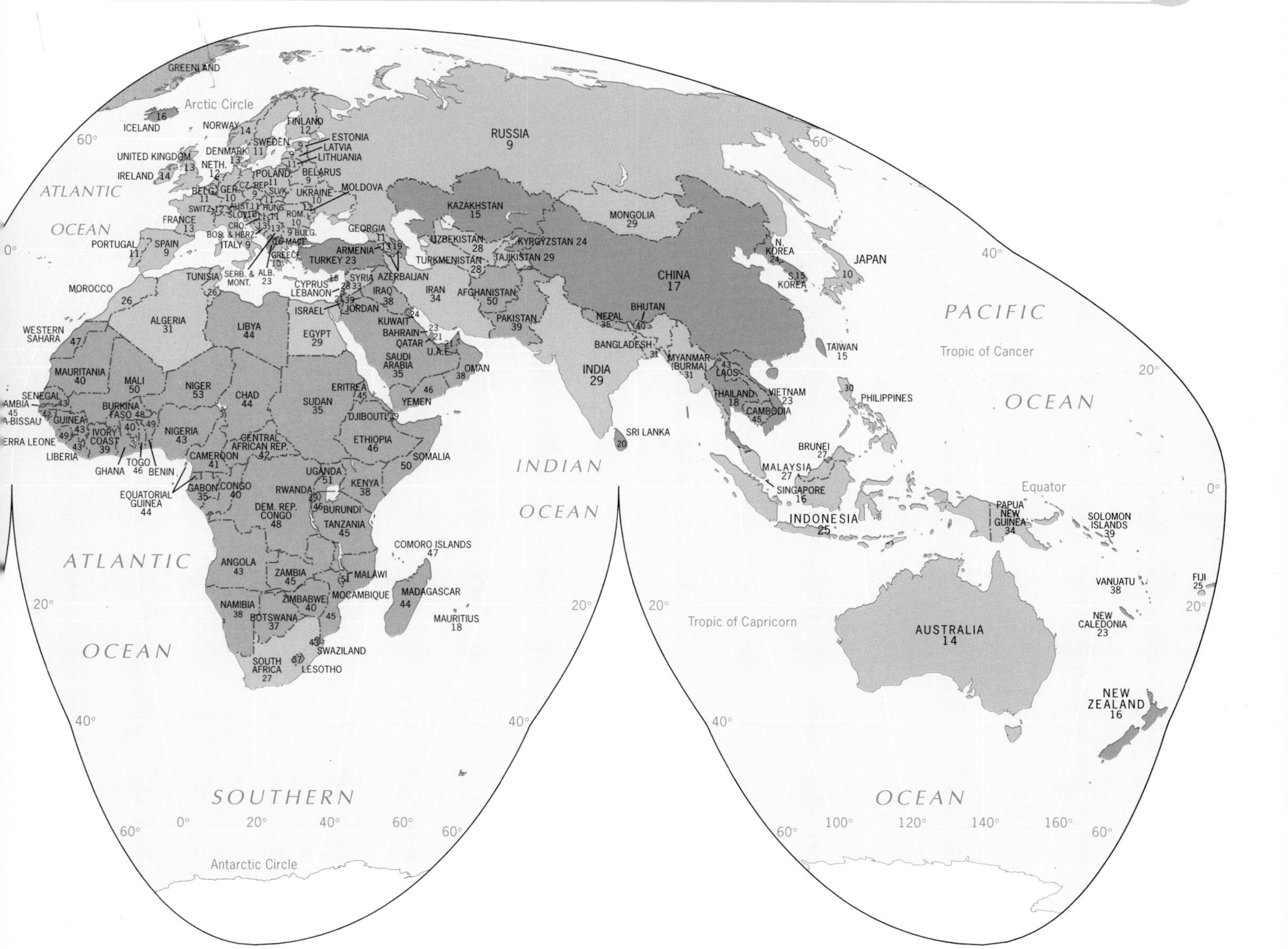

Today, TFRs are falling almost everywhere on Earth, and in some countries they are declining dramatically. Kenya's TFR is now down to 4.3; China's fell from 6.1 to 1.7 in just 30 years. The experience of Iran, where the TFR fell from 6.8 in 1980 to 2.7 in 2000, forms a reminder that such reductions are indeed possible under traditional Islamic rule when the government allows family planning and supports reproductive rights. Even Bangladesh, with many poor social indicators, has seen its TFR drop from 6.4 in 1980 to 2.9 in 2000.

These are encouraging data, for the TFR is a good indicator of future population change. Here is an important datum to remember: a TFR of 2.1 is required to keep a population stable over time without immigration. But at the beginning of this century, more than 60 countries, containing 45 percent of the world's population, had fallen below this replacement level. A substantial number of countries today, including some in the intermediate economic category, have TFRs lower than that of the United States. With TFRs falling globally, the world's population's doubling time may lengthen faster than has been anticipated.

The Death Rate

The crude death rate (CDR) is the number of deaths per thousand people in a given year. Also called the mortality rate, this figure has declined more dramatically than birth and fertility rates (Fig. 5-7). During the global population explosion, the widening gap between still-high birth rates and falling death rates signaled the rapid growth of the total human population.

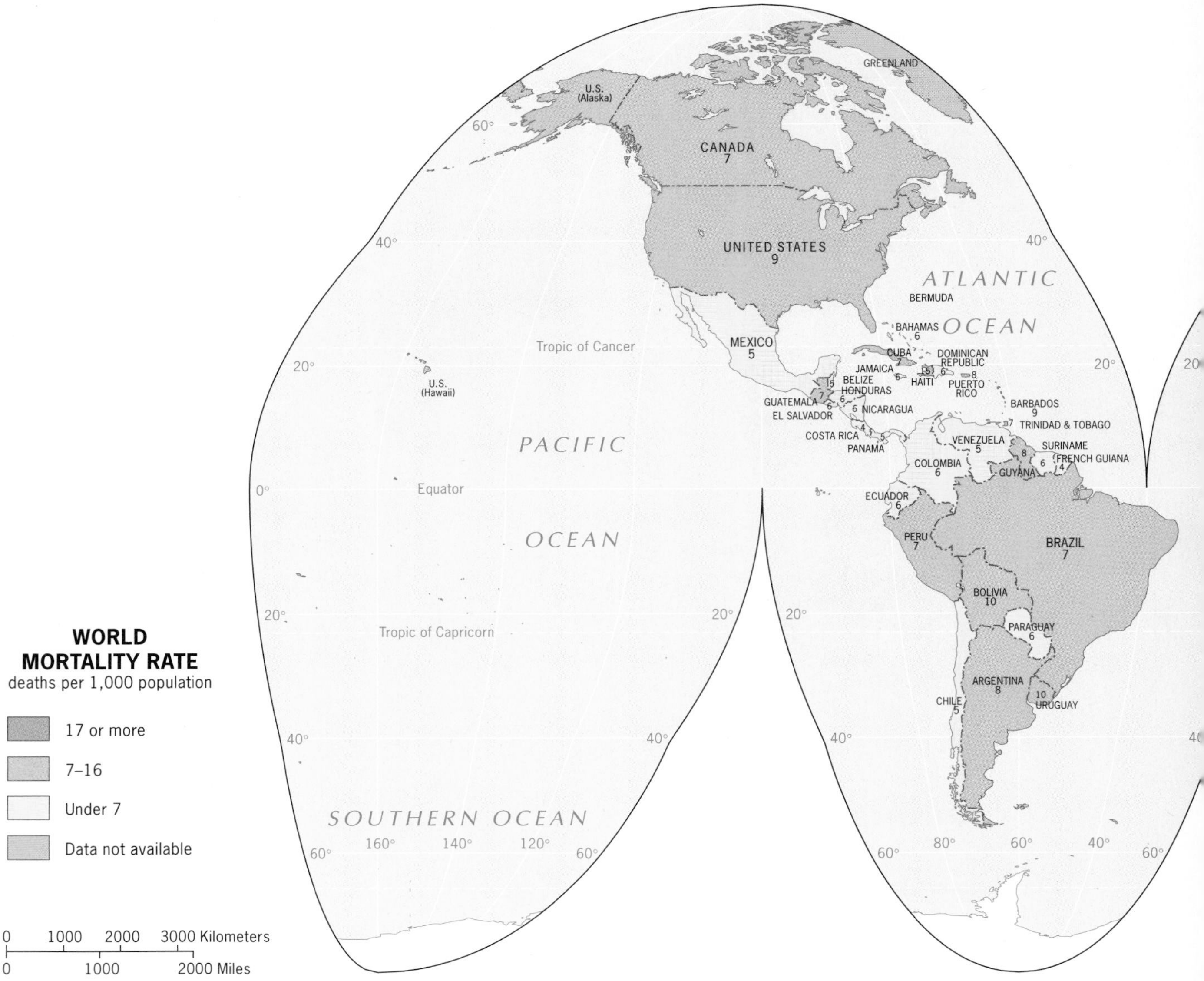

Figure 5-7 World Mortality Rates. World death rates by country. *Source:* Based on data from several sources.

As Figure 5-7 shows, death rates are highest in tropical Africa, where they are still above 20 per thousand in several countries. They are lowest in North America and most of South America, parts of Europe, Japan, China, and Australia. Also noteworthy are the low CDRs of several Southeast Asian countries. Here the correlation between economic development and low or declining death rates is less evident than appeared to be the case with birth rates. Otherwise we would not find Sri Lanka, Vietnam, or Paraguay recording lower rates. Figure 5-7 testifies not only to the role of economic development but also to the diffusion of health facilities and medicines, hygienic practices, pesticide use, and improved nutrition to less developed countries.

Crude death rates should be viewed in the context of ***infant mortality***. Many children (more than 1 in 10 in many countries) die before reaching their first birthday, so high CDRs tend to reflect high infant mortality. We will discuss this topic in detail in Part Nine, where we study medical geography, health, and nutrition.

◆ POPULATION CHANGES IN THE PAST

Because of the population explosion of the twentieth century, we have become accustomed to thinking of population change in terms of growth. But there have been times when populations have declined, sometimes

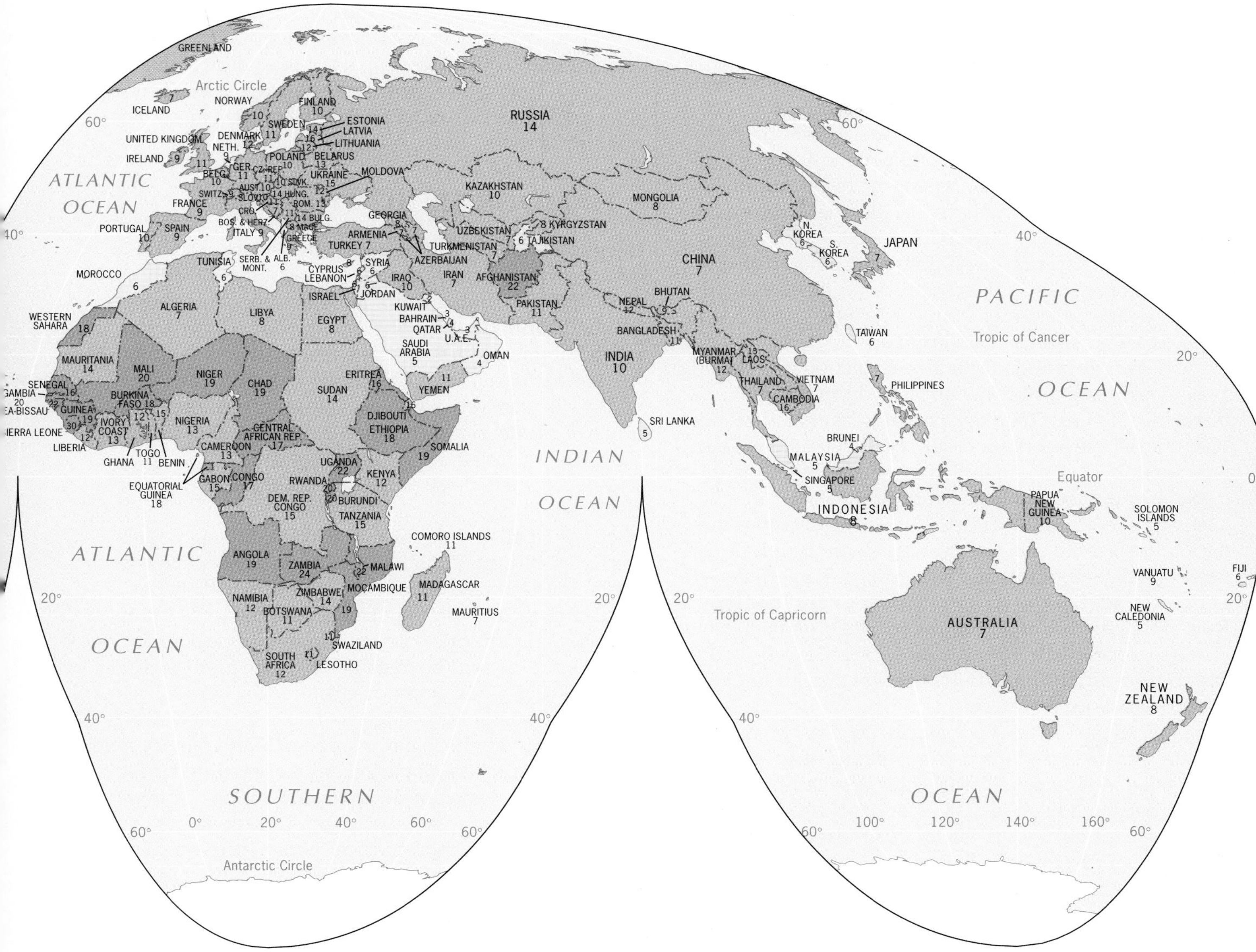

dramatically, and the number of deaths per thousand far exceeded the number of births in certain regions.

Limits on Population Growth

We noted earlier that the world's population increased slowly until the early nineteenth century. What were the reasons for this slow growth? A significant factor was epidemics and plagues, which often claimed hundreds of thousands of lives. Between 1348 and 1350 Europe was ravaged by the bubonic plague, and it is estimated that one-quarter of the population died. In this epidemic and its aftermath, many cities and towns were left with fewer than half of their inhabitants. It is believed that the population of England, which totaled nearly 4 million when the plague began, was just over 2 million when it was over. Clearly, a student of population change in the second half of the fourteenth century would have been more likely to talk of annual population decrease than of growth.

Famines also limited population growth. There are records of famines in India and China during the eighteenth and nineteenth centuries in which millions of people perished. Nor was Europe safe from such disasters. From Britain to Russia, unusual weather conditions periodically caused crops to fail, resulting in famine (the Little Ice Age had a major impact). At other times population gains were largely wiped out by destructive wars. Thus the apparent slow and steady increase of the world's population from 250 million at A.D. 0 to 500 million in 1650 and 1 billion in 1820 does not reflect countless unrevealed ups and downs. Birth rates were high, but death rates were also high, and there were times when there were many more deaths than live births.

The Second Agricultural Revolution and the Industrial Revolution

Eventually things began to change. In Europe there was a marked increase in the growth rate during the eighteenth century, and this time there was no major setback to erase the gains. This was the time of the Second Agricultural Revolution, when farming methods improved, crop yields increased, storage capacities were expanded, and distribution systems were improved. The Continental European Industrial Revolution of the nineteenth century also had a major impact: sanitation facilities made the towns and cities safer from epidemics, and modern medical practices became widespread.

Disease prevention through vaccination introduced a new era in public health. Death rates declined markedly. Before 1750 they probably averaged 35 per 1000 (births averaged under 40), but by 1850 the death rate was about 16 per thousand. Consider what this means in terms of natural growth: if in 1750 the birth rate was 39 per thousand and the death rate 35 per thousand, the rate of natural increase was 4 per thousand, or 0.4 percent. In 1850 birth rates were still high, perhaps 36 per thousand, but the death rate was 16 per thousand. Now the rate of natural increase was 2.0 percent. The change is especially spectacular when viewed in the context of doubling time. In 1750, it was about 150 years; in 1850, it was only 35 years.

One effect of this increase in the rate of natural growth was increased migration. Millions of people left the squalid, crowded industrial cities (and farms as well) to emigrate to other parts of the world—North and South America, Australia, South Africa, and elsewhere. They were not the first to make this journey. Adventurers, explorers, merchants, and colonists had gone before them. Those early immigrants had decimated native populations through conquest, slavery, and the introduction of diseases against which the local people had no natural immunity. However, when European colonization began in earnest during the nineteenth century, the Europeans brought with them their newfound methods of sanitation and medical techniques, and these had the opposite effect. In Africa, India, and South America death rates began to decline as they had in Europe, and populations that had long been caught in cycles of gains and losses began to grow—and to grow at increasing rates.

We can only speculate about the native populations of the Americas, Africa, Asia, and Australia before the arrival of the Europeans. At about the time of the first European contact, there were probably fewer than 25 million people in all of North and South America; in Africa south of the Sahara there may have been 70 million. (Some recent estimates place these totals somewhat higher.) In China in the mid-seventeenth century, the population may have been less than 200 million; India probably had fewer than 100 million inhabitants. In North America and Australia the European impact on the indigenous population was devastating, but elsewhere colonial rule reduced the impact of periodic calamitous checks on population growth through the introduction of technologies that reduced the effects of natural hazards and diseases.

◆ DEMOGRAPHIC CHANGE

The population of a country (or other unit area such as a State, province, or city) changes as a result of four conditions; births and inmigration (immigration), which add to the total; and deaths and outmigration (emigration), which subtract from it. Births (fertility), deaths (mortality), and migration are the three demographic variables.

To calculate demographic change in a country or region, we use the simple formula

$$TP = OP + B - D + I - E$$

where ***TP*** (total population) equals ***OP*** (original population) plus ***B*** (births) minus ***D*** (deaths) plus ***I*** (immigration) minus ***E*** (emigration). As noted earlier, only births and deaths are used in calculating a population's natural increase. You can calculate the natural increase for various countries by subtracting figures on the map of world mortality (Fig. 5-7) from those of births (Fig. 5-6).

The demographic change formula explains why calculations based only on births and deaths do not capture the entire picture. Population change, as recorded in Figure 5-1, does not take into account emigration and immigration. Obviously, the world population figures referred to previously represent the natural increase for the world as a whole because our planet does not (yet) experience immigration or emigration.

The Demographic Transition

Demographers who have studied population growth in various parts of the world believe that the high rates of increase now occurring in many less developed countries are not necessarily permanent. In Europe, for example, the situation is very different today than it was a century ago. In the United Kingdom in 1997, the crude birth rate was 13 and the crude death rate was 11, producing a rate of natural increase of just 0.2 percent. In the preindustrial period there also was a small difference between birth and death rates, but both rates were high; now both are low. It is in the intervening stage, when birth rates remained high but death rates fell rapidly, that Britain's population explosion took place. It is not difficult, then, to discern four stages in the United Kingdom's demographic cycle: (1) high birth rates and high death rates and a low rate of growth; (2) continuing high birth rates, but declining and low death rates and a high rate of growth; (3) declining and low death rates but a still sub-

From the field notes

"'There is more to Bordeaux than wine,' said my colleague from the local university as we walked the streets of this historic and storied city. But no other major city has a name so closely identified with wine, and perhaps none has an agricultural hinterland so wealthy and thriving. I had just flown here from Dakar, Senegal via Paris after several weeks in Subsaharan Africa, and what struck me more than the well-being of the people in the street was their age—after having been surrounded by youngsters for so long, this place looked like an old-folks' home by comparison. When I asked where the children were as I was taking these photographs, my host actually pointed and said 'there goes one now!' But in fact, in Bordeaux, in Paris, in all of France and in most of Europe, children are fewer and populations are aging."

stantial growth rate; and (4) low birth and low death rates and, thus, a low rate of growth.

This sequence of stages has been observed in the population records of several European countries, and on this basis demographers have defined what they call the ***demographic cycle*** or ***demographic transition***. Its four stages (Fig. 5-8) are:

1. ***High stationary stage***, with high fertility (births) and high mortality (deaths) and variable population, but little long-term growth.
2. ***Early expanding stage***, with high fertility and declining mortality.
3. ***Late expanding stage***, with declining fertility but, as a result of already-low mortality, continuing significant growth.
4. ***Low stationary stage***, with low fertility and low mortality, and a very low rate of growth.

The *demographic transition* is represented by stages 2 and 3, during which high birth and death rates decline. The initial rapid drop in death rates is not matched by lowered birth rates, so a period of high natural increase results. The dimensions of the expansion depend on the size of the base population and the rate of decline in the death rate.

This is what happened in the United Kingdom and in much of Europe. Europe as a whole currently has a population growth rate of close to zero. It appears, therefore, that the population "bomb" may eventually fizzle out and that in due course the European model of low birth and death rates and a nearly stable population will prevail everywhere—or will it?

Demographic Change in Developing Countries

In Europe the birth rate declined largely because of the effects of industrialization, urbanization, and general modernization. In contrast, in much of the developing world, the majority of the people have not been greatly affected by such changes. Moreover, there are quantitative differences between the situation in Europe during the nineteenth century and that prevailing in certain parts of the world today. When Europe's population revolution began, the base was small. Britain had between 6 and 7 million residents; Germany had 7 million; France, Belgium, and the Netherlands combined had 18 million. Asia's major population clusters were already much larger when the population revolution began there. China may have had over 200 million inhabitants and India over 100 million. If you superimpose the growth rates of the second and third stages on these large bases, the resulting population increases take on astronomical proportions.

Therefore, it may be unwise to assume that all countries' demographic cycles will follow the sequence that occurred in industrializing Europe or to believe that the still-significant growth currently taking place in Bangladesh, Mexico, and numerous other countries will simply subside. Nonetheless, agencies monitoring global population sometimes suggest that most (if not all) countries' populations will stop growing at some time during the twenty-first century, reaching a so-called ***stationary population level (SPL)***. This would mean, of course, that the world's population would stabilize and that the major problems to be faced would involve the aged rather than the young.

Such predictions require frequent revision, however, and the anticipated dates for population stabilization are often moved back. In the late 1980s, for example, the World Bank predicted that the United States would reach SPL in 2035 with 276 million inhabitants. Brazil's population would stabilize at 353 million in 2070, Mexico's at 254 million in 2075, and China's at 1.4 billion in 2090. India, destined to become the world's most populous country, would reach SPL at 1.6 billion in 2150.

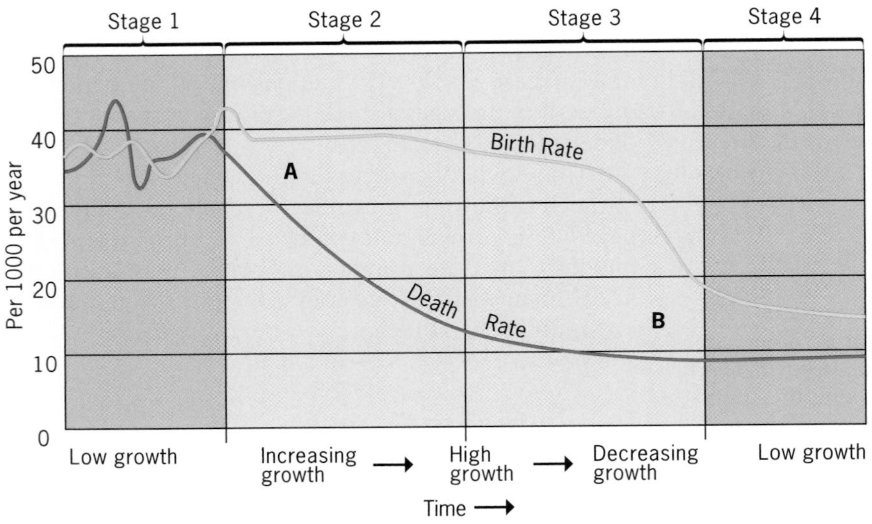

Figure 5-8 The Demographic Transition Model. Four stages of the demographic transition.

Today those figures seem unrealistic. China's population passed the 1.2 billion mark in 1994; India's reached 1 billion in 1998. If we were to project an optimistic decline in growth rates for both countries, China's population would "stabilize" at 1.7 billion in 2070 and India's at 2.0 billion in the same year. But population increase is a cyclic phenomenon, and overall declines mask lags and spurts (not to mention regional disparities).

There are some hopeful signs, however. In Sri Lanka, the birth rate is declining, and so is the overall growth rate—*without* the kind of economic development that is usually considered a prerequisite for such a decline. A similar noteworthy reduction in the population growth rate has been recorded in the Indian State of Kerala, where the growth rate now stands at 1.1 percent compared to 1.9 percent for India as a whole. It is interesting that the literacy rate for Kerala is about 90 percent of the population, compared to just over 50 percent for all of India. Yet there still is no proof of a permanent, worldwide reversal in population expansion. Hence, even though there are some grounds for optimism, population expansion remains a very real issue as we enter the twenty-first century.

◆ KEY TERMS ◆

age-sex pyramid
crude birth rate (CBR)
crude death rate (CDR)
demographic transition (cycle)
demography
doubling time
exponential growth
infant mortality
linear growth
natural increase
population composition
population explosion
population structure
stationary population level (SPL)
total fertility rate (TFR)

◆ APPLYING GEOGRAPHIC KNOWLEDGE ◆

1. The debate over population growth and food supply, started by Malthus 200 years ago, still continues. Neo-Malthusians argue that what Malthus wrote about Britain two centuries ago can be applied to the world as a whole today—recent gains in global food supplies notwithstanding. Take a pro- or anti-Malthusian position and argue your case, using your geographic knowledge of population distribution, urbanization, resource availability, and demographic processes.
2. Some argue that the demographic transition model (see Fig. 5-8) is not necessarily an appropriate tool for understanding likely future population trends in Subsaharan African countries. What is different about those countries now and the Western European countries at the time they went through the demographic transition? Are those differences likely to render the demographic transition model inapplicable to Subsaharan Africa? If so, why? If not, why not?

Chapter 6

Where and Why People Move

From the field notes

"Human mobility takes many forms, and commuting is one way activity space is defined. But the daily commute in Delhi, India, is a bit unlike that in, say London or Chicago. I watched the trains roll in during the early morning rush hour, most without doors or windows, with people literally hanging out of the cars as they passed by. Uncomfortable as this may be, especially during the monsoon season, but these commuters share in India's economic growth, and they are willing to accept it. Their activity space is measured in miles; take the train out of Delhi for a half hour, and you reach villages where life is confined to the few hundred yards between room and paddy."

KEY POINTS

◆ Many factors stimulate the migration process. They include conflict, economic conditions, political strife, cultural circumstances, environmental change, and technological advances.

◆ Voluntary migrations, such as the movement toward the Sunbelt in North America, are stimulated by "pull" as well as "push" factors.

◆ Not all migrations involve long-term relocation; cyclic and periodic movements are common as well.

◆ Forced migrations result from the imposition of power by stronger peoples over weaker ones. A modern example is the repatriation of illegal migrants by governments that are unwilling to accept them.

◆ The voluntary migration of Europeans to the New World, the forced migration of Africans to the Americas, and the migration of Europeans to their overseas colonial empires are among migration streams that have transformed the world.

◆ Internal migrations, involving major population shifts, have occurred in the former Soviet Union, the United States, China, and other large countries. Mobility is among the qualities that define the character of a culture, and American society today is the world's most mobile.

◆ Among the important contributors to contemporary population movements are refugees fleeing their place of residence in the face of international conflict, ethnic strife, or environmental disaster.

What impelled our African ancestors to leave their familiar abode for the unknown, to cross into Arabia, eventually into India, and ultimately into Australia? What could have persuaded early *Homo sapiens* to venture into the cold regions of Pleistocene Europe? To cross the Bering land bridge from Asia to America? To risk survival in flimsy boats on the open sea?

These questions go to the heart of a basic human behavior. Throughout history humans have sought new frontiers—new islands and continents. Risks have been taken and lives lost, but the search for new frontiers has continued and still continues today. Our efforts to reach the Moon stemmed from the same urge that dispersed *H. sapiens* in the first place.

The U.S. population is the most mobile in the world. More than 5 million people move from one State to another every year, and nearly seven times as many—an average of 35 million—move within their State, county, or community. On average, an American citizen moves once in about every six years.

Human mobility is of central interest in human geography because it is an inherently spatial process. Human movement speeds the diffusion of ideas and innovations; it intensifies spatial interaction and transforms regions; and as we will see, it is often closely linked to environmental conditions. ◆

◆ PERCEPTION AND MIGRATION

Human movement often results from a perception that conditions are better, safer, freer, or in some way superior at some distant destination. In Part One we noted the role of perception in human geography, illustrating this notion with maps of the "attractiveness" of American States in the view of university students. When it comes to the decision to migrate, such mental constructs play a crucial role. As we will see, the perception or image of a distant locale is often distorted, leading to dashed expectations and, in some cases, another decision—to return to the more familiar place left behind.

Earlier we discussed the notion of absolute and relative location, the former involving a global grid and the latter referring to the situation of a place with reference to other places with which it is connected. In the context of migration, ***distance*** has a similar dichotomy.

The ***absolute distance*** between two places (for example, the origin and destination of a migrant), measured on a globe or map by part of a great circle or a straight line, is the distance "as the crow flies." That distance may be perceived to be much shorter than the effective, ***relative distance*** the migrant must travel. A suburban resident may point from her backyard to the high-rises of a city's downtown and say, "I'm only seven miles from the city center." But in fact, she has to travel on a back road to the beltway, leave that ring road after several exits, and join a winding radial road into the central city. The commute will be a lot longer than seven miles.

Research has shown that people's perception of distance—whether relocating or commuting—is often quite distorted. This means that decisions by home buyers, travelers, and migrants are frequently based on inadequate information. Add to this people's tendency to have an incomplete geographic picture of the places and areas to which they plan to relocate, and it is understandable that a sizeable percentage of the movers eventually return to their original home.

◆ EXTERNAL AND INTERNAL MIGRATION

In Chapter 5, we noted that the growth of a country's population involves not only natural increase but also the immigration of outsiders. In some countries that would otherwise have negative population growth, these immigrants create the positive balance. In the case of the United States, the immigration of millions of people from virtually all parts of the world but especially (recently) from Middle America sustains a total growth rate far above that of most European countries—and much higher than the low natural increase of 0.6 percent.

The process of ***migration*** involves the long-term relocation of an individual, household, or larger group to a new locale outside the community of origin. When migrants move from one country to another and therefore cross an international boundary, they become part of the vital statistics of the country they leave as well as the one they enter. Their ***emigration*** from country A makes them part of the negative factors in the formula we stated in Chapter 5, and their ***immigration*** into country B adds them to the overall (not the natural) growth rate. But countries also experience ***internal migration***, often in well-defined streams that change over time. Early in the twentieth century, a major migration stream took tens of thousands of African-American families from the South to the industrializing cities of the Northeast and Midwest. Today, major movements are carrying migrants from East to West and from North to South, the latter marked by the "Sunbelt" attractions of warmer States. In present-day China, a major internal migration is bringing millions of workers from rural areas into the burgeoning cities of its Pacific Rim.

From the field notes

"When I first saw China's Great Wall, I felt that this was more than a wall: it was a giant building, complete with towers and roadways. It had taken us nearly three hours from central Beijing to get here (today a four-lane highway cuts that time to less than one hour), and along the way you can see collapsed sections of the various walls China's early rulers built. During Mao Zedong's regime, parts of the Great Wall were torn down to provide building materials for collectives, but the current government is restoring it. As a result the wall—built to keep Chinese farmers in and Mongol horsemen out—now generates its own population movement; an endless stream of tourists who throng the section nearest the capital. The Great Wall stretches from the Yellow Sea to Xinjiang, up mountain slopes and across plains, perhaps humanity's greatest effort ever to control population movement."

◆ THEORIES ABOUT MIGRATION

Under what circumstances do people migrate? This question has intrigued researchers for more than a century. Studies indicate that the intensity of a migration flow varies with such factors as the degree of difference between the source and the destination, the effectiveness of the flow of information from the destination back to the source, and the physical distance between the source and the (ultimate) destination.

As long ago as 1885, the British demographer Ernst Ravenstein studied internal migration in England. On the basis of his data he proposed several "laws" of migration. These generalizations are still relevant today.

1. ***Net migration amounts to a fraction of the gross migration between two places.*** Every migration flow generates a "return" or "counter" migration, so the actual migration is the volume of the original flow minus that of the return flow.
2. ***The majority of migrants move a short distance.*** Average migration distance undoubtedly has increased since Ravenstein's time, but step migration still prevails.
3. ***Migrants who move longer distances tend to choose big-city destinations.*** London was the great magnet in Ravenstein's time, and other British cities were mushrooming as a result of migration.
4. ***Urban residents are less migratory than inhabitants of rural areas.*** In England in Ravenstein's time, urbanization was drawing people toward towns and cities. The same phenomenon can be observed today in the developing countries.
5. ***Families are less likely to make international moves than young adults.*** Throughout the world young adults are the most mobile population group.

Ravenstein also posited an inverse relationship between the volume of migration and the distance between source and destination; that is, the number of migrants declines as the distance they must travel increases. This proposal anticipated the ***gravity model***, a measure of the interaction of places. The gravity model predicts this interaction on the basis of the size of population in the respective places and the distance between them. It states that spatial interaction (such as migration) is directly related to the populations and inversely related to the distance between them. In mathematical terms, the model holds that interaction is proportional to the multiplication of the two populations divided by the distance between them. Variants of this notion are applicable in many areas of human geography, especially economic geography.

◆ CATALYSTS OF MIGRATION

What specific factors impel people to pull up stakes and leave the familiar for the uncertain? Research has shown that usually it is not just one factor but a combination of factors that leads to the decision to move. In this section we look briefly at several key factors.

Economic Conditions

Poverty has driven countless millions from their homelands and continues to do so. Perceived opportunities in destinations such as Western Europe and North America impel numerous migrants, both legal and illegal, to cross the Mediterranean, the Caribbean, and the Rio Grande in search of a better life.

Political Circumstances

Throughout history oppressive regimes have engendered migration streams. More than 125,000 Cubans left their country in 1980 on the "Mariel Boatlift" to escape communist dictatorship. Desperate "boat people" fled Vietnam by the hundreds of thousands after communist insurgents took control of the country. In 1972 Uganda's dictator, Idi Amin, expelled 50,000 Asians and Ugandans of Asian descent from his country. Migrations driven by politics are therefore marked by both escape and expulsion.

Armed Conflict and Civil War

The dreadful conflict that engulfed the former Yugoslavia during the 1990s drove as many as 3 million people from their homes. Many of those people became permanent emigrants, unable to return home. During the mid-1990s a civil war engulfed Rwanda in Equatorial Africa, a conflict that pitted militant Hutu against the minority Tutsi and "moderate" Hutu. The carnage may have claimed as many as 600,000 lives and produced huge outmigrations into neighboring Zaire (now Congo) and Tanzania. It is estimated that more than 2 million Rwandans fled their homeland.

Environmental Conditions

A major example of migration induced by environmental conditions is the movement of hundreds of thousands of Irish citizens from Ireland to the New World during the 1840s. Prolonged excessive rains rotted the country's potato crop, creating a famine. The famine was exacerbated by a set of political conditions for which the British government has recently apologized—a reminder that environmental conditions rarely operate in a social vacuum. But this migration with an environmental component permanently altered the demographics of both Ireland (the source) and the northeastern region of the United States (the chief destination).

Environmental crises such as earthquakes and volcanic eruptions also stimulate migrations. For example, every major earthquake in California is followed by a surge in emigration. But because many of the emigrants return, the net outflow generated by such momentary crises is comparatively small.

Culture and Traditions

People who fear that their culture and traditions will not survive a major political transition, and who are able to migrate to places they perceive as safer, will often do so. When British India was partitioned into a mainly Hindu India and an almost exclusively Muslim Pakistan, millions of Muslim residents of India migrated across the border to the new Islamic state. Similarly, in the 1990s after decades of Soviet obstruction, more than 2 million Jews left the former USSR for Israel and other destinations. And turbulent political conditions in South Africa during the mid-1990s impelled many whites to emigrate to Australia, Europe, and North America.

Technological Advances

For many migrants emigration is no longer the difficult and hazardous journey it used to be. While many migrants still move by simple and even difficult means, millions more now use modern forms of transportation whose availability can itself encourage migration. Moreover, technological innovations have made certain parts of the planet more attractive to migrants. For example, it has been suggested that the growing availability of air conditioning greatly reduced return migration from the Sunbelt back to the North, resulting in a larger net flow of migrants within the United States.

From the field notes

"A truly ugly sight, this spiked, barbed-wire fence along the waterfront of (then-still Portuguese) Macau. To the right, the beach belonged to China; the road to the left lies in Macau. To stop Chinese from leaving the communist state and entering the former colony, the two governments erected barriers like this (the border between formerly British Hong Kong and China was reinforced in a similar way). When China took over control of both Hong Kong and Macau, barriers to migration were not removed overnight. Strict rules still apply when it comes to who has the right to live in these "Special Administrative Regions," and barriers to migration remain in place."

Flow of Information

Gone is the time when would-be emigrants waited months, even years, for information about distant places. News today travels faster than ever, including news of job opportunities and ways to reach desired destinations. Television, radio, and telephone have stimulated millions of people to migrate by relaying information about relatives, opportunities, and already established communities in destination lands. Thus Turks quickly heard about Germany's need for immigrant labor. Algerians knew where the most favorable destinations were in France. Haitians knew that a "Little Haiti" had sprung up in the Miami area.

"Push" and "Pull" Factors

Geographers who study human migration describe the conditions and perceptions that tend to induce people to leave their abodes as ***push factors***, whereas the circumstances that effectively attract people to certain locales from other places are termed ***pull factors***. The decision to migrate usually results from a combination of push and pull factors—and these can play out differently depending on the circumstance and the scale of the migration (see A Sense of Scale Box). Because a migrant is likely to be more familiar with his or her place of residence (source) than with the locale to which he or she is moving (destination), push factors are likely to be perceived more accurately than pull factors. Push factors include individual considerations

A SENSE OF SCALE

Factors Influencing Migration

Economic conditions, political circumstances, and environmental factors help explain why people throughout the world move to other parts of the world. Yet it is important to remember that migration occurs on a variety of scales. People not only move from one continent or country to another; they also move between regions within countries, and even between neighborhoods in a city. Many of the factors influencing migration on the global scale help explain local movements of people, but the circumstances of individual places can profoundly influence where and why those movements occur.

Compare, for example, patterns of mobility within the United States with those in Peru. The fact that the United States is a relatively prosperous country with a diverse, flexible economy means that patterns of mobility are quite complex. The past few decades have seen substantial numbers of people move to economically dynamic regions such as the Sunbelt and the Far West, the movement of people from both large cities and rural areas to medium-sized cities, and the colonization of environmentally attractive rural areas by individuals ranging from the wealthy to those seeking alternative lifestyles. Moreover, interregional migration in the United States is influenced by a variety of social and demographic factors, including age, marital status, and cohort size (the size of a group of a similar age level). Thus geographers have found that in recent decades there has been an inverse relationship between cohort size and mobility; when large numbers of "baby boomers" reached their early 20s in the mid-1970s, mobility among young adults decreased. This is presumably because the large young adult cohort faced stiffer competition for jobs—and was aware of that fact.

Internal migration in Peru is also influenced by economic factors, but the resultant pattern is much simpler. For decades a single migration stream has dominated: that between rural, small-town Peru and the burgeoning metropolis of Lima. As a country where external pressures have exposed small-scale enterprises to intense competition and where investment capital is concentrated in the dominant capital city, Lima represents the only major focus of economic opportunity for a rural population with diminishing economic prospects. As such, not only is Lima the recipient of the vast majority of Peru's migrants, but also the migration stream to the Peruvian capital is less sensitive to matters of age, marital status, or cohort size. So when considering influences on migration, it is important to recognize that general economic, political, and social forces must be seen in the context of the spaces and places that define migration patterns.

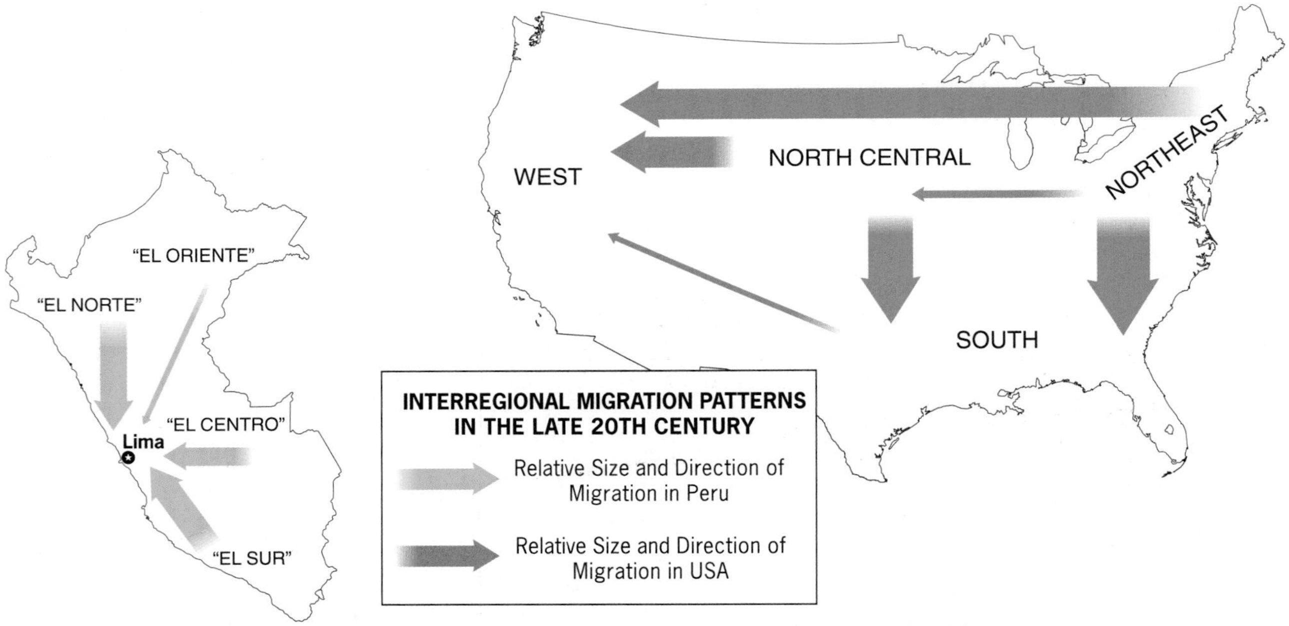

Dominant migrations patterns in Peru and the United States. *Source:* Schematic Peru map based in part on data from D. Collier, Squatters and Oligarchs (Baltimore, Md.: Johns Hopkins University Press, 1976 and schematic U.S. map based on data from W. A. V. Clark, Human Migration (Beverly Hills, CA: Sage, 1985).

such as work or retirement conditions, cost of living, personal safety and security, and, for many, weather and climate. Pull factors tend to be more vague and may depend on several visits to the destination. Many migrants move on the basis of excessively positive images and expectations regarding their destinations.

Distance Decay

The principle of ***distance decay*** comes into play here (Fig. 6-1). Prospective migrants are likely to have more complete and accurate perceptions of nearer places than of farther ones, which confirms the notion that the intensity of human activity, process, or function declines as distance from its source increases. Since interaction with faraway places decreases as distance increases, prospective migrants are likely to feel much less certain about distant destinations than about nearer ones. This leads many migrants to move less far than they originally contemplated. Indeed, many migration streams that appear on maps as long, unbroken routes in fact consist of a series of stages, a phenomenon known as ***step migration***. A peasant family in Brazil, for example, is likely to move first to a village, then to a nearby town, later to a city, and finally to a metropolis such as São Paulo or Rio de Janeiro. At each stage a new set of pull factors comes into play.

Intervening Opportunity

Not all migrants complete all of these steps. When 1000 people leave a village and migrate to a town in a given year, most, if not all, of them may dream of making it to—and in—the "big city." But only about 500 may actually move from town to city, and of these, only 200 eventually reach the metropolis that impelled them to move in the first place. Along the way the majority are captured by intervening opportunity. This is what happened when African-Americans migrated northward after World War I to seek work in growing cities like Chicago and Cleveland. Many found employment in St. Louis and Cincinnati; that is, they encountered ***intervening opportunities*** along their northbound routes.

Like distance decay, intervening opportunity is a geographic principle that is relevant to the study of migration as well as other human activities. A special kind of temporary migrants—tourists—also respond to intervening opportunities. Other things being equal, cost-conscious vacationers will choose a nearer, and hence cheaper, resort over a more distant one (e.g., Vermont instead of Maine for New Yorkers). Intervening opportunity is the constant worry of every resort that depends on attracting visitors from distant places.

Figure 6-1 Distance Decay.

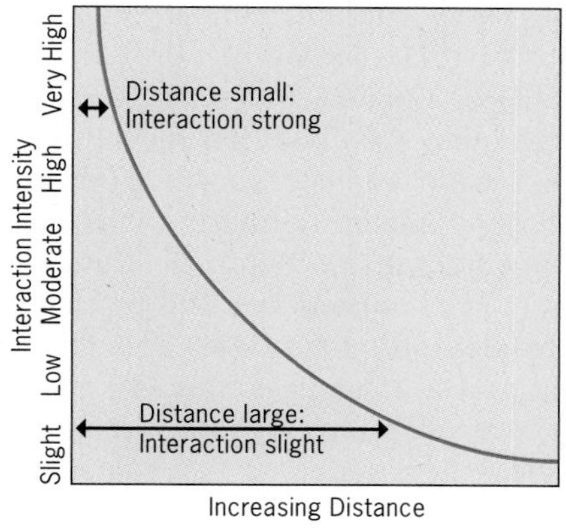

◆ VOLUNTARY AND FORCED MIGRATIONS

Our final look at the incentives that induce people to migrate focuses on a pair of opposites: the luxury of choice and the fear of compulsion. The former leads to ***voluntary migration***, relocation by choice; the role of push and pull factors is relevant here. The latter involves the imposition of authority or power, producing ***forced migrations*** that render theoretical issues irrelevant.

In truth, the distinction is not always clear-cut. The enormous European migration to the United States during the nineteenth and early twentieth centuries is often cited as a prime example of voluntary migration, but the conditions created by British colonial rule over Ireland—and not only the infamous potato famine—can be construed as a force factor. The key difference, however, is that voluntary migrants have an option; forced migrants do not.

The largest and most devastating forced migration in the history of humanity is the North Atlantic ***slave trade***, which carried tens of millions of Africans from their homes to the Americas, with huge loss of life (Fig. 6-2). How many Africans were sold into slavery will never be known (estimated to range from 12 million to 30 million), and Figure 6-2 can only be an approximation and display their destinations. As the map shows, the vast majority of Africans were taken to the Caribbean region, to coastal Middle America, and to Brazil; in 1900, the black population of the young United States was just 1 million. Neither will it be possible to gauge the full and lasting impact of the slave trade on the African societies from which they were forcibly taken, often by African raiders in the pay of European shippers.

Nothing in human history compares to the North Atlantic slave trade, but other forced migrations have also changed the world's demographic map. For 50 years beginning in 1788, tens of thousands of convicts were shipped from Britain to Australia, where they had a lasting impact on the continent's population geography. In the 1800s, thousands of Native Americans were forced onto

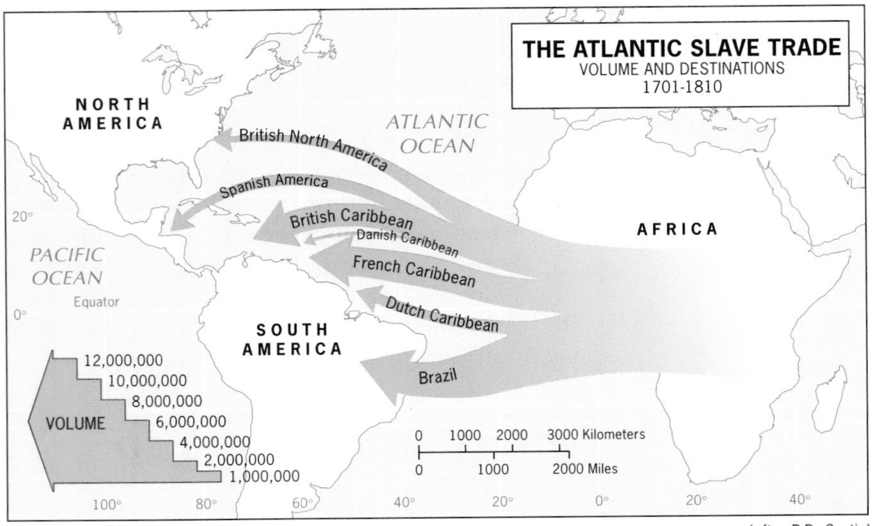

Figure 6-2 The Atlantic Slave Trade. Dimensions of the Atlantic slave trade. *Source:* After a map in P. Curtin, The Atlantic Slave Trade (Madison: University of Wisconsin Press, 1969), p. 57.

reservations—some far from their traditional homelands. In the then-Soviet Union during Stalin's ruthless rule earlier in this century, many millions of non-Russians were forcibly moved from their homes to remote parts of Central Asia and Siberia for political reasons. Nor is forced migration unknown today. It continues to occur in the form of ***counter migration***, in which governments send back migrants caught entering their countries illegally. In the 1990s the United States repatriated Haitian arrivals from Florida. Vietnamese escapees have been expelled from Hong Kong. By comparison, other migration streams—whatever their causes—are benign.

Whenever we observe migrations, we should realize that the flow of migrants represents only a small fraction of the population at the source; the migrants have made a choice that is not available to those who were moved forcibly. Another contrast lies in the "return" migration. All voluntary migration flows generate a return, or counter, migration. For example, some Soviet-Jewish emigrants have returned to Russia. Some Canadians find that they cannot adjust to life in Florida and return home. In short, any voluntary migration flow represents the numbers going from the source to the destination minus those returning from the destination to the source. This cannot be said of forced migrations.

◆ TYPES OF MOVEMENT

Human mobility takes several forms. Although we focus on migration and its consequences in the present chapters, we should take note of other types of movement as well because such mobility affects the potential for migration. Increased mobility broadens a society's perspectives, and widening horizons enhance the likelihood of relocation.

The great majority of people have a daily routine that takes them through a regular sequence of short moves. These moves create what geographers call ***activity*** (or ***action***) ***space***. The magnitude of activity space varies in different societies. North Americans' activity space, on average, is very large compared to that of, say, Africans or Southwest Asians. Millions of American commuters travel a greater distance each day than many Chinese village dwellers do in a year. Technology has vastly expanded daily activity spaces, as reflected by the continuous shuttle flights between major cities such as Washington, D.C., and New York City.

It is useful to categorize movement into three types. We are all familiar with the first: ***cyclic movement***, which defines your daily activity space. You may go to classes every weekday and perhaps to a job as well, creating an action space that is relatively confined and stable, diversified by shopping trips and social activities. Thus cyclic movement involves journeys that begin at our home base and bring us back to it. Suburb-to-city ***commuting***, involving trips of several hours and transport modes ranging from cars to trains, is a form of cyclic movement. Quite a different form of it is ***seasonal movement***. Every autumn, hundreds of thousands of travelers leave their homes in northern parts of the United States or Canada and seek the winter sun in Florida and other "Sunbelt" States, returning in the spring. This seasonal transfer has huge economic consequences in depopulated northern towns and burgeoning tourist centers in the South. Still another type of cyclic movement is ***nomadism***. This practice, dwindling but still prevalent in parts of Asia and Africa, is sometimes envisaged as an aimless wandering across steppe and desert by small groups of rootless roamers. Actually, nomadic movement tends to take place along long-familiar routes repeated time and again, so that the nomads and their animals visit water sources and pastures that have served them for centuries. Weather conditions may affect the timing of the circuit, but barring obstacles such as fenced international borders or the privatization of long-used open country, nomads engage in cyclic movement.

When movement involves less back-and-forth mobility but a longer period of residence away from the home base, it is referred to as ***periodic movement***. When you leave home to attend a college far away, you may not return for nine months or more, and if you go to summer school as well, you may be back only for brief holidays. Although you may retain a home address in your place of origin, you now spend the great majority of your time in your new abode, and your mobility cannot be categorized as cyclic. Again, periodic movement takes on other forms; ***military service*** is a form of it: In a given year as many as 10 million citizens of the United States, including military personnel and their families, are moved to new locations where they will spend tours of duty that can last years. Still another type is ***migrant labor***, involving millions of workers in the United States and tens of millions worldwide. The need for migrant labor in the farm fields of California, Florida, and other parts of the United States creates a large flow of cross-border movers, many of whom eventually become immigrants. A specialized form of periodic movement is ***transhumance***. This term refers to a system of pastoral farming in which livestock and their keepers move according to the seasonal availability of pastures. This is a periodic form of movement because it involves a long period of residential relocation (unlike classic nomadism). In Switzerland, for example, cattle are driven up the mountain slopes to high, fresh pastures during the summer; farm families follow the herds, taking up residence in cottages that are abandoned during the cold winter. In the "Horn" of Northeast Africa, hundreds of thousands of people follow their livestock from highland to lowland and back in search of pastures renewed by seasonal rainfall.

When movement results in permanent relocation across international borders, it is classified as ***migratory***. As has been noted earlier, migratory movement leads to a smaller but sometimes significant ***return migration*** by those unable to adjust to life in the place of destination, but the net influx is usually substantial and can change demographic indices. We turn now to this most consequential form of human mobility.

◆ THE MIGRATION PROCESS

Human history is the history of migration: of movement out of Africa into Eurasia, Australia, and the Americas, of transoceanic journeys and treks into the unknown. As you read this section, hundreds of thousands of people will be on their often perilous migrant adventure. Countless migration streams have transformed the human mosaic and continue to do so. Some of these momentous movements have had a crucial and lasting impact.

Major Modern Migrations (pre-1950)

The past five centuries have witnessed human migration on an unprecedented scale, much of it generated by events in Europe. Pre-1950 major modern migration flows are shown in Figure 6-3. They include movements

Figure 6-3 Human Migrations in Modern Times (pre-1950). Major routes of migrants.

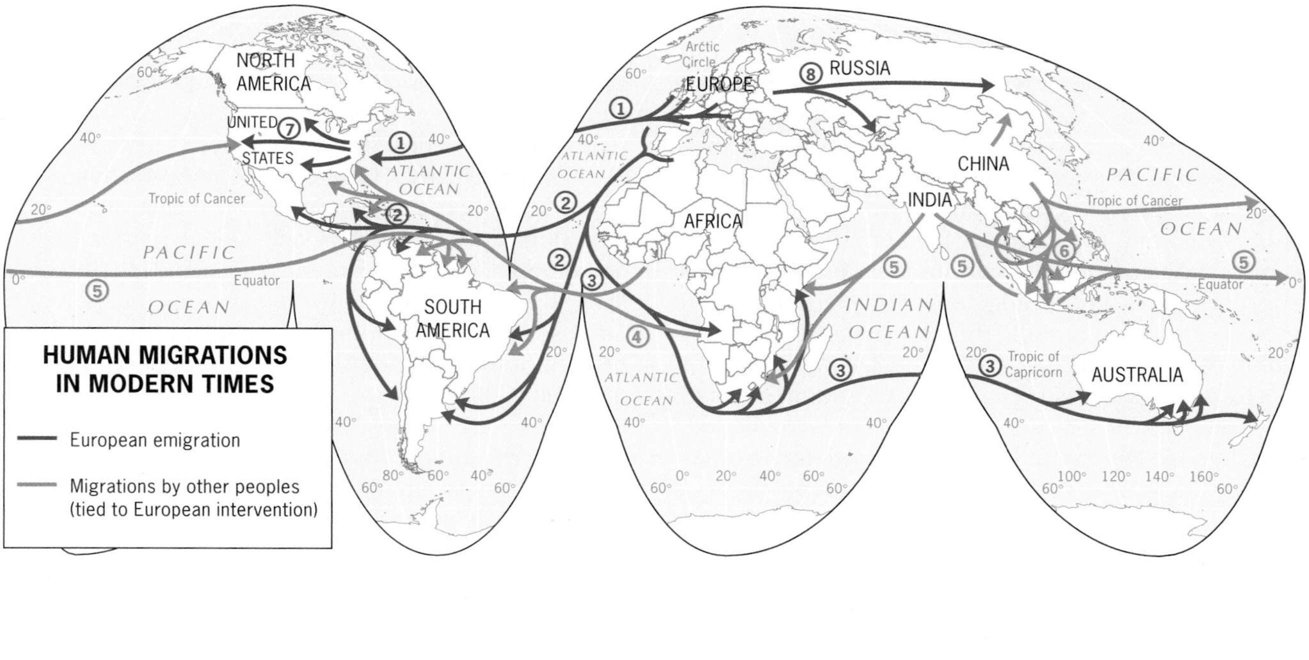

from Europe to North America (1); from Southern Europe to South and Middle America (2); from Britain and Ireland to Africa and Australia (3); from Africa to the Americas during the period of slavery (4); from India to eastern Africa, Southeast Asia, and Caribbean America (5); from China to Southeast Asia (6); from the eastern United States westward (7); and from western Russia eastward (8). These last two migrations are internal to the United States and Russia. Our map does not show some other significant internal migrations, for example, the south-to-north movement of black Americans during the twentieth century. We return to these great population shifts later in the chapter.

European Emigration

Among the greatest human migrations in recent centuries was the flow from Europe to the Americas. When we discussed the period of explosive population growth in nineteenth-century Europe (Chapter 5), we did not fully account for this process, which kept the total increase far below what it might have been. The great emigration from Europe (1 and 2 in Fig. 6-3) began slowly. Before the 1830s, perhaps 2.75 million Europeans left to settle overseas. After that, however, the rate of emigration increased sharply; between 1835 and 1935, perhaps as many as 75 million departed for the New World and other overseas territories. The British went to North America, Australia, New Zealand, and South Africa (3). From Spain and Portugal, many hundreds of thousands emigrated to Middle and South America. Early European colonial settlements grew, even in such places as Angola, Kenya, and Java. Although millions of Europeans eventually returned to their homelands, the net outflow from Europe was enormous.

African Forced Migration

This European emigration has had no counterpart in modern world history in terms of size and numbers, but it is not the only major migration flow that has occurred in recent centuries. As we saw in Chapter 6, the Americas were the destination of another mass of immigrants: African slaves. This forced migration began during the sixteenth century, when Africans were first brought to the Caribbean. In the early decades of the seventeenth century, they arrived in small numbers on the plantations that were developing in coastal eastern North America. They were among the very first settlers in this country (4).

The terror and destruction of slave raiding afflicted large areas of Africa. Most of West Africa was exploited, from Liberia to Nigeria and from the coast to the margins of the Sahara. So many Africans were taken from the area that is now Benin to Bahia in Brazil that significant elements of the local culture remained intact in the transition. Today there are strong ties between Bahia and Benin, and cultural exchanges are growing stronger. The entire Equatorial African coastal region was victimized as well, and Portuguese slave traders raided freely in the Portuguese domains of Angola and Moçambique. Arab slave raiders were active in East Africa and the Horn, penetrating Equatorial Africa and often cooperating with the Europeans. Zanzibar, off the coast of mainland Tanzania, long was a major slave market.

In combination, these forced migrations inflicted incalculable damage on African societies and communities, and changed the cultural and ethnic geography of Brazil, Middle America, and the United States. Although it is mapped as just one of the eight major migrations in Figure 6-3, its immense and lasting impact on both sides of the Atlantic sets it apart from all the others.

Even as the Atlantic slave trade was in progress, the European impact was generating other major migrations as well. The British, who took control over South Asia, transported tens of thousands of "indentured" workers from present-day India, Pakistan, and Sri Lanka to East and South Africa (see symbol (5) on Figure 6-3). Today, "Indian" citizens form substantial minorities in South Africa, Kenya, and Tanzania and, until their forced migration from Uganda, in that country as well. Their disproportionate share of commerce and wealth in their African abodes is now a major source of ethnic friction.

Long before the British arrived in India, Hindu influences had radiated into Southeast Asia, reaching Java (Indonesian Java) and Bali in force. Later the British renewed the Indian migration stream, bringing South Asians to the Malay Peninsula (including Singapore) and to their Pacific holdings including Fiji (Fig. 6-3).

The British were also instrumental in relocating Asians, mainly from India, to such Caribbean countries as Trinidad and Tobago and Guyana (the trans-Pacific stream marked 5 in Fig. 6-3). The Dutch brought many Javanese from what is today Indonesia to their former dependency of Suriname along the same route. Meanwhile, the colonial occupation of Southeast Asia presented opportunities for the Chinese to function as middlemen, and many Chinese immigrated to this region (Fig. 6-4). Chinese minorities in Southeast Asian countries (Fig. 6-4) account for substantial portions of national populations: 14 percent in Thailand, 32 percent in Malaysia, and no less than 76 percent in Singapore. The Chinese minority in Indonesia accounts for only about 3 percent of the total population, but Indonesia has more than 200 million people, so its Chinese minority is one of Southeast Asia's largest clusters. Several twentieth-century governments in Southeast Asia discouraged and restricted Chinese immigration. Like the Asians in East Africa, the Chinese minorities in Southeast Asia tend to be urban and to engage in trade, commerce, and finance.

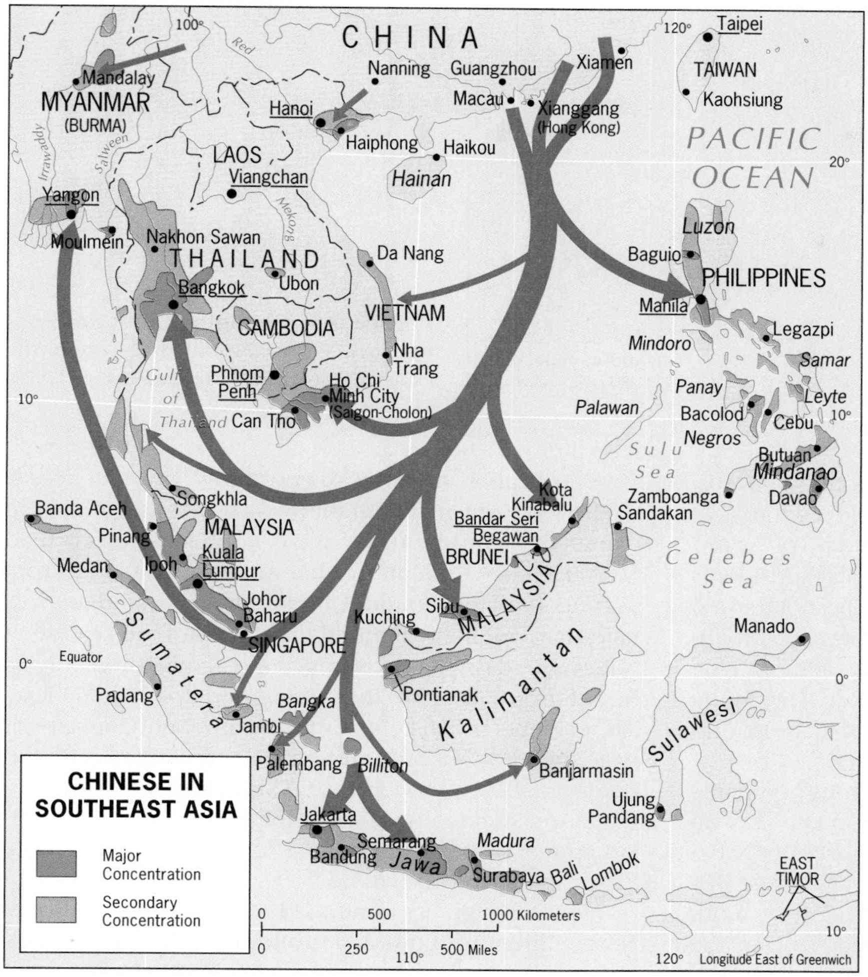

Figure 6-4 Chinese in Southeast Asia. The great majority of Chinese emigrants left from southeast China.

◆ EXTERNAL AND INTERNAL MIGRATIONS

Every one of the migrations we have discussed so far may be referred to as ***interregional migrations***: not only did the migrants cross international borders, but they moved (or were moved) from one geographic realm to another (that is, from Europe to the Americas, Africa to South America, India to Africa). As Figure 6-3 shows, however, two of the world's major population movements occurred within countries, not between them. Although the term ***migration*** should technically refer to cross-border movements only, it is also used to refer to such domestic relocations. It is therefore appropriate to distinguish between ***external*** and ***internal*** migrations, and on Figure 6-3 we take note of two significant internal cases. In the United States, a massive migration stream has for more than two centuries carried the center of population westward (and more recently also southward, as Fig. 6-5 shows). This internal migration, (7) on Figure 6-3, numerically exceeded another important internal stream, which carried millions of African-Americans from south to north. This northward movement gathered momentum during World War I, when immigration from Europe was interrupted and northern labor markets grew rapidly. It continued during the 1920s, declined during the depression years of the 1930s, and then resumed its upward climb. In 1900, only about 10 percent of the U.S. black population lived outside the South; in 2000, the proportion exceeded 50 percent. Thus the African-American sector of the population urbanized even more rapidly than the white population did because the vast majority of those who migrated to the industrializing North came from rural areas in the South.

Starting in the 1970s, census data began to reveal a surprising trend: more African-Americans were leaving the North and returning to the South than were leaving the South for northern destinations. This reversal of a trend that had continued for many decades appeared to have several causes. Undoubtedly, it resulted in part from changed civil rights conditions in the South. Disillusionment with living conditions in the urban North and

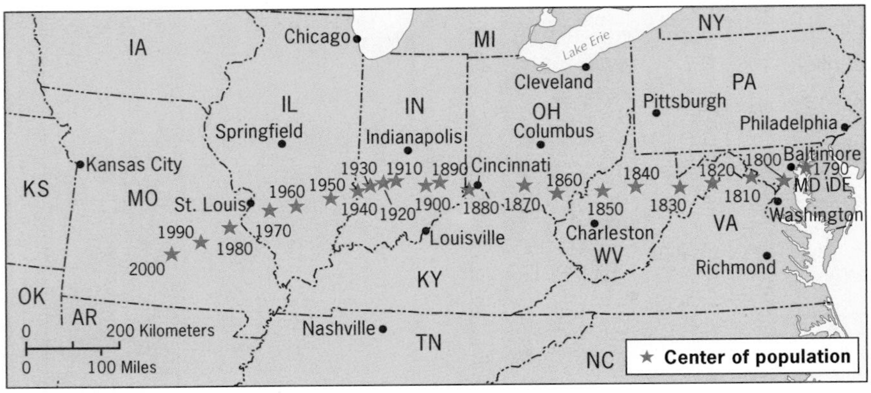

Figure 6-5 Changing Center of Population. *Source:* From U.S. Bureau of the Census, Statistical Abstract, 2001.

West was another factor. Perceived economic opportunities in the growing cities of the South played a role as well. One effect of this new situation could be observed in the growth statistics of southern cities. Black residents of northern cities migrated to southern cities, not to rural areas. Thus, the rural black Southerner became urbanized in the North and then relocated to a southern city. On the map, this adds up to a rural-to-urban flow in the South, which is now experiencing one of its most dramatic periods of growth.

The internal migration shown on Figure 6-3 marks the eastward movement of the Russian population from the heartland of the Russian state to the shores of the Pacific. Numerically, this migration did not match those discussed previously but its significance in forging the modern map of Eurasia cannot be overstated. During the czarist as well as communist periods, Russian rulers sought to occupy and consolidate Russia's (and the Soviets') far eastern frontier, moving industries eastward, building railroads and feeder lines, and establishing Vladivostok on the Pacific Coast as one of the world's best-equipped naval bases. This had the effect of opening up southern Siberia, incorporating numerous ethnic minorities under Russian and Soviet rule, and containing China. As Figure 6-3 indicates, part of Russia's eastward migration stream was diverted into Moscow's Central Asian sphere, where toward the end of Soviet control as many as 30 million Russians had moved. That number has been rapidly declining following the Soviet collapse, but the map will long carry the impact of Russia's eastward expansionism.

◆ POST–1945 EXTERNAL MIGRATIONS

Although the second half of the twentieth century witnessed no external migrations comparable to those shown on Figure 6-3, several major population movements in the aftermath of World War II and in the context of the Cold War had a major impact on the international order.

A migration stream with enormous consequences is the flow of Jewish immigrants to Israel. At the turn of the twentieth century, there were probably fewer than 50,000 Jewish residents in what was then Palestine. From 1919 to 1948 the United Kingdom held a mandate over Palestine, originally under the auspices of the League of Nations, and Britain encouraged the immigration of Jews from Europe. By 1948 there were perhaps 750,000 Jewish residents in Palestine, and the independent state of Israel was established through UN intervention and the partition of the area (Fig. 6-6). This in turn led to another migration stream: the displacement of 600,000 Palestinian Arabs who sought refuge in neighboring Jordan, Egypt, Syria, and elsewhere.

Jewish migrants continued to arrive from Europe, North America, South Africa and, even before the collapse, from the former Soviet Union. Today Israel's population of 6.4 million (including about 1 million Arab citizens) continues to grow through immigration as well as substantial natural increase.

The presence of a vigorous and growing Israel near the heart of the Muslim Arab realm has become one of the flashpoints in the modern world, with issues ranging from the fate of Jerusalem to the future of Jewish settlements on the conquered West Bank and in teeming Gaza (Fig. 6-6). It is probably true that no one involved in the establishment of the Jewish state foresaw the intensity of the crisis that lay ahead or the dimensions of the population movements it would generate.

Another conflict-induced population movement of major proportions occurred after the end of World War II, when as many as 15 million Germans migrated westward from their homes in Eastern Europe, either voluntarily or because they were forced to leave. Before the Berlin Wall went up and the Iron Curtain was lowered, several million Germans fled Soviet-controlled East Germany into what was then West Germany. And millions of migrants left Europe altogether to go to the United States (1.8 million), Canada (1.1 million), Australia (1 million), Israel (750,000), Argentina (750,000), Brazil (500,000), Venezuela (500,000), and other countries. As many as 8

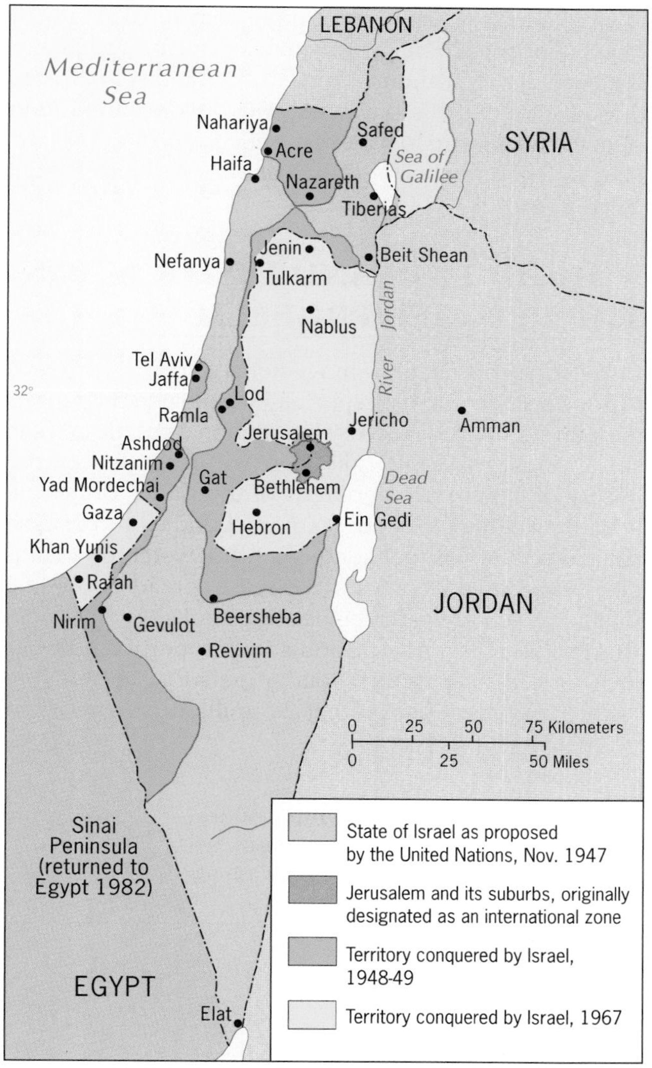

Figure 6-6 Different Boundaries of Israel. *Source:* From a map in M. Gilbert, Atlas of the Arab-Israeli Conflict (New York: Macmillan, 1974), p. 38.

Table 6-1 Legal Immigration to the United States' 1991–1998 (thousands)

Realm	Country	Total
Africa		301.6
	Nigeria	52.6
	Etheopia	41
	Egypt	37.8
	Ghana	27.6
	S. Africa	18.2
Asia		2427.4
	Philippines	432.1
	Vietnam	373.9
	China	346.7
	India	311.1
	Korea	142.6
Europe		1086.3
	Poland	150.7
	Ukraine	115.3
	United Kingdom	114.7
	Russia	98.5
	Ireland	56.8
N. America		3301.2
	Mexico	1929.9
	Dominican Rep.	305.6
	El Salvador	180.3
	Haiti	142.9
	Jamaica	142.7
S. America		442.3
	Colombia	106.5
	Peru	87.8
	Guyana	64.9
	Ecuador	59.9
	Brazil	41.4

Source: U.S. Department of Commerce, Bureau of the Census, Statistical Abstract of the United States: The National Data Book (2000), 120th edition (Washington, D.C., 2000), p. 10.

million Europeans emigrated from Europe in this postwar stream.

Recently, an even larger immigration stream reached the southwestern United States from Mexico (Table 6-1). So much of this movement has been unauthorized that demographers cannot estimate its magnitude even within hundreds of thousands. During the 1990s, legal immigration from Mexico approached 2 million; since 1961 it has surpassed 3 million. This migration stream has transformed the southwestern borderland of the United States.

As Table 6-1 shows, immigration from Asia during the 1990s approached that from Middle America. Nearly 2.5 million Asians entered the United States legally. The Philippines was the leading source country, followed closely by Vietnam, China and India. Europe, once the primary U.S. source area, contributed only 10 percent of the immigrants in the period from 1960 to 2000.

This massive emigration had political as well as economic consequences. European countries, rebuilding their economies with the help of the U.S.-sponsored Marshall Plan, now found themselves in need of laborers. Not only did this stimulate a substantial intra-European migration as workers from poorer countries moved to richer ones, but additional millions of foreign workers immigrated from North Africa (the majority to France) and Turkey (mostly to Germany) as well as from the Caribbean region, India, and Africa (many to the United

Kingdom). Not only the ethnic but also the religious mosaic of Europe changed in the process, and the growing presence of Islam in Europe produced social as well as political problems.

Migrations to North America

A set of major population movements during the second half of the twentieth century targeted the United States, not from Europe but from two other areas of the world: Middle America and East and Southeast Asia.

Even before Cuba became a communist state, thousands of Cuban citizens applied annually for residency in the United States. During the 1960s, this migration stream intensified and was formalized as the Cuban Airlift, an authorized movement of persons desiring to escape from a communist government. The great majority of the Cuban immigrants arrived and remained in the greater Miami area. In southern Florida they developed a core of Hispanic culture, and in due course Dade County declared itself bicultural and bilingual (Fig. 6-7).

Throughout the 1960s and 1970s, Cubans continued to arrive in the United States as refugees until in 1980 another massive, organized exodus occurred during the Mariel Boatlift, which brought more than 100,000 Cubans to U.S. shores; the migrants qualified for refugee status under U.S. regulations. The Cuban influx persisted throughout the 1980s, but in the 1990s diplomatic efforts to stem the tide began to have some effect. Still, by 2000, the official, legal number of Cuban arrivals had exceeded a half million.

◆ MIGRATION AND DISLOCATION: THE REFUGEE PROBLEM

Large-scale population movements tend to produce major social problems, especially when such migrations happen suddenly, forced by international conflict, ethnic strife, or environmental disaster. We have all seen the misery on television: hundreds of thousands of people streaming along dirt roads, carrying bundles and babies; squalid camps without adequate food, water, or amenities; desperate relief efforts as disease spreads, dooming infants and children and emaciating adults.

The world's refugee population proportionately has grown even faster than its total population. In 1970, the United Nations reported that 2.9 million persons were

Figure 6-7 Legal Immigration from Middle and South America to the United States, 1981–2000. *Source:* Based on data in U.S. Department of Commerce, Bureau of the Census. Statistical Abstract of the United States: The National Data Book (2000), 120th edition (Washington, D.C., 2000), p. 10.

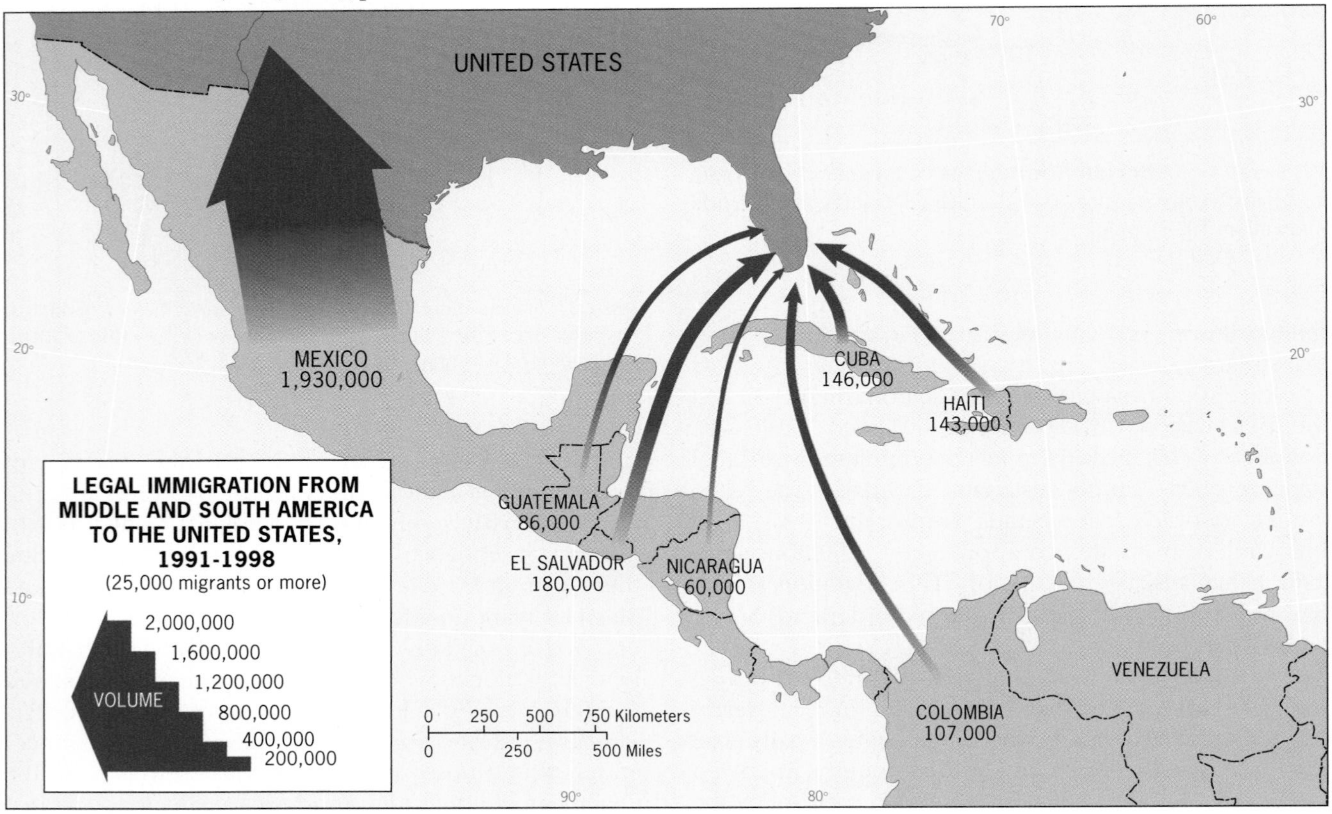

From the field notes

"This public war of words seen in Perth, Australia, was a reminder that immigration can raise social tensions and produce ugly reactions. Australia was among countries that agreed to accept a limited number of Indochina's "boat-people"; subsequently, several boatloads of Chinese would-be migrants arrived at the port of Darwin and appealed for refugee status. Australia's Asian population still is small but growing, and in the country's more politically conservative areas, extremist organizations such as the Australian Nationalist Movement proclaimed their opposition in various ways. I saw posters such as this not only in Perth but also in several smaller towns in Western Australia and in Queensland."

refugees, the majority of them Palestinian Arabs dislocated by the creation of the state of Israel and the armed conflicts that followed. In 1980 the refugee total had nearly tripled, to over 8 million, and in 1990 the estimated number approached 17 million. In 2000, the Office of the United Nations High Commissioner for Refugees (UNHCR) reported that 24 million people around the world were refugees, forced from their homes and unable to return.

Uncertain Dimensions

The United Nations agency that monitors the refugee problem is the key organization supporting dislocated persons. It organizes and funds international relief efforts and negotiates with governments and regimes on behalf of the refugees. But UNHCR is not alone in tracking this global problem; other offices often contradict UNHCR's data, arguing that the situation is even worse than the United Nations suggests.

Why the dispute? First, there are different definitions of what constitutes a ***refugee***. The UNHCR defines a refugee as "a person who has a well-founded fear of being persecuted for reasons of race, religion, nationality, membership of a particular social group, or political opinion." Countries interpret this definition in different ways; the phrase "well-founded" leaves much room for judgment. Second, refugees often flee into remote areas where it is difficult to count them, let alone provide help. Third, governments and regimes sometimes manipulate refugee numbers to suit their political objectives. Also note that the UNHCR definition says nothing about displacement resulting from environmental disaster.

Perhaps the biggest problem with the UN definition has to do with internal refugees—that is, people who have been displaced within their own countries, do not cross international borders as they flee, and tend to remain undercounted (if not almost invisible). In 2000, UNHCR estimated that as many as 25 million people (in addition to the 24 million official refugees) might be displaced, forced to abandon their homes. Thus the United Nations distinguishes between ***international refugees***, who have crossed one or more international borders during their move and have encamped in a country other than their own, and ***intranational refugees***, who have abandoned their homes but remain in their own countries. Resettlement efforts tend to be more successful with the latter because those fleeing their countries altogether often resist repatriation.

Because the status of refugee has an official, internationally sanctioned basis, UNHCR and other agencies must make difficult decisions when they distinguish between genuine refugees and migrants who may be just as poor or desperate but who do not qualify for refugee status. When a refugee meets the official criteria, he or she becomes eligible for assistance, including possible asylum, to which other migrants are not entitled. Such assistance can extend over decades and become the very basis for a way of life, as has happened in the Middle East. In Jordan, Palestinian refugees have become so integrated into the host country's national life that they are regarded as ***permanent refugees***, but in Lebanon other Palestinians wait in refugee camps for resettlement and still qualify as ***temporary refugees***.

Although it is not always easy to distinguish between a refugee and a voluntary (if desperate) migrant, refugees can be identified by at least three characteristics, individual or aggregate:

1. ***Most refugees move without any more tangible property than they can carry or transport with them.*** When the United States and its allies began their retaliatory bombing in Afghanistan following the terrorist attack on New York and Washington in September 2001, tens of thousands of Afghan refugees climbed across mountain passes to reach the relative safety of Pakistan, unable to bring any but the barest personal belongings.
2. ***Most refugees make their first "step" on foot, by bicycle, wagon, or open boat.*** In other words, the technological factor that facilitates modern migration is inoperative here. Refugees are suddenly

displaced, limiting their options, and the great majority have few resources to invest in their journey.

3. ***Refugees move without the official documents that accompany channeled migration.*** External refugees almost without exception migrate without authorization and often carry few or no identifying papers.

Regions of Dislocation

The refugee situation changes frequently as some refugees return home, conditions permitting, and as other, new streams suddenly form. Yet the overall geography of refugees has a certain continuity. In the late 1990s, Africa south of the Sahara had the largest number of refugees in the world as well as the greatest potential for new refugee flows. The second-ranking geographic realm in terms of refugee numbers was Southwest Asia and North Africa, the realm that includes the Middle East, Iran, and Afghanistan. South Asia, as a result of Pakistan's proximity to Afghanistan, ranked third (Fig. 6-8).

Subsaharan Africa Africa's people are severely afflicted by dislocation—and not just in terms of the 8 million "official" refugees accounted for by international relief agencies. Many millions more are intranational refugees.

During the last decade of the twentieth century and the first years of the twenty-first, several of the world's

Figure 6-8 Location of Refugees 2000. This map shows the number and areas of international and intranational refugees. *Source:* United Nations High Commission for Refugees, 2000; United States Committee for Refugees, 2000.

largest refugee crises occurred in Subsaharan Africa. The renewed outbreak of hostilities between cultural groups based in Hutu and Tutsi ethnicity in Rwanda and The Congo led to a disastrous exodus of refugees directly and indirectly involving millions, a genocide that killed hundreds of thousands and the collapse of order in the country then known as Zaire. Refugee flows entered not only The Congo but also Tanzania and Uganda; Tutsi-Hutu strife also engulfed Burundi and dislocated tens of thousands. In Sudan, which for decades has been Africa's worst refugee locale, a continuing conflict between the Muslim, Arabized north and the animist, African south continued to condemn more than 4 million people to refugee status. In 2001, just as there emerged some hope that the long-running war might see a negotiated end, the discovery of major oil reserves in tribal areas near the north-south frontier led to the expulsion of thousands from their homes, creating a new crisis. In West Africa, civil wars in Liberia and Sierra Leone sent columns of hundreds of thousands of refugees streaming into Guinea and Ivory Coast; in 1997 the UNHCR reported more than 1.5 million refugees in this small corner of Africa. And Angola, strife-torn ever since the days of the Cold War, still has well over 1 million intranational refugees (some estimates put the total nearer 2 million).

North Africa and Southwest Asia This geographic realm, extending from Morocco in the west to Afghanistan in the east, contains some of the world's long-lasting and most deeply entrenched refugee problems. A particularly significant set of refugee problems center on Israel and the displaced Arab populations that surround it. Decades of UN subventions have more or less stabilized this situation, but many refugees are still in

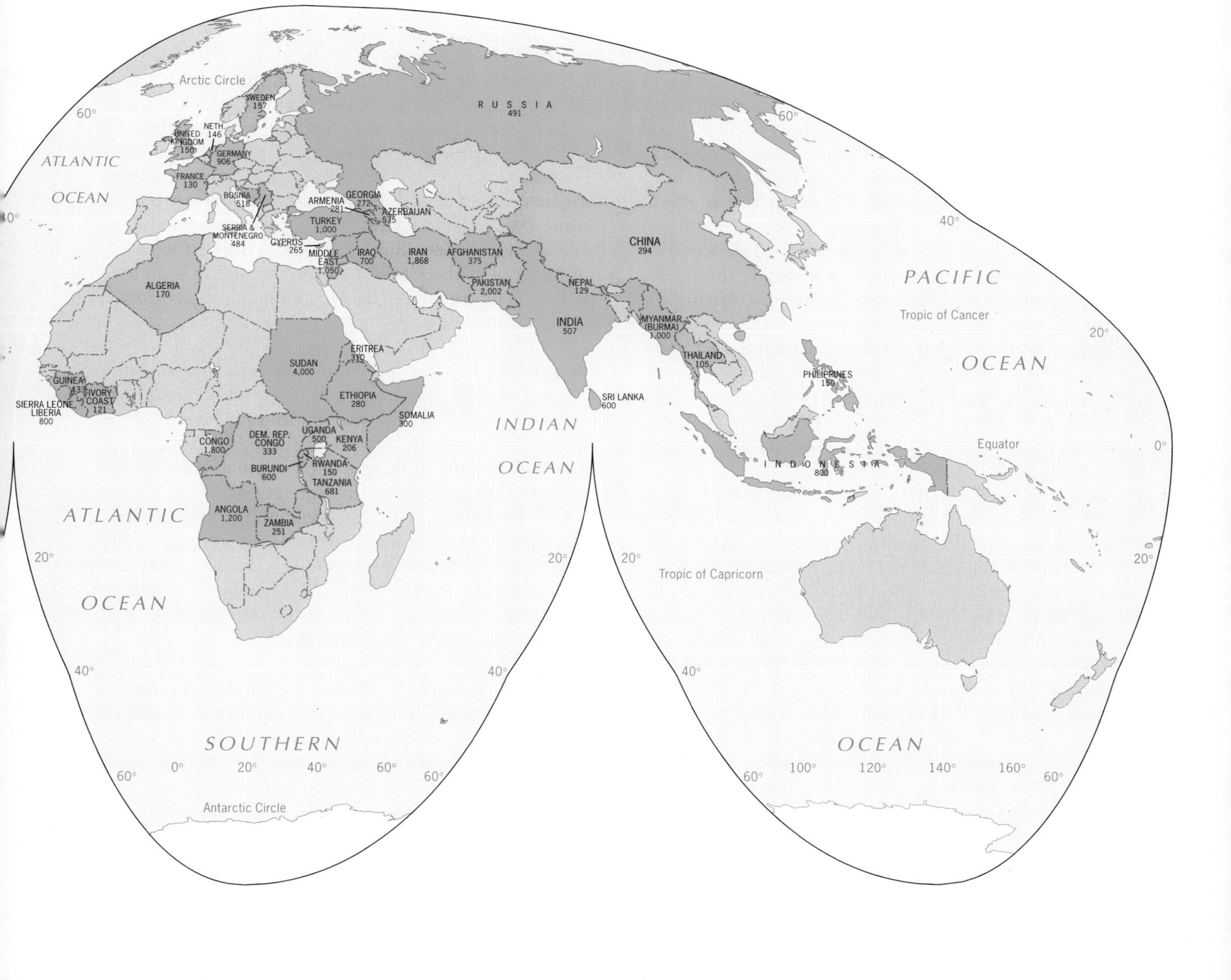

camps, and other crises elsewhere have tested the United Nations' capacity to provide relief. For example, in 1991, in the aftermath of the Gulf War that followed Iraq's invasion of Kuwait, a significant percentage of the Kurdish population of northern Iraq, threatened by the surviving military apparatus and under Baghdad's control, abandoned their villages and towns and streamed toward and across the Turkish and Iranian borders. The refugee movement of Iraq's Kurds involved as many as 2.5 million people and riveted world attention to the plight of people who are condemned to such status through the actions of others. It led the United States and its allies to create a secure zone for Kurds in extreme northern Iraq in the hope of persuading displaced Kurds in Turkey and Iran to return to their country. But this effort was only partially successful. The Kurdish people of Iraq were severely dislocated by the events surrounding the Gulf War; as Figure 6-4 shows, many remain refugees in Turkey as well as Iran.

During the 1980s Afghanistan was caught in the Soviets' last imperialist campaign and paid an enormous price for it. The Soviet invasion of Afghanistan at the end of 1979, in support of a puppet regime, and Afghan resistance generated a double migration stream that carried millions westward into Iran and eastward into Pakistan. At the height of the exodus, 2.5 million Afghans were estimated to be living in camps in Iran, and some 3.7 million gathered in tent camps in Pakistan's northwestern province and in southern Baluchistan. The Soviet invasion seemed destined to succeed quickly, but the Russian generals underestimated the strength of Afghan opposition. U.S. support for the Muslim forces in the form of weapons supplies helped produce a stalemate and eventual Soviet withdrawal, but this was followed by a power struggle among Afghan factions. As a result, most of the more than 6 million refugees in Iran and Pakistan—about one-quarter of the country's population—stayed where they were.

In 1996, an Islamic Fundamentalist movement, spawned in Pakistan, emerged in Afghanistan and took control of most of the country, imposing strict Islamic rule and suppressing the factional conflicts that had prevailed since the Soviet withdrawal. Although several hundred thousand Pashtun refugees did move back to Afghanistan from Pakistan, the harsh Taliban rule created a counter migration and led to further refugee movement into neighboring Iran, where their number reached 2.5 million. Eventually, Afghanistan became a base for anti-Western terrorist operations, which reached a climax in the attack on the United States on September 11, 2001. Even before the inevitable military retaliation began, and despite efforts by both Pakistan and Iran to close their borders, tens of thousands of Afghan refugees flooded across, intensifying a refugee crisis that is now nearly a quarter-century old.

South Asia In terms of refugee numbers, South Asia is the third-ranking geographic realm, mainly because of Pakistan's role in accommodating Afghanistan's forced emigrants. During the Soviet intrusion in the 1980s, the UNHCR counted more than 3 million refugees; during the 1990s, the total averaged between 1.2 and 1.5 million. That number rose when allied retaliation against terrorist bases began in October 2001.

The other major refugee problem in South Asia stems from a civil war in Sri Lanka. This conflict, arising from demands by minority Tamils for an independent state on the Sinhalese-dominated island, has cost tens of thousands of lives and has severely damaged the economy. The United Nations reports that about 1 million people (out of a population of 19 million) are now intranational refugees.

Southeast Asia Southeast Asia is a reminder that refugee problems can change quickly. Indochina was the scene of one of the twentieth century's most desperate refugee crises—the stream of between 1 and 2 million "boat people" who fled Vietnam in the aftermath of the long war that ended in 1975. In the early 1990s, it was Cambodia that produced an exodus of 300,000 refugees escaping from their country's seemingly endless cycle of violence, ending up in refugee camps on the Thailand side of the border. Today, the largest refugee camps in this realm are intranational refugees in Burma (Myanmar), victims of the repressive rule of the generals who are seeking to subjugate the country's minorities. But as the UNHCR states, that figure is an estimate only; information from Myanmar's closed society is difficult to secure.

Europe The collapse of Yugoslavia and its associated conflicts created the largest refugee crisis in Europe since the end of World War II. In 1995, the UNHCR reported the staggering total of 6,056,600 refugees, a number that some observers felt was inflated by the Europeans' unusually liberal interpretations of the United Nations' rules for refugee recognition. Nevertheless, even after the cessation of armed conflict and the implementation of a peace agreement known as the Dayton Accords, the UNHCR still reports as many as 1.6 million intranational refugees in the area—people dislocated and unable to return to their homes.

Elsewhere As Figure 6-8 shows, the number of refugees in other geographic realms is much smaller. In the Western Hemisphere, only Colombia in 1997 had a serious refugee problem, caused by the country's chronic instability associated with its struggle against narcotics. Large areas of Colombia's countryside are vulnerable to armed attack by "narcoterrorists" and paramilitary units; these rural areas are essentially beyond government control, and thousands of villagers have died in the crossfire.

Hundreds of thousands more, as the map indicates, have left their homes to seek protection as refugees.

People who abandon their familiar surroundings because conditions there have become unlivable perform an ultimate act of desperation. In the process, the habits of civilization vanish as survival becomes the sole imperative. The Earth's refugee population is a barometer of the world's future.

◆ KEY TERMS ◆

absolute direction
absolute distance
activity (action) space
commuting
counter migration
cyclic movement
distance decay
emigration
external migration
forced migration
gravity model
internal migration
international refugees
interregional migration
intervening opportunity
intranational refugees
migration
nomadism
permanent refugees
pull factors
push factors
refugee
relative distance
seasonal movement
slave trade
step migration
temporary refugees
voluntary migration

◆ APPLYING GEOGRAPHIC KNOWLEDGE ◆

1. A recent newspaper headline read as follows: POPULATION GROWTH CAUSES MIGRATION. The article beneath this headline described current global population growth trends and suggested that the pressure on people to migrate would not end until population growth had declined. Write a letter to the Editor commenting on this issue from a geographic perspective.

2. The world's refugee population (counting both internal and external refugees) is at an all-time high today. Account for the factors that explain this situation. What conditions and circumstances might cause the number of dislocated people to increase even more? Wherein lies the hope for improvement?

Chapter 7

Policy Responses to Demographic Changes

From the field notes

"Beijing is a city transformed, and if the forest of skyscrapers does not convince, then look around you as people stroll across Tienanmen Square or along what is reputed to be the world's longest main street. I must confess that the symbolism in this photograph only manifested itself after I had taken the picture—an obviously well-to-do local couple walking toward me, their (probably) only child, a son, in tow, all under the watchful eye of the police."

KEY POINTS

- **For practical purposes population data are reported by country. But demographic variation within countries can be very large as, for example, in India.**

- **During the twentieth century national governments pursued three kinds of population policy: expansive, eugenic, and restrictive.**

- **International agreements on population policies are difficult to reach, in part because religious ideologies and governmental goals may be incompatible.**

- **The most dramatic population-policy reversal in recent decades was carried out by communist China.**

- **Many governments have sought to control immigration through laws limiting the number or type of people who can cross borders and become citizens, but few countries have succeeded in controlling immigration effectively.**

The foregoing chapters contain ample evidence of an inescapable reality: try as they might, governments are unable to effectively control population change. The populations of some countries continue to grow far more rapidly than their administrations would like. And in other countries where populations are declining and aging, governments are hard put to get families to have more youngsters than they choose to have. In addition, despite their best efforts, governments are unable to control the flow of migrants across their borders.

Indeed, national governments even find it difficult to deal with population issues *within* their borders. We noted earlier in Part Two that national statistics on population can be deceptive: they do not reveal regional variations within individual countries. In India, for example, the population increase in some southern States is close to the world average of 1.4 percent—but in India's northeast some States record nearly *triple* the world average. In the demographic arena, such regional variations complicate efforts to forge effective population policies.

In this chapter we take a look at national and international population policies in spatial as well as temporal context. Much has changed over the past century or so: there was a time when governments could openly favor one ethnic group over another, close their borders to persons of particular racial ancestry, even segregate their own people based on race. Although various forms of more subtle discrimination still occur, these worst excesses have been terminated, in part through international pressure and action. But governments continue to see ways to constrain excessive population growth, to deal with the problems arising from population decline, and to control immigration. ◆

◆ ROLE OF THE UNITED NATIONS

Population change is a global issue, and the United Nations organizes conferences and meetings to address the problem on a regular basis. The most revealing conferences are the Population Conferences held every 10 years since the first one in Bucharest, Romania, in 1974.

It is interesting to read the record of this meeting. The population explosion was in full force, global hunger and dislocation were being forecast, and controlling population growth seemed to be a worldwide priority. But the minutes of the 1974 Conference paint quite another picture, and they remind us of the cost of the Cold War and of the difficulty in reaching international agreement on any issue as sensitive as population. China, still in the aftershocks of its costly Cultural Revolution, put the Marxist view bluntly: population control was a capitalist plot designed to hamper the growth and power of communist societies, and the Chinese would not agree to any multinational plan to limit growth. On the contrary, the Chinese applauded the (then) Soviet policy of giving special recognition and awards to women who had borne 10 children or more.

The Bucharest gathering was the first in a series of UN-sponsored conferences on population issues. Although it was marred by ideological disputes, the great majority of the world's governments agreed on the urgency of the population issue. China and the Soviet Union took similar positions for different reasons: China saw family planning as a capitalist plot, whereas the Soviet Union promoted births because its population had not fully recovered from the enormous losses it suffered during World War II. The Soviet Union encouraged large families because it saw its huge domain as underpopulated (a situation to which Stalinists had contributed by exterminating more than 30 million farmers, political opponents, and other dissidents during the 1930s). Nonetheless, the problems of spiraling population growth were evident to most of the participating states, communist and noncommunist alike.

The UN Population Conference of 1984, held in Mexico City, had a very different tone; gone were the sense of urgency and the depth of ideological animosity. The Green Revolution had narrowed the food gap, and the specter of global famine, predicted by so many scientists, was receding. China, now in its post-Mao era, had reversed its position on population growth. It had now embarked on a severely restrictive population policy, and its growth rate had declined dramatically—so much so that the Beijing regime had been awarded a United Nations medal for achieving rapid reduction in the national birth rate. In addition, during the Reagan (Republican) era the United States did not take an active role in support of family planning. It kept a relatively low profile at the conference, and no major confrontations like those at Bucharest occurred.

During the 1994 conference, held in Cairo, Egypt, a new and potentially crucial division emerged among the 180 countries represented. The great majority of these states wanted to endorse a plan to be known as the "Cairo Strategy," a program that would combine family planning with sex education in schools, along with other initiatives to achieve reduced population-growth rates in developing countries. But a relatively small group of conservative Roman Catholic and Muslim countries, strongly supported by the Vatican, blocked final agreement on this program. These countries refused to approve proposals to educate school-age youngsters on matters of sex and to make contraceptives more readily available. Roman Catholic countries such as Argentina, Nicaragua, and Guatemala argued that the program should endorse parental control over children's sex education rather than high school training (which had been proposed by Mexico). Muslim countries asserted that population-control measures of any kind were inconsistent with Islamic precepts (which was the basis for Saudi Arabia's refusal to participate at all).

From the field notes

"Searing social contrasts abound in India's overcrowded cities. Even in Bombay, India's most prosperous large city, hundreds of thousands of people live like this, in the shadow of modern apartment buildings. Within seconds we were surrounded by a crowd of people asking for help of any kind, their ages ranging from the very young to the very old. Somehow this scene was more troubling here in well-off Bombay than in Calcutta or Madras, but it typified India's urban problems everywhere." (Note: the names of Bombay and Madras were changed after this field note was written.)

Thus the Cairo Conference may have opened a new chapter in the ongoing struggle to constrain population growth; Cold War ideological conflict has now been replaced by strife between religious fundamentalism and secularism. The 2004 Conference will undoubtedly continue the debate begun in Cairo, where a number of delegations denounced secular society. These arguments pushed into the background a key to reducing population growth: the education of women and the strengthening of their rights in all societies (see Chapter 31). When women have access to education and paid employment, birth rates decline and development accelerates. Data from the World Bank indicate that women without some high school education have an average of seven children; the average drops to three for women who attend high school. And because there is more time between births, the health of women and children also improves, saving medical costs for the society as a whole.

Religious fundamentalism can work against the interests of women in societies of all kinds. Many observers argue that the poverty associated with rapid population growth is best combated by improving the status of women in traditional society. On this matter the conference made little progress.

◆ NATIONAL POPULATION POLICIES

Over the past century, many of the world's governments have instituted policies designed to influence the overall growth rate or ethnic ratios within the population. Certain policies directly affect the birth rate via laws that range from subsidization of abortion to forced sterilization. Others influence family size through taxation or subvention. These policies fall into three groups: expansive, eugenic, and restrictive.

The former Soviet Union and China under Mao Zedong led other communist societies in ***expansive population policies***, which encourage large families and raise the rate of natural increase. Ideological, anticapitalist motives drove those policies, now abandoned. But today, some countries are again pursuing expansive population policies—because their populations are aging and declining. We have already taken note of the situation in Europe, where France has embarked on a policy to encourage (through tax incentives and by other fiscal means) families to have more children. Another case is Singapore, where, shortly after its secession from Malaysia (1965), the government instituted a restrictive population policy. Sterilization was encouraged, abortion was legalized, and families with more than two children were fiscally punished. So successful was this policy that the population stopped growing and started aging. At this point, the government reversed itself, instituting an expansive population policy. Singapore's experience underscores the difficulties governments face when trying to constrain population growth: the island's city-state population is small (4.1 million), well-educated, and tightly ruled by an autocratic government—and still its population policies had unintended consequences.

In the past, some governments engaged in ***eugenic population policies***, which were designed to favor one racial or cultural sector of the population over others. The ultimate example of "eugenics" was Nazi Germany, but other countries also pursued such strategies, though in more subtle ways. Up until the time of the Civil Rights movement, some accuse the United States of pursuing social policies tinged with eugenics that worked against the interests of African-Americans; Japan's nearly homogeneous culture is sometimes said to result from deliberately eugenic social policies. Eugenic population policies can be practiced covertly through discriminatory taxation, biased allocation of resources, and other forms of racial favoritism.

Today the majority of the world's governments seek to reduce the rate of natural increase through various forms of ***restrictive population policies***. These policies range from toleration of officially unapproved means of birth control to outright prohibition of large families. As we note later in this chapter, China's "one-child-only" policy, instituted after the end of the Maoist period, had spectacular effect, reducing China's growth rate from one of the world's fastest to one of the developing world's slowest. But again the policy had unintended consequences and has been relaxed somewhat in recent years.

Limitations Many governments have learned that changing circumstances tend to overtake their carefully constructed population policies; the case of Singapore is one among these. Urbanization and industrialization inhibit population growth more effectively than restrictive population policies can; the liberation and education of women in traditionally male-dominant societies does more than sex education and condoms. Restricting the immigration of foreign workers will do more to age a population than any population policy can. Cultural tradition (especially religion) can neutralize the best-formulated strategies. Still, governments must keep trying because population continues to grow.

Contradictions No one who has looked carefully at the map of world population growth (Fig. 5-1) will have failed to note that natural increase is at its lowest in the very heart of the Roman Catholic world. (Italy's population is actually declining today.) Adherence to Catholic doctrine, it would appear, is far stronger in areas remote from the Vatican than within the Catholic core. Another case in point is in the Philippines, Asia's only Roman Catholic country (population: 84 million). Here, the still-powerful church opposes the use of artificial contraceptives, and church and state have been locked in a battle over birth control. Abortion is prohibited by the country's constitution. When Manila's cardinal demanded that the Philippine government boycott the Cairo Conference on Population and Development in 1994, the issue roiled the nation. But the Philippines is a democracy, and while Manila did send a delegation to Cairo, the government could not afford to ignore the pronouncements of the church. In the first decade of the twenty-first century, population growth in the Philippines remained one of Asia's highest at 2.2 percent, with a doubling time of only 31 years.

In the Islamic realm, the geographic situation seems to be the opposite. Saudi Arabia, home of Mecca and the heart of the Muslim world, has one of the globe's fastest growth rates (3.0 percent; doubling time 23 years). But in far-off Indonesia (the Philippines' neighbor), the government in 1970 began a nationwide family-planning program. When fundamentalist Muslim leaders objected, the government used a combination of coercion and inducement to negate their influence. Eventually, Indonesia's family-planning program came to be regarded as the most successful in the Muslim world: in 1970 the country's rate of natural increase was over 2.5 percent; by 2000 it was down to 1.6 percent, far below that of the Philippines. Doubling time rose from 28 to 44 years.

◆ THREE CASE STUDIES

The governments of three countries in Asia which, in combination, account for 40 percent of the world's population have had quite different experiences in their efforts to institute policies to limit and control population growth. The consequences of their efforts have varied widely—and have had a crucial impact on global prospects.

Japan

The Japanese experience is a prime example of success—perhaps too much success—in population control. During Japan's nineteenth- and early twentieth-century era of modernization, expansion, and military victories, families were encouraged to have several children. However, Japan also had growing urban centers, which tended to somewhat reduce the birth rate. This combination of circumstances helped stabilize the rate of population growth.

At the end of World War II, hundreds of thousands of Japanese nationals returned from the colonies. Soldiers came home and rejoined their families. During the American occupation medical services and public health were improved. The net result was an unprecedented increase in the birth rate and a simultaneous drop in death rates. Japan's rate of growth, which over the decades had averaged about 1.3 percent, suddenly rose to 2.0 percent per year. That represents a doubling time of 35 years, and with Japan's population already about 70 million at the time, it created a crisis.

In 1948 the Japanese government took action, and the results can be seen in the population pyramid in Figure 5-5. The ***Eugenic Protection Act*** legalized abortions for "social, medical, and economic reasons." Contraceptives were made available, and family-planning clinics were set up throughout the country. Although contraception and female sterilization (also made widely available) helped reduce the birth rate, it was the enormous number of abortions that really brought it down. So many abortions were performed—perhaps 7 to 8 million in a decade—that the Japanese authorities began to worry about their effect on the well-being of the nation. They then began to use propaganda and educational programs to encourage contraception.

As a result of these measures, the birth rate, which had been over 34 per 1000 in 1947, had fallen to 18 per thousand just one decade later and was reduced to 13 per thousand by 1985. Meanwhile, the death rate declined from 14.2 in 1948 to 7.5 in 1958 to 6.0 in 1985. Thus in the early 1980s Japan's population, growing at less than 1 percent per year, increased by about 1 million annually. Immigration contributed little to population growth, and emigration also had little effect.

In the 1990s, Japan's demographic situation became a matter of growing concern for its leaders. The country's fertility rate had fallen to a new low of just over 1.5, far below the 2.1 needed to maintain the population without loss. (This is still higher than the prevailing TFR in West Germany just before reunification, which was below 1.3.) The effects of this decline can be seen in projections of Japan's future population, which will reach a peak of approximately 127 million in 2007 and then begin a slow but accelerating decline down (by some projections) to 70 million by 2060.

In 1991, the Japanese government increased the benefits available to parents and embarked on an expansionist population policy. But under the special conditions of Japanese life it will be difficult to reverse the trend just described. Japan is a small country, about the size of Montana. It is among the world's most highly urbanized, industrialized, and regimented societies. Living space is at a premium; living costs are high. The financial and social burdens of raising a child are great, and parents are well aware that some child benefits will not be much help. So Japan, like Germany, faces an aging population, a dwindling workforce, and a shrinking tax base at a time when welfare and pension costs are rising.

What alternatives are available? Labor immigration is one possibility, but the Japanese refuse to allow large numbers of foreign workers into their nearly homogeneous island nation. A Singapore-style campaign to reverse the downward population spiral is not likely in Japan, nor would it be likely to work. For the time being, Japan will probably turn to an old ally—technology. It still is possible to turn over more work to robots and other advanced technologies in order to increase productivity. Some observers also suggest that many more women will enter the skilled workforce in the early twenty-first century.

None of this, however, will ultimately protect Japan from the social and economic adjustments that must accompany less-than-zero or ***negative population growth***. With its borders effectively closed to immigration, its future problems will be substantially self-imposed, proving again that in this age of interaction and interconnection, cultural isolation is no guarantee of a secure future.

India

Demographers predict that sometime during the first half of the twenty-first century India will overtake China as the world's most populous country—if India's political framework holds together. In the late 1990s, India's population was still growing at a rate of about 1.9 percent, adding over 18 million per year to a population approaching 1 billion.

The problems involved in carrying out a coordinated population policy in a country as culturally complex as India are enormous. India is a federation of 28 States and 7 so-called Union Territories, and the individual States differ greatly both culturally and politically. As in all true federations, the will of the federal government cannot be forcibly imposed on the States.

Earlier we mentioned the regional variation in India's rate of population growth (Fig. 7-1). From a demographic standpoint, in fact, there are several Indias. Population growth is most rapid (and still explosive) in Assam and neighboring states adjacent to Bangladesh. In Nagaland and Mizoram, the rate of natural increase during the 1970s actually exceeded 4.5 percent, one of the world's highest. It has been about 2.5 percent in India's great eastern population cluster in the lower Ganges-Brahmaputra Basin. As Figure 7-1 shows, the growth rate in the southern peninsula has been below the national average. The national average for population growth does not reveal these internal spatial variations. When the food situation was less secure than it has been in recent years, hunger often afflicted the east at a time when food was adequate in the west.

Population planning began on a shoestring budget in the 1950s, not long after India became independent. Limited funds were made available for family-planning

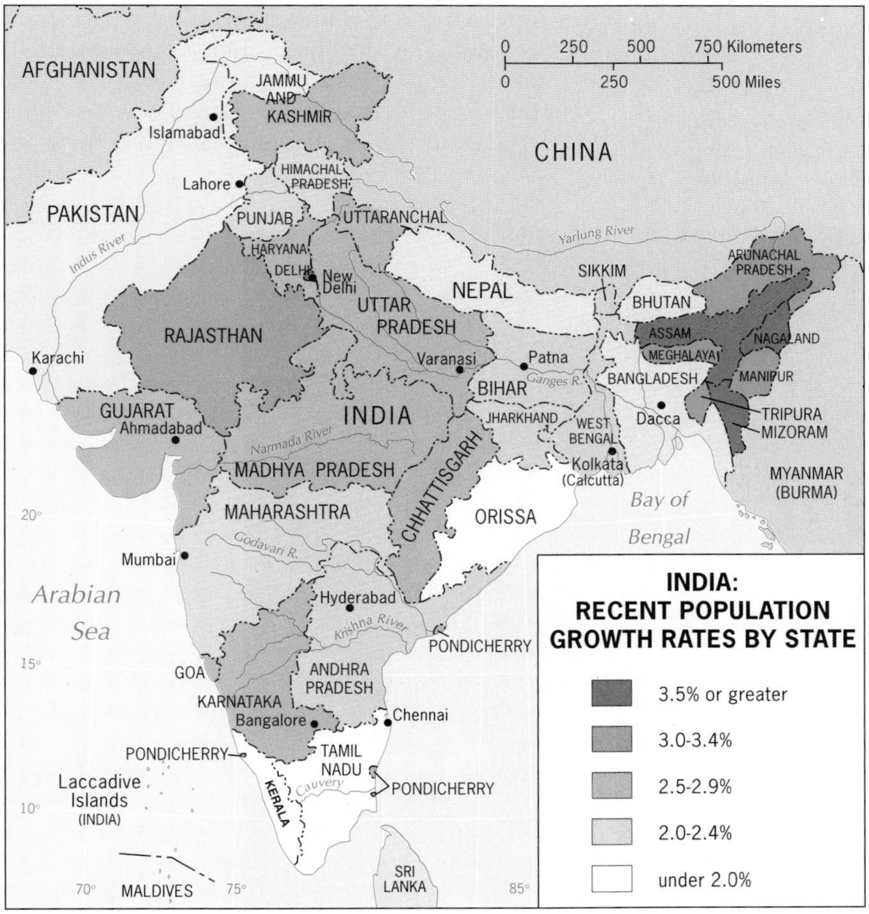

Figure 7-1 Recent Population Growth Rates in India. Data from census of India since 1970 and from demographic reports of individual State agencies were used to derive yearly population growth rates.

clinics and programs, but government leaders themselves were not aware of the real dimensions of the population explosion in progress at the time. In the 1960s, however, India's official census left no doubt, and the government's investment in population planning increased. A national program was instituted, and the States were encouraged to join.

Despite this national effort, rapid population growth continued, especially in the eastern States. Also, social problems arose in some of the States where the campaign was pursued most vigorously. The State of Maharashtra instituted a plan that required sterilization of anyone with three children or more. Public opposition led to rioting and the program was abandoned, but not before 3.7 million people had been sterilized. Other States also engaged in compulsory sterilization programs, but the social and political costs were heavy. Eventually, a total of 22.5 million people were sterilized, but this form of population control could not be sustained for long.

Today Indian State governments are using advertising and persuasion to encourage families to have fewer children. Almost everywhere one can see posters urging people to have small families, and a network of clinics has been established to aid women even in the remotest villages. As Figure 7-1 indicates, progress has been made in some areas, not only in the better educated areas of the south but elsewhere as well. We should keep in mind that several of India's States have 100 million inhabitants or more, which would put them among the world's larger countries. Any reduction in population growth rates in such States is a major achievement. However, India does not have enough resources to achieve a significant decline in population growth rates in the nation as a whole.

From the field notes

"China's communist regime could institute a one-child-only policy and enforce it, but India is a democracy, and India's States have considerable autonomy. Above this entrance to a suite of medical offices was some evidence of recent disputes over family planning in the State of Maharashtra: GOVERNMENT APPROVED URBAN FAMILY PLANNING CENTRE IS CLOSED FROM 1.1/1996, says one notice; FREE FAMILY PLANNING STERILISATION OPERATION NOW NOT CONDUCTED HERE FROM 1.1/1996, says another. These notices mark the outcome of decisions by the Maharashtra government to overrule federal family-planning initiatives; here is one reason why India's rate of population growth remains comparatively high."

China

For nearly 30 years after the communist government took power, China's demography was a mystery to the outside world. Estimates of China's population and its rate of natural increase varied widely. In 1978 the World Bank's ***World Development Report*** estimated the Chinese population at 826 million. Shortly thereafter the Chinese government announced that the 1 billion mark had been passed. Guesses about China's population had been wrong by as much as 200 million!

If there were doubts about the size of China's population, the political and social regime of Mao Zedong left no doubts about its views on family planning. At the 1974 Bucharest Conference, as noted earlier, the Chinese representative denounced population policies as imperialist tools designed to sap the strength of developing countries.

After Mao's death in 1976, China's new leaders expressed very different views. If China was to modernize, they said, population growth would have to be brought under control. In 1979 they launched a policy to induce married couples to have only one child. This would have stabilized China's population at about 1.2 billion by the end of the century.

The ***one-child policy*** was applied loosely at first, but when it had less than the desired effect, it was enforced more strictly. The results were dramatic. In 1970, China's population was growing at a rate of 2.4 percent (as estimated by China's own planners); by 1985, it was down to 1.1 percent. In 1983, by which time the growth rate had been reduced to 1.2 percent, the United Nations gave China (along with India) its first Family-Planning Award.

These statistics are encouraging, but they conceal the stresses the policies impose on families. After 1982, the government made it mandatory for women to use contraceptive devices after they had their one child. If a second child was born, one of the parents would have to be sterilized. Only members of China's recognized minorities (less than 3 percent of the total population) were exempt from these rules.

Such rules imposed severe hardships, especially on farming families. Many hands are needed to do farm work, and large families are common in many rural areas. Therefore, many Chinese families defied the authorities: they kept pregnant women out of sight, did not register births, and prevented inspectors from visiting villages.

In response, the government took drastic action. Those who violated the rules were fired from their jobs, had their farmlands taken away, lost many benefits, and were otherwise put at a disadvantage. In some parts of China the punishment was even worse: pregnant women known to have one or two children were arrested at work, in the fields, or at home and taken to abortion clinics to have their babies aborted—sometimes after more than six months of pregnancy. The national policies were imposed more harshly in some provinces than in others. Southeast China appears to have been targeted most severely.

China's Ministry of Public Health estimates that during the first six years of the population-control campaign, nearly 70 million abortions were performed in the country (where abortion was regarded as murder just a generation earlier). In addition, during the 1980s more than 20 million persons were sterilized ***annually*** (three times as many women as men), according to government reports.

The effectiveness of the Chinese population policies was ensured, not only by government incentives and punishments, but also through the actions of Communist Party officials and members. Through promises of advancements and cash payments for local compliance, party members became, in effect, the birth-control police. No village, neighborhood, factory, or collective escaped constant scrutiny.

But China is changing. In 1984, in response to a rising tide of complaints from rural areas, the government relaxed its one-child policy in the countryside. A couple whose first child was a daughter were allowed to have a second child after a four-year wait. Then the Party-imposed system of controls began to break down as enforcement weakened, people found more effective ways of circumventing the rules (sending an illegally pregnant woman to distant family members to await the birth, for example), and peasants with rising incomes could afford to pay the fine for unauthorized births. Corruption, an endemic problem in China, also enabled some people to evade punishment for violations. Briefly China's growth rate moved upward again, and China's census revealed that its goal for the end of the twentieth century—a stable population of 1.32 billion—had not been achieved; its total had been exceeded by 80 million. But the official data for the year 2000 are more optimistic: a growth rate of only 0.9 percent (see Table in Resource B).

China's one-child-only policy has had a major social impact in a society where sons carry on the family name. In the cities a one-child policy was feasible. In the tradition-bound countryside, however, where large families have long been the norm, the notion of one (possibly female) child was not acceptable. Observers reported that the one-child policy led to female infanticide and that hundreds of thousands of such killings went unreported at the height of the one-child-only campaign. Demographers estimated that the number of surviving male children exceeded females by 300,000 annually. China's own population experts have expressed concern over this imbalance. In the future males will greatly outnumber females, with unpredictable social consequences.

Thus China's relentless drive for zero population growth eroded the traditions of Chinese society and brought misery to millions of people. Chinese government and Communist Party officials admit that the policy, when strictly applied, was severe. But they argue that in a country with 100 million excess births, many millions of people will be mired in stagnation and poverty. To get ahead, they argue, the country cannot allow its material gains to be negated by an ever-growing population.

China's experience underscores the depth of the population dilemma. Even with an authoritarian government backed by party machinery, strict policies could not be enforced over the long term. Significant short-term gains were quickly wiped out, and population growth once again became an obstacle to modernization. Given China's experience, India's regional progress is all the more remarkable.

◆ POLICIES TARGETING MIGRATION

The control of immigration, legal and illegal, the problem of asylum seekers, genuine and fraudulent, and the fate of cross-border refugees, permanent and temporary, have become hot issues around the world. In Europe, right-wing political parties whip up anti-immigrant sentiment. In California, the state government demands federal help to provide services for hundreds of thousands of illegal immigrants; if the federal government cannot control its borders, the argument goes, the States should not have to foot the bill. In Cuba, the Castro regime has used migration as a threat: in August 1994, Castro threatened to open Cuba's doors to a flood of emigrants that "will make the Mariel Boatlift look like child's play." And in the United States the government faced reproach for preventing tens of thousands of Haitians from entering Florida.

Efforts to restrict migrations are nothing new, however. Media coverage, democratic debate, and political wrangling only make it seem so. China's Great Wall was built in part as a defensive measure but also as a barrier to emigration (by Chinese beyond the sphere of their authorities) and immigration (mainly by Mongol "barbarians" from the northern plains). The Berlin Wall, the Korean DMZ (demilitarized zone), the fences along the Rio Grande—all evince the desire of governments to control the movement of people across their borders.

Legal Restrictions

Usually, however, the obstacles placed in the way of potential immigrants are legal, not physical. Restrictive legislation made its appearance in the United States in 1882, when Congress approved the Oriental Exclusion Acts (1882 to 1907). These ***immigration laws*** were designed to restrict the immigration of Chinese people to California. In 1901 Australia's government approved the Immigration Restriction Act, which terminated all nonwhite immigration into the newly united Commonwealth. This act, too, was aimed primarily at Japanese and Chinese immigrants (but it included South Asians as well). It also had the effect of prohibiting immigration by South Pacific islanders who had entered Australia to work on the large sugar plantations. These workers, the Kanakas, were the target of a provision that facilitated their deportation by the end of 1906. The White Australia Policy was one of the issues on which the Australian colonies were united prior to the establishment of the Commonwealth, and it remained in effect until it was modified in 1972 and again in 1979.

In the United States, restrictive legislation affecting European immigrants was passed in 1921. The balance of European immigration had been shifting from Western Europe to Southern and Eastern Europe, and many immigrants had no training or resources—at a time when industry's need for skilled labor was declining. The 1921 legislation was a quota law. Each year each European country could permit the emigration to the United States of 3 percent of the number of its nationals living in America in 1910. This had the effect of limiting annual immigration to about 357,000 Europeans, most of them from Western Europe. In 1924 the Immigration Act lowered the quota to 2 percent and made 1890 the base year; this further reduced the annual total to 150,000 immigrants.

The National Origins Law took effect in 1929. It sustained the limit of 150,000 immigrants per year, but it also tied immigration quotas to the national origins of the U.S. population in 1920. This law had the effect of preventing the immigration of Asians. Immigration slowed to a trickle during the 1930s, and in some years emigration actually exceeded immigration.

After 1940, the restrictions on immigration to the United States were modified. In 1943 China was given equal status with European countries, and in 1952 Japan received similar status. A new Immigration and Nationality Act (1952) was designed to incorporate all preceding legislation, establishing quotas for all countries and limiting total immigration to under 160,000. However, far more immigrants entered the country as displaced persons (refugees), thereby filling quotas for years ahead. Estimates vary, but more than 7 million immigrants may have entered the United States as refugees between 1945 (the end of World War II in Europe) and 1970. The 1952 law was acknowledged to be a failure, and in 1965 the quota system was abolished. New limits were set: 170,000 immigrants per year from countries outside the Western Hemisphere and 120,000 from countries in the Americas. Nevertheless, in the 1970s and 1980s the number of Cuban, Haitian, and Mexican arrivals far exceeded these limitations.

The United States and Australia are not the only countries that have restricted immigration. Many countries practice selective immigration, in which individuals with certain backgrounds (criminal records, poor health, subversive activities) are barred from entering. Other countries have specific requirements. For example, South Africa long demanded "pure" European descent; New Zealand favored persons of British birth and parentage; Brazil preferred people with a farming background; and Singapore courts financially secure persons of Chinese ancestry. Today South American countries place limits on the number of immigrants who may cross their borders, and quota systems are being instituted. Thailand has restricted Chinese immigration, and Myanmar (Burma) limits immigration from neighboring India.

In France, problems associated with the large and growing Arab population from North Africa have resulted in calls for repatriation of those without residency permits and for restrictions on further immigration from the former French North African colonies (Algeria, Morocco, and Tunisia).

As the world's population mushrooms, the volume of migrants will likewise expand. In an increasingly open and interconnected world, neither physical barriers nor politically motivated legislation will stem tides that are as old as human history. Migrations will also further complicate an already complex global cultural pattern. What are some of the principal features of the global cultural pattern, and what is the significance of those patterns? We turn to these questions in the next two parts.

◆ KEY TERMS ◆

eugenic population policy
Eugenic Protection Act
expansive population policy
immigration laws
negative population growth
one-child policy
restrictive population policy

◆ APPLYING GEOGRAPHIC KNOWLEDGE ◆

1. For many years population geographers and others have been concerned over the continuing rapid growth of the world's population. But some countries, having traversed the demographic transition, now confront the reality of stable or even declining populations. What are the impacts of negative population growth on countries' cultural and economic geographies?
2. Population policies designed to influence the growth of national populations tend to have regional ramifications; that is, their impact varies regionally. Working at the national and subnational scale, demonstrate how this statement applies to three countries that have adopted population policies.

Part Two

POPULATION PATTERNS AND PROCESSES

At Issue: Revisited

How serious a problem is population growth? Should lowering the world's population growth rate be a global objective? Any attempt to address the hard questions about population growth must begin with the fundamental geographical concept of scale. Continued rapid global population growth presents troubling problems for the twenty-first century, but look regionally instead of globally and it is clear that numbers aren't the only issue. As we confront the population issue, different regions face different challenges. No place, however, can afford to exempt itself from those challenges, for in the mix of expanding numbers, consumption, economic development, technology, and women's rights lies the future of the Earth's environments and the people who inhabit them.

◆ SELECTED REFERENCES ◆

Part Two **Population Patterns and Processes**

Agozino, B. *Theoretical and Methodological Issues in Migration Research* (London: Ashgate Publishing, 2000).

Appleyard, R. ed. *Emigration Dynamics in Developing Countries* (Series) (London: Ashgate Publishing, 1999–2000).

Association for the Advancement of Science. *Atlas of Population and Environment* (Berkeley: University of California Press, 2000).

Blavo, E. Q. *The Problem of Refugees in Africa: Boundaries and Borders* (London: Ashgate Publishing, 1999).

Boserup, E. *Population and Technological Change* (Chicago: University of Chicago Press, 1981).

Brown, L. et al. *Beyond Malthus: Sixteen Dimensions of the Population Problem.* (Worldwatch paper 143, 1998).

Brown, L. R., et al. State of the World (New York: W. W. Norton, Annual).

Chessum, L. *From Immigrants to Ethnic Minority* (London: Ashgate Publishing, 2000).

Clark, W. A. V. *Human Migration* (Beverly Hills, Calif.: Sage, 1986).

Clark, W. A. V. *The California Cauldron: Immigration and the Fortunes of Local Communities* (New York: Guilford Press, 1998).

Curtin, P. D. *Death by Migration: Europe's Encounter with the Tropical World in the Nineteenth Century* (New York: Cambridge University Press, 1989).

Ehrlich, P., & Ehrlich, A. *Healing the Planet: Strategies for Resolving the Environmental Crisis* (Reading, Mass.: Addison-Wesley Publishing Co., 1991).

Goldscheider, C., ed. *Population, Ethnicity, and Nation-Building* (Boulder, Colo.: Westview Press, 1995).

Gould, W. T. S., & Findlay, A. M., eds. *Population Migration and the Changing World Order* (New York, N.Y.: John Wiley, 1994).

Grossman, J. R. *Land of Hope: Black Southerners and the Great Migration* (Chicago: University of Chicago Press, 1989).

Hampton, J. *Internally Displaced People: A Global Survey.* (London: Earthscan, 1998.)

Heer, D. M., & Grigsby, J. S. Society and Population (Englewood Cliffs, N.J.: Prentice-Hall, 2nd ed., 1992).

Hornby, W., & Jones, M. *An Introduction to Population Geography* (New York: Cambridge University Press, 2nd ed., 1993).

Kane, H. *The Hour of Departure: The Forces That Create Refugees and Migrants* (Washington, D.C.: Worldwatch Institute, 1995).

Kershen, A. J. ed. *Language, Labor and Migration* (London: Ashgate Publishing, 2000).

Lewis, G. *Human Migration: A Geographical Perspective* (New York: St. Martin's Press, 1982).

Malthus, T. R. *An Essay on the Principles of Population.* Edited by A. Appelman (New York: W.W. Norton, 1976).

Mortimore, M. *Adapting to Drought: Farmers, Famines, and Desertification in West Africa* (Cambridge, U.K.: Cambridge University Press, 1989).

Newman, J., & Matzke, G. *Population: Patterns, Dynamics, and Prospects* (Englewood Cliffs, N.J.: Prentice-Hall, 1984).

Nyiri, P. *New Chinese Migrants in Europe* (London: Ashgate Publishing, 1999).

Ogden, P. E. *Migration and Geographical Change* (Cambridge, U.K.: Cambridge University Press, 1984).

Pandit, K. and Davies Withers, S. (eds). *Migration and Restructuring in the United States* (Lanham: Rowman and Littlefield, 1999).

Peters, G. L. & Larkin, R. P. *Population Geography: Problems, Concepts, and Prospects, Sixth Edition.* (Dubuque: Kendall/Hunt Publishing Company, 1998.)

Plane, D. A. "Demographic Influences on Migration," *Regional Studies* 27 (1993), 375–383.

Plane, D. A., & Rogerson, P. A. "Tracking the Baby Boom, the Baby Bust, and the Echo Generations: How Age Composition Regulates US Migration," *The Professional Geographer* 43, no. 4 (1991), 416–430.

Population Reference Bureau. 1997 *World Population Data Sheet* (Washington, D.C., 1997).

Preston, S. H., ed. *World Population: Approaching the Year 2000.* Special edition of the *Annals of the American Acadamy of Political and Social Science,* July 1990, Vol. 510.

Pries, L. ed. *Migration and Transnational Social Spaces* (London: Ashgate Publishing, 1999).

Roberts, G. *Population Policy: Contemporary Issues* (New York: Praeger, 1990).

Sharma, M. B. "Population in Advanced Placement Human Geography," *Journal of Geography,* 99, 3/4 (2000), pp. 99–110.

Simon, R., & Brettell, C., eds. *International Migration. The Female Experience* (Totowa, N.J.: Rowman & Allanheld, 1986).

Swann, M. M. *Migrants in the Mexican North: Mobility, Economy, and Society in a Colonial World* (Boulder, Colo.: Westview Press, 1989).

Teitelbaum, M. S., & Winter, J. M., eds. *Population and Resources in Western Intellectual Traditions* (Cambridge, U.K.: Cambridge University Press, 1989).

United Nations High Commissioner for Refugees. *The State of the World's Refugees.* (New York: Oxford, 2000).

Wang, G. T. *China's Population: Problems, Thoughts and Policies* (London: Ashgate Publishing, 1999).

White, P., & Woods, R., eds. *The Geographical Impact of Migration* (London: Longman, 1980).

Wood, W. B. "Forced Migration: Local Conflicts and International Dilemmas." *Annals of the Association of American Geographers,* 84, no. 4 (1994), 607–635.

World Bank. *World Development Indicators 2000* (Washington: International Bank for Reconstruction and Development, 2000).

World Bank. *World Development Report 1990: Poverty* (New York: Oxford University Press, 1990).

World Bank. *World Development Report 1994* (New York: Oxford University Press, 1994).

Part Three

THE GLOBAL LINGUISTIC MOSAIC

At Issue

Language is one of the cornerstones of national identity, cultural unity, and community cohesion. Old languages with historic roots, and languages spoken by threatened minorities, are nurtured and fostered by their speakers. But language also can be a weapon in cultural conflict and in political strife. In the United States, the growth of the Spanish-speaking population has led to demands for the use of Spanish in public affairs; this movement, in turn, has spawned national countermovements called "English Only" and "English First." In Quebec, a campaign for political independence from Canada was accompanied by the official demotion of English in favor of Quebec's distinctive version of French. Language is a powerful component of local nationalisms in many areas. The issue now is: *Why do regimes in multilingual countries seek to promote a single national language? What are the consequences of such initiatives?*

English, global lingua franca? Dubai, Arabian Peninsula

Part Outline

Chapter 8

A Geography of Language

From the field notes

"Efforts to maintain and nurture indigenous and precolonial languages continue to multiply and can often be seen in the cultural landscape. Here in Ireland, official signs give the names of towns and other geographic features in Gaelic as well as English. I started to take notes, and soon I had a list not only of Gaelic equivalents of English place names, but also of geographic features such as, on this sign on the outskirts of Kilkenney, 'city center'."

KEY POINTS

- ◆ **Language is at the heart of culture, and no culture exists without it. When a people's language is threatened, the response often is passionate and protective.**
- ◆ **States often try to promote a standard language backed by national institutions and official state examinations. Such initiatives play a key role in distinguishing what we think of as a language from what we think of as a dialect.**
- ◆ **Languages are constantly in flux. Standard languages can slow the rate of linguistic change, but in the modern world where innovations diffuse rapidly, change is inevitable.**
- ◆ **More people speak languages belonging to the Indo-European language family than languages in any other family. Indo-European languages are also more widely distributed than any others.**
- ◆ **Chinese is spoken by more people than any other language, but English has become the principal language of cross-cultural communication, economics, and science.**
- ◆ **The present distribution of languages, as revealed on maps, is useful in understanding prior cultural diffusions and present cultural patterns.**

People tend to feel passionately about their language, especially when they sense that it is threatened. Language is at the heart of culture, and culture is the glue of society; without language, culture could not be transmitted from one generation to the next.

Such passion is not the exclusive preserve of small groups whose languages are threatened by extinction (of which there are many). It is also exhibited by cultures whose languages are spoken by the tens, even hundreds, of millions. Many French citizens, for example, are fiercely, even aggressively protective of their language. A former French president, Georges Pompidou, once stated that "It is through our language that we exist in the world other than as just another country."

More than 25 years ago these words were given the force of law: in 1975 the French government banned the use of foreign words in advertisements, television and radio broadcasts, and official documents unless no French equivalent could be found. In 1992, France amended its constitution to make French the official language of the Republic. In 1994 still another law was passed to stop the use of foreign (mainly English) words in France, with a hefty fine imposed for violators. The French, said the government, would have to get used to saying something other than le meeting, le corner, le drugstore, and le hamburger.

Such legislation is unlikely to stop the "pollution" of French. In our modern, interconnected world, where innovations diffuse rapidly, words will be borrowed and languages will change. But French is in no danger of disappearing. Many communities that perceive a real threat to their culture's survival will protect it even more forcefully.

Preliterate societies (peoples who speak their language but do not write it) are at a disadvantage. Although they can transmit their culture from one generation to the next, they do not have a written literature that can serve as a foundation for cultural preservation. Like endangered species, there are languages that are on the verge of extinction, and others that are threatened. The language mosaic of the world is constantly changing.

Linguists estimate that between 5000 and 6000 languages are in use in the world today, some spoken by many millions of people, others by a few hundred. As we will note in Chapter 9, there are many unanswered questions about the origins and diffusion of all these languages; clearly, however, the same migrations that led to spatial isolation among early human communities also led to linguistic differences. Modern research is reconstructing the paths of ***linguistic diversification*** and throwing new light on ancient migrations. ◆

◆ DEFINING LANGUAGE

The term ***language*** has been defined in numerous ways. Webster's Dictionary defines it as "a systematic means of communicating ideas or feelings by the use of conventionalized signs, gestures, marks, or especially articulate vocal sounds." Communication of sound (vocalization) is the crucial part of this definition. Such communication is symbolic; that is, in each language the meanings of sounds and combination of sounds must be learned.

The definition is correct in stating that other means of communication also constitute "language." Nonhuman primates such as chimpanzees can also communicate through signs, such as combinations of gestures and sounds that alert the group to the presence of a predator or the availability of food. Elephants and dolphins, too, use sounds to communicate. But only humans have developed complex vocal communication systems that change over time and space. How these systems first emerged remains an unanswered question. We do know that the vocal systems of nonhuman primates are so basic and static that they are unlikely to have been forerunners of human language.

This means that human languages, even those spoken in preliterate societies, are fundamentally different from those of nonhuman primates. The Khoisan-speaking peoples of southwestern Africa may not have a word for helicopter, but they have the symbols that they can use to describe this piece of unfamiliar technology. The potential vocabulary of any language is infinite, whether it is spoken by large-scale industrialized societies or by nonindustrial peoples like the San or the Yanomami of the Amazonian rainforest.

Languages are not static but change continuously. A vital culture requires a flexible language. If you read a few pages from one of Shakespeare's plays, you will realize how much English has changed over several centuries. Today we can see changes in American English; the computer revolution, for example, has greatly expanded the vocabulary of commonly used words. In this chapter we examine fundamental geographic aspects of the world's language mosaic—their distribution and spread. This will prepare us for an introduction to the fascinating study of language origins and diffusion, the subject of Chapter 9. In Chapter 10 we will look at some topics of special interest, including the language of place names.

Standard Language

Technologically advanced societies are likely to have a ***standard language***, whose quality is a matter of cultural identity and national concern. The standard language may be sustained by official state examinations for teachers, civil servants, and others. The phrase "the King's English" is a popular reference to the fact that the English spoken by well-educated people in London and its environs is regarded as British Received Pronunciation (BRP) English—that is, the standard.

Who decides what the standard language will be? Not surprisingly, the answer has to do with influence and power. In France, the French spoken in and around Paris was made the official, standard language during the sixteenth century. In China, standard Chinese is the Northern Mandarin Chinese heard in and around the capital, Beijing. Although this is China's official standard language, the linguistic term "Chinese" actually incorporates many variants. This distinction between the standard language and other versions of it is not unique to China; it is found in all but the smallest societies. The Italian of Sicily is very different from that spoken north of Venice, and both tongues differ from the standard Italian of Latium, the region around Rome.

Dialects

As we will see, the distinction between a language and a dialect is not always clear, but ***dialects*** can generally be thought of as regional variants of a standard language. Differences in vocabulary, syntax (the way words are put together to form phrases), pronunciation, cadence (the rhythm of speech), and even the pace of speech all mark a speaker's dialect. Even if the written form of a statement adheres to the standard language, an accent can reveal the regional home of a person who reads the statement aloud. The words "horse" and "oil" are written the same way in New England and in the South, but to the Southerner, the New Englander may be saying "hahse," while to the New Englander the Southerner seems to be saying "all."

More often, however, dialects are marked by actual differences in vocabulary. A single word or group of words can reveal the source area of the dialect used. Linguistic geographers map the areal extent of particular words, marking their limits as ***isoglosses*** (Fig. 8-1). An

Figure 8-1 Isoglosses. Isoglosses move over time. In this hypothetical case, the use of "herd" has receded in favor of "flock," but some outliers of "herd" remain.

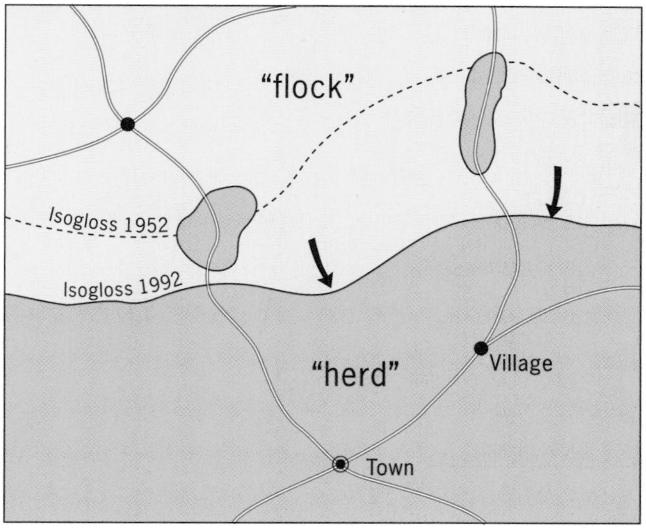

isogloss is a geographic boundary within which a particular linguistic feature occurs, but such a boundary is rarely a simple line. Usually there are outlying areas of usage, as in Figure 8-1. This may signify either that use of the dialect has expanded or that it has contracted, leaving the outliers as dwindling remnants. A series of large-scale maps over time will tell the story of that dialect's advance or retreat.

◆ CLASSIFICATION AND DISTRIBUTION OF LANGUAGES

In the context of cultural geography, we are interested in how languages are distributed throughout the world, what processes created this distribution, and how the present pattern is changing.

Before we view maps of language distribution, however, let us briefly consider the problem of language classification. This obviously relates to the definition of language: What is a language and what is a dialect? That issue is a complex one. Some scholars have classified Quebecois French as a language, whereas others insist that it is a dialect of European French. In regions of Africa where Bantu languages are spoken, many of those languages are closely related and share major portions of their vocabulary.

What is clear is that the distinction between a language and a dialect is not based on an objective measure of mutual intelligibility; if it were, Chinese would not be

Figure 8-2 Language Families of the World. Generalized map of the world distribution of language families. *Source*: Based on a map prepared by Hammond, Inc., for the first edition, 1977.

considered one language, whereas Norwegian and Danish might be. Instead, we must recognize that what we consider a language is a function of society's view of what constitutes a cultural community—a matter that in turn is influenced by historical developments in the political arena. The ability of the Chinese political elite to build and sustain a state encompassing speakers of different, albeit closely related, Sino-Tibetan tongues helps explain why we think of Chinese as one language. By contrast, the disintegration of the Danish and Swedish empires is partly responsible for our tendency to recognize several distinct languages in Scandinavia. As such, it is not too much of an exaggeration to say that a language is a dialect with an army behind it.

Given the complexities of distinguishing languages from dialects, the actual number of languages in use remains a matter of considerable debate. The most conservative calculation, which would recognize the maximum number of dialects, puts the number at about 3000. Most linguistic geographers today would recognize between 5000 and 6000 languages, including more than 600 in India and over 1000 in Africa alone.

In classifying languages we use terms that are also employed in biology, and for the same reasons: some languages are related and others are not. Languages that are grouped in ***language families*** are thought to have a shared, but fairly distant, origin; in a ***language subfamily***, their commonality is more definite. Subfamilies are divided into ***language groups***, which consist of sets of individual languages.

Figure 8-2 shows the distribution of 20 major language families. On this map, only the Indo-European language family is broken down into subfamilies (greater detail for Europe is shown in Figure 8-3). Spatially, the

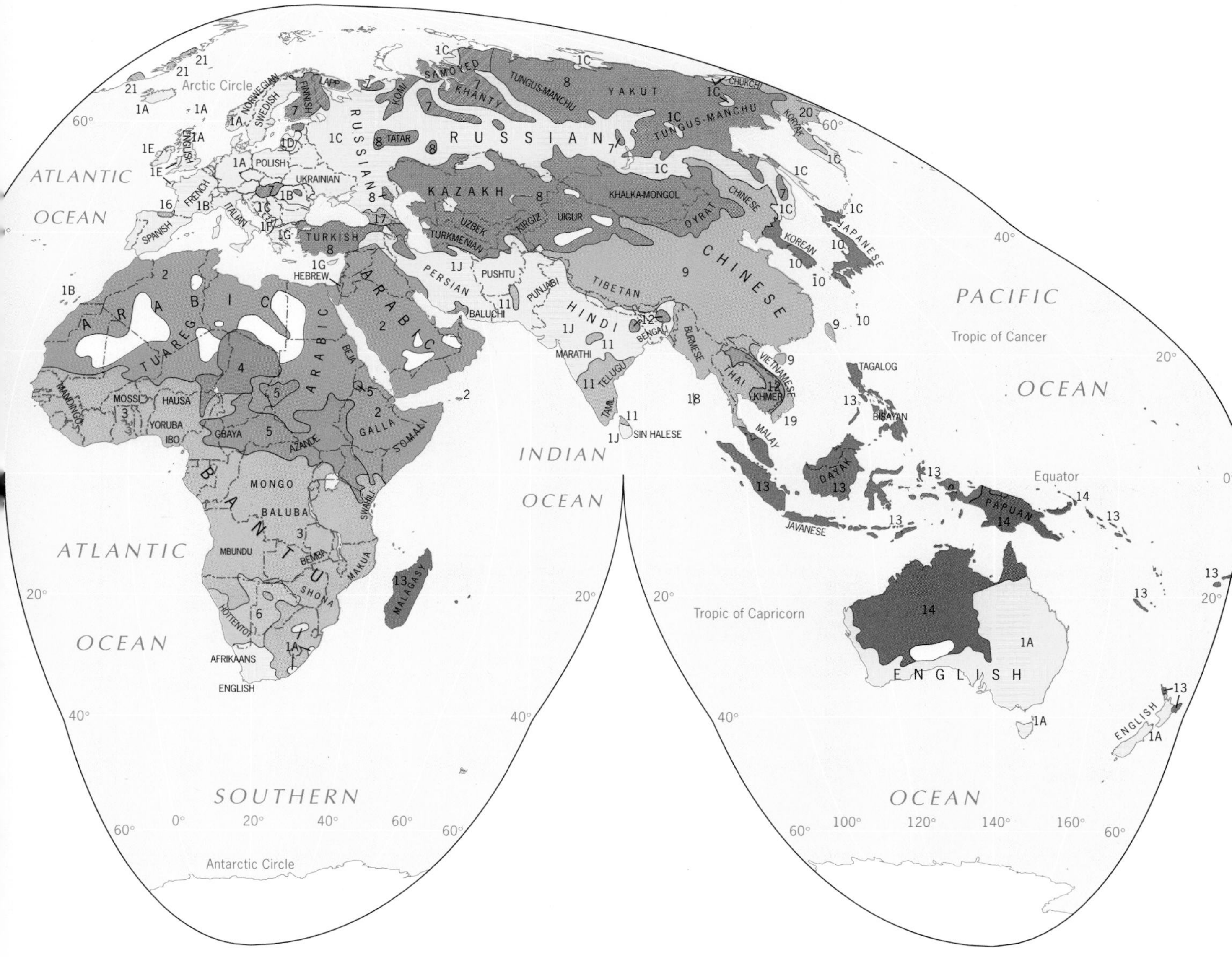

Figure 8-2 map

LANGUAGES OF EUROPE
0 200 400 600 Kilometers
0 100 200 300 Miles
Arctic Circle
Icelandic
Norwegian Sea
Faeroese
ATLANTIC
OCEAN
Scots Gaelic
English
Irish Gaelic
English
Welsh
English
North Sea
Norwegian
Swedish
Saami
Saami
Samoyedic
Karelian
Finnish
Russian
Estonian
Latvian
SWEDISH
Lithuanian
Danish
Frisian
Dutch
German
Polish
Belarusian
Ukrainian
Czech
Slovak
Hungarian
Romanian
Slovene
Serbo-Croatian
Bulgarian
Macedonian
Albanian
Greek
Turkish
Black Sea
Alsatian
Breton
French
Provençal
Italian
Galician
Basque
Spanish
Portuguese
Catalan
Catalan
Mediterranean Sea
Major Indo-European Branches
Germanic group
WESTERN GERMANIC
1 Dutch
2 German
3 Frisian
4 English
NORTHERN GERMANIC
5 Danish
6 Swedish
7 Norwegian
8 Icelandic
9 Faeroses
Romance group
10 Portuguese
11 Spanish
12 Catalan
13 Provençal
14 French
15 Italian
16 Rhaeto-Romance
17 Romanian
Slavic group
WEST SLAVONIC
18 Polish
19 Slovak
20 Czech
21 Sorbian
EAST SLAVONIC
22 Russian
23 Ukrainian
24 Belarusian
SOUTH SLAVONIC
25 Slovene
26 Serbo-Croatian
27 Macedonian
28 Bulgarian
Other Indo-European Branches
Celtic group
BRITTANIC
29 Breton
30 Welsh
GAULISH
31 Irish Gaelic
32 Scots Gaelic
Baltic group
33 Lativian
34 Lithuanian
Hellenic
35 Greek
Thracian/Illyrian group
36 Albanian
Thracian/Illyrian group
37 Romani
Uralic Language Family
Finno-Ugric group
38 Ginnish
39 Karelian
40 Saami
41 Estonian
42 Hungarian
Samoyedic group
44 Samoyedic
Altaic Language Family
Turkic group
45 Turkish
Other Languages
Basque
46 Basque
Areas with significant concentrations of other languages (usually adjacent national languages).
Boundary between languages.
Boundary between Indo-European and non-Indo-European languages.

Figure 8-3 Languages of Europe. Generalized map of language-use regions in Europe. *Source*: Based on a map in A. B. Murphy, "European languages," T. Unwin, ed., *A European Geography*. London: Longman, 1998, p. 38.

Indo-European languages are the most widely dispersed language family. As Figure 8-2 indicates, the Indo-European language family dominates not only in Europe but also in significant parts of Asia (including Russia and India), North and South America, Australia, and portions of Southern Africa. ***Indo-European languages*** are spoken by about half the world's peoples, and English is the most widely used Indo-European language.

Geolinguists theorize that a lost language (or set of languages) they call Proto-Indo-European existed somewhere in the vicinity of the Black Sea or east-central Europe (see the discussion in the next chapter) and that the present languages of the Indo-European family evolved from it. As Indo-European speakers dispersed, vocabularies grew and linguistic differentiation took place. Latin arose during this early period and was disseminated over much of Europe during the rise of the Roman Empire. Later, Latin died out and was supplanted by Italian, French, and the other Romance languages.

As Figure 8-2 indicates, the Indo-European language family includes not only the major languages of Europe and the former Soviet Union but also those of northern India and Bangladesh, Pakistan, Afghanistan, and Iran. This reflects the probable route of ancient migration from the west to South Asia. More modern migrations carried Indo-European languages (principally English, Spanish, Portuguese, and French) to the Americas, Australia, and Africa.

Table 8-1 The Major World Language Families

Language Family	Major Language	Number of Speakers (Millions)
Indo-European	English	445
	Hindi	366
	Spanish	340
	Bengali	207
	Portuguese	176
	Russian	167
	German	100
	French	77
	Italian	62
	Urdu	60
Sino-Tibetan	Chinese	1211
	Burmese	32
	Thai	23
Japanese-Korean	Japanese	125
	Korean	78
Dravidian	Telugu	69
	Tamil	66
Altaic	Turkish	61
Afro-Asiatic	Arabic	211
Malay-Polynesian	Indonesia	154

◆ THE MAJOR WORLD LANGUAGES

Although more of the world's peoples speak Indo-European languages than languages in any other family, Chinese is the single most important language in terms of number of speakers (Table 8-1), with English ranking second. The numbers in Table 8-1 should be viewed as approximations. English, for example, is not only spoken by 280 million North Americans, 60 million Britons and Irish, more than 20 million Australians and New Zealanders, and millions more in countries with smaller populations; it is also used as a second language by hundreds of millions of people in India, Africa, and elsewhere. French is the first language of 77 million people (some sources report as many as 100 million), but it is also widely used as a second language. Note also that some of the numbers in Table 8-1 are based on population data that are not reliable. The regional languages of India (Indo-European as well as Dravidian) are among the most used, but exact data on the number of speakers are not available.

Table 8-1 does not list any languages spoken south of the Sahara as major world languages. One reason can be seen in Figure 8-2: the African language map is highly fragmented. Subsaharan Africa still has a relatively small population (647 million people in 2002), but more than 1000 languages are spoken there. These languages are grouped into four families (3, 4, 5, and 6 in Figure 8-2). In terms of number of speakers, Hausa is estimated to be the most important Subsaharan African language, with perhaps as many as 50 million speakers. Hundreds of African languages have fewer than 1 million speakers.

Figure 8-2 also shows other language families that are spoken by dwindling, often marginally located or isolated groups. Austro-Asiatic languages (11), spoken in interior locales of eastern India and in Cambodia (Khmer) and Laos, are thought to be survivors of ancient languages spoken before modern invasions and cultural diffusion took place. Some scholars place Vietnamese in this family, but others do not. The Papuan and indigenous Australian languages (13), though numerous and quite diverse, are spoken by fewer than 10 million people. The languages of Native Americans (14) remain strong only in areas of Middle America, the high Andes, and northern Canada. Languages of the Eskimo-Aleut family (20) survive on the Arctic margins of Greenland, North America, and eastern Asia.

If we look carefully at the map of world languages, some interesting questions arise. Consider, for example, the island of Madagascar off the East African coast. The primary languages spoken on Madagascar belong not to an African language family but to the Malay-Polynesian family, the languages of Indonesia and its neighbors. How did this happen on an island so close to Africa? Actually, the map reveals a piece of ancient history that is

From the field notes

"Approaching the orthodox Jewish neighborhood for Meah Shearim in Jerusalem, I was drawn to a large sign specifying guidelines for how one should dress when entering the neighborhood. The call for covered arms and skirts below the knee was interesting, but so was the language in which the call was made. Jerusalem is a cosmopolitan city, with people from all corners of the earth. But when the local community seeks to communicate with those from the outside, they resort to one (and only one) language: English."

The Languages of Europe

The language map of Europe (Fig. 8-3) shows that the Indo-European language family prevails in this region, with pockets of the Uralic family occurring in Hungary (the Ugric subfamily) and in Finland and adjacent areas (the Finnic subfamily), and a major Altaic language—Turkish—dominating Turkey west of the Sea of Marmara. Indo-European tongues were brought into Europe by Celtic peoples who spread across the continent during the first millennium B.C.. Celtic speech still survives at the western edges of Europe, but in most places Celtic tongues fell victim to subsequent migrations and empire building. These historical developments led to the creation of a European linguistic pattern characterized by three major subgroups: Romance, Germanic, and Slavic.

The Romance languages (French, Spanish, Italian, Romanian, and Portuguese) lie in areas once dominated by the Roman Empire where the dominant form of speech was not subsequently overwhelmed by immigrants. The Germanic languages (English, German, Danish, Norwegian, and Swedish) reflect the expansion of peoples out of northern Europe to the west and south. Some Germanic peoples spread into areas dominated by Rome, and at the northern and northeastern edges of the Roman Empire their tongues gained ascendancy. Other Germanic peoples spread into areas that had never been a part of an ancient empire (e.g., present-day Sweden, Norway, Denmark, and the northern part of the Netherlands). The Germanic character of English bears the imprint of a further migration—that of the Normans into England in 1066, bringing a Romance tongue to the British Isles. The essential Germanic character of English remained, but many new words were added that are Romance in origin. The Slavic languages (Russian, Polish, Czech, Slovak, Ukrainian, Slovenian, Serbo-Croatian, and Bulgarian) came as Slavic people migrated from a base in present-day Ukraine close to 2000 years ago. Slavic tongues came to dominate much of eastern Europe over the succeeding centuries. They too overwhelmed Latin-based tongues along much of the eastern part of the old Roman Empire—with the notable exception of an area on the western shores of the Black Sea, where a Latin-based tongue either survived the Slavic invasion or was reintroduced by migrants. That tongue is the ancestor of the modern-day Romance language: Romanian.

A comparison of Europe's linguistic and political maps shows a high correlation between the languages spoken and the political organization of space. The Romance languages, of Romanic-Latin origin, dominate in five countries, including Romania. The eastern boundaries of Germany coincide almost exactly with the transition from Germanic to Slavic tongues. Even at the level of individual languages, boundaries can be seen on the political map: between French and Spanish, between Norwegian and Swedish, and between Bulgarian and Greek.

not well understood. Long ago, seafarers from the islands of Southeast Asia crossed the Indian Ocean. They may have reached the East African coast first and then sailed on to Madagascar, where they settled. Africans had not yet sailed across the strait, so there was no threat to the Indonesian-Malayan settlements. The settlements grew and prospered, and large states evolved. Later, Africans began to come to Madagascar, but by that time the cultural landscape had been established. If you compare the names of Madagascar's places to those across the water in Africa, you can see evidence of a fascinating piece of geographic history.

Although Figure 8-3 shows a significant correlation between political and linguistic boundaries, there are some important exceptions. The French linguistic region extends into Belgium, Switzerland, and Italy, but in France itself it coexists with a Celtic tongue in the Bretagne (Brittany) Peninsula. The Celtic languages survive not only in Brittany (Breton) but also in Wales (Welsh), western Ireland (Irish Gaelic), and Scotland (Scots Gaelic), where they constitute remnants of an early period of European history before modern languages displaced them toward the realm's westernmost fringes. The use of Romanian extends well into Moldavia, signifying a past loss of national territory. Greek and Albanian are also Indo-European languages, and their regional distribution corresponds significantly (though not exactly) with national territories. Figure 8-3 underscores the complex cultural pattern of Eastern Europe: there are German speakers in Hungary; Hungarian speakers in Slovakia, Romania, and Yugoslavia; Romanian speakers in Greece and Moldavia; Turkish speakers in Bulgaria; and Albanian speakers in Serbia.

Although the overwhelming majority of Europeans and Russians speak Indo-European languages, the Uralic and Altaic language families are also represented in this realm. Finnish, Estonian, and Hungarian are major languages of the Uralic family, which, as Figure 8-2 shows, extends across Eurasia to the Pacific coast. The Altaic family to which Turkish belongs is equally widespread and includes Turkish, Kazakh, Uigur, Kyrgyz, and Uzbek, among other languages. Not all students of linguistic geography view the Uralic and Altaic languages as distinct language families, and indeed there are reasons to group them together. It is believed that they both spread into Europe between 7000 and 10,000 years ago and later were overtaken in most places by the Indo-European languages. Their source area may have been a longitudinal zone along the Ural Mountains from which migrations occurred both westward into Europe and eastward into Asia. Whatever their origins, Uralic languages survive as the national languages of Finland and Hungary, and an Altaic language is the national language of Turkey.

The Languages of India

The mosaic of languages in India (Fig. 8-4) includes four language families, but only two of these—the

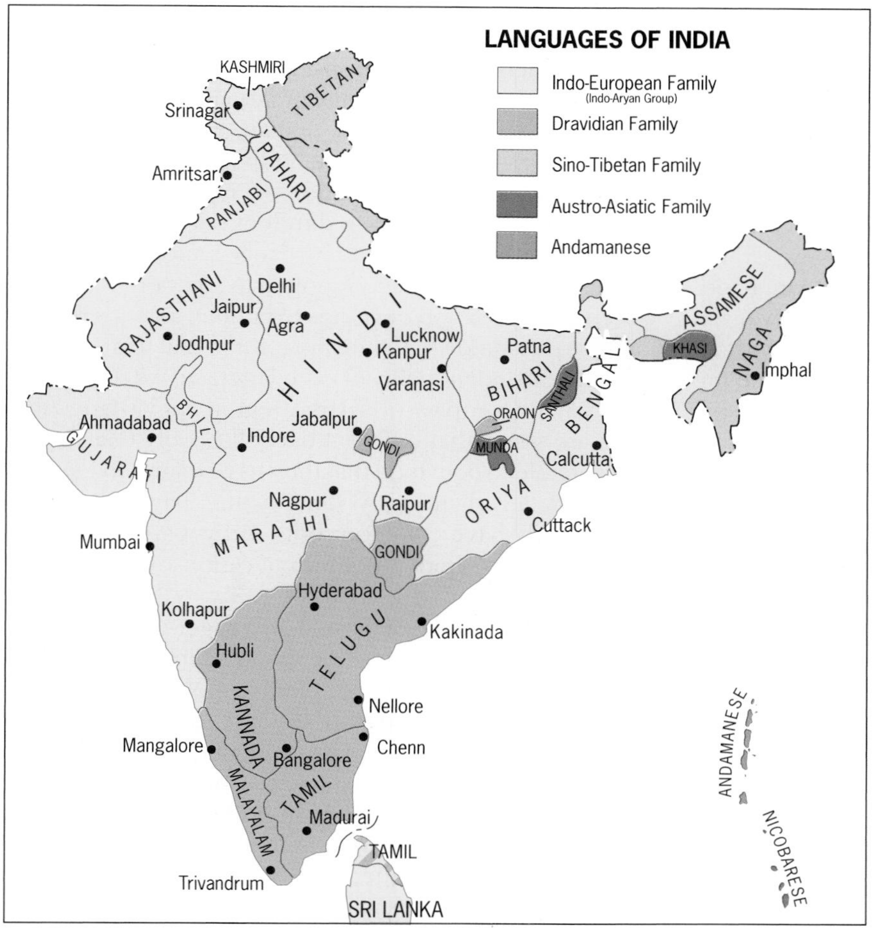

Figure 8-4 Languages of India. Major languages of the Indian subcontinent. *Source*: From a map prepared by Hammond, Inc., for the first edition, 1977.

Indo-European family and the Dravidian family—have significant numbers of speakers among India's nearly 1 billion inhabitants. In the Karakoram Mountains of Jammu and Kashmir (the far northwest) there are small numbers of Tibetan speakers, and along the border with Myanmar (Burma) in the east lies a cluster of Naga (Burmese) speakers. Also in the east are small groups of Austro-Asiatic speakers. Otherwise, the people of India speak about 15 major languages, all but 4 of them Indo-European, and more than 1600 lesser languages, some of which are spoken by only a few thousand persons.

As Figure 8-4 indicates, the four Dravidian languages are all spoken in a compact region in the south of the Indian Peninsula. The map suggests that these languages and the cultures they represent were "pushed" southward by the advancing Indo-European speakers. The Dravidian languages are older, although their origins are unclear. Some scholars believe that Dravidian emerged in India. Others suggest that Dravidian speakers arrived thousands of years ago from Central Asia and that Dravidian is related to Ural-Altaic languages. Still others link the Dravidians with the ancient Indus civilization that arose in what is today Pakistan. Indeed, there is a cluster of about 350,000 speakers of a form of Dravidian in north-central Pakistan.

Today the largest Dravidian language, with about 69 million speakers, is Telugu, the language of the Indian state of Andhra Pradesh. Tamil, with its rich literature, is spoken by approximately 66 million persons in Tamil Nadu. Kannada (also called Kanarese), the language of Karnataka, has approximately 35 million speakers, about the same number as Malayalam, which is spoken in the State of Kerala.

The close relationship between regional languages and political divisions in southern India also prevails in the north. Indeed, a comparison of Figure 8-4 with an atlas map of India's federal system underscores the important role of languages in the development of this spatial structure. Hindi, the principal Indo-European language with approximately 366 million speakers, extends across several north-central Indian States. But east as well as west of India's Hindi-speaking core lie States where other languages prevail: Orissa (Oriya), Bihar (Bihari), West Bengal (Bengali), Punjab (Punjabi), Rajasthan (Rajasthani), Gujarat (Gujarati), and Maharashtra (Marathi). In the northeast the linguistic map is especially complex, as is reflected in the existence of seven comparatively small states.

In addition to more than a dozen major languages, India has hundreds of lesser languages, both Indo-European and Dravidian, that cannot be shown on a map on the scale of Figure 8-4. Nevertheless, for such a large population the Indian language mosaic is not as intensely fragmented as Africa's. Instead, like that of Europe, it is dominated by several major regional languages with more speakers than many national tongues.

The Languages of Africa

As noted earlier, more than 1000 languages are spoken in Subsaharan Africa, and linguists have been working to record many of these; most are unwritten. The resulting data offer significant insights into Africa's cultural past.

The languages of Africa (Fig. 8-5) are grouped into four families, the largest of which is the Niger-Congo family, which extends from West Africa all the way to the south. This family can be subdivided into five subfamilies. One of these, the Bantu subfamily, encompasses the languages spoken by most of the people near the equator and south of it. The languages spoken in West Africa are of the Atlantic, Voltaic, Guinea, and Hausa subfamilies. The oldest languages of Subsaharan Africa are the Khoisan languages, which include a "click" sound. Among these is the language of the San, spoken by only a few thousand people in southwestern Africa. Perhaps the Khoisan languages were once the main languages of much of Africa, but they have been reduced to comparative insignificance by the Bantu invasion, just as the Celtic languages were in Europe.

How can languages help us reconstruct the cultural development of Africa? Consider what has happened in Europe, where the subfamily of Romance languages has differentiated into French, Italian, Spanish, and Portuguese. Even within these individual languages we see evidence of differentiation—for example, between forms of Italian spoken in different parts of Italy or between Northern and Southern French and Walloon (the traditional form of French spoken in southern Belgium). Such differentiation develops over time, and it is reasonable to assume that the more time that elapses, the greater the individuality of each language will be. Therefore, if the peoples of a large region speak languages that are somewhat different but still closely related, it is reasonable to conclude that they have migrated into that region relatively recently. On the other hand, languages that clearly have common roots and yet are very different must have undergone modification over a lengthy period.

Among the languages of the Niger-Congo family, those of the Bantu subfamily are much more closely related than those of other subfamilies. We can therefore deduce that the Bantu peoples and cultures of Central and Southern Africa are of more recent origin than those of West Africa. This is reflected in African names. The word "Bantu" should actually be written BaNtu (people), with the Ba being a prefix. Sometimes the prefix is retained in common usage, sometimes not. The Watusi, for example, are now usually called Tutsi. The people of

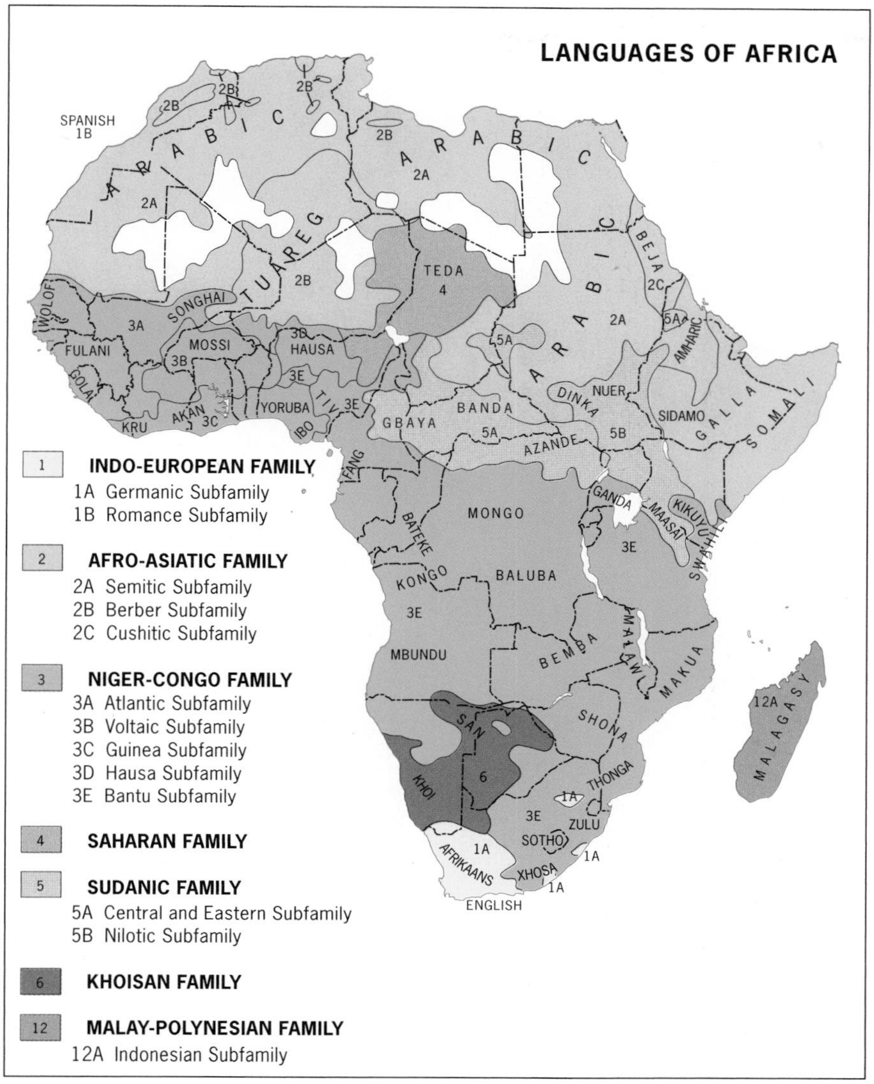

Figure 8-5 Languages of Africa. Regional classification of African languages. *Source*: From a map prepared by Hammond, Inc., for the first edition 1977.

southeastern Uganda are the BaGanda or Ganda. The Zulu of South Africa are actually the AmaZulu. Stories about Zimbabwe often mention the MaShona or Shona. Remember Basutoland, now called Lesotho? It was originally named after the Sotho, and BaSotholand became Basutoland. *Ba*, *Ma*, *Wa*, and *Ama* are not very far removed linguistically, and they reveal close associations between languages and peoples spread across Africa from Uganda to Kwazulu-Natal.

It is not just a matter of prefixes, of course. Bantu languages reflect their close relationships in vocabulary and in numerous other respects. Geolinguists have traced the changes that occur over space in a single word and have found that thousands of miles away a word is often quite close to its original form. Consider the familiar Swahili greeting, *jambo*, used in coastal East Africa. In the eastern Transvaal of South Africa and Swaziland, people will recognize *jabo*.

The situation in West Africa is quite different. Some of the languages there are closely associated, but the major languages of the West African subfamilies are much more discrete. Of course, there are other kinds of evidence supporting the conclusion that the peoples of Bantu Africa have a shorter history in that area than those of West Africa, but the primary evidence is linguistic.

Chinese: One Language or Many?

The map of China's ethnolinguistic areas (Fig. 8-6) should be compared to the map of world population distribution (Fig. 4-1). That comparison will reveal that the great majority of China's people speak Mandarin, either Northern or Southern. Chinese is one of the world's oldest languages and is spoken by the greatest contiguous population cluster on the Earth.

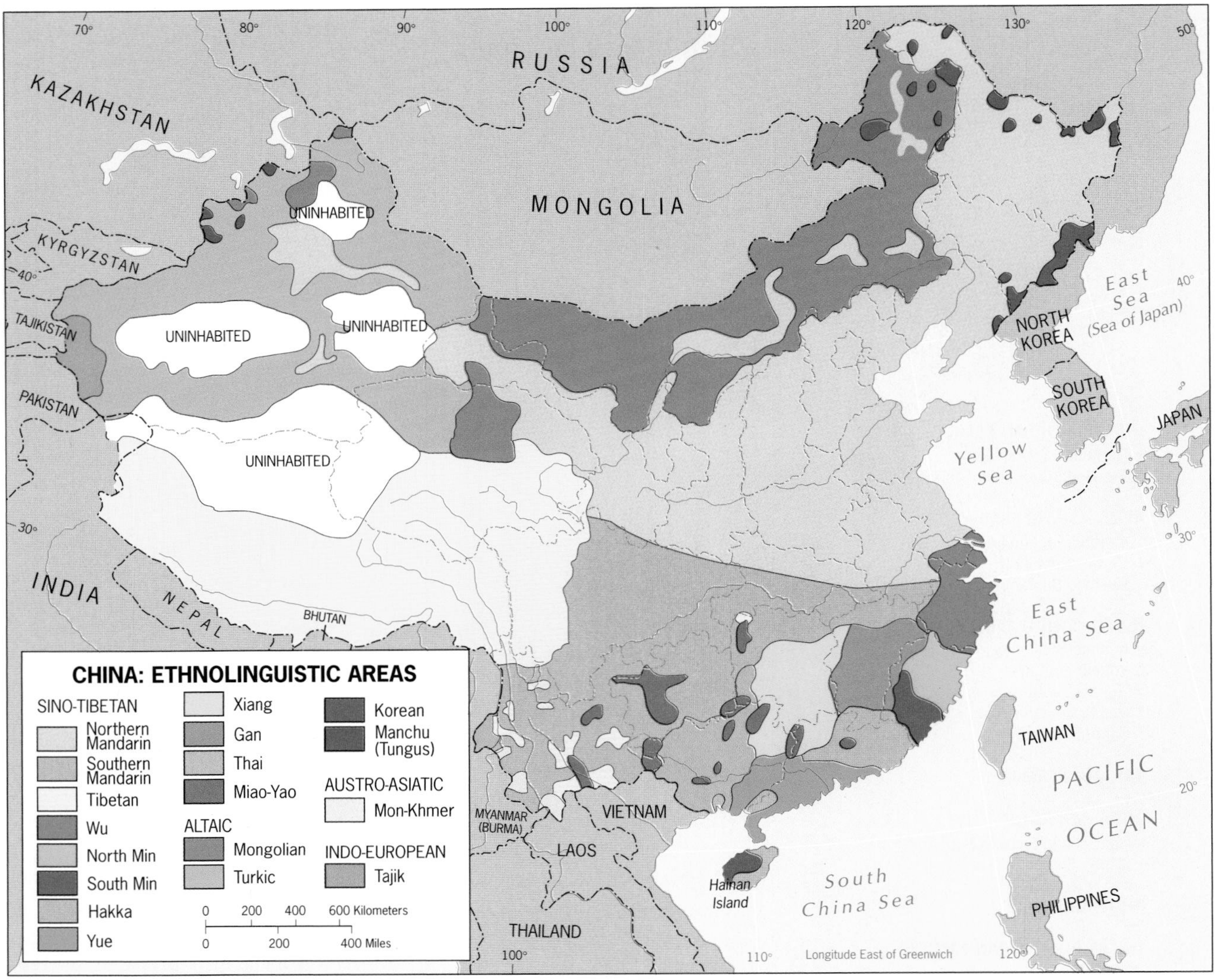

Figure 8-6 Ethnolinguistic Areas of China. Major languages zones of China. *Source*: From several sources including Academia Sinica, Republic of China Yearbook.

As the map shows, a number of Chinese dialects prevail in large areas of the country, notably in the south. Most of these dialects are mutually unintelligible, and some scholars therefore argue that Chinese is not one but several languages, among which Mandarin dominates with about 874 million speakers. Wu Chinese ranks next with over 75 million, and Yue (Cantonese) is third with about 71 million.

In mid-1997, when the government of China took over control of Hong Kong from the British, Beijing's leaders all made their speeches in Northern Mandarin, and the Cantonese familiar to the great majority of Hong Kong's population was never heard. Thus China's rulers used language to underscore the nature of the new authority to which the local people would now be subject.

During the twentieth century several efforts were made to create a truly national language in China. The latest of these efforts is the so-called pinyin system, a phonetic-spelling system based on the pronunciation of Chinese characters in Northern Mandarin, China's standard language. But China's population contains many minorities, as Figure 8-6 reminds us, and as a result linguistic integration may never be achieved.

One of the most interesting and challenging dimensions of the geography of language is the reconstruction of the routes of diffusion of peoples and their languages. While linguists attempt to establish the family tree of languages, geographers focus on the spatial implications of this effort: the routes of migration and linguistic diffusion. We turn next to this complicated topic, about which new information is constantly emerging.

◆ KEY TERMS ◆

dialect	language family	linguistic diversification
Indo-European languages	language group	preliterate society
isogloss	language subfamily	standard language
language		

◆ APPLYING GEOGRAPHIC KNOWLEDGE ◆

1. Why is the language spoken by more people in this world than any other not the language of international trade and communication? What factors put another language in this position? Can you foresee a twenty-first-century scenario that might alter the balance?
2. In 1997 several dozen "Francophone" countries convened in Hanoi, Vietnam, to discuss ways to promote the use of French and to (in the words of the conference report) "reverse the deterioration" of the language. In the social, economic, and political geography of the world today, why do French-speakers feel a threat to their language?
3. In terms of the geographic pattern (not the origins) of language, what do Subsaharan Africa and New Guinea have in common?

Chapter 9

The Diffusion of Languages

From the field notes

"Gibraltar lies at the southern tip of the dominantly Spanish-speaking Iberian Peninsula and a few miles across from Arabic-speaking North Africa. But this remnant of the British Empire speaks English, and makes it a point to do so, evincing the diffusion of Anglophones near and far. I ran into this loud demonstration by Moroccans objecting to their treatment by the British and Gibraltar governments, but when I went over to talk to the fellows in charge of this display, I found that we could only communicate in French—they spoke none of the English on these posters. Who wrote all this stuff? They told me that they had hired several locals to translate and print their opinions. When the newspaper people come to photograph all this, they said, the world should be able to read it, and to reach the world you have to say it in English."

KEY POINTS

◆ **The search for the origins of language goes back tens of thousands of years. It has yielded information not only about how language changes but also about the environments where early languages were spoken.**

◆ **Geolinguistic scholars group languages into different families based on similarities in structure and vocabulary. Some believe that major language families evolved out of distinct agricultural hearths, but this is a contested theory.**

◆ **Languages change through divergence, convergence, and replacement, making the spatial search for origins problematic.**

◆ **The number of language families in the Western Hemisphere is much greater than in the Eastern Hemisphere despite the relative recency of human migration in the Americas. This apparent anomaly is not well understood.**

◆ **Writing, technology, and political organization play a key role in the diffusion of individual languages.**

◆ **Indo-European languages were spread throughout much of the world during the European colonial period.**

The world today is a Babel of languages, a patchwork of tongues. Nevertheless, it is possible to identify some languages that are related, such as Spanish and Portuguese, which are so similar that their common origin and recent divergence are beyond doubt. In fact, there is a historical record of this process. It reveals how the Latin of Roman times gave rise to the Romance languages of today (the major ones being Italian, Spanish, Portuguese, French, and Romanian). In just a few centuries Latin, which had been spoken in territories extending from Britain to the Bosporus, was replaced by a set of derivative languages.

Given the speed and thoroughness of this process, can we hope to unlock the mysteries of much earlier languages and retrace the evolution of modern languages from what linguists call the Mother Tongue, the first language spoken by *Homo sapiens sapiens* perhaps as long as 200,000 years ago? That remains an elusive goal, but with the help of computers, remarkable progress is being made in the reconstruction of ancient languages and their paths of diffusion. This chapter focuses on the relevance of linguistic theory and research to historical geography. ◆

◆ TRACING LINGUISTIC DIVERSIFICATION

The diversification of languages has long been charted through analysis of ***sound shifts***. Take the Latin word for milk (*lacte*) and note that it becomes *latta* in Italian, *leche* in Spanish, and *lait* in French. Or the Latin for the number eight (*octo*), which becomes *otto*, *ocho*, and *huit*, respectively. Even if the Latin roots for these words had never been known, linguists would have been able to deduce them.

This technique of backward reconstruction is crucial to linguistic research. If it is possible to deduce a large part of the vocabulary of an extinct language, it may be feasible to go even further and re-create the language that preceded it. This technique, called ***deep reconstruction***, has yielded some important results. It takes humanity's linguistic family tree back thousands of years.

More than two centuries ago William Jones, an Englishman living in South Asia, undertook a study of Sanskrit, the language in which ancient Indian religious and literary texts were written. Jones discovered that the vocabulary and grammatical forms of Sanskrit bore a striking resemblance to the ancient Greek and Latin he had learned while in college. "No philologer [student of literature] could examine all three," Jones wrote, "without believing them to have sprung from some common source, which, perhaps, no longer exists." In the late eighteenth century this was a revolutionary notion indeed.

During the nineteenth century Jacob Grimm, a scholar as well as a writer of fairy tales, suggested that sound shifts might prove the relationships between languages in a scientific manner. He pointed out that related languages have similar, but not identical, consonants. (Consonants are formed by the constriction of the sound channel.) He believed that these consonants would change over time in a predictable way. Hard consonants, such as the **v** and **t** in the German word *vater*, would soften into va**d**er (Dutch) and **f**ather (English). Looking backward, we should expect to find the opposite: a hardening of consonants.

From Jones's notions and Grimm's ideas came the first major linguistic hypothesis, which proposed the existence of an ancestral ***(Proto) Indo-European language*** (or closely related languages), the predecessor of Latin, Greek, and Sanskrit, among other ancient languages. This concept had major implications because the proposed ancestral language(s) would link not only the present and past Romance language but also a number of other languages spoken from Britain to North Africa and South Asia.

Several research tasks followed from this hypothesis. First, the vocabulary of the proposed ancestral language must be reconstructed. Second, the hearth or source where this language originated, and from which it spread, must be located. Third, the routes of diffusion by which this dispersal took place should be traced. And fourth, researchers should attempt to learn about the ways of life of those who spoke this language.

◆ THE LANGUAGE TREE

Proto-Indo-European gave rise to more than Latin, Greek, and Sanskrit. As Figure 8-2 reminds us, the Indo-European language realm includes not only languages derived from Latin but also the Slavonic (Slavic) languages, including Russian, Ukrainian, Polish, Czech, Slovak, Bulgarian, and Slovenian, and the Germanic languages, including German, Swedish, Danish, and Norwegian. These, too, must have had common ancestors, branches of the Proto-Indo-European "tree."

Divergence

The first scholar to compare the world's language families to the branches of a tree was August Schleicher, a German linguist. In the mid-nineteenth century he suggested that the basic process of language formation is ***language divergence***, that is, differentiation over time and space. Languages would branch into dialects; isolation would then increase the differences between dialects. Over time, dialects would become discrete languages, as happened with Spanish and Portuguese and is now happening with Quebecois French. Although aspects of this idea were later challenged, it essentially stood the test of time, and the language-tree model remains central to language research (Fig. 9-1).

Convergence

A complicating factor, however is human mobility. While languages diverged, people migrated as well. Languages did not merely diffuse through static populations; they were also spread by relocation diffusion (see Chapter 2). Sometimes such diffusion caused long-isolated languages to make contact, fostering ***language convergence***. Such instances create special problems for researchers because the rules of reconstruction may not apply or may be unreliable.

Replacement

A further complication should be considered in view of modern cultural events. We know that the languages of traditional, numerically smaller, and technologically less advanced peoples have been replaced, or greatly modified, by the languages of invaders. This process of ***language replacement*** goes on today, and there is every reason to believe that it has happened ever since humans began to use language. (In the next chapter we discuss the process of *creolization*, a form of language replacement now occurring in the Caribbean region and elsewhere.)

Reconstructing even a small branch of the language tree, therefore, is a complicated task. Look again at the language map of Europe (Fig. 8-3). If only all the languages were members of the same family, the same branch of the tree! But things are not that simple. Hungarian, completely surrounded by Indo-European languages, is not in the same family as any of its neighbors. Finnish is another non-Indo-European language and apparently is distantly related to Hungarian but mapped as a member of a discrete subfamily. Estonian is more closely related to Finnish, as the map suggests. But a tantalizing enigma is presented by Basque, a language belonging to a distinct language family that is now isolated in a small region of northern Spain and southwestern France. What ancient proto-language gave rise to Basque? Similar questions arise in hundreds of places throughout the world, where linguistic islands survive despite later waves of language diffusion.

◆ THEORIES OF LANGUAGE DIFFUSION

Although linguists reconstructed Proto-Indo-European vocabulary, human geographers and other scholars searched for the source of Proto-Indo-European. Identifying this hearth would enormously increase their understanding of Eurasian historical geography.

The linguists' research produced many valuable clues. Reconstructions by scholars working independently

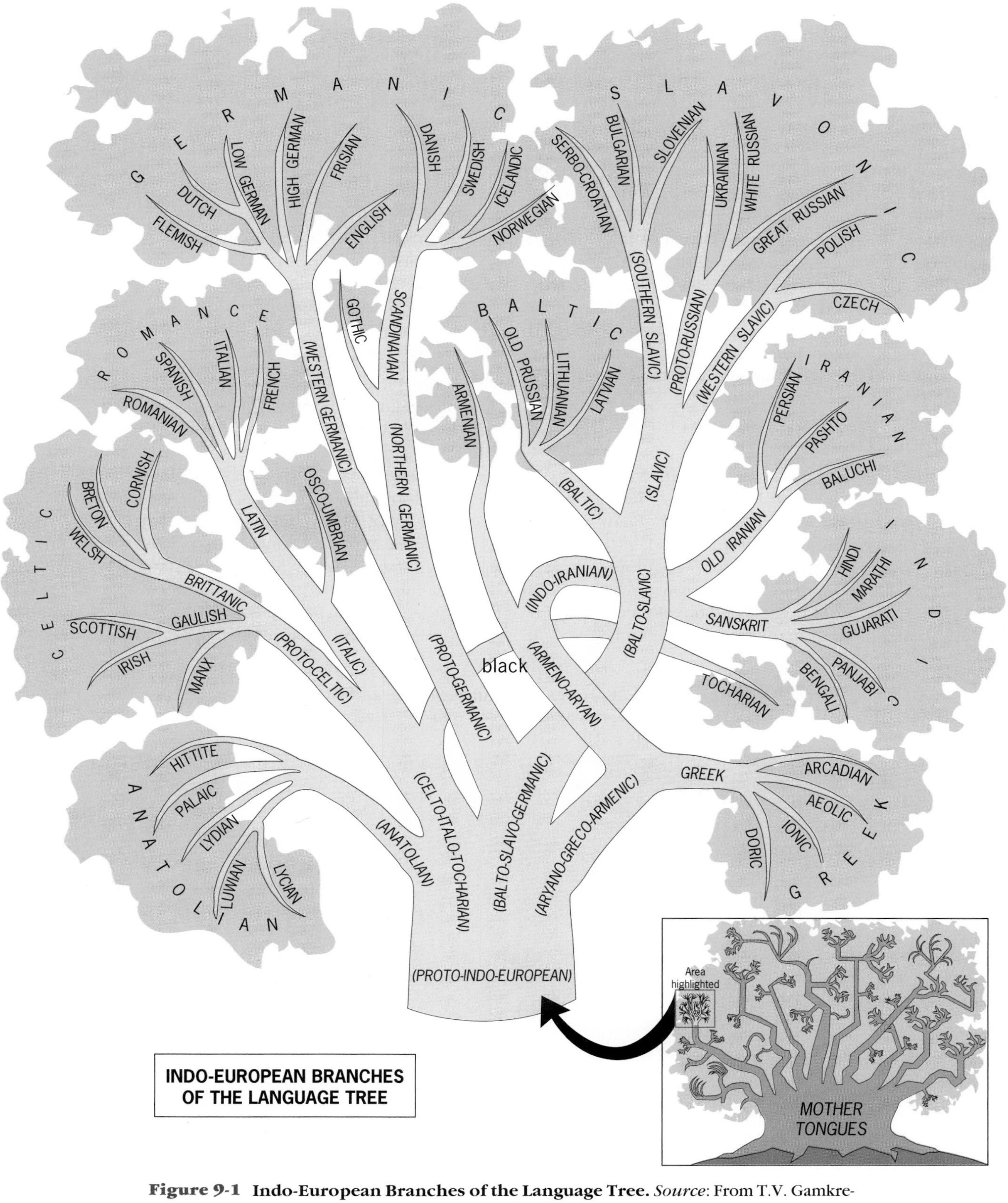

Figure 9-1 Indo-European Branches of the Language Tree. *Source*: From T.V. Gamkrelidze and V.V. Ivanov. "The Early History of Indo-European Languages," *Scientific American,"* March 1990, p. 111.

often produced remarkably similar results. The proto-language(s) had words for certain landforms, trees, and other features of the natural landscape, but it lacked others. Such information helps reveal the environment in which a language may have developed. For example, if a reconstructed language has no word for snow, this suggests a tropical or equatorial origin. If there is no word for palm tree, the language is likely to have emerged in a cold region. More specifically, if a certain type of vegetation (oak, pine, beech, birch, tall or short grass) is part of the vocabulary, the search for the environment where the language developed can be narrowed down—although researchers must factor in a time dimension, as environments have changed even during the Holocene. Time is less an issue when vocabulary refers to physiographic features of the landscape. If there are many words for mountains and hills but few for flat land, we can conclude that the source area was mountainous.

Conquest Theory

Analyses of this kind produced a tentative answer to the geographic question. The Proto-Indo-European homeland source, it seemed, lay somewhere north of the Black Sea in the vast steppes of present-day Ukraine and Russia. The time, it was suggested, was more than 5000 years ago, and judging from the reconstructed vocabulary, the people used horses, had developed the wheel, and traded widely in many goods. The logical conclusion seemed to be that these early speakers of Proto-Indo-European spread westward on horseback, overpowering earlier inhabitants and beginning the diffusion and differentiation of Indo-European tongues.

This ***conquest theory*** of language dispersal in Europe west of the Russian plains was long supported by a majority of archeologists, linguists, and human geographers. The sound shifts in the derivative languages (*vater* to *vader* to *father*, for example) seemed to represent a long period of westward divergence. The location of older Indo-European languages on western margins (Breton in France, Scottish Gaelic and Welsh in Britain, and Irish Gaelic in Ireland) appeared to be due to the arrival of newer languages from the east.

Agriculture Theory

But not all scholars were convinced. As the archeological record in Europe became better known, other hypotheses were proposed. Luca Cavalli-Sforza and Robert Ammerman suggested that it was the spread of agriculture, not conquest, that diffused the Proto-Indo-European language through Europe. This, of course, meant that the source area of the ancient language would have had to lie in an area of agricultural innovation, not in the Ukrainian-Russian grasslands where pastoralism was the prevailing way of life. But where was this hearth? Was it in the Fertile Crescent of the Middle East? Apparently not, because the vocabulary of Proto-Indo-European has few words

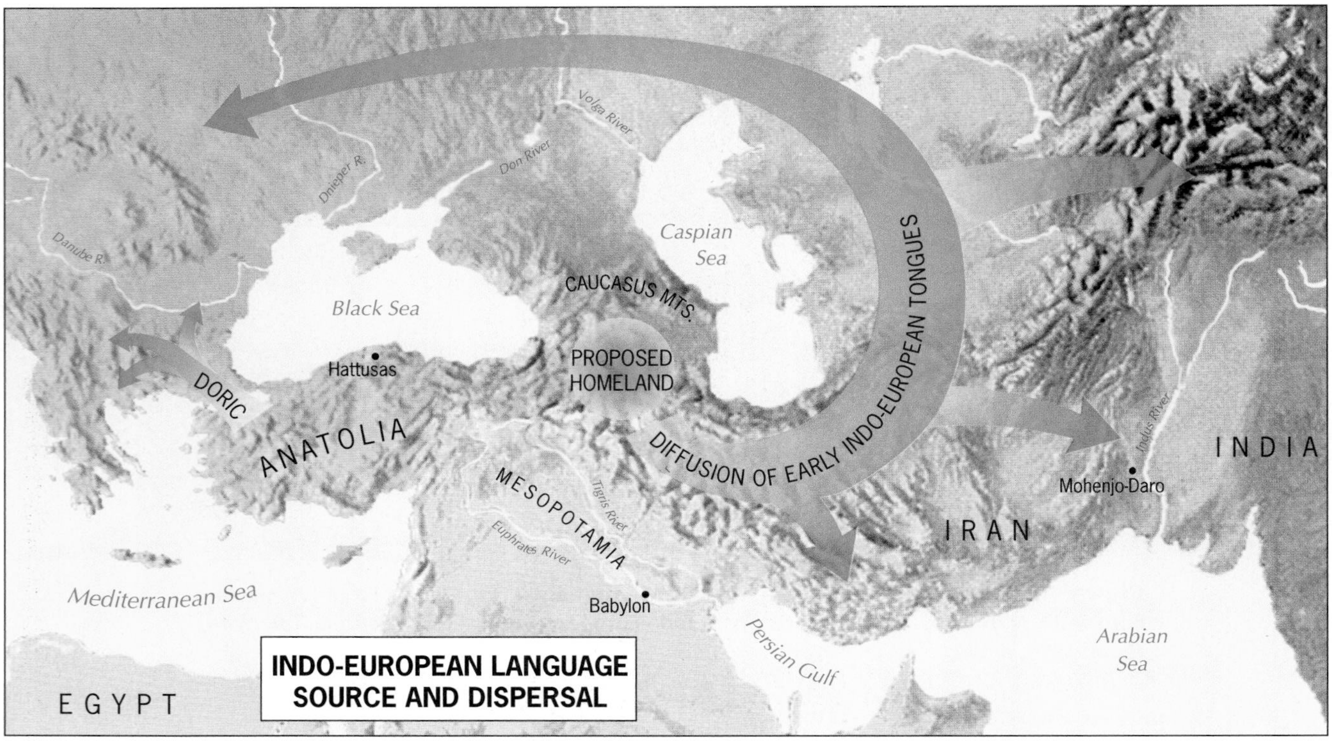

Figure 9-2 Proposed Indo-European Language Source and Dispersal. Postulated diffusion of an Indo-European proto-language. *Source*: From T.V. Gamkrelidze and V.V. Ivanov, *Scientific American,* March 1990, p. 112.

for plains but many terms for high and low mountains, valleys, mountain streams, rapids, lakes, and other high-relief landforms.

In 1984 the Soviet scholars Thomas Gamkrelidze and Victor Ivanov, who reconstructed much of the known vocabulary of Proto-Indo-European, published a book in which they reported that these terms were supplemented by words for trees such as mountain oak, pine, fir, willow, and ash. The language also had names for animals such as lions, leopards, and monkeys—none of which lived in the plains north of the Black Sea. Thus arose the ***agriculture theory*** (as opposed to the conquest theory) and its proposed source area: the mountainous, well-watered terrain of Anatolia in modern Turkey. The archeological record indicates that there, between 7000 and 9000 years ago, the horse had been domesticated and the wheel was in use. The realm's leading hearth of agricultural innovation lay in nearby Mesopotamia.

Support for the Theory In 1991 the agriculture theory received support from analyses of the protein (that is, gene) content of individuals from several thousand locations across Europe. This research confirmed the presence of distance decay in the geographic pattern: certain genes became steadily less common from southern Turkey across the Balkans and into Western and northern Europe. This pattern was interpreted as showing that the farming peoples of Anatolia moved steadily westward and northward. As they did so, they mixed with nonfarming peoples, diluting their genetic identity as the distance from their source area increased. Archeologists Robert Sokal, Neal Olden, and Chester Wilson argued that farming led to an unprecedented increase in population and that this in turn stimulated migration. As a result, a slow but steady wave of farmers dispersed into Europe.

The agriculture theory can be used to explain a number of features of the language map of Europe. Ammerman and Cavalli-Sforza proposed that for every generation (25 years) the agricultural frontier moved approximately 18 kilometers (11 miles). This would mean that the European frontier would have been completely penetrated by farmers in about 1500 years, which is close to what the archeological record suggests. But some of the nonfarming societies in their path held out, and their languages did not change. Thus Etruscan did not become extinct until Roman times, and Basque survives to this day as a direct link to Europe's pre-farming era.

Drawbacks of the Theory The agriculture theory has some drawbacks, however. The Anatolian region is not an ideal environment for farming, and there is no strong archeological evidence for an agricultural culture hearth there. In addition, despite the genetic gradient identified in Europe, some language geographers continued to prefer the dispersal hypothesis, which holds that the Indo-European languages that arose from the proto-language(s) were first carried eastward into Southwest Asia, next around the Caspian Sea, and then across the Russian-Ukrainian plains and on into the Balkans (Fig. 9-2). As is so often the case, there may be some truth in both hypotheses. If Anatolia were the source, the diffusion of Indo-European languages (that is, dialects of Proto-Indo-European) could have spread both westward across southern Europe and in the broad arc shown in Figure 9-3.

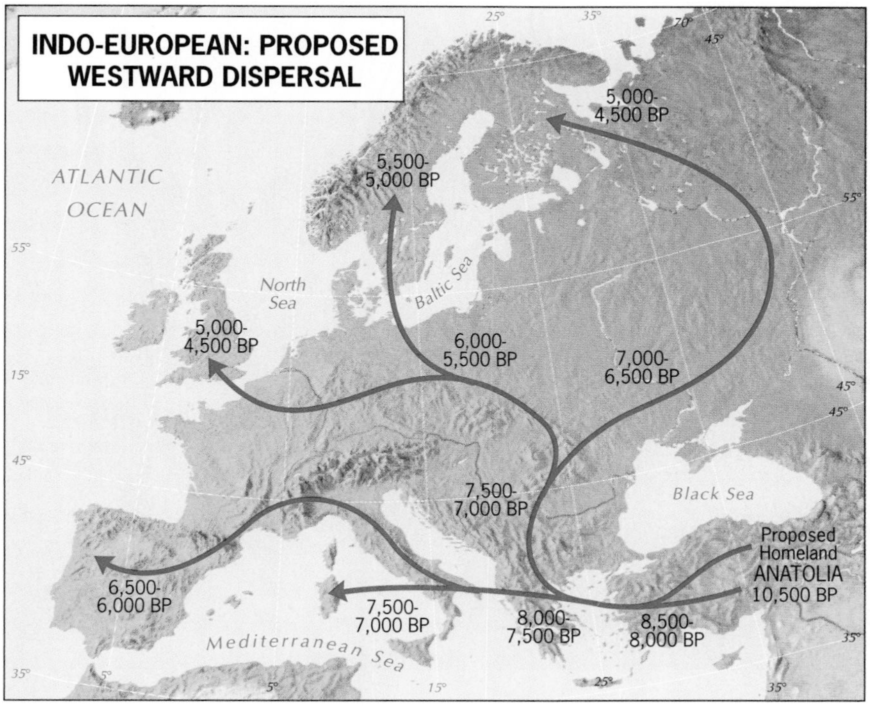

Figure 9-3 Indo-European: Proposed Westward Dispersal. Approximate timings and routes for the westward dispersal of the Indo-European languages.

In any case, an eastward diffusion must have occurred in view of the relationships between Sanskrit and Ancient Latin and Greek described by William Jones.

The geographic story of Proto-Indo-European is still unfolding, but this has not deterred researchers from going back even further. What was the ancestral language for Proto-Indo-European?

◆ THE SEARCH FOR A SUPERFAMILY

The evolution and diffusion of Proto-Indo-European occurred over a period of, at most, 9000 years. But language development and divergence have been going on for 10 times as long or more; we have just dissected a thin branch of an old, gnarled tree (Fig. 9-4).

This does not discourage modern linguists or language geographers, however. The British scholar Colin Renfrew carried the agriculture theory a step further by proposing that not just one but three agricultural hearths gave rise to language families (Fig. 9-5). From the Anatolian source diffused Europe's Indo-European languages; from the western arc of the Fertile Crescent came the languages of North Africa and Arabia; and from the Fertile Crescent's eastern arc ancient languages spread into present-day Iran, Afghanistan, Pakistan, and India, later to be replaced by Indo-European languages.

Russian scholars have long been in the forefront of research on ancient languages, but their work was not well known in the West until recently. The work of two scholars in particular has had great impact. Starting in the 1960s, Vladislav Illich-Svitych and Aharon Dolgopolsky tackled a daunting problem: deep reconstruction of the language that was ancestral to Proto-Indo-European. Using words that are assumed to be the most stable and dependable parts of a language's vocabulary (such as those identifying arms, legs, feet, hands, and other body

Figure 9-4 Schematic Diagram of Language Sources. *Source*: After a diagram in Philip E. Ross, "Hard Words," *Scientific American*, April 1991, p. 139.

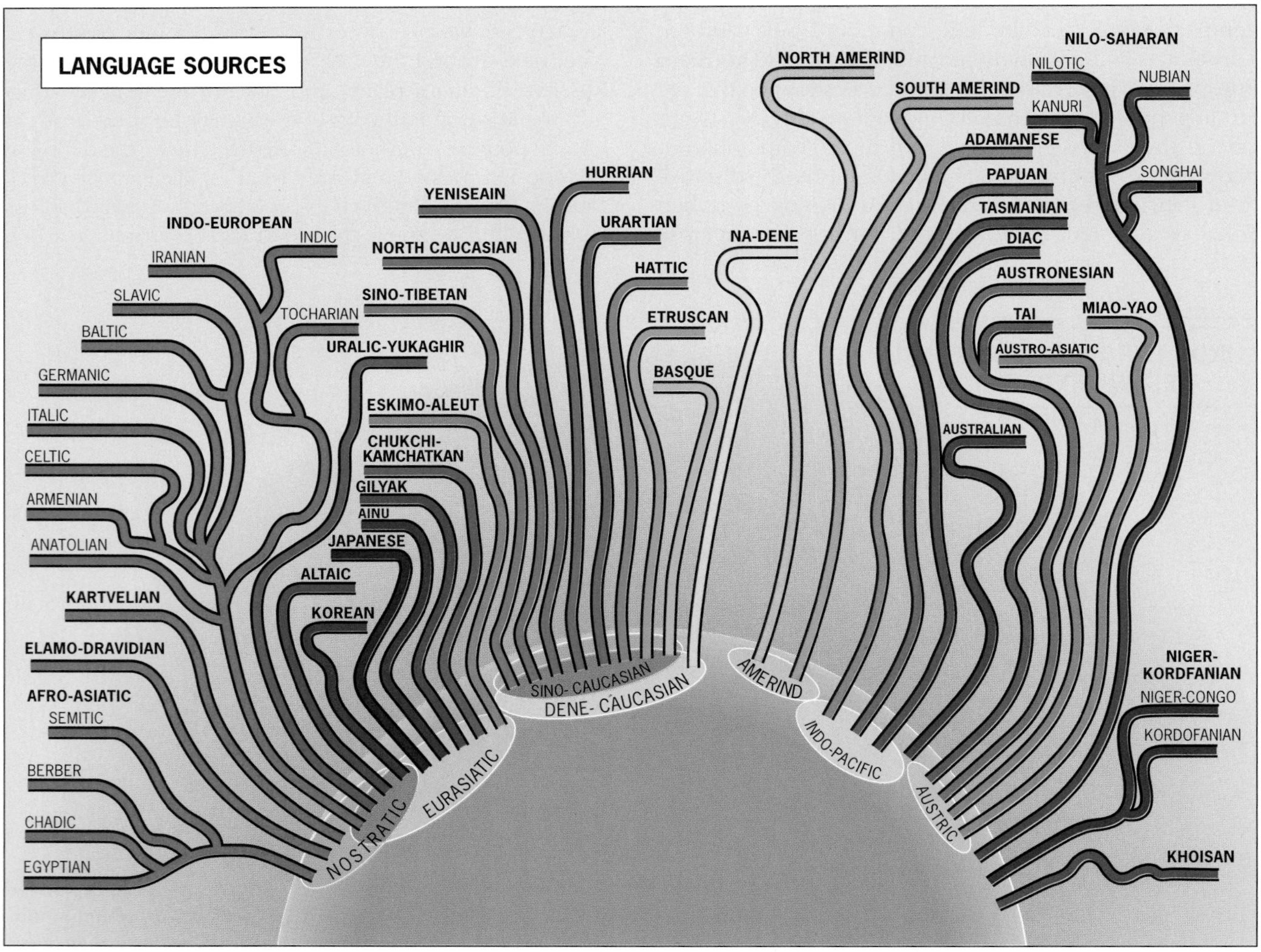

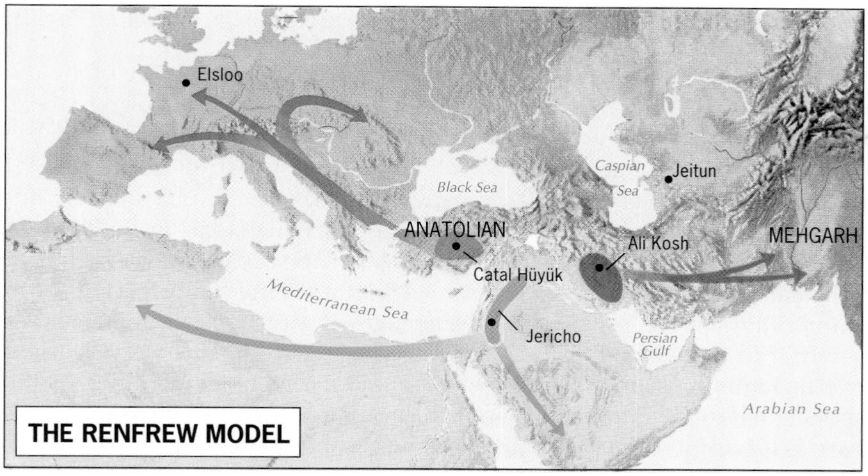

Figure 9-5 The Renfrew Model. The Renfrew Model proposes that three source areas of agriculture each gave rise to a great language family. *Source*: From "The Origins of Indo-European Languages," *Scientific American*, 1989, p. 114.

parts, and terms for the Sun, Moon, and other elements of the natural environment), they reconstructed an inventory of several hundred words. What was most remarkable is that they did this independently, each unaware of the other's work for many years. When they finally met and compared their inventories, they found that they were amazingly similar. They agreed that they had established the core of a pre-Proto-Indo-European language, which they named ***Nostratic***.

As with Proto-Indo-European, the evolving vocabulary of the Nostratic language revealed much about the lives and environments of its speakers. There apparently were no names for domesticated plants or animals, so Nostratic-speakers were hunter-gatherers, not farmers. An especially interesting conclusion had to do with the words for dog and wolf, which turned out to be the same, suggesting that the domestication of wolves may have been occurring at the time. The oldest known bones of dogs excavated at archeological sites date from about 14,000 years ago, so Nostratic may have been in use at about that time, well before the First Agricultural Revolution.

Nostratic is believed to be the ancestral language not only of Proto-Indo-European, and thus the Indo-European language family as a whole, but also of the Kartvelian languages of the southern Caucasus region (16 in Fig. 8-2), the Uralic-Altaic languages (which include Hungarian and Finnish, Turkish and Mongolian), the Dravidian languages of India (Fig. 8-5), and the Afro-Asiatic language family, in which Arabic is dominant.

How long before 14,000 years B.P. (Before the Present) it may have been in use has not yet been established. The same is true of Nostratic's geography. Where Nostratic was born, and what tongues gave rise to it, are unanswered questions. However, Nostratic links languages that are separated even more widely than those of the Indo-European family today. Some scholars have suggested that Nostratic (and its contemporaries, variously named Eurasiatic, Indo-Pacific, Amerind, and Austric) is a direct successor of a proto-world language that goes back to the dawn of human history, but this notion is highly speculative. The inset in Figure 9-1 reminds us how little of the human language tree we know with any certainty.

◆ DIFFUSION TO THE PACIFIC AND THE AMERICAS

The final stages of the dispersal of the older languages—before the global diffusion of English and other Indo-European languages—occurred in the Pacific realm and in the Americas. One would assume that the historical geography of these events would be easier to reconstruct than the complex situation in western Eurasia. After all, the peoples who canoed across the Pacific brought their languages to unpopulated islands. Similarly, there was no linguistic convergence with preexisting languages in the Americas. Therefore, if we needed a testing ground for linguistic divergence without "noise," the Pacific islands and the Americas would seem to be fine natural laboratories. But when we examine the debates over Pacific and American native languages, we find that the problems involved are not simple at all.

Pacific Diffusion

In our discussion of human dispersal, we noted how late people first arrived in the Pacific islands; Polynesians reached New Zealand little more than 1000 years ago. On the other hand, Australia was reached between 50,000 and 60,000 years ago, and New Guinea's first human population must have arrived even earlier because the route to the southern landmass passed through it. Papuans as well as Native Australians were hunter-gatherers, although there is archeological evidence that root-crop cultivation began in New Guinea as long as 6000 years ago, leading to population growth and the expansion of Papuan populations eastward into the

Solomon Islands and westward into present-day Indonesia. This expansion brought farmers into contact with foragers, and as a result the language mosaic of New Guinea and nearby islands is extremely complex.

Yet the diffusion of peoples and their languages into the Pacific north of Indonesia and New Guinea did not begin from these areas. Instead, it began in coastal China, where farming was well established. The languages of China and Southeast Asia had undergone several transitions; the sequence probably was similar to that from the pre-farmers' Nostratic to the farmers' Proto-Indo-European. An ancestral language gave rise to the Austro-Tai family of languages, and out of this family arose ***Austronesian***. Language geographers believe that speakers of this language (with many words for rice, field, farm, water buffalo, plow, and canoe) reached Taiwan about 6000 years ago. Several centuries later, Austronesian speakers managed to reach the Philippines. This movement resulted in the division of Austronesian into two dialects that later developed into major subfamilies. One of these, ***Malayo-Polynesian***, became the forerunner of a large number of languages, including those spoken by the first settlers of Madagascar, the islands of Melanesia and Micronesia, Fiji (where ***Fijian*** was a discrete Malayo-Polynesian offshoot), and New Zealand, whose Maori people speak ***Polynesian***, another derivative of this branch.

Considering the water-fragmented nature of the Pacific realm, this process of diffusion took place remarkably quickly. We may wonder why it took so long for the Agricultural Revolution in East Asia to stimulate emigration onto the islands off Asia's coast; but then the migrants rapidly spread from Madagascar in the west to Easter Island in the east. The whole eastern region of Polynesia was settled within several centuries (Fig. 9-6).

Although the lineages of Austronesian languages are better understood today, much remains to be learned about the reasons behind the complexity of the Pacific language map. Did successive waves of invasion stimulate divergence among the Malayo-Polynesian languages? Or was differentiation due to isolation? And there remains the question of Austronesian ancestries. Linguists do not have a model similar to Nostratic for the languages of the Asian mainland. Thus the Pacific language arena is anything but simple.

Diffusion in the Americas

As Figure 8-2 indicates, the current language map of the Americas is dominated by Indo-European languages.

Figure 9-6 Stages in the Austronesian Expansion. Bellwood's Pacific realm model shows the stages in the expansion of Austronesian lanuages. *Source*: Adapted from P. Bellwood, "The Austronesian Dispersal and the Origin of Languages," *Scientific American*, 1991, p. 88.

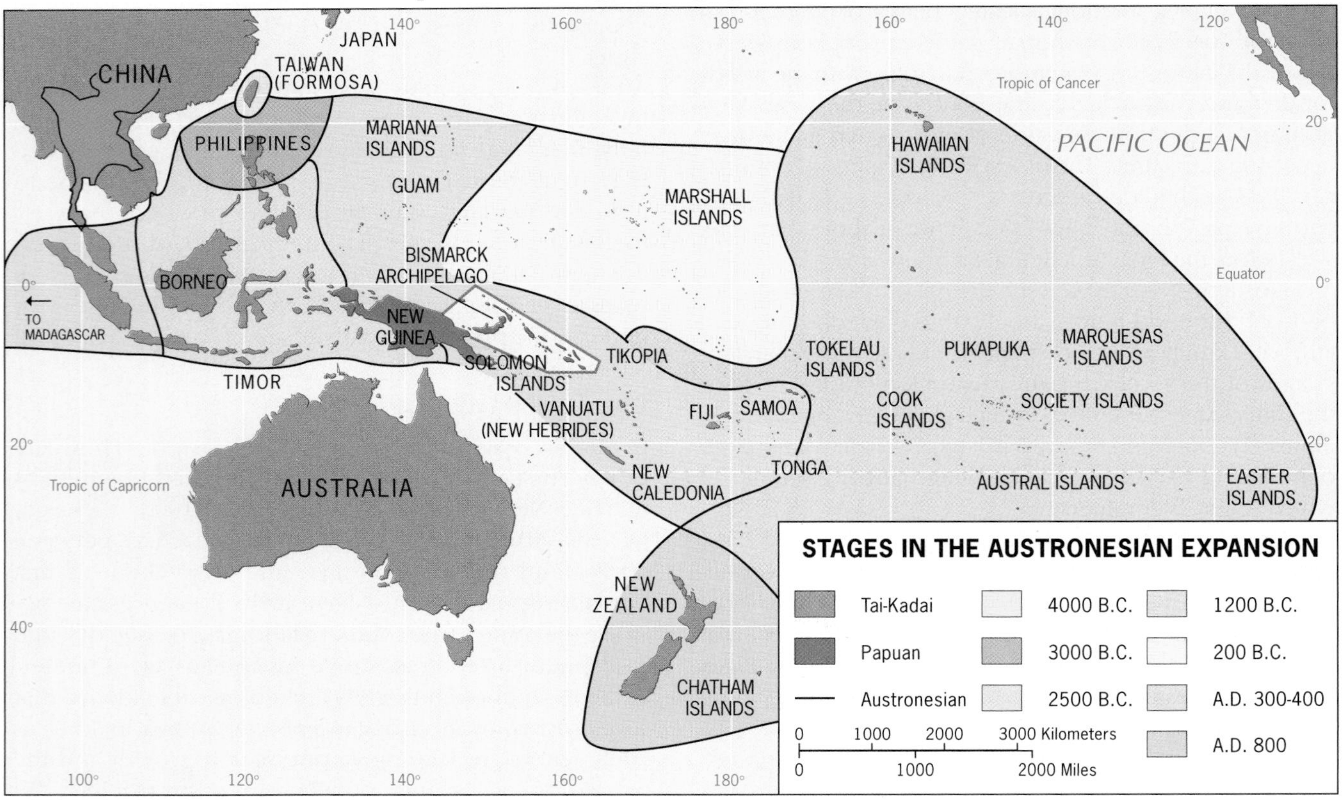

These have engulfed the languages spoken in America for thousands of years—the languages of Native Americans.

The Native American population never was very large by modern standards. Estimates of its pre-Columbian population have increased over the years as anthropologists have learned more about these peoples, but even the highest estimate puts the number of Native Americans at 40 million just before the European invasion. As noted previously, it was long believed that the Native Americans arrived via the Bering land bridge from Asia and that the earliest immigrations occurred just 12,000 to 13,000 years ago. Given the modest numbers of people involved and their recent arrival, one would assume under this scenario that the linguistic situation should be fairly simple. There were no preexisting peoples to be absorbed and no lifeways to be transformed. At the very least, the pattern should be much simpler than that of Eurasia.

These conclusions may be wrong, however. While some 40 language families have been recognized in the Old World, linguists have identified as many as 200 Native American language families, each different from the others. It thus appears that the first American languages diverged into the most intricately divided branch of the human language tree—within a very brief period if one accepts the Bering land bridge hypothesis.

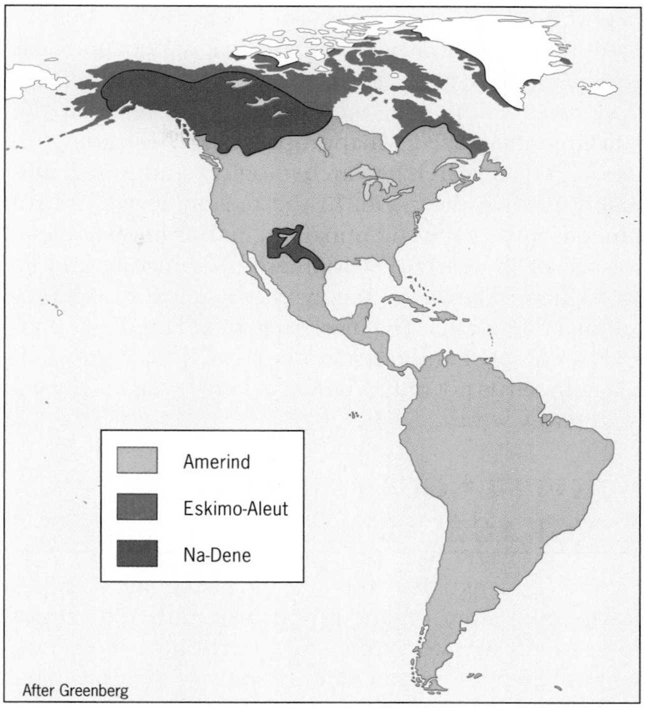

Figure 9-7 Greenberg's Three Indigenous Language Families. Greenberg's indigenous language families include Amerind, Eskimo-Aleut, and Na-Dene. *Source*: From R. Lewin, "American Indian Language Dispute," *Science* 242, 1988, p. 1633.

The Greenberg Hypothesis

Or did they? Not all linguists agree. In *Language in the Americas* (1987), Joseph Greenberg proposed that there are three families of indigenous American languages, each corresponding to a major wave of migration into the Western Hemisphere (Fig. 9-7). The oldest, largest, and most widely distributed family is the ***Amerind*** superfamily, which is spread from the shores of Hudson Bay to the coast of Tierra del Fuego. The next oldest, next largest, but much less widely diffused family is the ***Na-Dene***, which encompasses languages spoken by Native Americans of northwest Canada and part of Alaska as well as by the Apache and Navajo (the outlier in the southwestern United States shown in Figure 9-7). Last to arrive in North America were speakers of the ***Eskimo-Aleut*** family of languages, who are still concentrated along Arctic and near-Arctic shores.

Critics of Greenberg's hypothesis contended that Greenberg did not follow proper procedures of reconstruction. Rather than studying sound shifts and other details, he compared similar-sounding words in contemporary languages. Similar work in Africa produced the map shown in Figure 8-5, which also came under heavy fire when it was first published. Today, however, that map is widely accepted.

The implications of Greenberg's hypothesis are far-reaching. If the Amerind languages are indeed members of the same family, their divergence must have occurred during a period of more than the 12,000 to 13,000 years allowed for by the dating of the first immigration. That would require a revision of the long-held view of the peopling of the Americas.

In the late 1980s and early 1990s, new archeological data gave support to such a revision. A rock shelter in Pennsylvania produced artifacts dated at about 16,000 years B.P., and a site in Chile yielded material tentatively dated at 33,000 B.P.. If the latter date can be confirmed, the first wave of migrants may have crossed the Pacific more than 40,000 years ago. Crucial evidence may come to light in the next several years, but at the moment the archeological evidence for very early American immigration is still tentative.

Stronger support has come from other directions. For many years Christy Turner studied dental variation among Native Americans. On the basis of dental data he concluded that the Americas were peopled in three waves of immigration that occurred over a longer period than 12,000 years. Genetic studies are also producing results consistent with the Greenberg hypothesis: the Native American speakers appear to belong to one large group whose languages have diverged over a lengthy period.

The Continuing Controversy A majority of linguists still doubt the three-wave hypothesis and the three-family map of American languages. They believe that the ultimate family relationships will eventually become clear from careful reconstruction of individual languages. They also believe that drawing conclusions from the data Greenberg used is inappropriate and misleading.

Genetic research and archeological studies will ultimately resolve the issue. In the meantime we are reminded of the gaps still remaining in our knowledge—not just of the early development of humanity and its acquisition of language but even of its most recent precolonial migrations. The modern map of languages conceals a complex and fascinating past whose unraveling will help tell us not only where we were but also why we are the way we are.

◆ INFLUENCES ON INDIVIDUAL LANGUAGES

Each of the languages in the world's language families has its own story of origin and dispersal. We cannot hope to tell the story of even a fraction of these languages here, but we can identify some of the critical influences on the diffusion of individual tongues. First, it is clear that speakers of nonwritten languages will not retain the same language very long if they lose contact with one another. This is what led to the proliferation of languages before the advent of writing. By the same logic, the diffusion of a single tongue over a large area occurs only when people remain in contact with one another and continue to rely on a common linguistic frame of reference.

Beyond opportunities for contact, the changing character of the world's linguistic mosaic has been influenced by three fundamental forces: literacy, technology, and political organization. Literacy is critical because texts are the primary means by which language can become stabilized. Technology is important because it influences both the production of written texts and the interaction of distant peoples. Political organization is key because it affects both what people have access to and which areas are in close contact with one another.

With these influences in mind, we can begin to see how the global linguistic pattern has changed over the past several millennia. Just a few thousand years ago most habitable parts of the Earth's surface were characterized by a tremendous diversity of languages—much as one finds in interior New Guinea today. There were no literate societies and no means of bringing together peoples who were separated even by short distances.

With the rise of larger-scale, more technologically sophisticated literate societies, some languages began to spread over larger areas. By 2000 years ago certain languages (notably Chinese and Latin) had successfully diffused over entire subcontinents. This was possible because these languages were associated with political systems that knit together large swaths of territory—although it should be noted that the dominant languages often coexisted with local languages, leading to regional differences within imperial realms. Not surprisingly, then, when large-scale political systems disintegrated—as happened in the case of the Roman Empire—linguistic divergence took place.

Given the importance of literacy, technology, and politics for the diffusion of languages, two developments in the late Middle Ages were of particular importance to the emergence of the modern language pattern: the invention of the printing press and the rise of nation-states. The printing press was invented in Germany in 1588, and during the next hundred years it spread to other parts of Europe and beyond. The printing press allowed for an unprecedented production of written texts. Many of the early printed texts were religious, and these helped determine the standard form of various languages. The Luther Bible played this role for German, as did the King James Bible for English.

The rise of nation-states was equally important, for these political entities had a strong interest in promoting a common culture, and in some cases they asserted their interests in faraway places as well. Political elites

From the field notes

"Lucca, Italy, 2000. Standing in the oval plaza that still retains the shape of the Roman arena that once stood here, the signs on most of the commercial establishments reminded me of how language can change over time. Some words brought back memories of the Latin I had studied in school, and then there were the stores bearing signs in completely foreign tongues. Benetton is an Italian company, but its sign is in English—a reflection of its global ambitions. By adopting this linguistic strategy, Benetton is helping to promote English as a global lingua franca."

brought peoples together and played a key role in distributing printed texts. Moreover, as the leaders of countries such as England and Spain sought to expand their influence overseas, they established networks of communication and interaction that brought distant areas into closer contact than would have been conceivable just a few centuries earlier. In the process, certain languages came to be spread over vast portions of the Earth's surface.

As interesting as the historical geography of language is, the problems of language in the modern world are many and urgent. Language is a powerful component of ethnicity and lies at the heart of many current conflicts. It can be a barrier to advancement, a source of misunderstanding, and a divisive force. Governments manipulate language to bridge cultural and ethnic chasms; traders modify it to facilitate business. We consider these matters in the next chapter.

◆ KEY TERMS ◆

agriculture theory
Amerind
Austronesian
conquest theory
deep reconstruction
Eskimo-Aleut
Fijian
language convergence
language divergence
language replacement
Malayo-Polynesian
Na-Dene
Nostratic
Polynesian
(Proto)Indo-European language
sound shifts

◆ APPLYING GEOGRAPHIC KNOWLEDGE ◆

1. Language divergence involves the differentiation of languages over time and space. Where in North America is language divergence in progress today? What geographic factors contribute to this process here and elsewhere in the world?
2. After perhaps as many as 200,000 years of diffusion, the final phase of language dispersal (before the modern colonial period) occurred in the Americas and the Pacific. Explain how the distribution and content of indigenous languages in the Americas are analyzed to help in the reconstruction of the human settlement of this last frontier. Archeological and linguistic evidence are not always in agreement—why?

Chapter 10

Modern Language Mosaics

From the field notes

"Place names often provide insights into the history of towns and regions, but for Llanfairpwllgwyngyllgogerychwyrndrobwllllantysiliogogogoch, Wales, it is much more than that. The town with the self-proclaimed longest name in the world attracts hordes of tourists each year to a place whose claim to fame lies largely in its name. Why don't other places have such names? The answer to my question was provided by a local shopkeeper whom I engaged in conversation. This name is not an old name, I was told. Instead, it was coined by a local innkeeper a little over a hundred years ago in the hope of drumming up business from travelers. The innkeeper clearly realized something of importance. Language is not just about communication; when cleverly used and marketed it can make or break a place."

KEY POINTS

- **English, an Indo-European language that diffused throughout the world during the era of colonialism, has become the dominant international language of education, commerce, and business.**
- **Virtually no country is truly monolingual today, and in some countries serious ethnic discord exists between peoples speaking different languages.**
- **Some multilingual countries solve the problem of intercultural communication by making a foreign tongue their official language.**
- **In several areas of the world, linguistic convergence due to trade has produced languages of mixed origin. Some of these have developed into major regional languages.**
- **The study of place-names (toponymy) can reveal a great deal about the contents and historical geography of a cultural region.**
- **In their structure and vocabulary and in their ability (or inability) to express certain concepts and ideas, languages reflect the way people think about and perceive their world.**

Over the last decade a language debate has been raging in the United States. Large-scale immigration of Hispanic (primarily Mexican) people is changing the country's cultural composition. In less than three decades the ethnic balance of States from Florida to California has been transformed. In little more than a decade from now, Hispanics will constitute the largest minority in the country. America's ethnic character is once again changing.

With the growing Hispanic presence has come an expanded role for Spanish in many places. This—together with the sheer numbers of Spanish-speaking immigrants—has generated strong reactions, official as well as unofficial. Some state and local governments have sought to reaffirm the primacy of English. Organizations such as English First and English Only have spread their own message in the media. One of their oft-repeated arguments reminds Americans of their nation's history of admitting immigrant groups with foreign tongues: Germans, Italians, Swedes, and, most recently, hundreds of thousands of Asians from Vietnam and elsewhere. They ask why Spanish should be treated any differently.

To understand the special character of the recent Hispanic migration, one need only point to the map. Not only are Hispanic numbers growing faster than those of any other major ethnic community in the country, but the regional concentration of Hispanics in several Southern, Southwestern, and Western States is marked. In this mobile, migrating nation, where ethnic Easterners have moved westward, black Southerners have moved northward, and white Midwesterners have moved southward, the Hispanic sector has begun to redefine the southern tier of the United States because it is anchored there. True, large Hispanic communities have grown in cities from New York to Denver, and the Hispanic presence is growing rapidly in the Pacific Northwest. But the "Hispanicization" of America remains primarily a regional phenomenon, and from this comes the community's cultural strength in the national mosaic.

More than ethnic pride is at stake. Those who oppose giving special status to Spanish point to the problems faced by bilingual (two-language) countries such as Canada and Belgium, where linguistic differences create strong regional divisions. Supporters of greater recognition for Spanish argue that in bilingual countries suppression of minority languages has led to conflict, whereas promotion of multiple languages has kept minority cultures from being submerged by dominant ones.

Nevertheless, the issue has also divided Hispanic communities themselves. In 1990 a national Hispanic policy organization published the results of a study that showed that well over half of all Hispanic adults were functionally illiterate in English and that the educational attainment of Hispanics was declining compared to the national average. Some Hispanic educators saw in this data the clear need for Spanish speakers to learn English. Others argued that the data reflected the disadvantaged socioeconomic position of Hispanics. Still others pointed out that in the nineteenth and early twentieth centuries, many European immigrants did not learn English very well either. They viewed the current outcry over Spanish as a matter of cultural insecurity and even racism, and suggested that it was promoting anti-English sentiments among second-generation Spanish speakers. To support their argument, they cited the many cases around the world where legal efforts to mandate language use have backfired because the learning of another language is seen as a concession to the dominant society. ◆

◆ LANGUAGE AND CULTURE

Debates of this kind are ongoing in many countries. Note that the issue is not the preservation of the English language so much as its primacy in the national culture. Command of English undoubtedly is an advantage throughout the world. English has become the primary medium of international communication, especially in business, and for many the advantages of being able to use English outweigh cultural considerations. That, at least, is the position of several governments.

In Malaysia, for example, for four decades after independence the government promoted the Malay language, Bahasa Melayu. (This was less a reversal of the norms introduced by the former colonizer, Britain, than a boosting of the Malay language as opposed to Chinese, spoken by about one-third of the country's population.) But in 1994, the government of Malaysia announced that university courses in scientific and technical fields would henceforth be taught in English, not Bahasa Melayu. Malaysian nationalists were outraged, but the government held its ground. Proficiency in English, it argued, was essential to the country's economic competitiveness. Lack of such proficiency was creating a bottleneck for foreign investors and for Malaysians involved in international trade.

There was another problem as well. Malays learning English as a second language in the country's state schools were not doing nearly as well as Chinese citizens of Malaysia, many of whom were going to private schools where English was taught rigorously. Greater command of English among educated Malays would improve their competitiveness at home, too.

As we will see, some countries have made English (or another foreign language) their official language, giving indigenous languages secondary status. This provokes charges of neocolonialism or favoring the interest of educated elites. Again we see that emotional attachment to language is not just a matter of protecting threatened tongues. It is also a practical issue.

From the field notes

"The government of the Indian State of Maharashtra wasted no time once it had decided to scrap the name of its largest city! Even before all the legalities had been completed, the old signs showing Bombay were taken down and new ones erected. I saw this one near the harbor entrance, and asked a uniformed guard about it. 'It's the Hindu party, all politics,' he said. 'Bombay was a world name, but Mumbai refers to some Hindu goddess that is supposed to have lived here centuries ago. A lot of people in the city don't like it.' The guard was a Muslim, but he said that the city's large Sikh community also opposed the change. But a group of commuters at the railroad station were pleased. Bombay, they said, was a colonial name derived from the Portuguese, inappropriate in modern times. What was wrong with Mumbai? 'This is a Hindu country!' "

◆ LANGUAGE AND TRADE

As we saw in the previous chapter, the position of traditional native languages has changed greatly over the past several centuries—not for linguistic but for political reasons. The European subfamily of Indo-European spread rapidly over much of the globe, replacing and modifying local languages virtually everywhere. Then the world developed a boundary system that confined the speakers of many languages within specific territories. Although these borders often separated people speaking the same language, they more often threw together peoples with mutually unintelligible tongues. This created a host of difficulties both between and within states—problems that persist today.

The Esperanto Experiment

Early in the twentieth century a major effort was launched to create a world language, an artificial tongue that would eventually become the first or second language of all peoples everywhere. Called ***Esperanto***, this invented language was based on Latin and a combination of words from modern European languages. European schools introduced Esperanto, and Esperanto societies were formed in many countries during the interwar period. Even the League of Nations endorsed the idea, and by the late twentieth century as many as two million people claimed some acquaintance with Esperanto. But Esperanto was not a global tongue. It was another Indo-European language, and therefore its applicability was limited. Moreover, Europeans were becoming increasingly multilingual, and few wanted to learn another language that did not have obvious practical utility. Indeed, the latter issue is the critical one, for it is difficult to convince large numbers of people to invest the time and effort it takes to learn another language unless they are convinced that many others will do so as well. Yet to date no one has figured out how to create a sufficiently widespread commitment to learning Esperanto so that it becomes an appealing alternative to learning a language already spoken by substantial numbers of people. Hence, Esperanto is a theoretically attractive solution to cross-cultural communication, but the obstacles to its widespread adoption are truly formidable.

Lingua Franca

Where language planners failed, traders succeeded. Long before the rise of the global economy, centuries before the global diffusion of English, and before the invention of Esperanto, people speaking different languages were forced to find ways to communicate for trade. This need resulted in the emergence of a ***lingua franca***.

The term comes from the Mediterranean Sea and its numerous trading ports during the period following the Crusades. As sea-borne commerce in the Mediterranean expanded, traders from the ports of southern France—the Franks—revitalized the ports of the eastern Mediterranean. But the local traders did not speak the seafarers' language. Thus began a process of convergence in which the tongue of the Franks was mixed with Italian, Greek, Spanish, and Arabic. This mixture was known as the Frankish language, or *lingua franca*, and it served for centuries as the common tongue of Mediterranean commerce.

Today the term *lingua franca* is still used to denote any common language spoken by peoples with different native tongues. Arabic became a lingua franca during the expansion of Islam, and English did so in many areas during the colonial era. Indeed, the position of English has become so dominant globally that some people wonder whether it is positioned to become a truly global language (see Looking Ahead Box). But the term *lingua franca* is most appropriate for languages that are products of linguistic convergence. One of the best modern examples is Swahili, the lingua franca of East Africa. Over centuries of contact and interaction, Swahili developed from African Bantu languages, Arabic, and Persian. Although not a tone language like many other African languages, Swahili has a complex vocabulary and structure. It has become the Esperanto of a region that extends from southern Somalia to northern Moçambique and from coastal Kenya and Tanzania to Uganda and the East African Great Lakes region; it is even used in eastern Congo.

During the period when West Africa's interior kingdom thrived and trade between the arid north and the moist, forested coast was intense, a lingua franca emerged in the cities and bustling markets of the Sudanic zone extending from northern Nigeria westward to Senegal. That language, Hausa, is still a regional tongue used by speakers of other languages to communicate. Hausa is heard today not only in Nigeria but also in western Chad, southern Niger, and even Burkina Faso and eastern Mali (Fig. 10-1).

Creolization

When relocation diffusion sends speakers of a language far from their homeland, their language is likely to change, if not grammatically, then in terms of pronunciation, rhythm, and speed. Australian English is not very different from standard English in vocabulary, but its cadence makes it unmistakable. English as spoken in India and South Africa also sounds quite different from standard English.

In some instances, however, a language changes much more radically. Through contact with other languages, it can be simplified and modified to become what linguists call a ***pidgin***. In the Caribbean region, for example, English speakers met peoples speaking African languages, and before long a form of pidgin English developed. Ordinary people—not the colonialists or the elites—communicated in this pidgin, which diffused throughout the islands. It even reached mainland South America, not only in English-speaking Guyana but also in Dutch-speaking Suriname.

Over time a pidgin language may itself become the mother tongue as the original languages of its speakers are forgotten. African languages heard in the Caribbean in the years following the first involuntary migration faded away and were replaced by an ever more complex pidgin. This important form of language replacement is known as ***creolization***. The original pidgin becomes a lingua franca and is referred to as a ***creole*** language. A process similar to that just described occurred in the western Pacific region, where Melanesian pidgin is evolving into a regional creole language that was originally based on English but is now quite distinct. In coastal West Africa, a pidgin language called *Wes Kos* is also continuing to develop. Swahili, on the other hand, cannot be classified as a pidgin or a successor to a creole language. Because of its complex structure and vocabulary, it is a full-fledged, distinct Bantu language. A former

Looking Ahead

English as a Global Language?

What will the global linguistic mosaic look like 50 years from now? There is little doubt that more and more people are using English in a variety of contexts. English has become the standard language of international business and travel, much of contemporary popular culture bears the imprint of English, and the computer and telecommunications revolution has relied heavily on the use of English terminology. Does this mean that English is on its way to becoming a global language?

If "global language" means the principal language people use around the world in their day-to-day activities, the geographical processes we have examined so far emphatically do not point to the emergence of English as a global tongue. Population growth rates are generally lower in English-speaking areas than they are in other areas, and there is little evidence that people in non-English speaking areas are willing to abandon their mother tongue in favor of English. Indeed, since language embodies deeply held cultural views and is a basic feature of cultural identity, there is often active resistance to switching to English. In France, for example, a prestigious government-supported body known as the Académie Française has adopted rules forbidding the use of English on signs and in public documents, and it has sought to encourage the use of French-language equivalents for English terms that are creeping into use.

Yet if "global language" means a common lingua franca used around the world, the picture looks rather different. Although not always welcomed, the trend throughout much of the world is to use English as a language of cross-cultural communication—especially in the areas of science, technology, travel, and business. Korean scholars are likely to communicate with their Russian counterparts in English, Japanese scientific journals are increasingly published in English, Danish tourists visiting Italy use English to get around, and the meetings of most international financial and governmental institutions are dominated by English. Under these circumstances, it seems likely that the role of English as an international lingua franca is only likely to grow.

We must be careful, in this conclusion, however. Anyone looking at the world 200 years ago would have likely predicted that French would be the international lingua franca of the future. Times are different now, of course. The role of English in the computer revolution alone makes it hard to imagine a fundamental shift away from the dominance of English in international affairs. Yet economic and political influences on language use are always in flux, and nothing is inevitable. Moreover, in significant parts of the world other languages already function as regional lingua francae. Examples include parts of West Africa, where French functions as the lingua franca, and much of the Middle East and North Africa, where standardized Arabic plays that role. In these and other cases, there is likely to be considerable resistance to the adoption of English as a medium of cross-cultural communication. Hence, although English is likely to continue to expand its dominance as an international lingua franca, the global picture is likely to remain geographically patchy for a long time to come.

Despite official efforts to the contrary, English words can still be found on the streets of Paris, France.

president of Tanzania, Julius Nyerere, proved the depth and capacity of Swahili by translating Shakespeare's plays into that language.

Pidgin and creole languages are important unifying forces in a linguistically divided world. They tend to be simple and accessible, and therefore disseminate rapidly. In Southeast Asia a trade language called *Bazaar Malay* can be heard from Myanmar (Burma) to Indonesia and from the Philippines to Malaysia; it has become a lingua franca in the region. A simplified form

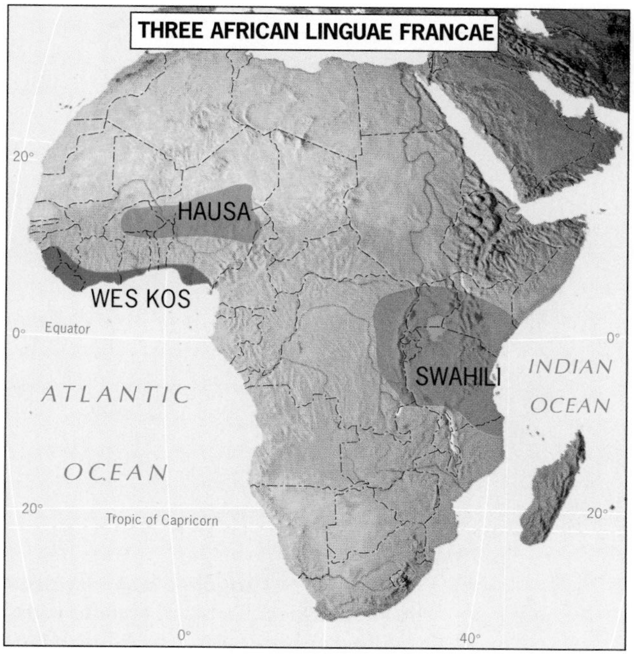

Figure 10-1 Three African Linguae Francae. The three African linguae francae are Swahili, Wes Kos, and Hausa.

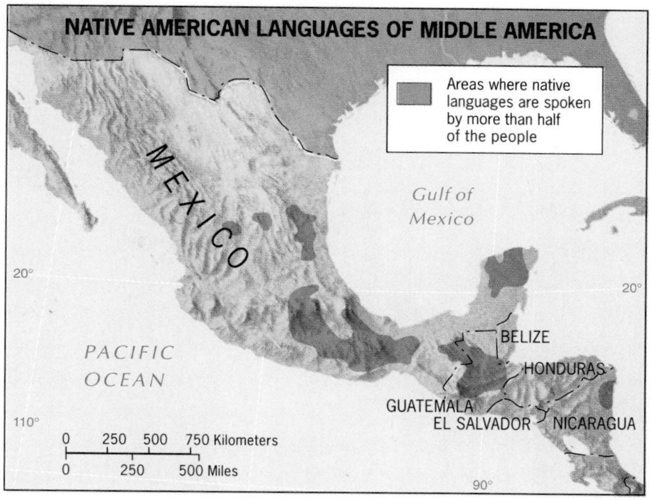

Figure 10-2 Native American Languages in Middle America. This map shows areas where native languages are spoken by more than half of the people.

of Chinese also serves as a language of commerce even beyond the borders of China.

Sometimes the difference between a dialect and a pidgin or creole language becomes blurred. As mentioned in the preceding chapter, some linguists regard Quebecois French as a dialect, but others consider it a distinct language derived from French. It is not a creole language; neither is Afrikaans, originally a dialect of Dutch spoken in South Africa but now generally regarded as a distinct language with Dutch, French, and even Malay components.

◆ MULTILINGUALISM

At the beginning of the chapter we touched on the sensitive issue of language and status. Languages, including pidgin and creole forms, can promote understanding and interaction between different peoples, but they can also divide. There are only a few ***monolingual states***—countries in which only one language is spoken. They include Japan in Asia; Uruguay and Venezuela in South America; Iceland, Portugal, and Poland in Europe; and Lesotho in Africa. Even these countries, however, have small numbers of people who speak other languages; for example, more than a half-million Koreans live in Japan. In fact, there is no truly monolingual country today. English-speaking Australia has more than 180,000 speakers of aboriginal languages. Predominantly Portuguese-speaking Brazil has nearly 1.5 million speakers of Native American languages.

Countries in which more than one language is in use are called ***multilingual states***. In some of these countries linguistic fragmentation reflects strong cultural pluralism as well as divisive forces. This is true in former colonial areas where peoples speaking different languages were thrown together, as happened in Africa and Asia. This also occurred in the Americas. As Figure 10-2 shows, Native American languages are spoken by more than half of the people in large areas of Guatemala and Mexico, even though these countries tend to be viewed as Spanish speaking.

Multilingualism, therefore, takes several forms. In effectively bilingual Canada and Belgium, it is reflected in regional divisions; that is, the two major languages each dominate in particular areas of the country. In multilingual Switzerland there are four such regions (Fig. 10-3). In Peru, centuries of acculturation have not erased the regional identities of the Native American tongues spoken in the Andean Mountains and the Amazonian interior, and of Spanish, spoken on the coast. We noted previously the jigsaw of languages in India, where entire States correspond to linguistic majorities.

But multilingualism has another dimension. In some countries (far fewer), there is less regional separation of speakers of different languages. For example, members of the white (European) community of South Africa speak two majority languages (Afrikaans and English) and several other tongues. Although Afrikaans remains the dominant language in part of South Africa's rural interior, the country does not have distinctive linguistic regions comparable to those of Canada or the former Czechoslovakia, where Czech was the language of the west and Slovak that of the east. In addition to the European languages spoken in South Africa, there are many African languages, of course, but their spatial interlocking is nonetheless noteworthy. Kwazulu-Natal and especially the city of Durban have large English-speaking minorities; Cape Town and

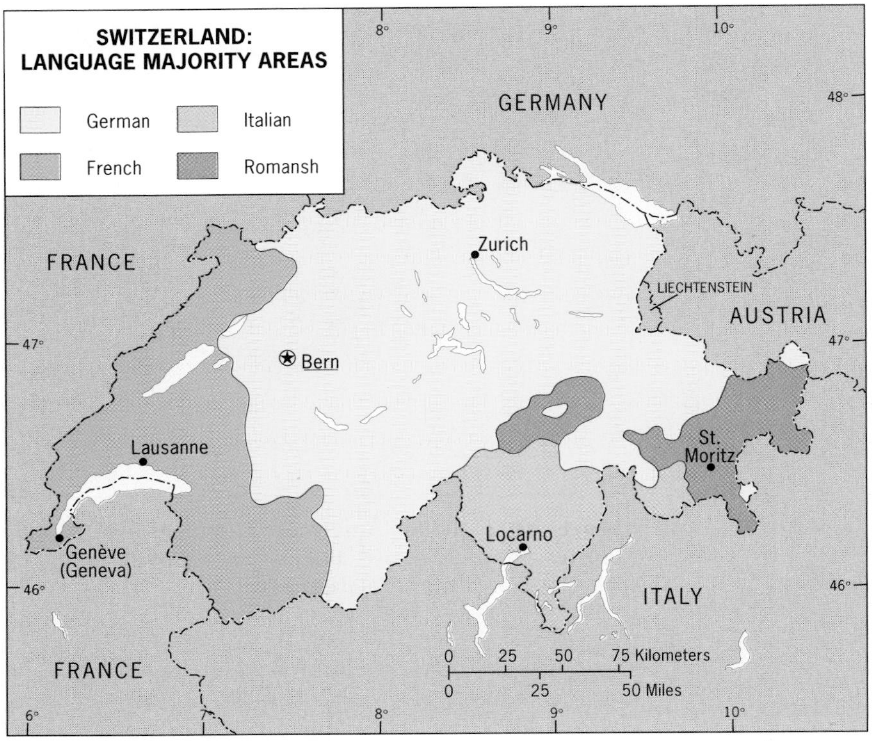

Figure 10-3 Language Majority Areas in Switzerland. German, French, Italian, and Romansh are spoken in different areas of Switzerland. *Source*: From a map in W. A. D. Jackson, *The Shaping of Our World*. New York: Wiley, 1985, p. 224.

Figure 10-4 Cyprus's Majorities before 1974. This map shows Greek and Turkish areas and British bases. *Source*: From a map in D. Downing, *An Atlas of Territorial Border Disputes*. London: New English Library, 1980, p. 30.

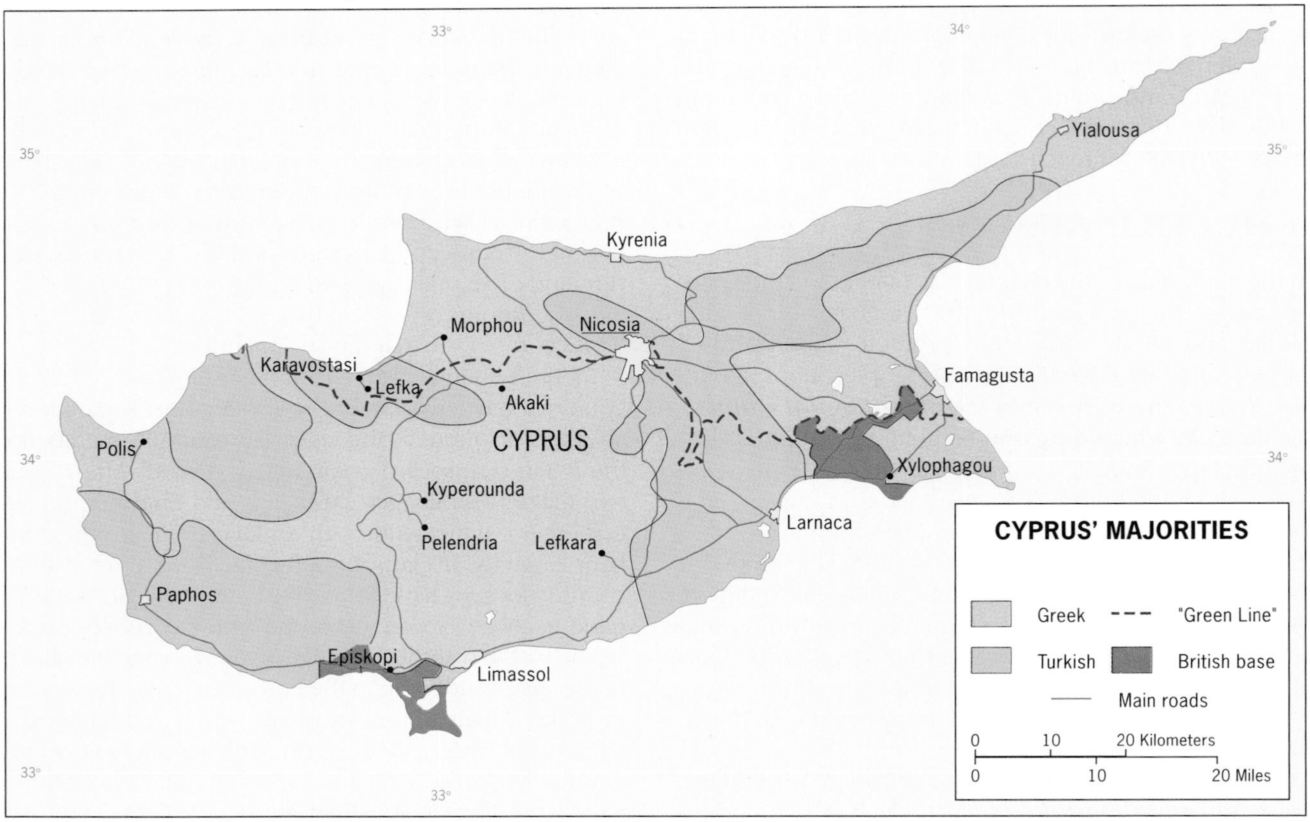

the Western Cape Province have large numbers of Afrikaner speakers. But neither group excludes the other.

This is the pattern Soviet planners had in mind when they organized the communist state after the Russian Revolution: Russian would become the lingua franca of the USSR, and the diffusion of Russians and their language would create a state in which linguistic communities retained their identities while "Russification" progressed around them. But today the region is a patchwork of ethnolinguistic areas, in many of which the local language is being promoted and supported.

Another country in which a multilingual experiment failed is Cyprus, where Greeks and Turks shared a small but comparatively prosperous island. Although the Greek majority and the Turkish minority were often at odds, there was much mingling between the two groups in the years after the country gained independence in 1960, as Figure 10-4 shows. But a political crisis in 1974 led to armed intervention by Turkey. Cyprus was partitioned, and both Turks and Greeks became refugees in their own country. Virtually all the Turks moved north of the "Green Line" shown in Figure 10-4, whereas all the Greeks were confined to the south of it. The partition of Cyprus did not simply reflect differences over language, of course; significant ethnonational divisions were at play. But in this and many other cases, language was an important symbolic element dividing the two communities.

Canada

The modern state of Canada is the product of a sequence of events that had the effect of combining a large, dominantly French-speaking territory, Quebec, with an even larger, mainly English-speaking area centered on neighboring Ontario. Under the British North America Act of 1867, which created the Canadian federation, Quebec was given important guarantees: the French civil code was sustained, and the French language was protected in Parliament and in the courts.

More than five generations later Canada is still a divided society, and language lies at the heart of the division. More than 85 percent of Quebec's population of over 7 million speak French at home, but that still leaves a significant minority of non-French speakers (Fig. 10-5). Many Québecois feel threatened by this situation. In 1977 the Quebec provincial Parliament passed a law that compelled all businesses in the province to demonstrate that they functioned in French. Canada's Supreme Court overturned this legislation, but in 1988 Quebec enacted a law that not only reinstated the legislation, but also added a regulation that made it illegal to exhibit any outdoor commercial sign in a language other than French in the entire province.

Predictably, such actions caused counteractions elsewhere in Canada. With fewer than 700,000 French-speaking Canadians living outside Quebec, other provinces reconsidered the costs of Canada's official policy of bilingualism. If English could be treated the way it was in Quebec, should French be accorded equality in, say, Alberta or Saskatchewan?

In this way the language issue, embedded in larger disputes over history and culture, tore at Canada's political fabric during the last decades of the twentieth century. Language is a potent force in national affairs, and

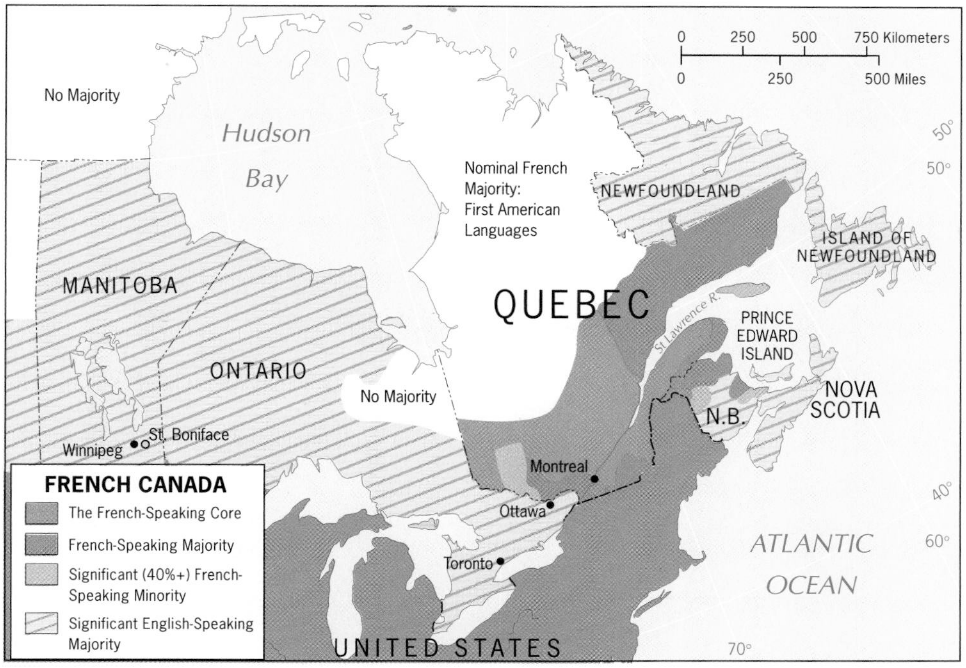

Figure 10-5 French Speakers in Canada. *Sources*: Canada Census, Statistics Canada. *The National Atlas of Canada* (1985), and *The Canada Year Book*.

the strongly regional character of bilingualism in Canada poses a daunting challenge to that country.

Belgium

A contemporary map of Belgium (Fig. 10-6) shows the country divided into a Dutch-speaking region in the north (Flanders) and a French-speaking region in the south (Wallonia). Near the center of the country, just inside of Flanders, is the officially bilingual—but majority French-speaking—capital of Brussels. These language regions reflect the fact that Belgium straddles the line separating the Romance and Germanic branches of Indo-European. Language has been a divisive issue in Belgium almost since its founding in 1830, but it has not always been associated with regionalism. The formal language regions of Belgium had little significance throughout most of the nineteenth century. Historically, the country had never been organized along linguistic lines, and differences in dialect made communication difficult among all but an elite—particularly in the northern part of the country.

During the nineteenth century the effort to build an integrated state led the largely French-speaking elite to make French the language of government and commerce. This left the speakers of Dutch dialects (called Flemish) in a disadvantaged position—a situation that eventually produced a language movement spearheaded by the elites of several northern cities. The leaders of that movement initially sought linguistic rights (the right of Dutch speakers to use Dutch in public affairs, court proceedings, schools, etc.), but when that effort failed they began demanding protection for Dutch in areas where Dutch or Flemish speakers dominated. Further frustrations led to more radi-

Figure 10-6 Divided Belgium and Its Neighbors. Dutch, French, and German dominate in different administrative areas in Belgium. *Source*: From a map in A. B. Murphy, "Belgium's Regional Divergence along the Road to Federation," in G. Smith, ed., *Federalism: The Multiethnic Challenge*. London: Longman, 1995, p. 82.

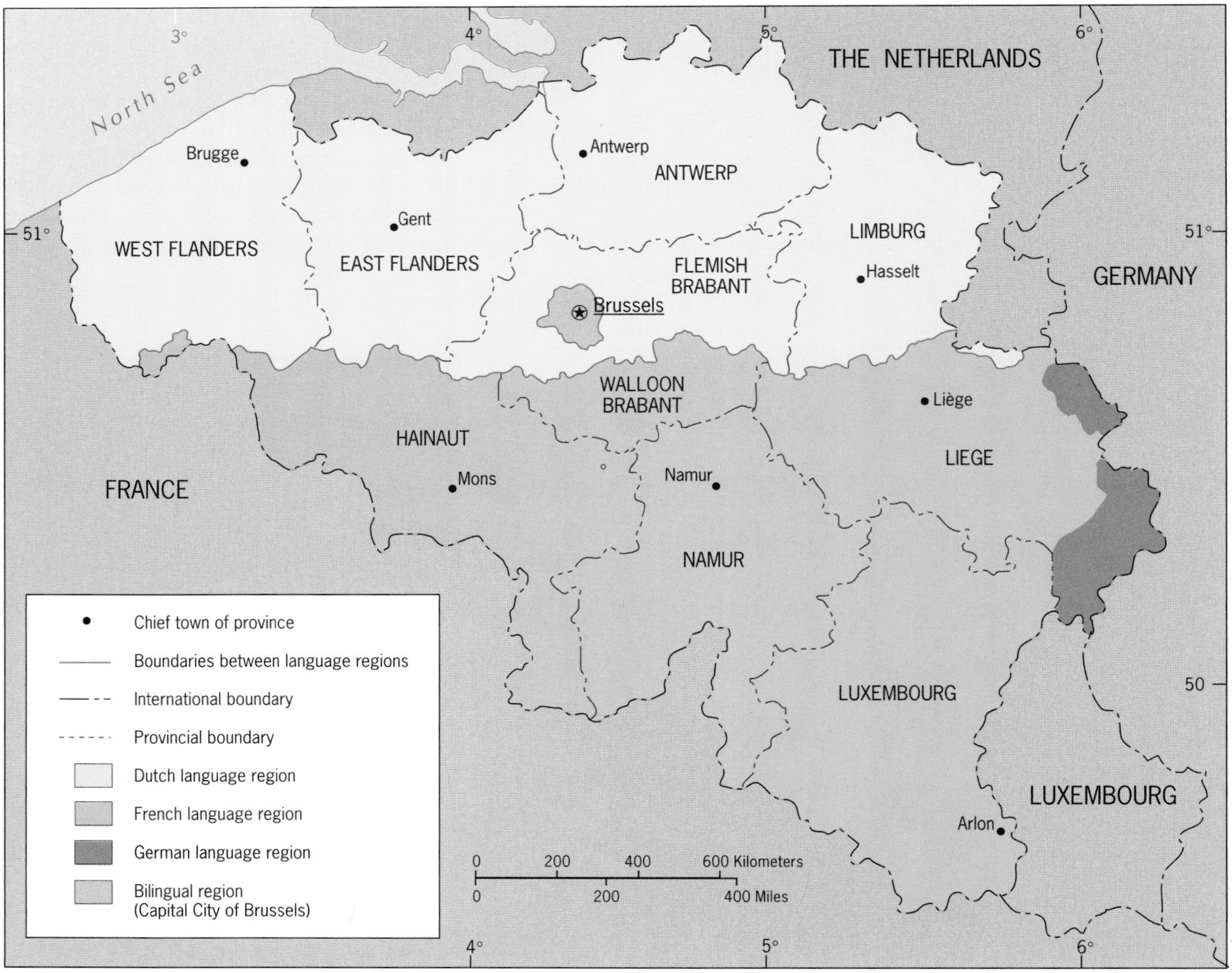

cal demands, and by the 1920s a growing cadre of activists began calling for the country to be partitioned along linguistic lines so that Dutch-speaking peoples could control their own affairs. These demands gradually became reality in the mid-twentieth century.

The upheavals produced by the partitioning process helped forge a sense of Flemish identity, and this in turn fueled a countermovement among Belgium's French speakers—the Walloons. With language-group identity on the rise, conflicts between linguistic "communities" became an increasingly central feature of Belgian political life. The conflict has been largely nonviolent, but it has led to the fall of several governments and has dominated the political agenda on numerous occasions. It is also responsible for Belgium's recent changeover from a unitary to a federal state. (The language regions shown in Figure 10-6 are the constituent units of the federation.)

The partitioning of Belgium along language lines does not signal the end of linguistic conflict. With the country divided between two major language regions, many issues are cast in regional linguistic terms—even issues that are not overtly cultural. Thus the language regions of Belgium are not just a product of the coalescence of language communities; their existence actually tends to foster regionalism. Some even wonder whether Belgium will follow Czechoslovakia's lead and split into two countries. This is not entirely unthinkable, but the situation of Brussels works against it. Both Flanders and Wallonia have a vested interest in Brussels, so neither would abandon it lightly. And the French-speaking majority in Brussels has little interest in casting its lot with the region in which it is situated—Flanders. Thus, for the time being, Belgium is likely to continue to look for the compromises that have kept the language issue alive

A SENSE OF SCALE

Linguistic Transition Zones

Behind many of the neat lines on language maps lie complicated, at times contentious, linguistic transition zones. This is certainly the case in Belgium, where the language regions shown on Figure 10-6 hide complexities that are evident only when language patterns are considered at the local scale. Brussels, the capital of Belgium, lies north of the line separating the two major language regions of Belgium. Most maps show the city as an officially bilingual area—and indeed many of its inhabitants can speak both French and Dutch. But the internal situation is more complicated than that—and it is fraught with political significance.

For centuries Brussels was a Flemish city dominated by a Germanic dialect related to Dutch. In the eighteenth century when French was the language of international politics and culture in Europe, a process of "Frenchification" began. Official promotion of French, together with the use of French in government in this heavily administrative city, led to a growing use of French during the nineteenth century. By the mid-twentieth century, a majority of the city's residents spoke French.

Bilingual signs in Brussels, Belgium

Brussels' linguistic history placed it at the center of Belgium's struggles over language. For the Dutch-speaking peoples of northern Belgium, the Frenchification of the city became a symbol of the creeping dominance of French. Their efforts to combat that process were interpreted by Belgium's French-speaking population as confrontational and undemocratic. An uneasy compromise now accords the city a bilingual status and places strict limits on the use of French in surrounding communes. Behind these legal arrangements lies a complex urban-cultural geography. No one knows precisely where speakers of French and Dutch live—language questions became so sensitive that they were banned from the Belgian census after 1947—but some areas are clearly dominated by one group or the other. As such, social and economic inequalities that reflect these patterns of dominance often take on larger meaning. Similarly, any departure from the principle of bilingualism can generate heated exchanges and, if official in nature, can have wide-ranging political repercussions.

Brussels is but one of many cities around the world where language communities come together. From Montreal to Jerusalem to Johannesburg, the local geography of language use is a matter that is imbued with larger cultural significance. The spatial distribution of language groups and the controversies that rage over language use in public spaces help to define the character of such places, as well as the ways that different groups view themselves and one another.

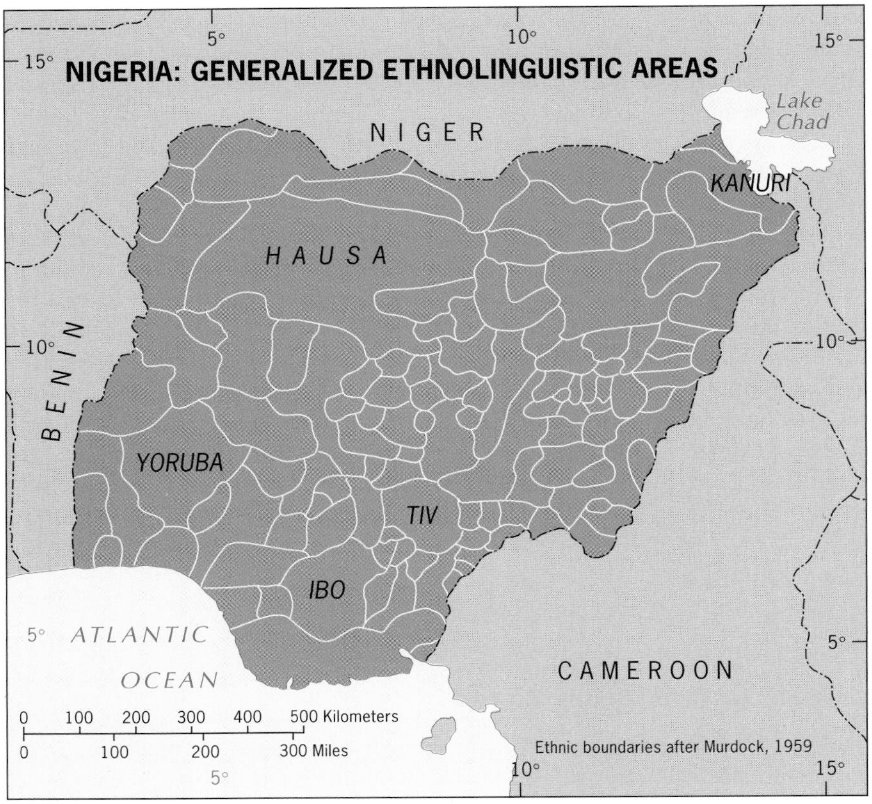

Figure 10-7 Generalized Ethnolinguistic Areas of Nigeria. This map is actually a simplification of the ethnolinguistic mosaic of Nigeria. *Source*: Detail from a map in G. P. Murdock, *Africa: It's Peoples and Their Culture History*. New York: McGraw-Hill, 1972.

for so long, but have also kept it from spilling over into violence.

Nigeria

Nigeria's multilingualism is much more complicated than that of either Canada or Belgium. Nigeria, with a population of over 100 million, is a former colony characterized by almost unimaginable linguistic diversity. It has three major regional languages—more than a dozen major local languages spoken by 1 to 5 million people, and 230 lesser tongues (Fig. 10-7). The three major regional languages—Hausa (the old lingua franca of the north, now spoken by some 35 million northerners), Yoruba (the leading language of the southwest, with 25 million speakers), and Ibo (the major language of the southeast, spoken by more than 20 million people)—are strongly associated with regional cultures and thus are unsuitable as national languages. Upon becoming independent, Nigeria decided to adopt English as its "official" language, as India had done earlier. When Nigeria's 20 million schoolchildren go to school, they first must learn English, which is used for all subsequent instruction.

Certainly, the use of English has helped Nigeria avoid cultural conflicts based on language, but Nigerian educators are having second thoughts about the policy. Upon entering school, children who have grown up speaking a local language are suddenly confronted with a new, unfamiliar language. The time and energy that must be spent learning the lingua franca are taken away from the learning of other important subjects. Moreover, for many students knowledge of English is irrelevant if they emerge from school (as many do after only six years) unable to function in local Nigerian society. Nigeria thus is having serious doubts about its relationship with the lingua franca brought there by the colonists who established their multiethnic country in the first place.

◆ OFFICIAL LANGUAGES

India and Nigeria are not the only countries that have chosen to use an "umbrella" language. Several dozen countries have embraced the concept of an ***official language***. In theory, an official language, already used by the educated and politically powerful elite, will enhance communication and interaction among peoples who speak different traditional languages.

As Table 10-1 shows, many former African colonies have adopted English, French, or Portuguese as their official language, even though they have gained independence from former imperial powers. Thus Portuguese is the official language of Angola, English is the language of Nigeria and Ghana, and French is the language of Côte d'Ivoire.

Such a policy is not without risks. As we noted in the case of Nigeria, the long-term results of using a foreign

Table 10-1 Official Languages of Selected Countries, 2002

Country	Language (s)
Angola	Portuguese
Benin	French
Botswana	English
Brunei	English, Malay
Burundi	French
Cameroon	French, English
Canada	English, French
Central African Republic	French
Chad	French
Congo	French
Djibouti	French, Arabic
Dominica	English
Equatorial Guinea	Spanish
Fiji	English, Fijian
Gabon	French
Ghana	English
Guinea	French
India	English, Hindi
Indonesia	Bahasa, Indonesian
Ivory Coast (Côte d'Ivoire)	French
Kenya	Swahili
Lesotho	English, Sesotho
Madagascar	French, Malagasy
Malawi	English, Chichewa
Mali	French
Mauritania	French, Arabic
Moçambique	Portuguese
Niger	French
Nigeria	English
Peru	Spanish, Quechuan
Philippines	English, Pilipino (Tagalog)
Rwanda	French, Kinyarwanda
Senegal	French
Seychelles	French, English
Sierra Leone	English
Singapore	English, Malay, Chinese, Tamil
Somalia	English, Somali
South Africa	English, Xhosa and 9 others
Suriname	Dutch
Swaziland	English, SiSwati
Tanzania	English, Swahili
Togo	French
Uganda	English
Zimbabwe	English

language may not always be positive. In some countries, including India, citizens objected to using a language that they associated with colonial repression. In response, some former colonies chose not just one but two official languages: the European colonial language plus one of the country's own major languages. As Table 10-1 shows, English and Hindi are official languages of India. Similarly, English and Swahili are official languages of Tanzania. In Mauritania, French and Arabic are official languages. But this solution was not always enough. When Hindi was given official status in India, riots and disorder broke out in non-Hindi areas of the country. Kenya, which at first made English and Swahili its official languages, decided to drop English in the face of public opposition to "archaic" rules requiring candidates for public office to pass a test of their ability to use English.

Further inspection of Table 10-1 reveals some noteworthy relationships. French and English are both official languages in the African country of Cameroon because an English-speaking province was welded to the French-dominated colony shortly after independence. In Peru, Spanish and the Native American (Amerindian) language Quechuan have official status and are found in distinct regions. In the Philippines, English and a creolized Spanish, Pilipino, are both official languages. Tiny Singapore, the city-state at the tip of the Malay Peninsula, has four official languages: English, Chinese, Malay, and Tamil, an Indian tongue. South Africa has the largest number of official languages—eleven.

As would be expected, Canada recognizes both English and French not only as official languages but as equals in all governmental settings. The United States, on the other hand, has never proclaimed an official language, although there have been many demands that it do so.

◆ TOPONYMY

Place-names can tell us much about the historical migration of peoples and the views they held about the places they inhabited. The systematic study of place-names is known as ***toponymy***. In the United States, a classic work on the topic is George Stewart's *Names on the Land: A Historical Account of Place-Naming in the United States* (1958). There are also numerous studies dealing with the significance of place-names in individual states or regions.

Place-names can reveal much about a culture area even when time has erased other evidence. A cluster of Welsh place-names in Pennsylvania, French place-names in Louisiana, or Dutch place-names in Michigan not only reveals national origins but may also provide insight into language and dialect, routes of diffusion, and ways of life. For example, amid the Portuguese place-names of Santa Catarina State, Brazil, lies the town named Blumenau. If you check more closely, you will discover that German immigrants played major roles in the development of this southern Brazilian state. The fondness for flowers reflected in so many German place-names (Blumberg, Blumenhof, Blumenort, Blumenthal, Blumenstein) is reflected on the map in this part of South America.

Toponyms (place-names) make reading a map a fruitful and sometimes revealing exercise. A careful eye will spot Roman names on the map of Britain, German names on the map of France, and Dutch names in Australia. Sometimes the links are harder to find. The Brazilian State of Bahia has a number of place-names that seem to have originated in West Africa, especially Benin and Nigeria. Indeed, these two areas were linked by the forced migration of enslaved Africans.

Two-Part Names

Many place-names consist of two parts, sometimes connected and sometimes separate: a specific (or given) part and a generic (or classifying) part. For example, the capital of the Netherlands, Amster/dam, refers to the city's major river (the Amstel) and the dam that made possible the settlement of the site. The name Battle Creek (Michigan) consists of a reference to an event (specific) and a landscape feature (generic). Johns/town, Pitts/burgh, Nash/ville, Chapel Hill, and Little Rock are among the many additional examples that could be cited.

Such generic names can sometimes be linked to each of the three source areas of U.S. dialects and their westward diffusion. In the North, towns and cities were typically laid out by compass directions. To this day, foreign visitors are impressed by the use of these directions to show the way ("go four blocks east, then three blocks north"). This led to the naming of adjacent settlements by direction as well: East Lansing (Michigan), West Chester (Pennsylvania), North Chicago (Illinois), South St. Paul (Minnesota). This pattern is mainly (though not exclusively) a northern phenomenon.

Classification of Place-Names

Many approaches are used in naming places, but the University of California, Berkeley, English professor George Stewart recognized that certain themes dominate. He developed a classification scheme focused on 10 basic types of place-names:

descriptive names (Rocky Mountains)

associative names (Mill Valley, California)

incident names (Battle Creek, Michigan)

possessive names (Johnson City, Texas)

commemorative names (San Francisco)

commendatory names (Paradise Valley, Arizona)

folk-etymology names (Plains, Georgia, or Academia, Pennsylvania)

manufactured names (Truth or Consequences, New Mexico)

mistake names, involving historic errors in identification or translation (such as Lasker, North Carolina, named after the state of Alaska!)

so-called **shift** names (relocated names; double names for the same feature—for example, Alpine Mountain)

Each of these categories is rooted in cultural geography. For example, the capital of Russia has an associative place-name. Moscow is actually spelled *Moskva* in Russian, but *kva* is Finnish for water. A check on other toponyms in the Moscow region confirms the ancient presence of Finnish peoples in what is now the Russian heartland. Another example is the southern tip of South America, Cape Horn, which can be categorized as a mistake name. The Dutch named this area Cape Hoorn, after a Dutch town. The English interpreted this as Cape Horn, which the Spanish, in turn, translated into *Cabo Hornos*—meaning Cape of Ovens!

Changing Place-Names

Like language itself, the names of places can elicit strong passions. When African colonies became independent countries, one of the first acts of many of the new governments was to change the names of places that had been named after colonial figures. Not only were the names of cities and towns changed, but also several countries were renamed: Upper Volta to Burkina Faso, Gold Coast to Ghana, Nyasaland to Malawi, Northern and Southern Rhodesia to Zambia and Zimbabwe, respectively, and many more. New names such as Sri Lanka (Ceylon), Bangladesh (East Pakistan), and Indonesia (Netherlands East Indies) appeared on the map of Asia.

Some years after General Mobutu Sese Seko seized control of the former Belgian Congo in Equatorial Africa, he renamed the country Zaïre. At first other governments and international agencies did not take this move seriously, but Mobutu's decision eventually had to be recognized. Maps and atlases were changed. The Congo's money, the franc, became the newly printed zaïre. Even the fabled Congo River was renamed the Zaïre.

In 1997, when the revolutionary leader Laurent Kabila ousted Mobutu and established his regime in the capital, Kinshasa, one of his first acts was to rename the country. It became the Democratic Republic of the Congo, and Zaïre thus got its colonial name back—at least in its short form. Renaming countries after revolutionary successes or military coups has become increasingly common. In 1989 the generals who had taken over the government of Burma changed their country's thousand-year-old name to Myanmar. This name, too, is hotly contested and may not outlast the next revolution.

Some embattled locales have more than one name at the same time. Argentinians refer to the Islas Malvinas, a small archipelago in the southwest Atlantic that the

British call the Falkland Islands. In 1982 Argentina's invasion of the Malvinas was repelled by British forces, and the Falklands remained under the British Crown. The war ended in a matter of weeks, but the underlying dispute lingers, and so do both names.

In the western Pacific, between Japan's Okinawa and Taiwan, lies a group of eight uninhabited islands that are claimed both by China, which calls them the Diaoyu, and by Japan, which calls them the Senkakus. In 1996 a band of Japanese nationalist activists built a lighthouse and memorial on one of the islands, enraging Chinese authorities. This issue is far from settled, and both names will remain on maps for years to come.

Changes in the names of cities and towns, however, often evoke stronger reactions than changes in the names of territories. Some governments have carried this campaign further than others, changing not only European names but even indigenous names that were thought to have a colonial tinge. Thus Leopoldville (named after a Belgian king) became Kinshasa, capital of the Congo; Salisbury (Zimbabwe), named after a British leader, was renamed Harare; and Lourenço Marques, commemorating a Portuguese naval hero, became Maputo. On the other hand, Etoile (the Congo), Colleen Bawn (Zimbabwe), and Cabo Delgado (Moçambique) remained on the postcolonial map.

The relatively recent round of name-changing occurred during and after the collapse of the Soviet Union. Thousands of places named after Soviet-era personalities or slogans were renamed—sometimes to their earlier Czarist-era names. Leningrad reverted to St. Petersburg, Sverdlovsk went back to Yekaterinburg (its name under the Czars), and Stalingrad was renamed Volgograd. Reformers, nationalists, and unreformed communists argued bitterly over these changes, and many people continued to address their mail according to the older usage.

Today, the government of South Africa is wrestling with pressures for and against place-name changes. It has restructured the country's administrative framework, creating nine provinces out of four and giving some of the new ones African names (Mpumalanga for the new Eastern Transvaal, Gauteng for a new central province). One of the old provinces, Natal, has become Kwazulu-Natal. Some names of towns and villages have been changed, but South Africa's map still includes many names from the Boer-British and Apartheid periods. Name changes can evoke strong reactions, and the government is trying to move slowly and carefully to avoid arousing emotions in this still-divided country.

◆ LANGUAGE AND THE GLOBAL CULTURAL MOSAIC

Obviously, language provides a wide range of opportunities for research and study. It is a vital element in the reconstruction of past cultures. The transmittal of oral literature and its interpretation opens up whole new possibilities. The professional storyteller in an African village is not just a picturesque figure; the storyteller's tales contain the history and psyche of a people. The study of dialects and the spatial character of word changes can tell us much about the movement of people, their external contacts or isolation, their former distribution, and more.

Language can also reveal much about the way people view reality. In their structure and vocabulary and in their ability (or inability) to express certain concepts and ideas, languages reflect the way people think about and perceive their world. There are African languages that have no word or term for the concept of a god. Some Asian languages have no tenses, no system for reporting chronological events. Given our own culture's preoccupation with dating and timing, it would be difficult for us to understand how speakers of those languages perceive the world about them.

Language and religion are two cornerstones of culture. Ethnic consciousness is aroused as deeply by religious fervor as it is by issues of language. Like language, religion has ancient roots that are not well understood. From a cluster of sources, the world's great religions diffused widely—a process that continues today. We turn next to this vital dimension of human culture in a spatial context.

◆ KEY TERMS ◆

creole	lingua franca	official language
creolization	monolingual states	pidgin
Esperanto	multilingual states	toponymy

◆ APPLYING GEOGRAPHIC KNOWLEDGE ◆

1. Over the more than two centuries of its existence, the United States has been a largely English-speaking country. For African-Americans, European-Americans, and Asian-Americans, English became the first (often the only) language. Today, Spanish is challenging this English monopoly. Geographic factors play a major role in this process. Explain how and why.

2. You have been put in charge of a group of Peace Corps volunteers who are going to Kenya to assist in the country's schools. An intensive language-training period will form part of the volunteers' preparation, but the group will study only one of Kenya's numerous languages. How will you decide on the language to be studied? Should it be that of the most powerful political group that dominates the government in Nairobi? Should it be one of the languages spoken in the rural areas? Is there another option?

Part Three

At Issue: Revisited

Why do regimes in multilingual countries seek to promote a single national language? What are the consequences of such initiatives?

Countries often seek to promote a single national language to facilitate internal integration. If the language in question can be presented as a more-or-less neutral *lingua franca* that can simply function as an aid to communication, such initiatives can provide a bridge among linguistic communities. However, in situations where antagonisms have developed among different ethnolinguistic groups and where the language of one of those groups is the proposed national standard, the effort to promote a single national language can exacerbate existing social divisions. Language, then, is far from a neutral tool of communication; it is at the heart of cultural identity, and its status can greatly influence the nature of intercultural contact.

◆ SELECTED REFERENCES ◆

Part Three The Global Linguistic Model

Baron, D. *The English Only Question* (New Haven, Conn.: Yale University Press, 1990).

Bellwood, P. "The Austronesian Dispersal and the Origin of Languages," *Scientific American*, July 1991, pp. 88–93.

Brenton, R. J. L. *Geolinguistics: Language Dynamics and Ethnolinguistic Geography*. Translated by H.F. Schiffman (Ottawa: University of Ottawa Press, 1991).

Brunn, S. D. "Geography: The World Around the World," *Annals of the Association of American Geographers*, December (2000) 905, no. 4: 759–763.

Cavalli-Sforza, L. L. "Genes, Peoples and Languages," *Scientific American*, November 1991, pp. 104–110.

de Carvalho, C. "The Geography of Languages," in P. Wagner & M. Mikesell, eds. *Readings in Cultural Geography* (Chicago: University of Chicago Press, 1962), 75–93.

Cormack, M. "Minority Language Media in Western Europe: Preliminary Considerations" *Journal of Communication*, (March 1998) 13, no.1: 759–763.

Crystal, D. *The Cambridge Encyclopedia of Language*. 2nd ed. (New York: Cambridge University Press, 1997).

Crystal, D. *English as a Global Language* (New York: Cambridge University Press, 1997).

de Varennes, F. *Language, Minorities and Human Rights* (The Hague: Martinus Nijhoff Publishers, 1996).

Dixon, R. M. W. *Searching for Aboriginal Languages* (Chicago: University of Chicago Press, 1989).

Frazer, T. C. *Geolinguistics: Language Dynamics and Ethnolinguistic Geography* (Concord, N.H.: Paul & Company Publishers Consortium, 1992.

Gamkrelidze, T. V. & Ivanov, V. V. "The Early History of Indo-European Languages," *Scientific American*, March 1990, pp. 110–116.

Gamkrelidze, T. V. & Ivanov, V. V. *Indo-European and the Indo-Europeans: A Reconstruction of a Proto-Language and a Proto-Culture: The Text (Trends I)*. ed. W. Winter (NY: Mouton De Gruyter, transl. 1995).

Greenberg, J. *The Languages of Africa* (Bloomington: Indiana University Press, 1963).

Greenberg, J. *Languages in the Americas* (Bloomington: Indiana University Press, 1987).

Holdon, C. "U.S. Dialects Persist by Both Religion and Race," *Science*, 27 February, 1998, p. 1311.

Kaplan, D. H. "Population and Politics in a Plural Society: The Changing Geography of Canada's Linguistic Groups," *Annals of the Association of American Geographers* 84, no. 1, (1994): 46–67.

Kirk, J., et al., eds. *Studies in Linguistic Geography* (Dover, N.J.: Longwood, 1985).

König, M. "Cultural Diversity and Language Policy," *International Social Science Journal* no. 161 (1999): 401–408.

Kontra, M., Phillipson, R., & Skutnabb-Kangas, T. *Language: A Right and a Resource: Approaching Linguistic Human Rights* (Budapest: Central European University Press, 1999).

Krantz, G. S. *Geographical Development of European Languages* (New York: Peter Lang, 1988).

Laponce, J. A. *Languages and Their Territories* (Toronto: University of Toronto Press, 1987).

Lewin, R. "American Indian Language Dispute," *Science* 23 December 1988, pp. 1632–1633.

Moseley, C., & Asher, R. E., eds. *Atlas of the World's Languages* (New York: Routledge, 1994).

Murphy, A. B. "European Languages," in T. Unwin, ed., *A European Geography* (London: Longman, 1998).

Murphy, A. B. *The Regional Dynamics of Language Differentiation in Belgium: A Study in Cultural-Political Geography* (Chicago: University of Chicago Geographical Research Paper No. 227, 1988).

Pred, A. R. *Lost Words and Lost Worlds: Modernity and the Language of Everyday Life in Nineteenth-Century Stockholm* (Cambridge: Cambridge University Press, 1990).

Renfrew, C. *Archaeology and Language: The Puzzle of Indo-European Origins* (Cambridge: Cambridge University Press, 1988).

Renfrew, C. "The Origins of Indo-European Languages," *Scientific American*, October 1989, pp. 106–114.

Scwartzberg, J. *An Historical Atlas of South Asia* (Chicago: University of Chicago Press, 1978).

Sopher, D., ed. *An Exploration of India: Geographical Perspectives on Society and Culture* (Ithaca, N.Y.: Cornell University Press, 1980).

Stewart, G. *Names on the Globe* (New York: Oxford University Press, 1975).

Stewart, G. *Names on the Land: A Historical Account of Place-Naming in the United States* 4th rev. ed. (San Francisco: Lexicos, 1982).

Trudgill, P. "Linguistic Geography and Geographical Linguistics," in C. Board et al., eds., *Progress in Geography*, Vol. 7 (New York: St. Martin's Press, 1975), 227–252.

Tuan, Yi-Fu "Language and the Making of Place: A Narrative-Descriptive Approach," *Annals of the Association of American Geographers* 81, no. 4 (1991): 684–696.

Williams, C. H., ed. *Language in Geographic Context* (Clevedon, Avon, England and Philadelphia: Multilingual Matters, 1988).

Wixman, R. *Language Aspects of Ethnic Patterns and Processes in the North Caucasus* (Chicago: University of Chicago Geographical Research Paper no. 191, 1980).

Wurm, S., & Hattori, S., eds. *Linguistic Atlas of the Pacific Area* (Canberra, Australia: Australian Academy of the Humanities, 1982).

Part Four

THE GEOGRAPHY OF RELIGION

At Issue

Religious fundamentalism is resurgent throughout the world. From the pulpits of Alabama to the mosques of Algeria, there is a drive toward the foundations of the faith. Growing secularization and loss of local autonomy have fostered widespread feelings of cultural marginalization and alienation. In response, many people have refocused their attention on traditional religious ideas and practices. In some cases they have merged their religious beliefs with their views of how political societies should function—leading to conflicts between fundamentalists and nonfundamentalists on matters ranging from prayer in public schools to the rights of women and religious minorities. Here, then, is the key issue: *Can modern-secular and fundamentalist religious communities and countries coexist?*

Wealth and power of Islam far from its source: the Blue Mosque near Kuala Lumpur, Malaysia

Part Outline

Chapter 11

Religious Origins and Distributions

From the field notes

"I took the elevator to the top of the tallest hotel tower in the city, and was rewarded with a sweeping view over Singapore. At once I was reminded of two tenets of cultural geography: that small-scale maps of religious distributions obscure the intermixing of religions in much of the world, and that Christian religious institutions in non-Christian areas of the world often look prosperous and well-maintained (Muslim mosques in non-Muslim areas tend to display similar affluence). Here, Saint Andrew's Cathedral reflects such wealth: its spacious grounds occupy some of Singapore's most costly real estate between the commercial center and the hotel district in a city that is predominantly Chinese with Buddhist, Hindu, and Muslim minorities. Around the world, the competition for adherents never ceases."

KEY POINTS

- **Despite the urbanization and secularization of modern societies, religion still dominates the lives and behaviors of billions of people.**
- **The distinction between universalizing and ethnic religions is geographically significant, as the universalizing religion is much more likely to diffuse over a large area.**
- **The several faiths of Christianity, having been diffused through European colonialism and aggressive proselytism, constitute the largest and most widely dispersed religion today.**
- **Islam is the world's fastest growing major religion, but like other major religions it has more than one branch.**
- **Christianity and Islam together hold the allegiance of nearly half the world's population; no other faith comes close, and the third largest religion, Hinduism, is not a universalizing but an ethnic faith.**
- **Despite the continued importance of religion, secularism is an important trend in the world today—particularly in the urbanized, industrialized parts of North America, Europe, and East Asia.**

Religion and language lie at the foundation of culture; they are vital strands in the fabric of society. Like language, religion confers and reflects identity, albeit in a somewhat different way. In some societies—particularly those not dominated by modern technology—religion is the great binding force, the guiding rule of daily life. From eating habits to dress codes, religion sets the standards for how people behave.

Like languages, religions are constantly in flux. Although religious leaders and bureaucracies sometimes attempt to slow the pace of change, religions nevertheless change with the times. In the process, the great religions of the world have diffused across cultural barriers and language boundaries. Persuasion rarely leads people to change the language they speak, but it can induce them to convert to a new faith. Conversion still goes on as missionaries spread beliefs and people choose to adopt new faiths. The new climate of freedom in the countries in the former Soviet bloc, for example, has opened the door to religious revival in areas where, until the end of the 1980s, religious practice was carried on furtively and quietly.

The cultural landscape is marked by religion—most obviously by churches and mosques, cemeteries and shrines, statues and symbols. There are more subtle markers of religion in the landscape as well. The presence or absence of stores selling alcohol or of signs depicting the human form in particular ways reflect prevailing religious views. Religion is also proclaimed in modes of dress (veils, turbans) and personal habits (beards, ritual scars). In industrialized societies, such overt religious displays have generally declined, but they are still common in more traditional societies. In the Islamic Republic of Pakistan, the government proclaimed in 1991 that henceforth possessing a beard would be a condition for the appointment of judges.

In Part Four, we consider the sources, diffusion, and transformation of the world's great religions, their regional distribution, and their cultural landscapes. Again like language, religion can be a strong unifying force, but it can also divide and foster conflict. Such strife is occurring in Northern Ireland, the former Yugoslavia, the Middle East, India, Sudan, and elsewhere. The study of religion thus has many geographic dimensions. ◆

◆ THE GEOGRAPHY OF RELIGION

In many parts of the world, religion is such a fundamental part of culture that it is almost synonymous with culture. Thus it is not surprising that it is difficult to define exactly what a religion is. Religion manifests itself in so many different ways: in the worship of the souls of ancestors living in natural objects such as mountains, animals, or trees; in the belief that a certain living person possesses special abilities granted by a supernatural power; in belief in a deity or deities, as in the great world religions. In some societies, religion—at least in organized form—has become less significant in the lives of many people. However, in nonindustrialized societies in particular, religious tradition strongly influences behaviors during waking hours through ritual and practice, and even during periods of sleep in prescribing the orientation of the body. In places where religion is less all-pervasive, its expression is still evident in many practices and beliefs. Indeed, no matter what society you come from, what you eat, when you work, and what you are allowed to do are all likely to be influenced by religion.

If we cannot define religion precisely, we can at least observe some of its overt characteristics. There are, of course, sets of traditions and beliefs relating to a god or gods. There are also a number of rituals for expressing these beliefs. Such rituals may mark important events in people's lives: birth and death, attainment of adulthood, marriage. They are also expressed at regular intervals in a routine manner, as is done on Sundays in most of the Western world. A common ritual is prayer, whether at mealtime, at sunrise and sundown, at night upon retiring, or in the morning when arising. Moreover, ritual is likely to involve the religion's literature, if such a literature exists.

Most religions are characterized by complex organizational structures, which in the case of globe-girdling religions such as Christianity can be extraordinarily complex. Such bureaucracies often have a hierarchy of office holders and command a great deal of wealth. The Roman Catholic Church, for example, is organized into archbishoprics, bishoprics, and parishes, on a worldwide basis. Religious leaders can also exert a great deal of control over peoples' lives as they seek to maintain particular sets of standards and the code of ethics prescribed by the religion.

By now it should be clear how strongly a culture can be influenced by religious precepts. The idea that a "good" life has rewards and that "bad" behavior risks punishment has an enormous effect. Modes of dress, diet, commercial practices, and even the location and structure of houses may be determined by religious rules. For those living in the United States, the daily influence of religion can be seen in the calendar, the holidays that are observed, architectural landmarks, many place-names, and even the slogan "In God We Trust" on coins and currency. Even in societies that have actively sought to suppress religion, such as China, religion has continued to affect living conditions and cultural landscapes.

In short, organized religion has had powerful effects on human societies. It has been a major force in combating social ills, sustaining the poor, promoting the arts, educating the deprived, and advancing medical knowledge. However, religion has also blocked scientific study, encouraged the oppression of dissidents, supported colonialism and exploitation, and condemned women to an inferior status in many societies. Religion is, if nothing else, one of the most complex—and often controversial—aspects of the human condition.

Sources and Distributions

A geographic perspective on religion requires consideration of the locational characteristics of the major religions, source areas, distribution, and patterns of religious affiliation. The map in Figure 11-1 provides a global overview of the distribution of the world's major religions. The information on this map should be viewed as a generalization of a much more intricate set of distributions. There are three significant points to make here. First, minority religions in each of the areas shown are dominated by one religion or another. When you look at a place like India on the map, for example, you will see that it is depicted as a Hindu region (except in the northwest), but other religious faiths survive there, including Islam and Sikhism. Second, some of the regions shown as belonging to a particular religious realm are places where faiths have penetrated relatively recently and where traditional religious ideas influence the practice of the nominally dominant faith. Many "Christian" Africans, for example, continue to believe in traditional powers even as they profess a belief in Christianity. Finally, in a number of areas many people have moved away from organized religion entirely. Thus France appears on the map as a Roman Catholic country, yet a very significant number of French profess adherence to no particular faith. We will look at each of these "hidden" dimensions of the global language map later in the chapter.

First, however, we can learn much from the map itself, for despite its limitations, maps such as Figure 11-1 convey important aspects of the geography of religion. This figure reveals how widely the Christian religions have diffused, the significance of the dispersal of Islam, the connection between Hinduism and one of the world's major population concentrations, and the continued importance Buddhism plays in parts of Asia. Many factors help explain the distributions shown on the map, but all of the widespread religions share one characteristic in common: they are all ***universalizing religions*** (sometimes called global religions). These are religions that actively seek converts because they view themselves as offering belief systems of universal appropriateness and appeal. Christianity, Islam, and Buddhism all fall within this category, and their universalizing character helps to explain their widespread distribution. This is not to suggest that other factors are less important. As we will see, it is impossible to understand the wide distribution of Christianity without reference to the European colonial project. Yet the universalizing character of Christianity was one of the impetuses for European colonialism, and it ensured that the spread of Christianity would be an important consequence of colonialism.

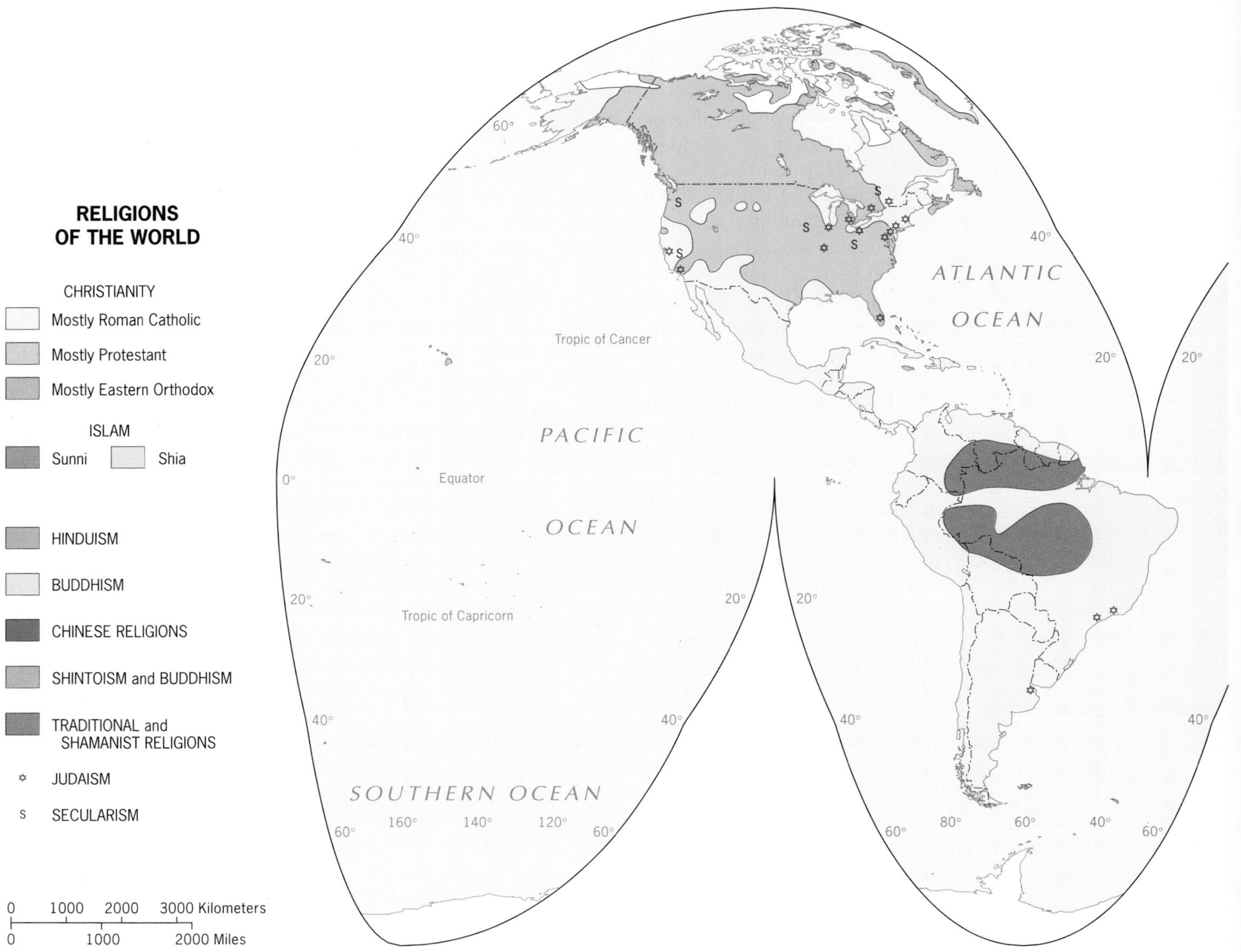

Figure 11-1 Religions of the World. This map shows the major religions of the world.
Source: From a map prepared by Hammond, Inc., for the first edition, 1977.

Universalizing religions are relatively few in number and of recent origin. Throughout much of human history, most religions have been cast as appropriate belief systems only for a particular cultural or ethnic group. These so-called ***ethnic religions*** (sometimes called cultural religions) generally do not seek converts outside of the group that gave rise to the religion. As a result, ethnic religions tend to be spatially concentrated—as is the case with Hinduism in South Asia or various traditional religions in Africa. The principal exception is Judaism, whose adherents are fairly widely scattered. The particular geographic pattern of this ethnic religion can be attributed to forced and voluntary migration—not the successful pursuit of universalizing practices—for Judaism and other ethnic religions do not actively seek converts.

To gain a richer appreciation of the character of the patterns depicted in Figure 11-1, it is useful to view it in conjunction with Table 11-1, which reports the latest available data on religious affiliation. Tables like this one should be viewed with caution, however, because the information on which they are based is not necessarily reliable. When you compare similar tabulations from other sources, you will find major discrepancies. This is due not only to undependable census data but also to problems of definition. Some census counts take a much broader view than others do. Consider, for instance, the table in the *Encyclopaedia Britannica Book of the Year 2000,*

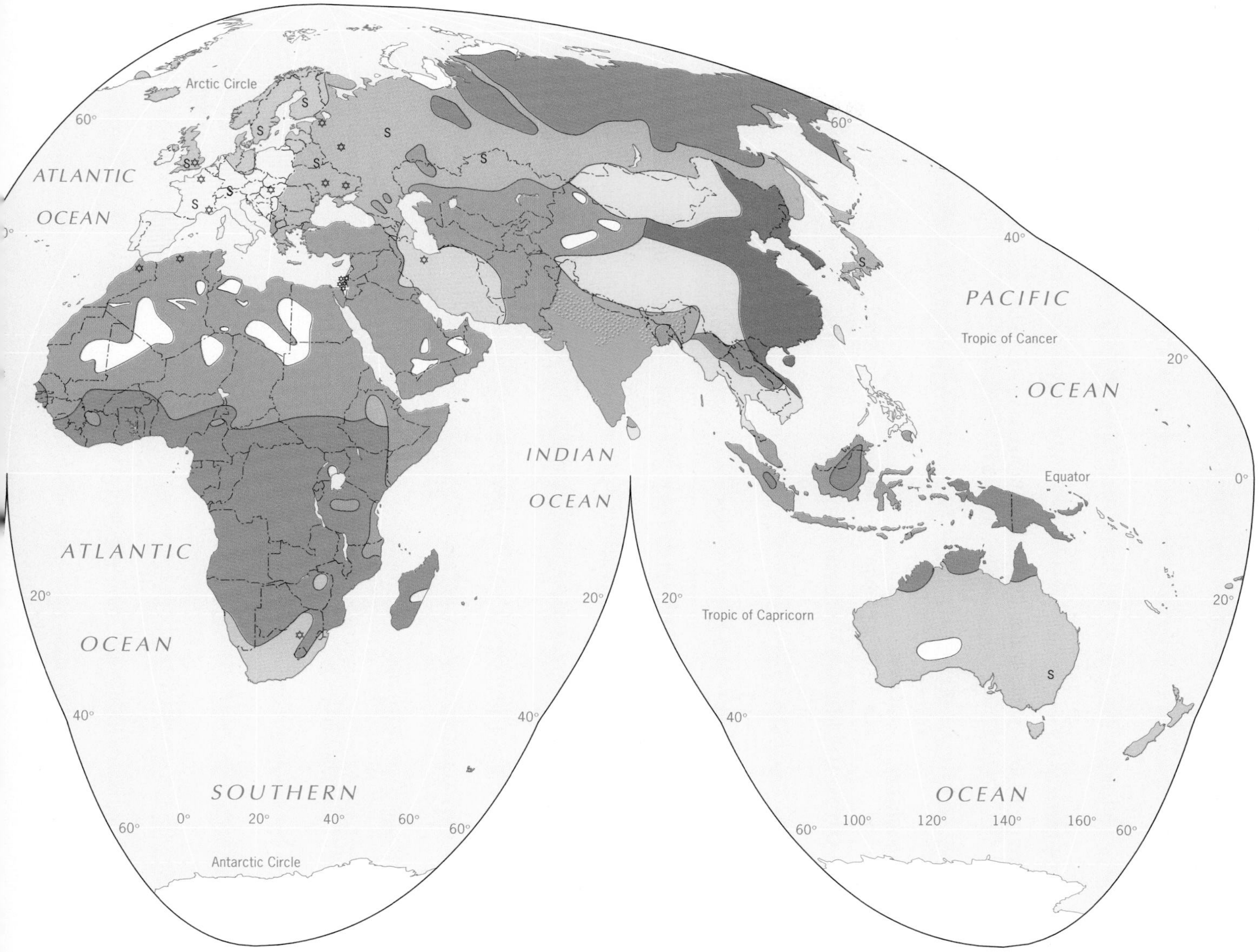

which reports the "religious population" of the world. It gives the number of Christians in North America (the United States and Canada) as 210,300,000. But the *1993 Yearbook of American and Canadian Churches* reports only 147,130,000 "members of religious groups" in North America. The larger estimate, therefore, includes a huge number of people "assumed" to be Christians, many of whom probably are agnostics or attend church rarely.

Table 11-1, therefore, should be seen as a very rough estimate. But certain conclusions are beyond doubt: the Christian religions have the largest number of adherents and are geographically the most widely dispersed. There are more than 1.5 billion Christians, including some 430 million in Europe and the former Soviet Union; approximately 355 million in North and Middle America; approximately 310 million in South America; perhaps 240 million in Africa; and an estimated 165 million in Asia. Christians thus account for nearly 40 percent of the members of the world's major religions. Islam, with more than 1 billion adherents, ranks second, and in fact there are about 300 million more Muslims than Roman Catholics.

Let us look a little more closely at the geographical distribution of the world's major religions as depicted in Figure 11-1.

Christianity As we note in more detail later, the world's religions are themselves divided. Roman Catholicism is the largest segment of ***Christianity***. Figure 11-1 reveals the strength of Roman Catholicism in Europe, areas of North America, and Middle and South America. The Protestant churches prevail in northern Europe and in

Table 11-1 Estimated Adherents to Major World Religions, by Geographic Realm, 2000 (in millions)*

Religion	*Americas* North	Middle	South	*Europe*	*Sub-saharan Africa*	*North Africa Southwest Asia*	Asia South	Southeast	East	*Russia*	*Pacific*	*Total*
Christianity	210.3	145.1	309.2	320.8	240.9	5.1	25.4	91	50	110.7	15.3	1523.8
Roman Catholic	74	129.9	263.9	162.1	98.7	0.4	5.4	69.9	13**	4.9	6.9	829.1
Protestant	130.2	15.1	45.1	100.5	112.8	4.3	20	21.1	37.2**	9.1	7.9	503.3
Orthodox	6.1	0.1	0.2	58.2	29.4	0.4	NA	NA	NA	96.7	0.5	191.6
Islam	4.1	0.7	0.7	15.4	187.1	402.7	330.2	182.7	29.7	3.2	0.2	1156.7
Sunni	4	0.7	0.7	13.4	179.3	261.5	323	180.2	29.7	3.2	0.2	995.9
Shiite	0.1	NA	NA	2	7.8	141.2	9.2	2.5	NA	NA	NA	162.8
Hinduism	1	0.3	0.4	0.7	1.9	2.3	743.7	6.3	0.3	NA	0.4	757.3
Buddhism	2.1	0.1	0.4	0.3	NA	0.1	22.9	169	151.5	0.9	NA	347.3
Chinese religions	0.1	NA	0.1	0.1	NA	NA	0.3	9.3	253	NA	NA	262.9
Sikhism	0.4	NA	NA	0.2	NA	NA	21.3	NA	NA	NA	NA	21.9
Judaism	6	0.2	0.7	2.1	0.1	5.1	NA	NA	NA	2.5	0.1	16.8

*Geographic Realms in Accordance with the de Blij/Muller definition.

**Official Count is 7.7 million Christians in state-sanctioned churches in East Asia, but counting unregistered Christian worshippers, the actual total may be about 50 million. Data from the *2000 Encyclopaedia Britannica Book of the Year.* Published Statistics vary widely, so these estimates must be viewed as rough approximations. This data includes people who claim to be a member of a religious group. Data extrapolated to 2000.

From the field notes

"Driving through the rugged countryside of southern Cyprus, I came across a little orthodox church sitting by itself. A priest noticed me looking around and came over to talk. 'Why is this church here,' I asked, and 'who comes to services?' The priest told me of the church's long history; he said that people come from a wide area to find peace and harmony within its walls. He painted a picture of a church that was as integral to the social landscape as its stone walls are to the physical landscape."

From the field notes

"Standing in the mist on top of the Rock of Cashel (Ireland), I could almost feel the presence of the monks of the early Middle Ages who kept Christianity alive at the edge of the European continent. This was no easy, hospitable environment for human habitation, but those who toiled away in the monasteries, copying books and producing religious art, set the stage for the eventual expansion of Christianity through Europe—and ultimately to the world beyond."

much of North America, as well as in Australia, New Zealand, and South Africa. The Eastern Orthodox churches have as many as 180 million adherents in Europe, Russia and its neighboring states, Africa (where a major cluster survives in Ethiopia), and North America.

Islam The fastest growing of the world's major religions, ***Islam*** dominates in Northern Africa and Southwest Asia, extends into the former Soviet Union and China, and includes clusters in Indonesia, Bangladesh, and southern Mindanao in the Philippines. Islam is strongly represented along the East African coast, survives in Bosnia and Albania, has an outlier at South Africa's Cape of Good Hope, and has substantial numbers of adherents in the United States and Western Europe. Islam too is divided—principally between Sunni Muslims (the great majority, as can be seen in Fig. 11–1 and Table 11-1) and the Shiah or Shiite cluster, which is concentrated in Iran. A comparison between Figure 11-1 and Table 11-1 shows that the largest Muslim country is Indonesia, with nearly 200 million believers.

As noted earlier, Islam has well over 1 billion followers, of whom more than half are outside the culture realm often called the Islamic World. There are 130 million Muslims in India, and approximately 190 million Muslims reside in Subsaharan Africa—including about 50 million in Nigeria alone (see Table 11-1). Southwest Asia and Northern Africa, however, remain the Islamic heartland, with well over 400 million adherents.

Hinduism In terms of number of adherents, ***Hinduism*** ranks after Islam as a world religion, but there are some important structural differences between Hinduism, Christianity, and Islam. The Hindu religion is not as centrally organized as Christianity and Islam, and it does not have two or three major branches. Instead, it is characterized by a great diversity of institutional forms and practices. Moreover, Hinduism lacks a central authority or a single prescriptive holy book like the Bible or the Qu'ran (Koran). Also unlike Christianity or Islam, Hinduism is an ethnic religion that is concentrated in a single geographic realm, its source region (it is regarded as the world's oldest organized religion). The vast majority of the world's 757 million Hindus live in India, although Hinduism extends into Bangladesh, Myanmar, Sri Lanka, and Nepal—and is carried farther afield by migrants from South Asia.

Buddhism Despite its historic roots in northern India, ***Buddhism*** is now a minority faith in that country but remains strong in Southeast Asia, China, and Japan. Buddhism's various branches have an estimated 347 million adherents. Although this is a strongly regional religion, as Figure 11-1 shows, its universalizing character ensured that it spread widely in that region. Like Christianity and Islam, Buddhism developed branches as it grew and diffused, although the divisions among branches are

From the field notes

"After a rather difficult (and, my colleague said, unsafe) trip from Phnom Penh we reached the temple complex at Angkor Wat in Cambodia. This extensive, walled structure, now suffering from neglect and destruction, marks the earliest period of Hinduism's diffusion into Southeast Asia and forms a reminder of six centuries of Khmer empire in this realm. Hinduism inspired magnificent architecture and art, and left its imprint not only on Cambodia but also on Jawa and Bali (Indonesia). But Buddhism supplanted Hinduism in Cambodia, and Islam did the same in Jawa."

less clear-cut than in some other religions. As we will see in the next chapter, a generalized distinction can be drawn between the Mahayana form of Buddhism in East Asia and the Theravada Buddhism of part of Southeast Asia. Yet behind these general terms lies a diversity of approaches to the religion, many of which reflect a mix between Buddhism and indigenous religions beliefs.

Shintoism One place where Buddhism is mixed with a local religion is Japan, where ***Shintoism*** is found. This ethnic religion, which is related to Buddhism, focuses particularly on nature and ancestor worship. It became the state religion of Japan in the nineteenth century, when the Japanese emperor was accorded the status of a divine-right monarch. World War II brought its dominance to an end, but Shintoism continues to attract numerous followers. Just how many is uncertain. The reported figures depend on varying definitions of who is a Shinto adherent. The number of registered worshipers is between 105 and 118 million, depending on the source. Suffice to say that the majority of Japanese people observe both Buddhism and Shintoism.

The Chinese Religions The ***Chinese religions*** also have elements of Buddhism mixed with local belief systems. The traditional Chinese religions never involved concepts of supernatural omnipotence. ***Confucianism*** was mainly a philosophy of life, and ***Taoism*** held that human happiness lay in maintaining the proper relationship with nature. Chinese Buddhism was a pragmatic version of what the Buddha originally preached (see Chapter 12). These faiths survive in China today, but there are no reliable data on the numbers of people adhering to them. The data given in Table 11-1 are rough estimates.

Judaism Our map shows that ***Judaism*** is distributed throughout parts of the Middle East and North Africa, Russia, Ukraine, and Europe, and parts of North and South America. Judaism is one of the world's most influential religions, but outside of Israel it is widely scattered. Today it has about 17 million adherents. The three main branches of Judaism are Orthodox, Conservative, and Reform. Significant differences in ideas and practices are associated with these three branches, but Judaism is united by a strong sense of ethnic distinctiveness.

Shamanism and Traditional Religions Finally, Figure 11-1 identifies large areas in Africa and several other parts of the world as "Traditional and Shamanist." ***Shamanism*** is a community faith in which people follow their *shaman*, a religious leader, teacher, healer, and visionary. A shaman appeared at various times to various peoples in Africa, Native America, Southeast Asia, and East Asia. These appearances had similar effects on the cultures of widely scattered peoples. Perhaps if these shamanist religions had developed elaborate bureaucracies and sent representatives to international congresses, they would have become more similar and might have evolved into another world religion. Unlike Christianity or Islam, the shamanist faiths are small and comparatively isolated.

Shamanism is a ***traditional religion***, an intimate part of a local culture and society, but not all traditional religions are shamanist. Traditional African religions involve beliefs in a god as creator and provider, in divinities both superhuman and human, in spirits, and in a life hereafter. Christianity and Islam have made inroads into traditional religions, but as the map indicates, they have failed to convert most African peoples, except in limited areas. Where Figure 11-1 shows that traditional religions continue to exist, their adherents remain in the majority.

◆ MINORITY RELIGIONS

At any scale above the local, it is difficult to find areas that are religiously homogeneous. Instead, minority religions abound within the major religious realms described here. Many of these religions are the result of migration or conversion. Some, however, are pockets of traditional religions that remain vital even as a major universalizing religion has taken hold around them (e.g., various Native American religions). Others are the product of the long-term fusion of different religious ideas in particular places. The Sikh religion of northwestern India is an example of the latter process. Founded around the turn of the sixteenth century, ***Sikhism*** contains elements of both Hinduism and Islam.

Most often, however, minority religions are the product of some combination of migration and conversion. Consider, for example, the case of Islam in the United States. Most of Islam's 6 million adherents in the United States are the product of a small, but recognizable, flow of migrants from Islamic parts of the world over the course of the past few decades. Yet Islam has even deeper roots in the United States—particularly among African-Americans. African Muslims were among the first slaves brought to the Americas, and some of them held onto their religion against seemingly impossible odds. More recently, Islam gained ground through a movement known as the ***Nation of Islam***. The movement was born in the 1930s and reflected the desire of American blacks to be freed from white oppression. Believing themselves to be members of a lost Islamic tribe, the so-called Black Muslims await the arrival of a messiah while subscribing to a doctrine of self-sufficiency. Fueled by charismatic leaders such as Elijah Muhammad, the movement grew from a few hundred adherents in 1930 to more than 100,000 by the 1970s. The movement has a history of factionalism, but among the million or more Islamic African-Americans today, the Nation of Islam has a clear presence.

Nonetheless, Islam is clearly a minority religion in the United States, as well as among its African-American population. As such, it often struggles for recognition and influence—and has experienced some of the tensions that often emerge between practitioners of minority and dominant religions. Tensions can also emerge between different minority religions. In the 1980s, for example, the anti-Semitic rhetoric of one of the leaders of the Nation of Islam, Louis Farrakhan, exacerbated tensions between certain American Muslims and Jews—and served to marginalize the Nation of Islam further from the American mainstream. More recently, however, the movement has been associated with more broad-based initiatives such as the 1995 Million Man March on Washington, D.C., encouraging male empowerment through self sufficiency and responsibility. The success of such initiatives suggests that Islam can experience further growth in the United States if polarization between different religions communities can be avoided.

Islam in the United States is but one example among many of religious coexistence. The larger point is that cultural intermixing is so pervasive that multiple religions are found in most places. As we will see in Chapter 13, this has sometimes led to conflict. Yet such conflict is often driven by a geographic fiction: that religiously homogeneous regions should be the normal state of affairs. This is clearly counter to the present reality.

◆ SYNCRETIC RELIGIONS

When Christianity moved into northern Europe in the eleventh and twelfth centuries, it encountered traditional Norse religions. Among other beliefs, followers of those religions thought that various animals—real and imaginary—possessed spirits with the power to shape the natural world and affect human destiny. Christianity gained a strong foothold in northern Europe by the thirteenth century, but if you visit one of the early wooden churches in the region, you are likely to find carvings near the door of the animal spirits worshiped by the followers of traditional Norse religions. Christianity may have been the driving force behind the construction of these churches, but those who were involved in their construction clearly weren't quite ready to leave former beliefs behind. Just in case, it made sense to these early Norse "Christians" to depict the forms of traditional protective spirits at the entrance to the church.

Since the early Christianity of northern Europe contained an intermixing of Christian and traditional Norse elements, it can be described as a ***syncretic religion***. Syncretism occurs when elements from different cultural sources are combined in distinctive ways—and this is clearly what was happening in northern Europe. In that particular case, the regional distinctiveness of Christianity gradually gave way to a more mainstream form of Christianity, which eventually lost almost all vestiges of the former syncretic mix when a form of Protestantism (Lutheranism) took hold in the region. Yet the larger point is that the religious intermixing that characterized the area was not unique to northern Europe. Instead, syncretic religions are often found where new, exogenous religions take hold in regions characterized by traditional religions. And the impact can be enduring, as in the case of Buddhism's encounter with different traditional religions in East Asia.

Modern examples of syncretic religions are especially prevalent in parts of Africa and Southeast Asia, where interesting amalgamations can be found between traditional religions and Christianity, Islam, and Buddhism. The complexities that can arise are exemplified by the South Korea case. Korea shows up on Figure 11-1 as an area dominated by Chinese religions because of the influence of Confucianism and Taoism on the character of Buddhism (the nominally dominant religion) in the region. Yet what really occurred here was a syncretic religious mix among these religions. Moreover, that mix was further complicated when Christianity was introduced to Korea at the end of the nineteenth century. Christianity developed some distinctive forms as a result of its contact with the preexisting amalgam of Buddhism, Confucianism, and Taoism—adding another dimension to the country's religious profile. The Korean case shows that behind the apparent religious uniformity shown on maps of world religions can lie many regionally distinct syncretic religious mixes that defy simple classification and cartographic depiction.

◆ THE RISE OF SECULARISM

Figure 11-1 might mislead us into assuming that populations in areas portrayed as Christian or Buddhist do in fact adhere to these faiths. This is not the case, as Table 11-1 emphasizes. Even the most careful analysis of worldwide church and religious membership produces a total of about 4 billion adherents—in a population of over 6 billion. Hundreds of millions of peoples are not counted in Table 11-1 because they practice traditional religions. But even when they are taken into account, it is clear that additional hundreds of millions do not practice a religion at all. Moreover, even church membership figures do not accurately reflect the number of active members of the church. These discrepancies underscore the rise of ***secularism***—indifference to or rejection of organized religious affiliations and ideas—in the modern world.

This should not surprise people in North America, where the church plays only a modest role in culture and society. However, in other countries antireligious ideologies have contributed to the decline of organized religion. Church membership in the former Soviet Union dropped drastically during the twentieth century under communist rule, rebounding, but to much lower numbers, after the collapse of the USSR. Maoist China's drive against Confucianism was, in part, an antireligious effort as well, and reports of religious persecution continue to emanate from China as we enter the twenty-first century. Elsewhere, communist regimes such as that in pre-1989 Poland found it necessary to accommodate powerful religious structures.

Secularism became more widespread during the past century, but the trend toward secularism can be traced back over the centuries. In the Christian world, for example, much of Western Europe was controlled by the Catholic Church in the Middle Ages: politics, science, farming, and all other spheres of life were dominated, if not directly managed, by the church. Following the rise of Protestantism, the priests became less powerful and the fortunes of the monasteries crumbled. The state took over functions that the church once held, and the realms of church and state became increasingly autonomous. Even in modern-day Rome, the center of Roman Catholicism, church and state exist side by side, each with its own bureaucracy and hierarchy.

With this separation came the freedom to choose—not only with whom to worship but whether to worship at all. People abandoned organized religion in growing numbers. Even if they continued to be members of a church, their participation in church activities declined. Traditions also weakened. For example, there was a time when almost all shops and businesses were closed on Sundays and the "seventh day" was a day of sermons, rest, and introspection. Today shopping centers are mostly open as usual, and Sunday is increasingly devoted to business and personal affairs, not church.

There are some exceptions to these developments, of course. Traditions are stronger in some culture regions than in others, and Sunday observance continues at a high level, for example, in the Mormon culture area of the United States. Moreover, Evangelical and other alternative churches are growing rapidly in some parts of the United States and Western Europe. However, in the Christian realms, from Canada to Australia and from the United States to Western Europe, the decline of organized religion as a cultural force is evident. This is so even in the strongly Roman Catholic regions of Southern Europe and Latin America. In Europe, many people are dissatisfied with religious rules regarding birth control. In Latin America, the church finds itself in a difficult position in the face of rapid social change.

The rise of secularism and the decline of church affiliation is not limited to the Christian realms; in South Korea, for example, half of the population does not profess allegiance to any particular religion. Yet other important trends are occurring elsewhere. In parts of the Muslim world, a newfound power based on oil revenues and a rejection of external influences has strengthened Islam's position. Moreover, although there may be an overall decline in adherence to the major faiths, several smaller religions are growing in importance. They include Baha'i, Cao Dai, Jainism, and the Spiritual Church of Brazil. The rise of secularism may be primarily a condition of industrialization and urbanization, reflecting the church's failure to adjust to modernizing society. In contrast, in more conservative, rural societies, the faiths remain strong.

◆ CENTRAL BELIEFS AND SOURCE AREAS

Despite the wide variety of religions found around the world, they are commonly classified into three categories based on their approaches to the concept of divinity. ***Monotheistic religions*** worship a single deity, a God or Allah. ***Polytheistic religions*** worship more than one deity, even thousands, as in the case of Hinduism. ***Animistic religions*** are centered on the belief that inanimate objects, such as mountains, boulders, rivers, and trees, possess spirits and should therefore be revered.

Throughout much of human history, virtually all religions were either animistic or polytheistic. Somewhere around the middle of the first millennium B.C., however, a monotheistic religion developed in southwest Asia called ***Zoroastrianism***. Some believe that the monotheism of late Judaism, Christianity, and Islam can be traced to Zoroastrian influences. Others believe that Judaism itself was the first monotheistic religion. Whichever is the case, the eventual widespread diffusion of religions influenced by monotheism—Christianity and Islam—diffused monotheistic ideas throughout much of the world—thereby marking a major theological shift given the long dominance of polytheistic and animist beliefs in most places.

Remarkably, all the major contemporary religions originated in a small area of the world stretching from the eastern shores of the Mediterranean Sea to the southwestern flanks of the Himalayas. Judaism and Christianity developed in what is today Israel and Jordan. Islam arose through the teachings of Muhammad, a resident of Mecca in western Arabia. The Hindu religion originated in the Indus region of what is today Pakistan, long before Christianity or Islam. Buddhism emerged from the teachings of Prince Siddhartha, who renounced his claim to his kingdom, located in northern India, to seek salvation and enlightenment in religious meditation.

These source areas coincide quite strongly with the culture hearths shown in Figure 2-6, and there can be no doubt that while other developments were occurring in these regions—urbanization, irrigated agriculture, political growth, increasingly complex social orders, and legal systems—religious systems became more sophisticated. Like technological innovations, the resulting faiths that possessed universalizing doctrines diffused far and wide. How and why they spread where they did, and their impacts on the cultural landscape, are the subjects of the next chapter.

◆ KEY TERMS ◆

animistic religion	Islam	Shintoism
Buddhism	Judaism	Sikhism
Chinese religions	monotheistic religion	syncretic religion
Christianity	Nation of Islam	Taoism
Confucianism	polytheistic religion	traditional religion
ethnic religion	secularism	universalizing religion
Hinduism	Shamanism	Zoroastianism

◆ APPLYING GEOGRAPHIC KNOWLEDGE ◆

1. You have been asked to guide a group of students from a Muslim country around the United States. You will point out that this is a society in which the separation of church and state is enshrined in the Constitution. Your guests, however, note that religion remains quite evident in the cultural landscape, in annual and weekly cycles of life, in daily transactions, in government and education—though more prominently in some parts of the United States than in others. Explain both the phenomenon and its geographic variability to a group of newcomers.

2. The map of world religions (Fig. 11-1) reveals that one geographic realm remains dominated by traditional and shamanist religions, while global and cultural religions dominate all others. What geographic factors contributed to this development? Considering precedents in other areas of the world, how might the African religious map change during the next century?

Chapter 12

Religions: Character, Diffusion, and Landscape

From the field notes

"I drove to this great memorial to Buddhist influence the hard way, from Semarang on Java's north coast rather than from Yogyakarta on the south, but the journey, past Mount Merapi and through countless bustling villages, was a great excursion all by itself. I had started at sunrise and Borobudur was still quiet when I got there, the crowds not yet around, allowing views like the one shown here. Built about 800 AD when Buddhism was spreading throughout Southeast Asia, Borobudur was abandoned and neglected after the arrivals of Islam and Christianity and lay overgrown until it was uncovered and restored under Dutch colonial rule in 1907-1911. The monument consists of a set of intricately carved, walled terraces; the upper terraces are open. There stand six dozen *stupas*, each containing a sculpture of the Buddha in meditation, visible when you peer through the openings. The upper terraces also afford a superb view over the verdant Javanese countryside."

KEY POINTS

- **Hinduism is the oldest of the world's major religions; it is an ethnic religion, strongly influencing Indian cultural landscapes.**
- **Buddhism, with fewer than half as many adherents as Hinduism, arose as a reaction to Hinduism and became a global religion. It continues to expand today.**
- **The more tolerant atmosphere in communist China today is reviving both the Chinese religions of old and the Christian and Islamic faiths; Confucianism and Taoism continue to shape Chinese society.**
- **Judaism is the oldest religion to arise west of the Indus River. With only about 18 million adherents, it has a global importance far greater than its numbers would suggest.**
- **Christianity's three major branches (Roman Catholicism, Protestantism, and Orthodoxy) have diffused throughout the world. The Orthodox churches are experiencing a revival in Russia.**
- **Islam, the youngest of the world religions, has two major sects, the majority Sunni and the minority Shiah. This division occurred almost immediately after the prophet Muhammad's death and took on regional overtones when Shiism became the state religion of Persia (now Iran).**

The major religions arose and diffused much later than the great language families. Even the oldest, Hinduism, emerged long after the First Agricultural Revolution had transformed the cultural landscape of Southwest Asia. Christianity appeared while the Roman Empire was at its height, and Islam was founded several centuries later. As a result, the historical geography of the global religions is better known than that of the earliest languages.

In this chapter we trace the causes and consequences of the spread of the belief systems that have contributed so strongly to the formation of modern culture regions. It is remarkable that, after tens of thousands of years of human development and migration, the great faiths all arose within just over a thousand years and within a few thousand kilometers of each other in South and Southwest Asia (Fig. 12-1). ◆

◆ HINDUISM

The Hindu religion is the oldest of the major religions and one of the oldest extant religions in the world. It emerged without a prophet or a book of scriptures and without evolving a bureaucratic structure comparable to that of the Christian religions. Hinduism appears to have originated in the region of the Indus Valley, perhaps as much as 4000 years ago. Its fundamental doctrine is ***karma***, which has to do with the transferability of the soul. According to Hindu doctrine, all beings have souls and are arranged in a hierarchy. The ideal is to move upward in the hierarchy and then to escape from the eternal cycle through union with the ***Brahman***. A soul moves upward or downward according to the individual's behavior in the present life. Good deeds and adherence to the faith lead to a higher level in the next life, whereas bad behavior leads to demotion to a lower level. All souls, those of animals as well as humans, participate in this process. The principle of ***reincarnation*** is a cornerstone of Hinduism. If you mistreat an animal in this life, chances are you will be that animal in a future life.

Hinduism's doctrines are closely bound to the Indian society's ***caste system***, for castes themselves are steps on the universal ladder. However, the caste system locks people into particular social classes and imposes many restrictions, especially in the lowest of the castes, the ***untouchables***. Until a generation ago, the untouchables could not enter temples, were excluded from certain schools, and were restricted to performing the most unpleasant tasks. The coming of other religions to India, the effects of modernization during the colonial period, and especially the work of Mahatma Gandhi loosened

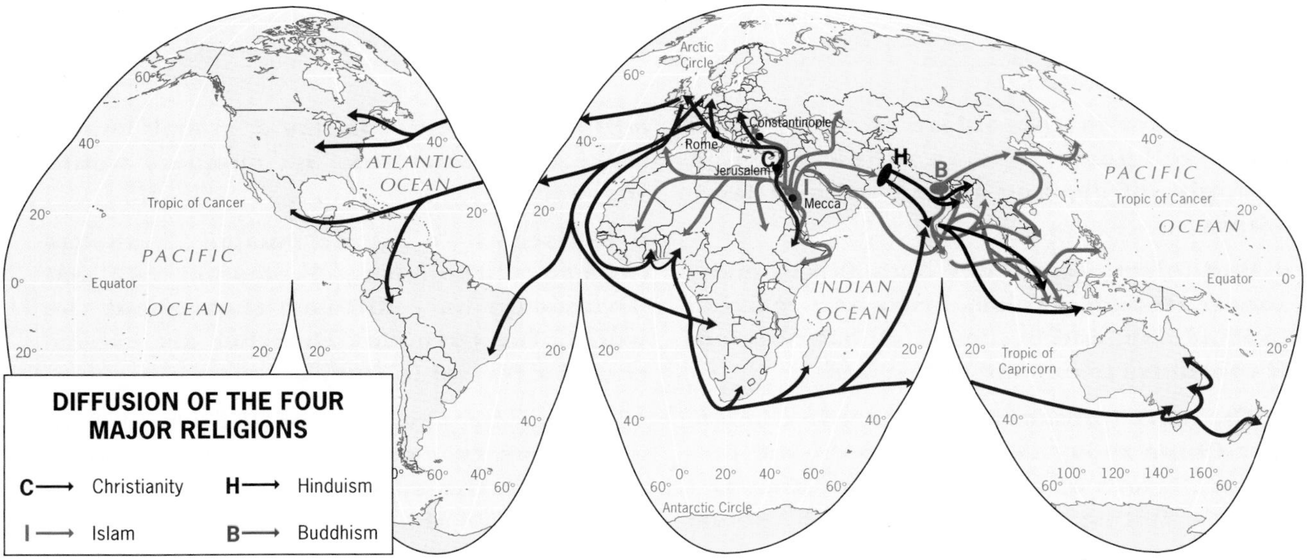

Figure 12-1 Diffusion of the Four Major Religions. Major routes of religious dispersal are shown on this map. It does not show smaller diffusion streams; Islam, for example, is gaining strength in North America, although its numbers are still comparatively small.

the social barriers of the caste system and somewhat improved the lot of the 80 million untouchables.

Diffusion

Hinduism was born in the western part of the Indian subcontinent and spread eastward through processes that are not well understood. Before the advent of Christianity, it had spread into Southeast Asia. It would first attach itself to traditional faiths and then slowly supplant them. Later, when Islam and Christianity appeared and were actively spread in Hindu areas, Hindu thinkers attempted to assimilate certain of the new teachings into their own religion. For example, elements of the Sermon on the Mount now form part of Hindu preaching, and Christian beliefs contributed to the weakening of caste barriers. In other instances, the confrontation between Hinduism and other faiths led to the emergence of a compromise religion. As we noted in the past chapter, the monotheism of Islam stimulated the rise of Sikhism, whose followers disapproved of the worship of idols and disliked the caste system, but retained the concepts of reincarnation and karma.

As Figure 12-1 shows, Hinduism evolved in what is today Pakistan, reached its fullest development in India, and spread into Southeast Asia. Given its character as an ethnic religion, it is not surprising that Hinduism has not been widely disseminated. However, throughout most of Southeast Asia, Buddhism and Islam overtook it. In overwhelmingly Muslim Indonesia, the island of Bali remains a Hindu outpost, however. This is because Bali became a refuge for Hindu holy men, nobles, and intellectuals during the sixteenth century, when Islam engulfed neighboring Java, which now retains only architectural remnants of its Hindu age. Since then, the Balinese have developed a unique syncretic faith, still based on Hindu principles but mixed with elements of Buddhism, animism, and ancestor worship. The caste system prevails, but the lower castes outnumber the higher castes by nearly ten to one—producing less divisiveness than in

From the field notes

"The various religions approach in different ways the disposition of the deceased. Those in the dominantly Christian, Western world are familiar with large, sometimes elaborate cemeteries. The Hindu faith requires cremation of the body. Wherever large Hindu communities exist outside India itself you will see this equivalent of the funeral parlor, pictured here in Mombasa, Kenya."

India. Religion plays an extremely important role in Bali. Temples and shrines dominate the cultural landscape, and participation in worship, festivals, and other ceremonies of the island's unique religion is almost universal. The religion is so much at the heart of Balinese culture that it is sometimes described as a celebration of life.

Outside South Asia and Bali, Hinduism's presence is relatively minor. During the colonial period in particular, Hinduism was brought to other areas as hundreds of thousands of Indians were transported to various parts of the world, including East and South Africa, the Caribbean, northern South America, and the Pacific islands (notably Fiji). This relocation diffusion did not result in new Hindu regions, however, and few non-Indians were converted to the faith.

Cultural Landscape

Traditional Hinduism is more than a faith; it is a way of life. Meals are religious rites; prohibitions and commands multiply as the ladder of caste is ascended. Pilgrimages follow prescribed routes, and rituals are attended by millions of people. Festivals and feasts are frequent, colorful, and noisy. Hindu doctrines include the belief that the erection of a temple, whether modest or elaborate, bestows merit on the builder and will be rewarded. As a result, the Hindu cultural landscape—urban as well as rural—is dotted with countless shrines, ranging from small village temples to structures so large and elaborate that they are virtually holy cities. The location of shrines is important because there should be minimal disruption of the natural landscape. Whenever possible, the temple should be in a "comfortable" position (for example, under a large, shady tree) and near water because many gods will not venture far from water and because water has a holy function in Hinduism. A village temple should face the village from a prominent position, and offerings must be made frequently. Small offerings of fruit and flowers lie before the sanctuary of the deity honored by the shrine.

Thus the cultural landscape of Hinduism is the cultural landscape of India, the culture region. Temples and shrines, holy animals by the tens of millions, distinctively garbed holy men, and the sights and sounds of long processions and rituals all contribute to a unique atmosphere. The faith is a visual as well as an emotional experience.

From the field notes

"To reach the capital of Myanmar (Burma) we had to transfer to a ferry and sail up the Rangoon River for several hours. One of Southeast Asia's most spectacular Buddhist shrines is the golden Shwedogon Pagoda in the heart of Yangon. The golden dome (or *chedi*) is one of the finest in the entire realm, and its religious importance also is superior: here are preserved eight hairs of the Buddha. Vast amounts of gold have gone into the creation and preservation of the Shwedogon Pagoda; local rulers often gave the monks their weight in gold—or more. Today, the pagoda is a cornerstone of Buddhism, drawing millions of faithful to the site. It also is slowly becoming a tourist attraction as Myanmar's door to the outside world is slightly ajar and foreign visitors are arriving again."

◆ BUDDHISM

Buddhism appeared in India during the sixth century B.C. as a reaction to features of Hinduism such as its strict social hierarchy that protected the privileged and kept millions mired in poverty. It was by no means the only protest of its kind. A rival South Asian religion known as ***Jainism*** is another, which bears certain similarities to Buddhism and became influential beyond its numbers because its adherents amassed great wealth through trade. Nonetheless, Buddhism ultimately emerged as the strongest and most effective rival to Hinduism.

Buddhism was founded by Prince Siddhartha, known to his followers as Gautama, the heir to a wealthy kingdom in what is now Nepal. Siddhartha was profoundly shaken by the misery he saw about him, which contrasted so sharply with the splendor and wealth in which he had been raised. The Buddha (enlightened one) was perhaps the first prominent Indian religious leader to speak out against Hinduism's caste system. Salvation, he preached, could be attained by anyone, no matter what his or her caste. Enlightenment would come through knowledge, especially self-knowledge; elimination of greed, craving, and desire; complete honesty; and never hurting another person or animal.

Diffusion

After the Buddha's death in 489 B.C. at the age of 80, the faith grew rather slowly until the middle of the third century B.C., when the Emperor Asoka became a convert. Asoka was the leader of a large and powerful Indian state that extended from the Punjab to Bengal and from the Himalayan foothills to Mysore. He not only set out to rule his country in accordance with the teachings of the Buddha, but he also sent missionaries to carry the Buddha's teachings to distant peoples. Buddhism spread as far south as Sri Lanka and later advanced west toward the Mediterranean, north into Tibet, and east into China, Korea, Japan, Vietnam, and Indonesia, over a span of about 10 centuries (Fig. 12-1). Although Buddhism diffused to distant lands, it began to decline in its region of origin. During Asoka's rule there may have been more Buddhists than Hindu adherents in India, but after that period the strength of Hinduism began to reassert itself. Today Buddhism is practically extinct in India, although it still thrives in Sri Lanka, Southeast Asia, Nepal, Tibet, and Korea. Along with other faiths, it also survives in Japan.

Buddhism is fragmented into numerous branches, the leading ones being Mahayana Buddhism and Theravada Buddhism. Theravada Buddhism is a monastic faith that survives in Sri Lanka, Myanmar (Burma), Thailand, Laos, and Cambodia. It holds that salvation is a personal matter, achieved through good behavior and religious activities, including periods of service as a monk or nun. Mahayana Buddhism, which is practiced mainly in Vietnam, Korea, Japan, and China, holds that salvation can be aided by appeals to superhuman, holy sources of merit. The Buddha is regarded as a divine savior. Mahayana Buddhists do not serve as monks, but they spend much time in personal meditation and worship. Other branches of Buddhism include the Lamaism of Xizang (Tibet), which combines monastic Buddhism with the worship of local demons and deities, and Zen Buddhism, the contemplative form that is prevalent in Japan.

Buddhism is experiencing a revival that started two centuries ago and has recently intensified. It has become a global religion and has diffused to many areas of the world. However, the faith has suffered in its modern hearth in Southeast Asia. Militant communist regimes have attacked the faith in Cambodia, Laos, and Vietnam. In Thailand also, Buddhism has been under pressure owing to rising political tensions. Nevertheless, the appeal of Buddhism's principles has ensured its continued diffusion, notably in the Western world.

Cultural Landscape

When the Buddha received enlightenment he sat under a large tree, the Bodhi (enlightenment) tree at Bodh Gaya in India. (The Bodhi tree now growing on the site is believed to be a descendant of the original tree.) The Bodhi tree has a thick, banyan-like trunk and a wide canopy of leafy branches. Because of its association with the Buddha, the tree is revered and protected. It is the object of pilgrimages to Bodh Gaya and other places where the Buddha may have taught beneath its branches. The tree has also been diffused as far as China and Japan and marks the cultural landscape of numerous villages and towns.

Buddhism's architecture includes some magnificent achievements, including the famed structures at Borobudur in central Jawa (Indonesia). The shrines of Buddhism include bell-shaped structures that protect burial mounds, temples that enshrine an image of the Buddha in his familiar cross-legged pose, and large monasteries that tower over the local landscape. The pagoda is perhaps Buddhism's most familiar structure. Its shape is derived from the relic (often funeral) mounds of old. Every fragment of its construction is a meaningful representation of Buddhist philosophy.

◆ THE CHINESE RELIGIONS

While the Buddha's teachings were gaining converts in India, a religious revolution of another kind was taking place in China. Confucius (551–479 B.C.) and his followers constructed a blueprint for Chinese civilization in almost every field—philosophy, government, education, and others. In religion, Confucius addressed the traditional Chinese cults that included belief in heaven and the existence of the soul, ancestor worship, sacrificial rites, and shamanism. He held that the real meaning of life lay in the present, not in some future abstract existence, and that service to one's fellow humans should supersede service to spirits.

Taoism

At the same time another school was influencing Chinese philosophy. The beginnings of ***Taoism*** are unclear, but many scholars believe that an older contemporary of Confucius, Lao-Tsu, published a volume titled *Tao-te-ching*, or "Book of the Way." In his teachings, Lao-Tsu focused on the proper form of political rule and on the oneness of humanity and nature: people, he said, should learn to live in harmony with nature. This gave rise to the concept of ***Feng Shui***—the art and science of organizing living spaces in order to channel the life forces that exist in nature in favorable ways. According to tradition, nothing should be done to nature without consulting the geomancers, who knew the desires of the powerful spirits of ancestors, dragons, tigers, and other beings occupying the natural world.

Among the Taoist virtues were simplicity and spontaneity, tenderness, and tranquility. Competition, possession, and even the pursuit of knowledge were to be avoided. War, punishment, taxation, and ceremonial ostentation were viewed as evils. The best government, according to Lao-Tsu, was the least government.

Taoism became a cult of the masses. Lao-Tsu himself was worshipped as a god, something of which he would have disapproved. People, animals, even dragons became objects of worship as well, and a sort of Taoist witchcraft emerged.

Confucianism

Like Taoism, ***Confucianism*** had great and lasting impacts on Chinese life. Appalled at the suffering of ordinary people at the hands of feudal lords, Confucius urged the poor to assert themselves. He was not a prophet who dealt in promises of heaven and threats of hell. He denied the divine ancestry of China's aristocratic rulers, educated the landless and the weak, disliked supernatural mysticism, and argued that human virtues and abilities, not heritage, should determine a person's position and responsibilities in society.

Despite these views, Confucius came to be revered as a spiritual leader after his death in 479 B.C. His teachings diffused widely throughout East and Southeast Asia. Temples were built in his honor all over China. From his writings and sayings emerged the Confucian Classics, a set of 13 texts that became the focus of education in China for 2000 years. In government, law, literature, religion, morality, and many other ways, the Confucian Classics were the guide for Chinese civilization.

Elements of Buddhism, introduced into China during the Han Dynasty, also formed part of the society's belief system. Buddhism's reverence for the aged, ancestors, and nature made it easily adaptable to Chinese philosophies. Thus elements of several existing religions were combined to create, if not a distinct faith, certainly a religious way of life. Over the centuries, Confucianism (with its Taoist and Buddhist ingredients) became China's state ethic, although Confucius' ideals were modified over time. (For example, worship of and obedience to the emperor became a part of Confucianism.)

Diffusion

As the name implies, the so-called Chinese religions are ethnic religions that are found in China. Confucianism diffused early into the Korean Peninsula, Japan, and Southeast Asia, however, where it has long influenced the practice of Buddhism. More recently, Chinese immigrants expanded the influence of the Chinese religions in parts of Southeast Asia and helped to introduce their principles into societies ranging from Europe to North America.

During the twentieth century, political upheavals in China led to reactions against the Chinese religions—first during the Republican period after 1912 and later under the communist regimes after 1949. However, Confucianism in particular has been China's beacon for a very long time, and the Chinese authorities, antireligion initiatives have had only limited success. In the 1950s, for example, the communist regime confronted Feng Shui. China's geomancers had long identified suitable gravesites for the deceased so as to leave the dead in perfect harmony with their natural surroundings. Burial mounds were an important part of rural Chinese communities, taking up much land that could have been farmed. The pragmatic communists had little regard for such practices, and they leveled burial mounds during the communalization program. This generated strong opposition by tradition-bound villagers, producing a reserve of deep resentment that was to explode much later and contribute to the revolutionary changes of the 1970s. Geomancy is still a powerful force in China today—even in areas undergoing urbanization.

Cultural Landscape

Confucianism and Taoism are not associated with particular landscapes distinct from Buddhism. Instead, they influence the character of certain Buddhist landscapes through concepts such as Feng Shui. Moreover, they have helped to expand the impact of Buddhist cultural influences because of their philosophical appeal. The presence of Buddhist temples and gardens in the United States, for example, is tied in part to the appeal of the Confucianist ideas that have diffused along with Buddhism.

◆ JUDAISM

Judaism grew out of the belief system of the Jews, one of several, nomadic Semitic tribes living in Southwest Asia in about 2000 B.C. The history of the Jews is filled with upheavals. Moses led them from Egypt, where they had been enslaved, to Canaan, where an internal conflict developed and the nation split into two branches, Israel and Judah. Israel was subsequently wiped out by enemies, but Judah survived longer, only to be conquered by the Babylonians and the Assyrians. The Jews regrouped to rebuild their headquarters, Jerusalem, but then fell victim to a series of foreign powers. The Romans destroyed their holy city in A.D. 70, at which time the Jews were driven away and scattered far and wide. They retained only a small presence on the eastern shores of the Mediterranean until the late nineteenth century (see below).

The roots of Jewish religious tradition lie in the teachings of Abraham, who united his people. Among the religions of the ancient Semitic tribes, that of the Jews was unique in that it involved the worship of only one god, who, the Jews believed, had selected them to bear witness to his existence and his works. However, the

Jewish faith also incorporated elements of other religions. From Zoroastrianism, which arose in Persia during the sixth century B.C., Judaism acquired its concept of paradise and hell, angels and devils, judgment day, and resurrection.

Modern times have seen a division of Judaism into many branches. During the nineteenth century, a reform movement developed with the objective of adjusting the faith and its practices to current times. However, many feared that this reform would cause a loss of identity and cohesion, and the orthodox movement sought to retain the old precepts. Between those two extremes is a sector that is less strictly orthodox but not as liberal as the reformers; it is known as the conservative movement.

Diffusion

The scattering of Jews after the Roman destruction of Jerusalem is known as the ***diaspora***—a term that now signifies the spatial dispersion of members of any ethnic group. Those Jews who went north into Central Europe came to be known as ***Ashkenazim***; those who scattered across North Africa and into the Iberian Peninsula were called ***Sephardim***. For centuries, both the Ashkenazim and the Sephardim were persecuted, denied citizenship, driven into ghettos, and massacred.

In the face of such constant threats to their existence, the Jews were sustained by extraordinary efforts to maintain a sense of community and faith. The idea of a homeland for the Jewish people, which became popular during the nineteenth century, developed into the ideology of ***Zionism***. Zionist ideals were rooted in the belief that Jews should not be absorbed into other societies. The horrors of the Nazi campaign against Jews from the mid-1930s through World War II—some six million Jews were exterminated, many in concentration camps—led Jews from all over the world to conclude that their only hope of survival was to establish a strongly defended homeland on the shores of the eastern Mediterranean. Aided by sympathetic members of the international community, the Zionist goal of a Jewish state became a reality in 1948, when Israel was created under UN auspices.

As Table 11-1 shows, the Jewish faith has about 18 million adherents, but the distribution of Jews proves that Judaism is indeed a world religion. Seven million Jews reside in North America and about 5 million in Europe and the former Soviet Union. The total for Asia, over 5 million, includes the Jewish population of Israel itself.

Cultural Landscape

Jewish cultural landscapes around the world are characterized by the presence of synagogues (places of worship and communal gathering) and by cemeteries. There is no single architectural style that characterizes synagogues around to world, but all have some kind of ark housing the Five Books of Moses (the Torah) written in Hebrew. The most distinctive element of Jewish cemeteries is the five-pointed star, which appears on most Jewish graves.

The most symbolically important landscape for Jews is the so-called Western Wall at the edge of the Temple Mount in Jerusalem. The Temple Mount was the site of the two great temples of the ancient Hebrew people. Occupying a site at the top of a modest hill where, according to the Bible, Abraham almost sacrificed his son Isaac, the temples were destroyed by invaders. The Western Wall is all that remains of the second temple, and Jews gather there to remember the destruction of the temples and to offer prayers. The nickname "Wailing Wall" evokes the sounds of mourning over the temple's demise made by visiting religious Jews.

◆ CHRISTIANITY

Christianity had its beginnings in the Jews' desire to be free from Roman oppression and in the appearance of Jesus. Many saw in Jesus a manifestation of God, but probably even a greater number hoped that he would be more than a spiritual leader and would lead them to freedom as well as salvation. Among Jesus's Apostles was Paul, a Jew who had received a Greek education and who, after the crucifixion, began offering the teachings of Jesus to non-Jews. Paul played a central role in organizing the Christian church and disseminating Jesus's teachings. But Paul's Christian church, with its center in Rome, was not the only Christian center. Alexandria, Constantinople, Damascus, and Jerusalem were also important centers.

After Paul's death, his church continued to grow but met the resistance of Roman authority. Christians were persecuted, and many lost their lives. A crucial event in the rise of Christianity was the conversion of the Roman Emperor Constantine in 312, after which Christianity was the Roman state religion. The Roman Empire soon declined and broke up, and the western half, centered on Rome, fell on hard times. The eastern half, with Constantinople (now Istanbul in Turkey) at its heart, became the new focus of the empire. Christianity thrived there and radiated into other areas, including the Balkan Peninsula. Today the Eastern or Orthodox Church is still one of the three major branches of the faith (Fig. 12-1)—despite the blows it suffered when Constantinople fell to the Turks and Islam invaded Eastern Europe (in the fifteenth century), and again when the church was threatened by the rise of communism in Russia (in the twentieth century).

In Rome, the papacy was established and the second branch of the faith, Roman Catholicism, arose. The power of the church was at its peak in the Middle Ages. Religious authorities often wielded their power in an au-

From the field notes

"In the light of dawn I looked toward the city of Bordeaux and saw a sight that must be representative of a Christian Europe that once was: the tower and steeple of a cathedral rising tall over the townscape. Today, the commercial skyscraper, not the symbol of the faith, tends to dominate urban landscapes."

tocratic manner and distanced themselves from the masses. The inevitable reaction came during the fifteenth and sixteenth centuries with the teachings of Luther, Calvin, and others. There followed widespread friction and open warfare among Christians holding different views. Nonetheless, the Protestant movement—the third major branch—grew steadily stronger.

Diffusion

The dissemination of Christianity occurred as a result of expansion combined with relocation diffusion. In Western Europe, Christianity went through a period of decline during the centuries immediately after the fall of the Roman Empire. Then a form of contagious diffusion took place as the religious ideas that had been kept alive in remote places such as coastal Ireland and Scotland spread throughout Western Europe. In the case of the Eastern Orthodox faith, contagious diffusion took place from religion's core in Constantinople to the north and northeast. Protestantism began in several parts of Western Europe and expanded to some degree through contagious diffusion. Much of its spread in northern and central Europe, however, was through hierarchical diffusion, as political leaders would convert—sometimes to escape control from Rome—and then the population would gradually accept the new state religion.

The worldwide dispersal of Christianity was accomplished during the era of European colonialism in the sixteenth century. Spain invaded Middle and South America, bringing the Catholic faith to those areas. Protestant refugees, tired of conflict and oppression, came to North America in large numbers. Through the efforts of missionaries, Catholicism made inroads in Congo, Angola, and Moçambique. A very small percentage of the people in formerly British India were converted to Christianity, but Catholicism scored heavily in the Philippines during the period of Spanish control.

Today Christianity is the largest and most widespread of the world religions, and although the numbers of its adherents may be declining in some places, it is still gaining adherents in many areas. The faith has always been characterized by aggressive and persistent proselytism, and Christian missionaries created an almost worldwide network of conversion during the colonial period (Fig. 12-1).

Cultural Landscape

The cultural landscapes of Christianity's branches reflect the changes the faith has undergone over the centuries. In Medieval Europe the cathedral, church, or monastery was the focus of life. Other buildings clustered around the tower, steeple, and spire of the church that could be seen (and whose bells could be heard) for miles in the surrounding countryside. In the square or plaza in front of the church, crowds would gather for ceremonies and festivals in which the church played a role whether or not the event was primarily religious. Good harvests, military victories, public announcements, and much else took place in the shadow of the symbol of religious authority.

The Reformation, the rise of secularism, and the decline of organized religion are reflected in the cultural landscape as well. The cathedral towns of Europe are reminders of Roman Catholicism's long-standing dominance. For Protestants, in contrast, a house of worship need not be large, imposing, or ornate. In Protestant regions, therefore, churches often blend into the local architecture and may be identified only by a sign.

In some large cities, cathedral and church now stand in the shadow of another kind of structure, the skyscraper—a symbol of the power of commerce and money. Churches are likely to be built outside the central business district, where land costs less. Except for some large-scale projects (such as the Washington Cathedral), most modern religious structures are not as impressive and elaborate as those of earlier times. Other kinds of symbols are needed to sustain the church in an age of television and automobiles.

Certain denominations have more durable cultural landscapes in which the authority and influence of the church remain visible. In the United States, the best example is the Mormon culture region. The Northeast is another, with its history of places dominated by Catholicism or particular combinations of Protestant denominations.

The cultural landscape also carries the imprint of death. It is appropriate to relate this topic to the cultural landscape of Christianity because no other faith has historically used so much land for burial. Hindus, Buddhists, and Shintoists cremate the dead, and it is noteworthy that this practice prevails in regions where living space and farmland are at a premium. However, Christian faiths traditionally buried their dead, often with elaborate rituals and in park-like cemeteries. Class differences are reflected here: some graves are marked by a simple tombstone, whereas others are elaborate structures. A more impressive aspect of this culture trait, how-

Figure 12-2 Major Religious Regions of the United States. A generalized map of religious regions in the United States shows concentrations of the major religions. *Source*: Modified from W. Zelinsky, *The Cultural Geography of the United States*, revised edition. Englewood Cliffs, N.J.: Prentice Hall, 1992, p. 96.

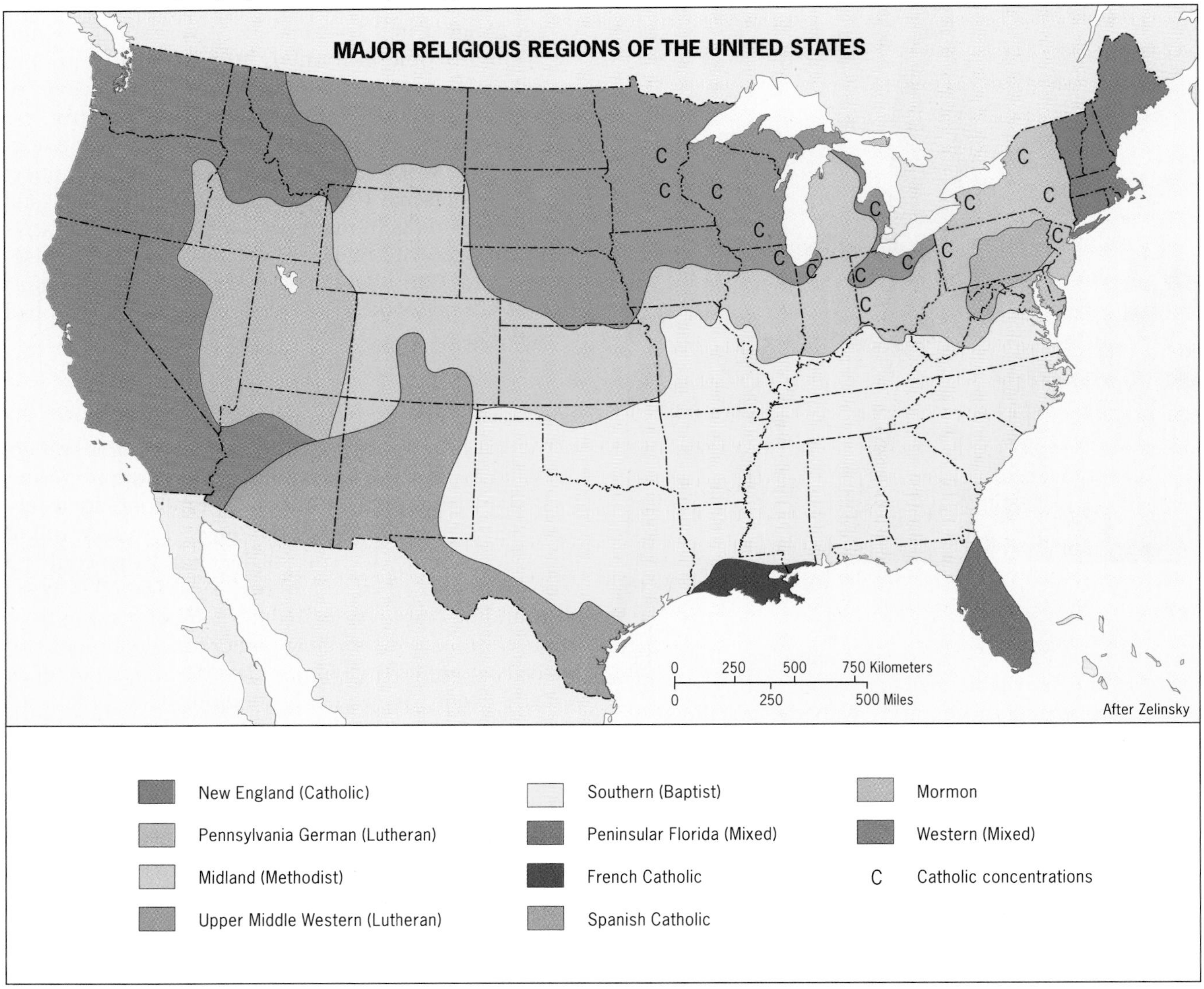

ever, is the amount of space that is devoted to graveyards and cemeteries, even in crowded urban areas where land prices have risen enormously. This is a reflection not only of the power of the church but also of the fact that cemeteries and funeral establishments constitute a significant economic enterprise in Western cultures. Even in Christianity, however, times are changing. With rising land-use pressures and associated costs of burial, cremation is becoming increasingly common—particularly in North America and Western Europe.

Religion and Culture Regions in the United States

The Mormon culture region is only one of several regions in the United States of which religion is a crucial cultural component. In *The Cultural Geography of the United States* (1992), Wilbur Zelinsky constructed a map of religious regions that identifies seven such regions. Figure 12-2 presents a modified version of Zelinsky's map. These religious regions shown on the map will be familiar to anyone who has even the most general impression of the United States. The New England region, for example, is strongly Catholic; the South's leading denomination is Baptist; the Upper Middle West has large numbers of Lutherans; and the Southwest is predominantly Spanish Catholic. A broad region extending from the Middle Atlantic to the Mormon region has a mixture of denominations in which no single church dominates; this is also true of the West. As Figure 12-2 shows, several of the major regions can be subdivided on the basis of local clustering, such as the French Catholic area centered in New Orleans and the mixed denominations of Peninsular Florida, where a large Spanish Catholic cluster has emerged in metropolitan Miami.

The culture regions of Christian denominations in the United States are better known and understood than similar regions in other geographic realms. Data on religious affiliation are more accurate and available for the United States, Canada, and Europe, but similar information for much of the rest of the world is unavailable. It is obvious that a great deal of research remains to be done in this interesting field.

From the field notes

"What is the Islamic World? Standing in front of the main mosque in Paris, France, the complexity of the question becomes clear. This is an important mosque—one of the larger and more elaborate I have visited. Its status as a prominent Paris landmark attests to the significance of Islamic in-migration over the past several decades. The global religions are not just found in neat geographical spaces; they are now found side-by-side all over the world."

◆ ISLAM

Islam, the youngest of the major religions, arose out of the teachings of Muhammad, who was born in A.D. 571. According to Muslim belief, Muhammad received the truth directly from Allah in a series of revelations that began when the prophet was about 42 years old. During these revelations Muhammad spoke the verses of the Qu'ran (Koran), the Muslims' holy book. Muhammad admired the monotheism of Christianity and Judaism; he believed that Allah had already revealed himself through other prophets (including Jesus). However, he also believed that he, Muhammad, was the real and ultimate prophet.

After his visions, Muhammad at first had doubts that he could have been chosen to be a prophet, but he was convinced by further revelations. He thereupon devoted his life to the fulfillment of the divine commands. In those days the Arab world was in religious and social disarray, with Christianity and Judaism coexisting with polytheistic religions. The political order was, at best, feudal. Muhammad's opponents, sensing his strength and purpose, began to combat his efforts. The prophet was forced to flee Makkah (Mecca), where he had been raised, for al Madinah (Medina), and he continued his work from this new base.

In many ways, the precepts of Islam constituted a revision of Judaic and Christian beliefs and traditions. The central precept is that there is but one god, who occasionally reveals himself through prophets. Jesus was such a prophet. Another key precept is that Earthly matters are profane; only Allah is pure. Allah's will is absolute; he is omnipotent and omniscient. All humans live in a world that was created for their use but only until the final judgment day.

Playing off the elitism of the Middle Eastern Christian Church and appealing to the common person, Islam spread relatively rapidly and brought to the Arab world not only a unifying faith but also a new set of values and a new way of life. Adherents were required to observe the "five pillars" of Islam (repeated expressions of the basic creed, frequent prayer, a month of daytime fasting, almsgiving, and at least one pilgrimage to Mecca). The faith dictated behavior in other spheres of life as well. Alcohol, smoking, and gambling were forbidden. Polygamy was tolerated if the man treated all of the women equally, although monogamy was preferred. Mosques were built in Islamic settlements, not only to observe the Friday prayer but also to serve as social gathering places. Mecca became the spiritual center of a divided, far-flung people.

The spiritual and political stimulus provided by Muhammad was so great that the Arab world was rapidly transformed. The prophet died in A.D. 632, but his fame continued to spread. Arab armies were formed. They invaded and conquered, and Islam was diffused throughout North Africa. By the early ninth century A.D., the Muslim world included emirates extending from Egypt to Morocco, a caliphate occupying most of Spain and Portugal, and a unified realm encompassing Arabia, the Middle East, Iran, and most of what is today Pakistan (Fig. 12-3). Muslim influences had penetrated France, Italy, and Turkestan in Central Asia as far as the Aral Sea. Ultimately, the Arab empire extended from Morocco to India and from Turkey to Ethiopia. The original capital

Figure 12-3 Areas under Muslim Rule at Certain Times. Islam continues to expand—particularly to the south—but it lost significant ground north of the Mediterranean over the last millennium.

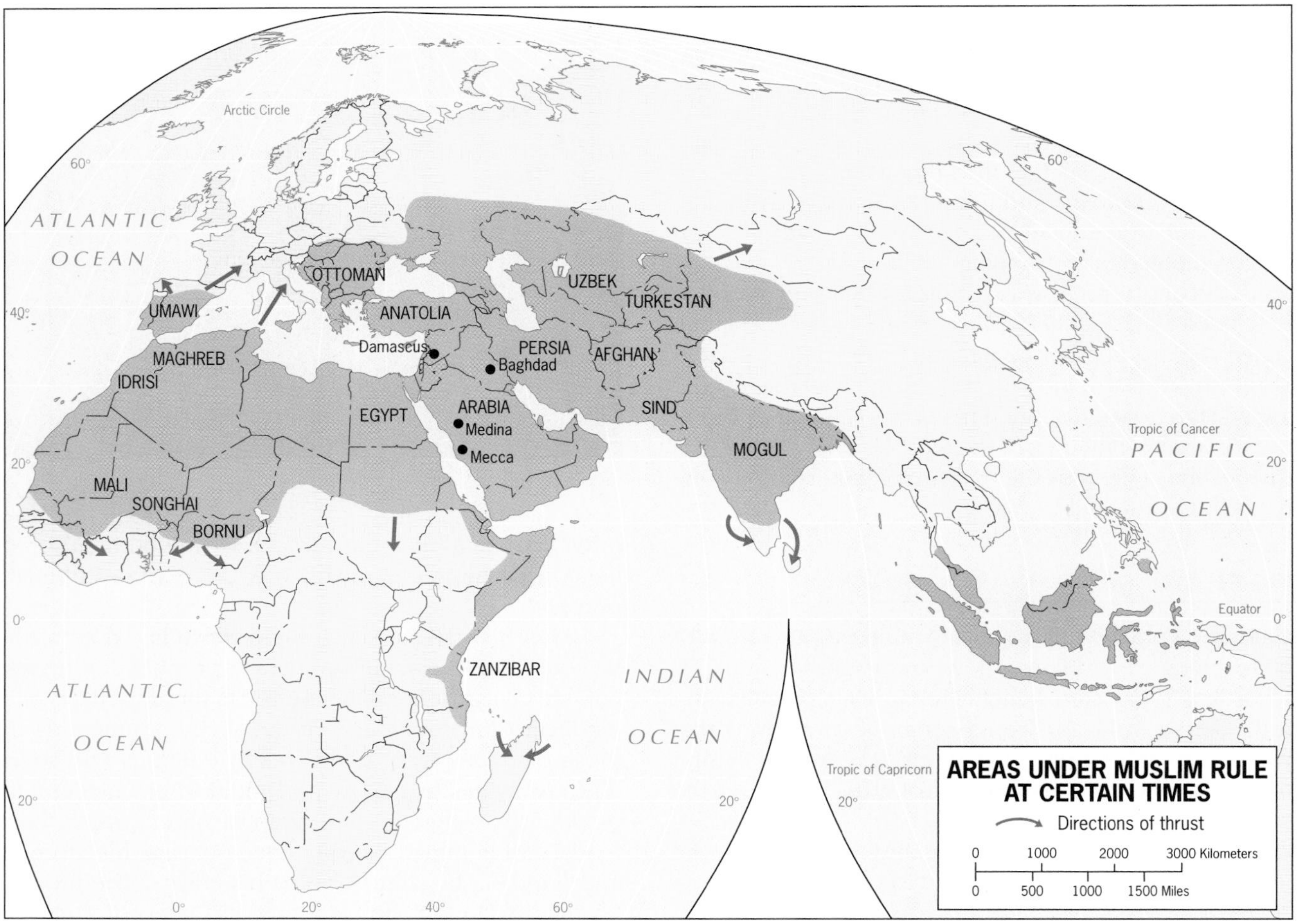

was at Medina, but in response to these strategic successes it was moved, first to Damascus and then to Baghdad. In the fields of architecture, mathematics, and science, the Arabs far overshadowed their European contemporaries, and they established institutions of higher learning in many cities, including Baghdad, Cairo, and Toledo (Spain). The Muslim faith had spawned a culture. Yet not all Arabs are Muslim; there are millions of Christians in the Arab world, as well as followers of smaller religious sects.

Regions and Sects

Islam is a divided faith (see Fig. 11-1). There are followers of many different sects of Islam, including Sufis, Alawites, Alevis, and Yazeedis. The religion's main division, however, occurred almost immediately after the prophet's death, and it was caused by a conflict over his succession. To some, the rightful heir to the prophet's ***caliphate*** (Muslim community) was Muhammad's son-in-law, Ali. Others preferred different candidates. The ensuing conflict was marked by murder, warfare, and lasting doctrinal disagreements. The orthodox ***Sunni*** Muslims eventually prevailed, but the ***Shiite*** Muslims, the followers of Ali, survived as small minorities. Then, early in the sixteenth century, an Iranian (Persian) ruling dynasty made Shiism (or ***Shiah***) the only legitimate faith of that empire—which extended into what is now southern Azerbaijan, eastern Iraq, and western Afghanistan and Pakistan. This gave the Shiite sect unprecedented strength and created the foundations of its modern-day culture region centered on the state of Iran (Fig. 12-3). Approximately 13 percent of all Muslims (about 160 million persons) are Shiites.

The differences between the Sunnis and the Shiites may be viewed as a matter of practicality and Earthly knowledge as opposed to idealism and the supernatural. Sunni Muslims believe in the effectiveness of family and community in solving life's problems; Shiites believe that the imam is the sole source of true knowledge. ***Imams*** are Shiite Muslim leaders whose appointments are regarded as sanctioned by Allah. They are thought to be without sin and infallible, and are therefore a potent social as well as political force. Shiite Muslim ceremonies can be especially passionate and emotional to Western Christian eyes—involving, on occasion, ritual processions in which marchers beat themselves with chains or cut themselves with sharp metal instruments.

Shiah Islam has influenced Sunni Islam in several ways. The passionate quality of the faith has diffused eastward into Pakistan, Afghanistan, and India, where Sunnis now engage in similar rituals. The veneration of Ali has diffused throughout Sunni Islam and is reflected in the respect shown to his family's descendants, the ***sayyids*** of East Africa and the ***sharifs*** of North Africa, by all Muslims. The revolutionary fervor of Iran during the late 1970s and 1980s stirred all of Islam, although it also produced violent conflict along the political-cultural boundary between Iran and its Sunni-dominated neighbor, Iraq.

Diffusion

The spread of Islam from its Arabian source area is a classic example of hierarchical diffusion. Islam reached across the Sahara largely as a result of the work of Arab traders from North Africa. Through their economic ties and cultural influence with leaders outside of Christian strongholds along the coasts, they were able to convert some of their trading partners from animist beliefs to Islam. Though entire kingdoms became officially Islamic with such conversions, it often took decades, and sometimes even hundreds of years, for Islam to make its way out to the "masses" in the periphery.

The diffusion of Islam into areas that had once been centers of Christianity sparked conflict between these two major religions. Islam spread into the Iberian Peninsula and, several centuries later, into southeastern Europe. These expansions led to protracted conflicts between Christianity and Islam. Ultimately, the Iberian Peninsula fell to the Christians (1492). Moreover, after significant expansion in southeastern Europe during the 16th–18th centuries, Islam declined in southeastern Europe—although it did not disappear.

It is important to note that conflict between Christians and Muslims was not limited to Europe. In response to Muslim control of Jerusalem and its surroundings, between 1095 and 1199 European political and religious leaders organized a series of ***Crusades*** to retake the so-called Holy Land. The first crusaders succeeded in capturing Jerusalem in 1099, and Christians ruled the city for almost 100 years. As the first crusaders made their way across what is modern-day Turkey on their way to Jerusalem, they also left a series of conquests in their wake—laying claim to the city of Antioch and a number of other strategically important sites. Some of the Crusaders returned to Western Europe, but many settled, mingled, and intermarried with the local people.

Muslims ultimately retook Jerusalem in 1187, and later crusaders did not succeed in reconquering it. They did, however, establish a Christian kingdom in the region that lasted for a century. Muslims also recaptured the areas in Turkey that had been taken by crusaders. But the Crusades opened the door for European expansion and influence in the Levant region, setting the stage for a troubled interreligious relationship that endures to this day (see Chapter 13).

Islam's dispersal to Malaysia, Indonesia, South Africa, and the New World resulted from relocation diffusion (Fig. 12-4). Unlike Hinduism, which also diffused through relocation, Islam attracted converts wherever it took hold, and new core areas became source areas for

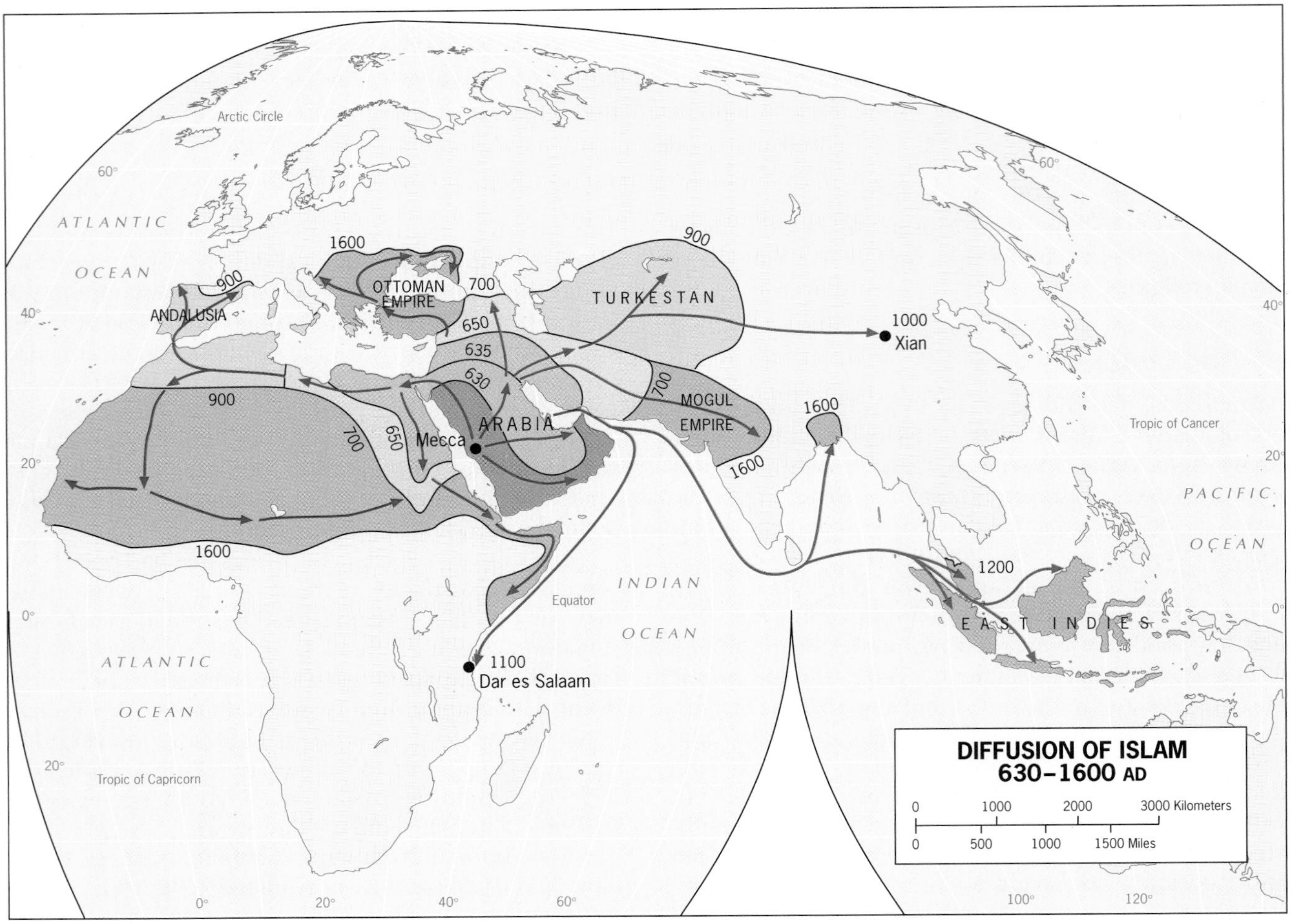

Figure 12-4 Diffusion of Islam. This map shows the diffusion of Islam from A.D. 630 to A.D. 1600.

further dispersal. As Figure 12-4 shows, Islam's regions include not only North Africa and Southwest Asia but also Bangladesh, Malaysia, and Indonesia—currently the country with the largest Islamic population in the world. Although Islam's adherents are concentrated mostly in Asia (nearly 540 million), Africa south of the Sahara (about 187 million), and Southwest Asia/North Africa (400 million), there are also about 41 million Muslims in the nations of the former Soviet Union north of Iran and Afghanistan, and perhaps 15 million in Europe and 6 million in the Americas (see Table 11-1). Islam is experiencing resurgence, and its expansion is likely to continue.

Cultural Landscape

Elaborate, ornate, sometimes magnificently designed mosques whose balconied minarets rise above the townscape dominate Islamic cities, towns, and villages. Often the mosque is the town's most imposing and most carefully maintained building. Five times every day, from the towering minarets, the faithful are called to prayer. The sounds emanating from the minarets fill the streets as the faithful converge on the holy place to pray facing Mecca.

At the height of Islam's expansion into eastern North Africa and southern Europe, Muslim architects incorporated earlier Roman models into their designs. The results included some of the world's greatest architectural masterpieces, such as the Alhambra Palace in Granada and the Great Mosque of Cordoba in Spain. Islam's prohibition on depicting the human form led to the wide use of geometric designs and calligraphy—the intricacy of which is truly astounding. During the eleventh century Muslim builders began glazing the tiles of domes and roofs. To the beautiful arcades and arched courtyards were added the exquisite beauty of glass-like, perfectly symmetrical cupolas. Muslim architecture represents the unifying concept of Islamic monotheism: the perfection and vastness of the spirit of Allah.

Islam achieved its greatest artistic expression, its most distinctive visible element, in architecture. Even in the smallest town, the community helps build and maintain its mosque. The mosque symbolizes the power of the faith and its role in the community. Its primacy in the cultural landscape confirms the degree to which, in much of the Muslim world, religion and culture are one.

This chapter has focused on the world's major religions, but to hundreds of millions of people, local variants of the global or regional faiths are more important. In the United States alone, for example, there are more than 60 Christian denominations, including such churches as the Christadelphians, the Evangelicals, the Moravians, the Schwenkfelders, and the Wesleyans. Some of these denominations, such as the Pentecostal Churches, encompass a dozen or more groups with memberships ranging from under 5000 people to over a half-million.

It is often said that "all politics is local"; the same may be said of church and faith. So when outside forces challenge the comfort and familiarity of religious routine, people often respond violently. Memories of past conflict or repression, or fear of future uncertainties, can make religion a source of strife. In the next chapter we conclude our overview of the geography of religion with a discussion of the problems of religious coexistence.

◆ KEY TERMS ◆

Ashkenazim	imam	Shiite (Shiah)
Brahman	Jainism	Sunni
caste system	karma	Taoism
Confucianism	reincarnation	untouchables
diaspora	Sephardim	Zionism
Feng Shui		

◆ APPLYING GEOGRAPHIC KNOWLEDGE ◆

1. Both urban and rural cultural landscapes carry the imprint of religion. But universalizing and ethnic religions differ in terms of the intensity of this impact, especially in the rural areas. Can you discern some geographic reasons for the differences?

2. Using your knowledge of diffusion processes, explain the spatial and temporal details shown in Figure 12-4. The diffusion of Islam continues worldwide; how is the map likely to change over the next 100 years?

Chapter 13

Religion, Culture, and Conflict

From the field notes

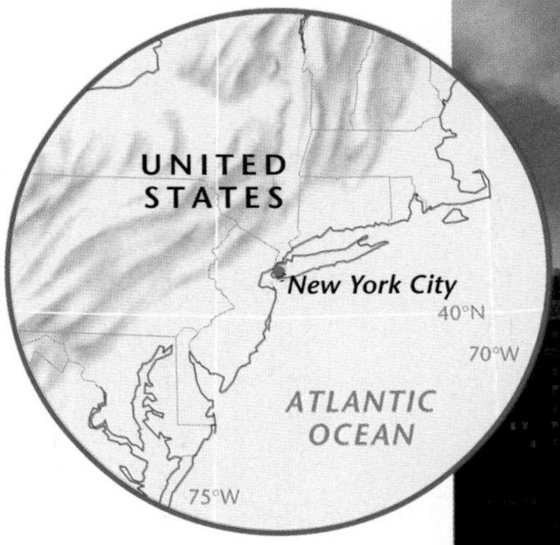

Unlike the other photos in this book, neither of us took this picture. But we watched—along with billions of others—as the events of September 11 unfolded. It is certainly not possible to reduce this horrific event simply to religion, but it cannot be divorced from religion either. Those behind the attack are the product of a revolutionary movement that sees America as a great enemy that all true Moslems must oppose. Indeed, they believe that the best hope for the future lies in a united, radicalized Islamic front. Most Moslems reject this vision, but it has significant historical roots and it has unquestionably become a focus of conflict in the contemporary world.

KEY POINTS

- ◆ **Boundaries between major religions that internally divide countries can be powerful sources of conflict.**
- ◆ **Conflicts among adherents to different branches of major religions can be as intense as conflicts between different religions.**
- ◆ **Religious fundamentalism is a worldwide phenomenon that affects virtually all religions, including Islam, Christianity, and Hinduism.**
- ◆ **Religious fundamentalism often develops in opposition to globalization, but it is also tied to a perceived breakdown in a society's mores and values and a sense of loss of control over local affairs.**
- ◆ **An extreme form of fundamentalism finds expression in terrorist activities. Recent international terrorist attacks by self-described Islamic fundamentalists are tied to the conviction that "infidels" have invaded the Islamic holy land's core over the past 80 years.**
- ◆ **The cultural cores of Christianity and Islam lie in close proximity in Europe and Southwest Asia/North Africa; the prospect of disharmony and conflict between them is growing.**

Language and religion are two of the most powerful forces shaping the geography of culture. In Part Three we noted the role of language as a unifying and culture-conserving force; a threat to the language is perceived as a threat to the culture as a whole. But language can also create a gulf between peoples otherwise united by cultural traits and traditions, and even by a political border. In many countries language disputes fuel the fires of division.

So it is with religion. Religious beliefs and histories can bitterly divide peoples who speak the same language, have the same ethnic background, and make their living in similar ways. Such divisions arise not only between people adhering to different major religions (as with Muslims and Christians in the former Yugoslavia) but also among adherents of the same religion. Some of the most destructive conflict has pitted Christian against Christian and Muslim against Muslim.

Religious conflicts usually involve more than differences in spiritual practices and beliefs. Religion functions as a symbol of a wider set of cultural and political differences. As we will see, the "religious" conflict in Northern Ireland is not just about different views of Christianity, and the conflict between Hindus and Sikhs in India has a strong political as well as religious dimension. Nevertheless, in these and other cases religion serves as the principal symbol around which conflict is organized. In this chapter we examine the role of religion in cultural strife and use our geographic perspective to gain insight into what the future may hold in particular places. ◆

◆ INTERFAITH BOUNDARIES

A comparison between Figure 11-1 and a political map reveals that some countries lie entirely within the realms of individual world religions, whereas other countries straddle ***interfaith boundaries***—the boundaries between the world's major faiths. Many countries that lie astride interfaith boundaries are subject to potentially divisive cultural forces—particularly when religious differences are treated as the source of the most basic social division within a country. This is the case in several countries in Africa that straddle the Christian-Muslim interfaith boundary (see Fig. 13-1). Among them is Nigeria, Africa's most populous state.

Nigeria

With about 110 million inhabitants, Nigeria is a multilingual country. Superimposed on its linguistic diversity is religious regionalism: the north is a Muslim zone, whereas Christianity prevails in the south along with local traditional religions. (see Figure 13-2)

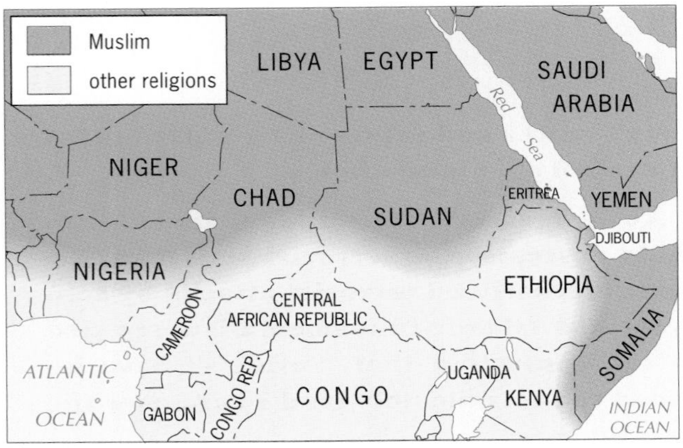

Figure 13-1 The African Transition Zone. Religious areas are shown across political boundaries in the African Transition Zone.

This north-south division puts the main ethnic group of the north, the Hausa-Fulani, in the Muslim camp. The two main culture cores of the south, the Yoruba of the southwest and the Ibo of the southeast, are in the Christian-animist sphere. These groups have shown considerable disdain for each other. Muslim Hausa sometimes say that Yoruba are godless and uncultured. Ibo at times characterize the Hausa as backward and uneducated. Northerners may see the Ibo as money-mad merchants who will do anything for a price.

When Nigeria conducts its census, people are not asked to state their religious preference. The numbers, however, are estimated as follows: Muslims, 55 million; Christians, 37 million; and others (chiefly animists), 12 million. A substantial number of Yoruba, perhaps 2 million, are Muslims. Islam has a moderate tone in Yorubaland, however, and some geographers describe the Yoruba as "middlemen" between Christian easterners and Muslim northerners, defusing the tensions that might long ago have led to religious conflict. In 1993 a Muslim Yoruba was elected president of Nigeria, but the military regime then in power would not allow him to take office.

Islam predominates in the north, but Christian communities do exist—and coexistence long was the rule despite sporadic skirmishes. During the past decade, however, Nigeria's fundamental religious division began to threaten the future of the state. In the north, Muslim preachers are calling for an "Islamic Republic," emboldened by the president's decision to allow Nigeria to join the Islamic Conference Organization (ICO), the global association of Islamic countries. In the south, Christian leaders are outraged by these developments. Calls for secession are being heard in the south, notably in the southeast (where the Ibo tried to secede once before, with disastrous results).

Will Nigeria's location astride an interfaith boundary ultimately destroy the country? The domination of national affairs by Muslims is becoming an issue in the south, and the aggressive expansion of Islam among smaller population groups adds to the problem. The potential for a fracture along religious lines is growing.

Any such development would have enormous social and political consequences. Nigeria is a crucible of West African culture, rich in literature and the arts. In the early 2000s Nigeria was OPEC's (Organization of Petroleum Exporting Countries) fourth largest oil producer. Nigeria's survival as a multicultural society is an achievement on a par with India's, and its Christian-Islamic coexistence has served as a model for other countries with two or more major religious groups within their borders. The breakup of Nigeria thus would have far-reaching implications.

Sudan

As Figure 13-1 shows, several other countries, including Chad, Sudan, and Ethiopia, straddle the Islamic–non-Islamic interfaith boundary in Africa. In Sudan the Muslim north and the Christian-traditional south have waged war since soon after the country gained independence. The conflict is more complicated than that, however. Sudan's northern provinces contain about 60 percent of the total population, but while this region is overwhelmingly Muslim, only about two-thirds of the northerners speak Arabic as their native language. These Muslim but non-Arab northerners have been targets of anti-Islamic propaganda from the south.

Intensifying the struggle between the north and the south was the decision by the Muslim-dominated regime in Khartum to impose Islam's ***sharia religious laws*** on the entire country. Sharia laws, especially the criminal code, are harsh (prescribing, for example, the amputation of hands or limbs for theft). In the south, where people are ethnically and culturally different from those in the Muslim north (there are few Arabs in the south), and where Christianity has made inroads among traditional religions, that action eliminated any prospect of a compromise.

The war in Sudan has caused immense damage. Millions of people have been dislocated, and hundreds of thousands have starved; both sides have interfered with the efforts of international agencies to help the refugees. In 1992 Nigeria sought to broker a peace, and in the Nigerian capital of Abuja the northerners promised to rescind the sharia regulations and allow freedom of belief and religious observance. But by 1994 the north seemed to have victory in its grasp and declined to honor these commitments. In the early twenty-first century, the war raged on.

The lesson of Sudan is not lost on Nigeria: the cost of religious conflict there would be immeasurable. Both Nigeria and Sudan underscore the risks shared by countries at the southern edge of the Sahara Desert that encompass interfaith boundaries.

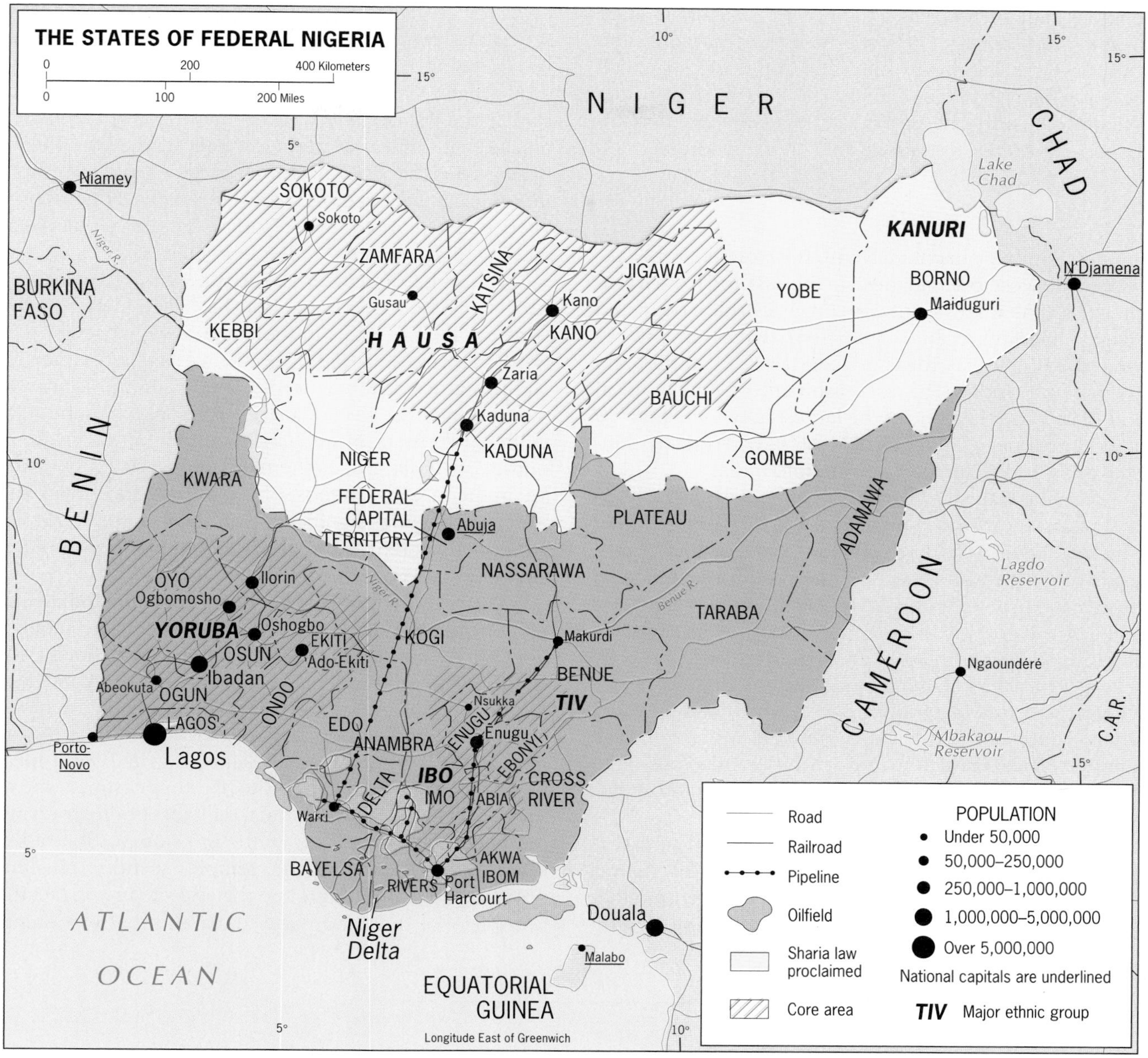

Figure 13-2 Nigeria. Twelve northern States of Federal Nigeria have proclaimed Islamic sharia law

The African Horn

Developments in the so-called Horn of Africa in the mid-1990s have changed the map. As Figure 13-1 shows, Ethiopia's religious map is even more complicated than that of Nigeria or Sudan. At the heart of the former mountain kingdom lies the cultural core area of Amharic (Coptic) Christians. From their nearly impregnable natural fortress, the Amharics controlled the lowlands in all directions. Islam won some adherents at the base of the mountains, but the Christian rulers maintained control (Fig. 13-1). When the last of Ethiopia's emperors fell in 1974, the Amharic rulers still controlled the Muslim Eritreans in the north, the Muslim Somalis in the east, and a huge arc-shaped region to the west and south. But a revolution was brewing, and in 1991 the military dictatorship that had overthrown the imperial dynasty was overthrown in its turn.

In the early twenty-first century, the future of Ethiopia remains uncertain. The revolution that destroyed the old order created a new state: Eritrea. With a significant Muslim population and a history of separate development during the period of Italian colonialism, there are clear cultural distinctions between Eritrea and the empire of which it was a part. But Eritrea's secession did not end Ethiopia's religious multiculturalism. Ethiopia still contains a large Muslim population of Somalis in its eastern zone; the south and west are non-Muslim; and Coptic Christians still cluster in their highland domain. The separation of Eritrea is likely to be only one step in a series of changes that underscore the perils of straddling an interfaith border.

South Asia

Britain's South Asian colonial empire extended from Pakistan in the west to Bangladesh in the east and from Kashmir to Sri Lanka. This giant domain lay astride a deep and divisive interfaith boundary. In 1947 that boundary became the political border between Islamic Pakistan and multicultural India. The establishment of that political boundary produced one of the largest human migrations of modern times as millions of Muslims crossed into Pakistan and Hindus moved eastward into India.

Whereas Pakistan became an almost exclusively Islamic state, India proclaimed itself a secular federation in which all faiths would be tolerated and freedom of religion would prevail. However, the region continued to experience problems created by the disjunction between political and cultural boundaries in South Asia. Conflicts have raged between India and Pakistan over the contested territory of Jammu and Kashmir in the north, where the terms of partition were much disputed and where Hinduism and Islam are mixed. Moreover, at a number of places within India's borders tensions have regularly bubbled over between large religious communities living in close proximity to each other.

For more than 30 years following independence, religious conflict in India was sporadic and relatively minor. During the 1980s, however, several events occurred that led to more intense conflict. The first was a campaign by Sikhs for greater independence. The Sikhs found themselves at a disadvantage in a nation that was dominated by Hindus and in which the Muslims were the most powerful religious minority. The Sikhs demanded a separate state in the Punjab. When this demand was not met, they reacted with militancy and terrorism. In 1984 the Indian Army raided the Sikhs' holiest shrine, the Golden Temple in Amritsar, causing more than 1000 deaths. Four months later India's prime minister, Indira Gandhi, was assassinated by Sikh members of her bodyguard.

The Sikhs' demand for a separate State (to be named Khalistan, if it ever comes about) is based in part on the concentration of Sikhs in the Panjab (Punjab) region of northwestern India (Fig. 13-3). As we saw in Chapter 11, Sikhism arose as a reaction to Hinduism and Islam. By world standards, it is not a large religion; it has about 20 million adherents, more than 90 percent of whom are in northwest India. But as the map shows, although Sikhs are in the majority in most of the districts of Punjab, the State also includes significant Hindu minorities. The situation bears certain parallels to that in Northern Ireland and may be even farther from a solution.

The second development that threatened India's stability occurred during the late 1980s, when the site of a holy shrine claimed by both Muslims and Hindus became a battleground. This struggle focused on a shrine at Ayodhya in the State of Uttar Pradesh. A building housing both a temple and a mosque sat atop a hill that was holy to both Hindus and Muslims, but in 1986 a local judge ruled it to be a Hindu site. Hindu pilgrims came to the site by the thousands, and a militant Hindu group announced plans to tear down the mosque portion of the building and expand the temple section. Muslims protested, but Hindus argued that the site was in fact the birthplace of the Hindu god Rama and that its original

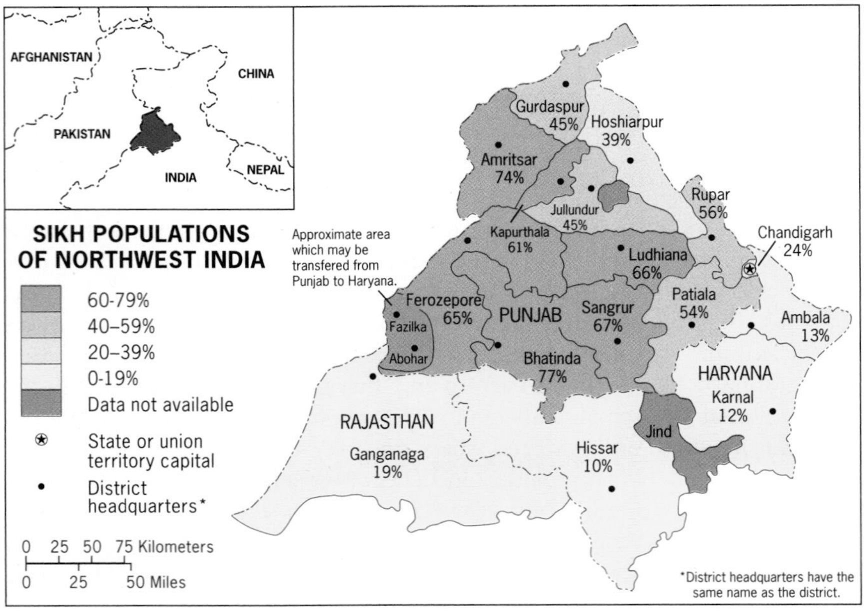

Figure 13-3 Sikh Populations of Northwest India. *Source:* From a map in M. I. Glassner and H. J. de Blij, *Systematic Political Geography,* 4th ed. New York: Wiley, 1989, p. 402.

temple had been torn down by the Muslims during the Moghul period. In 1989 the issue aroused religious passions throughout India, and the resulting clashes killed nearly 400 people.

Muslims eventually regained control of the site, but in late 1992 a mob of Hindu fundamentalists stormed the mosque and demolished it. Extensive communal violence soon erupted across the country, and some 2,000 people lost their lives—most of them Muslims. Plans to construct a temple were put on hold, but were not abandoned; March 15, 2002, became the new target date for construction.

In early 2002, with the date for construction rapidly approaching, new waves of violence erupted. A train carrying Hindu pilgrims from Ayodhya to their homes in Guyarat was set on fire by a Muslim mob and several dozen people lost their lives. This precipitated the deadliest outbursts of violence since the destruction of the Babri Mosque in 1992, leading to the death of more than 600 people.

The third threat to India's continuity arose in part from the kinds of skirmishes just described. For the first time in memory, Hinduism began to exhibit the sort of fundamentalism and militancy that had previously been associated with other faiths. The beginnings of this trend can be traced to 1983, when reactions to Sikh and Muslim militancy led to "Save Hinduism" marches across the country. Within a few years Hindu fundamentalism had become a major force in Indian politics.

The on-going conflict with anti-Indian militants from Pakistan has helped to fuel the fundamentalist movement. These militants have conducted a campaign of terror in India—murdering the families of Indian soldiers and even attacking the Indian parliament. In response, India has amassed a substantial army on the Pakistani border and demanded that Pakistan's leadership put an end to such incursions. The Pakistanis have claimed that they are seeking to bring the militants under control, but their willingness and ability to do this is not entirely clear. The resulting instability fosters extremism in both countries and raises the prospect of a major conflict between the two.

Conflicts have developed not just with Islam and Sikhism, but with Christianity as well. Hindu fundamentalism is strongest in the north-central region of the country, but it is spreading. To many observers, Hindu militancy and fundamentalism seem contradictory; Hinduism has never been an aggressive faith. But Hindu fundamentalist leaders share the passionate concern for tradition and reaction to external influence that has fueled militant fundamentalism elsewhere, and they are following suit.

The surge of Hindu fundamentalism is reflected on the map. In 1990 political leaders in the State of Maharashtra proclaimed that the city of Bombay would henceforth be named Mumbai (its precolonial name, after a Hindu goddess). The change was fiercely opposed by Muslims, Sikhs, and other communities in the giant city. Soon after the change was approved by the Indian government, Hindu leaders in Madras announced that their city would henceforth be known as Chennai. These developments show that fundamentalism is often tied to the rejection of outside influence—whether historical or contemporary.

The rise of fundamentalism is affecting virtually all religions today, and we will devote further attention to this development later in the chapter. The appearance of fundamentalism in India is evidence that returning to the "basics" of faith has worldwide appeal. The fundamentalist drive in India has slowed somewhat over the past few years, but the situation remains fragile and could easily gain new momentum if further interfaith conflict develops in India, or if the already strained relations between India and Pakistan deteriorate further.

The Former Soviet Union

When the Soviet Union was forged from the czar's empire three generations ago, the socialist planners faced the task of satisfying the territorial demands of dozens of diverse peoples. Most of these peoples had participated

From the field notes

"First trip to the Soviet Union, 1964. We are driven from Leningrad to Moscow. In every town we pass, and in many villages along the way, churches lie in ruins, their roofs collapsed, their steeples toppled. The bells are gone, stained-glass windows now are gaping holes. My host does not want me to photograph these churches. 'Why let them collapse?' I ask. 'Why not remove them altogether?' He points his finger. 'Religion causes conflict. We had many religions in the Soviet Union, and they set Soviet against Soviet. And the Orthodox Church opposed our communist victory. That's what these useless relics are for. They remind the people of our victory and their freedom.' I wondered what might be happening to the monumental mosques in Soviet Asia, and other great religious architecture now under Soviet sway."

in the revolution, and many were rewarded with territory, producing a multitiered political mosaic. The top tier consisted of the 15 Soviet Republics; other territories were of lower rank. Russia, the largest and dominant Soviet Republic, itself was divided into more than 70 territories, each of which had some degree of autonomy.

The Republics not only inherited more than 100 "nationalities" or ethnic groups with their languages, beliefs, and lifeways; they were also heir to parts of two great religious realms. Under the czars' rule, the Russian branch of the Eastern Orthodox Church had thrived, marking the Russian cultural landscape from Kiev to St. Petersburg (Leningrad). The czars also had subjugated the vast steppes and deserts of Central Asia, where Islam was the prevailing faith. East of the Caspian Sea, the Soviet empire included the physical and cultural landscapes of Southwest Asia.

Between the Caspian and Black seas, the Soviets acquired two neighboring territories that were strongly infused with religion. The Armenians, mainly on the Black Sea side, were Christians; the Azerbaijani, on the Caspian Sea side, were Shiite Muslims. The Soviet communists were determined to create an atheistic state, and so they discouraged religious practice on both sides of the interfaith boundary that extended from the Black Sea to the Chinese border. In Russia, they seized church bells and other religious paraphernalia and demolished many churches, converting others to secular uses. In the Soviet Muslim realm, they tolerated Islamic practice among the old but not among the young. Time, they believed, would erase the imprints of both Christianity and Islam.

In laying out an administrative framework, however, the Soviet planners proved to be poor geographers. In Armenia and Azerbaijan they tried to establish boundaries that would facilitate local control and discourage separatism. The result (Fig. 13-4) was a layout that could function as long as Soviet authorities controlled both "republics" but was a blueprint for religious conflict when that control diminished. A large ***exclave*** of Christian Armenia, called Nagorno-Karabakh, was created as an ***enclave*** within Muslim Azerbaijan. Azerbaijan was also divided through the creation of an exclave called Nakhichevan, which was established on the Iranian border.

When the USSR collapsed, the Soviet Republics became independent states, and ethnic strife broke out almost immediately. Azerbaijani Muslims, long cut off from their Iranian Shiite counterparts, broke through the southern border, acquiring weapons in the process. Soon Muslims and Christians were locked in combat, and Armenian refugees were streaming from Nagorno-Karabakh westward and even fleeing by boat across the Caspian Sea. More than 70 years of Soviet domination had done little to soften Armenian-Christian memories of Islamic oppression or to lessen the intensity of Azerbaijani-Muslim disdain for Christian unbelievers.

Another interfaith boundary extended across the vast region of Central Asia (see Fig. 11-1). There the Soviets subjugated a Muslim population numbering between 40 and 50 million. (Soviet census figures for this region were always suspect.)

The Soviet communist policy of promoting atheism applied to Central Asian Muslims as well as Russian Christians. But centuries of Muslim history and ideology could not quickly be stamped out, and when the Soviet Union collapsed, Islam quickly revived in the Central Asian republics. Most of Turkestan's Muslims adhere to Sunni Islam, although there are pockets of Shiism in the region. Simultaneously, the Russian Orthodox (Christian) Church is experiencing a resurrection in Russia and among Russians living in other countries; these events create the potential for friction.

Figure 13-4 Two Exclaves in Transcaucasia. This map shows two Transcaucasian exclaves: Muslim-Azerbaijan Nakhichevan, cut off by Christian Armenia, and Christian-Armenian Nagorno-Karabakh, surrounded by Muslim Azerbaijan.

The most serious problem could develop in Kazakhstan, the largest state in Central Asia. The Islamic-Christian interfaith boundary runs right across Kazakhstan, whose north is strongly Russified and whose south remains Islamic (Fig. 11-1). An estimated 47 percent of the population adheres to Islam, while about 17 percent now belong to the Russian Orthodox Church. Virtually all the Christians live in the north, and almost all the Muslims live in the south. There is a high degree of spatial separation between the Islamic and Christian communities, but Christians and Muslims do not have their own countries—unless the interfaith boundary becomes a political border at some future time. In the case of Kazakhstan, therefore, the religious map suggests that the future could be challenging if careful efforts are not made to balance the rights and needs of both religious communities.

Europe

No discussion of the impact of interfaith boundaries would be complete without some mention of the territories that made up the former Yugoslavia. Ever since the Ottoman Turks brought soldiers to their northwestern military frontier and converted some Slavic communities, the region has had Muslim pockets—and, hence, interfaith boundaries. In the former Yugoslavia these clusters were quite large in terms of both territory and population. They centered on Bosnia and its capital, Sarajevo, but they also could be found in southern Yugoslavia—particularly in the quasi-autonomous region of Kosovo within Serbia and in the Republic of Macedonia.

The scale of Figure 11-1 cannot illustrate the complexity of Yugoslavia's cultural map, but it can be imagined when one considers the fact that the Muslim-Christian interfaith boundary there lay in an area where an *intra*faith boundary also prevailed: a boundary between the Serbian Orthodox Church and the Catholic Church (Fig. 13-5). The Muslims were caught in the middle, and when Yugoslavia's political system collapsed in a conflict over different ethno-national territorial aspirations (see Chapter 17) that mirrored religious divisions, they were attacked by both Christian camps. The term ***ethnic cleansing*** came into use to describe the ouster of Muslims and others from their homes and lands—and

Figure 13-5 Religious distributions and historical boundaries in the former Yugoslavia. *Source:* From a map in M. Foucher, *Fragments d'Europe: Atlas de l'Europe Médiane et Orientale*. Paris: Fayard, 1993, p. 190.

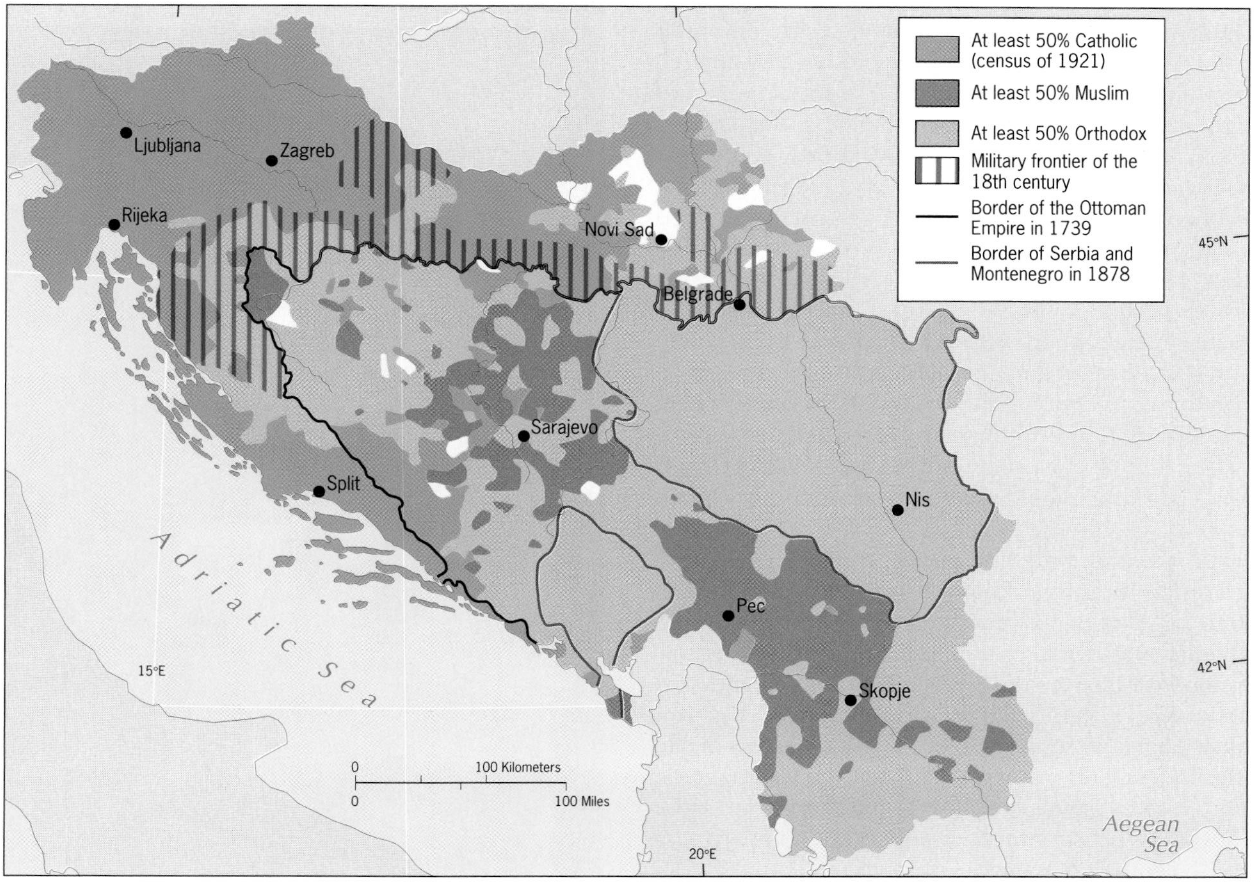

sometimes their slaughter. Serbs and Croats ousted Muslims, but they also sought to "cleanse" each other's territories. Where they could, Muslims drove their Christian adversaries away, but it was the Muslim minority that suffered most.

The case of Yugoslavia illustrates the risk an interfaith boundary poses to any state, if it mirrors important ethno-national divisions. Yugoslavia was a relatively young state, having been formed from the chaotic aftermath of World War I before 1920. But its 7 major and 17 smaller cultural groups had managed to live together for nearly three generations before disaster struck. During World War II, Nazi-supporting Croats fought anti-Nazi Serbs, but after 1945 Yugoslavia resumed its quest for stability under a special type of communist rule overseen by its strongman president, Tito. After Tito's death, and following an uneasy period of rule by committee, Yugoslavia was swept up in the winds of change produced by the disintegration of the Soviet Union. Urged on by a nationalistic leadership in the Serbian and Yugoslav capital, Belgrade, Yugoslavia's government made an effort to keep the state together through the construction of Serbian dominance over the country's different religious and cultural groups. The Yugoslav situation thus highlights how the mix between religion and nationalism can be particularly volatile—a theme to which we will return in Chapter 17.

The conflicts that raged in the 1990s were the worst that Europe had seen since World War II. Slovenia split off from Yugoslavia relatively peacefully—advantaged by location, external ties, comparative homogeneity, and Serbian distraction with other problems. But Croatia achieved independence only after bloody confrontations. It was Bosnia, however, that became the greatest focus of conflict—eventually erupting into a full-fledged civil war pitting Serbs, Croats, and Muslims against one another. More than 2.5 million Bosnians (mainly Muslims) were driven from their homes, and hundreds of thousands were injured or killed. The international community belatedly became involved, and a partition plan was put in place dividing the country between Croatian and Muslims and prompting many Serbs to leave for Serbia. The partition was secured by some 60,000 United Nations peacekeepers from Europe and the United States.

Even this did not bring peace to the region, however. During the second half of the 1990s the effort of Muslims of Albanian ethnic background in Kosovo to free themselves from continued erosion of their ethnic and religious rights led the Serbian nationalist leadership to undertake a campaign of oppression in Kosovo. Whole villages were razed, people were driven out in great numbers, and many were killed. The international community was once again slow to intervene, but under the auspices of an American-led NATO initiative, a bombing campaign against Serbia was eventually conducted that brought hostilities to a halt and paved the way for the introduction of a peacekeeping force. More recently, the defeat of Slobodan Miloševic—the Serbian leader who was behind the campaigns in Bosnia and Kosovo—has raised hopes that stability will return to what remains of the former Yugoslav state. Yet the situation in both Bosnia and Kosovo remains fragile, a reflection of how difficult it is to rebuild trust among communities under such circumstances.

Even as the uneasy, externally imposed peace hung on in Bosnia and Kosovo, another flash point emerged in Macedonia at the beginning of the twenty-first century. A quarter of the population of this former Yugoslav Republic is comprised of ethnic Albanian Muslims.

From the field notes

"Skopje, Macedonia, winter 2001. The two major religions of Macedonia are unmistakable as one walks the streets of Skopje. Eastern Orthodoxy may dominate, but in parts of the city Islam has an important presence. I took this photo as the first rumblings of armed conflict were being felt just a few miles to the west. Can Moslem and Orthodox Macedonians live together in peace? It is an open question, but one thing is clear: there is no hope for peace in this country if both societies do not feel that they have a stake in the country's future."

Their fears over domination by the Macedonian majority led to outbreaks of armed conflict in 2001. The situation remains highly volatile, but members of the international community—particularly the Europeans—sought to intervene at an early stage in the hope of averting another major outbreak of violence in the Balkans. The success of those efforts is not likely to be known for years to come.

The result of the events in parts of the former Yugoslavia has been disastrous not just for the lands and peoples of the region but for Europe generally. After World War II Europeans proclaimed that what had happened during the war would never happen again. In Yugoslavia Europe had a chance to prove that its collective power and influence would indeed prevent outrages like those that happened during World War II. But it failed to do so—at least in time to avert the bloodshed and psychological damages that occurred in Croatia and Bosnia—meaning that the case of Yugoslavia can truly be seen as Europe's tragedy. The open question is whether the effort to intervene earlier in Macedonia will be effective and can restore some faith in Europe as a stable realm.

Other Interfaith Boundaries

The problems of conflict between adherents of different major religions plague several other countries with various degrees of intensity. In populous Bangladesh, where the southern lowland regions are mainly Muslim and the interior is Hindu, interfaith conflict has been less intense than in India. Hindu fundamentalism has not yet made inroads here, and the level of Muslim militancy has until recently been relatively low. (In 1994, however, evidence of growing Muslim fundamentalism in Bangladesh came in the form of the arrest and forced exile of the author of a book that was deemed blasphemous by Islamic religious authorities.)

The future of the interfaith boundary in Bangladesh will depend on the religious situation in neighboring India. If India manages to accommodate its huge Muslim minority and if conflict with Islamic Pakistan can be avoided, Bangladesh is likely to remain calm. Should serious interfaith strife occur in India, Bangladesh will likely feel the effects.

Sri Lanka

Another neighbor of India, the island country of Sri Lanka, has experienced conflict with religious overtones. About 70 percent of Sri Lanka's 19 million inhabitants are Buddhists, but in the north and northeast a Tamil-speaking minority, ethnically Dravidian and religiously Hindu, has developed. Since 1984 this group has fought a war of secession in which religion has become an ever-stronger force. Buddhist shrines were targeted, and Hindu holy sites were attacked in retaliation. The Indian government tried to assist the Sri Lanka government to settle the issue, even through armed intervention. In India, Hindu fundamentalists protested this support for Buddhists against Hindus, and this may have led to the assassination of Prime Minister Rajiv Gandhi in 1991.

A series of attacks in the capital, Colombo, in 1997, exacerbated the situation, but in 2002 Norwegian mediators succeeded in working out a truce. The majority of Tamils appear ready to accept increased autonomy for their territory, but extremists continue to call for full independence. As such, the situation remains fragile.

Southeast and Southwest Asia

In Southeast Asia, an interfaith boundary between Islam and Christianity touches the southern Philippines. The southernmost islands of the Philippines have Muslim populations that are small minorities in a Catholic-dominated country (see Fig. 11-1). Although Muslims account for only about 5 percent of the population of the Philippines, they have campaigned vigorously, and sometimes violently, for improved status.

One of the most significant interfaith boundaries prevails in Southwest Asia, in Israel and between Israel and its neighbors. In the aftermath of World War I, the League of Nations recognized the creation of Palestine to be administered by the British under a mandate from the League. The British government set out to create, in Palestine, a national homeland for the Jewish people but with explicit assurance that the religious and civil rights of existing non-Jewish peoples in Palestine would not be prejudiced. The policy did not produce a peaceful result. Civil disturbances erupted almost immediately, and, by 1937–1938, there was open warfare between Jews and Palestinians.

In the wake of World War II, many more Jews moved to the region. Shortly after the war the British mandate ended, and the United Nations voted to partition Palestine—creating an independent Israeli state and a Palestinian state. Surrounding Arab states reacted violently against the new Jewish state. Israel survived, and during the ensuing conflict many Palestinians lost their lands, farms, and villages and were forced to migrate or flee to refugee camps. Agreement was never reached on the territorial parameters of a Palestinian state, and a series of conflicts culminated in 1967 with an Israeli occupation of Palestinian lands in Gaza, the West Bank, and the Golan Heights. The Jewish presence in Gaza has always been small, but Jewish settlements in the West Bank have complicated the Israeli-Palestinian situation and blurred the interfaith boundary between Israel and Jordan. Indeed, Israel's control over Gaza, the West Bank, and the Golan Heights put many miles of interfaith boundaries within that nation's jurisdiction.

From the field notes

"Golden domes and soaring minarets mark Islam's mosques from Morocco to Malaysia, and beautify townscapes from Casablanca to Kota Kinabalu. You can see this, Malaysian Sabah's most impressive mosque, from afar. But the airplane stands as a reminder that a modernized, secular world is never far away."

Events in the early- and mid-1990s began to change this religious-political mosaic as self-government was awarded to Gaza and to small areas inside the West Bank. Palestinian Arabs were empowered to run their own affairs within these zones. Stability and satisfactory coexistence could lead to further adjustments, some thought—and eventually a full-fledged Palestinian state. But Israel lies astride what may well be the world's most sensitive interfaith boundary. In the first years of the twenty-first century, the combination of Israel's policy of continuing to build settlements in the West Bank and Palestinian rejection of peace terms that would have created a substantial Palestinian state led to the complete abandonment of a framework for peace hammered out in Oslo in 1995 that many saw as the best hope for peace. The prospects for settlement once again dimmed, and continued outbreaks of violence show how difficult it will be to achieve a stable, long-term peace in the region.

◆ INTRAFAITH BOUNDARIES

Interfaith boundaries can threaten the stability of entire countries. Countries that contain ***intrafaith boundaries*** would seem to be less troubled.

In general, that is indeed the case. A number of Western European countries have Catholic as well as Protestant communities, and often these are reflected in the regional distribution of the population, as in the case of Switzerland (Fig. 13-6). In the early 2000s the great majority of these countries were not experiencing religious or ethnic conflict. The most notable exception is in Northern Ireland.

Northern Ireland

The single most intractable problem in Western Europe is Northern Ireland, where a Protestant majority and a Catholic minority are in conflict over their coexistence and their future. The issue stems from the centuries-long period ending in 1922 when all of Ireland was a British dependency. A substantial Protestant British population immigrated into Ireland during this colonial period, many from Scotland. Most settled in the northeastern corner of the island.

When the Catholic Irish rebelled against British colonialism, Ireland was partitioned so as to protect the Protestant minority in the northeast. But Northern Ireland also contained a substantial Catholic minority, which was left unprotected. In the 1920s, when the new map of Ireland was being drawn, it was assumed that time and economic development would soften the religious animosities in "the North" (Fig. 13-7).

This was not to be. The Protestant majority in Northern Ireland, constituting about two-thirds of the total population (about 1.6 million), held all the economic and political advantages. Charges of discrimination and repression of Catholics were underscored by terrorist acts, bringing British troops into the area. As time went on, economic stagnation worsened the situation. Although the Republic of Ireland was sensitive to the plight of Catholics in the North, no official help was extended to those who were engaging in violence.

An Anglo-Irish peace agreement, adopted in April 1998, raised hopes of a new period of peace in Northern Ireland. Yet the future of the accord hangs in the balance, with threats to the accord continuing to emerge. As with so many other religious conflicts, the clash in Northern Ireland is not simply—or even primarily—about religion; it is a conflict over access to opportunities, over civil rights, over political influence, and ultimately over nationalism. But religion and religious history are the banners beneath which the opposing sides march, and

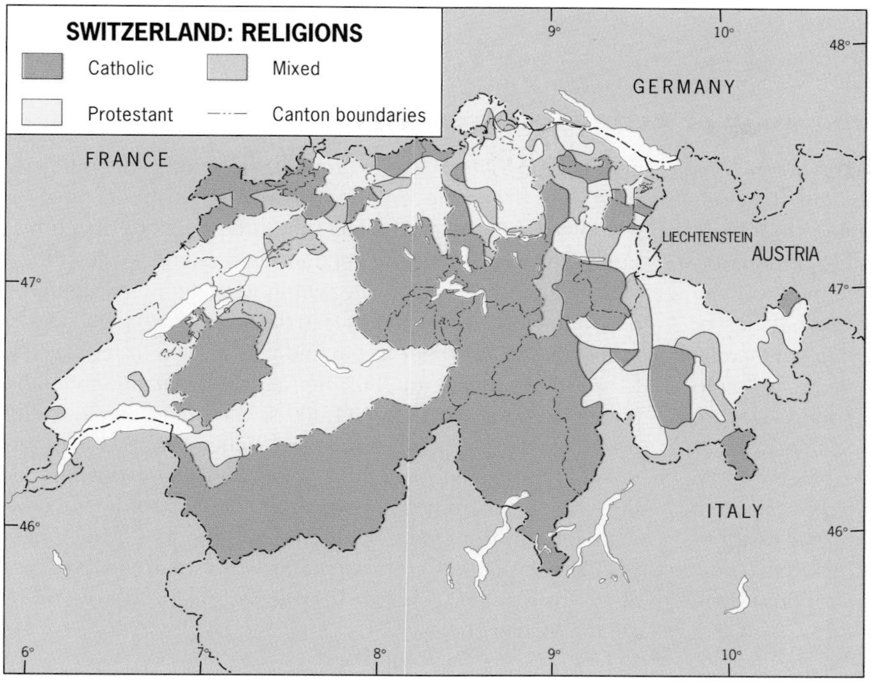

Figure 13-6 Religions of Switzerland. Switzerland includes Catholic, Protestant, and mixed religion areas. *Source*: From M. I. Glassner and H. J. de Blij, *Systematic Political Geography,* 4th ed., New York: Wiley, 1989, p. 535.

church and cathedral have become symbols of strife rather than peace.

The Islamic Realm

In the Islamic realm, conflicts between the majority Sunni and minority Shiite branches have pitted followers of Islam against each other. Undoubtedly the most destructive war of its kind in modern times, the Iran-Iraq conflict of the 1980s, was a battle between Sunni-dominated Iraq and Shiite-ruled Iran. The war began over a territorial issue, but religious enmity helped to sustain it. Although the Shiites constitute only about 12 percent of all Muslims, they proclaim themselves the true followers of

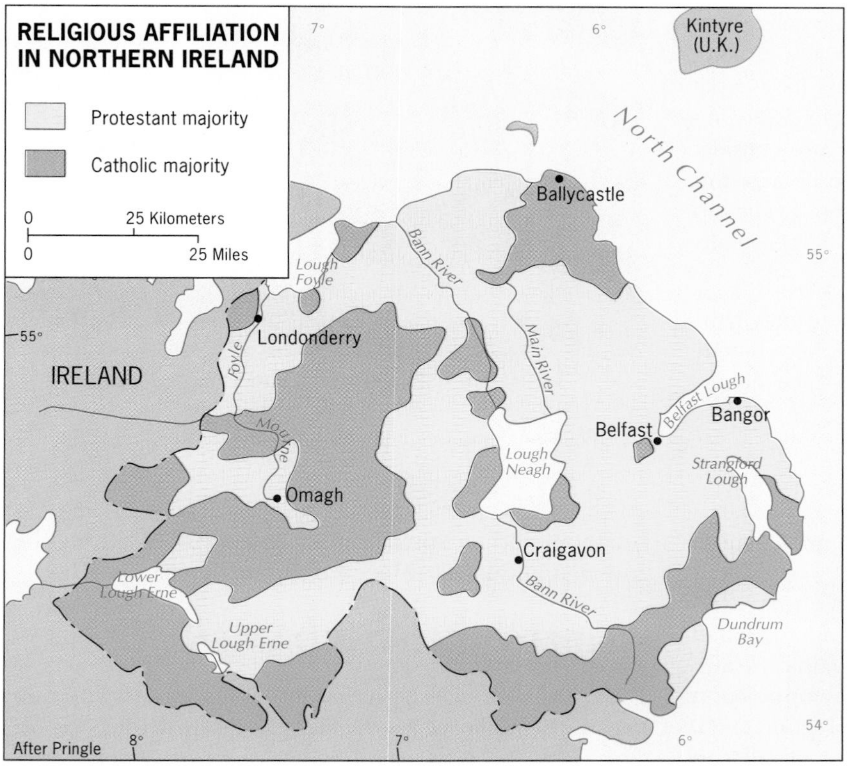

Figure 13-7 Religious Affiliation in Northern Ireland. Areas of Catholic and Protestant majorities are scattered throughout Northern Ireland. *Source:* From D. G. Pringle, *One Island, Two Nations?* Letchworth: Research Studies Press/Wiley, 1985, p. 21.

A SENSE OF SCALE

The Geography of Religious Diversity

The spatial scale of maps showing the distribution of religions throughout the world influences our understanding of the relative importance of a religion in a particular place or region. Figure 11-1, for example, shows the distribution of religions on a global scale. By looking at this small-scale map we may think that most of the United States is Protestant or that most of Western Europe is Catholic. Yet this understanding of the distribution of religions is adequate only when we are trying to identify patterns at a *macro* or global scale. As soon as we turn our attention to a more intermediate or *meso* scale, such as that depicted in Figure 12-2, a different picture emerges. The United States appears as a more culturally complex region. If taken a step further, a map showing the *micro*-scale distribution of religions in a city such as New York City would show some neighborhoods as predominantly Catholic, Protestant, or Jewish, and others as quite mixed.

A diversity of religions prevails in cities like New York, but no specific sites within the city are critically important to members of more than one religious group. In fact, in the whole of the United States virtually no sites are considered holy or otherwise essential to the identity of more than one religion. For example, the holy sites of Mormonism in Utah are critically important only to Mormons. Other sites of supreme importance to only one group are the Vatican City in Italy for Catholics and Mecca in Saudi Arabia for Muslims. However, throughout the world many sites are in some way claimed as holy or important to adherents of more than one religious faith. In India, for example, several locations are considered holy by Hindus, Buddhists, and Jains. Specifically, Volture Peak in Rajgir, India, is holy to Buddhists because it is the site where the Buddha first proclaimed the Heart Sutra, a very important canon of Buddhism. Hindus and Jains also consider the site holy because they consider Buddha to be a god or prophet. There has been no serious discord among religious groups over this site, however. Pilgrims of all faiths peacefully congregate there year after year.

Unfortunately, the same cannot be said of religious sites in the ancient city of Jerusalem. There sacred space has been bitterly contested among Jews, Christians, and Muslims since the seventh century, when Muslim armies took control over the city from the Byzantine Empire. Rivalry over the control of Jerusalem is based on the fact that three religions attach historic and religious significance to overlapping spaces in the city. The most contested site within Jerusalem (and arguably one of the most contested sites in the world) is the walled rise in the southeast corner in the Old City known to Jews as the temple Mount and to Muslims as *al-Haram al-Sharif* (the Noble Sanctuary). This 144,000-square-meter area is the place where Jews and Christians believe that God commanded Abraham to sacrifice his son, and where Muslims believe that Muhammad arrived from his extraordinary one-night journey from Mecca to Jerusalem. Attempts by members of different religious groups to control this small site have created tensions that echo far beyond Jerusalem to a world of great religious diversity.

Jerusalem's Western Wall and Temple Mount.

Muhammad and often resent the less dogmatic, more worldly Sunni.

The depth of this division was revealed in the aftermath of the Persian Gulf War, when the Sunni-controlled army of defeated Iraq immediately moved against the Shiite communities of the south to preclude any opposition or cooperation with neighboring Iran (see Figure 11-1). Shiite and Sunni factions have also been in conflict in Lebanon, and factional conflict has occurred during the annual pilgrimage to Mecca, claiming thousands of lives.

◆ RELIGIOUS FUNDAMENTALISM

Today, throughout the world, religious leaders and millions of their followers are seeking to return to the basics of their faith. This drive toward ***religious fundamentalism***

From the field notes

"The Lautoka Muslim School reminded me that communities try hard to maintain their traditions, no matter how far from their source areas they may be. Lautoka is a town on the northwest coast of Viti Levu, the most populous island of Fiji in the Pacific Ocean. This is a cosmopolitan place, on the boundary between Melanesia and Polynesia, with a large population of (South Asian) Indians brought here during (British) colonial times. Among these South Asians the Hindus are in the majority, but the smaller Muslim community is determined to protect its identity and ways of life. The Lautoka Muslim School is coeducational, though girls must wear elaborate dress that covers them from head to ankles while boys wear shorts and short-sleeved shirts—which, I am sure, is why the boys played ball on the field while the girls stood in the shade of the tent to the right. I asked a teacher about the relations between Muslim and Hindu communities in Lautoka, 'They are good,' he said. 'We keep to ourselves.' Then he told me where to find the town's largest mosque, and urged me to pay a visit."

is often born of frustration over the perceived breakdown of society's mores and values, loss of religious authority, failure to achieve economic goals, loss of a sense of local control, and a sense of violation of a religion's core territory.

People in one society often fear fundamentalism in other societies without recognizing it in their own. The attacks on the United States in September 2001 reinforced the tendency of many Americans to equate extreme fundamentalism with Islam. Yet Christian fundamentalism is a potent force as well—and other cultures view religious zealots' killings of physicians who are willing to perform legal abortions in this country as equally extreme. Fundamentalism and extremism are closely related, and their appeal is global.

Today the forces of globalization affect religions. Education, radio, television, and travel have diffused notions of individual liberties, sexual equality, and freedom of choice—but also consumerism and secularism. In the process, the extent and speed of cultural diffusion and innovation have accelerated. Some churches have managed to change with the times, allowing women to serve as priests and liberalizing their doctrines. Others have gone in the opposite direction, reaffirming fundamental dogma and trying to block modern influences and external cultural interference. Meanwhile, battle lines are being drawn. The drive toward fundamentalism in Christianity and Islam alike is creating a climate of mistrust that has already led to strife. On the other hand, fragmentation within the Christian and Islamic realms is more the rule than the exception, and members of different religious faiths are increasingly brought together as people migrate and bring their beliefs with them (see Looking Ahead Box).

Christian Fundamentalism

Among Christian religions, the Roman Catholic Church has resisted innovations deemed to be incompatible with the fundamentals of the faith. Among the issues giving rise to disputes are birth control, family planning, and the role of women in the religious bureaucracy. The major religions tend to be male-dominated, and few women have managed to enter the hierarchy. More important from a global viewpoint is the Roman Catholic Church's position on family planning. In a world of continuously expanding populations, the church continues to preach against the use of artificial means of birth control as well as abortion. During the September 1994 United Nations Conference on Population and Development, the Roman Catholic Church even sought to ally itself with Islamic countries against advocates of population control.

In the United States, however, Christian fundamentalism is most often associated with Protestant faiths. Preaching a doctrine of strict adherence to the literal precepts of the Bible, many Protestant Christian fundamentalists believe that the entire character of contemporary society needs to be brought into alignment with biblical principles. They have thus become increasingly active in political and social arenas—arguing for prayer in public schools, the teaching of "creationism" in science courses, a strict ban on abortion, and the adoption of laws outlawing homosexual liaisons. In the process, they have gained considerable influence. Indeed, countering religious fundamentalism entails political risks, as is evident in the care U.S. politicians take to avoid offending the "religious right."

Islamic Fundamentalism

Other major faiths must also confront the pressures of change. Not all Muslim communities, for example, ad-

Looking Ahead

The Changing Place of Religion

What will the global religious mosaic look like 50 years from now? It is difficult to predict with any certainty, but if present trends continue it will be increasingly difficult to describe the geography of religions as a "mosaic." Our current maps of religions show areas of Christianity, Islam, Judaism, Buddhism, and Hinduism, and the like—and of course we already understand that there is a great deal more religious intermixing than these maps suggest. As we look toward the future, however, religious intermixing is likely to become increasingly common. And the growth of New Age beliefs, fundamentalist religious variants, and secularization will make it even more difficult to think about the geography of religion as a pattern with discrete spaces dominated by individual religions.

Consider, for example, the areas in Figure 11-1 that are shown as Christian. Many of these areas are among the most common destinations of non-Christian migrants. This is having an impact on the cultures of both the migrants and the host cultures. Australia is the destination of many Buddhists, Hindus, and Muslims leaving Southeast Asia in search of economic opportunity, especially in the wake of the Asian economic crisis of the late 1990s. The United States continues to be the destination of migrants from around the world, and Christians of all denominations living and working with Jews, Muslims, Buddhists, Hindus, and others increasingly characterize American towns of all sizes.

Of all the Christian areas shown in Figure 11-1, Western Europe has seen the most dramatic increase in migrants practicing religions other than Christianity. Immigrants from Asia, southeastern Europe, and North Africa have created vibrant Muslim communities in cities throughout the region. In the process, new cultural forms have emerged as communities live and work together. Yet intercultural tensions can also appear, as seen most dramatically in the recent electoral successes of anti-immigrant political parties such as the National Front in France or the Flemish Bloc in Belgium.

No matter how vocal the opposition is, it will be very difficult to stem the forces that are producing more religious intermixing in Europe and beyond. Consequently, Figure 11-1 may become more and more of a historical artifact rather than a good representation of the geography of religion. Moreover, landscape and society will increasingly bear the imprint of the changing distribution of religions. This is already happening. The cultural landscape of American cities such as Detroit, Chicago, New York, and Los Angeles, for example, has already been modified by the presence of minarets rising up alongside church steeples. At the same time, many Muslim communities in these cities have adapted to the American workweek by allowing the traditionally obligatory Friday afternoon prayer at the mosque to be held on Friday evening or Sunday afternoon when families are freed from employment obligations.

Even as mutual adjustment and accommodation raises hope for peaceful relations among religions in the future, there are minorities of many faiths who seek separation, and even the fall of other religions. Their vision is fundamentally at odds with the changing geography of religion, but if their views gain strength and currency, the challenge of maintaining peace and stability in a world of growing religious intermixing will be great indeed.

here precisely to the rules of the Qu'ran such as the prohibition on the use of alcohol. The laws of Islam, which are very strict when interpreted literally, are not applied with equal force throughout the Muslim religious realm. Such inconsistency—along with concerns over external influence—produces a reaction, not only in the religious bureaucracies but also among many believers. The basic geographic dimension is often not difficult to find: conservatism is strongest in a tier of countries extending from Sudan to Pakistan, becoming weaker in Turkey to the northwest and Malaysia and Indonesia to the east, where a more laissez-faire Islam prevails.

Even in those "moderate" wings of Islam, however, fundamentalism is gaining ground. In Malaysia, the Chinese and other minorities reacted fearfully when the government considered demands for the general application of Sharia law. In Indonesia, a fundamentalist drive by Islamic preachers has found fertile soil, especially among rural people who remain remote from the changes affecting Indonesian society elsewhere.

As with Christian fundamentalism, countering Muslim fundamentalism entails political risks. When the former Shah of Iran tried to limit the power of the imams as he sought to integrate the state into the wider global economy, he provoked a religious movement that eventually led to his overthrow. (His overthrow was also tied to the autocratic regime he headed, which fostered much opposition.) During the revolution in Iran, the imams imposed the most basic of Shiite religious rules and practices upon their followers. After the Shah was replaced by an ***ayatollah***, a supreme religious leader, those rules and practices became law. Women, who had acquired greater freedoms under the Shah's regime, faced new restrictions. Those who had adopted Western modes of dress were arrested and required to wear Muslim headgear, veils, and long robes. Many lost positions in commerce and administration, and their political influence declined.

What happened in Iran during the 1970s and 1980s was one of the significant early manifestations of the trend toward fundamentalism. The process has, if anything, accelerated since then. Afghanistan under the Taliban provided a particularly striking example. The Taliban regime seized control of much of the country during the 1990s and asserted the strictest fundamentalist regime in the contemporary world. The leadership imposed a wide range of religious restrictions, sought to destroy all statues depicting human forms, required followers of Hinduism to wear identifying markers, and forbade women to appear in public with their head exposed. The Taliban also provided a haven for the activities of Islamic extremists who sought to promote an Islamic holy war, or ***jihad***, against the West in general, and the United States in particular.

One of the key figures in the extreme Islamic fundamentalist movement of the past decade—Osama bin Laden—helped finance and mastermind a variety of terrorist activities conducted against the United States. The beliefs of bin Laden and his associates are certainly not representative of Islam as a whole, but they are religious beliefs. Indeed, they can be traced to a form of Islam—known as Wahhabi Islam—that developed in the eighteenth century in opposition to what was seen as sacrilegious practices on the part of Ottoman rulers. The champions of the opposition movement called for a return to a supposedly pure variant of Islam from centuries earlier.

A variety of forces have fueled the violent path on which the extremist movement has embarked, but some of these forces are unambiguously geographic. Perhaps the most important is the widely held view among movement followers that "infidels" have invaded the Islamic holy land over the past 80 years. Of particular concern to the extreme Islamic fundamentalists are the presence of American military and business interests in the Arabian Peninsula, the establishment of the state of Israel, and the support that Israel has received from the outside. A principal goal of the movement, then, is to bring an end to what are seen as improper territorial incursions. A second geographically related concern of movement activists is the diffusion of modern culture and technology and its impact on traditional lifestyles and spiritual practices. Ridding the Islamic world of such influences is also a goal of extreme Islamic fundamentalists.

Those extreme Islamic fundamentalists who have resorted to violence in pursuit of their cause are relatively small in number. Yet one of the critical contemporary issues is the extent to which they can or will attract widespread support throughout the Islamic world. The potential for such support is greatest among those who feel that they are the losers in the contemporary global economic order and who feel that their cultures are fundamentally threatened. By extension, a key to avoiding the division of the world into mutually antagonistic religious realms is to promote an atmosphere in which such feelings do not become widespread. This, in turn, suggests the importance of non-Islamic cultures conveying an understanding of the gap between mainstream and fundamentalist Islam, and supporting the economic and political efforts of genuinely democratic forces in the Islamic core.

More broadly, like religion more generally, fundamentalism can constitute both a unifying and a divisive force. In the United States, fundamentalist "preachers" and their massive following have divided the Protestant churches, especially when the personal and financial excesses of certain evangelists became public knowledge. The debate over birth control within the Catholic Church has created a split between orthodox and liberal members. In Muslim societies, fundamentalism has stimulated the formation of political movements whose aim is to reverse the move toward secularization and, if possible, to seize political power.

In Algeria such a movement has come close to overthrowing the government. In 1991 a conservative Muslim political party was poised to win in the national elections, having appealed to voters who were eager to replace a corrupt secular administration with an Islamic regime. Rather than allowing the final round of voting to take place, the Algerian government canceled the election. The Muslim movement then began a campaign of violent opposition. Some saw a parallel with Iran, and Muslim leaders called for an ***Islamic republic*** in Algeria. Dozens of foreigners were killed; but thousands of Algerians lost their lives in a continuing exchange of reprisals. France, fearful of a mass exodus of Algerians to French shores, tried to mediate. But both the Algerian government and the Muslim fundamentalists rejected both French and European Union efforts to involve themselves in Algeria's internal struggle. Meanwhile, attacks on remote villages by unidentified bands of assailants cost tens of thousands of lives; the identity of the killers, and their goals, remained a mystery. The war between Islamists and secularists dealt Algeria a damaging setback.

The struggle in Algeria emboldened Muslim fundamentalists to challenge government authority elsewhere in North Africa. In Tunisia, Muslim clerics called for the end of secular government; in Egypt, Muslim radicals attacked foreign tourists, thus destroying one of the country's major sources of income. It was believed that disorder would generate dissatisfaction, and dissatisfaction would lead to the creation of an Islamic state.

It is often said that we live in an age of religious tolerance. But as the attacks on New York City and Washington, D.C., in September 2001 made clear, religious feelings can quickly be translated into hostility and conflict—particularly when they coincide with other social or political divisions. And when fundamentalism is an element as well, it is not surprising that conflicts involving religion can be among the most intractable of our day.

◆ KEY TERMS ◆

ayatollah	interfaith boundary	jihad
enclave	intrafaith boundary	religious fundamentalism
ethnic cleansing	Islamic republic	sharia religious law
exclave		

◆ APPLYING GEOGRAPHIC KNOWLEDGE ◆

1. In this chapter we focus on interfaith, as compared to intrafaith, boundaries in the cultural landscape. Select two of the world's countries, one astride an interfaith boundary and the other marked by an intrafaith boundary, and compare the level of conflict. Is such conflict inevitable when religious boundaries cross national territories?

2. One of the important consequences of the collapse of the Soviet Union has been the revival of religion, not only in Russia, but also in the former Soviet republics, notably in Turkestan. What cultural-geographic factors are contributing to this revival? Can you discern new or reemerging interfaith or intrafaith boundaries in what used to be the Soviet realm?

Part Four

At Issue: Revisited

◆ SELECTED REFERENCES ◆

Part Four The Geography of Religion

al Faruqi, I., & Sopher, D., eds. *Historical Atlas of the Religions of the World* (New York: Macmillan, 1974).

Benevenisti, M. *Sacred Landscape: The Buried History of the Holy Land Since 1948* (Berkeley and Los Angeles: University of California Press, 2000).

Bhardwaj, S. *Hindu Places of Pilgrimage in India: A Study in Cultural Geography* (Berkeley and Los Angeles: University of California Press, 1973).

Cooper, A. "New Directions in the Geography of Religion" *Area* 24, no.2 (1992): 123–129.

Curtis, J. "Miami's Little Havana: Yard Shrines, Cult Religion and Landscape," *Journal of Cultural Geography*, no.1 (1980): 1–15.

de Blij, H. J. "Islam in South Africa," in J. Kritzeck & W. H. Lewis, eds., *Islam in Africa* (New York: van Nostrand, 1970).

Eliade, M. *The Sacred and the Profane: The Nature of Religion* (New York: Harcourt, Brace & World, 1959).

Emmet, C. F. *Beyond the Basilica: Christians and Muslims in Nazareth* (Chicago: University of Chicago Press, 1995).

Finegan, J. *An Archaeological History of Religions of Indian Asia* (New York: Paragon House, 1989).

Gaustad, E. *Historical Atlas of Religion in America* (New York: Harper & Row, 1962).

Griffith, J. S. *Beliefs and Holy Places: A Spiritual Geography of the Pimeria Alta* (Tucson: University of Arizona Press, 1992).

Halvorson, P., & Newman, W. *Atlas of Religious Change in America, 1952-1990* (Washington, D.C.: Glenmary Research Center, 1994).

Isaac, E. "The Act and the Covenant: The Impact of Religion on the Landscape" *Landscape*, no.11 (1961): 12–17.

Khalidi, R. *Palestinian Identity: The Construction of Modern National Consciousness* (New York: Columbia University Press, 1997).

Kong, L. "Geography and Religion: Trends and Prospects" *Progress in Human Geography* 14 (1990): 12–17.

Korp, M. *The Sacred Geography of the American Mound Builders* (Lewiston, N.Y.: E. Mellen Press, 1990).

Levine, G. J. "On the Geography of Religion," *Transactions of the Institute of British Geographers* 11 (1987): 248–440,

Lewis, B., ed. *The World of Islam: Faith, People, Culture* (London, U.K.: Thames & Hudson, 1976).

Marty, M. E. *Pilgrims in Their Own Land: 500 Years of Religion in America* (Boston: Little, Brown, 1984).

Metcalf, B. D. ed. *Making Muslim Space in North America and Europe* (Berkeley: University of California Press, 1996).

Mitchell, G. *The Hindu Temple: An Introduction to Its Meaning and Forms* (New York: Harper & Row, 1977).

Noble, A. G., & Efrat E. "Geography of the Intifada," *The Geographical Review* (July 1990): 288–307.

Park, C. *Sacred Worlds: An Introduction to Geography and Religion* (London: Routledge, 1994).

Peters, F. E. *The Hajj: The Muslim Pilgrimage to Mecca and the Holy Places* (Princeton, N.J.: Princeton University Press, 1994).

Prorok, C. V. "The Hare Krishna's Transformation of Space in West Virginia," *Journal of Cultural Geography* 7, no.1 (1986) 129–140.

Romann, M., & Weingrod, A. *Living Together Separately: Arabs and Jews in Contemporary Jerusalem* (Princeton, N.J.: Princeton University Press, 1991).

Rowland, B. *The Art and Architecture of India: Buddhist, Hindu, Jain* (New York: Penguin, 1977).

Schwartberg, J. *An Historical Atlas of South Asis.* rev. ed. (Chicago: University of Chicago Press, 1978).

Scott, J., & Simpson-Housley, P., eds. *Sacred Places and Profane Spaces: Essays in the Geographics of Judaism, Christianity, and Islam* (Westport, Conn.: Greenwood Press, 1991).

Sheskin, I. M. "Jewish Metropolitan Homelands," *Journal of Cultural Geography* 13, no.2 (1993): 119–132.

Shortridge, J. R. "Patterns of Religion in the United States," *Geographical Review*, 66 (1976): 420–434.

Sopher, D. E. *Geography of Religions* (Englewood Cliffs, N.J.: Prentice-Hall, 1967).

Sopher,.D. E., ed. *An Exploration of India: Geographical Perspectives on Society and Culture* (Ithaca, N.Y.: Cornell University Press, 1980).

Stump, R. *Boundaries of Faith: Geographical Perspectives on Religious Fundamentalism* (Lanham, Md.: Rowman & Littlefield Publishers, 2000).

Weightman, B. A. "Changing Religious Landscapes in Los Angeles," *Journal of Cultural Geography* 14, no.1 (1993): 1–20.

Zelinsky, W. "An Approach to the Religious Geography of the United States," *Annals of the Association of American Geographers* 51 (1961): 139–167.

Zelinsky, W. *Cultural Geography of the United States*, rev.ed. (Englewood Cliffs, N.J.: Prentice Hall, 1992).

Part Five

THE POLITICAL IMPRINT

At Issue

The political world is in transition. Some scholars envisage the emergence of a multipolar world in which the United States, a unified Europe, Russia, and China constitute four power cores balanced to ensure a stable global system. The United States has emerged as the sole superpower, however. In the meantime, Europe has launched a common currency, Russia is struggling to find a new place in the world, and China is in ascendancy but in the grip of significant internal divisions and not yet a world force. In the face of such uncertainties, a new world order may be at hand, but its outlines are unclear. At issue is whether a variety of geopolitical transitions can be accomplished without serious instability. *Can Europe create a powerful economic/political union despite concerns about economic and political centralization? Can Russia overcome economic trauma and corruption to emerge as a major world power once again? Can China create the political and social institutions that can foster sustained growth and unity?*

Berlin. The new German capital rises as the old wall is removed

Part Outline

Chapter 14

Political Culture and the Evolving State

From the field notes

"I arrived in Ghana just after there had been an assassination attempt on the country's first President, Kwame Nkrumah. His statue had been draped in a hospital gown, his head bandaged. The end of colonialism in Africa seemed near, and hopes were high for the newly independent states. I knew no one who would disagree with the proclamations on Nkrumah's statue: 'To me the liberation of Ghana will be meaningless unless it is linked up with the liberation of Africa' and 'We prefer self-government with danger to servitude in tranquility.' But decolonization did not eliminate the economic and cultural problems faced by Africa's emerging states. President Nkrumah was to die in exile, his country ruled by the military, its economy severely damaged. The new African states found themselves in the periphery, their economies at the mercy of the core, their politics subject to Cold War competition between the superpowers, their peoples fragmented by tribalism. Now, nearly a half century later, African statecraft has some success stories, and Nkrumah's hope may not have been in vain."

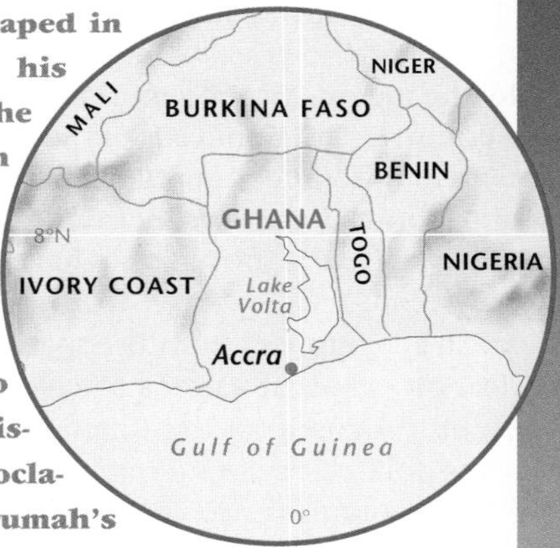

KEY POINTS

- **The world's living space is divided into nearly 200 states ranging in size from microstates to subcontinental giants.**
- **The modern state system is the product of a political-territorial order with European roots. At the core of the system is the concept of sovereignty and the idea of the "nation-state."**
- **The concepts of nation and state have different historical roots. The former refers to a group of people sharing common cultural and political perspectives, whereas the latter refers to a politically organized area. There are thus very few true nation-states.**
- **The European state model was exported through migration and colonialism, but it has not always worked well in the non-Western world.**
- **State territory varies in morphology as well as size; different territorial characteristics can present opportunities and challenges, depending on the historical and political-economic context.**
- **State territories are defined by international boundaries that mark the limits of national jurisdiction. Boundary lines on the ground mark the position of vertical planes that separate states; these planes cut through airspace as well as subsoil.**

Political activity is as basic to human culture as language or religion. It undoubtedly began when individuals first asserted themselves as leaders of villages or clans, when competition for such leadership roles, for territorial rights, or for other goals became a part of life. Ever since, political behavior by individuals, groups, communities, and nations has expressed the human desire for power and influence in the pursuit of personal and public goals. All of us are caught up in these processes, whose effects range from the composition of school boards to the conduct of war.

Political geography is the study of the political organization of the planet. Since political activity has spatial expression and focus, its outcome is revealed on the map. The present-day layout of the world political map is a product of endless accommodations and adjustments within and between human societies. Its most obvious feature is the mosaic of more than 200 countries and territories separated by boundaries shown on the typical map that hangs on the walls of many classrooms (Fig. 14-1). It is the most familiar and widely used map of the world—so widely used that we often fail to think about the patterns it contains. Yet even a brief examination of the nature and significance of the patterns on the political map provides valuable insights. It shows, for example, the inequality of countries in terms of territory (certain countries are hundreds of times larger than others) and great differences in relative location. For example, some countries are ***landlocked***, without coasts on the open sea, whereas the majority have direct access to the global ocean.

Political geographers study the spatial manifestations of political processes at various levels of scale. Some of their research focuses on the functioning of individual countries as political regions. From this research we have learned how countries are organized, how they overcome (or fail to overcome) divisive forces, how their boundaries function, and much more. In recent decades we have witnessed the collapse of colonial empires, and the problems of newly independent entities in the postcolonial era have taken political geography in new directions. In the meantime, some countries are banding together in international alliances, associations, and unions to further their common objectives. ◆

◆ POLITICAL CULTURE

From congressional district boundaries to international borders, the maps we draw reflect ***political culture***. And political cultures vary. People adhere to political ideas just as they profess a religion and speak a native language. Today, many political systems are designed to keep religion and politics separate, but other states are ***theocracies***: their leaders are deemed to be under divine guidance, their actions representing the will of a supreme being.

If contemporary political cultures have a common element, it lies in the centrality of territory to political life. Indeed, some have argued that the effort to control pieces of the Earth's surface for political and social ends is a fundamental dynamic in human affairs and must be a key component of geographical research. In a book published in 1986, Robert Sack used the term ***human territoriality*** to describe this effort. He sees human territoriality as a key ingredient in the construction of social and political spaces. Sack's approach to territoriality differs from that taken by the social anthropologist Robert Ardrey in *The Territorial Imperative* (1966). Ardrey argued that human territoriality is analogous to the instinct in animals to control and defend territory. Sack, by contrast, argues that human territoriality takes many different forms, depending on the social and geographical context, and that it should not be compared to an animal instinct. Instead, he calls for a better understanding of the human organization of the planet through a consideration of how and why different territorial strategies are pursued at different times and in different places.

Territoriality attracts so much attention because it is a key element of political culture. This trait manifests itself in different ways. At the village level, for example, land is held communally in some cultures and individually in others. Such differences also mark larger groups and even entire nations. Attitudes toward land and territory differ from one society to another and from one country to another.

The rise of the modern state system carried with it a distinctive view of territory as a fixed, exclusive element of political identification and group survival. As a result, few issues can agitate a people the way a perceived violation of territory can. A neighbor's annexation of even the smallest piece of land is likely to unify even the most divided society. Conversely, the prospect of having to yield any area over which a government has jurisdiction can cause violent opposition among otherwise peaceable citizens.

The long-standing issue of the Golan Heights provides a good example. This territory has been under Israeli control since the 1967 war, when it was captured from Syria. The prospect of its return to Syria has created deep division in Israeli society. But if Syria sought to annex any other part of Israel there would be no such division, and Israelis would be unified in opposition. Challenges to existing territorial arrangements thus remain a strong motivator for political, and even military, action in the modern world.

◆ STATE AND NATION

Up to now we have referred to national political entities as countries. The word *country* is derived from the Latin *contra*, which actually means "against" or "on the opposite side." That may seem to be a rather strange deriva-

From the field notes

"I have visited Berlin at least once in each of the last four decades. What changes I have seen! I took the photo on the top as a child—and what an impression it made. Not only was the city divided, but guards on the eastern side were mostly looking inward! I took my own children with me when I returned most recently during the summer of 2001. We tried to find traces of the old wall—sometimes without success. New buildings have sprung up, street patterns have been changed, and seemingly everything was under construction. But just off of Potsdamer Platz was a remnant of the old order that no one could miss: an old East German guard tower looming over a landscape being remade before our eyes. How long will this remnant remain? The wall is an ugly memory, but it is arguably a memory we should not lose."

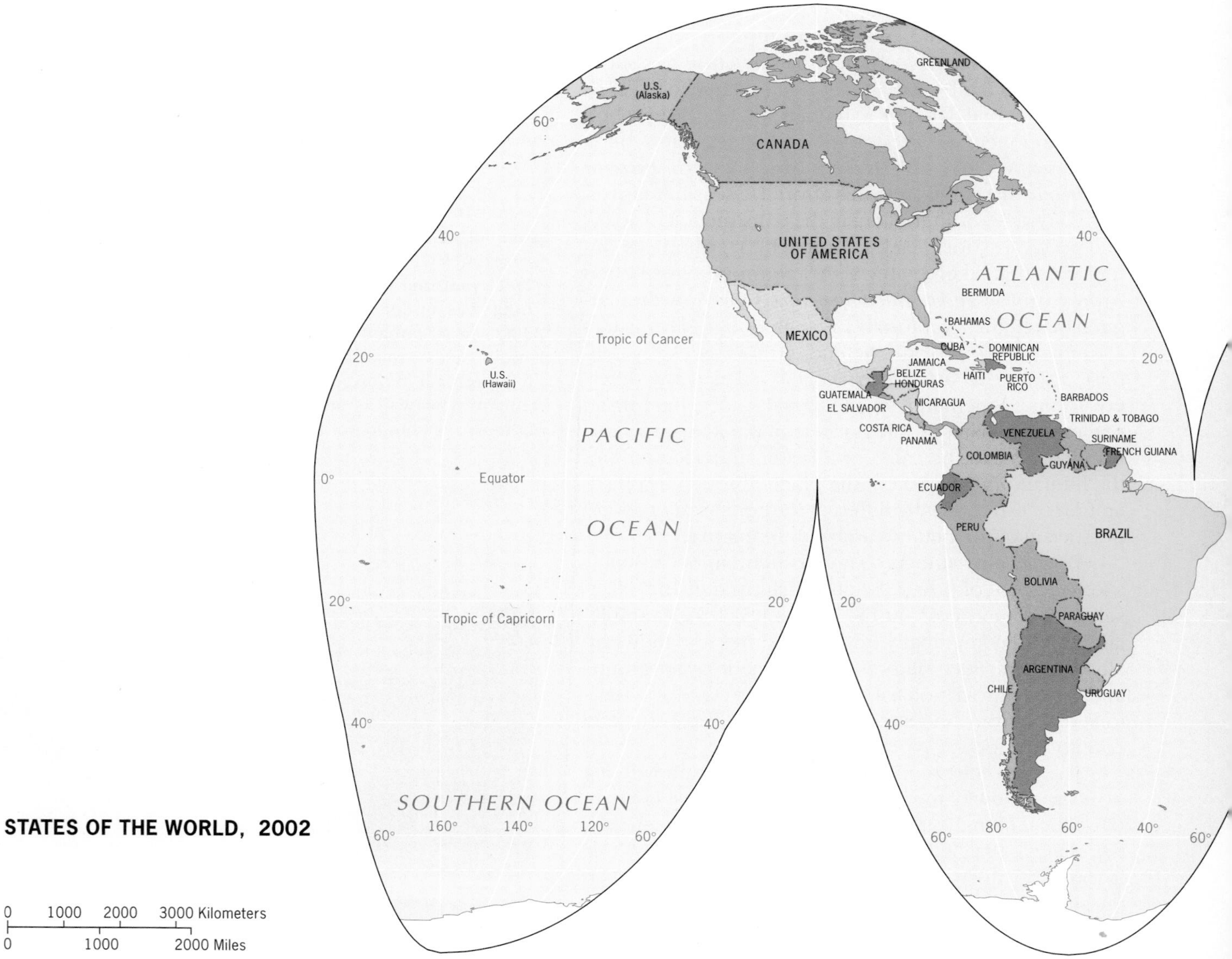

Figure 14-1 States of the World 2002. The building blocks of the international state system, 2002, are illustrated on this map. Only the smallest (micro-) states are not shown.

tion for a term denoting a political unit inhabited by a people of common nationality, but as we have noted before, the meaning of words often changes over time.

Because the term *country* is sometimes used to refer to any expanse of land, political geographers usually prefer the term ***state***, which comes from the Latin *status*, meaning "standing." This leads to a problem, however: certain countries have internal divisions that are also called states, as in the United States of America. The solution is to capitalize State when it refers to such an internal division, as in the State of Michigan or the State of Uttar Pradesh (India).

When used for the formally independent political units that appear in Figure 14-1, the terms *country* and *state* are essentially interchangeable, but the same is not true for the terms ***nation*** and *state* or *country*. This is one of the most common geographic errors you will see in the press and popular literature, and it is understandable because legally people in a state have a shared nationality. The term *nation,* however, has historic, ethnic, and often linguistic and religious connotations. It refers to a people's feeling of belonging to a cultural community that shares a sense of common history.

The perceptual dimension is of critical importance here, for all cultural communities are ultimately mixtures of different peoples. The French are often considered to be the classic example of a nation, but the most French-feeling person in France today is the product of a meld-

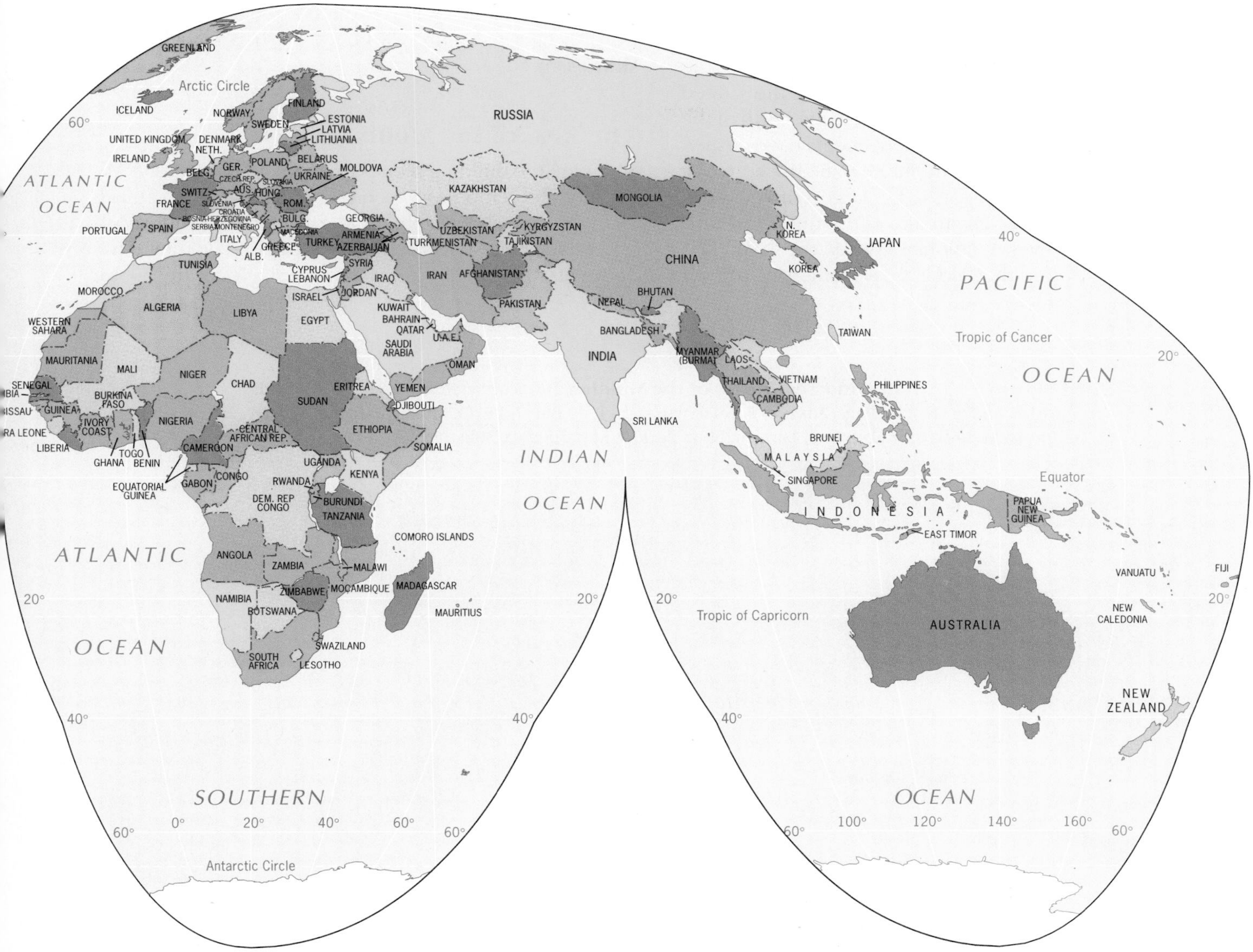

ing together of a wide variety of cultural groups over time, including Celts, Ancient Romans, Franks, Goths, and many more. So if the majority of inhabitants of modern France belong to the French nation—understood in cultural terms—it is because they *feel* that they are a nation, not that they are necessarily a primordial group that has always been distinct.

Historically, a sense of belonging to a nation has often developed among cultural groups occupying the same state territory. Yet a nation can sometimes be larger than the state that gave birth to it; the Chinese are often thought of as a nation, but many Chinese-speaking and Chinese-cultured people living outside China feel that they are part of the Chinese nation. In contrast, the people living in the former Yugoslavia never achieved nationhood in that sense. Millions of people of Yugoslav nationality (in the legal sense) always identified themselves as Slovenes, Croats, Serbs, or members of other ethnic groups. Yugoslavia thus was a state but never a nation, and eventually the state collapsed. Many other countries are states but not nations.

Stateless Nations

Still another complication is that some nations are stateless; that is, they do not possess a national territory even within a larger multinational state. In the 1990s the Palestinian Arabs gained control over fragments of territory that may form the foundations of a future state, but most of the 6.5 million Palestinians continued to live in Israel and several other countries, including Jordan (2.1 million), Lebanon (400,000), and Syria (350,000). A much larger stateless nation is that of the over 20 million Kurds who live in an area called "Kurdistan" that covers parts of six states (Fig. 14-2).

In the aftermath of the 1991 Gulf War, the United Nations established a Kurdish Security Zone north of the 36th parallel in Iraq, but subsequent events have dashed any Kurdish hopes that this might become the core of a future state. The Kurds form the largest minority in Turkey, and the city of Diyarbakir is the unofficial Kurdish capital; however, relations between the 10 million Kurds in Turkey and the Turkish government in Ankara have been volatile. Without the consent of Turkey, no Kurdish national state will be established anywhere in "Kurdistan."

The Rise of the Modern State

States are the building blocks of international society. Although contemporary economic and technological changes are undermining the traditional authority of states in some respects, nations still depend on their governments to represent them in the international arena—to

Figure 14-2 States and Territories of the Middle East. Kurdistan is a stateless nation divided under six state flags. *Source*: From a map in H. J. de Blij and P. O. Muller, *Geography: Regions, Realms, and Concepts*, 10th ed. New York: Wiley, 2002, p. 308.

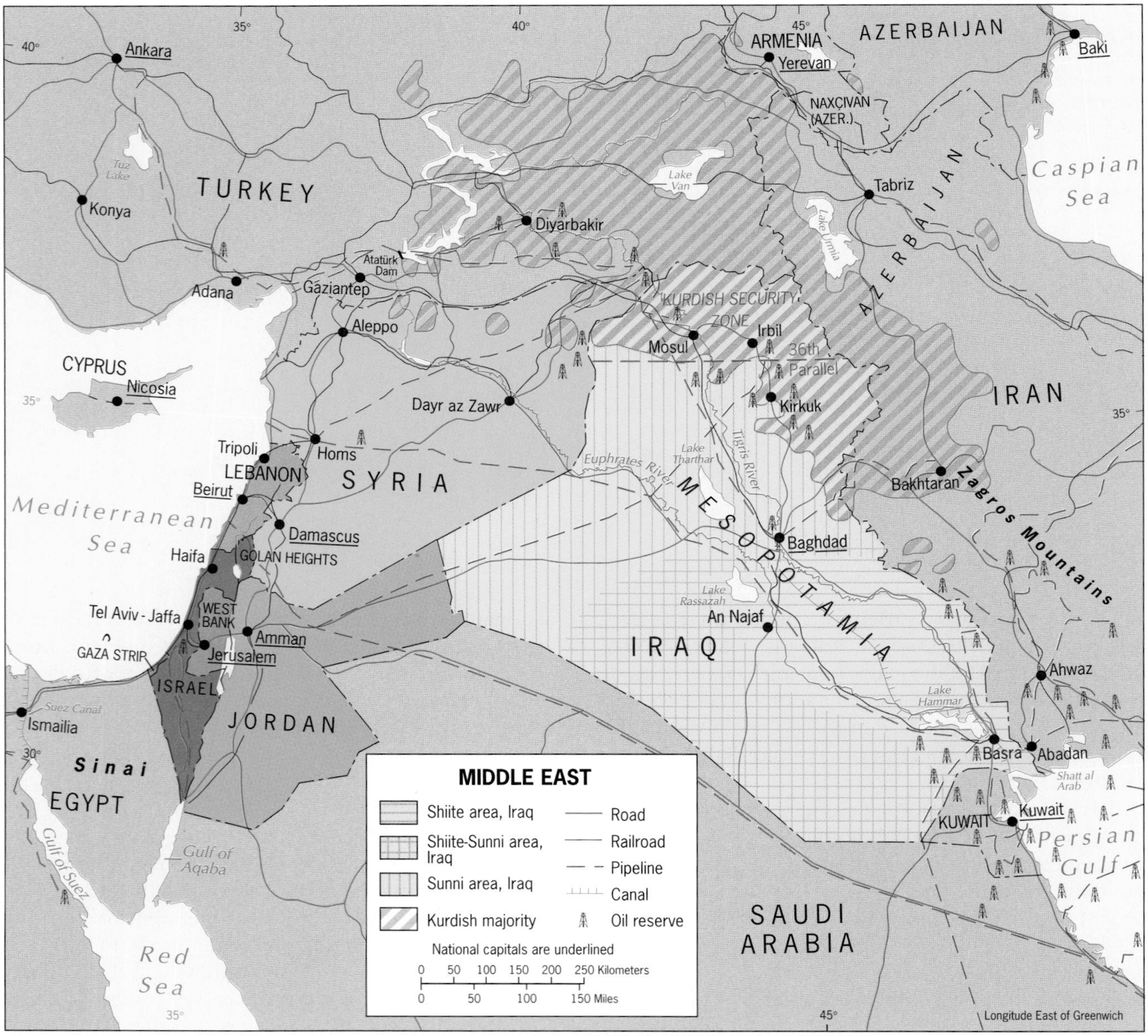

secure needed resources such as oil, to create markets for their products, to join in alliances in order to protect their security. Of course, governments are not always wholly representative of a state's inhabitants; minorities and oligarchies control some states. In such instances the state primarily serves the interests of a ruling class, which may be an ethnic minority. Outwardly, the state functions like any other, but its internal politics are likely to reflect major divisions, as we will see later in the chapter.

The European Model The European state idea deserves particular attention because it had the greatest influence on the development of the modern state system. The origins of the European state idea can be traced to developments several millennia ago near the southeastern shores of the Mediterranean Sea, where distinct kingdoms emerged within discrete territories. Ideas of political-territorial governance forged in these kingdoms diffused to Ancient Greece and later to Rome, which in turn carried the concept of statehood into the heart of Europe. There, in the post–Roman period of political fragmentation, these ideas lay dormant until feudalism gave way to reconsolidation.

The Norman invasion of England in 1066 was perhaps the most significant event in this process. The Normans destroyed the Anglo-Saxon nobility, created a whole new political order, and achieved great national strength under William the Conqueror. On the European mainland, the continuity of dynastic rule and the strength of certain rulers led to greater national cohesiveness. In present-day Germany, France, and Spain, sizable states began to emerge, and some of the trespass lines of the twelfth century were to become modern-day political boundaries (for example, the border between France and Spanish Aragon along the Pyrenees).

At the same time, Europe experienced something of an economic revival, and internal as well as foreign trade increased. Ports and other cities came back to life, and while much of the wealth went to the nobility and the rich merchants, the lifestyles of many more disadvantaged people improved. With its newfound wealth, invaders could be repelled and external forays such as the Crusades could be financed. Crucial technological innovations occurred as well. The horse collar, for example, enormously increased the efficiency of horses for plowing, transport, and other work. Windmills dotted the countryside. A period of stagnation was over, and a new Europe was emerging.

From a political-geographic perspective, the Peace of Westphalia can be seen as the first major step in the emergence of the European state. The treaties signed in 1648 at the end of Europe's most destructive internal struggle over religion—the Thirty Years' War—contained new language that recognized statehood and nationhood, clearly defined boundaries, and guarantees of security. Such agreements eventually were broken (and they continue to be broken today), but the language of the treaties laid the foundations for a Europe made up of national states. They provided a framework through which Spain, the Dutch United Provinces, France, and the Holy Roman Empire would gain regional stability.

In Western Europe, the strong monarchies began to represent something more than mere authority. Increasingly, they became the focal points of national consciousness. They developed increasingly integrated political economies focused on the capital city, in the process breaking down regionalisms and bringing people together in the pursuit of larger-scale political and military ends. The aristocracies, which had strongly opposed monarchical rule, were brought under control. In some places parliaments reappeared, although their power was limited. There was renewed interest in Greek and Roman achievements, in politics as well as in the sciences and arts.

Power and Primacy Europe's rebirth or ***Renaissance*** would not be painless. The emerging political nationalism was accompanied by economic nationalism in the form of mercantilism, which sought to acquire wealth through plunder, colonization, and the protection of home industries and foreign markets. Rivalry and competition intensified in Europe as well as abroad. Struggles among European states devastated not only Europe's towns and cities but also the parliaments and assemblies that had become a part of the political culture. In the end the monarchies benefited most. Louis XIV of France was the personification of the absolute rule that prevailed in Europe in the late Renaissance.

Thus the political-geographic map of Europe was slow in taking shape. In the mid-seventeenth century such states as the Republic of Venice, Brandenburg, the Papal States of central Italy, the Kingdom of Hungary, and several minor German states were all part of a complicated patchwork of political entities, many with poorly defined boundaries. Powerful royal families struggled for dominance in eastern and southern Europe. Instability was the rule, and strife occurred frequently. Repressive government prevailed. Europe was still far from achieving the ideal of the democratic nation-state, the state of and for the people.

Ultimately, the development of an increasingly wealthy middle class proved to be the undoing of absolutist rule. City-based merchants gained wealth and prestige, while the nobility declined. Money and influence were increasingly concentrated in urban areas, and the traditional measure of affluence—land—became less important. The merchants and businessmen demanded political recognition. In the 1780s a series of upheavals began that would change the sociopolitical face of the Continent. Overshadowing these events was the French Revolution (1789–1795), but this momentous event was only one in a series of political upheavals. Europe's political revolution continued into the twentieth century and is not over even now.

◆ THE NATION-STATE

Europe's political-geographic evolution was to have enormous significance because a particular variation of the European model of the state—the ***nation-state***—became at least the aspiration of governing elites around the world. Literally, a nation-state is a politically organized area in which nation and state occupy the same space. Since there are few examples of true nation-states, even in Europe, the importance of the nation-state concept lies primarily in the idea behind it. That idea involves more than bringing the map of nations and states into alignment. It also embodies the notion that ***sovereignty*** (final authority over a territory's political and military affairs) rests with the nation—that is, the people—and that each piece of territory belongs to one people or another.

Where did this idea come from? It is best understood as a fusion of the regime of sovereignty that emerged in central Europe after the Thirty Years' War and the ideas about the rights of nations that found expression in the French Revolution. Each nation, it was argued, should have its own sovereign territory, and only when that was achieved would there be true democracy and stability. The doctrine offered a potentially appealing political-geographic framework for governance, but it assumed the presence of reasonably well-defined, stable nations living within discrete territories. Very few places in the world come even close to satisfying this assumption, but in the Europe of the eighteenth and nineteenth centuries, many believed that the assumption could be met. Thus, in the name of the nation some states, such as France and Italy, abolished their monarchy altogether, whereas others, including the United Kingdom and the Netherlands, became parliamentary democracies, with the monarch remaining as titular head of state. And almost everywhere nationalism became the dominant political force—leading in some cases to efforts to integrate a country's population into an ever more cohesive national whole (e.g., France, Spain), in other cases to efforts to bring peoples with shared cultural characteristics within a single state (for example, Germany, Italy), and in yet other cases to successful separatist movements among nationally self-conscious populations living within states or empires (Ireland, Norway, Poland).

Europe's nation-states thus unified and nationalized large populations, and they did so within clearly defined territories. The modern map of Europe is still fragmented, but much less so than in the 1600s. As Europe went thought its periods of rebirth and revolutionary change, smaller entities were absorbed into larger units, conflicts were resolved (by force as well as by negotiation), and boundaries were defined. The new states became organized in other areas as well, including education, health, and the military. They possessed varying degrees of power, which enabled them not only to assert themselves in Europe but also to engage in colonial campaigns.

With Europe in control of so much of the world, Europeans defined the ground rules of the emerging international state system, and the modern European concept of the nation-state became the model that was adopted around the world. During the mid-nineteenth century, Japan reorganized itself on the European model, even moving its capital from Kyoto in the interior to Edo, renamed Tokyo, on the coast. Later, when colonial empires disintegrated, newly liberated peoples created "nation-states" on the European model—with their leaders purporting to speak on behalf of the "nation," no matter how diverse, or even antagonistic, internal populations might be. They did this because they hoped to forge nations from still-divided peoples, to secure their national territory, to develop economic (as well as other) systems of organization, and to assert national strength (sometimes, unfortunately, through excessive spending on military forces and equipment). On the map, former colonial provinces became new national states, with their administrative borders now transformed into international boundaries. Colonial administrative towns became national capitals in the image of London and Paris. Therefore, in countless ways, the European state became the world model.

Are There Real Nation-States?

To what extent can any state be thought of as a true nation-state? The answer, of course, depends fundamentally on how one defines nation. As we have seen, traditionally a nation was thought of in terms of measures of cultural homogeneity: a nation's people should speak a single language, adhere to the same religion, share a common sense of history, and be united by common political institutions. If these were the criteria for a nation, there would hardly be any true nation-states because virtually all states are characterized by internal cultural diversity—including many of the European states that gave birth to the idea of the nation-state. In only a handful of European cases do state territories largely coincide with the distribution of people who feel they are part of one nation. Iceland, Portugal, Denmark, and Poland are often cited as classic nation-states. These are rather exceptional cases, however, and it is even harder to find such cases outside Europe. Some good examples from the rest of the world are Japan, Uruguay, and Korea (if it were not divided).

There is, however, another way to look at the concept of nation. Even in culturally heterogeneous states the vast majority of the people can share a strong sense of "national spirit"—defined as emotional commitment to the state and what it stands for. One of Europe's oldest states, Switzerland, has a population that is divided along linguistic, religious, and historical lines, but Switzerland has endured because of a widespread commitment to the state ideal. This example suggests another way of viewing the concept of the nation: as a community with a shared commitment to a common political culture. It is an approach that departs from the historical meaning of the term ***nation***, but it offers a more realistic goal for most of the states around the world.

The problem, of course, is that few states have followed Switzerland's course of constructing a national political culture that is ethnically pluralist. In most cases, state elites emphasize the cultural norms of a particular (usually majority) ethnonational group—and this of course can produce feelings of exclusion on the part of minorities that do not share those norms. Thus, even adopting a more politically realistic notion of the term *nation*, we are far from living in a world of true nation-states, and many of our most intractable problems are the result of that reality. We will return to this thorny and widespread problem in Chapter 16.

◆ SPATIAL CHARACTERISTICS OF STATES

An outline map such as Figure 14-1 clearly shows that state territories are not all alike. There may be a "European model" of the nation-state, but even in Europe states differ in as many ways as they are similar. States vary in territorial size and morphology, demography, regime type, organizational structures, resources, development, power, and a host of other ways. We live in a world where one state has nearly 17 million square kilometers of territory (6.6 million sq mi) and several others exceed 7.5 million square kilometers (3 million sq mi), whereas some microstates do not even have 1000 square kilometers (400 sq mi). In terms of population, too, the contrasts are huge. China has over 1.3 billion people, Iceland 0.25 million.

The state is a complex system with many interacting parts. It is far more than a piece of territory inhabited by people; it is a region of cities, towns, and hinterlands, railroad and road networks, administrative subdivisions, schools, and hospitals. It is a maze of circulation and movement: of people, raw materials, finished products, foodstuffs, money, and ideas. It both provides services for the people and demands their taxes, their adherence to the law, and often their service in the armed forces. To succeed, it must foster a sense of legitimacy.

As we have seen, the inclusion of a body of people within a political boundary does not automatically make those people members of a nation. Instead, that happens through the development of a national attitude and an emotional attachment to the country and what it stands for. This attitude can be fostered in various ways; many states engage in programmed education and propaganda to encourage it. Periods of adversity or war can also strengthen national attachments, as became clear in the United States after the terrorist attacks on New York City and Washington, D.C., in September 2001. On the other hand, the spirit of nationhood is fragile and can be damaged by divisive issues. Efforts to promote a common sense of nationhood can backfire when peoples feel they are being forced to adopt an identity that is not their own. In the United States, the Vietnam War of the 1960s and early 1970s had a strong impact on commitment to the national ideal. In Canada, the national fabric has been frayed by efforts to make Quebec a separate nation. In Argentina, the costly invasion of the Falkland Islands caused observers to refer to that nation's "troubled soul."

As we have seen, the world political-geographic map reveals that a few states' boundaries enclose a single cultural nation. More often than not, however, state boundaries may either separate and divide peoples with shared cultural characteristics or throw culturally diverse peoples together. The language map of Europe (Fig. 8-3) reminds us of the former effect, whereas the colonial map of Africa is evidence of the latter. As will be noted later, boundaries often were established not by those whom they affected most directly but by outside forces. Imperial campaigns in Europe and colonial operations in Africa and Asia created boundary frameworks that often did not coincide with cultural divisions.

The European model of the nation-state has proven difficult to imitate even in Europe itself. Nevertheless, today a large majority of states possess all four of the main features of that model: a clearly defined territory, a substantial population, certain types of organizational structures, and some power. We focus next on the key geographic ingredient: territory.

◆ TERRITORY

No state can exist without territory, although the United Nations does recognize the Palestinians as a stateless nation. Within the state's territory lie the resources that make up the state. Yet a glance at a political map shows how different the world's states are in the amount of territory they control. Those differences, in turn, have translated into opportunities and challenges. The territorial character of states has long interested geographers, who have focused on matters of territorial size, shape, and relative location—together referred to as their ***territorial morphology***. Not long ago, in fact, efforts were made to draw broad generalizations about the advantages and disadvantages of a state with a large territory, a compact shape, and a strategic location. There is no question that the nature of a state's territory can have social and political significance, but we must be careful.

Focusing just on territory without considering other aspects of a state's geographical context can be misleading. Being small and landlocked can mean very different things for a state in a stable, prosperous region than it can for one in a poor region fraught by conflict.

Even though the territorial characteristics of states cannot be viewed in isolation, it is useful to recognize that different territorial circumstances can present opportunities and challenges. We can see this most clearly by focusing on the three classic attributes of territory noted earlier: size, shape, and relative location.

Size

It is tempting to assume that the more territory a state owns, the better off it is in all respects, especially in terms of raw materials. This is not necessarily the case, however. True, a state with several million square miles of territory has a greater chance of having a wide range of environments and resources within its borders than does a small state. However, much also depends on location with reference to the Earth's known mineral resources.

Large size has worked to both the advantage and disadvantage of countries. The United States' large size, large population, and abundant resources helped it emerge as a major global power. For the former Soviet Union, however, the vast distances over which people and resources were distributed presented a serious obstacle and helped bring about its collapse. At the other end of the spectrum lie states that are so small in size that they are referred to as ***microstates*** (e.g., Liechtenstein, Andorra, and San Marino). For many such states, small size does not mean poverty. The comparative wealth of the European microstates shows the importance of avoiding generalizations about the impacts of territorial size that are made without reference to the economic and political context within which states are situated.

Shape

Similar contrasts can be seen when the issue of shape or spatial form is considered. States take on a variety of forms, and these can each carry with them distinct advantages and disadvantages (Fig. 14-3). Particularly before the advent of modern transportation and communication, it was easier for a central government to knit together the territory of a ***compact*** state—one in which the distance from the geometric center to any point on the boundary did not vary greatly—than it was for states lacking this characteristic. Some states are ***fragmented***, consisting of two or more separate pieces; examples include the Philippines and East and West Pakistan before they were divided. This fragmentation makes certain kinds of interactions more difficult. Other states are ***elongated*** or attenuated (Chile, Vietnam), with historical consequences that are still evident today. Still others have a protruded area—one that extends out from a more compact core; this area sometimes has developed in different ways from the core (e.g., the southern portion of Thailand). Such states are sometimes called ***prorupt*** (protruded) states. Finally, a few states are ***perforated*** by another country (e.g., South Africa by Lesotho, Italy by San Marino and Vatican City).

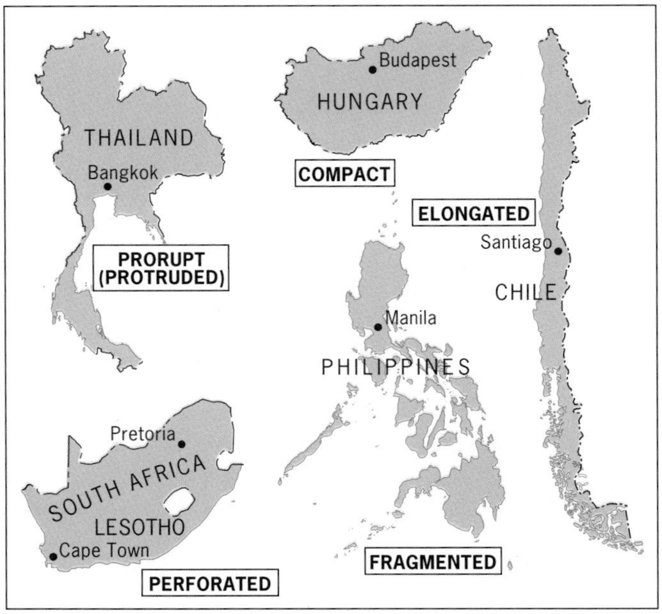

Figure 14-3 States with different territorial morphologies.

Relative Location

Territorial size and shape can influence the development of regions and states, but they do not determine their political, social, or economic well-being. Norway does very well despite its elongated shape, and Zimbabwe faces some serious internal tensions despite its relatively compact shape. The relative location of a state, however, can have more important effects. Most obviously, states in the global economic core are at a competitive economic and political advantage. States located in resource-rich regions can also be in an advantageous position. As we will discuss in Part Eight, however, not all such states are in a position to tap those resources for their own benefit (for example, Congo), and national wealth can be achieved even without a resource-rich territory—witness Switzerland and Japan.

Another important consideration is a state's situation in relation to global mainstreams of activity. Singapore's rise to global economic significance is tied to its position at the crossroads of some of the world's busiest shipping routes. Conversely, isolation from flows of goods and capital puts such states as Sierra Leone, Myanmar (Burma), and Suriname at a disadvantage.

Exclaves and Enclaves

A particularly interesting type of territorial irregularity occurs where historical circumstances have led to the existence of small outliers of territory that are separated from the state by the territory of another state. These ***exclaves*** can lie on coasts (e.g., the territory of Cabinda, which is part of Angola), but more often they are landlocked within another country, in which case they are known as ***enclaves*** within the country that surrounds them.

Figure 14-4 shows Nagorno-Karabakh, an exclave of Christian Armenia, lying totally within Muslim Azerbaijan. Soviet political planners, who designated specific homelands for sizeable ethnic or cultural minorities in the communist empire, created this situation. Christian Armenia was made a republic, and so was Muslim Azerbaijan. Awarding the Armenians their own territory but giving Azerbaijan the right to administer it solved the problem created by having a large cluster of Christian Armenians within Azerbaijan.

All this worked while Soviet rule kept the lid on potential conflict, but when the USSR collapsed, old animosities resurfaced. The Republic of Armenia demanded that Nagorno-Karabakh be included in its territory, if necessary by a corridor linking the exclave to the main territory. (They are separated by only about 16 kilometers, or 10 miles, of mountainous terrain.) As Figure 14-4 shows, Nagorno-Karabakh is not the only exclave in this region. Azerbaijan itself has a sizable exclave, Nakhichevan, which is separated from it by Armenian territory. But note that Nakhichevan is not an enclave; that is, it is not completely surrounded by one country. It has borders on Armenia to the north and Iran to the south.

Landlocked Countries

Landlocked countries in particular face locational challenges because they have no ready access to the seas. Landlocked Bolivia, for example, suffered considerably after a war with its neighbors ended its rights to use ports on the Pacific coast. The Czech Republic is also landlocked, but its isolation is far less serious because it is connected to the outside world by waterways and surface transport routes. In Asia, Mongolia and Nepal are severely landlocked, with distance, terrain, and limited communications all contributing to their condition. In Africa, the realm with the largest number of landlocked states of all, the resulting problems are especially severe. States in the Sahel are poorly linked to coastal entry points; in East Africa, Uganda has a rail link to the coast, but Rwanda and Burundi are among the world's most isolated places. To the south, Zimbabwe has access to the sea via South Africa and Moçambique, but Zambia and Malawi suffer from poor connections as well as from political instability in their coastal neighbors.

◆ LAND BOUNDARIES

The territories of individual states are separated by international boundaries. Boundaries may appear on maps as straight lines or may twist and turn to conform to the bends of rivers and the curves of hills and valleys. But a boundary is more than a line, far more than a fence or wall on the ground. A ***boundary*** between states is actually a vertical plane that cuts through the rocks below (called the ***subsoil*** in legal papers when countries argue about it) and the airspace above (Fig. 14-5). Only where this vertical plane intersects the Earth's surface (on land or at sea) does it form the line we see on a map.

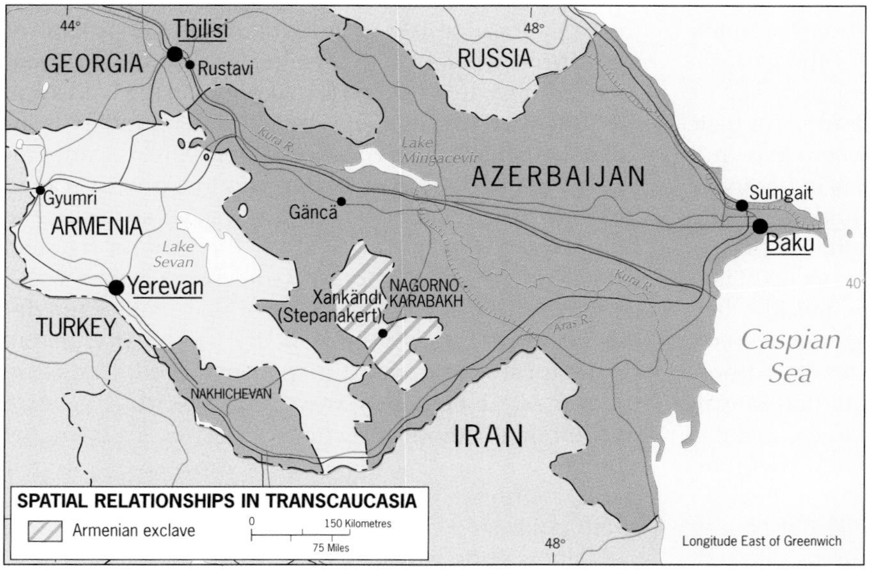

Figure 14-4 This map shows the political organization of territory in Transcaucasia. *Source*: From a map in H. J. de Blij and P. O. Muller, *Geography: Realms, Regions, and Concepts*, 10th ed. New York: Wiley, 2002.

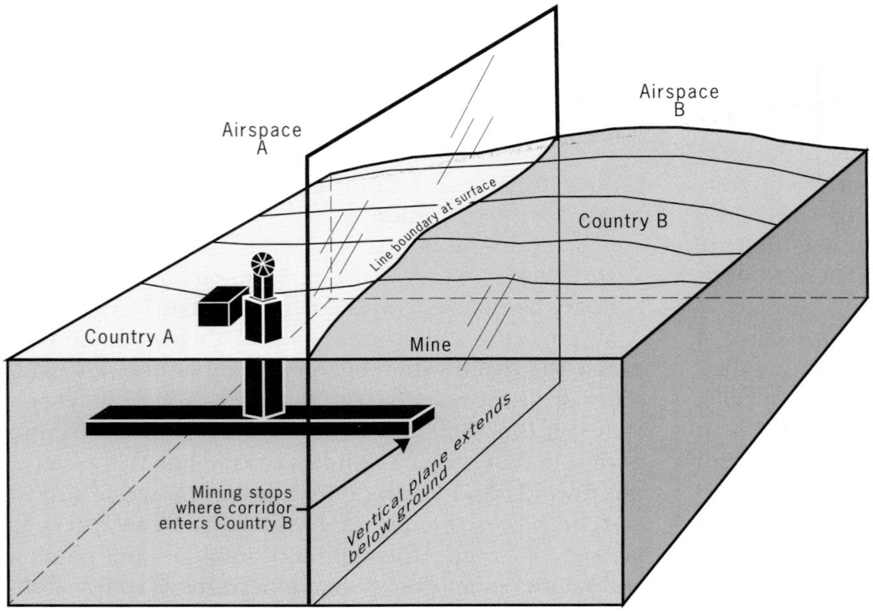

Figure 14-5 A political boundary is a vertical plane. It is not merely a line on the ground.

When boundaries were established, the resources below the surface were much less well known than they are today. As a result, coal seams extend from one country to another, oil reserves are split between states, and gas reserves are shared as well. Europe's coal reserves, for example, extend from Belgium underneath the Netherlands and on into Germany. Soon after mining began in the mid-nineteenth century, these three neighbors began to accuse each other of mining coal that did not lie directly below their own national territories. (The underground surveys that were available at the time were too inaccurate to pinpoint the ownership of each coal seam.)

During the 1950s-1960s, Germany and the Netherlands also argued over a gas reserve that lies in the subsoil across their boundary. The Germans argued that the Dutch were withdrawing so much natural gas that the gas was flowing from beneath German land to the Dutch side of the border. The Germans wanted compensation for their "lost" gas. Similarly, a major issue between Iraq and Kuwait, which led to Iraq's invasion of Kuwait in 1990, was the oil in the Rumaylah reserve, which lies underneath the desert and crosses the boundary between the two states. The Iraqis not only asserted that the Kuwaitis were drilling too many wells and draining the reserve too quickly; they also alleged that the Kuwaitis were drilling oblique boreholes that penetrated the vertical plane extending downward along the border. At the time that the Iraq-Kuwait border was established, however, no one knew that this giant oil reserve lay in the subsoil or that it would help create an international crisis (Fig. 14-6).

Above the ground, too, the interpretation of boundaries as vertical planes has serious implications. A state's "airspace" is defined by the atmosphere above its land area as marked by its boundaries, as well as by what lies beyond, at higher altitudes. But how high does that airspace extend? Most states insist on controlling the airline traffic over their territories, but they have not yet done the same in regard to satellite orbits. That time may come, however. In addition, air circulates from one airspace to another, often carrying the pollutants of one state across to another state. Acid rain (see Part Eleven) knows no political boundaries, but it can cause serious political disputes.

The Evolution of Boundaries

Boundaries evolve through three stages. First, agreement is reached on the rough positioning of the border. Then the exact location is established through the process of ***definition***, whereby a treaty-like, legal-sounding document is drawn up in which actual points in the landscape are described (or, where a straight-line boundary is involved, points of latitude and longitude). Next, cartographers put the boundary on the map in a process called ***delimitation***. If either or both of the states so desire, the boundary is actually marked on the ground by steel posts, concrete pillars, fences (sometimes even a wall), or some other visible means. That final stage is the ***demarcation*** of the boundary. By no means are all boundaries on the world map demarcated. There are thousands of miles where you could cross from one state into another without knowing it. Demarcating a lengthy boundary by any means at all is expensive, and it is hardly worth the effort in high mountains, vast deserts, frigid polar lands, or other places where there are few permanent settlements.

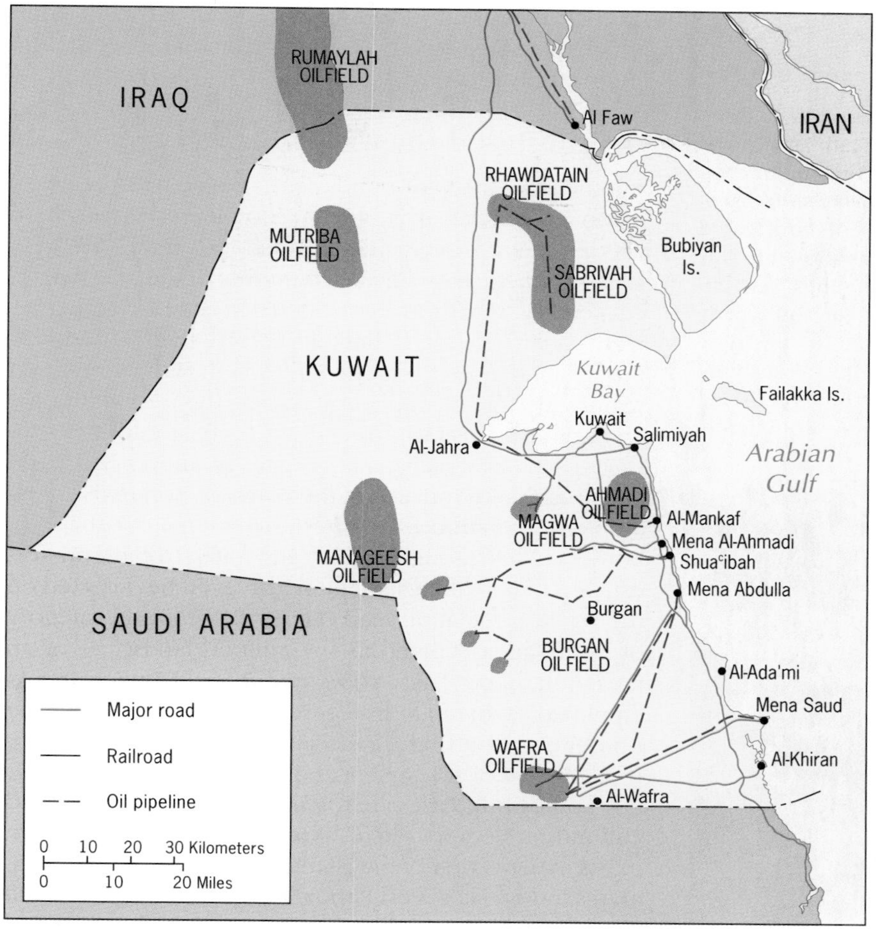

Figure 14-6 Relative Location of Kuwait. Kuwait's northern boundary was redefined and delimited by a United Nations boundary commission; it was demarcated by a series of concrete pillars 2 kilometers (1.24 miles) apart.

Types of Boundaries

Even the most casual glance at the world's boundary framework reveals that boundaries differ in morphological terms. Some conform to lines of latitude or longitude (Egypt occupies Africa's northeastern corner), others conform to natural features such as rivers, and still others separate societies with contrasting ethnic backgrounds or cultural characteristics. Political geographers use the term ***geometric boundary*** to identify straight-line boundaries such as that between the United States and Canada west of the Great Lakes. Such boundaries are totally unrelated to any aspects of the cultural or physical landscape. The colonial powers made extensive use of such boundaries in Africa.

Certain boundaries conform to physiographic features in the landscape, such as rivers or the crests of mountain ranges. These are referred to as ***physical-political*** or sometimes ***natural-political boundaries***, and many of them are modern versions of old trespass lines. The Rio Grande is an important physical-political boundary between the United States and Mexico; an older border follows crest lines of the Pyrenees between Spain and France. Lakes sometimes serve as boundaries as well—for example, four of the five Great Lakes of North America (between the United States and Canada) and several of the Great Lakes of East Africa (between Congo and its eastern neighbors). At first, national jurisdiction extended to the banks of rivers and the shores of lakes, but today the waters themselves are divided between riparian and littoral states.

Physical features sometimes make convenient political boundaries, but the nature and meaning of such boundaries change over time and space. Rivers can unify as well as divide, and a mountain range that separates two states now may not have done so in the past. But a combination of perception and practical circumstances has led to the creation of many physical-political boundaries. Some of these are stable (for example, the boundary between Switzerland and Italy in the Alps), and others are not (for example, the boundary between India and China in the Karakoram Range). Thus it is important to recognize that stability of boundaries often has more to do with local historical and geographical circumstances than with the physical character of the boundary itself.

From the field notes

"Unlike the Berlin wall of old, the so-called Green Line in Nicosia is not characterized by a swath of cleared land and a high concrete barrier. Instead, at the end of each street along the line one finds relatively make-shift barriers—piles of sandbags and barrels, sheets of corrugated metal, and the occasional viewing platform as shown in this photo. These barriers are strung between buildings, separating those on either side by a matter of a few feet. But what a separation it is! The barriers may be make-shift, but they have been there for decades. And guns project from windows nearby. The map at this point along the Green Line tells the story: an island once unified that is now completely divided."

Boundaries that mark breaks in the human landscape were formerly called anthropogeographic boundaries, but they are now known as ***cultural-political boundaries***. When communist planners laid out their grand design for the Soviet Union, they tried to create a patchwork of nationalities, delimiting many miles of cultural-political boundaries in the process. For example, the boundary between Christian Armenia and Muslim Azerbaijan mentioned earlier was a cultural-political boundary. The map of European languages and political borders (Fig. 8-3) suggests how common such boundaries still are. Cultural breaks in the human landscape tend to shift over time, which is one reason why cultural-political boundaries often lead to conflict. Nevertheless, when peacemakers tried to draw a new map of Bosnia to help end the conflict among Serbs, Croats, and Muslims there, their attempts were based on cultural-political principles. The proposed Muslim "safe zones" were essentially cultural enclaves. However, the intermixing of the population and the highly generalized maps from which the peacemakers worked made boundary delimitation highly problematic.

Origin-Based Classification

Another way to view boundaries has to do with their evolution or genesis. This genetic boundary classification was pioneered by Richard Hartshorne (1899–1992), a leading American political geographer of the mid-twentieth century. Hartshorne reasoned that certain boundaries were defined and delimited before the present-day human landscape developed. Although Hartshorne used mainly Western examples to illustrate this idea, its applicability is also illustrated elsewhere, for example, in Southeast Asia. In Figure 14-7A, the boundary between Malaysia and Indonesia on the island of Borneo is an example of this ***antecedent boundary*** type. Most of this border passes through sparsely inhabited tropical rainforest, and the break in settlement can even be detected on the world population map (Fig. 4-1). A second category of boundaries evolved as the cultural landscape of an area took shape. These ***subsequent boundaries*** are exemplified by the map in Figure 14-7B, which shows the border between China and Vietnam, the result of a long-term process of adjustment and modification.

Some boundaries are forcibly drawn across a unified cultural landscape. Such a ***superimposed boundary*** exists in the center of the island of New Guinea and separates Indonesia's West Papua from the country of Papua New Guinea (Fig. 14-7C). West Papua, which is peopled mostly by ethnic Papuans, was part of the Netherlands East Indies that did not receive independence as Indonesia did in 1949. After many tension-filled years, the Indonesians finally invaded this territory in 1962 to drive out the remaining Dutch. Following UN mediation and an eventual plebiscite, West Irian (as it was known) was formally attached to Indonesia in 1969—thereby perpetuating the boundary that the colonial administrators had originally superimposed on New Guinea in the early nineteenth century. The fourth genetic boundary type is the ***relict boundary***—a border that has ceased to function but whose imprints are still evident on the cultural landscape. The boundary between former North Vietnam and South Vietnam (Fig. 14-7D) is a classic example: once demarcated militarily, it has had relict status since 1976 following the reunification of Vietnam at the end of the Indochina War (1964–1975).

Frontiers

The term ***frontier*** is misused almost as often as nation. "Boundary" and "frontier" are used interchangeably, as though they were synonyms, but they are not. A frontier is a zone of separation, an area between communities, clusters, groups, and states. It is a sort of territorial cushion that keeps rivals apart. Such "cushions" may be

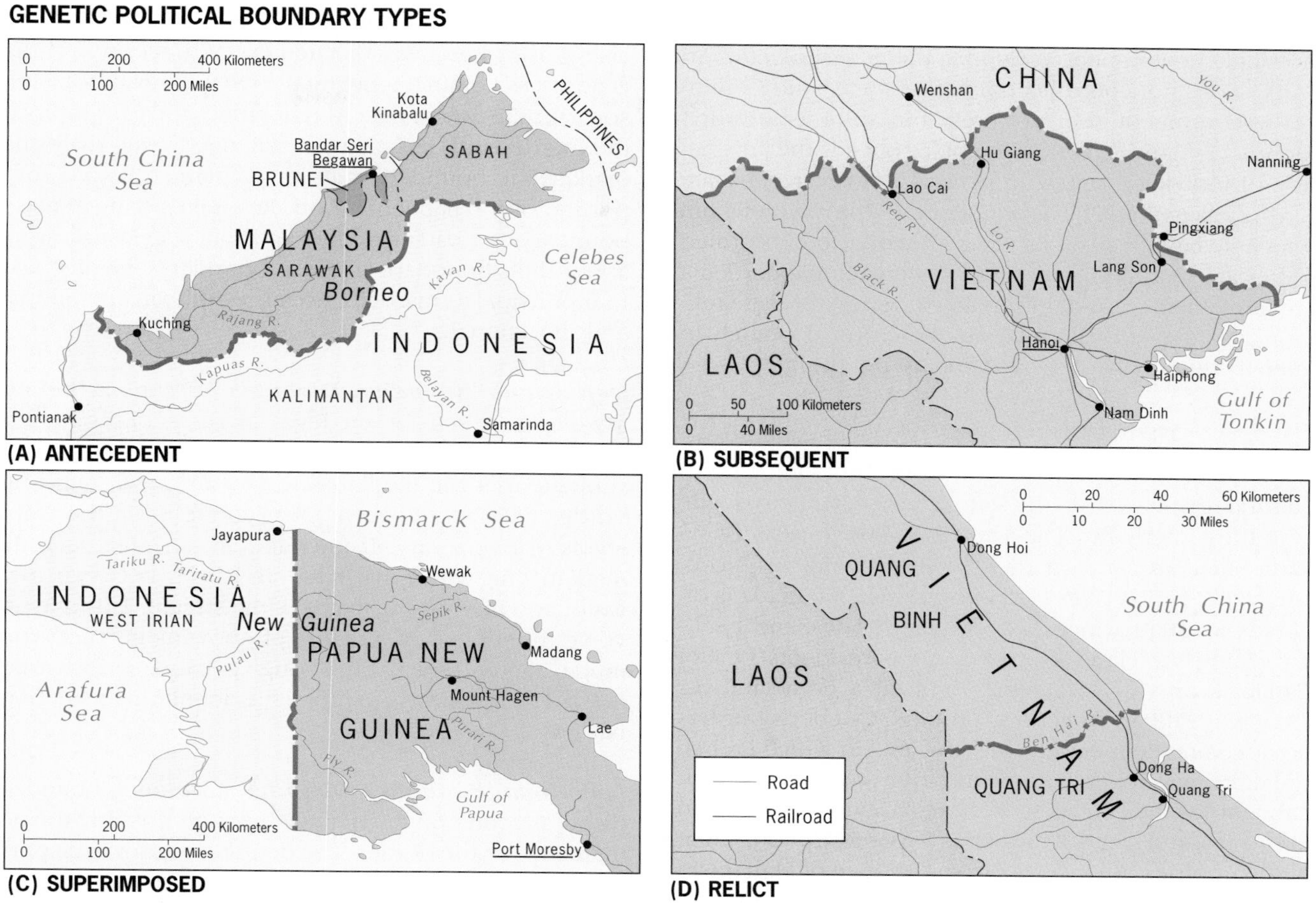

Figure 14-7 Genetic Political Boundary Types. Genetic political boundary types are (A) antecedent, (B) subsequent, (C) superimposed, and (D) relict. *Source*: From a map in H. J. de Blij and P. O. Muller, *Geography: Realms, Regions, and Concepts*, 10th ed. New York: Wiley, 2002.

swamplands, impenetrable forests, wide deserts, mountain ranges, or river basins. Before the present world boundary framework jelled, many societies were separated by such natural frontiers. Eventually, even the most remote parts of the planet were settled, and boundaries were drawn through the last frontiers—even in Antarctica, the Earth's last land frontier, and, as we will see later, in the seas and oceans.

◆ FUNCTIONS OF BOUNDARIES

There was a time when states and empires built walls to fortify their borders, to keep out adversaries, and, sometimes, to keep inhabitants from wandering too far from the seat of authority. China's Great Wall and Hadrian's Wall in Britain (built by the Romans) still stand as evidence of such intentions. Indeed, the notion that boundaries could serve as fortifications endured into the mid-twentieth century; during World War II there were several attempts to fortify boundaries. Boundaries continue to be reinforced in order to stop people from moving across them without authorization. The Berlin Wall was built in 1961 to keep East Germans from crossing into the Western enclave of West Berlin and seeking asylum from communist rule. More recently, the border between Mexico and the United States was walled and fenced in order to reduce illegal migration. Thus boundaries still serve defensive functions, though in a different context.

Today, boundaries mark the limits of state jurisdiction. They serve as symbols of state sovereignty. States often display maps of their national territory on the front pages of newspapers, on schoolbooks, on stamps, and even on flags. This contributes to the building of a national consciousness, a sense of inclusion that fosters ***nationalism***. Modern nationalism is a sense of national (often ethnic) consciousness and loyalty to nation and state, exalting it above all others and promoting its culture and interests over those of other nations. It is a potent force in the world today.

The governments of some states do not exert effective control over the entire territory of the state. There is no single government in Cyprus; the government of Sri Lanka does not control certain rebel areas; and Columbia's government does not prevail in all of its territory. Moreover, many activities take place outside the jurisdiction of individual states. In general, however, the state territory as outlined by its boundaries is the region within which its laws prevail, its taxes are collected, its armed forces are recruited or drafted, its educational curricula are implemented, and, in certain countries, the state religion is practiced. Boundaries, therefore, do much to keep the world divided—and not just politically.

Internal Boundaries

For administrative purposes, and sometimes to mark off cultural regions within the state, it is necessary to divide countries internally. The United States consists of 50 States that are in turn divided into counties (except Louisiana, which is divided into parishes). Canada is divided into 10 provinces, 2 federal territories, and 1 self-governing homeland set aside for Inuit residents. One of Canada's provinces, Quebec, is itself a homeland for French-speaking Canadians, although Quebec's borders do not coincide precisely with the area in which French speakers live. India, with nearly four times as many inhabitants as the United States, has 28 States and 6 union territories, and some of the States have more people than most countries. If you cross from the State of Maharashtra into Karnataka, you will hear a different language. India's internal boundaries represent more cultural variation than do many international boundaries.

Political geographers have identified another kind of internal boundary, a kind that does not show up on administrative maps. As we have seen, numerous countries are culturally divided. Take the case of the former Yugoslavia. Although there were internal "republics" for the country's Serbian, Croatian, Slovenian, Macedonian, and other major cultural components, this administrative structure did not accurately reflect the real situation. There were Serbs in Croatia, Croatians in Bosnia, and so on. Figure 14-8 is a simplification of the cultural mosaic of Yugoslavia before it was engulfed by civil war. Such internal boundaries can be seen in Belgium, Sri Lanka, Malaysia, Moldova, and a host of other countries, including many African states.

Boundary Disputes

Nations, like families and individuals, can become very territorial when they feel that their space has been violated. In suburban areas in the United States, quarrels over fence lines and surveys rank high among social disputes that must be solved by legal means. So it is with states. As noted earlier, the boundary we see as a line on an atlas map is the product of a complex series of legal steps that begins with a written description of the border. Sometimes that legal description is old and imprecise. Sometimes it was dictated by a stronger power that is now less dominant, giving the weaker neighbor a reason to argue for change. At other times the geography of the borderland has actually changed; the river that marked the boundary may have changed course, or a portion of it has been cut off. Resources lying across a boundary can lead to conflict. In short, states often argue about their boundaries. These boundary disputes take four principal forms: definitional, locational, operational, and allocational.

Definitional Boundary Disputes *Definitional* boundary disputes focus on the legal language of the boundary agreement. For example, a boundary definition may stipulate that the median line of a river will mark the border. That would seem clear enough, but the water levels of rivers vary. If the valley is asymmetrical, the median line will move back and forth between low-water and high-water stages of the stream. This may involve hundreds of meters of movement—not very much, it would seem, but enough to cause serious argument. The solution is to refine the definition to suit both parties.

Locational Boundary Disputes *Locational* boundary disputes center on the delimitation and possibly the demarcation of the border. The definition is not in dispute, but its interpretation is. Sometimes the language of boundary treaties is vague enough to allow mapmakers to delimit the line in various ways. For example, when the colonial powers defined their empires in Africa and Asia, they specified their international boundaries rather carefully. But internal administrative boundaries often were not strictly defined. When those internal boundaries became the boundaries of independent states, there was plenty of room for argument.

In a few instances, locational disputes arise because no definition of the boundary exists at all. An important case involves Saudi Arabia and Yemen, whose potentially oil-rich border area is not covered by a treaty.

Operational Boundary Disputes *Operational* boundary disputes involve neighbors who differ over the way their boundary should function. When two adjoining countries agree that cross-border migration should be controlled, the boundary functions satisfactorily. However, if one state wants to limit migration while the other does not, a dispute may arise. Similarly, efforts to prevent smuggling across borders sometimes lead to operational disputes when one state's efforts are not matched (or are possibly even sabotaged) by its neighbor's. And in areas where nomadic lifeways still prevail, the movement of people and their livestock across international borders can lead to conflict.

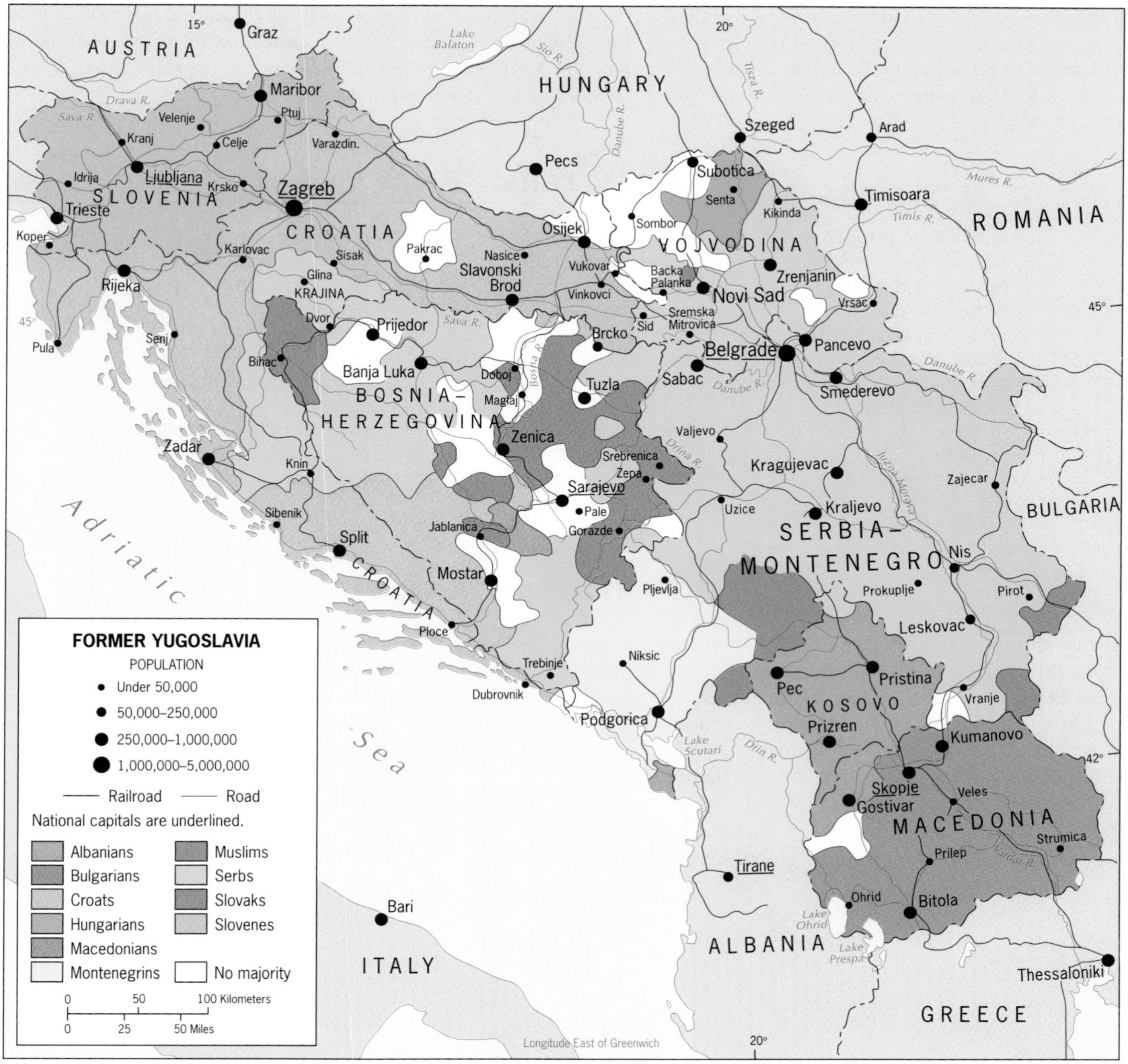

Figure 14-8 The Former Yugoslavia. The ethnic mosaic of the former Yugoslavia is illustrated on this map. *Source*: Based on maps drawn in the Office of the Geographer of the U.S. Department of State, Washington, D.C., 1991.

Allocational Boundary Disputes *Allocational* disputes of the kind described earlier, involving the Netherlands and Germany over natural gas and Iraq and Kuwait over oil, are becoming more common as the search for resources intensifies. Today many such disputes involve international boundaries at sea. Oil reserves under the seafloor in coastal waters sometimes lie in areas where exact boundary delimitation may be difficult or subject to debate. Another growing area of allocational dispute has to do with water supplies: the Tigris, Nile, Colorado, and other rivers are subject to such disputes. When a river crosses an international boundary, the rights of the upstream and downstream users of the river often come into conflict.

In this chapter we have examined various geographic aspects of the territory of states, including its development and its spatial limits. As we noted, the territorial attributes of states vary widely, as do the advantages of their relative locations. Whatever their territorial circumstances, however, states achieve strength, durability, and power by organizing their resources effectively. Some states have overcome severe geographic disadvantages and attained prosperity and security; others, with more available resources, have not. We turn next to the role of spatial organization in the functioning of states.

◆ KEY TERMS ◆

antecedent boundary
boundary
boundary definition
boundary delimitation
boundary demarcation
compact state
cultural-political boundary
elongated state
enclave
exclave
fragmented state
frontier
geometric boundary
human territoriality
landlocked
microstate
nation
nationalism
nation-state
natural-political boundary
perforated state
physical-political boundary
political culture
political geography
prorupted state
relict boundary
Renaissance
sovereignty
state
subsequent boundary
subsoil
superimposed boundary
territorial morphology
theocracy

◆ APPLYING GEOGRAPHIC KNOWLEDGE ◆

1. Just after the beginning of the twentieth century, the world numbered just 60 independent countries, and in 1946 there were 74. Today, the map shows almost 200 sovereign states. Has the proliferation of states reached a peak, or is the number of states likely to grow still further? What maps might you reference in support of your answer?
2. Political boundaries, it is often said, have become all but irrelevant in this world of global interaction and international cooperation. Still, boundary disputes continue in many parts of the world, and some countries (Cyprus, Somalia, Sri Lanka) threaten to split along newly delimited borders. Discuss the modern functions of boundaries and suggest ways in which such boundary roles may change during the twenty-first century.

Chapter 15

State Organization and National Power

From the field notes

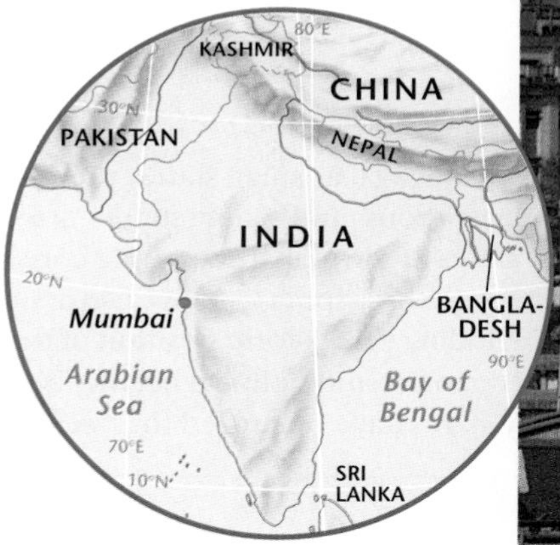

"China's Chairman Mao used to say that political power comes from the barrel of a gun. Of course there are other ways for a state to exercise power, but here in Mumbai, India, he seems to have been taken literally. This port is bristling with weaponry: aircraft carriers, cruisers, submarines, and dozens of other navy vessels. India aspires to be a global as well as a regional power, but the country has a history of conflict with two of its neighbors: Pakistan and China. The on-going dispute with Pakistan over Kashmir creates the potential for a devastating exchange between nuclear-armed neighbors."

KEY POINTS

◆ **The modern political-territorial order is characterized by great power differentials. Many of these have roots in a world order developed during the age of European colonialism.**

◆ **Understanding state power requires looking not just at the characteristics of individual states but at the relationships between and among states.**

◆ **Geopolitics, a century-old sub-field of political geography, is concerned with the influence of different geographical conditions and understandings on the exercise of power.**

◆ **The European state model had a centralized, unitary framework. Federal systems were developed in the New World and in former colonies elsewhere.**

◆ **The exercise of central government power within states is facilitated by a well-developed primary core area and a well-functioning capital city.**

◆ **The spatial organization of voting districts is a fundamentally geographically phenomenon that can have profound impacts on who is represented and who is not.**

◆ **States are held together by centripetal forces such as nationalism, education, circulation, and the institutions of government; but they are also subject to centrifugal forces in the form of ethnic disunity, cultural differences, or regional disparities.**

Many political geographers believe that the number of independent states will surpass 200 in the near future. These 200 countries will occupy the surface of a small planet of which over two-thirds is covered by water or ice! With such a large number of entities, some large and others very small, it is inevitable that equality will remain a mirage. Not only are there large as well as small states: there are also economically prosperous and poor states, stable and unstable states, states in the global economic core and states on the disadvantaged periphery. Many factors create this situation, including the historic position of the state in international economic and political networks. Also significant is the way states have organized themselves internally. ◆

◆ LARGE-SCALE INFLUENCES ON STATE POWER

Measuring the relative power of states is a complex and imprecise business. There is no question, however, that one of the most important long-term influences is the situation of a country in terms of global patterns of economic and political power. As noted in the previous chapter, several centuries ago part of Europe took advantage of an increasingly well-consolidated internal political order and newfound wealth to expand its influence to increasingly far-flung realms. Driven by motives ranging from economic self-interest to the desire to bring Christianity to the rest of the world, ***colonialism*** projected European power into the non-European world. The height of the colonial era came during the eighteenth and nineteenth centuries, when the British, French, Spanish, Portuguese, Dutch, and Belgians consolidated their overseas holdings (Fig. 15-1). The Germans and Italians were latecomers on the colonial scene. Spain and Portugal lost their American possessions even before the Berlin Conference in 1884–1885 laid out the colonial map of Africa, and early in the twentieth century it was evident that small European countries would not be able to control large, distant empires forever.

Elsewhere in the world, two other colonial powers built major empires: Russia and Japan. The Russian em-

From the field notes

"The Portuguese led the way. That is what this monument said to me as I visited the harbor at Lisbon (Portugal). Dedicated to the early Portuguese navigators and explorers, the monument is clearly a source of national pride. Yet it represents something quite different in other parts of the world. The legacy of European colonialism is surely a complicated and controversial matter, but one thing is for sure: it profoundly and irrevocably changed the world."

pire was vast, and unlike others, it was contiguous: only in what is today Alaska did Russia acquire an "overseas" domain—which it sold to the United States in 1867. Japan came late to the colonial scene, but in a few decades it acquired major holdings in East Asia.

The colonial powers were able to gain control over their empires by virtue of their economic, political, and military organization; when that organization failed, they lost their advantage. Russia's internal weaknesses were exposed by its losses in the Far East (Japan decisively defeated the Russian armies in 1905). But during the heyday of colonialism the imperial powers exercised ruthless control over their domains and organized them for maximum economic exploitation. The capacity to install the infrastructures necessary for such efficient profiteering is itself evidence of the power relationships involved: entire populations were regimented in the service of the colonial ruler. Flows of raw materials were organized for the benefit of the colonial power, and the tangible evidence of that organization (mines, railroads, ports, plantations) can still be seen. Moreover, these economic systems have survived the end of colonialism. In many cases raw material flows are as great as they were before the colonial era came to an end. And while the former colonies are now independent states, the influence of their former rulers continues, notably in the former French empire.

The long-term impacts of colonialism are many and varied. In conjunction with the colonial project, advances in health care, literacy, and the fight against some diseases diffused to parts of the colonial world. But one of the most powerful impacts of colonialism was the construction of a global order characterized by great differences in economic and political power. The European colonial enterprise gave birth to an ever more globalized economic order in which the European states and areas dominated by European migrants emerged as the major centers of economic and political power. There was much diversity within this realm. Large colonial empires did not necessarily guarantee economic or political dominance (e.g., Spain in the late seventeenth century), and enormous poverty persisted within the most powerful of states. Moreover, selected countries in other parts of the world emerged as important powers (e.g., Japan). But the concentration of wealth that colonialism brought to the Europe, and to parts of the world dominated by European settlers, is at the heart of the highly uneven global distribution of power noted above. Reinforcing the unevenness were the extraction of wealth from colonies and the subservient relationship that developed between colonizer and colonized.

When asking questions about the power and position of individual states, it is critical to consider where those states are situated within the larger global geography of power relations. Yet that larger geography is not simply reducible to a historical map of colonization. Instead, that map provides an important backdrop to the economic and geopolitical circumstances that affect interstate power relations.

Economic Dimensions of Power

In Part Eight we will look in some detail at the geographical dimensions of the world economy, but for present purposes it is important to recognize that the capacity of states to influence the economic trends, to buy and sell strategic commodities, and to control the assets of major international actors are integral to the exercise of political power on the world stage. A state can win concessions or reciprocal agreements with other states through its economic strength, and it can outbid other states in the competition for access to resources. As

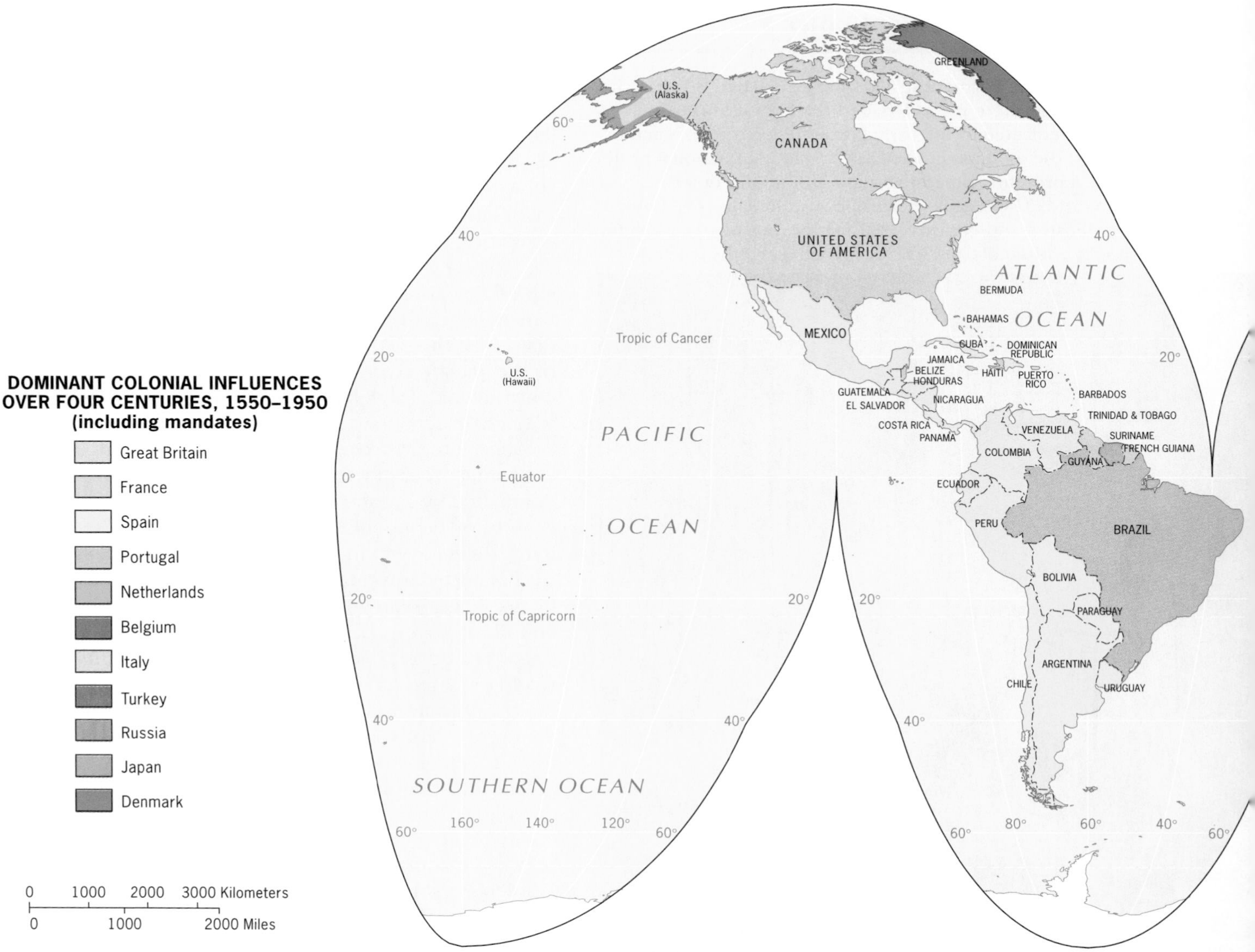

Figure 15-1 Dominant Colonial Influences over Four Centuries. Many areas of the world were under more than one colonial power. This map depicts the *dominant* colonial imprint over the four-century period 1550–1950.

such, it is critical to understand where states are situated in the global economy.

The forces of colonialism described earlier played a key role in knitting together the economies of widely separated areas—giving birth to an economic order that was both large-scale and highly differentiated. In many instances colonial countries were able to amass great concentrations of wealth, but being a colonial power is not a prerequisite to being an economic power. Countries such as Switzerland, Singapore, and Australia have significant global clout even though they were never classic colonial powers—and that clout is tied in significant part to their positions in the global economy. Those positions were gained, in turn, through the access those countries had to the networks of production, consumption, and exchange in the wealthiest parts of the world and their ability to take advantage of that access.

There are many different ways of understanding the significance of a country's position in the global economy for its projection of power. Comparing the size of different state economies is one common approach. Yet countries do not exist in isolation from one another, and what happens in one can greatly affect what happens in another; the cascading impacts of the Asian economic

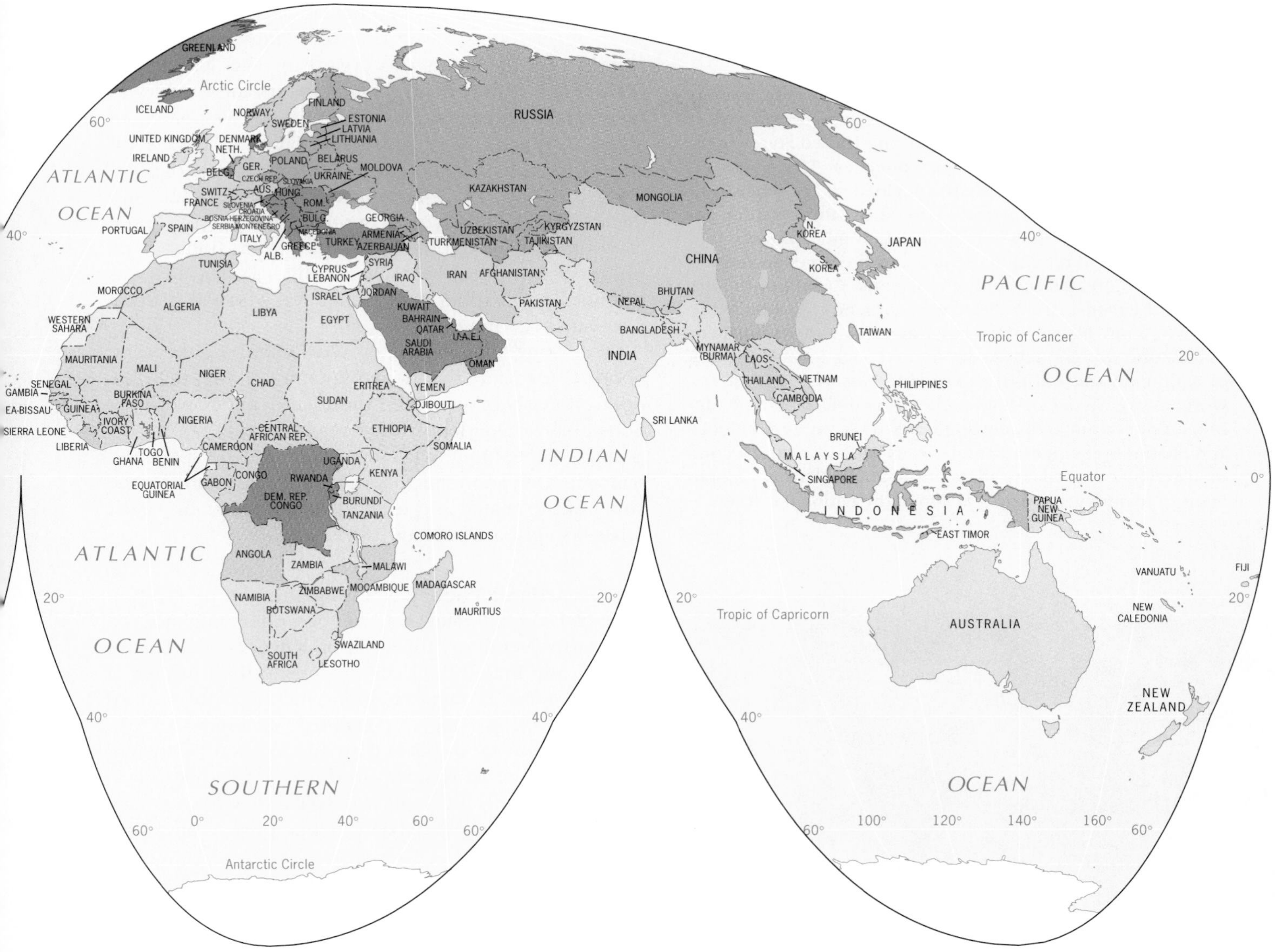

crisis of the late 1990s illustrate this point. Hence, the recent trend has been toward viewing states in relation to one another, as exemplified by ***World-Systems Analysis***. Building on the work of Immanuel Wallerstein, proponents of World-Systems Analysis view the world as an interlocked system of states. They argue that the situation of individual states must be seen in terms of their spatial and functional relationship to the emergence of a global capitalist economy, which began to develop around 1450. They posit a world divided into three basic tiers: a global economic core, which is in the driver's seat; a periphery, which has little economic autonomy or influence; and a semi-periphery which keeps the world from being polarized into two extremes. These tiers are not static, and countries can move in and out of different tiers over time, but a similar group of countries has dominated the core for much of the last century.

There is considerable debate about the categories associated with World-Systems Analysis, as well as its heavy emphasis on economic factors in political development. Nonetheless, it has encouraged many to see the world political map as a system of interlinking parts that need to be understood in relation to one another. As such, its impact has been considerable in political geography, and it has become increasingly commonplace to refer to the kinds of core-periphery distinctions suggested by World-Systems Analysis. This perspective also ties political geography more closely to economic geography, where core-periphery theories have also become widely used (see Part Eight).

From the field notes

"Symbol of power: the Panama Canal. You cannot traverse this marvel of twentieth-century engineering without being reminded of the power of the United States to intervene in the affairs of foreign countries. There was no Panama when the United States decided to try where the French had failed: this narrow stretch of land between Atlantic and Pacific waters belonged to Colombia. But the U.S. fomented a local rebellion, helped and then recognized the victors, and created not only the Panama Canal but the Republic of Panama itself. There was no need to colonize the country; control over the vital waterway and its adjacent Canal Zone was enough. As we looked back toward the city of Colon on the Caribbean sea side, we saw one of the world's largest ocean liners, the Queen Elizabeth II, approach the Gatun locks. Imagine: a two-way system of locks and channels engineered and built by 1914 can still accommodate most of the large ships of the 2000s. This is a monument to planning and organization in the national interest."

Geopolitics

What does it mean to control a particular space within the global political-territorial order? The first political geographer who studied this issue was the German professor Friedrich Ratzel (1844–1904). Ratzel focused on the spatial aspects of state behavior within a system of states. He postulated that the state resembles a biological organism whose life cycle extends from birth through maturity and, ultimately, decline and death. To prolong its existence, the state requires nourishment, just as an organism needs food. Such nourishment is provided by the acquisition of less powerful competitors' territories and their cultural contents. If a state is confined within permanent and static boundaries and deprived of overseas domains, Ratzel argued, it will atrophy. Space is the state's essential, life-giving force.

Ratzel's ***organic theory*** held that a nation, which is an aggregate of organisms (human beings), would itself function and behave as an organism. This was an extreme form of the environmental determinism that was to dominate human geography for decades to come, but it was so speculative that it would probably have soon been forgotten had it not given rise to a subfield of political geography called ***geopolitics***. Some of Ratzel's students translated his abstract writings into practical policies, and this led directly to the expansionist Nazi philosophies of the 1930s. One of Hitler's associates was a political geographer, Karl Haushofer, who was a strong advocate of geopolitics.

For some decades after World War II, the term ***geopolitics*** had such negative connotations that few political geographers, even those studying power relationships, would identify themselves as students of geopolitics. Time, along with more balanced perspectives, has reinstated geopolitics as an appropriate name for the study of the spatial and territorial dimensions of power relationships past, present, and future.

The Heartland Theory Not long after the publication of Ratzel's initial ideas, other geographers began looking at the overall organization of power on the Earth's surface and linked their conclusions to the fortunes of existing states. Prominent among them was the Oxford University geographer Sir Halford Mackinder (1861–1947). In 1904 he published an article titled "The Geographical Pivot of History" in the Royal Geographical Society's *Geographical Journal*. That article became one of the most intensely debated geographic publications of all time.

Mackinder was concerned with power relationships at a time when Britain had acquired a global empire through its naval supremacy. To many of his contemporaries, the oceans—avenues of colonial conquest—were the key to world domination, but not to Mackinder. He concluded that a land-based power, not a sea power, would ultimately rule the world. His famous article contained a lengthy appraisal of the largest and most populous landmass on Earth—Eurasia. At the heart of Eurasia, he argued, lay an impregnable, resource-rich "pivot area" extending from Eastern Europe to eastern Siberia (Fig. 15-2). This, he surmised, would become the base for world conquest, and the key to it was Eastern Europe.

Mackinder later renamed his "pivot area" the heartland, and his notion became known as the ***heartland theory***. In his book *Democratic Ideals and Reality* (1919) he stated the theory as follows:

> Who rules East Europe commands the Heartland
>
> Who rules the Heartland commands the World Island
>
> Who rules the World Island commands the World

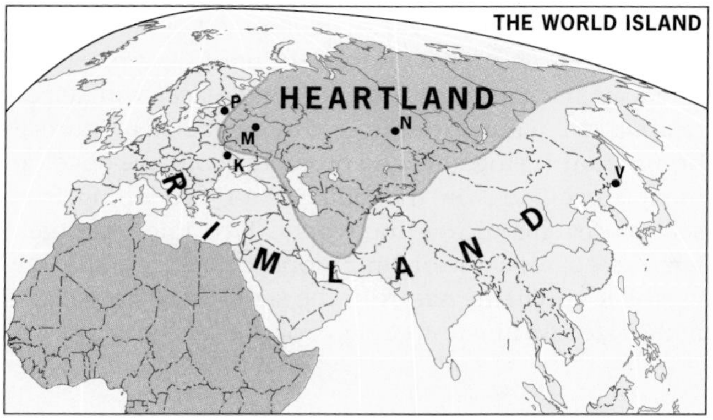

Figure 15-2 Eurasia. During the early part of the twentieth century, geopolitical theorists saw Eurasia as a "World Island" divided into heartland and rimland.

When Mackinder proposed his heartland theory, there was little to foretell the rise of a superpower in the heartland. Russia was in disarray, having recently lost a war against Japan (1905), and was facing revolution. Eastern Europe was fractured. Germany, not Russia, was gaining power. But when the Soviet Union emerged and World War II gave Moscow control over much of Eastern Europe, the heartland theory attracted renewed attention.

The Rimland Theory Not all political geographers agreed with Mackinder's assessment of the heartland. One of Mackinder's critics, the Yale professor of international relations Nicholas Spykman, coined a geographic term that is still in use: ***rimland***. Spykman argued that the Eurasian rim, not its heart, held the key to global power. In his book *The Geography of the Peace* (1944) he parodied Mackinder:

> Who controls the Rimland rules Eurasia
>
> Who rules Eurasia controls the destinies of the world

As Figure 15-2 shows, the rimland is a fragmented zone that is unlikely to fall under the sway of one superpower, as the heartland might. Spykman, who was more of a pragmatist than a theorist, saw a divided rimland as a key to the world's balance of power. Today the rimland is still divided, but it encompasses powerful states in Western Europe as well as a potential superpower: China.

Recent Developments In Chapter 17 we return to the topic of global geopolitics, but it is appropriate here to reflect on the evolving power relationships that will shape the world in the twenty-first century. When Mackinder foresaw a world dominated by a single superpower, that notion, too, was revolutionary. The nineteenth century had produced (or was in the process of producing) a large number of states seeking global influence: the United Kingdom, France, Germany, Russia, the United States, and Japan among them. This was a multipolar world that was soon engulfed in a global war (1914–1918) and then another (1939–1945). World War I was global as a result of the colonial empires of the combatants; German and Allied forces fought battles in East Africa and elsewhere. World War II was global for additional reasons: it spilled southward and eastward beyond the confines of Europe, and it involved the United States and Japan.

Out of World War II came two newly strengthened powers, the United States and the Soviet Union. The older powers in devastated Europe were losing their colonies and were in political and economic disarray. Although the United States aided Europe through its Marshall Plan and Japan through its enlightened postwar administration, no European or Asian power regained its former status. In the aftermath of World War II there were two clear superpowers. The world was a bipolar one divided into capitalist and communist camps. The Soviet Union dominated almost all of the heartland as Mackinder had defined it. The United States proved that Mackinder had underestimated the capacities of lands beyond his "world island" in Eurasia.

In the mid-1990s, after the collapse of the Soviet Union, the United States found itself the only surviving superpower. However, it was constrained by the growing power of extrastate institutions and organizations—most dramatically symbolized by the terrorist bombings of New York City and Washington, D.C., in September 2001, and by the unprecedented worldwide diffusion of weapons, including nuclear weapons. Briefly after World War II the United States, which used nuclear bombs to end that conflict, was the only state possessing the weapons that could have given it global supremacy. Today it is again the dominant force in world affairs, but this dominance is likely to be short-lived because the outlines of a new multipolar world are forming.

What are these outlines? Both Mackinder and Spykman might claim that their analyses were correct. A multipolar world is emerging in which the heartland and the rimland are represented by power cores. There are four potential foci of power on the "world island": (1) Russia, in disarray after the collapse of the Soviet Union but still possessing an enormous military complex and major resources; (2) Europe, if it can find a way to sustain its drive toward integration and unification; (3) China, now energized by the spectacular economic growth of its eastern provinces; and (4) the United States, facing China across a Pacific that has become a highway of trade and diffusion. So the world today shares some features with that in Mackinder's time: an unstable multipolar world with much potential for conflict.

◆ THE CHARACTER OF STATE TERRITORY

In *The Might of Nations* (1961), J. G. Stoessinger defines power as "the capacity of a nation to use its tangible and intangible resources in such a way as to affect the behavior of other nations." As we have seen, that capacity is shaped in significant part by a state's position in the global economic and political order. But the makeup and spatial organization of a state's territory can matter as well.

Determining how the particular geographical characteristics of a state affect its power is not an easy or straightforward matter, however. Consider the issue of population. We have already noted the differences in the amounts of territory controlled by different states. In terms of population, the range is even greater. Over half the world's states have populations below 5 million; nearly 50 have fewer than 1 million citizens. It might be tempting to assume that states with small populations can exercise very little power, whereas those with large populations have great international clout. At its extremes, such an assumption might be tenable; most states with very small populations have little power in a world where decisions are made by their larger neighbors, whereas India, China, the United States, or Indonesia cannot be ignored. Yet tiny Singapore exerts considerable international influence, and China's large population presents a great challenge for the country.

China has been undergoing dramatic economic growth, of course. Whereas economies in Western Europe and North America are experiencing growth of 1 to 3 percent annually, China has been reporting growth of 7 to 10 percent—such a high rate that Chinese rulers are trying to restrain it. At the beginning of the twenty-first century China's economy was the third largest in the world, behind the economies of the United States and Japan. Yet in 2002 the Chinese people were earning just a tiny fraction of what Americans or Japanese earn per capita. And with over 1.3 billion people, and adding almost 13 million every year, every economic measure must be divided by twelve hundred million. No matter how fast an economy grows, that kind of arithmetic will produce low per capita figures.

The point is that there is no "ideal" population size for a state; there is not even an ideal population in relation to a particular territorial size. With a territory the size of Montana and a limited natural resource base, Japan has one of the dominant economies on Earth. An "overpopulated" country such as the Netherlands thrives, while Liberia fractures. To understand this situation, we must consider people's capacities for organization in light of local circumstances—along with their position in the global political and economic order. Japan, Hong Kong, and Guangdong Province are examples of places where favorable shifts in the global economy worked together with a well-educated workforce to produce greater economic gains than those found among places with access to abundant natural resources. More generally, efforts to bring countries together and promote economic development are evident in the building of everything from school systems to road networks. Two important geographical clues to the organizational character of the state can be found in the nature of the state's core area(s) and in the size and functions of its capital city.

Core Areas

Several of the most influential European states grew over many centuries from a ***core area***, expanding into a regional entity and absorbing territory along their frontiers. Eventually, their expansion was halted when neighboring entities blocked them, boundaries were defined, and their internal organization matured.

In most cases the original nucleus of these states still functions as a core area. Many countries elsewhere in the world also have well-defined core areas, even though they are often much younger than their European counterparts. You can discern core areas even on a small-scale atlas map: here lie a country's major cities (usually including the capital), its largest and densest population cluster, its most intensive transport networks, and often its most intensively cultivated farmlands. Here the national economy is best developed and circulation is most efficient. If you travel away from the core area, you see smaller towns, fewer factories, and more open land.

Japan's Kanto Plain is one of the world's leading national cores, centered on the city of Tokyo. Note that intensive agriculture still plays a role in this highly urbanized heartland. France's Paris Basin is a more ancient core area, centered on one of Europe's greatest primate cities. In Egypt, the Cairo-Alexandria axis and the Nile delta form the national core, and in Chile, Santiago lies in what the Chileans call their country's *nucleo central.*

What role does a well-developed core area play in a state? The apparent answer is an important one. Countries without recognizable, well-integrated cores (Congo, Chad, Mongolia, Bangladesh) may have notable capitals, but these alone cannot easily provide a focus for the state. By contrast, countries with core areas characterized by a mix of urban settlements and land uses are often in a stronger position to promote a broad range of economic development initiatives.

States that possess more than one core area—***multicore states***—confront particular problems. If the primary core area is dominant or if there is a secondary core area that is not characterized by strong cultural discontinuities with the primary core, such problems may be slight. This is the case in the United States, where the primary core area still lies in the East and Northeast, and includes the federal capital and the country's largest city and commercial center. Many would regard coastal southern California as a secondary core area, but there are no strong cultural discontinuities with the East and Northeast. In Nigeria, by contrast, three core areas mark ethnically and culturally diverse parts of the state, and none is truly dominant. Nigeria's northern core area represents the Muslim heart of the country; the two southern cores center on two of its major population clusters.

Capital Cities

In most states, the ***capital city*** is the political nerve center of the country, its national headquarters and seat of government, and the center of national life. We recognize this special status by using the name of a country's capital interchangeably with that of the state itself; for example, a news report may say that "London's position has changed" or "Moscow is at odds with Ukraine."

The primacy of the capital is yet another manifestation of the European state model, one that has diffused worldwide. After they had gained independence, many former colonies spent lavishly on their capitals, not because this was essential to political or economic success but because the states were developing in the image of European states and capital cities such as London, Paris, Lisbon, or Brussels became the models.

In some countries the capital city is by far the largest and most economically influential city in the state, with a landscape designed to reflect a country's culture. Mexico City (Mexico), Jakarta (Indonesia), and Ouagadougou (Burkina Faso) all fit in this category. In none of these cases is there any other city that comes even close to rivaling the capital city in terms of size or influence. Cities of this sort are sometimes referred to as ***primate cities***—a concept to which we will return in Chapter 21. Such cities are particularly common in countries with dominantly agriculture-based economies (e.g., Bangladesh and Ethiopia), and those with a history of centralized colonial rule (e.g., Kenya and Sri Lanka).

Some newly independent states decided to relocate their capital cities, again at enormous expense. Several did so in order to move the capital from a geographically peripheral situation to a more central one. Until recently Nigeria's capital was Lagos, located on the coast in the southwest of the country. A new capital has been constructed at Abuja, nearer the geographic center of the state. Malawi moved its capital from Zomba, deep in the south, to more central Lilongwe. In Pakistan, the capital was moved from the colonial headquarters of Karachi to Islamabad in the far north.

More recently, Malaysia has been in the process of relocating its capital from Kuala Lumpur, the former British colonial headquarters, to a completely new center called Putrajaya about 40 kilometers (25 miles) to the south. This move was prompted by the Malaysian government's desire to build a brand-new, ultramodern capital to symbolize the country's rapid economic growth and modernization.

Capital cities are of interest to cultural as well as political geographers because they are occasionally used to focus a society's attention on a national objective. In Pakistan's case, the transfer of the capital to Islamabad was part of a plan to orient the nation toward its historic focus in the interior and toward the north, where the country narrows between Kashmir, China, and Afghanistan. In Brazil, the decision to move the capital from historic Rio de Janeiro to Brasília was made, in large part, to direct attention to the huge, sparsely populated yet poorly integrated interior. We have already noted Japan's transfer of its capital from Kyoto to Tokyo, a move that also had specific national objectives. The capital city thus can be used to achieve national aims and to promote change. Geographers sometimes refer to such cities as ***forward capitals***.

Berlin once served as such a forward capital. During the nineteenth century, when the German state was forming, its western boundaries (with the Netherlands, Belgium, and, until 1870, France) were relatively stable. To the east, however, lay the frontier. There the Germans confronted the Poles and other Slavic nations, and the growing empire expanded into much of what is today Poland.

This eastward march was underscored by the choice of Berlin as the capital. Berlin lies not far from the Oder River, whose basin was Germany's easternmost territory until the 1860s. Most of Germany lay to the west of Berlin, but the capital helped to solidify Germany's eastern orientation.

A century later Germany lay defeated and divided. West Germany chose a new capital, Bonn; East Germany, under Soviet control, was governed from East Berlin. The German empire had lost its entire eastern frontier, and Poland now extended to the Oder River, on Berlin's doorstep.

When Germany was reunified in 1990, Germans debated the choice of a new capital. Many favored Bonn, located near the country's western border and symbolic of its new role in Europe. Many others preferred a return to Berlin. Still others wanted to put the past behind them and argued for a totally new choice, such as Hanover, near the center of the country. In the end, Berlin was selected—raising fears among those who remembered the city's role during times of war. At the turn of the twenty-first century, a giant construction program that transformed Berlin and symbolized its new era was erasing those memories.

In general, the capital city symbolizes the state; its layout, prominent architectural landmarks, public art, historic buildings and monuments, and often its religious structures, reflect the society's values and priorities. The capital may be employed as a unifying force and can assert the state's values internally as well as externally. If its landscape images exclude important sectors of a state's population, however, it can also be divisive. This helps to explain why debates are so intense over new monuments in Washington, D.C., or new construction projects in the heart of Paris, France.

◆ INTERNAL POLITICAL-GEOGRAPHIC STRUCTURE

A well-integrated state consists of a stable, clearly bounded territory served by a well-developed infrastructure, an effective administrative framework, a productive core area, and a prominent capital. All states, however, confront divisive forces—some strong enough to threaten their very survival. The internal political organization of territory in a state can influence how these forces play out.

Unitary and Federal Systems

When the nation-state evolved in Europe, democracy as we now know it had not yet matured; governments could and did suppress dissent by forceful means. Most European governments were highly centralized; the capital city represented authority that stretched to the limits of the state. There were no clear efforts to accommodate minorities or outlying regions where the sense of national identity was weaker. Europe's nation-states were ***unitary states***, and their administrative frameworks were designed to ensure the central government's authority over all parts of the state. France, for example, was divided into more than 90 *départements*, whose representatives came to Paris less to express regional concerns than to implement governmental decisions back home.

European notions of the state diffused to much of the rest of the world, but in the New World these notions did not always work well. When colonies freed themselves of European dominance, many found that conditions in their newly independent countries did not lend themselves to unitary systems of government. In the United States, Canada, and Australia the newness of the culture, the absence of an old primate city, the lack of a clear core area, the vastness of the national territory, and the emergence of regionalism all required something other than highly centralized government. In Europe itself, some political philosophers had already theorized about alternatives to the unitary system, and regionalism in Scotland and Wales had become a concern in London. It was situations like these that led to the emergence of the ***federal state***.

Federalism accommodated regional interests by vesting primary power in provinces, States, or other regional units over all matters except those explicitly given to the national government. The Australian geographer K. W. Robinson described a federation as "the most geographically expressive of all political systems, based as it is on the existence and accommodation of regional differences . . . federation does not create unity out of diversity; rather, it enables the two to coexist."

In Europe, the only genuine, long-term federation was Switzerland, but conditions there were too different from those in the New World to allow it to serve as a model. For example, the choice of a capital city was a challenge for many federations. No region would agree to locate the capital in another region. As a result, federations often created new capitals, built on federal territories carved from one or more States. Thus the U.S. capital became neither New York nor Philadelphia, but Washington, D.C., built on a federal territory initially taken from Maryland and Virginia. The Australian capital became neither Sydney nor Melbourne but Canberra, established on federal territory taken from the State of New South Wales.

Federalism even spread to countries whose European settlers came from highly centralized unitary states. In Europe, few states were more strongly centralized than Spain and Portugal, yet Mexico and Brazil established federal systems. (Brazil moved its capital func-

From the field notes

"Singapore, a ministate that also is a city-state, is the product of organization as well as location. With an area of just 240 square miles (622 sq km) and a population of nearly 3 million, Singapore, the world's most urbanized state, has to be organized strictly in order to function. With the largest port in the world (in terms of number of ships served) and the third-largest oil refinery complex, Singapore is one of the Pacific Rim's economic tigers. This view, from the 68th floor of (then) Asia's tallest hotel, shows Singapore's still-evolving skyline, a reflection of its success."

tions from the primate city, Rio de Janeiro, to interior Brasília in the 1950s.)

Although the European colonial powers retained control over their empires in Africa and Asia, colonial rule mirrored the unitary system—only more so. Overseas domains were run with little or no consideration for local or regional cultures. When the colonial era came to an end, however, the federal idea seemed to hold promise for newly independent, ethnically and culturally divided countries. The British in particular attempted to create federal frameworks as the end of the empire approached. Their greatest success was India, where the transition to independence and the subsequent survival of the state may be attributed in large part to the federal framework created by British and Indian negotiators during the 1940s. In Africa, by contrast, the mechanisms of federation were put in place hastily and were based on contested territorial configurations (for

Figure 15-3 Regions of France. This map shows the 22 principal administrative regions of France, including Corsica. *Source*: From a map in H. J. de Blij and P. O. Muller, *Geography: Realms, Regions, and Concepts*, 10th ed. New York: Wiley, 2002, p. 74.

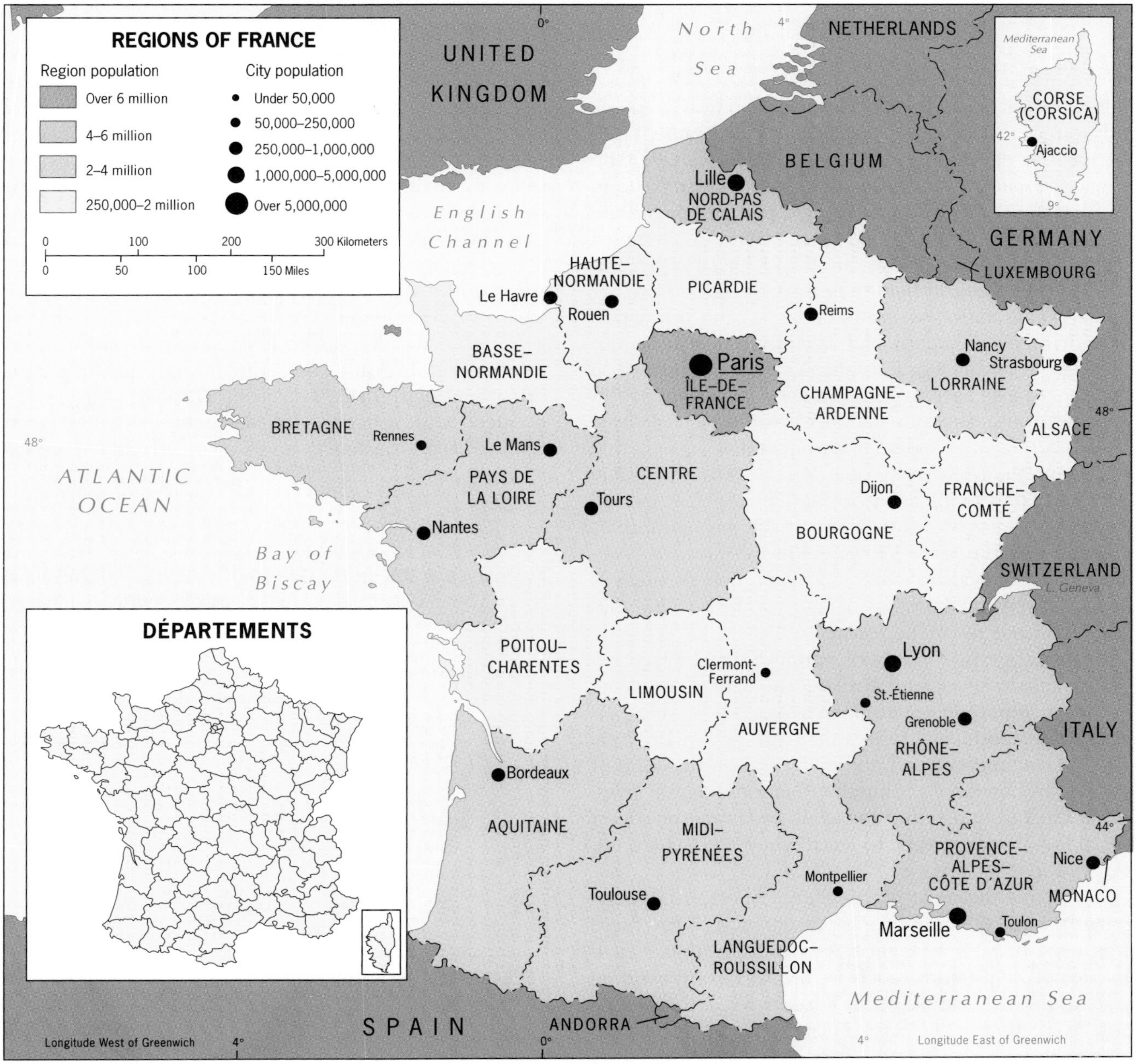

example, in Nigeria and Uganda). As a result, they failed to stabilize.

Today the divisive forces of regionalism are affecting not only recently formed federations but also the older unitary states of Europe. In response, European states are reconstructing their administrative frameworks; France, for example, has recognized 22 "regions," which consist of groupings of the 96 *départements* dating back to the time of Napoleon (Fig. 15-3). These regions are geographic evidence of France's attempt to decentralize governmental control. In similar ways, Spain, Italy, the United Kingdom, and other older unitary states are adjusting to new political-geographical circumstances—new to Europe but well known to federal governments elsewhere.

Electoral Patterns

"All politics is local," it is often said, and in truth a voter's most direct and important contact with government is at the local level. Voters who feel that they can have little impact on national elections but have a clear voice in local elections still feel that they are participating in the political system. This can be a crucial factor in building a sense of commitment to the nation and what it stands for.

Electoral geographers seek to understand how the spatial configuration of electoral districts and voting patterns that emerge in particular elections reflect and influence social and political affairs. Various countries use different voting systems to elect their governments. In the 1994 South African election we could observe how the leaders of that society formulated a system that would provide majority rule while awarding some power to each of nine newly formed regions. The overall effect was to protect, to an extent, the rights of minorities in those regions. In the United States, proportional representation prevails in the House of Representatives (Congress), while the rights of States with small populations are protected in the Senate.

The geographic study of voting behavior is especially interesting because it relates the way people vote to their geographic environments. Maps of voting patterns often produce surprises that can be explained by other maps, and GIS technology has raised this kind of analysis to new levels. Church affiliation, income level, ethnic background, education level, and numerous other social factors are studied to learn why voters voted the way they did.

Probably the most practical area of ***electoral geography*** is the geography of representation. When there are a certain fixed number of seats for representatives in an elected legislature (such as the 435 congressional seats in the U.S. House of Representatives), there must be a fixed number of electoral districts from which those representatives are elected. Since the congressional seats are based on State population totals, it is up to each State to draw a map of congressional districts from which representatives will be elected.

Or is it? Will States draw their districting maps fairly, giving minorities an opportunity to elect their own representatives? After all, if a State has a population that is 80 percent white, 10 percent African-American, and 10 percent Hispanic, an electoral district map could easily result in white majorities in all districts and no minority representatives at all. After the 1990 census, the U.S. government instructed all States with substantial minority populations to construct so-called majority–minority districts (districts within which a minority would have the majority of the voters). In the hypothetical State described here, this districting would lead to the election of at least one African-American and one Hispanic representative from among 10 districts.

Reapportionment of the total number of representatives among the States goes on all the time because the population shifts: some States gain seats, whereas others lose. As a result, redistricting also occurs after every census, and within States (for State legislatures) it occurs more frequently than that. Ideally, a State's congressional districts would, on the map, look relatively compact and contain roughly the same number of voters. In reality, our pluralistic society requires the construction of some oddly shaped districts in order to adhere to the majority–minority rule (Fig. 15-4).

Strange-looking districts that have been constructed to attain certain political ends are nothing new in American politics. In 1812, Governor Elbridge Gerry (pronounced with a hard G) of Massachusetts signed into law a district designed to give an advantage to his

Figure 15-4 Electoral Geography. Florida Congressional District No. 3 is an example of the spatial manipulation necessary to create majority-minority districts. In 1990, District 3 had about 310,000 African-American residents, 240,000 whites, and 16,000 Hispanics. In places, District 3 is no wider than U.S. Highway 90. *Source*: Map and data provided by Tanya de Blij, Geographer/Analyst for the Florida House of Representatives.

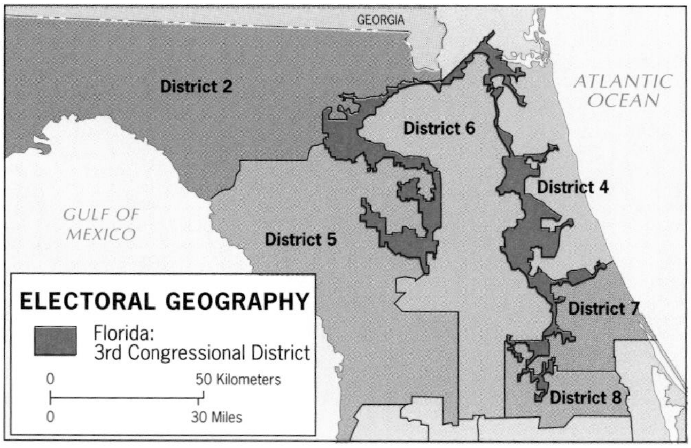

party—a district that looked so odd to artist Gilbert Stuart that he drew it with a head, wings, and claws. Stuart called it the "salamander district," but a colleague immortalized it by naming it a ***gerrymander***. Ever since, the term *gerrymandering* has been used to describe "redistricting for advantage." Certainly, many of the districts now on the U.S. electoral map may be seen as gerrymanders, but for an important purpose: to provide representation to minorities who, without it, would not be represented as effectively in the national legislature.

The larger point is that the spatial organization of voting districts is a fundamentally geographical phenomenon that can have profound impacts on who is represented and who is not—as well as peoples' notions of fairness. And that is only the beginning. The voting patterns that emerge from particular elections can help reinforce a sense of regionalism and can shape a government's response to issues in the future. Small wonder, then, that many individuals who have little general understanding of geography at least appreciate the importance of its electoral geography component.

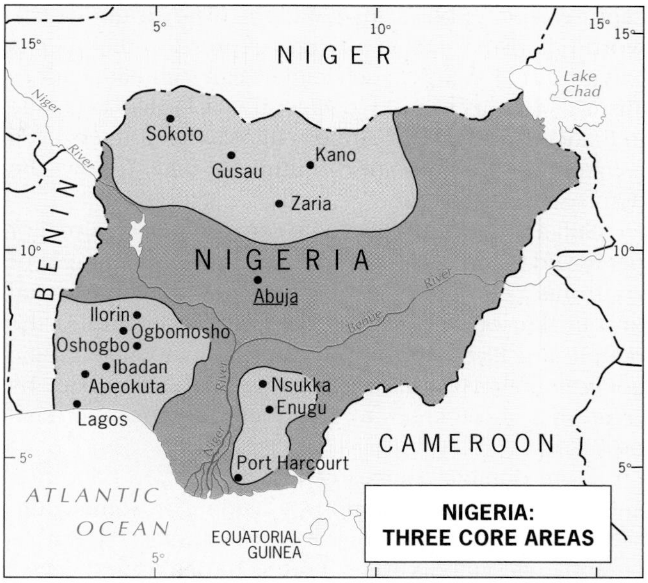

Figure 15-5 Nigeria's Three Core Areas. Nigeria is a multicore state; its northern core area lies in the Muslim realm, while the southern core areas lie in Christian influenced Africa. Nigeria's political survival is a major African political achievement. But pressures on Nigeria are rising, and disintegration remains a threat.

◆ FORCES OF FRAGMENTATION AND COHESION

All states confront in some measure forces that would tear the state apart, and all states possess unifying bonds. Strengthening these bonds to overcome actual and potential divisions is a principal concern of government. Analyzing the interplay between divisive and unifying forces can provide insight into state stability and prospects.

Centripetal Forces The forces that promote unity with states are often called ***centripetal forces***. Governments seek to promote such forces by, for example, changing the administrative structure of the state either to strengthen central authority or to assign more power to the provinces or regions. Although India is often cited as an example of successful manipulation of the federal framework, Nigeria is also a good example. When Nigeria became independent in 1960 after centuries of British colonial rule, it had a federal framework consisting of three regions based on the core areas shown in Figure 15-5. Soon a fourth region was added, but this was not enough to stave off a disastrous war that occurred when the Eastern Region's efforts sought to secede from the federation. After that war, it was clear to Nigerian leaders that the original regions had been too large; they were large enough to regard themselves as national entities capable of going it alone. They therefore decided to redivide Nigeria into a larger number of regions (and to call them States). The smaller States would be less able to mount separatist campaigns. Today, on paper, Nigeria is still a federation of 35 States, although successive military regimes have eroded their power and centralized the government. Given the religious division of Nigeria between a Muslim north and a non-Muslim south, the country's cultural fragmentation into some 200 peoples, and internal political-ideological struggles over regime type and orientation, the continued cohesion of the Nigerian federation is noteworthy.

Manipulating the system, however, may not be enough; after all, this approach failed to keep the Soviet Union, Yugoslavia, or Czechoslovakia together. Governments therefore seek to foster unity in other ways as well. Being a citizen of a country and carrying its passport are not enough to create an emotional commitment to the ideals for which the state stands. Such commitment is expressed as a sense of nationalism, an allegiance and loyalty that transcend other feelings of attachment. In a multicultural state such as South Africa, loyalties are divided: many people feel greater allegiance to their own ethnic group than to the state as a whole. In newly independent countries throughout Africa, ***tribalism*** has threatened "national" unity. Governments everywhere therefore seek to promote nationalism in order to overcome more local loyalties. One way to accomplish this objective is to ensure that minorities are represented in government.

Another centripetal force is the leadership of a charismatic individual who personifies the state and captures the public's imagination. (The origin of the word "charisma" lies in a Greek expression that means "divine gift.") At times such leaders can stimulate nationalism, as Juan Perón did in Argentina, Charles de Gaulle in France, and Marshal Tito in Yugoslavia. Conversely, a weakening of nationalist sentiment may follow the demise of such a leader.

Still another unifying force can come from a real or perceived external threat. When an aggressive neighbor confronts a country or the country loses something vital (a critical resource or access to the sea, for example), the people are likely to rally to the national cause. Some governments have taken advantage of this tendency by creating artificial crises to divert attention from internal problems.

More durable sources of nationalism are education and other national institutions, including, in some countries, the church. In all countries, the state's history and geography, its symbols and songs, its traditions and values are taught in the schools. This practice can build a sense of belonging that later translates into nationalism. Where the church still dominates everyday life, as in many Muslim countries and in some Roman Catholic societies, its contribution to national cohesion can be enormous.

Directly related to this institutional force is national ideology. All states seek to promote national ideology in one form or another, and this can lead to a positive desire to improve a country's well-being. Yet national ideology can easily take on negative characteristics as well. At the very least, the promotion and unquestioned acceptance of national ideology can lead to uncritical support for everything a state stands for and does. Examples of this phenomenon can be found in almost all states. At the extreme end of the spectrum, the Nazism of Germany in the 1930s and 1940s was a powerful ideological force that rallied the German nation; and communism as national ideology helped unify different peoples in states such as the Soviet Union and China—persuading them to make great sacrifices during particular periods even as millions of fellow citizens were put to death under its banner.

Communist states were walled off (literally in some instances) from the rest of the world, and when cracks opened in those walls, communist ideology alone was not enough to withstand the flow of ideas from the outside world. This underscores the importance of *circulation* as a nation-building factor. When a population is mobile, moving to and from various parts of a country and diffusing national norms in the process, regionalism and separatism often decline. The presence of economically depressed, isolated regions within a state is potentially divisive. Integration into the nation through effective circulation and communication systems reduces this threat if it is accompanied by policies of tolerance and inclusion. In a multilingual country, circulation enhances the likelihood that each language will be known and used by a substantial percentage of the population and will be regarded as part of the national culture. Low mobility, on the other hand, often reinforces the separateness produced by different languages.

Centrifugal Forces All states must deal with divisive or ***centrifugal forces***—the opposite of the centripetal forces described earlier. And when centrifugal forces outweigh centripetal ones, the state is in danger of collapsing. In recent times we have witnessed the disintegration of the world's largest colonial empires, including, in the late 1980s, the Soviet Union. We have seen the disintegration of Yugoslavia, where a quasi-federal system failed to withstand the forces of division. Czechoslovakia has broken up into two countries. Cyprus is divided. Sri Lanka is wracked by war. Eritrea has separated from Ethiopia.

At the dawn of the twenty-first century, centrifugal forces seem to be on the rampage. Many of these are the product of ethnic minorities' challenges to the norms of the modern state system. Others can be traced to the development of new networks of communication and interaction that cross state lines and bypass government control. Still others reflect deeply rooted regional inequalities. Taken together, they remind us that the map of states is not necessarily stable and that we always need to look at it in relation to other maps. In the last chapter of this part we will do just that, but first it is important to consider the large-scale political-territorial structures that exist to promote interstate cooperation. It is to this matter that we now turn.

◆ KEY TERMS ◆

capital city
centrifugal force
centripetal force
colonialism
core area
electoral geography
federal state
forward capital
geopolitics
gerrymander
heartland theory
multicore state
organic theory
primate city
rimland
tribalism
unitary state

◆ APPLYING GEOGRAPHIC KNOWLEDGE ◆

1. Virtually all states confront centrifugal (divisive) forces, some of them more or less permanent, others rising and ebbing over time. Consider the United States or Canada over the past half century, and identify (a) the centrifugal forces that have affected these countries continuously throughout that period and (b) centrifugal forces that have come and gone, testing the fabric of the state. Have any of these forces threatened the territorial integrity of the two countries?
2. Consider the heartland theory, a century after its publication. Is the kind of power analysis that undergirded Mackinder's construct, which focused on Eurasia as the key to global geopolitics in the future, still relevant today?

Chapter 16

Multinationalism on the Map

From the field notes

"The European Union is not a state, but it does have a flag: a circle of 12 yellow stars on a blue background. Although the flag was designed to mark the moment when the EU was expanded to include 12 states, three more states joined since that time and other states will become part of the Union in future years. In the case of the flag of the United States, the number of stars representing member States of the federation has increased each time new States were admitted. But the leaders of the European Union decided that no similar change would be made in the EU flag: it will remain a twelve-star circle even if the Union grows to double that number in member states. The EU flag can be seen flying in all the member countries. This particular display is one of hundreds in Maastricht, Netherlands—scene of the breakthrough conference that led to a key treaty on the route to unification.

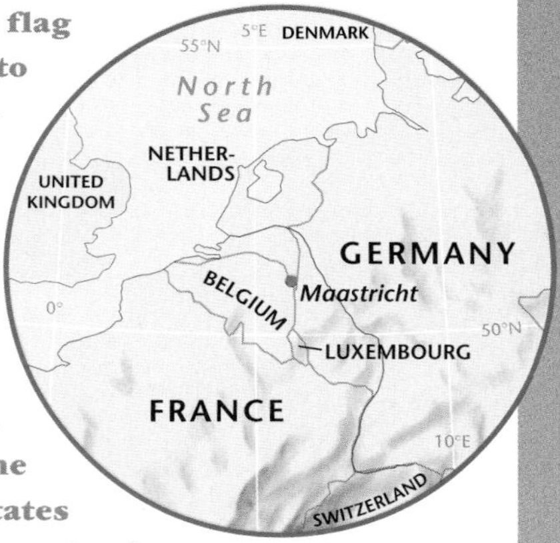

KEY POINTS

- ◆ **Supranational unions range from global organizations such as the United Nations and its predecessor, the League of Nations, to regional associations such as the European Union. All signify the inadequacy of individual states as spatial frameworks for dealing with many important issues and problems.**

- ◆ **Imposition of international sanctions and mobilization of peacekeeping operations are among the functions of the United Nations. Today the United Nations is active militarily in more than a dozen countries.**

- ◆ **Among many regional multinational associations, the European Union is the most complex and far reaching. Its 15 member states are likely to be joined by others within less than a decade.**

- ◆ **Economic prosperity and a shared security concerns are the strongest factors promoting international cooperation.**

- ◆ **The United Nations has channeled the extension of national claims over the oceans through its law of the sea.**

Ours is a world of contradictions. Over the past decade some Québecois have demanded independence from Canada even as Canada joins the United States in NAFTA (the North American Free Trade Agreement). At soccer games in Scotland, fans drown out "God Save the Queen" with a thunderous rendition of "Flower of Scotland," while in London Parliament debates Britain's entry into the European Monetary Union. At every turn we are reminded of the interconnectedness of nations, states, and regions, yet separatism and calls for autonomy are rampant. In the early years of the twenty-first century we appear to be caught between the forces of division and those of unification.

Despite the conflicts arising from these contradictory forces, today hardly a country exists that is not involved in some multinational association. There is ample evidence that such association is advantageous to the partners and that being left out can have serious negative effects on state and nation. In this chapter we look at the geographic dimensions of the progress that has been made toward unity and cooperation. ◆

◆ SUPRANATIONALISM

The phenomenon of interstate cooperation is quite old. In Ancient Greece city-states formed leagues to protect and promote mutual benefit. This practice was imitated many centuries later by the cities of Europe's Hanseatic League. The degree to which this idea has taken root in the modern world, however, is unprecedented. The twentieth century witnessed the establishment of numerous international associations in political, economic, cultural, and military spheres, giving rise to the term ***supranationalism***.

Technically, supranationalism refers to efforts by three or more states to forge associations for mutual benefit and in pursuit of shared goals. Today there are over 60 major supranational organizations, many of which have subsidiaries that bring the total to more than 100. The more states participate in such multilateral associations, the less likely they are to act alone in pursuit of a self-interest that might put them at odds with neighbors.

International Sanctions

These days we hear a great deal about ***international sanctions*** designed to induce states to change their behavior. Sanctions isolate a country that behaves in a way that is deemed inappropriate by the international community, and such isolation can be very costly. For example, in the 1980s sanctions were implemented against South Africa to put pressure on its minority government to abolish its apartheid policies. As a result, foreign firms left South Africa, and foreign investment almost dried up. How much the sanctions contributed to the ending of Apartheid is still debated, but their impact on the economy is beyond question. The sanctions imposed on Iraq following the Gulf War in 1991 had significant economic consequences for most Iraqis, producing a storm of protest across much of the Islamic world. For sanctions to succeed, international agreement is needed, and the Iraqi case shows how difficult it is to achieve such agreement. In cases where agreement is reached, it is a consequence of supranationalism.

From League of Nations to United Nations

The modern beginnings of the supranational movement can be traced to the conferences that followed the end of World War I. The concept of an international organization that would include all the states of the world led to the creation of the League of Nations in 1919. The United States, however, was among the countries that did not join this organization. In all, 63 states participated in the League, although the total membership at any single time never reached that number. Costa Rica and Brazil left the League even before 1930; Germany departed in 1933, shortly before the Soviet Union joined in 1934. The

Figure 16-1 The United Nations. This map shows charter members, members after 1945, and nonmembers of the United Nations. *Source*: From information provided by the United Nations, New York.

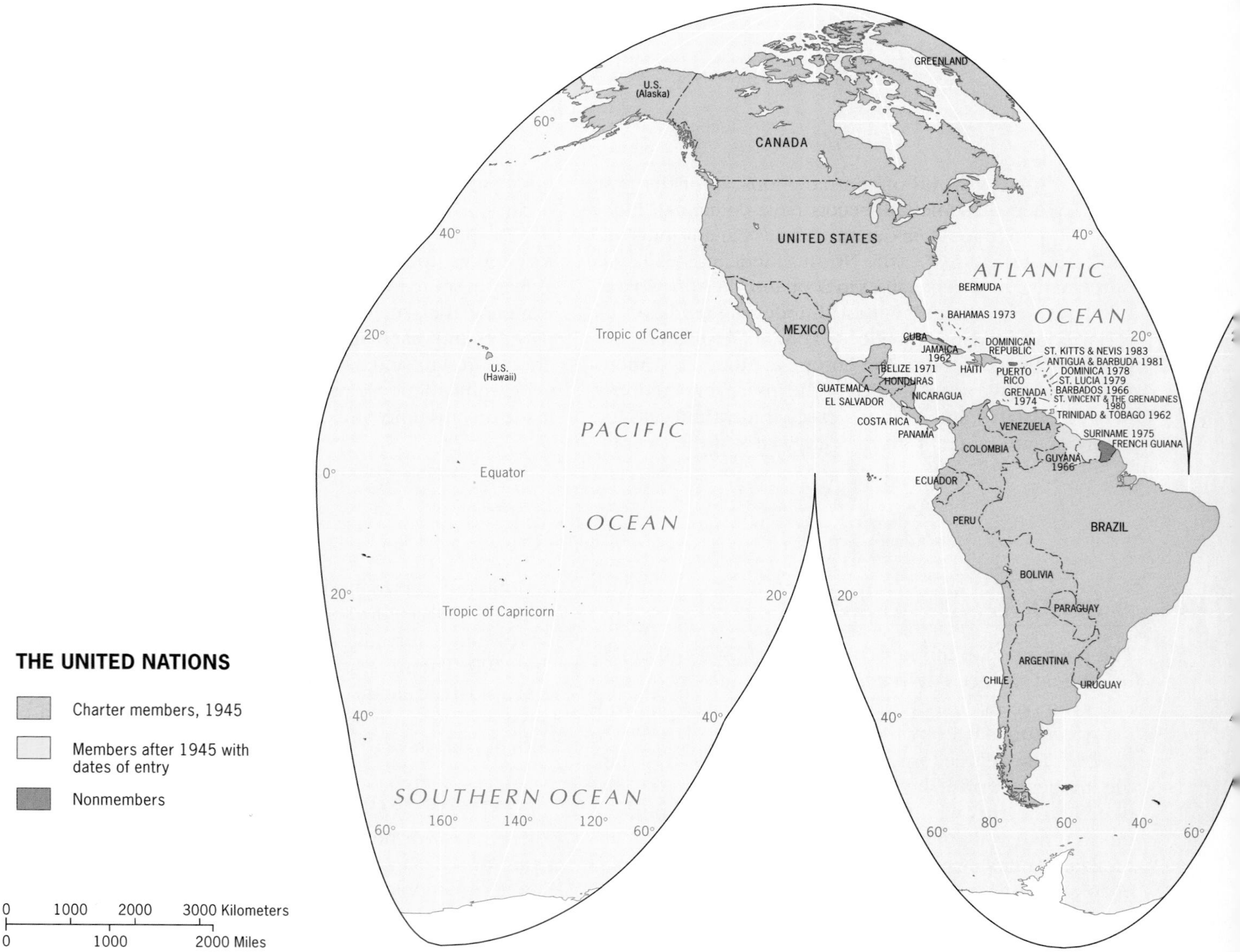

League was born of a worldwide desire to prevent future aggression, but the failure of the United States to join dealt the organization a severe blow. In the mid-1930s the League had a major opportunity when Ethiopia's Haile Selassie made a dramatic appeal for help in the face of an invasion by Italy, a member state until 1937. However, the League failed to take action, and in the chaos of the beginning of World War II it collapsed.

Nonetheless, the interwar period witnessed significant progress toward interstate cooperation. The League of Nations spawned other international organizations. Prominent among these was the Permanent Court of International Justice, created to adjudicate legal issues between states, such as boundary disputes and fishing rights.

The League of Nations also initiated international negotiations on maritime boundaries and related aspects of the law of the sea. The conferences organized by the League laid the groundwork for the final resolution of this problem decades later.

◆ THE UNITED NATIONS

After the end of World War II a new organization was formed to foster international security and cooperation: the United Nations. Just as the United Nations in many ways was a renewal of the League of Nations, so its International Court of Justice succeeded the Permanent Court of the interwar period.

The representation of countries in the United Nations has been more universal than it was in the League (Fig. 16–1). A handful of states still do not belong to the United Nations, but in 2002 the United Nations had 191 member

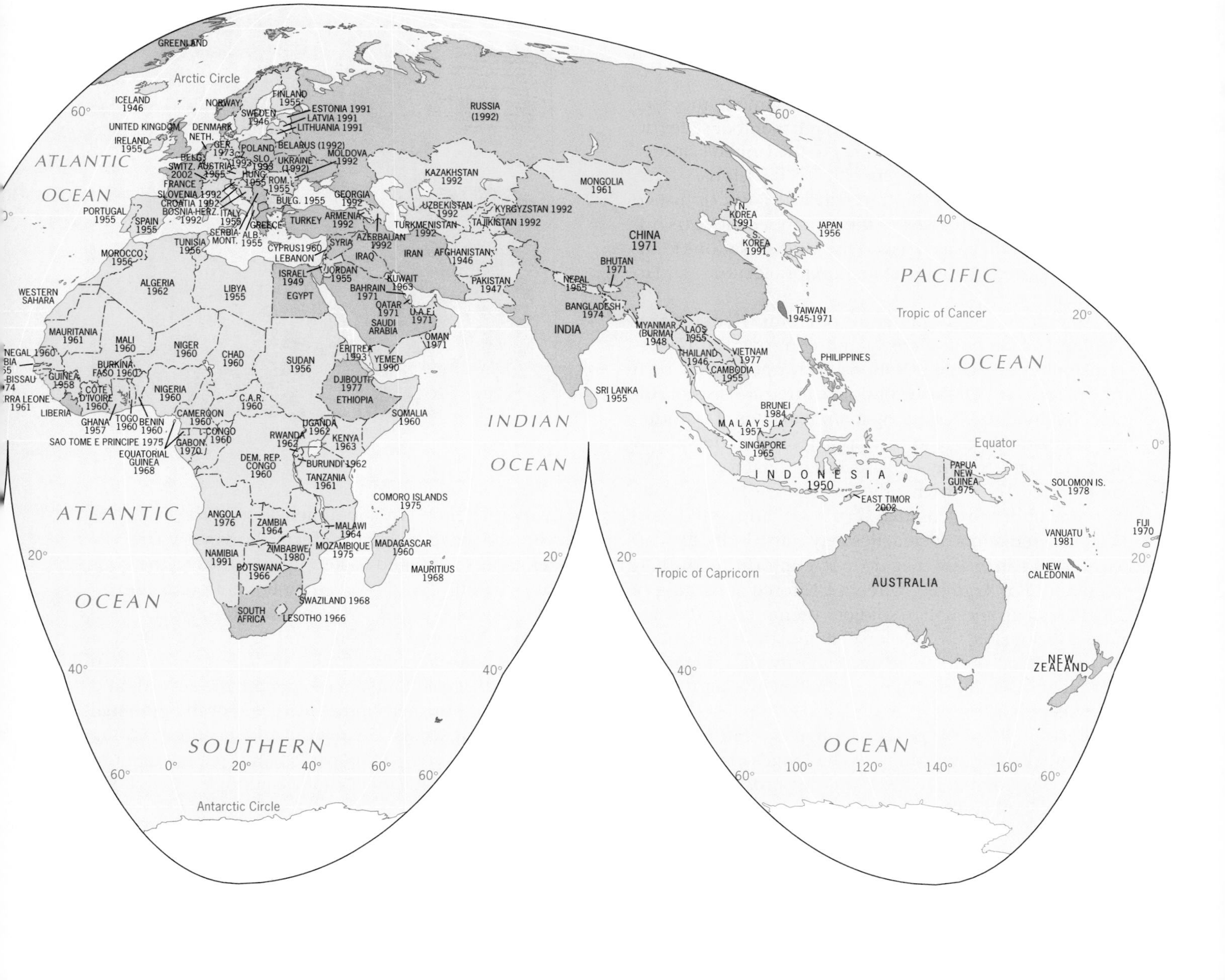

states (including the People's Republic of China, admitted in 1971). The UN's General Assembly and Security Council have overshadowed the cooperative efforts of numerous less visible but enormously productive subsidiaries, such as the FAO (Food and Agriculture Organization), UNESCO (United Nations Educational, Scientific and Cultural Organization), and WHO (World Health Organization). Membership in these organizations is less complete than in the United Nations as a whole, but their work has benefited all humanity.

Participation in the United Nations also serves to commit states to internationally approved standards of behavior. Many states still violate the standards, embodied in the UN Charter, but such violations can lead to collective action as, for example, in the cases of South Africa, Iraq, and North Korea. Even when censured or subjected to UN-sponsored military action, states do not withdraw from the organization. Membership is too valuable to lose; thus national governments develop an understanding of the advantages of international cooperation.

From the field notes

"Walking through The Hague I was attracted by a demonstration in the historic center of the city. Moving closer to find out what was happening, I saw posters of the sort depicted here, protesting the treatment of Kurds in Turkey. As I watched the demonstration, I was reminded of how truly international ethnic conflicts have become. Many are not confined to single countries, or even regions, and the pressure that is exerted from afar can at times be just as significant as that which happens at home."

Peacekeeping Operations

The United Nations is not a world government; member states participate voluntarily. Although member states do not formally yield any sovereignty to the United Nations, they may agree to abide by specific UN decisions, for example, those made by the International Court of Justice or those involving the law of the sea. In recent years, individual states have also asked the United Nations to intervene in internal conflicts, to monitor elections, and to care for refugees.

Among these and numerous other functions, peacekeeping has become a costly and controversial UN responsibility. The United Nations does not have its own armed force; any UN army or police force consists of soldiers assigned to UN duty by member states. This situation can sometimes lead to disputes over leadership. A multinational UN army consists of national forces, each commanded by its own officers. These officers, however, are under the command of a UN-appointed general. Disagreements over tactics may cause individual officers to act in ways that do not conform to the UN command. For example, when a UN force consisting of U.S., Pakistani, and Italian soldiers attempted to alleviate hunger in Somalia, the mission changed from humanitarian to political—and there were costly disagreements over tactics that led to many casualties among the UN peacekeepers.

Since 1994, UN peacekeeping operations have faced one of their most difficult challenges in the former Yugoslavia, where a civil war among Serbs, Croats, and Muslims, chiefly in Bosnia, long defied UN efforts to relieve the crisis. In Bosnia in particular, disputes over leadership and tactics weakened a mission that was already overwhelmed by the dimensions of the task. The mission did have positive effects, however. The UN peacekeepers managed to keep the parties to the conflict at bay until U.S. diplomatic intervention, achieved at Dayton, Ohio, in late 1995, produced a revised map of Bosnia. After the Dayton Agreement was signed, a large UN peacekeeping force, including more than 20,000 American soldiers, implemented the accords and helped rebuild Bosnia's infrastructure. But the potential for failure still exists. Suspicion and hostility among Muslims, Serbs, and Croats persist, and resettlement of refugees and political accommodation have not yet been achieved.

Despite these problems, the United Nations' peacekeeping role has continued to grow, and its successes have far outweighed its failures. In places such as East Timor and Kosovo, for example, UN peacekeepers have helped bring stability after upheavals in the late 1990s. By the middle of 2001, more than 40,000 peacekeeping troops from some 80 UN member states were serving in Bosnia, the Congo, Croatia, Cyprus, East Timor, Ethiopia and Eritrea, Georgia, Iraq/Kuwait, Kashmir, Kosovo, Lebanon, various parts of the Middle East, Sierra Leone, and Western Sahara. Considering the small size of most UN peacekeeping units and the enormity of their tasks, the organization's peacekeeping function provides major benefits to the international community.

Unrepresented Peoples

In Chapter 14 we noted the plight of stateless nations. Here, too, the United Nations provides an international forum and thus relieves tensions. In 1991 the United Nations created the Unrepresented Nations and Peoples Organization (UNPO), which by 2002 had 51 members and 13 applicants. Four former members (Armenia, Estonia, Latvia, and Georgia), having achieved full UN membership, no longer needed UNPO's help.

The roster of UNPO membership, and the appeals that arrive at UNPO's offices from would-be members, form a barometer of the world's political condition. Albanians in Greece, Tatars in the Crimea, Ogoni in Nigeria, the Ka Lahui in Hawai'i (Hawai'i's indigenous nation), North Dakota's Lakota Nation, Abkhazians in Georgia, Tibetans under China's rule, Zanzibaris hoping for independence from Tanzania, Basques in Spain, and dozens of other peoples seeking some form of redress or a stronger voice, all have approached UNPO for assistance.

UNPO cannot by itself solve the problems of stateless or otherwise "unheard" peoples, but it can give them a platform. In addition, UNPO ensures that appeals from its members, applicants, and others are channeled to appropriate agencies and are not lost in the UN bureaucracy. In so doing, it has already cleared up misunderstandings and forestalled conflict.

◆ THE LAW OF THE SEA

Another arena in which the United Nations has accomplished much is the ***law of the sea***. As noted earlier, the League of Nations led the way, but the international negotiations were continued under UN auspices until 1982, when a United Nations Convention on the Law of the Sea was achieved. National claims to adjacent waters (the ***territorial sea***) originated in Europe many centuries ago. A fourteenth-century Italian legal scholar is credited with the first formal proposal that states should be awarded sovereignty over a strip of water next to their coastlines; this proposal led to a lengthy legal debate over the width of that offshore zone. One suggestion was that this width should be determined by the distance a shore-based cannon could fire a cannonball; once within cannon-shot range, a ship would be in territorial waters.

Not surprisingly, various states chose different widths. Western European countries liked a 3-mile territorial sea. (Maritime distances are measured in nautical miles; about 1.15 statute mile equals 1 nautical mile.) Scandinavian countries preferred 4 nautical miles. Mediterranean states chose a 6-mile limit.

During the sixteenth and seventeenth centuries, some countries tried to broaden their maritime jurisdictions by closing off large bays with baselines (lines

From the field notes

"As we sailed from the port of Invergordon, Scotland, we could see a row of oil-drilling platforms under construction, in repair, or being towed out into the North Sea. The shallow, oil- and gas-rich North Sea subsoil has made it necessary to divide this maritime region through median lines. The wealth of energy resources off the Scottish coast has been a factor in the rise of Scottish nationalism and notions of greater autonomy or even independence."

drawn across the open mouths of bays) and claiming fishing grounds far from shore. But until the meetings of the League of Nations, territorial seas remained relatively narrow and the open oceans remained open or, to use the technical language, remained "high seas."

The League did get a hint of what lay ahead. The Soviet Union proposed widening the territorial sea to an unheard-of 12 nautical miles, which would mean that many straits could be closed off by the littoral states and that bays up to 24 miles wide could be closed as well. The matter of delimitation—exactly how maritime boundaries should be constructed on the map—also received much attention. In addition, participating states expressed the need for protection against smuggling, pollution, and other threats from the sea (not the least of which was concern over security). But World War II intervened, and no followup conference could be held.

The Truman Proclamation

Even before the newly formed United Nations could address these issues again, a critical event occurred. In September 1945 President Truman issued two proclamations pertaining to territorial waters. The first of these stated that the United States would henceforth regulate fish-

Figure 16-2 World Maritime Claims. The 200-mile EEZ dramatically reduces the area of the Earth's surface that falls outside the jurisdiction of individual states. *Source*: Based on a map prepared by the Office of the Geographer of the U.S. Department of State, 1980.

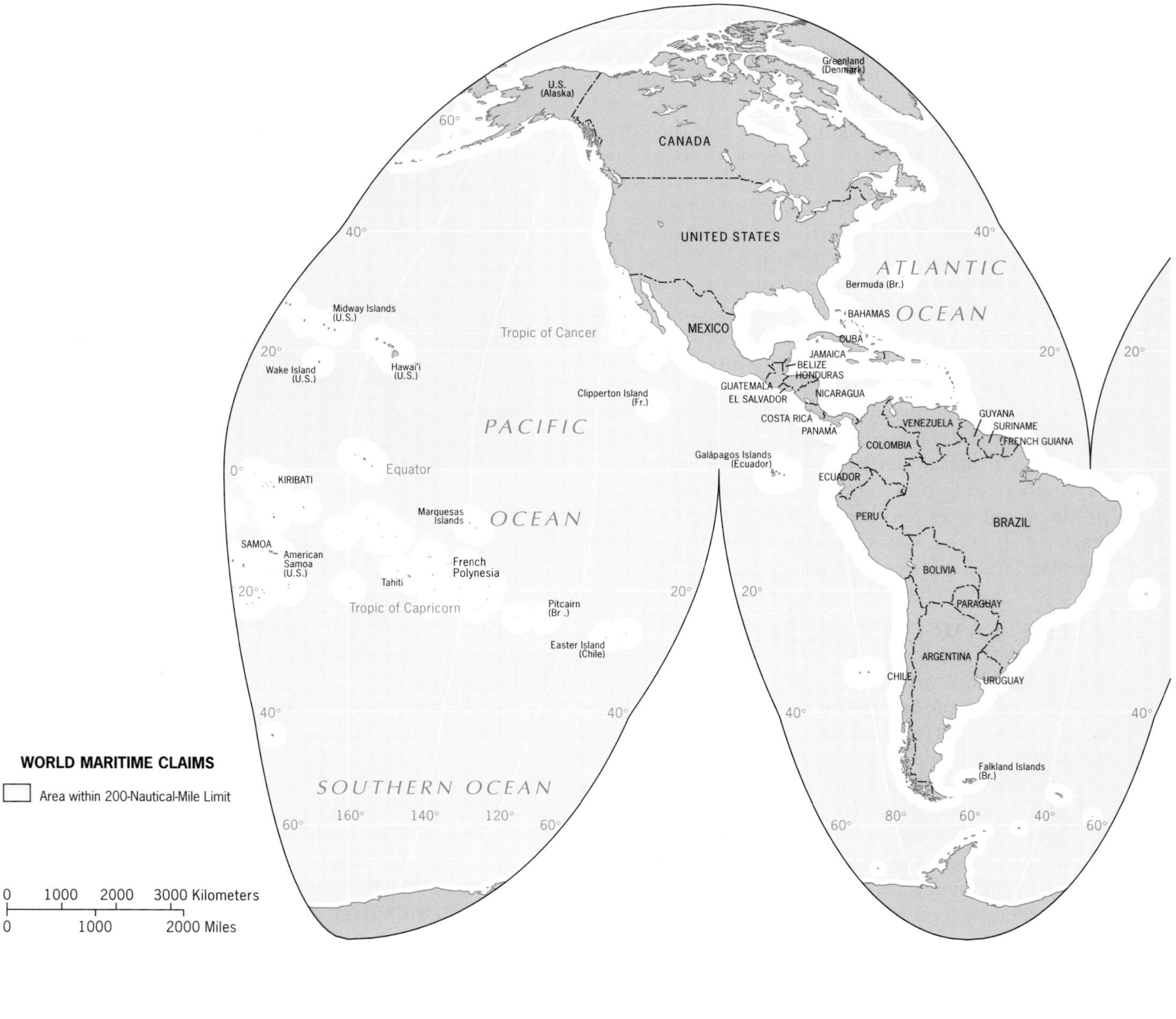

eries' activities in areas of the high seas adjacent to its coastlines but that in other respects these maritime regions would continue to function as free and open high seas. The second proclamation had a much greater impact. It announced, in part, that

> the Government of the United States regards the natural resources of the subsoil and seabed of the continental shelf beneath the high seas but contiguous to the coasts of the United States as appertaining to the United States, subject to its jurisdiction and control.

The ***Truman Proclamation***, as this pronouncement has since become known, specified that the United States' jurisdiction over the continental shelf and its contents would be limited to the region within the 600-foot isobath (line connecting points of equal depth). It also reconfirmed that the high seas above the continental shelf would remain open.

The Truman Proclamation focused world attention on the potential of the continental shelves. It also underscored the unequal distribution of shelf areas among the world's coastal countries. With its large eastern continental shelf, the United States gained more than 2.5 million square kilometers (900,000 square miles) of offshore territory. Neighboring Mexico, which shares the continental shelf off North America with the United States, was among the better-endowed countries, and it immediately claimed this region for itself. Next Argentina announced, in 1946, that it claimed not only its wide continental shelf but also the waters lying above it. This was a significant step because it closed an enormous area of high seas and designated them territorial waters instead.

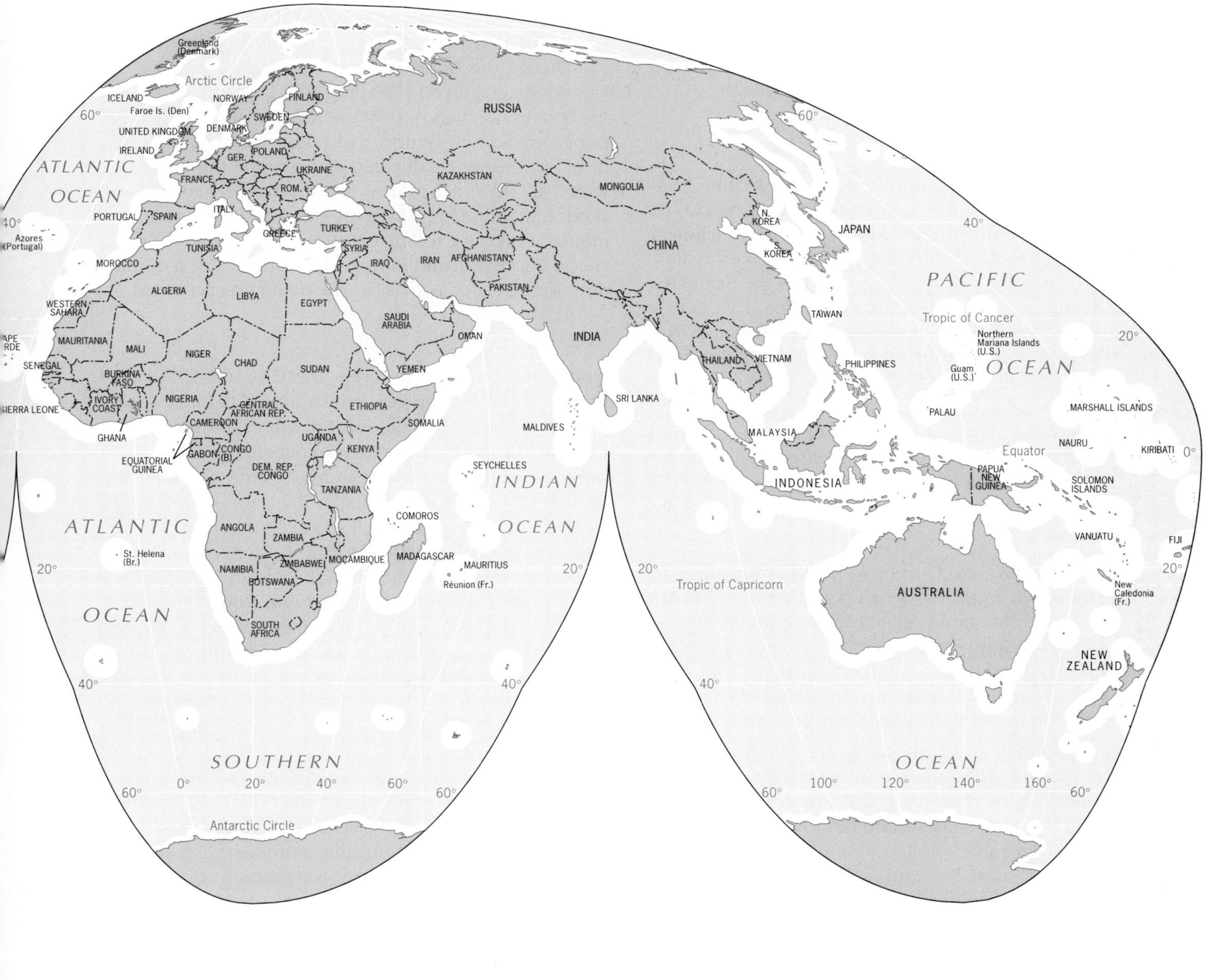

Widening Maritime Claims

States without extensive continental shelves now began to follow Argentina's example, claiming as much as 200 miles of territorial sea. In 1947, Chile and Peru took the lead, proclaiming that their seaward boundaries henceforth lay 200 miles into the Pacific Ocean. This had the effect of closing the rich fishing grounds of the Humboldt (Peru) Current to ships of countries other than Chile and Peru. Peru soon confirmed its control over its new maritime sphere by arresting fishing vessels and fining the companies and countries where they were based.

Thus economic motives have been the driving force behind the maritime expansion of coastal states. However, the situation was complicated by the end of the colonial era. After gaining independence, the former colonies could make their own decisions. Not surprisingly, many of them concluded that if narrow territorial waters were advantageous to the colonial powers, wider territorial seas would serve their own interests better. They were encouraged in this thinking by the former Soviet Union and by China, both of which claimed 12 miles when 3 miles was still the general rule.

The UNCLOS Process

This was the chaotic situation facing the first United Nations Conference on the Law of the Sea (UNCLOS I) when it convened in 1958. Although some technical matters were resolved during this meeting, key issues, such as the width of the territorial sea and the exclusive use of fishing grounds, remained unsettled. UNCLOS II met just two years later, and it, too, was unsuccessful. But then came UNCLOS III, beginning in 1973 and ending in 1982 with a convention opposed by only four countries (the United States among them) and signed by 157 states within two years of its completion. Although the United Nations had not yet established an enforceable law of the sea, it had created a consensus on what that law should contain. The key provisions were the following:

1. *The Territorial Sea.* The convention permits states to delimit their territorial seas up to 12 nautical miles (just under 14 statute miles) from their shorelines. State sovereignty in all its forms extends over this zone. Ships of other countries, however, have the right of passage through such territorial seas, so that narrow straits remain open to transit.
2. *The Exclusive Economic Zone (EEZ).* The convention recognizes a state's economic rights up to 200 nautical miles (just over 230 statute miles) from shore. Here the coastal state has the right to control exploration and exploitation of natural resources in the water, seabed, and subsoil below. All resources—fish, minerals on the seafloor, oil in the continental shelf—are the property of the coastal state and may be used or sold to foreign interests. If the continental shelf extends beyond 200 nautical miles from shore, the coastal state has exclusive rights to the resources it contains up to 350 nautical miles (400 statute miles) away.

Another provision, this one having to do with the remaining high seas and what lies beneath them, caused the United States not to sign or ratify the UNCLOS III Treaty. According to this clause, mineral resources beneath the high seas constitute a "common heritage of humankind," and their exploitation is subject to UN management. The purpose of this provision was to enable states without any coasts at all to derive some benefit from the Earth's marine resources. (The world's landlocked states are part of a UN group called the Geographically Disadvantaged States.) The United States and three other countries argued that a UN bureaucracy set up for this purpose might inhibit exploitation of such deep-sea resources by the only countries that could actually mine them, the technologically advanced states.

During the Carter (Democratic) administration the United States played a leading role in UNCLOS III, but the convention was not completed until the Reagan (Republican) administration had taken office (1980). The new administration decided against ratifying the treaty, which could not become law until one year after 60 states had ratified it. When the Clinton (Democratic) administration came to office in 1992, the prospect of ratification improved, and in June 1994, after some modification of the seabed provision, the treaty was accepted.

Median Lines

During the past two decades, the UNCLOS III Treaty's provisions have been generally adopted in international relations. Figure 16–2 shows the effect of the 200-mile EEZ on the high seas: huge expanses of ocean have been assigned to coastal countries, some of them mere specks of islands. What happens when countries lie closer than 400 nautical miles to each other, so that neither can have a full 200-mile EEZ? In such cases (for example, in the Caribbean, North, Baltic, and Mediterranean seas) the ***median-line principle*** takes effect. States on opposite coasts divide the waters separating them, creating an intricate system of maritime boundaries. Often such boundaries cross resource-rich zones, for example, in the North Sea between Norway and Britain, and allocational boundary disputes may arise as a result.

The effect of EEZ and median-line calculations can be seen on a map of Southeast Asia (Fig. 16–3), which also reminds us that the UNCLOS III Treaty may represent broad consensus but cannot prevent disputes. The South China Sea, in particular, is a problematic maritime region. The black line shows China's share of the South

Figure 16-3 Conflicting Maritime Claims in Southeast Asia. The potential for conflict over maritime claims in the seas of Southeast Asia remains strong. *Source*: From U.N., U.S., and Chinese maps as well as press reports.

China Sea based on its possession of numerous small islands there, including the Paracels. The red line represents China's published claims to the region, based on "historic" association with it. A key geographic element is the Spratly Islands, which are potentially rich in oil and are claimed by China and five other states.

This type of problem, however, is the exception, not the rule. The UN-sponsored conferences that led to the 1982 treaty rank among the great achievements of international diplomacy and stand as an example of what can be accomplished when states choose to cooperate for the common good.

◆ REGIONAL MULTINATIONAL UNIONS

The League of Nations and the United Nations are global manifestations of a phenomenon that is expressed even more strongly at the regional level. The past 50 years has been a period of growing cultural-regional awareness and assertiveness and intensifying economic competition. States have begun to join together to further their shared political ideologies, economic objectives, and strategic goals. In 2001 there were more than 60 such ***multinational unions***, many of them with subsidiaries focusing on particular issues or areas. Today, interstate cooperation is so widespread around the world that a new era has clearly arrived.

The first major experiments in interstate cooperation were undertaken in Europe, with the Netherlands, Belgium, and Luxembourg leading the way. It had long been thought that all three might benefit from mutual agreements that would reduce the divisiveness of their political boundaries. Certainly, they have much in common. Residents of northern Belgium speak Flemish, which is very close to Dutch, and residents of Luxembourg speak French, as do those of southern Belgium. Even more important, these countries complement one another economically. Dutch farm products are sold on Belgian markets, and Belgian industrial goods go to the Netherlands and Luxembourg. Would it not be reasonable to create common tariffs and eliminate import licenses and quotas? Representatives of the three countries thought so. Even before the end of World War II they met in London to sign an agreement of cooperation, creating what came to be known as ***Benelux***. Other European countries watched the experiment with great interest, and soon there was talk of larger economic unions.

This movement proved to be crucial to the reconstruction of postwar Europe, and it was given an enormous boost in 1947 when U.S. Secretary of State George Marshall proposed that the United States finance a European recovery program. A committee representing 16 Western European states plus (then) West Germany presented the U.S. Congress with a joint program for economic rehabilitation, and Congress approved it. From 1948 to 1952 the United States gave Europe about $12 billion under what became known as the Marshall Plan. This investment not only revived European national economies, with American encouragement, but it also spurred a movement toward cooperation among European states.

Toward European Union

Out of that original committee of 16 was born the Organization for European Economic Cooperation (OEEC), and this body in turn gave rise to other cooperative organizations. Soon after the OEEC was established, France proposed the creation of a European Coal and Steel Community (ECSC) with the goal of lifting the restrictions and obstacles that impeded the flow of coal, iron ore, and steel among the mainland's six primary producers: France, West Germany, Italy, and the three Benelux countries. This proposal was also implemented, but the six participants did not stop there. Gradually, through negotiations and agreement, they enlarged their sphere of cooperation to include reductions and even eliminations of certain tariffs and a freer flow of labor, capital, and nonsteel commodities. This led, in 1958, to the creation of the European Economic Community (EEC), also called the ***Common Market***.

The success of the EEC induced other countries to apply for membership. Denmark, Ireland, and the United Kingdom (which had initially declined to participate and formed EFTA, the European Free Trade Agreement) joined in 1973, Greece in 1981, and Spain and Portugal in 1986. The organization became known as the ***European Community*** (EC) because it was seen not only as an economic union but as a step toward a future United States of Europe. By the late 1980s the EC had 12 members: the three giants (Germany, France, and the United Kingdom); the four southern countries (Italy, Spain, Portugal, and Greece); and the five small states (the Netherlands, Belgium, Luxembourg, Denmark, and Ireland). These 12 members initiated a program of cooperation and unification that led to the formal establishment of a ***European Union*** (EU) in 1992. Subsequently, Austria, Sweden, and Finland joined the EU, bringing the total number of members to 15 (Fig. 16-4).

Under the EU's unification program, member states yield more power to the Union's central authority. Not all member countries were equally supportive of this plan. A major stumbling block was money: if the European Union were to have a single currency, other currencies would eventually have to be abandoned. Imagine France without its franc, the United Kingdom without its pound, and Germany without its mark! Many voters in the member countries were reluctant to let go of such national symbols; others did not wish to see their national parliaments subservient to that of the European Union. But the program of unification continued, and in the late 1990s the EU began preparing for the establishment of a single currency—the euro. First, all financial transactions were denominated in euros, and on January 1, 2002, euro coins and notes were introduced. Not all EU member states are currently a part of the so-called Euro-zone, but others may join soon and it is likely that the euro will be an increasingly visible, if potentially controversial, element of Europe's integration process.

The Future of European Supranationalism The integration initiative taking place within the European Union is the most significant development of its kind in

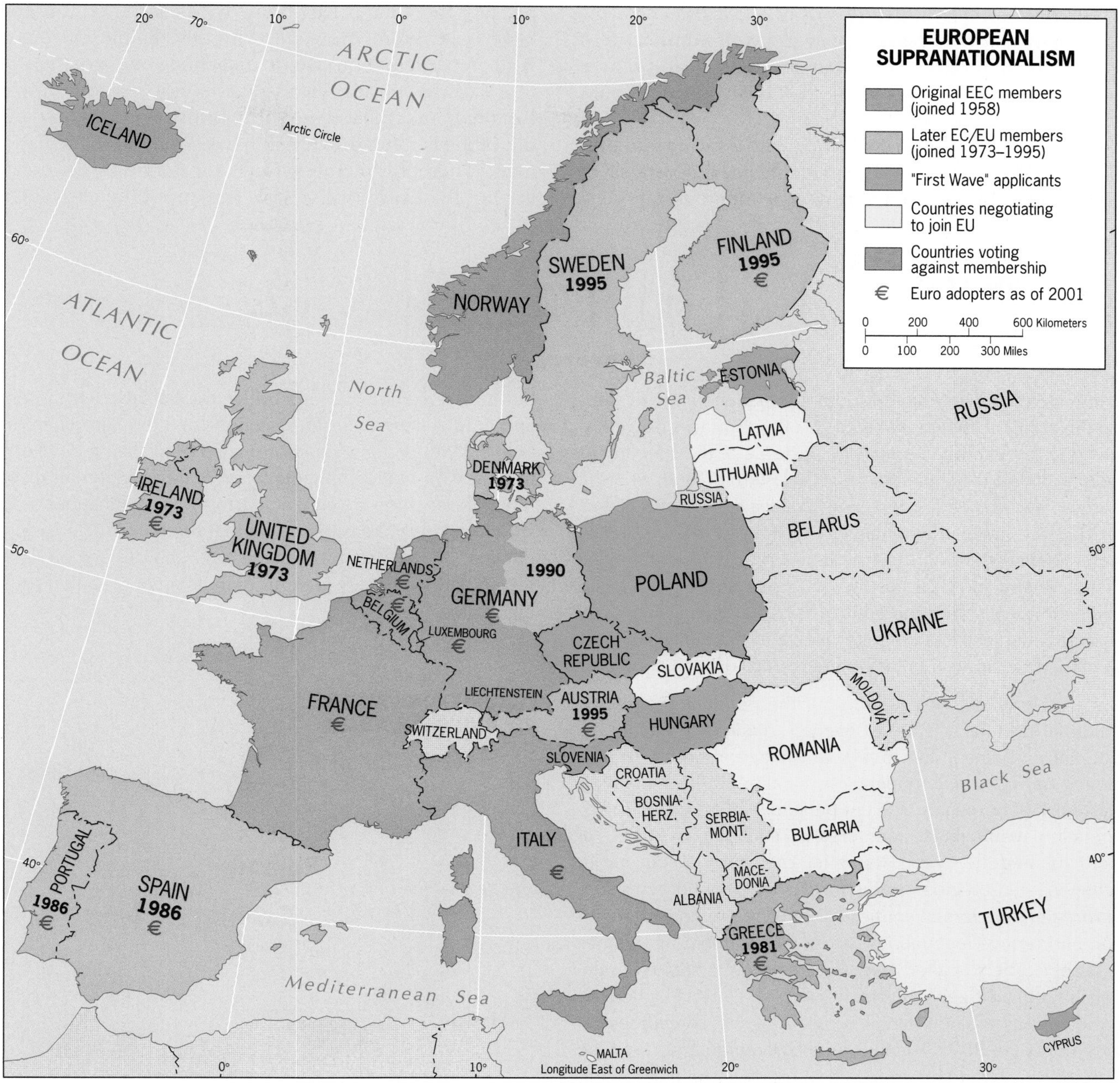

Figure 16-4 European Supranationalism. This map shows how the European states have aligned with supranationalist organizations.

the world today. At the same time, it is a difficult process in which the anticipated advantages are increasingly being weighed against concerns over the loss of local autonomy. Moreover, integration often requires painful adjustments because of the diversity of the European states. For example, agricultural practices and policies have always varied widely. Yet some general policy must govern agriculture throughout the European Union if the EU is to have real meaning. Individual states have found these adjustments difficult at times, and the EU has had to devise policies that accommodate regional contrasts and delays in implementation.

Another concern is the maintenance of a balance of power in the European Union. Germany is by far the most populous and economically powerful of the EU's members, and with a common currency it is increasingly able to exert great influence over fiscal matters. This, in turn, leads to worries that the traditional power balance between France and Germany will be upset. The Union is a patchwork of states with many different ethnic traditions and histories of conflict and competition. Economic success and growing well-being tend to submerge such differences, but should the Union face difficult economic or social times, divisive forces could well reassert themselves.

Such concerns have combined with a strong tradition of state autonomy to create significant differences of opinion over EU membership in some member states, especially the United Kingdom. Whereas other countries have held referendums allowing all eligible citizens to vote on participation (Denmark at first voted no, then yes in a second round), the issue was not put to a vote in Britain. Some polls suggest that British voters would pull out of the EU, but the decision has been left to the Parliament. There, EU membership is supported by the majority, but the Conservative government of the early 1990s

A SENSE OF SCALE

"Euroregions"

Economic globalization and suprastate nationalism are altering the political geographic context of local places as well as affecting the traditional functions and role of the state in Europe. Consider the situation in southwestern Poland, near the German and Czech borders. For decades the citizens of this region lived in an area dominated by Warsaw, although they were situated right across the border from then-communist East Germany and Czechoslovakia—countries that belonged to the same economic and political bloc as Poland. Yet, transboundary contact was not extensive, and planning decisions were made separately in the border regions of each country.

Since the collapse of communism, the political geographic situation has fundamentally changed. Anxious to encourage external investment and to take advantage of programs promoting transnational cooperation, local authorities in southwestern Poland began actively pursuing cross-boundary cooperation with their counterparts in adjacent parts of Germany and the Czech Republic. They soon succeeded in achieving "Euroregion" status for the transboundary region. ***Euroregions*** are formal entities designed to promote cooperation and reduce inequalities across international boundaries in Europe. The so-called Nysa Euroregion was created in the Polish-German-Czech border region in 1991. Plagued by some serious environmental problems—it is sometimes referred to as the Black Triangle—the Euroregion has paved the way for transboundary cooperation on environmental initiatives. In addition, a coordinated strategy has developed in the Nysa Euroregion to attract investment and encourage economic development. Poles, Germans, and Czechs in the region also engage in various forms of cross-border cultural activities (for example, music competitions) and sporting events (for example, track and field and soccer matches).

These developments have clearly transformed the political geography of the Polish-German-Czech border region. Most obviously, the inhabitants of the region no longer see themselves as living in an area fundamentally fragmented by national boundaries. Not only have new institutions emerged that link peoples and activities on different sides of the border, but also governmental authorities in Warsaw, Berlin/Bonn, and Prague have themselves encouraged the Euroregion initiative. With regionwide coordinated plans being developed to deal with matters ranging from land-use planning to historic preservation to enhancing the communications infrastructure, it is increasingly clear that the political geographic context of the Polish-German-Czech border region is no longer defined largely in terms of the map of so-called sovereign states.

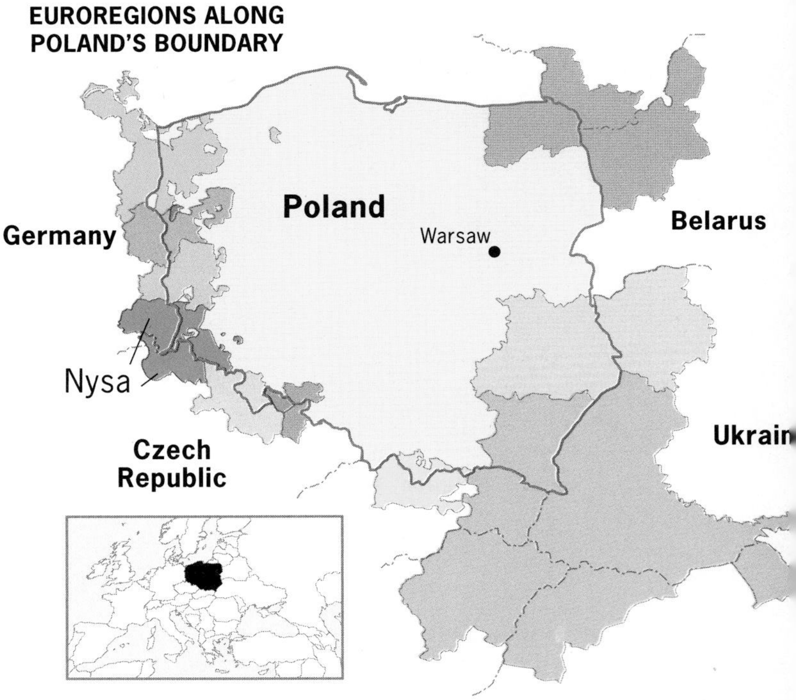

Euroregions. The Neisse Euroregion is but one of many that lie along Poland's boundaries, as shown in this map of existing and developing Euroregions around Poland. *Source:* PANORAMA EUROREGIONÓW/THE PANORAMIC OF EUROREGIONS, *Statistical Office of Jelenia Gora, Poland, 1997 p. 59*

resisted most initiatives designed to promote greater integration. The Labor government of recent years has taken a more conciliatory view toward a strengthened EU, but sharp divisions over the integration concept are still evident in Britain and are likely to come to the fore as the country faces a decision about joining the Euro-zone.

Expansion Still another problematic issue is the desire of many countries to join the Union at some future time. As long as these potential members are economically strong and politically stable, this does not pose a major problem. But as the EU expands eastward, perhaps someday including such states as Slovakia and Bulgaria and possibly Turkey, there will be powerful strains on the organization.

In late 1997, the EU authorized the initiation of membership negotiations with six prospective members: Estonia, Poland, the Czech Republic, Hungary, Slovenia, and Cyprus. Other Eastern European states are hoping to follow their lead. Under the rules of the EU, the richer countries must subsidize (provide fixed subsidies to) the poorer ones; therefore the entry of Eastern European states will add to the burden this rule imposes on the wealthier Western and northern European members. An even more difficult problem will involve Turkey. Some Western Europeans would like to see Turkey join the EU, thereby widening the organization's reach into the Muslim world. Turkey has indicated its interest in joining, but a referendum in Greece showed that more than 90 percent of voters there were opposed to Turkey's admission. Other EU members have expressed concern over Turkey's human rights record, specifically its treatment of the Kurdish minority, which would not meet the standards set by the Union. Behind these claims lies an unspoken sense among many that Turkey is not "European" enough to warrant membership. In early 1998, Turkey's hopes for membership were dashed by the EU's decision to consider and prioritize all applications—except Turkey's.

Even as the debate over expansion goes on, the center of the EU is experiencing other stresses. Many of the goals set during a key meeting in the Dutch town of Maastricht in 1992 are proving to be elusive; enthusiasm for the Union is not very high in key countries, notably France. But progress toward supranational goals tends to be cyclical. Visions of a political United States of Europe may be sustained by the maturing of a European Parliament and growing EU activism in international affairs, but progress toward European unification continues to depend more on economics than anything else. Hence, the fortunes of the euro are likely to have a significant impact on how the EU experiment fares in the years ahead.

Supranationalism Elsewhere

The notion of international association for mutual benefit is a worldwide phenomenon. As noted earlier, the EU originated in efforts to reduce economic barriers. Economic motives also lay behind the formation of the original North American Free Trade Agreement (NAFTA), formalized on January 1, 1994, which linked Canada, the United States, and Mexico in an economic community. The goals of NAFTA, however, are far more modest than those of the European Union—partly because the economic disparities between the United States and Mexico are much greater than those between EU member states. The lowering and eventual elimination of trade barriers is but one of the many goals of the EU; others include the free movement of labor, a centralized fiscal policy, and even a coordinated foreign policy. NAFTA has no comparable financial or political dimensions, and it does not look forward to a NAFTA Parliament or a single monetary unit.

Nevertheless, supranationalism is active in the Americas. The majority of the Caribbean island-states, with Belize in Middle America and Guyana in South America, are linked in the Caribbean Community (CARICOM), an evolving common market in the region. CARICOM has grown into an organization called the Association of Caribbean States (ACS), which includes not just Belize and Guyana but all interested states around the edge of the Caribbean. Also developing is the Central American Common Market, with seven members extending from Guatemala to Panama.

In South America, two major supranational groups have been established: the Andean Group and the Southern Cone Community Market (MERCOSUR). The Andean Group links Venezuela, Colombia, Ecuador, Peru, and Bolivia, and hopes to achieve shared economic objectives through open markets. The second group, MERCOSUR, consists of giant Brazil, struggling but economically significant Argentina, comparatively prosperous Uruguay, and developing Paraguay. Chile and Bolivia may join MERCOSUR, which is on track to become a full-fledged customs union (eliminating customs charges on goods moving between them) early in the twenty-first century.

Economic objectives also were the key to the formation of ECOWAS, the Economic Community of West African States. With far fewer fiscal assets than most multinational organizations and many divisive forces in the region, ECOWAS nonetheless supports economic cooperation and integration, joint development efforts, and a reduction in tariff and other barriers in West Africa. It played an important role when Liberia was engulfed in civil war in 1990. Several West African states organized a multinational peacekeeping force and sent it to Liberia, thus helping to end this costly conflict.

So numerous are the various economic unions that they represent a new force on the world map. From APEC (Asia-Pacific Economic Council) to CIS (Commonwealth of Independent States), an organization composed of most of the former republics of the USSR, countries are joining, treaties are being drawn up, and new associations are emerging. Not all of these alliances are successful, of course, but economic supranationalism is a sign of the times, a grand experiment still in progress.

Other Forms of Supranationalism

The main motives for supranational cooperation are economic, but they are not the only ones. Often the formation of one supranational union stimulates the creation of another (either a rival or a cooperative one). The development of economic supranationalism in Europe was paralleled by the formation of a ***military alliance***, the North Atlantic Treaty Organization (NATO). This, in turn, led to the creation of the Warsaw Treaty, which combined the USSR and its Eastern European satellites into an opposing military alliance. Today the Warsaw Treaty is defunct, and NATO is expanding eastward into the former Soviet sphere. In 1997 Poland, the Czech Republic, and Hungary were admitted to the alliance, and Romania and Slovenia, whose applications were denied, appeared likely to be invited in the next round.

The growth of NATO was a major concern to Russia, where this has become a leading political issue. Russia's sense of encirclement on the Eurasian landmass has always been a factor in Russian nationalism. One of the consequences of the September 11, 2001, terrorist attacks on the United States, however, has been the reorientation of Russian Policy. In 2002, Moscow became a "junior partner" in NATO.

Like economic unions, military alliances come and go. Among those that no longer exist are the Baghdad Pact, a Western-oriented alliance of Middle Eastern states, and SEATO (Southeast Asia Treaty Organization). Both alliances were dissolved in response to changing national policies. Military alliances are especially significant because they normally require member states to allow other members' forces to establish bases and facilities on their territory, which involves surrendering some sovereignty. This is a more significant dimension of supranationalism than economic cooperation; military forces symbolize power and intrusion, and their presence on foreign territory can be a sensitive matter.

Other supranational organizations are based on cultural objectives, although the distinction between cultural and political goals is sometimes blurred. The Organization of African Unity, now called the African Union, (AU) is often described as a cultural alliance to promote shared goals and resolve disputes, but the AU also has clear political objectives (among which was the ending of Apartheid in South Africa). Most African states are members of the AU. Another ***cultural organization*** with political overtones is the Arab League, a multinational alliance of Muslim states in North Africa and Southwest Asia. Founded in 1945, it is still a major force in regional affairs, but it has been rocked by divisions over such matters as the Gulf War, the recognition of Israel's right to exist, and cooperation with the United States and its European allies in the struggle against terrorism.

Some supranational organizations are primarily political. Europe's Parliament is the political manifestation of the EU's overall unification effort. Without economic underpinnings, however, ***political unions*** tend to be short-lived or inconsequential. The Commonwealth of Nations (successor to the British Commonwealth) is little more than a relic of Britain's imperial past, its economic benefits weakened by the United Kingdom's involvement in the European Union. The French Community has also lost much of its political relevance. The Federation of the West Indies is long forgotten. Nothing in the

From the field notes

"NATO's presence in Macedonia is welcomed by some—but certainly not all. Graffiti is not an uncommon site in Skopje, and it often has political connotations. The juxtaposition of NATO with the Nazi symbol leaves no doubt about what this wall writer wanted to convey. Even if NATO is there to help keep the peace, those who feel disadvantaged can turn around and equate NATO with the worst totalitarian excesses of the twentieth century. When it comes to politics, perception is the name of the game."

political arena matches the economic unions functioning today. The many manifestations of supranationalism all point to one important reality: the sovereign state alone cannot meet all the needs of its people in modern times. We still recognize the state as an extraordinarily important unit of political-geographical organization, since states are still the principal actors in the international arena. All over the world, however, states are joining supranational unions to further economic, strategic, or other aims. This situation reflects the changing position of the state in international affairs. Has the state system run its course and will something else replace it? It is too early to tell, but the answer is likely to depend on the ability of existing institutions to deal with the myriad social, cultural, and political forces remaking the world—the subject of the next chapter.

◆ KEY TERMS ◆

Benelux
Common Market
cultural organization
European Community
European Union
Euroregions
Exclusive Economic Zone (EEZ)
international sanctions
law of the sea
median-line principle
military alliance
multinational union
political union
supranationalism
territorial sea
Truman Proclamation

◆ APPLYING GEOGRAPHIC KNOWLEDGE ◆

1. The lengthy process that has led to the formation of the still-expanding European Union often is cited as the most significant example of supranationalism in world history. How does the EU compare to NAFTA in terms of its social, economic, and political geography?
2. The United Nations has managed to control and channel many conflicts that might otherwise have had serious consequences. One of these involved the world's oceans and seas: a United Nations Law of the Sea now exists. One feature of UNCLOS regulations is the so-called Exclusive Economic Zone (EEZ). How has the EEZ functioned to expand as well as inhibit states' maritime activities? What has been the impact on marine resources?

Chapter 17

The Changing Global Political Landscape

From the field notes

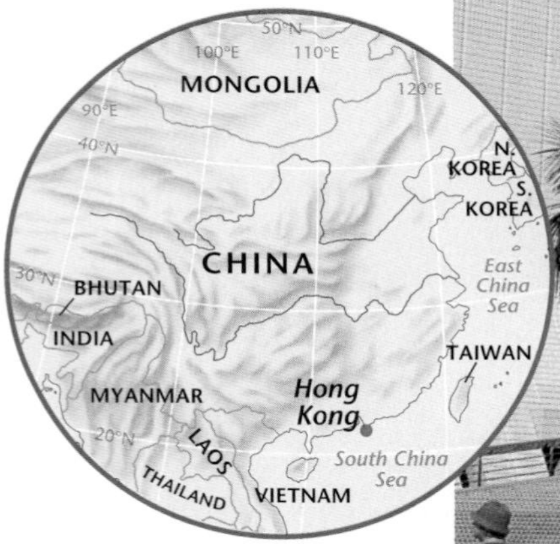

"In front of the exhibition hall on Salisbury Road in Hong Kong stood a display that was supposed to advertise an exhibit of Chinese art, but it seemed symbolic of something much more consequential than that: the red star rising over the western Pacific. This was Hong Kong before the 1997 takeover, and I went inside to ask whether this edifice was intended to do more than advertise an exhibit. 'They (the communist Chinese) insisted on this design,' said one of the staff members. 'You may look at it as a red star rising over us. But there *is* another way of looking at it.' I didn't ask, but I suppose he had in mind the reverse process. Obviously not everyone in Hong Kong was enthusiastic about what lay ahead."

KEY POINTS

◆ **Devolution, the disintegration of a state along regional lines, is occurring in a growing number of countries, old and young, large and small, wealthy and poor.**

◆ **Visions of local and regional autonomy, notions of democracy and participation, concepts of religious fundamentalism, and economic globalization are changing the territorial order based on distinct, sovereign states.**

◆ **The breakup of the former Soviet Union dramatically changed the international political order, leading to the creation of a host of new states and setting in motion lasting political and economic consequences.**

◆ **The world today must confront a weakening state system and an antiquated boundary framework. Yet the state remains a powerful presence on the international scene.**

◆ **Since the collapse of the Cold War order, the United States has emerged as the sole global superpower. Long-time allies and foes alike are concerned about American hegemony, and they are looking for ways to promote a multipolar geographical configuration.**

As the twenty-first century begins to unfold, consider how the world has changed over the past 100 years: its human population has quadrupled; hundreds of thousands of species of animals and plants have become extinct; two world wars have been fought; weapons of mass destruction have been invented; colonial empires have collapsed; the United States has become a superpower; the Soviet Union has disintegrated; Europe has unified; Japan has achieved economic eminence; the Pacific Rim has emerged as a new force in world affairs. Add to these developments the countless breakthroughs in science and technology (notably the invention of the computer and the beginning of space travel) and medicine, and it is no exaggeration to say that in the past century the world has been transformed.

Where does the world of political geography fit in that transformation? During the early 1990s, after the collapse of the Soviet Union and the end of the bipolar world we had known for so long, there was optimistic talk of a ***New World Order***, a world in which the balance of mutual opposition and nuclear terror between two superpowers would no longer determine the destinies of states. Supposedly this New World Order would be shaped by forces that connect nations and states, by supranational unions like the European Union, and by multinational action should any state violate international rules of conduct. The risks of nuclear war would recede, and negotiation would replace confrontation. When Iraq was driven out of Kuwait by a UN coalition of states led by the United States in 1991, the framework of a New World Order seemed to be taking shape. Russia, which a few years earlier might have led the Soviet Union in support of Iraq, endorsed the UN operation. Arab as well as non-Arab forces helped repel the invaders.

Soon, however, doubts and uncertainties began to cloud hopes for a New World Order. Although states were more closely linked to each other than ever before, national self-interest still acted as a powerful centrifugal force. For all its faults and changed circumstances, the state continued to function as a central building block in the new global framework. At the same time, a variety of nonterritorially specific forces seemed to be increasingly challenging the traditional dominance of all fixed territorial entities in the international arena. Some of these forces were tied to the emergence of economic and social networks that are not spatially bounded. Others are tied to the growing influence of groups with political agendas that are not channeled through states—and are often far-flung and spatially disaggregated.

In this chapter we focus on the forces that are changing the global political landscape. These are forces with which everyone must contend. They affect travelers, consumers, government officials, business representatives, and students. To be aware of these forces is to be better prepared to cope with them.

When we study the changes taking place in the world's political framework, we once again confront the field of ***geopolitics***. As its name implies, this field combines geography with some aspects of political science. Whereas political science tends to focus on governmental institutions, systems, and interactions, geopolitics brings locational, environmental, and territorial perspectives to the fore. As such, geopolitics is a wide arena that helps us understand the arrangements and forces that are transforming the map of the world. ◆

◆ FORCES OF DEVOLUTION

In the last chapter we noted how states are seeking common economic, political, and cultural ground by joining in supranational unions created to benefit the participants and, by definition, to disadvantage outsiders. The European Union is designed, in part, to enhance its members' competitiveness in the world at large. Many major European countries have replaced their historic currencies—the franc, mark, and lira—with a common currency called the euro. The euro, it is hoped, will be a stronger counterweight to the dollar than were the individual national currencies in the past.

Such supranational unions might be expected to form an important component in any emerging new world political order. That is likely to be the case, but these unions also have a reverse effect on the state. When a state's government joins a supranational union, it does so on behalf of all its people, majorities and minorities alike. In some cases minorities are heartened by this development, for it gives them a political identity beyond the state. But minorities (or parts of a state such as a region or a province) can feel disadvantaged as well, even threatened. Paradoxically, then, supranationalism can result in stronger centrifugal forces within states.

Yet this is but one type of centrifugal force working on states today—and like other forces it plays out against the backdrop of very diverse types of states. Some states (China, Egypt) are products of millennia of political-geographical evolution; others, including many European states, have matured over centuries; still others are much younger, having evolved from colonial empires only a few decades ago. Revolution, civil war, and international conflict accompany the evolution of states; the United States is a case in point. Even the oldest and apparently most stable states are vulnerable to a process that is the reverse of evolution, propelled by forces that divide and destabilize. That process is called ***devolution***.

Devolutionary forces can emerge in all kinds of states, old and young, mature and emergent. These forces arise from several sources. They can be generated by a government's decision to join a supranational union, as noted earlier. When the United Kingdom moved to join the European Union, some Scottish nationalists argued that Scotland would be disadvantaged by such a move. Within the United Kingdom, Scotland was a major player, one of the four territorial components of the state. But with the United Kingdom being just one member of a European Union, some feared that Scotland would be relegated to third-level status. Thus London's decision helped to revive devolutionary forces in Scotland. There were calls for independence for the Scots; if Denmark, with a population and territory not greatly different from that of Scotland, could be a full-fledged, first-rank member of the European Union, why not Scotland?

During the 1990s the Scottish National Party engaged in a campaign to underscore Scotland's disadvantaged position even within the United Kingdom. If Scotland were independent, it was claimed, oil and natural gas revenues would flow from its North Sea Exclusive Economic Zone to Edinburgh, not London; Scottish taxpayers' funds would serve Scotland, not the United Kingdom as a whole. In 1997 the newly elected Labor Party gave the Scots (and the Welsh) the opportunity to vote—not for independence, but for greater autonomy, to be embodied in regional parliaments. Both Scotland and Wales voted in favor, and a major devolutionary step was taken in one of Europe's oldest and most stable unitary states.

Interestingly, Scotland's new autonomous status has not necessarily fueled greater calls for independence. Instead, Scotland's new Parliament is coming in for its share of criticism—raising doubts among some about whether Scotland would truly be better off as an independent entity. Moreover, in the wake of the European Union's efforts to provide greater recognition and support of regions, some Scottish nationalists now see supranationalism as a positive development for Scotland—offering a political framework for the country that is not always based on London. What all of this shows is just how complicated devolution can be. At the heart of most devolutionary movements, however, is a strong sense of ethnonational or economic difference—and when these coincide with conflicting senses of territory, the results can be explosive.

From the field notes

"In 1990, Scottish nationalist activism seemed to be rising; I saw make-shift booths like this in several cities and towns, urging people to sign up for 'democracy' (that is, autonomy) for Scotland. 'Scotland should be independent,' the group's representative told me. 'We have our own culture, our own history and language, and we can maintain our economy if we get control over the oil and gas in the North Sea that are really ours. We have just as much right to be an independent nation as the Danes.' Talking to political leaders in Edinburgh and Glasgow, I found only one of them to be unwilling to discuss any accommodation for the Scots: the Conservative Party leader. And the Conservative Party was in control in London! Unless the political landscape changes, Scottish aspirations will have to wait." (Note: in 1997, following the Labour Party's victory over the Conservatives, Scotland was given the opportunity to vote on a first devolutionary step: the creation of a Scottish National Assembly with limited rights. A majority voted in favor. While this option may not satisfy those demanding full independence, a significant devolutionary move has been made. Voters in Wales also approved the establishment of an assembly, but by a narrower margin).

Ethnonational Forces

When peoples share a well-developed sense of belonging to the same cultural group, we describe them as an ***ethnic group***. Ethnicity is often based on cultural commonalities, but those commonalities that are singled out as significant is a product of social understandings that develop in particular situations. In some cases shared language can be the key to ethnic differentiation; in other cases religion can be the key; and in yet other cases lifestyles, diet, appearance, or agricultural practices matter most. The important point is that peoples sharing a strong sense of ethnicity feel that they are part of a group with a similar origin and cultural history—and ethnicity thus becomes an important way people distinguish "us" from "them."

Ethnic differences are manifest in a variety of different ways and at a variety of different scales. As we will see in subsequent chapters, different parts of cities are sometimes divided by a sense of ethnic difference, and at larger scales variable senses of ethnicity can complicate efforts to achieve social consensus within states. In some cases, however, ethnic differences within states can threaten the territorial integrity of the state itself. This occurs in situations where ethnic groups see themselves as distinct nations with a right to autonomy or independence in a territory of their own. ***Ethnonationalism***, then, can be a fundamental force promoting devolution.

Not all states with ethnonationalist movements are at risk of breaking apart. Britain, for example, has confronted ethnonationalism in Wales and Scotland, but English, Scottish, and Welsh histories have long been intertwined, and devolutionary tendencies are therefore not particularly acute. A much stronger sense of ethnocultural fragmentation, however, is at the root of many states' devolutionary problems. Most of the world's nearly 200 states have multicultural populations, and conflict among different groups can promote ethnonationalism, which in turn can lead to devolution. This is especially true when multiculturalism is regionally expressed—that is, where people of particular cultural backgrounds cluster in certain parts of the country. Consider, for example, the Canadian province of Quebec and its predominantly (though not exclusively) French-speaking population. If French speakers were distributed relatively evenly across the country, devolution would not be a threat, even if the minority objected to the government's policies. But the concentration of French-speaking Canadians in one province (with some spillover into neighboring ones) is a devolutionary force that poses a constant threat to Canada's stability.

The variety of devolutionary forces that exist in Europe reminds us that they can be found in older as well as younger states (Fig. 17-1). Not all of Europe's devolutionary movements have an ethnonational base, but several do. A prominent example is Spain, where demands for greater autonomy have come from the Basque area in the north, notably the region of Vascongadas, and from the eastern province of Catalonia. In 1979 the Spanish government signed autonomy agreements with Basque and Catalonian leaders, allowing both areas to have their own parliaments, giving their languages official status, and transferring some taxation and education powers from the capital to the respective provinces. Later the government reorganized its administrative structure, creating 17 so-called Autonomous

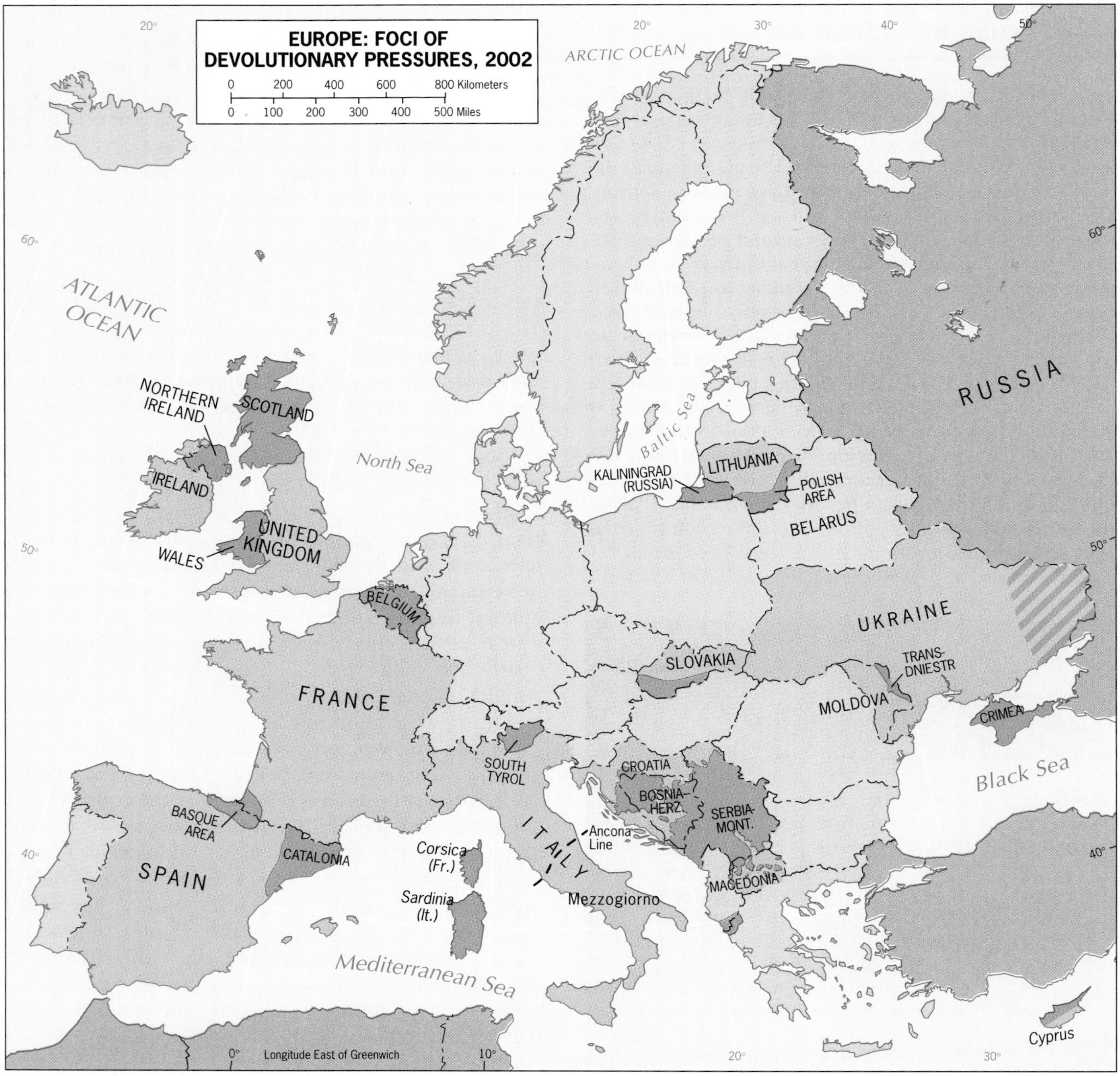

Figure 17-1 Devolutionary Pressures in Europe. Centrifugal forces have resulted in devolutionary pressures in various places in Europe. *Source*: From a map in H. J. deBlij and P. O. Muller, *Geography: Realms, Regions, and Concepts*, 10th ed. New York: Wiley, 2002, p. 61.

Communities and further decentralizing power. This plan reduced devolutionary pressures in strongly nationalistic Catalonia, but it was not enough for the most extreme elements in the Basque country, where a campaign of violence against Spanish targets (and even moderate Basque leaders) continues.

Devolution also threatens Belgium, and here, too, its roots are cultural. In Chapter 10 we discussed Belgium's Flemish (Dutch) and Walloon (French) subcultures and their strong spatial expression (see Fig. 10-6). By European standards Belgium is not an old state, but it was a founding member of Benelux and the EEC, and it is a charter member of the European Union, whose executive headquarters are in Brussels. None of this has been enough to overcome the centrifugal forces arising from cultural differences.

The capacity of ethnocultural forces to stimulate devolutionary processes is especially evident in Eastern Europe. Parts of the Eastern European map have changed quite drastically over the past decade, and two countries—Czechoslovakia and Yugoslavia—succumbed to devolutionary pressures. In the case of Czechoslovakia, the process was peaceful: Czechs and Slovaks divided their country along a new international boundary. As Figure 17-1 shows, however, one of the two new states, Slovakia, is not homogeneous: about 11 percent of the population is Hungarian, and that minority is concentrated along the border between Slovakia and Hungary. The Hungarian minority, facing discriminatory policies involving language and other aspects of its culture, has at times demanded greater autonomy to protect its heritage in the new state.

The conflict surrounding the breakup of Yugoslavia was the great tragedy of Europe in the second half of the twentieth century. Centrifugal forces broke apart a multinational, multicultural state that had survived seven decades of turmoil and war. Yugoslavia ("Land of the South Slavs") lay between the Adriatic Sea to the west and Romania to the east, and between Austria and Hungary to the north and Bulgaria and Greece to the south. Thrown together on maps after World War I, Yugoslavia was home to 7 major and at least 17 smaller ethnic and cultural groups. The north, where Slovenes and Croats prevailed, was Roman Catholic; the south, Serbian Orthodox. Several million Muslims lived in enclaves surrounded by Christian populations. Two alphabets were in use.

No Yugoslav nation existed except in the legal sense. This was a zone of divergent influences that were first held together by the Royal House of Serbia and later by a communist regime under the war hero Marshal Tito. But as nationalist sentiments became stronger, the various subgroups began fighting each other: Nazi-supporting Croats against anti-Hitler Serbs during World War II; Serbs, Croats, and Muslims against one another after the communist system collapsed and some nationalists sought to advance the interests of their ethnic nation. Ambitious leaders, often backed by the military, promoted the view that the peoples of the region were first and foremost Serbs, Croats, Slovenes, Muslims, Macedonians, or members of other, smaller ethnocultural groups.

As a result, the Yugoslavia of old is no more. When the communists ruled the country, they divided it into six internal "republics" on the Soviet model—all except Bosnia dominated by one major group. Now most of these republics are independent countries. Out of the collapse of Yugoslavia have come the newly recognized states of Slovenia, Croatia, Bosnia, and Macedonia. What remains as Yugoslavia is only Serbia and Montenegro.

From the field notes

"The battles fought with paint on church walls along the language line in eastern Belgium send a clear message: Belgium is not a nation-state in the traditional sense of the term. Disputes over the spatial extent and autonomy of the country's language regions are played out in the press every day, and even though no one has died over this ethnolinguistic clash, the Belgian landscape reminds us that the conflict is very real—and may challenge the integrity of the Belgian state in the decades ahead."

In early 1995 the devolution of Yugoslavia was centered in Bosnia. As Figure 17-2 shows, Bosnia is shaped like a triangle with only one point touching the sea; for all intents and purposes, Bosnia is landlocked. About 44 percent of its population of 3.8 million is Muslim; 31 percent are members of the Serbian Orthodox Church; and 17 percent are Croatian Catholics. In the civil war, Muslim Bosnians and Catholic Croats fought together against the Bosnian Serbs, who were aided—and often encouraged—by the Serbs in Serbia proper (capital Belgrade). When a stalemate occurred in late 1994, the Serbs had control of about 70 percent of Bosnia and the Muslims controlled a fragmented territory west of their capital, Sarajevo.

In 1995 the United States sponsored a conference in Dayton, Ohio, to redraw the map of Bosnia. It was agreed that the country (somewhat smaller than West Virginia but with similar mountainous and hilly terrain) had to be partitioned among the Serbs, concentrated in the east and north, and the Muslims and Croats, who prevail in the center, south, and west. On a large-scale map spread out on the conference table, the conferees

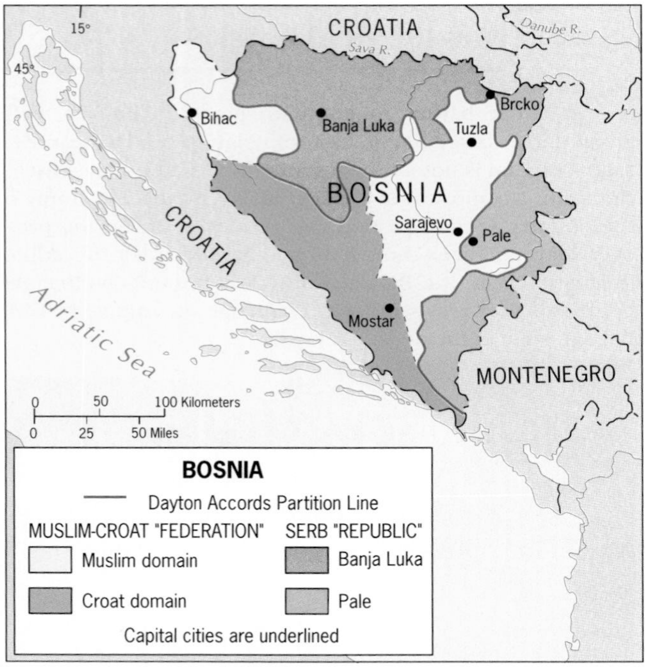

Figure 17-2 The Partition of Bosnia. The Dayton Accords Partition Line separates Serb from non-Serb entities.

drew a tortuous dividing line that created a Serb "Republic" on one side and a Muslim-Croat "Federation" on the other (Fig. 17-2). This 621-mile-long, 4-mile-wide barrier runs from Bosnia's northwestern corner to its southwestern one, almost cutting the country in half near the northern town of Brcko on the Sava tributary of the Danube River.

The Dayton Accords were achieved because all the participants saw immediate or potential advantage in them. Serb-dominated territory would be reduced to 48 percent of the country. Muslims as well as Croats each got domains in their "Federation." Sarajevo was made part of the non-Serb sector of Bosnia.

But the map also contained the seeds of further trouble. In effect, it created two Serb entities, linked by the most tenuous of corridors, and the two Serbian communities had their own differences. The east (centered on Pale) was far more closely aligned to Serbia proper than the north (centered on Banja Luka). And Muslims and Croats were by no means unified in their "Federation." Add to this Bosnia's landlocked situation (the Dayton Accords provided no corridor to the Adriatic), and it is clear that further devolution could occur in the future. Once cultural differences become a source of conflict, the cycle of violence is not easily stopped.

Recognition of this point explains why developments in Macedonia beginning early in 2001 raised such widespread concern. As we saw in Chapter 13, ethnic Albanian Muslims in Macedonia began rebelling against what they saw as ethnocultural hegemony on the part of the country's Macedonian majority. Violence broke out, and even though those behind the violence were relatively few, there was great concern that the situation would become polarized—leading to widespread conflict between groups. With the Bosnian example in mind, the international community was quicker to intervene in the Macedonian case than it had been in Bosnia—with military support from NATO and an active effort to promote negotiation. The situation remains fragile, however, and could easily deteriorate if strongly pluralist institutions do not take hold.

Compared to the constituent units of the former Yugoslavia, other countries shown in Figure 17-1 have dealt with devolutionary pressures more peacefully. Among these are Czechoslovakia, Lithuania, and Ukraine. Elsewhere in the world, however, ethnocultural fragmentation has produced costly wars. Ethnocultural differences lie at the heart of the decades-long conflict between the Muslim North and the non-Muslim South in Sudan, Africa. Similar forces have given rise to a seemingly endless civil war in Sri Lanka (South Asia), where the Sinhalese (Buddhist) majority has been unable to suppress or to accommodate the demands of the Tamil (Hindu) minority for an independent state. Moreover, devolutionary forces are gaining momentum in places that have long looked stable from the outside; China's far west is a case in point, where an Uyghur separatist movement is gaining momentum. The point is that ethnonational differences are weakening the fabric of many states in today's global political framework, and if anything the trend is in the direction of more, rather than fewer, calls for autonomy, or even independence.

Economic Forces

Devolutionary pressures often arise from a combination of sources. In Catalonia, for example, ethnocultural differences play a significant role, but Catalonians also cite economics: with about 6 percent of Spain's territory and just 17 percent of its population, Catalonia produces some 25 percent of all Spanish exports by value and 40 percent of its industrial exports. Such economic strength lends weight to devolutionary demands based on ethnonationalism.

Economic forces play an even more prominent role in Italy and France. In Italy demands for autonomy for Sardinia are deeply rooted in the island's economic circumstances, with accusations of neglect by the government in Rome high on the list of grievances. But Italy faces serious devolutionary forces on its mainland peninsula as well. One is the growing regional disparity between north and south. The Mezzogiorno region lies to the south, below the Ancona Line (an imaginary border extending from Rome to the Adriatic coast at Ancona). The richer, industrialized North stands in sharp contrast to this poorer, agrarian South. Despite the large subsidies granted to the Mezzogiorno, the development gap between the North, very much a part of the European core, and the South, the embodiment of the periphery, has been widening. Some politicians have exploited widespread impatience with this situation by forming organizations to promote northern interests, including devolution. The most recent of these organizations was the Northern League, which raised the prospect of an independent state called Padania in the part of Italy lying north of the Po River. After a surge of enthusiasm, the Padania campaign faltered. But it did push the Italian government to give more rights to the country's regions, moving it toward a more federal system. Although the Northern League's efforts fell short, the fundamental reasons behind its temporary attainments have not disappeared, and Italy will confront devolutionary forces again.

Even France, often cited as the model nation-state, must cope with devolutionary forces. Its chief problem lies on the island of Corsica, where a small minority of the population of slightly over 250,000 are engaged in a campaign for goals ranging from outright independence to greater autonomy. When this campaign began more than 25 years ago, it might have been called an ethnonationalist crusade; the activists published pamphlets that described Corsica (taken by the French from the Genoese in 1768) as a colony. Over time, however, nationalism seems to have given way to pragmatism: in return for abandoning their violent tactics, the activists want power and money. And the economy has become the key issue.

Corsica has been a significant problem for France. In 1996 bombs planted by Corsicans damaged a courthouse in Aix-en-Provence and destroyed the offices of the mayor of Bordeaux. In Corsica itself there were over 600 bomb attacks that year, and the island's tourist economy was devastated. Two years later one of France's top governmental officials was assassinated in Corsica. The fear of a more serious spillover of violence onto the mainland compelled the French government to intensify its search for a solution—and in 2001 the French Parliament passed a law giving Corsica's elected regional assembly special powers and allowing island schools to teach the Corsican language. The extent to which these new steps will quiet the situation remains to be seen.

Europe is not alone in confronting devolutionary forces with an economic dimension. During the 1990s a devolutionary movement arose in Brazil that was rooted in economic differences. As in northern Italy, a separatist movement arose in a well-defined region of the country (the three southernmost States of Rio Grande do Sul, Santa Catarina, and Parana). Southerners, complaining that their tax money was being misspent by the government on assistance in Amazonia, found a leader, manufactured a flag, and demanded independence for their Republic of the Pampas. The government responded by outlawing the separatists' political party, but the issue continues to affect Brazilian politics. It seems that no country is immune from devolutionary pressures.

Spatial Influences

We have seen how political decisions and cultural and economic forces can generate devolutionary processes in states. Devolutionary events have at least one feature in common: they most often occur on the margins of states. Note that every one of the devolution-affected areas shown in Figure 17-1 lies on a coast or on a boundary. Distance, remoteness, and peripheral location are allies of devolution. Thus the areas most likely to be affected are those that lie far from the national capital. Many are separated by water, desert, or mountains from the center of power, and adjoin neighbors that may support separatist objectives.

Note also that many islands are subject to devolutionary processes: Corsica (France), Sardinia (Italy), Taiwan (China), Singapore (Malaysia), Zanzibar (Tanzania), Jolo (Philippines), Puerto Rico (USA), Mayotte (Comoros), and East Timor (Indonesia) are notable examples. As this list indicates, some of these islands became independent states, while others were divided during devolution. Insularity has obvious advantages for separatist movements.

It is therefore not surprising that the United States faces its most serious devolutionary pressures on the islands of Hawai'i. Although the United States has not experienced devolutionary stresses of the kind faced by Canada, it is not immune to these forces. There is a small but vocal pro-independence movement in Puerto Rico, and some people in the Northwest occasionally broach the notion of a "Cascadia" that would consist of Oregon, Washington, and the Canadian province of British Columbia. The first real brush with devolution may come in Hawai'i. In 1993, the hundred-year anniversary of the U.S. annexation of Hawai'i, a vocal minority of native Hawai'ians and their sympathizers demanded the return of rights lost during the "occupation." These demands included the right to reestablish a Hawai'ian state (before its annexation Hawai'i was a Polynesian kingdom) on several of the smaller islands. The idea is that ultimately the island of Kauai, or at least a significant part of that island, which is considered ancestral land, would become a component of this parallel Hawai'ian state.

At present, the native Hawai'ians do not have the numbers, resources, or influence to achieve their separatist aims. The potential for some form of separation

From the field notes

"As I drove along a main road through a Honolulu suburb I noticed that numerous houses had the Hawai'i State flag flying upside down. I knocked on the door of this house and asked the homeowner why he was treating the State flag this way. He invited me in and we talked for more than an hour. 'This is 1993,' he said, 'and we native Hawai'ians are letting the State government and the country know that we haven't forgotten the annexation by the United States of our kingdom. I don't accept it, and we want territory to plant our flag and keep our traditions alive. Why don't you drive past the royal palace, and you'll see that we mean it.' He was right. The Iolani Palace, where the Hawai'ians' last monarch, Queen Liliuokalani, reigned until she was deposed by a group of American businessmen in 1893, was draped in black for all of Honolulu to see. Here was a touch of devolutionary stress on American soil."

between Hawai'i and the mainland United States does exist, however. The political geographer S. B. Cohen theorized in 1991 that political entities situated in border zones between geopolitical power cores may become ***gateway states***, absorbing and assimilating diverse cultures and traditions and emerging as new entities, no longer dominated by one or the other. Hawai'i, he suggests, is a candidate for this status.

Spatial influences, then, can play a significant role in starting and sustaining devolutionary processes. They decidedly contributed to the devolution of Yugoslavia. Remote frontiers and isolated valleys helped forge the complex cultural mosaic of the area in the first place, and during the country's breakup these same locales served as refuges for the adversaries who destroyed the state. Basic physical-geographic and locational factors can thus be key ingredients in the devolutionary process.

◆ THE DEVOLUTION OF THE SOVIET UNION

Devolutionary pressures, as we have seen, are present throughout the world. Governments have tried various methods to deal with the forces that drive the process; the methods range from suppression to accommodation.

In most of the affected states, the problem remains largely domestic in the sense that it has little impact on the world at large. But we must take note of one exception. When a powerful combination of political, cultural, and economic forces caused the devolution of the Soviet Union, the world was transformed.

For nearly a half century the Soviet Union had been one of the world's two superpowers, so that, geopolitically, the world was bipolar. In the second half of the twentieth century the world order was determined by the relationship between Moscow and Washington. This relationship was largely competitive. In what became known as the Cold War, each superpower tried to hamper the other against a dangerous background of nuclear armaments. One aspect of the Cold War was a relentless arms race.

In the late 1980s an explosion of centrifugal forces in the multicultural, multinational, economically troubled Soviet Union created the conditions for rapid devolution. The first geopolitical result was the weakening of Moscow's control over the countries of Eastern Europe. The consequences were far-reaching: the Berlin Wall, symbol of communist oppression, came down, communist-ruled East Germany collapsed and was reunited with West Germany, and communist parties from Poland to Bulgaria lost their primacy.

Some of the most dramatic developments, however, occurred in the Soviet Union itself. Devolutionary forces grew rapidly throughout the realm, and its component parts asserted their independence (Fig. 17-3). In reality, the Soviet Union had been a Russian empire, and now Russia itself, along with its 14 peripheral republics, emerged as new, independent states. As the map shows, the Soviet Union's rapid devolution affected a huge swath of Eurasia from the Baltic Sea to the Soviet Union's border with China.

Even as the Soviet Union broke up, Russian leaders tried to replace the Soviet framework with a supranational entity called the Commonwealth of Independent

States (CIS) with headquarters in Minsk (capital of Belarus). After some initial hesitation, all but the three Baltic states and Georgia joined the CIS (and Georgia later joined after Russia intervened to end its civil war). But when the Soviet flag was lowered for the last time on Christmas Day 1991, the CIS was but a skeleton organization, unable to replace what had been a cohesive empire.

The process of devolution did not stop here. Although the 15 Soviet republics had become independent states, most of them also confronted centrifugal forces arising from ethnic, historic, cultural, and economic circumstances. The newly independent states had to deal with significant economic adjustments as they coped politically with their new status. Large ethnic Russian minorities remained in each republic, as did Russian soldiers. Minorities that had been exiled by communist dictators demanded to be allowed to return home—where others had taken their homes and land. And old ethnic animosities came to the surface. Soon Muslim Azerbaijan and Christian Armenia, both in Transcaucasia (between the Black and Caspian seas), were in a state of armed conflict. Tensions between former Soviet republics in Central Asia also rose, involving cross-border minorities (for example, Uzbeks in Tajikistan), border issues, and resources such as oil and gas reserves.

The Changing Russian Periphery

When the Soviet Union collapsed, as many as 25 million Russians found themselves living outside the border of Russia proper, many as long-term settlers, some as Communist-Party representatives or "developers" of local resources on behalf of Moscow, and others as soldiers. A wide zone of northern Kazakhstan, for example, was so Russified that it was much more integrated with the Soviet north than with the rest of that republic.

Initially the new government in post-Soviet Russia had a strong interest in these Russian outposts, even describing the former Soviet sphere as the Russian ***Near Abroad*** and implying a right to intervene if they were threatened. But that concern quickly waned, partly because of troubles inside Russia itself and partly because any such threat failed to materialize. Indeed, although several million Russians left the republics because their jobs had disappeared and Moscow no longer paid their salaries, the new governments in the "Near Abroad" realized that the remaining Russian presence could be helpful to them in several ways.

In the first place, these new governments tended to mirror the authoritarianism of the Soviet system that had preceded them, and they took over the apparatus that had kept Soviet rulers in power. So the new rulers appointed experienced Soviets in key administrative positions, which served to protect the interests of remaining Russians in the republics. Uzbekistan, a Central Asian republic in a key location in Turkestan (the old name for this region, now reactivated), soon became a dictatorship in all but name, with close ties to Moscow. Secondly, the end of Soviet political power in the region created an opportunity for Islamic revival, which challenged the new governments in several Central Asian states. In Tajikistan the Russians took heavy losses in their efforts to help the government combat Muslim-inspired rebellions that became a full-scale civil war.

In geopolitical terms, Turkestan, and to a certain extent also Transcaucasia, changed from a Soviet empire to a Russian "near abroad" to an acknowledged Russian sphere of influence. The international community tacitly recognized this Russian primacy while sometimes criticizing Russian support for autocratic regimes and, in the case of Georgia, encouraging local opposition to less-cooperative governments. As we will see, events within Russia itself were shaping Moscow's policies in Turkestan; the Russians faced Islamic militants on their own ground even as they helped others confront them.

This was the situation in September, 2001, when, in the aftermath of the terrorist attacks in the United States, American and allied forces needed the cooperation of several Central Asian republics in their campaign in Afghanistan. Russian acquiescence was crucial; had Moscow objected, the republics would not have permitted their territories to be used as they did. Turkestan may culturally be witnessing a revival of Islam, but geopolitically it remains sphere of influence.

Devolution in Russia

The Soviet national planners who laid out the boundary framework on Russia's colonial periphery also devised a complex system to accommodate its minorities at home. At the top of the administrative hierarchy were 16 so-called republics created to recognize minorities such as the Tatars (Tatarstan), Kalmyks (Kalmykiya), and Buryats (Buryatiya). As soon as the Soviet flag was lowered, other minorities without such exalted status began to agitate for similar recognition, and within four years the new Russian Parliament had recognized five additional "republics," one of which, Chechno-Ingusheta, was later divided into two, Chechniya and Ingushetiya.

Initially the Muslim Tatar Republic created devolutionary problems, its leaders envisioning a level of independence not in Moscow's plans. But the real challenge came from the Caucasian frontier between the Caspian and the Black Seas, where Chechen Muslim extremists began a campaign for secession from Russia

from mountain hideouts. The Russian government sought to quell this movement by employing massive military force, but as in Afghanistan previously, the Russians took heavy losses. The Chechniyan capital, Groznyy, was almost totally demolished—precipitating a cycle of violence. In an incident that attracted global attention, Chechen separatists (they were never found) planted explosives in three of the capital's apartment buildings and killed more than 300 residents. Over the past ten years, thousands of Russian soldiers and many more civilians have perished in a campaign that, in mid-2002, was still at a stalemate.

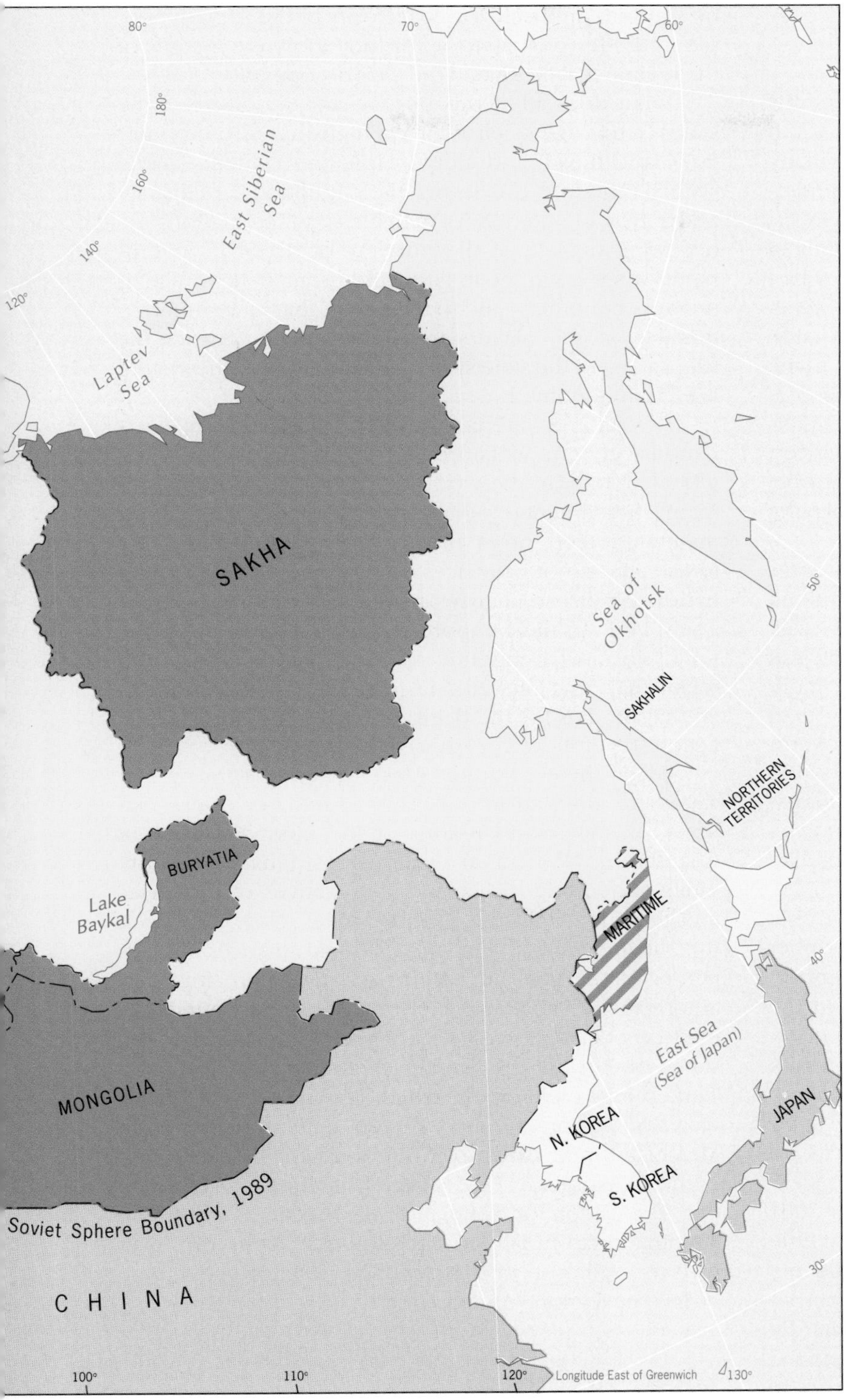

Figure 17-3 Devolution of the Soviet Union. Devolution occurred in all parts of the Soviet Union during the 1990s. *Source*: From a map in H. J. de Blij and P. O. Muller, *Geography: Realms, Regions, and Concepts*, 8th ed. New York: Wiley, 1997.

It is a measure of the importance of the Soviet Union's devolution that this giant country, territorially the largest in the world and with a population that ranked third, after China and India, broke into 15 parts of which the largest, Russia, still has more land than any other—but whose population now ranks sixth, after those of the United States, Indonesia, and Brazil. Russia today has turned inward, trying to reorganize and to control the disruptive forces of devolution. It still possesses a large arsenal of weapons, but its power to influence world affairs has dwindled—a casualty of the devolutionary events set in motion in the late 1980s.

◆ THE STATE IN THE NEW WORLD ORDER

As we have seen, the state, the crucial building block in the global international framework, is vulnerable to many destructive forces. The challenge to the state is underscored by the growing power of regions, provinces, States, and other internal entities to act independently of the national government. With or without the approval of central governments, provinces such as Catalonia, Quebec, Baden-Württemberg (Germany), Lombardy (Italy), Tatarstan (Russia), and many others have gained much more than internal autonomy: they have become economic, and to some degree political, actors on the international stage. And the cities that anchor these provinces, such as Barcelona, Stuttgart, Milan, and Lyon in Europe, Mumbai in India, and Guangzhou in China, are playing an increasingly autonomous role in the world.

Powerful provinces and their thriving urban cores engage in their own foreign commercial policies and, in some cases, pursue their own political goals as well. France's second city, Lyon, is a good example. Lyon is at the center of the Rhône-Alpes region; today it does more than twice as much business with northern Italy than with other parts of France. Moreover, Lyon's city government has opened nearly a dozen legations around the world, from Toronto and Seattle to Shanghai and Singapore. Quebec has a mission in Paris called *Maison Quebec* that draws more visitors than the official Canadian embassy in that city.

Yet the complexities do not end here. The terrorist attack on the United States of America in September 2001 provided a stark reminder of the growing importance of extrastate networks and organizations in the contemporary world. When the attack occurred, many commentators made an analogy with the Japanese attack on Pearl Harbor that brought the United States into World War II. There was a fundamental difference, however. When Pearl Harbor was bombed, there was no question what that meant: war with Japan—and by extension Germany. In the wake of the September 2001 terrorist attacks, however, the map of states was of little use in analyzing the situation. Afghanistan was deeply implicated in the activities of the terrorists who perpetrated the attack, of course, but Afghanistan could hardly be cast as the principal enemy because those behind the attack were, in no meaningful sense, synonymous with Afghanistan. Yes, the ruling regime at the time—the Taliban—apparently aided and abetted the operation of the terrorists behind the attack, buy many Afghans did not even regard the Taliban as a legitimate government. Instead, they saw the Taliban for what it was: an offshoot of the resistance movement that grew in the wake of the Soviet invasion of Afghanistan at the end of the 1970s and that seized power in the late 1990s. As such, it made no sense to implicate a vast majority of the Afghan people in the terrorist attacks, for they too were victims of the regime that facilitated the terrorist operation.

What does all of this portend for the future of the state? In this age of information highways, cross-border trade and travel, and global capital movements, many state boundaries are losing their traditional relevance and a growing number of activities and interactions are occurring outside of the purview of national governments. As we will see in Part Nine, some of these activities are economic—and to the extent that major international economic players are able to operate outside the framework of the state system, the integrity of the system itself is undermined.

In a different arena, however, national capitals and national governments are still key components of the global system. In the world of geopolitics, the state remains fundamental. States, not provinces or regions, maintain armed forces and use them in the national interest. States, not provinces or regions, enter into multinational military alliances to pursue common security goals. Perhaps most important, states continue to be the units we most frequently use to divide up the world when analyzing international issues and problems—with all that implies for the decisions that are made and the actions that follow from those decisions.

Given these contradictions, it is not surprising that states are entering into a growing number of associations, alliances, and unions of the kind discussed in Chapter 16. Multilateral relationships enhance security while supporting the economic initiatives of provinces and regions within the member states. Note, however, that the great majority of supranational alliances bind together states that lie within geographic realms, not among them. The European Union's national boundaries may be overshadowed by economic interests, but the states of Europe are having great difficulty accepting Turkey into their union, which (rightly or wrongly) is viewed as belonging to a different cultural realm. From Mercosur (South America) to the Southern African Development Community (SADC) and from the Arab League to the Association of Southeast Asian Nations (ASEAN), supranationalism is a growing force. This, in turn, may give us a glimpse into the coming political geographic order (see Looking Ahead box).

Forces of Change

Devolution is the direct result of a vision that has diffused throughout the world: a vision of greater autonomy or independence for ethnic or cultural groups wishing to overcome real or perceived threats to their well-being or security. From native Hawai'ians to New Zealand's Maori, from Canada's Cree to Australia's Aboriginal peoples, communities are seeking previously expanded rights and freedoms. National governments

From the field notes

"The long line of cars waiting to cross from Germany into Poland provides a strong reminder of what borders once were like in western Europe—but are no longer. And the Polish car stacked high with household goods symbolizes the attempts of eastern Europeans to adjust to a rapidly changing world. Many take goods produced cheaply in Eastern Europe to sell in open markets in the West, and then return with products that are difficult to obtain or expensive in the home country."

often misjudge the power of such movements or lack adequate means for dealing with them. The "window" for negotiation may be very small, and once a demand translates into violent action, it is very difficult to end the cycle of conflict.

Other major transformations are also changing our world. Prominent among these are globalization, notions of democracy, and the growing influence of religion.

Globalization As will be discussed in more detail later in the book, the last century witnessed a vast spatial expansion of economic, social, and cultural interactions. These interactions affect some places more than others, but they impact such large portions of the Earth's surface that they are often grouped together under the term ***globalization***. Globalization is most commonly seen as an economic phenomenon. Financial and trade links now tie together peoples in distant places, and economic developments in one part of the globe can have an immediate impact on areas thousands of miles away. At the same time, the state's ability, or at least willingness, to exert control over increasingly globalized economic relations is constrained. Multinational corporations operating in a transnational legal and political environment have assumed major roles in human affairs. Financial instruments seamlessly move across international boundaries. Investments made on one continent can and do affect the economic prospects of others.

States play an important role in these developments. They provide the territorial foundation from which producers and consumers still operate, and they continue to exert considerable regulatory powers. However, economic globalization makes it ever more difficult for the state to control economic relations. States are responding to this situation in a variety of ways, with some giving up traditional regulatory powers and others seeking to insulate themselves from the international economy. Still others are working to build supranational economic blocs that they hope will help them cope with an increasingly globalized world. The impacts of many of these developments are as yet uncertain, but it is increasingly clear that states now compete with a variety of other forces in the international arena.

The state's traditional position is being further eroded by the globalization of social and cultural relations. Networks of interaction are being constructed in ways that do not correspond to the map of states. When unrest breaks out in southern Mexico, for example, activists use the Internet to contact interested people throughout the world. Scholars and researchers in different countries work together in teams. Increased mobility has brought individuals from far-flung places into much closer contact than before. Paralleling all this change is the spread of popular culture in ways that make national boundaries virtually meaningless (see Chapter 29). Jennifer Lopez is listened to from Iceland to Australia; fashions developed in northern Italy are hot items among Japanese tourists visiting Hawai'i; Thai restaurants are found in towns and cities across the United States; countless Russian women hurry home to watch the next episode of soap operas made in Mexico; and movies produced in Hollywood are seen on screens from Mumbai to Santiago.

Globalization has produced economic, social, and cultural geographies that look less and less like the map of states. At the same time, the traditional sovereign authority of the world's 200-odd states is being increasingly eroded. The state system is unlikely to disappear anytime soon, but we are apparently headed for a world in which the spatial distribution of power is more complex than suggested by the traditional map of states. Describing that spatial distribution will be a challenge for geographers for generations to come.

Notions of Democracy Although it is defined and practiced in various ways, the idea of ***democracy*** is found throughout the world. Visions of a democratic China led to the disastrous Tiananmen Square massacre in June 1989, in which communist authorities crushed a pro-democracy movement of students and workers. South Africa achieved a triumph for democracy when it held universal elections in April 1994, soon after the dismantling of Apartheid. From Mexico to the Philippines and from Poland to Argentina, democracy has taken significant strides forward over the past decade.

Not all regions of the world are equally affected: representative government has made little progress in the North African-Southwest Asian realm, for example. Moreover, the vision and practice of democracy are often two different things. Some African ruling elites see no contradiction in the term *one-party democracy*, arguing that the multiple parties in many Western countries cover a narrower political spectrum than a single African party does. Elsewhere, as in Singapore, those in control place strict limits on democratic practice. However, even in countries where little progress has been made toward representative government (North Korea, Saudi Arabia, Myanmar), the idea of democracy still stirs the hopes of millions.

Yet, it is important to remember that antidemocratic practices can be found even in long-established democracies. Few countries are without voters or groups of voters who feel underrepresented or even disenfranchised. Such voters do not believe that their votes can affect the course of affairs. As we saw in Chapter 15, by manipulating the system, a national government can deny minority voters an opportunity to influence the outcome. By the same token, governments can construct political frameworks that promote voter participation and empowerment, thereby involving voters who otherwise might feel alienated.

The Growing Influence of Religion Another global phenomenon with major implications for a future world order is the revival of religion as a force in global affairs. In Chapter 12 we noted the continuing diffusion of the major faiths, especially Islam, and the renaissance of the Russian Christian churches in the post-Soviet era. This is another contrast in a world of contradictions: even in an era of science and secularism, millions of people are turning to religion to make sense of their lives and goals.

When the move to religion is associated with fundamentalist ideas—and when those fundamentalist ideas are rooted in notions of historical marginalization—the results can be explosive. Bolstered by a sense of righteousness rooted in Christian fundamentalist ideas, an individual wreaked havoc in Oklahoma City in the late 1990s. That act sent shockwaves throughout the United States, but it did not have large-scale geopolitical implications.

A variety of other acts perpetrated in the name of ***religious fundamentalism*** have had such effects. Fundamentalist ideas have prompted Jews to settle in Israeli-occupied territories, fueling territorial conflicts in the region. An upsurge of Shiite fundamentalism, led by an exiled ayatollah, ousted the Shah of Iran and transformed the political geography of a wider region. In Algeria, Islamic fundamentalists were poised to gain majority rule through democratic elections in 1992, and the country faced the prospect of an Islamic republic that would dismantle democratic institutions. The elections were canceled, and Algeria has been wracked by violence ever since. In Egypt, Islamic fundamentalists have attacked the government for what they regard as godless excesses and oppression, and have sought to destabilize the state by destroying its tourist industry. In Sudan, the Islamic regime extended Islam's severe *sharia* criminal law to both Muslim and non-Muslim communities, causing a devolutionary conflict. In Malaysia, calls for the implementation of sharia law have been heard in Parliament. And then of course there is the wave of international terrorist activities done in the name of fundamentalism. These began in the 1990s but came to dominate the international scene in the latter part of 2001.

Some speculate that the divisions that are emerging in the wake of recent events could lead to a new bipolar international system pitting the Islamic world against the Judeo-Christian world. This is the scenario posited in a controversial book, *The Clash of Civilizations and the Remaking of World Order*, by Harvard historian Samuel Huntington. Huntington's thesis has been strenuously challenged for its failure to recognize the extraordinary diversity within the Islamic and the Judeo-Christian realms and for its role in promoting stereotypes that do not represent the heterogeneous character of different religious traditions. Moreover, as we have seen, migrations and religious conversions over the past several decades have produced such an extensive interpenetration of peoples that it is increasingly difficult to assign single religious labels to large swaths of territory. Nonetheless, there are those who see the world in bipolar religious terms—including terrorists who seek to promote large-scale intercultural conflict. Prospects for future stability would thus seem to be strongly tied to the ability to promote intercultural understanding.

A New World Order?

If a New World Order (as opposed to disorder) is to come into being, it must do so in an environment of multiple, and often conflicting, pressures. Although subnational groups strive for independence, economic and social relations are being organized at ever larger scales; notions of democracy are gaining strength in some, but not all, places; and religious forces are influencing political and social conditions. These conditions all reflect challenges to the state system. Both supranationalism and devolution are signs of a search for alternatives, but neither process is likely to dominate the international scene. Most supranational unions remain weak and do not require member states to give up much sovereignty. The products of devolution (Slovakia, Croatia, Eritrea,

Looking Ahead

Geopolitics in the Twenty-First Century

Today only one state can be described as a superpower, but if history is any guide American dominance will not last forever. Yet it is difficult to see the United States disappearing as a major power. Hence, some believe that we may be looking toward a geopolitical order focused on four centers of gravity: the United States, a united Europe, a stable Russia, and a developing China—and the new quadripartite order will be characterized by a balance of power among these four.

It is difficult to predict such a framework with any confidence, however. Among these four powers, only the United States is not undergoing a major political or economic transition. Europe is facing a variety of challenges associated with the expansion of the EU to the east and the uncertain implications of its new single currency. The Russian Federation, still a superpower in terms of armaments, shows signs of serious political weakness at its center and is confronting an enormously powerful organized criminal network. Even the fate of China is uncertain; a serious bump on the road to economic liberalization or instability caused by economic or cultural differences could greatly complicate the leadership challenges the country already faces. Expectations of a four-power international geopolitical order in the twenty-first century would therefore seem premature.

Such predictions also assume that individual states will continue to be the dominant actors in the international arena. Yet with the traditional powers of the state under increasing strain, it seems likely that other geopolitical arrangements need to be taken more seriously. Chief among these are clusters of former states bound together by history, tradition, common economic interests, and perceptions of mutual geopolitical advantage. An alternative, and perhaps more likely, version of a multipolar world would be one composed of as many as five or six such clusters, each under the sway of one or several dominant powers. Moreover, within these clusters the power of traditional states may well be increasingly supplemented by the power of regions—whether sub-state or trans-state.

The European Union is clearly the great experiment currently underway in this direction, and much will be learned in the course of its development over the next couple of decades. Its success might well spawn supranational initiatives that are currently far less advanced in other parts of the world—which, in turn could promote the emergence of a multipolar world based on supranational blocs. Not all of the world's states would likely belong to strong regional blocs, however. In particular, the states of Africa and South America might well lie outside a global geopolitical system of blocs dominated by China, India, Russia, Europe, and the United States. During the Cold War, African and Latin American states became arenas of conflict fueled by the United States and the Soviet Union, and so-called proxy wars that did huge amounts of damage. In the future, these states could again become battlegrounds for conflicts between major powers—belying the notion that a multipolar world would necessarily be a more stable or politically benign world.

Moldova) in most cases do not appear to be viable alternatives to the state as we know it.

Another factor standing in the way of a New World Order is the world's antiquated boundary framework. We are entering the twenty-first century with a boundary system rooted in the nineteenth, which is a recipe for disorder. Changes in the social and economic geographies of entire regions have made existing boundaries irrelevant or worse. Decolonization and the demise of Soviet communism turned administrative borders into international boundaries. Many cannot function as such, yet the notion that conflicts must be resolved "within established borders" still prevails.

We have already noted the impact of cross-border migrations and the media-driven flow of ideas and images. Also significant is the flow of weapons and the diffusion of nuclear arms in the modern world. During the Cold War, both superpowers supplied their allies with weaponry, and numerous smaller arms manufacturers contributed further to the diffusion of weapons. As a result, when a subnational group wishes to pursue its political goals by violent means there is no shortage of weapons to use in doing so. This obviously poses a grave threat to any future world order; any failure to agree can quickly escalate into armed conflict by groups with easy access to remarkably sophisticated weaponry.

Another development of great significance is the ongoing diffusion of nuclear technology. Nuclear weapons give even small states the ability to inflict massive damage on larger and distant adversaries. Combined with missile technology, this may be the most serious danger the world faces, which is why the United Nations insisted on the dismantling of Iraq's nuclear capacity after the 1991 war and why North Korea's apparent progress in the nuclear arms arena in the 1990s caused President Clinton to threaten military action. Although it was always known that the former Soviet Union and several Western powers possessed nuclear bombs and the missiles to deliver them to enemy targets, the nuclear capabilities of other countries have been carefully guarded secrets. Thus in 1977, when reports of Iraq's nuclear program reached Israel, the Israelis attacked. But Israel itself is believed to possess a nuclear arsenal; South Africa was building one during the Apartheid period; India and Pakistan have recently joined the nuclear club; and there are concerns over Iran's potential as a nuclear power. As nuclear weapons became smaller and "tactical" nuclear arms were developed, the threat of nuclear weapons sales had to be taken seriously. It is now possible for a hostile state to purchase the power with which to blackmail the world.

The foregoing discussion underscores how elusive a New World Order may be. We live on a small, crowded, environmentally changing, economically disparate, politically unstable planet. To understand its geography is to marvel at its diversity, capacity, and continuity. Five billion years ago, the Earth was about to be born. Five million years ago, our ancestral lineage had been established. Five thousand years ago, the first cities worthy of the name, and the first complex states, had come into existence. Five hundred years ago, Europe made its fateful contact with the Americas. Fifty years ago, the world emerged from its most devastating war. Five years ago, the world was reorganizing in the aftermath of the Cold War. Where will the world be five years from now—and beyond? Any serious effort to answer this question must take into account the ways humans are using and transforming the surface of the Earth, and it is to such matters that we now turn.

◆ KEY TERMS ◆

democracy	ethnonationalism	globalization
devolution	gateway state	New World Order
ethnic group	geopolitics	religious fundamentalism

◆ APPLYING GEOGRAPHIC KNOWLEDGE ◆

1. You are a member of the staff of a multinational corporation doing business in several European countries. Your management has been used to dealing with governments in the capitals of several countries, including Portugal, the Netherlands, Poland, and Hungary. Now there are plans to expand operations into Spain at Barcelona, Belgium at Antwerp, the United Kingdom at Edinburgh, and France at Ajaccio. What advice will you provide, based on your knowledge of devolution?

2. Globalization and devolution are changing the role of the state in the world of today—and of the future. Using your knowledge of political geography and geopolitics, try to do what Mackinder did a century ago: formulate a model for the world of the next century. Do globalization and devolution preclude the emergence of superpower states? Can you envisage circumstances that might reverse these two processes and strengthen the state? Is Eurasia still the key, as Mackinder and Spykman argued?

Part Five

At Issue: Revisited

Can Europe create a powerful economic/political union despite concerns about economic and political centralization? Can Russia overcome economic trauma and corruption to emerge as a major world power once again? Can China create the political and social institutions that can foster sustained growth and unity? There are multiple obstacles to the creation of a stable, multipolar international order. These obstacles do not relate solely to international difficulties faced by Europe, Russia, and China in a quest for superpower status. Creating new superstars also ushers in new international issues and problems. The establishment of a strong European currency could pit the United States against Europe in a destabilizing international fiscal confrontation. The rise of a strong Russia could raise serious concerns among neighbors who have only recently extracted themselves from the Soviet shadow. The ideological gap between the United States and China, which has been overlooked for a time in pursuit of economic interests, could once again come to the fore as China's regional and global influence broadens. All of this suggests that the end of the Cold War did not signal the end to large-scale threats to stability. Instead, one of the critical challenges for the future is to manage changing global power relations through peaceful channels.

◆ SELECTED REFERENCES ◆

Part Five The Political Imprint

Agnew, J. A. *Place and Politics: The Geographical Mediation of State and Society* (Boston: Allen & Unwin, 1987).

Agnew, J. A. *Geopolitics: Re-visioning World Politics* (New York: Routledge, 1998).

Agnew, J. A., ed. *Political Geography: A Reader* (London: Arnold, 1997).

Anderson, J., Brook, C., & Cochrane, A., eds. *A Global World?: Re-ordering Political Space* (Oxford, U.K.: Oxford University Press, 1995).

Ardrey, R. *The Territorial Imperative* (New York: Antheneum, 1966).

Barakat, H. *The Arab World: Society, Culture, and State* (Berkeley: University of California Press, 1993).

Barton, J. R. *A Political Geography of Latin America* (London: Routledge, 1997).

Boateng, E. A. *A Political Geography of Africa* (Cambridge, U.K.: Cambridge University Press, 1978).

Booth, J. A., & Walker, T. W. *Understanding Central America.* 3rd ed. (Boulder, Colo.: Westview Press, 1999).

Boyd, A. *An Atlas of World Affairs.* 10th ed. (New York: Routledge, 1998).

Bremmer, I., & Taras, R., ed. *New State, New Politics: Building the Post-Soviet Nations* (Cambridge: Cambridge University Press, 1997).

Connor, W. *Ethnonationalism: The Quest for Understanding* (Princeton, N.J.: Princeton University Press, 1994).

Crossette, B. *India: Facing the Twenty-first Century* (Bloomington: Indiana University Press, 1993).

Davidson, B. *The Black Man's Burden: Africa and the Curse of the Nation-State* (New York: Times Books/Random House, 1992).

Dawson, A. H. *The Geography of European Integration: A Common European Home?* (New York: Belhaven, 1993).

Demko, G. J., & Wood, W. B. *Reordering the World: Geopolitical Perspectives on the 21st Century.* 2nd ed. (Boulder, Colo.: Westview Press, 1999).

Dink, N., & Karatnycky, A. *New Nations Rising: The Fall of the Soviets and the Challenge of Independence* (New York: John Wiley & Sons, 1993).

Esposito, J. L. *The Islamic Threat: Myth or Reality?* (New York: Oxford University Press, 1992).

Finkelstein, N. *The Separation of Quebec and the Constitution of Canada* (North York, Ontario: York University Centre for Public Law and Public Policy, 1992).

Glassner, M. I. *Neptune's Domain: A Political Geography of the Sea* (Boston: Unwin Hyman, 1990).

Glassner, M. I. *Political Geography.* 2nd ed. (New York: John Wiley & Sons, 1996).

Guéhenno, J. M. *The End of the Nation-State*, trans. V. Elliott (Minneapolis: University of Minnesota Press, 1995).

Hancock, M. D., & Welsh, H., eds. *German Unification: Process and Outcomes* (Boulder, Colo.: Westview Press, 1993).

Held, C. C. *Middle East Patterns: Places, Peoples, and Politics.* 3rd ed. (Boulder, Colo.: Westview Press, 2000).

Herb, G., & Kaplan, H. D. *Nested Identities: Nationalism, Territory and Scale* (Lanham, Md.: Rowman & Littlefield Publishers, 1999).

Huntington, S. P. *The Clash of Civilizations and the Remaking of World Order* (New York: Simon & Schuster, 1996).

Jackson, P., & Penrose, J. *Constructions of Race, Place and Nation* (Minneapolis: University of Minnesota Press, 1994, c 1993).

Johnston, R. J. *Geography and the State: An Essay in Political Geography* (New York: St., Martin's Press, 1983).

Johnston, R. J., Knight, D. B., & Kofman, E., eds. *Nationalism, Self-Determination, and Political Geography* (New York: Croom & Helm, 1988).

Johnston, R. J., Shelley, F. M., & Taylor, P. J. *Developments in Electoral Geography* (New York: Routledge, 1990).

Johnston, R. J., Taylor, P. J., and Watts, M. J., eds. *Geographies of Global Change: Remapping the World in the Late Twentieth Century* (Oxford: Blackwell, 1995).

Lewis, R. A., ed. *Geographic Perspectives on Soviet Central Asia* (New York: Routledge, 1992).

Mackinder, H. J. "The Geographical Pivot of History," *Geographical Journal* 23 (1904): 421–444.

Mackinder, H. J., *Democratic Ideals and Reality: A Study in the Politics of Reconstruction* (New York: H. Holt & Company, 1919).

Mikesell, M. A., & Murphy, A. B. "A Framework for Comparative Study of Minority-Group Aspirations." *Annals of the Association of American Geographers* 81, no, 4 (1991): 581–604.

Muir, R. *Political Geography: A New Introduction* (New York: John Wiley & Sons, 1997).

Muni, S. D. *Pangs of Proximity: India and Sri Lanka's Ethnic Crisis* (Newbury Park, Calif.: Sage Publications, 1993).

Murphy, A. B. "The Sovereign State System as Political-Territorial Ideal: Historical and Contemporary Considerations." In T. Biersteker & C. Weber, eds., *State Sovereignty as Social Construct* (Cambridge: Cambridge University Press, 1996), 81–120.

Nahaylo, B., & Swoboda, V. *Soviet Disunion: A History of the Nationalities Problem in the USSR* (New York: Free Press, 1990).

Nijman, J. *The Geopolitics of Power and Conflict: Superpowers in the International System, 1945–1992* (London: Belhaven, 1993).

O'Loughlin, J. V., & Van der Wusten, H., eds. *The New Political Geography of Eastern Europe* (New York: Belhaven/Wiley, 1993).

O'Tuathail, G. *Critical Geopolitics: The Politics of Writing Global Space* (Minneapolis: University of Minneapolis Press, 1996).

Painter, J. *Politics, Geography, and "Political Geography": A Critical Perspective* (London: Arnold, 1995).

Prescott, J. R. V. *Political Frontiers and Boundaries* (London: Allen & Unwin, 1987).

Ratzel, F. "Laws of the Spatial Growth of States." In R. E. Kasperson & J. Minghi, eds., *The Structure of Political Geography*, trans. R. L. Bolin (Chicago: Aldine, 1969).

Robinson, K. W. "Sixty Years of Federation in Australia," *Geographical Review* 51 (1961): 1–20.

Rumley, D., & Minghi, J. V., eds. *The Geography of Border Landscapes* (New York: Routledge, 1991).

Sack, R. D. *Human Territoriality: Its Theory and History* (Cambridge: Cambridge University Press, 1986).

Spykman, N. J. *The Geography of the Peace* (New York: Harcourt, Brace, 1944).

Stoessinger, J. *The Might of Nations* (New York: Random House, 1961).

Taylor, P. J. *The Way the World Works: World Hegemony to World Impasse* (New York: John Wiley & Sons, 1996).

Taylor, P. J., ed. *Political Geography of the Twentieth Century: A Global Analysis* (New York: Halsted Press, 1993).

Taylor, P., & Flint, C. *Political Geography: World Economy, Nation-State, and Locality*, 4th ed. (New York: John Wiley & Sons, 2000).

Van Dyke, J. M., et al. *Freedom for the Seas in the 21st Century: Ocean Governance and Environmental Harmony* (Washington, D.C.: Island Press, 1993).

Vasciannie, S. C. *Landlocked and Geographically Disadvantaged States in the International Law of the Sea* (New York: Oxford University Press, 1990).

White, G. *Nationalism and Territory: Constructing Group Identity in Southeastern Europe* (Lanham, Md.: Rowman & Littlefield, 2000).

William, C. H., ed. *The Political Geography of the New World Order* (New York: Halstead Press, 1993).

Part Six

LAND AND LAND USE IN THE RURAL SECTOR

At Issue

The farmers on the land produce what the consumers in the cities need, but it is the consumers, not the producers, who dictate what the farmers will be paid. This core-periphery relationship prevails at global as well as regional levels: North Americans and Europeans determine the prices of bananas grown in the Caribbean and Central America; food prices are kept artificially low by governments in African capitals for political reasons, and the farmers suffer. Now the World Trade Organization is sweeping away the last vestiges of price support for poor-country farmers, and economies from St. Lucia to Mauritius face adversity. *Should poor-country commercial farmers be protected against the avarice of the rich markets?*

What are the chances for this Egyptian farmer's cotton crop on the world market?

Part Outline

Chapter 18

Traditional Livelihoods of Rural Peoples

From the field notes

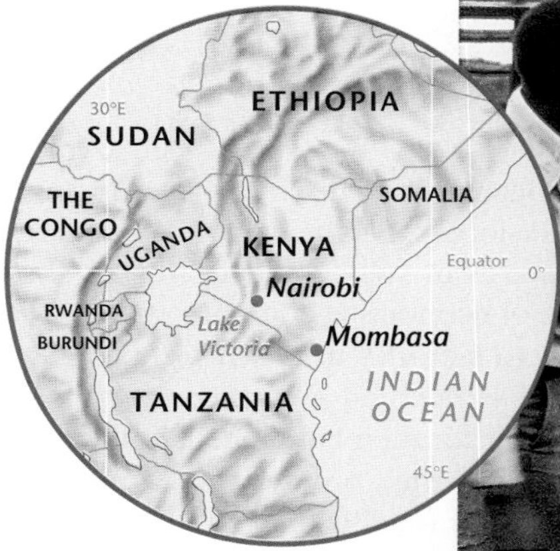

"Attempts to tame wildlife started in ancient times, and still continue. At Hunter's Lodge on the Nairobi-Mombasa road we met an agricultural officer who reported that an animal domestication experiment station was located not far into the bush, about 10 miles south. On his invitation, we spent the next day observing this work. In some herds, domestic animals (goats) were combined with wild gazelles, all penned together in a large enclosure. This was not working well; the gazelles continued all day to seek escape. By comparison, these eland were docile, manageable, and in good health. Importantly, they also were reproducing in captivity. Here, our host describes the program."

KEY POINTS

◆ **Rural life has long been dominated by primary economic activities—particularly farming and fishing.**

◆ **Agriculture, the deliberate tending of crops and livestock to produce food and fiber, may be less than 12,000 years old and emerged sequentially in several different world regions. Whether agriculture diffused from one hearth to another, or was an independent innovation in the different hearths, is an open debate.**

◆ **The First Agricultural Revolution occurred when plants were first domesticated. The Second Agricultural Revolution involved improved methods of cultivation, production, and storage. The Third Agricultural Revolution (now in progress) is based on research and technology in plant genetics.**

◆ **The process of animal domestication, set in motion more than 8000 years ago, still continues.**

◆ **Subsistence agriculture, which produces little or no surplus, still prevails in large regions in Africa, Asia, and the Americas.**

◆ **J. H. von Thünen developed one of the earliest rural land-use models. It accounted for agricultural patterns around urban market centers.**

When we examined the problems involved in attempts to define culture, it was obvious that this term encompasses the full range of human thought and activity, from belief systems to technological implements. Human geographers are especially interested in the imprints made by human culture on the landscape. These include not only the marks of religion and language, but also the impress of economic and political activities.

It is not difficult to visualize the cultural landscapes of farming. Agriculture transforms whole countrysides. The range of agricultural landscapes is enormous, from the vast, rolling wheatlands of the Great Plains in America to the terraced hillslopes of Asia; from the vineyards of France to the pastures of New Zealand. In Part Six, we begin a discussion of economic geography that will carry us from farmlands to factories to urban complexes. Economic geography is concerned with the various ways in which people provide for their basic needs and with how the goods and services they produce and consume are spatially expressed and organized. It is also concerned with the impacts of the spatial organization of economic activity on society, politics, and the environment. ◆

◆ CLASSIFYING ECONOMIC ACTIVITIES

Economic activities range from the simple to the complex and from the ancient to the modern. One way to classify those activities is to distinguish among different types of activities. For a long time three basic types of economic activities were recognized: primary, secondary, and tertiary.

Primary Activities

Hunting and gathering, farming of all kinds, livestock herding, fishing and aquaculture, forestry and lumbering, mining and quarrying are all primary activities. What unites these activities is that they are all concerned with extracting something from the Earth. As such, workers and the natural environment come into direct contact in the primary sector. When such activities are carried on at a large scale, the environment sometimes suffers.

Secondary Activities

Economic activities concerned with the conversion of raw materials into intermediate or finished products are termed secondary activities. These manufacturing industries date from the time stones and bones were first shaped into tools. Major stages in human history are based on various forms of conversion of raw materials (the Bronze Age and the Iron Age are examples). Today secondary activities include the production of an almost infinite range of commodities. Toys, warships, pottery, steel, chemicals, buildings—all are products of secondary activities.

Tertiary Activities

Today hundreds of millions of workers are employed in the so-called service industries. The people in the offices, banks, hospitals, and shops in the downtown of an American city represent the tertiary sector. They connect producers to consumers, thus facilitating commerce and trade; as lawyers, doctors, dentists, teachers, and librarians, they provide essential services in a complex society.

Quaternary (and Quinary) Activities

As we will see in Part Eight, the tertiary sector has become so complicated that specialized service activities are now often grouped into quaternary and quinary categories. The term quaternary is used for economic activities concerned with information and the exchange of money or capital. The term quinary refers to the spheres of research and higher education. We will return to these categories in due course.

Grouping economic activities into categories helps us discuss and analyze them, but it is evident that such categories are actually points on a continuum. Take the case of farming. Most farm products are marketed in the form in which they are harvested (rice, oranges, potatoes), but some are cooked, dried, salted, or otherwise converted before distribution. These latter products may be classified as secondary manufactures, since raw materials have been converted into different commodities. Nevertheless, all farming industries, from subsistence rice growing on small plots to commercial wheat cultivation on huge estates, are generally regarded as primary activities. These activities are the focus of this chapter.

◆ THE PERSISTENCE OF AGRICULTURE

In this part of the book we focus on ***agriculture***, the deliberate tending of crops and livestock in order to produce food and fiber. Yet in the United States this activity has involved fewer and fewer people. In 1994 the U.S. Bureau of the Census announced that the number of farmers in the United States had fallen below 2 million. Not since the mid-nineteenth century, when the American population was barely over 20 million, had the Census Bureau counted so few farming families.

Does this mean that farming is no longer a major component of the U.S. economy? Hardly. Total agricultural production is at an all-time high. But the nature of farming has changed: mechanization and farm consolidation have driven millions of small farmers off the land. The transformation of the U.S. economy from an agricultural to an industrial and technological one has altered the pattern of employment. Still, American farm output is enormous and remains among the world's largest.

In the chapters that follow, we will move our focus from farming to industry and technology, but it is well to remember that in the majority of countries agriculture remains the leading employment sector. Indeed, in some societies people continue to live and work as they did thousands of years ago. The revolutionary changes that are so commonplace to us have barely touched the existence of many millions of people in Asia and Africa. We may be witnessing the beginnings of a postindustrial age, but they are not. The first half of this chapter, therefore, focuses on the way these people make their living.

◆ ANCIENT LIVELIHOODS IN A MODERN WORLD

The processes whereby food is produced, distributed, and consumed form a fundamental part of every culture. The way in which land is allocated to individuals or families (or bought or sold), the manner in which it is used for food production, the functions of livestock, and the consumption of food from crops and animals are all aspects of culture. In earlier chapters we noted that food consumption is often related to religious influence and ideology. Adherents of Islam and Judaism avoid pork; Hindus do not consume beef (Fig. 18-1). Yet culture influences diet in far less obvious ways. Offer an American a dish of dog or horse meat, and you are likely to encounter a strong negative reaction. The point is that various forms of partial or total abstinence occur among human cultures, including periodic fasts. Such rules, like the cultural ideas that generate them, tend to be old and persistent, and change only slowly. In other cases food avoidance is due to intolerance for particular substances, such as dairy products, eggs, or fish.

Before Farming

Most of the food eaten by humans comes, directly or indirectly, from the soil. ***Farming*** therefore has long been the basis of existence all over the world. However, there was a time before the invention of agriculture when human existence was based on methods other than farming. Viewed in the context of human history as a whole, farming is a very recent innovation (its begin-

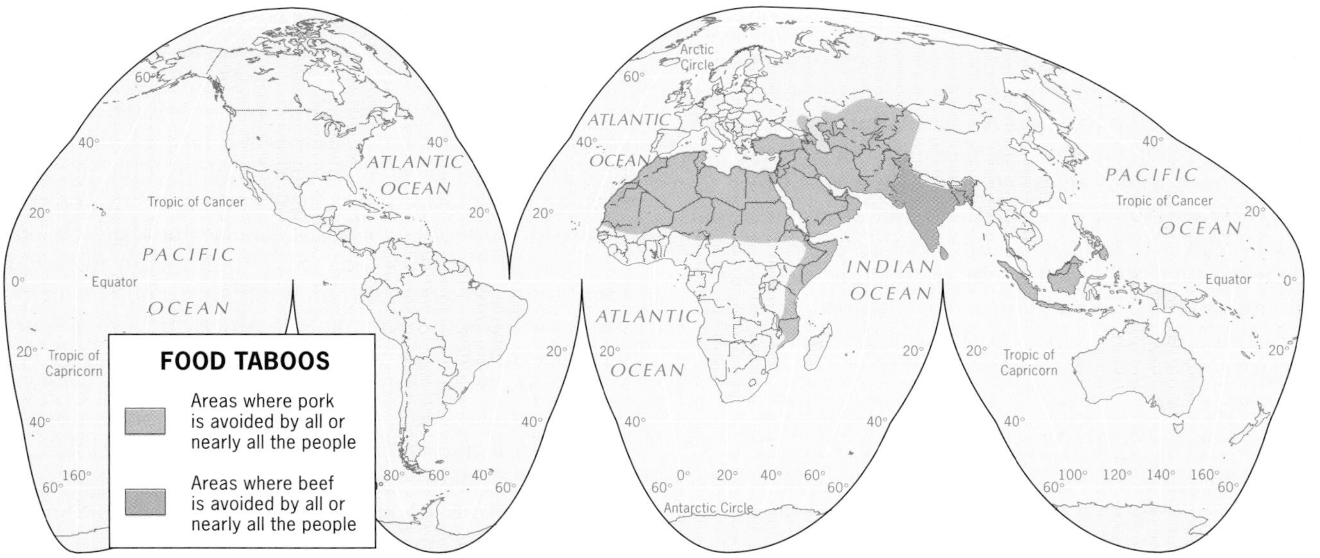

Figure 18-1 World Areas of Food Taboos. Prohibitions and bans against certain foods affect diets in many areas of the world. Here only the major taboos are mapped.

nings date back a mere 12,000 years at most). Even today, a few small societies survive much as they did before agriculture was developed: by ***hunting and gathering*** whatever food nature has to offer and sometimes by fishing.

From the field notes

"It was harvest time on the North China Plain, and everywhere you looked, farm workers by the thousands were cutting the wheat, carting it in, threshing it, piling up the chaff. Not a sign of any machines: it was all done by hand. What will all these workers do when Chinese agriculture mechanizes?" (This note written at a collective near Anyang in 1981; today the question is: How many of these workers are employed by Beijing's building boom or in the factories of the Pacific Rim?)

Peoples who still subsist in this way have been pushed into difficult environments by more powerful competitors (as the San of Southern Africa were by the Bantu and the white invaders), and their survival seems to involve one crisis after another. Cyclical drought is often a serious enemy. It withers vegetation, kills or drives off wildlife, and cuts off natural water supplies such as springs. Still, the San of Southern Africa, the aboriginal peoples of Australia, the Native Americans of Brazil, and several other groups in the Americas, Africa, and Asia manage to survive in the face of great odds. They do so by knowing and fully exploiting their environment. Local knowledge of seeds, roots, fruits, berries, and insects is quite extraordinary, and these societies depend on that knowledge for survival.

Hunting was traditionally done with poisoned spears, bows and arrows, clubs, and sticks—but in the modern era it is not unusual to find hunters and gatherers using rifles, jeeps, and other vehicles in their hunting activities. Those without access to such technologies continue to follow long-established practices. In the case of the San, these include poisoning water holes that the people themselves do not depend on so they can follow animals that have drunk there until they succumb. Such practices ensure that the community is on the move much of the time. Groups practicing traditional hunting and gathering cannot become too large, nor can settlements be permanent. However, without agriculture and the storage of food for the future, life is often difficult. It was easier where the land was more productive, but most of the surviving hunting-and-gathering peoples have been driven into dry, cold, and otherwise less hospitable environments.

We should not assume that the hunting-and-gathering groups that survive today are entirely representative of early hunter-gatherer communities. When Europe's plains opened up after the most recent glacial retreat, immigrant peoples hunted mammoth and other plentiful wildlife. They set elaborate traps and cooperated in driving wildlife to areas where it would be vulnerable. Communities were much larger than present-day San clans. Very early on, there were peoples who subsisted on hunting and gathering and fishing who had learned to specialize to some extent in some area of production. The oak forests of parts of North America provided an abundant harvest of nuts, sometimes enough to last more than a full year; so Native American communities collected and stored this food source. Others living near the Pacific Ocean became adept at salmon fishing. The buffalo herds of interior North America provided sustenance for centuries before being virtually wiped out by overhunting with the coming of Europeans. In more northerly regions, people followed the migrations of the caribou herds. The Aleut and the Ainu (now confined to northern Japan) developed specialized fishing techniques.

We can deduce to some extent the means by which our preagricultural ancestors survived. Undoubtedly, some hunting-and-gathering communities found themselves in more favorable locations than others. For example, people living on the forest margins could gather food in the forest when hunting yielded poor results and return to hunting when the opportunities improved again. Possibly those communities could stay in one place for some time, creating a more or less permanent settlement. That is one of the key contributions of agriculture: it permitted people to settle permanently in one location with the assurance that food would be available in seasons to come.

Terrain and Tools

The capacity of early human communities to sustain themselves was enhanced by their knowledge of the terrain and its exploitable resources, as well as by their ability to improve on their tools, weapons, and other equipment. Such technological advances came slowly, but some of them had important effects. The first tools used in hunting were simple clubs, tree limbs that were thin at one end and thick and heavy at the other. These were not only used to strike trapped animals but also thrown at hunted wildlife. The use of bone and stone and the development of spears made hunting far more effective. The fashioning of stone into hand axes and, later, handle axes was a crucial innovation that enabled hunters to skin their prey and cut the meat. It now was possible to cut down trees and build even better shelters and tools.

The controlled use of fire was another important early achievement of human communities. The first opportunities to control fire were offered by natural conditions (lightning, spontaneous combustion of surface-heated coal). Excavations of ancient settlement sites suggest that attempts were made to keep a fire burning continuously once it was captured. Later it was learned that fire could be generated by rapid hand rotation of a wooden stick in a small hole surrounded by dry tinder. Fire became the focal point of the settlement, and the campfire became a symbol of the community. It was a means of making foods digestible and was used to drive animals into traps or over cliffs. This greatly enhanced the capacity of ancient communities to modify the natural landscape.

In the meantime, tools and equipment were developed as well. Perhaps the first transportation tool ever devised was a strong stick carried by two men; over the stick might hang the limp body of a freshly killed gazelle. Simple baskets were fashioned to hold berries, nuts, and roots. Various kinds of racks, packing frames, and sleds were developed to transport logs, stones, firewood, and other heavy goods. Fishing became a more important means of survival for communities situated along rivers or on shorelines, and primitive rafts and canoes soon made their appearance. (Controlled use of fire made the dugout canoe possible.)

Even before the domestication of animals and plants, rudimentary forms of metalworking had emerged, although true ***metallurgy***, the technique of separating metals from their ores, came later. There is evidence that fragments of copper, nuggets of gold, and pieces of iron from meteorites were hammered into arrowheads and other shapes. Equipment made of stone also went far beyond simple knives and axes. Stone pots and pounders, grinders, and simple mills were developed to prepare seeds, grains, and other edible foods. Meat was roasted and other foods were cooked; dietary patterns and preferences began to develop. Thus, long before animal and plant domestication, preagricultural human communities were characterized by considerable complexity not only in forms of shelter, but also in tools, utensils and weapons, food preferences and taboos, and related cultural traits.

Fishing

It is quite likely that our distant ancestors added dried fish to their diets during the warming period that accompanied the melting of the latest of the Pleistocene glaciers. Perhaps 12,000 to 15,000 years ago, as the glaciers melted, sea levels began to rise. Coastal flatlands were inundated as the seawater encroached on the continental shelves. Until this time, coastal waters over much of the Earth had been cold and rough, and shorelines were often steep cliffs. Therefore, most coastal areas were not hospitable to humans, and marine life was not nearly as plentiful as it was to become later.

When glacial melting began and water levels rose, the continental shelves became shallow seas, full of coastal lagoons and patches of standing water. The sun warmed these thin layers of water very quickly, and soon marine fauna flourished. Coastal regions became warmer and more habitable, and communities moved to the water's edge. There people were able to harvest all kinds of shellfish, and they learned to trap fish by cutting small patches of standing water off from the open sea. And they invented tools for catching fish: harpoons for spearing larger fish, and baskets suspended in streams where fish were known to run.

In several regions, human communities achieved a degree of permanence by combining hunting and fishing with some gathering and by making use of the migration cycles of fish and animal life. Native American peoples along the Pacific coast and on Arctic shores, the Ainu of Japan and coastal East Asia, and communities in coastal Western Europe caught salmon as they swam up rivers and negotiated rapids and falls. (Huge accumulations of fish bones have been found at prehistoric sites near such locations.)

When the salmon runs ended, people stalked deer during their annual spring and fall movements, trapping them where they crossed rivers or in narrow valleys. The summer salmon runs and the wildlife migrations of fall and spring provided food for all the year except winter. People had learned, however, that dried meat could remain edible for months, and the winter cold provided natural refrigeration.

The early fishers and hunters had their bad years as well as good ones. Sometimes winter brought hunger and death. The riverside dwellers were forced to abandon their settlements and pursue distant herds.

Along with the development of fishing as a means of subsistence came the invention of a wide range of tools. Among the earliest means of catching fish and other aquatic life was a simple stone trap used in tidal channels. Stones would be removed during the incoming tide, permitting fish to enter an inlet; the stones would be replaced at high tide. When the next low tide drained the closed-off pool, water could seep out between the stones, but the fish would be trapped. Crescent-shaped stone traps on a tidal flat had the same effect, but eventually traps were refined by the creation of basket-like wicker devices that could be used in stream channels and nets of rough twine that could be stretched across an inlet or placed off a shoreline.

The fishing spear was to fishing what the arrow was to hunting, and various kinds of spears were invented, ranging from simple pointed sticks to more refined harpoon-like spears. The use of hooks and bait led to the invention of hooks made from wood, bone, horn, and seashells. Most important, however, was the invention of boats. From the first simple rafts were developed more elaborate canoes and sailing boats. The role of these innovations in the worldwide diffusion of humans is obvious.

From the field notes

"At the time of my arrival at La Coruna on the northwest coast of Spain, the Spanish and the British were engaged in one of their periodic quarrels over fishing rights and practices in the waters off Western Europe. The Spanish press denounced the British for claiming that Spain's fishermen were violating international agreements, and there were angry posters all over town. Of course La Coruna had a special stake in this matter: it lies along the limited Spanish coastal window on the Bay of Biscay between France and Portugal, and among Spanish fishing fleets its boats are closest to the action. Any obstruction to Spanish fishing would be severely felt here."

◆ THE FIRST AGRICULTURAL REVOLUTION

Plant Domestication

We noted in Part One that the domestication of plants and animals may have begun nearly simultaneously in several parts of the world. The first conscious cultivation of plants may have involved root crops and may have occurred in South and Southeast Asia. Not long afterward—possibly as long as 12,000 years ago—the ***First Agricultural Revolution*** was in progress. By applying simple agricultural techniques, the First Agricultural Revolution allowed humans to increase the carrying capacity of the Earth, and it fundamentally transformed human understanding and use of the environment. Wherever it took hold, this First Agricultural Revolution was accompanied by a modest population explosion, the outmigration by farmers with their new techniques, and the absorption of foraging peoples

As we saw in Chapter 3, the geographer Carl Sauer was keenly interested in ***agricultural origins***. He postulated that ***plant domestication*** began in an area north of the Bay of Bengal when people began cultivating plants that can regenerate when some part of the plant itself is buried and tended (i.e., a root plant, as opposed to a seed plant). This is sometimes called the vegetative reproduction of root crops. Sauer also proposed other early agricultural hearths (Fig. 18-2)—some associated with root crops (e.g., the regions in South America) and others with seed crops (e.g., Southwest Asia). He left open the question of whether these hearths represented the diffusion of agricultural ideas from the areas north of the Bay of Bengal, or developed independently.

Sauer's ideas about the origin and diffusion of plant domestication are not universally accepted, but the general pattern of early agricultural hearths that he proposed has been widely adopted. Moreover, we know that the First Agricultural Revolution did not begin simultaneously in all of the agricultural hearth areas. Archeological evidence confirms that agricultural techniques developed much later in the Americas than in Southeast and Southwest Asia, and the European and African hearths also postdate the early Southeast and Southwest Asian hearths.

Figure 18-2 highlights the truly global nature of plant domestication hearths. In *Cultural Geography* (1969), where this map first appeared, cultural geographers Joseph Spencer and William Thomas emphasized that local groupings of plants formed the basis for each regional agricultural zone. For example, in the Mesoamerican region (Region 6 in Fig. 18-2), the basic plants were maize (corn), squashes, and several kinds of beans. In Southeast Asia (Region 1), on the other hand, taro, yams, and bananas were the leading food plants. In Southwest Asia (Region 4), plant domestication centered on wheat, barley, and other grains.

Agricultural origins in central China (Region 7) have recently attracted greater attention because they may have occurred earlier than was long believed—so early, in fact, that Chinese farmers may have been among the world's first. The resulting food surpluses and population increases produced the wave of emigration that peopled Taiwan, the Philippines, the Pacific islands, and perhaps even the Americas.

Another agricultural source region lies in West Africa (Region 9). This region was recognized quite late, and it is not certain that agriculture developed independently there. As Table 18-1 indicates, however, secondary domestication clearly did take place in West Africa.

Table 18-1 is worth careful attention, if only because it reveals the enormous range of crops that were cultivated around the world. At various times and in different locales, particular groups of crops became the mainstays of life. Soon the knowledge needed to farm such crops diffused outward from these agricultural hearths. It is thought that millet, a small-seed grain, was introduced to India from West Africa, and sorghum, another grain crop, from West Africa to China. The watermelon spread from West Africa, first to nearby regions but eventually all over the world.

Figure 18-2 World Areas of Agricultural Innovations. Cultural geographer Carl Sauer identified 11 areas where agricultural innovations occurred. *Source:* From C. O. Sauer, *Agricultural Origins and Dispersals*. New York: American Geographical Society, 1952, p. 24.

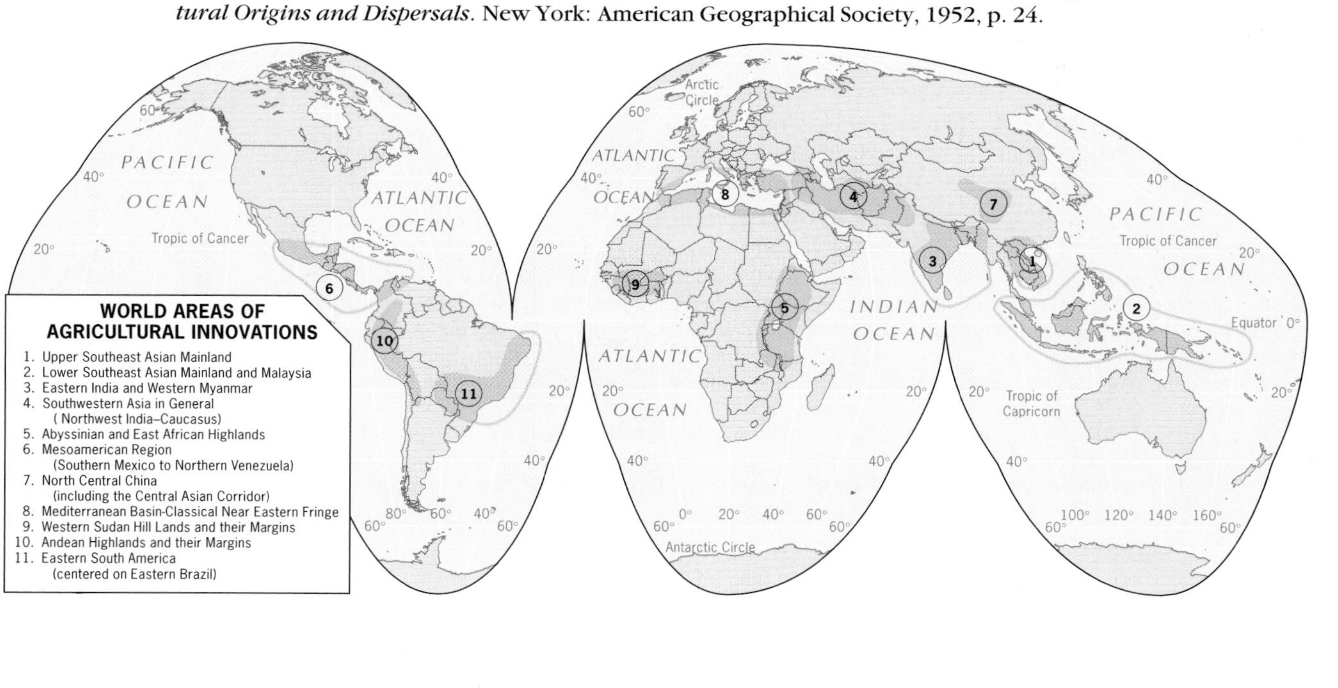

Table 18-1 Chief Source Regions of Important Crop Plant Domestications (after J. E. Spencer and W. L. Thomas)

A. Primary Regions of Domestications

1. The Upper Southeast Asian Mainlands

Citrus Fruits*	Bamboos*	Yams*	Rices*	Eugenias*	Lichi	Teas	Ramie
Bananas*	Taros*	Cabbages*	Beans*	Job's tears	Longan	Tung oils	Water chestnut

2. Lower Southeast Asian Mainland and Malaysia (including New Guinea)

Citrus fruits*	Taros*	Pandanuses	Breadfruits	Lanzones	Vine peppers*	Nutmeg	Areca
Bananas*	Yams*	Cucumbers*	Jackfruits	Durian	Gingers*	Clove	Abaca
Bamboos*	Almonds*	Sugarcanes	Coconuts	Rambutan	Brinjals*	Cardamom	

3. Eastern India and Western Burma

Bananas*	Beans*	Millets*	Grams	Vine peppers*	Mangoes	Safflower	Lotus
Yams*	Rices*	Sorghums*	Eggplants	Gingers*	Kapok*	Jute	Turmeric
Taros*	Amaranths*	Peas*	Brinjals*	Palms*	Indigo	Sunn Hemp	

4. Southwestern Asia (Northwest India-Caucasus)

Soft wheats*	Peas*	Rye*	Beets*	Hemp	Soft Pears*	Pomegranates	Walnuts
Barleys*	Oil seeds*	Onions	Spinach	Apples	Cherries*	Grapes*	Melons
Lentils*	Poppies	Carrots*	Sesames	Almonds*	Plums*	Jujubes*	Tamarind
Beans*	Oats*	Turnips	Flax	Peaches*	Figs	Pistachio	Alfalfa

5. Ethiopian and East African Highlands

Hard wheats*	Sorghums*	Barleys	Beans*	Oil seeds*	Melons*	Coffees	Okras
Millets*	Rices*	Peas*	Vetches	Cucumbers*	Gourds*	Castor beans	Cottons*

6. Meso-American Region (Southern Mexico to Northern Venezuela)

Maizes	Taros*	Tomatoes*	Avocados	Muskmelons	Cottons*
Amaranths*	Sweet potatoes	Chili peppers	Sapotes	Palms*	Agaves
Beans*	Squashes	Custard apples	Plums*	Manioc	Kapok

B. Secondary Regions of Domestications

7. North-Central China (including the Central Asian corridor)

Millets*	Soybeans	Naked oat*	Mulberries	Bush cherries*	Peaches*
Barleys*	Cabbages*	Mustards	Persimmons	Hard pears*	Jujubes*
Buckwheats	Radishes*	Rhubarb	Plums*	Apricots	

8. Mediterranean Basin—Classical near eastern Fringe

Barleys*	Lentils*	Grapes*	Dates	Parsnips	Lettuces	Carrots*	Sugar beet
Oats*	Peas*	Olives	Carobs	Asparagus	Celeries	Garlic	Leek

9. Western Sudan Hill Lands and Their Margins

Sorghums*	Rices*	Yams*	Peas*	Melons*	Oil palms	Kola nut
Millets*	Fonio	Beans*	Oil seeds*	Gourds*	Tamarind*	

10. Andean Highlands and Their Margins

White potatoes	Tomatoes*	Beans*	Quinoa	Cubio	Ulluco
Pumpkins	Strawberries	Papayas	Oca	Arrocacha	

11. Eastern South America (centered on Eastern Brazil)

Taros*	Peanuts	Cashew nut	Cacao	Cottons*
Beans*	Pineapples	Brazil nut	Passion fruits	Tobaccos

Source: J. E. Spencer and W. L. Thomas, *Introducing Cultural Geography:* 1978. Reproduced by permission from John Wiley & Sons.

*The asterisk indicates domestication of related species or hybridized development of new species during domestication in some other region or regions. Some of these secondary domestications were later than in the original region, but evidence of chronologic priority seldom is clear-cut.

The plural rendering of the crop name indicates that several different varieties/species either were involved in initial domestication or followed thereafter,

The term *oil seeds* indicates several varieties species of small-seeded crop plants grown for the production of edible oils, without further breakdown.

In regions 2 and 3 the brinjals refer to the spicy members of the eggplant group used in curries, whereas in region 3 the eggplants refer to the sweet vegetable members.

None of the regional lists attempts a complete listing of all crop plants/species domesticated within the region.

The table has been compiled from a wide variety of sources.

In many cases what we now think of as centers of production of particular crops are not the places where those crops were originally domesticated. Corn (maize) spread from Middle America into North America. After the Portuguese brought it across the Atlantic, it became a staple in much of Africa. Even more strikingly, the white potato came originally from the Andean highlands, but was then brought to Europe where it became a staple from Ireland to the eastern expanses of the North European Plain. The banana came from Southeast Asia, as did a variety of yams. Dispersal occurred slowly for many thousands of years, but it was greatly accelerated by the worldwide trade and communications networks established with the colonial expansion of Europe. Now, many of the world's bananas come from South America.

Animal Domestication

While our distant ancestors were learning to plant crops, they were also beginning to keep animals as livestock. As we saw in Chapter 9, the Nostratic proto-language word for wolf also meant dog, suggesting that domestication was in progress as long as 14,000 years ago.

Perhaps ***animal domestication*** became possible when communities became more sedentary. Animals were kept as pets or for other reasons (e.g., for ceremonial purposes). Quite possibly, animals attached themselves to human settlements as scavengers and even for protection against predators, thus reinforcing the idea that they might be tamed and kept. Any visitor to an African wildlife reserve can observe that when night falls, permanent camps are approached by animals such as gazelle, zebra, and monkeys, which spend the night near and sometimes even within the camp. At daybreak the animals wander off, returning at nightfall. Similar behavior probably brought animals to the settlements of the ancient forest farmers. Hunters might bring back the young offspring of an animal that had been killed in the field and raise it. The concept of animal domestication probably developed out of such events.

Just when this happened is still a subject of debate. Some scholars believe that animal domestication began earlier than plant cultivation, but others argue that animal domestication began as recently as 8000 years ago—well after crop agriculture. In any case, goats, pigs, and sheep became part of a rapidly growing array of domestic animals, and in captivity they changed considerably from their wild state. Archeological research indicates that when animals such as wild cattle are penned in a corral, they undergo physical changes as time goes by. Protection from predators led to the survival of animals that would have been eliminated in the wild, and modifications that nature would have wiped out were preserved through inbreeding. Our domestic versions of the pig, the cow, and the horse differ considerably from those first kept by our ancestors.

How did the ancient communities select their livestock, and for what purposes were livestock kept? It is thought that wild cattle may originally have been domesticated for religious purposes, perhaps because the shape of their horns looked like a crescent moon—a sacred celestial object in some cultures. Apparently, cattle were strongly associated with religious ritual from the earliest times, and they remain holy animals in some societies today. However, those religious functions may also have led to the use of cows as draft animals and suppliers of milk. If cattle could pull sled-like platforms used in religious ceremonies, they could also pull plows. If cattle whose calves were taken away continued to produce milk, and in fact needed to be milked, cattle could be kept for that purpose as well.

As with plant domestication, it is possible to identify certain regions where the domestication of particular animals occurred. In Southeast Asia, the presence of several kinds of pigs led to their domestication, along with the water buffalo, chickens, and some other bird species (ducks, geese). In South Asia, cattle were domesticated and came to occupy an important place in the regional culture. Later, the Indian elephant was domesticated, to be used as a ceremonial animal, a beast of burden, and a weapon of war. However, elephants were never successfully bred in captivity, and some scholars argue that the elephant never really became a domesticated animal. In Southwest Asia and adjacent areas of Northeast Africa, domesticated animals included the goat, sheep, and camel. In inner Asia, the yak, horse, some species of goats and sheep, and reindeer were domesticated. In the Mesoamerican region (including the Andes from Peru northward and Middle America up to central Mexico), the llama and alpaca were domesticated, along with a species of pig and the turkey.

Although we can identify regions of domestication like those just described, they should be regarded with caution. When animal domestication began, there were numerous species of fauna, and they may have been domesticated almost simultaneously in different places. The water buffalo, for example, was probably domesticated in both Southeast and South Asia during the same period. Camels may have been domesticated in inner Asia as well as in Southwest Asia. The pig was domesticated in numerous areas. Different species of cattle were domesticated in regions other than South Asia. Dogs and cats attached themselves to human settlements very early (they may have been the first animals to be domesticated) and in widely separated regions. Specific sources can be identified for only a few animals, including the llama and the alpaca, the yak, the turkey, and the reindeer.

As in the case of crops, the dispersal of domesticated animals—first regionally and later throughout the world—blurred the original spatial patterns of domestication. Successful domestication depended on the presence of wild animals suitable for domestication. The great majority of these inhabited Eurasia; far fewer species were available in the Americas, Australia, or Africa. Among Africa's numerous wild animals, only the guinea fowl was domesticated early. All other species resisted domestication. This greatly affected Subsaharan Africa's cultural and economic development, leaving Africans without the kinds of dependable livestock that benefited societies in Eurasia.

Africans became cattle herders only after cattle were introduced via Southwest Asia. Other livestock spread worldwide. Chickens can now be found in virtually every rural village, from Indonesia to Ecuador. Donkeys (probably first domesticated in Southwest Asia) serve as beasts of burden around the world. Goats and sheep, cattle and horses, and dogs and cats are globally distributed. Even the Asian elephant made its appearance not only in China but also in ancient Europe as part of Hannibal's forces.

Efforts to domesticate animals continue today. Now it may be possible to domesticate some African species as livestock. An example is the eland, a potential source of meat in a region where one is greatly needed. Several experiment stations in the savannalands are trying to find ways to breed the region's wildlife. They have had some success with a species of eland but less with various species of gazelles, and they have been unable to domesticate the buffalo. Indeed, throughout the world only about 40 species of higher animals have been domesticated—and most of these were domesticated long ago.

Thus the process of animal domestication, set in motion more than 8000 (and perhaps as long as 14,000) years ago, still continues. Communities that were able to combine the cultivation of plants and the domestication of animals greatly reduced their dependence on limited food resources. This was a critical step in the evolution of human civilization.

◆ SUBSISTENCE FARMING

We tend to think of agricultural geography in terms of cash cropping (i.e., farming for sale and profit): plantations, ranches, mechanization, irrigation, the movement of farm products, and so on. When we associate certain crops with particular countries, these are usually cash commodities: Brazilian coffee, Colombian tobacco, Egyptian cotton, Australian wool, Argentinean beef. But large numbers of farmers are not involved in commercial agriculture at all. Hundreds of millions of farmers grow only enough food to survive. They are ***subsistence farmers***. Some stay in one place, but many others move from place to place in search of better land. The latter engage in a form of agriculture known as ***shifting cultivation.***

Shifting cultivation is found primarily in tropical and subtropical zones, where traditional farmers had to abandon plots of land after the soil became infertile. Once stripped of their natural vegetative cover and deprived of the constant input of nutrients from decaying vegetative matter on the forest floor, soils in these regions can quickly lose their nutrients as rain water leaches out organic matter. Faced with these circumstances, farmers would move to another parcel of land, clear the vegetation, turn the soil, and try again. This practice of shifting cultivation, like hunting and gathering, still goes on today. In tropical areas, where the redness of the soil signifies heavy leaching of soil nutrients and yet natural vegetation thrives, a plot of cleared soil will carry a good crop at least once and perhaps two or three times. Then, however, the land is best left alone to regenerate its natural vegetative cover and replenish the soil with nutrients lost during cultivation. Several years later, the plot may yield a good harvest once again.

Shifting cultivation is a way of life for many more people than hunting and gathering. Between 150 million and 200 million people still sustain themselves in this way in Africa, Middle America, tropical South America, and parts of Southeast Asia. At one time this was the chief form of agriculture. As a system of cultivation, it has changed little over thousands of years. It goes by various names: slash-and-burn agriculture, milpa agriculture, patch agriculture, and others.

The term *slash-and-burn agriculture* reflects the major role that the controlled use of fire plays in shifting agriculture. Trees are cut down and all existing vegetation is burned off. The resulting layer of ash contributes to the soil's fertility. In these cleared patches are planted crops that are native to the region: tubers in the humid, warm tropical areas, grains in the more humid subtropics, and vegetables and fruits in cooler zones. Shifting cultivation gave ancient farmers opportunities to experiment with various plants, to learn the effects of weeding and crop care, to cope with environmental vagaries, and to discern the decreased fertility of soil after sustained farming.

The process of shifting agriculture thus involves a kind of natural rotation system in which areas of forest are used without being destroyed. It does not require a nomadic existence. Usually there is a central village surrounded by parcels of land that are worked successively. When the village grows too large and the distance to usable land becomes too great, part of the village's population may establish a new settlement some distance away. This implies, of course, that population densities in areas of shifting agriculture cannot be very high. However, high population densities were rare in ancient times, and today shifting agriculture continues only in areas where population densities are far lower than in crowded regions like the Nile delta or the Ganges Valley.

Through the eyes of those used to seeing agricultural landscapes in the United States, shifting agriculture might appear wasteful and disorganized. There are no neat rows of plants, carefully turned soil, or precisely

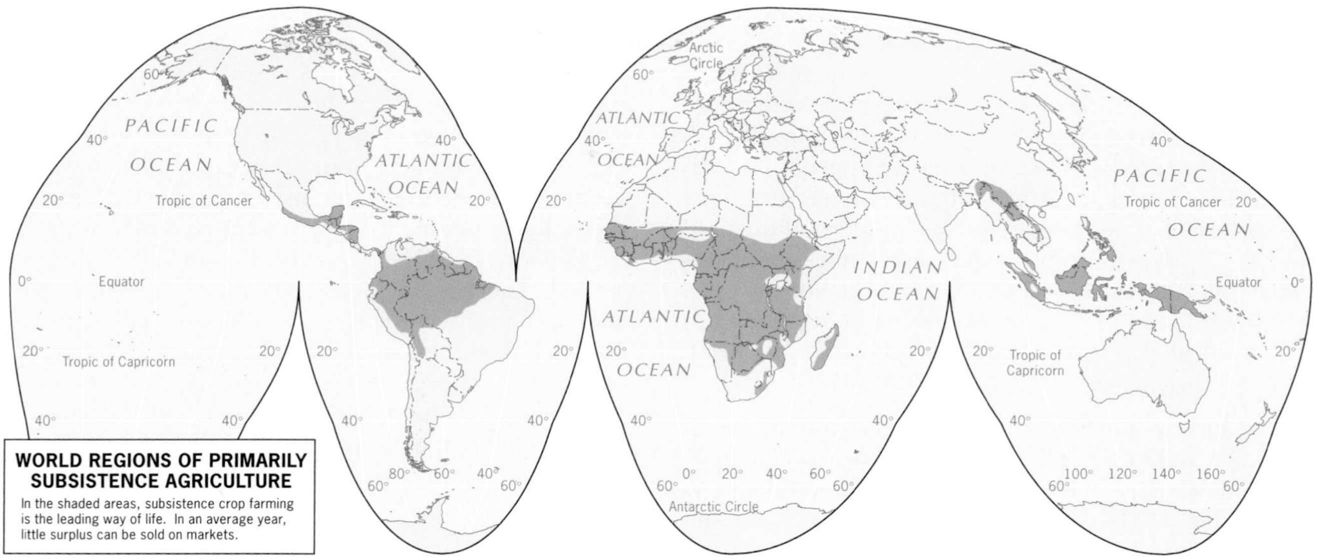

Figure 18-3 World Regions of Primarily Subsistence Agriculture. Definitions of subsistence farming vary. India and China are not shaded because farmers sell some produce on markets; in equatorial Africa and South America, subsistence allows little of this.

laid-out fields. In fact, however, shifting agriculture conserves both forest and soil; its harvests are substantial given the environmental limitations; and it requires better organization than one might assume. It also requires substantially less energy than more modern techniques of farming.

Shifting cultivation is not the only form of subsistence farming, however. In many areas, subsistence farmers cannot migrate but are confined to a small field of more fertile soil that they farm intensively year after year. Very likely, they do not own the soil they till.

The term *subsistence* is sometimes used in the strictest sense of the word—that is, to refer to farmers who grow food only to sustain themselves and their families, find building materials and firewood in the natural environment, and do not enter into the cash economy at all. This definition fits farmers in some societies where shifting agriculture is practiced, for example, in remote areas of South and Middle America, Africa, and South and Southeast Asia (Fig. 18-3). Yet there are many farm families that are living at the subsistence level but that sometimes sell a small quantity of produce (perhaps to pay taxes). They are not subsistence farmers in the strict sense, but the term *subsistence* is surely applicable to societies where farmers with small plots sometimes sell a few pounds of grain on the market but where poverty, indebtedness, and (sometimes) tenancy are ways of life. For the Native American peoples in the Amazon Basin, the sedentary farmers of Africa's savanna areas, villagers in much of India, and peasants in Indonesia, subsistence is not only a way of life but a state of mind. Experience has taught farmers and their families that subsistence farming is very often precarious and that times of comparative plenty will be followed by times of scarcity.

Marginalization of Subsistence Farming

European powers seeking to "modernize" the economies of their dependencies often tried to end subsistence practices by integrating farmers into colonial systems of production and exchange. Sometimes their methods were harsh: by demanding that farmers pay some taxes, they forced subsistence farmers to begin selling some of their produce to raise the necessary cash. They also compelled many subsistence farmers to devote some land to a cash crop such as cotton, thus bringing them into the commercial economy. The colonial powers also provided genuine assistance by conducting soil surveys, building irrigation systems, and establishing lending agencies that would provide loans to farmers. In addition, the colonial powers sought to make profits, yet it was difficult to squeeze very much from subsistence-farming areas. Forced cropping schemes were designed to solve this problem. If farmers in a subsistence area cultivated a certain acreage of, say, corn, they were required to grow a specified acreage of a cash crop, such as cotton, as well. Whether this crop would be grown on old land that was formerly used for grain, or on newly cleared land, was the farmers' decision. If no new land were available, the farmers would have to give up food crops for the compulsory cash crops. In many areas, severe famines resulted and local economies were disrupted.

Many scholars have considered the question of how "to tempt [subsistence farmers] into wanting cash by the availability of suitable consumer goods," as agricultural specialists A. N. Duckham and G. B. Masefield wrote in *Farming Systems of the World* (1970). In the interests of "progress" and "modernization," subsistence farmers are pushed away from their traditional modes of livelihood. Yet some aspects of subsistence farming may be worth preserving. Changing farmers' attitudes could result in a less cohesive society. Subsistence farmers often hold land in common; surpluses are shared by all the members of the community; accumulation of personal wealth is restricted; and individual advancement at the cost of the group as a whole is limited. As economist A. H. Bunting wrote in *Change in Agriculture* (1970):

> To allocate the land or manage the seasonal migrations, and to survive through hardship and calamity these societies have to be cohesive, communal and relatively little differentiated socially and economically: the chiefs, elders or elected headmen may be little richer than their fellows—to many of whom they are in addition linked by ties of relationship within the extended family. Mutual dependence, imposed by the environment and the state of the agricultural art, is maintained and reinforced by genetic relationships. The community is enclosed socially and may even tend to be isolated culturally. Landlords and feudal rulers are unknown; the cultivators are poor but free.

This description could also be applied to the human communities that first developed agriculture as a way of life and have shown such amazing durability. Changing the economic system could lead to unpredictable changes in the social fabric.

Such changes are occurring. Subsistence land use is giving way to more intensive farming and cash cropping—even to mechanized farming in which equipment does much of the actual work. In the process, societies from South America to Southeast Asia are being profoundly affected. Land that was once held communally is being parceled out to individuals for cash cropping. The system that ensured an equitable distribution of resources is breaking down. And the distribution of wealth has become stratified, with poor people at the bottom and rich landowners at the top.

◆ THE SECOND AGRICULTURAL REVOLUTION

We sometimes regard the Industrial Revolution as the beginning of a new era of development and modernization. In doing so, we lose sight of another revolution, which began even earlier and had an enormous impact on Europe and other parts of the world. This was the ***Second Agricultural Revolution***. Although it was less dramatic than the Industrial Revolution, it had far-reaching consequences nonetheless.

The Second Agricultural Revolution began slowly during the latter phase of the so-called Middle Ages. At first it took hold in a few widely scattered places. Its origins and diffusion cannot be readily traced, but it seems clear that, after centuries of comparative stagnation and lack of innovation, farming in seventeenth- and eighteenth-century Europe underwent significant changes. Tools and equipment were modified. Methods of soil preparation, fertilization, crop care, and harvesting improved. The general organization of agriculture, food storage, and distribution was made more efficient. Productivity increased to meet rising demands. Europe's cities were growing, creating problems for existing food supply systems. But by the time the Industrial Revolution gathered momentum, progress in agriculture made possible the clustering of even larger urban populations than before.

Agriculture and the Industrial Revolution

The Industrial Revolution helped sustain the Second Agricultural Revolution. Tractors and other machines took over the work that for so long had been done by animals and humans. In some regions the cultural landscape of commercial agriculture changed, as did much of the urban landscape of industrializing cities. Fields of wheat and other grains, sown and harvested by machine, cloaked entire countrysides. Even where tradition continued to prevail—in the vineyards of France's Bordeaux and the rice fields of East Asia, for example—the impact of modernization was felt in the form of research leading to improved fertilizers and more productive crop strains.

Farming obviously is not possible everywhere. Vast deserts, steep mountain slopes, frigid polar zones, and other environmental obstacles prevent farming in many parts of the world. Where farming is possible, the land and soil are not put to the same uses everywhere. The huge cattle ranches of Texas represent a very different sort of land use than the dairy farms of Wisconsin or the paddies of Taiwan.

Within a few miles of the subsistence farms of Middle America lie rich plantations whose products are shipped to North American markets by sea. We can observe such differences around our own cities: if you travel by car or train from Chicago, Cincinnati, or St. Louis into the countryside, you can see how land use changes. Close to the city, the soil is used most intensively, perhaps for vegetable gardens yielding crops that can be sent quickly to nearby markets. Farther away, the fields are larger and time becomes less important. The cornfields of Iowa are dotted with grain elevators, and some of the grain stored in them may be consumed not in Chicago or St. Louis, but in India or Bangladesh.

Still farther from the Midwestern cities, we enter the pasturelands of the Great Plains, almost the opposite of the vegetable garden. Here land is measured in hundreds of square miles rather than by the acre. Distance from the market is a powerful factor in shaping the country's economic geography.

Understanding the Spatial Layout of Agriculture

What factors have combined to produce the spatial distribution of farming systems? This is a very complicated question. One of the first economic geographers to consider it in a systematic way was Johann Heinrich von Thünen (1783–1850). Von Thünen experienced the Second Agricultural Revolution firsthand: he farmed an estate not far from the town of Rostock, in northeast Germany. Studying the spatial patterns of farming around towns such as Rostock, von Thünen noted that one commodity or crop gave way to another in Rostock's hinterland—without any visible change in the soil or climate or terrain. When he mapped this pattern, he found that each town or market center was surrounded by a set of more-or-less concentric rings within which particular commodities or crops dominated.

Nearest the town, farmers produced commodities that were perishable and commanded high prices, such as dairy products and strawberries and similar specialized crops. In von Thünen's time the town was still surrounded by a belt of forest that provided wood for fuel and building; but immediately beyond the forest the ring-like pattern of agriculture continued. In the next ring the crops were less perishable and bulkier, including wheat and other grains. Still farther out, livestock raising began to replace field crops.

Von Thünen used these observations to build a model of the spatial distribution of agricultural activities. As with all models, he had to make certain assumptions. For example, he assumed that the terrain was flat, that soils and other environmental conditions were the same everywhere, and that there were no barriers to transportation to market. Under such circumstances, he reasoned, transport costs would govern the use of land. He reasoned that the greater the distance to market, the higher the transport costs that had to be added to the cost of producing a crop or commodity. At a given distance to market, then, it would become unprofitable to produce high-cost, perishable commodities—and market gardens would give way to field crops such as grains and potatoes. Still farther away, livestock raising would replace field agriculture.

Von Thünen's model (including the ring of forest) is often described as the first effort to analyze the spatial character of economic activity (Fig. 18-4). He published it as part of a monumental series of works called *Der Isolierte Staat* (The Isolated State), which, in many ways, constitutes the foundation of the geographic field known as location theory. Today ***Thünian patterns*** are discerned in many parts of the world. But often such patterns are not solely the result of the forces modeled by von Thünen. Consider the hinterland of Chicago. If you take the train to Denver, you cannot miss a certain concentric zonation that puts dairying and market gardening nearest the city, cash grains such as corn (plus soybeans) in the next "ring," more extensive grain farming and livestock raising beyond, and cattle ranching in the outermost zone. This clearly has something to do with von Thünen's ideas, but it also reflects soil quality and climate changes.

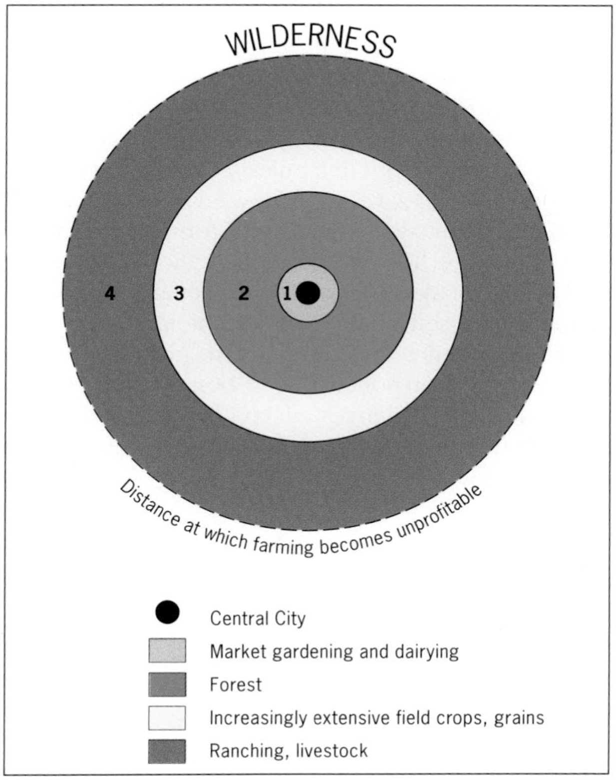

Figure 18-4 Von Thünen's Model.

The logic of von Thünen's model, then, is only partially reflected in what we actually observe. This does not undermine the fundamental logic of the model, however; it simply shows that there are things that can change the model's assumptions. And even when agricultural patterns do not appear at all to conform to the concentric rings of von Thünen's model, his underlying concern with the interplay of land use and transportation costs is frequently still determinative. The fresh flowers grown in the Caribbean for sale in New York City could be viewed as the application of the von Thünen model at a larger scale, for it is less expensive to grow flowers in the Caribbean and ship them to New York City than it is to grow them in other locations.

When looking at patterns of agriculture at the global scale, however, it is important to recognize that von Thünen's concerns with the interplay of market location, land use, and transportation costs can reveal only one part of the picture. We must also consider the effects of different climate and soil conditions, variations in farming methods and technology, and the economic dominance of the United States, Canada, and Europe. Decisions made by colonial powers in Europe led to the establishment of plantations from Middle America to Malaysia. The plantations grew crops not for local markets but for consumers in Europe; similarly, U.S. companies founded huge plantations in the Americas. Over the past few centuries the impact of this plantation system transformed the map of world agriculture. The end of colonial rule did not merely signal the end of the agricultural practices and systems that had been imposed on the former colonial areas. Even food-poor countries must continue to grow commercial crops for export on some of their best soils where their own food should be harvested. Long-entrenched agricultural systems and patterns are not quickly or easily transformed.

◆ FORCES OF CHANGE

The early twentieth century saw an intensification of the Second Agricultural Revolution with the development of harvesting machines, tractors, and other farming technology that heightened the role of technology in crop and animal production, facilitated the growth of commercial agriculture, and reduced the need for human labor in the agricultural sector. This paved the way for a third major phase in the evolution of agriculture, which is associated with intensive mechanization and the use of biotechnology. This so-called ***Third Agricultural Revolution*** is still in progress. It is based on new, higher-yielding strains of grains and other crops developed in laboratories using modern techniques of genetic engineering. Where it has taken hold, it has often blurred the distinctions between primary, secondary, and tertiary activities in the rural sector, as farmers become involved in a combination of plant and animal cultivation (a primary activity), food processing (a secondary activity), and marketing (a tertiary activity).

From the field notes

"Growing crops is one thing; marketing them is another. As I approached one of the Ancient temples of southern Korea, I saw a group of women waiting patiently in the hopes of selling something to passerbys. On my way to the temple I had traveled through a landscape dominated by large paddies. But here the forces of change in the agriculture sector seemed distant indeed. These women sit here all day selling the modest output from their own market gardens. The agricultural sector is indeed in transition, but in many places the old and the new sit side by side."

The changes unfolding in the wake of the last phase of the Second Agricultural Revolution and the Third Agricultural Revolution are of such magnitude that they require separate examination. We take up this subject in Chapter 20. First, however, it is important to gain some understanding of the cultural landscapes and practices associated with the development of agriculture. Thus we turn next to a discussion of rural settlements and lifestyles.

◆ KEY TERMS ◆

agricultural origins
agriculture
animal domestication
farming
First Agricultural Revolution
hunting and gathering
metallurgy
plant domestication
Second Agricultural Revolution
shifting cultivation
subsistence farmers
Third Agricultural Revolution
Thünian patterns

◆ APPLYING GEOGRAPHIC KNOWLEDGE ◆

1. It may be said that in most countries where subsistence agriculture still forms the way of life of a substantial number of people, governments seek ways to improve these farm families' lives. What impels governments to do so? What methods have they used to convert subsistence farming into cash agriculture? What are the rewards—and the risks—to the subsistence farmers?
2. The Earth has witnessed three Agricultural Revolutions; each had enormous impact on human civilization. Geographically, each occurred in a distinct area (or group of areas) of the world, and each had a technological dimension. Explain the spatial settings of the three Agricultural Revolutions in cultural, environmental, and technological contexts.

Chapter 19

Landscapes of Rural Settlement

From the field notes

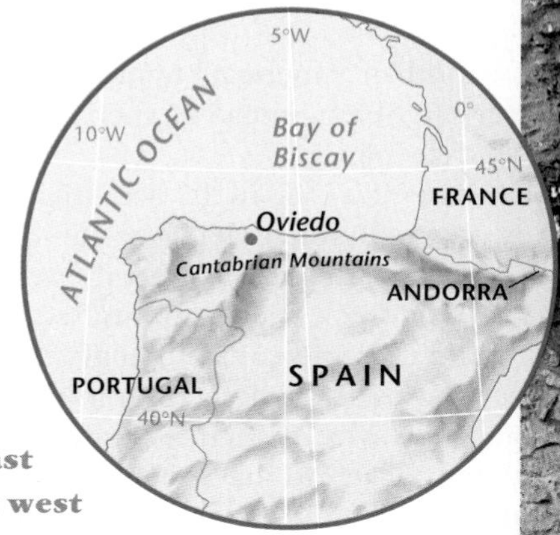

"Driving along the northern coast of Spain just west of Oviedo I came across a scene that a traveler could have found a hundred years ago: two women sitting in front of a stone farmhouse, surrounded by the milk cans and animals of the farm. It is sometimes said that things are slower to change in the countryside, and that certainly seemed true here. It was almost a timeless scene, and I watched the women from a distance engage in a quiet, good natured exchange. Yet I also realized that I was witnessing something that is becoming harder to find in Western Europe. Most people's lives have become easier, but something can be lost in the process as well."

KEY POINTS

- **About half of the world's population still resides in rural areas.**
- **The forms, functions, materials, and spacing of rural dwellings reveal much about a region and its culture—including social and economic opportunities and needs and the culture's relationship to the natural environment.**
- **Village forms reflect historical circumstances, the nature of the land, and economic conditions. They range from linear and clustered to circular and grid-patterned.**
- **In some parts of the world—particularly the more industrialized regions—the distinctions between rural and urban are becoming increasingly blurred as people commute from traditional villages to towns or cities for work and as part-time farming has increased.**
- **Among the greatest influences on patterns of settlement and land use are social norms concerning land ownership and distribution.**
- **The North American landscape has been profoundly influenced by the survey systems that were used to divide and allocate land.**

Shelter ranks high on the list of human needs. Throughout the world, in the coldest regions as well as in the warmest, in the rainiest areas as well as in deserts, people build dwellings that are the focal points of their daily lives. These dwellings have several functions, and protection against cold, wind, and precipitation is only one of them. In residential quarters people find privacy, a certain degree of comfort, a place to store belongings, and even an opportunity to display their values and achievements.

Geographers have many reasons to be interested in the nature of human settlements. A house reveals much about a region and its culture: the building materials that are available, the social and economic needs as well as the cultural traditions of the occupants, and the natural environment that the house must withstand. In the *form* of houses, we can sometimes see one culture give way to another. If you were to take a trip southward on a Nile riverboat, you would see the square, flat-roofed Arab houses of Egypt and northern Sudan yield to the round, steep-roofed African houses of southern Sudan and Uganda. House types thus can be valuable indicators of cultural traditions and transitions.

In the layout and *function* of houses, we get an impression of social values and economic needs: in parts of rural Eastern Europe, for example, people and some of their livestock live under the same roof, so that the building is part house and part barn. Consider the contrast with a suburban American home, in which different rooms serve different purposes such as cooking, bathing, eating, and sleeping.

The *materials* used in the construction of dwellings in many areas still reflect local availability and purpose. In the cold, forested areas of northern Europe, the log cabin, with its thick walls and pitched roof, developed to withstand extreme cold and heavy snowfalls. In low-lying tropical areas, cold weather is not a problem, and you will find leaves, branches, and matting used in the construction of traditional dwellings. Today it is easier to transport building materials from one place to another, so local availability is not as important as it was in the past. Nevertheless, there are still many places where location significantly influences the types of materials used.

We are also interested in the character and pattern of villages. There is a relationship between the density of houses and the intensity of crop cultivation, but that relationship can vary. In the U.S. Midwest, for example, individual farmhouses lie quite far apart in what we call a ***dispersed settlement*** pattern: the land is intensively cultivated but by machine rather than by hand. In the populous Indonesian island of Jawa, villages are located every half-mile or so along a rural road, and settlement there is defined as nucleated. Land use is just as intense, but the work is done by people and animals. Hence, when we consider the density of human settlement as it relates to the intensity of land use, we should keep in mind the way the land is cultivated.

Nucleated settlement is by far the most prevalent rural residential pattern in agricultural areas. When houses are grouped together in tiny clusters or hamlets, or in slightly larger clusters we call villages, their spatial arrangement also has significance. Sometimes it is possible to identify the prevailing culture just by looking at the ground plan of a village. In parts of Africa where cattle herding is the primary means of existence, the houses in a village are arranged in a circle (that of the chief or headman will be larger and somewhat separated from the others) surrounding a central corral where the livestock are kept at night. In the low-lying areas of Western Europe, the houses of a village are often situated on a strip of higher ground (such as a dike or a levee). When you look at the map of such a village, it is simply a row of evenly spaced units, perhaps on two sides of a road but often on only one side.

In such different regions as Eastern Europe, western Nigeria, and northern Spain, the houses of older villages are not regularly arranged but are closely clustered together, a defensive measure that included the construction of a surrounding outer wall. The need for such defenses has disappeared, but the traditional village is still part of the landscape and people continue to build new villages similar to those of bygone centuries. The arrangement of houses in villages therefore takes many different forms. Tradition, political organization, physical characteristics of the land, and many other factors underlie the development of the villages we see today. ◆

◆ HOUSING AND LANDSCAPE

We may assume that early humans lived in bands containing from a dozen to 50 or 60 individuals, which moved from place to place, setting up a temporary campsite in each place. We can only speculate on the appearance of these campsites because nothing very permanent was built. Perhaps holes were dug and covered with branches and leaves to serve as shelters. Later, these burrows may have been improved and enlarged, with posts to support rafters. In any case, it is unlikely that the earliest dwelling was the cave, despite the many myths and stories about "cave men." Our ancestors lived in many parts of the world, including those where no convenient natural housing was available. Efforts were made to construct shelters wherever the earliest human communities clustered.

Functional Differentiation

Such communal living gave way to family structures as human society developed, and dwellings came to accommodate single families rather than larger groups. As the capacity to domesticate animals, grow crops, and store food increased, so did the size and complexity of human groupings. Communities became larger and more highly organized, and they developed rules governing marriage, inheritance, food allocation, domestic duties, and so on. It also became necessary to construct buildings other than those used for living. The chief or headman's residence must appear more imposing than others, and facilities were needed for the storage of food and implements, for guest quarters, and for the sheltering of livestock. Thus we begin to see some ***functional differentiation*** in buildings.

An example of functional differentiation can be seen in a comparison of lifestyles and dwellings in Africa. In the Kalahari Desert, some San bands probably resemble those of the distant past: their shelters are often mere windbreaks made of a few branches across which an animal skin is stretched. Campsites are occupied only temporarily, for the people must hunt wandering animals in their constant struggle for survival. In contrast, the villages of cattle-raising peoples in the eastern highlands are permanent, and larger communities construct centralized buildings that reflect the increasing complexity of society.

Environmental Influences

There is ample evidence that human communities existed in widely separated areas as early as 100,000 years ago, occupying warm as well as cold regions, moist as well as dry zones, coastal as well as interior locations, and river valleys as well as uplands. Early migrations propelled human groups into unfamiliar environments, and conflict and war drove others into new and sometimes difficult situations. From the beginning humans were confronted by variable environmental conditions—floods, storms, severe cold, and heavy winter snows—and began to build shelters for protection against the elements. The physical structures built by ancient human groups differed in form and function, starting traditions that in some cases have survived for thousands of years. People in flood-prone areas learned to construct stilt houses. Where heavy snow prevailed, the steep-sided roof offered protection against the enormous weight of a winter's accumulation. Nomadic peoples needing lightweight, transportable shelters developed various kinds of tents. Among the truly amazing adaptations was the invention of the igloo by Inuit peoples in the frozen northlands, using as building material the very snow and ice against which they sought to protect themselves.

Thus the diversity of dwellings around the world has ancient origins. The distribution pattern was further complicated by migration, which diffused building practices along numerous routes. Sometimes the introduction of new construction techniques led to the abandonment or modification of existing practices. During the period of European colonial expansion, this occurred in many parts of the Americas, Africa, and Asia. In other cases, societies retained their building methods even when they were displaced. Some builders of stilt houses, for instance, continued to construct elevated dwellings even after they had been relocated to areas where floods were not a threat. Building on stilts had become an integral part of their culture.

Cultural geographers have tried to reconstruct the diffusion of building forms, a task that has at times proved to be extremely difficult. Barns and other outbuildings, and even fences, have been the subjects of such studies, and influences have been traced halfway around the world. (For example, historical linkages from Western Europe to New England to California, and ultimately to Hawaii, have been identified.) The dynamic geography of ***domestic architecture*** is a complex and fascinating field.

From the field notes

"Between the Tana River and the Somali border, the bush becomes thinner and building materials are less easy to come by. Still, some houses here are very substantial, requiring a large amount of wood for their frames. This house not far from Ijara is ready for roofing (thatch will be used) and wall construction. The walls are made of a mixture of pebbles and soil mixed with termite-mound clay, dried and hardened by the sun."

◆ CHANGING RESIDENTIAL TRADITIONS

Although cultural traditions promote continuity in building types and styles, time does bring change. In certain parts of the world, dwellings appear much as they did centuries ago. In portions of Africa, for example, dwellings in rural areas and even in some cities are still built according to centuries-old patterns. You can walk some of the streets of Kano, Nigeria, and readily imagine that you are in another age. On the other hand, the effects of modernization can be seen even in the African bush, where many houses have corrugated metal instead of thatch roofs. Today, the floor plan of a house may remain the same, but the building materials are no longer limited to those available in the region. Thus we can classify dwellings into four groups: (1) unchanged-traditional, (2) modified-traditional, (3) modernized-traditional (where change affects both building materials and floor plan), and (4) modern.

Unchanged-Traditional Dwellings

Unchanged-traditional houses (both permanent and temporary) are those in which layout, construction, and appearance have not been significantly altered by external influences over the past century. Such houses may be modified over time—but as a result of changes within

From the field notes

"A large number of buildings in the town of Torshavn (Faroe Islands) display a characteristic Scandinavian feature: a sod-covered roof. It conserves warmth during the cold winter, but it does present rot problems (judging by the repairs under way all over town) in the supporting wood."

the culture, not borrowing from other cultures. Such is the domestic architecture seen in Arab towns, African villages, rural settlements in China, and other places that are remote from or resistant to foreign influences. Villages all over the world contain a mixture of traditional and modified housing, but unchanged-traditional dwellings survive as well. These range from wood-framed, mat-walled, thatch-roofed Micronesian houses to rough-stone structures in Native American areas of Andean South America; also included are mud-brick houses of Native Americans in the Southwestern United States, mud-walled houses in China, and cloth tents in North Africa.

Traditional houses of European and other Western cultures also belong in this category of domestic architecture. Log houses with sod roofs in Scandinavia, single-story stone houses with thatched roofs in Ireland, and barrel-tiled, whitewashed houses in Spain all represent local or regional traditions. In Canada, two types of houses—the French-Canadian house of Quebec and the British-Canadian house of Ontario—typify modernized-traditional domestic architecture. The French-Canadian house tends to be more elaborate, with curved rooflines, attic or dormer windows, and a raised balcony across the front; attached to one side is a summer kitchen that is closed off during the winter. The British-Canadian house is most common in Ontario, and it is more compact and austere. Stone and brick are used in the construction of these two traditional house types.

In the United States, several types of traditional houses of European cultural origin can be identified: most notably the New England, Middle Atlantic, and Southern styles. The New England house, unlike its Canadian counterparts, is of wood-frame construction (Fig. 19-1A). Sometimes called a "saltbox" house, it exemplifies a style that dates from colonial times and became gradually more elaborate over time. The Middle Atlantic style originated as a one-room log cabin with a stone chimney and fireplace at one end. Later, additional rooms, a porch, and a second floor were added (Fig. 19-1B). In the South, the size and construction of houses reflected the modest means of most of their builders and the comparative warmth of the climate. Smaller than New England houses, traditional Southern dwellings had only one story (sometimes with a small attic room) and a characteristic porch. Often the house was built on a raised platform to reduce interior heat. In low-lying areas, houses were built on raised stone foundations to guard against flood damage (Fig. 19-1C).

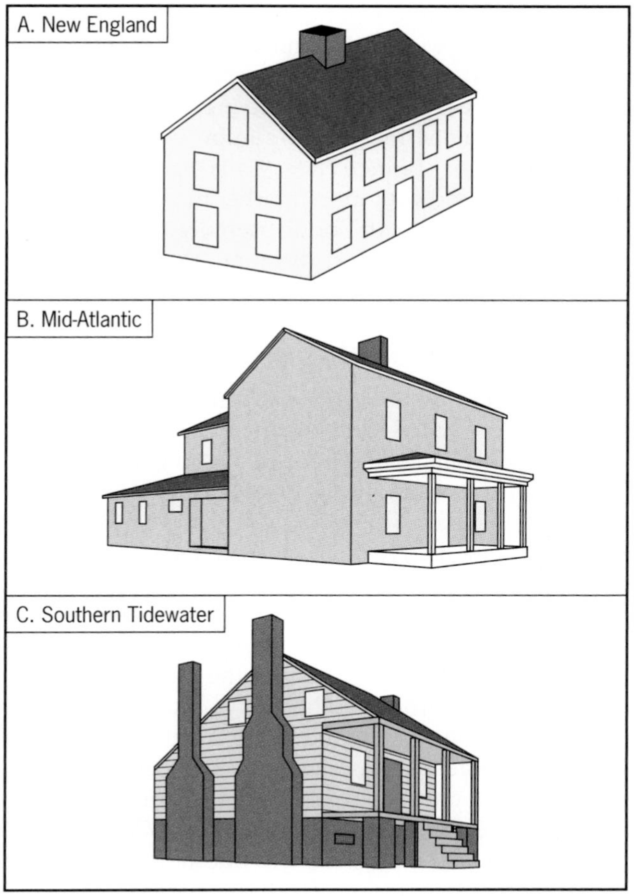

Figure 19-1 Traditional American House Types *Source*: Based on figures in F. B. Kniffen, "Folk Housing: Key to Diffusion," *Annals of the Association of American Geographers* 55, 1965, pp. 559, 563, and 570.

Modified-Traditional Dwellings

As noted earlier, traditional houses the world over have been modified in many ways. In modified-traditional dwellings, new building materials have been used or elements added that do not fundamentally alter their original structure or layout. The use of corrugated iron as a roofing material, for example, has diffused to many areas of the world and has affected housing everywhere. From Polynesia to West Africa, traditional thatch-roofed dwellings stand next to houses with corrugated-iron roofs. Through the eyes of some, this can look incongruous, and the tendency for the iron sheeting to rust can make houses appear unkempt from the outside. Yet the iron roof provides better protection against rain and moisture, cannot be infested by disease-carrying vermin or insects, and often serves as a catchment for fresh water.

Other modifications of traditional houses include the addition of windows and wooden doors. The wall openings are especially important in village houses in Africa, where fires burn inside closed dwellings and smoke-related diseases are prevalent. Improved air circulation helps reduce the negative effects of the smoke, particularly for newborns and young children. Another modification of traditional dwellings is the raised floor. Without changing the basic structure, the practice of raising the floor has the effect of decreasing the amount of moisture inside the dwelling, thus reducing discomfort and disease. Colonial governments therefore encouraged builders of traditional dwellings to raise their floors. Still other modifications are less obvious, yet also important. Thatched roofs were improved through the use of wire mesh and metal ties. Walls made of sun-dried brick were coated with mortar rather than smeared with mud. Although these did not materially change the appearance of the traditional dwelling, they did result in better protection and greater durability.

Modernized-Traditional Dwellings

In the case of modern-traditional house types, the modifications are more far-reaching, involving not only building materials but also the floor plan and general layout. Elements of the traditional house persist, but modernization has overtaken tradition. When the New England house type emerged (from European traditions), it had a single bathroom quite unlike those of today, no two-car garage, and almost none of the interior specialization found in modern versions. Remnants of traditional styles still exist—for example, in the Cape-Dutch facades of South Africa, upturned rooflines of Japan, and "Mediterranean" forms in Central and South America—but these are mere vestiges of the originals. European styles have also changed traditional housing in former colonies, where the idea of multiple rooms and specialized facilities has produced imitations of Western houses displaying a mixture of modern and traditional forms and building materials.

Modern Dwellings

The modern house type is most common in the United States but is increasingly common elsewhere as well. This category reflects advanced technology, upward mobility, practicality, comfort, and hygiene—and large-scale suburbanization. There was a time when the two-story house symbolized a family's socioeconomic status and well-being, but the practical advantages of the ranch-style house (once called the "California bungalow") overtook such considerations. Originating in the designs of Elbert Hubbard in Buffalo and Frank Lloyd Wright and his associates in Oak Park, outside Chicago, the ranch-style house took root in Southern California and diffused in various forms to suburbs, where it was much less practical, with its low-angle roof, screened porches and patios, pool and deck, barbecue pit, and other space-demanding, energy-consuming features.

Modern domestic architecture in the United States may be less aesthetically pleasing than other dwelling forms, but there are compensations. With its plumbing and electrical systems, temperature- and humidity-control mechanisms, kitchen and bathroom facilities, and automated equipment ranging from garage-door openers to pool-maintenance devices, many would say that the modern American house makes up in technology for what it lacks in style.

Modern domestic architecture tends to sacrifice tradition for practicality and efficiency. Modern house types in Tokyo, Sydney, Nairobi, São Paulo, and Vancouver are far more similar to each other than to the traditional houses in and around these cities. Clearly, tradition remains strongest in the domestic architecture of rural areas.

◆ STRUCTURE AND MATERIALS

Dwellings may also be studied from the viewpoint of their physical structure, their complexity, and the materials from which they are constructed. Cultural geographers sometimes classify dwelling types according to these criteria. At one end of the scale are the caves still occupied by people in some parts of the world, as well as the windbreaks of wandering food-gathering peoples, the pit dwellings, and the simplest huts, which can be little more than stacked-up sticks, branches, grass, and leaves. At the other end are imposing mansions in the wealthy suburbs of Western cities, as well as millions of simpler single-family homes. Between these two ends of the scale are dozens of intermediate dwelling types, ranging from the beehive-shaped Zulu house to the complex houses of several cultures of South, Southeast, and East Asia.

Particular dwelling-structure types are associated with particular regions. In China, for example, farmhouses as well as village houses are now most often built of baked-mud walls and thatch roofs, but older villages contain houses with walls of brick and tile roofs (Fig. 19-2). Most such villages are in the hinterland of Shanghai in the Chang Jiang's middle basin. The many less durable dwellings reflect the scarcity of building materials and the explosive population growth of recent times, which created widespread housing shortages.

In Africa, the transition from the Arab dwelling of the north to the traditional African house of the mid-continent region has already been noted. The existence of Arab and African structures side by side in the transition zone shows how the two culture regions penetrate each other in that zone.

In South America, a map of house structures would reveal not only the diffusion of modern and modernized-traditional forms but also the persistence of older styles such as the rough-stone houses of the Andean Indians, the mud-walled dwellings of the west and south, and the Amazonian Indians' structures of branches and leaves. Maps of this kind have been drawn for local regions, but not for entire geographic realms. However, as in the case of languages, it is often difficult to distinguish what is truly traditional from what has been introduced—the original from the modified.

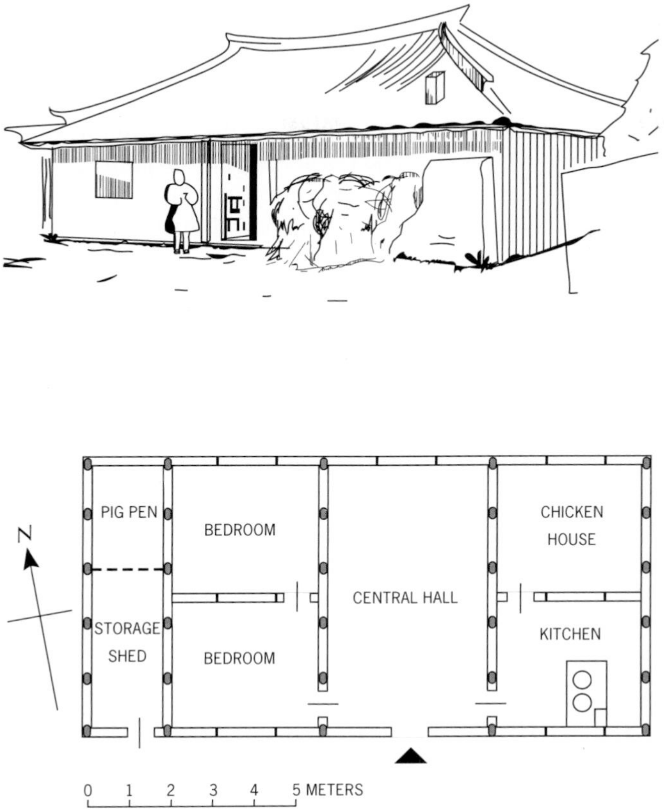

Figure 19-2 Traditional House from Jiangsu Province, China. *Source*: From R. G. Knapp, *China's Traditional Architecture*. Honolulu: University of Hawaii Press, 1986, p. 80.

Building Materials

Another way of studying dwellings is to examine the materials from which they are constructed. In this section we will examine several of the most common types of building materials, bearing in mind that a wide variety of other types are used as well.

Wood Houses made principally of wood still reveal some links to the distribution of forests, although, of course, wood is shipped to all parts of the world today. The log house, which probably originated in the cold forest zones of northern Europe, was brought by early European settlers to northern North America, where forests were plentiful and the cold was at least as severe. Comparatively few log houses are constructed today, except as recreational homes. Wood buildings are common, however, as modern sawmills produce cut lumber that makes building with wood comparatively easy.

Houses made primarily of wood are found in a zone that extends across Eurasia from central Scandinavia and Eastern Europe through Russia to the Pacific coast, including Korea and Japan as well. Wood-frame houses prevail throughout North America from New England to California and from Florida to Alaska. In South America, wood is the primary material for houses in southern Chile and southeastern Brazil, where local forests yield wood for building. Wood is also important in the domestic architecture of Australia and New Zealand.

Brick Where wood is not readily available, houses are likely to be built of ***brick***. We tend to define a brick as a hard, cement, and oven-baked block that comes in various standard sizes. Elsewhere in the world, however, bricks are made from different raw materials. In the Middle East (as well as in the southwestern United States and Mexico), wet mud is mixed with straw, poured into wooden frames, allowed to dry briefly, and then placed in the sun to harden. These bricks are then used in wall construction. Moister mud is used as mortar, and after the newly built structure dries out, the walls are smeared with mud. To construct the roof, a frame of sticks, branches, and straw is covered with mud. In arid regions such dwellings provide good protection against both heat and cold; however, the infrequent heavy rains can create havoc because the sun-baked mud bricks never become as hard or resistant as oven-baked bricks and tiles used in other parts of the world.

Sun-dried brick is widely used as a building material. It is the main component of traditional dwellings, not only in the Middle East and the Arab culture realm

From the field notes

"I drove northward from Bergen, Norway, and then inland. Roads narrowed from four lanes to two, then to one, and turned from asphalt to dirt. Houses became simpler. Here, near Stalheim, is a house that well represents the area, where the building materials are in ample supply. Wood forms the walls; large slabs of slate create the roof."

generally, but also in much of Middle and South America (especially west of the Andes and south of Brazil), the savannalands of Africa, and northern India. The mud-brick house is also common in timber-poor, fairly dry northern China, and some scholars believe that the homebuilding method used there may have diffused from the Middle East.

The fired or baked brick, a more modern innovation, has become a major element of modern construction all over the world. Traditional houses in a Mexican village are made of sun-dried brick, but homes in the towns and cities are built with oven-baked bricks. So it is in the cities of the Arab realm, Africa, and South America (although traditional dwellings cluster on the outskirts of the modern towns). In a few parts of the world, notably Southern Africa and central China, the use of fired brick developed as a traditional building method before modern building technologies were introduced.

Stone Houses also are built of natural stone. In the high Andes of Peru, house-builders pile rough stones on top of each other without mortar, caulk the remaining openings with mud, and add a thatched roof.

From the field notes

"The countryside in Armenia between Yerevan and Lake Sevan is dry and rocky, and the rocks are piled up to mark lot and field lines. They are also used in the construction of houses. As we approached the lake near the town of Akhta you could see the same house form in all directions. The stones are only roughly cut square, and then used to build thick walls with much cement. Windows are small, roofs not very steep (not much rain here). Many residents were changing their roofs from stripped-down tarpaper over wood to corrugated iron sheeting."

Traditional European homes, such as English cottages, also are made of natural stone with cement mortar and have thatched roofs. Southern and interior Egypt, where natural building stone is plentiful, is another area where stone houses are common. Building with available stone developed as traditional architecture in central and southern India, Xizang (Tibet) and neighboring areas of western China, Yucatan and adjacent parts of Mexico, and south-central Africa (where the great ruins of Zimbabwe provide evidence of the higher level of technology achieved in stone building). Overall, however, wood and mud brick are far more common building materials.

Wattle We use the term ***wattle*** to refer to houses built from poles and sticks, which are woven into a tight network and plastered with mud. In fact, these dwellings are built of a combination of wood (the poles and sticks) and the same material from which mud bricks are made. Many African houses are constructed this way, with a thick thatched roof to protect against the occasionally heavy rains.

Regions where poles, sticks, bamboo, bark, leaves, and similar materials are used for building purposes obviously correspond to zones where these materials are readily available. In terms of population, Southeast Asia is the leading region in this category; the traditional houses of Indonesia, the Philippines, and the mainland countries south of China and east of India are made of wattle. In Africa, these materials prevail along the west coast and throughout the lowland basin. And in South America, the sparsely populated Amazon Basin provides ample building material for traditional Native American settlements.

Grass and Brush Between the wattle dwellings of the equatorial rainforest areas and the earthen construction of the drier subtropical zones lie the low-latitude regions where grass and brush are the most common building materials. The African savannalands, including interior West Africa south of the Sahel, East Africa's highlands, and upland South Africa, form the major region of this type, but many traditional dwellings on the Africa savanna also contain sun-dried mud. Grass-and-brush construction also prevails in the Brazilian and Venezuelan highlands to the south of the forested Amazon Basin. Northern Australia's indigenous peoples also build their simple dwellings from vegetation growing on the savanna.

Our enumeration of building materials is by no means complete. The Zulu's beehive-shaped dwellings are made almost exclusively of African tall grass. The tents of nomadic peoples are made of cloth or skins. Even blocks of ice are used as building materials. Bamboo is used as a building material in parts of Southeast Asia. In northernmost Europe, sod may be piled on the roof to enhance insulation, and in summer you can see goats grazing on the new grass that grows up there. People live permanently on boats and in trailers. The variations are almost infinite.

◆ DIFFUSION OF HOUSE TYPES

Around the world, houses display great variety in form and layout. When people migrate, they carry with them notions of how a home should be planned and constructed, but in new environments those ideas may need to be modified. Differences in available materials and new environmental conditions cause changes that contribute to the development of new styles.

A good example of this process comes from the eastern seaboard of the United States. Fred Kniffen, who conducted extensive research on house types and their diffusion in North America, concluded that the three principal types appeared more or less simultaneously in New England, the Middle Atlantic region, and the "Tidewater South" of lower Chesapeake Bay (Fig. 19-3). From these sources, the diverse building styles diffused westward and southward in several parallel streams. By the middle of the nineteenth century, these streams had created three distinct ***folk-housing regions*** (see the inset in Fig. 19-3).

We have only to look around us to see how things have changed since about 1850. In the Midwest and the South and elsewhere, we still find many single-family houses that are structural variations of the Atlantic-coast types described by Kniffen. However, we also find L-shaped ranch houses, T-shaped homes with the bedrooms separated in the two wings of the T, and U-shaped houses with a patio and perhaps a pool in the enclosed courtyard.

The present cultural landscape thus is a composite of older and newer forms. Figure 19-3 shows the ***diffusion***

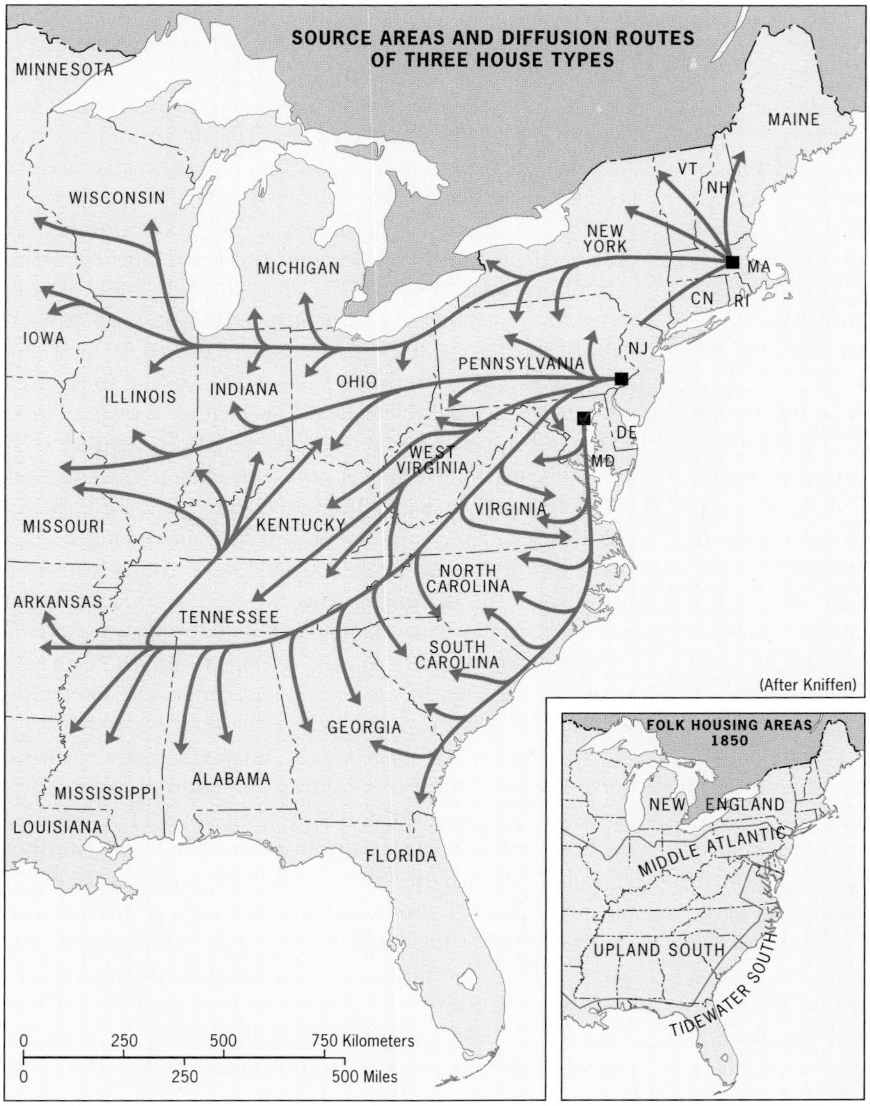

Figure 19-3 Source Areas and Diffusion Routes of Three House Types. This map shows New England, Middle Atlantic, and Southern house styles and their diffusion. *Source*: From F. B. Kniffen, "Folk Housing: Key to Diffusion," *Annals of the Association of American Geographers* 55, 1965, p. 560.

routes of the three original types into the U.S. interior. Note that the New England house type was confined to a northern corridor, whereas the Middle Atlantic and Lower Chesapeake types spread more widely. What the map does not show is the eastward diffusion of ranch-style houses from the West. This house style evolved during the 1920s in California and became a cultural symbol of a lifestyle. Expansion diffusion had carried Eastern styles westward, but now Western styles diffused in the opposite direction, first along the Sunbelt corridor and then more widely. But the ranch house is designed for a balmy climate and outdoor living; its single-story, open construction is not really suitable for climates with greater extremes of temperature. Nevertheless, ranch houses are now found virtually everywhere in the United States, even in areas where they are not appropriate. This results from a period of ***maladaptive diffusion*** in which image took precedence over practicality. There are many other examples of such diffusion. To cite just one, the New England style diffused as far as Hawaii, where clusters of these houses still stand—strangely out of place in a tropical environment.

◆ VILLAGES

We now turn our attention from individual dwellings to settlements: purposely grouped, organized clusters of houses and nonresidential buildings. The smallest such clusters are known as ***hamlets*** and may contain only about a dozen such buildings. The largest clustered settlements, of course, are cities, the subject of Part Seven of this book. Here we are interested in the smallest settlements—hamlets and villages.

Before proceeding, we should note that the definition of a ***village*** varies. We have a mental picture of a village as a small settlement without high-rise buildings or large commercial enterprises, but it is difficult to be precise. What is the upper limit of a village's population? When does a village become a town? In Canada, the official definition of a village limits it to 1000 people; in the United States, the limit is 2500. In India, a place can have up to 5000 residents and still be officially classified as a village. And in Japan a settlement cannot be called an "urban" place until it has 30,000 inhabitants or more. International statistics reporting "rural" (village) and "urban" (city) populations, therefore, are meaningless unless standardized definitions are used.

Since numbers alone are not particularly revealing, scholars have traditionally looked to social and organizational criteria for defining villages. Traditionally, a village was defined as a settlement in which the majority of the population was involved in primary activities and in which there was relatively little investment in public infrastructure. In traditional villages, relatively few people had narrow, specialized jobs; instead, most people did a variety of things to keep themselves and the community going. Defining villages in these terms provided a useful means of distinguishing rural from urban throughout much of human history—and it continues to be helpful in many parts of the world. Yet in some parts of the world—particularly the more industrialized regions—the distinctions between rural and urban are becoming increasingly blurred as people commute from traditional villages to towns or cities for work and as part-time farming has increased. In these places, it is increasingly difficult to define what constitutes a village in any precise way—so the tendency is to revert simply to numbers.

Village Forms

Traditionally, the people who lived in villages either farmed the surrounding land or provided services to those who do the farming. Thus they were closely connected to the land, and most of their livelihoods depended, directly or indirectly, on the cultivation of nearby farmland. As such, they tended to reflect historical and environmental conditions. Houses in Japanese farming villages, for example, are so tightly packed together that only the narrowest passageways remain between them. This reflects the need to allocate every possible square foot of land to farming; villages must not use land where crops could grow.

In the hilly regions of Europe, villages frequently are clustered on hillslopes, leaving the level land for farming. Often an old castle sits atop the hill, so in earlier times the site offered protection as well as land conservation. In many low-lying areas of Western Europe, villages are located on dikes and levees, so that they often take on linear characteristics (Fig. 19-4A). Where there is space, a house and outbuildings may be surrounded by a small garden; the farms and pasturelands lie just beyond. In other cases a village may take on the characteristics of a cluster (Fig. 19-4B). It may have begun as a small hamlet at the intersection of two roads and then developed by accretion. The European version of the East African circular village, with its central cattle corral, is the round village or *rundling* (Fig. 19-4C). This layout was first used by Slavic farmer-herdsmen in Eastern Europe and was later modified by Germanic settlers.

In many parts of the world, farm villages were fortified to protect their inhabitants against marauders. Ten thousand years ago, the first farmers in the Fertile Crescent faced attacks from the horsemen of Asia's steppes and clustered together to ward off this danger. In Nigeria's Yorubaland, the farmers would go out into the surrounding fields by day but retreat to the protection of walled villages at night. Villages, as well as larger towns and cities in Europe, were frequently walled and surrounded by moats. When the population became so large that people had to build houses outside the original wall, a new wall would be built to protect them as

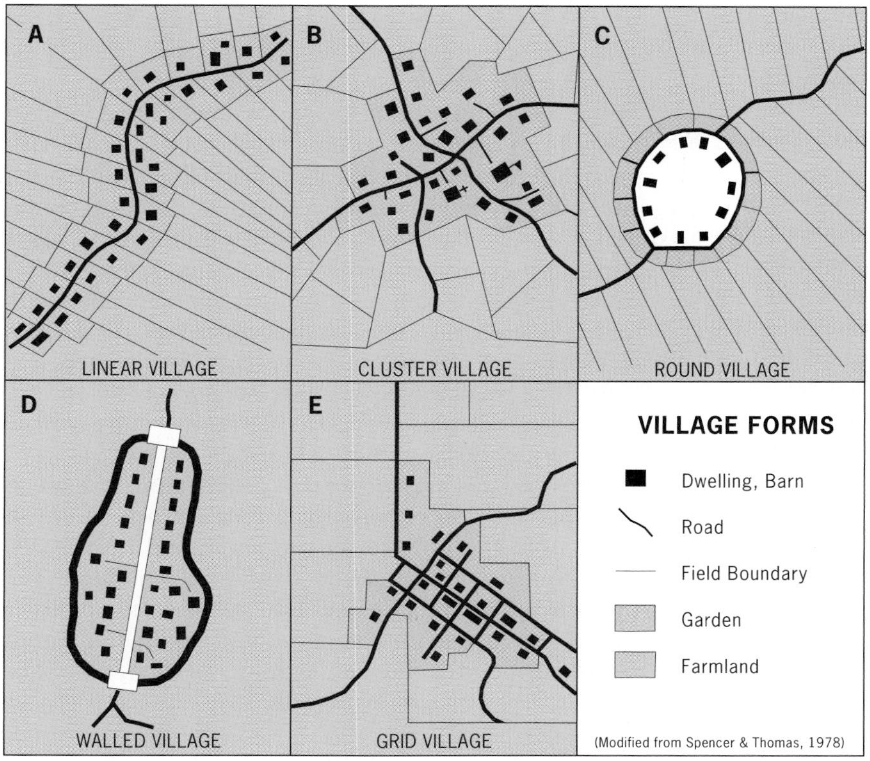

Figure 19-4 Village Forms. Five different representative village layouts are shown here. *Source*: From J. E. Spencer and W. H. Thomas, *Introducing Cultural Geography*. New York: Wiley, 1978, p.154.

well. Walled villages (Fig. 19-4D) still exist in rural areas of many countries, reminders of a turbulent past.

More modern villages, notably planned rural settlements, may be arranged on a grid pattern (Fig. 19-4E). This is not, however, a twentieth-century novelty. Centuries ago the Spanish invaders of Middle America laid out grid villages and towns, as did other colonial powers elsewhere in the world. In urban Africa, as we will see in Part Seven, such imprints of colonization are pervasive.

Although the twentieth century has witnessed unprecedented urban growth throughout the world, half of the world's people still reside in villages and rural areas. In China alone, some 800 million people (in a country of over 1.2 billion) inhabit villages and hamlets. In India, with a population approaching 1 billion, three out of four people live in villages. Small rural settlements are home to most of the inhabitants of Indonesia, Bangladesh, Pakistan, and other developing countries, including those in Africa. Thus the agrarian village remains one of the most common form of settlement on Earth despite the industrial and technological revolutions.

Regional Contrasts

Village life varies from one region to another. The modern comforts of a farm village in Wisconsin, with its paved streets, electricity, water supply, and other urban amenities, are a far cry from the dusty, isolated, poverty-ridden village of eastern India. In some areas, modernization has reached all but the remotest rural areas, and on most of the farmlands mechanization prevails. As we noted earlier, it is hard even to say what is rural anymore—what with farmers or farm families often splitting their time between the farm and occupations in nearby towns and cities. In other areas, however, farm villages lie far removed from the sources of change, and there are few material comforts. In South Asia there may be as many as 1 million farm villages, most with fewer than 1000 inhabitants. From a distance, many appear picturesque, rising from emerald-green rice fields or clinging to rocky slopes. However, a closer look often reveals poorly fed, underdressed children, the absence of sanitation, and inadequate housing.

Clearly, it is not easy to generalize about village life. Villages in areas where subsistence modes of life prevail share certain qualities, whether they lie in South Asia, Subsaharan Africa, or Middle America. Karl Marx once remarked that such places confine the human mind within the narrowest possible bounds, but he failed to understand the inner strength of the inhabitants—their relationship with God or Allah, their confidence in ultimate salvation. Villages in regions where commercial agriculture prevails share a more materialistic orientation, whether they exist in Western Europe, Japan, or the U.S. Midwest. Villages may be viewed as lying along a continuum from the most communal (the multiple-family "long-house" communities of some Pacific, Native

American, and Asian cultures) to the most individualistic (the affluent villages of rural North America). Between these extremes are forms of communal agrarian living (Israel's kibbutzim); closely knit farm villages in Asian, African, or Native American societies; and looser clusters in rural Europe.

Despite these differences, villages everywhere display certain common qualities, including evidence of social stratification and differentiation of buildings. The range in size and quality of houses, representing their owners' wealth and standing in the community, reflects social stratification. Material well-being is the chief determinant of stratification in Western commercial agricultural regions, where it translates into more elaborate homes. In Africa, a higher social position in the community is associated with a more impressive house. The house of the chief or headman may not only be more elaborate than others but may also stand in a more prominent location. In India, caste still strongly influences the overall quality of daily life, including village housing; the manors of landlords, often comprising large walled compounds, stand in striking contrast to the modest houses of domestic servants, farm workers, carpenters, and craftspeople. The poorest people of the lowest castes live in small one-room, wattle-and-thatch dwellings.

Functional Differentiation Within Villages

The functional differentiation of buildings within farm villages is more elaborate in some societies than in others. Protection of livestock and storage of harvested crops are primary functions of farm villages, and in many villages where subsistence farming is the prevailing way of life, the storage place for grains and other food is constructed with as much care as the best-built house. Moisture and vermin must be kept away from stored food; containers of grain often stand on stilts under a carefully thatched roof or behind walls made of carefully maintained sun-dried mud. In India's villages, the paddy-bin made of mud (in which rice is stored) often stands inside the house. Similarly, livestock pens are often attached to houses or, as in Africa, dwellings are built in a circle surrounding the corral or *kraal.*

The functional differentiation of buildings is greatest in Western cultures, where a single farmstead may contain as many buildings as an entire hamlet elsewhere in the world. A prosperous North American farm is likely to include a two-story farmhouse, a stable, a barn, and various outbuildings, including a garage for motorized equipment, a workshop, a shed for tools, and a silo for grain storage. The space these structures occupy often exceeds that used by entire villages in Japan, China, and other agrarian regions where space must be conserved.

◆ PATTERNS OF SETTLEMENT AND LAND USE

At the beginning of this chapter we noted that villages range from dispersed to nucleated, but there are also great differences in the distribution of villages across the land. As we will learn in Chapter 23, under ideal conditions one might assume an even distribution of villages. Such an idealized pattern rarely occurs, however, because settlement patterns are always influenced by cultural preferences, physical circumstances, and even chance historical occurrences. Yet traditionally there is at least some regularity to the spacing among villages, for agricultural villagers needed to be within relatively close proximity to the lands they cultivated.

Beyond this most general of observations, the greatest influences on patterns of settlement and land use come from the physical environment and from social rules concerning land ownership and distribution. The physical environment places limitations on the types of agriculture that can be practiced and on the number of people that agriculture can support; as such, the space

From the field notes

"The Dingle Peninsula in Ireland was long one of the more remote parts of the country, and even its largest town—Dingle—was primarily an agricultural village just a few decades ago. Dingle still has a special, rural charm, but signs of an outside, urbanized world are not hard to find. As I walked the streets of the town, I was particularly struck by this intersection, where the colorful inns and houses of the older town were set off by signs of commercial and tourist influences. It is easy to be nostalgic for the old, but poverty abounded, and the young frequently left. Dingle today is a vibrant place. Like so many other places, the challenge it faces is to hang onto the character that makes it special while adapting to a changing world."

between villages tends to be much greater in mountainous areas than it is in fertile plains. But the most dramatic differences in the rural landscape from place to place can be attributed to social norms.

Property ownership is one of those norms, and it is symbolized by landscapes where parcels of land are divided into neat, clearly demarcated segments. The size and order of those parcels is heavily influenced by rules about property inheritance. In systems were one child inherits all of the land—such as the Germanic system of ***primogeniture*** in which all land passes to the eldest son—parcels tend to be larger and farmers tend a single plot of land. This is the norm in northern Europe and in the principal areas of northern European colonization—the Americas, South Africa, Australia, and New Zealand.

In areas where land is divided among heirs, however, considerable fragmentation can occur over time. The latter is the norm throughout much of Asia, Africa, and southern Europe—meaning that farmers living in villages are tending a variety of scattered small plots of land. In some places land reform initiatives have rationalized landholdings to some degree, but fragmentation is still common in many parts of the world.

A related influence on patterns of settlement and land use is the prevailing ***cadastral system*** that delineates property lines. These systems were adopted in places where settlement could be regulated by law, and land surveys were crucial to their implementation. One of the most notable of these systems is the ***rectangular survey system*** adopted by the U.S. government after the American Revolution as part of a cadastral system known as the ***township-and-range system***. Designed to facilitate the dispersal of settlers evenly across farmlands of the U.S. interior, the system imposed a rigid grid-like pattern on the land. The basic unit was the 1 square mile *section*—and land was bought and sold in whole, half or quarter-sections. The section's lines were drawn without reference to the terrain, and they thus imposed a remarkable uniformity across the land. The influence of the rectangular survey can be seen in everything from the dispersal of farms across the countryside to the straight rural roads that follow section lines.

The imprint of the rectangular survey system is evident in Canada as well, where the government adopted a similar cadastral system as it sought to allocate land in the prairie provinces. There are portions of the United

Figure 19-5 Dominant land survey patterns in the United States. Based on Edward T. Price, *Dividing the Land: Early American Beginnings of our Private Property Mosaic* (Chicago: University of Chicago Press, 1995), p. 8 and several other sources.

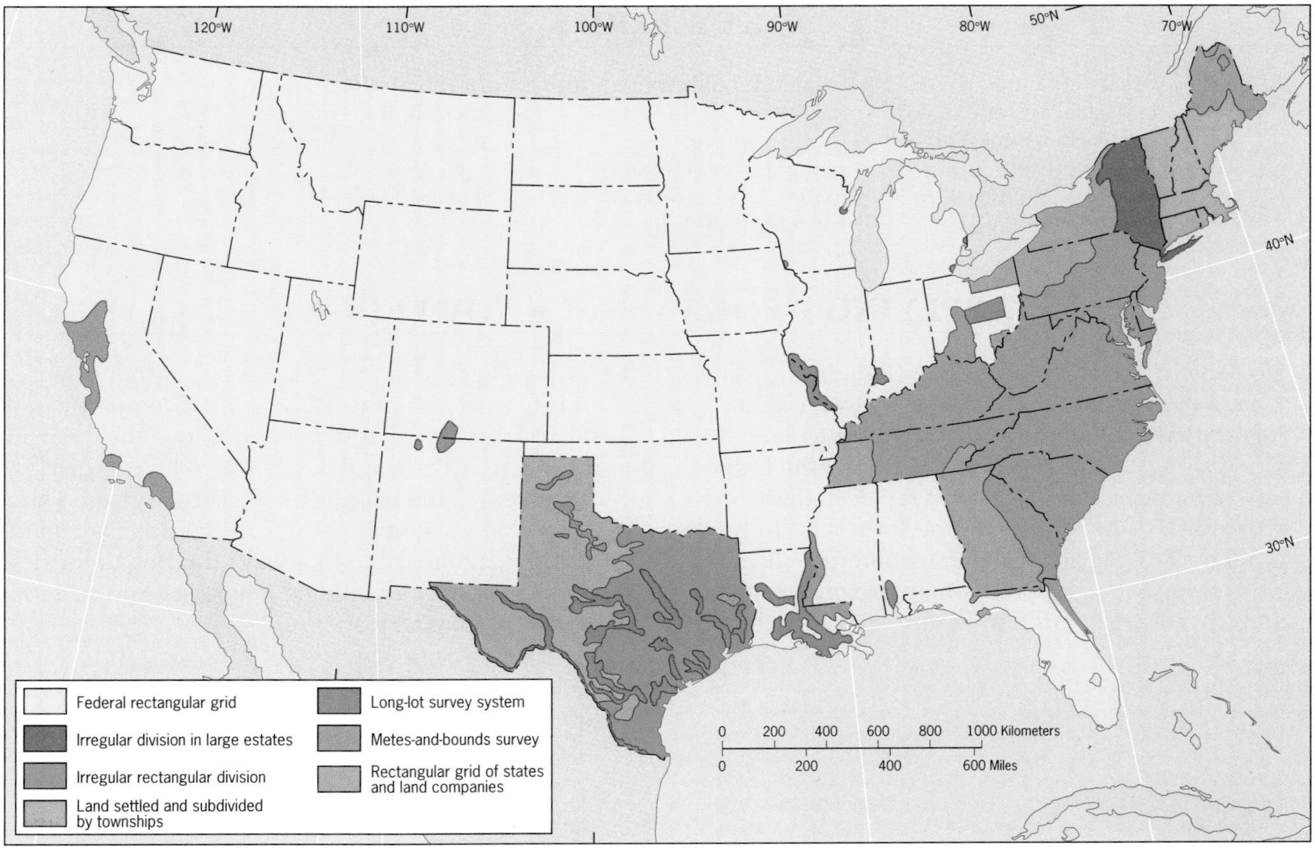

States and Canada where different cadastral patterns predominate, however (Fig. 19-5). These reflect particular notions of how land should be divided and used. Among the most significant are the ***metes and bounds survey*** approach adopted along the eastern seaboard, in which natural features were used to demarcate irregular parcels of land. One of the most distinct regional approaches to land division can be found in the Canadian Maritimes and parts of Quebec, Louisiana, and Texas where a ***long-lot survey*** system was implemented. This system divided land into narrow parcels stretching back from rivers, roads, or canals. It reflects a particular approach to surveying that was common in French America.

◆ THE DIVERSITY OF THE RURAL SECTOR

Rural landscapes in different parts of the world exhibit great variations. The one unifying theme is agricultural; until recently, the great majority of rural residents made their living by farming. Their settlements typically contain barns, storage sheds, and other buildings related to farming. Villages are also likely to include a place of worship, perhaps a medical clinic, a school, and a public gathering place; in larger villages one may find professional people such as teachers, doctors, and ministers, as well as shopkeepers and mechanics. However, all of these people serve a population whose major tie is to the surrounding land—except in industrialized areas where rural life is changing rapidly.

Throughout this book we take note of various core-periphery contrasts our world presents. Such contrasts are prominent in rural as well as urban areas. Traditional farm-village life is still common in India, Subsaharan Africa, China, and Southeast Asia. In the world's core areas, however, agriculture has taken on a very different form, and true farm villages, in which farming or providing services for farmers are the dominant activities, are disappearing. In India, farming, much of it subsistence farming, still occupies nearly 70 percent of the population. In the United States, where farming once was the leading economic activity, only some 2 percent of the labor force remains engaged in agriculture. The small farmer, it is often said, is a disappearing species.

In the next chapter we examine the spatial features and cultural landscapes of the kind of farming that has come to dominate in the world's economic core areas and in isolated places in the periphery as well: commercial farming. This is the farming of huge corporate grain producers and cattle ranches, mechanized equipment and factory-type labor forces, plantations and profit. As we will see, it is a world apart from the traditional farms of Asia and Africa.

◆ KEY TERMS ◆

brick
cadastral system
diffusion routes
dispersed settlement
domestic architecture
folk-housing region
functional differentiation
hamlet
long-lot survey
maladaptive diffusion
metes and bounds survey
nucleated settlement
primogeniture
rectangular land survey
township-and-range system
village
wattle

◆ APPLYING GEOGRAPHIC KNOWLEDGE ◆

1. Do some research on a rural dwelling in the hinterland of the city or town in which you live. Is there evidence that traditional use of local resources (such as wood shingles for the roof, cut stone for the foundation) continues? If not, what has replaced these materials? In the area where you perform this study, do older houses display consistently different characteristics from newer ones? If so, approximately when, and why, did the transition occur?
2. Farm villages are disappearing in the industrialized world, where less than 5 percent of the population still resides in such settlements; but they remain prevalent in Africa and South Asia, where as many as 70 percent of the people inhabit them. What do farm villages in these contrasting core-periphery regions have in common? In what ways do they differ? Use your knowledge of cultural landscape and religious geography in your response.

Chapter 20

Commercialization and the Transformation of the Rural Sector

From the field notes

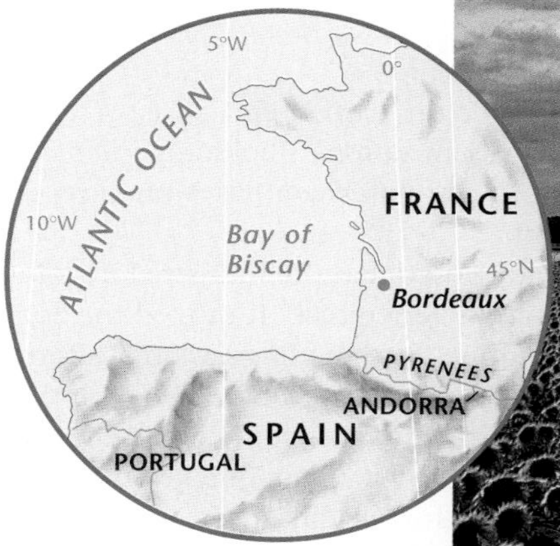

"Seeing the enormous fields of sunflowers southeast of Bordeaux brought home the enormity of the changes sweeping through the French agricultural landscape. Long a country of modest-sized, individually owned farms, French agriculture is increasingly dominated by large commercial interests. There is much talk in France about the impacts of the English language on French culture. But as I looked over this field I couldn't help wondering if the greater catalyst for change is not coming from elsewhere. France's culinary tradition—its breads, cheeses, and meats—is deeply rooted in the countryside. Yet traditional marketing and consumption practices are clearly being challenged by commercialization. Will France find the right balance between cultural preservation and adaptation to a changing world?

KEY POINTS

- **Modern commercial agriculture developed out of a global system of commodity exchange with roots in the European colonial era.**
- **Suitable natural environments and plentiful labor led colonial powers to establish plantation- and luxury-crop agriculture that persists today largely because poorer countries need the cash generated by these crops.**
- **In general, the world's two key grain crops represent different societies: wheat tends to be grown on large landholdings by mechanized means in the richer countries, whereas rice is grown labor-intensively on small plots in poorer countries.**
- **Mediterranean agriculture, a specialized form of farming in a dry-summer climate, yields typical crops in five regions where these conditions prevail.**
- **The Green Revolution has allowed agricultural production to keep up with expanding population, but controversies have developed over the social and environmental impacts of genetically modified foods.**
- **Much food production in wealthier parts of the world has come to be dominated by agribusiness, which has blurred the lines between agriculture and manufacturing and between the meaning of rural and urban.**

The roots of modern ***commercial agriculture*** can be traced to the vast colonial empires established by European powers in the eighteenth and nineteenth centuries. Europe became a market for agricultural products from around the world but with an added dimension: European countries manufactured and sold in their colonies the finished products made from imported raw materials. Thus cotton grown in Egypt, Sudan, India, and other countries colonized by Europe was bought cheaply, imported to European factories, and made into clothes—many of which were then exported and sold, often in the very colonies where the cotton had been grown in the first place.

Obviously, much has happened to alter the patterns established during the colonial era. The evolution of a worldwide transport network with ever-greater capacity and efficiency changed the competitive position of various agricultural activities. The beef industry of Argentina, for example, secured a world market when the invention of refrigerated ships made it possible to transport a highly perishable commodity over long distances. Yet global agricultural patterns are still influenced by the fact that European colonial powers required farmers in their colonies to cultivate specific crops. Ghanaians still grow cacas. Moçambiquans still raise cotton. Sri Lankans still produce tea. Moreover, the continued production of cash crops by poorer countries is perpetuated by loan and aid requirements imposed on former colonies by industrialized countries—either on a unilateral basis or through nongovernmental organizations including the World Trade Organization, the International Monetary Fund, and the World Bank.

We have already noted that the Industrial Revolution had a major impact on agriculture. It moved the Second Agricultural Revolution into high gear and ultimately paved the way for the Third Agricultural Revolution. It also revolutionized transportation and communication—making it possible to ship products quickly and cheaply over vast distances and for agricultural conglomerates to develop that could control crop and animal production in distant places. When we attempt to describe the relationships between the urbanized and agricultural areas, we should view those urban centers as urban-industrial cores, not merely as markets. To these urban-industrial cores, in Europe, North America, Japan, and Russia, flow agricultural (and industrial) raw materials and resources from virtually all parts of the inhabited world—and those cores, in turn, rework products for export and control much of the infrastructure and technology of shipment. This creates a world agricultural circulation of considerable complexity.

Understanding the basic features of global food circulation is critical to the agricultural regions shown on maps of world agriculture (Fig. 20-1). To make sense of that system, we need to examine its components in some detail. ◆

From the field notes

"This field trip through the Oregon wine country brings to mind a comment by a colleague to the effect that the vineyard is the most commercial of agricultural landscapes. That may be an exaggeration (think of terraced paddies and wheat fields extending to the horizon), but certainly the carefully tended, bright-green rows of evenly spaced vines create an unmistakable cultural landscape wherever they stand. Here at Tualatin Vineyards, as elsewhere in the Willamette Valley, we could see orchards retreating and vineyards advancing, led by the well-adapted Pinot Noir, the great red grape that made Burgundy famous. Rapid expansion of vineyards planted to this varietal, here being studied by our team of geographers, has made Oregon one of the world's leading producers of high-quality Pinot Noir wines. Winegrowing is a high-risk but also a high return enterprise, and the industry continues to diffuse worldwide, aided by global warming, consumer prosperity, and biotechnology."

◆ GLOBAL PATTERNS OF COMMERCIAL AGRICULTURE

Figure 20-1 reveals that virtually all countries have more than one kind of agricultural economy. Even at the small scale required by a global view, it is clear that numerous countries are divided into subsistence farming areas and commercial-crop production zones. Later, when we investigate secondary and tertiary economic activities, we will see similar regionalisms. In China, for example, the eastern provinces along the Pacific coast have strongly commercial economies, whereas much of the interior remains largely subsistence-based.

Cash Crops and Plantation Agriculture

Nonsubsistence farming in many poorer countries is a leftover from colonial times. Colonial powers implemented agriculture systems to benefit their needs, and this has tended to lock poorer countries into production of one or two "cash" crops. Cash farming continues to provide badly needed money, even if the conditions of sale to the urban-industrial world are unfavorable. In the Caribbean region, for example, whole national economies depend on sugar exports (sugar having been introduced by the European colonists centuries ago). These island countries naturally wish to sell the sugar at the highest possible price, but they are not in a position to dictate prices. Sugar is produced by many countries in various parts of the world, as well as by farmers in the technologically advanced countries (Fig. 20-1). Thus it is the importing countries that set tariffs and quotas, not the exporters, although regional and global agreements limit what can be done in this respect.

The extent of the importers' power can be seen in the case of Cuba. During its ideological quarrel with Cuba, the United States cut off all imports of Cuban sugar. Although Canada and the Soviet bloc continued to buy sugar from Cuba, loss of the U.S. market was a staggering blow to the Cuban economy. The wealthy importing countries can threaten the very survival of the economies of the producers—much like the farmers in von Thünen's Isolated State, who were at the mercy of decisions made by the buyers in the central-city marketplace.

There are occasional signs that the producing countries are seeking to form a cartel in order to present a united front to the importing countries, as the oil-producing states did during the 1970s. Such collective action is difficult, for several reasons. First, the wealthy importing countries can make deals with countries that are not members of the cartel. Second, the withholding of produce by exporting countries may stimulate domestic production among importers. For example, although cane sugar accounts for more than 70 percent of the commercial world sugar crop each year, farmers in the United States, Europe, and Russia produce sugar from sugar beets. In Europe and Russia these beets already yield 25 percent of the annual world sugar harvest. Collective action by countries producing sugarcane could easily cause that percentage to increase.

When cash crops are grown on large estates, we use the term ***plantation agriculture*** to describe the production system. Plantations are colonial legacies that persist in poorer, primarily tropical, countries along with subsistence farming. Figure 20-1 shows that plantation agriculture (7 in the legend) continues in Middle and South America, Africa, and South Asia. Laid out to produce bananas and sugar, coffee and cocoa in Middle and South America, rubber, cocoa, and tea in West and East Africa, tea in South Asia, and rubber in Southeast Asia, these plantations have outlasted the period of decolonization and continue to provide specialized crops to wealthier markets. Many plantations in former colonies are still owned by European or American individuals or

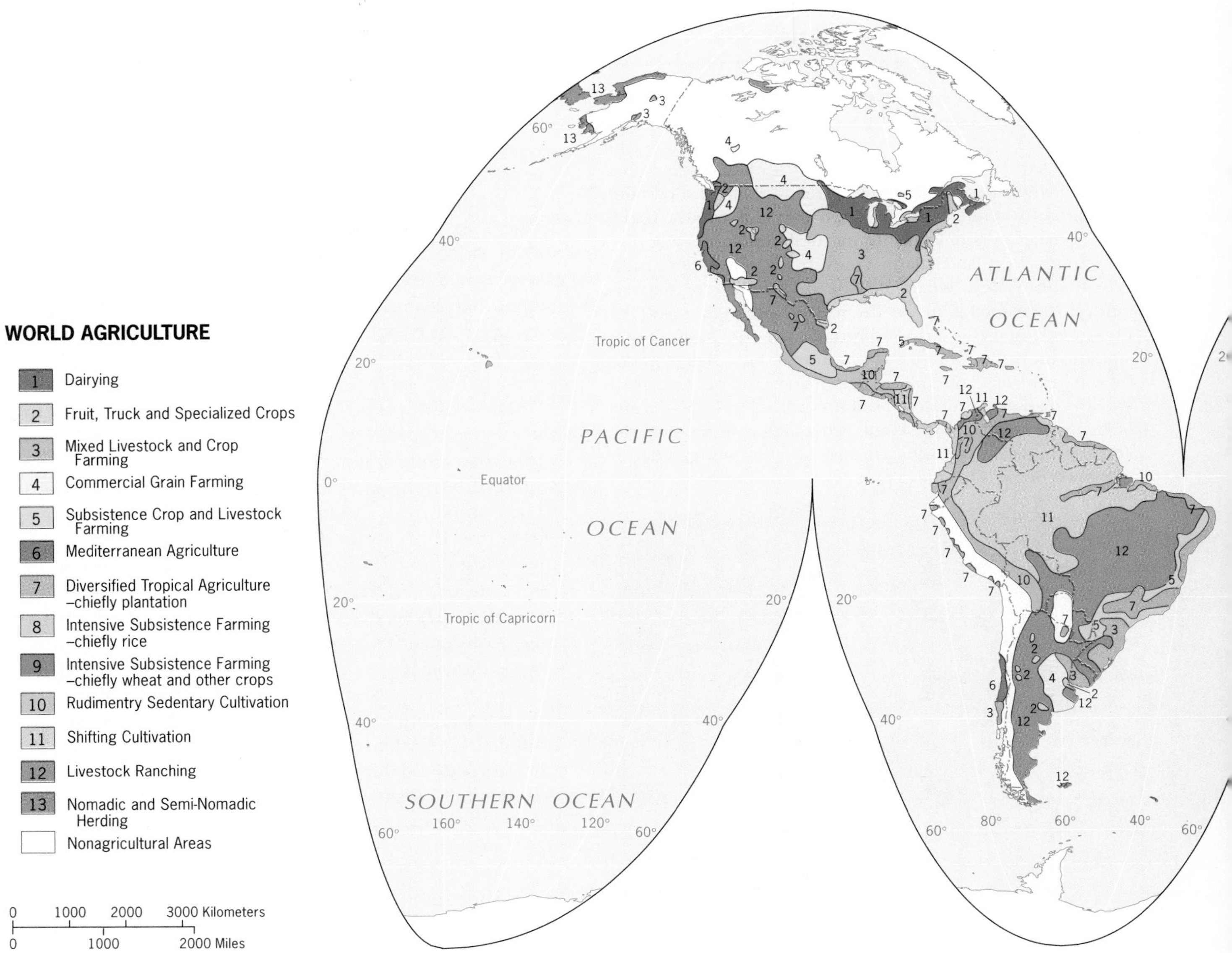

Figure 20-1 World Agriculture. Different kinds of agricultural areas are shown throughout the world. *Source*: From a map prepared by Hammond, Inc. for the first edition, 1977.

corporations, but even where they have been taken over by the governments of newly independent countries, they have often been kept in operation—because they are an important and immediate source of income.

Multinational corporations have tenaciously protected their economic interests in plantations. In the 1940s and 1950s, the Guatemalan government began an agrarian reform program. In part, the plan entailed renting unused land from foreign corporations to landless citizens at a low appraised value. The United Fruit Company, an American firm with extensive holdings in the country, was greatly concerned by this turn of events. The company had close ties to powerful individuals in the American government, including Secretary of State John Foster Dulles, CIA director Allen Dulles (the two were brothers), and Assistant Secretary of State for Inter-American Affairs John Moors Cabot. In 1954, the United States supported the overthrow of the government of Guatemala because of stated concerns about the spread of communism. This ended all land reform initiatives, however, leading many commentators to question the degree to which the United Fruit Company was behind the coup. Indeed, with the exception of President Eisenhower, every individual involved in the decision to help topple Guatemala's government had ties to the company. This example illustrates the inextricable links between economic and geopolitical circumstances—and it raises questions about the degree to which multinational

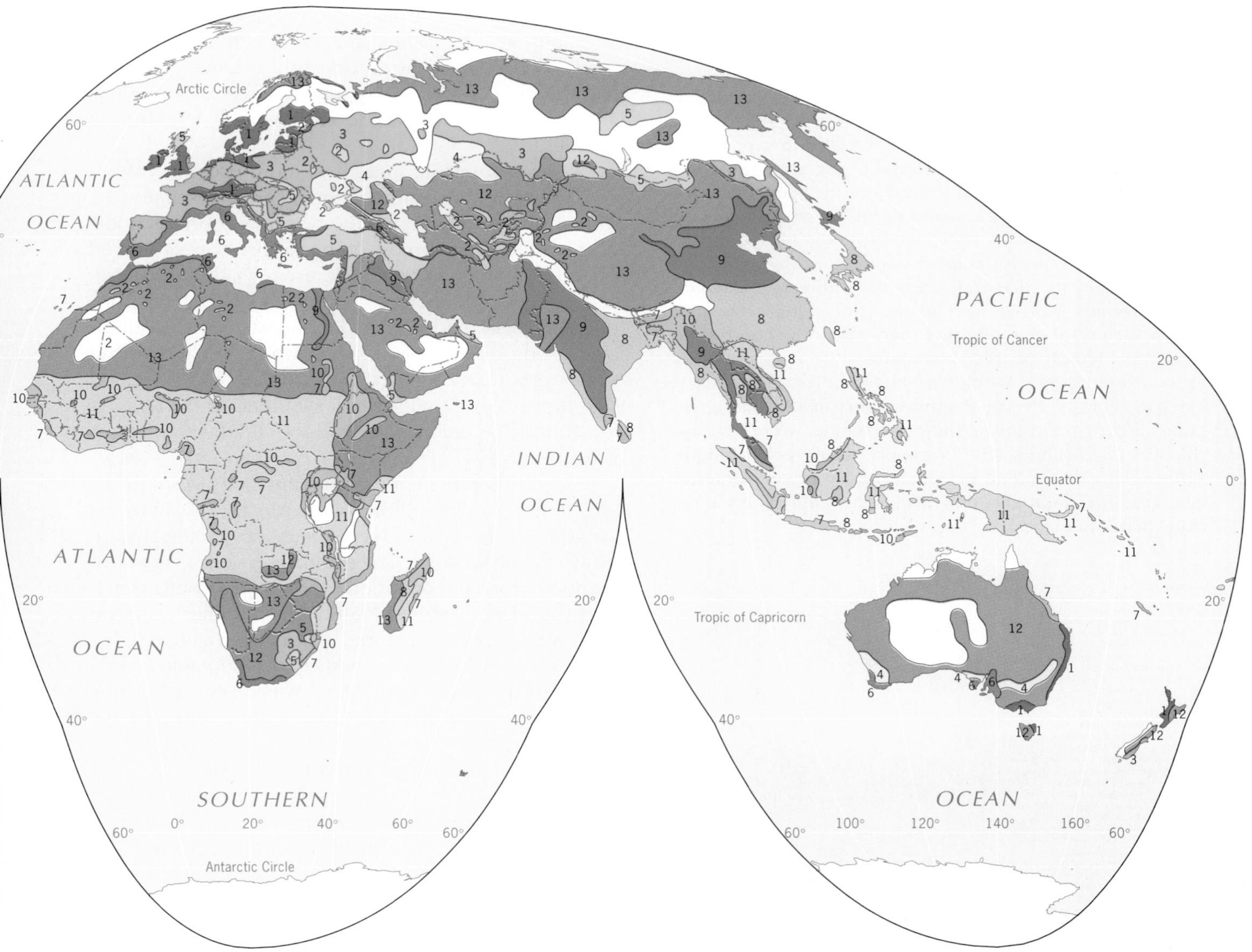

corporations based in wealthy countries influence decisions about agriculture in distant locations.

Cotton and Rubber Two of the most significant contemporary cash crops are cotton and rubber. Cotton production is not grown solely in former colonial areas; cotton is a major product in the southern United States and northeastern China, as well as several Central Asian Republics. But the colonial imprint is still recognizable. India, for example, began producing cotton on a large scale under the influence of British colonists. However, cotton cultivation was promoted on a smaller scale in numerous other countries: in Egypt's Nile delta, in the Punjab region shared by Pakistan and India, and in Sudan, Uganda, Mexico, and Brazil.

Cotton cultivation expanded greatly during the nineteenth century, when the Industrial Revolution produced machines for cotton ginning, spinning, and weaving that increased productive capacity, brought prices down, and put cotton goods within the reach of mass markets. As with sugar, the colonial powers laid out large-scale cotton plantations, sometimes under irrigation (e.g., the famed Jezira Scheme, in the triangle between the White Nile and Blue Nile rivers in Sudan). The colonial producers received low prices for their cotton, and the European industries prospered as cheap raw materials were converted into large quantities of items for sale at home and abroad.

Today many of the former colonial countries have established their own factories to produce goods for the domestic market, and synthetics, such as nylon and rayon, compete with cotton. Still, the wealthier countries have not stopped buying cotton, and cotton sales remain important for some former colonies. But they compete

From the field notes

"I had driven from Nairobi to Kisumu to visit a graduate student working on Luo markets in the Lake Victoria lowland, and headed back east via Kericho toward Maasai Mara. As the elevation rose and the topography took on a gentle roll, vast expanses of a meticulously maintained crop came into view—what a contrast to the crowded small-farm landscape on the plain! These were the tea plantations established by the British colonists and, more than a generation after Kenya's independence, still yielding important export revenues. I drove over to the processing center and talked to the (Kikuyu) manager there about the contrast between the densely peopled lowland and these open, luxury-crop covered slopes. Wouldn't it be better for these acres to carry food crops? He said that his country needed foreign income; apart from tourism, the opportunities were few, and this was one of them. In this respect, Kenya is not unique. An economy dependent, even in a small way, on plantation crops cannot simply abandon this land use and expect something better in place of it."

with cotton being grown in East Asia and North America. Much of the cotton purchased by Japan, the United Kingdom, and Western Europe, for example, comes from the United States.

The case of rubber is more complicated. Initially, rubber was collected from rubber-producing trees in equatorial rainforests, mainly in the Amazon Basin in northern South America. In those days, around 1900, the town of Manaus on the Amazon River experienced a rubber boom. Rubber companies in the Congo Basin in Africa experienced a similar period of prosperity. The boom in wild rubber was short-lived, however. Rubber-tree plantations were created to make rubber collection easier and more efficient. Seedlings of Brazilian rubber trees were planted elsewhere, and they did especially well in Southeast Asia. Within two decades nearly 90 percent of the world's rubber came from new plantations in colonial territories in Malaya, the Netherlands East Indies (now Indonesia), and neighboring colonies.

As time went on, more and more uses for rubber were found, and consumer demand grew continuously. The advent of the automobile was an enormous boost for the industry, and most of the rubber now produced is used to manufacture vehicle tires. World War II created a need for alternative sources of rubber, since Japan had occupied much of Southeast Asia. This stimulated the production of synthetic rubber. In 2001, world rubber production totaled approximately 17.7 million tons, more than 10 million of it synthetic; of the remainder, almost 70 percent was produced on the plantations of Southeast Asia.

The development of rubber plantations in Southeast Asia, rather than in sections of the Amazon Basin or the Congo Basin, is due less to environmental factors than to the availability of labor. The colonial powers were aware that Southeast Asia combined conditions of tropical environment and labor availability that neither Amazon South America nor Equatorial Africa could match. Eventually, a large-scale rubber industry developed in Liberia (West Africa), but in the 1990s it was destroyed during the country's disastrous civil war. Lately, efforts have been made to introduce the plantation system along the Amazon River in the heart of northern Brazil.

Luxury Crops Similar conditions—a combination of suitable environment and available labor—led the European colonial powers to establish huge plantations for the cultivation of ***luxury crops*** such as tea, cacao, coffee, and tobacco. Coffee was first domesticated in the region of present-day Ethiopia, but today it thrives in Middle and South America, where approximately 70 percent of the world's annual production is harvested. The United States buys more than half of all the coffee sold on world markets annually, and Western Europe imports most of the rest.

Coffee is one of the best examples of the colonial legacy's impact on present-day agricultural practices. In the early eighteenth century, coffee was virtually unknown in most of the world. After petroleum, coffee is now the second most valuable traded commodity in the world. The best-known image of coffee production in North America is probably that of Juan Valdez, who is portrayed as a simple yet proud Colombian peasant who handpicks beans by day and enjoys a cup of his own coffee by night. This image is quite contrary to the reality of much coffee production in Latin America, however; in many cases coffee is produced on enormous, foreign-owned plantations, where it is picked by local laborers who are hired at very low wage rates. Most coffee is sent abroad; and if the coffee pickers drink coffee, it is probably of the imported and instant variety.

Compared to coffee, tea is consumed in greater quantities in areas where it is grown: India, China, Sri Lanka, and Japan. Whereas coffee is cultivated and consumed mainly in the Americas, tea is the dominant beverage in Eurasia. It goes from the Asian-producing areas to the United Kingdom and the rest of Europe. Tea is a rather recent addition to the Western diet. It was grown in China perhaps 2000 years ago, but it became popular in Europe only during the nineteenth century. The colonial powers (mainly the British) established enormous tea plantations in Asia and thus began the full-scale flow of tea into European markets.

Commercial Livestock, Fruit, and Grain Agriculture

By far the largest areas of commercial agriculture (1 through 4 in the legend) lie outside the tropics. ***Dairying*** (1) is widespread at the northern margins of the mid-latitudes—particularly in the northeastern United States and in northwestern Europe. Fruit, truck, and specialized crops (2), including the market gardens von Thünen observed around Rostock, are found in the eastern and southeastern United States and in widely dispersed small areas where environments are favorable. (Major oases can be seen in the Sahara and in Central Asia.)

Mixed livestock and crop farming (3) is widespread in the more humid parts of the mid-latitudes, including much of the eastern United States, Western Europe, and western Russia, but it is also found in smaller areas in Uruguay, Brazil, and South Africa. Commercial grain farming (4) prevails in the drier parts of the mid-latitudes, including southern prairie provinces of Canada, in the Dakotas and Montana in the United States, as well as in Kansas and adjacent areas. Spring wheat (sown in the spring and harvested in the summer) grows in the northern zone, and winter wheat (sown in the autumn and harvested in the spring of the following year) is used in the southern area. An even larger belt of wheat farming extends from Ukraine through Russia into Kazakhstan. The Argentinean and Australian wheat zones are smaller in area, but their exports are an important component of world trade.

Even a cursory glance at Figure 20-1 reveals the wide distribution of ***livestock ranching*** (12). The raising of cattle for meat and of sheep for meat and wool developed in the wake of European colonization on vast tracts of natural pasture. In addition to the large cattle-ranching areas in the United States, Canada, and Mexico, much of eastern Brazil and Argentina are devoted to ranching, along with large tracts of Australia and New Zealand, as well as South Africa. You may see a Thünian pattern here: livestock ranching on the periphery and consumers in the cities. Refrigeration has overcome the problem of perishability, and high volume has lowered the unit cost of transporting beef, lamb, and other animal products.

Rice Growing

Note that commercial rice growing does not appear as a separate item in the legend, although it certainly exists. The United States is the world's leading exporter of rice, followed by Thailand and Vietnam. The reason has to do with the nature of most rice production. Wheat farming is carried out on huge landholdings with large machines that sow and harvest the grain. Rice, in contrast, is grown on small plots and is labor-intensive, so that subsistence and export production (at least in Southeast Asia) occur side by side. Despite the region's significant rice exports, most Southeast Asian farmers are subsistence farmers. Thus Southeast Asia appears on the map as primarily a subsistence grain-growing area.

Mediterranean Agriculture

Only one form of agriculture mentioned in the legend of Figure 20-1 refers to a particular climatic zone: ***Mediterranean agriculture*** (6). As the map shows, this kind of specialized farming occurs only in areas where the dry-summer Mediterranean climate prevails: along the shores of the Mediterranean Sea, in parts of California and Oregon, in central Chile, at South Africa's Cape, and in parts of southwestern and southern Australia. Here grows a special combination of crops: grapes, olives, citrus fruits, figs, certain vegetables, dates, and others. From these areas come many wines; these and other commodities are exported to distant markets because Mediterranean products tend to be popular and command high prices.

Illegal Drugs

One important crop that cannot be easily mapped is one that is turned into illegal drugs. Because of the high demand for drugs—particularly in wealthier parts of the world—farmers in poorer countries often find it more profitable to cultivate poppy, coca, or marijuana plants than to grow standard food crops. Cultivation of these plants increased steadily through the 1980s and 1990s, and they now constitute an important source of revenue for parts of the global economic periphery. Coca, the source plant of cocaine, is grown widely in Colombia, Peru, and Bolivia. Over half of the world's cultivation of coca occurs in Colombia alone. Heroin and opium are derived from opium poppy plants, grown predominantly in Southeast and Southwest Asia. According to the United Nations Office for Drug Control and Crime Prevention, over 90 percent of illegal opium production worldwide comes from Afghanistan and Myanmar. Cultivation of plants used for drugs is by no means limited to poorer countries, however; there are places in the United States where marijuana cultivation brings in substantial revenue.

◆ ENVIRONMENTAL IMPACTS OF COMMERCIAL AGRICULTURE

As we will examine in more detail in Part Eleven, agriculture has long been associated with significant environmental change. Travel to Mediterranean Europe today and you will see a landscape that reflects the clearing of forests in ancient times to facilitate agriculture and trade. Look carefully at many hillslopes and you will see evidence of terraces cut into the hills many centuries ago. Yet the industrialization and commercialization of agriculture has accelerated the pace and extent of agriculture's impact on the environment. More land has been cleared, and the land that is under cultivation is ever more intensively used. The result is an agricultural environment that not only supports an entirely different mix of plants and animals from what it might have supported if humans had never developed agriculture; the ecological fundamentals of agricultural areas are often radically altered.

Many ingredients to this alteration go far beyond the simple clearing of land. They range from soil erosion to changes in the organic content of soils to the presence of chemicals in soils and ground water. The impacts can be particularly severe when commercial agriculture expands into marginal environments. This has happened, for example, with the expansion of livestock herding into arid or semiarid areas (see the map of world climate, Figure 3-3). The natural vegetation in these areas cannot always sustain the herds, especially during prolonged droughts. This can lead to ecological damage and, in some areas, to desertification.

Looking Ahead

Organic Agriculture

One of the more remarkable recent trends in agriculture is the expansion of the production of "organic" products. ***Organic agriculture*** refers to crops produced without the use of synthetic or industrially produced pesticides and fertilizers. In wealthier parts of the world, the demand for organic products has risen exponentially in recent years. Sales of organic food in the United States, for example, went from under $200 million in 1980 to $1.5 billion by the early 1990s to some $4 billion by the late 1990s. This is still only a small percentage of all food sales in the country, but the growth rate is so strong that some predict organic sales will approach 10 percent of total U.S. food sales within a decade. Parts of Western Europe are already approaching that figure—notably Denmark, Sweden, Finland, and parts of Germany.

There are fields devoted to organic agriculture in both wealthy and less wealthy parts of the world. The crops receiving the most attention are coffee, tea, cacao, fruits and vegetables, nuts, oils, and spices. Compared to all land devoted to agriculture, the organic segment is still quite small, but a farmer who can gain organic certification from an internationally recognized third party has some prospect of developing a lucrative business. Yet unless the farmer is located in the United States, Western Europe, or Japan, he or she cannot expect to sell organic products locally. This is because the marketing and consumption of organic products are heavily concentrated in the countries that make up the global economic core.

Organic agriculture, then, has a very specific geographical character. It is an increasingly important part of agricultural production and consumption in wealthier countries, but it is only a (relatively minor) production issue in most poorer countries. Moreover, the position of organic agriculture in the latter countries mirrors the cash crop circulation system with roots in European colonialism, for production is almost entirely for export to the global economic core.

The organic movement has some clear environmental benefits, particularly in the prospect of reducing levels of synthetic chemicals in soil and water. Moreover, some organic farmers have extracted themselves to some degree from the control of large, external corporate interests. And the health and taste advantages of organic produce are likely to ensure the continued growth of the organics movement in parts of the world. Twenty years from now we can expect to see more land devoted to organic production and an expanding presence for organic products on the shelves of stores in the more affluent parts of the world.

None of this means that we are on the cusp of a major revolution in agriculture, however. The costs of organic production are likely to remain relatively high, and this type of agriculture will thus have relatively little impact on 80 percent of the world's peoples. A telling sign is that the organic movement has had little effect on the production of the staple foods on which billions of people depend. In addition, large corporate entities are playing an increasingly prominent role in the organic movement—raising controversies about standards and rendering illusory the ideal of the independent organic farmer engaged in sustainable agriculture.

In short, there are powerful economic forces that are working a large-scale shift away from traditional commercial agriculture. Looking ahead, then, we can expect organic agriculture to occupy only a somewhat specialized, if growing, niche in the larger agricultural picture.

In recent years the popularity of fast-food chains that serve hamburgers has led to the deforestation of wooded areas in order to open up additional pastures for beef cattle, notably in Central and South America. Livestock ranching is an extremely land- water- and energy-intensive process. Significant land must be turned over to the cultivation of cattle feed, and the animals themselves need extensive grazing areas. By stripping away vegetation, the animals can promote the erosion of river banks, with implications for everything from water quality to wildlife habitat.

In places where large commercial crop farms dominate, the greatest concerns often center around the introduction of chemical fertilizers and pesticides into the environment—as well as soil erosion. And the movement toward genetically modified crops (see below) carries with it another set of environmental concerns. Yet in some parts of the world there is a growing movement to alter some of the ways in which agriculture is practiced (see Looking Ahead Box—Organic Agriculture). The impacts of this movement are still spatially limited, but they are growing.

◆ THE THIRD AGRICULTURAL REVOLUTION

As we saw at the beginning of this Part Six, 12,000 years ago momentous developments were taking place in a few small areas of Southwest Asia. These involved sowing seed and harvesting grain, and they produced the First Agricultural Revolution. Three hundred years ago, a Second Agricultural Revolution occurred as improved equipment, better farming methods, and other innovations greatly increased the productivity of European farming. The Industrial Revolution stimulated the modernization of farming and helped spread it around the world. Over the past several decades, a ***Third Agricultural Revolution*** has been in progress. It has occurred in laboratories and plant nurseries. It is the product of the age of ***biotechnology***.

The Green Revolution

The Third Agricultural Revolution began in the 1960s, when scientists at a research institution in the Philippines crossed a dwarf Chinese variety of rice with an Indonesian variety and produced IR8. This "artificial" rice plant had a number of desirable properties: it developed a bigger "head" of grain, and it had a stronger stem that did not collapse under the added weight. IR8 produced much better yields than either of its "parents," but the researchers were not satisfied. In 1982 they produced IR36, which was bred from 13 parents to achieve genetic resistance against 15 pests and a growing cycle of 110 days under warm conditions, thus making possible three crops per year. By 1992, IR36 was the most widely grown crop on Earth, and in September 1994, scientists developed a strain of rice that was even more productive than IR36.

The so-called ***Green Revolution*** represented by the hybrid rice initiative had its roots in the 1930s, when agricultural scientists in the American Midwest began experimenting with technologically manipulated seed varieties to increase crop yields. By the 1940s, American agriculturalists were exporting their ideas to Mexico, and the success of the endeavor led to the blossoming of the Green Revolution in the 1960s. In addition to the hybrid rice initiative, new high-yield varieties of wheat and corn were developed and were diffused to other parts of the world—particularly South and Southeast Asia.

Coming at a time of growing concern about global hunger, the successes of the Green Revolution were truly extraordinary. The disastrous famines of the past have been avoided as a result of increased yields of grains. India became self-sufficient in grain production by the 1980s, and Asia saw a two-thirds increase in rice production between 1970 and 1995. Such achievements were not simply the product of new seed varieties; they also required fertilizers, pesticides, irrigation in some places, and significant capital improvements. This meant that the social and environmental consequences of the Green Revolution were not always benign. Higher inputs of chemical fertilizers and pesticides can lead to a reduction of organic matter in the soil and to groundwater pollution. Moreover, many small-scale farmers lack the resources to acquire genetically enhanced seeds and the necessary fertilizers and pesticides. Hence, these farmers are in a poor competitive position, and some are being driven off their lands. In addition, the need for capital from the West to implement Green Revolution technologies has led to a shift away from production for local consumers toward export agriculture.

Whatever the downside, the Green Revolution is clearly here to stay, for there would be a massive hunger problem if farmers turned away from technologically enhanced food production. The geographical impact of the Green Revolution is highly variable, however. Its traditional focus on rice, wheat, and corn means that it has had only limited impact throughout much of Africa, where agriculture is based on different crops and where lower soil fertility makes agriculture a less attractive external prospect for external investment.

New Genetically Modified Foods

An entire field of biotechnology has sprung up in conjunction with the Third Agricultural Revolution, and the development of genetically modified foods is its principal orientation. Some of the work continues to focus on traditional Green Revolution crops. Researchers at the International Rice Research Institute, for example, are working to breed a genetically modified "super rice" that will not have to be transplanted as seedlings but can be seeded directly in the paddy soil. It will have the virtues of its predecessors but will yield nearly twice as much rice per acre than the average for strains in current use.

The charting of the genome of rice (the 12 chromosomes that carry all of the plant's characteristics) is under way, so it may also be possible to transform rice genetically so that it will continuously acquire more desirable properties. Not only could yields improve; so could resistance to diseases and pests.

Increasingly, researchers are turning their attention to new agricultural products, and this could expand the geographical impact of the Green Revolution. Research has already led to methods for producing high-yield cassava and sorghum—both of which are grown in Africa. And beyond Africa, research on fattening livestock faster and improving the appearance of fruits is having an impact in North and South America.

The promise of such developments in a world in which almost a billion people are malnourished—and in which population continues to expand—is evident. Yet much controversy surrounds the development of genetically modified food. Of course, farmers have been involved in some genetic modification for millennia; cross breeding and selective breeding are age-old approaches to enhancing quality and quantity. What is controversial is the application of modern technology in the service of genetic modification. The concern is that gene manipulation could create health risks and produce environmental hazards. It was found, for example, that the consumption of soybeans that contain brazil nut proteins could produce allergic reactions in some people—and some worry that if this had not been recognized, people could have been harmed. Moreover, some environmentalists have speculated about the impacts of pollen dispersal from genetically modified plants and the potential for disease-resistant plants to spur the evolution of super-pests.

One of the difficulties of assessing the situation at present is that developments are occurring so fast that it is not easy to keep up with them. Not all the available evidence is negative, however. Plants that are genetically modified to reduce susceptibility to disease can reduce the use of toxic pesticides, and there are no known instances of people being harmed by genetically modified food. As a result, some parts of the world are moving rapidly to embrace genetically modified food. China, for example, is growing an increasing amount of genetically modified tomatoes, rice, and cotton—and in North

A SENSE OF SCALE

The Impact of Changing Agricultural Practices

Recent shifts from subsistence agriculture to commercial agriculture have had dramatic impacts on rural life. Land-use patterns, land ownership arrangements, and agricultural labor conditions have all changed as rural residents cope with shifting economic, political, and environmental conditions. Interestingly, changes in agricultural practices have affected different parts of the world in different ways. In the more industrialized realms, we have witnessed increased mechanization, consolidation of smaller farms into larger corporate units, and increased crop specialization. In the less industrialized world, changes in agricultural practices have had a variety of impacts.

In Latin America, dramatic increases in the production of export crops (or *cash crops* like fruits and coffee) have occurred at the expense of crop production for local consumption. In the process, subsistence farming has been pushed to ever more marginal lands. In Asia, where the "Green Revolution" has had the greatest impact, the production of cereal crops (grains such as rice and wheat) has increased for both foreign and domestic markets. Agricultural production in this region remains relatively small in scale and quite dependent on manual labor. In Subsaharan Africa, total commercialized agriculture has increased but overall agricultural exports have decreased. As in Asia, farm units in Subsaharan Africa have remained relatively small and dependent on intensified manual labor.

What this regional-scale analysis does not tell us is how these changes have affected local rural communities. These changes can be environmental, economic, and social. A recent study in the small country of Gambia (West Africa) by geographer Judith Carney has shown how changing agricultural practices have altered not only the rural environment and economy, but also relations between men and women. Over the last 30 years international developmental assistance of Gambia has led to ambitious projects designed to convert wetlands to irrigated agricultural lands, making possible production of rice year-round. By the late 1980s, virtually all of the country's suitable wetlands had been converted to year-round rice production. This transformation created tensions within rural households by converting lands traditionally used by women for family subsistence into commercialized farming plots. In addition, when rice production was turned into a year-round occupation, women found themselves with less time for other activities crucial for household maintenance. This situation underscores the fact that in Africa, as in much of the rest of the less-industrialized world, agricultural work is overwhelmingly carried out by women. In Subsaharan Africa over 85 percent of all women in the labor force work in agriculture, while in China the number is close to 75 percent and in India 70 percent. A geographical perspective that is sensitive to scale helps to shed light on how changes in agricultural practices throughout the world not only alter rural landscapes but also affect family and community relationships.

America the amount of land area given over to genetically modified crop production is expanding rapidly.

The geography of genetically modified food production and consumption is variable, however. Many of the poorer countries of the world do not have access to the necessary capital and technology. Moreover, ideological resistance is strong in some places—particularly Western Europe. Agricultural officials in most West European countries have declared genetically modified foods to be safe, but there is a strong public reaction against them based on combined concerns about health and taste. Such concerns have spread to less affluent parts of the world as well, and debates are currently raging in India, for example, about the acceptability of planting genetically modified cotton.

Whatever opposition may exist, the continuing challenge of feeding the world's expanding population will likely fuel continued investment in biotechnology—and we can therefore expect that controversies over genetically modified foods will continue. Feeding the world's hungry is not solely a production problem, however. There is currently enough food to go around, but the political will and social infrastructure to get it to many who need it are lacking. Biotechnology can play a role in addressing the problem of hunger, but it cannot solve the problem.

◆ AGRIBUSINESS AND THE CHANGING GEOGRAPHY OF AGRICULTURE

The commercialization of crop production and associated applications of technology has not just changed what is grown; it has profoundly altered the very nature of agriculture. Most obviously, it has transformed farms into corporate-like units—giving rise to the term ***agribusiness***. The impetus for this change comes from large-scale social, economic, and technological developments, which in turn are transforming the character of rural life at the local scale (see Sense of Scale box). Agribusiness serves to connect local farms to a spatially extensive web of production and exchange. At the same time, it fosters the spatial concentration of agricultural activities. Both of these trends are revealed in the development of the poultry industry in the United States.

Early in the twentieth century, poultry production in the United States was highly disaggregated—with many farmers raising a few chickens as part of a multifaceted farming operation. Over the past 50 years, however, poultry production has fundamentally changed. In an article on modern agriculture, geographer David Lanegran summarizes the impact of this transformation as follows:

> Today, chickens are produced by large agribusiness companies operating hatcheries, feed mills, and processing plants. They supply chicks and feed to the farmers. The farmers are responsible for building a house and maintaining proper temperature and water supply. Once a week the companies fill the feed bins for the farmers, and guarantee them a price for the birds. The companies even collect market-ready birds and take them away for processing and marketing. Most of the nation's poultry supply is handled by a half dozen very large corporations that control the process from chicks to chicken pieces in stores.

Lanegran goes on to show how selective breeding has produced faster growing, bigger chickens, which are housed in enormous broiler houses that are largely mechanized. These are concentrated in northwestern Arkansas, northern Georgia, the Piedmont areas of North Carolina, and the Shenandoah Valley of Virginia. He shows that in many respects the "farmers" who manage these operations are involved in manufacturing as much or more than farming. They are as likely to spend their time talking to bank officers, overseeing the repair of equipment, and negotiating with vendors as they are tending their animals. As such, they symbolize the breakdown between the rural and the urban in some parts of the world—as well as the interconnections between rural places and distant markets.

Agribusiness is shaping the world distribution of commercial agricultural systems and their relationship to subsistence agriculture. Through time, many factors

From the field notes

"The technology of refrigeration has kept pace with the containerization of seaborne freight traffic. When we sailed into the port of Dunedin, New Zealand, I was unsure of just what those red boxes were. Closer inspection revealed that they are refrigeration units, to which incoming containers are attached. Meats and other perishables can thus be kept frozen until they are transferred to a refrigerator ship."

have affected that relationship. History and tradition have played important roles, as have environment and technology. At times governments have encouraged their citizens to limit family size in an attempt to lift the population above the subsistence level. Some governments have sought to maintain the privileges of large landowners, whereas others have initiated bold land reform programs. Communist governments, notably those of the former Soviet Union and Maoist China, have tried to control agricultural output by creating collective farms and agricultural communes—a giant experiment that resulted in significant displacement of rural peoples and mixed results in terms of output. (Today farming reprivatization is under way in both countries.)

Most of all, the map of global agricultural regions reveals the capacity of markets to influence the activities of farmers. The range and variety of products on the shelves of urban supermarkets in the United States is a world away from the constant quest for sufficient, nutritionally balanced food that exists in some places. A global network of farm production is oriented to the one-fifth of the world's population that is highly urbanized, wealthy, and powerful. Few farmers in distant lands have real control over land-use decisions, for the nations in the global economic core continue to decide what will be bought at what price. The colonial era may have come to an end, but, as Figure 20-1 reminds us, its imprint remains strong.

◆ KEY TERMS ◆

agribusiness
biotechnology
commercial agriculture
dairying
Green Revolution
livestock ranching
luxury crops
Mediterranean agriculture
organic agriculture
plantation agriculture
Third Agricultural Revolution

◆ APPLYING GEOGRAPHIC KNOWLEDGE ◆

1. For many years, Caribbean islands such as St. Lucia have been exporting bananas to markets in North America and Europe, with their industries protected by preferential trade agreements. Now those agreements are ending as trade barriers fall all over the world, and the single-crop economies of the Caribbean are in trouble. What are the options for the farmers of St. Lucia and its neighbors? Can the small-island economies be diversified? Relate your answer to core-periphery contrasts in the modern world.
2. Why is it difficult for producing countries in the periphery to create and sustain cooperative cartels that might protect their joint interests on markets of countries in the global economic core?

Part Six
LAND AND LAND USE IN THE RURAL SECTOR
At Issue: Revisited

Should poor-country commercial farmers be protected against the avarice of the rich markets? The liberalization of trade has fostered an extraordinary global movement of agricultural products. The beneficiaries of this trade range from consumers in wealthier parts of the world to the owners of lands on which high-value crops are produced. But the economic fortunes of many commercial farmers in the poor parts of the world are vulnerable to the whims of the international market, and the environmental costs of shifting to large-scale commercial farming are often high. It is difficult to confront such issues without protective measures, yet the major players in the international economy show no signs of abandoning the free trade principle. As pressure grows on the economies and environments of farmers in less well-off areas, steps for improvement will become increasingly necessary. Effective measures will require cooperation among farmers and the political/business elite in poorer parts of the world—a difficult prospect given the vested interests of much of that elite in the status quo.

◆ SELECTED REFERENCES ◆

Part Six Life in the Rural Sector

Blaikie, P. *The Political Economy of Soil Erosion in Developing Countries* (London: Longman, 1985).

Blaikie, P., & Brookfield, H. *Land Degradation and Society* (London: Methuen, 1987).

Boserup, E. *The Conditions of Agricultural Growth: The Economics of Agrarian Change under Population Pressure* (Chicago: Aldine, 1966).

Bowler, I. R., ed. *The Geography of Agriculture in Developed Market Economies* (New York: Wiley, 1992).

Bunting, A. H. ed. *Change in Agriculture* (New York: Praeger Publ. 1970).

Carney, J. A. "Converting the Wetlands, Engendering the Environment: The Intersection of Gender with Agrarian Change in Gambia," in R. Peet & M. J. Watts, eds., *Liberation Ecologies* (London: Routledge, 1996).

Dalal-Clayton, D., ed. *Black's Agricultural Dictionary.* 2nd rev. ed. (Totowa, N.J.: Barnes & Noble, 1986).

de Blij, H. *Wine: A Geographic Appreciation* (Totowa, N.J.: Rowman & Allanheld, 1983).

de Blij, H. *Wine Regions of the Southern Hemisphere* (Totowa, N.J.: Rowman & Allanheld, 1985).

de Souza, A. *World Space-Economy.* 2nd rev. ed., (Columbus, Ohio: Charles E. Merrill, 1989).

Duckham, A. N., & Masefield, G. B. *Farming Systems of the World* (New York: Praeger, 1970).

Goodman, D., & Redclift, M. *Refashioning Nature: Food, Ecology, and Culture* (London: Routledge, 1991).

Gourou, P. *The Tropical World: Its Social and Economic Conditions and Its Future Status.* 5th rev. ed., trans. S. Beaver (London and New York: Longman, 1980).

Grigg, D. *Population Growth and Agrarian Change* (London: Cambridge University Press, 1980).

Grigg, D. *An Introduction to Agricultural Geography.* 2nd ed. (London: Routledge, 1995).

Gritzner, J. A. *The West African Sahel: Human Agency and Environmental Change* (Chicago: University of Chicago Geography Research Paper No. 226, 1988).

Harris, D., ed. *Human Ecology in Savanna Environments* (New York and London; Academic Press, 1980).

Hart, J. F. *The Land That Feeds Us: The Story of American Farmers* (New York: W. W. Norton, 1991).

Heiser, C., Jr., *Seed to Civilization: The Story of Food* (Cambridge, Mass.: Harvard University Press, 1990).

Horvath, R. "Von Thünen's Isolated State and the Area Around Addis Ababa, Ethiopia," *Annals of the Association of American Geographers* 59 (1969): 308–323.

Ilbery, B. W. *Agricultural Geography: A Social and Economic Analysis* (Oxford: Oxford University Press, 1985).

Ilbery, B. W., et al., eds. *Agricultural Restructuring and Sustainability: A Geographical Perspective* (New York: CAB International, 1997).

Keen, E. A. *Ownership and Productivity of Marine Fishery Resources* (Blacksburg, Va.: McDonald & Woodward, 1988).

Klee, G., ed. *World Systems of Traditional Resource Management* (New York: Halsted Press N.H. Winston, 1980).

Knox, P., & Agnew, J. *The Geography of the World Economy.* 2nd ed. (London: Edward Arnold, 1994).

Lanegran, D. A. "Modern Agriculture in Advanced Placement Human Geography." *Journal of Geography* 99, no.3/4 (2000): 132–141.

Levi, J., & Havinden, M. *Economics of African Agriculture* (Harlow, U.K.: Longman, 1982).

Little, P. D., & Watts, M. J. *Living under Contract: Contract Farming and Agrarian Transformation in Sub-Saharan Africa* (Madison: University of Wisconsin Press, 1994).

Moris, J. R., & Thom, D. J. *Irrigation Development in Africa: Lessons of Experience* (Boulder, Colo.: Westview Press, 1990).

Nelson, T. "Urban Agriculture." *World Watch* 9 (1996): 10–17.

Sauer, C. O. *Agricultural Origins and Dispersals.* 2nd rev. ed. (Cambridge, Mass.: MIT Press, 1969).

Spencer, J., & Horvath, R. "How Does an Agricultural Region Originate?" *Annals of the Association of American Geographers* 53 (1963): 74–82.

Spencer, J. E. and William H. Thomas *Cultural Geography: Introduction to Our Humanized Earth.* (Artography by R. E. Winter (New York: Wiley, 1969).

Troughton, M. J. "Farming Systems in the Modern World," in M. Pacione, ed., *Progress in Agricultural Geography* (1986), pp. 90–97.

Von Thünen, J. H. *Der Isolierte Staat,* trans. C. M. Wartenberg, in P. Hall, ed., *Von Thünen's Isolated State* (Elmsford, N.Y.: Pergamon, 1966).

Whittlesey, D. "Major Agricultural Regions of the Earth." *Annals of the Association of American Geographers* 26 (1936): 199–240.

Yellen, J. E. "The Transformation of the Kalahari !Kung," *Scientific American,* April 1990, pp. 96–105.

Part Seven

THE URBANIZING WORLD

At Issue

During the post–World War II era, a house in the suburbs became the American ideal, and suburbanization pulled an ever-larger number of residents from central cities to the outskirts. A single spacious home, a two-car garage, a patio, perhaps a pool, separation, and privacy were the attractions of suburban life. In the decaying inner cities, push factors abounded: deteriorating schools, disintegrating neighborhoods, declining services, frightening crime. Suburbanization has robbed the central city of much of its tax base, leaving city governments without the means to reverse the tide. In the United States today, the future of the urban core is in question. *Should the central city be saved, and should suburbanites, who commute downtown every day to earn their salaries, help pay for this? Or should it be left to be transformed by the forces that are reshaping America's urban areas?*

Pull factor for urbanites the world over: spacious, leafy suburbia. Hobart, Tasmania

Part Outline

Chapter 21

Civilization and Urbanization

From the field notes

"The Greek Island of Delos is a window on a time when this was a pivotal place in the Aegean Sea, and indeed in a much larger maritime region. Delos was the Hong Kong of the Mediterranean, a place of magnificent temples, sculptures, theaters, and aqueducts. It had a bustling harbor at least 3,000 years ago, an entrepot that housed and transferred slaves, wild animals, and goods from Africa and Asia. Delos fell to the Greeks and later to the Romans, and for a time was a free port. But the foci of trade in the region changed, and Delos collapsed. All this happened before the birth of Jesus; later, this magnificent site was quarried for building stone by, among others, Venetians and Turks. Today Delos is a national monument, uninhabited, to preserve what remains of a creative and turbulent past."

KEY POINTS

- ◆ **Urbanization and the formation of states transformed egalitarian societies into stratified, functionally specialized ones. This process occurred independently in several regions, probably first in the Fertile Crescent.**

- ◆ **The ancient Greeks assimilated concepts of urban life from Mesopotamia as well as Minoa. They produced the most highly urbanized society of their time, 2500 years ago.**

- ◆ **The ancient Romans combined local traditions with Greek customs in building an urban system that extended from Britain to Mesopotamia. All of the urban centers of the Roman Empire were linked together by a network of land and water routes.**

- ◆ **Southwest Asians and Europeans did not hold a monopoly over the process of urbanization. Cities evolved in other culture regions as well, including East Asia, West Africa, and Mesoamerica.**

- ◆ **Greek and Roman concepts of urbanization diffused into Western Europe, but Europe's preindustrial cities were poorly organized, unsanitary, overcrowded, and uncomfortable places to live for the majority of their inhabitants.**

- ◆ **Cities evolve in stages. The traders' mercantile city gave way to the factory-dominated manufacturing center, and the automobile enabled the evolution of the suburbanized modern city. Today's "postmodern" cities reflect the age of high technology.**

Virtually everywhere in the world, people are moving from the countryside to towns and cities. This migration is happening so fast that the various agencies that monitor it, such as the United Nations and the World Bank, cannot agree on the pace. In 1994, one such bureau announced that by its observations, the world's urban population was about to outnumber the rural one. Newspapers and television newscasts marked this as a momentous occasion: from 1994 on, more people would live in towns and cities than in rural areas. Other tabulators disagreed, however, and reported that the 50 percent benchmark would not be reached until early in the twenty-first century. The problem of undependable census data (Chapter 4) and inconsistent definitions (Chapter 19) made agreement all but impossible. Nevertheless, every indicator pointed to the same conclusion: in the twenty-first century, the world will be predominantly urban.

Urbanization is not evenly distributed around the globe, however. In Western Europe, the United States, Canada, and Japan, four out of five citizens live in cities or towns. In India and China, the figure is closer to three out of ten. Yet even where urbanization remains low, people are moving to towns and cities. The city of Shenzhen in China was the world's fastest-growing urban area during the second half of the twentieth century; its population increased from about 20,000 to 2.5 million in three decades. When a major development project was announced in Shanghai, nearly 3 million people rushed to the area, hoping to find work. Two of the world's fastest-growing cities, Calcutta and Mumbai (Bombay) in India, also rank among the 10 largest.

It is difficult to think of a human world without cities. Cities are the centers of political power and industrial might, higher education and technological innovation, artistic achievement and medical advances. They are the great markets, centers of specialization and interaction, sources of news and information, suppliers of services, and providers of sports and entertainment. Cities are the anchors of modern culture: the urban system and its spokes form the structural skeleton of society.

And yet, the rise of the city is a very recent phenomenon in human history. If human communities have existed for 100,000 years, they did not cluster into towns until more than 90,000 years had passed. Humans migrated far and wide, glaciations came and went, and cli-

mates warmed and cooled. But not until about 8000 years ago did some human settlements begin to grow into larger places.

In Part Seven we trace the evolution of urbanization in geographic context, identify the factors that influenced the location and growth (or decline) of cities, investigate the internal structure of cities in various cultural settings, and note the serious problems created by rapid urban growth. We start by looking back at the beginnings of urbanization. ◆

◆ ANCIENT CITIES AND EARLY CIVILIZATIONS

In earlier chapters we noted the beginnings of the diffusion of agriculture between 10,000 and 12,000 years ago. Populations grew and people migrated outward from the early agricultural hearths, carrying their knowledge of farming with them. Settlements became more sedentary; languages diffused and diversified.

For several thousand years those settlements remained true villages. They were small and did not vary much in size. The households they contained had about the same amount of possessions and status. Apparently, no governmental authority existed beyond the village. There were no public buildings and no workshops. ***Egalitarian societies*** persisted long after agriculture was introduced.

Scholars are fairly certain that this was the situation in the region of the Fertile Crescent and the areas into which agricultural innovations diffused. There is evidence that the same conditions prevailed in other, later hearths of agricultural innovation. In Southwest Asia things began to change in about 6000 B.P. as agricultural societies became more complex with the introduction of irrigation and larger-scale farming. There is also evidence that social inequality was developing. The size of houses began to vary. Some people had more property than others and were buried with the best of their Earthly belongings. Specialization developed as some people remained farmers, whereas others were craftspeople or became involved in government. Government buildings and workshops appeared, and the village became more diversified.

Cities and States

None of this made a city out of a village, but now an important political development occurred. As some villages grew larger and increasing specialization took place in the work that people did, there was a greater need for political systems and structures. Thus it is not surprising that groups of settlements came under the control of a central authority. This was the beginning of the formation of the ***state***, a process that was to lead to the rise of ancient Egypt, Greece, the Roman Empire, and ultimately, the modern state.

The rise of the earliest states is closely linked to the evolution of the first cities. But when did a group of villages controlled by a central government become a state? In a 1975 article, anthropologists Henry Wright and Gregory Johnson proposed that the existence of an early state can be deduced from the presence of a centralized political hierarchy with at least three levels of administration. They analyzed an area in present-day southwestern Iran that contained evidence of more than four dozen settlements. The great majority of these settlements were small villages, but four larger "towns" could be identified, and one center was even larger than these towns. So there was a dominant urban center, the probable capital, where the power likely was concentrated, and two levels of settlement below it. This suggests that a state had arisen there more than 5000 years ago.

The period between about 7000 B.P. and 5000 B.P. is called the ***formative era*** for both the development of states and urbanization—the two obviously went hand in hand—in Southwest Asia. Toward the end of that period, there was a large state in the lower basin of the Tigris-Euphrates (Mesopotamia) with a number of cities, including Ur. Sumer's cities had impressive temples on high artificial mounds, as well as imposing public buildings, army barracks, numerous workshops, and dwellings of various sizes. The egalitarian society had become a ***stratified society***. Now there were priests, merchants, administrators, soldiers, farmers, craftspeople, and slaves. The city had become the focus of the culture.

Function and Location

The ancient city was also the organizational focus of the state. Agriculture had to be planned so as to guarantee a flow of food into the city—a task that became even more complicated when irrigation systems developed. Some scholars believe that the earliest civilizations emerged from the need for organization that arose when irrigation was invented. The collection of taxes and tribute from an expanding region under the city's control also had to be organized. Soon the city needed to be protected against enemies, and this required collective action—for example, to build fortified walls.

The geographic advantages of certain locations, as well as the organization of the community, influenced the growth of ancient towns and cities. Not only proximity to productive farmlands but also the availability of water and the defensibility of the site contributed to the durability of certain towns. Towns in Mesopotamia enjoyed secure food supplies (see Fig. 3–3). In the Indus Basin, the first cities were served by carefully maintained stone-lined wells (see Harappa and Mohenjo-Daro in Fig. 21–1). Also significant was the position of towns on ancient travel and trade routes. Where such routes converged on an urban place, there were contact, interaction, and growth. Less accessible, more isolated places were at a disadvantage.

Urban growth tested the ingenuity of the town's leaders. Food not only had to be acquired and stored but also distributed. This required an ***urban elite***, a group of decision makers and organizers who controlled the resources, and sometimes the lives, of others. An urban elite could afford to devote time to such pursuits as religion and philosophy. Out of such pursuits came the concept of writing and recordkeeping. Writing made possible the codification of laws and the preservation of traditions. It was a crucial element in the development of systematic administration in Mesopotamia and in the evolution of its religious-political ideology. The rulers in the cities were both priests and kings, and the harvest brought by the peasants to be stored in urban granaries was a tribute as well as a tax.

Archeologists, often teaming up with anthropologists and geographers, have learned much about the ways ancient Mesopotamian cities functioned. The ancient Mesopotamian city was usually protected by an earthen wall that surrounded the entire community, or, sometimes, the cluster of temples and shrines at its center. Temples dominated the urban landscape, not only because they were the largest structures in town but also because they were built on artificial mounds often over 100 feet (30 meters) high.

Priests and other authorities resided in substantial buildings, many of which might be called palaces. Ordinary citizens lived in mud-walled houses packed closely together and separated only by narrow lanes. Facing these lanes were shops and the workplaces of craftspeople. On the outskirts of the city were the homes of the poorest inhabitants. These were little more than tiny huts, often with mud-smeared reed walls. Slaves were held in prison-like accommodations, sometimes outside the city wall.

Lacking waste-disposal or sewage facilities, ancient cities were far from sanitary. Mesopotamians threw their

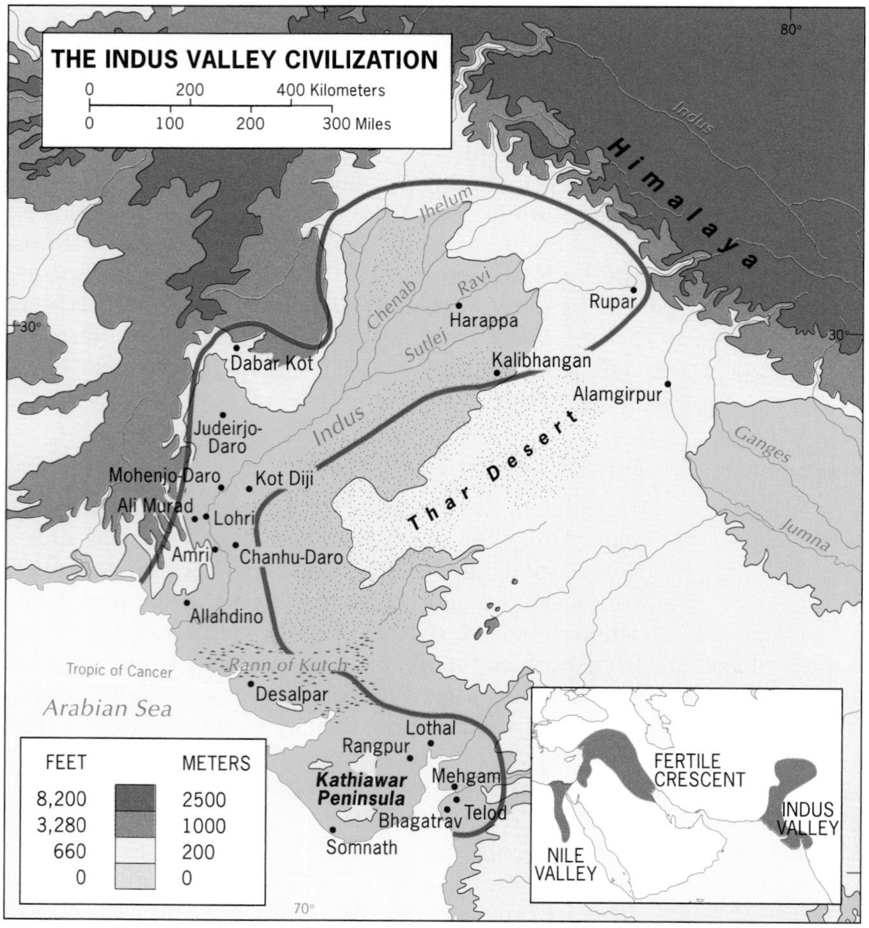

Figure 21-1 The Indus Valley Civilization. The Indus Basin was a crucible, a hearth of culture whose innovations diffused into India.

garbage and refuse into the streets and other open spaces, and in some places layers of this waste accumulated to a depth of several yards. In a way this was fortunate because archeologists have been able to sift through the garbage for clues to life in the ancient city. Not surprisingly, disease was among the reasons the populations of ancient cities remained small.

Thus ancient cities had several functions. As centers of power, they became the headquarters of the first state-like entities the world had seen. As religious centers, their authority was augmented by the presence of priests, temples, and shrines. Many ancient cities were ***theocratic centers*** where rulers were deemed to have divine authority and were, in effect, god-kings. Examples include the great structures of Yucatan, Guatemala, and Honduras built by the Maya Indians (including Tikal, Chichén-Itzá, Uxmal, and Copán) (Fig. 21–2). As economic centers, they were the chief markets, the bases from which wealthy merchants, land and livestock owners, and traders operated. As educational centers, their residents included teachers and philosophers. They also had handicraft industries, which attracted the best craftspeople and inventors. Therefore, ancient cities were the anchors of culture and society, the focal points of power, authority, and change.

As noted earlier, urbanization did not occur simultaneously in all culture hearths. Figure 21–3 shows that it probably occurred first in Mesopotamia and neighboring areas; in the Nile Valley the formative era came less than a millennium later. The formation of cities in China and in the Indus Valley may have occurred at about the same time. European and West African urbanization came later, and in Mesoamerica the formative era probably began during the middle of the third millennium B.P.

As the principal centers, crossroads, markets, places of authority, and religious headquarters, the earliest towns drew talent, trade, and travelers from far around. Where else would metallurgy have developed? Where would a traveler, tradesman, priest, or pilgrim rest before continuing the journey? Towns had to have facilities that would not be found in farm villages: buildings to entertain visitors, package food, process raw materials, provide a place for worship, and house those who defended the town.

How large were the ancient cities? We have only estimates because it is impossible to judge from excavated ruins the dimensions of a city at its height, or the number of people who might have occupied each residential unit. By modern standards, the ancient cities were not large. The cities of Mesopotamia and the Nile Valley may have had between 10,000 and 15,000 inhabitants after nearly 2000 years of growth and development. That, scholars conclude, is about the maximum size that could have been sustained by existing systems of food gathering

Figure 21-2 Maya and Aztec America. Early centers of culture in Maya and Aztec America.

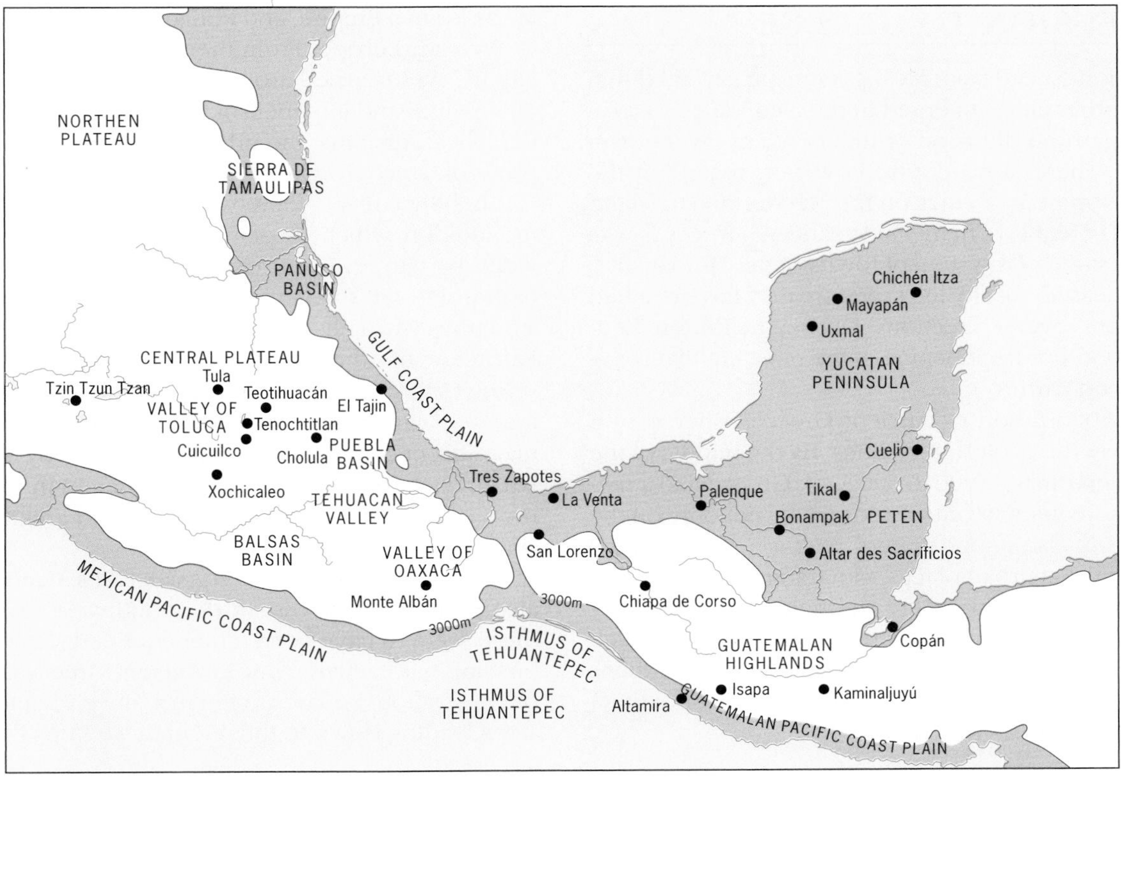

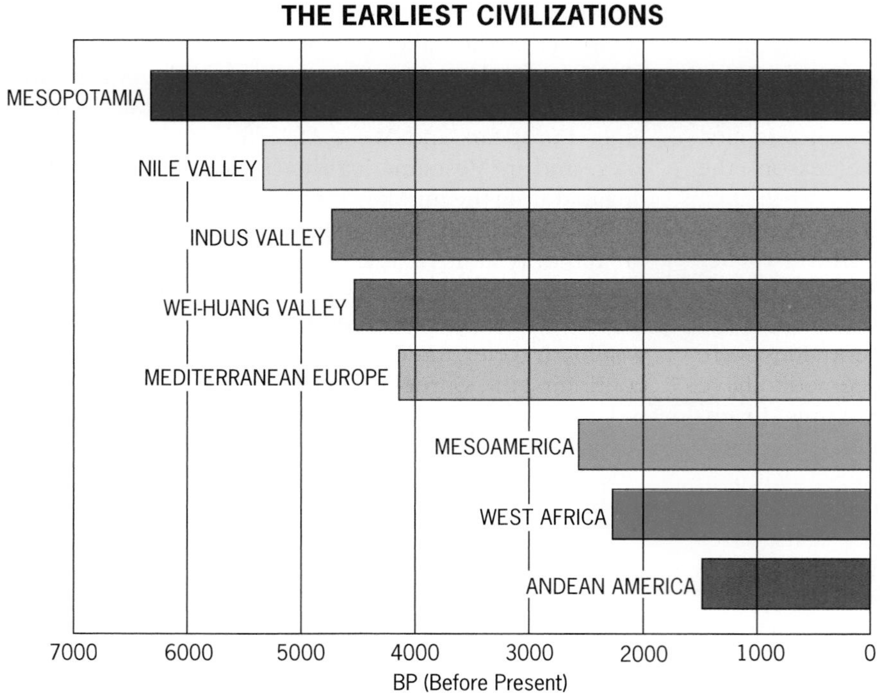

Figure 21-3 The Earliest Civilizations. Approximate dates of origin of the world's early civilizations are shown.

and distribution, and by social organization. These urban places were geographical exceptions in an overwhelmingly rural society. Urbanized societies such as those we know today did not emerge until several thousand years later.

◆ DIFFUSION TO GREECE

Urbanization spread from Mesopotamia in several directions. Whether cities emerged in the Nile Valley as a result of expansion diffusion or independent invention is uncertain. There is no doubt, however, regarding the early development of cities on the Mediterranean island of Crete. There, more than 3500 years ago, Knossos was the cornerstone of a system of towns of the Minoan civilization. Ideas about city life therefore may have reached Greece from several directions. During the third millennium B.P., Greece became one of the most highly urbanized areas on Earth.

The urbanization of Ancient Greece ushered in a new stage in the evolution of cities. By the middle of the third millennium B.P. (600 to 500 B.C.), Greece had a network of more than 500 cities and towns, not only on the mainland but also on the many Greek islands. Seafarers connected these urban places with trade routes and carried the notion of urban life throughout the Mediterranean region. Athens and Sparta, often vying with each other for power, were Greece's leading cities. Athens may have been the largest city in the world at the time, with an estimated 250,000 inhabitants.

We should remember that 2500 years ago urbanization was also occurring in several other parts of the world, including China, South Asia, and Mesoamerica, but the developments in Ancient Greece had a global, not just regional, impact. Greece inherited Southwest Asian innovations. It transmitted its own urban traditions to the Roman Empire, and Roman urban culture diffused to Western Europe. From there, "Western" concepts of city life were carried around the world on the wings of colonialism and imperialism. From Washington, D.C., to Canberra, Australia, the urban landscape shows the imprints of Greco-Roman urban culture.

In hilly Greece, there was no need to build earthen mounds on which to perch temples; these were provided by nature. Every city had its ***acropolis*** (*acro* = high point; *polis* = city), on which the most impressive structures—usually religious buildings—were built. The Parthenon of Athens remains the most famous of all, surviving to this day despite nearly 2500 years of war, earth tremors, vandalism, and environmental impact. This magnificent columned structure, designed by the Athenian architect-engineer Phidias, was begun in 447 B.C.; its rows of tapering columns have inspired architects ever since.

Like the older Southwest Asian cities, Greece's cities also had public places. In the Southwest Asian towns these seem to have been rather cramped, crowded, and bustling with activity, but in Ancient Greece they were open, spacious squares, often in a low part of town with steps leading down to them. On these steps the Greeks

From the field notes

"The rocky, hilly peninsulas of Greece provided every ancient Greek city with its *acro* (high point). We waited for the sunrise on the most famous acropolis of all, the acropolis of Athens, still crowned by the great Parthenon, standing after nearly 25 centuries *(above)*. As daylight spread across the modern city, it revealed the commanding position on which the Parthenon was built; in all directions you could see how remnants of the old stand among the urban sprawl of the present *(below)*. Athens was the greatest city of ancient Greece; today it is the capital of a modern state, an unbroken urban tradition of nearly three millennia. You can't help thinking about the philosophers, scholars, artists, architects who walked these same hills and streets."

debated, lectured, judged each other, planned military campaigns, and socialized. As time went on, the ***agora*** (meaning market) also became the focus of commercial activity.

Greece's cities also had excellent theaters, another innovation that was transmitted to the Romans. But while the aristocracy attended plays and listened to philosophical discourses, for many people life was miserable. Housing for ordinary people was no better than it had been in the Mesopotamian cities thousands of years earlier. Sanitation and health conditions were poor. And much of the grandeur designed by Greece's urban planners was built by hundreds of thousands of slaves.

◆ THE ROMAN URBAN SYSTEM

The great majority of Greece's cities and towns were located near the Mediterranean Sea, linking peninsulas and islands. When the Romans succeeded the Greeks as rulers of the region, their empire incorporated not only the Mediterranean shores but also a large part of interior Europe and North Africa (Fig. 21–4). The Roman ***urban system*** was the largest yet. The capital, Rome, was the

From the field notes

"When you think of Roman ruins, visions of the Coliseum or the Forum in Rome usually come to mind. Yet just outside of Nimes (France) I visited what has to be one of the most impressive structures from the Roman period: an enormous aqueduct built over 2000 years ago. This is no ruin, either. It is remarkably intact—even though it is an uncemented masonry construction. And despite its formidable character, it is only a small part of an engineering project that brought water to Nimes from 50 km away. The Romans achieved a level of technological sophistication that was far advanced for its time. When the Roman Empire collapsed, it took well over a thousand years for anyone to match some of the Romans' greatest engineering feats."

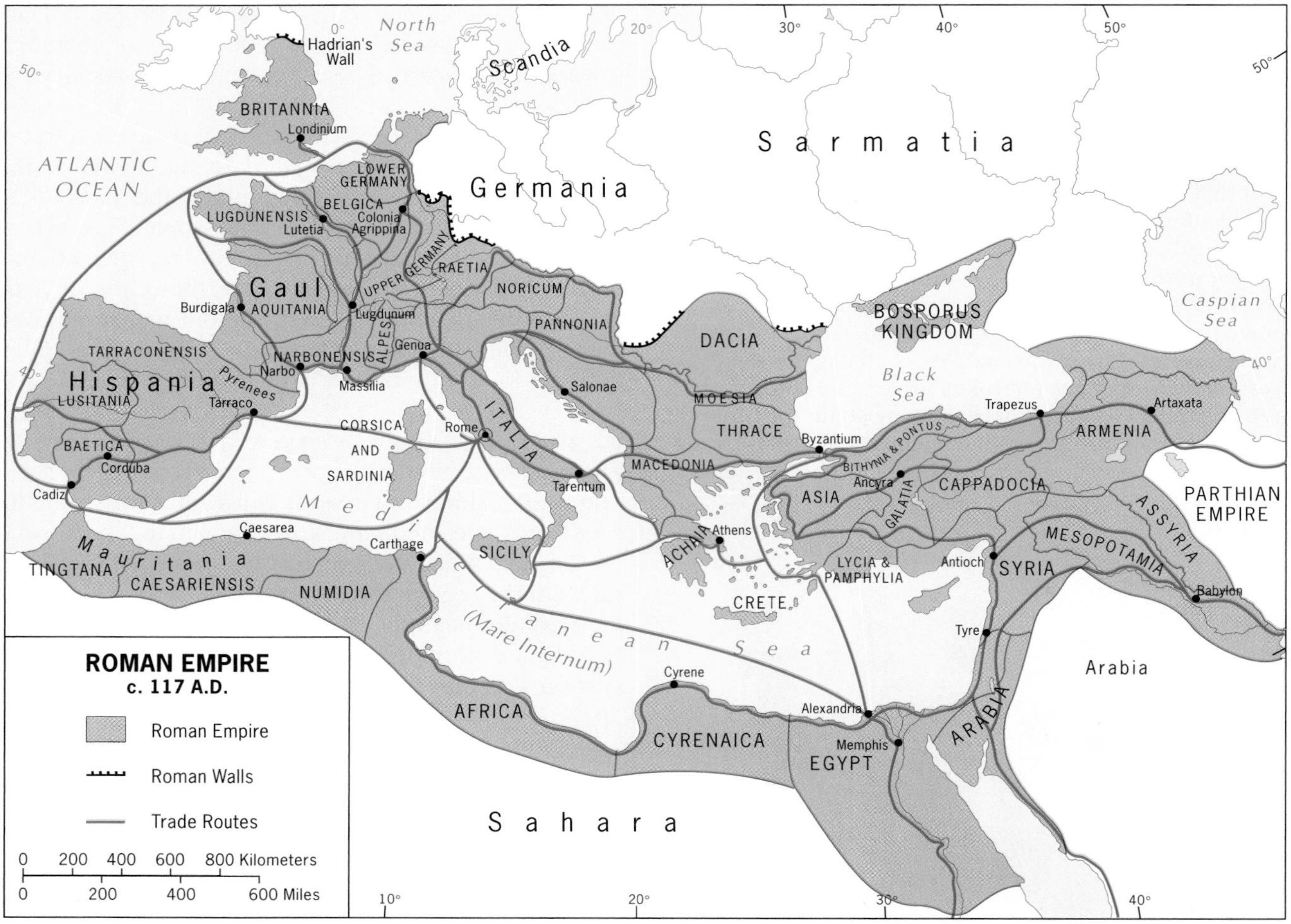

Figure 21-4 The Roman Empire, circa 114 A.D. The Romans established a system of cities linked by a network of land and sea routes. Many of the Roman cities have grown into modern metropolises.

apex of a hierarchy of settlements ranging from small villages to large cities. A ***transport network*** linked these places by road, river, and sea. Roman regional planners displayed a remarkable capacity for identifying suitable locales for settlements. They also chose surface routes, many of which still serve European motorists today. Efficiency was a Roman hallmark: urban places were positioned a modest distance from each other so that they could be reached in a reasonable amount of time. Roman road builders created a grid of communications to link the empire together.

An urban tradition already existed on the Italian peninsula before Rome emerged. The Etruscans built cities centered on temples. These cities, which still are not well understood by researchers, served as nodes for a thriving agricultural and commercial civilization. Etruscan cities extended from present-day Tuscany into the valley of the Po River; thus the Etruscan state occupied much of what was to become the heart of the Roman Empire. The Romans, therefore, had domestic as well as foreign traditions on which to build.

Greek imprints on the layout of Roman cities are unmistakable. The Greeks had learned to plan their colonial cities in a rectangular grid pattern (the early cities of mainland Greece were jumbled and congested). The Romans adopted this plan wherever surface conditions made it possible. The notion of an open market found expression in the Roman city's Forum, the focus of public life. The Romans expanded on the Greek theater to build the world's first great stadium, the Colosseum in Rome. (All Roman cities of any size had such an arena in which competitions, war games, ceremonies, and other public events took place.) Wild animals imported from Africa were killed before crowds of onlookers in the Colosseum. After Christianity was diffused to Rome, Christians were forced into the Colosseum to be attacked and eaten by hungry lions as thousands watched.

The Roman city was a place of cultural contrasts: of monumental buildings, impressive villas, spacious avenues, ingenious aqueducts and baths, and sewage systems built of stone and pipe. The Roman city also was home to the most wretchedly poor, who were crammed into overcrowded tenements. Even worse off were the slaves, many from North Africa. The Roman city, like the city of today, was home to both rich and poor and reflected both the greatest achievements and the worst failings of Roman civilization.

The Post–Roman Decline

The collapse of the Roman Empire was accompanied by the disintegration of its urban system and the decay of many of its cities. The empire failed because of misrule, corruption, external attack, and environmental degradation. Trade and transport networks broke down, the social order fell apart, and once-vibrant cities went to ruin. Between about A.D. 500 and 1000, little was left of the urban tradition Rome had bequeathed to its empire. The weakness of the now-fragmented empire was evident in the invasion of Iberia by the armies of the Moorish Empire of North Africa, where culturally and scientifically flourishing Islam brought order, scholarship, and magnificent architecture into what had been one of Rome's principal provinces. The glory of Al-Andalus (Spanish Andalusia today) is a testament to the significance and grandeur of the Islamic presence in Iberia.

Urban Growth Elsewhere

Elsewhere in the world, however, the growth of cities was proceeding vigorously. China's urban system was developing rapidly, and Xian was known as the Rome of East Asia. In West Africa, trading cities were developing along the southern margin of the Sahara. By 1350, Timbuktu was a major city—a seat of government, a university town, a market, and a religious center. In the upper valley of the Nile River, Meroë was a leading center of metallurgy, specializing in the smelting of iron and the manufacture of weapons. Trade routes from a wide region focused on this populous city.

Significant urban growth was also taking place in the Americas. In the Maya civilization of the Yucatan Peninsula and adjacent areas (Mexico and Guatemala), urbanization was under way. On the Mexican Plateau to the northwest, even larger urban centers emerged. Mexico's largest pre-Columbian city, the Aztec capital of Tenochtitlán, may have had more than 100,000 inhabitants and was growing vigorously while many European cities lay in ruins.

◆ POST–ROMAN, PREINDUSTRIAL EUROPE

The Roman-European urban traditions were weakened, but they were not extinguished. The Muslim invasion helped galvanize Europeans into action; the invaders were halted as they were about to enter southern Italy after penetrating southern France and Sicily, and the Christian counterthrust began. Soon the Crusades carried the battle to the heartland of Islamic power, and old trade routes were reopened.

Earlier in this book we warned of the dangers of environmental determinism, but many scholars have pointed out that Western Europe's resurgence coincided with a salubrious environmental period, the so-called Medieval Optimum. Warmer times expanded farmlands and pastures, opened northern waters for fishing, and enabled permanent settlement in Iceland and Greenland. Of course, it was not climate alone that "determined" Europe's recovery, but it clearly played a role in making it possible. In the cities the pulse of commerce picked up; there was work to be had, and population growth resumed. "The twelfth and thirteenth centuries," writes archeologist historian Brian Fagan in a book titled *The Little Ice Age* (2000), "were golden years of architects, masons, and carpenters, who moved from cathedral to cathedral, taking their evolving ideas with them. They created works of genius: Notre Dame (Paris) . . . Canterbury Cathedral (England) . . . Sainte-Chapelle, completed in 1248."

Thus Paris, Amsterdam, Antwerp, Lisbon, Venice, Naples, and many other cities and towns revived. It is important to remember that these cities were still small by today's standards. By the middle of the fifteenth century, London had perhaps 80,000 inhabitants and Paris had 120,000. Around the beginning of the nineteenth century, while riches poured into Europe from the colonies, London still had fewer than 1 million residents and Paris only 670,000.

Urban Environments

What were the preindustrial cities like as places to live and work? Well, the adage of the "good old days" hardly applies. If today's cities are no bargain for many of their residents, neither was preindustrial Ghent or Warsaw. With more efficient weapons and the invention of gunpowder, cities faced threats that they had not confronted before. Walls and moats could no longer withstand armies, so cities developed more extensive fortifications at a time when they were also required to accommodate growing numbers of people. Once built, the new fortifications could not simply be moved outward. The only way to house greater numbers of people was to build upward, and four- and five-story tenements made their appearance in the urban landscape.

The great days of Europe's medieval cities were numbered. To what extent the sudden climatic reversal know as the *Little Ice Age* can be blamed for this remains a much-debated question, but during the fourteenth century much of Europe (and, from the evidence, many places around the world) turned colder, got drier, and made life for farmers as well as city-dwellers very difficult. Farmlands dwindled, pastures shrank, crops failed, and desperate peasants fled the

From the field notes

"When you arrive by ferry at St. Petersburg they let you off on the so-called Vasilyevsky side of the city, but it's worth the long walk to the first bridge across the Neva to get to the Admiralty side. That is the heart of this historic, monument-studded city where seemingly every turn produces another memorable cityscape. The communist period saw the destruction of many historic buildings in the Soviet Union, including many churches, but most of central Leningrad (as the city was then called) was spared, including the magnificent Church of the Annunciation, dating from 1720. Turned into a Soviet museum and badly neglected, the church was undergoing restoration when I first saw it in 1992, and the surrounding area, just off the famous Nevsky Prospekt, also has seen much renovation. The newly burnished spires and cupolas characteristic of Russian Orthodox churches symbolize the new Russian era."

barren countryside for the cities. By the seventeenth century, as the cold of the Little Ice Age deepened, Europe's cities were slum-ridden, unsanitary, and depressing. Epidemics, fires, crime, and social dislocation prevailed. Picturesque four-story merchants' homes overlooked the sparkling canals of Amsterdam and the lush green parks of London, but their residents were the fortunate few who controlled the labor force and the lucrative overseas commerce. For the ordinary people, the overcrowded cities were no place to be. When the chance came, many decided to leave for America, Australia, and other parts of the world.

Models of Urban Places

Obviously, preindustrial cities in Renaissance Europe were quite different from preindustrial cities in India or China, and the cities of Roman Europe differed from those of medieval times. Scholars have tried to develop a general model of preindustrial urbanism that would account for the different characteristics of cities at various times in history and in different societies. Among the most widely discussed models was that proposed by Gideon Sjoberg in *The Preindustrial City: Past and Present* (1960). Sjoberg argued that cities should be viewed as products of their societies and, as such, could be divided into four categories: (1) ***folk-preliterate***; (2) ***feudal***; (3) ***preindustrial***; and (4) ***urban-industrial***.

This view places cities on a continuum reflecting the nature of their societies at each stage of their development. Thus during feudal times a European city was little more than a town, its houses modest and its streets unpaved. The landlords' estates and the monasteries were more imposing. The medieval revival brought the first stage in the rise of the preindustrial European city. The consolidation of political power and the expansion of states were reflected in the growth of the cities, now the focal points of a new order. Architecture and the arts, as well as commerce and trade, moved forward, but the dominant aspect of the preindustrial city, as we saw earlier, was the imposing complex of religious and governmental structures at its heart. Much later, when Europe entered its urban-industrial age, the high-rise buildings of financial and commercial organization took over the dominant position in the urban cores.

Primate Cities

Focusing on preindustrial cities around the world, Sjoberg suggested that prior to the industrial age almost all cities shared certain basic characteristics. Whether in medieval Europe, West Africa, East Asia, the Islamic culture realm, or the Americas, preindustrial cities were similar in form, function, and "atmosphere." Eventually, however, one of these cities would become preeminent, the leading urban center for the culture. Thus Sjoberg recognized what the geographer Mark Jefferson had earlier called the ***primate city***. Jefferson's Law of the Primate City, as he titled an important article in urban geography, defined the primate city as "a country's leading city, always disproportionately large and exceptionally expressive of national capacity and feeling." It refers, obviously, to cities representing national cultures of modern times, but the notion can be extended to earlier periods. As Sjoberg stated, cities of preindustrial, feudal, and preliterate societies were products as well as reflections of their cultures.

Although Jefferson's notion is rather imprecise, it is supported by numerous cases, past and present: Kyoto as the primate city reflecting old Japan and Tokyo the new; Paris as the reflection of France; and London, where the culture and history of a nation and empire are deeply etched in the urban landscape. In Europe, such cities as Athens, Lisbon, Prague, and Amsterdam may no longer be disproportionately large, but they remain self-consciously expressive of the cultures they represent.

From the field notes

"From the Eiffel Tower, one can see why Paris is one of the world's best-defined primate cities. The historic old city contains numerous military, political, and religious icons. Several of these can be seen on this photograph, notably the Arc de Triomphe rising above the townscape."

Generalizations about preindustrial cities are always open to debate. Clearly, not all preindustrial cities were structured as Sjoberg suggested. In Muslim cities, with their impressive central mosques, the surrounding housing is less variable than in Europe's preindustrial cities, and commerce and crafts are concentrated within a bazaar that is without an equivalent in European cities. In the theocratic states of Middle America, the city centers, with their great temples, served as ceremonial sites where thousands of people were present during rituals, but at other times they were vacant. In Africa, no religious or governmental structures dominated the townscape the way they did in preindustrial European or Muslim cities. Nevertheless, Sjoberg's thesis provides a useful basis for comparison.

Another viewpoint holds that the term *preindustrial* is inaccurate because so-called preindustrial cities of various historic periods (Roman, medieval European) and in various realms (Africa, South Asia, China) were so different in form that they cannot be grouped together. For example, "preindustrial" cities did have industries. These were not modern manufacturing industries, but they were industries nonetheless. In the urban places of Japan and India, for example, there was much handicraft industry. Thus the preindustrial city's character was shaped by activities of an industrial type. The industries were small, but they often were quite numerous. Some geographers, therefore, avoid the adjective "preindustrial" entirely; others use it only in referring to the Western city before the Industrial Revolution.

The Global Spread of Urbanization

While European cities were growing and changing, urban places were arising and developing elsewhere in Eurasia as well. Oases and resting places along the Silk Route between Europe and Asia grew into towns, and some, such as Bukhara and Samarqand, became major cities. Chinese styles of city-building diffused into Korea and Japan; Seoul was a settlement 2000 years ago and a full-fledged city by A.D. 1200, and Kyoto, Japan's historic capital, grew rapidly after the turn of the ninth century. Urban geographers refer to a giant ***urban banana***, a crescent-shaped zone of early urbanization extending across Eurasia from England in the west to Japan in the east and including cities from London and Paris, Venice and Constantinople (Istanbul today), and Tabriz and Samarqand to Kabul and Lahore, Amra and Jaunpur, Xian and Anyang, Kyoto and Osaka.

Note that many of the cities of the "urban banana" are located in the interior (as was the case in West Africa and indigenous America). Interior trade routes such as the Silk Route and the caravan routes of West Africa sustained these inland cities and, in many cases, helped them prosper. All that was to change, however, when European maritime exploration and overseas colonization ushered in an era of oceanic trade. From about 1500 on, the dominance of interior cities in the "urban banana" declined, and other cities, many of them in coastal situations, gained prominence. The era of the great seaports had arrived—not only in Europe, but also in the rest of the world. In Asia, such names as Bombay (now Mumbai), Madras (Chennai), Singapore, Batavia (Jakarta), and Tokyo came to the fore. As the colonial period went on, the key cities in international trade networks now were Cape Town, Salvador, Lima-Callao, and New York—among others.

These still-famous names overshadowed numerous smaller coastal cities whose impact was nevertheless powerful. In West Africa before about 1500, urbanization was concentrated in a belt extending along the southern margin of the Sahara, including such cities as Timbuktu, Niani, Gao, Zaria, Kano, and Maiduguri. Here cross-desert caravan traffic met boat traffic on the River Niger (or, as the saying went, "camel met canoe,") and goods from northern deserts were exchanged for those from coastal forests. But then maritime trade disrupted this whole system: coastal ports became the leading markets and centers of power, and the African cities of the interior began a long decline.

The trade networks commanded by the European powers (including the slave trade) brought unprecedented riches to Europe's burgeoning medieval cities. To such places as Amsterdam, London, Lisbon, Liverpool, and Seville they brought revival and even prosperity. Successful merchants built ornate mansions and patronized the arts. They participated in city governance and supported the reconstruction of city centers. As a result, the ***mercantile city*** took on similar properties whether it was Antwerp, Copenhagen, Lisbon, or Genoa. A central square became the focus of the mercantile city, fronted by royal, religious, public, and private buildings evincing wealth and prosperity, power and influence. Streets leading to these central squares formed arteries of commerce and the beginnings of what we today call "downtown."

During the sixteenth and seventeenth centuries, these European mercantile cities became the nodes of a widening network of national, regional, and global commerce. So wealthy and powerful were the merchants that, supported by their rulers, they were able to found and expand settlements in distant lands. Cities such as Dakar (Senegal, West Africa), Lourenco Marques (now Maputo, Moçambique), and Saigon (now Ho Chi Minh City, Vietnam) were endowed with the ornate trappings of the mercantile cities of Europe, including elaborately inlaid sidewalks, tree-lined avenues, and neo-gothic architecture.

When the Industrial Revolution made its appearance during the last decades of the eighteenth century, therefore, a new and global distribution of cities was already in place. In Europe, the eighteenth century brought bitter cold during the worst years of the "Little Ice Age," and once again the now-mercantile cities were engulfed by desperate immigrants. These masses formed a ready labor pool when industries needed them, but none of Europe's cities could have been prepared for what lay ahead: an avalanche of changes that ripped the fabric of urban life. Cities had to adapt to the mushrooming of factories and supply facilities, the expansion of transport systems, and the construction of tenements for the growing labor force. They bulged—and sometimes broke—at the seams. The ***manufacturing city*** now emerged, first in the British Midlands and soon in Western Europe. Some European cities, such as Paris and Amsterdam, managed to retain the character of their historic centers, but many others were totally or partially destroyed. Cities became unregulated jumbles of activity. Private homes were engulfed by factories. Open spaces became refuse dumps. Elegant housing was converted into overcrowded slums. Ugly railroad tracks knifed through long-stable neighborhoods. Sanitation systems failed, and water supplies were inadequate and often polluted.

And yet, people migrated to the manufacturing cities, not only in Europe but wherever factory towns emerged. Living conditions were dreadful for the workers, and working conditions were shocking. Children worked 12-hour shifts in textile mills. Health conditions were worse than they had been in medieval times; the air was polluted and the water contaminated. The grimy, soot-covered cities of the English Midlands were appropriately called the "black towns."

In time, conditions in the European manufacturing city improved as a result of government intervention, legislation, the introduction of city planning and zoning, and the recognition of workers' rights. Many manufacturing cities in the New World never suffered as much as their European predecessors, although living and working conditions for factory workers (and "blue-collar" workers generally) were far from satisfactory. During the late nineteenth and early twentieth centuries, the American manufacturing city grew rapidly, often with inadequate planning and excessive inmigration leading to the development of slums and ghettoes. Thus the American manufacturing city did not altogether escape the problems of its European predecessors.

During the second half of the twentieth century, the great manufacturing cities swelled by the Industrial Revolution stopped growing. As we will note in more detail later, the nature of manufacturing changed, as did its location: many factories were repositioned away from congested, overcrowded, expensive urban areas. Large numbers of manufacturing plants were simply abandoned, making "rust belts" out of once-thriving industrial districts. Many of them still stand there today, overgrown by weeds, with broken windows and cracking walls. And so the all-powerful, leading cities, including manufacturing centers, still rank at the top of the list, but New York, London, Paris, Chicago, and other top-ten cities at midcentury have been eclipsed. In 2001, the United Nations Population Fund published a list of the world's largest cities at the turn of the century, along with projections for the year 2015. According to its calculations (other agencies produce slightly different figures, but all agree on the overall pattern), there will be 23 cities with populations over 10 million by the year 2015, with Mumbai, India, challenging Tokyo for the top spot. In 1975, there were only five cities with 10 million or more inhabitants. The global urban scene is undergoing another major transition.

While cities in the developing world have been growing at unprecedented rates, the now-demographically stagnant cities of the industrialized Western world have been changing in quite different ways. Modern means of transportation and elaborate road construction have permitted the dispersal of urban population in a process that made suburbanization the hallmark of the ***modern city*** in American life. (European cities are much less far-flung, in general, than North American cities, but suburbanization is happening there too.)

Today the U.S. city is a sprawling, expanding urban region with many parts and functions, from downtown to suburb, from shopping mall to business park. It is a reflection of an entrepreneurial culture, a showplace of technology, but also a place of sharp contrasts between rich and poor, high culture and street culture, cosmopolitanism and parochialism.

The modern city has not stabilized. Some urban geographers see what is often referred to as ***postmodernism*** in the cities of technologically advanced societies. They use this term because at least parts of such cities are increasingly divorced from their own historical roots and the industrial past that long shaped their development. Instead, they are pastiches of architectural and design elements developed for purposes of entertainment and the promotion of consumption rather than the facilitation of production. To shed light on some of the forces at work in the changing geography of cities, we now turn to the structuring and spacing of urban centers in different parts of the world.

◆ KEY TERMS ◆

acropolis	manufacturing city	stratified society
agora	mercantile city	theocratic center
egalitarian society	modern city	transport network
feudal city	postmodernism	urban banana
folk-preliterate city	preindustrial city	urban elite
formative era	primate city	urban-industrial city
Little Ice Age	state	urban system

◆ APPLYING GEOGRAPHIC KNOWLEDGE ◆

1. Since the onset of the Industrial Revolution, cities have grown and urbanized areas have expanded almost continuously, their populations today reaching unprecedented numbers—even in countries whose populations remain mostly agricultural. Is this growth phase a continuation of preindustrial trends, or have cities undergone periods of growth and subsequent decline in the past? How do you view the demographic and economic prospects of today's megacities in the future?
2. A number of governments today are repositioning their capital cities away from the very primate cities that embody the national culture, or did so during the twentieth century (Brazil, Australia, Nigeria, Malaysia, and others). What cultural-geographic considerations might motivate a government to take this action?

Chapter 22

Location, Pattern, and Structure of Cities

From the field notes

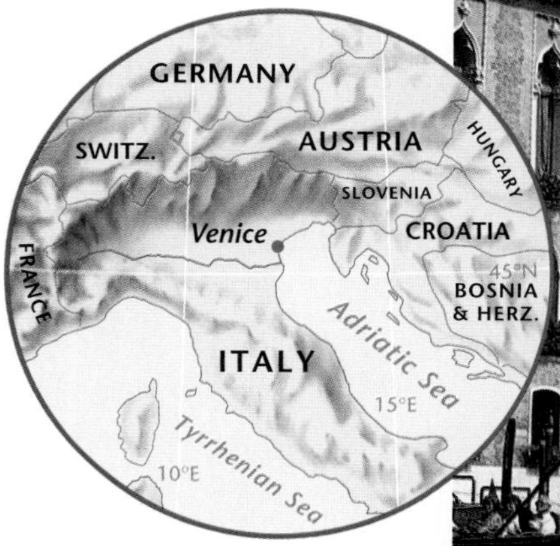

"The Grand Canal of Venice has to be one of the most amazing sites on Earth. On an marshy site in the middle of a lagoon, the early Venetians built a city that was destined to become one of Europe's premier economic and political centers of the late Middle Ages. Is any city more a product of its physical environment and locational setting? The former gave the city a character unlike any other, and the latter is deeply implicated in Venice's rise to dominance. For if Venice did not sit in a strategic position at the northern end of the Adriatic or at the mouth of a rich agricultural valley, the town's citizens could not possibly have amassed the wealth and power that made Venice, for a time, the envy of much of the Western world."

KEY POINTS

◆ **Urban geography is the study of the way cities function, their internal structures and systems, their impact on their surroundings, and the external influences on them.**

◆ **The development of cities is influenced both by the physical character of the places they occupy (their site) and by their position in relation to other places and networks (their situation).**

◆ **Models of urban structure reveal how the forces that shape the internal layout of cities have changed, transforming the single-center city with one dominant downtown into the polycentric metropolis with several commercial nodes.**

◆ **Cities are shaped by economic forces, technology, government policy, and sociocultural attitudes about how land should be used and who should live where.**

◆ **In the United States, the urban system evolved through five stages of development determined by prevailing modes of transport and industry; today's period of high technology, still in the process of transforming the modern city, dates from the 1970s.**

◆ **Central place theory helps explain why, under ideal circumstances, small urban places such as villages lie close together while larger cities lie far apart.**

The study of urban settlements encompasses a broad range of approaches and interests. Geographers have long recognized that the relationships between cities and surrounding countrysides can be measured and mapped. Every city and town has an adjacent region within which its influence is dominant. Farmers in that region sell many of their products on the city's markets, and customers from smaller towns and villages come to the city to shop and to conduct other business. The city's newspapers are read and its television stations watched in the surrounding region. The city's dominance can be seen in many other areas of life as well. The term ***hinterland***, a German word meaning the land "behind" the city, is used in referring to such a region.

When cities lie some distance apart, where does the hinterland of one city end and that of the other begin? That question leads us to investigate the factors that influence the spacing of cities. In general, large cities tend to lie farther apart than smaller ones; towns lie still closer together, and villages are separated by even shorter distances. What forces influence the evolution of this pattern? Can von Thünen's method of model-building be used to interpret what the map shows?

This chapter takes up these questions. As we will see, they lead quite naturally to the anatomy of the city itself, its internal structure and functions. A city's spatial organization can reveal much about its efficiency and productivity, and hence about its capacity to compete not only for dominance over a large hinterland but also for more distant linkages. Today, some regional cities are so successful and powerful that their leaders can afford to bypass their own government and do business with foreign countries as though they were independent entities (Barcelona is a case in point). At the same time, some once-thriving cities with international connections have lost their vigor (as in the case of Liverpool). There are usually geographic explanations for such contrasts.

In Chapter 21 we traced the evolution of cities from their origins in Southwest Asia to modern times, combining cultural and historical geography in the process. The study of how cities function, their internal systems and structures, and the external influences on them, is the field of ***urban geography***. Urban geographers want to know how cities are arranged, what they look like, how their circulation systems function, how commuting patterns develop and change, how and why people move from one part of a city to another. What is it that attracts millions of people to cities every year, even while millions of others "escape" from the city to the suburbs?

Cities, too, display spatial variation; that is, they possess internal regional contrasts. Urban regions (such as the "downtown" or the "inner city") can be better understood if they are clearly delineated. Urban geographers therefore conduct detailed studies of economic, cultural, political, and other aspects of cities. Such studies show that the layout of Western cities contrasts quite sharply with that of many East Asian, African, or South American cities. ◆

◆ RANKING URBAN CENTERS

Before proceeding, we should deal with a problem of terminology. Terms such as "city," "town," "village," and even "urban" do not have consistent, universally accepted meanings. Inconsistent use of these terms can lead to confusion and invalid comparisons.

Take, for example, the term *urban*. Earlier we compared the dispersed settlements of rural areas to clustered urban settlements. If clustering is the hallmark of urbanization, even a hamlet is an urban settlement, although it may contain only 100 residents. At what point does a hamlet become a village, a village a town, and a town a city?

One way to approach this question is to use the notion of ***urban hierarchy*** and consider the functions of clustered settlements in addition to their size. Take the case of the hamlet. If a hamlet is a group of farmers' dwellings, it offers no services, such as a gas station, general store, or coffee shop—in short, it has no ***urban function***. But if a hamlet provides some basic services for the people living there and for some of those living nearby, it is an urban place on the bottom step of the urban hierarchy.

A village, the next larger urban settlement, is likely to offer several dozen services. The key here is specialization. Stores sell certain goods; gas stations sell competing brands. As an urban center, the village serves a larger area and more people than a hamlet.

A town is not merely larger than a village; its functions reveal a higher level of specialization. Bank and postal services, medical services, educational institutions (school, library), and stores selling such goods as furniture, appliances, and hardware are among the functions of towns. Rather than relying solely on population size, we define a town as a place where a certain assemblage of goods and services is available, with a ***hinterland*** (surrounding service area) that includes smaller villages and hamlets. The hinterland reveals the economic reach of each settlement, the maximum distance from the town or village at which people are still attracted to it for business purposes. A settlement's functions as well as its economic reach produce a measure of its centrality, its economic power relative to that of competitors.

The city is next in the urban hierarchy. Not only does a city have more functional specialization than a town, but it has a larger hinterland and greater centrality. To distinguish between town and city, we also should look at the urban layout. A city has a well-defined commercial center, a so-called central business district (CBD). A town may have outskirts, but a city has suburbs—subsidiary urban areas surrounding and connected to the central city. Many suburbs are exclusively

From the field notes

"I took the elevator to the top of the tallest building in sight to get a sense of the dimensions of what was the fastest-growing city in the world: Shenzhen, China. Just a fishing village one generation earlier, Shenzhen is now a city with about 3 million inhabitants, and still expanding. Geographic location boosted Shenzhen's fortunes. It lies right across the border from Hong Kong, and when the Chinese government established a Special Economic Zone (SEZ) here, business and industry mushroomed. Hundreds of industries moved from Hong Kong to Shenzhen, attracted by lower labor costs; many foreign corporations set up factories and outlets in Shenzhen. Hundreds of thousands of workers moved to the SEZ. Everything you see in this photograph is less than 25 years old; all of it stands where duck ponds and paddies lay less than three decades ago. As my Chinese colleague said as we surveyed this scene, Shenzhen has three great advantages: location, location, and location."

residential, but others have their own commercial centers or shopping malls.

Urban areas that are larger than cities have various names. The term *metropolis* is sometimes used, and in television weather forecasts you may hear the term *metropolitan area.* In many parts of the world, large metropolises are coalescing to create megacities called ***megalopolises***—a term used to describe multiple cities that have grown together to create a single urban expanse. One such megalopolis stretches along the U.S. East Coast from Boston to beyond Washington, D.C.—this is the so-called Bosnywash megalopolis. Obviously, its economic reach is not just regional but global.

◆ PLACE AND LOCATION

In Guangdong, a province in southern China, there is a city named Shenzhen. Less than three decades ago, Shenzhen was a fishing village with perhaps 20,000 inhabitants and few services. Thatch houses and duck ponds marked the distinctly nonurban scene. Today, Shenzhen has a population of 3.1 million and is the world's fastest-growing urban area (Fig. 22–1). The thatch houses are long gone; skyscrapers tower over the townscape.

Urban Situation

What has propelled Shenzhen to megacity status? The answer is geography. Shenzhen happens to lie next to one of the world's most successful economic centers, Hong Kong. Shenzhen's relative location—its ***situation,*** as urban geographers call it—has enabled it to benefit immensely from commerce and trade, and rapid growth has ensued.

When it comes to explaining the growth and success of certain cities, situation often is the key. A city's situation describes its position relative to much-traveled transport routes, productive farmlands, manufacturing complexes, other towns and cities—in short, its near and distant surroundings. Indeed, the size, growth, and character of a city are reflections of its situation.

A city's situation can change. The world's largest and most enduring cities have seen their situation improve with the times. In Paris, for example, settlement may

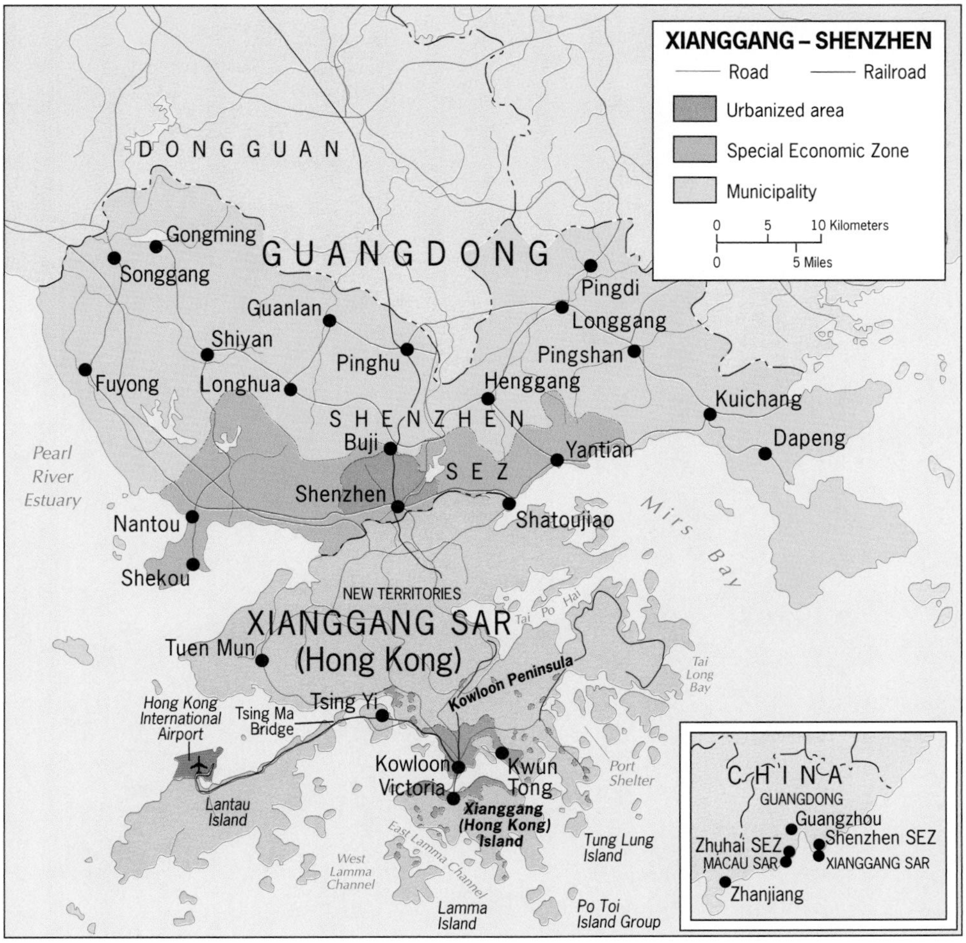

Figure 22-1 Xianggang-Shenzhen. Shenzhen, China's most successful Special Economic Zone, lies adjacent to Xianggang (Hong Kong), one of the economic "tigers" of the Pacific Rim. This proximity has propelled Shenzhen's SEZ ahead of all others. *Source:* From a map in H. J. de Blij and P. O. Muller, *Geography: Realms, Regions, and Concepts*, 10th ed. New York: Wiley, 2002, p. 468.

have begun in pre-Roman times, long before the Seine River became a major transport route and before the Seine Basin became one of Europe's most productive areas. Over time the city's situational advantage grew. As its hinterland prospered, so did the city. Paris became increasingly multifunctional—a religious center, a crucible of culture, a political capital, an industrial giant, a focus of high technology. Centrally situated not only in relation to the prosperous Seine Basin but also in relation to the country as a whole, Paris eclipsed every other city in France. Today, with a population of 10 million, it is a ***megacity***, a vast metropolitan area (Fig. 22–2). The next largest city in France, Lyon, is only one-seventh the size of Paris.

Figure 22-2 Paris Region. *Source:* From a map drawn for H. J. de Blij and P. O. Muller, *Geography: Regions and Concepts,* 2nd ed. New York: Wiley, 1978.

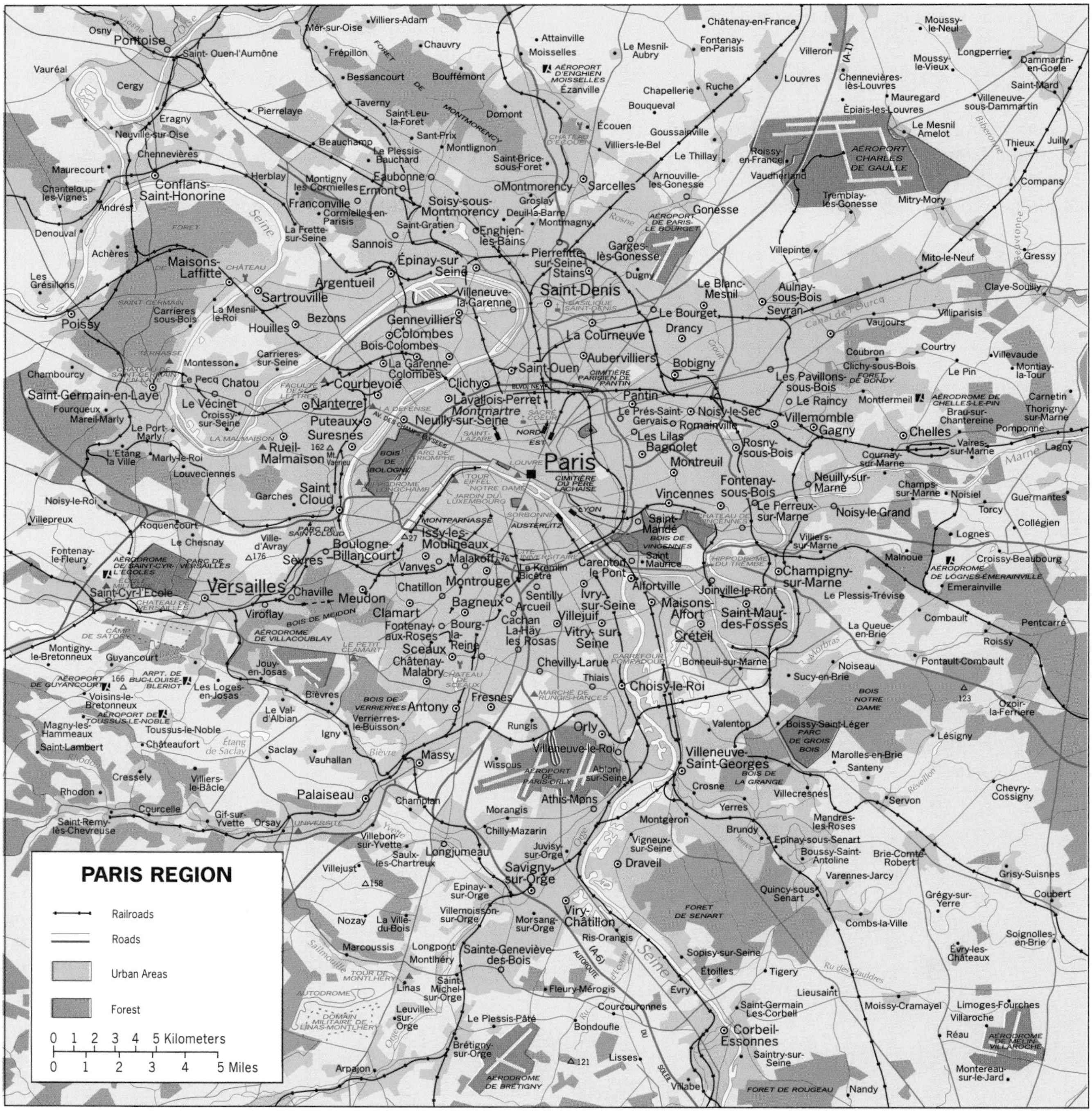

Closer to home, we can observe the effect of a long-term favorable situation on the growth of the Chicago urban area. Chicago lies at the landward end of the Great Lakes waterway, where it meets the water routes of the Mississippi system; it lies where the western end of the country's largest manufacturing belt yields to the vast farmlands of one of the world's most productive agricultural zones; it is situated at an ideal location for the convergence of rail, road, and air routes; and it has major natural resources in its vast and populous hinterland. Chicago has long been the dominant city of the North American interior, a place with unparalleled situational advantages.

A city's situation can also deteriorate over time. When parts of the U.S. northeastern manufacturing belt began to decline, the downturn was reflected in many cities and towns. Exhaustion of resources, repeated crop failure, climatic change, and political developments all can change a city's situation. Berlin suffered severely not only from its destruction during World War II but also from the subsequent division of Germany, which deprived the city of much of its hinterland. At a different level of scale, note what happens to the busy commercial center of a small town when a new expressway bypasses it. Gas stations, restaurants, and other services feel the effects as traffic through the town decreases.

Urban Site

A second locational factor affecting the development of cities and towns is their ***site***. This term refers to the actual physical qualities of the place a city occupies: whether it lies in a confining valley, on a coastal plain, on the edge of a plateau, or perhaps on an island. It was site, more than situation, that led to the founding of Paris. The first settlement was built on an island in the middle of the Seine River, where security and easy defense were available, where the river could be easily crossed—and the cross traffic controlled. This island, *Ile de la Cité*, soon proved to be too small, and Paris spread onto both banks of the Seine (Fig. 22–3).

Paris was fortunate; no physical obstacles stood in the way of the city's expansion. Other cities have seen their growth stunted by site problems of various kinds or have experienced environmental deterioration resulting in part from site factors. Consider another large urban area, Mexico City, which lies in a mountain-flanked

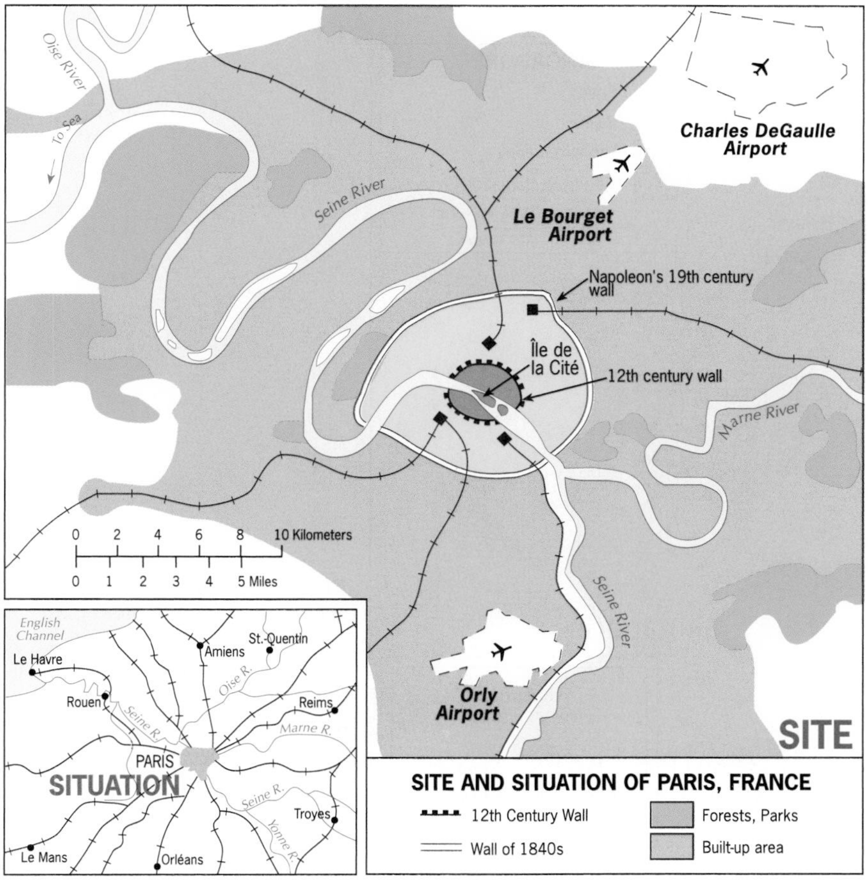

Figure 22-3 Site and Situation of Paris, France. The Île de la Cité was—and remains—at the heart of Paris.

basin at an elevation of more than 2100 meters (7000 feet). Underlain by the now-dry bed of a former lake, the city is vulnerable to earthquakes, is chronically short of water, cannot dispose of its wastes effectively, and has smog-choked air. Once one of the most gracious and attractive cities in the Americas, with magnificent public and private buildings and tree-lined avenues, Mexico City today is a noisy, crowded, traffic-congested central city dominated by high-rises and encircled by hundreds of slums, beyond which lies a ring consisting of some of the most squalid squatter camps in the world. It is probably true that no physical site could have accommodated Mexico City's rapid growth (the city receives about 1000 immigrants each day to add to a natural increase of about the same number, creating an annual total growth of about 750,000 inhabitants). But Mexico City's site has greatly complicated an already difficult set of urban problems.

Other fast-growing cities in developing countries confront site problems of various kinds. Bangkok (10 million), the capital of Thailand, lies on the delta of the Chao Phraya, the major river in this part of the country. Fresh water is provided by numerous wells. The pumping of water from the wells has contributed to a serious site problem: southern Bangkok is sinking into the Gulf of Thailand at a rate of more than 2 centimeters (nearly 1 inch) per year. Already the city is honeycombed by countless canals that form, in effect, a second network of streets. Millions of people stand to lose their homes if the subsidence continues. Add to this the fact that on an average day Bangkok's air is even more polluted than that of Mexico City, and the enormity of the problem comes into focus.

The role of site in the development of cities obviously has changed over time. The Ancient Romans, who founded many of Europe's cities, often chose a site that was easy to defend; that function is no longer relevant. A city's site can still play a role in political struggles, however. Geographers often use Singapore to illustrate the advantages of a favorable situation. Singapore's situational advantages helped it emerge as one of the successful "economic tigers" on the Pacific Rim. But in 1965, when Chinese-dominated Singapore opted to secede from Malay-dominated Malaysia, it was Singapore's site that helped make this step feasible. Singapore lies on an island separated from the Malaysian mainland by the Johore Strait (Fig. 22–4). That clear site definition created geographic identity; without it, Singapore probably would not have seceded from Malaysia. Whenever we study a major city, therefore, site as well as situation should be investigated for clues to its development.

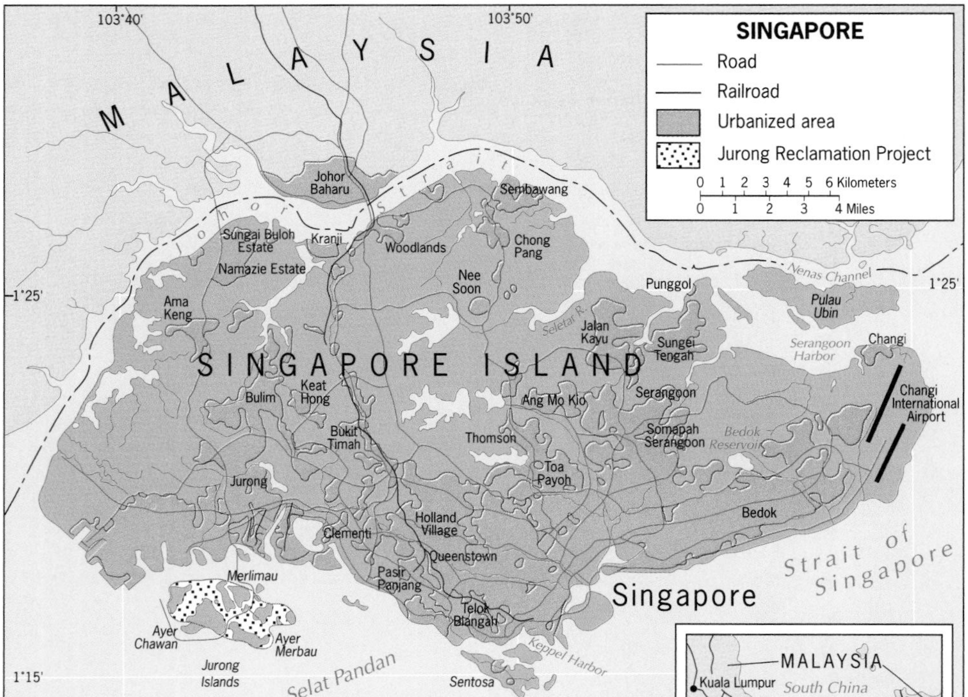

Figure 22-4 Singapore. Singapore's physiographic separation from the Malayan Peninsula facilitated its secession from the Malaysian Federation. The city-state's relative location (inset) helped boost its economy. *Source:* From a map in H. J. de Blij and P. O. Muller, *Geography: Realms, Regions, and Concepts,* 10th ed. New York: Wiley, 2002.

From the field notes

"Although many miles of Bangkok's canals *(khlongs)* have been drained and replaced by roads, a large part of the right bank of the Chao Phraya, the city's major river, still is honeycombed by waterways. And on the left bank, a network remains for use by 'river taxis.' I asked the driver of my boat to go slowly so that I could map the many waterfront businesses along the *khlongs;* they ranged from laundries to grocery stores, the latter often displaying a wide range of goods, here including one with a familiar logo. But the site of canal-riddled Bangkok is presenting serious problems: it is sinking relative to sea level, and the sea is not far away. Already, many waterfront structures show signs of flooding and deterioration. The future of the 'Venice of Southeast Asia' is in doubt."

◆ THE CHANGING CITY

All of us are aware that cities have what might be called personalities—a special "feel" that is sometimes expressed anecdotally as "brash" (New York) or "laid-back" (San Francisco) or "mile-high" (Denver) or "easy" (New Orleans). And there is no doubt about it: even in this era of convergence, cities have different "atmospheres." Boston and Miami, Cleveland and San Diego, Pittsburgh and Phoenix are studies in contrast, even if all are American and all have high-rise skylines.

Such atmosphere takes time to accumulate, but once established it tends to survive, even when cities change and modernize. Architecture, street layout, economic function, political history—all these are imprinted in the urban scene. Geographers have analyzed these imprints in historic context, as John Borchert did in 1967, when he recognized four stages in the evolution of the American metropolis: (1) the Sail-Wagon Epoch, 1790–1830, when transoceanic and coastal trade were by sailing vessel and land connections by wagon; the Iron-Horse Epoch, 1830–1870, when the steam-powered locomotive and spreading rails brought the early industrial age; the Steel-Rail Epoch, 1870–1920, when the full impact of the Industrial Revolution came to bear on the American city, headed by the steel industry; and the Auto-Air-Amenity Epoch (1920 to the 1960s), driven by the gasoline-powered internal combustion engine. Today we would add a fifth, High-Technology Epoch (1970 to the present) when service and information industries are contributing to an ever-greater dispersal of urban populations.

Note the role of technology—particularly transportation technology—in each of these epochs. In America's older cities, each epoch left its mark on the urban landscape; one reason younger cities tend to look so modern is that their development was not constrained by distant legacies. St. Louis, "the westernmost Eastern city," is quite distinct from Kansas City, the "easternmost Western city," despite the fact that both are interior river cities. Of course, much of the old has been lost—American culture until relatively recently did not place much value on what seemed to be old and in the way of modernization. Nevertheless, cities continue to carry the imprints of history, and these imprints are now the subject of much geographic research.

Some of this research involves the creation of models of urban development, and it is to this that we now turn.

◆ MODELS OF URBAN STRUCTURE

Cities are not simply random collections of buildings and people. They exhibit ***functional structure***: they are spatially organized to perform their functions as places of commerce, production, education, and much more. What are the spatial components in the layout of a city? How and where are the various residential and nonresidential sectors of the city positioned with respect to each other? If certain forces govern the distribution of central places on the landscape, then surely there are forces that affect the way cities are organized. It is not difficult to think of one of these forces: the price of land. This tends to be highest in the downtown area and declines as one moves outward from the center; one would not expect to find a spacious residential area in the central business district.

Before proceeding, let us define some terms that are commonly used in referring to parts of the city—particularly those in North America. The ***central business district (CBD)*** (or "downtown") is the core of the city. High land values, tall buildings, busy traffic, converging highways, and mass transit systems mark the American CBD. An urban zone is a sector of a city within which land use is relatively uniform (an industrial or residential zone, for example). The term ***central city*** is often used to denote the part of an urban area that lies within the outer ring of residential suburbs. In effect, it refers to the older city as opposed to the newer suburbs. A ***suburb*** is an outlying, functionally uniform part of an urban area, often (but not always) adjacent to the central city. Most suburbs are residential, but some have other land uses, including schools, shopping malls, and office parks.

Just by using such terms as residential area and central business district, we acknowledge the existence of a regional structure within cities. When you refer to downtown, or to the airport, or to the municipal zoo, you are in fact referring to urban regions where certain functions prevail (business activity, transportation, and recreation, in the three just mentioned). All of these urban regions or zones, of course, lie near or adjacent to each other and together make up the metropolis. But how are they arranged? Is there any regularity or recurrent pattern in the location of the various zones, perhaps reflecting certain prevailing growth processes? In other words, do the city's regions constitute elements of a metropolitan structure that can be recognized in every metropolis, perhaps with modifications related to a city's particular site, size, shape, and relief?

One way to attack this problem is to study the layout of a large number of cities, compare the resulting maps, and determine which features recur. If we were to do this in North America, we would find that cities generally have central zones, consisting mainly of the CBD, and outer zones where lower-density suburbs and their new business and shopping centers lie. Between the central and outer zones, one may sometimes discern a middle zone, an ill-defined, often rather mixed and disorganized area. This zone is characterized by change, as in the aging of housing and the development of slums.

Modeling the North American City

As cities evolved, urban geographers attempted to construct models that would account for their geographic layouts. Three of these models, in particular, reveal not only some alternative interpretations of urban structure, but also its increasing complexity over time (Fig. 22–5). The concentric zone model (Fig. 22–5A) resulted from sociologist Ernest Burgess's study of Chicago in the

Figure 22-5 Three Classical Models of Urban Structure. The three classical models of urban structure are the concentric zone model, the sector model, and the multiple nuclei model.

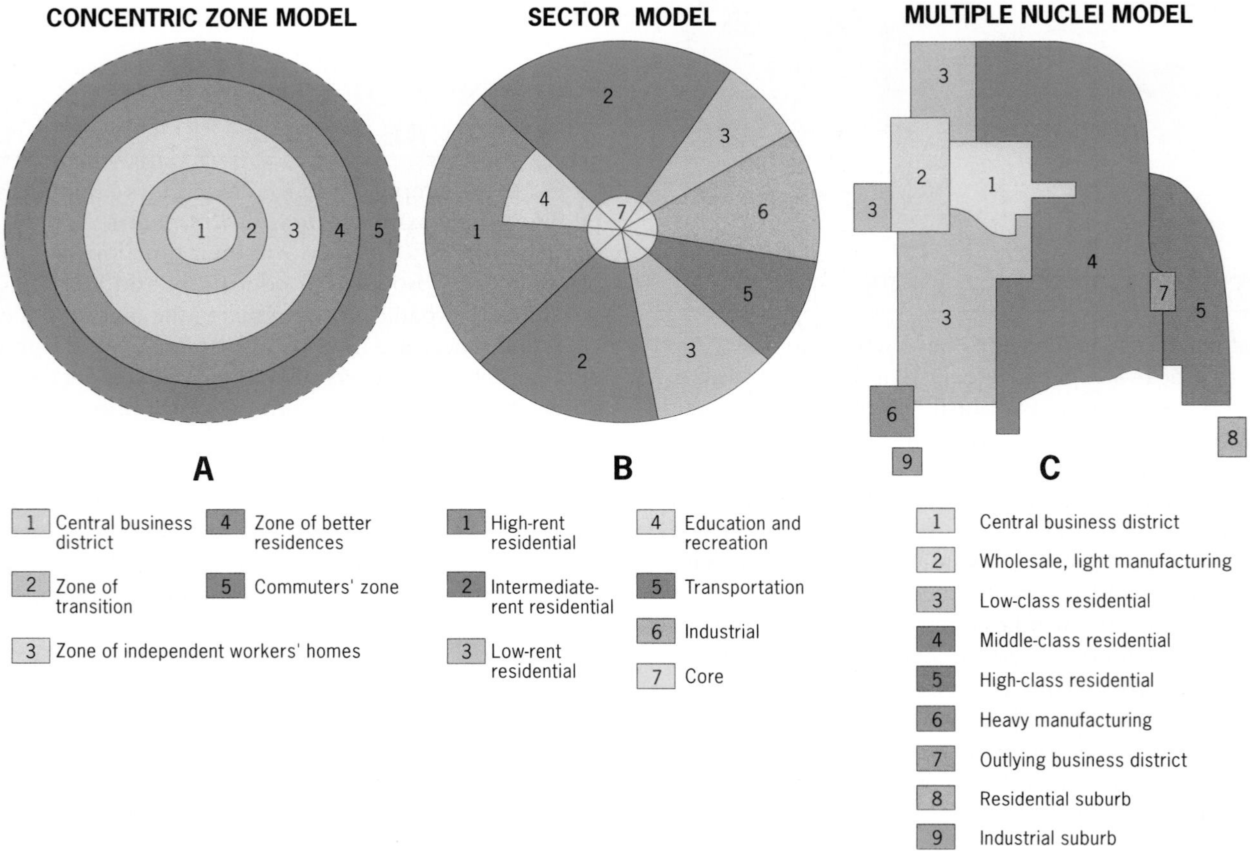

1920s. He recognized five concentric functional zones. At the center was the CBD (1), itself subdivided into several subdistricts (financial, retail, theater, etc.). The zone of transition (2) was characterized by residential deterioration and encroachment by business and light manufacturing. Zone 3 was a ring of closely spaced but adequate homes occupied by the blue-collar labor force. Zone 4 consisted of middle-class residences, and zone 5 was the suburban ring. Burgess described his model as dynamic: as the city grew, inner zones encroached on outer ones, so that CBD functions invaded zone 2 and the problems of zone 2 affected the inner margins of zone 3.

In the late 1930s Homer Hoyt published his sector model (Fig. 22–5B), partly as an answer to the drawbacks of the Burgess model. Hoyt argued that growth alone created a pie-shaped urban structure. From the concentric zone model we would conclude that rent paid for residential use would increase steadily from the tenements of zone 2 to the suburbs of zone 5. But in reality, Hoyt discovered, a low-rent area could extend all the way from the CBD to the city's outer edge, as in sector 3; the same could be true for a high-rent sector (1). Transport (5) and industrial (6) sectors also did not reflect the concentric character proposed by Burgess.

In fact, we can recognize both concentric and sector layouts in the urban structure of many cities. In the 1940s Chauncy Harris and Edward Ullman, arguing that neither of the earlier models adequately reflected city structure, proposed the multiple nuclei model (Fig. 22–5C). This model was based on the notion that the CBD was losing its dominant position as the nucleus of the urban area. Several of the urban regions shown in the figure therefore have their own subsidiary but competing "nuclei."

As manufacturing cities became modern cities and modern cities became increasingly complex, the construction of explanatory models became more complicated. Today's megacities are regions in themselves, and cities-within-cities make models such as those in Figure 22–5 seem simplistic. Today urban geographers recognize what they call ***urban realms***, components of giant conurbations that function separately in certain ways but are linked together in a greater metropolitan sphere.

In the early postwar period, rapid population dispersal to the outer suburbs not only created distant nuclei but also reduced the volume and level of interaction between the central city and these emerging suburban cities. This situation made the new outer cities of the suburban ring more self-sufficient as locational advantages produced an ever-greater range of retailing and employment activity. By the 1970s, outer cities were becoming increasingly independent of the CBD to which these former suburbs had once been closely tied, and they began to duplicate certain functions of the central city. In the 1980s, the increasingly complex American metropolitan area revealed combinations of the classic models described previously, as well as a redistribution of activities and zones in the urban fringe. Regional shopping centers in the suburban zone were becoming the CBDs of the outer nuclei. Business and industrial parks were locating outside the central city as well (Fig. 22–6). The term *urban realm* came into use to describe the spatial components of the metropolis of the 1990s, each a separate and distinct economic, social, and political entity within the larger urban framework.

The realm structure is readily apparent in metropolitan Los Angeles. Five discrete urban realms have emerged around the central city (Fig. 22–7), creating a suburban ring that extends as far as 50 miles (80 kilometers) from the CBD. Clockwise from the west, these are:

1. The *West Realm*, typified by Santa Monica, Beverly Hills, and the ribbon extending along the coast toward Santa Barbara.
2. The *Northwest Realm*, the San Fernando Valley between the Santa Monica and the San Gabriel Mountains.

From the field notes

"Our field trip focused on the degeneration of what Burgess would have called St. Louis's middle zone, west of the CBD. Here at Wellston, off Page Boulevard, stood a symbol of decay on the urban fringe: the gutted frame of a once-thriving electrical manufacturing plant. Surrounded by a tall chain-link fence with a locked gate and posted warnings that the site was dangerous because of severe PCB pollution, this wreckage was nevertheless flanked by housing in all directions—some of the poorest housing in the St. Louis area. It was a world (but just a few miles) away from the city center, ballpark, and famous Arch."

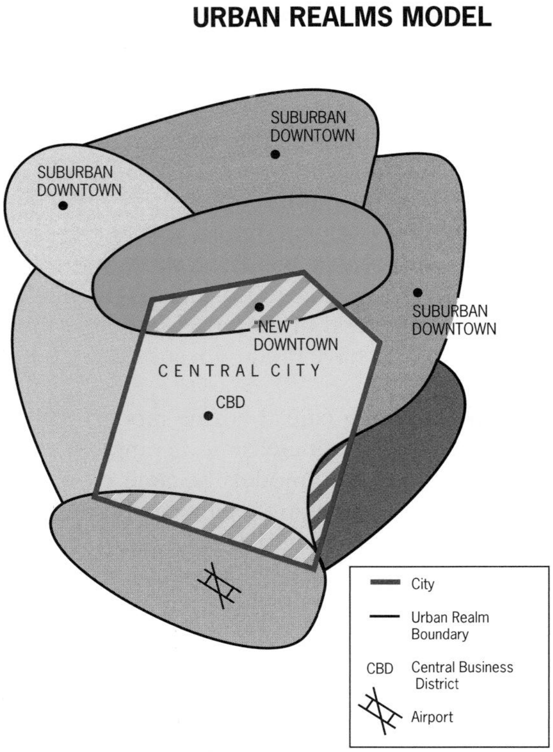

Figure 22-6 Urban Realms Model. The Urban Realms Model includes central business district, central city, new downtown, and suburban downtown. *Source:* From T. Hartshorn and P. O. Muller,"Suburban Downtowns and the Transformation of Metropolitan Atlanta's Business Landscape," *Urban Geography* 10 (1989), p. 375. Reproduced by permission of *Urban Geography*.

3. The *East Realm*, which follows the San Gabriel Valley eastward to the desert margin.
4. The *Southeast Realm*, Orange County, one of America's fastest growing urban areas, centered on Costa Mesa and Anaheim.
5. The *Southwest Realm*, straddling the San Diego Freeway from near Inglewood in the north to Long Beach in the south, and dominated economically by Los Angeles International Airport (LAX) and aerospace activities.

Approximately in the middle lies the sixth urban realm, Central Los Angeles, which is located at the hub of the freeway network but serves more as a crossroads than as a regional core. The CBD itself does contain a cluster of high-rise commercial buildings and a group of cultural and sports facilities, but it is overshadowed economically by Orange County.

The growth of the outer cities has been the hallmark of American urbanization since the 1960s. The federal government facilitated this development through the construction of super highways as mandated in the National Defense Highways Act of 1956. For a time the new highways actually reinforced the positions of downtowns, while promoting the development of close-in suburbs. With the construction of ring roads and other arteries in the 1970s and 1980s, however, suburbanization exploded around the new transportation corridors. As early as 1973, American suburbs surpassed the central cities in total employment. By the mid-1980s, the suburbanization of a critical mass of jobs (greater than 50 per-

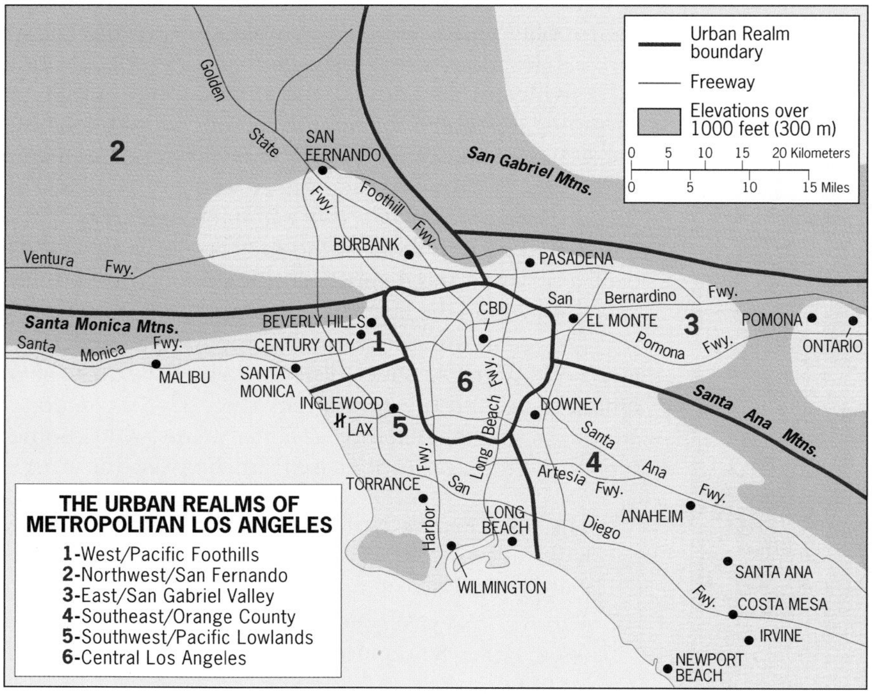

Figure 22-7 The Urban Realms of Metropolitan Los Angeles. *Source:* From a map in H. J. de Blij and P. O. Muller, *Geography: Regions and Concepts*, 10th ed. New York: Wiley, 2002, p. 164, designed by P.O. Muller.

The United States Census

Every 10 years since 1790, the government of the United States has undertaken the task of collecting information on the country's inhabitants. The last census occurred in 2000. Census forms were mailed to 105 million homes in the 50 states, each of the country's Indian Reservations, the District of Columbia, and Puerto Rico. Even though people are required by law to provide information to the Census Bureau, some do not comply and some are difficult to track down. Census workers attempt to count those who do not live in permanent residences, but this is a difficult task given, for example, the number of homeless people in cities such as Detroit, St. Louis, and Seattle.

The most important original purpose of the census was to determine the number of representatives each State was entitled to send to the House of Representatives. Over the course of the nation's history, however, statistics gathered from the census have become vital in determining the allocation of federal, State, county, and municipal funds for education, social services, health care, and infrastructure.

A variety of types of data are collected from the census, including information about age, race, gender, language, education, employment, income, and housing. Census data are tabulated and presented at six geographical scales: (1) National, (2) State, (3) County (or Parish in Louisiana), (4) Census Tract, (5) Block Group, and (6) Census Block. The first three categories are self-explanatory. The smallest level of census information is the Block—usually the size of one city block. A Block Group is a collection of several Blocks. Census Tracts, the most commonly used level of information, are at the approximate scale of an urban neighborhood and average about 4000 inhabitants. The Census Bureau also aggregates statistics for Metropolitan Statistical Areas (formerly Standard Metropolitan Statistical Areas). These encompass the 258 major urban areas of the United States and include "outlying counties" where those are viewed as integral to the urban area.

The census provides a wealth of information that helps us understand geographic developments and changes. Economic statistics provide insight into patterns of wealth and poverty income levels. Residential statistics offer evidence of mobility or stability in different communities. The census can be a source of pride and of controversy. Cities in economically depressed regions sometimes boast when a new census reveals a rise in population. Controversies, however, are more common. Neighborhoods, municipalities, and States can lose funds and political clout when their census numbers go down, so questions about the accuracy of the count often arise—particularly when it comes to poor or minority populations. Moreover, local governments have the power to design census districts, and controversy sometimes surrounds the decisions that are made.

The U.S. Census Bureau is one of the largest employers of geographers in the United States. Advancements in the field of Geographic Information Science (GIScience) have allowed massive amounts of data to be analyzed in new and creative ways. Useful and attractive maps constructed with census data have helped to promote awareness of the nation's changing geography and are an increasingly important tool for policymakers.

cent of the urban-area total) could be seen even in some major metropolises in the Sunbelt.

After about 1970, as the outer city grew rapidly and became more functionally independent of the central city, new suburban downtowns emerged to serve their new local economies. Often located near key freeway intersections, these multipurpose activity nodes developed mainly around big regional shopping centers and attracted industrial parks, office complexes, hotels, restaurants, entertainment facilities, and even major league sports stadiums to locate nearby. They became so-called ***edge cities***. As these new outer city downtowns flourished, they attracted tens of thousands of nearby suburbanites—offering workplaces, shopping, leisure activities, and all the other elements of a complete urban environment—thereby loosening remaining ties not only to the central city but to other suburban areas as well.

Thus the urban realms model constitutes the latest step forward in the interpretation of urban structure. It clearly demonstrates that today's outer cities are not satellites of the central city; they have become equal partners in the shaping of the polycentric metropolis.

◆ SOCIOCULTURAL INFLUENCES ON CITIES

Urban models tend to emphasize the generalized impacts of economic, technological, and demographic factors on the geography of cities. Behind these influences, however, lie powerful sociocultural forces that shape the character of particular parts of the city and that influence who lives where. As will become clear when we look at cities in other parts of the world, some of these forces are manifest at the scale addressed by most urban models, but they are manifest at the neighborhood scale as well. Wander through a typical middle-class American residential neighborhood with your eyes open, and you will find yourself surrounded by landscape indicators of social and cultural preferences. These are found not just in the existence of separate houses or particular styles of

A SENSE OF SCALE

Social and Economic Change Incite the Los Angeles Riots

On April 29–30, 1992, the city of Los Angeles, California, became engulfed in the worst incident of widespread civil unrest in U.S. history. During the two days of rioting 43 people died, 2383 people were injured, and 16,291 people were arrested. Property damage was estimated at approximately $1 billion, and over 22,700 law enforcement personnel were deployed to quell the unrest. According to the media, the main catalyst for the mass upheaval was the announcement of a "not-guilty" verdict in the trial of four white Los Angeles police officers accused of using excessive force in the videotaped arrest of Rodney King, a black motorist. To the general public, the Los Angeles riots became yet another symbol of the sorry state of race relations between blacks and whites in the United States. Yet a geographical perspective on the Los Angeles riots

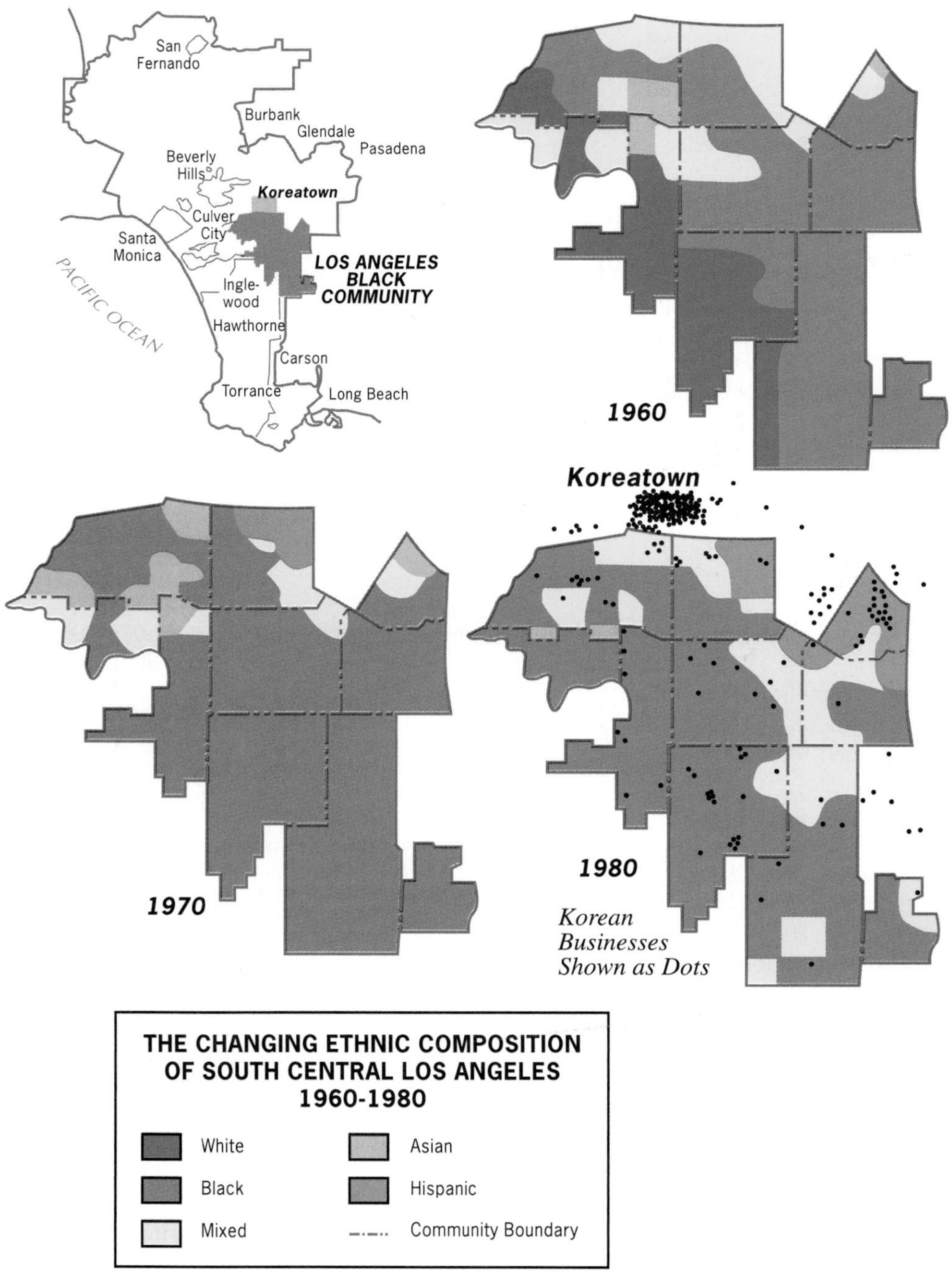

The Changing Ethnic Composition of South-Central Los Angeles, 1960–1980. *Source:* J. H. Johnson, Jr., C. K. Jones, W. C. Farrell, Jr., & M. L. Oliver. "The Los Angeles Rebellion: A Retrospective in View," *Economic Development Quarterly* 6 (4) (1992), pp. 356–372.

suggests that they were more than a snap response to a single event; they were localized reactions to sweeping economic, political, and ethnic changes unfolding at regional and even global scales.

Cities like Los Angeles have witnessed dramatic changes in their physical form, economic function, and social composition over the last century. Many of these changes are responses to shifting economic conditions and dramatic technological advances, including the invention of the automobile and the advent of telecommunications. They affect not only the economic health of cities and their hinterlands, but also the social composition and stability of neighborhoods within those cities. This is certainly the case in post-1970 south-central Los Angeles, which experienced a substantial decrease in the availability of high-paying, unionized manufacturing jobs as plants closed and relocated to the city's periphery and beyond. Indeed, over 70,000 manufacturing jobs were lost in south-central Los Angeles between 1978 and 1982 alone.

An interest in understanding the significance of this development led geographer James Johnson and his colleagues to explore its impact on the ethnic and social geography of south-central Los Angeles. Johnson et al. found that while the population of south-central Los Angeles was over 90 percent African American in 1970, it had become evenly split between Latinos and African Americans by 1990. They also found that this change was accompanied by a steady influx of Korean residents and small-business owners who were trying to find a niche in the rapidly changing urban area.

Armed with this information, Johnson and his colleagues argued that the Los Angeles riots were more than a spontaneous reaction to a verdict. They were also rooted in the growing despair and frustration of different ethnic groups competing for a decreasing number of jobs in an environment of declining housing conditions and scarce public resources. Their work shows the importance of looking beyond the immediate catalysts of particular events to the local, national, and international geographical contexts in which they unfold.

construction; they are also found in the distance between houses, the nature and style of vegetation around houses, the distance between the houses and the streets, the amount of space devoted to automobile movement and storage, and much, much more.

Sociocultural perspectives also help explain the internal ethnic geography of cities. As we will see when we look at life in cities (Chapter 28), most urban areas have distinct ethnic neighborhoods. These are not simply the product of the desire of people sharing a particular ethnic background to live together—although that can be a factor. Ethnic neighborhoods are primarily the result of the attitudes and practices of dominant groups within cities. The segregation between blacks and whites in many American cities is a case in point.

Until the 1960s, there were no significant legal obstacles to racial discrimination in the urban land market, and the desire of many whites to keep African-Americans out of their neighborhoods led to the development of clearly defined racial ghettos. There were also important economic forces and institutions behind the racial patterns that developed in cities. Financial institutions in the business of lending money would engage in a practice known as ***redlining.*** They would identify what they considered to be risky neighborhoods in cities and refuse to offer loans to those in the districts (marked by red lines on a map). This practice worked against those living in poorer neighborhoods and helped to precipitate a downward spiral in which poor neighborhoods became increasingly rundown because funds were not available for upkeep.

Real estate agents also contributed to ghettoization. Real estate agents would sometimes seek to interest a member of the African-American community in a house in a white neighborhood by offering it at a very low price. When that person moved in, efforts would be made to convince the neighboring white population that the neighborhood was going downhill—producing the so-called white flight to the suburbs. This practice, known as ***blockbusting***, led to a significant turnover in housing, which of course benefited real estate agents through the commissions they earned. It also prompted landowners to sell their properties at low prices, which in turn allowed property developers to subdivide lots and turn them into tenements.

Blockbusting became illegal in the 1960s, but more subtle forms of ***racial steering*** continued. Realtors would encourage whites and blacks to look for housing in areas that would promote changing ghetto boundaries—and therefore real estate turnover. Such practices have diminished in the face of increasing legal activism, but efforts to promote more generalized concerns about the dangers of urban life have led to the proliferation of ***gated communities*** which feature a variety of covenants and restrictions ensuring that the communities are at least relatively homogenous in socioeconomic and lifestyle terms. Even the look of many such places bespeaks their homogeneity—rules govern everything from house size and color to allowable vegetation around dwellings.

A variety of recent influences on urban life have led to changes that are further complicating the internal character of cities (see Sense of Scale Box). These influences are so intertwined with recent economic and cultural developments that we will hold off examining them until Part Nine (Chapter 28). To gain a better understanding of the urban context in the twenty-first century, we also need to look at cities in relation to one another.

◆ PATTERNS OF CITIES

When we look at an atlas map of the United States or Canada, or at a road map of a State or province, we see an array of places of different sizes, with varying distances between them. The map looks like a jumble, yet each place is where it is because of some decision, some perception of the site or its situation, or perhaps some incident that led to settlement at that particular place.

The Rank-Size Rule

Even a general map provides an impression of the sizes and locations of settlements in an area. There are many villages with unfamiliar names, a number of towns named in larger print and situated on highways, several cities where transportation routes converge, and perhaps one familiar, dominant city. We can conclude that the larger places become, the fewer there are: there is only one dominant metropolis, but there are several large cities, a greater number of towns, and many villages. We discern not only the hierarchy of urban places but also the so-called ***rank-size rule***. This rule holds that in a model urban hierarchy, the population of a city or town will be inversely proportional to its rank in the hierarchy. For example, if the largest city has 12 million people, the second city will have about 6 million (that is, half the population of the largest city); the third city will have 4 million (one-third); the fourth city 3 million; and so on. Note that the differences between cities become smaller at lower levels of the hierarchy so that the tenth-largest city would have 1.2 million inhabitants.

The rank-size rule does not apply in all countries, especially countries with dominant primate cities, such as France or Mexico, but it does seem to apply in several countries with complex economies, such as the United States. However, the map tells us little about the reasons behind the distribution of places at various levels in the hierarchy. We can use our knowledge of site and situation to speculate about the dominance of Boston compared to, say, Portland, Maine. What governs the distances among many cities of similar size or from village to village?

Urban Functions

Before we try to answer this question, we should note the functions performed by cities and other urban places. Every city and town has an ***economic base***. Geographers classify the activities of workers in cities according to their purpose: a percentage of workers produce goods or services to satisfy demand in the hinterland or in markets even farther away, while others do things that keep the city itself going. For example, workers in a manufacturing plant that produces microwave ovens (the first category) are in the city's ***basic sector***; their work produces goods for export and generates an inflow of money. On the other hand, workers who maintain city streets, clerks who work in offices, and teachers who teach in city schools are responsible for the functioning of the city itself. They constitute the ***nonbasic sector*** (also called the service sector). Many people who work in a city, of course, do some of each. An attorney may serve clients from a village in the city's hinterland, where there is no lawyer's office, but may also serve city residents.

The ratio of basic to nonbasic workers gives an impression of the city's economic base. The number of nonbasic workers is always greater than the number of basic workers, and this ratio tends to increase as a city grows. Therein lies a danger: when the products or services exported from the basic sector fail to find a market and jobs in the basic sector are lost, many more jobs in the nonbasic sector are affected.

Functional Specialization

Data on the number of people employed in basic and nonbasic jobs (the ***employment structure***) can help us discern the primary functions of a city. Note that all cities have multiple functions, and the larger the city, the larger the number of functions. As we saw at the beginning of the chapter, however, some cities are dominated by one particular activity. This ***functional specialization*** was a characteristic of European cities even before the Industrial Revolution, but the Industrial Revolution gave it new meaning. To most of us, the associations between the names of cities and their functional specialties have little relevance today, but there was a time when many cities were closely identified with certain products. Nonetheless, even when automobile production was Detroit's dominant function, other functions also made important contributions to the city's economic base.

In 1943 Chauncy Harris published a detailed study of the distribution of U.S. cities according to their dominant functions. In an article titled "A Functional Classification of Cities in the United States," he described the concentration of manufacturing-dominated cities in the Northeast, the wide dispersal of retail centers, and the western diffusion of cities that were already so diversified that no primary or dominant function could be discerned from the employment data (Fig. 22–8).

The three maps included in Figure 22–8 reveal a situation that no longer exists. Only slightly more than a dozen northeastern cities could still be mapped as manufacturing centers, including such cities as Flint, Michigan; Gary, Indiana; and Wilmington, Delaware. Most of the other northeastern cities on Harris's maps have become diversified centers. Retail-dominated cities are fewer still; they include Phoenix, Arizona; San Antonio, Texas; and Orlando, Florida. Thus growing size has brought greater diversification.

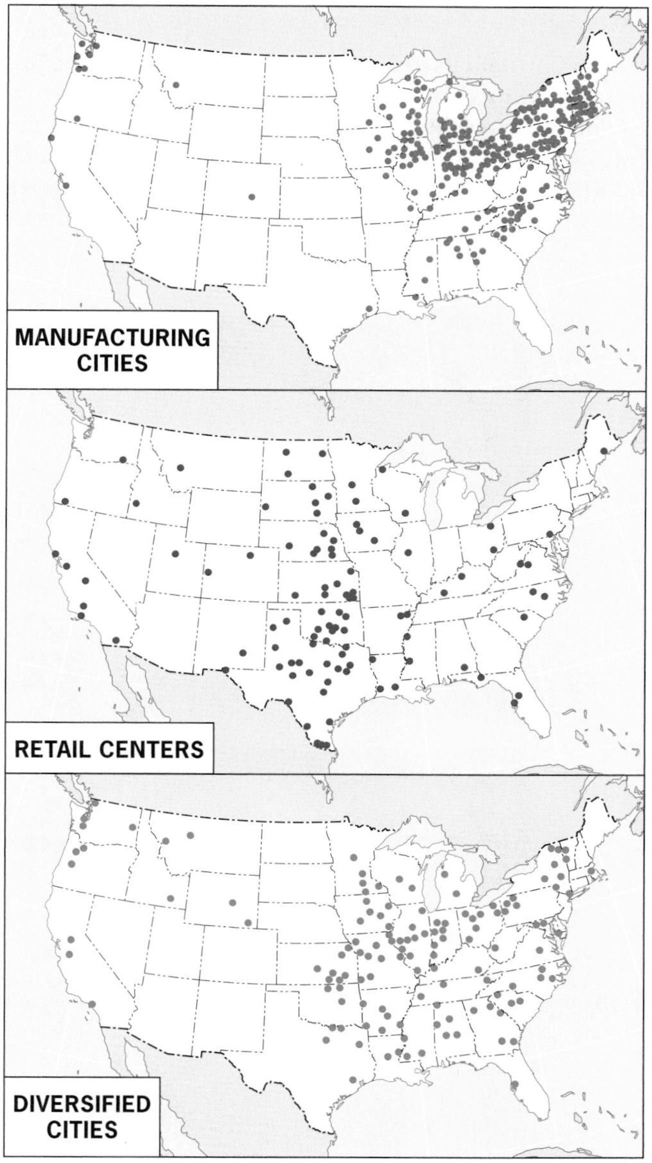

Figure 22-8 Distribution of Cities According to Function. This map shows the distribution of cities according to function: manufacturing, retail-dominated, and diversified cities in the early 1940s. *Source:* From C. Harris,"A Functional Classification of Cities in the United States," *The Geographical Review* 33 (1943), p. 88.

This is not to say that specialization no longer exists. As noted at the beginning of the chapter, we can still identify educational centers (Boston), gambling cities (Las Vegas, Atlantic City), resort and retirement towns (Vero Beach, Florida), government headquarters (Augusta, Maine), and mining centers (Leadville, Colorado). But many of these places remain small—or their main industry is unusually dominant. As urban centers grow, they tend to lose their functional specialization.

Another implication of urban growth emerges from the ratio between workers in the basic sector and those in the nonbasic sector. This ratio is about the same (1 to 2) for most large cities. When a business is established with 50 production (basic) workers, it adds 100 nonbasic workers to the workforce. Economic expansion of this kind therefore has a ***multiplier effect***, not only on the workforce but also on the urban population as a whole, because most workers have dependents who also consume goods and services.

Central Places

Earlier we encountered the notion of a *hierarchy* of urban settlements ranging from hamlets to metropolises. That hierarchy is based not only on population but also on functions and services. These functions and services attract consumers not just from the urban areas themselves but also from areas beyond the urban limits. Thus every urban center has a certain ***economic reach*** that can be used as a measure of its centrality.

From the field notes

"Looking down on Cuzco, Peru, from the rim of the surrounding mountains, I was struck by the sheer density of human habitation of a site over 11,000 feet (c. 3350 meters) above sea level. What does it mean for the environment to pack 100,000 people into a small opening between mountain peaks? The impacts on the city's site itself, and on surrounding vegetation, were clear enough. But what about problems of waste disposal and air pollution in this fragile environment? The challenges are formidable indeed, but they are not new. People have been living here since Incan times, and Cuzco had already developed into a substantial urban center by the seventeenth century."

Centrality is a characteristic of urban situations that is crucial to the development of urban places and their service areas. For these hinterlands, towns and cities are central places; even a village is a central place for its small surrounding area. How do service areas relate to each other? Do they overlap? Do towns of approximately the same size lie about the same distance away from each other? What rules govern the arrangement of urban places on the landscape? These questions are important if we are to understand the structuring of urban hierarchies. Let us therefore take a closer look at the arrangement of urban places.

◆ CENTRAL PLACE THEORY

In a 1933 book titled *The Central Places in Southern Germany,* Walter Christaller laid the groundwork for the ***central place theory***. He attempted to develop a model that would show how and where central places in the urban hierarchy (hamlets, villages, towns, and cities) would be functionally and spatially distributed. In his effort to discover the general forces that govern this distribution, Christaller began with a set of assumptions. The surface of the ideal region would be flat and have no physical barriers. Soil fertility would be the same everywhere. Christaller also assumed an even distribution of population and purchasing power and a uniform transportation network that permitted direct travel from each settlement to the other. Finally, he assumed that a constant maximum distance or range for the sale of any good or service produced in a town would prevail in all directions from that urban center.

Christaller's idea was to calculate the nature of the central place system that would develop under such conditions, and then to compare that model to real-world situations and try to explain any variations and exceptions. Some places, he realized, would have more centrality than others. The central functions of larger towns would cover regions within which several smaller places with lesser central functions and service areas were nested. What was needed, he reasoned, was a way to calculate the degree of centrality of various places. In order to do this, Christaller defined central goods and services as those provided only at a central place. These are the goods and services that a central place makes available to its consumers in a surrounding region—as opposed to services that might be available anywhere or are produced for distant markets. Next came the range of sale of such central goods and services: the distance people would be willing to travel to acquire them. The limit would lie halfway between one central place and the next place where the same product was sold at the same price because under the assumptions Christaller used, a person would not be expected to travel 11 miles to one place to buy an item if it were possible to go only 9 miles to purchase it at another place.

Hexagonal Hinterlands

In Christaller's ***urban model***, each central place has a surrounding complementary region, an exclusive hinterland within which the town has a monopoly on the sale of certain goods because it alone can provide such goods at a given price and within a certain range of travel. From what has just been said, we would expect

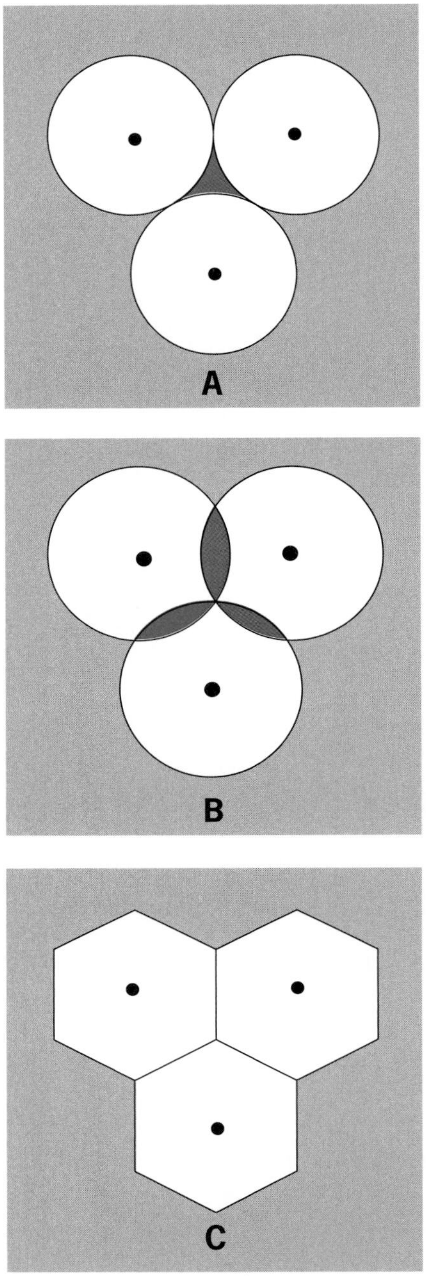

Figure 22-9 Christaller's Hexagonal Trade Areas Surrounding Urban Centers. Constructing Christaller's hexagonal trade areas surrounding urban centers involves: (A) unserved areas shown in purple; (B) purple areas indicate places where the conditions of monopoly would not be fulfilled; and (C) hexagons completely fill an area without overlap.

such complementary regions to be circular. However, when we construct the model on that basis, problems arise: either the circles adjoin and leave unserved areas, or they overlap; in the latter situation the central place no longer has a monopoly. These two problems are resolved by a model consisting of perfectly fitted hexagonal regions, as shown in Figure 22–9.

The logical extension of this conclusion is shown in Figure 22–10. If the hexagonal complementary region shown in Figure 22–9 is centered on a hamlet, where the fewest goods and services are available, that hamlet and its region must form a part of the complementary region of a village. And that village and its complementary region would be part of a town's complementary region. The central place system thus reveals a nesting (region-within-region) pattern; each larger complementary region is centered on a higher-order urban place.

Like von Thünen, whose economic-geographic model was also based on a series of assumptions, Christaller knew that conditions would be different in the real world. His model yielded a number of practical conclusions, however. First, he showed that the ranks of urban places do in fact form an orderly hierarchy of central places in spatial balance. If one component is removed, the whole system will move toward a new equilibrium. Second, Christaller's model implied that places of the same size with the same number of functions would be spaced the same distance apart. Third, larger cities would be spaced farther from each other than smaller towns or villages. What the model confirmed, therefore, was that the general pattern on the map is not an accident but a product of specific forces that tend to create regular rank-size patterns.

The Real World

If you fly over the rural landscape of southern Germany or any other countryside, you are reminded that Christaller's proposed hexagonal pattern is a model, not reality. Physical barriers, uneven resource distributions, and other factors create modifications of the spatial pattern. Because of such modifications, geographers were divided on the relevance of the model. Some saw hexagonal systems everywhere; others saw none at all. Soon attempts were made to alter the model and relate it to specific parts of the world. Christaller himself joined the debate: in 1950, he published an article, "The Foundations of Spatial Organization in Europe," in which he insisted that he had been correct all along:

> When we connect the metropolitan areas with each other through lines, and draw such a network of systems on the map of Europe, it indeed becomes eminently clear how the metropolitan areas everywhere lie in hexagonal arrangements.

Christaller received support from geographers who applied his ideas to regions in Europe, North America, and elsewhere. In China, both the North China Plain and the Sichuan Basin display the kind of uninterrupted flatness assumed by Christaller's model. When G. William Skinner examined the distribution of villages, towns, and cities there in 1964, he found a spatial pattern closely resembling the one predicted by Christaller's model. Studies in the U.S. Midwest suggested that while the square layout of the township-and-range system imposed a different kind of regularity on the landscape, the spatial forces at work there tended to confirm Christaller's theory.

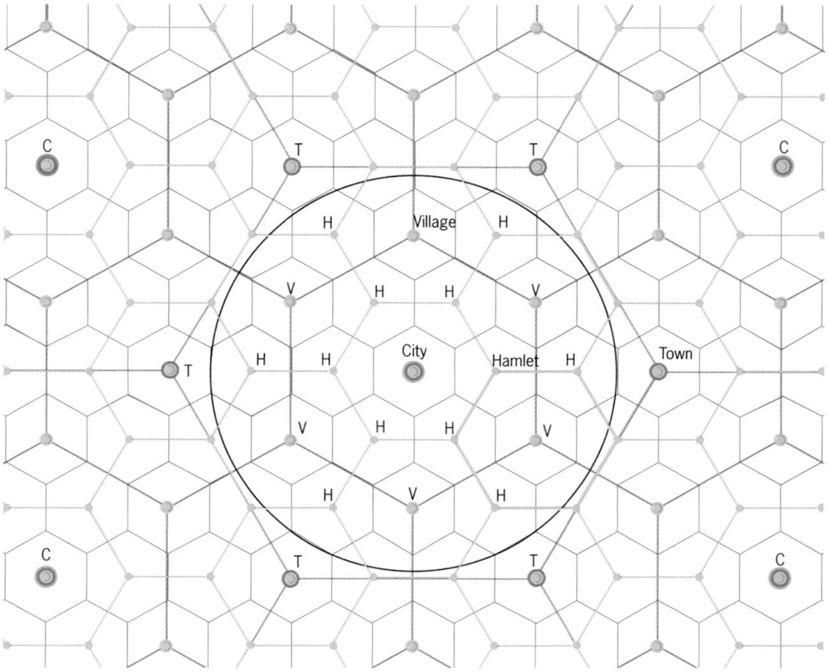

Figure 22-10 Christaller's Hierarchy of Settlements and Their Service Areas. Christaller's interlocking model of a hierarchy of settlements and their service areas include: T = town; C = city; H = hamlet; V = village.

Christaller's main contribution was the stimulus he gave to urban and economic geography in general and to location theory in particular. Since the 1950s, many studies have been published in which geographers have attempted to refine Christaller's model or use it as starting point to highlight the forces that are creating irregular distributions. In the process, our understanding of the functioning of urban places and the forces that influence their distribution has been strengthened.

◆ CHANGING REALITIES

When Christaller worked on his spatial model and projected central place theory to help explain the distribution of urban places, the world was a simpler (and much less populated) abode than it is today. As many urban geographers have pointed out during the debate that followed Christaller's publications (and those of his disciples), new factors, forces, and conditions not anticipated by his models and theories make them less relevant today.

As geographer Larry Ford has stressed, however, central place notions still have their role in explaining current developments. Take, for example, the so-called *Sunbelt* phenomenon of the past three decades—the movement of millions of Americans from northern and northeastern States to the South and Southwest. This is not just an internal, voluntary migration made possible by social security funds and retirement plans; it also results from deliberate governmental economic and social polices that favor "Sunbelt" cities through federal spending on military, space, and research facilities. And even as northerners moved southward, millions of Middle and South American migrants moved northward—into the same urban centers already growing for domestic reasons.

The overall effect of all this was to create a changed ***urban hierarchy*** in the Sunbelt region. Central place theory would predict that some existing cities would respond by increasing their production of higher-order (technological) goods and services, increasing their economic reach and bypassing others. And this is what happened: Atlanta, Dallas, and Phoenix became headquarters cities for large regions, moving up in the urban hierarchy. Charlotte, Tampa, San Antonio, and Tucson also rose, but took secondary status. Other centers participated less in the new spatial economy and remained where they were on the urban ladder.

As Ford emphasized, central place theory can still add, in his words, analytical power to the understanding of patterns of urban growth, even in this era of fast and long-distance transportation, suburbanization, and multiple urban functions.

This chapter has focused to a considerable extent on American and European cities and the models and theories spawned by their structures and distributions. But urbanization is a global phenomenon, and in the next chapter we take a worldwide perspective on what may truly be called an urbanizing planet.

◆ KEY TERMS ◆

basic sector
blockbusting
central business district (CBD)
central city
centrality
central place theory
economic base
economic reach
edge cities
employment structure
functional specialization
functional structure
gated communities
hinterland
megacity
megalopolis
multiplier effect
nonbasic sector
racial steering
rank-size rule
redlining
site
situation
suburb
Sunbelt
urban function
urban geography
urban hierarchy
urban model
urban realm

◆ APPLYING GEOGRAPHIC KNOWLEDGE ◆

1. The growth of towns and cities is boosted by the multiplier effect, one of the linkages between basic and nonbasic employment in any urban area. What are the implications of the multiplier effect when basic employment in a city declines?
2. The popular image of a city still tends to be dominated by the impressive, skyscraper-dominated skyline that symbolizes the supremacy of the "downtown." Behind that image lies a changing reality. How is the downtown-dominant model of the American city changing? Relate the new model to the North American city you know best.
3. You are a geographer on a corporate team that is going to a city in China to position and build a factory. You will need maps to assess the site of this factory as well as its situation in the urban area. At what scales will you request that maps be made available to you? What kind of maps will you want to consult?

Chapter 23

Global Urbanization

From the field notes

"Urban regions are defined by particular features: high-rise buildings in the city center, commercial-residential mixes in the middle zones, open spaces in the suburbs. Major cities are often characterized by their most prominent buildings, as was New York City by the twin towers of the World Trade Center before their destruction on 11 September 2001, and as is Chicago by its Sears Tower, Kuala Lumpur by the Petronas Towers, Shanghai by its Pearl Television Tower, Sydney by its Opera House, and San Francisco by the Transamerica Tower. But behind and beneath these impressive and often towering facades, modern city centers have lost much of their long-term character and atmosphere and have acquired a sameness that belies their individualities. This photograph happens to show a part of downtown San Francisco, but it is really a view of the modern central city anywhere, and surely does not reflect the popular image of one of America's most vibrant cities."

KEY POINTS

- **As a percentage of total population, urban dwellers are most numerous in Western Europe, North America, Japan, and Australia. However, urbanization is occurring rapidly elsewhere, especially in Subsaharan Africa.**
- **World urbanization is accelerating, and by some estimates well over 50 percent of our planet's inhabitants now live in urban settings, a percentage that may rise to 67 by 2050.**
- **The largest urban agglomerations exist in the less developed world, and the leading cities of the 1950s, such as London and Paris, do not even make the top 25 today.**
- **Several of the world's great urban complexes, notably in eastern North America, Western Europe, and Japan, are the products of megalopolitan coalescence. The fastest-growing megacities, however, are in South and East Asia.**
- **South American, Southeast Asian, and Subsaharan African cities reflect their colonial beginnings as well as more recent domestic developments.**

At the outset of Part Seven we noted that people are moving to cities and towns all over the world. Although definitions of what constitutes an urban area vary, and estimates of the rate of urbanization differ, all observers agree that the process continues to speed up. This acceleration varies from region to region, as it has historically. Today, the fastest rates of urbanization are occurring in the least urbanized parts of the world, such as Subsaharan Africa and China. A half century ago, Europe and North America were urbanizing rapidly. In this chapter we examine the process of urbanization in global perspective. ◆

◆ EUROPE IN THE VANGUARD

When the medieval and mercantile cities of Europe were transformed by the forces of the Industrial Revolution, a new regional map was being forged. Europe has old and famous cities, but its population around 1800 still was overwhelmingly rural. Two centuries later, Western Europe is about 80 percent urban, and if all the remaining farmers moved to the cities this year, it would not make much difference. Western Europe is an urban region.

Europe's rapid ***urbanization*** was the beginning of a worldwide process set in motion by the globalizing forces of colonialism and the power of the Industrial Revolution, exported to the farthest corners of the planet. Australia, essentially a European outpost, today is 85 percent urban. Cities founded as colonial headquarters in Asia and Africa grew slowly at first, their development controlled by the imperial powers; today these cities are experiencing a population explosion fueled by inmigration.

The growth of urbanization in Western Europe and in the world as a whole is charted in Figure 23–1A and B, respectively. In the case of Western Europe, Figure 23–1A shows that as recently as 1950, only slightly more than 50 percent of Western Europeans lived in cities and towns with 5000 inhabitants or more. Still, Europe's greatest cities ranked among the dozen largest in the world, and at the time no major world region was more urbanized than Western Europe was.

By some measures, Western Europe is even more highly urbanized than Figure 23–1A suggests. As noted in Chapter 19, various countries use different criteria for defining urban residents. Some regard almost any clustered settlement, even a village of a few hundred people, as an urban area; others put the limit higher; and

From the field notes

"Floating along the Thames River through London on my way to the great observatory in Greenwich, I marveled at the urban scene unfolding before me. Here is a city that has been a dominant presence on the European scene for centuries. It has evolved from hub of the British Empire to major global financial node—benefiting both from its position as capital of the country where the Industrial Revolution was born and from its role in the emerging world economy. The symbols of its power and status are scattered throughout the urban landscape—ranging from the dome of St. Paul's cathedral to the steel and glass towers of recent decades."

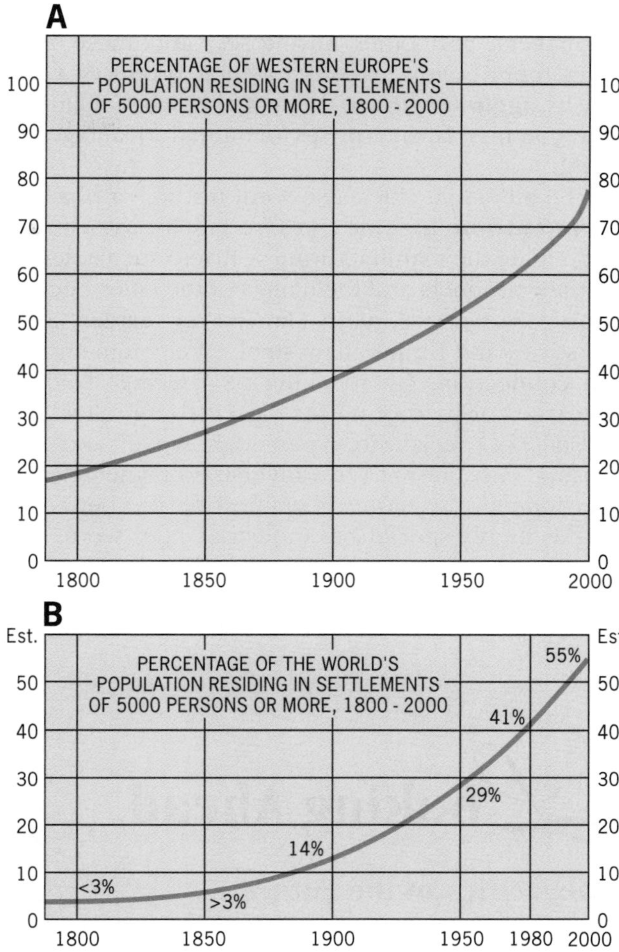

Figure 23-1 Percentage of Population Residing in Settlements of 5000 + Persons. Data on urbanization vary by country; the level of 5000 residents for a settlement to qualify as urban is arbitrary.

still others use employment as the chief criterion. Since the criteria vary, so do the resulting statistics. Figure 23–1A uses the limit of 5000, which gives a regional estimate of urbanization of about 75 percent. This limit is arbitrary, however. By other calculations, urbanization in Western Europe exceeds 85 percent.

The same caveat applies to Figure 23–1B, which shows the growth of urbanization worldwide. Some agencies, including the Population Reference Bureau and the American Association for the Advancement of Science (the latter in its *Atlas of Population and Environment,* published in 2000), estimate that global urbanization still is below 50 percent. Other agencies, including the United Nations, calculate it as high as 55 percent. Whatever the basis, it is clear that the world as a whole has now reached the approximate level of Western Europe just before 1950. Will the rest of the world also reach 80 percent urbanization or more in the coming half century? That is unlikely, but it is not improbable that two out of three inhabitants of our planet will be living in urban centers by midcentury.

The impetus toward urbanization in the less developed regions of the world is quite different from that which propelled the process in industrializing Europe. During the Industrial Revolution, relative location played a major role in the fortunes of cities; some cities were favorably located with respect to natural resources and other essentials, and had an advantage that moved them upward in the urban hierarchy. Others were so large that their markets and services sustained them, even if major industries did not dominate their economies. Still others could not keep pace, and some even declined, losing population and economic reach under the withering competition brought about by industrialization.

In the growing manufacturing cities, raw materials were consumed at enormous rates, and products poured forth from the factories in ever greater quantities. Industrialists found that there was an advantage in sharing the services of raw-material suppliers, transporters, builders, glassmakers, and other businesses, and these businesses found ready markets for their products. Cities grew by ***agglomeration***, the spatial process of clustering by commercial enterprises for mutual advantage and benefit.

The industrial cities also went through a phase of ***specialization***. In some cities, certain industries grew to dominate the manufacturing sector to such a degree that their products and the names of the cities became almost synonymous, as in Manchester textiles, Sheffield silver, and Birmingham steel. (We commemorate such connections by speaking of carrying "coals to Newcastle" or by rooting for the Pittsburgh Steelers.) This stage of specialization passed, however, and most industrial cities now have a diversified manufacturing base. Indeed, the more diversification the better: famous as highly specialized industrial cities were, they also faced heightened risk. Eventually, in Europe as well as America, such cities and towns proved vulnerable to changing economic conditions. Specialized textiles are a good example: names like Manchester and Burlington once stood for brand and quality, but now the mills stand empty and the towns have faced wrenching adjustments.

Europe's largest cities, however, thrived, and for a very long time London and Paris ranked among the world's 10 largest cities. In 1950, when New York was not only the largest city in the world but the only one with more that 10 million residents, London (8 million) and Paris (6 million) ranked number 2 and 4, respectively. Tokyo, with 7 million, ranked third. Shanghai, Buenos Aires, Chicago, Moscow, Calcutta (now Kolkata), and Los Angeles, all with populations between 4 and 6 million, completed the top 10. By 1975, however, the global picture had changed significantly. At that point there were five cities with more than 10 million people, none of them in Europe and only one in the United States. New names on the list included Mexico City, Mumbai (Bombay), São Paulo, and Lagos (Nigeria). As we look to the future, more changes can be anticipated (see Looking Ahead Box and Table 23–1).

Looking Ahead

Megacities of the Future

According to a report entitled *The State of the World Population*, published by the United Nations Population Fund in 2001, over 2.8 billion people lived in cities at the turn of the century (a low estimate compared to estimates from other sources). By 2015, the report states, that number will have risen to 3.9 billion, with nearly 75 percent in the developing world. The number of megacities with more than 10 million inhabitants will have risen from 5 in 1975 to 23 in 2015. The top 23 will not include a single European city (Table 23–1). Tokyo will remain the largest city in the world, about to be overtaken by Mumbai. Moreover, there will be many new names on the 2015 list: Lagos, Dhaka (Bangladesh), Karachi (Pakistan), Jakarta (Indonesia).

Table 23–1 makes clear that the pattern of world urbanization is undergoing dramatic change. Carrying UN projections beyond 2015, we can expect that by 2035 as many as 15 cities will have populations between 20 and 30 million, and as many as 5 will have more than 30 million. Thus several of these huge megacities will be larger than some of the magalopolitan conurbations of Europe and the United States.

Table 23–1 also indicates how fast individual megacites in poorer countries are growing compared to conurbations in richer states. The New York–New Jersey conurbation is being overtaken by a growing number of cities in the periphery; at the turn of the century it had dropped from first place (1950) to ninth (2000), and it is projected to occupy the nineteenth position by 2015. Meanwhile, burgeoning centers such as Mumbai and Kolkata will move up rapidly. Between them, Mumbai and Kolkata gained about 9 million inhabitants during the 1990s alone; Tokyo and New York combined increased by just 2 million.

All of this suggests that the greatest challenges posed by global urbanization still lie ahead. The challenges will be great indeed—ranging from the economic to the social to the environmental. As we will discuss in some detail in Chapter 28, many cities are already facing serious strains on infrastructure and social services, and as millions of new urban dwellers arrive, municipal authorities will have to find increasingly creative and dynamic ways of coping—or risk having their cities dissolve into chaos. Indeed, if urbanization trends continue at present rates, there is the very real prospect that huge cities could become the principal incubators of social unrest in the decades ahead.

Avoiding that outcome will place great strains on municipal and state authorities during the twenty-first century. Planning will become increasingly essential if the basic resource and housing needs of burgeoning urban populations are to be met and if cities are to retain some degree of functional coherence, livability, and aesthetic appeal. Increasingly active municipal governments will be needed to keep pace with the changes—meaning that the city halls of megacities are likely to become increasingly significant loci of power and decision making as the twenty-first century unfolds.

Table 23-1 **Populations of the World's Largest Conurbations**

1975		2000		2015	
Tokyo	19.8	Tokyo	26.4	Tokyo	26.6
New York	15.9	Mexico City	18.1	Mumbai	26.1
Shanghai	11.4	Mumbai	18.1	Lagos	23.2
Mexico City	11.2	São Paulo	17.8	Dhaka	21.1
São Paulo	10	Shanghai	17	São Paulo	20.4
		New York	16.6	Karachi	19.2
		Lagos	13.4	Mexico City	19.2
		Los Angeles	13.1	New York	17.4
		Kolkata	12.9	Jakarta	17.3
		Buenos Aires	12.6	Kolkata	17.3
		Dhaka	12.3	Delhi	16.8
		Karachi	11.8	Manila	14.8
		Delhi	11.7	Shanghai	14.6
		Jakarta	11	Los Angeles	14.1
		Osaka	11	Buenos Aires	14.1
		Manila	10.9	Cairo	13.8
		Beijing	10.8	Istanbul	12.5
		Rio de Janeiro	10.6	Beijing	12.3
		Cairo	10.6	Rio de Janeiro	11.9
				Osaka	11
				Tianjin	10.7
				Hyderabad	10.5
				Bangkok	10.1

Population in millions. Source: UN Population Fund, *The State of World Population 2001* (New York, 2001), p. 33.

◆ WORLD URBANIZATION

A productive way to examine world urbanization is to map urban population as a percentage of total population by country (Fig. 23–2). A state or region may not contain any of the world's largest cities, but it may be more highly urbanized than states or regions with ***megacities***. Compare India, which has several of the world's largest cities as ranked in Table 23–1, and Germany, which has none. Yet Germany is 86 percent urbanized, and India only 28 percent (as of the year 2002).

Figure 23–2 reveals not only the high level of urbanization in the core regions of Western Europe, North America, Australia, and Japan but also the remarkably high percentages of urbanization in several countries in the periphery. Taking 70 percent and higher as the highest category, we find Mexico and Cuba to be on a par with France. In fact, Mexico's level of urbanization is higher than that of several Eastern European countries.

Seventy years of communist rule and industrialization raised levels of urbanization throughout most of the former Soviet Union. Today Russia's population is 73 percent urbanized; in Ukraine the figure is just below 70 percent. In Transcaucasia urbanization exceeds 55 percent, although Armenia is well ahead of Georgia and Azerbaijan. The former Soviet colonial domain in Central Asia is the least urbanized of the former Soviet realms, ranging from 63 percent in strongly Russified Kazakhstan to a mere 27 percent in remote and poorer Tajikistan.

The progress of urbanization in South America is also obvious from the map. Not only are the three countries of the South American "cone" (Argentina, Chile, and Uruguay) highly urbanized, but Brazil and Venezuela also rank high. In late 2002 only the landlocked countries (Paraguay and Bolivia) lagged well behind their neighbors, but the lowest levels of urbanization were reported by the three countries on the north coast, Guyana, Suriname, and French Guiana. These "three Guianas" with their Caribbean (and otherwise non-Iberian) cultural characteristics stand apart from the rest of South America in other geographic ways as well.

At the beginning of the new century, the Subsaharan African geographic realm included countries with some

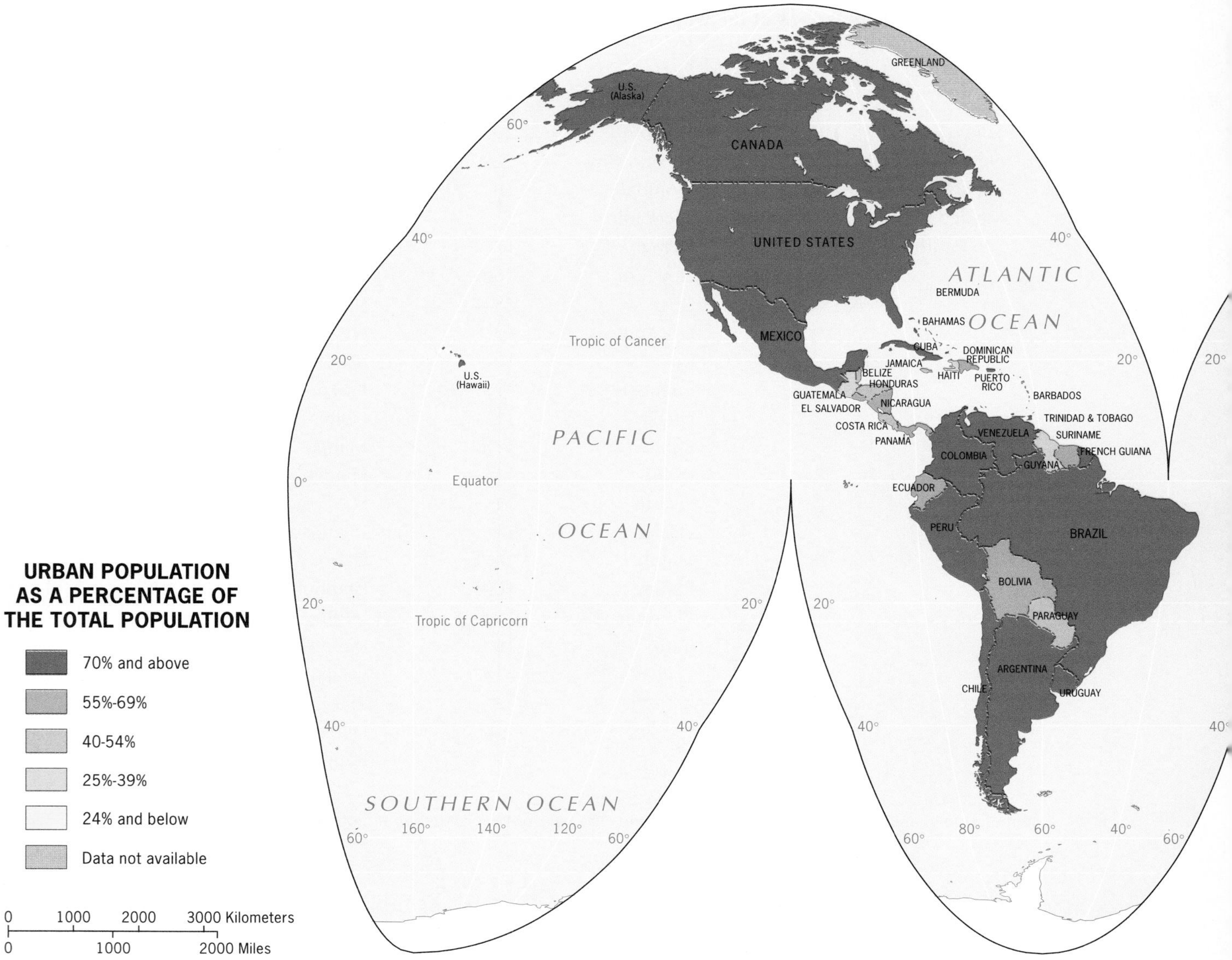

Figure 23-2 Urban Population as a Percentage of the Total Population. *Source:* Data from Population Reference Bureau, World Population Data Sheet 2001. Washington, D.C., 2001.

of the world's lowest levels of urbanization. Nigeria was just 36 percent urban in 2002. Even lower percentages were reported by Ethiopia, the Democratic Republic of Congo, and Moçambique—all populous countries in the African geographic realm. Indeed, in tropical Africa, where the majority of the people still are farmers, most countries remain under 40 percent urbanized. Outside the tropics, South Africa in 2002 was at the 57 percent level, but that figure should be seen in light of that country's strong regional diversity. The mining-industrial heartland is highly urbanized, approaching Western European levels, but beyond this core area the country is predominantly rural and resembles tropical Africa.

The culturally and economically diverse realm of Southwest Asia and North Africa displays remarkable variation in levels of urbanization. This variation is related to differences in national economies and cultures. Much of the realm, the Middle East and the Arabian Peninsula, is quite highly urbanized. ***Nucleation*** resulting from the oil industry has much to do with this situation, although this does not explain the urbanization of Jordan, where the urban tradition is old. At the southern end of the Arabian Peninsula, urbanization has not reached high levels because industrialization and the exploitation of energy resources have not altered traditional livelihoods as much as in Iraq and Saudi Arabia.

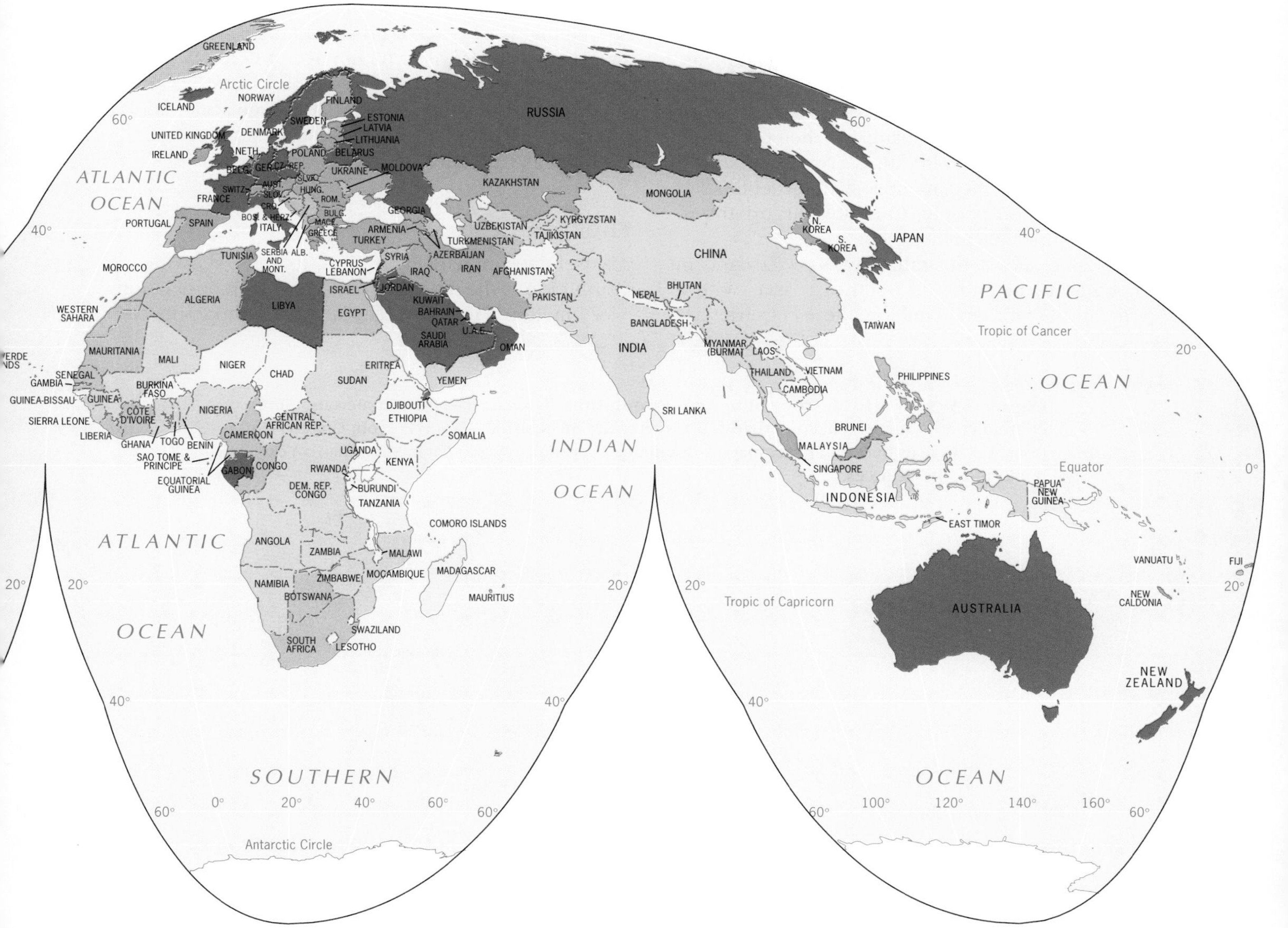

To the east and west similar variations occur: note the low level of urbanization in resource-poor Afghanistan and the high level in oil-rich Libya.

Despite the presence of great cities such as Mumbai and Kolkata (Calcutta), urbanization in South Asia remains low. For the realm as a whole, urbanization is still well below 30 percent. India today is about 28 percent urbanized, Pakistan 33 percent, and populous Bangladesh only 20 percent. As noted earlier, farming (including subsistence farming) remains the dominant way of life in this realm, and this condition is reflected in the level of urbanization.

Southeast Asia includes the only country in the world that is 100 percent urban: the city-state of Singapore. Overall, however, this geographic realm is marked by low levels of urbanization. In addition to Singapore, Brunei, the ministate on the Island of Borneo, and Malaysia are more than 50 percent urbanized. Elsewhere the figures are more characteristic of the developing world: Myanmar (26 percent), Vietnam (24), and Thailand (31). Indonesia, the fourth most populous country in the world, is only 39 percent urbanized.

These days we hear a great deal about the rapid rate of economic growth on the western Pacific Rim and the explosive growth of urban centers there (such as Shenzhen). Yet only Japan, South Korea, and Taiwan are highly urbanized here. As a whole, East Asia is only about 36 percent urbanized, and in China, despite its great cities, barely over one in four citizens lives in urban centers. Shanghai and Beijing between them have about 25 million inhabitants, and there are many other major cities in this country, including one that the Chinese allege is the world's largest, whose boundaries were redrawn to incorporate a large and densely peopled hinterland, creating a "city" of 30 million inhabitants. Chongqing proper may have as many as 9 million, making this a city on a par with Tianjin; other large Chinese cities include Wuhan and Shenyang, but their combined population is not enough to lift China's overall urbanization level much above 30 percent. Still, consider this statistic: with 1.3 billion people, China has an urbanized population of about 400 million.

Figure 23–2 shows Australia and New Zealand in sharp contrast to neighboring Southeast Asia. With a total population of under 24 million, these countries are 85 percent urban; neighboring Indonesia, with about 220 million, is 39 percent urbanized, only slightly more than the Southeast Asian realm as a whole. Australia's economy depends strongly on pastoralism and farming, but the industry is mechanized and large-scale. Southeast Asia may have larger cities, but subsistence farming still plays a leading role in most people's lives.

The Great Cities

It is useful to compare Figure 23–2 to a map showing the distribution of the more than 300 cities with populations over 1 million (Fig. 23–3). The latter map shows the con-

Figure 23-3 World Metropolitan Area Population. Based on data from numerous, often contradictory, sources (data on urban centers often are inconsistent). *Source:* From United Nations, U.S. Census Bureau, Encyclopaedia Britannica Yearbooks, World Bank, Statesman's Yearbook, and other sources.

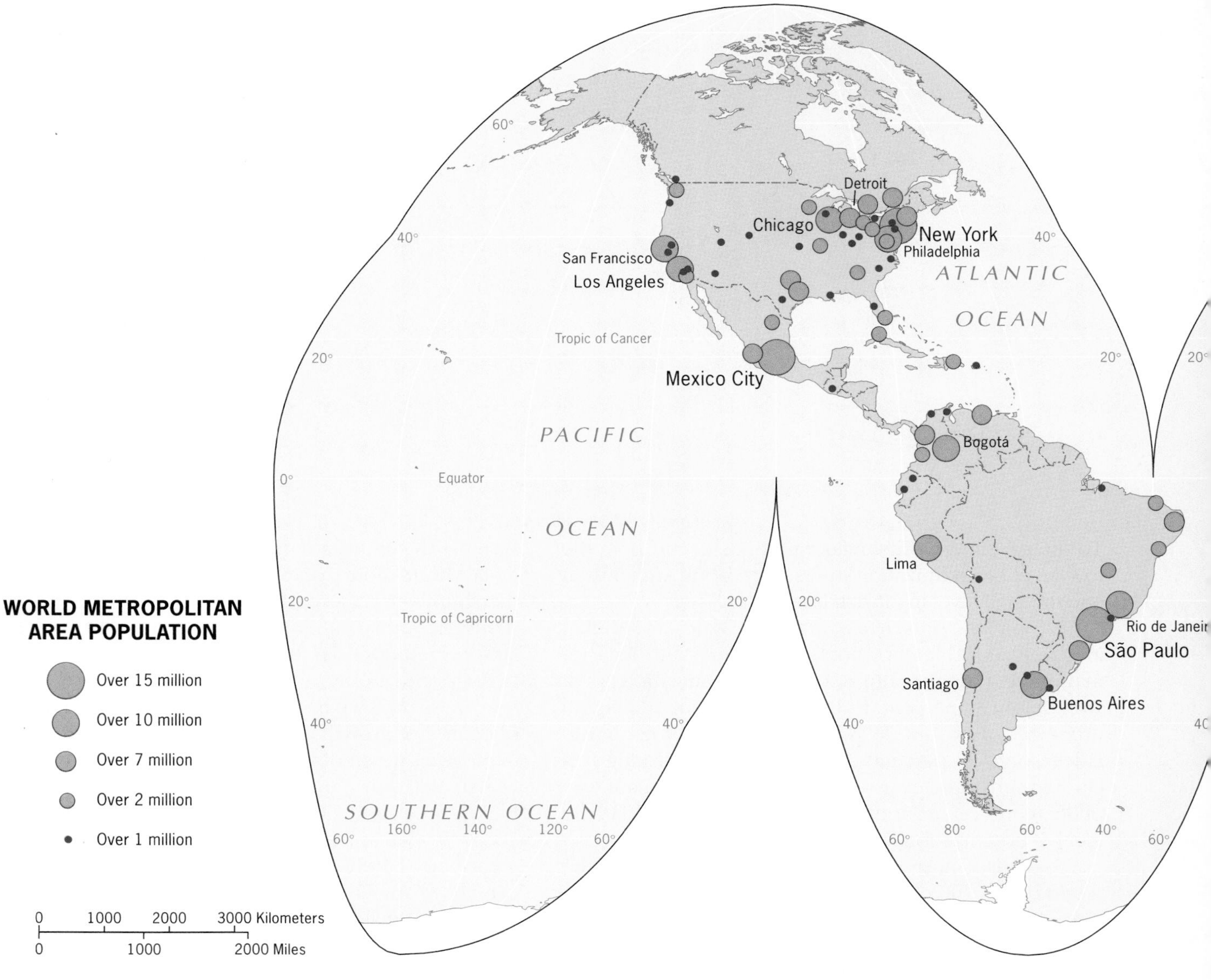

centration of large cities in eastern North America, Western Europe, East Asia (notably Japan), and to a somewhat lesser extent Latin America. Africa's low level of urbanization is clearly evident.

North America displays the anchors of several megalopolitan regions (Fig. 23–4). These include the Boston–Washington, D.C., Chicago–Detroit–Pittsburgh, San Francisco–Los Angeles–San Diego, and Montreal–Toronto–Windsor conurbations. Yet another, in Florida, is still marked only as a set of discrete, comparatively small cities, but as a result of recent population growth a regional megalopolis is developing quickly. Centered on Miami–Fort Lauderdale–West Palm Beach, it is growing northward along the Atlantic coast toward Jacksonville and westward across central Florida.

In England, a major megalopolitan region is developing around London. That city and its environs lie at the center of an expanding population cluster of nearly 20 million, and the industrial cities of South Wales and the Midlands are now just a short distance away. On the European mainland, a major urban complex is emerging in western Germany in the Ruhr–Rhine zone, which includes such cities as Düsseldorf, Essen, and Cologne. In Belgium, an urban complex is developing centered on Brussels and Antwerp. In the Netherlands, planning for a triangular megalopolis (Amsterdam–Rotterdam–The Hague) is high on the national agenda. An attempt is being made to make this ***megalopolis***, called Randstad (edge or / "ring-city"), a model megacity, complete with parks, spacious housing, good communications and public transportation, and well-distributed social services.

Other major urban agglomerations in Europe include the region centered on Paris, the rapidly developing Po Plain of northern Italy, and the Central Euro-

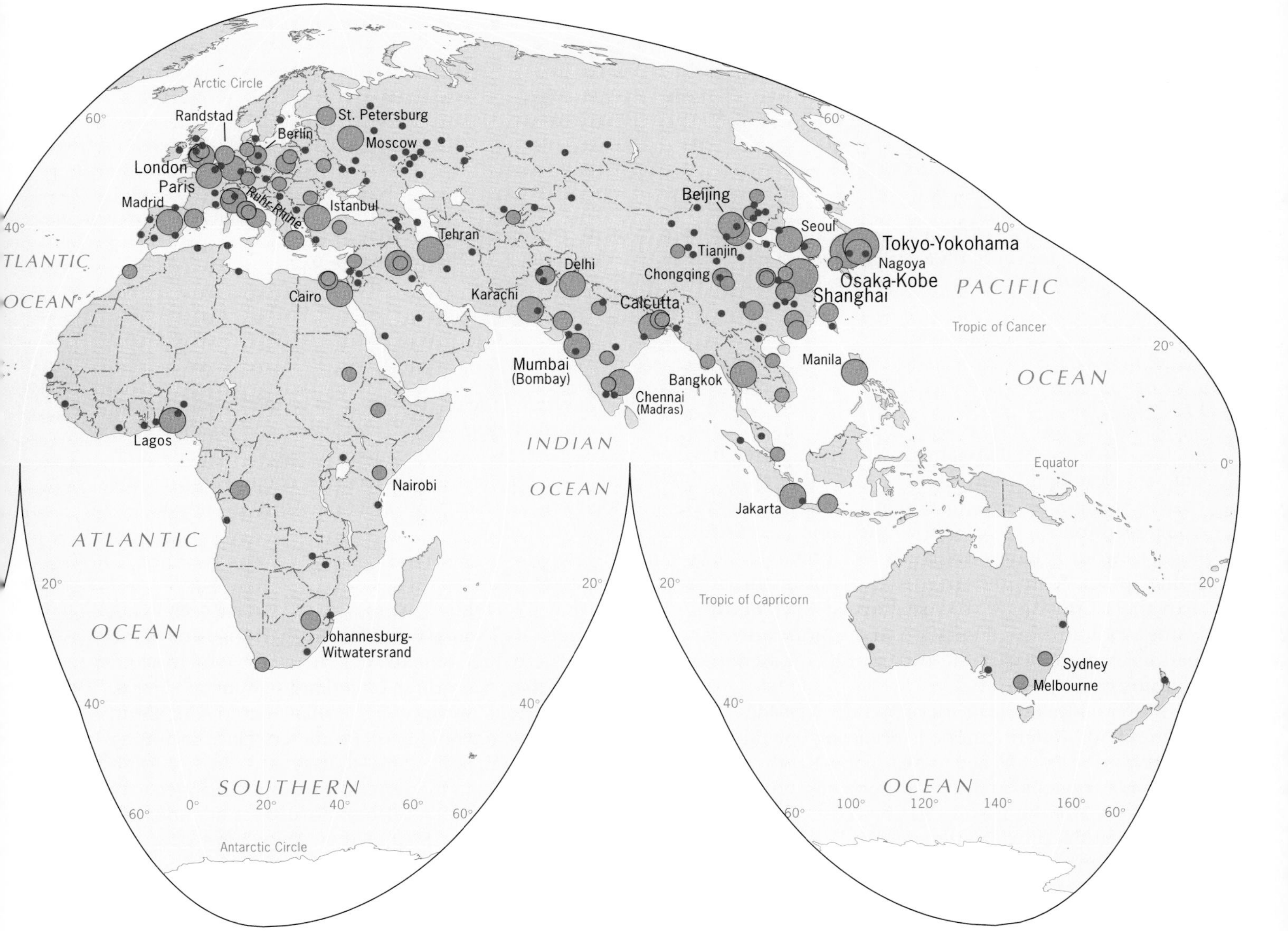

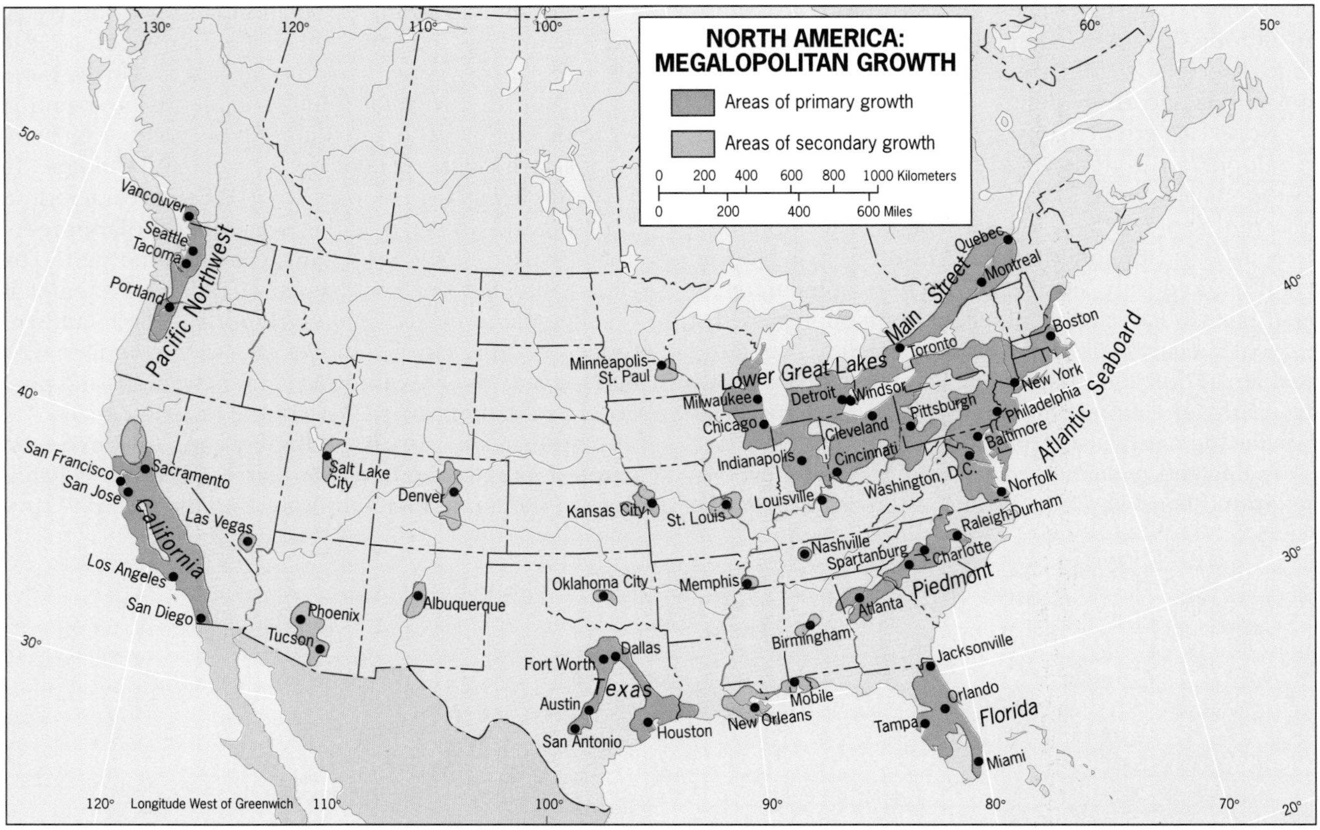

Figure 23-4 North American Megalopolitan Growth. This map shows evolving megalopolises in North America. *Source:* From a map in H. J. de Blij and P. O. Muller, Geography: Realms, Regions, and Concepts, 10th ed. New York: Wiley, 2002.

pean complex that extends from Saxony in Germany to Silesia in Poland. Elsewhere, there are major cities, such as Moscow, St. Petersburg, and Madrid, that have not yet developed into multicity urban regions. Of course, we should keep the dimensions of these developments in perspective. The whole urbanized area of Europe, from Britain's Midlands to Germany's Ruhr–Rhine region, extends over an area not much larger than the North American megalopolis. Yet Europe's historic political fragmentation and cultural diversity lead us to identify discrete urban units on a country-by-country basis.

Major megalopolitan development outside North America and Western Europe is occurring only in Japan. The Tokyo–Yokohama and Osaka–Kobe–Kyoto conurbations are enormous, and they are growing toward each other along Honshu Island's Pacific coast. This is not to suggest that the urbanizing trend that has generated the Bosnywash megalopolis and Randstad–Holland cannot be seen in other parts of the world. Johannesburg in South Africa, for example, lies at the center of a substantial megalopolis that includes several medium-sized cities in the Witwatersrand region. However, in general, conurbanization outside Europe, the United States, and Japan has not yet reached massive proportions. A high level of urbanization does not necessarily produce conurbation, as the widely spaced cities of Australia and Argentina reveal.

Megacities

As Table 23–1 shows, many of the world's evolving megacities are located in the less prosperous parts of the world. These huge human agglomerations tend to stand alone in their vast rural hinterlands. Mumbai, Lagos, Dhaka, Karachi, Mexico City, Kolkata, and Delhi are in this category, and some less prominent cities including Hyderabad, Bangkok, Lima–Callao, and Ho Chi Minh City (Saigon) are in the process of joining this megacity group. Other megacities also stand alone, but under different circumstances: Shanghai on China's fast-developing Pacific Rim, São Paulo as Brazil's economic headquarters; Buenos Aires as Argentina's primate city.

As we noted in Part Two, people continue to migrate to cities in response to "pull" factors that are often

From the field notes

"An unusual itinerary: directly from St. John's, Newfoundland, to St. John, New Brunswick. Canadian cities and towns, including those of the Atlantic Provinces, also have experienced central-city problems. Here in the east, factory closings and the decline of the fishing industry have hurt cities and towns. In St. John, New Brunswick, old warehouses have been converted into shopping malls, and the wharf now is a tourist attraction; the city even invites visits from cruise ships. The economic base is changing."

more imaginary than real; their expectations of a better life mostly fail to materialize. Particularly in the less developed realms, but in the industrial cities of Europe and North America as well, the new arrivals (and many long-term residents, too) are crowded together in overpopulated apartment buildings, dismal tenements, and teeming slums. New arrivals come from other cities and towns and from the rural countryside, often as large families; they add to the cities' rate of natural growth. Housing cannot keep up with this massive inflow. Almost overnight huge shantytowns, mostly without the barest amenities, develop around these cities. These do not deter additional urban immigration, and as a result millions of people spend their entire lives in urban housing of wretched quality.

Despite the miserable living conditions of large numbers of urban immigrants, the cities continue to beckon. During the 1990s, Africa had the world's fastest growing cities, followed by those in South Asia and mainland East Asia and South and Middle America. In contrast, the cities of North America, southern South America, and Australia were growing more slowly, and those of Western Europe were barely growing at all. Figure 23–3 therefore shows much change in the poorer parts of the world and relatively little in the richer regions. In less well-off countries, villages are becoming towns, towns are growing into cities, and cities are expanding into metropolises. There was a time when New York was the world's largest city, its skyline of skyscrapers a symbol of the economic power of the Western world. Then Tokyo's population overtook New York's. For a time Mexico City appeared poised to become the world's most populous city, a vast agglomeration of slums and squatter settlements encircling a deteriorating central city. But then Mumbai, São Paulo, and Shanghai challenged Mexico City's ascent, and UN projections put Mexico's capital behind a half-dozen larger or faster-growing cities.

Cities in poorer parts of the world generally lack enforceable ***zoning*** laws, which are drawn up to ensure that space is used in ways that the society at large deems to be culturally and environmentally acceptable. Thus a fast-food franchise could not occupy a corner lot in a residential U.S. suburb because all the lots in that suburban block would be zoned exclusively for single-family residences. In cities in less developed countries, zoning practices are often minimal, ineffective, or unenforced. In Chennai (Madras) and other Indian cities, open space between high-rise buildings is often occupied by squatter settlements. In Bangkok, elementary schools and noisy, polluting factories stand side by side. In Nairobi, hillside villas overlook some of Africa's worst slums. Over time such incongruities may disappear, as is happening in many cities in East Asia. Rising land values and greater demand for enforced zoning regulations are helping transform the central cities there. But in South Asia, Subsaharan Africa, Southwest Asia and North Africa, and Middle and South America, unregulated, helter-skelter growth continues.

Perhaps the most obvious characteristic of megacities in these realms is the stark contrasts they display. Actually, sharp contrasts between wealthy and poor areas can be found in megacities all over the world, but their intensity and scale are greater in some places than in others. If you stand on the roof of the Nile Hilton Hotel in Cairo, Egypt, overlooking the square and avenues leading into it, you see what appears to be a modern, Mediterranean-European metropolis. But if you get on a bus and ride it toward the city's outskirts, that impression fades almost immediately as paved streets give way to dusty alleys, apartment buildings to harsh tenements, sidewalk coffee shops to broken doors and windows. Traffic-choked, garbage-strewn, polluted Cairo is home to an estimated 12.5 million people, about one-fifth of Egypt's population; the city is bursting at the seams. And still people continue to arrive, seeking the better life that pulls countless migrants from the countryside year after year.

◆ MODELING THE MODERN CITY

As megacities have multiplied and cities with a million inhabitants or more can be counted in the hundreds, it has become increasingly difficult to model, classify, or typify urban centers. Less than a half century ago, it was possible to identify "colonial" cities as European transplants dominated by Western styles and layouts and to point to "indigenous" cities that still remained remote from globalizing influences and, as we noted in Chapter 22, various forms of the Western city. Today's postcolonial megacities, many of them founded as colonial headquarters but now engulfed by massive inmigration, defy generalization. Even indigenous cities deep in continental interiors (such as those in West Africa's Sahel and in Central Asia) have been exposed to the forces of modernization and inmigration, and in the process they have been transformed.

Any attempt to identify some consistent spatial framework in the cities of the world regions beyond those of Europe and North America must be based on exceptions to the circumstances just described. In Middle and South America, Mexico City and São Paulo are now the kinds of megacities that make analysis difficult. But South American cities have been endowed with strong Iberian cultural imprints that define a certain common social-spatial geography. In Subsaharan Africa some former colonial cities have retained the spatial components lost in stupendous agglomerations like Lagos and Kinshasa (The Congo). And in Southeast Asia some middle-sized cities continue to exhibit a fairly consistent pattern.

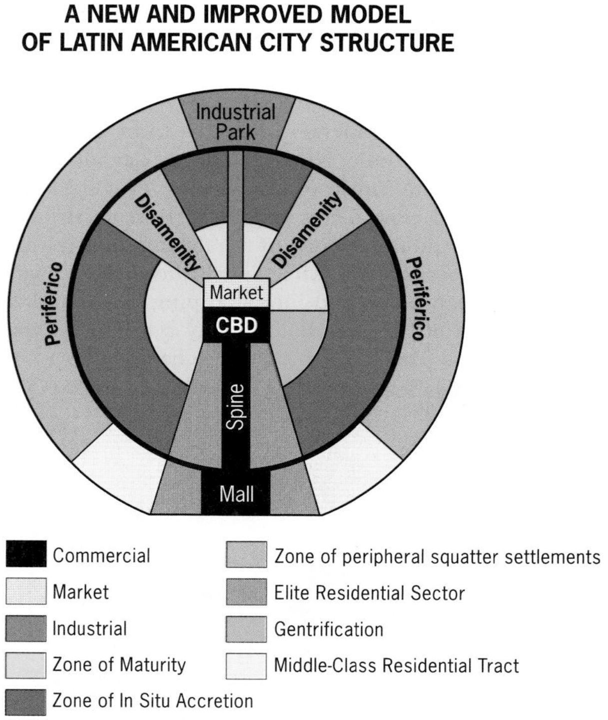

Figure 23–5 A Generalized Model of Latin American City Structure. This model includes commercial/industrial zones, elite residential sector, zone of maturity, zone of *in situ* accretion, and zone of peripheral squatter settlements. *Source:* From L. Ford, "A New and Improved Model of Latin American City Structure," *The Geographical Review* 86 (1996), p. 438.

The Ibero-American City

South and Middle America are urbanizing rapidly, and cities are growing fastest in those countries where Iberian ("Latin") cultures dominate. In those countries, urban population grew from 41 percent of the total in 1950 to 77 percent in 2002. Although the urban experience has been a varied one—a function of diverse historical, cultural, and economic influences—many common threads exist. These commonalities form the basis of the model of the Latin American city proposed by Ernst Griffin and Larry Ford in 1980 and revised by Ford in 1996 (Fig. 23–5).

The basic spatial framework, which blends traditional elements of Latin American culture with the forces of modernization that are reshaping the urban scene, combines radial sectors and concentric zones. Anchoring the model is the thriving CBD, which, like its European counterpart, remains the city's primary business, employment, and entertainment focus. The CBD is divided into a traditional market sector and a more modern high-rise sector. Adequate public transit systems and nearby affluent residential areas assure the dominance of the CBD. Emanating outward from the urban core along the city's most prestigious axis is the *commercial spine*, which is surrounded by the *elite residential sector*. This widening corridor is essentially an extension of the CBD. It features offices, shopping, high-quality housing for the upper and upper-middle classes, restaurants, theaters, and such amenities as parks, zoos, and golf courses. At the end of the elite spine sector lies an incipient edge city shown as "mall" on the model and flanked by high-priced residences. This reflects the emergence of suburban nodes on the North American model in South America's cities.

The remaining concentric zones are home to less well-off residents (the great majority of the urban population). Socioeconomic levels and housing quality decrease markedly with greater distance from the city center. The zone of *maturity* in the inner city contains the best housing outside the spine sector, attracting the middle classes, who invest sufficiently to keep their solidly built but aging dwellings from deteriorating. The adjacent zone of *in situ accretion* is one of much more modest housing. Interspersed with it are unkempt areas, which represent a transition from inner-ring affluence to outer-ring poverty.

From the field notes

"It was not easy to gain permission to go to the roof of the building overlooking Lima's Plaza de San Martin, one of the Peruvian capital's most impressive public squares. The political situation was tense; the orange tent on the grass was a police post. Only in the company of an armed guard was I able to survey the square, which is flanked by some of the city's architectural treasures, several of them recently restored. The great plazas of Middle and South America's major cities often are named (as this one is)after revolutionary heroes and are flanked by cathedrals and churches as well as public buildings."

The residential density of this zone is usually quite high, reflecting the uneven assimilation of its occupants into the social and economic fabric of the city. The outermost *zone of peripheral squatter settlements* is home to the impoverished and unskilled. Although this ring consists mainly of teeming, high-density shantytowns, residents here are surprisingly optimistic about finding work and improving their living conditions.

A structural element of many Latin American cities is the ***disamenity sector***, which contains relatively unchanging slums known as *barrios* or *favelas.* The worst of these poverty-stricken areas often include large numbers of people who are so poor that they are forced to live in the streets. There is little in the way of regular law enforcement within such communities, and drug lords often run the show—or battle with other drug lords for dominance. Such conditions also prevail in places beyond the ring highway or *periférico*, now a feature of most South American cities.

Finally, the Griffin Ford model displays two smaller sectors: an industrial park, reflecting the ongoing concentration of industrial activity in the city, and a gentrification zone, where historic buildings are preserved. Gentrification remains much less common in South American cities than in North America, but it is an emerging phenomenon.

To what extent is the Griffin–Ford model a realistic portrayal of the Ibero-American city? In truth, the cities of South and Middle America display so much diversity that no simple model can represent all of their aspects. Elements of sector development can be seen in many large South American cities, for example, and the concentricity suggested by the model seems to be breaking down. Nevertheless, this model remains a useful abstraction of the "Latin" American city.

◆ THE SOUTHEAST ASIAN CITY

When we think of urbanization in Southeast Asia, we tend to focus on Singapore as the prime example. Other cities in this geographic realm also are growing and

From the field notes

"Ho Chi Minh City, called Saigon by all but a few local bureaucrats, in many ways is the quintessential Southeast Asian city. I have watched the transformation of the city from this vantage point atop the Rex Hotel for more than a decade, and much of the French colonial layout and architecture remain (including the former city hall, left foreground). But modern times are intruding, as reflected by the Prudential Tower in the background, in 2003 still the tallest building in town. Situated on the right bank of the Saigon River, Saigon still has no bridge to the left bank, creating a noteworthy (and undoubtedly temporary) contrast in economic landscapes on the opposite sides. In the outskirts of Saigon lies Cholon, the city's huge and bustling Chinatown. Just downriver lies a growing free-trade zone, although Vietnam's communist regime has not embraced the market economy the way their neighbors in China have. Still compartmentalized in the terms of the model regional city formulated in McGee's model, Saigon needs improved internal circulation."

modernizing, however, and some of them are surpassing Singapore in certain respects. Anyone who has not seen Kuala Lumpur, the capital of Malaysia, in recent years is in for a surprise: the city is a complex of high-rise development (including the 1483-foot-tall Petronas Towers, now the world's tallest buildings). The Malaysian government is building an entirely new, $30 billion capital at Putrajaya, 40 kilometers (25 miles) to the south.

Southeast Asian cities are also growing rapidly, and this realm's first megalopolis is emerging centered on the capital of Indonesia, Jakarta. This conurbation, called Jabotabek by locals, also includes the cities of Bogor, Tangerang, and Bekasi. Also fast-growing are Saigon-Cholon, Bankole, and Manila. Urbanization in this geographic realm in 2002 was just 36 percent.

Many of Southeast Asia's medium-sized cities, according to urban geographers studying their development, still exhibit similar land-use patterns. These patterns were identified and summarized by T. G. McGee as long ago as 1967 in *The Southeast Asian City* (Fig. 23–6). The old colonial port zone is the city's focus, together with the largely commercial district that surrounds it. Although there is no formal central business district, its elements are present as separate clusters; within the belt beyond the port: the government zone, the Western commercial zone (practically a CBD by itself); the alien commercial zone, usually dominated by Chinese merchants whose residences are attached to their places of business; and the mixed land-use zone that contains miscellaneous economic activities, including light industry. The other nonresidential areas are the market-gardening zone at the urban periphery

Figure 23-6 A Generalized Model of Land Use Areas in the Large Southeast Asian City. A model of land use in the large Southeast Asian city includes port zone, government zone, mixed land use zone, high-class zone, new high-class zone, middle-density residential zone, zone of new suburbs and squatter areas, market gardening zone, and new industrial zone. *Source:* From T. G. McGee, *The Southeast Asian City*, London: Bell, 1967, p. 128. Reprinted by permission of the publisher.

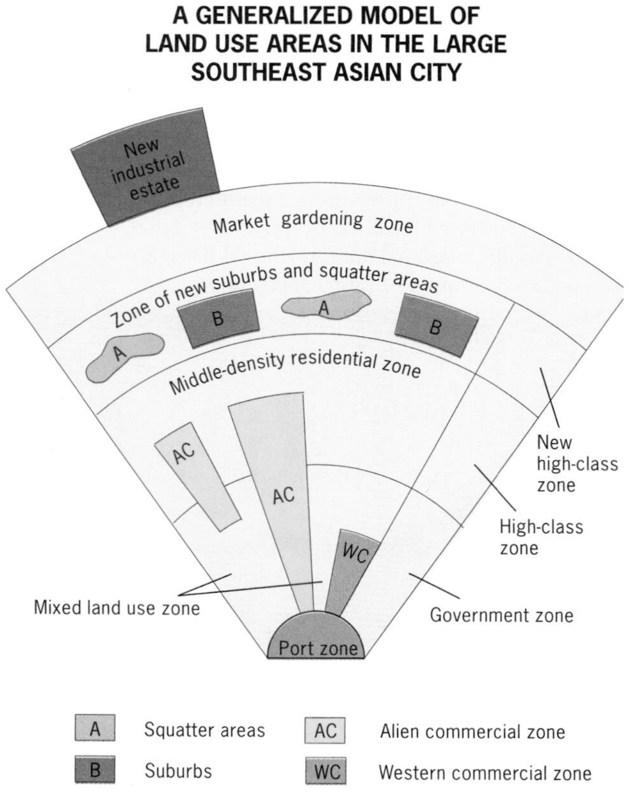

From the field notes

"Cities in the developing world sometimes seem to be a jumble of inadequate housing and poorly maintained (or absent) facilities. But despite their appearance, clusters of housing such as those shown in this photo are far superior to the rudimentary shacks of newly arrived squatters on the outskirts. This view over a part of Lagos, Nigeria, was just two blocks from the port and on the very edge of the city center. High-rise development was overtaking this area, reflecting the dual geographies of so many urban centers in such countries. This group of houses was occupied by a set of extended families; recent arrivals had been accommodated among them."

and, still farther from the city, a recently built industrial park or "estate." The residential zones in McGee's model are similar to those in the Griffin–Ford model of the Latin American city (Fig. 23–5). Among the similarities between the two are the hybrid structure of sectors and zones, an elite residential sector that includes new suburbs, an inner-city zone of middle-income housing (with new suburban offshoots in the McGee model), and peripheral low-income squatter settlements. The differences are relatively minor and are partly accounted for by local cultural and historical variations.

◆ THE AFRICAN CITY

Africa South of the Sahara is both the least urbanized and the most rapidly urbanizing realm in the world, with the single exception of the islands of the Pacific realm. At present, only Lagos is emerging as a world-class megacity, soon to rank, according to the United Nations Population Fund, as the world's third largest.

As in Southeast Asia, the imprint of colonialism can be seen in many African cities. In Africa, the traditional city occurs mainly in the Muslim zone in the west. Kano, Kaduna, Zaria, and other cities in this zone retain their precolonial structures in part because of their remoteness from the routes of European colonial invasion.

But it was the Europeans who laid out such prominent urban centers as Kinshasa, Nairobi, and Harare in the interior, and Dakar, Abidjan, Luanda, Maputo, and other ports along the coast. Africa even has cities that are neither traditional nor colonial. South Africa's major urban centers (Johannesburg, Cape Town, and Durban) are essentially Western, with elements of European as well as American models, including high-rise CBDs and sprawling suburbs.

As a result of this diversity, it is difficult to formulate a model African city that would account for all or even most of what we see. Studies of African cities indicate that the central city often consists of not one but three CBDs (Fig. 23–7): a remnant of the colonial CBD, an informal and sometimes periodic market zone, and a transitional business center where commerce is conducted from curbside, stalls, or storefronts. Vertical development occurs mainly in the former colonial CBD; the traditional business center is usually a zone of single-story buildings with some traditional architecture; and the market zone tends to be open-air, informal, yet

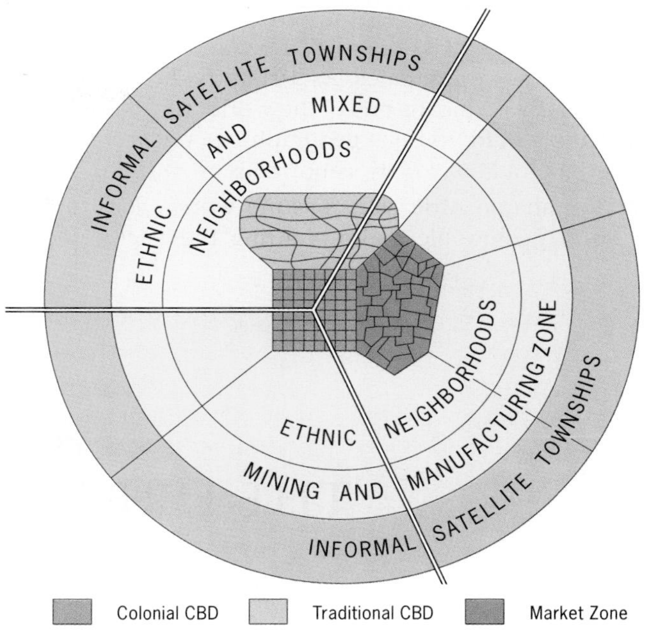

Figure 23-7 A Model Subsaharan City. One model of the African city includes colonial CBD, traditional CBD, and market zone.

still important. Sector development marks the encircling zone of ethnic and mixed neighborhoods (often characterized by strong ethnic identities); manufacturing or mining operations are found next to some parts of this zone. Finally, many African cities are ringed by satellite townships; these are, in effect, squatter settlements.

In Part Seven, we have viewed the evolution and maturation of the city from ancient to modern times, and we have seen that the Industrial Revolution brought the most far-reaching transformation to the cities it affected. Coupled with this urban transformation was an economic one: not just cities but entire regions were drastically changed. Raw materials that previously had no value became critical resources. Formerly remote countries found that they possessed fossil fuel and mineral reserves over which powerful empires would fight wars. We turn next to this industrial and technological transformation and the regions and landscapes it has generated.

◆ KEY TERMS ◆

agglomeration
disamenity sector
megacity
megalopolis
nucleation
specialization
urbanization
zoning

◆ APPLYING GEOGRAPHIC KNOWLEDGE ◆

1. Mexico City is one of the Americas'—and the world's—largest cities. As a country, however, Mexico is by no means one of the world's most populous. How would you use geographic perspectives to account for Mexico City's enormous growth?
2. Subsaharan Africa ranks as the world's least urbanized geographic realm—barring the Pacific Ocean realm. Yet it has the world's highest rate of urbanization. Use your geographic knowledge to explain these apparently contradictory circumstances.
3. Models are useful in explaining the location, growth, and structuring of cities. Why has model-building become so much more difficult than it was in Christaller's day?

Part Seven
THE URBANIZING WORLD
At Issue: Revisited

Should the central city be saved, and should suburbanites, who commute downtown everyday to earn their salaries, help pay for this? Or should it be left to be transformed by the forces that are reshaping America's urban areas: The exodus to the suburbs has slowed in many American cities, and in a few places there is even some movement back into the central city. But these trends have not been of sufficient magnitude to offset the problems of the urban core. Moreover, the continuing dispersal of economic activity is working together with the telecommunications revolution to undermine the original purpose of the central city. Yet millions of Americans continue to live and work in inner cities, and these areas also contain significant elements of our cultural life and historical heritage. Since many urban cores cannot be kept alive and vibrant solely by taxing those who live there, subsidies from suburbanites using the central city are one of the few alternatives to stagnation and decline. The willingness to implement and sustain such subsidies will tell us much about the social and landscape priorities of Americans in the years ahead.

◆ SELECTED BIBLIOGRAPHY ◆

Part Seven The Urbanizing World

Adams, J., ed. *Contemporary Metropolitan America,* 4 vols. (Cambridge, Mass.: Ballinger, 1976).

Andersson, H., et al., eds. *Change and Stability in Urban Europe* (Burlington, Vt.: Ashgate, 2001).

Berry, B.J.L. *Comparative Urbanization: Divergent Paths in the Twentieth Century.* 2nd rev. ed. (New York: St. Martin's Press, 1981).

Borchert, J. "American Metropolitan Evolution." *Geographical Review* 57 (1967): 301–332.

Bourne, L. S., & Ley, D., eds. *The Changing Social Geography of Canadian Cities* (Montreal, Quebec: McGill-Queen's University Press, 1993).

Burgess, E. "The Growth of the City," in R. Park et al., eds., *The City* (Chicago: University of Chicago Press, 1925), pp. 47–62.

Burnett, J. A. *A Social History of Housing, 1815–1970* (North Pomfret, Vt.: David & Charles, 1978).

Carter, H. *The Study of Urban Geography.* 4th ed. (New York: Edward Arnold, 1995).

Castells, M., & Hall, P. *Technopoles of the World: The Making of Twenty-First-Century Industrial Complexes* (New York: Routledge, 1994).

Chant, C., & Goodman, D., eds. *Pre-Industrial Cities and Technology* (London: Routledge, 1999).

Christaller, W. "The Foundations of Spatial Organization in Europe." *Frankfurter Geographische Hefte* 25 (1950).

Christaller, W. *The Central Places in Southern Germany,* trans. C. Baskin (Englewood Cliffs, N.J.: Prentice-Hall, 1966 [originally published 1933].

Chudacoff, H. *The Evolution of American Urban Society.* 4th rev. ed. (Englewood Cliffs, N.J.: Prentice-Hall, 1994).

Clay, G. *Close-Up: How to Read the American City* (Chicago: University of Chicago Press, 1980 [reprint of 1973 original].

Costa, F. J., et al. *Asian Urbanization: Problems and Processes* (Berlin: Gebruder Bomtraeger, 1988).

Deckker, T., ed. *The Modern City Revisited* (New York: Routledge, 2000).

Fagan, B. *The Little Ice Age* (New York: Basic Books, 2000).

Ford, Larry R. *Cities and Buildings: Skyscrapers, Skid Rows, and Suburbs* (Baltimore, Md.: Johns Hopkins University Press, 1994).

Ford, Larry R. "A New and Improved Model of Latin American City Structure," *Geographical Review* 86 (1996): 437–440.

Ford, Larry R. "Cities and Urban Land Use in Advanced Placement Human Geography." *Journal of Geography* 99, no. 3–4 (2000): 153–168.

Gaubatz, P. R. *Beyond the Great Wall: Urban Form and Transformation on the Chinese Frontiers* (Palo Alto, Calif.: Stanford University Press, 1996).

Gilbert, A., & Gugler, J. *Cities, Poverty and Development: Urbanization in the Third World.* 2nd ed. (New York: Oxford University Press, 1992).

Gugler, J., ed. *The Urbanization of the Third World* (New York: Oxford University Press, 1988).

Guldin, G. E., ed. *Urbanizing China* (Westport, Conn.: Greenwood Press, 1992).

Hall, T. *Urban Geography*. 2nd ed. (New York: Routledge, 2001).

Harris, C. D. "A Functional Classification of Cities in the United States," *Geographical Review* 33 (1943): 86–99.

Harris, C. D., & Ullman, E. L. "The Nature of Cities" *Annals of the American Academy of Political and Social Science* 242 (1945): 7–17.

Hartshorn, T. *Interpreting the City: An Urban Geography*. 2nd ed. (New York: John Wiley & Sons, 1992).

Hoyt, H. *The Structure and Growth of Residential Neighborhoods in American Cities* (Washington, D.C.: U.S. Federal Housing Administration, 1939).

Jefferson, M. "The Law of the Primate City." *Geographical Review* 29 (1939): 226–232.

Jones, G. W., ed. *Urbanization in Large Developing Countries* (London: Oxford University Press, 1998).

Kim, W. B., ed. *Culture and the City in East Asia* (New York: Oxford University Press, 1997).

King, L. *Central Place Theory* (Beverly Hills, Calif.: Sage Publications, 1984).

Knox, P. L. *Urbanization: An Introduction to Urban Geography* (Englewood Cliffs, N.J.: Prentice-Hall, 1994).

Knox, P. L., & Taylor, P. J., eds. *World Cities in a World-System* (Cambridge, U.K.: Cambridge University Press, 1995).

Knox, P. L., ed. *The Restless Urban Landscape* (Englewood Cliffs, N.J.: Prentice-Hall, 1993).

Lea, J., and Connell, J. *Urbanization in the Pacific* (New York: Routledge, 2001).

Ley, D. *A Social Geography of the City* (New York: Harper & Row, 1983).

Ley, D. *The New Middle Class and the Remaking of the Central City* (Oxford, U.K.: Oxford University Press, 1996).

McGee, T. G. *The Southeast Asian City: A Social Geography of the Primate Cities of Southeast Asia* (New York: Praeger, 1967).

McGee, T. G., & Robinson, I. R., eds. *The Mega-Urban Regions of Southeast Asia* (Vancouver, BC: UBC Press, 1995).

Muller, P. O. *Contemporary Suburban America* (Englewood Cliffs, N.J.: Prentice-Hall, 1981).

Olds, K. *Globalization and Urban Change* (London: Oxford University Press, 2001).

Pacione, M., ed. *Britain's Cities: Geographies of Division in Urban Britain* (New York: Routledge, 1997).

Portnov, B. A., & Erell, E. *Urban Clustering* (Burlington, Vt.: Ashgate, 2001).

Rotenberg, R., & McDonogh, G., eds. *The Cultural Meaning of Urban Space* (Westport, Conn.: Bergin & Garvey, 1993).

Scott, A. J., ed. *Global City—Regions* (London: Oxford University Press, 2001).

Short, John R. *The Urban Order: An Introduction to Cities, Culture, and Power* (Oxford: Basil Blackwell, 1996).

Sjoberg, G. *The Preindustrial City: Past, and Present* (Glencoe, Ill.: Free Press, 1960).

Skinner, G. W. "Marketing and Social Structure in Rural China." Part I, *Journal of Asian Studies* 24 (1964): 3–43.

Slater, T., ed. *Towns in Decline, AD 100–1600* (Burlington, Vt.: Ashgate, 2000).

Smith, D. W. *Third World Cities*. 2nd ed. (New York: Routledge, 2000).

Smith, M. P. *Transnational Urbanism: Locating Globalization* (Oxford: Basil Blackwell, 2000).

Stilgoe, J. R. *Borderland: Origins of the American Suburb, 1820–1939* (New Haven, Conn.: Yale University Press, 1988).

Stren, R. E., & White, R. R., eds. *African Cities in Crisis: Managing Rapid Urban Growth* (Boulder, Colo.: Westview Press, 1989).

United Nations Population Fund. *State of World Population 2001* (New York: United Nations, 2001).

Wright, H. T. & G. A. Johnson. "Population Exchange and Early State Formation in Southwest Asia" *American Antrhopologist* 77 (1975): 267–289.

Yeates, Maurice. *The North American City* (New York: Longman, 1998).

Part Eight

THE ROOTS AND CONSEQUENCES OF INDUSTRIALIZATION

At Issue

Near the beginning of the twentieth century, average incomes in Argentina were the equal of many of the world's wealthier countries, but the twenty-first century opened with a dramatic collapse of the country's economy. Argentina had attracted substantial foreign investment during the closing decades of the twentieth century, but it also suffered from government deficits, widespread tax evasion, little internal entrepreneurial development, and uncompetitive wages. As the country's economy began to spiral downward, the size of the country's external debt problem grew, and international lending institutions began insisting on higher taxes and lower government spending. This made it increasingly difficult for the government to support long-standing social programs, and popular resentment increased. A downward spiral ensued that eventually went out of control. *How can countries with weak internal business sectors and large debt-service obligations move forward—and to what degree should wealthier parts of the world assist them in their struggles?*

Facing the challenges of a rapidly changing economy. Marrakech, Morocco.

Part Outline

Chapter 24

Industrial Activity and Geographic Location

From the field notes

"Large ports provide many advantages for industry. They are transport hubs at the center of water, rail, and often air networks. They tend to have dependable energy supply because the ingredients (coal, oil) arrive here first, before national distribution. They are likely to have ample labor availability. The port area of St. Petersburg, Russia, is a growing industrial complex today. Trains and ships exchange goods ranging from raw materials to finished products."

KEY POINTS

- **Location theory helps explain the spatial positioning of industries and their success or failure.**
- **Weber's least cost theory accounted for the location of a manufacturing plant in terms of transportation, labor, and agglomeration (shared talents, services, and facilities).**
- **Transportation costs played a key role in the location of heavy industries; raw-material acquisition and finished-product distribution determined the options.**
- **Other factors influencing the location of industries include labor costs, energy availability, infrastructure, and the location of similar industries.**
- **The growth or decline of secondary industries is also influenced by factors that are not accounted for by models, such as political changes and environmental fluctuations.**

Few dimensions of human occupance of the planet are as dramatic as industrialization. Industrialization paved the way for many of the material goods that shape peoples' lives today, and it facilitated a fundamental shift away from the agricultural sector. At the same time, it also brought with it enormous environmental transformations and greatly exacerbated the gap between rich and poor. In this part, we look at some of the basic geographic dimensions of industrialization—the industrial patterns that characterize our world and the role of industrialization in creating differential patterns of wealth. First, however, we turn our attention to the rise of the industrial era and some of the basic influences on the location and industrial activity.

In Chapter 18 we noted that economic activities can be categorized according to their purpose, their relationship to the natural resources on which they are based, and their complexity. The primary or extractive industries exist to feed and supply. They develop where the resources are: the soils to be farmed, the minerals to be mined, the forests to be cut. Secondary and tertiary economic activities function to convert raw materials into finished products and facilitate trade and other interactions between producers and consumers. Not only are these manufacturing and service industries more complex than primary industries, but they are also much less closely tied to the location of natural resources. During the second half of the twentieth century, Hong Kong developed one of the world's most powerful economies on the basis of secondary and tertiary industries. It could never have done so on the basis of a primary industry.

Economic geographers investigate the reasons behind the location of economic activity. What made Hong Kong an economic tiger? The Portuguese colony of Macau was nearby, but Macau never came close to matching Hong Kong's meteoric rise. Today the world is a vast panorama of primary economic activity within which are clusters of secondary industries—symbolized by the great manufacturing belts of Japan, the United States, Europe, and Russia. What geographic factors created this arrangement, and what will happen next?

Answers to such questions come from the field of ***location theory***, which attempts to explain the locational pattern of an economic activity in terms of the factors that influence this pattern. But before we look at current circumstances, let us take note of the past. The modern map of world industries carries imprints of a time, long before the Industrial Revolution, when manufacturing centers had already become established in many parts of the world. ◆

◆ THE "PREINDUSTRIAL" WORLD

It is accurate to describe our modern age as one of industrial intensification. Industrial development did not begin with the Industrial Revolution. Instead, it accelerated during that period and diffused from certain areas of innovation to other parts of the world. But long before that time industries existed in many parts of the world, and trade in their products was widespread.

For example, in the towns and villages of India, workshops produced goods made of iron, gold, silver, and brass. India's carpenters were artists as well as artisans, and their work was in demand wherever it could be bought. India's textiles, made on individual spinning wheels and hand looms, were considered the best in the world. These industries were sustained not only by local aristocrats, but also by international trade. So good were India's textiles that British textile makers rioted in 1721, demanding legislative protection against imports from India.

China, too, possessed a substantial industrial base long before the Industrial Revolution, and so did Japan. Even European industries, from the textile makers of Flanders and Britain to the iron smelters of Thüringen, had developed considerably, but in price and quality Europe's products could not match those of other parts of the world.

What Europe's products lacked in quality, its merchants more than made up for in aggressiveness. Commercial companies, such as the Dutch and British East India Companies, laid the groundwork for Europe's colonial expansion. They gained control over local industries in India, Indonesia, and elsewhere, profited from political chaos, and played off allies against enemies. British merchants could import about as many tons of raw fiber for the textile industries as they wanted, and all they needed to do was find ways to mass-produce these raw materials into finished products. They would then bury the remaining local industries in Asia and Africa under growing volumes and declining prices. Even China, where local manufactures long prevailed over inferior and more expensive European goods, would eventually succumb.

◆ THE INDUSTRIAL REVOLUTION

During the eighteenth century European markets were growing, and there was not enough labor to keep pace with either local or overseas trade. Better machines were urgently needed, especially improved spinning and weaving machines. The first steps in the ***Industrial Revolution*** were not so revolutionary; the new machines were still driven by water running downslope. However, James Watt and others succeeded in developing a steam-driven engine, and this new invention was adapted for various uses. At about the same time, it was realized that coal could be transformed into high-carbon coke, which was far superior to charcoal in the smelting of iron.

These innovations had dramatic effects. The power loom revolutionized the weaving industry. Freed from their dependence on charcoal, iron smelters could be located near the coalfields—the same fields that supplied fuel for the new textile mills. One invention led to another, with each being applied to more and more industries. Pumps could keep water out of mines. Engines could move power looms. There was plenty of capital available for investment because British industrialists had been drawing wealth from the overseas empire for many years.

The Industrial Revolution also affected transportation and communications. The first railroad in England was opened in 1825. In 1830 Manchester was connected by rail to the nearby port of Liverpool, and in the next several decades thousands of miles of iron and then steel track were laid. Ocean shipping also entered a new age when the first steam-powered vessel crossed the Atlantic in 1819. Now Britain enjoyed even greater advantages than it had at the beginning of the Industrial Revolution. Not only did it hold a monopoly over products that were in demand around the world, but it alone possessed the skills necessary to make the machines that manufactured them. Europe and America wanted railroads and locomotives; England had the know-how, the experience, and the capital to supply them. Soon British influence around the world was reaching its peak.

Meanwhile, the spatial pattern of modern Europe began to take shape. In Britain, densely populated and heavily urbanized industrial regions developed in the "Black Country" near the coalfields. The largest such region was (and remains) the Midlands of north-central England. In mainland Europe, a belt of major coalfields extends from west to east, roughly along the southern margins of the North European Lowland—across northern France and southern Belgium, the Netherlands, the German Rühr, western Bohemia in the Czech Republic, and Silesia in Poland. Iron ore is dispersed along a similar belt, and the industrial map of Europe reflects the resulting concentrations of economic activity (Fig. 24-1). Nowhere on the continent, however, were the coalfields, iron ore deposits, and ports located in such close proximity as they were in Britain.

As Figure 24-1 shows, the Industrial Revolution rapidly diffused eastward. Some industrial regions emerged because of their raw material combinations (such as the Rühr, Saxony, Silesia, and the Donbas); others were based on enormous urban markets (such as London and Paris). These urban centers became, and remain, important industrial complexes for other reasons besides availability of resources.

The Industrial Revolution transformed the world's economic map, but while it had dramatic impact in certain areas, it totally bypassed others. Understanding the forces and factors that shaped the world's industrial layout is a prime objective of economic geographers.

◆ THE LOCATION DECISION

Industrial activity takes place in certain locations and not in others. We have already accounted for the spatial character of primary industries: the location of resources

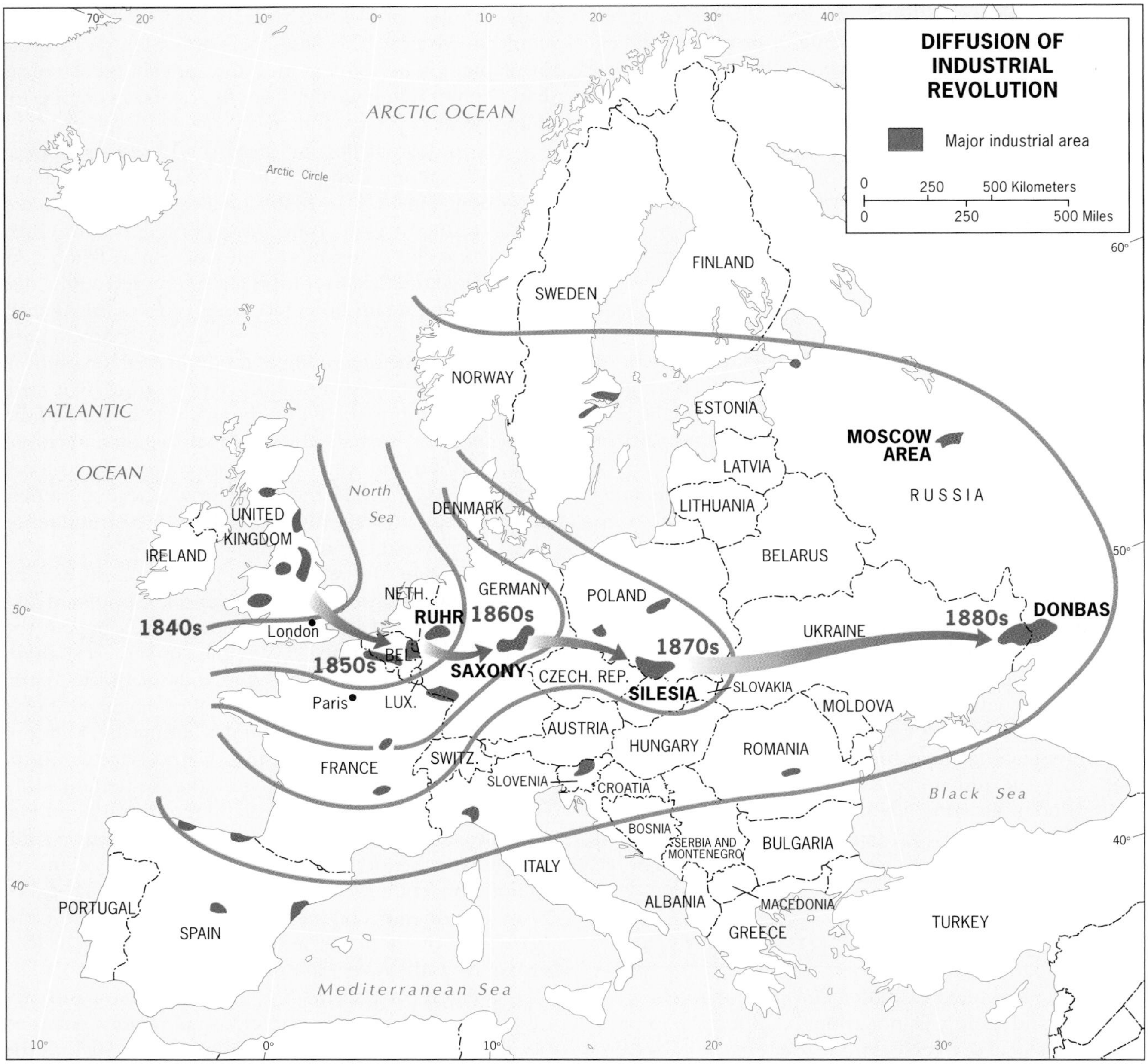

Figure 24-1 Diffusion of the Industrial Revolution The eastward diffusion of the Industrial Revolution occurred during the second half of the nineteenth century.

is the determining factor. ***Secondary industries*** are less dependent on resource location. Raw materials can be transported to distant locations to be converted into manufactured products—if the resulting profits outweigh the costs.

Any attempt to establish a model for the location of secondary industry runs into complications much greater than those confronting von Thünen, who dealt only with primary industries. The location of secondary industries depends to an important extent on human behavior and decision making, on cultural and political as well as economic factors, even on intuition or whim. Since models must be based on assumptions, economic geographers have to assume that decision makers are trying to maximize their advantages over competitors, that they want to make as much profit as possible, and that they will take into account ***variable costs*** such as energy supply, transport expenses, labor costs, and other needs.

In calculating efforts to maximize advantages, one of the key issues is the ***friction of distance***. This refers to the increase in time and cost that usually comes with increasing distance. If a raw material has to be shipped hundreds of miles to a factory, rather than being manufactured right next door, the friction of distance becomes apparent.

A corollary to the concept of the friction of distance is what geographers call ***distance decay***. This concept is based on the idea that the impact of a function or activity will decline as one moves away from its point of origin. What this means, for example, is that manufacturing plants will be more concerned with serving the markets of nearby places than more distant places. This basic principle is of importance in efforts to understand the locational dynamics of a variety of phenomena—including economic activities such as industrialization.

Weber's Model

The German economic geographer Alfred Weber (1868–1958) did for the secondary industries what von Thünen had done for agriculture: he developed a model for the location of manufacturing establishments. Europe's rapid industrialization during the nineteenth century had attracted the attention of economic geographers at an early stage. Much of this pioneering research was incorporated into Alfred Weber's *Theory of the Location of Industries* (1909). Like von Thünen before him, Weber began with a set of assumptions in order to minimize the complexities of the real world. However, unlike von Thünen, Weber dealt with activities that took place at particular points rather than across large areas. Manufacturing plants, mines, and markets are located at specific places, so Weber created a model region marked by sets of points where these activities would occur. By eliminating labor mobility and varying wage rates, he was able to calculate the "pulls" exerted on each point in his theoretical region.

Weber's ***least cost theory*** accounted for the location of a manufacturing plant in terms of the owner's desire to minimize three categories of costs. The first and most important of these categories was transportation: the site chosen must entail the lowest possible cost of moving raw materials to the factory and finished products to the market. The second cost was that of labor. Higher labor costs reduce the margin of profit, so a factory might do better farther from raw materials and markets if cheap labor made up for the added transport costs. (The late-twentieth century economic boom on the Pacific Rim was based largely on low labor costs, which caused industries to move from Japan and Taiwan to China and Vietnam.)

The third factor in Weber's model was what he called ***agglomeration***. When a substantial number of enterprises cluster in the same area, as happens in a large industrial city, they can provide assistance to each other through shared talents, services, and facilities. All manufacturers need office furniture and equipment; the presence of one or more producers in a large city satisfies this need for all. Thus agglomeration makes a big-city location more attractive, perhaps overcoming some increase in transport and labor costs. Excessive agglomeration, however, leads to high rents, rising wages, circulation problems (resulting in increased transport costs and loss of efficiency), and other problems. These may eventually negate the advantages of agglomeration. Such factors have led many industries to leave the crowded urban centers of the U.S. eastern megalopolis and move to other locations—a process known as deglomeration.

In developing this model, Weber discerned various factors that affect industrial location. For example, he drew attention to what he called "general" factors that affect all industries, such as transportation costs for raw materials and finished products, as well as "special" factors specific to particular industries, such as the perishability of foods. Weber singled out transportation costs as the critical determinant of regional industrial location. He suggested that the site where transportation costs are lowest is the place where it would be least expensive to bring raw materials to the point of production and distribute finished products to consumers.

Like von Thünen's model, Weber's least cost theory gave rise to a long and spirited debate among economic geographers. Some argued that Weber's model did not adequately account for variations in costs over time. For example, when relative labor costs decline or when land rent goes down, an industry can sustain an increase in transport costs. Although Weber's model might indicate that a location had become unprofitable, this ***substitution principle*** suggests otherwise. Also, the model suggests that one particular site would be optimal for a manufacturer's location, but in reality the business might be quite profitable within a larger area. Other factors that are not accounted for by the model, such as taxation policies and changes in consumer demand, also complicate the picture.

Despite these criticisms, Alfred Weber set in motion a debate over the spatial aspects of economic activity that continues today. Other economic geographers later extended Weber's theories. A major contribution was made by August Lösch, whose 1940 book on the spatial structure of the economy was published in English translation in 1954 as *The Economics of Location*. Lösch countered Weber's studies of least cost location by seeking ways to determine maximum profit locations. He inserted the spatial influence of consumer demand, as well as production costs, into his calculations. Lösch's work was a major step forward in the analysis of factors shaping the economic landscape.

Factors of Industrial Location

Our discussion of models of industrial location is based on circumstances prevailing in commercial economies—that is, economies guided by market mechanisms and relationships between supply and demand. However, some important industrial regions evolved under state planning, which tolerated large losses for the sake of rapid industrialization. As we saw earlier, the Industrial Revolution reached Ukraine and Russia before the Soviet

Union was created. But Soviet economic policy changed the direction of industrial growth, so that by the end of the Soviet era (1991) the imprints of the old commercial era were mingled with those of the era of state planning. Today Russia has once again turned toward the market, but it has been distorted by the huge Russian black market and the influence of entrenched interests. The Soviet framework persists, hampering efforts at reform.

One of the first decisions faced by the capitalists who built the great iron works of Europe had to do with the need to move either coal to the iron ores or iron ore to the coalfields. As you can see from any map of the time, the iron smelters were built near the coalfields of the British Midlands (the Black Towns were aptly named for the soot that hung permanently in the air and coated the entire landscape). The practice of moving the iron ore to the coal spread throughout Europe's industrial axis, but it is only one of three options. The other two are (1) to move the coal to the iron ore reserves or (2) to transport both materials to an intermediate location. (The planned economy of the former Soviet Union offered still another option: steel mills were built on the coalfields as well as on the iron ore reserves, and trains carried coal in one direction and iron ore in the other.)

In commercial economies, iron ore is usually transported to the coalfields, often after some waste and impurities have been removed. This is because, in a coal-powered manufacturing plant, it takes more coal to produce steel than it does iron. But there are exceptions. Large quantities of coal are transported to France's iron-rich Lorraine region, where coal is scarce. When an industrial complex develops near a coalfield and the coal is used up, it may be less expensive to import coal than to relocate the factories. Even when both coal and iron ore are shipped over large distances to some intermediate site, the iron ore usually travels farthest.

From the field notes

"The great Kennicott copper mining operation in the heart of Alaska's Wrangell St. Elias National park was once one of the most important of its kind in the world. From 1911–1938, it owners made a net profit of $100,000,000 on the high-grade ore mined in the nearby hills. Finding an old window through which I could enter, I wandered through the now-quiet remains and imagined the noise and bustle of the operation when hundreds of people were employed to mine and process a product more valuable than all of the gold discovered in the Yukon Gold Rush. How things change! These buildings have now lain quiet for more than 60 years. When the most accessible veins had been mined and copper ore could be extracted and processed more cheaply elsewhere, the Kennicott mine was abandoned—a testament to the shifting forces affecting industrial location."

Raw Materials Numerous factors enter into location decisions; these factors are of great interest to economic geographers who seek to discover the processes whereby manufacturing activity organizes and adjusts economic space. Obviously, the resources involved—that is, ***raw materials***—play a major role. One example is the location of steel plants along the U.S. northeastern seaboard. Those industrial facilities were built there largely because they used iron ore shipped from Venezuela, Labrador, Liberia, and other overseas sources. Instead of transferring these materials from oceangoing ships onto trains and transporting them inland, the plants used them right where they arrived—practically at the point of unloading at such huge steel-mill complexes as Sparrows Point, near Baltimore, and Fairless, near Philadelphia. So in this case distant ore deposits affected the location of industry in the United States. Thus transport costs affect the location of industry in important ways. (Transportation is discussed in a separate section because this factor involves finished products as well as raw materials.)

In the case of raw materials, we have already noted the spatial relationships between Europe's zone of coalfields and iron ores and the spread of manufacturing throughout the region. However, not all of the world's great industrial regions lie near major sources of raw materials. Japanese industries must import raw materials from distant sources because Japan's domestic resource base is quite limited. This has not prevented Japan from developing into one of the world's great industrial nations, but it does present special problems of availability and cost. Japan's early industrial progress was based on its own manufacturing traditions and, initially, on its own resources. The rapid depletion of these raw materials was among the motives that led Japan to embark on its expansion into East Asia, where Korea and Northeast

China became Japanese dependencies and sources of raw materials for Japanese industries.

Even after Japan lost its colonial empire, its industries continued to be sustained by a large, highly skilled labor force (which, before recent wage increases, was relatively cheap). Japanese products dominated markets around the world and allowed Japanese industries to purchase needed raw materials virtually anywhere. Australia, for example, became one of Japan's leading suppliers. For many decades European countries also controlled sources of raw materials through colonization. (Britain's example had much to do with Japan's colonial expansion for similar purposes.) In the postcolonial era, materials have continued to flow from the source countries to manufacturers in Europe and areas settled by Europeans. This not-so-new pattern of trade spells disadvantage for former colonies, since they must sell their raw materials in order to secure foreign capital even when commodity prices fall because of oversupply or recession. The former colonial countries, on the other hand, can keep prices low by shifting from one supplier to another. When a source country loses customers for its raw materials, the effect on its economy may be disastrous.

Countries at a disadvantage in this global network of trade have tried to band together in cartels in order to control vital commodities, but such efforts have had only sporadic success. Usually the buyers are in a stronger position than the sellers because they can find other sources (including countries that have not joined the cartels). When OPEC (the Organization of Petroleum Exporting Countries) took control of world oil supplies in the 1970s, it succeeded in driving up the price of petroleum. But countries that did not join OPEC increased their production and gave the developed countries a chance to break OPEC's hold; oil supplies recovered, prices collapsed, and the producers—not the consumers—were again the losers. OPEC had some greater success in controlling global production and oil pricing at the turn of the twenty-first century, but political tensions among and between OPEC countries continue to erode the cartel's ability to maintain a consistent, long-term position.

Labor One of the three fundamentals of Weber's least cost model was ***labor***, and availability of cheap semiskilled labor has had an immense impact on regional industrial development. Even in an era of automated assembly lines and computerized processing, the prospect of a large, low-wage, trainable labor force continues to attract manufacturers.

As noted earlier, Japan's postwar success was based in large measure on the skills and the low wages of its labor force, which allowed manufacturers to flood foreign markets with low-priced goods. Into the 1950s Japanese goods had little reputation for quality but were known for their affordability. But then Japan's factories began to excel in quality as well. This in turn led to higher prices, higher wages, and, inevitably, competition from countries where cheaper labor could be found. Taiwan and South Korea competed with Japan in goods ranging from electronics to automobiles, and in the mid-1990s Japan was in a recession while Taiwan and South Korea boomed.

The next stage of economic transformation on the Pacific Rim was already under way in the 1980s. This was the entry of China with its huge labor force. In 1994 the daily wage of a factory worker in Shanghai's Pudong district was one-fortieth that of a Japanese worker in a similar job and one-thirtieth that of a Taiwanese worker. These low wages, coupled with favorable tax regulations, are attracting thousands of enterprises to China's Special Economic Zones, transforming cities and towns in the region.

What is happening on China's Pacific Rim is nothing new; similar developments are affecting Thailand and Malaysia. And like South Korea and Japan before it, China will feel the effects of cheaper labor when Vietnam enters the picture. Similar developments are occurring elsewhere as well. Before the United States, Canada, and Mexico joined in the North American Free Trade Agreement (NAFTA) in 1994, there was intense debate over the relocation of industries from the United States across the border to Mexico, where wages were lower and profits would be higher. Thus the cost of labor still looms large in the location of industry.

Transportation As Weber noted, ***transportation*** facilities and costs are crucial in industrial location. A huge market may exist for a given product, but if that market is not served by an efficient transportation system, much of the advantage is lost. The maps in Chapter 25 underscore the fact that highly industrial areas are also the places that are served most effectively by transportation facilities. Industrialization and the development of modern transport systems go hand in hand. In a sense, the Industrial Revolution was a transportation revolution—a revolution that is still going on. Every year more freight is carried by air, and in the United States trucks increasingly haul goods that were formerly carried on trains.

Efficient transportation systems enable manufacturers to purchase raw materials from distant sources and distribute finished products to a widely dispersed population of consumers. Manufacturers desire maximum transport effectiveness at the lowest possible cost. They will also consider the availability of alternative systems in the event of emergencies (e.g., truck routes when rail service is interrupted). An important innovation in bulk transport was the development of container systems that facilitated the transfer of goods from one type of carrier to another (from rail-to-ship and ship-to-truck). This change lowered costs and increased flexibility, permitting many manufacturers to pay less attention to transportation in their location decisions.

For most goods, truck transport is cheapest over short distances; railroads are cheapest over medium distances;

and ships are cheapest over the longest distances. However, numerous aspects of transportation must be taken into account when location decisions are made. For example, when goods are hauled, costs are incurred at the terminal where trucks, trains, and ships are unloaded. These costs are much higher for ships than for trucks. Then, of course, there is the actual cost of transportation itself. This increases with distance, but at a decreasing rate, making long-distance transportation cheaper per mile and allowing manufacturers to reach out to distant suppliers of raw materials and also to sell to faraway customers. Still another factor has to do with the weight and volume of the freight. Certain goods may be light but occupy a lot of space inside railroad cars or ships' holds; thus they may still be expensive to transport.

Infrastructure When Weber considered the role of agglomeration in location decisions, he could not foresee the dimensions of urban areas or industrial complexes a century hence. In his time, the world population was about the size of China's today; few cities had more than 1 million inhabitants. Today's urban populations are much larger—and so are the problems and benefits of agglomeration. If you wished to build a factory in Shanghai to benefit from low-cost labor, you would have many needs, ranging from transportation facilities to markets both in China and overseas to telephones and utilities such as electricity and water supply. All these facilities, and others such as banks, postal and messenger services, hotels, and social services, are collectively referred to as ***infrastructure***. Airports, roads, docks, railways, and taxis are also included.

Infrastructure is an important factor in industrial location decisions. One reason the communist regime in China has tried to slow the rate of industrialization along the Pacific Rim lies in the inadequacy of local and regional infrastructures: the demand for such facilities as telephones and administrative assistance far exceeds what is available. Factories are having difficulty importing raw materials; market distribution systems cannot yet meet the demand. Public utilities are also inadequate. (Shanghai recently brought a major new coal-burning power plant on line, but demand is expected to overtake supply in a few years.)

Given such shortcomings in infrastructures, why does the influx of enterprises continue? The answer is not found in any formal economic-geographic model. It has to do with the perception of future disadvantage. Not to gain a place on the new industrial frontier is to risk falling behind in the future. So the Chinese economic hot spots continue to grow and prosper, even with inadequate infrastructures.

Vietnam (which some observers regard as the next economic "tiger" on the Pacific Rim) has an even weaker infrastructure than China. For all its advantages (self-sufficiency in food, good relative location, large educated labor force, and domestic market of nearly 80 million), Vietnam has infrastructure problems that will not soon be overcome. Inadequate power and water supply and a poor surface transportation network are just two of these weaknesses.

In many Western cities, the disadvantages of excessive agglomeration are driving firms away from crowded and decaying urban areas, despite their highly devel-

From the field notes

"I stood for more than an hour on a bridge overlooking this open-air laundry in Mumbai, India, one of several of this kind in the vast urban area, but the closest to my hotel and thus reachable on foot. As I watched hundreds of workers toil in the hot and polluted atmosphere of this burgeoning city I was reminded of Weber's least-cost model and the role of labor in it. A passing Sikh fellow stopped to chat and told me that this scene had not changed 'for about a century' and that I could forget about the workers in this laundry moving up the technological ladder. These jobs, he said, had been held by fathers and grandfathers and were not about to yield to mechanization or automation. 'For them, this is security,' he said. 'Look at your shirt, sir. You're sweating right through it. You'll need these people tomorrow!' He was right, at least about my shirt. But this scene seemed to be from another era, a glimpse of the colonial past in a globalizing city."

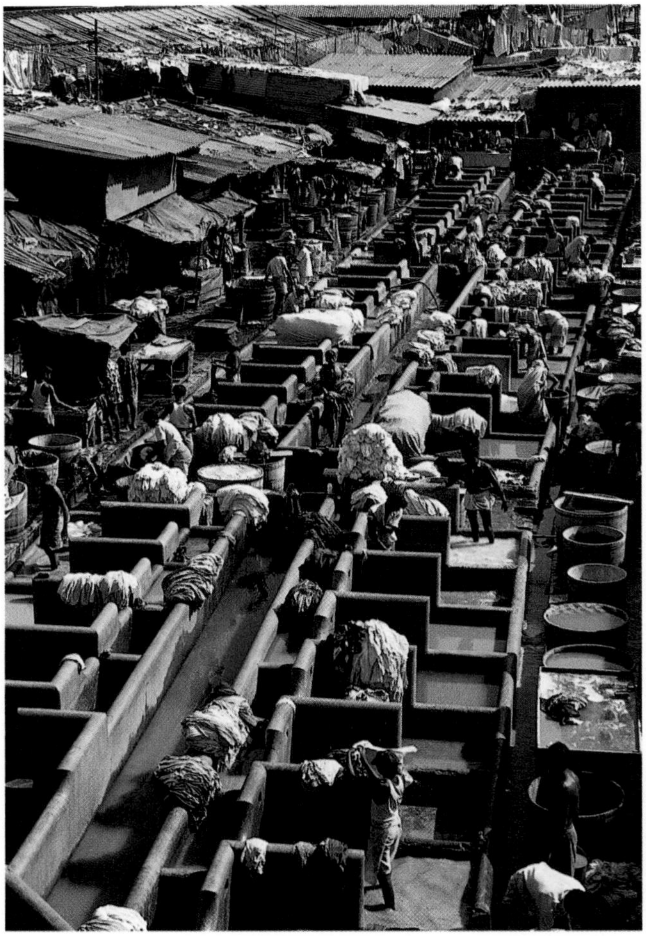

oped infrastructures. Meanwhile, industries are entering non-Western cities in the expectation that their infrastructures will improve. Thus the economic landscape is constantly shifting.

Energy Another factor in the location of industry is the availability of an ***energy*** supply. This factor used to be much more important than it is today. The early British textile mills, because they depended on water rushing down hillsides to drive the looms, had few choices in deciding where to locate. The same can be said of the early mills in the northeastern United States. However, today power comes from different sources and can be transmitted via high-voltage electrical lines over long distances. Manufacturers are therefore able to base location decisions on considerations other than power. Exceptions occur when an industry needs very large amounts of energy—for example, certain metallurgical (aluminum and copper processing) and chemical industries (fertilizer production). Such industries are attracted to sites where abundant energy is available, as is the case near hydroelectric plants. In the United States, the growth of aluminum production in the Pacific Northwest and the Tennessee Valley is based mainly on the ready availability of cheap electricity; this is also the case in Canada's Saint Maurice and Saguenay River Basins.

A SENSE OF SCALE

Locational Interdependence

Many of the influences on industrial location that we examine in this chapter are ones that play out at a fairly large spatial scale. Raw materials, transportation lines, and population concentrations are all things that are often recognizable at regional, and even national scales. But smaller scale influences can matter as well. One of the most important of these is the location of similar or competing industries—that is, industries supplying the same good or service.

An economist by the name of Harold Hotelling (1895–1973) sought to understand the issue of ***locational interdependence*** by posing the question of where two ice cream vendors might stand on a beach occupied by people distributed evenly along its stretch. In choosing a simple, one-dimensional space, Hotelling was able to simplify the analysis. He concluded that the two vendors might start at locations somewhat distant from one another so that they could each be as close to as many customers as possible. As the two vendors sought to maximize sales, however, Hotelling argued that they would seek to constrain each other's sales territory as much as possible. This would lead them to move ever closer to the center of the beach, until they were standing back-to-back. And once they reach those positions, they are likely to stay there because a decision by one of them to move can only hurt profitability.

DIAGRAMMATIC REPRESENTATION OF ECONOMIC INFLUENCES ON BUSINESS LOCATION

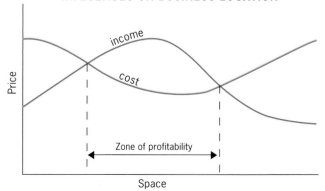

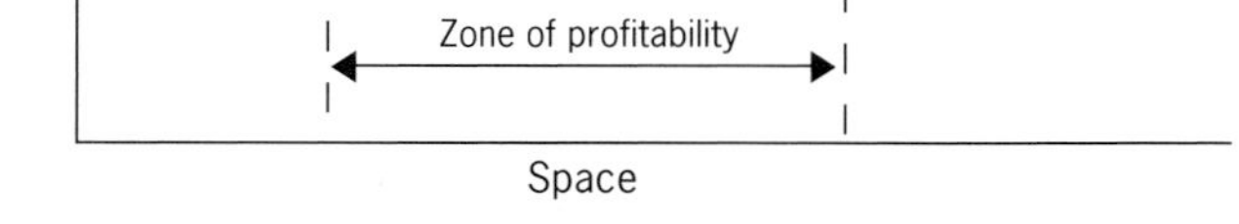

The point of Hotelling's analysis is to show that the location of an industry cannot be understood without reference to the location of other industries of like kind. But in the example of the ice cream vendors, only one variable is considered: the effort to maximize the number of sales. What fails to recognize is that the costs for some of the consumers will be greater if the two sellers cluster at the center of the beach—for those at the edges will have to walk farther to buy ice cream than if the two vendors were each located close to the center of each half of the beach. Moreover, more consumers may be aware of the ice cream vendors if they are spread out.

It was a concern with such complexities that led August Lösch to emphasize profit-maximization in his locational analyses—and Lösch's theories play out at small, as well as large, scales. Determining the point of maximum profit is often difficult, but as the figure accompanying this box suggests, firms will usually try to identify a zone in which some kind of profit can be expected. To the left and right of the zone, distance decay will make sales unprofitable. Hence, firms will try to situate themselves away from the margins of that zone. Of course, other businesses can always come along and change the configuration of that zone—and this is one element that can cause economic turnover in a capitalist system. Yet the development of an agglomeration can also give the entire area a competitive advantage over more distant areas. This can work to the advantage of old and new businesses alike by giving the area the kind of image that will lead people to come from distant locations to acquire the product(s) being sold.

The role of energy supply as a factor in industrial location decisions has changed over time. Whereas during the Industrial Revolution manufacturing plants were often established on or near coalfields, today major industrial complexes are not found near oil fields. Instead, a huge system of pipelines and tankers delivers oil and natural gas to manufacturing regions throughout the world. For some time during and after the global oil supply crises of the 1970s, fears of future rises in oil costs led some industries that require large amounts of electricity to move to sites where the environment is moderate and heating and air-conditioning costs are low. When the crisis waned, national energy-conservation goals were modified, and in the early 2000s the United States' reliance on foreign energy resources was even greater than it had been in the 1970s. So just as energy supply has become a less significant factor in industrial location, so energy security had lessened a national priority.

Other Factors

Factors other than those we have identified may also influence industrial location decisions. Some concern the specific location of similar competing businesses (see "Sense of Scale" Box). Others relate to political stability and receptiveness to investment. Industries are frightened away when there are signs of uncertainty in a country's political future, or when a government indicates that it intends to nationalize industries owned by foreigners. Taxation policies can also play a role. Some countries try to attract industries by offering huge tax exemptions over long periods.

Influential industrialists sometimes decide to locate a major plant in a particular area for personal reasons, ignoring the principles of industrial location. The directors of multinational corporations can affect the course of regional industrial development in many countries almost at will. Moreover, some industries are located where they are because of environmental conditions. The film industry is concentrated in Southern California because of the large number of clear, cloudless days there—an environmental factor that has also attracted aircraft manufacturers, which need good weather for flight-testing new planes.

Much as we may theorize, therefore, the location and success of industries may depend on unanticipated, even unaccountable factors as well. In hindsight we can explain Hong Kong's success in terms of its location, but when the colony was just a river-mouth trading port there was little to suggest its phenomenal future growth. Then China was ostracized for its role in the Korean War, and Hong Kong's links to the mainland were cut. Manufacturers had to look for new products and markets, and textiles were the answer. The political situation ensured a huge supply of labor at low wages, and the textile industry, based on imported raw materials and exported clothing, thrived. The money made in the textile industries was invested in the development of other manufactures, and the rest is—geography.

But Hong Kong would not have achieved what it did without another advantage. China, isolated as it was, needed a back door to the outside world, a route along which to funnel finances, crucial imports, and messages. That route lay through Hong Kong. As the door opened wider, Hong Kong prospered and even spawned a "twin": Shenzhen across the border.

As we have seen throughout this chapter, explaining industrial location and predicting its growth are complex matters. This point will become even clearer when we turn to global patterns of industrialization.

◆ KEY TERMS ◆

agglomeration
distance decay
energy
friction of distance
Industrial Revolution
infrastructure
labor
least cost theory
location theory
raw materials
secondary industries
substitution principle
transportation
variable cost

◆ APPLYING GEOGRAPHIC KNOWLEDGE ◆

1. Invention, industrial intensification, and diffusion are among the processes that propelled the Industrial Revolution. What geographic factors help explain the locational aspects of this momentous process and its dissemination around the world? Has it run its course, or is industrialization still continuing?
2. Although the location of raw materials, labor, and markets still plays a role in the decision-making processes that determine where industrial plants will be situated, these factors have less influence today than in the past. What are the circumstances—economic as well as political—that allow more leeway in the location of industries?

Chapter 25

Resources and Regions: The Global Distribution of Industry

From the field notes

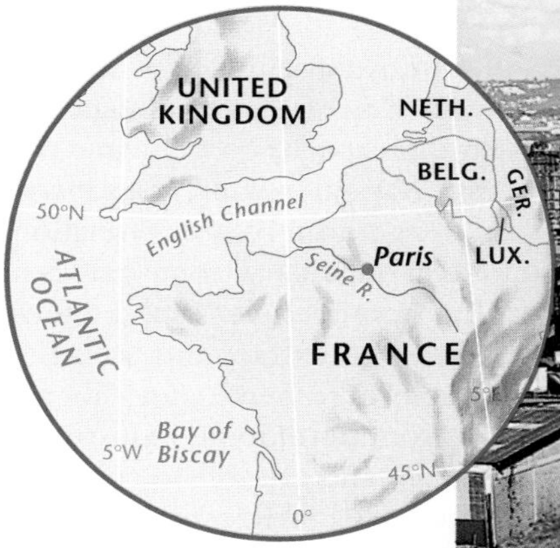

"Paris and the Paris Basin form the industrial as well as agricultural heart of France. The city and region are served by the Seine River, along which lies a string of ports from Le Havre at the mouth to Rouen at the head of navigation for ocean-going ships. Rouen has become a vital center on France's industrial map. As we approached on the river, you could see the famous cathedral and the city's historic cultural landscape to the left (north), but on the right bank lay a major industrial complex including coal-fired power facilities (although France leads Europe in nuclear energy), petrochemical plants, and oil installations. It is all part of the industrial region centered in Paris."

KEY POINTS

- **The global industrial pattern is dominated by those areas that first industrialized and were able to take advantage of their position in the developing global economy.**
- **Four major industrial regions have emerged, all in the Northern Hemisphere: Western and Central Europe, Eastern North America, Russia-Ukraine, and Eastern Asia.**
- **The location of Europe's primary industrial regions still reflects the spatial diffusion of the Industrial Revolution. An axis of manufacturing extends from Britain to Poland and the Czech Republic, and onward to Ukraine.**
- **North America's manufacturing complex, anchored by the American Manufacturing Belt, is the largest in the world today.**
- **Industrial regions in East Asia are the fastest growing in the world. The Asian Pacific Rim includes several of the most rapidly expanding economies, recent setbacks notwithstanding.**

In Chapter 24 we focused on some of the general principles of geographic location. In this chapter we turn our attention to the actual distribution of industry around the world. The global industrialization pattern is highly uneven—a reflection of historical circumstances, global power relations, and geographical context. The location of Europe's primary industrial regions can still be traced to the spatial diffusion of the Industrial Revolution, with an axis of manufacturing extending from Britain to Poland and the Czech Republic, and onward to Ukraine (Fig. 25-1). In other parts of the world, the distribution of industry is often related to the legacy of European colonialism, with former centers of commerce having developed into places of modern industry, especially in Southeast Asia. In other cases, ***growth poles***—that is, industries designed to stimulate growth through the establishment of various supporting industries—have attracted people and money to particular regions.

In industry, as in so much else, place matters. Each place has a unique mix of natural, technological, and human resources with the capacity to influence the industrialization process. Natural resource endowment can be important, but there is no absolute correlation between natural resources and industry. Some places have an abundance of natural resources, yet lack the technological or human resources to extract and utilize them (e.g., The Congo). A paucity of resources does not necessarily preclude an area from developing industry and a strong economy if its inhabitants are able to exert significant power and influence (e.g., Switzerland and Japan). What is clear, then, is that the global distribution of industry cannot be understood solely by reference to the types of variables highlighted by Weber. Instead, consideration must be given to historical inertia and to the position of places in the global economic picture. ◆

◆ MAJOR INDUSTRIAL REGIONS

The world map of major regional-industrial development reveals that only a small minority of countries have become major industrial economies. Many factors help explain this situation, including resource endowment, relative location, political circumstances, economic leadership, labor costs, and levels of education and training. The legacy of the Industrial Revolution is evident in many older industrial complexes, such as Germany's Rühr, Poland's Silesia, and Ukraine's Donbas. Major industrial centers are also emerging in such countries as India, Brazil, and China.

Figure 25-1 Europe's Core and Regions. This map shows core and urban areas as well as industrial districts.

When industrial concentrations are mapped, four ***primary industrial regions*** stand out:

1. Western and Central Europe
2. Eastern North America
3. Russia and Ukraine
4. Eastern Asia

Each of these regions consists of one or more core areas of industrial development with subsidiary clusters some distance away. Although the older manufacturing regions are quite entrenched, notable shifts are occurring. This is especially evident in East Asia, where Japan's dominance is being challenged. In Europe, the Rühr is being affected by a southward shift of German industry. In North America, the old eastern core of industries is still dominant, but the balance is shifting toward subsidiary clusters to the west and south.

A useful way of looking at global patterns of industrialization is to see how these patterns developed over time. Toward that end, we look first at the industrial concentrations that developed from the early days of the Industrial Revolution through World War I. The focus here is primarily Europe and the United States. We then consider the global expansion of industry throughout the mid-twentieth century. We conclude with a consideration of the changing character of the global industrial pattern over the past few decades.

◆ FIRST-ROUND INDUSTRIALIZATION: THROUGH WORLD WAR I

Any consideration of the development of global patterns of industry must begin with Europe, for it is here that the Industrial Revolution was launched. The manufacturing regions of Europe (Fig. 25-1) are the continent's historical and contemporary heartland. The areas in the region of the map labeled Western Europe are largely those that were transformed between the late-eighteenth and early-twentieth centuries by the diffusion of the Industrial Revolution in Europe. Not surprisingly, these areas are at the heart of the evolving European Union.

As we have seen, Britain was the first to industrialize. By the early nineteenth century, industrialization had given Britain an enormous ***comparative advantage*** over others areas—leaving it in a position of global dominance. Britain was able to use and expand its colonial empire in building an industrial economy—and in the process it laid the foundations for the development of a world economy characterized by sharp differences in levels of development (see Chapter 26). Britain's early industrialization was focused on the Midlands and northern England, where coal and iron were available, but soon it diffused to London because of the concentration of people, money, and transportation infrastructure in and around the British capital.

When the Industrial Revolution spread to mainland Europe, it first took root in southern Belgium, where coal and iron were available. Soon, however, major markets would attract industrial concerns. Paris was already continental Europe's greatest city, but it did not have coal or iron deposits in its immediate vicinity. Nevertheless, Paris was the largest local market for manufacturers for hundreds of miles around, and when a railroad system was added to the existing network of road and waterway connections, the city's centrality was further strengthened. Like London, Paris soon began to attract major industries, and the city, long a center for the manufacture of luxury items (jewelry, perfumes, and fashions), experienced substantial growth in such industries as metallurgy and chemical manufacturing. With a ready labor force, an ideal regional position for the distribution of finished products, the presence of governmental agencies, a nearby ocean port (Le Havre), and France's largest domestic market, Paris's development as a major industrial center was no accident.

Europe's principal coal deposits lie in a belt across northern France, Belgium, north-central Germany, the northwestern Czech Republic, and southern Poland—and it was along this zone that industrialization expanded in mainland Europe. Three manufacturing districts lay in Germany: the Rühr, based on the Westphalian coalfield, the Saxony district, near the border of the former Czechoslovakia, and Silesia (now part of Poland). Germany still ranks among the world's leading producers of both coal and steel and remains Europe's leading industrial power (Table 25-1).

From the field notes

"Driving through the industrial district of Silesia in southern Poland, I came across several out-dated or abandoned factories. But there was evidence of new industrial vigor as well. Why build this plant here? The answer is the same as it was when the region first industrialized in the eighteenth century: the region's vast coal deposits make energy cheap. That—combined with labor availability and market accessibility—is the key. The challenge now is to build on the industrial legacy in a way that does not exacerbate the already serious environmental and social problems of the region."

Table 25-1 World Production of Raw Steel, 2001 (Thousands of Net Tons)

China	148,900
Japan	102,900
United States	90,100
Russia	59,000
Germany	44,800
South Korea	43,900
Brazil	26,700
Italy	26,700
Ukraine	33,100
India	27,300
United Kingdom	13,700
Canada	15,300
France	19,300
Turkey	15,000
Mexico	13,300

Source: International Iron and Steel Institute, *Annual Statistical Report 2001*.

Western Europe's industrial success was not based solely on the local availability of raw materials, however. The colonial empires of France, Britain, and the Low Countries gave it access to resources around the world. Moreover, Europe itself possessed a comparatively skilled labor force, and the high degree of specialization achieved in various industrial zones led to an intensive exchange of products. Natural transport routes, augmented by artificial ones, facilitated this exchange.

By the early twentieth century, industry began to diffuse far from the original European source areas to such places as northern Italy (now one of Europe's major industrial hearths), Catalonia (anchored by Barcelona) and northern Spain, southern Sweden, and southern Finland. These and other European industrial zones are just districts within the continent's massive industrial structure; yet each would stand out as a major center of manufacturing activity in most other parts of the world.

By the beginning of the twentieth century, the only serious rival to Europe came from a realm heavily settled by Europeans with particularly close links to Britain: North America. Manufacturing in North America began in New England as early as late colonial times, but the Northeastern states are not especially rich in mineral resources. Still, this oldest manufacturing district produced high-quality light manufactures—a tradition that continues to this day. Industrialization also began early in New York, which today is at the heart of the Bosnywash megalopolis and home to tens of thousands of industrial establishments. An early start, large urban growth, and agglomeration played roles in this development. The New York area is not especially well endowed with mineral resources but, like Paris and London, it is a large market. It also has a huge skilled and semiskilled labor force, is the focus of an intensive transport network, and has long been one of the world's great ports, a major ***break-of-bulk*** location. This term refers to the transfer of transported cargo from one kind of carrier (e.g., a ship) to another (truck or train). Such transfers generate much economic activity and wealth.

The expansion of industrialization in North America was facilitated by the continent's natural resources and supported by networks of natural as well as artificial transportation systems. Ample capital (much of it initially from Britain), specialization, and diversification marked the robust growth of this region in the decades leading up to World War I. North America benefited from the capacity of its companies to acquire needed raw materials from overseas sources. It did not need to go overseas for the raw materials to produce energy, however. Coal was the chief fuel for industries at the time, and there was never any threat of a shortage of coal. U.S. coal reserves are among the world's largest and are widely distributed—from Appalachian Pennsylvania to the northwestern Great Plains (Fig. 25-2). Indeed, the United States still vies with China as the world's largest coal producer.

On the eve of World War I, Europe had already developed a major industrial base, and North America was rapidly catching up. Industrialization elsewhere, however, was proceeding slowly at best. There were a few exceptions; the Industrial Revolution had diffused to the Donetsk Basin (Donbas) region of eastern Ukraine by the end of the nineteenth century (see Fig. 25-1), and industrial pockets could be found in other parts of the world—particularly those settled by Europeans (e.g., Australia). Most of the world was left behind, however. The stage had been set for a highly uneven pattern of industrial development that persists to this day.

◆ MID-TWENTIETH-CENTURY INDUSTRIALIZATION

The earlier industrialization of parts of the United States and Europe gave those regions an enormous advantage in the unfolding industrial picture. Certain other parts of the world entered the fray as well—most notably those that were not dealing with a recent colonial past. Before turning to the regional patterns that developed, however, it is important to comment on the key resources on which twentieth-century industrialization was built: oil and natural gas.

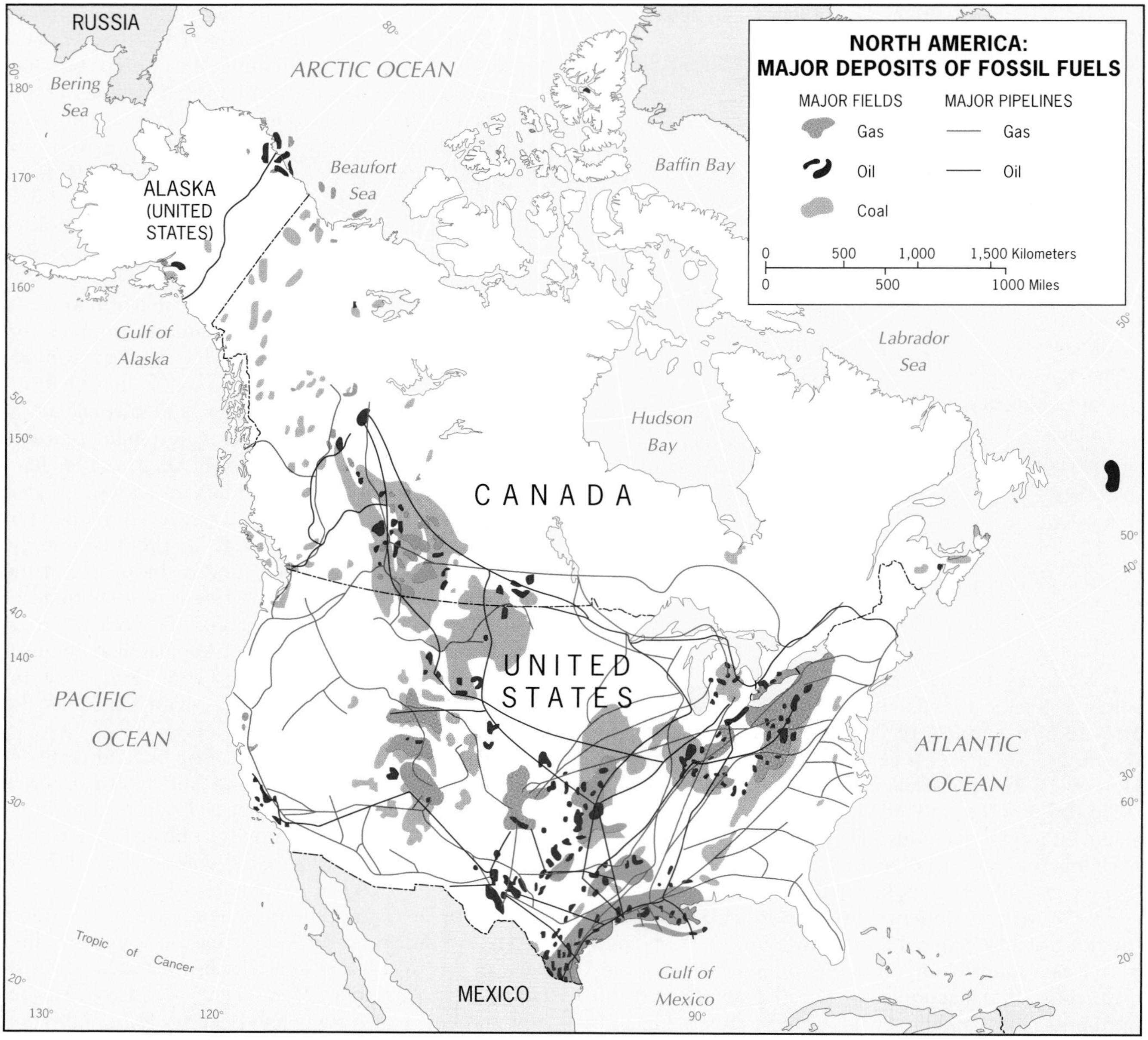

Figure 25-2 North America's Major Deposits of Fossil Fuels. The world's largest energy consumer, North America is also endowed with substantial energy resources.

Oil and Natural Gas

During the mid-twentieth century, the use of coal as an energy source in industry increasingly gave way to the use of oil and gas. Nowhere was this more true than in the United States. U.S. consumption of petroleum and natural gas today is about 27 percent and 37 percent, respectively, of the annual world total. In the early 1990s, the United States required no fewer than 17 million barrels of petroleum per day to keep its power plants, machinery, vehicles, aircraft, and ships functioning. However, U.S. production of oil in recent years has averaged about 18 percent of the world total, and, even including the known Alaskan potential, U.S. oil reserves are estimated to amount to only about 4 percent of the world total. The result is heavy dependence on foreign oil supplies, with all the uncertainties that involves.

Petroleum is not the only energy source for which the United States leads world demand and consumption. As Figure 25-2 shows, natural gas often occurs in association with oil deposits. The use of natural gas has increased enormously since World War II. In the 1990s, the

United States consumed about 37 percent of the natural gas used in the world, and even this was barely enough to meet the demand. One result of the increased use of natural gas is the proliferation of pipelines shown in Figure 23-2. In North America in 2002, there were over 2.5 million miles (4 million kilometers) of pipelines, including parts of a new pipeline designed to carry Alaskan natural gas across Canada to the U.S. market.

Dependence on external fuel supplies affects three of the four world industrial regions that were the principal regions of industrial development during the mid-twentieth century. Despite discoveries of oil and gas in the North Sea, Europe still depends on foreign shipments of petroleum. The United States has two neighbors with substantial fossil fuel reserves (Mexico's oil and gas may rank among the world's largest), but its own supplies remain rather limited. Japan is almost totally dependent on oil from distant sources.

On the other side of the coin, countries with large reserves of oil and natural gas—Saudi Arabia, Kuwait, Iraq, Russia, and others—occupy a special position in the global economic picture. None of these except Russia is a major industrial power, but they all played a key role in the industrial boom of the twentieth century. And while oil has brought wealth to some in the Middle East, it has also ensured that outside powers such as the United States and Great Britain are involved and invested in what happens in the region. This has often produced an uneasy relationship between countries in the Middle East and the major industrial powers of the "West." Such geopolitical concerns—along with accompanying concerns over long-term supply and environmental change —are now pushing countries to consider alternative energy sources (see Looking Ahead Box).

Let us turn now to the major industrial regions that developed during the middle of the last century.

Looking Ahead

The Future of Oil

Oil is a finite resource. It is not a question of *if* the world's oil supply will run out but *when*. Because discoveries of new reserves continue to be made, and because the extraction of fossil fuels is becoming ever more efficient, it is difficult to predict exactly how much longer oil will remain a viable energy source. Many suggest that the current level of oil consumption can be sustained for up to 100 years, although some argue for much shorter or much longer time frames. Despite the range of opinion, the majority of scientists believe that, by the middle of this century, alternative sources will have to be developed.

When one considers that oil could become an increasingly scarce commodity within the lifetimes of many college students today, the importance of finding alternative energy sources becomes apparent. Adding further urgency to the quest are the pollution problems associated with the burning of fossil fuels and the geopolitical tensions that arise from global dependence on a resource concentrated in one part of the world. Moving away from a dependence on oil carries with it some clear positives, but it could lead to wrenching socioeconomic adjustments as well.

The effects of a shift away from oil will certainly be felt to some degree in the industrial and postindustrial countries, where considerable retooling of the economic infrastructure will be necessary. It is the oil-producing countries, however, that will face the greatest adjustments. More than half of the world's oil supply is found in the Middle Eastern countries of Saudi Arabia, Iraq, Kuwait, the United Arab Emirates (UAE), and Iran. In each of these countries, the extraction and exportation of oil account for at least 75 percent of total revenue and 90 percent of export-generated income. What will happen to these countries when their oil reserves run dry?

Consider the case of Kuwait—a country in which the incomes of 80 percent of the wage earners is tied to oil. Kuwait's citizens are currently guaranteed housing, education, and health care, and each adult couple receives a one-time stipend when a child is born. All of these programs are provided tax free, and when workers retire, their pensions are close to the salaries they earned as active members of the workforce.

Concerns over the long-term implications of a decline in oil revenue in Kuwait have led to efforts to find an alternative source of wealth: potable water. In a part of the world that can go for months without rain, water is a most precious resource. Some people in Kuwait joke that for each million dollars is spent in the quest for sources of fresh water, all that is found that is a billion dollars worth of oil! But where fresh water cannot be found, it can potentially be made, and Kuwait has begun to position itself to become one of the world's leaders in the field of desalinization (the conversion of salt water to fresh water). This is currently a very expensive process, but Kuwait is able to devote some of its oil revenues to research and development on the desalinization process. Absent a major technological breakthrough, in the short term income generated by desalinization will amount to only a tiny fraction of the income provided by oil production. The long term may be a different story, though. If it is not, Kuwait—and other countries in its position—will be facing a socioeconomic adjustment of enormous proportions.

North America

In the decades after World War I, the United States emerged as the world's preeminent industrial power. Having escaped the destruction that World War I brought to much of Western Europe, the United States could capitalize on its newfound global political stature, its developed infrastructure, and its highly trained workforce to build an industrial economy that was second to none. The Great Depression that began in 1929 was an enormous setback, of course, but only in absolute terms. The effects of the Depression were felt worldwide, and if anything, the United States came out of it with an expanded industrial dominance. That dominance would grow even greater after World War II, when once again the United States avoided destruction within its own boundaries and yet received a major industrial boost from the wartime effort. Canada, too, was in a strong position, and a major American Manufacturing Belt emerged in the rectangular region shown in Figure 25-3.

The American Manufacturing Belt

The American Manufacturing Belt extends from the northeastern seaboard to Iowa and from the St. Lawrence Valley to the confluence of the Ohio and Mississippi rivers. At the belt's northeastern edge, the light industries of New England and New York give way to heavier manufacturing. Here lies the Southeast Pennsylvania district, centered on metropolitan Philadelphia and encompassing the Baltimore area. Throughout much of the twentieth century, iron ores shipped from distant locations like Canada and South America could be smelted right on the waterfront in tidewater steel mills. Major chemical industries (notably in northern Delaware), pharmaceutical industries, and lighter manufacturing plants were established there as well.

Farther west lies the well-defined Upstate New York district, extending from Albany, on the Hudson River, to Buffalo, on the shore of Lake Erie. Growth there was originally stimulated by the Erie Canal, which was dug in the early nineteenth century to connect the East Coast to

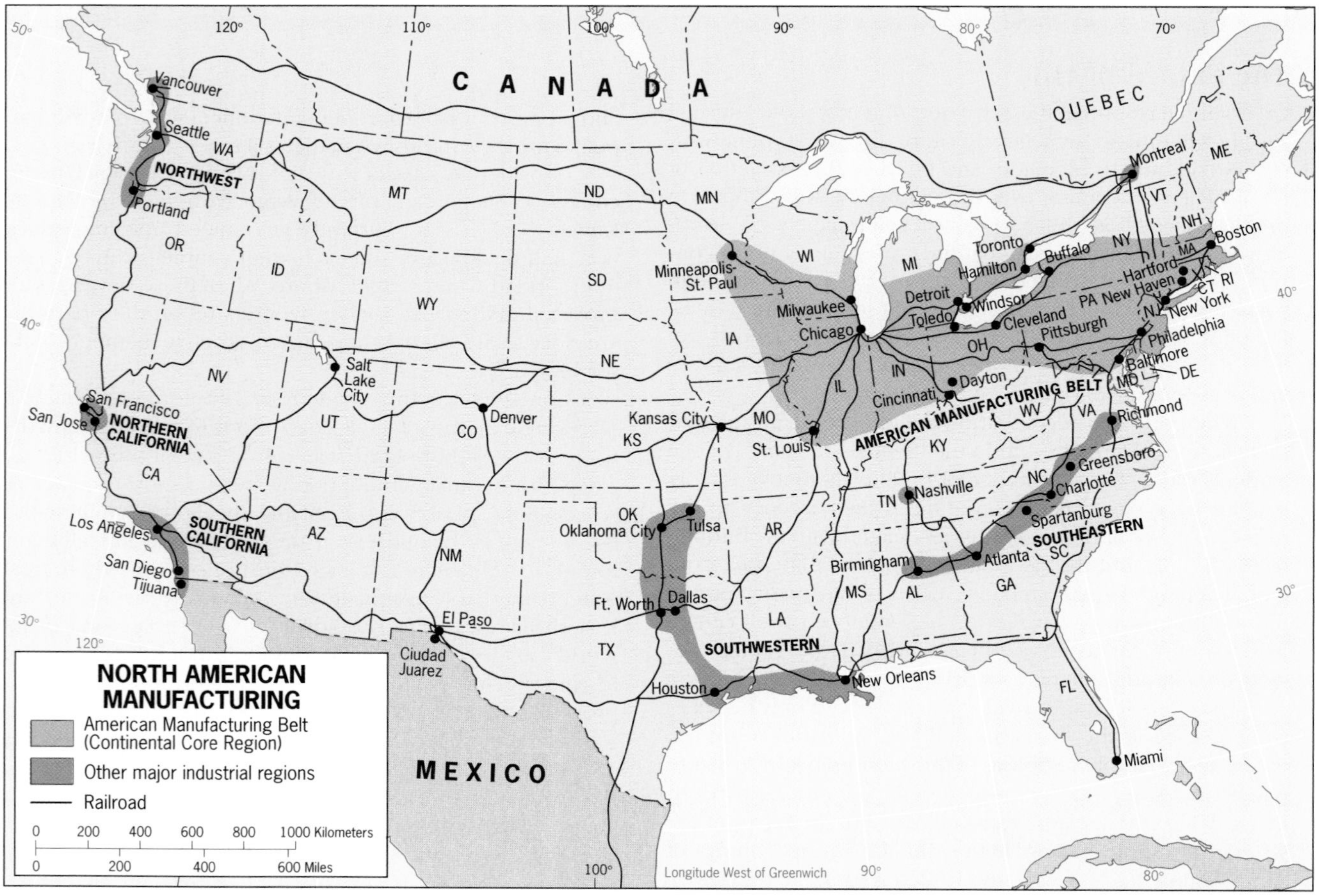

Figure 25-3 North America's Major Manufacturing Regions. North American manufacturing has dispersed westward and southward, but the eastern core area remains dominant.

the Great Lakes. During the mid-twentieth century, specialty manufactures developed in this region. Rochester came to be known for cameras and optical products, Schenectady for electrical appliances, and Buffalo for steel.

Canada's Southern Ontario district extends from the western end of Lake Ontario to the industrial zone at the western end of Lake Erie. As Figure 25-3 shows, this district links two parts of the U.S. Manufacturing Belt anchored by Buffalo and Detroit; the most direct route between these two industrial cities is through Ontario.

Canadian and U.S. manufacturing complexes meet in two great horseshoe-shaped zones around the western ends of Lakes Ontario and Erie. In the Northeast is the so-called Golden Horseshoe, which curls from Oshawa through Toronto and Hamilton to Buffalo. Westward, around the western end of Lake Erie, is the "Erie Horseshoe," which extends from Windsor in Ontario through Detroit and Toledo to Cleveland. The first of these zones is mainly Canadian, and the second is largely American.

Figure 25-3 shows that the Montreal area along the upper St. Lawrence River also forms part of the Canadian industrial zone. This area is no match for the Ontario district, but it has one big advantage: cheap hydroelectric power. Aluminum-refining and papermaking industries therefore are located there.

Westward lies the remainder of the U.S. industrial heartland. This comprises the interior industrial district, with nodes such as the Pittsburgh–Cleveland area, the Detroit–Southeast Michigan area, Chicago–Gary–Milwaukee, and smaller areas centered on Minneapolis, St. Louis, Cincinnati, and other areas. There industrial power truly transformed the landscape during the twentieth century as Appalachian coal and Mesabi iron ore were converted into autos, bulldozers, harvesters, armored cars, and tanks.

Other North American Regions

Figure 25-3 reminds us that the industrial heartland is not the only significant industrial region in the United States. Other important industrial areas developed during the twentieth century. The Southeastern district extends from Birmingham, Alabama, to Richmond, Virginia. The name of Birmingham has long been associated with iron and steel. Local raw materials sustained this industry for many years. Atlanta, the regional focus of the South, developed an industrial economy around cotton, tobacco, and furniture. Later, high-tech industries changed the industrial structure of this region, but many older industries are still found there.

On the Gulf of Mexico, a Southwestern district also began to emerge, centered on the thriving urban areas of Houston and the Dallas–Fort Worth "Metroplex" and extending along the Gulf coast to New Orleans. The region's industrialization has its roots in meat packing and flour milling, but the growing importance of oil as a source of energy is the main story behind the emergence of this region as a major industrial center.

Among industrial districts in the western half of the United States, three stand out. The two California districts were originally based on agricultural products. The Northwest district, extending from Seattle northward to Vancouver, Canada, and southward to Portland, Oregon, became the focus of America's aerospace industry. As we will see, these districts received a significant boost in the late twentieth century with the rising economic importance of the Pacific Rim.

Europe

Like North America, Europe had a head start in the industrialization arena, and its access to global resources continued to be facilitated by its colonial empires. Hence, European industry recovered relatively quickly from World War I and began to expand rapidly. The expansion was in part spatial; new industrial areas began to develop in Italy, Spain, and Scandinavia. But the biggest story was the growth of industry in the European core.

The Rühr became Europe's greatest industrial complex. Named after a small tributary of the Rhine River, the Rühr reveals the combined advantages of high-quality resources, good accessibility, and proximity to large markets. When local iron ore reserves became depleted, ores could be brought in from overseas. The Rühr was already undergoing industrialization in the closing decades of the nineteenth century, but by the 1930s the river basin had become one of the most important industrial regions in the world, pouring forth the products of heavy industry, including tanks and other weapons for Hitler's armies.

Saxony, on the other hand, was always oriented toward specialized lighter manufactures. Anchored by Leipzig and Dresden, it became known for such products as optical equipment and cameras, refined textiles, and ceramics. Farther east, the industrial district of Silesia was originally part of Germany but now lies in Poland and extends into the Czech Republic (Fig. 25-1). The development of the Silesian district was based on high-quality coal resources and lesser iron ores that were later supplemented by imports from Ukraine.

The sophistication of European industry ensured that World War II would be the most destructive conflict ever fought, but the war ended up destroying much of the continent's industrial infrastructure in the process. This outcome created considerable challenges in the decade following the war, but from an industrial standpoint it was not altogether a minus. German industry had been reduced to rubble, but with American aid new factories sprang up that incorporated the latest technology. In time, such factories had a competitive edge over older industrial establishments in North America and less-hard-hit parts of Europe.

By the late 1950s, European industry had rebounded throughout much of the continent. The colonial empires of European countries were disintegrating, but Europe's economic and political influence was sufficiently great that it could withstand that change without losing its privileged position in the global industrial picture. Other rivals were emerging, however—most notably to the east in the Soviet Union and its satellite countries.

The Former Soviet Union

As we saw previously, prior to its incorporation into the Soviet Empire, the western part of the former Soviet Union, particularly Ukraine, had been affected by the Industrial Revolution before the end of the nineteenth century. After World War I, the rich resources and industrial potential of Ukraine were called upon to help the Soviet Union become an industrial power. Ukraine produced as much as 90 percent of all the coal mined in the then Soviet Union, and, with iron ores from the Krivoy Rog reserve and later from Russia's Kursk Magnetic Anomaly, it grew into one of the world's largest manufacturing complexes during the mid-twentieth century.

The Soviet effort to develop its industrial potential led to aggressive efforts to nurture industry in western Russia—particularly around Moscow and Leningrad (now St. Petersburg) (Fig. 25-4). The strong role of the state could have overridden classic industrial location influences, but in fact the state largely supported industry where it would have been likely to develop anyway. In the case of Moscow, the city and its hinterland offered an important local market, converging transport routes, a large labor force, and strong centrality—just like Paris and London. Light manufacturing could already be found in this district during Tsarist times, but under communist rule heavy industries were added. Nizhni Novgorod (then named Gorkiy), with its huge automobile factories, became the "Soviet Detroit."

The St. Petersburg area is one of Russia's oldest manufacturing centers. It was chosen by Tsar Peter the Great not only to serve as Russia's capital but also to become the country's modern industrial focus. The skills and specializations that Peter the Great nurtured with the help of Western European artisans still mark the area's key industries: high-quality machine building, optical

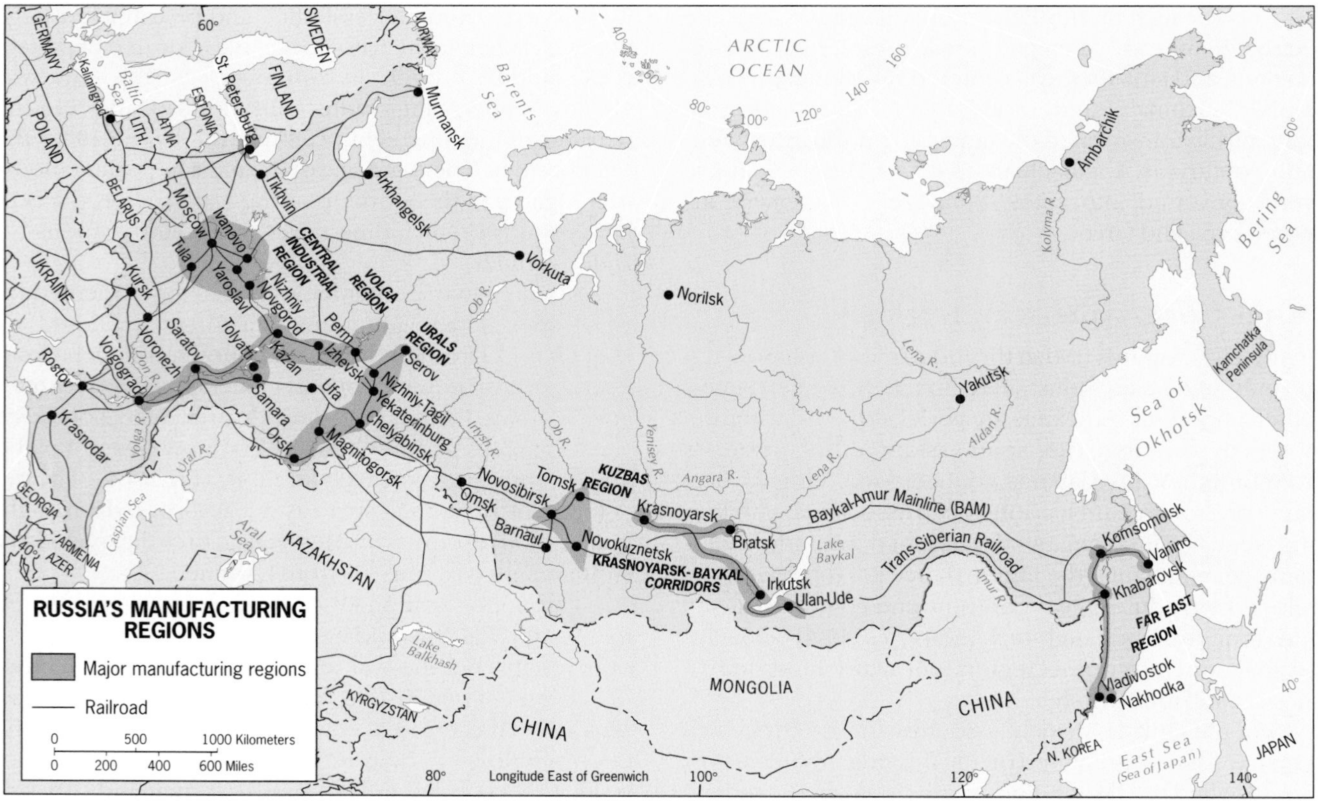

Figure 25-4 Russia's Major Manufacturing Regions. The major manufacturing regions of Russia reflect the dominance of the west in the country's economic geography.

products, and medical equipment. But St. Petersburg has become a large metropolis, and industries such as shipbuilding, chemical production, food processing, and textile making are also located there.

The Volga experienced major development beginning in the mid-1930s, where the combination of accessible raw materials and ease of transport facilitated its development. When the Ukraine and Moscow areas were threatened by the German armies in World War II, whole industrial plants were dismantled and reassembled in Volga cities—protected from the war by distance. Samara (formerly Kuibyshev) even served as the Soviet capital for a time during World War II. This was part of a more general eastward shift of industry that occurred during World War II, when Russia was invaded from the west.

After the war, the industrialization program continued. A series of dams, constructed on the Volga River, made electrical power plentiful. Known oil and natural gas reserves were larger than anywhere else in the former USSR. Canals linked the Volga to both Moscow and the Don River, making it easy to import raw materials. The cities lining the Volga, spaced at remarkably regular intervals, were assigned particular industrial functions in the state-planned economy. Samara became an oil refinery center, Saratov acquired a chemical industry, and Volgograd became known for its metallurgical industries. The Volga was set on a course that has allowed it to remain one of Russia's dominant industrial regions to this day.

East of the Volga region lies the Urals region. This area also developed rapidly during World War II. The Ural Mountains yield an enormous variety of metallic ores, including iron, copper, nickel, chromite, bauxite, and many more. The only serious problem is coal—there is not enough of it, and the little it has is of poor quality. So coal is shipped in by rail from reserves near Novosibirsk to the east. In the cities of the Urals district, metals, metal products, and machinery are produced in great quantities. Together with the Siberian centers, the Urals district now produces more than half of all the iron and steel made in Russia.

In the wake of World War II, areas in Siberia also emerged as key industrial regions. About 1900 kilometers (1200 miles) east-southeast of the Urals is the Kuznetsk Basin, or Kuzbas. In the 1930s this area supplied raw materials, especially coal for the Urals, but this function diminished as local industrial growth accelerated. The original plan was to move coal from the Kuzbas to the Urals, with returning trains carrying iron ore to the coalfields. However, good iron ores were later discovered in the Kuznetsk Basin itself.

Between the Kuzbas and Lake Baykal lies the Krasnoyarsk–Baykal Corridors region. Served by the Trans-Siberian Railroad and several important rivers, this 1600-kilometer-long (1000-mile-long) region contains impressive resources, including coal, timber, and water. During the mid-twentieth century, large hydroelectric facilities were developed at Krasnoyarsk, Irkutsk, and Bratsk to supply power to factories producing mining equipment, chemicals, aircraft, and railway rolling stock.

Finally, there is the Far East region, long focused on the Pacific port of Vladivostok and more recently on the new port of Nakhodka. This region began to be developed during the mid-twentieth century, but as we will see later, it has become a major zone of industrial development in the last few decades.

Eastern Asia

Aside from the eastern Soviet Union, Japan and China were the most significant areas of Asia that had avoided direct European colonization—and these are the Asian countries where large-scale industrialization first took root. Of the two, Japan was clearly the early dominant player.

From the field notes

"Sail up Japan's Inland Sea toward Kobe, and its seems as though the country's entire waterfront has been turned into one vast system for unloading raw materials and loading finished products. Large freighters can be offloaded in just a few hours by massive cranes that lift out hold-sized containers, empty them into trucks and return them to the ship. A never-ending lineup of railroad cars and flatbed trucks circulates through the port of Kobe (seen here), picking up incoming freight and delivering goods for export. Such infrastructure and efficiency have combined to help make Japan's one of the most competitive economies in the world."

Japan In less than a century after the beginning of the Industrial Revolution, Japan became one of the world's leading industrial countries. This accomplishment is all the more remarkable when one realizes that Japan has limited natural resources. Much of what Japan manufactures is made from raw materials imported from all over the world. Japan's national territory is just one twenty-fifth the size of the United States, and its population is less than half the U.S. total. Its transformation into the world's second-largest economy has often been described as a miracle.

Japan's economic development began during the second half of the nineteenth century, when it embarked on a campaign of modernization and colonization. Under the banner of the Meiji Restoration, reformers modernized Japan's domestic industries, moved the capital from the interior to the coast, organized its armed forces, and obtained advice from British experts on issues ranging from education to transportation (which is why the Japanese drive on the left side of the road). The Japanese also established colonies, and soon raw materials were flowing to Japan from an expanding colonial empire in Korea, Taiwan, and mainland China.

The 1930s and early 1940s brought triumph and disaster: triumph in the form of a military campaign that included vast conquests in the Pacific, East Asia, and Southeast Asia and a surprise attack on Pearl Harbor in Hawaii, and disaster when Japanese forces were driven back with great loss of life. The war ended with the destruction of two Japanese cities by atomic bombs. When U.S. forces took control of Japan in 1945, the nation's economy was in shambles. Yet a few decades later Japan had not only recovered but become a global economic power.

Four key industrial districts emerged in the country (Fig. 25-5):

- *The Kanto Plain* Japan's dominant region of industrialization and urbanization is the Kanto Plain, which contains about one-third of the population and includes the Tokyo-Yokohama-Kawasaki metropolitan area. This gigantic cluster of cities and suburbs (the second biggest metropolis on Earth, behind only Mexico City) forms the eastern anchor of the country's core area. The Kanto Plain possesses a fine natural harbor at Yokohama and is centrally located with respect to the country as a whole. It has also benefited from Tokyo's designation as the nation's capital, when Japan embarked on its planned course of economic development. Many industries and businesses chose Tokyo as their headquarters in order to be near government decision makers. During the mid-twentieth century, the Tokyo-Yokohama-Kawasaki metropolitan area became Japan's leading manufacturing complex, producing more than 20 percent of the country's annual output.
- *The Kansai District* Japan's second largest industrial complex extends from the eastern end of the Seto Inland Sea to the Nagoya area and includes the Kobe-Kyoto-Osaka triangle. This, the Kansai district, comes close to rivaling the Kanto area: it is a vast industrial region with steel mills, a major chemical industry, automobile manufacturing, shipbuilding, textile factories, and many other types of production. The urban agglomeration here is often called the Tokaido megalopolis.
- *The Kitakyushu District* The Seto Inland Sea is Japan's pivotal waterway, and the Kansai district has benefited from its location at the eastern end of it. During the nineteenth century, raw materials from Korea and later from Northeast China moved in large quantities along this route. At the western entrance to the sea lies the focus of Japan's third industrial district, called Kitakyushu—a conurbation of five northern Kyushu Island cities. Japan's first coal mines were located there, as well as its first steel mills, which for many years remained the largest in the country. But during the mid-twentieth century, heavy industry came to dominate, with shipbuilding and steel-making in the lead, supplemented by a large chemical industry and numerous lighter manufacturing plants.
- *The Toyama District* Only one manufacturing district in the area depicted by our map lies outside the belt extending from Tokyo in the east to Kitakyushu in the west. It is the secondary district centered on Toyama, on the Sea of Japan. Its advantage—cheap electricity from nearby hydroelectric stations—led to a cluster of industries developing there: paper manufacturing, chemical industries, and textile plants.

Of course, our map gives an inadequate picture of the variety and range of industries that developed in Japan, many of them oriented to local markets. Thousands of manufacturing plants were established in cities and towns other than those shown on the map, even on the cold northern island of Hokkaido.

China

Although some industrial growth occurred in China during the period of European colonial influence, and later during the Japanese occupation, China's major industrial expansion occurred during the communist period. When the communist planners took over in 1949, one of their leading priorities was to develop China's resources and industries as rapidly as possible.

China is a vast country and has a substantial resource base. The quality of its coal is good, the quantity enormous, and many of the deposits are near the surface and easily extracted. China's iron ores are not so produc-

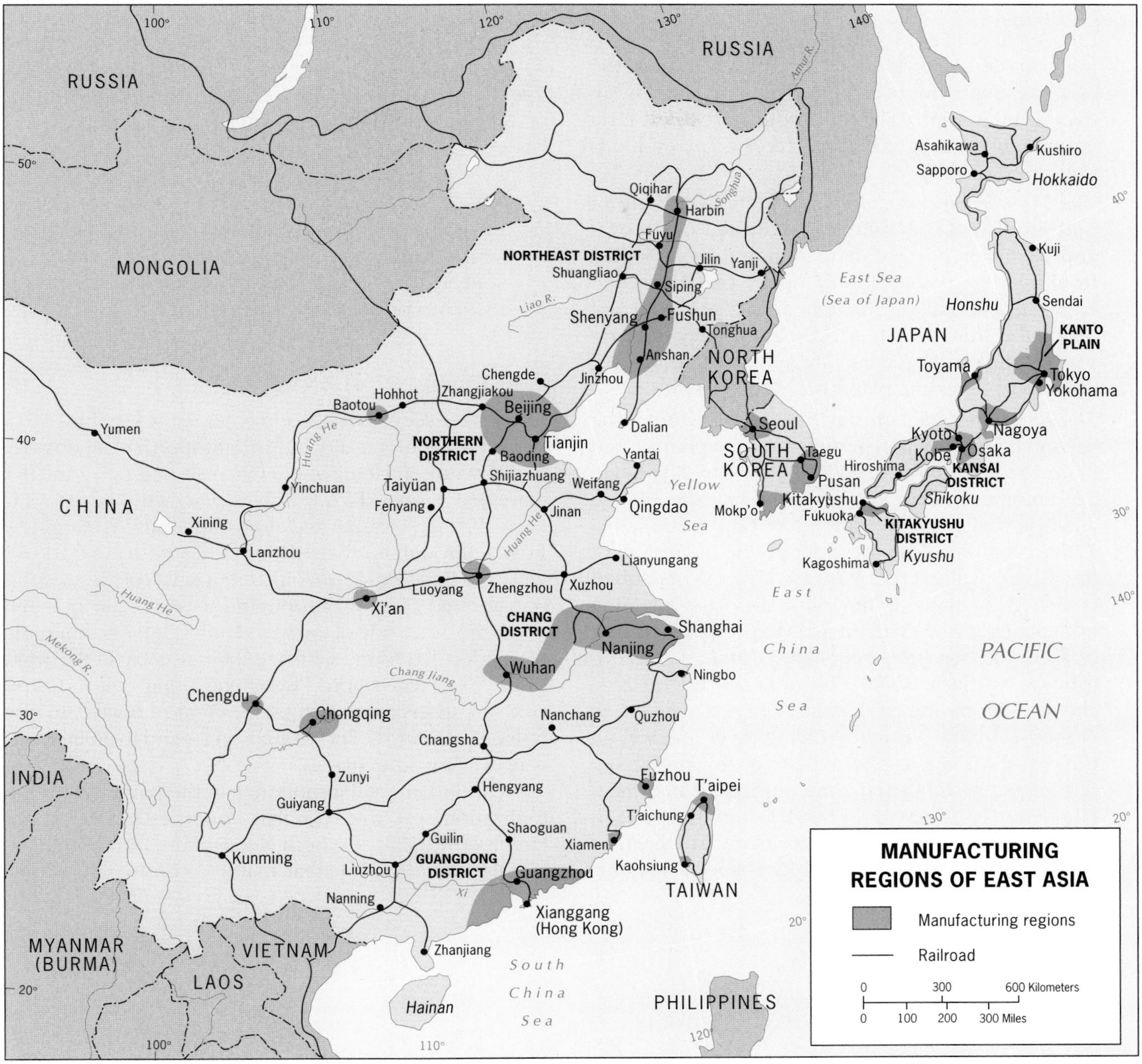

Figure 25-5 East Asia's Major Manufacturing Regions. For decades, the Northeast was China's most rapidly growing industrial area. Now the Chang District is taking the lead.

tive and are generally of rather low grade, but new finds have regularly been made.

Until the early 1960s, China's communist-era industrial development was aided by Soviet planners. It was spatially constrained by the location of raw materials, the development that had taken place before the 1949 communist takeover, the pattern of long-term urbanization in the country, the existing transport network, and the eastern clustering of the population. Like their then-Soviet allies, China's rulers were determined to speed the industrialization of the economy, and their decisions created several major and lesser industrial districts.

- *The Northeast District* Under state planning rules, the Northeast district (formerly known as Manchuria and called Dongbei in China today) became China's industrial heartland, a complex of heavy industries based on the region's coal and iron deposits located in the basin of the Liao River. Shenyang became the "Chinese Pittsburgh," with metallurgical, machine-making, engineering, and other large factories. Anshan, to the south, emerged as China's leading iron- and steel-producing center. Harbin to the north (China's northernmost large city, with more than 2 million inhabitants) produced textiles, farm equipment, and light manufactures of many kinds (Fig. 25-5).

◆ *The Northern Industrial District* The Northern industrial district was established around the capital and its major port, Tianjin. Although it benefited from nearby coalfields, an ample labor force, and large agricultural production, this district did not match the Northeast in any respect. Heavy industry was located in the Tianjin area, and textile-making and food-processing plants handled local products.

◆ *Shanghai and the Chang (Yangzi) District* The second largest industrial region in China developed in and around the country's biggest city, Shanghai. The communist planners never allowed Shanghai to attain its full potential, often favoring the Beijing–Tianjin complex over the great port at the mouth of the Chang called the Yangtzi River in its lower course. Nevertheless, the Chang district, containing both Shanghai and Wuhan, rose to prominence and, by some measures, exceeded the Northeast as a contributor to the national economy. As Figure 25-5 shows, still another industrial complex developed farther upstream along the Chang River focused on the city of Chongqing. Whether we view the Chang district as one industrial zone or three, it became a pacesetter for Chinese industrial growth, if not in terms of iron and steel production, then in terms of its diversified production and local specializations. Railroad cars, ships, books, foods, chemicals—an endless variety of products come from the thriving Chang district.

◆ *The Guangdong District* In the south, the Guangdong industrial district was slower to develop. China's rulers tended to favor northern provinces over southern ones, and China's uneasy relationship with Hong Kong, located on the estuary of the Pearl River, further diminished Beijing's interest in the south. In the absence of major mineral or fuel resources, the Guangdong industrial zone could not rival the complexes of the north.

The Larger Context

As we have seen, as the world entered the last third of the twentieth century, major industrialization had taken place in the Northern Hemisphere in a resource-rich zone that extended eastward from Britain, across the heart of Europe, through Ukraine and along the southern margins of Russia, through northern China, and across the U.S. Midwest and East (Fig. 25-6). Industrialization of the kind that transformed Central Europe and its cities did not fully reach the other side of the world until China's communist rulers decided to industrialize their country in the wake of the 1949 revolution. Elsewhere, significant industrial concentrations were spotty at best—most notably in Australia, South Africa, and Hong Kong—and in an incipient way in a few other places.

Of fundamental importance to the pattern of industrialization was the role that countries played in the larger world. The Northern Hemisphere Industrial Zone largely encompassed areas that had considerable politi-

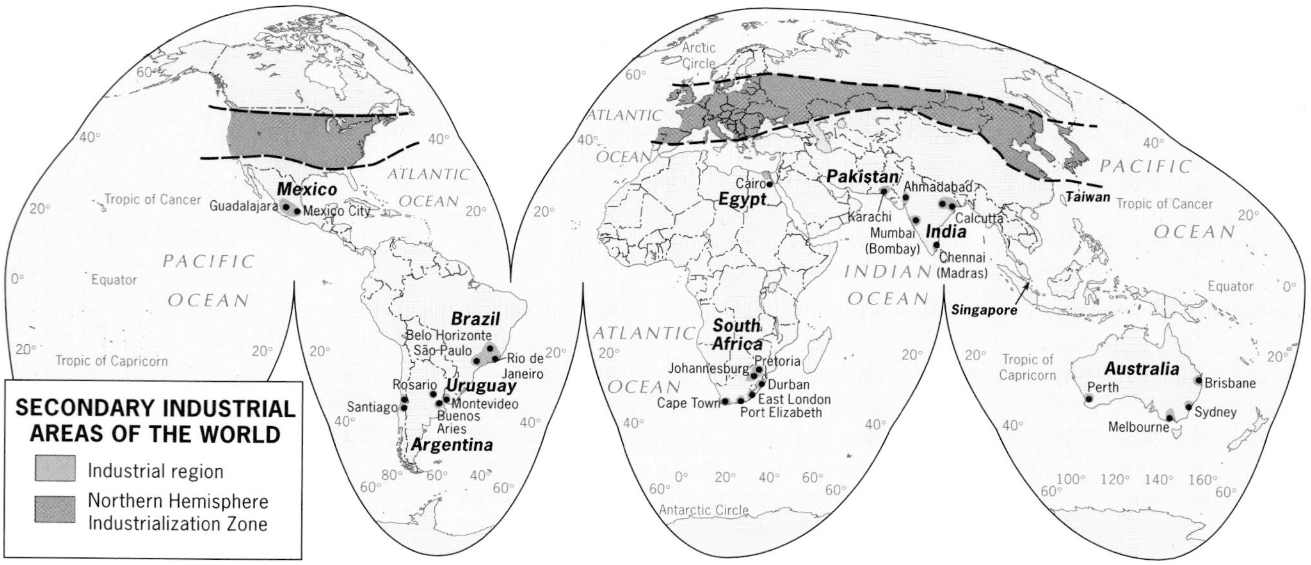

Figure 25-6 Secondary Industrial Areas of the World.

cal and economic strength. The presence of raw materials helps to explain the pattern, but it was not determinative. Japan emerged as a significant industrial economy even though it lacked raw materials of its own. And in other parts of the world, significant resources could be found, but local populations lacked the technology and capital to exploit them for their own interests.

◆ THE LATE TWENTIETH CENTURY AND BEYOND

The past 40 years has seen some fundamental shifts in the global industrial picture. Two dominant pieces of that picture can be identified: (1) deindustrialization along with a growing service sector in some traditional industrial areas and (2) the expansion of industry into new places. The first of these topics is sufficiently vast that it requires extended treatment of its own. We thus take it up in Chapter 27—the first chapter of a part focused on globalization. But to conclude our account of industrial patterns, we need to look at the global expansion of industrialization in recent decades. Perhaps the most dramatic story in this regard occurred along the eastern edge of Asia.

The "Four Tigers"

Until about two decades ago, Japan's economic dominance of East Asia was beyond doubt. Other nodes of manufacturing existed, but these were no threat, and certainly no match, for Japan's industrial might.

Over the past 20 to 30 years, however, Japan has been challenged. Although it remains the undisputed leader, it has faced growing competition from the so-called Four Tigers of East and Southeast Asia: South Korea, Taiwan, Hong Kong, and Singapore—and more recently from China. The forces behind the rise of the Four Tigers are complex; as we will see in Chapter 27, they are tied to the shift of labor-intensive industries to areas with lower labor costs. They are also the product of government efforts to protect developing industry and to invest in education and training.

Among the Four Tigers, South Korea emerged as the largest industrial power. Three significant manufacturing districts export products ranging from automobiles and grand pianos to calculators and computers. One of these is centered on the capital, Seoul (with 10 million inhabitants), and the two others lie at the southern end of the peninsula, anchored by Pusan and Kwangju, respectively (Fig. 25-5). If the two Koreas were reunited, the combination of the North's heavy industries and the South's major manufacturing would create a formidable industrial power just a few miles from Japan.

To the south lies the island of Taiwan. Although the island is neither large nor populous (it has just under 23 million inhabitants, compared to 48 million in South Korea), its industrial power is growing. In recent years, Taiwan's economic planners have been moving the secondary sector away from labor-intensive manufacturing toward high-technology industries, thus meeting Japanese competition head-on. Personal computers, telecommunications equipment, precision electronic instruments, and other high-tech products flow from Taiwanese plants, which benefit from a skilled labor force. The capital, Taipei (with 7.7 million inhabitants), is the focus of the country's industrial complex, which is situated on the northern and northwestern zone of the island.

Just a trading colony five decades ago, Hong Kong exploded onto the world economic scene during the 1950s with textiles and light manufactures. The success of these industries, based on plentiful, cheap labor, was followed by growing production of electrical equipment, appliances, and other household products. Hong Kong's situational advantages have contributed enormously to its economic fortunes. The colony became mainland China's gateway to the world, a bustling port, financial center, and ***break-of-bulk*** point. In 1997 China took over the government of Hong Kong from the British, and a showplace of capitalism came under communist control. This has raised questions about the future of this "Tiger," but the Chinese can ill afford to undercut its economic dynamism.

The industrial growth of Singapore also was influenced by its geographical setting. Strategically located at the tip of the Malay Peninsula, Singapore is a small island inhabited by a little over 4 million people, mostly ethnic Chinese but with Malay and Indian minorities. Fifty years ago, Singapore was mainly an entrepôt (transshipment point) for such products as rubber, timber, and oil; today the bulk of its foreign revenues come from exports of manufactured goods and, increasingly, high-technology products. Singapore is also a center for quaternary industries, selling services and expertise to a global market.

Rapid economic growth entails risks. To varying degrees, East and Southeast Asia's economies expanded under circumstances that contained potential for trouble. Autocratic governments protected banks and state-owned industries that could not survive without help; the banks lent too much money. Those same governments engaged in sometimes-grandiose construction projects requiring huge loans. Cronyism (giving special favors such as mining permits and import licenses to family and friends) and corruption were not uncommon, their costs hidden by the economic boom until the crisis. Legal systems to protect foreign businesses on Asian soil were in some ways inadequate. Currencies (the money of the countries) were weakened by the resulting pressures, and some were seriously overvalued against, say, the U.S. dollar and the British pound.

In 1997, the region suffered a severe economic setback resulting from these circumstances. Thailand's currency collapsed, followed by its stock market; banks closed and bankruptcies abounded. Soon Malaysia and Indonesia were affected, and by early 1998 one of the Four Tigers, South Korea, required a massive infusion of dollars (provided by the International Monetary Fund, a Washington-based bank) to prevent economic chaos.

These economic troubles on the Pacific Rim have not marked the end of the region's economic expansion. The reforms required to overcome them have served to strengthen East and Southeast Asia's economies, and the Four Tigers continue to exert a powerful regional—and international—economic role.

Other Parts of the Pacific Rim

The forward march of the Four Tigers is just a piece of the fast-changing Pacific Asian industrial picture. Two centuries after the onset of the Industrial Revolution, East Asia is the cauldron of industrialization. From Japan to Guangdong and from South Korea to Singapore, the islands, countries, provinces, and cities fronting the Pacific Ocean are caught up in a frenzy of industrialization that has made the geographic term *Pacific Rim* synonymous with economic opportunity. In Chinese cities such as Dalian, Shanghai, Zhuhai, Xiamen, and Shenzhen, pollution-belching smokestacks rise above a smog-choked urban landscape. Streets are jammed with traffic ranging from animal-drawn carts and overloaded bicycles to trucks and buses. Bulldozers are sweeping away vestiges of the old China; cottages with porches and tile roofs on the outskirts of the expanding city must make way for (often faceless) tenements. Decaying vestiges of the old city stand amid glass-encased towers that symbolize the new economic order.

Not all of the Pacific Rim displays such symptoms. China's coastal provinces are industrializing, but the process shows signs of having run its course in Japan and Singapore. Taiwan and South Korea are in an intermediate stage, and Vietnam lags behind China. But taken as a whole, East Asia is becoming the world's most productive cluster of industrial regions. China's economy is now the world's third largest (after the United States and Japan), and many are looking with a combination of amazement and concern at what lies ahead. The country's economic ambitions are symbolized by the construction of the gigantic Three Gorges Dam in the middle course of the Chang River. This project is destined to change the economic and environmental landscape of the Chang industrial district in ways that can only be imagined.

The communist regime is still in control in China, but it has chosen to pursue a market-driven economic course. Certain cities and areas facing the Pacific coast have been designated as ***Special Economic Zones (SEZs)***, "open cities," and "open coastal areas" to encourage foreign investment. Shanghai is no longer closed to the outside world: a gigantic development project is transforming the right bank of the Huangpu into an industrial complex (named Pudong) that is expected to rival Hong Kong. In the meantime Shenzhen, across the border from Hong Kong, has undergone massive industrialization and become the world's fastest-growing urban area. Once-dormant Guangdong Province has become a major contributor to China's export economy.

At the same time, the Northeast has become China's rustbelt. Many of its state-run factories have been sold or closed, or are operating below capacity. Unemployment is high, and economic growth has stopped. Eventually, the Northeast is likely to recover because its resources and its geography favor it. But under the new economic policies the dynamic eastern and southern provinces are producing their own industrial revolution and changing the map of this part of the Pacific Rim.

In the late 1990s, Japan's economy experienced a downturn—not because of changes in the country's energy or raw-material supply, but as a result of government mismanagement (Japanese industry is tightly regulated and controlled by the Japanese bureaucracy) and financial mistakes. Japan's problems posed a risk to the global economic system because world economies are interconnected. But Japan remains one of the most economically powerful countries on Earth, and its fortunes are thus inextricably linked to the fortunes of the Pacific Rim as a whole.

The Russian Far East is also part of the Pacific Rim, and today industrial growth is occurring in the hinterlands of such cities as Komsomolsk (the first steel producer in the region) and Khabarovsk (with metal and chemical industries). The region's rich raw materials are finally being extracted, and there is enormous potential for development beyond the low-grade coal and iron ore found to date. Already the zinc and tin deposits mined here constitute Russia's largest sources of these metals. As the region becomes more economically confident, questions are being asked about the role that Moscow, 10 time zones away, should play in its political and economic future.

The Pacific Rim is generally understood to encompass the eastern edge of the Pacific Ocean as well—or at least the northern part of the eastern edge—and this brings the western edge of Canada and the United States into the picture. The overall dynamism of the Pacific Rim has facilitated the development and expansion of industry along the North American west coast. In the process, cities such as Los Angeles, San Francisco, Portland, Seattle, and Vancouver have become increasingly important players in the global economy.

Secondary Industrial Regions

Today we can identify a ***secondary industrial region*** south of the world's primary industrial region (Fig. 25-6). Thailand, Malaysia, Indonesia, and Vietnam (and possibly the Philippines), in particular, are sharing in the economic growth of the Pacific Rim. Elsewhere, however, industrialization is proceeding more slowly. In the Western Hemisphere, only Brazil and Mexico have substantial manufacturing industries: Brazil in the São Paulo–Rio de Janeiro–Belo Horizonte triangle (with output ranging from automobiles and weapons to chemicals and textiles) and Mexico in the Mexico City–Guadalajara complex. In Africa, some industrialization is occurring in the hinterland of Cairo and in South Africa, principally in Gauteng Province centered on Johannesburg.

As noted earlier, political decisions as well as economic forces shape industrialization patterns, and this is certainly true of the emergence of secondary industrial areas. Consider, for example, the secondary manufacturing zone that has developed in northern Mexico just south of the border with the United States. A manufacturing zone began developing here several decades ago in response to the creation of a so-called ***maquiladora*** district where manufactured products could be sent to the United States free of import tariffs. This led many U.S. companies to establish plants that were designed to transform imported, duty-free components or raw materials into finished industrial products. At least 80 percent of these goods were then to be reexported to the United States.

Although the maquiladora process started during the 1960s, it did not really take off until the 1980s, when it was stimulated by expanding wage differences between U.S. and Mexican workers and by changed political conditions. Today about 2000 assembly plants employ more than 600,000 workers, accounting for over 20 percent of Mexico's entire industrial labor force. The maquiladora plants produce such goods as electronic equipment, electrical appliances, automobiles, textiles, plastics, and furniture. Such plants have given the region an industrial character, but they are controversial as well because they are sites where American manufacturers can avoid the employment and environmental regulations that are in force just a few miles to the north. A frequent practice, then, is to hire young women for low pay and put them to work in repetitive jobs without access to many benefits—and sometimes in environmentally questionable conditions.

The establishment of the ***North American Free Trade Agreement (NAFTA)*** on January 1, 1995, promoted further industrialization of the area. In addition to manufacturing plants, NAFTA has facilitated the movement of tertiary-sector industries from the United States to Mexico, including data processing operations. Most of the

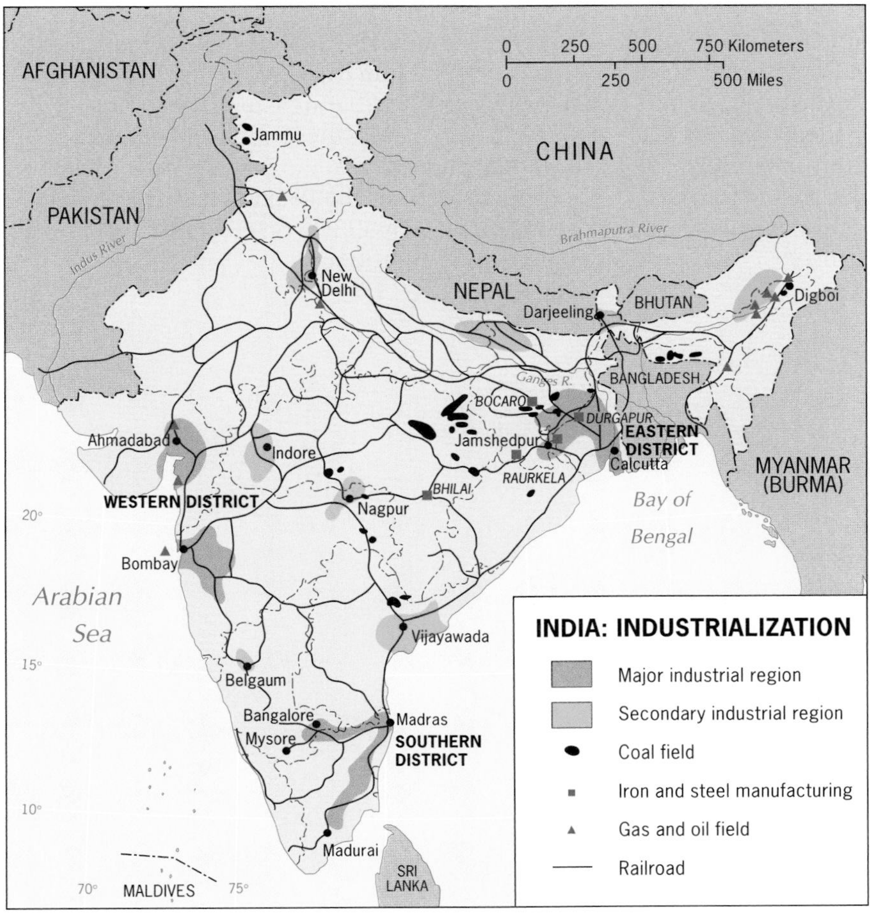

Figure 25-7 India's Major Industrial Areas. India's industrial areas are widely dispersed. India has large coal deposits, but its oil reserves are small.

new plants are located in two districts: Tijuana on the Pacific coast, linked to San Diego across the border, and Ciudad Juarez on the Rio Grande across from El Paso, Texas.

Even more significant is the recent industrial development taking place in India (Fig. 25-7). Although small in the context of India's huge size and enormous population, India's economy now ranks as the eighth largest in the world, and industrialization is expanding as a result of recently changed economic policies. Industrialization in India still reflects its colonial beginnings, but major industrial complexes are developing around Calcutta (the Eastern district, with engineering, chemical, cotton, and jute industries, plus iron and steel based on the Chota Nagpur reserves), Mumbai (the Western district, where cheap electricity helps the cotton and chemical industries), and Chennai (the Southern district, with an emphasis on light engineering and textiles). India has no major oil reserves, so it must spend heavily on energy. On the other hand, India has much hydroelectric potential and ample coal, and its Bihar and Karnataka iron ore reserves may be among the largest in the world. With a large labor force and a location midway between Europe and the Pacific Rim, India may yet become a participant in the last wave of the Industrial Revolution.

To complete our understanding of the global industrial picture, it is critical to see how differential patterns of development are implicated in the evolving economic picture. We turn to this issue in the next chapter. At the beginning of the next Part, we then consider some of the sweeping changes that have occurred in the global economy during the twentieth century. These changes have affected most parts of the planet and account for the shifting economic character of some older manufacturing regions and the types of recent industrial developments we have considered at the end of this chapter.

◆ KEY TERMS ◆

break-of-bulk
comparative advantage
growth pole
maquiladora
North American Free Trade Agreement (NAFTA)
primary industrial region
secondary industrial region
Special Economic Zone (SEZ)

◆ APPLYING GEOGRAPHIC KNOWLEDGE ◆

1. After a surge of nuclear power-plant building and plans for a growing substitution of coal-fired power plants by nuclear facilities, the drive toward nuclear power in the United States slowed and then virtually stopped. In other countries, however, the expansion of nuclear power generation continued; France has the lead in Europe. What factors explain the differences between the United States and France?

2. Most of North America's manufacturing industries remain concentrated in the core area shown in Figure 25-6, but other industrial areas are developing. Unlike the massive core area, these subsidiary areas tend to be specialized around some product or combination of products. Explain the locational characteristics of the subsidiary areas shown on the map in the context of their particular products.

Chapter 26

Concepts of Development

From the field notes

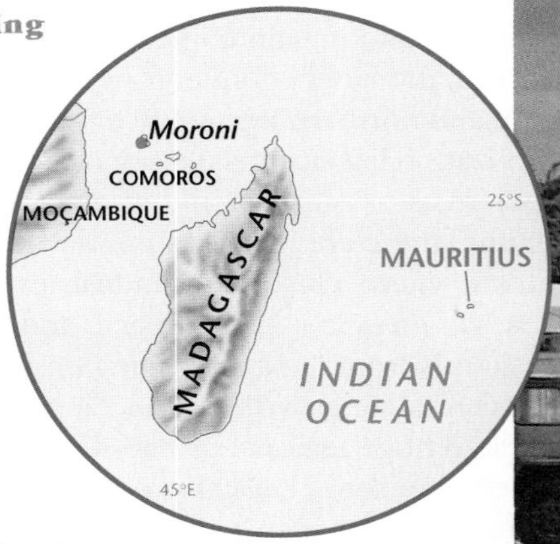

"Why do some economies forge ahead while others do not? I spent a morning at the port of Moroni in the Federal Islamic Republic of the Comoros just after having visited the bustling economic hub of Mauritius. A boatload of wheat flour was being offloaded, bag by bag; several broke and the flour dusted the dock. Meanwhile, workers waiting to unload a cargo of wood sat motionless, unable to get started until the single crane became available. With poor infrastructure, negligible natural resources, and limited education, the Republic of the Comoros is one of the world's poorest countries. But Mauritius was very poor also, and has progressed remarkably since it began to attract foreign investment in its textile and other manufactures. Here in the Comoros, the sole opportunity may be tourism."

KEY POINTS

◆ **The global economic picture is characterized by enormous gaps between rich and poor countries, but the geography of economic well-being also reveals regional disparities within countries.**

◆ **Economic disparities are usually believed to be due to different levels of development, but in reality development is more complex and cannot be reduced to simple categories.**

◆ **Underlying economic disparities is a core-periphery relationship among different regions of the world. This affects how economies develop in both the core and the periphery.**

◆ **As the twenty-first century unfolds, some states are still subsistence-based and poor, whereas others are industrializing rapidly.**

◆ **Rapid development is taking place under widely different political systems; it is often associated with democratization, but it is also occurring under authoritarian regimes.**

In 2000, the per capita ***gross national product*** (GNP) in Japan in U.S. dollars was $32,350. In the United States it was $29,240. In the European Union it averaged $26,348. But in India it was $440, in Nigeria it was $300, and in Indonesia, the world's fourth most populous country, it was $640. This enormous range reflects the often-searing contrasts between the rich world and the poor (Table 26-1).

The economic and social geography of the contemporary world is a patchwork of almost inconceivable contrasts. On the simple fields of shifting cultivators in equatorial American and African forests, root crops are still grown using ancient methods and the most rudimentary tools. On the Great Plains of North America, in Ukraine, and in eastern Australia, modern machines plow the land, seed the grain, and harvest the wheat. Toolmakers in the villages of Papua New Guinea still fashion their implements by hand, as they did many centuries ago, while the factories of Japan disgorge automobiles by the shipload for distribution to markets thousands of miles away. Between these extremes, the range and variety of productive activities are virtually endless.

Despite the worldwide impact of the Industrial Revolution, there are areas even within the industrialized countries where change is slow in coming. Parts of the rural South in the United States still experience significant poverty and remain comparatively remote from the effects of national economic growth. In remote areas of western and northern Japan, life has changed little while modernization has occurred elsewhere in the country. In Europe, areas of isolation and stagnation persist. At the same time, there are places in poorer, less industrialized countries where clusters of industries have emerged, rapid urban growth is taking place, and local conditions differ sharply from those prevailing in surrounding areas. Recent economic growth on the Pacific Rim of East Asia has created huge regional disparities in economic conditions between some coastal provinces of China and distant interior provinces. Such regional contrasts have significant social as well as political consequences, and China is by no means the only country affected. Regional economic disparities are increasing throughout the world. ◆

◆ CONCEPTS AND APPROACHES

Economists and geographers use a variety of approaches to describe the wide disparities in the global economy. Traditionally, countries with high levels of urbanization and industrialization and high standards of living were referred to as ***developed countries***, in contrast to ***underdeveloped countries***. This approach divides the world into two major categories, but it is also based on the idea that all countries are at some stage of ***development***. However, the concept of development is a complicated one. How should development be measured? The GNP index provides one commonly used, if increasingly controversial, approach.

Table 26-1 Per Capita GNP for Selected Countries, 2002 (in U.S. $)

Europe	United Kingdom	21,410
	Sweden	25,580
	France	24,210
	Germany	26,570
	Hungary	4,510
	Italy	20,090
	Spain	14,100
	Greece	11,740
North America	Canada	19,170
	United States	29,240
Middle America	Mexico	3,840
	Costa Rica	2,770
	Nicaragua	370
	Haiti	410
South America	Argentina	8,030
	Brazil	4,630
	Bolivia	1,010
	Guyana	780
	Peru	2,440
East Asia	China	750
	Japan	32,350
	South Korea	8,600
South Asia	India	440
	Bangladesh	350
	Pakistan	470
	Sri Lanka	810
Southeast Asia	Indonesia	640
	Malaysia	3,670
	Singapore	30,170
	Thailand	2,160
Southwest Asia/ North Africa	Egypt	1,290
	Kuwait	15,000
	Morocco	1,240
	Qatar	20,300
	Saudi Arabia	6,910
	UAE	17,870
Subsaharan Africa	Nigeria	300
	Ethiopia	100
	Kenya	350
	Moçambique	210
	Gabon	4,170
	Sierra Leone	140
	South Africa	3,310

Sources: Averages from various World Bank and United Nations Sources. Figures for Kuwait and Qatar from the CIA Factbook, 2001.

The GNP index was developed by economists who wanted to compare countries on the basis of certain standardized measures. Such comparisons are also difficult because the criteria one chooses for comparison will influence the outcome. There is also the problem of data reliability; statistics for many countries are inadequate, unreliable, and incompatible with those for other countries, or simply unavailable.

Despite those complications, a number of standard measures are widely used to gauge levels of economic development—and the GNP index is the most common of these. GNP is a measure of the total value of the officially recorded goods and services produced by the citizens and corporations of a country in a given year. It includes things produced both inside and outside the country's territory, and it is therefore broader than gross domestic product, which encompasses only goods and services produced within a country during a given year.

Since countries are widely variable in size, comparative studies usually focus on GNP per capita, which involves dividing a country's total GNP by the total population. Using GNP per capita to compare countries has many shortcomings, however. Most obviously, it says nothing about the distribution of wealth. Consider, for example, the GNP data for such countries as Kuwait and the United Arab Emirates (UAE). In 2002 the per capita GNP (GNP divided by the population of the country) of both countries was over $15,000. This figure is larger than those of many countries that are regarded as part of the developed world, including several European countries. Also note the high per capita GNPs for such countries as Qatar. Are these "developed" countries in an economic and social sense? The answer is that large amounts of money derived from the sale of a single product (in this case oil) do not automatically or even quickly result in overall national development. Thus the bare figures give us no hint of the degree of overall participation in the country's economy or the average citizen's material standard of living. National statistics (such as population data) can conceal enormous regional and demographic diversity.

Beyond these matters, GNP is a limited measure because it includes only transactions in the formal economy. Quite a few countries have a per capita GNP of less than $400 per year—a figure so low that it might seem impossible to survive in those countries. The explanation for this apparent dilemma lies in the informal economy, which includes everything from a garden plot in a yard to the black market and the drug trade. Collectively, these are quite significant elements of the economic picture in many areas, but they are entirely omitted from GNP statistics.

Finally, GNP does not reflect any negative spinoffs to economic activity, such as resource depletion or environmental pollution. It may even treat such externalities as a plus. For example, the sale of cigarettes augments

GNP—and if the cigarettes cause sickness and hospitalization is required, the GNP figure is boosted further. Conversely, the use of energy-efficient devices can actually lower GNP.

The limitations of GNP have prompted some analysts to look for alternative measures of economic development. These include:

1. *Occupational Structure of the Labor Force* This is the percentage of workers employed in various sectors of the economy. A high percentage of laborers engaged in the production of food staples, for instance, signals a low overall level of development.
2. *Productivity per Worker* This is the sum of production over the course of a year, divided by the total number of persons in the labor force.
3. *Consumption of Energy per Person* Those using this measure equate the greater use of electricity and other forms of power with higher levels of economic development. To some extent, this data must be viewed in the context of climate.
4. *Transportation and Communications Facilities per Person* This measure reduces railway, road, airline connections, telephone, radio, television, and so forth to a per capita index—and reflects the amount of infrastructure that exists to facilitate economic activity.
5. *Consumption of Manufactured Metals per Person* Development is sometimes measured by the quantity of iron and steel, copper, aluminum, and other metals utilized by a population during a given year.
6. *Dependency Ratio* A measure of the number of dependents, young and old, that each 100 employed people must support. A high dependency ratio can result in significant economic and social strain.
7. *Social Indicator Rates* A number of measures are employed, including literacy rates, infant mortality, life expectancy, caloric intake per person, percentage of family income spent on food, and amount of savings per capita.

Many countries come out in approximately the same position no matter which of these measures is used, but it is important to recognize the limitations of any one of them. In particular, all are national averages, so they share with GNP an inability to capture differences within countries. Moreover, each measure reflects particular ideas about what is important—and they are therefore the product of particular value systems. Social indicator rates such as infant mortality and life expectancy are among the more value neutral, but here data problems are often significant.

Importantly, none of these approaches produces a clear dividing line between developed and underdeveloped countries. Instead, countries lie along a development continuum, and any division between them is arbitrary. The problem of classifying countries into two categories of development became even more acute in the 1960s and 1970s, when some countries traditionally classified as underdeveloped, such as South Korea and Taiwan, began shooting ahead. Hence, the term ***developing countries*** came into use to describe a third category of development consisting of countries that show evidence of moving toward the developed category as measured by the indices of development described above.

The term *underdeveloped* has such a negative connotation, however, that no country wanted to be so classified. The term came to be seen as condescending, conveying the notion that a country was poor culturally as well as economically. Such sensitivity is understandable when one realizes that ideas about development tend to come from scholars in the so-called developed world. Moreover, terms such as developed and underdeveloped also mean rich and poor, haves and have-nots—which carry with them emotionally laden notions of advantaged and disadvantaged. Hence, the term *underdeveloped* was used less and less, and the developed–underdeveloped distinction was largely replaced by a developed–developing distinction. The latter had the advantage of sounding more optimistic, and it could encompass countries such as South Korea and Taiwan. But it was also misleading because it suggested that all countries were achieving higher levels of socioeconomic prosperity when that was not the case.

Beyond problems of terminology, the very effort to classify countries in terms of levels of development has come under increasing attack during the last three decades. One concern is that a scale of development suggests that all countries have moved or will move through the same process of development. Hence, like the demographic transition model (see Chapter 5), the development model does not take geographical differences very seriously. Just because Japan moved from a rural, agrarian state to an urbanized, industrial one does not mean that Sudan will—or at least that it will do so in the same way. Others criticize the development model because of the Western bias in the way development is conceptualized. They argue that some of the measures taken in poorer countries that are viewed as progress (attracting industry, mechanized agriculture, etc.) can lead to worsened social and environmental conditions. Still others criticize the development model because it does not reflect the ways in which some parts of the world influence socioeconomic changes in others. Instead, the model treats countries as autonomous units moving through a process of development at different speeds.

The Core-Periphery Model

In light of these criticisms, a growing number of scholars have argued for a new approach to describing global economic disparities—one that is more sensitive to geographical differences and the relationships among development processes occurring in different places. They propose that the geography of the world economy can be understood in terms of a ***core-periphery model***. This model, which is also used in discussions of political power, views the world as characterized by a ***core***, a ***semi-periphery***, and a ***periphery***. Core regions are those that have achieved high levels of socioeconomic prosperity and are dominant players in the global economic game. By contrast, periphery regions are poor regions that are dependent in significant ways on the core and do not have as much control over their own affairs. The semi-periphery, as the name implies, consists of regions that exert more power than peripheral regions but are dominated to some degree by the core regions. Since the core-periphery model focuses attention on the economic relationships among places, it is a key component of many theories that treat the global economy as a large system. As we saw in Part Four, the best known of these theories—***World Systems Theory***—was pioneered by Immanuel Wallerstein, whose work has done much to promote the core-periphery concept.

Dividing the world into cores, semi-peripheries, and peripheries might seem to do little more than replace developed–developing–underdeveloped with a new set of terms. But the core-periphery model is actually quite different because it makes the power relations among places explicit and does not assume that socioeconomic change will occur in the same way in all places. It also has the advantage of being able to describe developments at any spatial scale, be they local, regional, national, or global. Thus a core-periphery relationship can exist within a region (Los Angeles can be described as the economic and social core region of Southern California); within an individual country (the Johannesburg area can be described as the economic core region of South Africa); or in a global context (Japan can be described as an economic core region of the world).

Patterns on the Map

The core-periphery model is a useful frame of reference for understanding the geography of modern economic change. All the same, development concepts are still widely used, and despite their limitations, they provide a useful indication of the character and extent of economic disparities at the scale of the state. These disparities can be seen vividly in Figure 26-1. This map is based on four categories of development used by the World Bank, the Washington, D.C.-based agency that is involved in global development projects. The World Bank groups countries into four categories based on income: low-income economies, lower-middle-income economies, upper-middle-income economies, and high-income economies. The low-income countries are concentrated in Africa and South, Southeast, and East Asia. At the beginning of the twenty-first century, the countries with the world's lowest incomes were Tajikistan in Asia and Niger, Eritrea, Malawi, Ethiopia, Sierra Leone, Burundi, and the Democratic Republic of the Congo in Africa. In all, some 56 of the world's countries are still designated as low-income states; four of them—Guyana, Haiti, Honduras, and Nicaragua—are in the Western Hemisphere.

It is encouraging to note that middle-income countries outnumber the poorer states. According to World Bank statistics, there are 65 middle-income countries, including many in Middle and South America. Forty-seven of these are in the lower-middle-income group and 18 in the upper-middle-income group.

The high-income economies include oil-rich Southwest Asian states as well as prosperous Western European countries. When Figure 26-1 is compared to Table 26-1, some inconsistencies seem to arise. But remember that per capita GNP (Table 26-1) is only one criterion for development; Figure 26-1 is based on a wider range of indicators, as discussed earlier.

◆ MODELS OF DEVELOPMENT

What processes dictate the rate and extent of economic development? In the last few decades, various models have been proposed to describe the economic processes that facilitate or inhibit a country's drive toward material and social prosperity. These models are of two broad types: liberal and structuralist.

Liberal models are based on the ideas about development discussed earlier. They assume that all countries are at the same stage along a development trajectory and that economic disparities between countries are the result of short-term inefficiencies in local or regional market forces. Over the long term, liberal models assume that all countries are capable of development. On the other hand, ***structuralist models*** view regional economic disparities as a structural feature of the global economy. Disparities exist because things have come to be organized or structured in a certain way that cannot be changed easily. For many structuralist theorists, the development of the global economy brought into being a set of large-scale orders or structures—the concentration of wealth in certain areas, unequal relations among places, and so forth—that make it very difficult for poorer regions to improve their situation. Hence, they believe that it is misleading to assume that all areas will go through the same process of development.

The Modernization Model

One of the most influential liberal models was formulated by the economist Walt Rostow in the 1960s and is referred to as the ***modernization model***. Rostow's

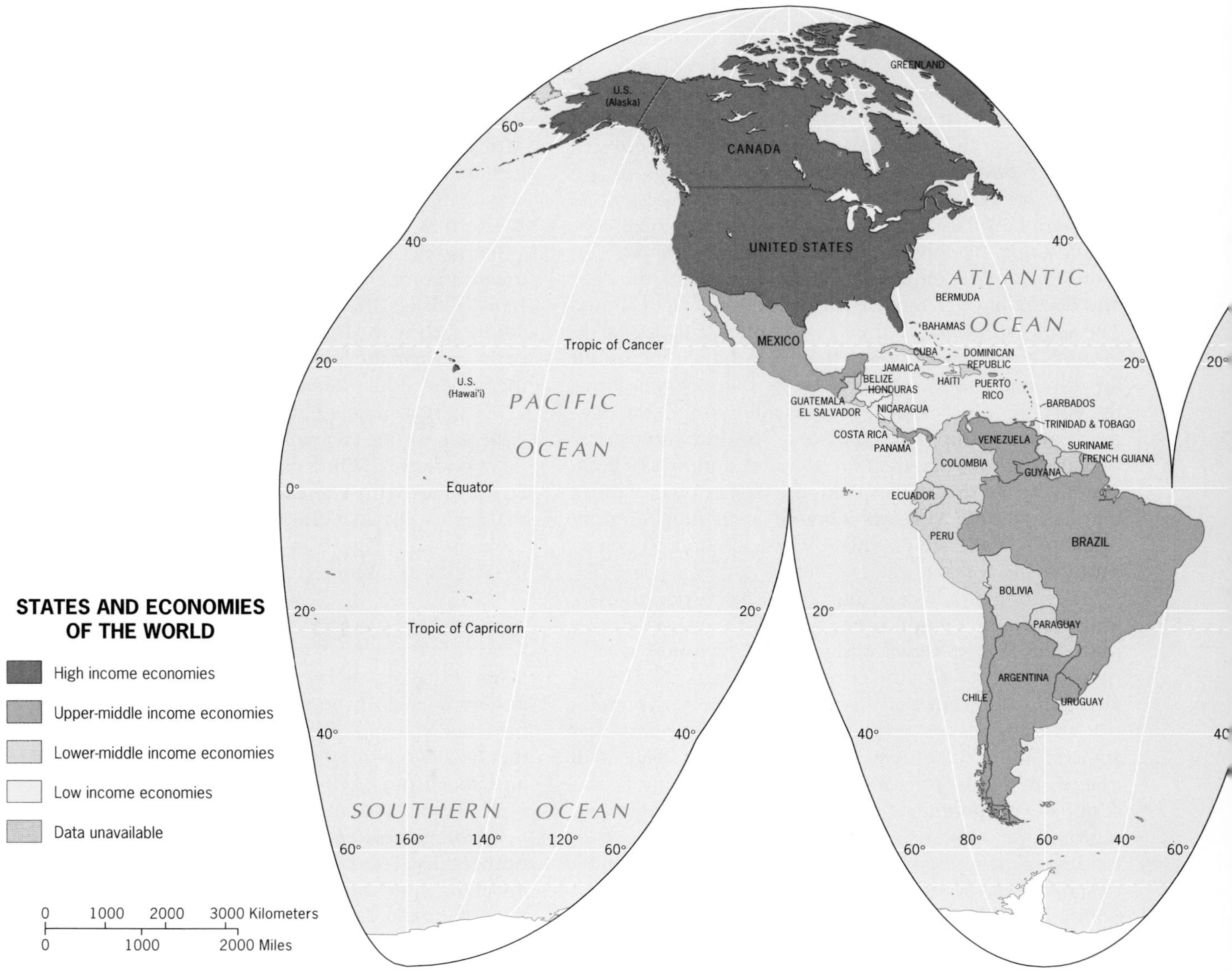

Figure 26-1 World Economies. *Source*: Based on data from the World Bank, *World Development Report 2000/2001*. Oxford: Oxford University Press, 2001, p. 273.

model suggests that all countries follow a similar path through five stages of development.

In the first stage, the society is *traditional* and the dominant activity is subsistence farming. The social structure is rigid and unchanging, and there is much resistance to technological change.

The second stage brings the *preconditions of takeoff.* Progressive leadership moves the country toward greater flexibility, openness, and diversification.

This, in turn, will lead to the third stage, *takeoff.* Now the country experiences something akin to an industrial revolution, and sustained growth takes hold. Urbanization increases, industrialization proceeds, and technological and mass-production breakthroughs occur.

Next, the economy enters the fourth stage, *drive to maturity.* Technologies diffuse, industrial specialization occurs throughout the nation, and international trade expands. Modernization is evident in the core areas of the country; the rate of population growth is reduced.

Some countries reach the final stage, that of *high mass consumption*, which is marked by high incomes and widespread production of many goods and services. A majority of workers enter the service sector of the economy.

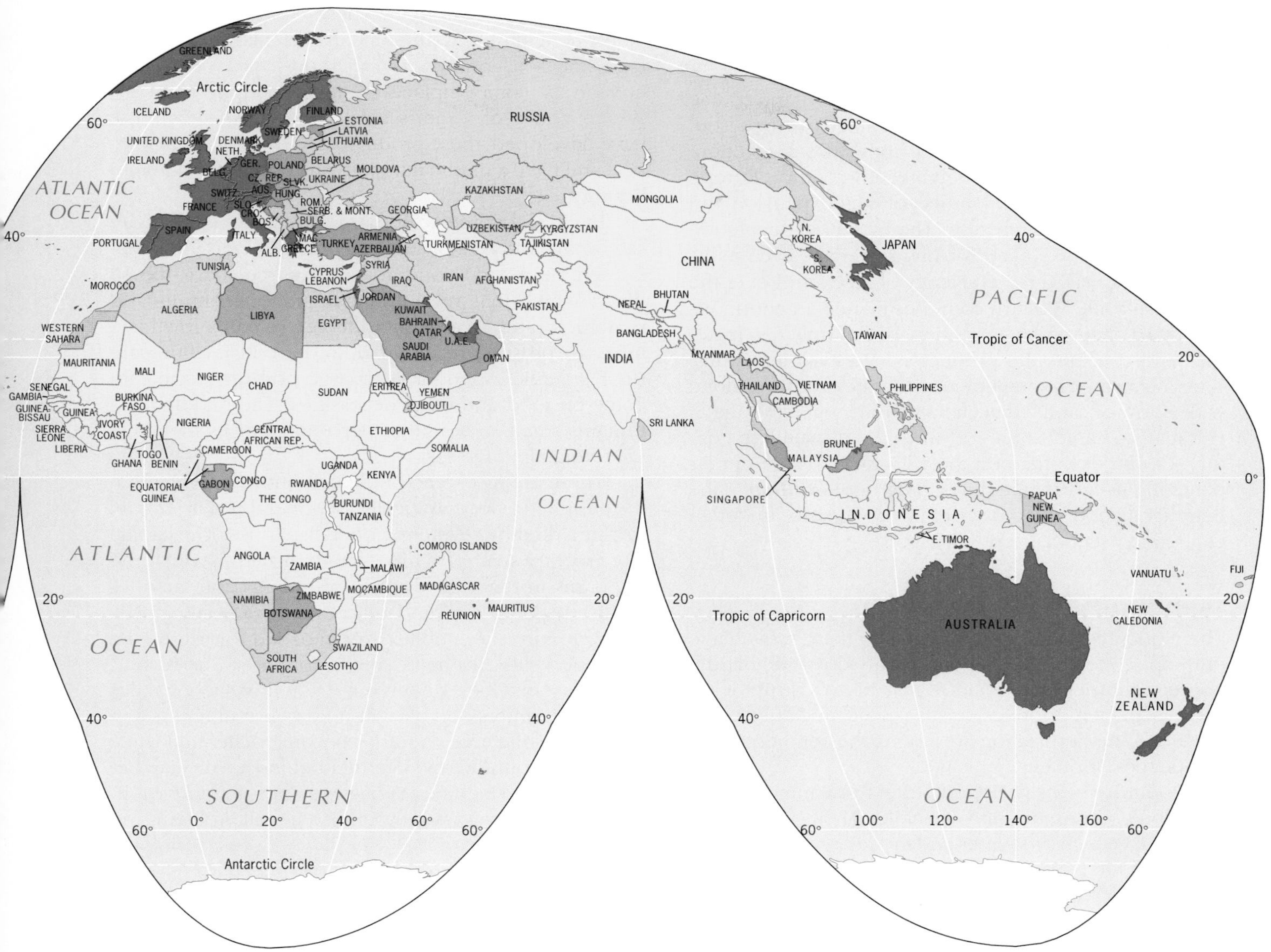

Dependency Theory

Rostow's model provides a useful view of how certain parts of the world have changed over time, but it has been criticized because it does not take into account the different constraints that regions face and because it suggests a single development path that is not influenced by cultural differences. The principal structuralist alternative to Rostow's model, known as ***dependency theory***, addresses some of these criticisms but not all. Dependency theorists hold that the political and economic relationships between countries and regions of the world control and limit the economic development possibilities of less well-off areas. They note, for example, that colonialism created political and economic structures that caused the colonies to become dependent on the imperial powers. They further argue that such dependency helps sustain the prosperity of dominant regions and the poverty of other regions.

Dependency theory thus sees very little hope for economic prosperity in regions and countries that have traditionally been dominated by external powers. This aspect of dependency theory has been criticized, since some traditionally "dependent" regions have made economic gains. Indeed, like modernization theory, dependency theory is based on generalizations about economic change that pay relatively little attention to geographical differences in culture, politics, and society. Although both models provide some insights into the development process, neither is greatly concerned with the spatial and cultural situation of places—central elements of geographical analysis.

◆ GLOBAL ECONOMIC DISPARITIES

Figure 26-1 is in large measure a reflection of the course of history. The sequence of events that led to the present divisions began long before the Industrial Revolution. Even by the middle of the eighteenth century, Europe had laid the foundations for its colonial expansion and global economic domination. The Industrial Revolution increased Europe's need for raw materials, even as its products increased the efficiency of its control over the colonies. While Western countries gained an enormous head start, their colonies continued to supply raw materials and consume the products of Western industries. Thus a system of international exchange was born, along with a flow of capital that changed little when the age of colonialism came to an end in the mid-twentieth century. Countries in the periphery accuse the core of perpetuating its advantage through ***neo-colonialism***—the entrenchment of the old system of dominance under an economic rather than a political guise.

Conditions in the Periphery

The world economic system works to the disadvantage of the periphery, but it is not the only obstacle that the poorer countries face. Political instability, corrupt leaders, misdirected priorities, misuse of aid, and cultural resistance to modernization are among the conditions that hamper development.

Countries in the periphery suffer from numerous demographic, economic, and social ills. Their populations tend to have high birth rates and moderate to high death rates, and life expectancy at birth is comparatively low (see Part Two). As much as half the population is 15 years old or younger. Infant mortality is high. Nutrition is inadequate, and diets are not well balanced; protein deficiency is a common problem. The incidence of disease is high, and many are without adequate health care. There is an excessively high number of persons per available doctor, and too few hospital beds are available. Sanitation is poor. Large numbers of school-age children do not go to school; illiteracy rates are high.

Many people live in rural areas, and surface communications are of low quality. Men and women often do not share equally in the work that must be done; women's workloads tend to be much heavier, and children are required to work. Landholdings are often fragmented, and the small plots are farmed with outdated, inefficient tools and equipment. The main crops tend to be grains and roots; little protein is produced because high protein crops typically have lower yields than grain crops. Moreover, little is produced for the local market because distribution systems are poorly organized and demand is low. On the farms, yields per unit area are low, subsistence modes of life prevail, and many families are constantly in debt. These conditions preclude investment of money and time in such luxuries as fertilizers and soil conservation methods. As a result, soil erosion is commonplace in most peripheral areas. Where zones of larger-scale, modernized agriculture have developed, these produce exports for foreign markets and have a minimal impact on conditions in neighboring areas.

In cities, overcrowding, poor housing, inadequate sanitation, and lack of services prevail. Unemployment is high. (Yet rural conditions are perceived to be so much worse that rural-urban migration continues at very high rates.) Per capita income remains low, savings per person are minimal, and credit facilities are poor. Families spend a very large portion of their income on food and basic necessities. The middle class remains small, and a large percentage of its members are foreign immigrants.

These are just some of the conditions prevailing in the periphery. Geographically, peripheral countries tend to be marked by severe regional disparities. The capital city may be a symbol of urban modernization, with thriving farms in the immediate surroundings and factories on the outskirts. Road and rail connect to a bustling port, where luxury automobiles are unloaded for use by the privileged elite. In the country's core area, the rush of "progress" may be evident, but if you travel a few miles into the countryside you will find a very different picture. Just as the core countries become richer and leave the poorer countries even farther behind, so the gap between progressing and stagnant regions within peripheral countries grows wider. This is a global problem, and it is growing worse.

Economic Options

Countries seeking to climb out of a peripheral position often look to industrialization programs. Many start from a weak industrial base, however. Certainly some industries exist in virtually all countries, however modest and local. These include the production of everyday items, or items that are expensive to transport, such as bread, cement, liquid beverages, basic textiles, and food processing. But developing large-scale, specialized industry is another matter. A successful industrialization program can have significant impacts, however. As noted earlier, development is tied to such factors as productivity per worker in the labor force, consumption of energy per person, quantity of metal used, and transport facilities that have been developed. These indicators are related to a country's industrialization because output per worker goes up when industry becomes mechanized, commercial energy is consumed in greater quantities, metals play a leading role in manufacturing, and transport networks are more highly developed.

Small wonder, then, that some countries seeking to accelerate their economic development have undergone massive industrialization. In the Soviet Union under Stalin, planners poured huge resources into industry. Similarly, countries from Indonesia to Egypt have built their own steel mills and national airlines to serve as symbols of "progress."

Not all poorer countries, however, have made this decision. Some have realized that economic progress is achieved not just through industrial growth, but through the transformation of an entire society. A steel mill or other symbolic industry will do little to speed that transformation. Some governments, therefore, have made agriculture, not industry, their main priority. Still others have turned to tourism.

All development strategies carry with them pros and cons—and this is well illustrated by the case of tourism. Peripheral countries in the Caribbean region of Middle America and in other parts of the world have become leading destinations for millions of tourists from richer nations. Tourism brings some wealth and employment to these countries (see Chapter 27), but the industry's contributions are often narrow in scope and time—and they may have serious negative effects on their cultures.

In economic terms, the investment that must be made by the "host" country is substantial. Often, imports of building materials and equipment strain the country's supply system, and funds are diverted to hotel construction that could have been spent on other needs such as housing for citizens. Moreover, many hotels and other tourist facilities are owned not by the host country but by large multinational corporations. These corporations earn enormous profits, most of which are sent back to headquarters in the home country.

Some countries do earn substantial income from tourism; they include Thailand, Kenya, Barbados, and Fiji, among others. However, that income does not greatly benefit local economies. Some of the income may result from tourists' consumption of scarce commodities such as food, water, and electricity. Much of it must be reinvested in the construction of airports, cruiseports, and other amenities. As for the creation of employment, neither the number nor the nature of jobs in the tourist industry is encouraging.

Tourism frequently strains the fabric of local communities. The invasion of poor communities by wealthier visitors sometimes creates hostility among the hosts. For some local residents, tourists have a "demonstration effect" that causes them to behave in ways that may please or interest the visitors but is disapproved of by the larger community. Free-spending, sometimes raucous tourists contribute to anger and resentment. Moreover, tourism can have the effect of debasing local culture, which is adapted to suit the visitors' taste. Many workers say that employment in the tourist industry is dehumanizing because it demands displays of friendliness and servitude that locals find insulting.

A flood of affluent tourists may be appealing to the government of a poor country (whose elite may have a financial stake in the hotels where they can share the pleasures of the wealthy), but local entrepreneurs usually take a different view. Powerful multinational corporations and national governments may intervene to limit the opportunities of local, small-scale operators in favor of mass, prearranged tour promotions that isolate the tourist from local society.

The cultural landscape of tourism is a study in harsh contrasts: gleaming hotels tower over modest, often poor housing; luxury liners glide past poverty-stricken villages; opulent meals are served in hotels while, down the street, children suffer from malnutrition. If the tourist industry offered real prospects for economic progress in the periphery countries, such circumstances might be viewed as temporary, unfortunate byproducts. However, the evidence indicates otherwise.

Nevertheless, tourist travel heightens knowledge and awareness and can promote intercultural contact and understanding. "Ecotourism" aims to inform about the natural environment, whereas "geotourism" involves scholars in tourists' travel experience. Such initiatives help improve the image of what is sometimes called the "irritant industry."

The challenge of turning tourism into an economic and social plus is one example of the many obstacles facing many peripheral countries as the twenty-first century unfolds. These obstacles arise not only from their own internal circumstances (rapid population growth, limited capital, etc.) but also from global economic conditions over which they have little control. The core countries constitute two-thirds of the market for all the products of the periphery combined, but market prices, tariffs, demand, and other conditions can change quickly and sometimes disastrously. When oil costs rose during the 1970s, poorer countries suffered severely. When inflation rose in the core, the periphery's exports were severely affected.

Complicating the picture further is the foreign debt crisis faced by many low- and middle-income countries. During the closing decades of the twentieth century, international financial institutions loaned massive amounts of money to peripheral countries for development projects of various sorts. The need to repay that debt can make it very difficult for countries to invest in further development projects. We will examine the debt situation in more detail in Chapter 27.

◆ A CHANGING WORLD

Today the world remains divided, but change is occurring almost everywhere. In many countries change continues to be localized, so that "national" statistics suggesting

From the field notes

"This journey across much of western India produced some stark contrasts. Some of India's States are doing well economically, but others are lagging, and it is evident that State governments have a lot of power when it comes to decisions affecting industrialization, privatization, and foreign investment. The small State of Goa, once a Portuguese dependency on the Indian Peninsula's west coast, remained a separate administrative entity after annexation and has become one of India's most prosperous entities. Although we had traveled south from Mumbai along crowded, slow-traffic roadways, we saw a major four-lane artery under construction. And from the hordes of tourists to the many factories, we saw the results of Goa's industry-friendly policies. Damage to the environment has been a federal as well as a State concern in India, and industrial enterprises make it a point to proclaim their sensitivity to this issue, as reflected by this billboard in Madgaon."

overall progress mask growing regional inequalities. Moreover, political geographic changes have created economic hardship in some cases—most notably in parts of the former Soviet Union. Not only has the collapse of the Soviet Union led to economic swings that have disadvantaged many; it has created a power vacuum that has all too often been filled by organized criminal elements. Moreover, it has led to the establishment of international boundaries where once they did not exist. When Ukraine became independent, Russia lost one of its key industrial heartlands, and with it a substantial Russian population living in Ukraine. One of the great challenges for Russian policymakers is to address the economic and social problems that arise from this situation.

The problems of Russia pale by comparison to some of the truly poor countries of the planet. Nevertheless, there are some grounds for limited optimism. In many countries significant indicators—rates of population growth, levels of education, percentages of workers in nonagricultural jobs—are showing improvement.

One reason for progress in countries such as Mexico, Brazil, Thailand, and Malaysia lies in major political and economic changes. Until the end of the 1980s there were three major political-economic blocs: the capitalist First World, the communist Second World, and an uncommitted Third World consisting mainly of mixed economies tending toward state control. Both the First and Second Worlds sought to influence the Third World by encouraging the adoption of their economic models. The results were often disastrous, as when Tanzania and Ethiopia imposed collective farming, which was not well suited to local conditions, or when the United States helped to keep corrupt leaders in power simply because they opposed communism. The collapse of the Soviet Union, however, ushered in a period of tumultuous transition whose outcome is still uncertain. But the distinctions and concerns associated with the previous divisions no longer apply, and the notion of a Third World is obsolete.

Although communist economics failed in the Soviet Union and Eastern Europe, the same cannot yet be said of China. In the early twenty-first century, China remains a bastion of socialist planning, having overcome the challenge of democratization by military force in 1989. In China, unlike Tanzania or Ethiopia, the collectivization of agriculture brought success in the war against famine. Also, unlike the Soviet Union, China did not experience a steadily worsening economy in the 1980s. So while communism was abandoned in Russia and its neighbors, China, along with North Korea and Cuba, became its last stronghold. Even in China, however, a process of market liberalization is producing rapid changes in some parts of the country and undermining the state's grip on all aspects of the economy.

Despite the current shift toward free-market practices, we should remember that there are many routes to development. Just as there always were hard-line communist states (such as Albania and North Korea) and less rigid systems (as in Yugoslavia and Hungary), so there are variations in capitalism. For example, the economic systems of Sweden and New Zealand are essentially capitalist, but many socialist principles prevail there as well. This is less true in the Netherlands and the United Kingdom, and still less true in the United States.

Politics and economics are closely intertwined. In the Soviet Union, the end of Communist Party domination was a precondition for economic as well as political change. In South Africa, the end of Apartheid and a changing political order were followed by significant economic changes. But the key question may well be this: Can China prove that communist political systems are able to coexist with capitalist economic practices? If the authoritarianism of China's political system survives the economic transition that is now under way, other countries may conclude that such a combination constitutes a model worth emulating. In that case the world could become polarized all over again.

Evaluating such questions requires looking beyond individual cases, however. It necessitates considering the globalizing tendencies that are evident in economic, social, and cultural realms. It is to these that we turn in the next Part.

◆ KEY TERMS ◆

core-periphery model
core region
dependency theory
developed country
developing country
development
gross national product (GNP)
liberal model
modernization model
neo-colonialism
peripheral region
semi-peripheral region
structuralist model
underdeveloped country
underdevelopment
World Systems Theory

◆ APPLYING GEOGRAPHIC KNOWLEDGE ◆

1. Group the countries of Asia into the following categories: (1) developed and developing, and (2) core, semi-periphery, and periphery. What criteria did you use in categorizing the countries in each of the two classifications? What are the strengths and weaknesses of the approach to categorization that you chose?
2. You are charged with drafting a report assessing whether a bank should make a loan to Indonesia to help finance a new road across Java. What would you look at in preparing your report? How might you use the figures showing changes in the gross national product of Indonesia since 1970? Why might those figures offer only limited insight into the economic performance of the country?
3. In this chapter we discuss some of the advantages and disadvantages of tourism as it affects countries—especially small countries. Identify a country in which tourism's advantages eclipse any disadvantages, and another country in which tourism has manifestly negative consequences. If you were to generalize from your cases, what would you say in terms of core-periphery relationships?

Part Eight

THE ROOTS AND CONSEQUENCES OF INDUSTRIALIZATION

At Issue: Revisited

How can countries with weak internal business sectors and large debt-service obligations move forward—and to what degree should wealthier parts of the world assist them in their struggles? The Argentine situation reveals the extraordinary challenges facing countries with weak economies that have accumulated large debts. In our interconnected world, the range of options available to turn economics around are limited. Hence, more cases of loan default and social unrest can be expected if adjustments are not made. The wealthier parts of the world can help countries in this position through some combination of debt relief and foreign aid—although internal corruption and a lack of commitment to the distribution of aid monies in recipient countries can limit the effectiveness of aid initiatives. Wealthier countries that built their own economies through the extraction of resources from the global economic periphery arguably have a moral obligation to provide assistance. Self-interest also argues against abandoning these countries. If a substantial number of countries were to default on their debts, a global financial crisis could ensue that would work to the detriment of everyone.

◆ SELECTED BIBLIOGRAPHY ◆

Part Eight The Roots and Consequences of Industrialization

Agnew, John. *The United States in the World Economy: A Regional Geography* (New York: Cambridge University Press, 1987).

Allen, J., & Hamnett, C., eds. *A Shrinking World? Global Unevenness and Inequality* (Oxford, U.K.: Oxford University Press, 1995).

Bailey, Adran J. "Industrialization and Economic Development in Advanced Placement Human Geography," *Journal of Geography* 99, no. 3/4 (2000): 142–152.

Bater, J. *Russia and the Post-Soviet Scene: A Geographical Perspective* (New York: John Wiley & Sons, 1996).

Berry, B. J. L., Conkling, E. C., & Ray, D. M. *The Global Economy in Transition*. 2nd ed. (Upper Saddle River, N.J.: Prentice-Hall, 1997).

Birdsall, S. S., & Florin, J. W. *Regional Landscapes of the United States and Canada*. 5th ed. (New York: John Wiley & Sons, 1999).

Blouet, B. W., & Blouet, O. M., eds. *Latin America and the Caribbean: A Systematic and Regional Survey*. 4th ed. (New York: John Wiley & Sons, 2002).

Borthwick, M. *Pacific Century: The Emergence of Modern Pacific Asia* (Boulder, Colo.: Westview Press, 1992).

Boserup, E. *Economic and Demographic Relationships in Development* (Baltimore, Md.: Johns Hopkins University Press, 1990).

Bryson, J. R. *The Economic Geography Reader: Producing and Consuming Global Capitalism* (Chichester : John Wiley & Sons, 1999).

Burks, A. W. *Japan: A Postindustrial Power*. 3rd ed. (Boulder, Colo.: Westview Press, 1991).

Chowdhury, A., & Islam, I. *The Newly Industrializing Economies of East Asia* (New York: Routledge, 1993).

Cole, J. P., & Cole, F. J. *The Geography of the European Community* (New York: Routledge, 1993).

Corbridge, S. *Debt and Development* (Cambridge, Mass.: Blackwell, 1993).

Dicken, P. *Global Shift: Transforming the World Economy* (New York: Guilford Press, 1998).

Dicken, P. *Global Shift: The Internationalization of Economic Activity*. 2nd ed. (London: Paul Chapman, 1993).

Drakakis-Smith, D. *Pacific Asia* (New York: Routledge, 1992).

Freeman, M. *Atlas of the World Economy* (New York: Simon & Schuster, 1991).

Gleave, M. B., ed. *Tropical African Development: Geographical Perspectives* (New York: Wiley/Longman, 1992).

Hanink, D. M. *The International Economy: A Geographical Perspective* (New York: John Wiley & Sons, 1994).

Hodder, R. *Development Geography* (New York: Routledge, 2000).

Hugill, P. J. *World Trade Since 1431: Geography, Technology, and Capitalism* (Baltimore, Md.: Johns Hopkins University Press, 1993).

Hussey, A. "Rapid Industrialization in Thailand, 1986–1991." *Geographical Review* 83 (1993): 14–28.

Knox, P., & Agnew, J. *The Geography of the World Economy: An Introduction to Economic Geography*. 3rd ed. (London: Edward Arnold, 1998).

Leeming, F. *The Changing Geography of China* (Cambridge, Mass.: Blackwell, 1993).

Lewis, R. A., ed. *Geographic Perspectives on Soviet Central Asia* (New York: Routledge, 1992).

Lösch, A. *The Economics of Location*. trans. W. Woglom & W. Stolper (New York: Wiley Science Editions, 1967; originally published in 1940).

Massey, D. *Spatial Divisions of Labor: Social Structures and the Geography of Production*. 2nd ed. (New York: Routledge, 1995).

Murphy, A. B. "Economic Regionalization and Pacific Asia: Problems and Prospects." *Geographical Review* 85, no.2 (1995): 127–140.

Murphy, R. T. The Weight of the Yen (New York: W.W. Norton, 1996).

Porter, P. W., & E. S. Sheppard. *A World of Difference: Society, Nature, Development* (New York: Guilford Press, 1998).

Pounds, N. J. G. *A Historical Geography of Europe, 1800–1914* (New York: Cambridge University Press, 1985).

Rostow, W. W. *The Stages of Economic Growth*. 2nd ed. (New York: Cambridge University Press, 1971).

Sheppard, E., & T. J. Barnes. *A Companion to Economic Geography* (Oxford: Blackwell, 2000).

Smith, D. M. *Industrial Location: An Economic Geographical Analysis*. 2nd ed. (New York: John Wiley & Sons, 1981).

Smith, N. *Uneven Development: Nature, Capital and the Production of Space* (New York: Blackwell, 1984).

Songqiao, Z. *Geography of China: Environment, Resources, and Development* (New York: John Wiley & Sons, 1994).

Stewart, J. M., ed. *The Soviet Environment: Problems, Policies and Politics* (New York: Cambridge University Press, 1992).

Szekely, G., ed. *Manufacturing Across Borders and Oceans: Japan, the United States and Mexico* (La Jolla, Calif.: Center for U.S.-Mexican Studies, University of California, San Diego, 1991).

Vogel, E. F. *The Four Little Dragons: The Spread of Industrialization in East Asia* (Cambridge, Mass.: Harvard University Press, 1991).

Weber, A. *Theory of the Location of Industries*, trans. C. Friedrich (Chicago: University of Chicago Press, 1929; originally published in 1909).

Wheeler, J. O. *Economic Geography*. 3rd ed. (New York: John Wiley & Sons, 1998).

World Bank. *World Development Report 2000/2001* (Oxford, U.K.: Oxford University Press, 2001).

Part Nine

FROM DEINDUSTRIALIZATION TO GLOBALIZATION

At Issue

We live in an age of heightened global interdependence. Decisions made in Tokyo can have an immediate effect on stock markets around the world. A Hollywood movie can produce lines at movie theaters from Fairbanks to Johannesburg. An e-mail virus started at a computer terminal in Mexico City can spread around the world in a matter of hours.

Interdependence has brought wealth to millions and rescued many more from poverty. It has hastened the development of science and technology, it has pried open long-closed political systems, and it has broadened the horizons of people in distant places. Interdependence has also highlighted the extraordinary gaps between rich and poor. It has led to greater levels of resource consumption, it has heightened some intercultural animosities, and it has eroded traditional modes of livelihood. *As we enter an age of unprecedented global interaction, can interdependence be made to work in the interests of human economic, social, and political betterment?*

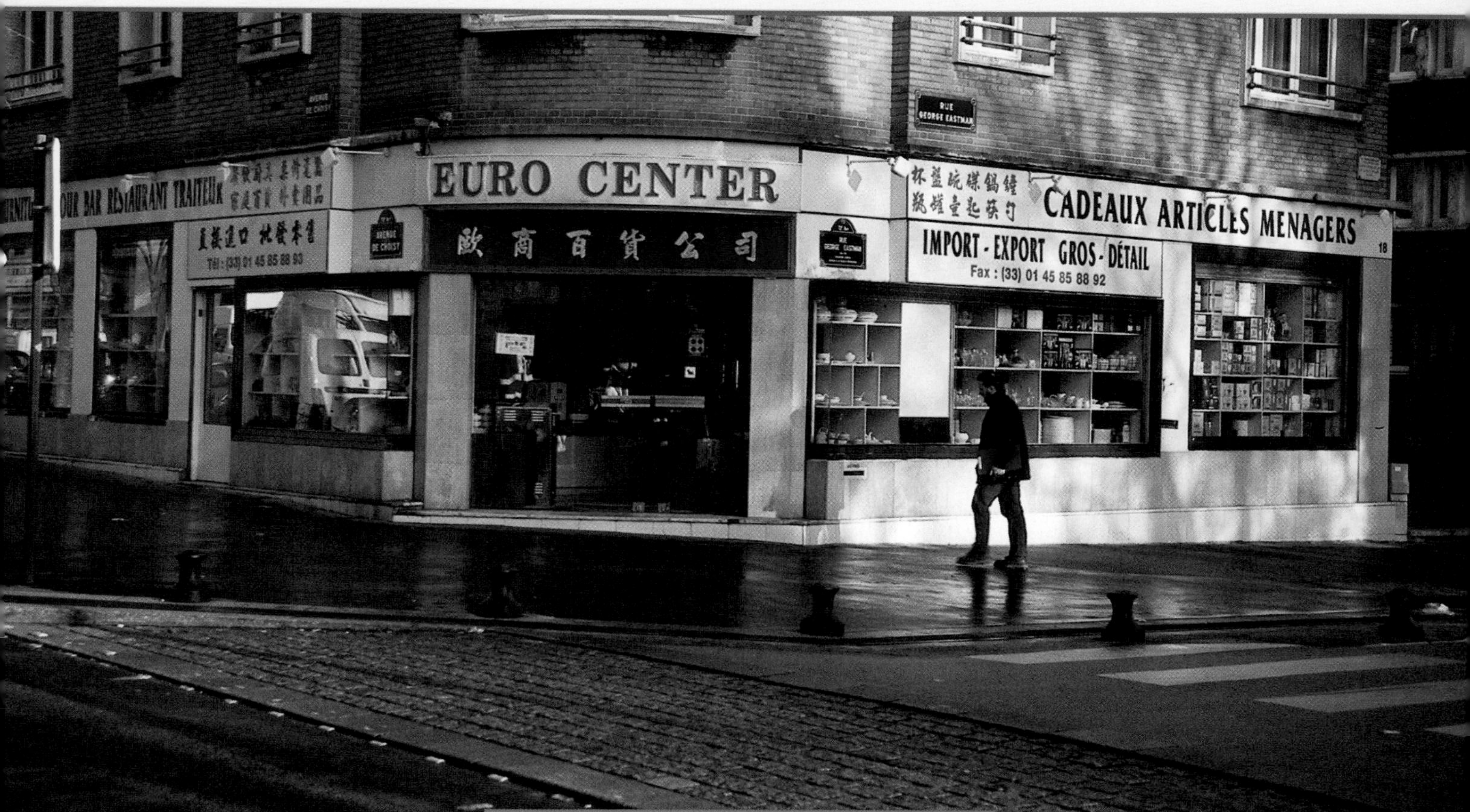

Economies, languages, and cultures come together on a street corner in Paris, France.

Part Outline

Chapter 27

Deindustrialization and the Rise of the Service Sector

From the field notes

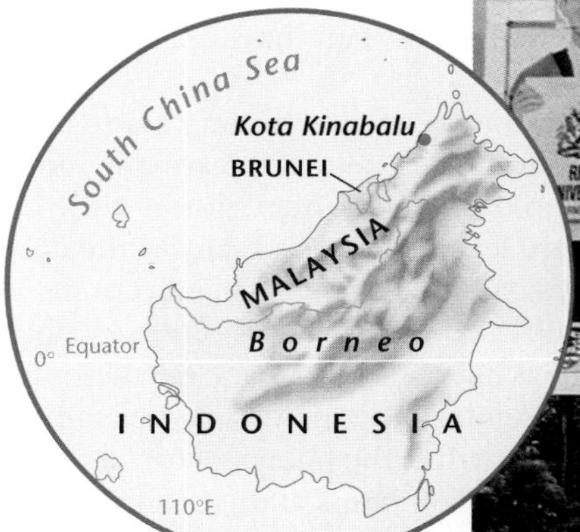

"Leaving the Eastern Malaysian city of Kota Kinabalu on my way to the town of Beaufort, I see some familiar names in a most unlikely place! Education is one of the major service industries, and like others (banking, finance, tourism) it is globalizing. University and college linkages around the world are multiplying, and it is a hopeful sign: out of such interaction comes intercultural understanding. It also will have an effect on the dissemination of English; this billboard stands in a country where Malays and Chinese make up most of the population, and where Malay is the official language."

KEY POINTS

◆ **The declining cost of transportation and communication, along with changes in the production process, led to an enormous expansion of the service sector in the twentieth century, particularly in the industrialized core.**

◆ **Deindustrialization in the core has not altered basic global patterns of economic well-being, but it has led to the growth of labor-intensive manufacturing in the periphery.**

◆ **The resulting new international division of labor has linked the world's economies more closely together, but it carries with it patterns of interaction that favor some areas over others.**

◆ **A global economic geography dominated by political states is giving way to one in which world cities and multinational corporations play an increasingly significant role.**

◆ **Developments such as the World Wide Web are accelerating the pace of life and changing the relationship among places.**

As we saw in Part Eight, ever since the Industrial Revolution the growing demand for resources, the expansion of manufacturing and trade, and technological innovation have worked together to produce an increasingly interconnected global economy. Almost all places are in some way part of the web of production, exchange, and consumption that make up that economy, which explains why this process is often referred to as ***globalization***. Moreover, the position of places in the globalization web has significant social consequences. Those in the developed core tend to be in the driver's seat, whereas those in the periphery have far less control. Someone living and working in the banana-producing part of Ecuador has little to say about the global price of bananas, and the banana-growing firms that dominate the economy may not even be locally owned. Yet what happens to banana prices on the global market, and the decisions that are made about that banana-growing firm, can have profound local consequences.

Tracing the historical geography of industrialization can tell us much about why some areas are in a more advantageous position than others, but that is not the entire story. Over the past several decades, many of the core industrial economies have experienced significant deindustrialization, accompanied by growth in service-related activities. This shift has its roots in dramatic decreases in the cost of transporting goods, the increasing mechanization of production, the growth of the public sector, and the rise of new information and communication technologies. The changes of the past 30 to 40 years have not fundamentally altered global patterns of economic well-being, but they have produced significant geographic changes in the global economic order. They have caused shifts in the locus of production, altered patterns of regional specialization, and fostered new centers of economic growth. ◆

◆ CATEGORIES OF SERVICE INDUSTRIES

The origins of the manufacturing boom of the twentieth century can be traced to early innovations in the production process. Perhaps the most significant of these innovations was the mass-production assembly line pioneered by Henry Ford, which allowed for the production of consumer goods at a single site on a previously unknown scale. So significant was Ford's idea that the dominant mode of large-scale manufacture that endured for much of the past century is known as ***Fordist***.

By the end of World War II, the increasing saturation of consumer markets, the tremendous growth in governmental activity, rising labor activism, and declines in the cost of transportation and communication began to challenge the Fordist order. The challenge shifted into high gear in the early 1970s, when a sharp rise in oil prices during a period of international financial instability and inflation produced a dramatic downturn in the global economy. Under these circumstances, it became increasingly difficult for the core industrial regions to sustain their competitive advantage without significant readjustment. The direction that readjustment would take was toward mechanization and the development of service and information industries. These changes worked together with the need for new markets and the growth of multinational concerns to bring about a "postindustrial" or "post-Fordist" economic order in many of the core economies.

Service industries (tertiary industries) do not generate an actual, tangible product; instead, they include the range of services that are found in modern societies. So many different types of activities can be thought of as service activities that, as we saw in Chapter 18, specialized aspects of the service economy were given their own designations: *quaternary industries* for the collection, processing, and manipulation of information and capital (finance, administration, insurance, legal services, computer services, etc.) and *quinary industries* for activities that facilitate complex decision making and the advancement of human capacities (scientific research, higher education, high-level management, etc.).

Distinguishing among types of services is useful, given the extraordinary growth in the size and complexity of the service sector. In the global economic core, service industries employ more workers than the primary and secondary industries combined, yet these service industries range from small-scale retailing to tourism services to research on the causes of cancer. Placing all of these in a single category seems unwarranted.

Specificity in terminology is also useful in highlighting different phases in the development of the service sector. In the early decades of the twentieth century, the domestic and quasi-domestic tertiary industries were experiencing rapid growth in the industrialized world. With the approach of World War II, the quaternary sector began expanding rapidly, and this expansion continued after the war. During the last three decades, both the quaternary and quinary sectors have experienced very rapid growth, giving greater meaning to the term *postindustrial*.

The expanding service sector in the core economies is only one aspect of the changing global economy. Accompanying, and in some cases driving, this expansion are several other developments that have already been mentioned: the increasing mechanization of production, particularly in manufacturing enterprises operating in the core; the growth of large multinational corporations; and the dispersal of the production process, with components for complex products such as automobiles and consumer electronics coming from factories in many different countries.

◆ GEOGRAPHICAL DIMENSIONS OF ECONOMIC ACTIVITY

The trends just outlined unfolded on a stage that was already characterized by wide socioeconomic disparities—disparities that shaped the changing economic geography of the planet. Only areas that had industry could deindustrialize, of course, and at the global scale the wealthier industrial regions were the most successful in establishing a postindustrial service economy. Thus we should not be surprised that deindustrialization did little to change the basic disparities between core and periphery that have long characterized the global economy. Indeed, even in the manufacturing realm, mechanization

From the field notes

"One of the more depressing sights of the former Soviet Bloc are the endless rows of cinderblock structures built to house the growing population. What must it be like to come home to one of these? Yes, they were minimally functional, but as I look at them I can't help but think of rabbit warrens. Such structures now house a population facing high unemployment as Poland privatizes or closes outdated industries in an effort both to decentralize its economy and shift its economic base from manufacturing to services and high technology."

and innovative production strategies allowed the core industrial regions to retain their dominance. In the first decade of the twenty-first century, eastern Asia, western Russia and Ukraine, Western Europe, and North America still account for well over 75 percent of the world's total output of manufactured goods.

Despite its continued dominance in the manufacturing arena, the developed core has experienced some wrenching changes associated with the economic shifts of the past three decades. Anyone who has ever spent time in northern Indiana, the British Midlands, or Silesia (southern Poland and northeastern Czech Republic) knows that there are pockets of significant hardship within the core. As we saw in Chapter 24, Britain's coal-fired industries produced a pattern of functional specialization that, for a time, had no equal in the world. Today that pattern has been diluted by diversification, relocation, and failure. Some aging plants are still operating, but it is difficult for them to maintain a competitive position because they are inefficient, expensive to run, slow, and wasteful.

With the relative decline of the manufacturing cities of the Midlands and northern England, industrial enterprises tend to relocate near London. This is the greatest

Figure 27-1 Increases in Value of Manufacturing Exports to OECD Countries. This map shows the percentage of increases in value of manufacturing exports to OECD countries from major low and middle-income trading partners, 1970–1992. *Source:* The World Bank. *World Development Report 1994. Infrastructure for Development*, Oxford: Oxford University Press, 1994.

domestic market of the British Isles, and it is therefore a great draw for local manufacturers. The changes in Britain's economic geography reflect the decreasing importance of coal in the energy-supply picture, the desire to start afresh with up-to-date machinery, and the fact that London, in addition to forming a huge domestic market, is also a good port through which to import raw materials.

The changes that have reshaped the industrial economy in Britain can be found in many other traditional industrial regions. Older factories simply could not compete against newer, mechanized competitors, leading to the shutdown of the older plants. Frequently, the newer factories were not even located in the same place, and even when they were they often required a labor force with different skills from those of the workers in the old factories. Moreover, it has been difficult for the local governments of such districts to respond to these circumstances. The closing of factories has drastically reduced the tax base of many areas, making it all but impossible to invest in economic restructuring.

To understand the economic shifts that have occurred over the past few decades, we must look beyond individual places to the global scale. However, as we have already seen, the hardships of an older industrial region are just one part of a much larger story. Part of that story involves changing business and investment practices and social arrangements, and much has been written about them by economists and sociologists. But geography is also central to the story, for some of its most fundamental elements can be seen in the changing

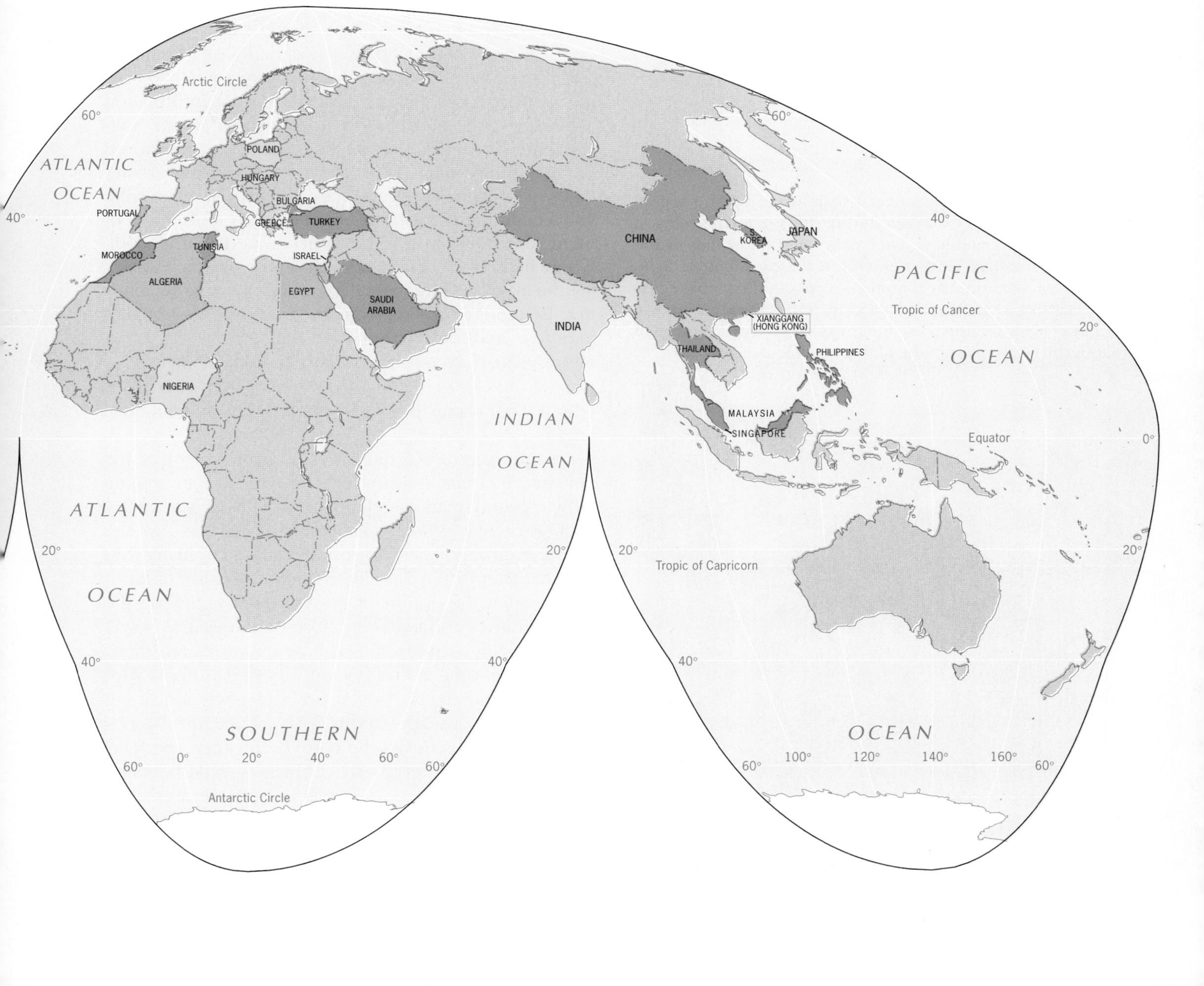

spatial structure of economic activity. Three matters are of particular importance: the rise of new economic relationships binding together different parts of the world; a shift in the locational features of certain industries and activities; and the emergence of specialized zones of economic activity. Let us look at each of these.

The New International Division of Labor

The phrase ***new international division of labor*** refers to the set of relationships that define the contemporary world economy. Whereas earlier in the century economic relations were defined by an industrialized core and a resource-exporting periphery, today the geography of the global economy is more complex. As we have seen, the traditional industrial core regions remain dominant, but important shifts have occurred in their relative importance, and new regions have emerged as major players. The countries and regions outside the core that have increased their manufacturing output most rapidly in recent decades are shown in Figure 27–1. Among the core areas, the United States and the United Kingdom are no longer as significant as they once were, whereas Japan's manufacturing base has grown dramatically. Even more striking is the emergence of new large-scale contributors to the global manufacturing base—especially the "Four Tigers" (discussed in Chapter 26), Brazil and Mexico in the Americas, as well as countries at the southwestern and southeastern edges of Europe.

Lying behind the patterns shown in Figure 27–1 is a set of developments and connections that give meaning to the phrase "new international division of labor." On the one hand, there is the shift away from heavy industry and toward the service sector that has occurred in parts of the traditional industrial core. On the other hand, there is the rise of labor-intensive manufacturing in new locations. Finally, there are the multinational corporations that have helped engineer the new international division of labor.

Some of the larger multinationals, such as General Motors, Philips, Union Carbide, and Exxon, are major global economic players, with annual earnings that exceed the gross national products of many smaller states. Taking advantage of low transportation costs, favorable governmental regulations, and expanding information technology, they have constructed vast economic networks in which different facets of production are carried out in different places in order to benefit from the advantages of specific locations (see "A Sense of Scale: Nike and Economic Globalization"). Research and development activities tend to be concentrated in the core, where high levels of education and access to technology are the norm. Technologically sophisticated manufacturing also tends to be situated in the core because both the expertise and the infrastructure are there. More labor-intensive manufacturing, particularly assembly activities, is more likely to be located in peripheral countries where labor is cheap, regulations are few, and tax rates are low.

Supporting the economic web at the heart of the new international division of labor are elaborate trading networks and financial relations. Trade itself is a tertiary economic activity of considerable importance to the global economy. Patterns of trade vary by industry, but the character of the new international division of labor ensures that the dominant flow of trade is among the core countries and between those countries and newly industrializing countries. The core countries are those with the highest levels of demand, as well as major suppliers of manufactured goods, and the newly industrializing countries are key exporters of manufactured goods used in the industries of the core. By contrast, the level of trade between peripheral countries—even between newly industrializing countries—is low because the dominant flow of exports is to the core, not to other peripheral countries. Indeed, some peripheral countries compete with each other in producing similar commodities destined for the core.

From the field notes

"What a change a decade can make! When I visited Alexander Platz in East Berlin during the 1980s, the signs of international economic activity were few. Returning in the late 1990s, the signs were everywhere. To many, high-tech industry now symbolizes economic success in the global economy, and in East Berlin the indicators of its arrival are unmistakable. The signs atop these buildings seem to proclaim to all that Berlin is now part of the global economic core."

A SENSE OF SCALE

Nike and Economic Globalization

Economic globalization and the new international division of labor are associated with very different local economic and social arrangements from those in prior eras. A U.S. shoe manufacturing concern 50 years ago might well have imported some materials, but its headquarters and production facilities would probably have been located in the same place, and it would have drawn a mix of skilled and un-skilled labor from the community. Some secondary industries still conform to this characterization, but a great many do not.

Consider, for example, the modern American athletic shoe manufacture, Nike. Nike was founded in Oregon in 1972 by a former competitive runner, and it has grown to be one of the giants of the shoe and apparel business. With headquarters in Beaverton, Oregon, a suburb of Portland, the company is far more than a Beaverton concern. Despite an Oregon work force of over 20,000 people, not a single individual in Oregon is directly involved in the process of putting a shoe together. Nike began by contracting with an Asian firm to manufacture its shoes. In 1974, Nike set up its first domestic shoe manufacturing facility in the small town of Exeter, New Hampshire. By the end of that year, Nike's work force was still modest in number, but the Oregon contingent focused on running the company and expanding sales, whereas the New Hampshire and the Asian contingents focused primarily on the production of athletic shoes.

As Nike grew to become the world's leading manufacturer of athletic shoes (with almost a 40 percent share of the world's athletic-shoe market), its employment numbers skyrocketed and many new manufacturing plants were established in Asia and beyond. This transformation did not translate into manufacturing jobs in Beaverton, Oregon, however. The employment opportunities now provided by Nike at its world headquarters are for the financial administrators, marketing and sales specialists, information technology directors, computer technicians, lawyers, and support personnel needed to run an international company with over $9 billion in annual revenues. Thus, the local social and economic geography of Beaverton bears little resemblance to what one might have expected in a town housing an important shoe company a few decades ago. Instead, it is a local geography influenced, and profoundly tied into, an elaborate network of international exchange. And each node of that network is functionally specialized, dependent on other nodes, and influenced by the niche it occupies in the network.

Nike Headquarters in the Portland, Oregon, where business and marketing decisions—but not shoes—are made.

The production of television receivers provides an example of how changing multinational networks function in a particular industry. Commercial production of television sets began after World War II. During the industry's early decades, a variety of small and medium-sized firms in Europe, Asia, and North America were involved in it, although the United States was the dominant producer. During the 1970s and 1980s a dramatic shift occurred, with a small number of large Asian producers—particularly in Japan—seizing a much larger percentage of the market and with a few European firms increasing their position as well. By 1990 ten large firms were responsible for 80 percent of the world's color television sets; eight of them were Japanese and two European. Only one U.S. firm—Zenith—remained, and its share of the global market was relatively small. Behind this rather simple picture lies a more complicated story.

The television production industry has three key elements: research and design, manufacture of components, and assembly. Research and design has always been located in the countries where the major television manufacturers were based. During the 1970s, the major firms began to move the manufacture of components and assembly "offshore." U.S. firms moved these functions to locations in Mexico (particularly the *maquiladora*, the special manufacturing districts described in Chapter 26); Japanese firms moved them to Taiwan, Singapore, Malaysia, and South Korea. The assembly stage was the most labor intensive, so it went not just to Mexico and newly industrializing Southeast Asian countries but to places such as China, India, and Brazil as well. The Southeast Asian countries began to develop their own competing consumer electronics industries but continued to supply components to major Japanese and European manufacturers. And then a move toward greater mechanization in the production and assembly process in the 1980s led the then-dominant Japanese producers, as well as some of their Pacific Asian counterparts, to locate a growing number of their offshore production sites in Europe and the United States—places where there was a combination of suitable infrastructure, skilled labor, and accessible markets. These developments brought with them a set of trade links that both reflect and define the relationships that characterize the new international division of labor.

Patterns of financial relations mirror those of trade but with some interesting twists. One key component of international finance is ***foreign direct investment***. A few of the largest economies in the core are responsible for an overwhelming percentage of that investment—notably the United States, Japan, Italy, Germany, France, and the United Kingdom. Most foreign direct investment goes to other core countries and the newly in-

Figure 27-2 External Debt Obligations. *Source:* The World Bank. *Global Development Finance 2001*. Washington, D.C.: The World Bank, 2001, pp. 2-4.

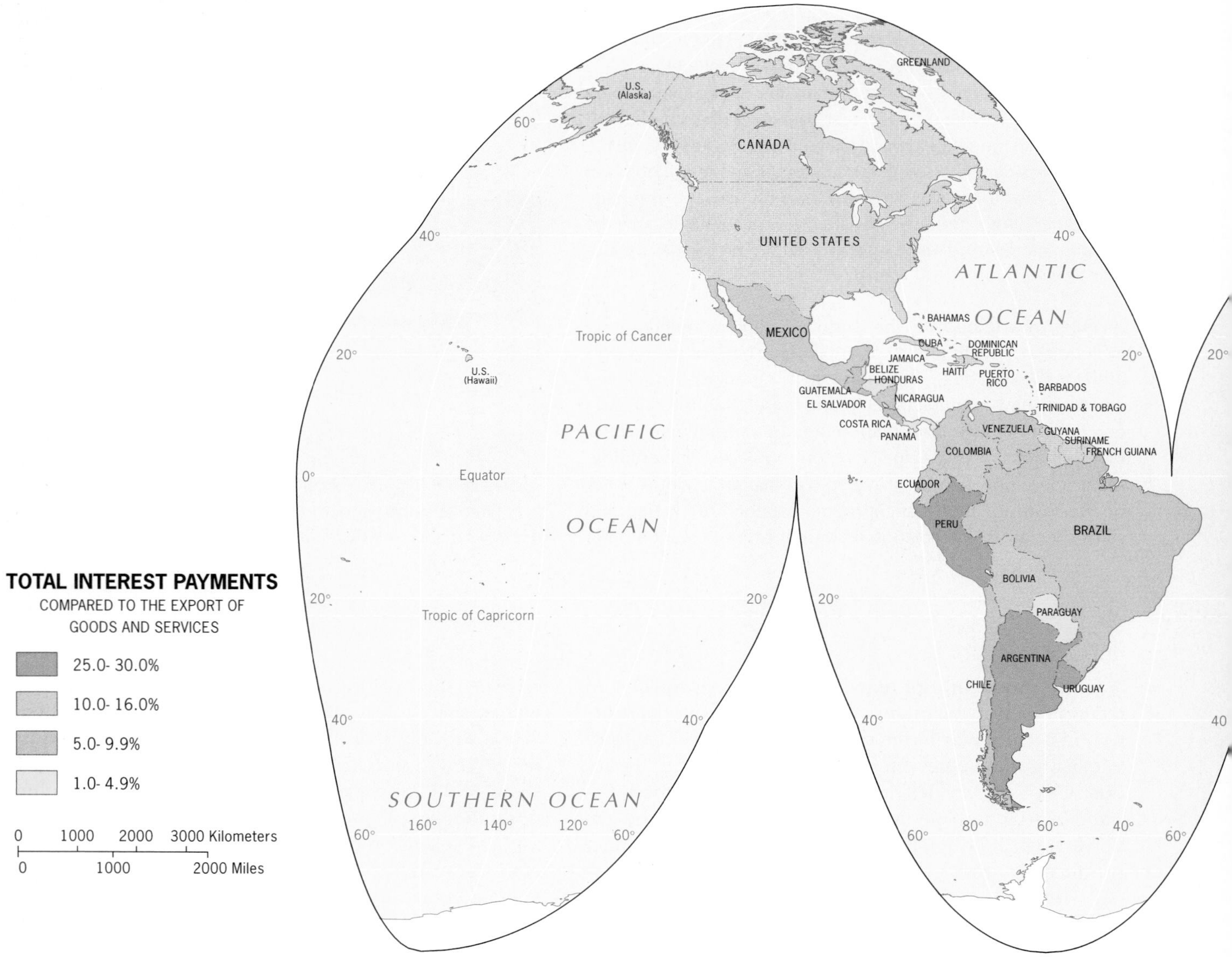

dustrializing periphery. The major exception to this pattern is the growth of foreign direct investment by multinational corporations based in newly industrializing countries such as Taiwan, Korea, and Singapore. Companies such as Tatung, Hyundai, and Samsung became increasingly significant actors in the global economic arena.

The other part of the finance picture is the pattern of loans and payments handled by banks. Recent decades have seen an extraordinary expansion of international banking, with the banks of Japan, the United States, and key European countries leading the way. The need for capital in the periphery led to significant borrowing, especially by governments seeking to promote development. The returns on development projects have often been much lower than anticipated, however, and this has led to a debt problem of global proportions. For many countries the cost of servicing their debts (that is, the cost of repayments plus interest) has exceeded revenues (Fig. 27–2). Many of these countries have been able to continue making interest payments, but the burden of these payments can become crushing. At the very least, such payments can make it difficult for countries to invest in their own development. The political crisis in Argentina at the end of 2001 demonstrates an even greater problem: the economic adjustments needed to make debt payments can lead to social meltdown. The only alternative in those circumstances is to default on the loan, but if a substantial number of countries were to follow that route, a global economic crisis could ensue that would work to the disadvantage of almost everyone. Moreover, defaulting countries find themselves in a severely disadvantaged position when it comes to attracting any future investment that can be critical for economic growth.

New Influences on Location

Despite changes in the global economic environment in the late twentieth century, location decisions continue to be driven by the factors of production discussed in Chapter 25. Yet with the striking growth of the service sector and information technologies, new factors have come into play that are affecting patterns of economic activity. Most obviously, many service industries are not tied to raw materials and do not need large amounts of energy. Hence, those factors of production are markedly less important for service industries than for manufacturing concerns. Market accessibility is more relevant for the service sector, but advances in telecommunications have rendered even that factor less important for some types of service industries.

To understand these new influences on the location of services, it is useful to go back to our distinction between tertiary, quaternary, and quinary industries. Tertiary services related to transportation and communication are closely tied to population patterns and to the location of primary and secondary industries. As the basic facilitators of interaction, they are strongly linked to the basic geography of production and consumption. Other tertiary services—restaurants, hotels, and retail establishments—are influenced mainly by market con-

Figure 27-3 Major World Cities. In 1995 John Friedman delineated the major world cities according to global financial, multinational, national, subnational/regional articulations. *Source:* J. Friedman, "Where We Stand in a Decade of World City Research," in P. C. Knox and P. J. Taylor, eds., *World Cities in a World System*. Cambridge: Cambridge University Press, pp. 21–47.

siderations. If they are located far from their consumers, they are unlikely to succeed.

The locational influences on quaternary services—high-level services aimed at the collection, processing, and manipulation of information and capital—are more diverse. Some of these services are strongly tied geographically to the locus of economic activity. Retail banking and various types of administrative services require a high level of interpersonal contact and therefore tend to be located near the businesses they are serving. Other types of quaternary services, however, can operate almost anywhere as long as they have access to digital processing equipment and telecommunications. When you send in your credit card bill, it is unlikely to go to the city where the headquarters of the issuing bank is located. Instead, it is likely to go to North Dakota, or Nebraska, or Colorado. Similarly, many "back-office" tasks related to insurance are performed in places such as Des Moines, Iowa, not Chicago or Hartford. These locational curiosities occur because technological advances in the telecommunications sector have made it possible for all sorts of quaternary industries to be located far away from either producers or consumers. What matters most is infrastructure, a workforce that is sufficiently skilled but not too expensive, and favorable tax rates.

Those working in the quinary sector tend to be concentrated around nodes of quinary activity—governmental seats, universities, and corporate headquarters. The latter tend to be in large metropolitan areas, but seats of government and universities can be found in places that were chosen long ago as appropriate sites for administrative or educational activities based on cultural values or political compromises. The American ideal of the university town

(which originated in Germany) led to the establishment of many universities at a distance from major commercial and population centers, in such towns as Champaign-Urbana, Illinois; Norman, Oklahoma; and Eugene, Oregon. Political compromises led to the establishment of major seats of government in small towns. Ottawa, Canada, and Canberra, Australia, are examples of this phenomenon. The point is that historical location decisions influence the geography of the quinary sector. And it is not just university professors and government officials who are affected. All sorts of high-level research and development activities are located on the fringes of universities, and a host of specialized consultants are concentrated around governmental centers. These then become major nodes of quinary activity.

Specialized Patterns of Economic Concentration and Interaction

Many more geographical changes have followed in the wake of the developments outlined here. We have already reviewed some of the most important of these—the growing connections between the developed core and the newly industrializing countries, the decline of older industrial areas, the emergence of assembly-style manufacturing in the periphery. Two other changes deserve attention, however, for they are altering the economic landscape of the contemporary world. One is the development of a set of links between ***world cities***—links that are in some respects more intense than the links between those cities and their hinterlands. The other is the rise of specialized economic zones devoted to particular types of activities.

World Cities The array of economic links that have developed between different parts of the globe can no longer be adequately described or understood solely in national terms. Corporate structures and flows of capital transcend national boundaries, and decisions about what happens in one corner of the world may well be made in a city thousands of miles away. In this new economic environment it is often as meaningful to look at the connections between cities in different countries as it is to focus on patterns of economic activity within a given country. This is particularly true with respect to the major urban centers of multinational business and finance—the world cities. John Friedmann, who popularized this term in the mid-1980s, calls world cities the control centers of the world economy. These cities are not necessarily the largest in terms of population, nor are they the greatest centers of manufacturing. Instead, they are the places where the world's most important financial and corporate institutions are located and where decisions are made that drive the world economy.

It is hard to come up with a definitive list of world cities, but Figure 27–3 shows the basic pattern. As the map reveals, most of the major world cities are located in the developed core. New York, London, and Tokyo are not only the dominant international actors but the focal points of the three major regional subsystems: Pacific Asia, Western Europe, and North America. The Southern Hemisphere is linked to the system primarily through Sydney and São Paulo.

Figure 27–3 is interesting not only for what it shows about the relationship among cities but also for what it implies about the world's changing human geography. Someone living and working in London may well be in closer contact and even feel greater affinity with people in New York and Tokyo than with people in Yorkshire. We must be careful not to overstate the case; these relationships and sensitivities are likely to be confined to people working in the quaternary and quinary sectors. Nevertheless, these are usually the people who exercise the most power, and their changing worldviews therefore are of considerable importance. In a different vein, people living far from the network of world cities can find it difficult to influence decisions made in that network. Note that these same points play out as one moves down the urban hierarchy. A map of connections in South America would show significant links between Buenos Aires and Santiago that are enormously influential in defining the regional economy of, say, northwestern Argentina.

From the field notes

"Looking back toward Sydney from near the shore (the ocean is behind us) confirms the dominance of this city in Australian and Southern Hemisphere affairs. This is a world-city skyline, and what you see here are the highrises of banks, financial institutions, hotels, and corporations—the embodiment of the service-sector economy."

Specialized Economic Zones Beyond the phenomenon of world cities, global economic change has produced specialized economic zones that did not exist before the late twentieth century. Specific economic activities have long been concentrated in particular places; for decades Detroit was synonymous with automobile production in the United States, and the Ruhr Valley with iron and steel production in Germany. With the increasingly global economy, we now see two new economic concentrations: special ***manufacturing export zones*** in poorer countries and ***high-technology corridors*** in wealthier countries.

In their efforts to attract manufacturing, the governments of many countries in the global economic periphery have set up special manufacturing export zones where favorable tax, regulatory, and trade arrangements are offered to foreign firms. By the early 2000s, more than 60 countries had established such zones, and many of these had become major manufacturing centers. Two of the best known of these zones were discussed in the last chapter: the Mexican maquiladora and the special economic zones of China. These are just two examples of a more widespread phenomenon. Such zones are often created in places with easy access to export markets—in Mexico, directly across the border from the United States; in China, near major ports. They typically play host to a mix of manufacturing operations that are suited to the skill levels of the labor force and the available infrastructure.

A related, but very different, type of development can be seen in the high-technology corridors that have sprung up in the global economic core. The catalyst for these corridors is technology: computers, semiconductors,

Looking Ahead

The Future of Tourism

Tourism has become such an economic giant because of trends that may well continue into the foreseeable future. These include rising salaries, longer paid vacations, earlier retirement, and increases in average life expectancy. In the wake of such developments, people are traveling more and more, and around the world billions of dollars are being spent on improving the infrastructure that supports tourism. In the past few years, worldwide hotel and resort capacity has increased by as much as 8 percent annually. In order to facilitate the continued growth of tourism, new airports, highways, and port facilities are continually being built or renovated. Denver, Hong Kong, Kuala Lumpur (Malaysia), and London all opened new airports in the 1990's, and plans for new airports are being contemplated in Chicago and Tokyo. Moreover, political barriers that once prevented the free movement of tourists are increasingly being loosened or removed. Even closed regimes such as Myanmar and Cuba now invite tourists to come and contribute to the local economy.

If current trends continue, the social and economic impacts of tourism could well be extraordinary in a few decades. With populations exceeding one billion people in China and India, imagine what would happen if a substantial middle class emerges with the tourism tastes and habits of the middle class in Japan, Australia, Western Europe, and North America. One implication, of course, would be the further expansion of an industry that already is one of the dominant economic activities of the world. More hotels, highways, and airports would follow those that have been constructed in recent years. Another implication would be an almost unimaginable level of congestion at major tourist destinations.

Signs of such congestion are already present. To visit one of the great art galleries of Florence, Italy—the Uffizi gallery—one can no longer just wander in. Except in the very quietest times of the year, your choice is to stand in line for as much as two to three hours, or make reservations well in advance. In the more popular National Parks of the United States, one can no longer arrive during the summer and expect to find a campsite without an advance reservation. To catch a glimpse of the famed Mona Lisa of Leonardo da Vinci now requires jostling for position with thousands of others on a typical day at the Louvre in Paris. Looking ahead, it seems likely that tourism management is going to become an increasingly challenging issue for many, if not most, major tourist destinations.

What is also clear is that the problems will not be limited to crowd control. The social- and physical-environmental implications of tourism are likely to be of increasing concern. Many people travel in search of some special place: a dramatic physical landscape, an encounter with a different culture, or a get-away rural retreat. Yet what happens when the press of tourism brings environmental despoliation and so alters the cultural environment that the very features that lured the tourist in the first place are no longer present? Herein may be found the circumstance that will cap the rise in tourism. If places become so changed that they no longer offer something special, the desire to see them will decline.

The challenge, of course, is not to reach this point. There are no easy answers; restricting access to places is often the only alternative, yet this is often complicated, unpopular, and (at least in the short term) economically disadvantageous. Yet in a world of over six billion people, it doesn't take more than a small fraction of tourists to overwhelm a particular tourist destination. As more and more people travel, tourism's social and environmental implications will have to be viewed alongside its economic potential.

telecommunications, sophisticated medical equipment, and the like. California's "Silicon Valley" is a well-known example of a high-technology corridor. Several decades ago a number of innovative technology companies located their research and development activities in the area around the University of California, Berkeley, and Stanford University. They were attracted by the prospect of developing links with existing research communities and the availability of a highly educated workforce. Once some of these businesses located there, others were attracted as well. The resulting collection of high-technology industries produced what Manuel Castells and Peter Hall call a ***technopole***. A similar sort of technopole developed outside Boston, where the concentration of technology-based businesses close to Harvard and the Massachusetts Institute of Technology gave rise to what is called the Route 128 high-technology corridor.

Technopoles can be found in a number of countries in Western Europe, Eastern Asia, North America, and Australia. Few are of the scale of Silicon Valley, but they are noticeable elements of the economic landscape. Many of these have sprung up on the edges of good-sized cities, particularly near airports. In Brussels, for example, the route into the city from the airport passes an array of buildings occupied by computer, communication, and electronics firms. Many of these firms are multinationals, and like their counterparts in

Figure 27-4 Access to the Internet. This map depicts Internet connected computers per 1000 population as of January 1997. *Source:* "Access to the Internet," Scientific American 277(1): July 1997, p. 26.

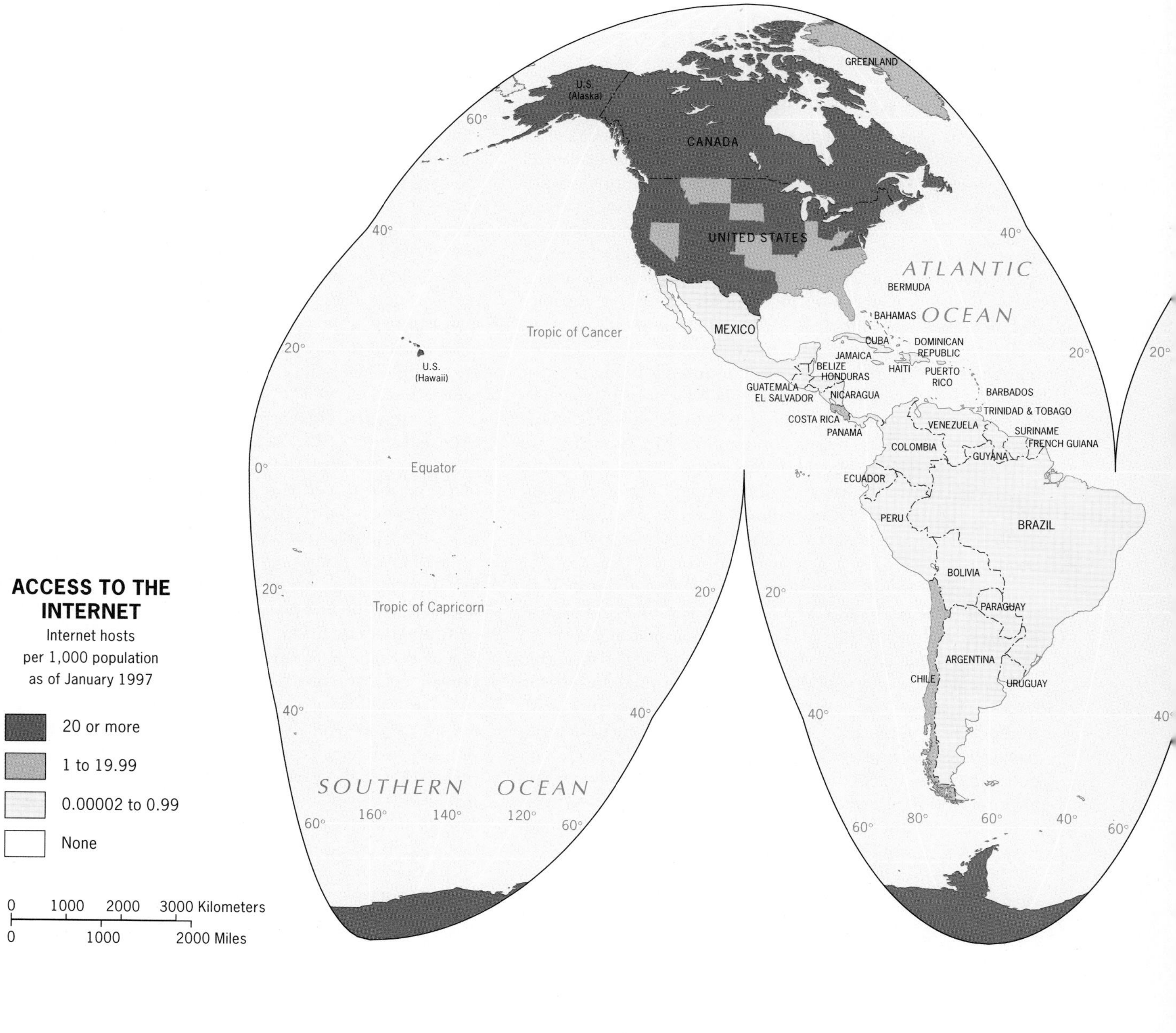

other countries, they function in an information environment and market their products all over the world. Being near raw materials or even a particular market is unimportant for these firms; what matters to them is proximity to major networks of transportation and communication.

High-technology industries have become such a symbol of the postindustrial world that local, regional, and national governments often pursue aggressive policies to attract firms in this sector. These industries are thought to be pollution free and to offer positive benefits for the communities in which they are located. Hence, bidding wars sometimes develop between communities seeking to attract such industries. High-technology industries do bring a variety of economic benefits, but they have some drawbacks as well. Communities that have attracted production facilities find that the manufacture of computer chips, semiconductors, and the like requires toxic chemicals and large quantities of water. And even more research-oriented establishments sometimes have negative environmental impacts in that land must be cleared and buildings constructed to house them. Despite these drawbacks, the high-technology sector is clearly here to stay, and areas that can tap into it are likely to find themselves in an advantageous economic position in coming years.

A Service Industry Giant: Tourism

The tourism industry deserves special attention because of its importance and its distinctive geographical character. Ask most people what the largest industry is in the world today, and you are likely to get a response such as computers or automobiles. Yet by almost any measure

you use—number of jobs, total value—the leading industry is tourism and travel. Tourism accounts for some 11 percent of all the jobs around the world, creating work for hundreds of million people.

Tourism grew dramatically during the second half of the twentieth century. The tourism boom began in the global economic core as incomes and leisure time increased for a rapidly expanding segment of the population. Over the past 20 years, the number of East and Southeast Asian tourists has risen much faster than the global average, reflecting the economic boom in many of the Pacific Rim countries. The combination of a weakening global economy and concerns over political stability caused a noticeable dip in travel in 2001–2002—particularly among those living in North America—but absent a major economic or geopolitical crisis, this is likely to be only a blip in the larger expanding tourism picture. Indeed, if current trends continue, tourism will be a true giant of the twenty-first century, bringing with it opportunities as well as problems. (See "Looking Ahead Box: The Future of Tourism.").

One of the fastest-growing segments of the tourist industry is cruising. Until the 1960s, oceangoing liners provided transportation rather than recreation, but the advent of the jet plane ended that era. Today, ships several times as large as their predecessors, up to 135,000 tons, carry as many as 3000 passengers on vacation cruises that begin and end at the same port. Only one liner still maintains an abbreviated Transatlantic schedule. One cruise ship carrying 2000 passengers on week-long cruises can accommodate 100,000 passengers per year and generate $100 million in gross revenues while keeping 1200 officers and crew employed.

The tourist industry has transformed downtowns, ports, hinterlands, parks, and waterfronts. High-rise, ultramodern hotels dominate urban skylines from Boston to Brisbane. The Port of Miami and Fort Lauderdale's Port Everglades have been reconstructed to serve the cruise industry, and many ports from Tokyo to Tampa have added cruise terminals complete with shopping malls and restaurants. Theme parks such as Disney's establishments near Orlando, Paris, Tokyo, and Los Angeles draw millions of visitors and directly and indirectly employ thousands of workers. Once-remote wildlife parks and nature reserves in East Africa and South Asia now receive thousands of visitors, requiring expanded facilities and sometimes causing ecological damage. Formerly isolated beaches are now lined by high-rise hotels and resorts; in the Caribbean and the Pacific, some entire islands have been taken over by tour operators.

The geographic impact of the tourist industry is far-reaching, and its economic influence on national economies grows every year. In 2000, the economic value of goods and services associated with tourism exceeded $4 trillion, or about 11 percent of the combined GNP of all the countries of the world. It is a dramatic example of the rise of the service sector in the world economy.

◆ TIME-SPACE COMPRESSION AND ITS IMPACT

A key theme reflecting the economic and social changes of the last few decades is that of ***time-space compression***. This phrase, coined by geographer David Harvey, refers to a set of developments that have dramatically changed the way we think about time and space in the global economic arena. It is an offshoot of the concept of ***time-space convergence***, which refers to a reduction in the importance of distance when, for example, a transportation innovation makes it possible for people or goods to move from one place to another more easily or more cheaply. A variety of developments during the twentieth century have promoted time-space convergence, especially technological developments that make possible faster, less expensive transportation and communication across significant distances. But Harvey argues that time-space convergence is too limited a term to encompass what has happened in recent decades. He believes that modern capitalism has so accelerated the pace of life and so changed the nature of the relationship between places that "the world seems to collapse inwards upon us."

Although there is some debate about the causes and extent of the compression Harvey has described, few would deny the basic concept. The transition away from a Fordist industrial system to a more flexible set of production practices has speeded up production, opened new markets, and brought places closer together in time and space than would have been imaginable at the beginning of the twentieth century. Fluctuations in the Tokyo stock market can have impacts in New York just hours, if not minutes, later. Overnight, marketing campaigns can turn a product innovation into a fad in far-flung corners of the globe. Apples picked in New Zealand yesterday can be in the lunch boxes of boys and girls in Canada tomorrow. And decisions made in London can make or break a fast-developing deal over a transport link between Kenya and Tanzania.

The rise of the World Wide Web plays into the time-space compression. It is too early to know what the full impact of the Web might be, but its role in reducing the importance of distance is self-evident. It also clearly plays a role in the decentralization of economic activity. Anyone with a computer and a network connection can establish a home page and a marketing enterprise with little up-front investment. There are no accurate estimates of the economic significance of the World Wide Web, but it is of growing importance. If those trends continue, it may be harder for traditional businesses to exert as much control over certain economic sectors as they have in the past.

These trends,though very important, must be interpreted with caution. First, the precise impact the World Wide Web will have is not known. Moreover, the geographical distribution of people with access to network connections closely mirrors the map of "haves" and "have-nots" (see Fig. 27–4). At the global scale, this means that the developed core will continue to exert a disproportionate influence on Web-based economic innovations. At the regional scale, it means that traditional centers of economic and political power—especially large cities—could strengthen their position relative to areas that are less well-off. Thus there are clear limits to the Web's ability to significantly alter the existing set of relationships that define the global economy.

The sensation of a shrinking world is so strong that a few commentators have proposed that we are entering an era characterized by the "end of geography." Alvin Toffler first suggested this idea in his *Future Shock* (1970). More recently, Richard O'Brien dealt with similar concepts in *Global Financial Integration: The End of Geography* (1992). Both Toffler and O'Brien argue that a combination of technological changes and developments in the global economy have reduced the significance of location and place to the point where they no longer matter much. There is no question that the nature and meaning of location and place have changed greatly in recent times, but the developments discussed in this chapter show that those changes have not created an undifferentiated world. Rather, they have reshaped the economic geography of the planet so profoundly and rapidly that they cry out for understanding and analysis. That is one reason why geography is attracting renewed attention and why geographical understanding will be increasingly critical in the years ahead. It is therefore important not just to appreciate the forces that are remaking the world's economic geography but to be aware of its impact on how people practice the cultures that frame their lives. It is to these matters that we turn in the next two chapters.

◆ KEY TERMS ◆

globalization
Fordism
foreign direct investment
high-technology corridors
manufacturing export zones
new international division of labor
technopole
time-space compression
time-space convergence
world cities

◆ APPLYING GEOGRAPHIC KNOWLEDGE ◆

1. Evaluate the strengths and weaknesses of the argument that buying a car from an American car manufacturer will support the workers of the United States and the U.S. economy.
2. Which of the world cities shown in Figure 27–3 would not have been on a map of world cities created 25 years ago? What helps to explain why they are on the map now? What cities not currently on the map would you expect to be there 25 years from now? Why?
3. In what ways has time-space compression affected your daily life? Think of at least five examples that you would cite to explain the concept of time-space compression to someone who was not familiar with it.

Chapter 28

The Changing Nature of the Civic Experience

From the field notes

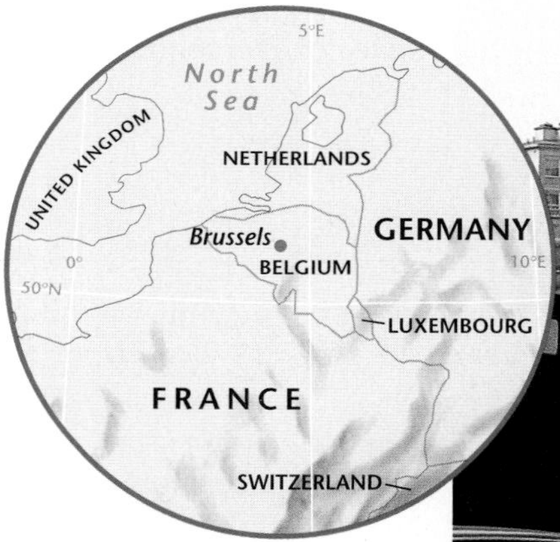

"Key elements of the changing urban scene come together on this Brussels (Belgium) street corner. Located in the so-called European district, where the landscape has been completely transformed by Brussels' ambition to be the new European capital, a few remnants of the older city can still be found. And even one of these—the Irish pub on the right—symbolizes the interpenetration of peoples and cultures in Europe. What must it be like to be one of the last residents to live in one of the old, four-story walk-ups? With most shops gone and with the district increasingly taking on the character of an office complex, it is hard to believe that these older establishments will hang on for long."

KEY POINTS

- ◆ **Older central cities as well as more recent shantytowns have ethnic neighborhoods, but the older districts are generally more stable and less troubled.**
- ◆ **In this era of globalization, events in a remote part of the world can have a major impact on cities thousands of miles away.**
- ◆ **In European cities where immigrants are assigned public housing on a sequential basis, ethnic segregation is less problematic than it is in areas where tenements are privately owned and illegal immigrants are numerous.**
- ◆ **In multicultural societies, urban-ethnic accommodation tends to reflect power relationships in the country as a whole.**
- ◆ **Urban inmigrants who populate the shantytowns ringing megacities survive in an informal economy.**
- ◆ **The emerging global economy is transforming former colonial cities, and the corporate era in some ways mirrors the colonial one.**
- ◆ **The North American city is marked by suburbanization and concomitant central-city deterioration as well as inner-city stagnation.**
- ◆ **In the mid-twentieth century about 25 percent of the world's population was urbanized; by 2050 it may be 75 percent. Although the process brings some benefits, it also carries with it serious environmental consequences.**

In Part Two we examined a process that is transforming the world: the annual migration of millions of people not only across international borders but also from rural areas to urban places and from smaller towns to larger ones. Even as Western cities are spreading outward and American, Canadian, and to a lesser degree European urbanites are moving from central cities to suburbs and to "edge" or "ring" cities, people arriving in the burgeoning megacities of other parts of the world crowd as close to the heart of the urban area as they can. In Part Seven, we chronicled the growing dimensions of those evolving megacities, whose populations must now be counted in the tens of millions. The inhabitants of individual cities such as Mumbai and Mexico City outnumber those of some Western megalopolises formed from the coalescence of several metropolitan areas. Only the Bosnywash Megalopolis of eastern North America can still claim first rank in this context, but let us be realistic. Bosnywash may include a tier of cities from Boston to Washington, but much of its regional continuity is suburban, with lots of open space. The "rural" areas around many non-Western megacities are more densely populated than the suburbs of Bosnywash. Life in the congested, jammed outskirts of Kolkata or Jakarta is nothing like life in the suburbs of Washington. ◆

◆ CITY AND CULTURE

In this chapter, therefore, we assess what life is like in the fast-changing cities of the world, for long-term residents as well as new arrivals, and in the non-Western as well as the Western world. In all urbanized societies, cities are crucibles of culture, arenas of transculturation and often difficult accommodation. The people who are drawn to cities (or who are forced off their land by push factors such as environmental adversity or simply not being able to make ends meet) represent countless histories and traditions, habits, and practices.

Ethnic Diversity in the United States and Europe

A common practice in the Western world is to acknowledge the geographic imprint of multiculturalism by calling certain urban districts "Chinatown," "Little Havana," or the "French Quarter." Behind such names lie tales of relocation that range from desperation (ask residents of Dade County's "Little Haiti") to a relatively easy adjustment to a social environment that bears some resemblances to home (as recent arrivals in Boston's "Little Italy" will tell you).

In older, relatively stable cities such neighborhoods are long-established and permanent, although their fortunes wax and wane as conditions change. In the age of globalization, the source of those changes may lie thousands of miles away, in another part of the world. Take the case of the Chinatown of Victoria, British Columbia. For many years this was a stable, slowly growing cluster of shops and homes a few blocks from the waterfront off the city's main artery (an ornate Chinese gate still welcomes visitors). In the 1980s and 1990s, however, political developments on the western Pacific Rim had an impact in Canada. The British had agreed to relinquish their colony of Hong Kong to China in 1997, and although the Chinese government promised to allow Hong Kong to go on as before, many Chinese residents of the colony were worried. Those who were financially well-off had the option of establishing an alternate residence in some other Commonwealth country, and thousands did—in Vancouver. As a result, Vancouver's already large Chinese community mushroomed and became a magnet, not just for Hong Kong Chinese but also for young Chinese residents of Victoria who were attracted by the opportunities Vancouver presented. Victoria's Chinatown quickly showed the effect in an aging and dwindling population.

Still, Victoria's Chinatown is not likely to disappear altogether. Already in the early 2000s, the boom in Vancouver has slowed as the fears that pushed many Hong Kong Chinese away from the former colony did not materialize. Over time, Victoria is likely to regain Chinese residents, and when it does, its Chinatown will be there to cushion their arrival.

Similar ups and downs mark the ethnic neighborhoods of other North American cities. Studies have shown that a change of status for Puerto Rico (where Statehood periodically is an election issue) would have a substantial impact on New York City's Puerto Rican community and neighborhood. The collapse of the former Soviet Union and the freedom of movement this entailed energized a number of Ukrainian, Armenian, Lithuanian, and other neighborhoods in America.

European cities, too, have durable ethnic neighborhoods ranging from the Algerian sectors of Paris and the Turkish districts of Frankfurt to the Moroccan community in Madrid and the Jamaican quarter of London. Like their American counterparts, European cities are growing but slowly, and what growth they do exhibit is tied to immigration. This immigration comes largely from countries in the global periphery, not from other countries in Europe, despite the greater freedom of movement enjoyed by citizens of the member states of the European Union. Such "Third-World" immigration into the cities has persuaded large numbers of European city-dwellers to depart the city cores for locales beyond the zones of immigrant neighborhoods that ring many central cities. This is changing the spatial-cultural geography of those cities: in the (often historic) center, Paris, Amsterdam, and other cities still present their "European" face. But in what Burgess would have (appropriately) called the Zone of Transition adjacent to the core, immigrants have settled in large numbers, and locals have moved out. In the process, these surrounding neighborhoods, with much of the real estate in public-housing projects, have taken on the cultural imprints of their non-European residents.

These imprints vary, and for several reasons. Some European countries, because of their colonial history, have attracted one dominant (though not exclusive) immigrant group. In France, for example, a significant majority of immigrants come from the "Maghreb" (Algeria and Morocco), although smaller minorities of other origins (West Africans, Southeast Asians, Caribbeans) have also moved permanently to this country. Maghrebis are by far the most numerous in the tough, hardscrabble immigrant neighborhoods around Paris, where unemployment is high, crime is widespread, resentment festers,

From the field notes

"The grand gate marking the entrance to Victoria's Chinatown promises rather more than the current neighborhood delivers. Events on the Pacific Rim have drawn many of the community's younger people to Vancouver, and the once-bustling city blocks, while still containing Chinese shops, restaurants, and other services operated by Chinese owners, have become diluted and have lost much of their cultural imprints."

and Islam provides solace. Walk along the tenement-lined, littered streets here, and the elegant avenues of historic Paris seem remote indeed—but they are not. A short subway ride takes you from one world to another.

Almost all immigrants gravitate to the cities, so that the challenge of adjustment and assimilation is essentially an urban one. Unlike immigration to France, immigration to the Netherlands has not created one dominant non-Dutch community. Indonesians, Turks, Surinamers, Moroccans, and others have come to Amsterdam and other Dutch cities, and as in the case of Paris, locals responded by leaving the Zone of Transition and moving outward. (Amsterdammers made Almere their "New Amsterdam.") But Amsterdam's immigrant neighborhoods are not defined by the sources of their immigrants, and instead present a multicultural picture. This is because legal immigrants are assigned homes on a sequential basis in the city's Zone of Transition, where some 80 percent of the housing stock is public housing. Thus a family from Suriname is as likely as not to find itself living next to an Indonesian family and a Moroccan family, not in a Surinamese neighborhood. Of course there are religious and other organizations that draw cultural groups together—the call to Friday prayer rings out all over the immigrant areas—but residential regulations have softened the cultural apartheid that marks many other European cities.

Note, however, that such a solution can apply only to legal immigration, and it is illegal immigrants who tend to cluster in areas where their cultural cohorts live. Illegal immigrants often move in with legal acquaintances, creating the very social conditions official policy is designed to counter. In recent decades, another kind of immigrant has become a factor in European immigration: the ***asylum seeker***. Asylum seekers are migrants who claim escape from armed conflict or political persecution as a way to attain legitimacy in the country they have entered. In many instances the claim is based on genuine circumstances, but in others it is fraudulent. Since documentation may not be available and claims cannot be easily checked, asylum seekers tend to be confined to special facilities to await their fate. This has become a contentious political issue in Europe, especially in the United Kingdom.

Cities in the Developing World

Many of the giant cities of Latin America, Africa, and Asia represent very different urban landscapes, but it would be a mistake to conclude that ethnic differentiation and clustering of the kind just described does not exist there. The vast, massive squatter settlements that encircle (and often spatially dominate) cities such as Cape Town, Nairobi, Lagos, Lima, Mumbai, Karachi, and Jakarta are anything but homogeneous despite their appearance. As the urban models discussed in Chapter 23 suggest, the older, colonial-era, inner zones of these cities still contain elements of historic ethnic neighborhoods such as Kolkata's Muslim district, Durban's Indian (South Asian) quarter, and Jakarta's Chinatown. Crowded and dilapidated, these neighborhoods are nevertheless functionally similar to the ethnic districts of European cities. But

From the field notes

"Mombasa, 1966. This is one of the world's most multicultural cities, with several African peoples, South Asians, Arabs, and Europeans represented in the urban area. The atmosphere in the Arab Old Town differs greatly from that of the Asian and European districts, but even the various African quarters exhibit architectural and organizational contrasts. If such a place reveals anything 'typical', it shows in the prosperous African district near the north of the island (above) and the two-story apartment housing preferred by South Asians, known as Indians (below). And there is a spatial contrast too: the Indian housing lies closer to the commercial center, where Indians control business, than the Africans' houses."

where the non-Western megacity's permanent buildings end, the sea of slum development begins, in some-cases engulfing and dwarfing the interior city. Stand on a hill outside Lima or overlooking the Cape Flats near Cape Town, and you see an unchanging panorama of makeshift shacks built of every conceivable material, vying for every foot of space, extending to the horizon. You are unlikely to see a single tree; a pall of smoke hangs over the scene. Narrow footpaths lead to the few and unpaved streets that in town lead, miles away, to the promised city.

To such baleful environs come millions of migrants ever year, their numbers uncertain because control is impossible and enumeration impractical. (Mexico City's population estimates vary by the millions; the city today houses between one-fifth and one-quarter of the country's entire population.) In Rio de Janeiro they build their dwellings on dangerous, landslide-prone slopes; in Port Moresby they sink stilts in the mud and build out over the water, risking wind and waves. In Kolkata countless thousands do not even try to erect shelters: there and in many other cities they live in the streets, under bridges, even in storm drains.

In the interior city, the immigrants contribute to crime and sometimes disorder, but better-off residents of the center have fewer options to relocate than do those of Western cities. Joblessness, hunger, and desperation make the urban experience something far different from the hopes that impelled most migrants to make their fateful move, and their collective impact on the city of their dreams can be devastating. City governments do not have the resources to adequately educate, medicate, or police their burgeoning populations, let alone to provide even minimal housing for most. Even countries that attempt to limit, if not control, urban inmigration altogether, such as China and Vietnam, confront such problems. Earlier we took note of the rapid growth of Shenzhen, adjacent to Hong Kong; this expansion was to some extent channeled by a Chinese regime pursuing a deliberate policy of economic development in this SEZ. During the 1990s, however, quite a different problem arose in Shanghai, where the announcement of the need for workers in the new Pudong district led to the arrival of some 3 million jobseekers from the countryside and temporary chaos. A massive repatriation project by city and state moved most of the immigrants back to their rural homes.

From the field notes

"Beijing, Shanghai, and other Chinese cities are being transformed as the old is swept away in favor of the modern. Locals, powerless to stop the process, complain that their neighborhoods are being destroyed and that their relocation to remote apartment complexes is a hardship. Urban planners argue that the 'historic' neighborhoods are often dilapidated, decaying, and beyond renovation. The housing shown above was demolished to make room for what is going up below—a scene repeated countless times throughout urbanizing China."

Power and Accommodation

The vast slums of cities in poorer parts of the world may appear homogeneous and multicultural, but in fact they contain their own ethnic neighborhoods where new arrivals are somehow accommodated and community interests promoted. Here, too, the more powerful exploit the less fortunate. As squatter settlements expand, they occupy land owned by previous residents, families that farmed what were once the rural areas beyond the city's edge. Perhaps favored by the former colonial administration, these people long ago moved into the city but kept ownership of their land. When the inmigrants' dwellings encroached, they allowed that to happen—but charged them rent. Having once established an owner–tenant relationship, the owners would steadily raise rents, threatening to destroy the squatters' flimsy shacks if they failed to pay. In this way the powerful long-term inhabitants of the urban area exploit the weaker, more recent arrivals. Since the former are from the city or its immediate environs and the latter tend to come from farther away, the newcomers are at a disadvantage that has ethnic implications.

An example of the potential consequences came from Nairobi during the autumn of 2001. The settlement known as Kibera is Nairobi's largest slum area (and one of Subsaharan Africa's worst in terms of amenities). As it happens, much of Kibera's once-rural land is owned by Nubians of Sudanese descent, who settled there during the colonial period but have in many cases become businesspeople in the city. The tenants in Kibera include large Luo communities from western Kenya and Luhya, a cluster of peoples to the northwest. When some tenants were unable to pay the latest increase in rents, landowners came to evict them, and in the fighting that followed, a number of people were killed. Groups of Luo, Luhya and others even took to fighting among themselves, and government intervention was needed to stabilize the situation. The latest rent increases were withdrawn, but the fundamental problems—crowding, unemployment, unsanitary conditions, hunger, lack of education—remain, and Kibera will not have seen its last outbreak of disorder.

Thus geography plays a major role in the relationships among ethnic components of a former colonial city. That was true even before the surge of urbanization the non-Western world witnessed during the last third of the twentieth century. In a study of the city of Mombasa during the 1960s, one of us (H. J. de Blij) found that the inner city (in effect the island on which central Mombasa was built) was informally partitioned among major ethnic groups. Apart from the Swahili, who occupied the Old Town and adjacent historic portions of the built-up area, the pattern of occupance reflected the status of the various ethnic groups in the country (Kenya) as a whole. The port of Mombasa, the country's largest, was the city's major employer, and the Kikuyu workers and their families lived closest to it—although the Kikuyu's historic heartland lies far away, in the highlands north of Nairobi. It was a privilege begun during colonial times. Another powerful group, the Kamba, occupied a zone farther outward. The locals, the Mijikenda, mostly had to come to work from off-island villages. The Asians, then still in control of all the city's commerce, were concentrated on the opposite side of the island, away from the port. By 2001, with Mombasa's population seven times as large as it was in the 1960s, elements of these early advantages could still be recorded in the cultural townscape. The latecomers in the immigrant population crowd the outer zone of the city, off-island.

How do the many millions of urban immigrants living in the slum-ridden rings and pockets of the poorer world's megacities survive? Extended families share and stretch every dollar they manage to earn; when one member of the family has a salaried job, his or her income saves the day for a dozen or more relatives. When a member of the family (or several members of a larger community) manages to emigrate to a Western country and makes good money there, part of that income is sent back home, and becomes the mainstay for those left behind. Hundreds of millions of dollars are transferred this way every year, ***remittances*** that make a critical difference in the poorer countries of the world. In those vast slums, barrios, and favelas, those who are jobless or unsalaried are not idle. Everywhere you look there are people at work, inside or in front of their modest habitats, fixing things, repairing broken items for sale, sorting through small piles of waste for salvageable items, trading and selling goods from makeshift stands. What prevails here is referred to as the ***informal economy***, and it can add up to a huge total in unrecorded monetary value. Of course, this worries city and national governments because the informal economy is essentially a recordless economy and no taxes are paid. Even the money sent back from overseas is usually delivered in

From the field notes

"There is a viaduct over the waterfront Marine Drive (Netaji Subhash Road) along Mumbai's Back Bay that is intended for vehicular traffic only, but it has a narrow walkway, probably intended for maintenance purposes. It looked as though that overpass would afford an unusual view of this globalizing metropolis, and I walked up, which seemed to require every vehicle that passed me to honk and many drivers to make a certain unmistakable gesture. But the view was rewarding: this is the image of Mumbai as the global city where, for a time during the 1990s, real-estate prices were the highest in the world."

cash, not via Western Union or a bank; it is more often carried by a trusted community member who might pay a comparatively small bribe at the airport when passing through immigration.

Even as the informal economy thrives among the millions in the shantytowns, the new era of globalization is making a major impact in the megacities founded or fostered by the colonial powers. The geographers Jan Nijman and Richard Grant (2002) have documented this transformation in former colonial port cities, including Mumbai. In this city, formerly called Bombay, colonial rule produced an urban landscape marked by strong segregation of foreign and local activities, commercial as well as residential (Fig. 28-1A), and high levels of functional specialization and concentration. Adjacent to the port area was a well-demarcated European business district containing foreign (mostly British) companies. Most economic activities in this European commercial area involved trade, transport, banking, distribution, and insurance. Zoning and building codes were strictly enforced to maintain an orderly European atmosphere. Physically separated from this European district were the traditional markets and bazaars of the so-called Native Town, a densely populated mix of commercial and residential land uses.

Now in the new era of globalization, a new spatially demarcated foreign presence has arisen. There is what may be called a Global CBD at the heart of the original British city, housing mostly foreign corporations and multinational companies and linked mainly to the global economy. The former European Town has a large presence of big domestic companies and a pronounced orientation to the national (Indian) economy. And the Native Town now has a high concentration of small domestic company headquarters and the strongest orientation to the immediate urban area (Fig. 28-1B).

Clearly, then, numerous forces are shaping the new megacities of the world, although these forces affect cities in different world regions in different ways. Lagos, rivalling Mumbai in terms of total population, has a

Figure 28-1 The Changing Character of Mumbai. *Source:* Jan Nijman and Richard Grant, "Globalization and the Corporate Geography of Cities in the Less-Developed World," *Annals of the Association of American Geographers,* 92,2 (2002).

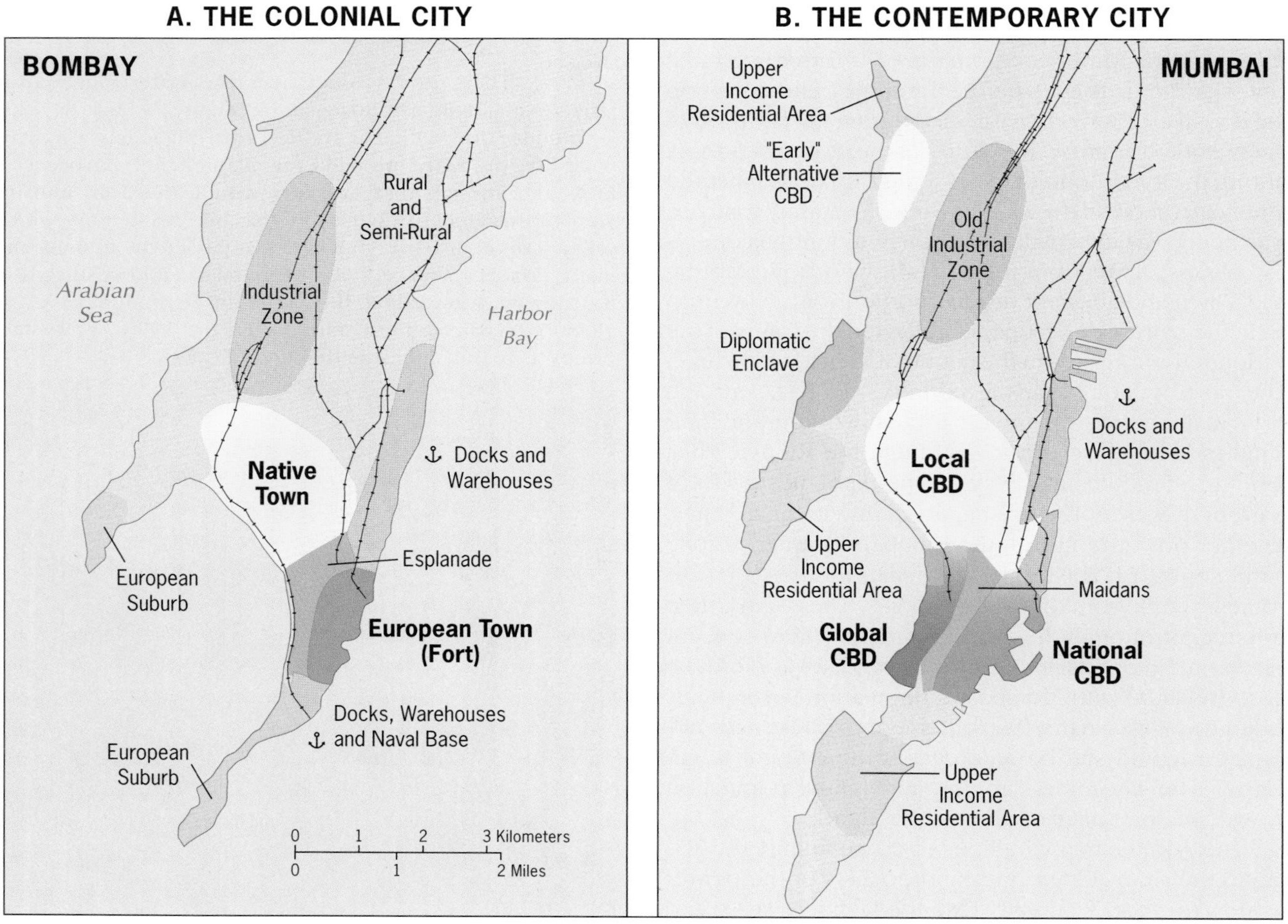

much weaker global presence and a weaker economy, reflecting Nigeria's comparative isolation from the global economy and the failures of its governments. Cities on China's Pacific Rim have a much stronger global presence than Mumbai's, again evincing government economic policies as well as locational advantages. As the world's megacities grow, their forms and fortunes will diverge.

◆ LIFE IN URBAN AMERICA

The American city, too, is a place of contradictions. Even as urban sprawl continues and cities are coalescing, residents by the millions have left the urban cores and moved to the suburbs. This suburbanization has at times perpetuated racial separatism: in the case of Washington, D.C., for example, the great majority of African-Americans moved east into Prince George's County, while whites moved west into Virginia. Meanwhile, CBDs lost their primacy against competition from outlying shopping malls; manufacturing employment in the urban heartland declined, and jobs were lost.

The growth of service functions (hotels, financial institutions, shops, etc.) compensated for this decline, but the recession that began in 2001 emphasized the weakness of these alternatives. Meanwhile, many of the so-called ***inner cities***, the rings and sectors between the CBD and the suburbs, remain problem-ridden zones where city governments, having lost tax revenues as residents moved to the suburbs, are unable to adequately fund schools, public housing, and social services. Efforts to lure wealthier families back to the CBD have had some success, and not all cities suffer to the same degree, but urban America presents a somewhat troubled picture.

In the older industrial cities, the inner city has become a landscape of inadequate housing, substandard living, and widespread decay. In New York City nearly 3 million people (plus a substantial number of foreigners who are not officially tabulated in the census), many of them ethnic minorities, are crowded into apartment buildings averaging five stories high that were built as walkups 75 to 100 years ago. Lots of these buildings are now worn out and unsanitary; many are infested by rats and cockroaches. These apartments are overfilled with people who cannot escape the vicious cycle that forces them to live there.

Yet something of value remains in many of the aging neighborhoods of New York and other "manufacturing belt" cities. In the squalid poverty of ghetto and slum life, there persists a sense of neighborhood, social structure, and continuity. Urban renewal in the form of anonymous high-rises and relocation of people to new neighborhoods may so disrupt this sense of community that the costs outweigh the benefits. Drug abuse, crime, vandalism, and other social problems afflict newer areas of the inner city as well as older ones. Relationships between communities and law enforcement officers usually are tense; a single incident can set off massive disturbances.

Smaller cities have been spared some of the worst problems of the largest cities, but the transformation of their central cores has been dramatic. The rise of suburban shopping malls has devastated the commercial core of many a modest-sized city, and without the sheer numbers of people and services of their larger counterparts, these cities' downtowns have become hollow reflections of what they once were. As people and money leave, it becomes very difficult to reverse the downward spiral.

During the 1990s, the deterioration of central cities became a major issue of public debate. Many CBDs are surrounded by blighted inner cities. Is the central city worth saving? Let us remember that the downtown area of larger cities still contains many of a city's crucial assets. Although many establishments and businesses have moved to the suburbs, others have not, at least not yet. Great museums, research libraries, world-renowned orchestras, leading universities, attractive recreational facilities, and other amenities still exist in the centers of many American cities. Crowds still fill the sidewalks of the cities each business day, and traffic jams evince their continuing vitality.

But this is a different kind of vigor than the one that first made the downtown the heart of the city. It is a residual vitality that is engendered by activities and facilities still based in or near the CBD. Central banks, old educational institutions, major museums, governmental agencies, and large hotels are among the kinds of organizations that remain, often because their physical facilities cannot be moved or replaced. But the former advantages of agglomeration are fading fast. Publishing companies, for example, formerly shared the pool of specialized services available in Manhattan, but now many of those services can be performed anywhere in the country and transmitted electronically. The high cost of a downtown location now outweighs the advantages of agglomeration, and publishing companies have moved from New York to as far away as Florida and Texas. Geographers call this process ***deglomeration***, and it is affecting older downtowns everywhere in America.

Revitalizing the Center

In recent years, city governments have taken a number of steps to counter the deterioration of the urban core. One of these steps involves new residential construction in the hope of luring middle- and upper-class residents (and their taxes and spending) back to the heart of the city. The number of people who have actually moved back downtown is relatively small, however. Most of the reinvestment was done by people who were already living in the central city, and a hoped-for "return to the city" movement by suburban dwellers never fully materialized.

Residential construction within and near the downtown has created some attractive high-rise buildings with modern amenities and advantageous locations, but it has not reversed the net outward flow of the urban population. However, the ***gentrification*** of rundown areas of the inner city has had a greater impact. Gentrification is the rehabilitation of deteriorated, often abandoned inner-city housing with favorable locations relative to the CBD and central-city places of employment. The growing interest in such inner-city housing results in part from the changing character of American society: the proportion of childless couples and single people in the population is growing, and for these urbanites, the suburbs do not look so attractive. Living within walking distance of the workplace, and very near the cultural and recreational amenities the central city still offers, attracts more residents every year. For them, the gentrified neighborhood is a good choice. For those displaced by gentrification, however, the consequences can be serious. Rising housing costs associated with gentrification have played a key role in the growing problem of homelessness.

Another program for inner-city revival is the ***commercialization*** of part of the downtown. Several cities, including Miami, New York, and Baltimore, have created waterfront "theme" areas to attract visitors. Such ventures have been successful in attracting tourists and generating business, but they have not substantially revived the downtowns because they cannot attract what the core of the city needs most: permanent residents with a stake in its future.

Does it matter over the long term? Sweeping changes have affected cities for 200 years, so if the time of downtown prosperity has come and gone, why try to stem the tide? Apparently, the answer is that it does not matter enough to change people's habits or governments' investment priorities. The office towers of Denver, Houston, and other cities contain thousands of suburban commuters whose only contact with the city is the short drive between the freeway exit and their building's parking garage. Again, the shining skyscrapers that were built to attract businesses (or keep them) downtown have not had a major effect on the social fabric of the CBD, and they have actually contributed to the abandonment of older commercial buildings, thus adding to the region's blight. Even more significant, the federal government has not provided nearly enough financial support to help the major cities reverse their decline. Services are being reduced, staff and workers in the nonbasic sector are being laid off, and the city's essential functions (sanitation, maintenance, security, transportation, and education) are suffering, affecting the downtown severely. As a result, the livability of many inner cities continues to decline, and its relevance in America's urban culture is diminishing.

The Suburban City

For many decades the attraction of country life with city amenities, reinforced by the discomforts of living in the heart of many central cities, has propelled people to move to the suburbs and more distant urban fringes. In postwar times, the automobile made possible mass commuting from suburban residences to downtown workplaces. As a result, the kind of suburbanization that is familiar to North Americans and other Westerners became a characteristic of urbanization in mobile, highly developed societies.

Suburbanization holds special interest for human geographers because it involves the transformation of large areas of land from rural to urban uses, affects large numbers of people who can afford to move to more expensive suburban homes, and rapidly creates distinct urban regions complete with industrial, commercial, and educational, as well as residential, components. In a sense, the suburbs reveal their occupants' idealized living patterns more accurately than any other urban zone because their layout can be planned in response to choice and demand. Elsewhere in the metropolis, there are too many constraints imposed by preexisting land-use arrangements. In a 1974 book titled *Suburban Growth*, J. H. Johnson suggests that in the suburbs "life and landscape are in much closer adjustment" than in the older parts of the urban area, providing geographers with a direct expression of the behavior of contemporary urban society. Suburban life also provides important clues about the nature of the urban future.

Among the most comprehensive geographic analyses of the rapid and dramatic changes affecting U.S. cities is a book by P. O. Muller, *Contemporary Suburban America* (1981). In it the author points out that suburbia has "now evolved into a self-sufficient urban entity, containing its own major economic and cultural activities, that is no longer an appendage to the central city." As such, suburban cities were ready not just to be self-sufficient but to compete with the central city for leading urban economic activities such as telecommunications, high-technology industries, and corporate headquarters.

In the current era of globalization, America's suburban cities are proving their power to attract such activities, thereby sustaining the suburbanizing process. In an article entitled, "The Suburban Transformation of the Globalizing American City" (1997), Muller shows that the urban realms model (see Chapter 22), which views today's suburbanized cities as polycentric metropolises consisting of "realms" of activity such as international company headquarters, telecommunications hubs, and communities of foreigners, describes the typical large American city today. "A new urban future is being shaped as fully developed suburbs become the engine driving metropolitan and world city growth," Muller writes.

The overall importance of suburban life in the United States is underscored by the results of the 2000 census, which indicated that no less than 50 percent of the entire American population resided in the suburbs (up from 37 percent in 1970); the remaining 50 percent were divided between the central cities (30.3 percent) and nonmetropolitan or rural areas (19.7 percent). Of the population living in metropolitan areas, 62.2 percent resided in the suburbs, which in 2000 had 141 million residents. Thus the suburbs have become the essence of the modern American city.

The Canadian City

When you fly into Toronto, Canada's largest city, or indeed any of Canada's major urban centers, you may get the impression that Canadian and American cities are pretty much alike. A cluster of skyscrapers creates an impressive CBD. Highways carry busy traffic. Tree-lined streets mark suburban neighborhoods. Groups of high-rises near major intersections mark suburban downtowns.

That impression, would be mistaken, however. Canada's major cities suffer far less from the problems that plague their American counterparts. Large as the Toronto urban area may seem, for example, it is much less dispersed than an American city with the same population. Urban population densities are higher; multiple-family dwellings are more common; and most important, suburbanization has not gone nearly as far as it has in the United States. This means that far more high- and middle-income workers have remained in the central city, resulting in a stronger tax base and, generally, better services, ranging from public transit to police protection.

Downtown Toronto still is the functional heart of the Toronto urban area (and the same is true for several other Canadian cities). Although not immune to the forces of globalization and the development of world cities, Canadian central cities have retained a larger share of overall economic activity than their U.S. counterparts have. The kinds of urban amenities that make a central city attractive have not moved to the outer ring of suburbs. In general, the suburbs of Canadian cities are neither as wealthy nor as far from downtown as their American counterparts. The severe decline of inner-city low-income housing that marks so many American cities is not seen in urban Canada. Indeed, Canadian cities do not display the sharp contrasts in wealth that are so evident in American cities.

All this should not suggest that Toronto and other Canadian cities do not share some of the problems affecting American urban areas. The integration of foreign-born residents has not always gone smoothly in Canada's cities. Violent crime, though much less serious than it is in the United States, also afflicts Canada's cities. Circulation in several cities, while eased by the general use of mass transit, is hampered by inadequate road building. Overall, however, Canada's cities have not (at least not yet) developed into competing urban realms. Stability and cohesion have produced an urban model that is beyond the reach of the politically and socially fragmented cities of the United States.

◆ THE EUROPEAN CITY

European cities are older than North American cities, but they, too, were transformed by the Industrial Revolution. Indeed, industrialization struck many of Europe's dormant medieval towns and vibrant mercantile cities like a landslide. But there are some differences between the European and the North American experience.

In terms of population numbers, the great European cities are in the same class as major North American cities. London (7.6 million) and Paris (9.6 million), like Rome, Berlin, Madrid, and Athens, are large cities by world standards. These, however, are among Europe's many historic urban centers, which have been affected but not engulfed by the industrial tide. The cities of the British Midlands and the megalopolis of Germany's Ruhr are more representative of the manufacturing era. Individually, these cities are smaller, but in a regional context they are major urban complexes.

The industrial cities have lost much of their historic heritage, but in Europe's largest cities the legacy of the past is better preserved. Large, dominant cities such as Paris, Athens, and Lisbon (many of which are primate cities) proved to be the most durable in the face of the impact of the Industrial Age. Wars have taken their toll, of course. In the London CBD, for example, historic and modern buildings vie for space. Many of the modern structures stand on sites where historic buildings were destroyed during World War II. In Paris, Madrid, Rome, and Lisbon, on the other hand, the historic cores are well preserved and protected.

Greenbelts

The central city of London contains residential sectors of varying quality that radiate outward from the CBD. It also contains the city's main industrial zones. But unlike American cities, London's central city is not flanked by a zone of expanding suburbs. The central city today is about the same areal size as it was in the early 1960s. The reason for this is the so-called Metropolitan Greenbelt, a zone of open country averaging more than 30 kilometers (20 miles) wide that contains scattered small towns but is otherwise open country. This had the effect of containing London's built-up area within its 1960 limits throughout the period of rapid suburbanization in the United States. Although there are some settlements within the greenbelt, suburbanization has had to proceed beyond it—a long train ride away from the CBD (Fig. 28–2).

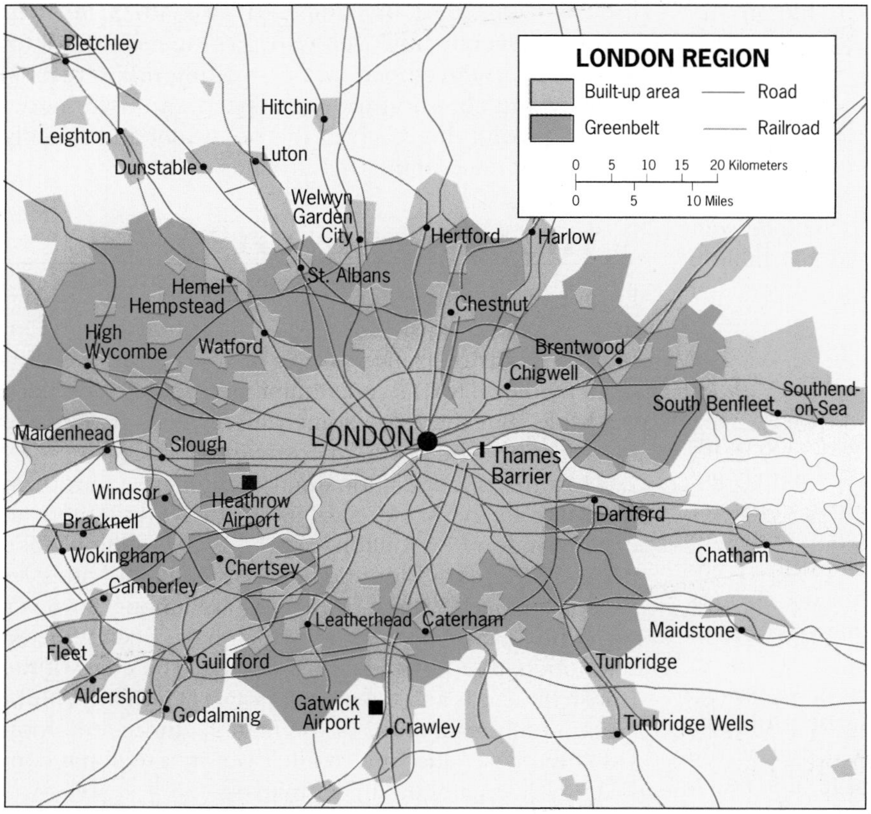

Figure 28-2 London Region. London's greenbelt and the built-up area adjacent are indicated on this map.

The ***greenbelt*** phenomenon is not unique to London; many European cities have a version of it. This preservation of near-urban open space is a legacy of governments' reaction to the impact of the Industrial Revolution during the nineteenth century. It has limited not only urban sprawl but also suburbanization. Beyond the greenbelt, suburbs are too far away from the CBD for commuting. And since the cost of gasoline is as much as three times higher in Europe than in the United States, people have an incentive to use rapid transit. This makes it more practical to cluster homes close together, and as a result the suburbs of European cities tend to be high-density villages or towns set in open countryside.

As in the United States, the outlying smaller towns in the urban hinterlands of cities such as London, Paris, and Frankfurt have attracted high-tech industries, corporate headquarters of multinational firms, and other activities typical of the modern ***world city*** (see Chapter 27). In general, however, the suburban towns around Europe's major cities do not yet compete with the urban center as American suburban cities do. European governments make every effort to sustain the dominance of their central cities; a prime example is the massive La Défense business district in the heart of Paris, west of the historic CBD. The largest project of its kind in Europe, La Défense is a symbol of the world city. Glass-fronted high-rises tower over wide avenues, huge parking garages, and every modern amenity—all within sight of the Arc de Triomphe. La Défense has become the hub of greater Paris, far outpacing all of its suburban competitors combined.

For reasons such as this, cities in Western Europe tend to be even more compact than Canadian cities. Highway and beltway development still lag, with mixed results: the central cities are clogged with cars, but mass transit, bicycles, and walking are the primary means of getting to work. Zoning rules are restrictive and strictly enforced. As a result, the European city remains clustered and crowded—which is good for the financial health of its CBD.

Microdistricts

Note that we are referring to Western Europe here. Just as there are significant differences between American and Canadian cities, so the cities of Europe show regional contrasts. The cities of Eastern Europe, many of which are old primate cities, were affected by communist planning that tended to neglect their cultural and historic heritage and attempted to reorganize urban life into so-called ***microdistricts***. This plan entailed the creation of a huge, dominant square at the center of the city and wide, radiating avenues flanked by ugly apartment blocks. Assemblages of these apartment blocks, generally 7 to 11 stories high, were designed to form microdistricts with workplaces, schools, recreational facilities, stores, and other amenities either within them or nearby. Thus there was no need for a large CBD, for the districts were supposed to be largely self-sufficient. Neither would there be suburbanization, mass commuting, class contrasts in neighborhoods, or traffic congestion. The emptiness of those vast, multilane avenues became a hallmark of the "socialist city."

In Eastern Europe the impact of communist city planning varied. Prague and Budapest were less severely affected than Bucharest (Romania), where the communist regime destroyed much of the city's historic townscape and replaced it with the faceless apartment blocks that make socialist cities so monotonous and dull. Today the cities of Eastern Europe are undergoing still another transformation as glass towers, reflecting the global economy, rise above the city.

◆ URBANIZATION AND ENVIRONMENT

Ours is an urbanizing world. Only about 25 percent of the world's population lived in urban settings at the middle of the past century; by the middle of the present one, as many as 75 percent may be concentrated in cities and towns. On the face of it, one might conclude that this is a positive development: fewer people in rural areas would seem to be good for forests, wildlife, marginal environments, and soils. Moreover, urban life tends to reduce family size, increase the likelihood that women will receive better education, and improve children's access to adequate health care (for example, inoculation programs are more effective where children are clustered than in remote areas where they live widely dispersed).

Some scholars argue that these positives, over the long term, will outweigh the negatives for reasons such as these. Others calculate that urbanization of the kind the world is experiencing will have a detrimental impact on the planet. Their major concerns are these:

1. *Hazards of Site.* Millions of migrants moving to urban areas are occupying land that was never intended to be part of the built-up area and thus expose themselves to landslides, floods, storms, and earthquakes. No amount of investment, even if it were available, could create the infrastructure needed to protect these residents; but there is no way to persuade them to leave and no alternate space to relocate them. Thus the megacities of the global economic periphery (and the smaller cities to which many rural inhabitants make their first move) are involuntarily acquiring a permanent liability of huge dimensions.
2. *Loss of Land from Expansion.* A much-debated issue centers on the loss of farmland resulting from urban expansion everywhere—suburbanization in North America and shantytown development in developing-world megacities. At a small scale, this seems to be inconsequential, but at larger scales the loss of farmland is considerable. In the United States, the process consumes about 400,000 ha (1 million acres) a year; in China, the total approaches three times as much. Since some of the world's best soils lie in the immediate environs of large settlements, this is a serious and growing depletion.
3. *Changed Land Cover.* When cities expand, more land is paved over, roads and parking lots are built, and, in geographic terminology, the natural landscape becomes cultural. The vast shantytowns consist of roofed dwellings and hardened roads and paths, and they, too, contribute to runoff. Less rainfall permeates downward; more of it, laden with pollutants, washes into streams. All cities affect the courses of rivers they adjoin—fast-expanding cities all the more so.
4. *Impact of Pollution.* Rapid urban and industrial growth create growing volumes of contaminants in air as well as water. Earlier we referred to the pall of

From the field notes

"This is not postcard Ireland, but it is a growing reality for the Emerald Isle. The country's recent economic surge has made separate houses affordable for more and more people, and that—combined with substantial immigration—has led to a construction boom. This new housing estate in County Cork was built on land where sheep grazed just a decade ago. With more and more such developments taking place, Ireland is facing a growing challenge to traditional ways of life. The amenities are the attraction, but they carry with them social and environmental costs that cannot be ignored."

smoke that hangs over the megacities' shantytowns; places like Mexico City, Delhi, São Paulo, and Bangkok rank among the world's most smog-ridden. Studies of Jakarta (and the entire Jabotabek conurbation) show that burning garbage and automobile exhausts combine to make its air severely polluted throughout the year. This affects all residents, but children especially.

5. *Production of Waste.* In many developing-world megacities burning, smoking mountains of garbage can be found—not remote and out of sight, but right in the heart of the urbanized area. Day and night the mounds grow larger; people living in the vicinity breathe some of the world's most polluted air. In such cities as Manila and Jakarta people actually live in the waste dumps, looking for salvageable items. Add to this the lack of sewer facilities for countless millions (in the Mexico City area, some 3 million shantytown residents are not connected to any sewer system), and the production of waste and its disposition loom as a century-long and growing predicament.
6. *Larger Demand for Water.* Urbanization brings with it a higher demand for water. A rural villager who gets by with a bucket of well water a day becomes a consumer requiring five or more times as much water in the city—if and when he or she gets a salaried job, a permanent abode, and modern household facilities. While in the shantytowns, urban residents face water shortages that create health risks and daily discomfort. Already, riverfront cities are contributing not only to downstream pollution but also to so much water use that some rivers (such as the Nile and the Yellow) barely reach the sea. The implications for water consumption of rising urbanization are critical.
7. *Changing Consumption Habits.* Not only do urban residents consume more water than most of their village counterparts, but they also change their diets, their dress modes, and their recreation habits. They also demand more energy as they turn on lights and equipment and ride scooters or drive cars. All these changed behaviors have impacts far beyond the limits of the city. The rice- or wheat-eating villager may now want meat (as we will see in the next chapter, McDonald's ranks as a leading "pull" image among young migrants); the sandal-wearer wants leather shoes; the walker wants a motorized vehicle and hence gasoline. To satisfy growing demand, meat producers need expanded pastures, threatening the very forests where land pressure was supposed to be relieved by the departure of farmers for the city. The accelerating growth of urbanization will put greater stress on rural areas than would otherwise be the case.

It is well known that the urbanized inhabitants of the industrialized world place enormous demands on the planet's resources and contribute massively to the pollution of the planet. Now major regions of the rest of the world are adding theirs, and the question is whether the benefits of ongoing urbanization can ever be expected to compensate for its detriments.

◆ KEY TERMS ◆

asylum seeker
commercialization
deglomeration
gentrification
greenbelt
informal economy
inner city
microdistrict
remittances
suburbanization
world city

◆ APPLYING GEOGRAPHIC KNOWLEDGE ◆

1. A city may be affected strongly by events occurring elsewhere. Use your geographic skills to assess the impact on the Greater Miami urban area of a normalization of political and economic relations between the United States and Cuba.

2. You are a member of a planning group charged with the task of lessening social tensions in an immigrant sector of a large European city. What kinds of maps, and at what level of scale, will you ask for? How will these contribute to the plan you and your team will design?

Chapter 29

Cultural Change in an Era of Globalization

From the field notes

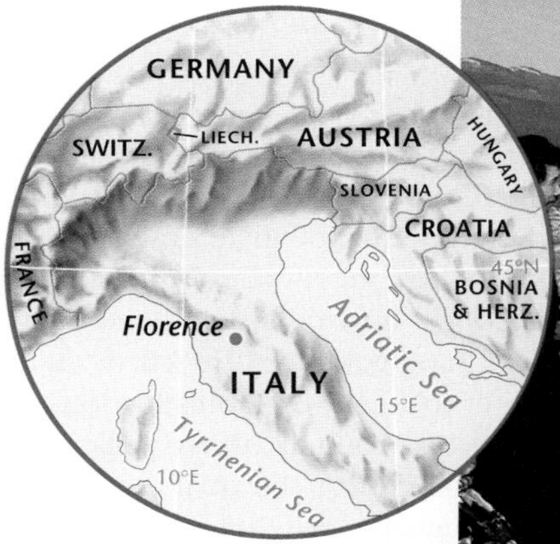

"Florence, Italy, December 2001. On a clear, cold day I went up to the Piazza Michelangelo for the traditional panoramic view of the city. The city's skyline turned out to be only one item of interest. I also found myself surrounded by 8 or 9 Chinese brides and grooms, together with many family and friends. My colleague from Milan told me that a modest-sized Chinese immigrant community could be found not far from Florence, and we had by chance chosen the day for our excursion when a number of young couples had decided to celebrate their weddings. Melding Chinese and Western traditions in a celebration overlooking one of the cradles of modern European civilization, here was a memorable example of the growing cultural complexity of our planet."

KEY POINTS

- ◆ **Cultures have affected one another throughout history, but the extent and scale of interaction has greatly increased over the past century.**
- ◆ **The globalization of culture has eroded the distinction between folk culture and popular culture while fostering the development of new identity communities that cut across traditional cultural lines.**
- ◆ **Cultural products produced in a small number of places exert an influence greatly disproportionate to their size, but the geographic pattern of this influence is highly uneven.**
- ◆ **Economic and cultural globalization are closely linked, and that link has increasingly led cultural products to be seen as commodities to be bought and sold.**
- ◆ **The twin impacts of economic and cultural globalization make it increasingly important to see individual places not in isolation but in relationship to other places and to processes unfolding at extra-local scales.**
- ◆ **The globalization of culture has threatened the distinctiveness of individual places, leading to efforts to protect endogenous cultural products.**

In the 1990s, it was said that more people around the world knew who Michael Jordan was than any other individual—living or dead. At first glance, this might seem to be little more than a curious bit of trivia, but of course it is indicative of much more. People in far-flung places not only know the name Michael Jordan, but many millions of them spend time playing the game that made him famous. They recognize the brand name he wears on his basketball shoes, and they often make efforts to acquire shoes made by the same manufacturer. They watch movies and advertisements with references to Michael Jordan, and when he makes a comeback they read magazines filled with stories detailing his every move.

With your newfound awareness of geography, you might assume that all of this can be attributed to Michael Jordan's interest in geography during his college years (yes, Michael Jordan was a geography major at the University of North Carolina). But what this really symbolizes is the globalization of culture. As we have seen, globalization is a complicated concept; nothing is truly globalized because there are always places that are much less affected than others by the spread of innovations or ideas. Yet the world of the early twenty-first century is one in which the global scale is of increasing importance in a variety of arenas—including the cultural. Indeed, cultures are affecting one another at unprecedented rates across extraordinary distances. Moreover, the flow of ideas and beliefs is not just in one direction. For example, even as American music finds its way into popular culture in places all over the world, there is a surge of interest in Buddhist philosophy in the United States.

To understand culture change in an era of globalization, we must return to the concept of culture itself. Early in the book, we noted just how complex the concept of culture is. Even in common parlance, the word "culture" is used variably to refer to a level of sophistication (a cultured person), the artistic products of particular groups of people (literature, music, etc.), the attributes that help distinguish peoples (language, religion, ethnicity, etc.), and the whole way of life of a people. If we are to grasp the interconnections between cultural change and globalization, it is important to recognize that not one of these approaches to the concept of culture is adequate by itself. Globalization affects, and is affected by, everything from the spread of popular music to the ways in which economic contacts between cultures influence daily lives and preferences. The fundamental point is that cultural change in an era of globalization is about the ways that a variety of place-specific cultural ideas and practices both shape globalization and are shaped by globalization.

To illustrate what the last sentence means, consider the mushrooming interest in trekking in the Himalayas in recent decades. That interest has been driven by the desire of people living in certain regions (particularly urban areas in North America, Europe, and Australia) to have a particular type of experience in a place thought to be remote and exotic (a cultural aspiration). It has been facilitated by the expansion of an increasingly wealthy middle class in those regions, which in turn is tied to a progressively more globalized economy based on particular (culturally rooted) ideas about how to organize production, exchange, and consumption. At the same time, trekkers have headed to the Himalayas in such numbers that they have fundamentally altered the economy of Nepal, which now relies on tourist spending for approximately one-sixth of its foreign earnings. In the process, they have brought profound changes to the lives of many inhabitants of the Nepalese highlands. The lives of many in Nepal have been altered not just by the importation of new ideas and practices by the trekkers, but by the social and environmental changes that have accompanied trekking. They have learned to adapt to a cash economy, to begin producing cultural artifacts primarily for sale to outsiders (rather than for ceremonial purposes or exchange), and to cope with the deforestation that has occurred in order to satisfy the demand for trekking lodges with hot showers, warm food, and washing machines. The point is that, in this case as well as in countless others, place-based cultural ideas and practices are deeply implicated both in the creation of a certain type of globalization and in the impacts of that globalization on particular people and places. ◆

◆ THE CHANGING SCOPE OF CULTURAL INTERACTION

As is clear from much of what we have studied so far, there is nothing new about cultures affecting one another. Virtually all cultures at all times have been the product of cultural interactions among diverse peoples. Three hundred years ago, a small fishing village along the Norwegian coast might have seemed like a fairly isolated, homogeneous place, and in some respects it was. But that place came into being through complex interactions among a variety of Scandinavian peoples—and between those peoples and more distant cultures; the intermixing of peoples that occurred during Viking times was, for example, quite extensive. At the same time, the very character of the town would have signaled its ties to an outside world. There would likely be a Lutheran church in the town—a symbol of a clear link to a far-flung religious realm that originated in an entirely different world region. The street patterns, housing styles, and dietary preferences would reflect the town's ties to a wider Western cultural heritage. Even in its comparative isolation, some trade and travel would bring villagers into contact with an outside world on a relatively regular basis.

Even though virtually all places experience cultural interaction, the extent and scale of interaction has not been uniform across time or space, and in some cases it has produced far greater changes in a short time than in others. Historically, change has tended to be the greatest in the face of rapid developments in the technology of communication or warfare (e.g., the invention of the printing press or firearms) and in cases where an expansionist society has come into contact with a society with a markedly less advanced level of technological development (e.g., the Russians' expansion eastward across Siberia). A further, special case of rapid change has occurred when a society brings new diseases into an area where the inhabitants lack resistance to those diseases (e.g., as occurred when Europeans arrived in the Western Hemisphere). These circumstances help to explain why colonialism was more than a political and economic affair; it had profound cultural impacts as well. Those cultural impacts were so great, and so widespread, that culture change can be thought of as occurring at a very large scale well before the twentieth century (see Chapter 15).

For all the magnitude of cultural change prior to the contemporary period, however, certain groups still maintain much of their traditional lifestyle. Such groups are traditionally termed ***folk cultures***—defined as largely self-sufficient, somewhat isolated groups with longstanding traditions that change comparatively slowly through time. Juxtaposed against the notion of a folk culture is that of a ***popular culture***—a term that usually refers to the rapidly changeable, nontraditional heterogeneous ideas and practices of urban industrial societies. Popular culture is mass culture, regional culture, even national or international culture. Its defining attributes and landscape symbols have diffused far and wide.

We can infer from the above definitions that folk cultures are a fading phenomenon in the industrialized core countries of the world—and they are increasingly disappearing in the global economic periphery as well. Indeed, the scope and sweep of globalization in the modern era raises questions about how meaningful the distinction is between folk and popular cultures. It is difficult to find any culture that has not been affected in some significant way by what was traditionally known as popular culture. Moreover, the effort to identify distinct folk cultures in an era of globalization is fraught with difficulties. The search for "authentic" folk cultures implies an effort to identify peoples who are seemingly untouched by change or external influence. Yet since all cultures are dynamic, and since almost all have been touched by external influences throughout their existence, such a search involves an inherent contradiction: the object of the search (an "authentic" folk culture) is ascribed properties (lack of change, lack of influence) that themselves are inauthentic.

From the field notes

"Driving from Jerusalem to Tel Aviv, the rest stop I chose turned out to be a veritable shrine to Elvis Presley. The owner was apparently an Elvis fan of serious proportions, and the statue of Elvis on the outside was only the beginning. Inside, every possible item of Elvis memorabilia was either on display or for sale. From the place where I stood to take this photograph, Elvis almost seemed to be carrying the Israeli flag. Elvis in the Holy Land—the ultimate proof of the ubiquity of popular culture!"

At the heart of the blurring of folk and popular culture are the extraordinary changes that have occurred over the past century in the time it takes for people, innovations, and ideas to spread around the globe. We saw in earlier chapters that the idea of cultivating crops took millennia to diffuse around the world. In much more recent times, the diffusion of developments such as the printing press or the Industrial Revolution could be measured over the course of 100 years or more. During the past century, however, the pace of diffusion shrank to months, weeks, days, and in some cases even hours; witness the impacts of a bank collapse in Japan on the London stock market a few hours later. Simultaneously, the spatial extent of diffusion has tended to expand, so that more and more parts of the Earth's surface are affected by ideas and innovations from far-away places.

A variety of political, economic, and technological developments lie behind this remarkable decline in the distance decay of innovation diffusion. The stage was set by the development of an increasingly integrated world political order with its roots in the European colonization of much of the rest of the world. On this stage, an increasingly globalized economy was built, linking people's fates to one another across vast distances (Chapter 27). Accompanying and propelling it was a series of technological innovations that have radically altered the cost, pace, and scope of interaction: automobiles, airplanes, telephones, radios, televisions, satellites, personal computers, the Internet, fiber-optic cables, and much more. These developments have worked together to facilitate the rapid movement of the products, ideas, and people that are the heart of contemporary culture change.

These developments have even fostered a fundamental shift in the very notion of a cultural community. One hundred years ago, cultural communities were thought of primarily as contiguous communities of peoples sharing the types of cultural characteristics we examined in Parts Three and Four. The extraordinary technological and social changes of recent decades have both heightened awareness of different dimensions of culture and made it possible for close contacts to emerge among peoples living in distant places. As a result, the way that many people define their cultural communities has changed. In places that have been strongly affected by economic and cultural globalization, local, regional, and national cultural identities now coexist—or are sometimes even supplanted—by identities based on commonalities in gender, sexual identity, and even commitment to particular political causes.

Even as we marvel at the cultural fluidity of the modern world, it is important to remember that there are significant geographical differences in the access people have to the things that facilitate the movement of cultural products, ideas, and people—as well as in the impacts that mobility has on individual places. As a result, some peoples and places are able to exert a much greater external influence than are others. At the global scale, North America, Western Europe, and East Asia are arguably exerting the greatest global cultural influence at present. At the regional scale, there is a hierarchy of influence among and between these world regions that changes with the issue under consideration. North America influences Western Europe and Japan in fast food, Japan influences North America and Western Europe in electronic games, Western Europe influences North America and Japan in certain realms of art and philosophy, and so on. And there is a geography of influence at ever smaller scales—with urban centers tending to exert greater influence over rural areas and certain urban neighborhoods influencing others.

Influence does not always lead to acceptance, as we will see when we look at some of the reactions to instances of cultural globalization later in this chapter. Moreover, flows are rarely one-sided, even when one side has much more influence or power than the other. The impact of Latin music, dance, and food in the United States today is a case in point. Indeed, even in cases where there is clearly one dominant source of influence—such as the United States in the world of television—trends can start in other places that come to play a very important role in the place of origin of the influence. Thus, the so-called Real TV phenomenon in the United States today has its roots in the United Kingdom and Sweden. In a curious twist on the globalization of culture theme, it was a Swedish production called "Expedition Robinson" that gave birth to shows such as "Survivor" in the United States. But of course the very name for the Swedish show comes from an English novel published in the early eighteenth century!

◆ IMPACTS OF THE GLOBALIZATION OF CULTURE

"The trouble with French music is that it is all English." This comment, innocently offered by an 11-year-old American boy after spending a few months in France, sums up one of the most obvious consequences of cultural globalization: the increasing dominance around the world of particular cultural forms produced in specific places. This is most evident in popular music, television, and film, where American, and to a lesser extent British, products can now be seen and heard around the world. Turn on the television in Harare, Zimbabwe, and you can easily find reruns of a 10-year old American television show—or a contemporary CNN broadcast. Walk down the street in Seoul, South Korea, and you might well hear a radio broadcasting a song recorded by the Beatles, Madonna, or Brittany Spears. Go to a cinema in Santiago, Chile, and you are likely to be able to choose among several recently released American films.

There are, of course, other important nodes where these cultural forms are being produced. Brazilian soap operas are followed in distant places, the French cinema has carved out a special niche in the film world, and the Japanese exert extraordinary influence over television programming for children. The larger point here is that the cultural forms produced in a relatively few places exert an influence greatly disproportionate to their size—and with clear cultural impacts. Most obviously, the values and priorities of the creators of the cultural products are brought to millions, if not billions, of people. More subtly, it is often difficult for those outside of one of the principal nodes of cultural production to compete against the dominance of exogenously produced cultural products—thus limiting or stifling the development of alternative cultural forms. Sensitivity to this latter issue is evident in the heavy subsidies provided by the French government to its domestic film industry; French television stations, for example, must turn over 3 percent of their revenues to the French cinema. This initiative has helped the French film industry to some degree, but in countless other cases, governments and cultural institutions lack the means or the will to promote local cultural productions.

The overarching theme bridging the foregoing examples is the threat of cultural homogenization. The point is not that cultures around the world are necessarily all becoming alike. This is far from the case, and there is much evidence that individual cultural productions are interpreted and understood in very different ways, depending on the cultural context in which they are viewed. Recent American war movies, for example, have been viewed in very different ways around the planet—as entertainment, as symbols of an excessive patriotism, as efforts to assert the importance of American values, and so on. Yet differences in interpretation do not negate the possibility that cultural diversity can suffer when a narrow range of cultural forms exerts an extraordinary degree of dominance. This is clearly occurring not just in the realms described here, but in arenas where multinational corporations have developed the power and reach to shape tastes, buying practices, and even social customs around the globe. Terms such as Coca-Colonization, McDonaldization, and Disneyfication have been coined to symbolize this process.

The Link Between Economic and Cultural Globalization

The spread of McDonald's hamburger outlets around the world offers a prominent example of the cultural implications of this phenomenon. From a small fast-food chain in the United States, McDonald's outlets are now spread over six continents. Their success is not based primarily on tourists looking for a familiar place to eat. Instead, local consumers, particularly young people, largely sustain them. In most places they have competed successfully against local businesses—with clear implications for the range of restaurant options available in those places. Moreover, they have introduced a fairly standardized fare—albeit with some variations to reflect local tastes (beer in German establishments, warm goat cheese sandwiches in French establishments, lamb hamburgers in India, etc.). Beyond the impacts this may have on dietary preferences, there are social impacts as well. Many of these places become "hang-outs" where young people meet and talk and where parents bring their children for birthday parties—thus even changing the way that some people observe celebrations. Invariably, too, they alter the character of the cultural landscape as well.

The foregoing example shows the depth of the links between economic and cultural globalization. Among the most far-reaching consequences of this link is the tendency for a growing number of things to be thought of, and treated as, commodities to be exchanged for money. This process, sometimes termed ***commodification***, involves taking something (a good, an idea, even a person) that previously was not regarded as an object to be bought and sold, and turning it into something that has a particular price and that can be traded in a market economy. In its simplest form, this can occur when family farmers in a peasant society begin producing food for sale, rather than for self-consumption, gift giving, or nonmarket exchange. In this case, the food has gone through a process of commodification. But ideas can be commodified as well. Many societies have no tradition of treating an idea about how to create a new tool as something to be bought and sold. When such ideas come to be seen as items with monetary value, however, they too can be said to be commodified. The concept even extends to individuals themselves when, for example, they start working in someone's field as agricultural laborers for a wage rather than simply growing crops for the household. An extreme case of the commodification of individuals would be something like prostitution—which involves the commodification of women's bodies.

The geographic point of all this is that the development of an increasingly globalized market-based economy, with its expanding reach into places all over the globe, has promoted the commodification process—with

Figure 29-1 Skyscrapers around the World. This map shows the countries and cities with the world's tallest buildings, as compiled by the Council on Tall Buildings and Urban Habitat at Lehigh University. *Source:* Zaknic, I., M. Smith, and D. Rice. *100 of the World's Tallest Buildings.* Mulgrave, Australia: Images Publishing, 1998, and updates at http://www.lehigh.edu/~inctbuh.

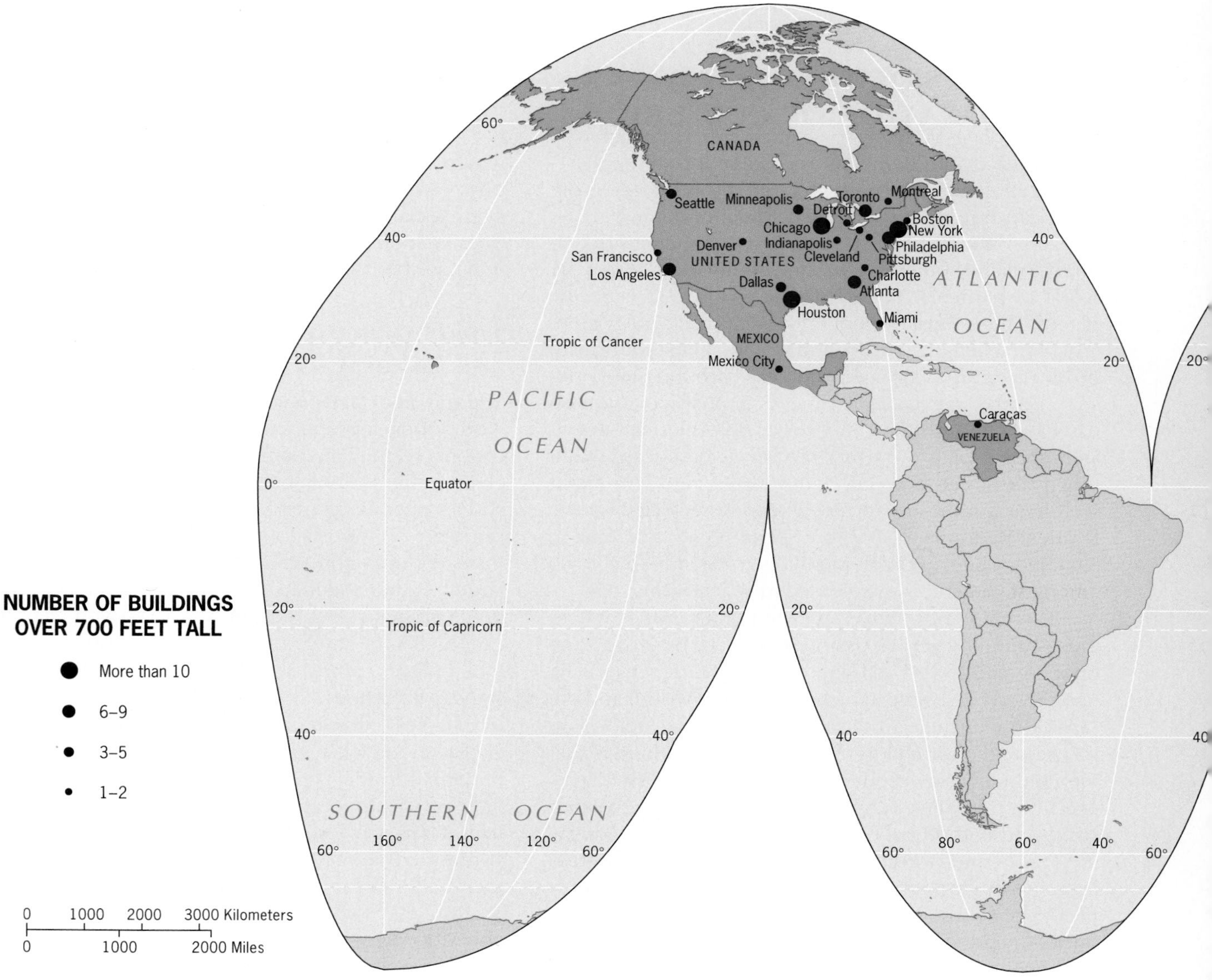

important economic, social, *and* cultural consequences. On the explicitly cultural side, those consequences can range from changes in the ways people view their environment to adjustments in values and preferences. The desire, for example, to acquire blue jeans and T-shirts is now something found all over the world; it is thus a clear consequence of the intersection between culture and economy in an era of globalization. Even cultural traditions of celebration are becoming globalized. In just the past few years, the once distinctly North American way of celebrating All Saints Day, Halloween, has diffused to various parts of the world—particularly Western Europe. Fueled by entrepreneurs looking for new markets for the costumes, masks, candy, cards, and other items associated with the holiday, Halloween has not simply changed the mix of products available in European stores in late October; it is increasingly becoming a part of the celebratory tradition in parts of Western Europe.

The Evolving Cultural Landscape

The most concrete expression of the homogenizing tendency of cultural globalization can be found in the cultural landscape. As we saw in the previous chapter, a certain landscape convergence has occurred in, for example, the commercial centers of large cities around the world. This convergence has three dimensions. First, there are particular architectural forms and planning ideas that have diffused around the world. Second, there are individual businesses and products that have become so widespread that they now leave a distinctive landscape stamp on far-flung places. Third, there is wholesale borrowing of idealized landscape images that, while not necessarily fostering convergence, at least promote a blurring of place distinctiveness.

The global diffusion of the skyscraper provides a clear illustration of the first point (Fig. 29–1). From Singa-

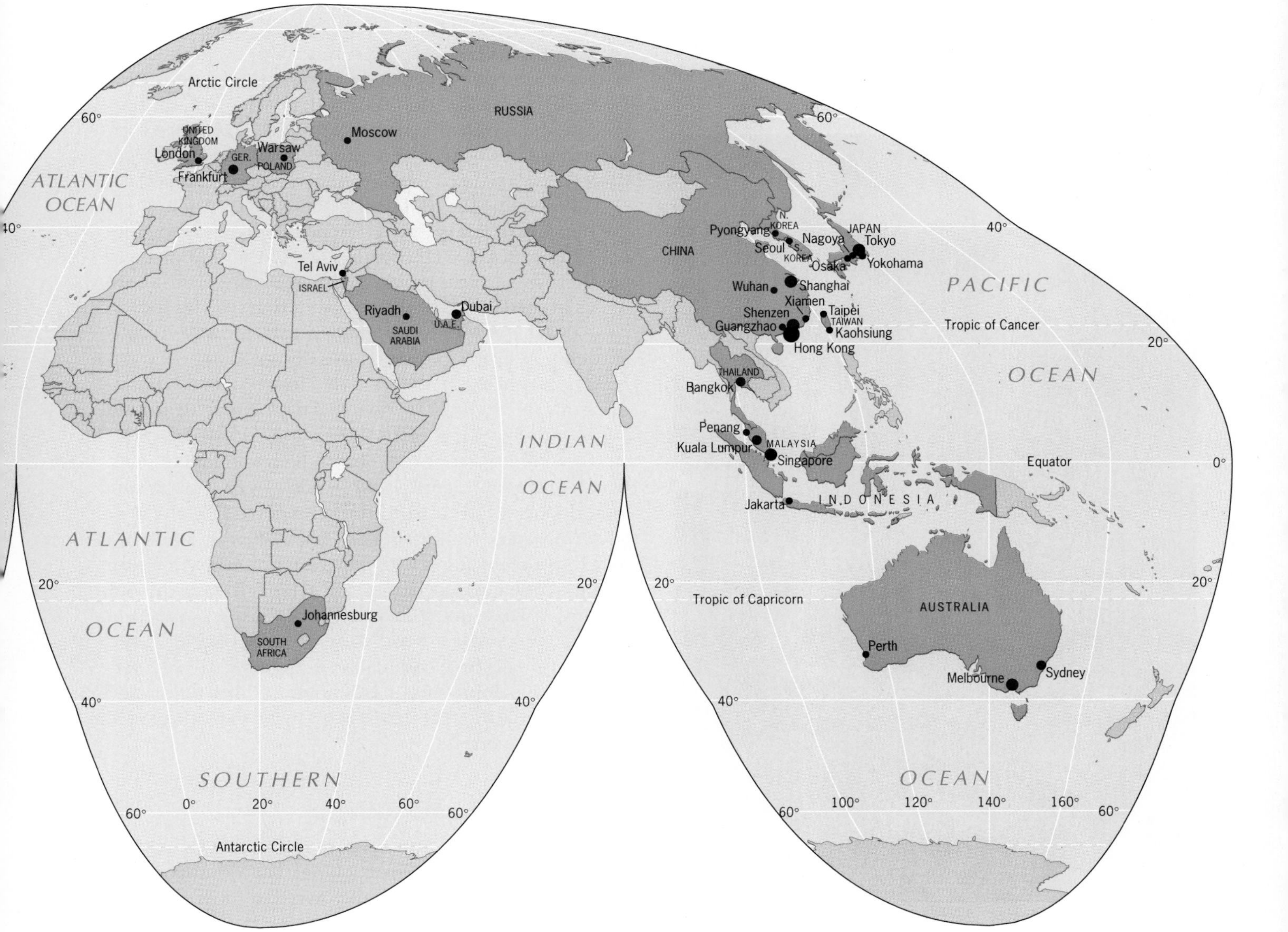

pore to Johannesburg and Caracas to Toronto, the commercial centers of major cities are dominated by tall buildings, many of which have been designed by the same architects and engineering firms. Moreover, the functional requirements of these "cities within cities" have impacts beyond the immediate buildings themselves. They are often associated with substantial land clearing in the vicinity of individual buildings, the construction of wide, straight streets to promote access, and the reworking of transportation systems around a highly centralized model. Skyscrapers are only one example of the globalization of a particular landscape form. Marked landscape similarities can be found in everything from international airports to shopping centers. Indeed, it is not unusual for the same group of planners to be involved in the construction of such facilities in places separated by many thousands of miles.

From the field notes

"A little bit of New York in Vegas. As I walked down the famous strip, icons from the corners of the Earth greeted me. What a juxtaposition: the New York skyline, the Paris Opera, and an Egyptian pyramid all within a few blocks of one another—sitting in the Nevada desert. It's a blatant, caricatured example of a widespread contemporary process: the borrowing of landscape elements from one place to give character to another. At least there is no pretending here—unlike some suburbs in the American Southwest where residents seem motivated in an almost unconscious way to recreate New England in the desert."

The McDonald's example described earlier illustrates the impact that individual businesses can have on widely dispersed places—and of course landscape change is among the more important of those influences. Whether one is sitting in the square in front of the cathedral in Cologne, taking in the sites of the Ginza in Tokyo, or strolling along the beaches of Rio de Janeiro, McDonald's is an unmistakable part of the cultural landscape. Compromises are often made; McDonald's had to reduce the size and prominence of its signature golden arches before the French authorities would permit the company to open a store along the prestigious Champs d'Elysée in Paris in the 1970s. But large fast-food chains, transnational retail outlets, car companies, and even large financial institutions have left a common imprint on the landscapes of very different places. Moreover, advertisements for these businesses, and the products they sell, furthers that imprint. From Moscow to New Delhi to Mexico City, the images of Coca-Cola, Kentucky Fried Chicken, Hard Rock Cafés, and Marlboro cigarettes are hard to miss.

Completing the triumvirate of factors contributing to the blurring of landscape differences is the growing tendency to transpose landscape ideals from one place to another—regardless of whether there is any tie to those ideals in the culture of the recipient region. The strip in Las Vegas, Nevada, represents an extreme case of this tendency, with various structures designed to evoke different parts of the planet. Yet in a less obvious way, indiscriminate cultural borrowing is happening all around the world. Shopping malls are built in North American cities with a (supposed) Latin flair—complete with plazas and roaming mariachi bands—even though one would be hard pressed to find any place in Central or South America with a similar look. Cities in Southeast Asia have set up alleys with little restaurants that evoke a (highly caricaturized) image of a French café district. Moving down a notch in scale, suburbs are planned in the American desert Southwest to model an idealized image of small-town colonial New England. These ***post-modern*** developments (see Chapter 21) both reflect and shape the culture of places in ways that can work against local distinctiveness.

The Changing Meaning of "Local"

As we have seen, the impacts of globalization on cultural change are many and far-reaching. The homogenizing impacts of all of this are highly variable, however, and

From the field notes

"Walking through central Vienna I marveled at the elaborate detail of the neoclassical architecture. But what once was distinctly Viennese is now punctuated by the symbols of modern economic internationalism. Häagen-Dazs is an American company that traces its roots to a vendor who sold ice cream from a horse-drawn wagon in the Bronx. According to the company website, the Häagen-Dazs name was chosen 'to convey an aura of the old-world traditions and craftsmanship to which he (the founder) remained dedicated.' And now that name decorates—and in some respects defiles—the heart of one of Europe's most extraordinary cities."

even where they are strong we cannot speak of cultural convergence in any meaningful sense. Aside from the reactions that homogenization produces, the same cultural form or process will not have the same impact in different places because the culture of those places differs to begin with. This, in turn, means that the understanding of, and reactions to, seemingly uniform cultural products will differ from place to place. Hence, we are looking at processes that can erode distinctiveness and can even threaten the survival of particular cultural forms and practices, but they are certainly not bringing us rapidly toward a mono-cultural world. By extension, the concept of local differences is still both meaningful and important.

Yet the trends described here also point to the importance of understanding the world as something more than a mosaic of individual places with distinctive characteristics. This, indeed, is a fundamental limitation of the popular conception of geography as a discipline concerned with identifying "place facts." Individual places are not worlds unto themselves; they exist in relationship to events and processes that unfold at larger scales. As many of the foregoing examples show, developments coming from individual places influence larger-scale processes, and those processes in turn shape the social and landscape character of individual places. As such, understanding what is happening in different locales requires looking at the intersection between particular place characteristics and the larger regional and even global forces with which they are in constant, dynamic interaction.

This idea is behind the concept of the ***global-local continuum***. This notion emphasizes that what happens at one scale is not independent of what happens at other scales. Following this line of reasoning, we see that human geography is not simply about documenting the differences between places. It is also about understanding the processes unfolding at different scales that produce those differences. This means recognizing that "the local" is rarely truly local. Yet it also means seeing individual places not simply as the product of larger-scale processes. The character of place—and hence of the Earth's surface—ultimately comes out of a dynamic interaction between local distinctiveness and larger-scale events and influences.

◆ REACTIONS TO CULTURAL GLOBALIZATION

Consider the following diverse set of developments. When the Taliban controlled much of present-day Afghanistan, it engaged in an active effort to shut off the country's people from the wider world. People from all over the world are flocking to Disneyland Paris in record numbers—fueling a recent expansion of the amusement park. Protestors are converging on meetings of the World Trade Organization, demonstrating not just against the environmental and economic impacts of free trade, but against their cultural impacts as well. International educational exchange is growing by leaps and bounds, with more and more students going to foreign countries for extended periods of study. Substantial numbers of voters are favoring candidates for election with strong anti-immigration views in Belgium, Austria, and Italy—even as these countries have adopted a common currency.

Each of these developments is in some way tied to the link between globalization and culture. When considered together, they highlight the remarkable diversity and complexity of reactions that link is producing. Cultural globalization is both rejected and embraced. Some people look for ways to exploit it to maximum advantage, whereas others erect barriers to its advancement. Many adopt a stance somewhere between these extremes—looking for ways to buy into globalization selectively without entirely subverting traditional practices. From a geographical perspective, the important point is that the range of reactions—often working together in the same place—is shaping the character of places and landscapes.

At the heart of the reaction to cultural globalization is a tension that juxtaposes the appeal/irresistibility of external ideas and innovations against concerns over the loss of local distinctiveness and identity. It is easy to understand the allure of external cultural forms and processes. They can broaden horizons, offer new experiences, and provide possibilities for economic and social advancement. They can also be irresistible—not simply in the sense of people not wanting to resist them, but of people not being in a position where they can resist them. Returning to the example of trekkers in Nepal, we find that the economic and cultural adjustments of the Nepalese to the surge of foreign trekkers are as much a product of people being forced to adjust to changed circumstances associated with, for example, deforestation, as they are with any desire to embrace external cultural-economic norms. Frequently, some combination of desire and necessity is at play, as when Native peoples in the United States establish gambling casinos that provide a means of meeting basic needs while also offering intercultural connections and luxury goods that are appealing to many. Not surprisingly, internal disagreement about what to do in these circumstances is not uncommon.

From the field notes

"Take away the sign in French, and I could have been walking past a Halloween display in Philadelphia, Chicago, or San Francisco. But this was Brussels, Belgium, and the signs of Halloween were everywhere. When I lived in this city in the mid-1980s, Halloween was a foreign concept. Now it is an increasingly visible part of the fall social—and economic—calendar."

Concerns over the Loss of Local Distinctiveness

It is the very appeal of external cultural forms that promotes concerns about their implications for local distinctiveness and identity. Human beings define themselves in significant part by the communities and places to which they feel a sense of attachment or belonging, and cultural globalization can often represent a threat to those feelings. It can represent a challenge to the cultural forms and behaviors that have a high degree of symbolic importance in societies, and it can undermine the position of the institutions and individuals tied to those cultural forms and behaviors. At times this might seem like a good thing, as when it undermines institutions that have supported oppressive or despotic political regimes. Yet it can also disrupt long-standing traditions, promote behaviors that accelerate human alteration of the environment, and threaten the richness of a region's cultural diversity.

Concern over the loss of local distinctiveness and identity is not limited to particular cultural or socioeconomic settings. We find such concern among the dominant societies of the global economic core, where it is reflected in everything from the rise of religious fundamentalism to the establishment of semi-autonomous communes in remote locations. We find this concern among minorities (and their supporters) in the global economic core, where it can be seen in efforts to promote local languages, religions, and customs by constructing barriers to the influx of cultural influences from the dominant society. We find it among political elites in the global economic periphery seeking to promote a nationalist ideology that is explicitly opposed to cultural globalization. And we find it among social and ethnic minorities in the global economic periphery who seek greater autonomy from regimes promoting acculturation or assimilation to a single national cultural norm.

The motivations behind resistance are equally wide ranging. The stated motive of those supporting limitations on free trade and a variety of ethnic autonomy movements is the preservation of democracy, the environment, and human rights. The desire to maintain power and social position in the face of external influences is a motivating factor in, for example, attacks on foreigners in Germany and the pursuit of isolationist policies by the regime ruling North Korea. Apprehension or fear of the unknown can be a motive in everything from the Burmese government's effort to exclude large numbers of foreigners from entering the country to the efforts of fundamentalist religious leaders to ban the books, films, and music produced by others. And some combination of active dislike of particular cultural influences and cultural/national pride is at work in, for example, the official resistance mounted by a variety of governmental authorities to the influence of American cultural products and language.

Impacts of Resistance

Even though forms of resistance to the globalization of culture are widespread and often vehement, their success is tempered by the power and allure of cultural globalization itself. As a result, resistance has been truly successful in relatively few instances—at least as measured by the stated objectives of those who are mounting the resistance. Minority groups seeking to distance themselves from *exogenous* cultural influences have had only modest success in achieving a degree of autonomy. Anti-immigration initiatives have rarely stemmed the flow of migrants for long, and the music, dress, and language emanating from centers of popular culture innovation have diffused widely despite efforts to limit their impact. Even in cases where political regimes actively seek to isolate countries from external cultural influences, pressures tend to mount against isolationism over time. Such pressures are very much at play today in countries such as Iran, China, Burma (Myanmar), and Albania.

Despite the limited impacts of resistance, cultural globalization is not proceeding unchecked because, as we have seen, globalizing influences become geographically differentiated as they encounter differences from place to place. Moreover, much of that encounter does not juxtapose active proponents and vehement opposers of cultural globalization. Instead, it involves people simply trying to lead their lives in a rapidly changing cultural milieu. These people are adapting to external cultural norms as needed or are required to go about their lives, but they do so against the backdrop of preexisting cultural ideas and practices. The result is a kind of ***syncretism*** in which elements from different cultural sources are combined in novel ways to create something new. The term *syncretism,* originally developed in anthropology, is increasingly used by cultural geographers to denote the hybrid cultural characteristics and landscapes that define most places today. It is important to remember that some degree of ***hybridity*** has characterized most cultures and landscapes throughout human history. Yet the scope and scale of hybridity has greatly expanded in recent decades, and the rapidity of change has accelerated substantially.

What all of this has produced is an extraordinary intermixing of cultural elements from all over the world that becomes manifest in individual places. On a street corner in Paris, France, you can find a restaurant serving a mixture of French and American dishes named after a prominent figure of the American West—with a huge advertisement looming over it promoting a Korean-made cellular telephone to facilitate communication to far-flung places. In a farmer's field on the outskirts of Cairo, Egypt, you can find traditional agricultural tools leaning up against a house with a European design. On the streets of a village in Malawi without electricity or running water, you can hear the strains of Michael Jackson or Madonna coming from battery-powered cassette disks being played inside houses. On a back street of a poor neighborhood in Skopje, Macedonia, you can find little boys playing basketball using a beaten-up backboard displaying a faded Nike "swoosh."

Which brings us back to Michael Jordan. The fact that one American basketball star can become the most recognized person on Earth tells us something about the spatial sweep of globalization, the cultural influence of particular regions, and the variable impacts of globalization. Studying the geographical character of cultural globalization shows us that many places are undergoing rapid change. Yet it also demonstrates that, from place to place, those changes are neither of the same intensity nor the same kind. Unraveling the nature and diversity of those changes is a fundamental geographic challenge that can offer critical insights into where places have come from and where they are going.

From the field notes

"Walking through a relatively poor neighborhood in Skopje (Macedonia) with the midday Muslim "call to prayer" ringing in my ears, the last thing I expected to see was something from my home State. But here it was—the unmistakable Nike "swoosh" on a backboard where the local kids play pick-up games of basketball. Economic and cultural globalization is not just about downtowns and big stores; it finds its way into many of the world's nooks and crannies."

KEY TERMS

commodification
folk culture
global-local continuum
hybridity
popular culture
postmodern
syncretism

APPLYING GEOGRAPHIC KNOWLEDGE

1. You are asked to develop a plan and pick sites for six new outlets for an American fast-food chain in Paris, France. Make a list of five key factors you will want to consider if you want to minimize negative cultural reactions to the new outlets. Provide a brief explanation of each factor you identify.
2. Identify a good example of what you consider to be a folk culture. In what ways has that culture been affected by the globalization of culture? To what extent is it still useful to think of that culture as a folk culture?
3. Look under "restaurants" in the Yellow Pages of the local telephone book and make a list of each of the restaurants offering foreign cuisines. Which types of cuisine are most represented? Is there a correspondence between the most widely available "foreign" restaurants and the source-country of migrants who have moved to your community? If not, why not?

Part Nine
FROM DEINDUSTRIALIZATION TO GLOBALIZATION

At Issue: Revisited

As we enter an age of unprecedented global interaction, can interdependence be made to work in the interests of human economic, social, and political betterment? Interdependence can bring with it many positives, but there is no law that guarantees this outcome. Making interdependence work in the interests of humanity requires recognizing that more interaction is not always better interaction—and that people, cultures, and the environment can be hurt in the process. The scale of our political institutions has not caught up with the scale of our interactions, making it difficult to harness interdependence for the good of the greatest number of people. If we are to rise to the challenges that are posed by interdependence, expanding links between people, economies, and cultures will have to be matched by institutions and policies with a corresponding geographical reach.

SELECTED BIBILIOGRAPHY

Part Nine From Deindustrialization to Globalization

Awotona, A., ed. *Housing Provision and Bottom-Up Approaches* (Burlington, Vt.: Ashgate, 1999).

Blakeley, E. J., & Stimson, R. J., eds. *New Cities of the Pacific Rim,* Monograph 43 (Berkeley: University of California, Institute of Urban and Regional Development, 1992).

Brown, L. R., et al. *State of the World 2001* (New York: W. W. Norton, 2001).

Castells, M. *The Power of Identity.* 3 vols. Vol. II, *The Information Age: Economy, Society and Culture* (Malden, MA: Blackwell, 1997).

Castells, M. *The Rise of the Network Society* (Oxford: Blackwell Publishers, 1996).

Castells, Manuel; Hall, Peter; Hutriyk, John. "Technopoles of the World: The Making of 21st Century Industrial Complexes" *The Sociological Review* 43, no. 4: 895–900.

Castles, S. "Globalization and Migration: Some Pressing Contradictions." *International Social Science Journal* 156 (1998): 179–199.

de Blij, H. J. *Mombasa: An African City* (Evanston, Ill.: Northwestern University Press, 1968).

Domosh, M. "Cultural Patterns and Processes in Advanced Placement Human Geography." *Journal of Geography* 99, no. 3/4 (2000): 111–119.

Duncan, J. S., and Ley, D. *Place/Culture/Representation* (London and New York: Routledge, 1993).

Featherstone, M. "Global Culture: An Introduction," in Mike Featherstone, ed., *Global Culture: Nationalism, Globalization and Modernity,* 1–14 (London, Newbury Park: Sage in association with *Theory, Culture & Society,* 1990).

Friedmann, J. "The World City Hypothesis." *Development & Change* 17 (1986): 69–83.

Glasmeier, A. K., & Howland, M. *From Combines to Computers: Rural Services in the Age of Information Technology* (Albany: State University of New York Press, 1995).

Graham, S., & Marvin, S. *Splintering Urbanism* (New York: Routledge, 2001).

Grant, R., & Nijman, J. "The Corporate Geography of Cities in the Less Developed World." *Annals of the Association of American Geographers* 92, no. 2 (June 2002).

Harvey, D. *The Condition of Postmodernity: An Enquiry into the Origins of Cultural Change* (Cambridge, Mass.: Blackwell, 1989).

Herb, G., and Kaplan. D. *Nested Identities: Nationalism, Territory, and Scale* (Lanham, Md.: Rowman & Littlefield Publishers, 1999).

Ioannides, D. and Debbage, K., eds. *The Economic Geography of the Tourist Industry: A Supply-Side Analysis* (London and New York: Routledge, 1998).

Jackson, P. *Maps of Meaning: An Introduction to Cultural Geography* (London and New York: Routledge, 1994).

Jameson, F., and Miyoshi, M., eds. *The Cultures of Globalization, Post-Contemporary Interventions* (Durham, N.C.: Duke University Press, 1998).

Johnson, J. H., ed. *Suburban Growth: Geographical Perspectives at the Edge of the Western City* (London and New York: John Wiley & Sons, 1974).

Johnston, R. J., et al. eds. *Geographies of Global Change* (Oxford: Blackwell, 1995).

Kelly, P. *Landscapes of Globalization* (New York: Routledge, 2000).

Kiely, R., and Marfleet, P. *Globalisation and the Third World* (New York: Routledge, 1998).

King, A. D. *Culture, Globalization, and the World-System: Contemporary Conditions for the Representation of Identity.* [Rev.] ed. (Minneapolis: University of Minnesota Press, 1997).

King, R., et al. *Writing across Worlds: Literature and Migration* (London and New York: Routledge, 1995).

Knight, D. B. "People Together, Yet Apart: Rethinking Territory, Sovereignty, and Identities," in George J. Demko and William B. Wood, eds., *Reordering the World: Geopolitical Perspectives on the Twenty-First Century,* 200–225. (Boulder, Colo.: Westview Press, 1999).

Knox, P., & Taylor, P. J., eds. *World Cities in a World-System* (Cambridge, U.K.: Cambridge University Press, 1995).

Kotler, P., et al. *Marketing Places: Attracting Investment, Industry, and Tourism to Cities, States, and Nations* (New York: Free Press, 1993).

Massey, D. B. *Space, Place, and Gender* (Minneapolis: University of Minnesota Press, 1994).

Muller, P. O. "The Suburban Transformation of the Globalizing American City." *Annals of the American Academy of Political and Social Science* 551 (May 1997): 44–58.

Muller, P. O. *Contemporary Suburban America* (Englewood Cliffs, N.J.: Prentice-Hall, 1981).

O'Brien, R. *Global Financial Integration: The End of Geography* (New York: Council on Foreign Relations Press, 1992).

Pacione, M. *Urban Geography* (New York: Routledge, 2001).

Sassen, S. *Losing Control?: Sovereignty in an Age of Globalization, University Seminars/Leonard Hastings Schoff Memorial Lectures* (New York: Columbia University Press, 1996).

Smith, A. D. *Nations and Nationalism in a Global Era* (Cambridge, Mass.: Polity Press, 1995).

Storey, J. *Cultural Studies & the Study of Popular Culture* (Athens: University of Georgia, 1996).

Timmons Roberts, J., & Hite, A. *From Modernization to Globalization* (Oxford: Blackwell, 2000).

Toffler, A. *Future Shock* (New York: Random House, 1970).

Wallerstein, I. M. *Geopolitics and Geoculture: Essays on the Changing World-System* (Cambridge, England: Cambridge University Press, Editions de la Maison des Sciences de l'Homme, 1991).

Waters, M. *Globalization, Key Ideas* (London and New York: Routledge, 1995).

Part Ten

SOCIAL GEOGRAPHIES OF THE MODERN WORLD

At Issue

Ours is a world divided by differences in people's health and well-being, as well as by race, ethnicity, and gender. We are all too familiar with large-scale economic differences, which profoundly influence patterns of food consumption and access to health care. Yet the social divisions created by societies also affect the lives and livelihoods of the world's peoples. Some groups have used differences in physical appearance to justify discrimination and even murder.

Ethnic conflicts have caused enormous loss of life in recent decades. Gender-based inequalities are evident not just in the economic and social constraints still present for women in our own society; in some places they even result in female infanticide and the merciless exploitation of girls. *Can the smaller world created by transport, information, and communication technologies help overcome some of these divisions?*

Will her life change for the better? Saigon, Vietnam

Part Outline

Chapter 30

Global Disparities in Nutrition and Health

From the field notes

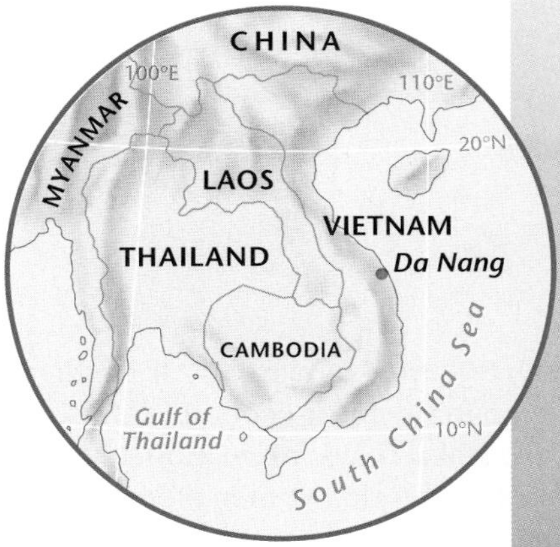

"AIDS may have originated in Africa, but today this disease is a worldwide threat. Countries in the global economic periphery do not have adequate resources to cope with it, but wherever you go, posters and billboards warn people of the risk of exposure. I saw this one on the heavily traveled road from Da Nang to Hue in Vietnam—near a beach where an international corporation is building a large resort. Obviously the lesson of Thailand has been learned here."

KEY POINTS

◆ **Daily calorie consumption varies from high levels in the richer countries such as the United States and Canada, European states, Japan, and Australia to very low levels in poorer countries in Africa.**

◆ **Although global food production is sufficient to feed the world's people (if it were evenly distributed), concerns are rising that a food emergency may develop as a result of population growth, rapid urbanization, climate change, and energy costs.**

◆ **The mitigation of a future food crisis depends on policies and practices ranging from family planning and women's rights to improvement of distribution systems and expansion of farmlands.**

◆ **Average life expectancy maps conceal the greater life expectancies of women virtually everywhere, but they do underscore the aging of many populations.**

◆ **Tropical areas are zones of intense biological activity and hence are the sources of many disease-transmitting viruses and parasites.**

◆ **Certain major diseases remain contained within tropical or near-tropical latitudes, but others have spread into all parts of the world; AIDS originated in tropical Africa and is now a global pandemic.**

◆ **Densely populated urban shantytowns with inadequate sanitation and contaminated water supplies are highly susceptible to outbreaks of disease; the South American cholera epidemic of the 1990s began in the slums of Lima, Peru.**

◆ **Despite the worldwide attention focused on AIDS, the leading killers in the Western world are the chronic diseases, including heart disease, cancer, and strokes.**

Much as we hear and read these days about growing globalization, the emergence of a global economy, the shrinking of our world into a "global village," and the homogenization of culture, the reality for billions of people on this planet is quite different. Hundreds of millions of people (estimates range from 780 million to 1.2 billion, mostly youngsters) do not get enough to eat or have seriously imbalanced diets. An even larger number do not have access to adequate medical care. While life expectancies in the rich countries approach 80 years, in parts of Africa they are falling below 40. Even in the most economically developed countries, women still face discrimination. In the less developed regions of the world, women often confront far worse conditions. And ethnic minorities everywhere encounter racism, prejudice, and disadvantage. Ours is a world of inequality and disparity, of contrast and imbalance. In Part Ten we focus on geographic aspects of three particular forms of inequality: health and well-being, race, and gender. ◆

◆ MIRACLE OR DEBACLE?

In this first chapter we consider the question of health and well-being. As we have noted in earlier chapters, developments in genetic engineering of grain crops, including so-called ***miracle rice***, have increased staple-food production enormously and closed the gap between demand and supply. The ***Green Revolution***, part of the Third Agricultural Revolution in history, raised the prospect that famine and hunger would no longer threaten humanity, even during a time of still-rapid population growth. As we noted in Part Six, however, the Green Revolution is also yielding ethical problems. To whom does an "engineered" strain of highly productive wheat belong? Should a research firm be able to demand an annual payment from a farmer using seed it modified to produce a larger harvest?

Beyond such issues lies a practical one: how to ensure that the food produced reaches all those who need it. Divide annual global food production by the number of people alive today, and you can prove that there is enough to provide every human being with adequate nourishment, calculated in daily calories. And yet around one-sixth of the Earth's population is seriously malnourished. Three fundamental causes lie behind this picture: (1) the failure of distribution systems, (2) the inability of people to pay the cost, and (3) traditional cultural practices that favor males and disadvantage women and especially children.

Distribution systems fail for various reasons. Many countries lack transport networks that reach all people in need, especially where demand may suddenly rise because of environmental crises. Inept and rapacious governments sometimes obstruct the flow of food to ethnic groups they want to punish, thus using food as a weapon. They may even refuse emergency aid, as has recently been done by regimes in Sudan and North Korea, preferring millions to go hungry.

Where food does reach the needy, its price may be unaffordable. Hundreds of millions of people subsist on the equivalent of one dollar a day, and, as we saw in Chapter 28, many in the vast shantytowns encircling the world's megacities must pay rent to landlords who own the plots on which their dwellings are built. Too little is left for food, and it is the children who suffer most.

We might conclude that those remaining in the countryside, where the food is grown or raised, would be better off, but in fact the majority of the world's malnourished population live in rural areas. Village life in much of Africa and Asia is harsh and competitive. Farmers must sell more of their harvests than they should in order to make ends meet; too little is left over to feed every family member adequately and to diversify diets for better health. Males and male children fare much better in the allotment of calories than females and girls.

◆ NUTRITION AND DIET

A balanced diet includes carbohydrates (derived from staples such as rice, corn, wheat, and potatoes), proteins (from meat, poultry, fish, eggs, and dairy products), vitamins (from fruits and vegetables as well as other sources), fats, and minerals. Proteins are a critical element and may be derived from plant sources, including soybeans, peas, peanuts, and wheat as well as from meat and dairy products.

Food intake is measured in terms of calories, which are units of "fuel" for energy production in the body. Calorie requirements are not the same among the population. Males, for example, need more calories, on average, than females: young adults need more calories than children or old persons; larger people require more calories than smaller people.

Figure 30–1 reveals the wide range of ***caloric intake*** throughout the world. Various agencies monitor this index, but their categories differ, and, in recent years, the urgency of their reporting has diminished. As the map indicates, countries are usually grouped into four ranks ranging from high intake (usually over 3000 calories daily) to very low, or under 2000, but there is no agreement about adequacy. The World Bank regards 2500 calories as adequate, while the United Nations uses 2360 as its boundary between adequate and low intake. Such discrepancies (there are others when additional sources are consulted) should raise a caution when you consult Figure 30–1, which is based on the latest data available in early 2002. The map may effectively portray the global situation by country in general terms. What the map does *not* reflect is also important: there are nutritional disparities *within* countries that cannot be shown at this level of scale. For example, diets in western India are superior to those in eastern India; the intake in northern parts of Sudan is substantially higher than in its unstable south.

Another factor not shown on Figure 30–1 is ***dietary balance***. With few exceptions, the countries where caloric intake is low are also those where protein is in short supply. Recent studies have indicated that the first six months of life are critical in this respect: inadequate protein intake can damage brain and body for life. Moreover, the food sources that are richest in proteins—meat, fish, and dairy products—are in short supply where they are most needed. It takes food to raise the animals that produce meat, and that food cannot be spared to feed animals when it is needed to sustain the people themselves. And while fish may be obtainable in coastal areas, it becomes less available (and more expensive) in interior Africa and Asia. Thus even people whose caloric intake is marginally adequate may still be malnourished, and what is often called ***hidden hunger*** occurs even in areas mapped as having "adequate calories."

Figure 30–1 shows that the comparatively rich countries also are the best-fed and that Subsaharan Africa is currently in the worst position, with numerous countries in the lowest category. In Part Six we noted the still-limited impact of the Green Revolution in Africa; agricultural production in this realm has actually declined over the past two decades and continues to drop. A combination of circumstances causes this reduction in locally grown food, ranging from environmental crises to the failures of African governments and from the ravaging impact of diseases to the disadvantages faced by farmers in national and global economies. But with the exception of Subsaharan Africa, the overall situation reflected by the map is one of improvement as many countries (when they are not embroiled in conflict, misgoverned, or in the grip of environmental crisis as in Afghanistan,

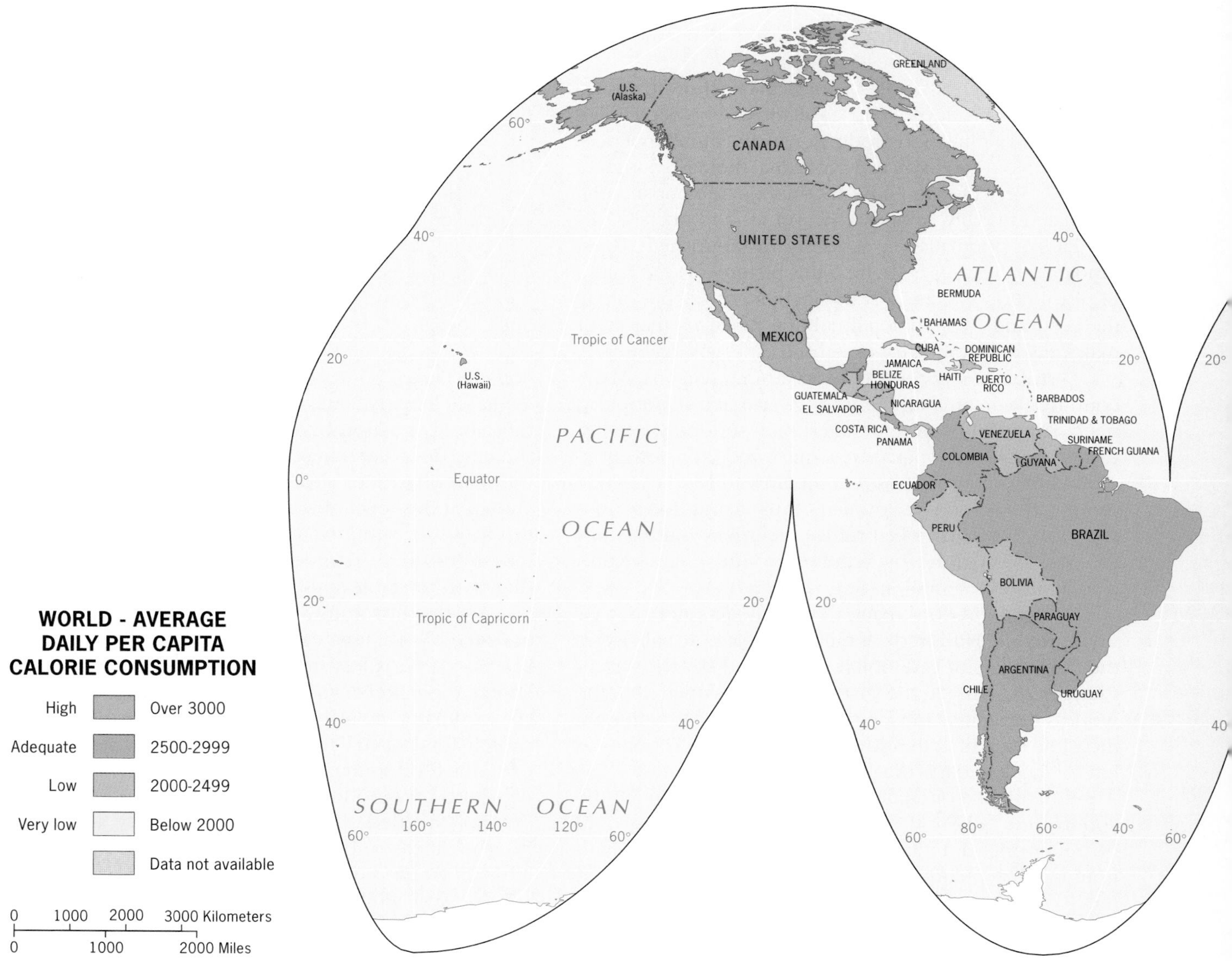

Figure 30-1 Average Daily per Capita Calorie Consumption, early-2000s. Data for several countries are not available. *Source:* FAO Food Balance Sheets, Britannica Book of the Year 2001.

North Korea, and Mongolia, respectively, in 2002) are better fed than they were in the 1970s and 1980s.

When we consider the data shown on Figure 30–1, however, we should not lose sight of a key but hidden factor: the disproportionately negative impact of malnourishment on children, especially in rural areas. When food supply in a village dwindles, the social order frequently falls apart and children are the first and most vulnerable victims. Protein deficiency in the first three years of life, when the brain grows to about 80 percent of its adult size, does permanent damage; both mental capacity and physical growth are impaired by inadequate nutrition. Infants born into an environment of deprivation face lifelong handicaps—if they survive the experience. As we noted in Part Two, maps showing high death rates in the poorer countries to a large extent reflect high infant and child mortality. Figure 30–1 provides one insight into the underlying causes.

◆ MITIGATING THE RISKS

Even at a time when the global food situation is relatively favorable, there is reason for concern about the future of the global food supply (see "Looking Ahead Box: Food in the Future"). Under the circumstances, national and international action should be taken to reduce the likeli-

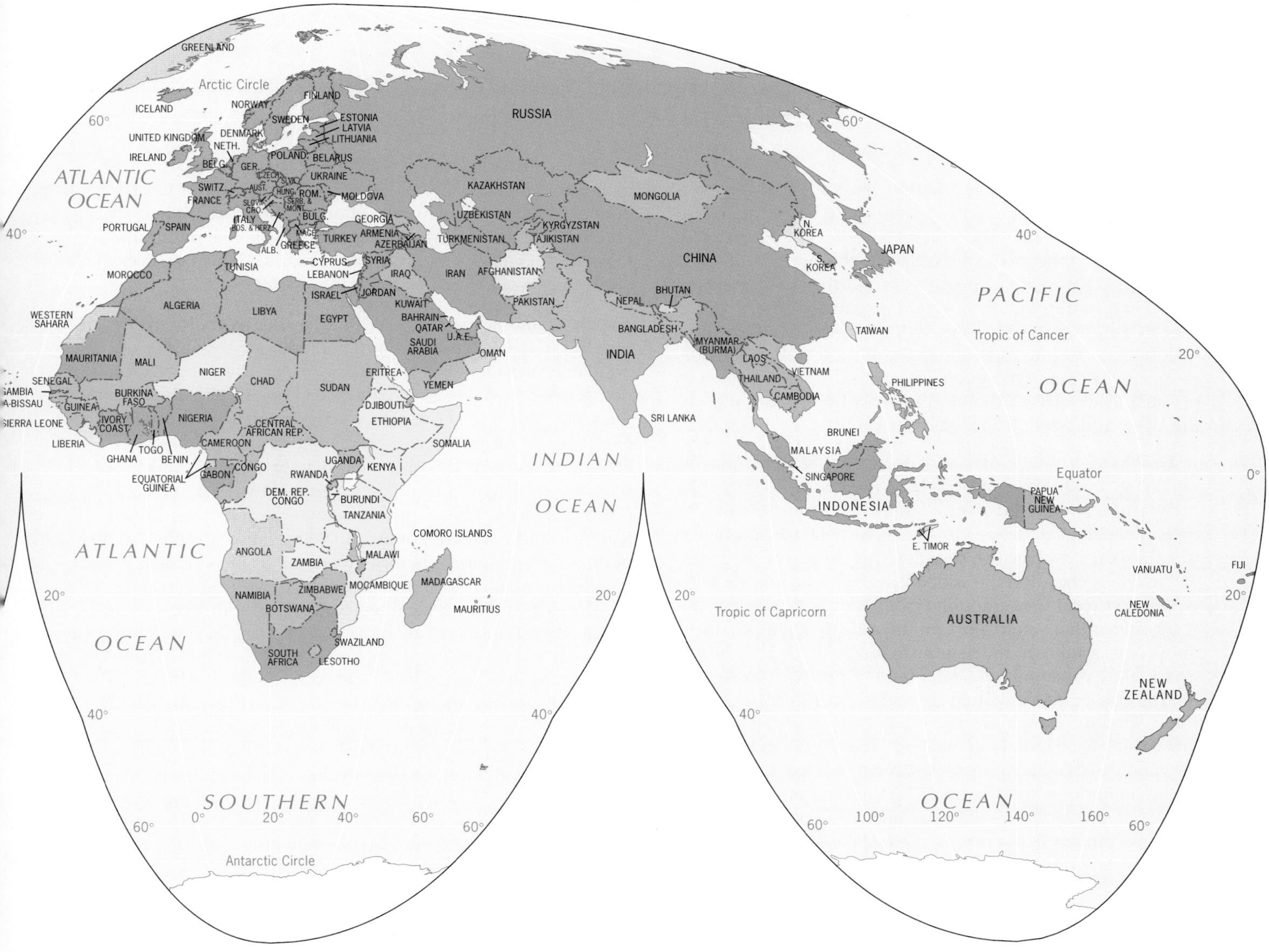

hood of a food crisis. Here are 10 arenas in which such action either is being taken or might be taken:

1. *Formulate Population Policies.* Today this goes beyond family planning; the aging or "graying" of populations in developed countries such as Germany and Japan poses challenges as well. For the time being, however, the greatest need for family-planning help is in the poorer countries.
2. *Sustain the Green Revolution.* Dramatic progress continues to be made, but opposition to "GM" (genetically modified) products is growing, in part because certain public figures, notably including Britain's Prince Charles, have joined the cause (see the discussion of this issue in Chapter 20).
3. *Expand Farmlands.* Some experts calculate that the amount of land presently under cultivation could be greatly expanded, even doubled, through heavy investments in organic and inorganic fertilizers that would virtually reconstitute infertile soils. Studies proposing such action tend, however, to give insufficient attention to water needs and to the dangers of deforestation and loss of biodiversity.
4. *Stimulate Local Production.* A surprisingly large percentage of farm produce comes from small gardens and tiny plots cultivated with great care by people who often use household waste and compost to improve their patch of soil and who know just what to plant on it. These initiatives should be supported wherever possible.

Looking Ahead

Food in the Future

"The world's food production," states the World Bank's *World Development Indicators 2000,* "has outpaced its population growth, except in Subsaharan Africa." So is the world safe from famine and food emergencies for the foreseeable future? Geographers who specialize in this area are divided on the question. With the prospect of a further and significant slowdown in the growth of world population, there would seem to be grounds for optimism. But even today, as many as one billion people and perhaps more are not adequately nourished. Pessimists argue that it would not take much to create a food crisis of the kind forecast by the naysayers of the 1950s and 1960s. Where do the risks lie?

Population Change. The rate of population increase may be declining, but in the first decade of the twenty-first century the world is still adding over 70 million people annually. As long as nothing interferes with the growth of farm production recorded over the past two decades, this alone will not generate an emergency. But the added factor of rapid urbanization is creating food-consumption habits that will increase demand more than mere population growth would. It takes about twelve times as much grain to feed a single head of cattle for meat consumption as it would to provide the equivalent nourishment directly in just the form of bread or porridge. Already today only about half of all the staple grains grown are food grains consumed directly by people; the other half are feed grains to raise livetock for meat. Once part of the hamburger culture, consumers rarely return to leaner diets. Satisfying this growing demand (in which Western countries already lead the world) entails risks for the future.

Climate Change. As we learn more about the rapid, even vicious swings of climate during the Little Ice Age, it is becoming clear that climate change also constitutes a risk factor. If the predictions of some physical geographers are correct, the primary environmental problem of the first quarter of the twenty-first century may not be drought but, rather, wide fluctuations in weather conditions that may bring storms, floods, freezes, heat waves, and other extremes capable of destroying crops and farm lands. These extremes may be related to the warming trend that led climatologists to believe that human activity was raising global temperatures. There are signs that nature itself is getting ready for one of its cyclic changes. If so, sustaining food production, let alone increasing it as required, may become more difficult.

Water Supply. Water is a renewable resource, but there are limits on its availability. Farmers are prodigious users of water, diverting streams and drilling wells to irrigate their crops. But rivers are drying up, water tables are falling, and per-capita water use keeps rising. It is a formula for future trouble.

Energy Costs. Concern is also rising over the possibility that the cost of energy will rise again, as it did during the last major food crisis. When energy costs rise, so does the cost of fertilizers. Farmers also need to be able to buy fuel to run irrigation pumps and other equipment. The impact of the last energy crisis has faded from memory; in the United States it is remembered mainly as a shortage at the gasoline pump. But for farmers in many other countries a renewed increase in energy prices would be disastrous.

Failure of Alternative Sources. Still another worry for the future lies in the apparent failure of alternative sources as dependable providers of calories and dietary balance. As the demand for food has grown and technologies have become more efficient, one of the planet's last bounties—fish, a valuable source of protein—is declining rapidly. From mid-century to the late 1980s, the fish harvest from oceans and seas increased fivefold, and there seemed to be no limit to it. Nations quarreled over fishing rights, poor nations leased fishing grounds to richer ones, and fleets of trawlers plied the oceans. International attempts to regulate these industries failed. Meanwhile, there were signals that overfishing was destroying fish stocks. Several regional fishing industries, such as the cod fisheries on Canada's Grand Banks off Newfoundland, collapsed. In 1975 biologists estimated the Atlantic bluefin tuna population at 250,000; today there may be about 20,000 left, and the species may be placed on the endangered species list. From ocean perch and king crabs off Alaska to rock lobsters and roughies off New Zealand, fish and shellfish populations are depleted. The total annual catch is also declining and may already be beyond the point of recovery. Now much of the damage has been done, and fishing industries in many parts of the world report dwindling harvests and missing species.

Persistence of Colonial Systems. Yet another concern lies in the persistence of colonial systems (sometimes called neocolonialism) in countries that gained independence from imperial powers. Trapped in a world economic order they cannot change, they have maintained the cash-crop estates and plantations of the colonial period. There, often on the country's best soils, crops are produced to be sold on foreign markets. Senegal's peanuts, Angola's coffee, Zimbabwe's tobacco, Kenya's tea, and Sudan's cotton still flow to those markets, even while food production is inadequate to feed those countries' own populations. In any future global food crisis, the failure to restructure production in such areas will have serious consequences.

Loss of Farmland. In Chapter 28 we discussed the impact on farmland of expanding and suburbanizing cities—not only in the wealthiest countries but also in the poorer ones, where urbanization is speeding up. Although this loss seems small in statistical terms, much of the lost acreage consists of the best, most fertile soils. Many cities were originally established amid productive farmlands that could supply the needs of their inhabitants. Now they are absorbing those farmlands as they expand. The American Farmland Trust, for example, reported in 1993 that twelve U.S. areas are severely affected, including California's Central Valley, South Florida, California's coastal zone, North Carolina's Piedmont, and the Chicago-Milwaukee-Madison triangle in Illinois-Wisconsin. These twelve areas represent only 5 percent of U.S. farmland, but they produce 17 percent of total agricultural sales, 67 percent of all fruit, 55 percent of all vegetables, and one-quarter of all dairy products. Figures for other countries in the richer parts of the world (such as Japan) as well as for poorer countries (such as Egypt) prove that this is a global problem with serious implications for the future.

Changing Food Preferences. As demand for beef, pork, and chicken rises in cities and towns of the developing world, and more grain is being used to raise livestock rather than to feed people, food producers will be hard pressed to satisfy the wants of the world's urbanizing population. In China alone, tens of millions of new city-dwellers are altering the country's needs, and it has been suggested that Chinese (and other) urban consumers may insist on their food options in the same way American consumers insist on cheap energy, forcing the Chinese government to intervene to ensure continued supply in case of global shortages. In any case, the structure of food consumption continues to change worldwide, and this may be the greatest risk of all.

5. *Encourage Land Reform.* Farmers who own their land tend to cultivate it more carefully and productively than those who work someone else's land. Huge tracts of land still are owned by rich proprietors (who often live in the city) and farmed by tenants, often in desultory fashion because of the lack of incentives. Legal and cooperative land reform in Japan, Mexico, and Egypt has shown positive results.
6. *Improve Food Distribution Systems.* Famine and hunger, as we noted earlier, may be a matter of distribution, not availability of food. Helping poorer countries improve their transport infrastructures makes them better prepared for the next food crisis.
7. *Develop Alternative Food Sources.* A prominent alternative source is **aquaculture,** the raising of fish and shellfish in ponds and controlled saltwater hatcheries. Food scientists are also working toward what they call a "Food Revolution" in the laboratory, seeking to make food from grass, leaves, algae, even oil.
8. *Strengthen Controls over Ocean Fishing.* On the principle that late is better than never, the world's fishing industries must be more strongly regulated. Several rich countries (including Japan and Norway) have violated international agreements; the sanctions regime should be strengthened.
9. *Reduce Meat Consumption.* This is an important arena of action. Meat consumption by people in the wealthier countries puts an enormous strain on economies and ecologies elsewhere. Apart from the fact that reducing consumption of red meat is good for health and well-being, such reduction has good effects in a wider sphere by reducing the amount of grain used to feed livestock and limiting the conversion of forest into pasture in poorer countries where beef cattle are raised cheaply to provide meat for wealthier markets.
10. *Promote Social Change.* In many parts of the world, notably Subsaharan Africa and South and East Asia, food emergencies afflict women more severely than men. Among the children, too, the male tends to be favored in the allocation of food. In certain rural African societies, it is not uncommon for women not only to be more severely malnourished than men, but to be responsible for hoeing the croplands, making the family's clothing, walking endless miles for water and firewood, cooking the meals, and accomplishing numerous other tasks, in addition to bearing the children. Men do not take nearly the share of work that they could, and often they abandon the family and go to the city. It is obviously unrealistic to expect rapid change in traditions that are nearly as old as those societies themselves. However, it is possible to direct aid primarily to women and children.

Although the specter of hunger has receded and newspaper headlines no longer refer to looming global famines, we have no guarantee that the conditions shown on Figure 30–1 will continue to improve. A major perturbation in global climate alone could reverse the favorable trends of the past quarter century. Then a rising tide of world hunger would threaten world order. Even the most selfish interests in the best-fed countries thus have a stake in the war on malnutrition.

◆ THE DISTRIBUTION OF HEALTH

Food and well-being are inextricably linked, and good health, like adequate food, is unevenly distributed across the world. The study of health in geographic context is called ***medical geography***. Many diseases have their origin in the environment. They have source (core) areas, spread (diffuse) through populations along identifiable routes, and affect clusters of populations (regions) when at their widest distribution. Mapping disease patterns can produce insights into relationships between disease and environment. Associations between natural environments and ***contagious diseases*** (diseases that can be transmitted) are of special interest to medical geographers, since geography deals with natural (physical) as well as human problems. Medical geographers also concern themselves with the location of health-care facilities for people who need them. If a poor country receives funding to establish 25 clinics, where should those clinics be located so as to serve the greatest number of potential patients?

◆ INFANT AND CHILD MORTALITY

When we examine the distribution of disease, we must return to the issue of nutrition as well because regions where ***malnutrition*** prevails are also areas of poverty, inadequate medical services, poor sanitation, and substandard housing. It is difficult to identify the specific effects of malnutrition on people's susceptibility to disease because so many other factors are present. However, there is little doubt about the effects of malnutrition on growth and development. The impact on children is especially important.

Figure 30-2 World Infant Mortality. Infant deaths per 1000 live births throughout the world are shown on this map. *Source:* Based on data from Population Reference Bureau, World Population Data Sheet 2000. Washington, D.C., 2000.

Infant Mortality Rates

As noted earlier, a key measure of the human condition is the ***infant mortality rate (IMR)***. Infant mortality is recorded as a baby's death during the first year following its birth (unlike child mortality, which records death between ages 1 and 5). Like other population statistics, infant mortality is normally given as the number of cases per thousand, that is, per thousand live births.

Infant and child mortality reflect the overall health of a society. High infant mortality has a variety of causes. The physical health of the mother is a key factor. In societies where women bear a large number of babies, those women also tend to be inadequately nourished, exhausted from overwork, suffering from disease, and poorly educated. Many infants die because they are improperly weaned. Demographers report that more children die because their parents do not know how to cope with the routine childhood problem of diarrhea than because of epidemics. This, together with malnutrition, is the leading killer of children throughout the world. Poor sanitation is yet another threat to infants and children. It is estimated that more than one-fifth of the world's population lacks ready access to clean drinking water or hygienic human waste-disposal facilities.

The map showing the world distribution of infant mortality (Fig. 30–2) reveals the high rates in many poorer countries. The map shows infant mortality patterns at five levels ranging from 100 or more per thousand (one death for every eight live births) to fewer than 15. When you compare this map to that of overall crude

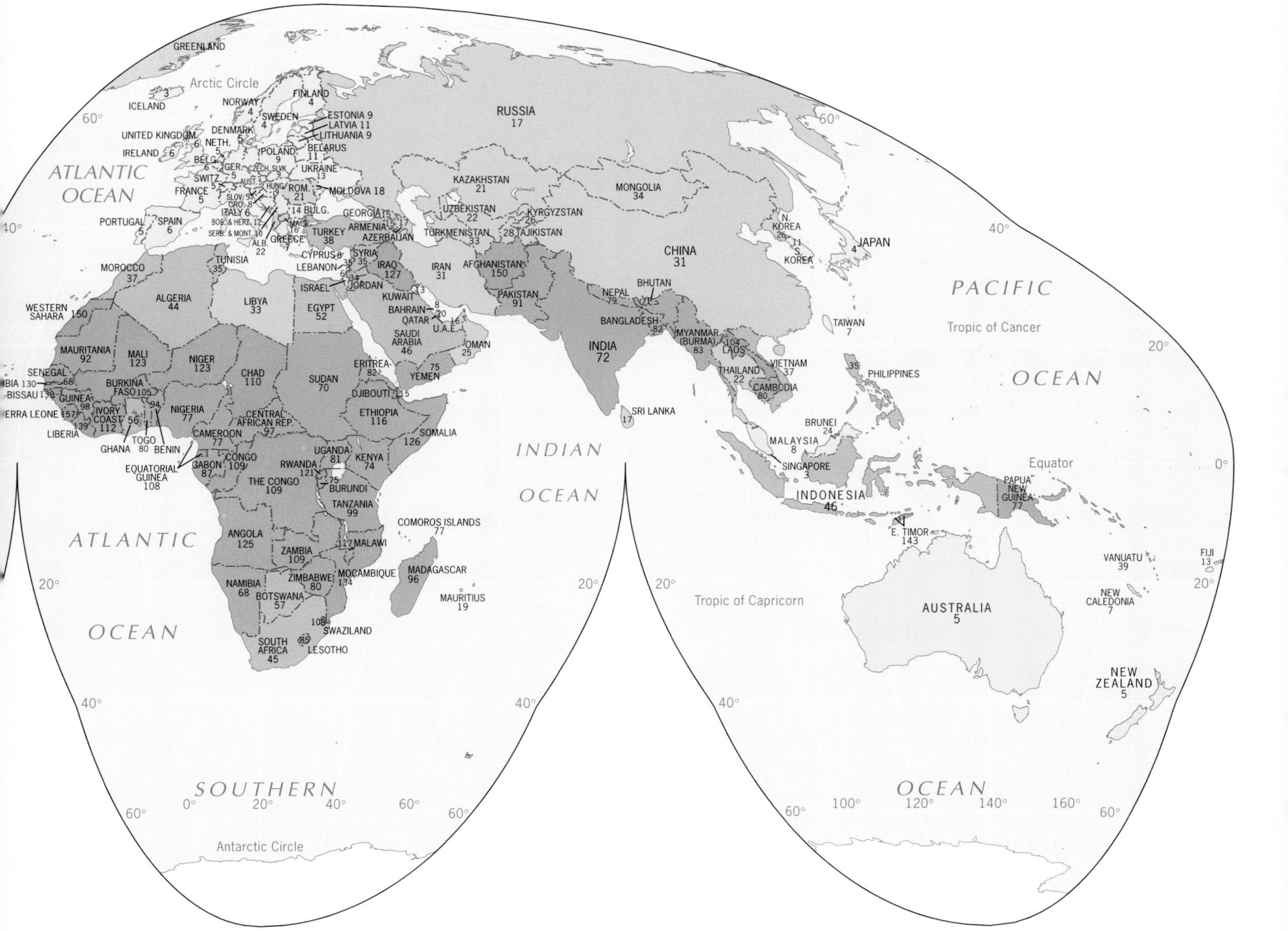

death rate (CDR) in Figure 5–7, the role of infant mortality in societies with high death rates is evident.

The lowest infant mortality rate among larger populations has long been reported by Japan, with 4.0 deaths per 1000 live births. (Singapore matches Japan, and Sweden reports 4.2.) Japan's achievement is related to its stability, strong social fabric, and prosperity. The infant mortality rate is also quite uniform throughout the country, for Japan does not have any significant ethnocultural minorities with different growth rates. As is so often the case, a map based on national statistics conceals internal regional, ethnic, or other variation, but not in Japan.

In the United States, on the other hand, infant mortality rates are higher in some sectors of the population than in others; the national IMR of 7.0 represents an average. To take a more extreme case, the IMR of South Africa is an average of those of several nations within that country's borders. The IMR for South African whites is near the European average; for black Africans it is nearer the African average; and for the Coloured and Asian population sectors it lies between these two figures. The reported average of 45 per thousand therefore does not tell the "national" story as Japan's does.

In the first decade of the twenty-first century, 27 countries still reported an IMR of 100 or more (including one in the Western Hemisphere, Haiti), and of these 11 had rates of 125 or higher—that is, one death or more among every eight newborns. Dreadful as these figures are, they are a substantial improvement over the situation 20 or even 10 years ago (although they are not much improved since 1997). Globally, infant mortality has been declining, even in the poverty-stricken regions of the world. Still, the situation in many African and some Asian countries remains grim.

Figure 30–2 should be inspected carefully; it contains some remarkable data. Note, for example, the contrast between Greece and Turkey, neighbors on Europe's rim; Mexico and the United States, neighbors in the Americas; Indonesia and Australia, neighbors on the Pacific Rim. Given the demographic transition in progress in Middle and South America, several IMRs there remain surprisingly high.

Malnutrition and Child Mortality

Infants who survive their first year of life still do not have a long life expectancy in the poorer areas of the world. The ***child mortality rate (CMR)***, recording the deaths of children between the ages of 1 and 5, remains staggeringly high in much of Africa and Asia, notably in the protein-deficient tropical and subtropical zones. ***Kwashiorkor***, a malady resulting from a lack of protein early in life, afflicts millions of children; ***marasmus***, a condition that results from inadequate protein *and* insufficient calories, causes the deaths of millions more.

Table 30–1 reveals the global range of CMRs, by country, across the world's geographic realms, by gender.

Table 30-1 Child Mortality (Deaths per thousand, Ages 1–5), By Gender, for Selected Countries, 2000

Geographic Realm/Country	Males	Females
Europe	7	6
Netherlands	5	6
Sweden	7	6
Spain	29	25
Russia		
Russian Federation	24	18
North America		
Canada	7	6
United States	8	8
Middle America		
Mexico	37	31
Haiti	111	96
Cuba	12	6
Honduras	55	44
South America		
Brazil	50	38
Venezuela	25	20
Peru	61	50
Chile	15	12
NorthAfrica/Southwest Asia		
Egypt	49	49
Saudi Arabia	26	23
Turkey	56	42
Iran	40	45
Kazakhstan	62	42
Subsaharan Africa		
Nigeria	130	130
Senegal	107	102
Congo (DR)	136	120
Kenya	109	98
Moçambique	236	212
South Africa	107	95
South Asia		
India	79	92
Pakistan	121	135
Bangladesh	88	97
Sri Lanka	30	16
Southeast Asia		
Indonesia	55	43
Myanmar	141	124
Thailand	32	19
Philippines	40	30
East Asia		
China	38	45
Japan	5	4
South Korea	10	9
Mongolia	88	83
Austral		
Australia	7	6
Pacific		
Papua New Guinea	81	88

Source: United Nations Population Fund, The State of World Population 2001 (New York, UN 2001), pp. 70–72.

In some countries more than one in five children still die between their first and fifth birthdays, a terrible record in this twenty-first century. (In the more fortunate countries one in 100 is the norm.) Note, too, the gender situation. A number of the countries recorded in Table 30–1 show a higher male than female mortality. Later in Part Ten we look into the social causes behind these statistics.

◆ LIFE EXPECTANCY

Another indicator of a society's well-being lies in the ***life expectancy*** of its members at birth, the number of years, on average, someone may expect to remain alive. Life expectancies can change in relatively short order. In the former Soviet Union, and especially in Russia, life expectancies of males dropped quite precipitously following the collapse of communism, from 68 to 62 years. (Today, Russia's life expectancy is 61 for males; female life expectancy also declined, but only slightly from 74 to 72, recovering to 73 today.) In Subsaharan Africa, the spread of AIDS over the past two decades has lowered life expectancies in some countries below 40, a level not seen for centuries.

Figure 30–3 shows the average life expectancies of populations by country and thus does not take account of gender differences. Women outlive men by about four years in Europe and East Asia, three years in Subsaharan Africa, six years in North America, and seven years in South America. In Russia today, the difference may be as much as 12 years.

Regional Contrasts

Given this variation by sex, the map also reveals huge regional contrasts. At the start of the century, world average life expectancy was 68 for women and 64 for men. Not only are these levels exceeded in the wealthy countries of the Western world, but great progress has also been made in East Asia, where Japan's life expectancies are among the highest in the world, those of South Korea and Taiwan are high as well, and China's have risen to 69 for males and 73 for females. By contrast, tropical Subsaharan African countries have the lowest range today.

Age Contrasts

These life expectancy figures do not mean that everyone lives to those ages. The figure is an average that takes account of the children who die young and the people who survive well beyond the average. Thus the dramatically lower figures for the world's poorer countries primarily reflect high infant mortality. A person who has survived beyond childhood is likely to survive well beyond the recorded life expectancy. The low life expectancy figures for the food-short countries remind us again how hard hit children are in poorer parts of the world.

Life expectancies have increased significantly over the past half-century. More progress has been made toward reducing death rates than toward lowering birth rates, and as a result life expectancies are slowly rising—even in the global economic core, where they are already high. It has been predicted that life expectancies may soon reach 85 years but that they will then level off because of the natural failure of vital organs in the aging body. In the meantime, we should expect a continued increase in life expectancies in poorer countries as improvements in medical facilities, hygiene, and drug availability suppress death rates.

Even now, the effects of these improvements can be observed from maps showing life expectancies (that is, remaining years of life) at advanced ages (for example, 20 and 40 years). Such maps show much less contrast between core and peripheral countries. As we will note later, although infant mortality has been dramatically reduced in better-off societies, much less progress has been made in combating the diseases of middle and advanced age. The great contrast between economically advantaged and disadvantaged countries lies at the base of the population pyramid, in rates of survival in the first few years of life.

We have discussed in earlier chapters the serious implications of the "graying" of the world's populations. Today there are nearly 600 million people age 60 or above, and this number is growing rapidly. Rising life expectancy is a symbol of national well-being, but it is also a harbinger of social problems ahead.

◆ THE DISTRIBUTION OF DISEASE

We all know that people in certain regions of the world are more (or less) susceptible to particular diseases than others. Certain kinds of natural environments harbor dangerous disease carriers, and diseases have ways of spreading from one population to another. Certain artificial environments, such as crowded, unsanitary shantytowns, make large numbers of people vulnerable to diseases lurking in polluted water. The study of diseases, their sources, carriers, diffusion, and mitigation, their environmental linkages and social settings, form part of the arena of the field of medical geography.

Medical geographers today use geographic information systems as well as traditional cartographic methods to analyze spatial aspects of disease outbreaks, to predict diffusion patterns, and to help mobilize responses. For example, a map showing the location and extent of an outbreak of diarrheal diseases can provide an early warning of the development of kwashiorkor. Maps showing the distribution of unvaccinated populations in urban areas can assist in preparation for crisis situations.

Major Types of Diseases Let us begin by classifying the types of diseases we will discuss in the remainder of the chapter:

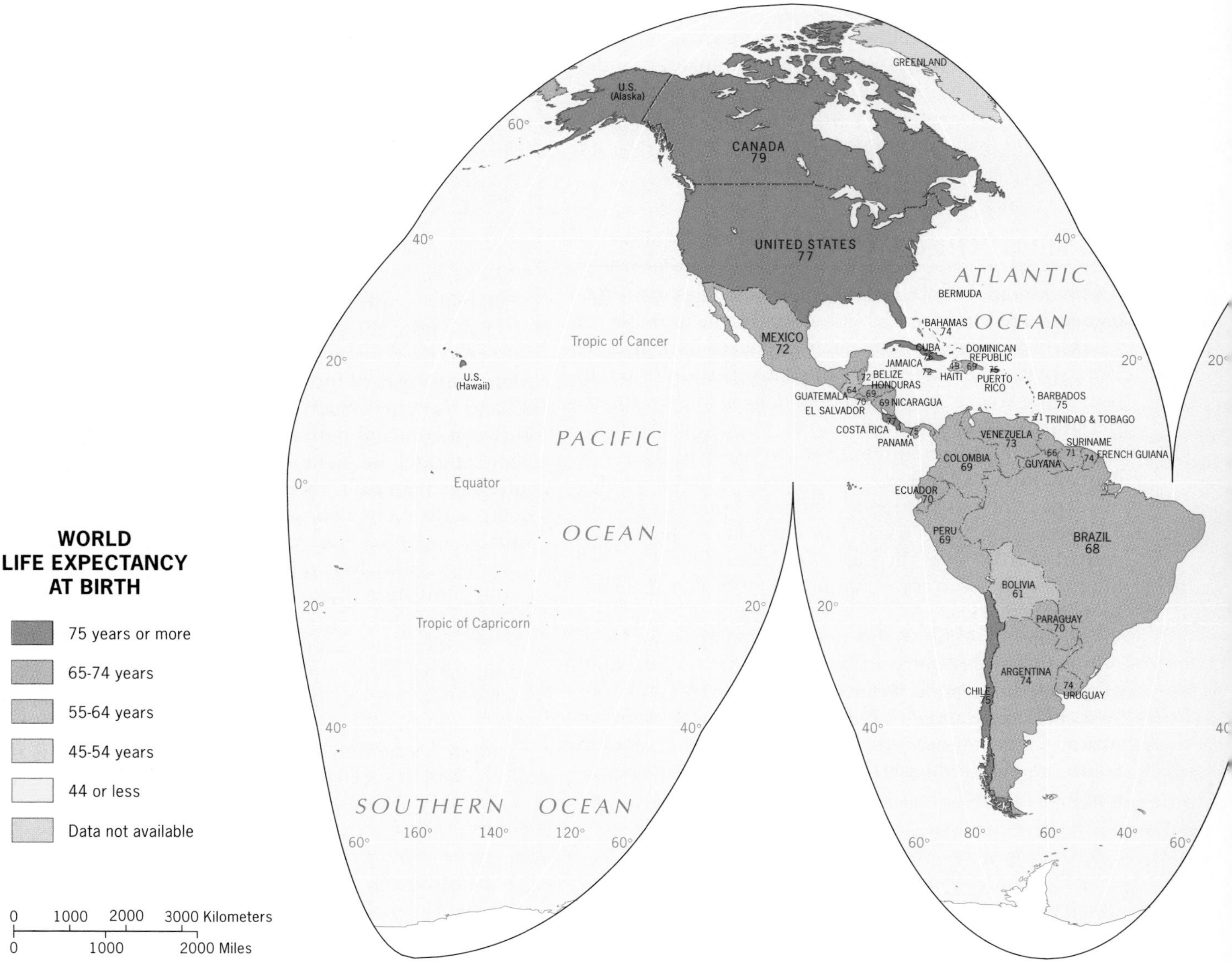

Figure 30-3 Life Expectancy at Birth. *Source:* Based on data from Population Reference Bureau, *World Population Data Sheet 2000.* Washington, DC., 2000.

1. *Infectious Diseases* About 65 percent of all human illnesses are of the infectious type. They result from an invasion of parasites and their multiplication in the body. Malaria is an example.
2. *Chronic or Degenerative Diseases* These are diseases of longevity or age. They do not kill instantly; instead, they cause long-term deterioration of the body. Cancer and heart disease are common chronic diseases in our society.
3. *Genetic or Inherited Diseases* Certain diseases can be traced directly to genetic factors. Hemophilia, sickle-cell anemia, and lactose intolerance are among these inherited maladies.

Some diseases occur in confined regions; others spread throughout the world. When a sudden outbreak leads to a high percentage of cases and a large number of deaths in a region, it is called an ***epidemic***. When the outbreak spreads around the world, as various forms of influenza have done since the beginning of the twentieth century, a ***pandemic*** develops. Many diseases have a limited range, however, because the organisms that transmit them are restricted by environmental conditions.

Certain diseases become established in a population without a spectacular epidemic or pandemic. Even today, many people in the United States have a venereal disease of some kind, sometimes without being aware of

it. Such a situation, in which a disease is carried by many people (or ***hosts***) without leading to a rapid and widespread death toll, means that the disease is ***endemic*** to that population. This is not to suggest that an endemic disease has no effect on the well-being of those who have it. General health does deteriorate, and energy levels are lowered; in addition, susceptibility to other diseases may rise. On college campuses, a malady called mononucleosis is sometimes described as endemic to the population of students (and some have it without being aware of it).

How Diseases Spread ***Infectious diseases*** are spread by disease-causing organisms ranging from microscopic, one-celled protozoa to parasitic worms and insects. The list of ***agents***, as these organisms are called, is almost endless and includes worms, such as hookworms and tapeworms; insects that burrow under the skin; and viruses, bacteria, and other microorganisms that can invade the body or contaminate the environment. The viruses are a unique group of infectious agents. They are smaller than bacteria and are composed of a core of nucleic acid and layers of protein and, in some instances, fatty substances. Viruses can infect animal cells and cause diseases such as measles, influenza, polio, and probably certain forms of cancer.

When we are afflicted by an infectious disease, we are hosts to a particular disease organism. When a population contains a large number of hosts, a ***reservoir*** has been formed from which the disease may expand or diffuse. Those to whom it spreads become additional hosts, strengthening the disease reservoir.

From the field notes

"Along the road east from Colombo (Sri Lanka) I was reminded repeatedly how far even a relatively well-off country like Sri Lanka still has to go to provide adequate medical care to all its citizens. Small, poorly equipped and supplied, often-unhygienic clinics are the only recourse for those needing medical care. Government oversight is minimal and, as shown here, maintenance is lacking. And, locals told me, things are far worse in the Tamil-majority parts of the country, where civil war has had had devastating impact on health facilities."

Diseases spread in several ways. Some agents are transmitted from one person directly to another by contact. In this case, the disease is carried from one host to the next without any intermediate host. A handshake, a kiss, or some other form of touching can transmit the agents. Even standing close enough to a person so that tiny moisture particles from exhaled air reach you can have the same effect. Diseases that are transmitted in this way are termed *nonvectored diseases;* examples are the common cold, measles, venereal diseases, and mononucleosis.

When a disease is carried from one host to the next by an intermediate host, the disease is said to be *vectored.* The intermediate host or ***vector*** plays a critical role in the transmission process because the parasite (the agent) undergoes change in the host's body. For example, no one can contract malaria by touching a person who has the disease. A mosquito is essential to the transmission process. Moreover, it is not just a case of the mosquito biting the infected person and then biting the new host. Rather, a parasite must go through a significant change as part of its life cycle while it inhabits the mosquito and before it is injected into the new host. Insects (including various kinds of mosquitoes, flies, and ticks) are the most common vectors, but worms, snails, and larger animals, such as house pets, can also serve as vectors.

Disease organisms are also transmitted by water, soil, food, and feces. These are nonbiological vectors, sometimes called mechanical vectors, or ***vehicles***. In this case, the agent does not necessarily undergo a biological change between the infected host and the new host, but the vehicle sustains it between hosts.

Infectious diseases can thus be grouped according to whether they are vectored or nonvectored. These categories are not mutually exclusive. Some diseases can be transmitted either directly or through a vector or vehicle; humans themselves can serve as vectors. Still, the differentiation between nonvectored and vectored diseases is useful because geographic contrasts are associated with it. Cholera, a vehicle-vectored disease, spread throughout the world during several nineteenth-century pandemics. Malaria, on the other hand, is a vectored disease whose spread is limited by the environmental constraints on the mosquito that transmits it.

Data on population numbers, growth rates, and demographic structures do not provide a complete picture of the degree of well-being of the people they represent. Hundreds of millions of people, especially in equatorial and tropical regions, face a combination of undernourishment, malnutrition, and prevalent disease. Let us therefore take a closer look at some of the more common diseases affecting people in various parts of the world.

Vectored Infectious Diseases

As noted earlier, tropical (and especially equatorial) environments enhance biological activity. Vectors and agents abound in such environments, and infectious diseases spread rapidly through host populations.

Malaria As Figure 30–4 shows, ***malaria*** occurs throughout the world, except in higher latitudes and altitudes, and drier environments. Although people in the tropical portions of Africa suffer most from this disease, malaria also prevails in India, Southeast Asia, China, and the tropical Americas.

There are several types of malaria, some more severe than others; not only human beings but also various species of monkeys, rats, birds, and even snakes can be affected by it. Malaria's virulence results from the effectiveness of its vectors, three African mosquitoes (*Anopheles gambiae, A. arabiensis,* and *A. funestus*). The role of these mosquitoes in the diffusion of the disease was not determined until the late eighteenth century, but the sequence is now well known. The mosquito stings an infected host and sucks up some of the disease agents. In the mosquito's stomach, the parasites reproduce and

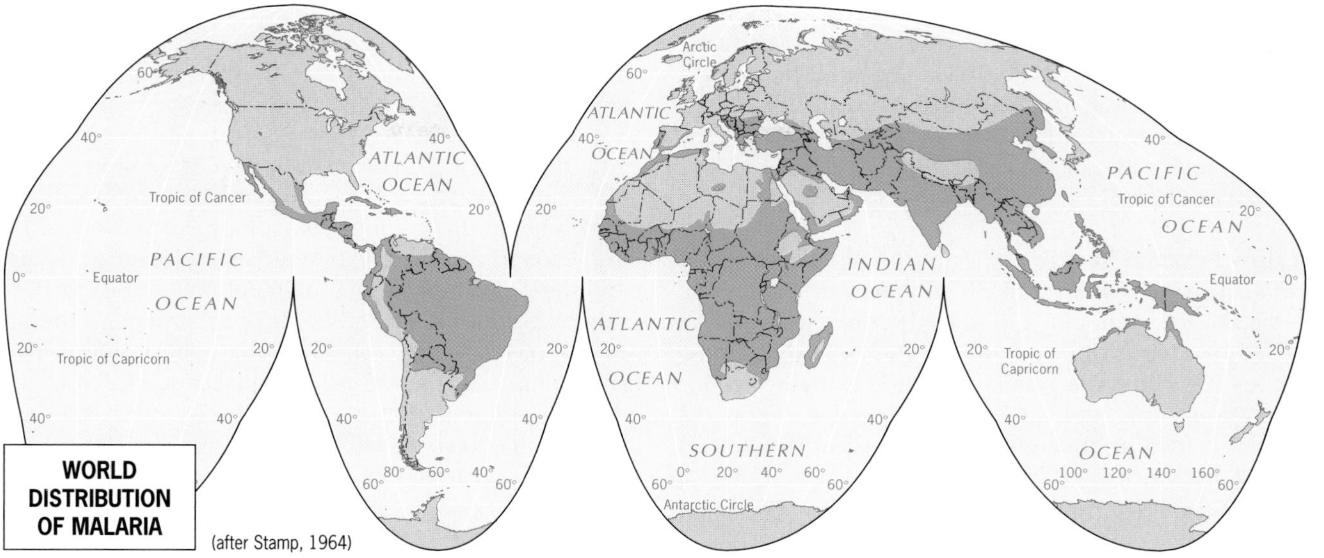

Figure 30-4 World Distribution of Malaria. Forty years ago, malaria's global distribution was similar to today's; the battle against it is a stalemate. *Source:* From L. D. Stamp, *The Geography of Life and Death.* Ithaca: Cornell University Press, 1964, p. 132.

multiply, eventually reaching its saliva. When the mosquito stings the next person, some of the parasites are injected into that person's bloodstream. Now the person who has been stung develops malaria and becomes a host.

Malaria still kills between two and three million people every year and incapacitates many more. It is a major factor in infant and child mortality. Most of the victims are children age 5 or younger. If they survive, they develop a certain degree of immunity, although someone infected by malaria is likely to be weak and lack energy. Whole populations are afflicted, and entire regions have been abandoned because of the prevalence of the disease. The abandonment of ancient irrigation systems and apparently fertile lands, sometimes ascribed to climatic change, was in some instances probably due to the spread of malaria.

Malaria manifests itself as a recurrent fever and chills, with associated symptoms such as anemia and an enlarged spleen. The victim is not only deprived of energy, but also faces an increased risk of other diseases taking hold in the weakened body. Antimalarial drugs exist, but to defeat malaria it is necessary to eliminate the vector, the mosquito. In 1955 the World Health Organization launched a massive worldwide program against malaria following a remarkably successful campaign in Sri Lanka (then Ceylon). As Figure 30–4 shows, Sri Lanka was freed of malaria in the mid-1940s, when a massive attack on the mosquito was launched with the aid of a pesticide called *dichloro diphenyl trichloroethane* (DDT). The results were dramatic; the mosquito was practically wiped out, and the rate of deaths attributable to malaria fell. In 1945, Sri Lanka's death rate overall had been 22 per 1000; in 1972, it reported a death rate of only 8 per 1000. The figure was further reduced to 6 per 1000 by 1985. Malaria had been defeated.

The conquest of malaria produced other problems, however. DDT proved to be highly carcinogenic and to have negative health and environmental consequences of its own. Also, the birth rate did not decline—it was 32 per 1000 in 1945, and in 1972 it was still 30 per 1000. Thus, while malaria was eradicated, the population growth rate rose substantially, creating new problems for Sri Lanka. By the time the birth rate dropped, the island had experienced a population explosion.

Success in combating major diseases often is only temporary. Following the Sri Lanka experiment, a massive assault was initiated against the malaria mosquito in India, and the number of new cases of the disease declined dramatically. But 10 years later India reported that 60 million people were infected with malaria, more than half the number who had the disease before the antimalaria campaign began. This proved the mosquito population's ability to rebound quickly after even the most intensive application of insecticides. Today the war against malaria is taking a new tack: genetic interference with the mosquito so that its capacity to transmit the malaria parasite, *Plasmodium,* is destroyed. By introducing "engineered" mosquitoes into the general population, it is anticipated that those that cannot transmit malaria will eventually replace A. *gambiae.*

The fact remains, however, that malaria is mainly a scourge of the poorer peoples of the world. When an American tourist contracts malaria during an East African safari and succumbs, a rare event, it makes the headlines in the person's hometown. The millions who die in Asia and Africa do not make the news. The wealthier world has not mobilized against malaria as it has against cancer or, after it penetrated the West, AIDS. Those who continue to suffer do not have the clout to change global medical priorities.

Yellow Fever ***Yellow fever*** is now confined to tropical and near-tropical areas (Fig. 30–5), but in past centuries its distribution was much wider. The disease, which is caused by a virus transmitted by various kinds of mosquitoes, has killed vast numbers of people. In the Americas, devastating epidemics and serious outbreaks erupted in the Caribbean Islands, in tropical Middle and South America, and as far north as Boston. The southern United States was repeatedly invaded by yellow fever; the last major outbreak struck coastal cities, especially New Orleans, as recently as 1905. Europe, too, experienced severe attacks of yellow fever; not even England and France were spared.

Today yellow fever has been driven back to the areas where it has long been endemic, and a vaccine is available that can provide long-term immunity. Eradicating the disease is difficult, however, since yellow fever also affects monkeys and several species of small forest animals. In the tropics, therefore, immunization of humans is the only solution.

Yellow fever contributed to the failure of Ferdinand de Lesseps, the builder of the Suez Canal, in his first attempt to cut a canal across Panama's mosquito-infested swamps in 1876. Not until a massive campaign of eradication had been waged could a second attempt at building the Panama Canal be made. This was done in 1905, but yellow fever and malaria still took a heavy toll among the workers.

The onset of yellow fever, which occurs some days after the bite of the vector mosquito, is marked by high temperatures. The fever is accompanied by headache, backache, and vomiting. Sometimes unchecked vomiting leads to death. In less acute cases jaundice occurs, and the deposition of bile pigment colors the eyes and skin quite yellow. Since there is no treatment for the disease, it has to run its course. In areas where yellow fever is endemic, people have developed a degree of immunity. Still, there is always a sufficient reservoir of susceptible people to sustain a severe outbreak, and the threat of yellow fever continues for millions of people.

Sleeping Sickness The diffusion of ***sleeping sickness*** from a source area in West Africa is thought to have begun about A.D. 1400 (Fig. 30–6).

The tsetse fly, of which Africa has many species, is the vector. The fly sucks blood from an infected animal or person and in doing so ingests the single-celled agents or trypanosomes. These trypanosomes reproduce in the fly's body and eventually reach the insect's salivary glands. When the fly next bites a person or an animal, it spreads the infection to new hosts.

Africa's immense wildlife population acts as a reservoir for sleeping sickness because antelope are among the carriers of the disease (Fig. 30–7). The fly infects livestock as well as people, limiting the development of herds in places where meat and milk would improve

Figure 30-5 World Distribution of Yellow Fever. This maps shows the approximate areas in Africa and South America where yellow fever has long been endemic.

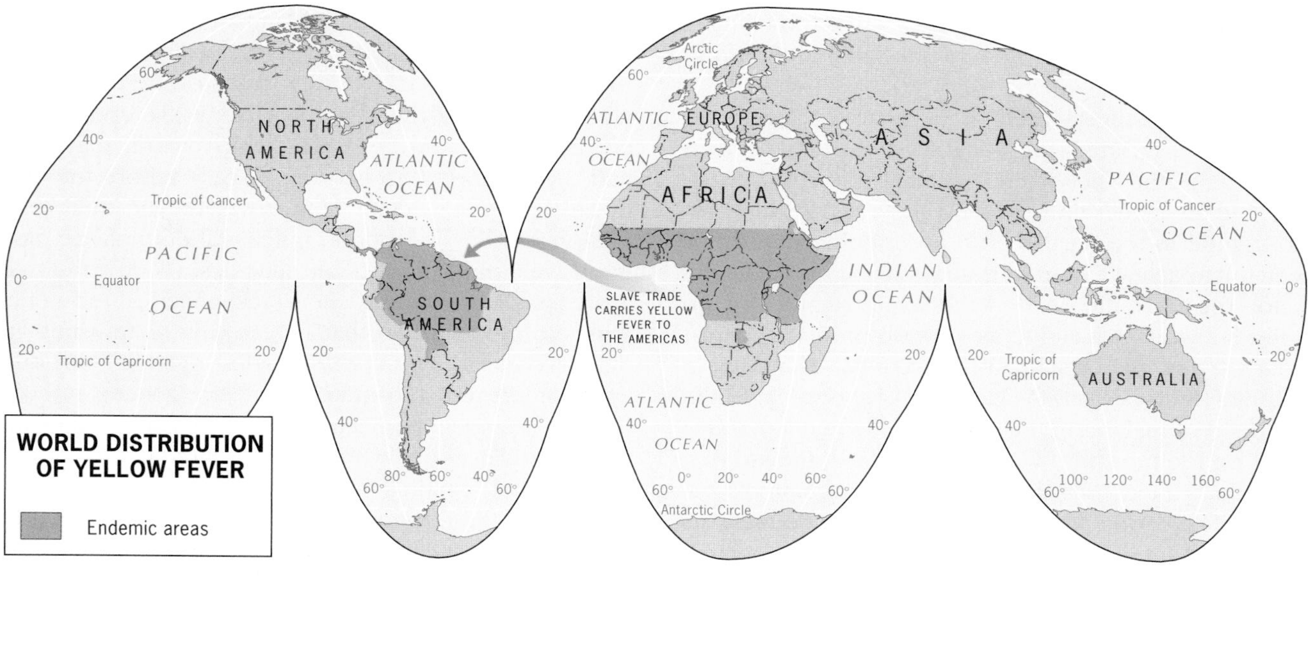

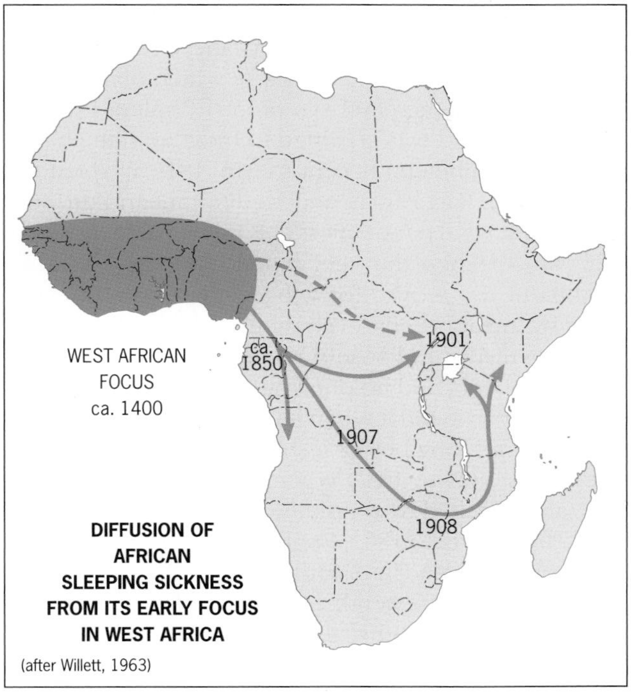

Figure 30-6 Diffusion of African Sleeping Sickness. African sleeping sickness diffusion from its early focus in West Africa is illustrated here. *Source:* From K. C. Willett, "Trypanosomiasis and the Tsetse Fly Problem in Africa," *Annual Review of Entomology,* Vol. 8, 1963, p. 197.

diets that are seriously imbalanced. It also prevented the adoption of the animal-drawn plow and cart before Europeans arrived in Africa. In addition, it channeled the diffusion of cattle into Eastern and Southern Africa through corridors that were free of tsetse flies, destroying herds that moved into infested zones nearby. Most of all, it ravaged the population.

In humans, sleeping sickness begins with a fever, followed by swelling of the lymph nodes. Next the inflammation spreads to the brain and the spinal cord, producing the lethargy and listlessness that give the disease its name. Death may follow. The impact on livestock is equally severe: sick animals wither away and die within a year of infection. In some areas the disease is accompanied by a grotesque swelling of the limbs, which soon cannot be controlled. The animal stumbles about, becomes crazed, and then dies.

Although progress has been made in combating this dreaded disease, much of Africa is still affected by it (Fig. 30–8). The most promising line of attack is at the vector—killing tsetse flies in massive eradication campaigns. Sometimes whole villages have been moved from infested areas to tsetse-free zones. Killing of infected wildlife, destruction of the bush that the tsetse fly needs as its habitat, and other methods have been attempted. Africa is large, however—some 11.7 million square miles

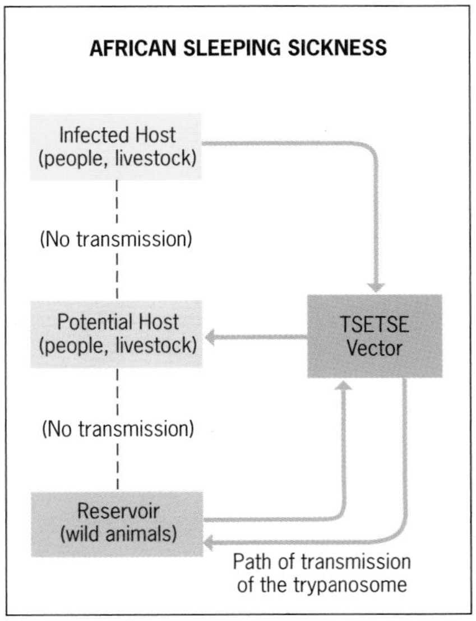

Figure 30-7 Transmission of African Sleeping Sickness.

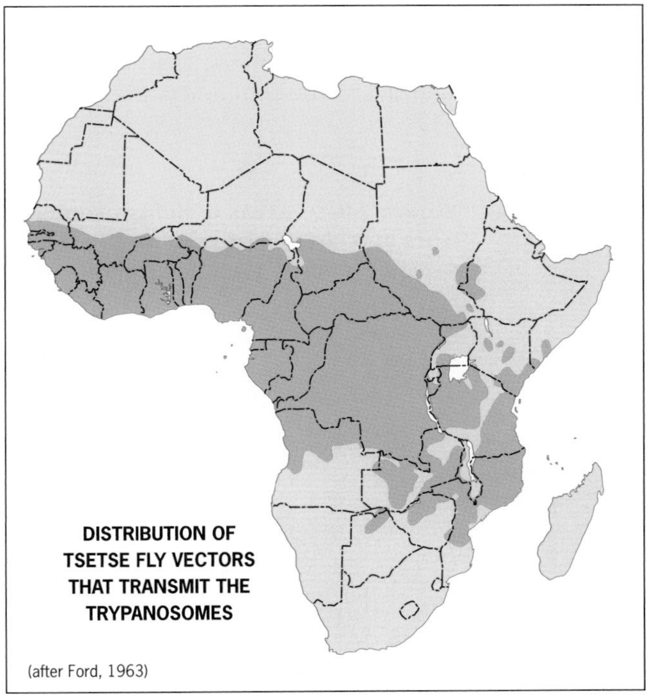

Figure 30-8 Distribution of Tsetse Fly Vectors. This map shows the distribution of tsetse fly vectors that transmit the trypanosomes. *Source:* From J. Ford, "The Distribution of the Vectors of African Pathogenic Trypanosomes," *Bulletin of the WHO,* Vol. 30, 1963, p. 655.

(over 30 million square kilometers)—and so the tsetse fly is still prevalent over much of the continent.

Malaria, yellow fever, and sleeping sickness are just three of dozens of vectored infectious diseases that occur in tropical regions. A fourth is schistosomiasis, also known as ***bilharzia***, a debilitating disease transmitted by freshwater snails. The vector sends infected larva into still or slow-moving water, and when these penetrate the skin, they develop into mature, egg-laying worms. The eggs wreak havoc in the liver and other organs. When fast-moving streams in tropical areas were dammed for electricity-generating or agricultural purposes, the dams became ideal environments for the snails that transmit schistosomiasis, and local people paid the price. Figure 30–9 shows world areas at risk from three forms of this disease.

Still another vectored disease is *onchocerciasis* or ***river blindness***, so named because it afflicts people living in river valleys in West Africa and elsewhere. The vector is a fly; the parasite eventually reaches the eyes and the victim goes blind.

Nonvectored Infectious Diseases

Direct transmission of an infectious disease takes place through (1) close bodily contact, as in the case of venereal diseases and mononucleosis; (2) contamination of water and food by fecal material, which spreads diseases like cholera and infectious hepatitis; and (3) contamination of air when tiny droplets of saliva are expelled by infected persons and inhaled by others, as in the case of tuberculosis, influenza, and the common cold.

Cholera Perhaps the most frightening disease in this group is ***cholera***, also called Asiatic cholera, a term used to denote a set of diseases in which diarrhea and dehydration are the chief symptoms. Cholera is an ancient disease and was confined to India until the beginning of the nineteenth century. In 1816 it spread to China, Japan, East Africa, and Mediterranean Europe in the first of several pandemics. This initial wave abated by 1823, but by then the very name cholera was feared throughout the world, for it had killed people everywhere by the hundreds, even thousands. Death was horribly convulsive and would come in a matter of days, perhaps a week, and no one knew what caused the disease or how to avoid it when it invaded.

It was not long before a second pandemic struck. It lasted from 1826 to 1837, when cholera crossed the Atlantic and attacked North America. During the next pandemic, from 1842 to 1862, England was severely hit, and cholera again spread into North America (Fig. 30–10). But during this mid-nineteenth-century pandemic, a medical geographer named John Snow, working in a district of London, confirmed a link between contaminated water and cholera victims that was to save millions of lives.

Dr. Snow and his students drew a street map of London's Soho District, marking all water pumps (then still the way people got their water supply for home use) with a P (Fig. 30–11). When the pandemic that began in 1842 reached England in the 1850s, Soho was severely affected, and on his street map (dated 1854) Snow located every cholera death by marking the residence of each victim with a dot. Approximately 500 deaths occurred in Soho, and as the map took shape, it became evident that

Figure 30-9 Areas of Schistosomiasis Risk. Areas where people are at risk from three types of schistosomiasis (bilharzia) are shown here. *Source:* From G. Pyle, *Applied Medical Geography.* Silver Spring, Md.: Winston/Halsted, 1979, p. 47.

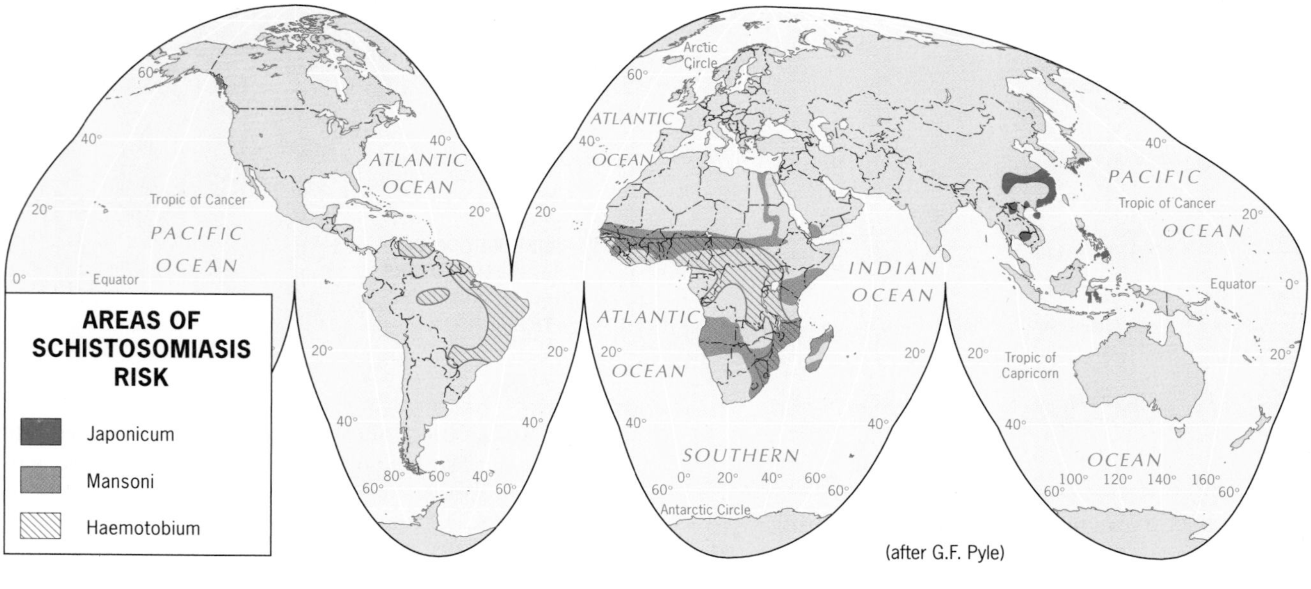

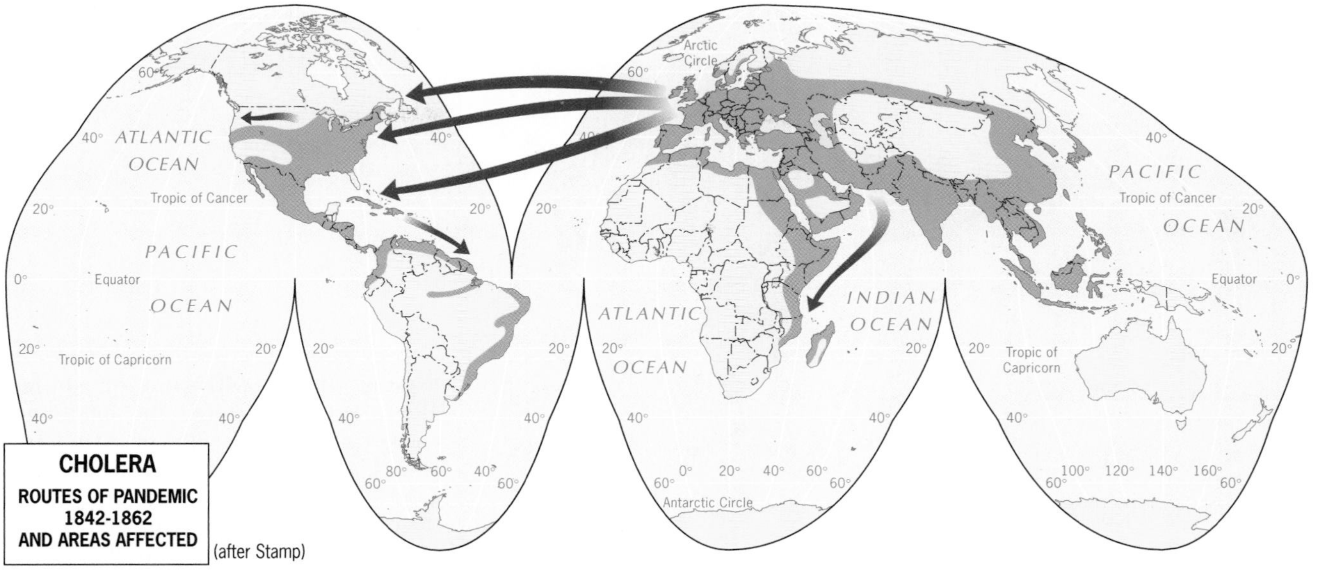

Figure 30-10 Routes of Cholera Pandemic, 1842–1862. The areas affected by the 1842–1862 cholera pandemic and the routes it took are depicted here. *Source:* From L. D. Stamp, *The Geography of Life and Death* (Ithaca: Cornell University Press 1964).

an especially large number of those deaths were clustered around the pump on Broad Street. At the Doctor's request, city authorities removed the handle from that pump, making it impossible to draw water there. The result was dramatic: almost immediately the number of reported new cases fell to nearly zero. Snow's theory about the role of water in the spread of cholera was confirmed.

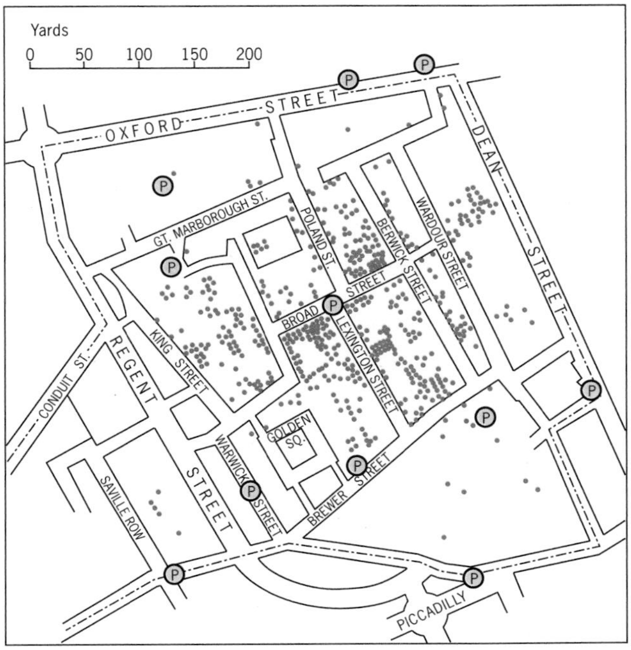

Figure 30-11 Cholera in the Soho District of London in 1854.

Of course, Dr. Snow and his colleagues advised people to boil their water, but it would be a long time before his advice reached all those who needed to know, and in any case many people simply did not have the ability to do so. Meanwhile, the 1842 pandemic raged on, affecting large parts of the United States (Fig. 30–12).

When the last great cholera pandemic struck in 1865, spreading from New Orleans and the East Coast to Detroit and Chicago, its impact was moderated by people's awareness of the risks of possibly contaminated water. While Asia and parts of East Africa were severely affected, Europe suffered less and cholera never did reach the U.S. West Coast before this pandemic abated in 1875.

Cholera has not yet been totally defeated, however, and in some ways the risks have been rising in recent years rather than falling. In the teeming shantytowns of the growing megacities of the developing world, and in the refugee camps of Africa and Asia, cholera remains a threat. Until the 1990s, major outbreaks remained few and limited (after remaining cholera-free for a half century, Europe had its first cholera reappearance in Naples in 1972), and Africa reported most cases. But an outbreak in the slums of Lima, Peru, in December 1990 became a fast-spreading epidemic that, while confined to the Americas, touched every country in the hemisphere, infected more than 1 million people, and killed over 10,000.

Hygiene prevents cholera, but contaminated water abounds in much of the tropical world's cities. A cholera vaccine exists, but it remains effective for only six months, and it is costly. Dr. Snow achieved a victory through the application of geographical reasoning, but the war against cholera is not yet won.

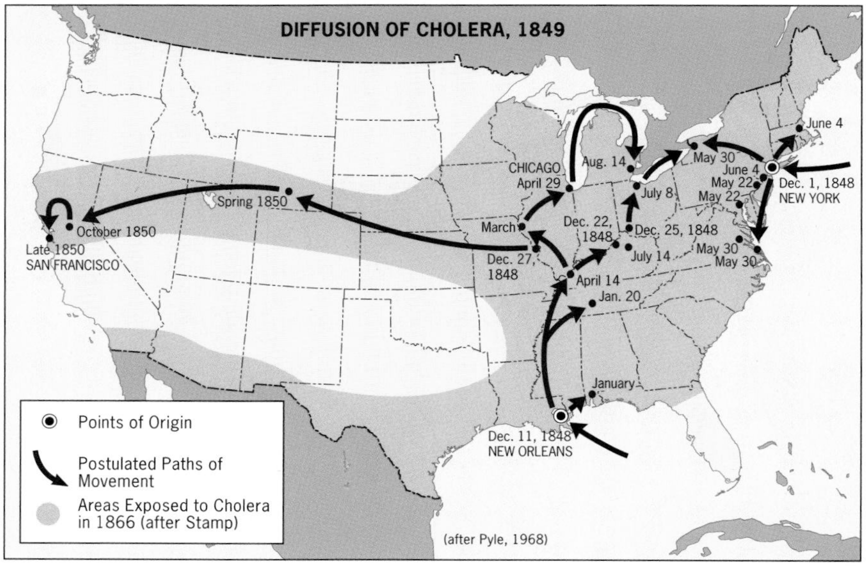

Figure 30-12 Diffusion of Cholera, 1849. This map shows the diffusion of cholera in the United States in 1849. *Source:* From L. D. Stamp (see Figure 30-10), 1964, and G. F. Pyle, "The Diffusion of Cholera in the United States in the 19th Century," *Geographical Analysis,* 1, 1969, p. 59.

Influenza Every year tens of thousands of people succumb to the "flu," a malady that strikes millions of people throughout the world. The great majority recover, but many do not. In the United States in a typical year, ***influenza*** is the cause of death for some 20,000 people. Older people and those who are weak are especially susceptible.

Flu outbreaks are much worse in some years than in others. In 1918, a worldwide pandemic killed between 20 and 30 million people after an especially virulent strain of the virus diffused throughout the world. Once a new strain of influenza has begun to spread, the disease is transmitted when people inhale the airborne virus, and it diffuses rapidly. A single infected person in an airplane or bus can transmit it to dozens of others.

Why do new epidemics and pandemics of influenza occur? The answer apparently lies in the life cycle of the influenza A virus, which comes from China (hence the names given to recent pandemics, such as "Chinese flu" and "Hong Kong flu"). There the virus resides in birds, especially waterfowl. The virus cannot be transmitted directly from birds to people, but it is transmitted from birds to pigs and from pigs to humans.

Chinese farming practices put ducks (major carriers of the influenza A virus) in close proximity to pigs and in turn to people. People with the flu can transmit the virus to pigs. Medical geographers therefore believe that the pig is host to strains of influenza A virus from both birds and humans. This means that new strains of the virus can form in the host and be transmitted to people, perhaps causing an epidemic or pandemic (Fig. 30–13).

In late 1997, a new strain of influenza, apparently originating in chickens (and possibly other fowl), broke out in Hong Kong, causing much alarm worldwide. All poultry and ducks in Hong Kong were destroyed, and imports from China were stopped. Although only a few dozen cases of the "chicken flu" appeared in humans, and human-to-human transmission was minimal, the new and unfamiliar strain raised much concern.

Influenza therefore has a vector at its source, but once it spreads away from its core area, it is diffused by contact. As noted previously, the distinction between vectored and nonvectored infectious diseases is not always hard and fast.

AIDS As we have noted earlier, tropical Africa has been the source of numerous infectious diseases whose vectors thrive in its equatorial environments. In the early 1980s, a nonvectored disease that would spread in a pandemic was identified in Africa: ***AIDS*** (Acquired Immune Deficiency Syndrome). Undoubtedly AIDS had taken hold in Africa years earlier, perhaps decades earlier. But its rapid diffusion worldwide began in the 1980s and created one of the great health catastrophes of the twentieth century. Nowhere was its impact greater, however, than in Africa itself.

Medical geographers estimate that in 1980 about 200,000 people were infected with HIV (Human Immunodeficiency Virus, which causes AIDS), all of them Africans. By 2002, the number worldwide exceeded 40 million according to the World Health Organization, more than 28 million of whom were Africans. In 2001, 5 million new cases were reported, and 3 million patients died. Of those, 93 percent were Africans.

AIDS is a debilitating disease that weakens the body and reduces its capacity to combat other infections. It is spread through bodily contact that involves the exchange of bodily fluids such as blood and semen. Sexual

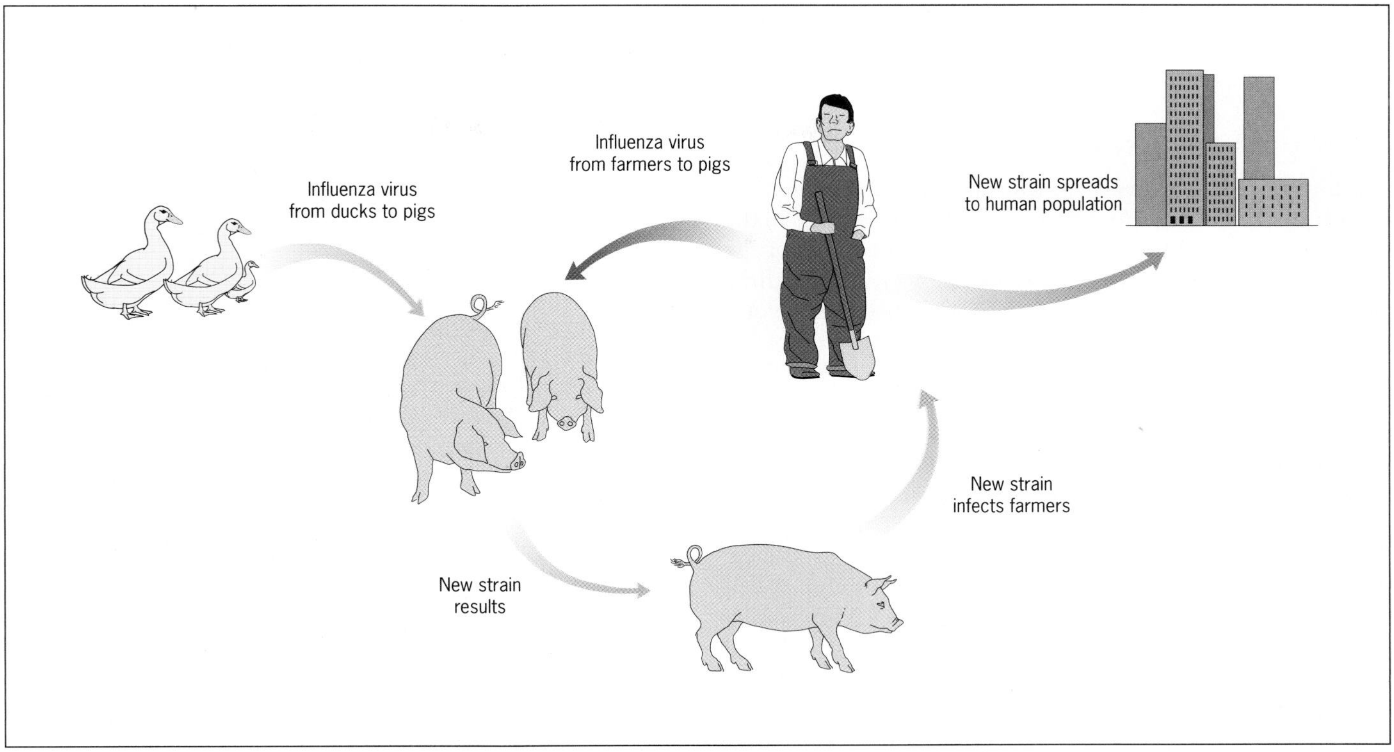

Figure 30-13 The Life Cycle of a New Strain of Influenza Virus.

activity can transmit it but so can blood transfusions. Over a period of years, a person's immune system is impaired, weight loss and weakness set in, and other afflictions, such as cancer or pneumonia, may hasten an infected person's demise.

Over the past two decades, the AIDS pandemic has reached virtually all parts of the world, but its full dimensions are unknown. People infected by HIV do not immediately display visible symptoms of the disease; they can carry the virus for years without being aware of it, and during that period they can unwittingly transmit it to others. In its earliest stages a blood test is needed to confirm HIV's presence, but millions go untested. Add to this the social stigma that attaches to this malady, and it is evident that official statistics on AIDS lag far behind the reservoir's real numbers.

That is true not only in Africa but in other parts of the world as well; both India and China, for example, long denied that AIDS presents a serious health threat to their populations. Now China is reporting more than 1 million infected, and the number in India may be even larger. Estimates of the number of cases in the United States surpass 1 million; in Middle and South America, nearly 2 million are infected. But after Africa, the worst-afflicted geographic realm is Southeast Asia, with as many as 6 million cases.

Nowhere is AIDS having the impact it has had upon Subsaharan Africa, however. In 2002, more than 25 percent of people aged 15 to 49 were infected in Zimbabwe and Botswana, about 20 percent in Zambia, and about 15 percent in South Africa. These are the official data; medical geographers estimate that 20 to 25 percent of the entire population of several tropical African countries is infected. A United Nations report published in 2000 indicated that more than 10 million people had died of AIDS in Africa between 1990 and 1998. The geographer Peter Gould, in his book *The Slow Plague* (1993), calls Africa a "continent in catastrophe," and the demographic statistics confirm his viewpoint. Life expectancy in Botswana has gone from over 60 to under 40; in Swaziland it is 37, in Zimbabwe, 39. In a continent already ravaged by other diseases, AIDS is the leading cause of death.

There are few positives to report. Uganda, once Africa's worst afflicted country, has slowed the growth of AIDS through an intensive, government-sponsored campaign of propaganda and action—notably the distribution of condoms in even the remotest part of the country. In the world's wealthier countries, remedies have been developed that can stave off the effects of AIDS for many years. But African countries cannot afford such luxuries. UN calculations suggest that Subsaharan Africa annually needs between $8 and $10 billion to combat its AIDS pandemic; currently, about $500 million is available. The impact of AIDS will be felt in African economies and on African demographics for generations to come. The "slim disease," as some Africans call it, will constrain African economic development and require world intervention to overcome.

Chronic Diseases

Although AIDS has become the leading cause of death in Subsaharan Africa, the number of fatal AIDS cases in the rest of the world remains far smaller than those of the ***chronic diseases***: heart disease, cancer, stroke, lung ailments, and others. These chronic diseases always have been the leading cause of death in one form or another: in the United States 100 years ago, tuberculosis, pneumonia, diarrheal diseases, and heart diseases (in that order) were the chief killers. Today, heart disease and cancer head the list, with cerebral hemorrhage (stroke) next and accidents high on the list as well (Table 30–2). At the turn of the century, tuberculosis and pneumonia caused 20 percent or all deaths; today, they cause fewer than 5 percent. The diarrheal diseases, which were so high on the old list, are now primarily children's maladies. Today, these diseases are not even on the list of the 10 leading causes of death. The modern deadly diseases are the afflictions of middle and old age, reflecting higher life expectancies.

Table 30–2 reflects other realities, some of which are not encouraging. Although the diseases of infancy have been largely defeated and such infectious diseases as tuberculosis and pneumonia are less serious threats than they were, the battles against cancer and heart disease are far from won. Recent decades have brought new lifestyles, new pressures, new consumption patterns, and exposure to new chemicals, and we do not know how these affect our health. People often smoke cigarettes because they find it relaxing, but lung cancer—a major modern killer—is linked to smoking. In order to distribute adequate food supplies to populations in huge urban areas, we add various kinds of preservatives to foods without knowing exactly how they will affect our health in the long run. We substitute artificial flavoring for sugar and other calorie-rich substances, but some of those substitutes have been proven to be dangerous. The map of cancer and heart disease shows that these problems are as heavily concentrated in the urban, industrial core as some of the major infectious diseases are prevalent in the periphery (Fig. 30–14).

Table 30-2 Leading Causes of Death in the United States, 1999

Cause	Total	Percent
1. Heart Disease	724,269	31.0
2. Cancer	538,947	23.1
3. Stroke	158,060	23.1
4. Lung Diseases	114,381	4.9
5. Pneumonia and Influenza	94,828	4.1
6. Accidents	93,207	4.0
7. Diabetes Mellitus	64,574	2.8
8. Suicide	29,264	1.3
9. Kidney Diseases	26,295	1.1
10. Liver Diseases	24,936	1.1

Source: National Center for Health Statistics, Washington, D.C.: U.S. Department of Health and Human Services, 2001.

The chronic diseases are also known as degenerative diseases and tend to be associated with old age. Arteriosclerosis involves the narrowing and sometimes the blocking of arteries carrying blood to vital organs, including the heart, brain, and kidneys. This appears to be the result of long-term accumulation of fatty material and calcium on the interior walls of arteries; the risk increases with age. High-cholesterol diets over long periods contribute to the blockages, and the sedentary habits of urban life apparently are also partly responsible.

At the opposite end of the life cycle, children confront new dangers. As everyone knows, small children will chew on almost anything—toys, utensils, and whatever else is in reach. In the poorer areas of the cities and towns, where many families live in substandard housing, paint peels off the walls and children pull at the slivers and chew on them. The paint contains lead, and it is now known that many children contract lead poisoning in this way, as well as from drinking water that has flowed through old lead pipes. Lead poisoning has several negative effects, including brain damage.

In addition, in many parts of the country drinking water contains substances that may be conducive to the development of cancer. Chlorine and fluoride are added to water to reduce the risk of contamination, and other chemicals are used to treat water pollution of various kinds. We are not sure of the long-term effects of consuming treated water, however, and we may be substituting one risk for another. It is one thing to start using treated water at middle age, but it is another to begin consuming it at birth. When something is consumed from birth, damaging substances have a long time to build up. Water treatment on the scale at which it occurs today is a relatively new phenomenon, and only the most recent generation has been using chemically treated water from birth. The results in terms of disease and mortality are not yet known.

Genetic Diseases

The origins of genetic or inherited diseases lie in the chromosomes and genes, and these maladies can be transferred from one generation to the next. Genetic diseases are not well understood, although some, such as sickle-cell anemia, have been studied intensively.

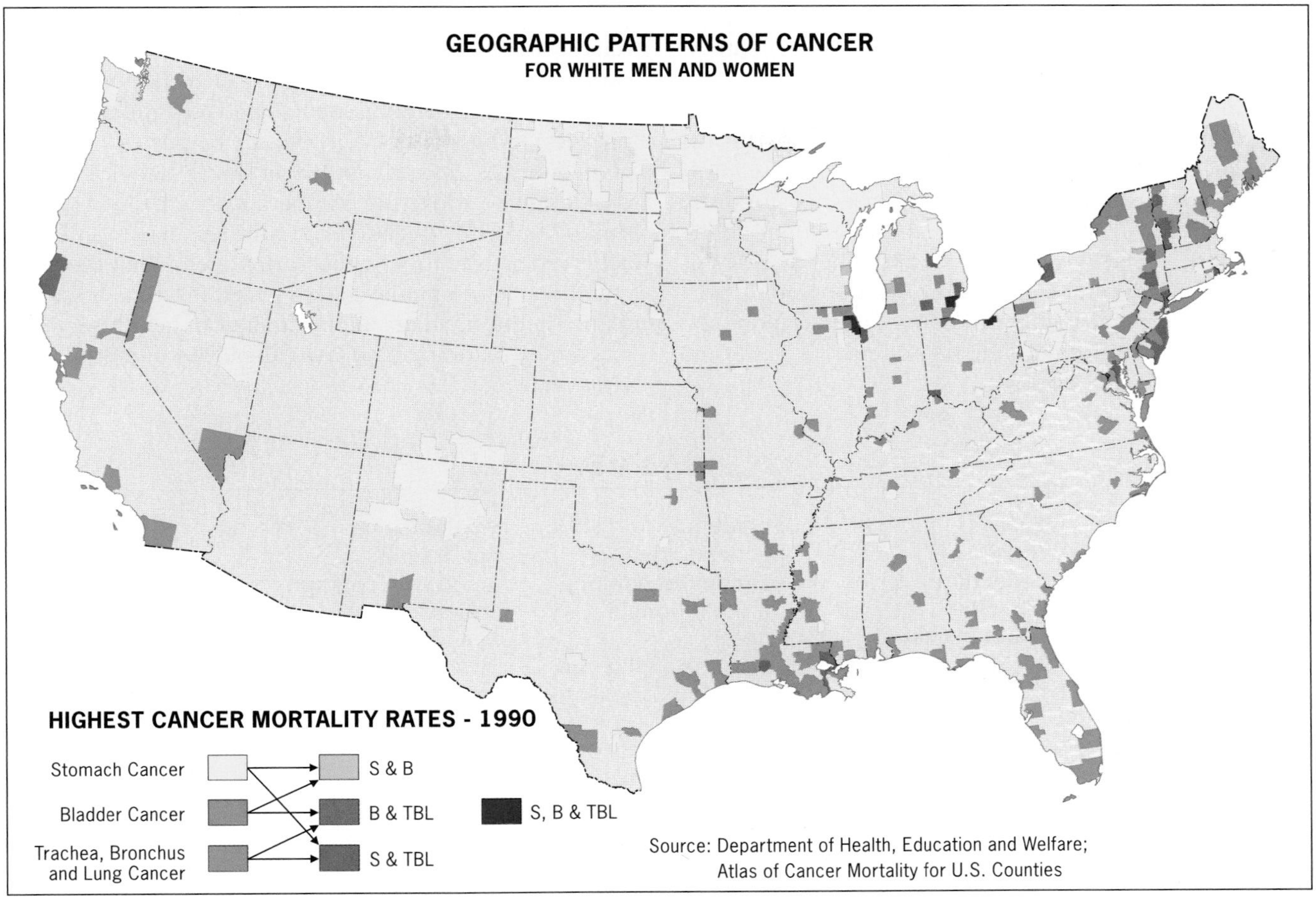

Figure 30-14 Highest Cancer Mortality Rates, 1990. The regional aspects of cancer incidence in the United States as of 1990 are illustrated in this map. *Source:* Department of Health, Education and Welfare; Atlas of Cancer Mortality for U.S. Counties.

Genetic diseases result from gene mutations or accidents to the chromosomes. In some cases, a mutation may occur in the fetus before birth and affect the child even if both parents are completely normal; Down's Syndrome is an example. Radiation and viruses may also damage a parent's chromosomes, but the role of drugs in gene mutations is still uncertain. From a geographic standpoint, other forms of inherited disease are of greater interest. Certain genetic diseases are concentrated in specific populations, and others appear to be associated with particular natural environments. *Phenylketonuria,* for example, occurs mostly among Europeans. People who have this disorder cannot convert one kind of amino acid into another, and unless it is diagnosed and treated early, mental retardation results.

Metabolic problems—the inability to process all elements of the diet—are a major category of genetic diseases. Enzymes facilitate critical reactions within the body, and failure to produce an adequate quantity of a particular enzyme (or to produce any at all) leads to metabolic malfunction. Such a disorder can be inherited. A prominent example is primary adult lactose intolerance. People who suffer from this disorder lack an adequate supply of an enzyme needed to break down the milk sugar lactose. When it is severe, this "milk allergy," or ***galactosemia***, leads to damage of the liver and spleen; young children display swelling of the abdomen, face, hands, and feet due to the accumulation of fluid. Mental retardation can result, but this effect is rare. The symptoms are more likely to be mild, including stomach and intestinal pain after milk is consumed or foods containing lactose are eaten. People who experience such discomfort will reduce or eliminate their intake of milk.

People who cannot comfortably consume milk and other foods containing lactose may suffer from deficiencies in nutrients that these foods contribute to the body, especially calcium. This has led to some unusual supplementing of diets, including the ancient custom of earth-eating, or *geophagy*. In West Africa this time-honored practice involves the eating of clay for medicinal and dietary reasons.

Lactose intolerance does not occur randomly. For example, it is much more prevalent among African-

Americans than among whites. In India, primary adult lactose intolerance is the rule rather than the exception. (About 80 percent of India's population probably has some intolerance, and in China the figure may be even higher.) In Africa, the peoples of the forest zone, who do not have livestock that give milk, are highly lactose intolerant, while those of the savanna, who are pastoralists, have much lower intolerance. As these regional differences illustrate, lactose intolerance and other diseases of metabolic origin can be studied from a geographic perspective, in terms of migration routes, acculturation (see Chapter 2), natural environments, ethnic distributions, and other spatial phenomena.

This chapter has focused on only a few of the topics related to the health of the world's population. The problems of medical geography should not be viewed in isolation from other issues related to population. Improved medical systems in poorer countries may prevent diseases from claiming as many lives as in the past—only to add to the numbers who will die of starvation. Even the wealthier countries have still not achieved satisfactory health-care systems, but the poor countries in particular need programs that combine planning efforts in nutrition, sanitation, health services, and family planning. The tasks ahead are numerous and enormous.

◆ KEY TERMS ◆

agent
AIDS
aquaculture
bilharzia
caloric intake
child mortality rate
cholera
chronic disease
contagious disease
dietary balance
endemic
epidemic
genetic diseases
Green Revolution
hidden hunger
hosts
infant mortality rate
infectious disease
influenza
kwashiorkor
life expectancy
malaria
malnutrition
marasmus
medical geography
miracle rice
pandemic
reservoir
river blindness
sleeping sickness
vector
vehicle
yellow fever

◆ APPLYING GEOGRAPHIC KNOWLEDGE ◆

1. Two northeast corners of continents, Africa and South America, periodically suffer from climatic extremes (mainly droughts, but also floods) and resulting food shortages. In Brazil's northeast, the government never has been able to forestall starvation; in Somalia, a relief effort under UN auspices ended in failure. Compare these two areas from environmental, cultural, and political standpoints and explain why they continue to defy attempts to reduce their problems.
2. As a geographer, you have been asked by a government to assist in promoting land reform as a partial solution to food shortages. But the task is difficult and sensitive: some of the large landholdings targeted for reform produced not only food harvests, but also cash crops for which the government receives taxes. How will your advice attempt to balance the losses and gains inherent in land reform, and project a favorable long-range outcome?
3. Despite improvements in sanitation and health care in Europe and North America over the past few decades, some infectious diseases are more rampant now than they were 40 years ago. What social, economic, and technological changes help explain this circumstance?
4. You are a member of a team of medical geographers working on AIDS. Your maps of the incidence of AIDS reveal different spatial patterns of transmission for different cultural realms of the world, and even for different societies within these realms. How are culture and AIDS interrelated?

Chapter 31

Geographies of Inequality: Race and Ethnicity

From the field notes

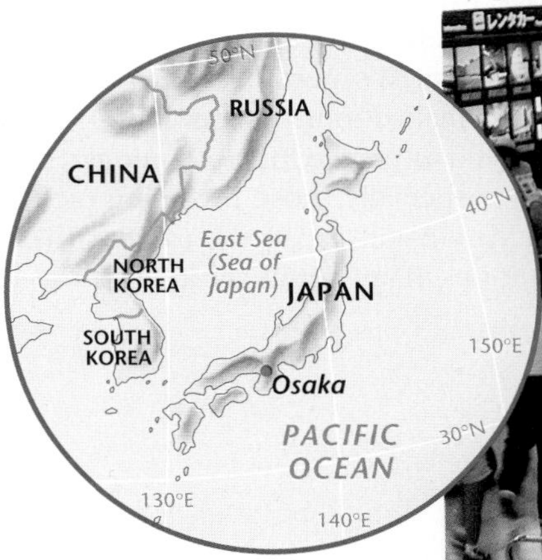

"Ethnicity can be a sensitive topic, but in some places more than others. Japan is the most ethnically homogeneous large country in the world, with tiny minorities of indigenous people (Ainu) and other East Asians (mainly Koreans) the sole exception to the rule. And Japanese nationality generally implies Japanese ethnicity. The international arrivals hall of the Osaka Airport leaves no doubt: who are the non-Japanese in this photo?"

KEY POINTS

◆ **All humanity constitutes one race, but humans differ physically from each other. Many societies have used these differences to create distinctions in status and opportunity among individuals.**

◆ **The idea that skin color is a particularly important way of dividing humans is rooted in cultural, as opposed to biological, understandings.**

◆ **Racism is often associated with a degree of segregation that promotes stereotypes and influences where people go and what they do.**

◆ **Ethnicity differs from race because it is based on notions of cultural history and lifestyles. Race and ethnicity can overlap, however, when race is treated as a symbol or source of cultural division among peoples.**

◆ **Ethnic islands can be eroded through processes of acculturation, but cultural linkages and networks can help sustain senses of ethnic identity.**

◆ **Ethnic conflict is often rooted in the frustrations of ethnic groups living in political territories that are defined and governed by the national ambitions of other ethnic groups.**

Ours is a world of inequalities—of unequal opportunities, advantages, and privileges. The disparities apply across the board, to entire countries, to majorities and minorities within those countries, and to individuals in those societies. Disadvantaged people in the peripheral regions look with envy at the material advantages of those located in the wealthy core. Dominant majorities in multicultural states create and sustain systems designed to protect their privileges. Members of minority groups find their upward path blocked by racial or ethnic discrimination. Women the world over suffer from mistreatment in male-dominated cultures.

In the next two chapters we focus on geographic aspects of inequality, especially those involving race, ethnicity, and gender. As we will find, these are sensitive topics; even the definitions of key terms are in dispute. ◆

◆ THE HUMAN RACE

When you enter a foreign country for a visit, you may be asked to fill out a questionnaire to be presented to the immigration office. As often as not, one of the questions will be "What is your race?" The answer, of course, is "human." All human beings belong to the same species. However, the answer "human" is not the one that is wanted. (In fact, it may get you into trouble.) What the questionnaire is asking is what kind of human being you are, that is, what recognizable group you belong to. The term *race* has become synonymous with something other than the human species. It focuses on differences rather than on similarities.

This terminology is as frustrating to biologists and anthropologists as the misuse of geographic terms such as state, nation, or frontier is to human geographers. Indeed, many anthropologists believe that the whole concept of human "races" should be abandoned. Yet we cannot avoid the fact that humans do not all look alike and that the differences are given varying emphases in different societies.

◆ A GEOGRAPHY OF RACE

Let us look at the positive side first. There is no doubt about the biological unity of the human species: no matter where we live and whatever our physical attributes, our genetic structures are similar. Our physical systems function in remarkably similar ways, and we have the capacity to interbreed and produce offspring.

We may think that humans have a wide range of appearances, but some other species display a much wider variation. Take dogs, for example. All dogs belong to the same species, but a Saint Bernard does not appear to have much in common with a fox terrier, or a wolf with a

Pekingese. But it is not appearance that is the key. Rather, it is the genetic makeup of the individuals. Within a species, the chromosomes of reproducing organisms are identical in number and size, and they carry very similar groups of genes.

Nevertheless, groups of individuals within a species display certain physical characteristics that tend to set them apart from others. In the human species, these groups (sometimes called subspecies or populations) exhibit regional variation. This variation results not from differences in the fundamental genetic makeup of each group but from differences in gene frequencies among populations. For example, some people are blue-eyed, others brown-eyed; the blue-eyed dominate in the populations of northern Europe, while the brown-eyed prevail in southern Europe. Another variation related to gene frequencies has to do with blood type. The O type dominates in Native American populations, while the A type prevails in Western Europe. These and other differences among human populations occur within the human race, not between races.

What has caused the regional variation in the appearance of humans in clustered populations? What is often called a race is in fact a combination of physical attributes in a population, the product of a particular genetic inheritance that dominates in that population (such as Australia's Aborigines, North Africa's Berbers, or Asia's Mongols). This inheritance varies from one population to another and probably results from a long history of adaptation to different environments. For this reason, use of the term *race* for such populations is in error.

Genetics and Inheritance

When Charles Darwin published his *Origin of Species* in 1859 (complete title: *The Origin of Species by Means of Natural Selection or the Preservation of Favoured Races in the Struggle for Life*), his critics seized upon a major weakness: Darwin failed to explain exactly how traits are passed from one generation to the next. But before the end of the nineteenth century, the broad principles of ***genetics*** were understood. This field was given its name by the English biologist William Bateson. The term *gene* was introduced to signify the physical basis of an inherited quality. Genes were defined as units of inheritance for certain traits (say, eye color or body size), which together form a ***genotype***. The expression of those traits (say, brown eyes or tall build) forms the ***phenotype***.

A century ago it was believed that groups of people of similar appearance (phenotype) would share, and therefore repeat, a single genotype. Today, however, it is known that all individuals except identical twins are genetically unique; each has his or her own "genetic fingerprint." This uniqueness makes it possible to identify a person through his or her DNA, which can be derived from even a small sample of blood, hair, or saliva.

Culture and Race

Unfortunately, our understanding of the biological concept of race does little to change how many people see race. This is the negative side: after tens of thousands of years of movement and migration, mixing, and intermarriage in our increasingly mobile world, human populations exhibit a wide array of characteristics, but many continue to see race as a simple way of dividing humans into a small number of groups based primarily on generalizations about skin color.

The idea that skin color is a particularly important way of dividing humans is rooted in cultural, as opposed to biological, understandings. Yes, there is a diversity of skin pigmentation among humans, and this broadly correlates with environmental factors. Sunlight stimulates the production of *melanin*, which protects skin from damaging ultraviolet rays; the more melanin that is present, the darker the skin will be. Many believe that this helps to explain why, over the millennia, humans living in low latitudes—from tropical Africa through southern India to Australia—developed darker skins. Another (not incompatible) theory holds that vitamin D production is stimulated by the penetration of ultraviolet rays, such that over the millennia, natural selection in areas with shorter days in winter and more oblique sun angles (i.e., the higher latitudes) favored those with the least amount of pigmentation that might block ultraviolet rays.

Understanding the relationship between environment and skin pigmentation can be of interest if, for example, one wants to comprehend past patterns of human migration. The indigenous population of Australia has much darker skin pigmentation than does the indigenous population of the Americas. This suggests that the diffusion route of the Australian Aborigines was tropical, so that even before their migration into Australia they had inhabited low latitudes for a very long time. The first Americans, however, probably came from higher latitudes.

Whatever may be said about the link between environment and the development of particular physical characteristics, it is important to recognize that skin color is *not* a reliable indicator of genetic closeness. The indigenous peoples of southern India, New Guinea, and Australia are as dark-skinned as native Africans, but black Africans, southern Indians, and Aboriginal Australians are not closely related genetically. Thus, there is no biological basis for dividing the human species into four or five groups based on skin color. Instead, this is the product of how particular cultures have *viewed* skin color. There are examples of societies drawing racial distinctions throughout human history, and many of them have involved drawing distinctions based on relatively minor variants in skin color. But in the contemporary world, more often than not such distinctions are based on broad categories with roots in the cultural histories of the dominant political and economic powers of the past few centuries. To understand how the very categories we use in defining race are the product of a particular history is to understand the degree to which race is indeed a cultural conception.

Let us keep one other reality in mind as we approach this sensitive topic. What is often called "racial" conflict is nothing of the sort. The disastrous breakdown of order in Rwanda in the 1990s is a case in point. The Western press implied that a genuine difference exists between the Tutsi and the Hutu "races" who killed each other by the hundreds of thousands. Although Tutsi and Hutu did fight over land and primacy in areas around Rwanda long ago, those distinctions had largely faded when the most recent civil war broke out. No one can discern a Tutsi from a Hutu just by physical appearance. The war was over status, advantage, and opportunity. The conflict was cultural or ethnic, not "racial." A culturally rooted sense of ethnicity transcends "racial" stereotype. Many of Rwanda's Hutu, through social success and/or intermarriage, had "become" Tutsi, taking on the habits and privileges of this advantaged minority. Many paid the price at the hands of other resentful Hutu.

So it is culture, not the misused notion of race, that often produces conflict among human groups. In the former Yugoslavia, the Bosnian Muslims and the Serbs, as well as the Croats, are Slavs. In Northern Ireland, no one can tell a Catholic from a Protestant, but the thousands of people who have died in that conflict were almost all of Irish or distant Scottish ancestry. In Israel, little distinguishes Jew from Palestinian except culture and associated feelings of ethnic distinctiveness.

◆ THE SCOURGE OF RACISM

Despite the evidence that humans are a single species, we continue to use appearance as a basis for dividing ourselves into separate groups and creating inequalities. The importance of race is reinforced every time a visa form is filled out or a report on voting emphasizes differences among "racial" groups. Against this backdrop, it is easy to forget that the traits that societies regard as indicating racial divisions are not fixed. The darkness of skin pigmentation is a basis for "racial" divisions in parts of Africa, but in the United States anyone of African descent is regarded as being part of a single race. Moreover, as the publicity surrounding the golfer Tiger Woods reminds us, the increased intermixing of the world's populations over the past century has produced a growing number of people who are difficult to classify in terms of any of the traditional racial categories.

These subtleties notwithstanding, many societies around the world *do* treat race as significant, and a large number of people believe that those of different races—however defined—are in some senses inferior. ***Racism*** is, therefore, part of the human condition, and it has both geographic expression and geographic consequences. Attacks on Turkish guestworkers in Germany are the product of a flow of people from one part of the world to another. Such attacks are concentrated in areas where social problems are more acute and nationalism has taken root among the young. In India, lighter-skinned families have for centuries enjoyed advantage and privilege as a result of a hierarchical system that came into being when Moghuls (Mongols) invaded the subcontinent. Some African-Americans in the United States find themselves with few opportunities for educational or social advancement. In these and many other cases, racism influences the organization of people and place in ways that have significant impacts on possibilities and opportunities.

From the field notes

"Whenever I am in a port city, I walk the docks to see what cargo is being shipped, and try to learn whether any significant changes are occurring. On this day at the port of Cape Town I learned a great deal more: these fellows were waiting for their assignments and told me about working conditions, job security, social life, and politics in the Western Cape. I asked whether they voted for the African National Congress, South Africa's dominant political party. 'People with shiny shoes don't vote ANC, man,' said the fellow in the uniform, 'we don't want the ANC running this place.' This led to much laughter about whose shoes were least scuffed and who was therefore best-paid and laziest (the photographer was elected). During the apartheid period, everyone in this photograph was officially classified as 'Coloured,' that is, neither African nor white, and this ethnic designation still identifies a minority of some 3 million at the Cape today. When I asked about their main concerns, they quickly agreed that immigration from the Eastern Cape, rising crime, and increasing costs of living troubled them most."

Racism in the United States

The United States has had a particularly complicated history of race relations because one "racial" group, Native Americans, were pushed to the side—and in some cases slaughtered—as the country was founded and built, and another group, African-Americans, arrived in a desperately unequal situation—as slaves. The latter led to a system of exploitation whose worst features were ended by the Civil War but whose effects are still manifest today in everything from the paucity of African-Americans in senior management positions to persistent inequalities in income. In recent decades, the United States has done much to guarantee equal protection of all people under the law—most clearly in the enactment of the Civil Rights Act of 1964. Yet in many of the places where Americans live and work, race continues to be a divisive factor in American society.

Race is a particularly notable feature of the internal geography of many American urban areas. Cities such as Chicago and Washington, D.C., are remarkably segregated along racial lines. The significance of segregation goes beyond who lives where. Segregation promotes stereotypes of racial neighborhoods, and it fosters arrangements and perceptions that affect what people do and where they do it. Many Americans carry images of African-American neighborhoods as dangerous places where crime is rampant. Although some neighborhoods conform to this image, many do not. And the impacts of the visible and invisible boundaries that separate neighborhoods are often striking. Blacks can be hesitant to venture into white areas, and vice versa, for fear of discrimination or worse. City planners, investors, and business entrepreneurs make decisions that consciously or unconsciously are influenced by assumptions about the distinctiveness of racially defined neighborhoods—decisions that in turn can promote further differences among neighborhoods. These geographic processes are a critical element of the social geography of American cities. Understanding racial patterns at various scales can reveal important aspects of the way human beings create communities and relate to one another.

Historical Geography and the Fallacy of Racial Superiority

Notions of racial supremacy are premised on the idea that groups with particular physical characteristics are more advanced, capable, or intelligent. White supremacists, for example, have bolstered their claims to superiority by noting that some of the most advanced technological cultures are based in the realm dominated by Europeans. Yet even the most cursory consideration of historical geographic arrangements puts the lie to such ideas. Civilizations in Asia and Africa developed sophisticated cultures long before most European societies managed to rise above simple tribal organization. For thousands of years the greatest achievements in administration, legislation, education, agriculture, construction, writing, and other fields were made in China, Southwest Asia, and North Africa—not in Europe. Looking at the world through the lenses of geography and history helps expose the fallacies of those who seek to equate race with capacity or intelligence.

We can condemn racial stereotypes, but we must come back to the inescapable fact that physical appearance, notably skin color, remains a critical factor in people's relationships and in their advantages and opportunities (or lack thereof). How many millions of conflicts, individual and collective, small and large, have begun because of this attribute? The "racial" stereotype remains a huge obstacle to social harmony.

◆ ETHNIC PATTERNS AND PROCESSES

Only a few decades ago, many social scientists treated ethnicity as a relic of the past that was rapidly giving way to "national" (i.e., state) loyalties and identities. Yet a look at any newspaper today reveals the significance of ethnicity in the contemporary world. Ethnicity is in many senses as important a category as race—sometimes even overlapping race. And ethnicity defies easy definition or description. Its defining characteristics differ from place to place, and a map showing all recognizable ethnic areas would look like a three-dimensional jigsaw puzzle of thousands of often-overlapping pieces, some no larger than a neighborhood, others as large as entire countries.

But size is no measure of the intensity of ethnic identity and solidarity. These feelings are the product of socially and historically rooted perceptions of distinctiveness based on shared cultural traits, a common history, a treasured cultural landscape, and real or potential threats to language or faith. "Racial" ancestry may or may not play a part in this, but ethnicity should not necessarily be equated with race-consciousness. As noted earlier, all the combatants in the former Yugoslavia are Slavs. In Equatorial Africa, the conflict is not simply between Hutu and Tutsi, both of whom are African peoples. It is between peoples who define themselves in terms of cultural history and lifestyles, and of course it is about power.

Where ethnic and racial conflict coincide, it is because mutually antagonistic groups perceive themselves to be of different ancestries as, for example, occurs between the Sinhalese and the Tamils in Sri Lanka. Race also functions as a symbolic divider between many indigenous peoples and later arrivals. The Native Peoples of the Americas—both North and South—have long suffered from discrimination along ethnic and racial lines. In New Zealand, where a growing Maori (Polynesian) community now numbers over 450,000 in a population of 3.9 million, race is implicated in a struggle over territory; growing ethnic awareness and identity have led the Maoris to launch a campaign not just to improve their position in New Zealand society but to regain control over about half of the country's territory. Asserting that the British settlers of New Zealand have violated the 1840 Treaty of Waitangi, the Maoris have gone to court to achieve this objective.

In these and other cases, race and ethnicity are inextricably intertwined, but the majority of ethnic conflicts have no racial basis. Instead, they are rooted in perceptions of distinctiveness based on actual or perceived differences in language, religion, lifestyle, or historical experience.

Ethnic Spaces and Places

We all use the term *ethnic* routinely: to describe a neighborhood, to identify a certain cuisine. In the American mosaic of cultures, ethnic enclaves are common and have names such as "Little Italy," "Chinatown," or "Little Havana." Such names signify clusters of people whose shared ancestry and cultures give them a special identity in a city's social mix. Ethnic heritage lingers in the countryside, too. Sometimes this is revealed in place-names—for example, Holland (Michigan), Denmark (Wisconsin), and Stockholm (North Dakota).

From the field notes

"Walking through the back streets of Taipei I noted the distinct identities of local neighborhoods: superficially they looked similar, but look more closely, and you saw variations in the kinds of stores, sorts of goods, types of activities (from repair shops to art studios), even the ways doors were marked and windows draped. And then I heard the sound of laughter and applause, and followed it to find a street theater in progress. The play went on for hours; pedestrians would stop and watch, other passersby got off their bikes and spent some time listening. By the time I left, the audience that was there when I arrived had been almost totally replaced. 'It's very local, very ethnic,' said a colleague whom I asked about this. 'These groups make some pretty biting criticisms of their neighbors!' Here, obviously, is one way ethnic identity is kept alive."

Such place-names—which also occur as neighborhood designations in American cities—record not only the origins but also the aspirations of some of America's immigrants. Note how many U.S. cities and towns have European names with the prefix "New"; undoubtedly, the ethnic groups clustering in such places not only called them "New" but hoped for a "better" Albany, Almelo, Bremen, Durham, Leipzig, Plymouth, Prague, and dozens more. The immigrants who came to North America's urban places from the crowded cities and awful sweatshop industries of industrializing Europe were familiar with city life, poverty, and insecurity. What they came for was jobs, and what they hoped for was the strength of numbers. So they, too, named their neighborhoods Ha(a)rlem, Brooklyn, Cicero, and Livonia, where they converged and helped each other succeed in a new setting.

Other groups of immigrants, however, came from rural areas and hoped to find comparable, perhaps familiar natural environments. It is thus not surprising that certain rural ethnic groups in America are concentrated in natural environs that are similar to those of their source areas: Scandinavians in Minnesota, Finns in northern Wisconsin, Germans in central and southern Wisconsin, Dutch (Hollanders mainly) in western Michigan, Italians in California.

These rural ***ethnic islands*** in the cultural mosaic reflect their inhabitants' perceptions of both the natural environment they left behind and the one they selected after arriving in America. Similar landscape and vegetation did not always mean similar climate and soils, and some communities could not adjust. But many more made a fortuitous choice, and from the German and English dairy farmers of Wisconsin to the Italian winegrowers of California, they brought prosperity to the places where they settled.

Exactly what are the origins of the term *ethnic*? It comes from the ancient Greek word *ethnos*, meaning "people" or "nation." In Latin, the adjective became *ethnicus*, and hence *ethnic*, also an adjective. Note, however, what happens when the term is used in the combined form, for example, ethnology and ethnogeny. In these terms race is a crucial component. The adjective *ethnic* thus refers to culture (traditions, customs, language, religion) and, in a much more general, often vague sense, to racial ancestry.

As noted earlier, this racial identity is largely a matter of self-perception. When the Yugoslavian republic of Slovenia declared its independence in 1991, local newspapers carried reports justifying that decision. Those reports frequently referred to the rights of the Slovenian "race" to control its own domain. But in the ethnic makeup of Slovenia, race is much less significant than cultural and natural environments. Slovenian is a discrete Slavic language (see the discussion in Part Three), and Slovenia lies to the northwest of the religious transition zone between Roman Catholicism and Eastern Orthodoxy that crossed the former Yugoslavia (see Part Four). Perceptions of the natural environment can also play a role in forging a sense of cultural distinctiveness. Slovenians refer to their country as an Alpine, not a Balkan, republic. Slovenian nationalists may have called upon race to bolster people's feelings of nationalism, but the strength of Slovenian ethnicity is based on other cultural traditions and customs.

Ethnicity thus arises out of different combinations of cultural traditions, racial backgrounds, and natural environments. In Northern Ireland there is no racial distinction between two ethnic groups that are locked in a tragic struggle: the dominant ethnic glue is a sense of national belonging that is symbolized by religion: Catholic for one group, Protestant for the other. In Belgium, the symbolic glue is linguistic. In Northern Belgium, the Flemings are an ethnolinguistic group made up of more than 6 million people. Heirs to the rich cultural history of Flanders, they speak a language derived from Dutch. Southern Belgium is the domain of nearly 4 million French-speaking Walloons. The capital, Brussels (Bruxelles in French, Brussel in Flemish), lies north of the ethnic division that splits Belgium, a division so deep that each language region has its own parliament. As in so many multiethnic countries, one ethnic group (most recently the Walloons, but historically the Flemings) fears domination by a larger or more powerful ethnic group within the national boundaries.

Cases such as Ireland and Belgium reveal the role of the political organization of space not just in fostering ethnic conflict, but in the creation of ethnic identity itself. The rise of ethnoreligious consciousness in Northern Ireland is inextricably tied to Great Britain's territorial ambitions in the modern era. In the Belgian case, Flemings and Walloons were not even self-conscious ethnolinguistic groups at the beginning of the nineteenth century. The development of Flemish identity was tied to the challenges faced by non-French speakers after Belgium gained independence in 1830, and Walloon identity grew up as a reaction to the Flemish movement. The twentieth-century decision to partition the state along language lines both reflected growing ethnic polarization and helped to promote feelings of ethnolinguistic difference.

Thus, like other aspects of culture, ethnicity is a dynamic phenomenon that must be understood in terms of the geographic context in which it is situated (see "Sense of Scale" box). Ethnic communities in American cities and towns often are quite small, sometimes having no more than a few thousand inhabitants. On a national scale, ethnic groups may have millions of members, as in the case of Yugoslavia and Belgium. And in many senses "nations" such as the French, the Russians, and the Chinese can themselves be thought of as ethnic groups, for they are communities that define their distinctiveness based on perceptions of shared culture, history, and lifestyle.

A SENSE OF SCALE

Chinatown in Mexicali

The ethnic patterns that attract the most attention sometimes obscure important smaller-scale patterns. This was the case when Czechoslovakia was breaking up; concerns with the Czech-Slovak relationship obscured the fact that a substantial Hungarian minority lives in Slovakia. The border region between the United States and Mexico provides another case in point. This border region is generally regarded as a bicultural Anglo-Hispanic meeting point. Yet a more detailed examination of the region reveals that members of a number of different ethnic communities have shaped the region over time. Settlers from Germany, Russia, India, China, and Japan established themselves in both cities and rural areas. While many have blended into the larger community over time, distinctive ethnic patterns persist.

Take, for example, the case of the Chinese in Mexicali, Mexico, the Baja California capital city lying just south of the State of California. Not far from the historic core of this city of 600,000 residents can be found one of the largest Chinatowns in Mexico. A 1995 study of the Mexicali Chinatown by geographer James R. Curtis showed that it has been the crucible of Chinese ethnicity in the Mexicali Valley throughout much of the twentieth century. Chinese began arriving in 1902, and by 1919 more than 11,000 Chinese were either permanent or temporary residents of the valley. They established a thriving Chinatown in the heart of Mexicali that served as the uncontested center of Chinese life in the region for decades.

The Chinese of Mexicali were prominent players in the social and economic life of the city during the twentieth century. They owned and operated restaurants, retail trade establishments, commercial land developments, currency exchanges, and more. By 1989 they owned nearly 500 commercial or service properties. Moreover, in an effort to sustain their cultural traditions and to add the cultural life of the city, they established the China Association, which plays an active role in Mexicali's social and civic life.

As a result of the aging infrastructure of Mexicali's Chinatown, together with the growing affluence of some members of the Chinese community, Chinese have dispersed to the edges of the city and beyond. Relatively few Chinese continue to live in

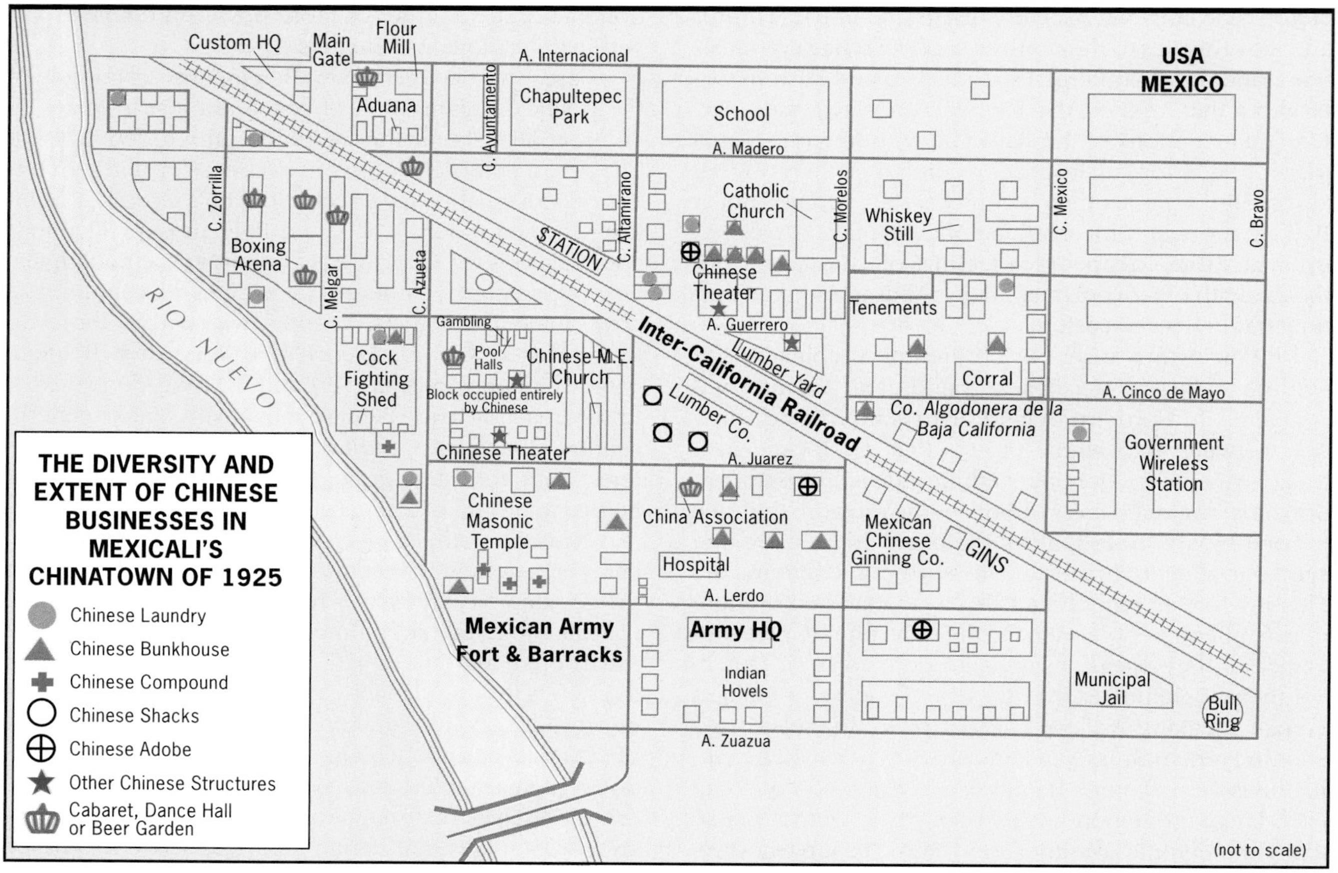

Mexicali, 1925. The diversity and extent of Chinese businesses in Mexicali's Chinatown of 1925 is shown in this map. *Source*: J. R. Curtis, "Mexicali's Chinatown," *The Geographical Review*. Vol. 85 (1995), p. 344.

the city's Chinatown; some have even moved across the border to Calexico, while retaining business interests in Mexicali. Yet Mexicali's Chinatown continues to play an important symbolic and functional role for individuals of Chinese ancestry in the area—people who are still shaping the region's social and economic geography. The story of these people reminds us that behind many national or regional scale generalizations about ethnic patterns lie "hidden" groups. Although they may be relatively small in number, they often make substantial contributions to the character of the places they inhabit.

Ethnic distributions at these multiple scales are affected by many factors. In some cases, distinct ethnic areas are the product of discrimination and oppression. The "homelands" of Apartheid South Africa were designed in part to confine African ethnic groups to particular areas. Some segregated neighborhoods in American cities were sustained by discriminatory attitudes and institutions. Yet not all segregations are pernicious; some find comfort and security in the familiarity of their "own" culture and cultural landscape. In smaller urban communities, group identity and cohesiveness offer certain advantages: they can provide a social network and a safety net. Members of a particular ethnic community may be especially successful in certain businesses and will help other members of the group succeed in such businesses. For new arrivals, an ethnic neighborhood can ease the transition with a familiar language, a shared church, and stores carrying products that are valued in the local culture.

Acculturation and Ethnicity in North America

As we saw in Chapter 28, many North American cities have distinct urban ethnic neighborhoods. Some, however, are being eroded by the process of ***acculturation***. This process is evident in Miami's Cuban neighborhoods, for example, in which ethnic identity is far stronger among the old than among the young. Miami's Little Havana was created by a transplanted community that is now a generation older. The Span-

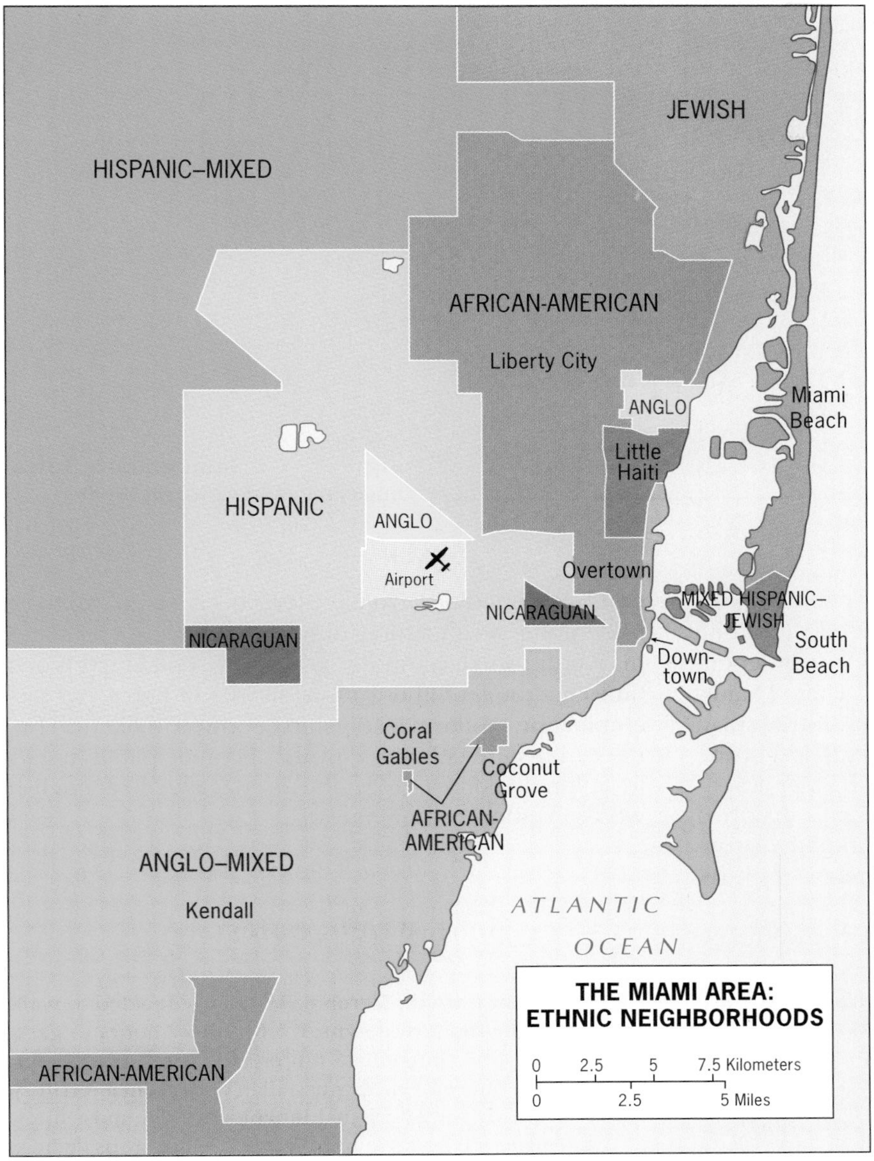

Figure 31-1 Ethnic Neighborhoods in the Miami Area. This map shows ethnic majorities in Miami-area neighborhoods in 1992. *Source*: Based on information provided by T. D. Boswell and I. M. Sheskin, University of Miami.

ish-speaking, aged domino players in the neighborhood's parks are a dwindling minority. The old values (strong family ties, regular Catholic church attendance, strict schooling) still prevail, but young Cuban Americans, born in Florida, are increasingly adopting dominant American cultural norms.

Does this mean that the Cuban ethnic neighborhood will disappear from Miami's urban scene? All ethnic communities go through transitions, and some disappear in the process. Yet many stabilize, and eventually Miami could well include established Cuban-American ethnic neighborhoods in addition to its other ethnic clusters (Fig. 31-1). Two basic factors promote stabilization in the face of acculturation pressures: cultural revival and growing awareness of cultural linkage.

Cultural revival takes several forms. In both urban and rural settings, people from similar ethnic backgrounds initially clustered in particular areas but later diffused outward, moving some distance from the community that served as a stepping stone during the difficult days of immigration (Fig. 31-2A). Over several generations these dispersed migrants increase in numbers, intermarry, and form a loose network of families that are still conscious of their shared ethnicity (Fig. 31-2B). As these families become more prosperous, funds sometimes become available for reviving their ties to the cultural source. The old neighborhood is reenergized by these renewed links (Fig. 31-2C). For example, newspapers published in various languages for particular ethnic communities have experienced increased circulation and broader regional distribution as a result of this process.

Renewed awareness of ***cultural linkage*** also tends to counter assimilation. Such awareness is strengthened by the enhanced flow of information through modern

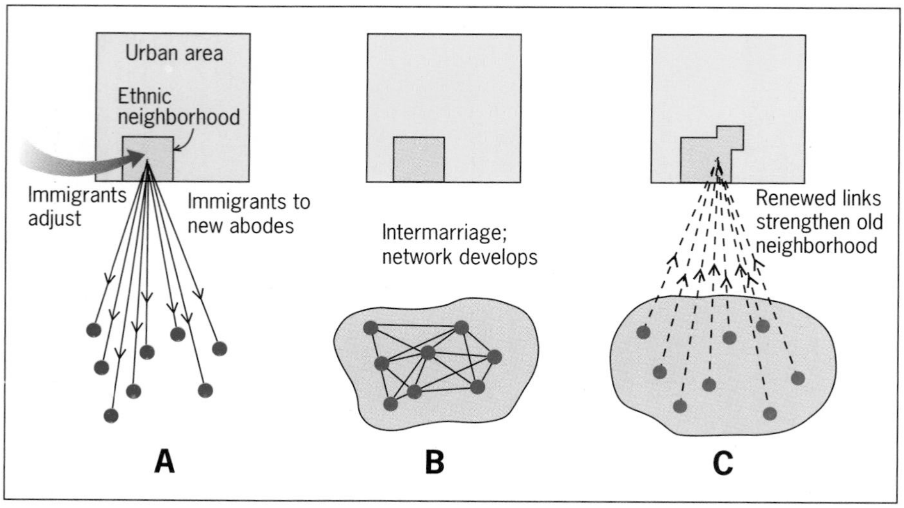

Figure 31-2 Immigration, Intermarriage, and Cultural Revival.

media. During the breakdown of the Soviet empire, for example, Lithuanian Americans marched on the White House in support of Lithuania's struggle for independence, and Ukrainian communities in the United States rallied for Ukrainian sovereignty. Serbian and Croatian neighborhoods in North America as well as in Europe were galvanized by the struggle in the former Yugoslavia. African-Americans in the United States marched in solidarity with black South Africans during the struggle to end Apartheid. Such emotional involvement revives ethnic consciousness and culture.

Finally, the cultural landscape can be a powerful element in promoting and sustaining ethnic distinctiveness. The dominant features of the cultural landscape are buildings—religious, public, private—and the layout of neighborhoods, villages, and towns. But the cultural landscape is more than buildings and layout. Signs in a particular language can be important, as can religious symbols. Clothing also makes a statement. Headgear and footwear and the wearing of jewelry and other ornaments contribute to a cultural landscape that promotes a sense of belonging and helps to maintain cultural boundaries.

◆ ETHNIC CONFLICT

Cultural revival and cultural linkage are cyclical processes. After Lithuania and Ukraine achieved independence, the common cause that aroused ethnic consciousness in American-Lithuanian and American-Ukrainian communities lost its urgency. But a conflict between Russia and Ukraine—for example, over the Crimean Peninsula—could quickly revive it.

Cultural consciousness also seems to ebb and flow without such external stimuli. Economic circumstances in a community vary over time, and prosperity plays a role in cultural perception and sensitivity. As a result, ethnic communities that have long been stable and have undergone acculturation during good economic times may erupt in disharmony and even separatism when times get tough. Other causes may lie in perceived discrimination, political leadership (a powerful political figure can inspire cultural revival), and anticipated threats to cultural identity (e.g., the growing use of English words in ethnic communities).

From the field notes

"Near Darwin, March 8, 1994. We decided to walk away from the modern downtown for a few hours to get a sense of the city's immediate hinterland. Darwin is a multicultural city, but remains an Australian outpost in a territory largely set aside for Aboriginal inhabitants. The most interesting places, we soon found, were the bus stops, where out-of-towners got off for work or social services. The man in the white shirt and his son had just arrived and allowed me to take their picture, but they spoke no English and our efforts at sign language caused much laughter among those waiting for the next bus."

Territory is at the root of ethnic conflict. As we saw in Part Five, the global political order is organized around so-called nation-states whose governments theoretically control the territory of the state in the name of the nation. But the concept of the nation itself is often tied to a particular sense of ethnic identity, which in turn can lead members of different ethnic groups to resist the control of national governments. This is especially likely to occur when governments seek to suppress or deny the existence of ethnic minorities within their territory. Those minorities, in turn, are likely to seek some territorial autonomy within, or separation from, the states in which they are situated. This process is at work among Kurds in Turkey, Basques in Spain, Tibetans in China, Ibos in Nigeria, Albanians in Serbia, and on and on. It even plays out in places where active suppression of minority groups is more a matter of history than of policy, yet intense ethnic regionalism is fueled by lingering feelings of domination. Canada and Quebec provide insight into such regionalism.

The Case of Quebec

Like the United States, Canada is a ***plural society***. Canada's population of over 31 million consists of several ethnic groups and includes people of British, French, Native American, Asian, Eastern European, and other ancestries. Territorially, Canada is even larger than the United States, although Canada's population is only slightly more than one-tenth that of the United States.

Canada is organized as a federal state. It is divided administratively into ten provinces, two territories, and the special territory of Nunavut, which has been set aside for the nation's indigenous peoples (Fig. 31-3). The

Figure 31-3 Canada's Provinces and Territories. Canada's provinces and territories and their capitals are illustrated here. The entity entitled Nunavut was proposed in 1992 to recognize the territorial rights of indigenous peoples in this area; it formally came into being in 1999.

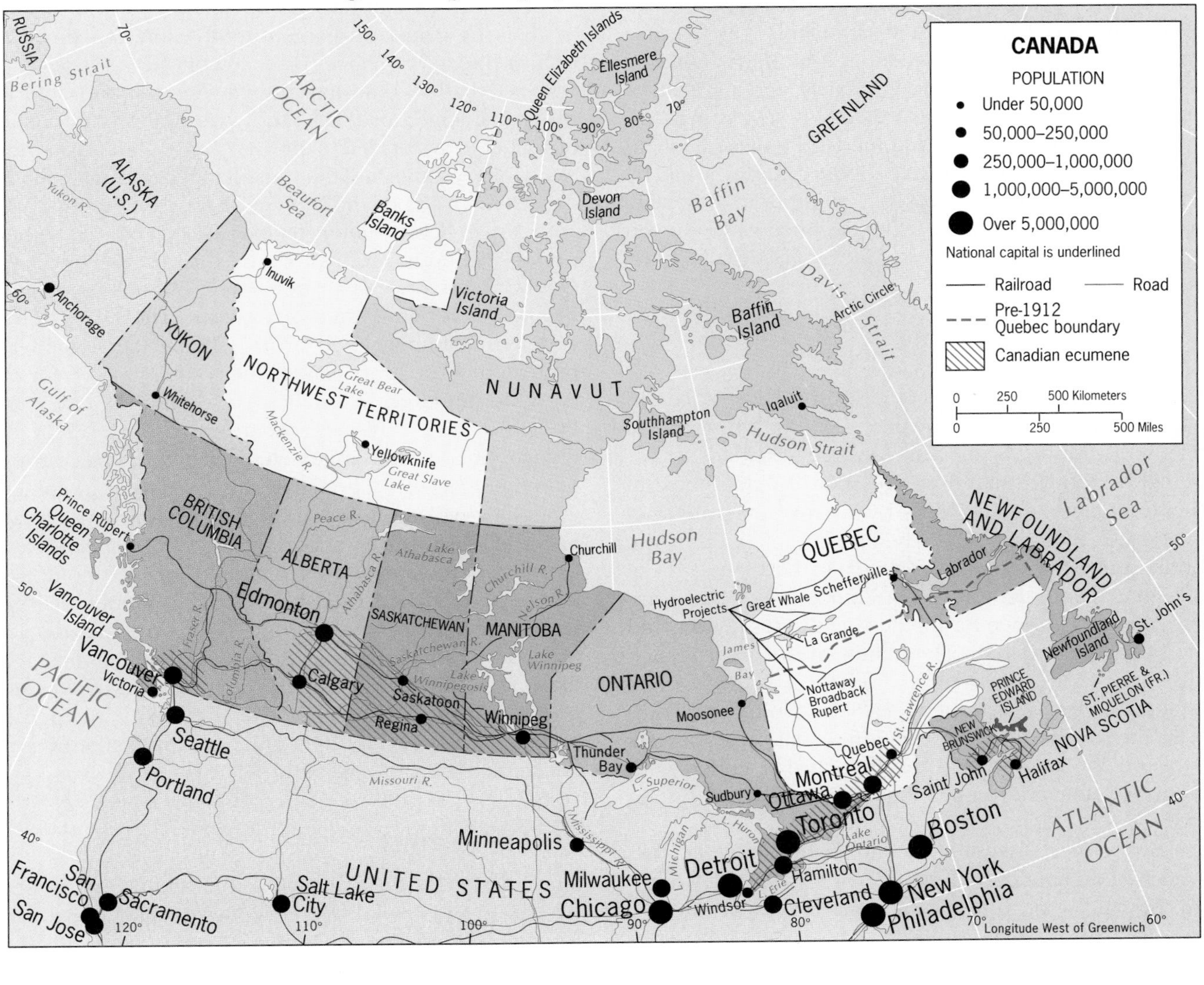

two territories, Yukon and the Northwest Territories, together occupy an area larger than Alaska and are inhabited by fewer than 100,000 people.

Canada's provinces range in size from tiny Prince Edward Island, the size of Delaware, to vast Quebec, more than twice as large as Texas. Each province has its own legislative assembly (Quebec calls this its national assembly) and premier. The country is also divided into 295 federal electoral districts, from which representatives to the House of Commons (Canada's House of Representatives) are chosen.

Canada faces diverse problems in its various provinces. The economies of the Atlantic Provinces have stagnated. In the far west, British Columbia's economy is growing rapidly—but so is its immigrant population, posing a social and cultural challenge. Such regional contrasts were anticipated in 1867, when the British North America Act established the Canadian federation. At the time, not all of present-day Canada joined; much of the West had yet to be organized. But the last province to join the federation was not a western one; it was Newfoundland, a holdout until 1949.

Modern, prosperous Canada would seem to have everything: a vast territory with a wealth of resources, a small, slowly growing population, a modern economy with high incomes by world standards, and a system of government that can accommodate regional differences. Canada's provinces are accustomed to a great deal of autonomy. Yet there have been periodic crises, sparked by changes in government policy, attempts to negotiate constitutional solutions to regional concerns, and even terrorism. At the heart of these crises are issues of ethnicity and ethnic revival.

French Canada

To understand the cultural stresses that have arisen in Canada, we should examine the federation's history and relative location. Eastern Canada was first settled by aboriginal people and later (c. A.D. 1000) by the Norse in Newfoundland, and possibly by Basque fishermen between A.D. 1000 and 1500. The French, followed by the British, entered present-day Canada in the 1530s. During the seventeenth century, New France grew to encompass the St. Lawrence Basin, the Great Lakes region, and the Mississippi Valley. (The names of the great French missionaries and explorers who led this advance are still on the map today: Marquette, La Salle, Duluth, and others.) The late 1680s saw the beginning of a series of wars between the English and the French that ended with France's defeat and the cession of New France to Britain in 1763.

By the time Britain took control of New France, the French had made considerable progress in their American domain. French laws, the French land-tenure system, and the Roman Catholic Church prevailed, and substantial settlements (including Montreal on the St. Lawrence) had been established. The British, anxious to avoid war and preoccupied with problems in other American colonies, gave former New France (the region extending from the Great Lakes to the mouth of the St. Lawrence) the right to retain its legal and land-tenure systems, as well as freedom of religion.

After the American War of Independence, the British were left with a region that they called British North America (the name Canada was not yet in use) but whose cultural imprint still was strongly French. The war drove many thousands of British refugees northward, and soon difficulties arose between the French and the English in British North America. In 1791, heeding appeals by British settlers, the British Parliament divided Quebec into two provinces: Upper Canada, the region upstream from Montreal and centered on Lake Ontario, and Lower Canada, the valley of the St. Lawrence. Upper and Lower Canada became, respectively, the provinces of Ontario and Quebec. Under the Parliament's plan, Ontario would become English-speaking and Quebec would remain French-speaking (Fig. 31-3).

This earliest cultural division did not work well, and in 1840 the British Parliament tried again, this time reuniting the two provinces in the Act of Union. Upper and Lower Canada would have equal representation in the provincial legislature. This, too, was a failure. Efforts to find a better system led to the 1867 British North America Act, which established the Canadian federation (initially consisting of Upper and Lower Canada, New Brunswick, and Nova Scotia, later to be joined by the other provinces and territories). Under this Act, Ontario and Quebec were once again separated, but this time Quebec was given important guarantees. The French civil code was left unchanged, and the French language was protected in Parliament and in the courts.

One hundred years later a significant event in French Canada's history occurred. The president of France, Charles de Gaulle, while visiting Canada during its centennial celebration, made open appeals to French ethnonationalism. Before a huge audience in Montreal, he ended a speech by shouting "Vive le Quebec Libre!" The thunderous response from the crowd left no doubt that he had touched a sensitive nerve in Quebec society. Quebecers did not have a strong Canadian champion, let alone an international one. Polls indicated that most felt like second-class citizens in their own country; that bilingualism meant that French-speakers had to learn English but not vice versa; and that Quebec was not getting its fair share of Canada's wealth.

Ethnic Revival

Since the 1960s, the intensity of ethnic feeling in Quebec has ebbed and flowed, despite government efforts to satisfy Quebec's demands. In the 1970s, a Quebecer was prime minister of Canada, and it seemed that a new constitution might satisfy those demands. In 1976 a political party calling for separatism finally came to power in Quebec, but in 1980 Quebec's voters rejected separation. Yet the new constitution did not satisfy Quebec, and polls indicated that, if given another chance, the voters would support separation from Canada. To prevent a crisis, Quebec was asked to present its terms for continued membership in the Canadian federation. Its key demand was recognition of Quebec as a "distinct society" within Canada. At a meeting at Meech Lake in 1987, the prime ministers of all of Canada's provinces agreed to these terms, which were to be ratified by their parliaments. However, when the deadline for ratification came, in 1990, the parliaments of Newfoundland and Manitoba had failed to ratify, and Quebec had reason to feel rejected. Immediate demands were heard for a new referendum on separation.

In the meantime, ethnic issues in Quebec, especially those involving language, became even more intense. Over 80 percent of Quebec's more than 7 million people speak French at home, but that still leaves a substantial minority of non-French speakers. In 1977 the Quebec Parliament had passed a law that compelled all businesses in the province to demonstrate that they functioned in French. As a result, many businesses and individuals moved to Ontario. Canada's Supreme Court ruled against Quebec's language legislation, but in 1988, Quebec enacted a law that not only reinstated the legislation the Supreme Court had overturned but added a regulation that made it illegal to exhibit any outdoor commercial sign in a language other than French.

Predictably, such actions caused reactions elsewhere in Canada. With fewer than 700,000 French-speaking Canadians living outside Quebec, other provinces reconsidered the costs of bilingualism. If English could be treated as it was within Quebec, should French be accorded equality under the law in, say, Alberta or Saskatchewan? Feelings of ethnicity increased among Canada's native peoples as well. Canada has more than 500,000 native inhabitants ("First Americans") in nearly 600 distinct bands. Their leaders pointed out that if the "distinct society" clause in the Meech Lake Accord could apply to French-speaking Quebecers, it certainly should apply to them. But the Meech Lake Accord says nothing about "distinct societies" of indigenous peoples.

Indeed, the ups and downs of *Quebecois* activism have had a significant impact on the ethnic consciousness of Canada's native peoples. Canada's First Americans look to the federal government to protect their rights. Quebec's Mohawks have made it clear that they do not wish to become subjects of a sovereign Quebec; the Cree, the peoples of Quebec's northern frontier, have repeatedly asserted their right to seek their own independence should their province's status change. Canada's federal government assigned administration of the Cree, whose domain extends over more than half of Quebec's territory, to Quebec's government as long ago as 1912. Should Quebec separate from Canada, the Cree would have a legal case to nullify that assignment and seek their own autonomy. The stakes would be high: the Cree's domain includes large parts of the enormous James Bay Hydroelectric Project, a vast scheme of dikes, dams, and artificial lakes that yields electric power for a vast market in Quebec and beyond.

Ethnic consciousness in the French community of Quebec may not be defused by such considerations, but in the early 2000s there were signs that its fervor was ebbing. The *Bloc Quebecois*, the political party that stands for separatism and independence, has been on a losing streak; in 1997 it gained 44 of 75 seats in Quebec's Parliament; in the 2000 election it won just 38. The Liberal Party, which dominates Ontario and governs Canada today, made significant gains not only among Quebec's English-speaking communities in and around Montreal, but even in French-speaking areas. The strength of separatism in Quebec was perhaps reflected by the level of support for the so-called Clarity Act, legislation based on a Canadian Supreme Court opinion on the question of Quebec's potential independence issued in 1998. Under the stipulations of the Clarity Act, the federal government would not be required to negotiate sovereignty with a Quebec government unless Quebec voters in a federally approved referendum clearly indicated their desire for independence. The Clarity Act was approved overwhelmingly throughout Canada, but the Quebec provincial government strenuously objected to it, arguing that it amounted to an unacceptable intrusion into Quebec's affairs. Still, in the Francophone province itself the Clarity Act received the endorsement of 58 percent of the voters, suggesting that a referendum on independence itself would result in a defeat for the separatists.

It may well be, as some observers argue, that *Quebecois* ethnic consciousness is on another temporary downturn and will revive again: ethnic revival and ethnic linkage are two of the province's key qualities. Francophone Quebec's emotional ties to France remain strong: in Paris, *Maison Quebec* (House of Quebec) beckons visitors and is a virtual embassy of the province. Moreover, it is suggested, the slumping of separatist strength is directly related to the recent robustness of the Canadian economy; when people do well, they are less likely to want to changes the *status quo*. When economic conditions worsen, goes the argument, Quebec's "disadvantageous" position in Canada will get the blame and support for independence will surge, as it has in the past.

We should consider two factors in this context, both related to earlier chapters in this book. First, Quebec's ethnic mix is changing through immigration. Francophone Quebecers cannot do anything about this; their province is as open to movement as any other part of the federal state and is not an ethnic island whose exclusivity can be protected the way Switzerland's or Japan's is. The immigrants, whether they are Anglophone Canadian businesspeople or Asian workers, are not likely to develop a commitment to the separatist cause; they have their own ethnic and cultural linkages. Second, there is the matter of *language*. The vast majority of immigrants want to learn and use English, the dominant language in the rest of North America. Canada is bilingual, and schools in Quebec teach both French and English, but English offers greater access to the world at large, and migrants view it as more useful, in the long term, than French. As a result, Quebec's Francophone character is gradually diminishing, and legislation cannot easily stem the tide.

Whether or not the decline of Quebec separatism continues, its failure to dismember the Canadian federation along ethnic lines reveals the effectiveness of Canadian governance in the face of an internal ethnic challenge. The province's grievances, ranging from unfair taxation to disproportional representation, have been heard, addressed, and largely resolved. Quebec's provincial government has been allowed to embark on cultural campaigns and tactics that would have been actively suppressed elsewhere—but at the cost of heightened resentment. Even when separatists briefly, but tragically, engaged in a campaign of violence, the Canadian government did not overreact. Political opportunity was never suppressed: for more than 30 of the past 50 years, Canada's prime minister has been a Quebecer.

Today there are signs that a growing majority of Quebecers agree that the advantages of membership in the Canadian federation and citizenship in a united Canada can be combined with Francophone ethnic identity without the need for separation. If those signs presage the future, Canada will stand as a beacon of hope for dozens of other countries confronting serious internal ethnic tensions. The clear lesson from the Canadian case, however, is that success does not come from denying or suppressing ethnic diversity; rather, it comes from working with self-conscious ethnic groups to forge a pluralist notion of common purpose.

◆ KEY TERMS ◆

acculturation	ethnic islands	phenotype
cultural linkage	genetics	plural society
cultural revival	genotype	racism

◆ APPLYING GEOGRAPHIC KNOWLEDGE ◆

1. Africans who were brought to North America on slave ships came from many different ethnic groups. Yet after their arrival, they came to be thought of collectively as members of a single ethnic group. What factors led to this transformation? To what extent does recent voluntary migration from Africa challenge the notion of African-Americans as a single, distinct ethnic group?

2. It is sometimes said that territorial identity is at the root of ethnic conflict. Explain how the meaning of this proposition might differ if one were looking at it on the scale of a State or province as opposed to the scale of a city.

Chapter 32

Gender Inequalities in Geographic Perspective

From the field notes

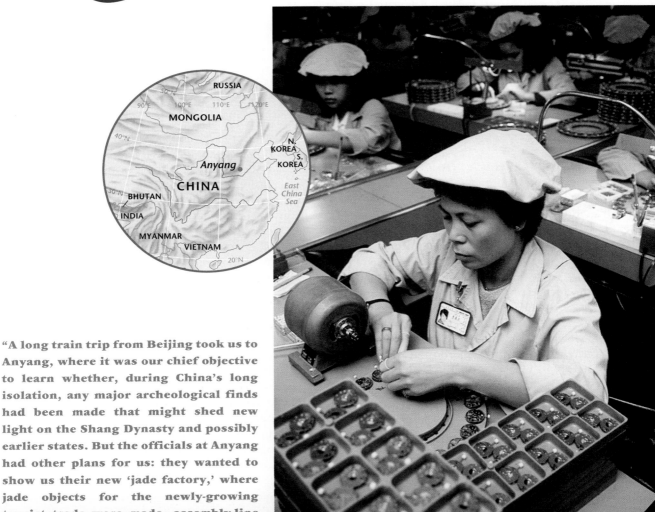

"A long train trip from Beijing took us to Anyang, where it was our chief objective to learn whether, during China's long isolation, any major archeological finds had been made that might shed new light on the Shang Dynasty and possibly earlier states. But the officials at Anyang had other plans for us: they wanted to show us their new 'jade factory,' where jade objects for the newly-growing tourist trade were made, assembly-line fashion, for sale at home and abroad."

KEY POINTS

◆ **Demographic statistics for individual countries (or divisions within countries) tend to conceal gender gaps—differences between females and males ranging from life expectancies to literacy rates.**

◆ **In all but three countries of the world, women outlive men for periods ranging from less than one year to ten years or more. In terms of life expectancy, the gender gap is widest in the richer countries and smallest in the poorer.**

◆ **Female infanticide and the abortion of female fetuses occur in a number of countries, most notably in India and China. Population-control policies are implicated in this human disaster.**

◆ **Work performed by women as unpaid labor in households and on the land would, if measured in monetary value, increase the world's total paid production by about one-third. In the poorer countries women perform much of the essential labor, producing more than half the food, transporting water and firewood, building dwellings, and performing numerous other tasks.**

◆ **The lack of good data on the conditions, roles, and contributions of women is itself a reflection on gender inequalities in the world today.**

◆ **The participation of women in governance has expanded over the past decade and a half, but only in the countries of northern Europe do women account for even a third of the seats in national parliaments.**

◆ A GEOGRAPHY OF GENDER

As we have seen, ours is a world of racial diversity, cultural variety, and economic disparity. We view these variations spatially, and we study ethnic homelands, culture hearths, and regional economic contrasts. There is another kind of inequality, however: inequality between the sexes, sometimes referred to by the term ***gender***—a term that connotes social situation, not just biology.

When topics such as population growth or migration or food production arise, they tend to be discussed in the aggregate. When a country's high population growth rate is cited as a threat to its future stability or its development potential, we may not consider the situation of the women who bear the children and raise them, who are confined to a village, probably for life, as their mothers and grandmothers were. Their husbands and brothers generally suffer fewer such constraints; men and women born and raised in the same village can live in completely different worlds.

So it is with migration. We read the total numbers: hundreds of thousands of people flee armed conflict in West Africa and Equatorial Africa; similar numbers try to escape war in Afghanistan. Behind those numbers lie vastly different, gender-related experiences. In refugee camps, women and female children are the worst off in the struggle for survival. In voluntary migrations, males tend to dominate the decision-making process and, in their new destinations, quickly form new social networks. Again, the man's and the woman's perspectives on the experience differ strongly, and male dominance remains the rule rather than the exception.

Education and economic development reduce inequalities between men and women, but even in settings such as Western Europe and North America, equality has not been achieved. Substantial wage differentials remain, barriers to economic and social advancement persist, and male physical violence against females continues. More subtly, male-dominated power relations in families, workplaces, and schools can work to the disadvantage of women and girls—marginalizing their concerns and channeling them toward prescribed roles and behaviors. In corporate, political, and domestic settings, then, maps of inequality can still be drawn.

Despite the persistence of gender inequality, women in urban, industrial societies have made enormous progress during the twentieth century—sometimes in stark contrast to what has occurred in other parts of the world. Yet the case of Saudi Arabia shows that wealth and economic prosperity do not automatically improve the rights and opportunities of women. In this oil-rich, high-income country, the rights of women are restricted on a number of fronts. For example, women are not permitted to drive automobiles. By itself, this might seem trivial, but it is indicative of a wider range of restrictions. During the Gulf War foreign troops, including female soldiers driving vehicles, entered Saudi Arabia. Perhaps emboldened by their presence, several dozen Saudi women, many of whom had been educated abroad, got into their families' cars and drove through the streets in defiance of the law. But they were arrested, and the ban on driving by women in Saudi Arabia was reaffirmed.

To gain an understanding of the geographic situation of women in the contemporary world, it is useful to begin by looking at the issue in global perspective. Adopting that perspective, in this chapter we assess the circumstances under which women live and work in five arenas: demography and health; family and social conditions; education and opportunity; economy and productivity; and politics and public life. At times we depend on anecdotal and subjective information because data on the conditions, roles, and contributions of women often are inadequate or incomplete. This insufficiency in itself is a reflection on gender inequality in the majority of the world's countries.

◆ DEMOGRAPHY AND HEALTH

Early in the book we noted that population pyramids for certain countries show that women outrank men, especially in the higher age categories. On average, women live about four years longer than men, but this differential varies spatially. In the economic core, the ***longevity gap*** widened from five years to seven years between 1950 and 2000. In *Women: A World Survey* (1985), Ruth Leger Sivard noted that this widening gap resulted not only from medical and other advantages associated with socioeconomic progress but also from the fact that

> women seem to have been less inclined to adopt some of the unhealthy habits often associated with affluence: cigarette smoking in particular, but also the excessive consumption of food and alcohol, fast driving (and high accident rates), high levels of stress. (p. 7)

However, as Sivard points out, the increased stresses imposed on women who are trying to deal with the competing demands of home and workplace, as well as lifestyle changes associated with modern times, may erode the gender-longevity gap.

In the early 2000s, women outlived men overall in every geographic realm of the world and in all but nine of Earth's 200-odd countries and territories (Fig. 32-1). The situation in 2002 reveals some noteworthy differences from that of 1998, when life expectancies for men and women were identical in India, Bangladesh, and Pakistan, and women outlived men in South Asia's other countries. Today, women live longer in India and Pakistan, but men outlive women in Bangladesh and Nepal—a significant reversal in both countries. Men also live longer in Afghanistan, where several years of Taliban rule had devastating impacts on women and girls, but this could well change in the years ahead.

The other key difference between 1998 and 2002 lies in Subsaharan Africa. In 1998, life expectancies were higher for women than for men in all countries of that realm, but by 2002, six countries reported that men were outliving women amid the general decline in life

From the field notes

"During a taping session on the Indonesian island of Bali, I saw a brick-making facility and visited it. Young boys were bringing the wet mud from a quarry near a creek and poured it from their wheelbarrows into wooden forms. Once the bricks begin to dry and harden in the sun, they must be turned to prevent cracking. This woman told me that she worked ten hours a day, stacking and restacking the bricks, six days per week. At about 45 cents (U.S.) per hour, she was better paid than some factory workers I had visited in Sumatera. But what about her quality of life?"

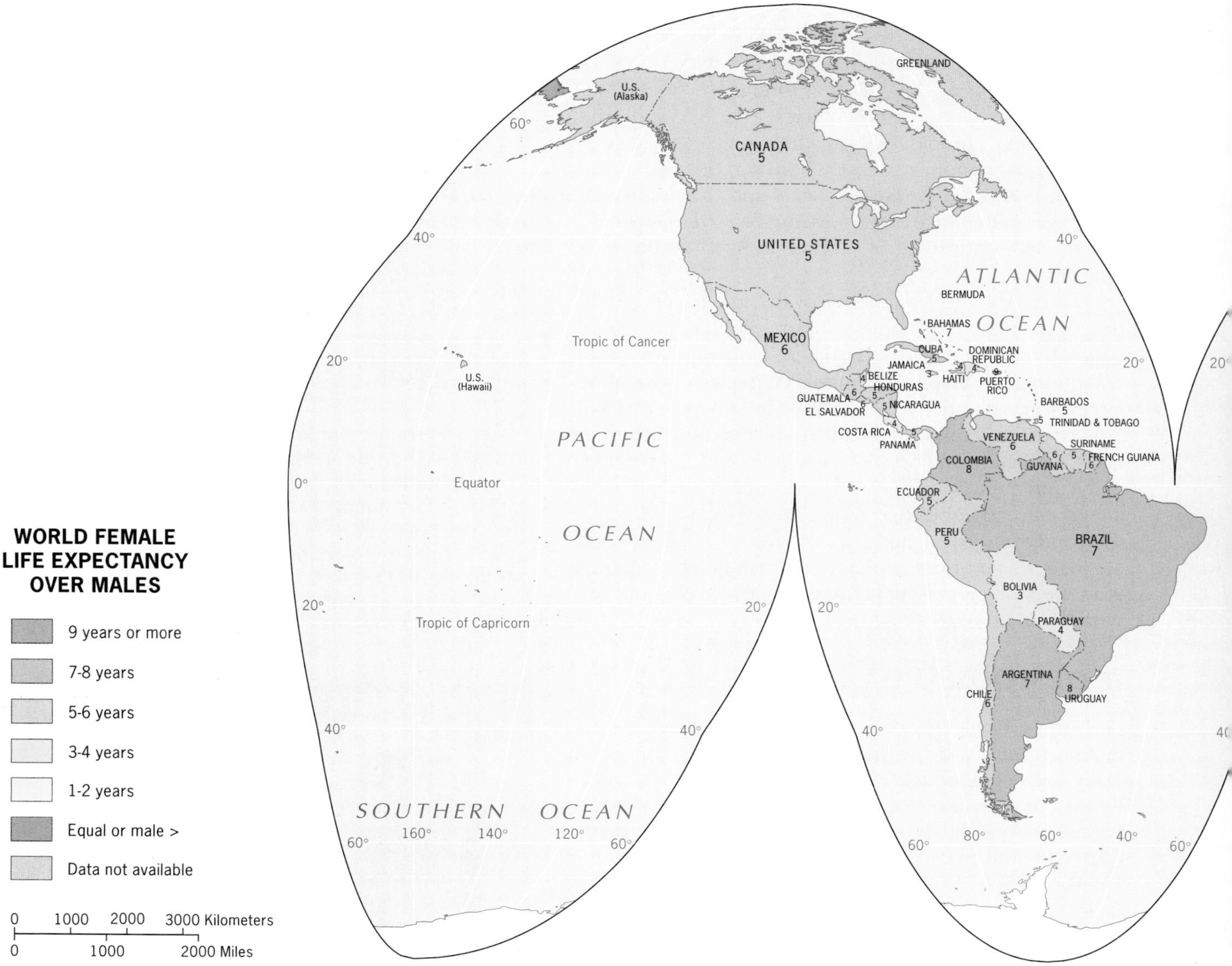

Figure 32-1 World Female Life Expectancy over Males. Generally female life expectancy is higher than that of males. This map depicts the differences in female life expectancy over males in years.

expectancies related to the AIDS pandemic. Three of these countries lie in West Africa: Mali, Burkina Faso, and Guinea-Bissau. The other three are in Southern Africa: Moçambique, Namibia, and Zimbabwe. The data reflect the perturbing effect of AIDS on women and families; millions of children are being orphaned, and girls have the lowest prospect of survival.

The global norm, however, is for women to outlive men, and quite substantially. In Europe, the gap is seven years; in Russia, twelve; in South America, seven; in Subsaharan Africa, despite the narrowing difference, two; in East and Southeast Asia, four; and in South Asia, one. Over time, the gap has been widening, notably in the wealthier countries.

In virtually all cultures, men tend to marry women who are younger than they are. Married women therefore can expect to outlive their husbands, sometimes by as much as 10 years. This statistic seems to favor women until we note that widows often lack adequate support. Hundreds of millions of women who have spent their lives sustaining their families die alone, in poverty, without sufficient support from their deceased husband's pension, the state, their children, or savings.

Quality of Life

Figures on life expectancy say nothing about quality of life. During their lifetimes, women's health problems and concerns differ from those of men. According to a UN study titled *The World's Women 1970–1990*, women in poorer realms who become pregnant face health risks

80 to 600 times greater than those faced by women in the richer countries. In this respect, South Asian women suffer the highest ***maternal mortality rate***, with approximately 650 maternal deaths per 100,000 births. The risk for African women is nearly as high. In the wealthier countries of the Western world, these deaths may number as few as 3 per 100,000. Inadequate medical services, an excessive number of pregnancies, and malnutrition are among the leading causes of maternal death in poorer countries (Fig. 32-2). Add to this the fact that an estimated 250,000 women die from illegal abortions each year and the extent of the problem becomes clear.

In Chapter 30, we discussed world nutritional patterns, using average calorie consumption as the key measure. Again, such averages conceal gender differences: in the global economic periphery, women are less well nourished than men, and female children are even worse off. World Health Organization (WHO) reports indicate that anemia, a consequence of malnutrition, affects the majority of women in these regions, as well as two-thirds of all pregnant women in Africa and South and Southwest Asia. During their reproductive years, women need nearly three times as much iron in their daily diets as men, but they are often unable to satisfy this dietary requirement.

Under these circumstances, it is all the more remarkable that women's life expectancies—even in poorer countries—exceed those of men. According to Sivard, women have a genetic advantage over men; they are inherently stronger. But as we have noted, the greater expectancy of women is not uniform, and it is affected by variations in the cultural-economic environment within which women work and bear children.

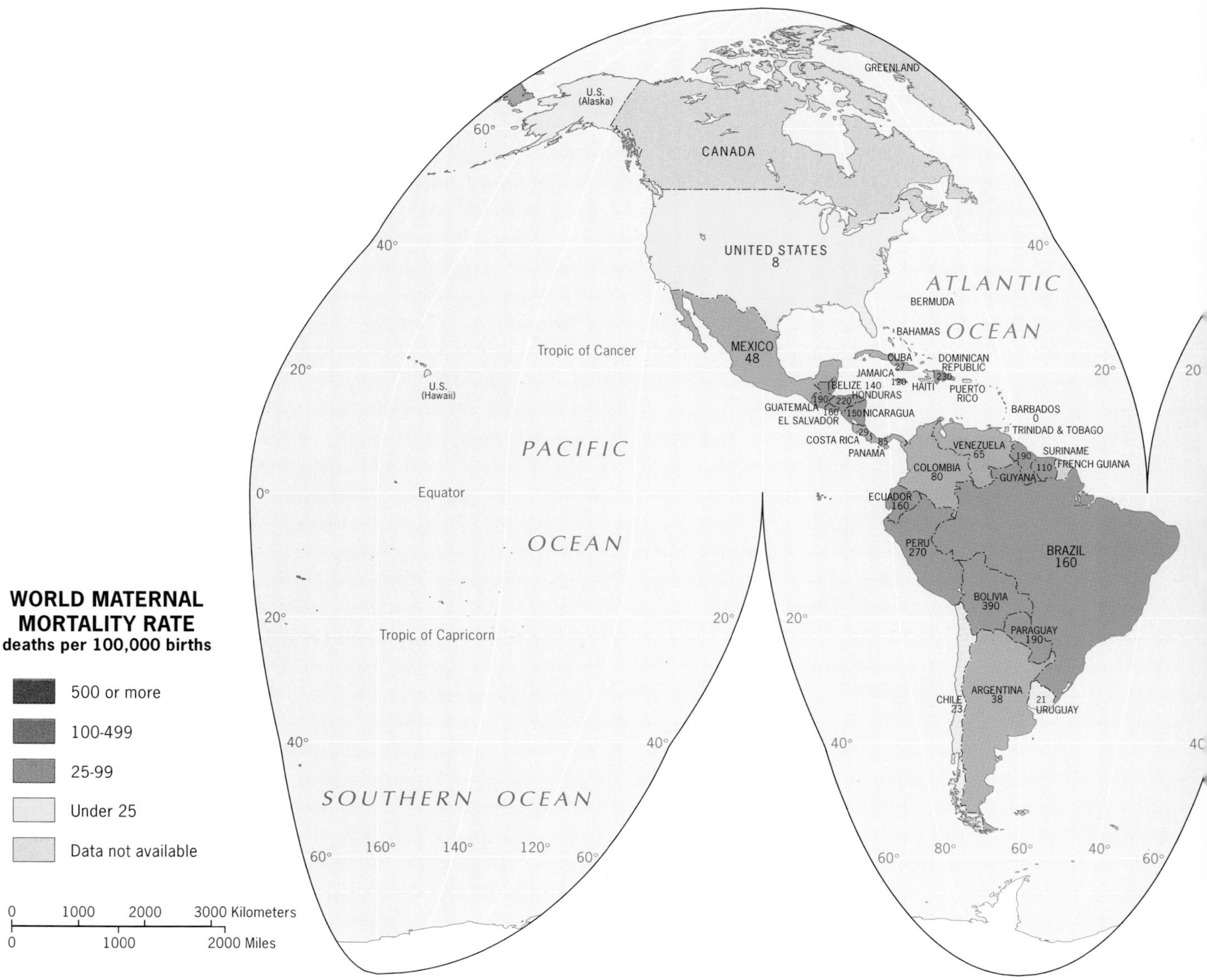

Figure 32-2 World Maternal Mortality Rate. Maternal mortality rate reflects the number of deaths per 100,000 live births. This map shows the maternal mortality rate throughout the world. *Source*: Data from United Nations, *The World's Women 2000*. New York: United Nations, 2000, pp. 79–83.

Female Infanticide

Women may live longer than men, and in the upper age categories women may outnumber men, but in early life it is another story. In October 1990 UNICEF published a disturbing report titled *The Lesser Child: The Girl in India.* It revealed that 300,000 more girls than boys die in India each year, and many more are never born—aborted after gender-detection tests.

As a result, the ratio of men to women in India continues to widen. During the twentieth century the gap has grown from over 970 women per thousand men to under 930. In Haryana, the State in which the capital, New Delhi, is located, the 1992 figure was 873 females for every 1000 males, a disproportion so extreme that it has been known to occur only in societies that have experienced the ravages of war. In 1994 the United Nations reported that India as a whole had 133 single men for every 100 single women.

The UNICEF report indicated that many thousands of female infants are killed each year. But the modern techniques of prenatal gender detection—ultrasound and amniocentesis—contribute far more to the imbalance between male and female. Women's groups have called for a federal law that would outlaw such tests, but in India it is difficult to counter any measure that contributes to population control. In July 1994 the Indian Parliament passed a law prohibiting prenatal tests solely to determine the sex

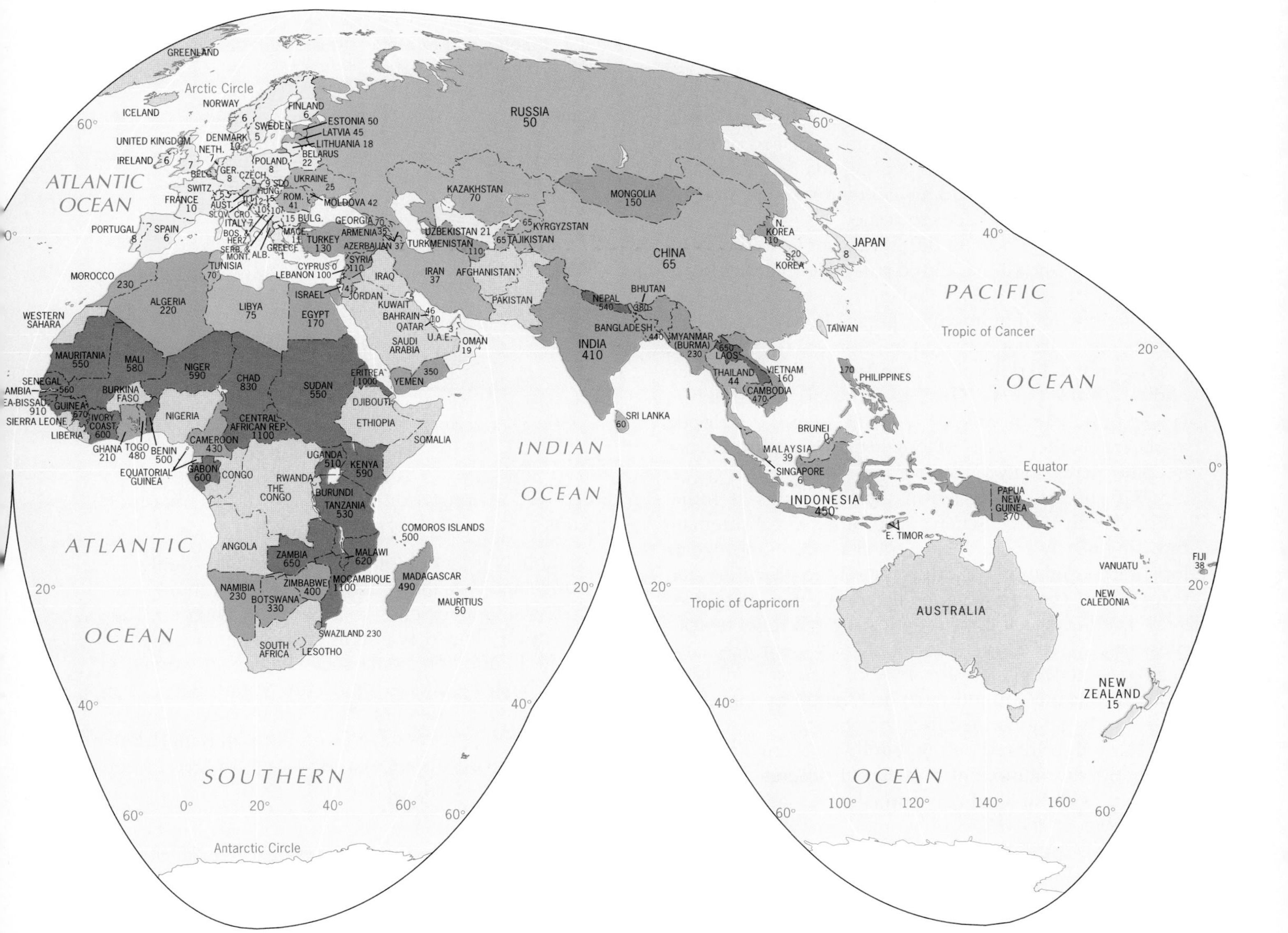

of a fetus. But a provision in the law punishes women for taking the test—even though they are often compelled to do so by male heads of families who want male heirs. Fathers want to see the family lineage preserved through males, for in Hindu society the oldest son lights the funeral pyre of the father. In addition, the supposedly outlawed, but widely practiced, tradition of dowry, by which families with sons receive payments from the brides' parents, makes male offspring valuable commodities in the marriage business, whereas daughters are liabilities.

Under such social conditions, will a law against prenatal testing work? When the debate on the issue was gaining momentum, three States (Maharashtra, Rajasthan, and Haryana) imposed a testing ban in advance of the federal law. Its effect was minimal. The clinics simply went underground, and since the required equipment can be moved easily, a thriving black market in gender detection developed. Laws against ***female infanticide*** and dowry payments are already on the books. If those laws are enforced (which they rarely are), the result will exceed anything a law against prenatal testing could achieve.

India is not alone in its traditional preference for male offspring. When China implemented its one-child-only policy (see Part Two), the overwhelming number of couples wanted a male child. Although the policy quickly brought the overall population growth rate down, it further widened the male-female ratio. In 1995 the Chinese government published figures indicating that, while the great majority of Chinese had married by age 30, nearly 10 million people in their thirties remained single—and in this age group men outnumbered women by more than 10 to 1. The number of abortions following gender-detection tests (which are legal in China) skyrocketed after the one-child-only policy was implemented. In addition, millions of Chinese babies die through food deprivation, denial of medical care, abandonment, and murder. These conditions are having some unanticipated consequences. It is projected that the number of males unable to find wives will double, even triple, during the present decade. Some Chinese scholars suggest that this situation could lead to social disorders ranging from increased prostitution to higher suicide rates among males, as well as other problems that could have a major impact on Chinese society in the decades to come.

There is an important difference between the problems in India and China. In India, female infanticide appears to be most prevalent in the poorest sectors of society, notably in remote rural areas. In China, female infanticide has long occurred in poor and remote areas, but the one-child policy has been most effective in urban and near-urban areas. This has led to a substantial increase in female infanticide in China's more developed areas, where the scarcity of female marriage partners has become increasingly acute.

Will the lot of women in such countries as India, China, South Korea (where male births exceed female births by nearly 15 percent), and elsewhere improve as lopsided population pyramids reflect the growing need for women? Governments could try to offer incentives such as educational opportunities and tax relief to couples who have girls. They could also enforce laws against practices that are biased against girls and women. But governments are dominated by men, and long-standing habits are difficult to change.

As we have noted before, family planning has been an important component of material progress in many societies. Without legal constraints and balanced incentives, however, its impact on women can be devastating.

◆ FAMILY AND SOCIAL CONDITIONS

To reiterate a key point, data on life expectancy and maternal mortality tell us nothing about women's quality of life. We can discern some aspects of this issue from more detailed statistics, for example, from mortality figures for children between the ages of 1 and 4 (Table 32-1). Under normal conditions, more boys than girls die during the early years. Yet that pattern is reversed in some cases—notably in the larger South Asian countries and in Egypt. If you had looked at these data five or ten years ago, you would have seen many more cases of reversal, so improvements have occurred. Yet the persistence of higher levels of female child mortality in large countries such as India and Pakistan cannot be ignored. Such discrepancies reflect a dreadful contrast in the treatment of girls and boys, a discrimination that, even if the girls survive these early years, puts females at a lifelong physical and emotional disadvantage.

The larger set of problems that girls and women face in many parts of the world was highlighted in a

Table 32-1 Child Mortality rates for Girls and Boys Aged 1-4, Selected Countries (annual deaths per 1000)

Country	Girls	Boys
Pakistan	9.6	8.6
Bangladesh	15.7	14.2
India	42.0	29.4
Philippines	2.5	2.8
Malaysia	0.6	0.8
South Korea	0.6	0.7
Iran	3.9	5.1
Egypt	6.6	5.6

Source: United Nations, *The World's Women 2000: Trends and Statistics* (New York, 2000), p. 57.

United Nations report on women (1991). As the report explains:

> Although girls contribute much to the family—in Africa and Asia they often work seven or more hours a day—many societies consider them a burden. They are discriminated against as children and married off early. In addition, some societies expect women to start having children at a very young age . . . in Mauritania, 39 percent of girls are married by age 15 and fifteen percent have given birth. In Bangladesh, 73 percent of girls are married by age 15, and 21 percent have had at least one child. (p. 67)

Other information about women's lives can be obtained from sources ranging from death certificates to hospital records, from local studies to newspaper reports. However, much of what happens in rural areas is simply not known. In Landscapes of the Home (1982) geographers Bonnie S. Lloyd, Janice J. Monk, and Arlene C. Rengert point out that men are traditionally associated with the outdoors. The cultural landscape, they argue, is created and dominated by males; the home is an indoor, female space, which is less studied and less well known. So we have only fragmentary knowledge of the quality of life of women in rural as well as urban settings.

What we do know is dismaying. Women are often victims of domestic violence. This is a global, cross-cultural phenomenon. It happens among the rich as well as the poor and in industrialized as well as traditional societies. Survey results indicate that the incidence of such violence is astonishingly high. A recent UN study investigated 1500 divorce cases in Austria; violence against the wife was cited in nearly 60 percent of these cases. In a study done in Thailand, more than 50 percent of women from a Bangkok slum area reported regular beatings by their husbands. A study from Brazil reported two dozen unpunished domestic murders in one state alone; it was said that the murdered wives had been killed by "justifiably" jealous husbands.

No society publicly condones domestic violence against women as a cultural right, but the same cannot be said of ***female genitalia mutilation*** (FGM). This procedure, sometimes called female circumcision, is performed on over 2 million girls under the age of 11 every year. It entails the complete or partial removal of the female clitoris and often leads to infection, infertility, and increased difficulties in childbirth. Although this custom is found more commonly in parts of Africa, it is also practiced in places in Southeast Asia, the Middle East, and Central and South America. In Somalia it is estimated that 70 to 90 percent of all women have been subject to FGM. Regarded as barbaric by most Westerners, FGM is defended in societies where it is common as an ancient ritual designed to ensure the virginity and suitability of women for marriage and to control women's attitude toward sex. Such arguments are hard for even an extreme cultural relativist to swallow, but movements to ban the practice reveal another conflict: who should determine what is permitted in a given society? Seen as a matter of fundamental human rights to some, this issue is treated as a matter of cultural sovereignty to others. Given the fact that no reciprocal procedure exists for males, however, no argument about cultural sovereignty can erase the inequality between the sexes that is represented by the practice of FGM.

Women in India

As one of the largest countries in the world, the contrasting circumstances of men and women in India deserve attention. In India, where Hinduism prescribes reverence for life, many girls are still forced into arranged marriages. In extreme cases, disputes over the bride price to be paid by the bride's family to the groom's father have led to the death of the bride, who may be punished for her father's failure to fulfill the marriage agreement. One might expect that such ***dowry deaths*** would be declining in recent decades, but official figures indicate otherwise. In 1985, the number was 999; in 1987, 1786 women died at the hands of vengeful husbands or in-laws; and in 1989, 2436 perished. These figures report only confirmed dowry deaths; many more are believed to occur but are reported as kitchen accidents or other fatal domestic incidents.

Indian governments (federal as well as State) have set up legal aid offices to help women who seek assistance, and in 1984 the national legislature passed the Family Courts Act, creating a network of "family courts" to hear domestic cases, including dowry disputes. But the judges tend to be older males, and their chief objective, according to women's support groups, is to hold the family together, that is, to force the threatened or battered woman back into the household. Hindu culture attaches great importance to the family structure, and the family courts tend to operate on this principle.

India is a multicultural country, and powerful communities sometimes seek to institute their own laws in place of those enacted in New Delhi. With the resurgence of Muslim fundamentalism came a controversy over the rights of divorced Muslim women in India. The (national) Indian Civil Code gives some rights and protections to women who have succeeded in obtaining a legal divorce, including child support. But representatives of Muslim communities argued that the Indian Code goes against Islamic law. They therefore proposed a separate Muslim Woman's Bill that would deny divorced Muslim women even the limited rights they would have under the Indian Civil Code.

Women in Islamic Countries

The circumstances of women in the majority of traditional Muslim societies are even more restrictive than in India, where legal help and aggressive women's movements have given support and visibility to the plight of women. The story of the Saudi women who were arrested for driving the family car is a sidelight to a far more serious situation: women in some Islamic countries live an existence of isolation and servitude. Many Muslim political and social leaders deplore this situation, and some Muslim women have succeeded in becoming doctors, lawyers, and other professionals. But in parts of the Islamic world there are significant restrictions on what women can do—and even on what they can wear; women may wear what they please in the privacy of their homes and compounds, but in public they must be cloaked and veiled.

The resurgence of Islamic fundamentalism, along with the severe Sharia laws in some Muslim societies, has had an especially strong impact on women. Before the Iranian Revolution, women were given significant freedoms, including the right to wear clothing of their choice in public. In the wake of the revolution led by the Ayatollah Khomeini, however, women were ordered to resume wearing the long cloaks of traditional Islamic society, as well as veils over their faces. Muslim men policed the streets to enforce this order, and many women were arrested; some, it is alleged, were even executed for flouting the fundamentalist dress code.

In 1997, the victorious Islamic Taliban movement, after taking control of the capital, Kabul, in Afghanistan, severely restricted the rights of women. A substantial number of women held professional jobs ranging from nurses to teachers; all were instructed to resign. Many women wore modern dress; all were told to don head-to-toe traditional clothing. Girls were banned from schools, and press reports described women being stoned to death for adultery. The downfall of the Taliban may signal a new era for Afghanistan's women, but many local and state leaders have little interest in promoting fundamental change for the country's female population.

As we will note later in the chapter, the circumstances under which African women live vary widely. In parts of West Africa, women control markets and commerce and have a powerful position in society. In most of the realm, however, men live more freely (and often more comfortably), eat better, do lighter work, and do less to support the children. As noted previously, gender inequality around the world differs only in degree, not in kind.

◆ EDUCATION AND OPPORTUNITY

Education offers a chance to escape from poverty and stagnation, improve one's circumstances, and fulfill one's potential. Where educational levels are higher, the conditions of women's lives are better. It is no accident that most of what has been said about India does not apply to the southern Indian State of Kerala, where women are better educated than elsewhere. In Kerala, the gender gap actually favors women; women's health is better and women have fewer children. Education is the key.

In North America it is normal for all girls and boys to attend school; in fact, it is the law. Imagine a situation in which the boys enter elementary school at the age of 5 or 6, but the girls stay home doing chores. In some parts of the world this is exactly what happens. Women's education is a lower priority, and women have much less access to education than men. This has produced an education gap that still exists today. In India, for example, the overall adult literacy rate is estimated to be 65 percent, but the United Nations and UNICEF estimate that between 65 and 75 percent of all Indian women are illiterate.

Figure 32-3 Women's Education as a Ratio of Men's. This map represents the average of data for primary and secondary levels of education during 1992–1997. *Source*: Data from United Nations, *The World's Women 2000*. New York: United Nations, 2000, pp. 103–107.

The situation is improving. Long-term education data show that the gender gap is narrowing throughout the world, that girls now go to school, at least elementary school, where previously they did not (or did in far smaller numbers), and that a growing number of women obtain some higher education. Experts predict that it will take several generations for the educational gender gap to disappear, however.

The progress that is being made varies spatially. In the late 1990s there were still nearly 600 million illiterate females and more than 350 million illiterate males (the great majority of them adults) in the world. Girls are now going to school in the same numbers as boys in many countries, not only in Europe, North America, and parts of East Asia but also in Middle and South America. But progress lags in South Asia and in Africa south of the Sahara. In addition, sharp contrasts remain between rural and urban areas. UN studies show that these contrasts may be strongest in Middle and South America, where 1 in 4 rural women aged 15 to 24 is illiterate, compared to only 1 in 20 in urban areas. (In Subsaharan Africa, the figures are more than 7 in 10 for rural areas and more than 4 in 10 for urban areas.)

Every relevant study shows that although substantial progress has been made in the past four decades, major obstacles remain. Women still are denied access to training in such fields as forestry, fishing, and agriculture; they still have difficulty breaking into male-dominated professions. Some societies still do not allow women to teach boys (although the teaching profession is generally open to women). In the urbanized industrialized realms, women have become physicians, lawyers, and other professionals, although they still face special job-related difficulties.

Figure 32-3 summarizes the global situation in a general but revealing way. A similar map was made by Ruth Leger Sivard more than a decade ago in her study,

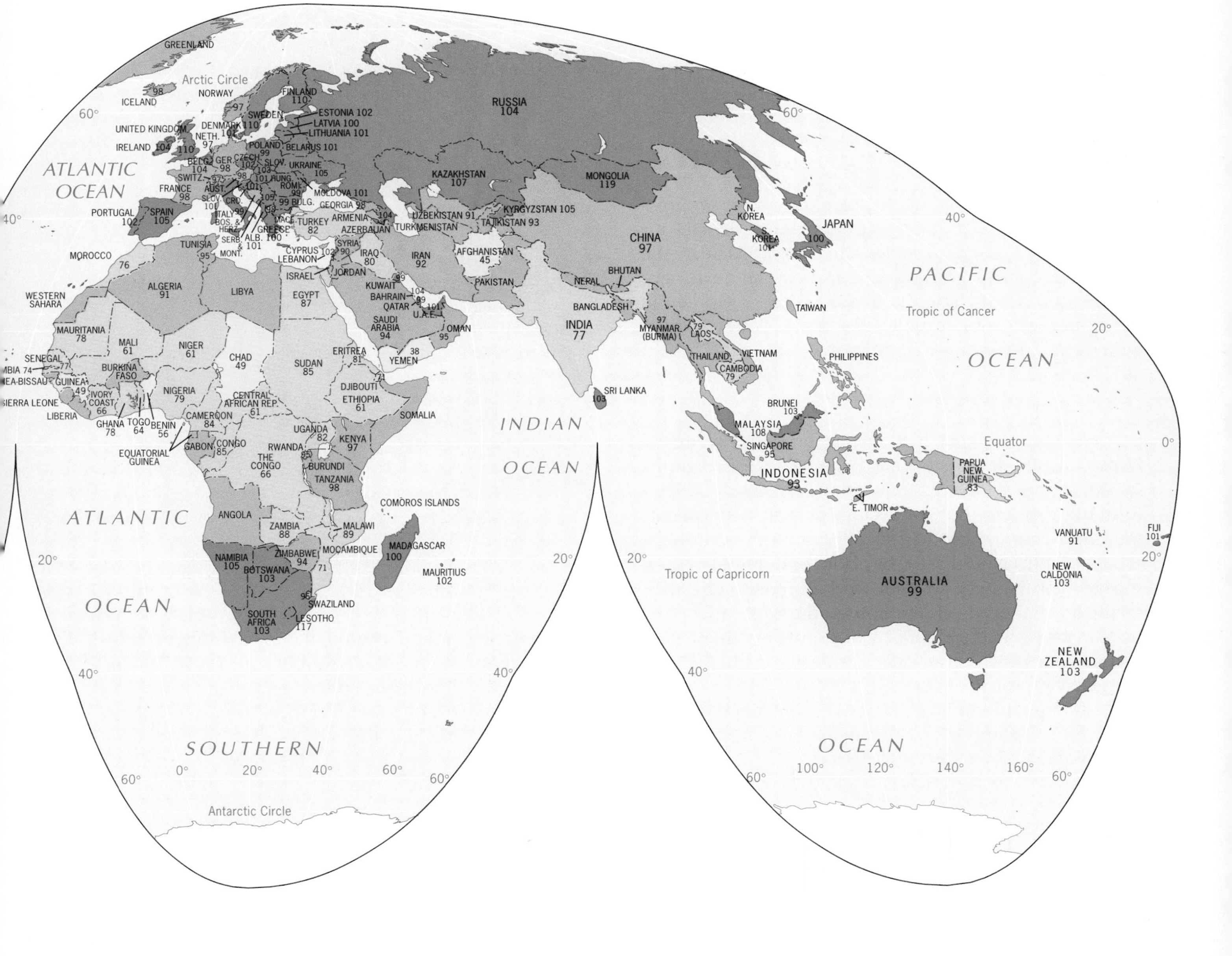

Women: A World Survey. It was based on the question, "If male education equals 100, where does female education stand on a scale of 1 to 100?" Our map is based on the ratio of female to male enrollment at all three levels of schooling and thus is a very general average for each country. Nevertheless, the spatial pattern tells us much about the regional status of women's education. Note that the gender gap is narrowing in Middle and South America but remains very wide in tropical Africa and South Asia as well as in parts of Southwest Asia and North Africa. Rapid population growth, limited budgets, and cultural and political barriers combine to cause the disparities shown in Figure 32-3.

When reading maps like this one, it is important to remember that the validity of the data may be questionable. Recent reports from Africa and Asia suggest that progress in women's education has been halted or even reversed. Especially in Africa, economic setbacks and armed conflicts have combined to erode education systems, and women's education suffers most under such conditions. While women's education has advanced in some Muslim countries, it has declined in others, for example in Afghanistan during the several years of Taliban rule.

◆ ECONOMY AND PRODUCTIVITY

Although women have made some long-term progress in the educational arena, the same cannot be said for their economic situation. When economists calculate the total annual production of goods and services in a country, they do not include the unpaid labor of women in the household, nor, usually, the work done by rural women in less developed countries.

Women's Productivity

Scholars estimate that if women's productivity in the household alone were given a dollar value (for example, by calculating what it would cost to hire people to perform these tasks), the world's total annual GNP (that is, the gross national product for all countries combined; see Part Eight) would grow by about one-third. In countries in the periphery, women produce more than half of all the food; they also build homes, dig wells, plant and harvest crops, make clothes, and do many other things that are not recorded in official statistics as being economically productive.

Although the circumstances of rural women in much of the global economic periphery are generally difficult, the situation of women in parts of Africa may be the worst. Apart from the areas in West Africa where women dominate local commerce, women in Africa south of the Sahara have heavy responsibilities and few rights. They produce an estimated 70 percent of the realm's food, almost all of it without the aid of modern technology. Their backbreaking hand-cultivation of corn and other staples is an endless task. As water supplies decrease, the exhausting walk to the nearest pump gets longer. Firewood is being cut at ever-greater distances from the village, and the task of hauling it home becomes more difficult every year. As the men leave for the towns—sometimes to marry other wives and have other children—the women left in the villages struggle for survival.

Even though a woman in this position becomes the head of a household, when she goes to the bank for a loan she is likely to be refused; banks throughout much

From the field notes

"She and her daughter came walking along the path to the village near Kanye, Botswana, carrying huge, burlap-wrapped bundles on their heads. I had seen them go earlier to fetch pails of water; in the early afternoon they were working in the field, weeding the maize (corn). Later I saw them with batches of firewood that must have weighed 60 pounds or more. In the evening, they would cook the meal. From the village I could hear men arguing, laughing."

of Africa do not lend money to rural women. Not having heard from her husband for years and having reared her children, she might wish to apply for a title to the land she has occupied and farmed for decades, but land titles usually are not awarded to women. Only a small percentage of African women have the legal right to own property.

Young girls soon become trapped in the cycle of female poverty and overwork. Often there is little money for school fees; what is available first goes to pay for the boys. As soon as she can carry anything at all, the girl goes with her mother to weed the fields, bring back firewood, or fetch water. She will do so for an average of perhaps 12 hours a day, seven days a week, during all the years she remains capable of working. But national statistics say nothing about her contribution to the economy.

Therefore, when we study the distribution of farming and crops, as we did earlier in this book, we should remind ourselves of distributions that are not revealed by available maps. In East Africa, cash crops such as tea are sometimes called "men's crops" because the men trade in what the women produce. But when the government of Kenya tried to stimulate the productivity of the tea plantations, it handed out bonuses—not to the women who did the harvesting but to the men who owned the land.

Although the quality of life for women may be lowest in parts of rural Africa, conditions are not much better in many other regions. Village life is similar for women in South Asia or Middle and South America. Yet their productivity also is immense: women produce an estimated 40 percent of all the food consumed in Middle and South America.

Women in the Labor Force

Despite these conditions, the number of women in the "official" labor force is rising. In 1990, the United Nations estimated that there were 828 million women in the labor force. All but one geographic realm showed increases between 1970 and 1990: in the global economic core, from 35 to 39 percent of the labor force; in Middle and South America, from 24 to 29 percent. In East and Southeast Asia the figure rose very slightly, to 40 and 35 percent, respectively. In Subsaharan Africa, the percentage of women in the labor force actually declined from 39 percent in 1970 to 37 percent in the 1990s. These statistics reveal that, in stagnating or declining economies, women are often the first to suffer from job contraction.

In most of Asia and virtually all of Africa, the great majority of wage-earning women still work in agriculture. In Subsaharan Africa, nearly 80 percent of wage-earning women work on plantations and farms; in Asia, the figure is over 50 percent. Although the number of women working in industries in these areas is comparatively small, it is rising. The increase has been slowed by the global economic downturn of the early 2000s, as well as by mechanization, which leads to job reductions and hence to layoffs of women workers. In the *maquiladoras* of northern Mexico (see Chapter 29), for example, women workers bore the brunt of the contracting labor market of 2001–2002.

As the foregoing discussion has highlighted, many women engage in "informal" economic activity—that is, private, often home-based activity such as tailoring, beer brewing, food preparation, and soap making. Women who seek to advance beyond subsistence but cannot enter the formal economic sector often turn to such work. In the migrant slums on the fringes of many cities, informal economic activity is the mainstay of the community. As with subsistence farming, however, it is difficult to assess the number of women involved, their productivity, or their contribution to the overall economy.

Wherever they work and at whatever job, women still face job discrimination, occupational segregation, and wage inequities, in both highly industrialized, economically wealthy countries and the countries of the global economic periphery. At the global scale, the world of economic gain and decision making remains a male-dominated one in which women's needs and contributions are undervalued.

◆ POLITICS AND PUBLIC LIFE

The United States is a society in which anyone can seek elected office. Approximately half the voters in the United States are women. Yet in 2002 only 13 of the country's 100 senators and 5 of its 50 governors were women. The number of women in the House of Representatives is somewhat larger (61), but it is nowhere near the number of men. How has this male dominance developed, and why does it persist?

The answer lies in the past as well as the present. Today the idea that anyone can vote may seem normal and routine, but women in the United States and Canada did not achieve full ***enfranchisement***—the right to vote—until 1920. This was a half-century after the U.S. government approved the Fifteenth Amendment to the Constitution, which granted the vote to all male citizens "without regard to race, color, or previous condition of servitude." By the time women became able to vote (and could seek office), male dominance of political institutions and networks was deeply entrenched.

Although the United States was not the first country to respond to women's demand for the right to vote (New Zealand did so in 1893 and Australia in 1902), it was among the earliest to do so. The map in Figure 32-4 underscores the fact that, for the most part, women were unable to vote before the twentieth century. Some Western countries did not fully enfranchise women until as recently as 1971 (Switzerland) and 1976 (Portugal). In some countries in Southwest Asia, women still cannot vote.

Figure 32-4 Women's Enfranchisement. The years in which women were enfranchised are shown on this world map. *Source*: Data from United Nations, *The World's Women 1970–1990*. New York: United Nations, 1991, p. 39 and from other sources including R. L. Sivard, *Women: A World Survey*. Washington, D.C.: World Priorities, 1985.

The legal right to vote does not immediately translate into political power or political representation. As Table 32-2 shows, women's participation in parliamentary bodies remains limited; nowhere has it yet come close to 50 percent. Currently, women's participation rates are the highest in northern Europe—reaching levels well above 30 percent, and in the case of Sweden above 40 percent. In most other industrialized countries it fails to reach 15 percent, although Canada, Australia, and New Zealand have rates in the low 20s. In the global economic periphery rates are generally lower but with some notable exceptions (notably Vietnam, Argentina, and China). And highly industrialized, wealthy Japan has a participation rate for women that is as low as many of the world's poorer countries.

Male-dominated power structures make it difficult for women to enter the political arena, although the overall situation is improving, (see Table 32-2). When the 2001 data (the latest available) are compared to those for 1987, a general increase in women's representation can be discerned. For example, women's parliamentary representation almost tripled in the United States during these 14 years, and it increased substantially in all northern European countries. It quadrupled in Australia, tripled in the United Kingdom, and more than doubled in New Zealand and Canada. And in a few countries women have become

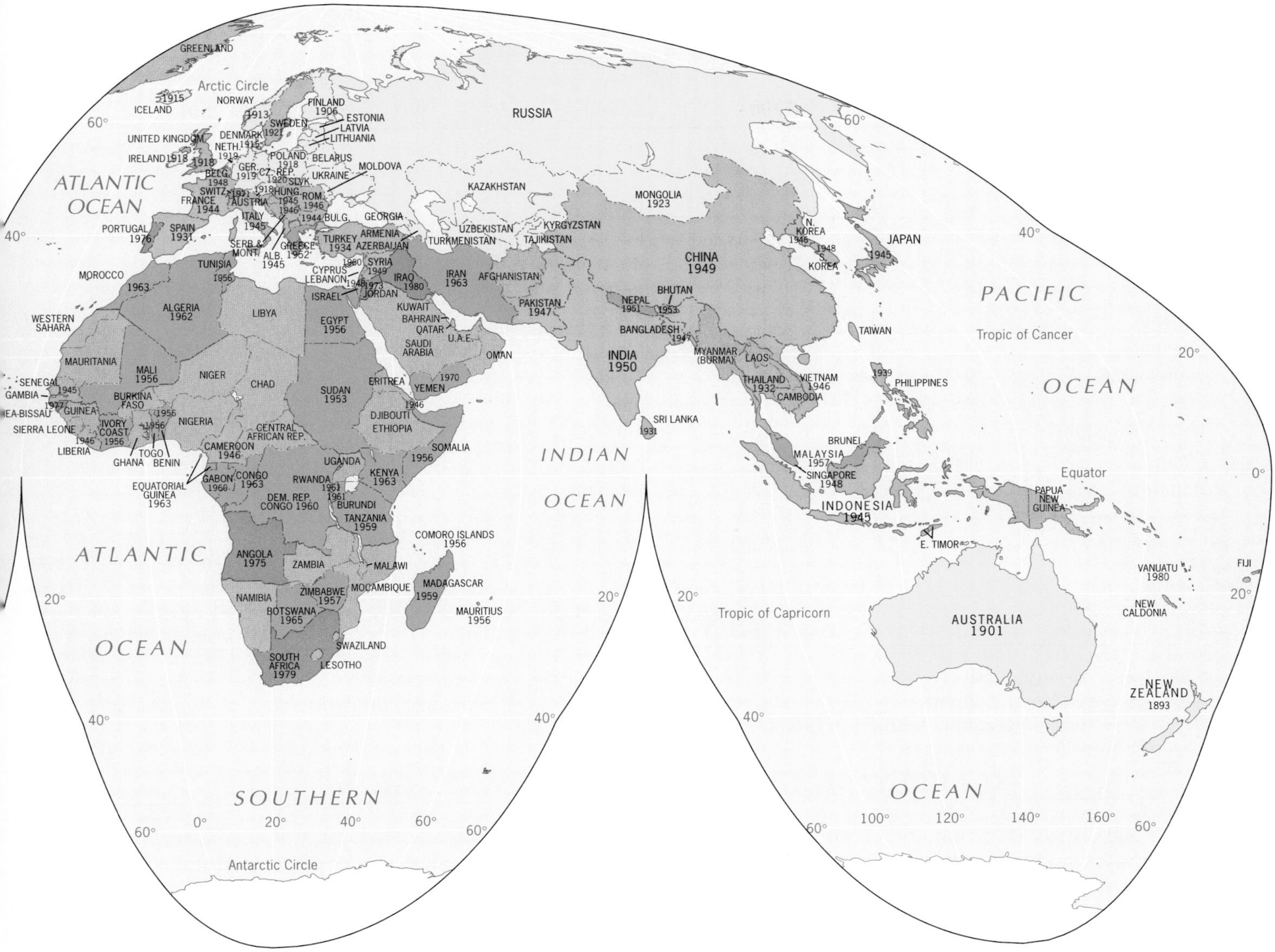

national leaders in recent decades: Corazon Aquino and Gloria Macapagal Arroyo (Philippines), Benazir Bhutto (Pakistan), Violeta Chamorro (Nicaragua), Tansu Ciller (Turkey), Indira Gandhi (India), Chandrika Bandaranaike Kumaratunga (Sri Lanka), Mary Robinson (Ireland), Margaret Thatcher (United Kingdom), Vaira Vike-Freiberga (Latvia), Tarja Kaarina-Halonen (Finland), and several others have attained their countries' highest office.

During the coming century women will likely achieve representative equality in government in many countries, and more women will become national leaders. What effect will this have on political interaction? Ruth Leger Sivard reminds us that

> the few women who have attained the highest positions in male-dominated governments have not avoided confrontational politics. Yet in broad opinion surveys women have revealed attitudes significantly different from men's. When women have had a chance to use power in settings where there is a deep feminist consciousness and social commitment to justice—as in the Nordic countries—government policies are noteworthy for their emphasis on equality, development, and peace (p. 6).

In the last two chapters we have dealt with the sensitive topics of race, ethnicity, and gender. What we have learned here can help us understand contrasting worldviews and divergent reactions to the same social environment. We should keep these matters in mind when we turn to human interaction with the physical environment in Part Eleven.

Table 32-2 Percentage of Seats in National Parliaments Occupied by Women, 1987, 1994, 2001 (rounded to closest whole number)

Country	1987	1995	2001	Country	1987	1995	2001
United States	5	11	14	Morocco	0	1	1
Canada	10	18	21	Egypt	4	2	2
Australia	6	10	24	Côte d'Ivoire	6	5	9
New Zealand	14	21	31	Kenya	2	3	4
Sweden	32	40	43	Zimbabwe	11	15	10
Norway	34	39	36	Brazil	5	7	6
Finland	32	34	37	Argentina	5	22	27
Denmark	29	33	37	Mexico	11	14	16
Netherlands	20	31	36	Turkey	1	2	4
France	7	6	11	Iran	1	3	3
United Kingdom	6	10	18	India	8	8	9
Japan	1	3	7	China	21	21	22
Algeria	2	7	3	Vietnam	18	18	26

Sources: United Nations, *The World's Women, 2000: trends and statistics*, posted on the world wide web at *www.un.org/depts/unsd/ww2000/table6a.htm*.

◆ KEY TERMS ◆

dowry deaths
enfranchisement
female genitalia mutilation (FGM)
female infanticide
gender
longevity gap
maternal mortality rate

◆ APPLYING GEOGRAPHIC KNOWLEDGE ◆

1. As we have seen, men outnumber women in many societies, including the world's most populous ones. Explain the factors that produce male numerical dominance in some countries, and discuss what changes would have to occur if that situation were to change.

2. Geographers Janice Monk and Arlene Rengert have argued that certain landscapes are created and dominated by men. Which landscapes in the community where you live fit this description? In what ways are those landscapes uninviting to women? Do those landscapes affect the activity patterns of women?

Part Ten
SOCIAL GEOGRAPHIES OF THE MODERN WORLD

At Issue: Revisited

Can the smaller world created by transport, information, and communication technologies help us overcome some of the divisions of race, ethnicity, and gender? Technological advances now make us more aware than ever of the social fragmentation of our world. Words and images of faraway atrocities can sometimes open possibilities for international pressure to be brought to bear on responsible parties—pressure that is organized through the use of airplanes, telephones, and computers. Those same words and images also make us aware of how deeply, even hopelessly, divided our world is. When one considers that patterns of access to modern technology reflect the geographies of inequality surveyed in this part, technology can look as much like a part of the problem as a solution. A challenge for the decades ahead, then, is to broaden access to technology and participation in its development. Such an undertaking offers the hope that technology can help us understand the true complexity of our differences—a first critical step toward overcoming them.

◆ SELECTED BIBLIOGRAPHY ◆

Part Ten Social Geographies of the Modern World

Adepoju, A., & Oppong, C., eds. *Gender, Work & Population in Sub-Saharan Africa* (London: J. Currey, 1994).

Agarawal, B. *A Field of One's Own: Gender and Land Rights in South Asia* (Cambridge, U.K.: Cambridge University Press, 1994).

Aslanbeigui, N., Pressman, S. & Summerfield, G., eds. *Women in the Age of Economic Transformation: Gender Impact of Reforms in Post-Socialist and Developing Countries* (London:Routledge, 1994).

Atkings, P. J., & Bowler, I. R. *Food in Society: Economy, Culture, Geography* (New York: Arnold, 2001).

Back, L., & Salomos, J. *Theories of Race and Racism: A Reader* (New York: Routledge, 2000).

Badran, M. *Feminists, Islam, and Nation: Gender and the Making of Modern Egypt* (Princeton, N.J.: Princeton University Press, 1995).

Bahvnani, K-K., ed. *Feminism and "Race"* (New York: Oxford University Press, 2001).

Barnett, T., & Blaikie, P. *AIDS in Africa: Its Present and Future Impact* (New York: Guilford Press, 1992).

Beneria, L., & Feldman, S., eds. *Unequal Burden: Economic Crises, Persistent Poverty and Women's Work* (Boulder, Colo.: Westview Press, 1992).

Biswas, M. R., & Gabr, M., eds. *Nutrition in the Nineties: Policy Issues* (New York: Oxford University Press, 1994).

Brooks, G. *Nine Parts of Desire: The Hidden World of Islamic Women* (New York: Anchor Books/Doubleday, 1994).

Brown, B. J., & LaPrairie, L. A. *Shades of Opportunity and Access: Ethnic and Gender Minority Issues in America with Global Reflections* (Boulder, Colo.: Department of Geography, University of Colorado, 1991).

Brown, L. R. *The Changing World Food Prospects: The Nineties and Beyond* (Washington, D.C.: Worldwatch Institute, 1988).

Brown, L. R. *Full House: Reassessing the Earth's Population Carrying Capacity* (Washington, D.C.: Worldwatch Institute, 1994).

Chatty, D., & Rabo, A., eds. *Organizing Women: Formal and Informal Women's Groups in the Middle East* (New York: Berg, 1997).

Clark, R. P. *Global Life Systems: Population, Food, and Disease in the Process of Globalization* (Lanham, Md.: Rowman & Littlefield, 2000).

Clarke, C., Ley, D., & Peach, C., eds. *Geography and Ethnic Pluralism* (London: George Allen & Unwin, 1984).

Cliff, A., & Haggett, P. *Atlas of Disease Distribution* (Oxford, U.K.: Basil Blackwell, 1989).

Cravey, A. J. *Women and Work in Mexico's Maquiladoras* (Lanham, Md.: Rowman & Littlefield, 1998).

Currey, B., & Hugo, G., eds. *Famines as a Geographical Phenomenon* (Boston: D. Reidel, 1984).

Currie, G., & Rothenberg, C., eds. *Feminist (Re)Visions of the Subject: Landscapes, Ethnoscapes, Theoryscapes* (Lanham, Md.: Rowman & Littlefield, 2001).

Curtis, J. A. "Mexicali's Chinatown." *Geographical Review* 85, no. 3 (1995): 335–348.

Delaporte, F. *The History of Yellow Fever*, trans. A. Goldhammer. (Cambridge, Mass.: MIT Press, 1991).

Despommier, D. D. *Parasitic Diseases.* 4th ed. (New York: Apple Trees Productions, 2000).

Devereux, S. *Famine in the Twentieth Century* (Brighton: Institute of Development Studies, 2000).

Domosh, M., & Seager, J. *Putting Women in Place* (New York: Guilford Press, 2001).

Dyck, I., Lewis, N., & McLafferty, S., eds. *Geographies of Women's Health* (New York: Routledge, 2001).

Flores, Rafael, & Gillespie, S. *Health and Nutrition: Emerging and Reemerging Issues in Developing Countries* (Washington, D.C.: International Food and Policy Research Institute, 2001).

Gatrell, A. G., & Löytönen, M., eds. *GIS and Health* (Philadelphia: Taylor & Francis, 1998).

Gesler, W. *Health Care in Developing Countries* (Washington, D.C.: Association of American Geographers, Resource Publications in Geography, 1984).

Gordon, A. A. *Transforming Capitalism and Patriarchy: Gender and Developments in Africa* (Boulder, Colo.: Lynne Rienner, 1996).

Gould, P. R. *The Slow Plague: A Geography of the AIDS Pandemic* (Oxford: Basil Blackwell, 1993).

Haddad, Y. Y., & Esposito, J. L., eds. *Islam, Gender & Social Change* (New York: Oxford University Press, 1998).

Haggett, P. *The Geographical Structure of Epidemics* (New York: Clarendon Press, 2000).

Hall, S. *Race: The Floating Signifier [Videorecording].* Media Education Foundation; Introduced by Sut Jhally, produced, directed & edited by Sut Jhally (Northampton, Mass., 1996).

Hanson, S., & Pratt, G. *Gender, Work and Space* (New York: Routledge, 1995).

Hartl, D. L., & Clark, A.G. *Principles of Population Genetics.* 3rd ed. (Sunderland, Mass.: Sinauer Associates, 1997).

Honari, M., & Boleyn, T., eds. *Health Ecology: Health, Culture, and Human-Environment Interaction* (New York: Routledge, 1999).

Howland, C. W. *Religious Fundamentalisms and the Human Rights of Women* (New York: Palgrave, 2001).

Hurrell, A., & Woods, N., eds. *Inequality, Globalization, and World Politics* (New York: Oxford University Press, 1999).

Jeffrey, R., & Jeffrey, P. *Population, Gender and Politics: Demographic Change in Rural North India* (Cambridge, U.K.: Cambridge University Press, 1997).

Jobin, W. *Dams and Disease: Ecological Design and Health Impacts of Large Dams, Canals, and Irrigation Systems* (New York: Routledge, 1999).

Johnson, L., Huggins, J., & Jacobs, J. *Placebound: Australian Feminist Geographies* (New York: Oxford University Press, 2000).

Jones III, J. P., Nast, H. J., & Roberts, S. M., eds. *Thresholds in Feminist Geography: Difference, Methodology, Representation* (Totowa, N.J.: Rowman & Allanheld, 1997).

Kahne, H., & Giele, J. Z., eds. *Women's Work and Women's Lives: The Continuing Struggle Worldwide* (Boulder, Colo.: Westview Press, 1992).

Lieberson, S., & Waters, M. C. *From Many Strands: Ethnic and Racial Groups in Contemporary America* (New York: Russell Sage Foundation, 1990).

Lloyd, B. S., Rengert, A. C., & Monk, J. J. "Landscapes of the Home," in A. C. Rengert & J. J. Monk, eds., *Women and Spatial Change: Learning Resources for Social Science Courses* (Dubuque, Iowa: Kendall-Hunt, 1982).

Marchand, M. H., & Runyan, A. S., eds. *Gender and Global Restructuring: Sightings, Sites and Resistance* (New York: Routledge, 2000).

Marty, M. E., & Appleby, R. S., eds. *Religion, Ethnicity, and Self-Identity: Nations in Turmoil* (Hanover, N.H.: University Press of New England, 1997).

Massey, D. *Space, Place and Gender* (Minneapolis: University of Minnesota Press, 1994).

McCall, L. *Complex Inequality: Gender, Class and Race in the New Economy* (New York: Routledge, 2001).

McDowell, L., & Sharp, J. P., eds. *Space, Gender, Knowledge* (New York: Arnold, 1997).

McKee, J. O. *Ethnicity in Contemporary America* (Lanham, Md.: Rowman & Littlefield, 2000).

Meade, M. S., & Earickson, R. J. *Medical Geography: A Geographical Appraisal.* 2nd ed.,(New York: Guilford Press, 2000).

Mikesell, M. W., & Murphy, A. B. "A Framework for Comparative Study of Minority-Group Aspirations." *Annals of the Association of American Geographers* 81 (1991): 581–604.

Miranne, K. B., & Young, A. H., eds. *Gendering the City* (Lanham, Md.: Rowman & Littlefield, 2000).

Momsen, J. H., & Kinnaird, V., eds. *Different Places, Different Voices: Gender and Development in Africa, Asia, and Latin America* (London: Routledge, 1993).

Momsen, J. H., & Townsend, J., eds. *Geography of Gender in the Third World* (Albany, N.Y.: SUNY Press, 1987).

Montagu, A. *Man's Most Dangerous Myth: The Fallacy of Race,* 5th rev. ed. (Cleveland: World, 1975).

Opdycke, S. *The Routledge Historical Atlas of Women in America* (New York: Routledge, 2000).

Palca, J. "The Sobering Geography of AIDS." *Science*, 19 April 1991, pp. 372–373.

Phillips, D. R. *Health and Health Care in the Third World* (Essex, U.K.: Longmans, 1990).

Pyle, G. *The Diffusion of Influenza: Patterns and Paradigms* (Totowa, N.J.: Rowman & Allanheld, 1986).

Roberts, L. "Disease and Death in the New World." *Science*, 8 December 1989, pp. 1245–1247.

Rose, H. M., & McClain, P. D. *Race, Place and Risk: Black Homicide in Urban America* (Albany: State University of New York Press, 1990).

Roseman, C. C., Laux, H. D., & Thieme, G., eds. *EthniCity: Geographical Perspectives on Ethnic Change in Modern Cities* (Lanham, Md.: Rowman & Littlefield, 1996).

Sachs, C. *The Invisible Farmers: Women in Agricultural Production* (Totowa, N.J.: Rowman & Allanheld, 1983).

Seager, J. *The State of Women in the World Atlas.* 2nd ed. (New York: Penguin Group, 1997).

Shannon, G. W., Pyler, G., & Bashshur, R. *The Geography of AIDS* (New York: Guilford Press, 1991).

Sheldon, K., ed. *Courtyards, Markets, City Streets: Urban Women in Africa* (Boulder, Colo.: Westview Press, 1996).

Shinagawa, L. H., & Jang, M. *Atlas of American Diversity* (Walnut Creek, Ca.: AltaMira Press, 1998).

Shortridge, B. G. *Atlas on American Women* (New York: Macmillan, 1987).

Singer, M., & Berg, P. *Genes and Genomes: A Changing Perspective* (Mill Valley, Calif.: University Science Books, 1990).

Sivard, R. L. *Women: A World Survey* (Washington, D.C.: World Priorities, 1985).

Sperling, V. *Organizing Women in Contemporary Russia* (Cambridge: Cambridge University Press, 1999).

Sowell, T. *Race and Culture: A World View* (New York: Basic Books, 1994).

Staudt, K., ed. *Women, International Development and Politics* (Philadelphia: Temple University Press, 1997).

UNICEF. *The Lesser Child: The Girl in India* (Geneva: United Nations, 1990).

UNICEF *The State of the World's Children 2001* (New York: United Nations/Oxford University Press, 2001).

United Nations. *The World's Women, 2000: Trends and Statistics.* 3rd ed.(New York: United Nations, 2000).

United Nations. *The World's Women, 1970–1990: Trends and Statistics.* (New York: United Nations, 1991).

Zouev, A. ed., *Generation in Jeopardy: Children in Central and Eastern Europe and the Former Soviet Union.* UNICEF (Armonk, NY: M. E. Sharpe, 1999).

Part Eleven

THE CHANGING ENVIRONMENTAL CONTEXT

At Issue

Environmental variation (spatial as well as temporal) is one of the Earth's crucial characteristics. Temperatures rise and fall, precipitation waxes and wanes. Forests flourish and wither, deserts expand and contract. Humanity has evolved during a series of alternately warm and cold phases of an ice age that is still in progress. But today humanity itself is part of the process. The Earth has been warming, and we may be contributing to some degree to this warm-up. The world's governments are trying to find ways to combat industrial pollution and the release of "greenhouse" gases. *At issue: Should all countries be subject to the same rules? Or should the poorer countries be exempt from some of the more costly regulations? And can an effective response be organized without undermining state sovereignty?*

Forged by the ice, occupied and shaped by humans. A glacial valley leading into the Sognefjord, Norway.

Part Outline

Chapter 33

The Planet and Humanity

From the field notes

"A helicopter flight over the coastal slopes of the Hawai'ian island of Maui provided a magnificent view of this mid-Pacific volcanic landscape and a reminder that the human imprint is modifying it even in this remote setting. Original vegetation has made way for farm fields; birds and other wildlife have been exterminated; roads lead along valleys; buildings make their appearance even here. Only the steepest of slopes hold off the human penetration, but not the human impact: ecological change reaches far beyond the frontiers of human settlement."

KEY POINTS

- **Throughout history, the Earth has experienced dramatic environmental shifts that have greatly affected the land, oceans, and atmosphere of the planet.**
- **Complex life appeared on Earth only recently in geologic time, and it has evolved through three environmentally induced mass extinctions.**
- **Glacial advances and recessions have occurred repeatedly; complex human societies emerged in the wake of the most recent major glacial retreat.**
- **Climatic fluctuations during the past 1000 years created environmental challenges that influenced the development of societies in both the Western and the Eastern Hemisphere.**
- **Human adjustments to further dramatic environmental shifts will be complicated both by the extraordinary growth of the human population over the past two centuries and by the expansion of humans into increasingly marginal environmental zones.**

The Earth is four thousand six hundred million years old: 4.6 billion years have passed since it congealed from an orbiting band of cosmic matter into a fiery ball of molten substance burning fiercely and emitting clouds of superheated gases that found its place in the solar system as the third planet among the nine revolving around the Sun. Millions of lightning strikes rained down upon the red-hot surface while, inside the globe, heavier matter settled toward the center and lighter material accumulated in the outer layers, all of it kept in motion by the intense heat.

And then, when the Earth was a mere 100 million years old, a cataclysmic event occurred that was to change it forever. In the continuing chaos of the evolving solar system, a large object—perhaps as large as Mercury or even Mars—approached our planet on a collision course. Even a thick atmosphere would not have protected the Earth from the devastating impact. It struck at a low angle, a glancing blow that briefly buried it in the molten mass of Earth's primordial shell. So great was the speed of the object, so huge was the collision, that much of it bounced outward again into space, weighted down now by a clump of Earthly matter.

That combination of mass, the slowed-down planetoid plus the Earth matter attached to it, was so heavy that its flight back into space was aborted. It could not escape the Earth's gravitational field, and it began to orbit the Earth as a satellite. The Earth had acquired its Moon.

Imagine the scene, 4500 million years ago. Just a few hundred miles above the Earth's surface hung an incandescent Moon that filled the night sky from one horizon to the other, seemingly so close to the Earth that you could touch it. A gaping craterlike depression marked the place where the impact had occurred, threatening for a time the very structure of the planet. The low-angle blow from the impact object set the Earth spinning on a wobbly axis, so fast that one rotation may have lasted only about four hours. The force of this rapid rotation set up wild currents of motion in its outer as well as inner layers.

But our planet held together, and the Moon's orbit grew progressively larger during the several hundred million years that followed. By about four billion years ago, the Earth's rotation had slowed significantly as well, so that our planet's day had lengthened to around 10 hours, and the Moon was nearly half as far away as it is today. (The Moon continues to move away from the Earth in very small but measurable increments.) At the same time, patches of the Earth's crust began to cool enough to harden molten material into the first solid rocks. Initially, these patches soon were melted down again by streams of hot lava, but eventually some of them survived. The Earth had begun to form a crust.

Consider these events in the context of humanity's arrival and impact on this globe. In Chapter 3 we noted that ***Homo sapiens*** emerged less than 200,000 years ago (and possibly not much more than 100,000 years ago). Virtually everything you have read about in this book—plant and animal domestication, state formation, urbanization, industrialization, high technology, space travel—has occurred over the past 10,000 years. It is interesting to compare Earth history to one's own. If you are about 20 years of age, every year of your life corresponds to around 240 million years of planetary history. One month represents some 20 million years, one week, somewhat less than 5 million years. One day in a young adult's life corresponds to roughly 700,000 years, and one hour, approximately 30,000 years.

This means that, by comparison, *Homo sapiens* appeared less than six hours ago, and the whole saga of modern human civilization, from irrigation to suburbanization, took place over just the past 20 minutes. The Roman Empire existed four minutes ago. The Industrial Revolution began less than 30 seconds ago, and we have been measuring temperature and other weather conditions instrumentally for only about 17 seconds.

This raises the question: how representative is the short-term present of the long-term past? Over the past century, geographers and other scientists have been embarked on a joint mission to reconstruct our planet's history on the basis of current evidence. One of them, the climatologist-geographer Alfred Wegener used his spatial view of the world to make a key contribution. Viewing the increasingly accurate maps of the opposite coastlines of the North and South Atlantic Oceans, he proposed a hypothesis that would account for the close "fit" of the shapes of the facing continents, which, he argued, would be unlikely to be a matter of chance. His continental-drift hypothesis required the preexistence of a supercontinent, which he called, ***Pangaea***, that broke apart into the fragments we now know as Africa, the Americas, Eurasia, and Australia (Fig. 33-1). As we noted in Chapter 1, Wegener's hypothesis engendered the later theory of plate tectonics and crustal spreading, and scientists now know that Pangaea and its fragmentation were only the latest episodes in a cycle of continental coalescence and splintering that spans billions of years. This latest Pangaean breakup, however, began only 180 million years ago (nine months ago in a 20-year-old 's lifetime!) and continues to this day. When you hear of earthquakes and volcanic eruptions, they are likely to have occurred along the boundaries of the crust's rocky plates.

In Part Eleven we touch on some complex subjects that are only beginning to be understood: the history of environmental change on Planet Earth, the current environmental picture, and the relationships between human society and activity and natural environments. During our brief presence on this planet, we humans have had a powerful impact on natural environs ranging from rainforests to tundras. Long before we became technologically proficient we exterminated wildlife by the millions and burned grasslands and forests by the hundreds of thousands of square miles. The twentieth-century population explosion magnified humanity's impact on the Earth in unprecedented ways. Adjectives such as "calamitous" and "catastrophic" are often used to describe this impact, but our planet has been the scene of calamities and catastrophes throughout its existence, beginning with the lunar collision. *Homo sapiens* has not dominated his world long enough to have much experience with such events (although, as we note later in this chapter, an occurrence about 73,000 years ago came very close to exterminating humanity altogether), but the natural environments with which we are familiar today result from long histories—and are temporary. Environmental change is a hallmark of Planet Earth, and understanding long-term change helps us cope with the present and prepare for the future. ◆

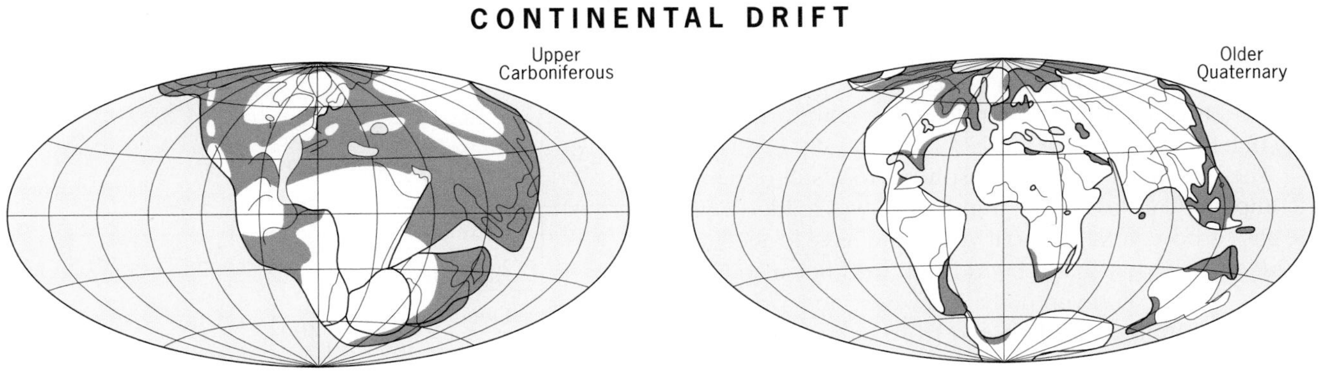

Figure 33-1 Wegener's hypothesis of continental drift. From his own sketch map in *The Origin of Continents and Oceans* (1914). His dates required revision, but were remarkably prescient.

Ocean and Atmosphere

The fall of the Berlin Wall in 1989 gave rise to a spate of books signaling the onset of a new era. Their titles were often misleading, such as *The End of History* by Francis Fukuyama, but none more so than one called *The End of Science*, which argued that all the great questions of science had been answered and that what remained, essentially, was a filling of the gaps. When it comes to global environments, however, some great questions remain open.

One of these relates to the oceans. Planet Earth today is often called the Blue Planet because more than 70 percent of its surface is covered by water and views from space are dominated by blue hues and swirls of white cloud, but in truth we do not know with any certainty how the Earth acquired its watery cloak, or exactly when. Some scientists hypothesize that the water was originally trapped inside the Earth during its formation and rose to the surface during the time when heavier constituents sank to form the core. Others calculate that most of the water that did reach the surface in this way would have been evaporated into space by the searing heat then prevailing, suggesting that another source must be identified. This has led to the comet hypothesis, which proposes that icy comets bombarded the Earth for more than a billion years while its atmosphere was still thin, accumulating fresh water from space that filled the basins in the formative crust.

Obviously, the "end of science" has not arrived when it comes to as crucial a question as this, and here is a related one: will the Earth retain its life-giving oceans permanently? Probes of our neighboring planet Mars produced some startling conclusions: Mars may have lost a global ocean more than 30 meters (100 feet) deep, and there are indications that Mars at one time had even more water (as a proportion of mass) than planet Earth. Why and how rapidly did Mars lose its ocean? And what may that loss portend for Earth?

The evolution of the atmosphere, too, still remains incompletely understood. Originally, it was loaded with the gas carbon dioxide, and if you could have looked up at the sky it would have been bright red because CO_2 scatters red light. Eventually, however, the primitive ocean, undoubtedly still heated from below, began to dissolve CO_2 in huge quantities, depositing limestone and other carbonate rocks and turning the sky a familiar blue. Yet it was to be a very long time before oxygen became a substantial gas in the atmosphere. Around 1500 million years ago, green algae started to spread across the Earth's ocean surfaces, and as their colonies grew, their ***photosynthesis*** (the conversion of carbon dioxide and water into carbohydrates and oxygen through the absorption of sunlight) raised the atmosphere's oxygen content. About 800 million years ago—our young adult would have been 16 already—the oxygen content in the atmosphere was about one-twentieth of its present strength or just 1 percent of the total. But that was enough to support the emergence of the first single-celled animals, the protozoa.

We report all this because it leads up to an environmental event of great significance. The protozoa appeared just before the Earth's atmosphere, and indeed the entire planet, went into a deep freeze, an ice age that was to be followed by many more (but none as severe as this one). Land and oceans alike appear to have been frozen over. According to the still-controversial ***Snowball Earth theory***, this glaciation perhaps resulted from a decrease in volcanism, a temporary decline in the Sun's radiative output, and/or a surge in the continuing precipitation of calcium carbonate on the ocean floor. The last would entail a sharp reduction in atmospheric CO_2 and a decrease in the evolving atmosphere's ***greenhouse effect***—the trapping of outgoing radiation from the Earth's surface—allowing global temperatures to

Table 33-1 Stages in Earth History

Era[a]	Period[b]	MYA	Epoch
Cenozoic	Quaternary		Holocene (Recent)[c]
		2	Pleistocene
	Tertiary	6	Pliocene
		24	Miocene
		36	Oligocene
		57	Eocene
			Paleocene
	K/T Boundary	65	
Mesozoic	Cretaceous	146	
	Jurassic	208	
	Triassic	250	
Paleozoic	Permian	290	
	Carboniferous	363	
	Devonian	409	
	Silurian	440	
	Ordovician	510	
	Cambrian	570	
	Precambrian	↓	

[a]The numbers represent millions of years ago and are very approximate, even for the Tertiary period.

[b]The second half of the Cenozoic era has been marked by the onset of a global ice age that prevailed throughout the Quaternary period.

[c]The Holocene epoch is merely the latest of many interglaciations (warm periods) during this ice age and has lasted only about 10,000 years.

drop. As is well known, ice ages are times of accelerated evolution. The single-celled protozoa evolved into multicelled, complex metazoa, and those with protective shells (there was plenty of calcium carbonate around) had a better chance of survival. When the ice retreated, life on Earth was set for its ***Cambrian Explosion***, the burgeoning of marine organisms in unprecedented diversity (Table 33-1).

Fire and Ice

When you consider that these history-making events occurred after the Earth had already existed for nearly four billion years (at age 17, therefore, in our 20-year-old's lifetime), the brevity of complex life on this planet comes into even sharper focus. What took so long? The causes are many: an inhospitable ocean, an oxygen-deprived atmosphere, perhaps a variably hot Sun, recurrent bursts of volcanism, repeated ice ages. The Earth was a challenging place for life.

Today a major volcanic eruption is rare enough to make the news. Krakatoa (1883), Mount St. Helens (1980), Pinatubo (1991), and Etna (2001) took lives, damaged property and in the case of Pinatubo, even changed global climate slightly. One billion years ago, however, the Earth's crust still was immature and subject to huge bursts of volcanic activity. Such episodes poured incalculable volumes of gases and ash into the atmosphere, causing ***mass depletions*** (loss of diversity through a failure to produce new species) and contributing to the three ***mass extinctions*** (mass destruction of most species) known to have occurred over the past 500 million years. The Earth's most recent experience with mass volcanism took place between 180 and 160 million years ago, when the supercontinent Pangaea began to fracture. Lava poured from fissures and vents as South America separated from Africa and India commenced its northeastward march. Skies were blackened, the atmosphere choked with ash. Animals responded as they always have in time of crisis: by migrating, fragmenting into smaller groups, and speeding up their adaptive, evolutionary response. Physical geographers hypothesize that the earliest phase of Pangaea's fragmentation was also the most violent, that the plate separations that started it all were driven by built-up, extreme heat below the supercontinent, but that the motion of the plates has since slowed down. The ***Pacific Ring of Fire***—that ocean-girdling zone of crustal instability, volcanism, and earthquakes—is but a trace of the paroxysm that marked the onset of Pangaea's breakup (Fig. 33-2). Yet, as we will see, natural events on that Pacific margin have cost millions of humans their lives and altered the course of history. Imagine what would have happened to humanity if there had been more than 6 billion of us on Pangaea.

And then there are the ice ages. Whether or not the Snowball Earth hypothesis turns into a tenable theory, there is no doubt that our planet plunges into frigid conditions time and again. When Pangaea still was a supercontinent, such an ice age cooled the Permian Period (see again the time chart on page 516) and may have contributed to—if it was not the cause of—the greatest known extinction crisis in the history of life on Earth.

Figure 33-2 Recent Earthquakes and Volcanic Eruptions. *Source*: From a map in H. J. de Blij and P. O. Muller, *Geography: Realms, Regions, and Concepts*, 10th ed. New York: Wiley, 2002, p. 10.

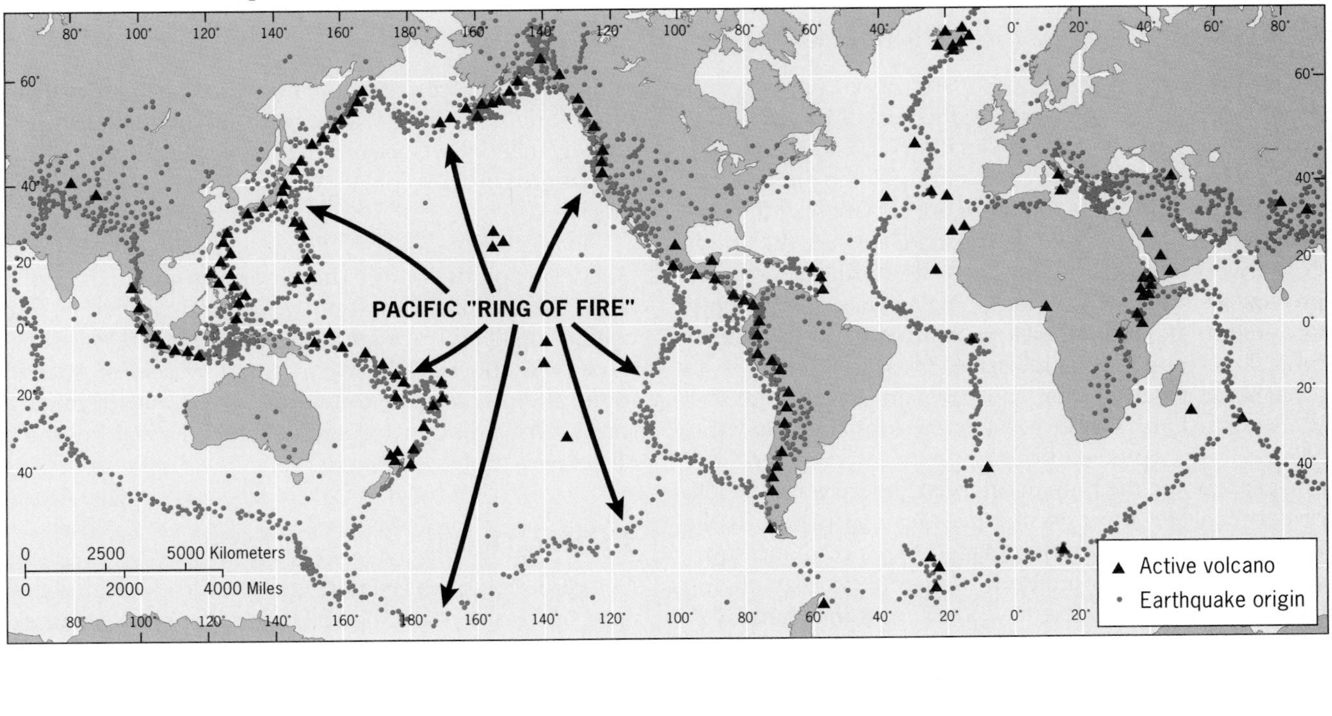

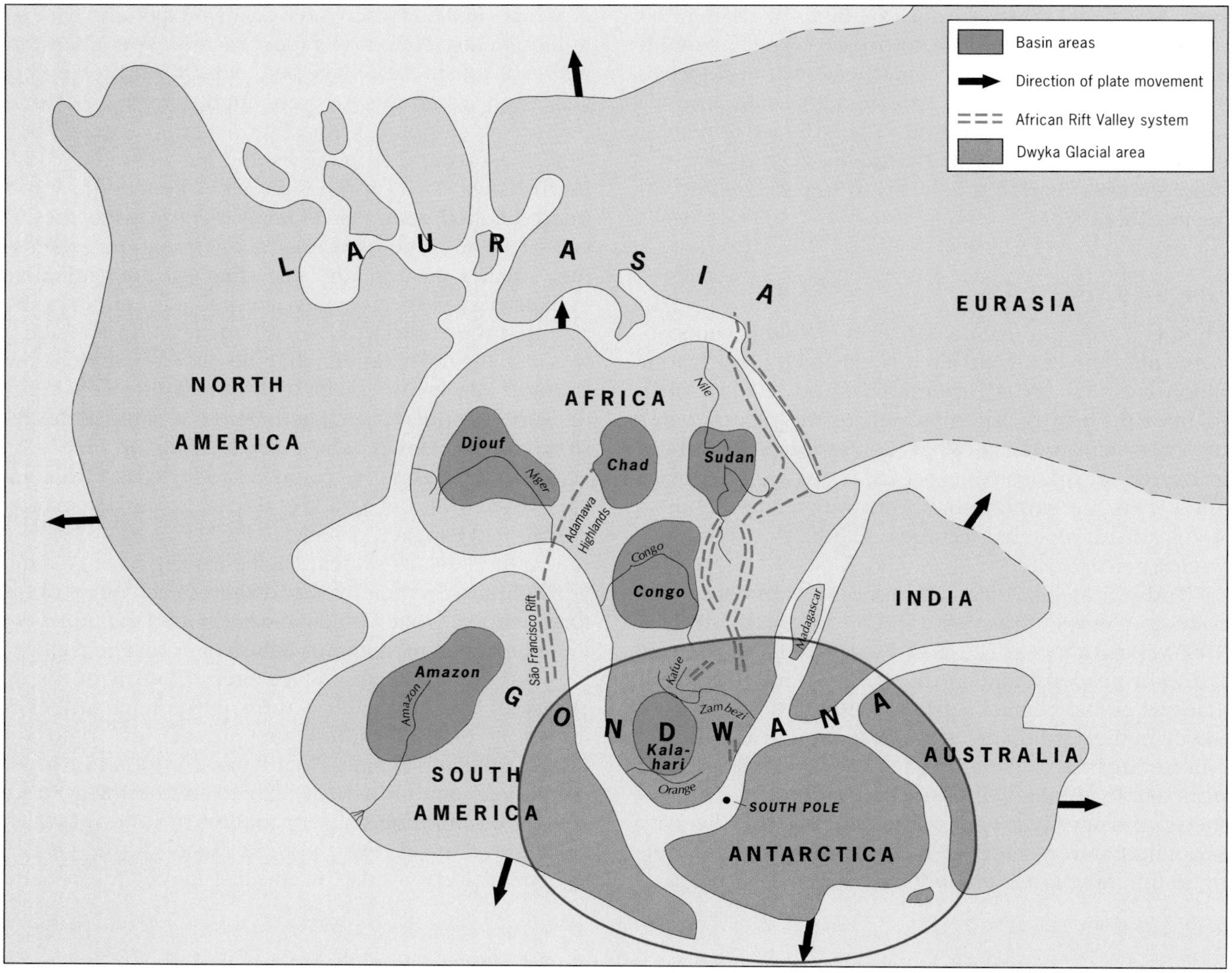

Figure 33-3 Pangea Reassembled. *Source*: From a map in H. J. de Blij and P. O. Muller, *Geography: Realms, Regions, and Concepts*, 10th ed. New York: Wiley, 2002, p. 339.

The ***Dwyka Ice Age***, as it is also known, is recorded most vividly in the southern landmasses of Pangaea, the group Wegener called Gondwana: Africa, South America, India, Australia, and Antarctica (although the present ice-covered condition of Antarctica conceals most of the evidence there). While Gondwana was glaciated, the South Pole was positioned not far from the southeast coast of present-day South Africa, and the glaciers spread deeply into central Africa, southeastern South America, southern India, and southern Australia (Fig. 33-3).

As we noted earlier, the Permian ended with the worst of the Earth's three great extinctions, and when the Mesozoic Era opened about 250 million years ago (just one year ago on the human calendar), there was little left of Permian life. But now the post-ice-age planet made up for it. Tropical warmth replaced Arctic cold, moisture and precipitation abounded, atmospheric oxygen increased as luxuriant forests spread, and the Earth was ready for the faunal exuberance of Jurassic Park. The age of the dinosaurs also saw the first birds, the first ***marsupials*** (animals whose females nurture their offspring externally in a pouch, not internally in a placenta), and the first ***angiosperms*** (plants whose seeds are encased in fruit).

Even the breakup of Pangaea during the Jurassic failed to spoil the party. The dinosaurs grew larger and larger, specializing into herbivores and carnivores and competing fiercely for survival. As the landmasses separated and the seas between them widened, species found themselves isolated and evolved into distinctive forms. Only another ice age, it seemed, could end the Mesozoic's profusion.

Sudden Death

As it turned out, the last period of the Mesozoic, the Cretaceous, ended not in a glacial whimper but with an extraterrestrial bang. About 65 million years ago, an object technically known as a carbonaceous meteorite, in orbit since the formation of the solar system, was on a collision course with Earth. Only about 6 miles (10 kilometers) in diameter but traveling at about 55,000 mph (90,000 kph), it approached from the southeast at a low angle, striking the planet a glancing blow. It hit what is today the northwestern edge of Caribbean Mexico's Yucatan Peninsula, not far from the present city of Merida and just to the east of the small port of Progreso, where a small, hand-painted sign along the road points to one of the most momentous locales on Earth: Chicxulub, the more than 100-mile wide, 40-mile deep crater formed by the impact, now filled with sediments.

At that moment life on Earth—or what was to remain of it after the cataclysm—took a new turn. As geologists have pointed out, the speed and angle of impact could not have been worse, and for North America the immediate consequences were catastrophic. At the time the comet struck, the impact area was a shallow sea with soft, deep sediments, and the blast sent a mass of debris hurtling thousands of miles into the heart of the continent and high into the atmosphere. The dinosaurs were killed, forests were flattened, ecologies devastated. Oceans and seas were thrown into great waves that destroyed coastal marine as well as terrestrial life. The most recent of the planet's great extinctions had begun.

North America was worst hit, but the impact affected the entire world, if not in the immediate aftermath of the collision, then in the years that followed. It is possible that some dinosaur species survived for a time in refuges in the Southern Hemisphere, but all expired during the first epoch of the Cenozoic, the Paleocene (the Cenozoic is divided into two periods, the Tertiary and the Quaternary, and these in turn into seven epochs; see Table 33-1). However, some smaller mammals, which had made their appearance during the Cretaceous, did manage to survive, migrating and adapting and setting the stage for what was to become the Age of Mammals. The so-called Cretaceous-Tertiary (***KT***) **boundary** marks the start of the sequence of events that led to the appearance of Homo sapiens on this planet.

Back to the Future

On the post-impact planet, however, there was little to suggest that an era of recovery and renewed biodiversity lay ahead. The collision released as much energy as 100 million megatons of high explosives and sent huge volumes of water vapor into the atmosphere along with carbonates from the bottom of the sea. This created an unprecedented greenhouse effect that outlasted the soot in the atmosphere and raised global temperatures to levels that killed many species that had survived the blast. The heat also destroyed numerous plant species; North America has been described as one "vast muddy field devoid of life" in the first years of the Tertiary. This is why, on charts showing the rise and fall of global temperatures, you will see a rise following the K/T boundary that continues throughout much of the Paleocene, when the planet was actually warmer still than it had been during the days of the dinosaurs. Then, in the early part of the Eocene, global temperatures began to drop. Even a rebound during the middle of the Eocene did not last. By the beginning of the Oligocene, about 36 million years (less than two months) ago, it would have been clear to any weather forecaster: the Earth was headed for another ice age (Fig. 33-4).

Soon the evidence began to accumulate: the early phase of the Oligocene witnessed the beginning of the formation of the Antarctic Ice Sheet even as South America and Antarctica were separating. (Remember: through all this activity, the continents continued to move on their crustal plates, the Atlantic Oceans, North and South, kept widening, and the distribution of land and water on the planet kept changing.) Even before the ice on Antarctica reached its shores, glaciers began to develop on the Earth's highest mountains, filling high-elevation valleys and sculpting a new, angular topography of sharp-edged peaks and ridges. Tree lines dropped to lower altitudes, vegetation shifted equatorward, and mammals everywhere, including the now-common primate forms, migrated and evolved rapidly.

From the field notes

"As we flew over the ice sheet, I imagined that this is what much of the world—at higher latitudes and altitudes—must have looked like during the most recent advance of the Late Cenozoic Ice Age. Whole expanses of continent, plateaus, plains, hills, as well as mountains, lay buried under thousands of feet of ice, only the highest crests protruding. It must have been a cold, forbidding world of climatic extremes, on the margins of which only the most adaptable of our ancestors survived."

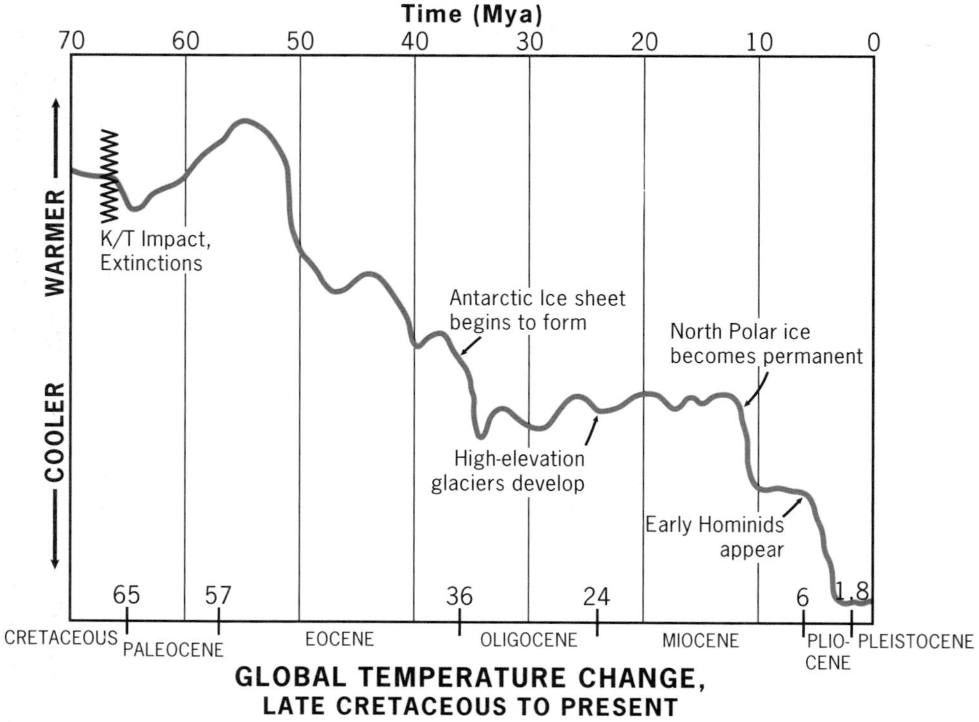

Figure 33-4 Global Temperature Change, Late Cretaceous to Present. *Sources:* C. Emiliani, *The Scientific Companion*, Second Edition, (New York: Wiley, 1995), p. 260; B. Fagan, *The Little Ice Age* (New York: Basic Books, 2001) *passim*.

Ice ages are not uniform cooling events: surges of coldness and advances of glaciers are interrupted by temporary warming spells long enough to reverse much of the glacial impact. So it was from about the middle of the Oligocene to the middle of the Miocene when, it seemed, the Cenozoic Ice Age had reached an equilibrium that (had weather and climate analysts been around in those days) might have been taken as a sign that the worst was over. Antarctica still had coastal zones clear of ice; the high-mountain glaciers advanced and receded as global climate cooled and warmed, and while the planet overall was cooler and drier than it had been during the age of the dinosaurs, there was plenty of environmental variety and related biodiversity. But then, about 14 million years ago, global cooling resumed with a vengeance. Antarctica's ice sheet not only reached the ocean all around its shores, but the ice floated from land onto water and cooled the Southern Ocean, affecting the entire global ocean in the process. Permanent ice appeared and rapidly thickened on the waters of the North Pole and environs. The temperature plunge continued into the Pliocene, just 6 million years (about eight days) ago, and glaciers appeared even on mountains in equatorial zones of the Andes, East Africa, and New Guinea. Early hominids had made their appearance in the late Miocene and scrambled for survival in rapidly changing environments and unreliable refuges; numerous lineages diverged and disappeared. And still it got colder. By the time the ***Pleistocene*** epoch opened, less than two million years ago, the planet was in a deep freeze.

In Chapter 3 we referred briefly to conditions during the Pleistocene, an epoch marked by long glaciations and short, warm ***interglacials*** (or interglaciations). In Africa, where the great drama of hominid evolution was proceeding, these phases were marked by fluctuating climates and variations in ecologies that guided natural selection. ***Homo erectus***, successor to ***Australopithecus***, was the most successful hominid, flourishing not only in Africa but spreading into Eurasia as well, a migration that reached present-day Indonesia, China, and Russia. *Homo erectus* managed to cope with forests that changed into savannas and back again, lakes that formed and evaporated, wildlife that varied from easy prey to difficult catch, and, as the fossil record shows, even with massive volcanic eruptions and earthquakes. Undoubtedly the numbers and distribution of *Homo erectus* also varied, but the species survived for perhaps as long as two million years and presaged the global dispersal of *Homo sapiens* to follow.

When the Pleistocene glaciations were most severe, permanent ice advanced deep into the landmasses of the Northern Hemisphere (Fig. 33-5). Plants, animals, and hominids saw their living space diminished, their refuges shrunk, their niches unusable. Such glaciations could last as long as 100,000 years, but eventually a warming spell would arrive, the ice would recede, and space as well as opportunity expanded again (Fig. 33-6). A warming

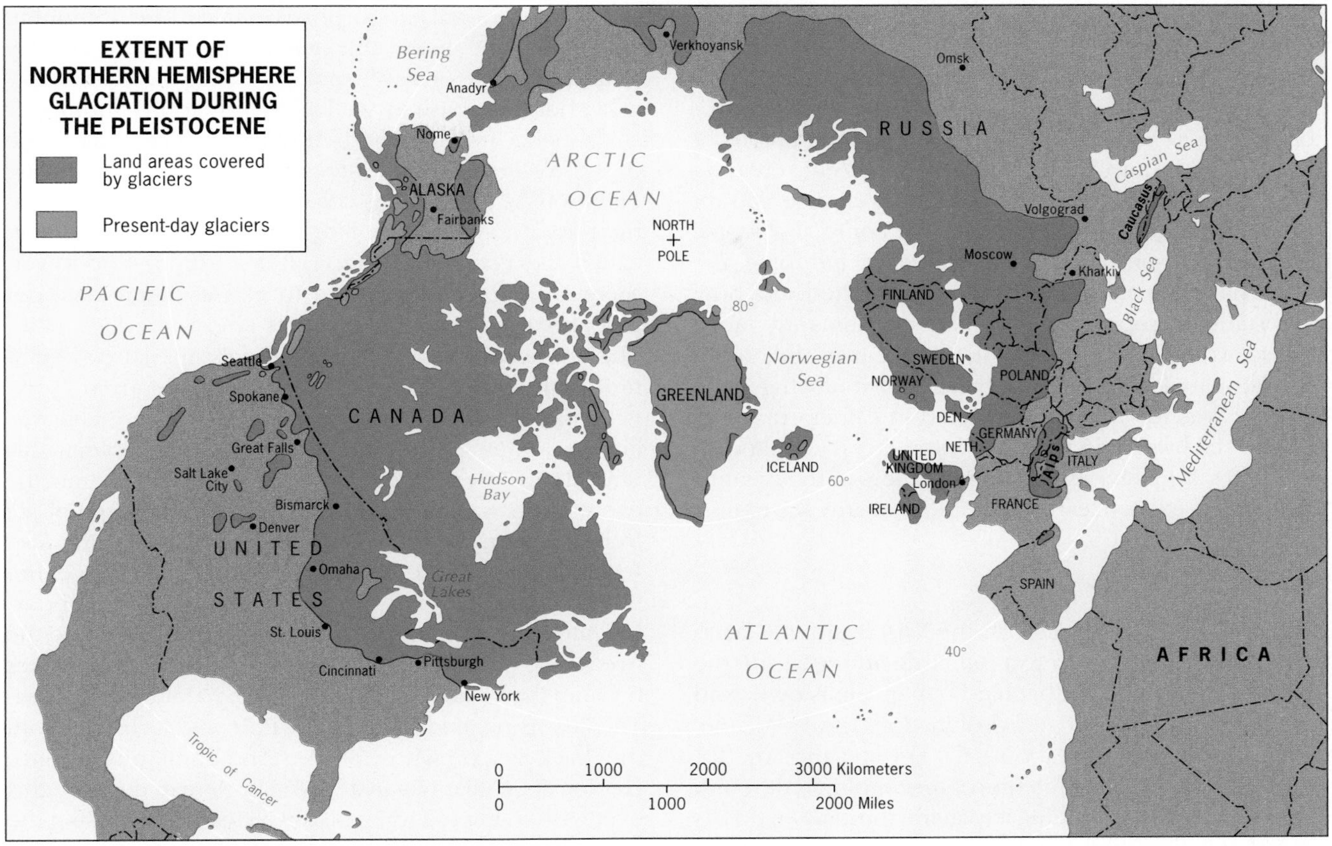

Figure 33-5 Extent of Northern Hemisphere Glaciation During the Late Pleistocene's Wisconsinan Glaciation. The evidence on which this map is based includes glacial deposits and the marks of glaciers' erosion on bedrock.

phase of this kind occurred between about 120,000 and 100,000 years ago, and some scientists suggest that this is the time when *Homo sapiens* appeared on the scene, perhaps contemporaneously with the species known as the ***Neanderthals***. According to this hypothesis, *Homo sapiens*, after emerging in Africa, spread rapidly into Eurasia and vanquished both *Homo erectus* and the Neanderthals in the process.

The most recent glaciation of the Pleistocene, the ***Wisconsinan Glaciation***, left its mark on much of the Northern Hemisphere (Fig. 33-5). But resourceful humans managed to survive where their predecessors could not, and there is ample evidence of human occupation in Europe ranging from cave art to tool kits. As noted earlier, even during a glacial advance there are brief periods of milder climate, and Figure 33-5 represents a glacial extreme, not the whole picture. So human communities, fishing, hunting, and gathering and using increasingly sophisticated tools (and probably means of verbal communication), exploited the milder times by expanding their frontiers.

Figure 33-6 Global Temperature Change Over the Last 600,000 Years of the Pleistocene. This scenario represents a composite of seven sources cited in the bibliography. Modifications continue, but the overall pattern is representative.

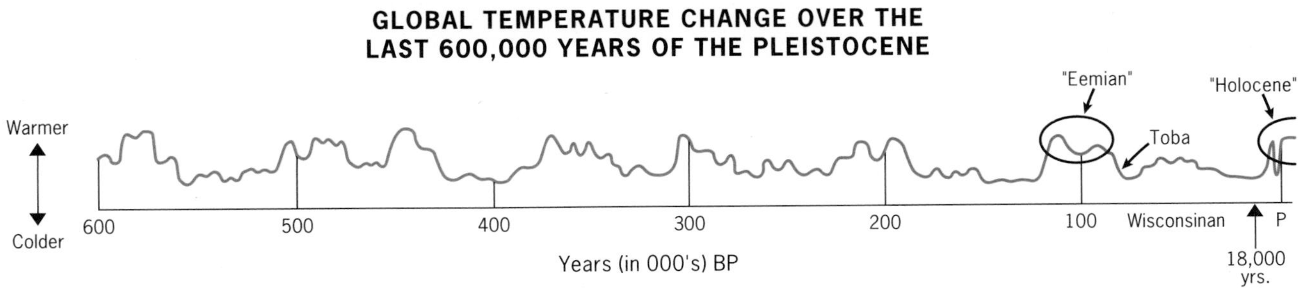

But then something happened that came close to exterminating humanity altogether. About 73,500 years ago a volcano erupted on the Indonesian island of Sumatera (Sumatra in the old spelling). This was not just an eruption: the entire mountain exploded, sending millions of tons of debris into orbit, obscuring the Sun, creating long-term darkness, and altering global climate. Mount Toba's detonation could hardly have come at a worse time. The Wisconsinan Glaciation was in full force, the Earth's habitable zone was already constricted, and now a substantial proportion of still-sparse humanity faced demise. Anthropologists refer to this event as humanity's "evolutionary bottleneck," suggesting that much genetic diversity was lost. Today, the filled-in caldera marking Toba's cataclysm is 55 miles (90 kilometers) long and 30 miles (50 kilometers) wide, silent witness to the greatest threat to our existence ever to come from any source.

The Holocene

Like its 20 or so predecessors, the Wisconsinan Glaciation eventually gave way to a full-scale ***interglacial***, the current warm interlude that has been given its own (and not altogether appropriate) designation, the Holocene. Global warming began about 18,000 years ago, and for the next 6000 years, temperatures rose rapidly. Although the ice sheets were thinning and giant, mud-laden floods sped down the Mississippi Valley, building the river's enormous delta, ice continued to cover most of northern North America as recently as 13,000 years ago.

To our Stone Age ancestors, who inhabited much of western and eastern Eurasia and may just have been entering the Americas (some scholars argue that Native Americans were here much earlier), this warming must have been a welcome experience. Slight temperature increases had happened before during the Wisconsinan Glaciation, but these were quickly followed by colder times. So persistent was this most recent warming that people ventured farther and farther poleward.

But nature still had surprises in store. Those thinning and melting ice sheets still covering much of present-day Canada became unstable; not only were they less heavy now, but their base as well as their margins and upper surfaces became liquefied. About 12,000 years ago, one of these ice sheets slid into the North Atlantic, causing disastrous waves along coasts and chilling the ocean right back to glaciation-like temperatures. This event, called the ***Younger Dryas*** after a tundra wildflower, seemed to forecast a return to glacial conditions, but global warming continued right afterward (Fig. 33-7). The Younger Dryas event, accordingly, marks the beginning of the Holocene on most geologic calendars.

That designation was established before much was known about still another North Atlantic cooling, this time about 7500 years ago, accompanied by a dramatic event in the basin of the Black Sea. A final surge of ice from northern North America plunged into the Atlantic, which had of course been rising—along with the entire world ocean—from the huge volumes of meltwater pouring into it. This time, the ice mass that collapsed into the ocean not only cooled it, but also sent a wall of water through the Strait of Gibraltar into the Mediterranean Sea. The fast-rising Mediterranean overflowed its barrier with the Black Sea, on whose shore stood numerous villages. Geologists William Ryan and Walter Pitman describe this event as having the force of 200 Niagara Falls, filling the Black Sea at the rate of 6 inches (15 centimeters) per day and forcing the coastal-plain inhabitants living near the shore to back away about 1 mile daily. Many sought refuge in the mountains along the present-day Turkish coast, but thousands of others must have abandoned their dwellings, boats, and fields and watched the flood swallow them up. By the time it was over, the surface of the Black Sea had risen 500 feet (145 meters) and, quite possibly, the biblical legend of the Great Flood was born.

The Holocene, therefore, was no uneventful transition to warmer and calmer times. Still, conditions did stabilize enough following the Black Sea crisis to allow

Figure 33-7 Northern Hemisphere Temperature Change Over the Last 18,000 Years. *Sources:* J. Grove, *The Little Ice Age* (London: Methuen, 1988); D. I. Benn, "Younger Dryas Stade" in P. L. Hancock and B. J. Skinner, *The Oxford Companion to the Earth*, pp. 1112–1116.

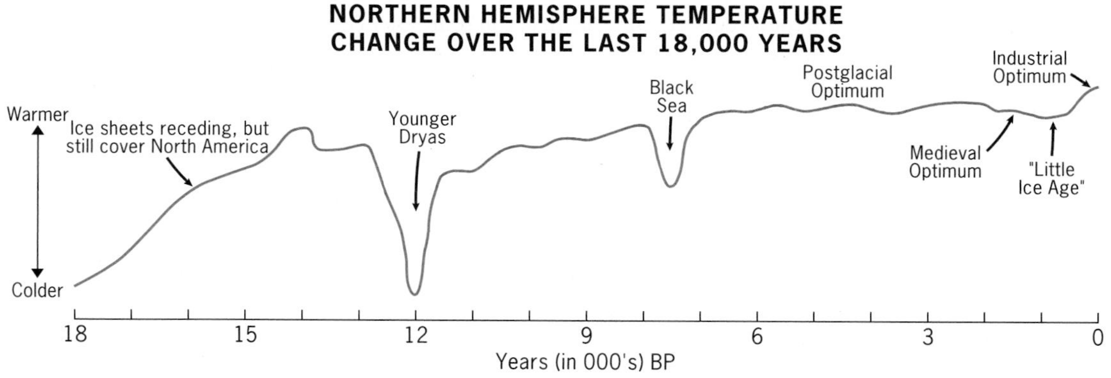

climatologists to talk of a ***Postglacial Optimum***. This started about 6000 years ago and marked the time when global environmental conditions became rather like those familiar to us today. This Postglacial Optimum transmuted into another salubrious period, the ***Medieval Optimum***, starting around 2000 years ago. This period witnessed the expansion of settlement in northern latitudes of Eurasia, the peopling of Iceland, and even the colonization of Greenland.

Not all was quiet during these climatically optimal times. About 3620 B.P. (Before the Present) the volcanic island of Thira (Santorini), to the north of Crete in the Greek archipelago now known as the Cyclades, blew up in a Toba-like eruption that covered a wide area of the eastern Mediterranean with a thick layer of poisonous ash. Days of darkened skies and seismic waves in the waters may have given rise to biblical allusions to darkness and parting waves (and perhaps to the legend of Atlantis), for when daylight returned, Thira was mostly gone. More consequential is what happened on Crete, where the powerful and culturally advanced Minoan civilization was based. Thira may have dealt it a fatal blow, opening the way to the regional dominance of ancient Greece.

Nor was this optimal period a time of invariably favorable climate. The impacts of ***deglaciation*** (the recession of ice and the opening of land to atmospheric conditions) continue long after the ice has disappeared; the poleward shift of climatic zones, the maturing of soils, the migration of plants and animals keep altering the environment for thousands of years. Some societies found themselves in favorable locales and converted their good fortune into security, expansion, and power. Others, including some early states and cities in what is today the Middle East, saw rivers dry up, deserts encroach, and livelihoods disappear. Was the innovation of irrigated farming a response to these challenges, as some scholars suggest, or had population pressure in stable environments led to it previously?

The Medieval Optimum certainly was a good time for two contemporaneous empires: the Roman in western Eurasia and the Han in eastern Eurasia. The Roman Empire unified Europe as never before (or since) and put an indelible cultural stamp on much of it. The empire of Han was China's formative dynasty and laid the foundation for a large and powerful state. The Han capital, then called Ch'angan (now Xian), was the Rome of China; Rome was the Ch'angan of the Mediterranean. The Silk Route not only transferred goods between East and West, but also tales of splendor and power.

And it was warm in Western Europe as well as in eastern Asia. The Romans planted grapevines in Britain and left behind a thriving wine industry. The agricultural frontier moved steadily northward in Scandinavia, and treelines and pastures moved upward on Alpine slopes. Meanwhile, Europe's medieval cities mushroomed as architects endowed them with some of their culture's major works: the Notre Dame Cathedral on an island in the Seine River in the heart of Paris; the cathedral at Chartres; the cathedral at Canterbury; and numerous other triumphs of Gothic styling and engineering. In China, the Tang Dynasty (618–907) brought a golden age of expansion and consolidation, architecture, and art. Superbly designed pagodas heralded the diffusion of Buddhism; Xian was the cultural capital and the largest city in the world. The ensuing Song Dynasty benefited from the unprecedented agricultural productivity of the North China Plain and the rice fields to the south. By the end of the dynasty, 1279, China had an estimated 100 million inhabitants. When the Mongols invaded China to establish their Yuan Dynasty, they, too, benefited for some time from the beneficent conditions of the Medieval Optimum.

But not for long. Had the Chinese and the Europeans been exchanging weather information the way we

From the field notes

"In coastal Alaska you can get a glimpse of the power and grandeur of great valley glaciers. We sailed slowly into Glacier Bay (something you couldn't do in the late eighteenth century, when the Little Ice Age had the entire basin filled with ice), past the Johns Hopkins Inlet, occupied by that glacier until the 1890s, toward the face of the Grand Pacific Glacier. But before we reached it, we began to hear what sounded alternately like thunder, gunshots, loud groans, and gusts of wind. All this came from the towering face of the Margerie Glacier to our left, a relatively small tidewater glacier that seemed to make up for its size with uproar. As its thick ice disgorged into Glacier Bay accompanied by booming and crashing sounds that echoed up the valley, huge columns of it collapsed into the water, making large waves and leaving car-sized chunks of ice floating in widening semicircles. And this glacier is still stable, neither advancing nor receding. Imagine, I thought, what it must be like when such glaciers, propelled by global cooling, push rapidly down their valleys, crushing all in their path."

do today, the Chinese would have been alarmed at what they were hearing from Europe. In the west, the mild and pleasant conditions that had prevailed for so long showed signs of ending. Winters got colder. May frosts, hardly known for centuries, became common. Early fall frosts led to local famines. Persistent droughts hit some parts of Europe; destructive floods struck elsewhere. Britain's wine industry was erased by cold in a matter of decades. By the turn of the fourteenth century, Alpine glaciers began to advance. Greenland's small settlement had long since disappeared, and Iceland was abandoned as well. Weather extremes abounded, not only in the form of record cold snaps but also as searing summer heat and raging storms. Nature seemed to be preparing for one of those climatic reversals so common during the Pleistocene. Was the Holocene itself coming to an end?

◆ THE LITTLE ICE AGE

To the farmers, winegrowers, and seafarers of the fourteenth century, it must have seemed so. Increasing cold, decreasing rainfall, frigid winds, and shortened growing seasons made for dwindling harvests, failing farms, and seas too stormy for fishing. Famines struck all over Europe, just at a time when more people were clustered in towns than ever before. The climatic record, pieced together from farmers' diaries (winegrowers' diaries are especially useful), tree ring research (dendochronology), ice cores, contemporary writings, illustrative paintings, and surviving sketches and drawings justify the designation of the post–1300 period as a shift in the direction of ***reglaciation***. We now know that this return to colder times, marked by advancing mountain glaciers and thickening Subarctic ice, would end in the mid-nineteenth century and that even the worst of it, starting in the late 1600s, did not lead to full-scale Pleistocene glaciation. Whatever was happening precipitated serious social disruptions in Europe and in other parts of the world as well, but of course those who experienced it were unaware of the long-term implications. Only when new methods of analysis became available did scientists realize what had happened—and then they gave the episode an inappropriate name. This temporary cooling was no ice age: it was a minor glaciation and not the first over the past 6000 years. But the name ***Little Ice Age*** certainly was more dramatic than "Minor Glaciation," and it stuck.

To those affected, it was anything but little or minor. Europe's climate fluctuated wildly, often suddenly, so that recovery would be followed by renewed famine; populations mushroomed and then collapsed again. In the fourteenth century, the human geography of eastern and western Eurasia became fatally interlocked. The salubrious conditions that enabled Mongol peoples to thrive and expand, leading to a Mongol dynasty in China, also facilitated their penetration westward. In the process, Mongol migrants and their horse caravans picked up the strain of bacteria that brings on the bubonic plague, and its vector, the flea, rode into Europe on rats and people ahead of their relentless advance. The Black Death swept over an already weakened Europe in waves that often killed half the population or more. Recovery, medical as well as environmental, did not start until the last quarter of the fifteenth century.

In China, meanwhile, the full impact of the Little Ice Age occurred after the end of the Mongol (Yuan) Dynasty (1368). The early Ming rulers inherited a populous state sustained by wheat in the north and rice in the center, linked by the Grand Canal and other busy waterways. Late in the fourteenth century the Ming rulers, exhorted by the legendary admiral Chung Ho, authorized the construction of an oceangoing fleet that would stake China's claim and enhance its reputation in the Indian Ocean and beyond. The fleet eventually numbered more than 6000 ships, the largest carrying as many as 500 men; these were 400 feet long, had four decks and nine masts, and carried sufficient fresh water and supplies to sail for 20 days. Nothing built in Europe even began to approach these vessels in terms of technology or capacity, and the first expedition, in 1405, involved 315 ships and 27,000 men. Later voyages reached the Persian Gulf and the Red Sea as well as East Africa, possibly as far south as Sofala. The Chinese seemed poised to round the Cape of Good Hope and enter the Atlantic.

But then disaster struck at home. The first onslaught of the Little Ice Age came later than it did in Europe, but it was no less severe. Interior rains failed, rivers dried up, the wheat crop shrank, famines broke out, and social disorder and epidemics raged. The Ming rulers ordered an end to the maritime expeditions, dictated the burning of all oceangoing vessels, and instructed the Nanjing shipyard, then by far the largest in the world, to build only barges that could navigate the Grand Canal with cargoes of rice, thus alleviating the plight of the colder, drier north. Environments do not determine the capacities of humans, but environmental events can certainly influence the course of history.

Crisis in Europe

The vicissitudes of Western Europe's Little Ice Age climate necessitated the onset of what cultural geographers refer to as the Second Agricultural Revolution. Farm implements were improved; field methods (planting, sowing, watering, weeding, harvesting) got better; transportation and storage of produce involved less waste and loss. New crops were tried (not always with good results); marketing in the growing urban areas became more efficient. All this was, literally, a matter of survival because toward the end of the sixteenth century there were signs that the Little Ice Age had even worse in store. The century closed with one of the most extreme decades in Europe's known environmental history. During the seventeenth century, conditions were worsened by a series of volcanic eruptions in Southeast Asia, precipitating colder spells in an already frigid region.

Some historical geographers call the period from about 1650 to 1850 the "real" Little Ice Age, noting that the environmental crisis that gripped Europe during those 200 years was much more severe than anything that had gone before. Indeed, between 1675 and 1735, the planet appears to have experienced the coldest cycle of the millennium. Growing seasons in parts of Europe were shortened by as much as six weeks; ports were blocked by ice; the Denmark Strait between Iceland and Greenland remained ice-choked and impassable even during the summers. Sea ice formed and remained in place over the North Sea as far as 35 miles (55 kilometers) from shore. Priests and their parishioners prayed at the edges of fast-advancing Alpine glaciers threatening villages and farms.

Was this indeed a global phenomenon? In his book *The Little Ice Age* (2000), archeologist Brian Fagan describes how the Franz Josef Glacier on New Zealand's South Island "thrust downslope into the valley below, smashing into the great rainforests . . . felling giant trees like matchsticks." In North America, our growing understanding of the Little Ice Age helps explain why the Jamestown colony collapsed so fast, a failure attributed by historians to ineptitude, lack of preparation, and racist attitudes toward the Native Americans in the area. The chief cause may well have been environmental. Geographer David Stahle of the University of Arkansas and his team, studying tree ring records that go back eight centuries, found that the Jamestown area experienced a seven-year drought between 1606 (the year before the colony's founding) through 1612, the worst in nearly eight centuries. European colonists and Native Americans were in the same situation, and their relations worsened as they were forced to compete for dwindling food and falling water tables. The high rate of starvation was not unique to the colonists. They, and their Native American neighbors, faced the rigors of the Little Ice Age as well.

In Europe, there was little respite. The 1780s brought one crisis after another. A gigantic volcanic eruption on Iceland in 1783 lasted eight months, ejecting an estimated 100 million tons of ash, sulfur dioxide, and other pollutants into the atmosphere. The Laki eruption lowered temperatures in North America by 7 degrees Fahrenheit and brought on a series of frigid winters in Europe, Russia, and even North Africa. In February 1784, ice blocked the entire lower Rhine River, producing the worst floods in recorded history and causing food shortages and general economic distress. Violent weather in Western Europe in 1788 included hailstorms that felled forests (one report refers to hailstones 15 inches in diameter) and storms that flattened crops. The French Revolution had other causes, of course, but its timing undoubtedly was related to the recurring food shortages in that dreadful decade. Nor was Napoleon Bonaparte fortunate in his timing when he marched against Russia in 1812. The period from 1805 to 1820 was one of the coldest in the "real" Little Ice Age, and when Napoleon's armies invaded Russia their biggest adversary was the bitter winter, with which Russian forces were more familiar.

Distant Threat

Just when it must have seemed that conditions could not get any tougher, they did—not because of an atmospheric event but as a result of a volcanic eruption on the other side of the planet.

On April 5, 1815, the Tambora Volcano on the island of Sumbawa in what was then the Dutch East Indies, located not far East of Bali, rumbled to life. Less than a week later it was pulverized in a series of explosions that could be heard a thousand miles away, killing all but 26 of the island's population of 12,000. When it was over, the top 4000 feet of the volcano were gone, and much of what is now Indonesia was covered by debris. Darkness enveloped most of the colony for weeks, and tens of thousands died of famine in the months that followed. Colonial reports describe fields covered by poisonous ash and powder, waters clogged by trees and cinders, air rendered unbreathable by a fog of acid chemicals.

Tambora's explosions rocketed tens of millions of tons of ash into orbit, darkening skies around the world. What began as a narrow equatorial band of ash and dust gradually widened into a globe-girdling membrane that blocked part of the Sun's radiation. By the middle of 1816, it was clear to farmers everywhere that this would be a year without summer, a growing season without growth. In Europe, food shortages were acute and grain prices rose rapidly, forcing governments to close their borders to prevent speculation. Food riots nevertheless broke out in the towns, and in the countryside armed gangs raided farms and stores. In the United States, the "year without summer" was especially difficult on the farms of New England, where corn would not ripen, grain prices escalated, and the livestock market collapsed. We can only guess at the impact of Tambora's eruption in other parts of the world, but there can be no doubt that 1816 was a desperate year in the Little Ice Age—a crisis that reminds us of the risks under which all of humanity lives.

The Human Factor

To put these chronological events in spatial perspective, we should remind ourselves of what was happening to the human world as the Little Ice Age came to its mid-nineteenth-century end. The Industrial Revolution was gathering steam; the colonial era was transforming societies and economies from Central America to Southeast Asia. Europeans were populating and dominating distant lands, fighting among themselves even as they exploited their imperial domains. And population growth was accelerating. Around the time of the Tambora eruption, the Earth's population was about 1 billion, perhaps twice what it was at the beginning of the Little Ice Age. In Part Two we note what happened next: the human population explosion coincided with the post–Little Ice Age warming that has been in progress with only one major interruption since about 1850. By 2015, two centuries after Tambora, the Earth will carry seven times as many people as it did when that volcano exploded, and more and more people will be living in marginal environmental zones. How would the world cope today with a "year without summer?" Or with a sudden return to colder conditions?

In the chapters that follow, we discuss the environmental systems and conditions on which we depend, as well as the impact of our huge numbers and insatiable appetites for resources. Since the 1850s, when the Little Ice Age waned and a slow but nearly persistent warming phase began, climatologists and other scientists have learned much about the workings of our planet, but they do not yet know enough to be able to make reliable predictions. We seem to be experiencing a phase similar to the Medieval Optimum, although this time the planet's warmth has been enhanced by human activity to an as yet uncertain degree. (Indeed, we might call the post–1850 phase the ***Industrial Optimum*** since it has coincided substantially with the Industrial Revolution and is affected by its emanations.) Once again, glaciers are in retreat, agricultural frontiers are expanding (the British wine industry is back!), seas are calmer, and storms are fewer—but there are also warning signals. The warming of the Industrial Optimum was interrupted between 1940 and 1970 just when the Industrial Revolution was in full gear, and the scientific as well as the popular literature of the 1950s and 1960s was full of forecasts of impending reglaciation. Warming resumed in the 1970s and has continued since, but we may be arrogant if we assume that human activity, even in the form of our prodigious atmospheric pollution and forest destruction, can override nature's design. As Brian Fagan states, it may be an illusion to suggest that humanity, through its technological prowess, will be able to adjust to the kinds of changes nature has on the record. "Climate change,"

From the field notes

"Walking toward the receding face of the Fox Glacier not far from the west coast of New Zealand's South Island is an unusual experience: a well-trodden footpath leads past a series of signs showing where the glacier stood in decades past. Glacial debris freshly exposed lies underfoot, and the ice at the face is soft and filled with sediment. Water streams from beneath the ice down the valley. It is global warming in action. The Fox and Franz Josef glacier nearby were products of the Little Ice Age. During the Medieval Optimum their high-altitude snowfields gave no indication of what lay ahead, but global cooling created reservoirs of ice that thrust downslope, carving U-shaped valleys into the rock and crashing, through the trees of the coastal rainforest. They might have reached the shore but for the warming that began in the nineteenth century, since when they have receded (and at times re-advanced). As the signposts show, retreats have outdistanced advances, and the glacier's lower valley now lies unoccupied. Flying up the glacier in a two-seater plane you can see its entire profile, from source to face. Will it disappear completely in the warmth of the Industrial Optimum?"

writes Eagan, "is almost always abrupt, shifting rapidly within decades, even years . . . it is unpredictable, and sometimes vicious. The future promises violent change on a local and global scale. . . . such cycles of change are frightening to contemplate in an overpopulated and heavily industrialized world."

These are considerations to keep in mind as you read the chapters that follow.

◆ KEY TERMS ◆

angiosperms	interglacial	Pangaea
Australopithecus	K/T boundary	Photosynthesis
Cambrian Explosion	Little Ice Age	Pleistocene
Deglaciation	marsupials	Postglacial Optimum
Dwyka Ice Age	mass depletion	Reglaciation
greenhouse effect	mass extinction	Snowball Earth Theory
Homo erectus	Medieval Optimum	Wisconsinan Glaciation
Homo sapiens	Neanderthal	Younger Dryas
Industrial Optimum	Pacific Ring of Fire	

◆ APPLYING GEOGRAPHIC KNOWLEDGE ◆

1. We live today during an interglacial period. The Earth is experiencing a warm phase: sea levels are already high, coastal plains lie partially submerged, climates are comparatively mild. Write a brief report for a real estate office describing how your (or your family's) place of residence would be affected by (a) a further and significant warming of the atmosphere or (b) a sudden return to glacial conditions.

2. Much of what is known about seasonal weather conditions during the Little Ice Age comes from the records of winegrowers. Where are wine grapes grown today compared to, say, 1500, and how might the present-day distribution give us insight into the Industrial Optimum? (*Note:* Include the Southern Hemisphere in your discussion.)

Chapter 34

Patterns and Processes of Environmental Change

From the field notes

"My first field experience in one of China's Autonomous Regions, the Guangxi-Zhuang A. R., designated for non-Han minorities, had mixed results. Land degradation here was more advanced than in any other part of China visited; desertification seemed to be in progress in many areas. The cause: overuse of the land, and the collapse of what appeared to have been sound terracing systems. My Chinese colleague told me that China's rules for population control *and* land use were relaxed in these Autonomous regions, often leading to ecological damage."

KEY POINTS

◆ **Human alteration of the environment has been taking place for millennia, but only recently have humans acquired the ability to affect environmental change at the global scale.**

◆ **Water is a renewable resource, but water shortages threaten in many areas of the world. Future conflict over water supplies may come to rival recent conflicts over oil supplies.**

◆ **Human activity has produced an unprecedented concentration of greenhouse gases in the atmosphere, raising concerns about the prospects for significant global warming.**

◆ **Deforestation, desertification, and soil erosion pose a triple threat to the Earth's environment.**

◆ **The rapid accumulation of solid, toxic, and radioactive wastes in the technologically advanced countries is producing an increasingly serious disposal problem.**

Just 15 years ago, the Soviet Union was still a formidable force in world affairs. South Africa was still in the grip of Apartheid. Iraq and Kuwait were at peace. China was still pursuing its Four Modernizations campaign. NAFTA did not exist. Yugoslavia was still unified, as was Czechoslovakia.

Consider how much the world has changed in just the past 10 years: the world map has been redrawn. New countries have arisen from old ones. New names by the hundreds have appeared on regional maps. New economic and political alliances have been formed. New industrial regions and new trade routes have emerged.

All this is going on against a background of global environmental change whose future is uncertain but troubling. A combination of natural cycles and human impacts may produce unprecedented climatic extremes. ◆

◆ THE HUMAN IMPACT

Biologists estimate that there may be as many as 25 million types of organisms on Earth, perhaps even more; most have not yet been identified, classified, or studied. *Homo sapiens* is only one of these, yet in 10 millennia our species has developed a complex culture that is transmitted from one generation to the next through learning and is also to some degree encoded in our genes. Humans are not unique in possessing a culture: gorillas, orangutans, chimpanzees, and dolphins have cultures too. Ours is the only species, though, with a vast and complex array of artifacts, technologies, laws, and belief systems.

No species, not even the powerful dinosaurs, ever affected their environment as strongly as humans do today. The dinosaurs (and many other species) were extinguished by a cometary impact at the Cretaceous/Tertiary (K/T) boundary. Some biogeographers suggest that the next great extinction may be caused not by asteroids but by humans, whose numbers and demands are destroying millions of species.

Alteration of Ecosystems

This destructiveness is not just a matter of modern technology and its capacity to do unprecedented damage, whether by wartime forest defoliation, peacetime oil spills, or other means. Humans altered their environment from the beginning, when they set fires to kill herds of reindeer and bison, or hunted entire species of large mammals to extinction. The Maori, who arrived in New Zealand not much more than 1000 years ago, inflicted significant destruction on native species of animals and plants long before the advent of modern technology. Elsewhere in the Pacific realm, Polynesians reduced the forest cover to brush and, with their penchant for wearing bird-feather robes, had exterminated more than 80 percent of the regional bird species by the time the first Europeans arrived. The Europeans ravaged species ranging from Galápagos turtles to Antarctic seals. European fashions had a disastrous impact on African species ranging from snakes to leopards. Traditional as well as modern societies have had devastating impacts on their ***ecosystems*** (ecological units consisting of self-regulating associations of living and nonliving natural elements) as well as on those of areas into which they migrated.

Human alteration of the environment continues in many forms today. For the first time in history, however, the combined impact of humanity's destructive and exploitive actions is capable of producing environmental changes at the global scale. Consider for a moment the history of human life on the Earth. Early human societies had relatively small populations, and their impacts on the physical environment were limited in both duration and intensity. With the development of agrarian and preindustrial societies, human alterations of the physical environment increased, yet the effects of these early activities were still limited in scale. Even the onset of urbanization and the development of urban centers, which concentrated large numbers of people in particular places, were relatively limited. Over the last 500 years, however, both the rate and scale at which humans modify the Earth have increased dramatically. Particularly during the last half-century, the very character of human alterations of the physical world has taken on global dimensions.

From the field notes

"Traveling through Poland in 1997, I witnessed first hand the effects of the devastating floods of that summer. The floods were a product not just of nature's fury, but of human alteration of the environment. Deforestation and the paving over of natural areas produced more rapid runoff, which in turn moved swiftly down channels sculpted by human hands. Downstream those channels were inadequate to handle the quantity of fast moving water flowing through them, producing scenes such as this."

From the field notes

"We drove north on Route 89 from Tucson, Arizona, across the desert. Drought rules the countryside here, and dams conserve what water there is. Snaking through the landscape are lifelines such as this, linking Coolidge Dam to distant farms and towns. In the vast, arid landscape, this narrow ribbon of water seems little more than an artificial brook—but to hundreds of thousands of people, this is what makes life possible in the Southwest."

Environmental Stress

The natural environment is being modified and stressed by human activity in many obvious ways and some less obvious ones. Among the more obvious actions causing ***environmental stress*** are the cutting of forests, the emission of pollutants into the atmosphere, and the spilling of oil into the oceans. Less obvious actions include the burying of toxic wastes that foul groundwater supplies, the dumping of vast amounts of garbage into the oceans, and the use of pesticides in farming. Humans have built seawalls, terraced hillslopes, dammed rivers, cut canals, and modified the environment in many constructive as well as destructive ways. All of these activities have a huge impact on the environment and have given rise to a number of key concerns. Among these are the future of water supplies, the state of the atmosphere, desertification, deforestation, soil degradation, and the disposal of industrial wastes.

◆ WATER

Economic geographers differentiate between resources that are replenished even as they are being used (***renewable resources***) and resources that are present in finite quantities and thus are nonrenewable. Water, the essence

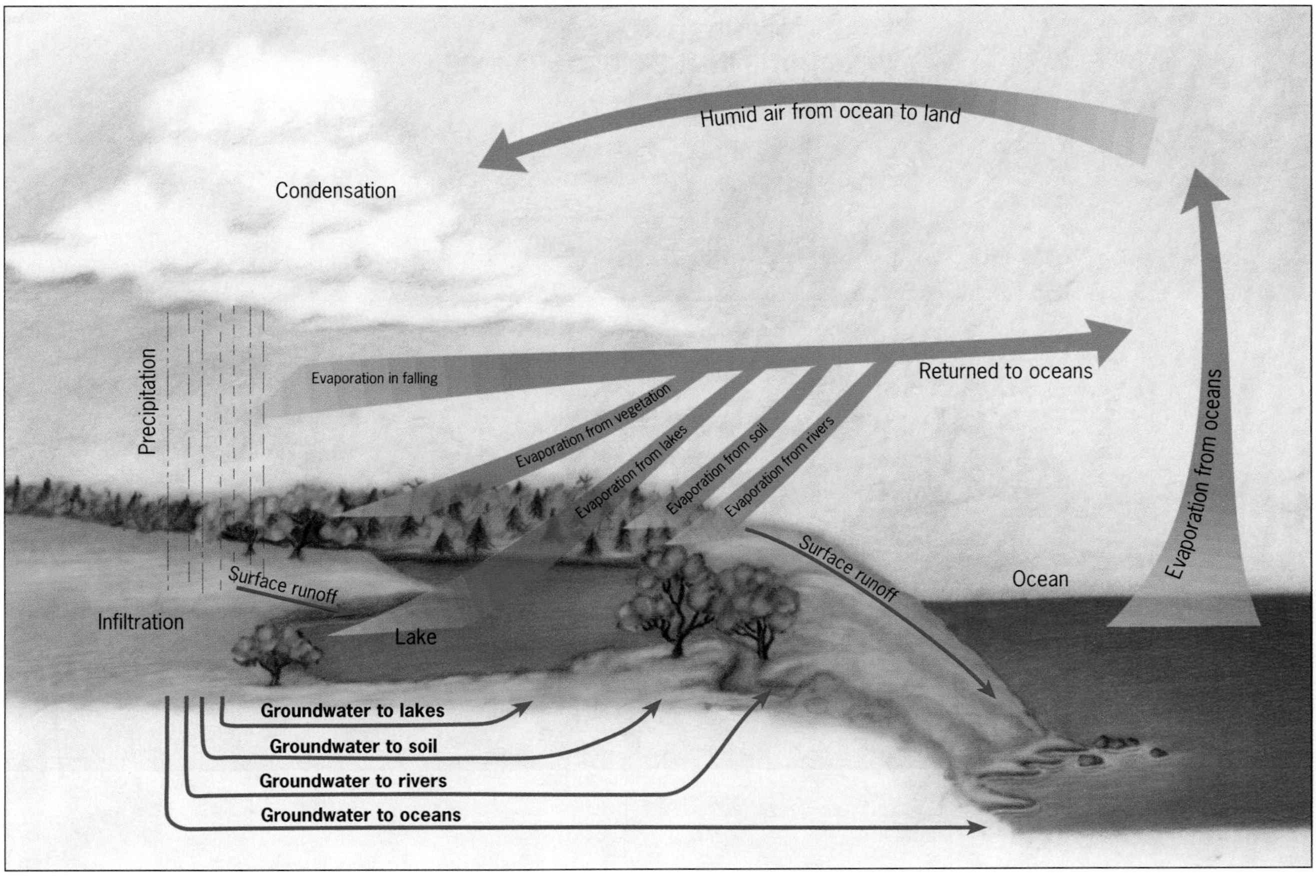

Figure 34-1 The Hydrologic Cycle. The hydrologic cycle carries moisture from the oceans and from other water bodies over the land, where precipitation, runoff, and evapotranspiration sustain the system.

of life, is a renewable resource. But the available supply of fresh water is not distributed evenly across the globe. Figure 1–5 shows the world distribution of precipitation, with the largest totals recorded in equatorial and tropical areas of Southeast Asia, South Asia, Central and coastal West Africa, and Middle and South America. That distribution is sustained through the ***hydrologic cycle***, which brings rain and snow from the oceans to the landmasses (Fig. 34-1). The volume of precipitation in the world as a whole is enormous; spread out evenly, it would cover the land area of the planet with about 33 inches (83 centimeters) of water each year. Much of that water is lost through runoff and evaporation, but enough of it seeps downward into porous, water-holding rocks called ***aquifers*** to provide millions of wells with steady flows. In the United States alone, it is estimated that there is 50 times as much water stored in aquifers as there is precipitation falling on the land surface every year.

Despite such favorable data, the supply of water is anything but plentiful (Fig. 34-2). Chronic water shortages afflict tens of millions of farmers in Africa and hundreds of thousands of city dwellers in Southern California; water rationing has been imposed in rainy South Florida and in Spain, which faces the Mediterranean Sea.

In many areas of the world, people have congregated in places where water supplies are insufficient, undependable, or both. In California with some frequency, people are not allowed to wash their cars or refill their swimming pools; these are minor inconveniences compared to the fate faced by millions of Sudanese trying to escape their country's civil war by fleeing to the parched borders of the Sahara. In Florida, whose urban population depends on the Biscayne Aquifer for most of its water, the long-term prospect is troubling: when seasonal rainfalls do not reach their projected averages, the Biscayne Aquifer is overused, and saltwater enters the aquifer from the nearby Atlantic Ocean. Such invasion can permanently destroy a freshwater aquifer.

It is interesting to compare Figures 1–5 and 4–1. Note how hundreds of millions of people still cluster along several of the Earth's great rivers. Indeed, nearly three-quarters of all the fresh water used annually is consumed in farming, not in cities. In California, where about 80 percent of available water is used for irrigation,

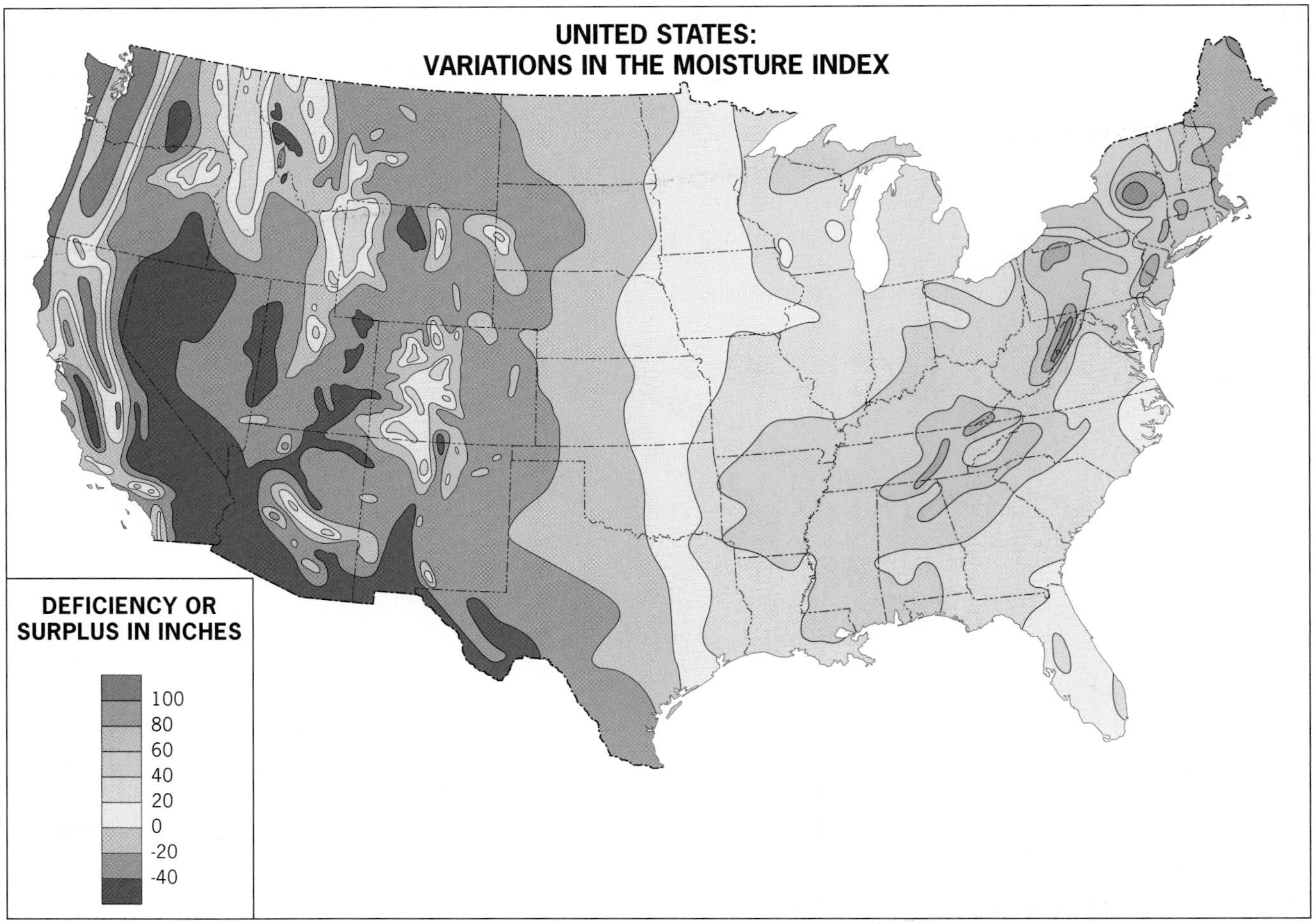

Figure 34-2 Variations in the Moisture Index in the United States. This map shows the variation in moisture surplus and deficiency in the United States. *Source*: From a map in E. A. Fernald and D. J. Patton, editors, Water Resources Atlas of Florida (Tallahassee: Florida State University, 1984) p. 6.

this has led to an intense debate: should cities be provided with ample water at the expense of Central Valley farms, and should fruits and vegetables be bought from elsewhere, even overseas, rather than be grown locally?

Industries use another 20 percent of the world's water supply, contributing heavily to pollution when the used water is returned to streams, lakes, and aquifers. When communist rule ended in Eastern Europe, tests indicated that the region's rivers and groundwater were among the most severely polluted in the world because industries there had not been adequately regulated.

As human populations have expanded, people have increasingly settled in arid regions. One of the great ecological disasters of the twentieth century occurred in Kazakhstan and Uzbekistan, whose common boundary runs through the ***Aral Sea***. Streams that fed this large body of water were diverted to irrigate the surrounding desert (mainly for commercial cotton production). Heavy use of chemical pesticide ruined the groundwater below, causing a health crisis that some observers describe as an "ecological Chernobyl." In the meantime the Aral Sea began to dry up, and by the mid-1990s it had lost more than three-quarters of its total surface area (Fig. 34-3).

Throughout the world, people have come to depend on water sources whose future capacity is uncertain. Rocky Mountain and Sierra Nevada snows feed the Colorado River and the aquifers that irrigate the California Central Valley. Aqueducts snake their way across the desert to urban communities. None of this slows the population's move to the Sunbelt (see Part Two), and the water situation there is becoming problematic. In coastal eastern Spain, low water pressures in city pipes often deprive the upper floors of high-rise buildings of water. In Southwest Asia and the Arabian Peninsula, growing populations strain ancient water supply systems and desalinization plants are a necessity. As oil did in the past, water may spark regional conflicts in the future.

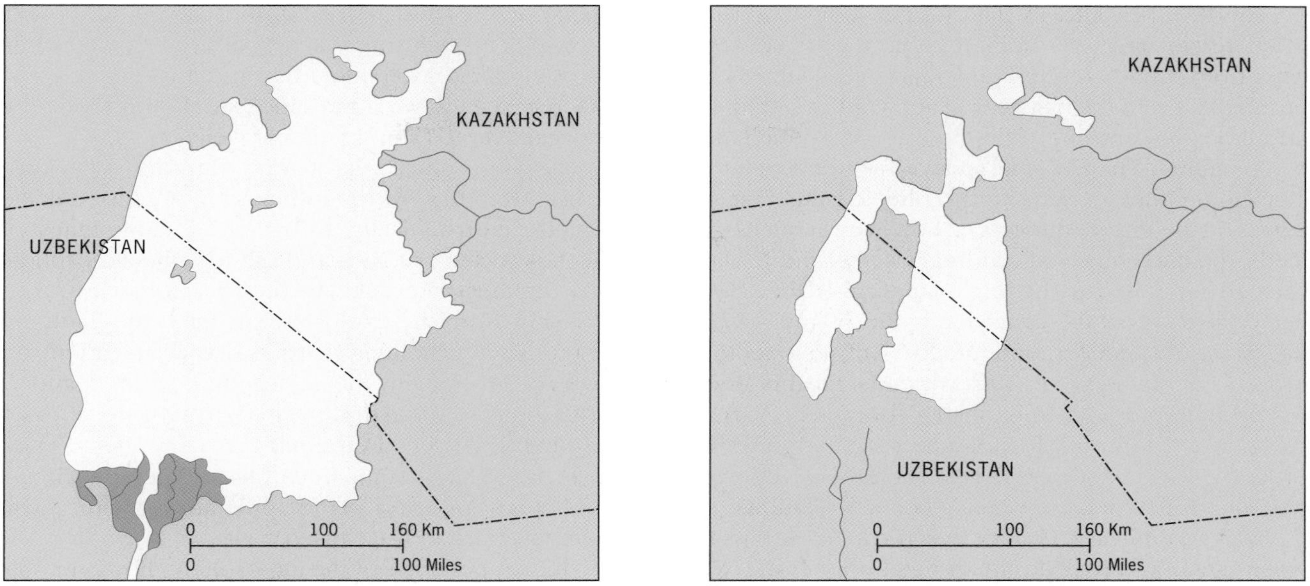

A Aral Sea, mid-1960s **B** Aral Sea, early 2000s

Figure 34-3 The Dying Aral Sea. Affected by climatic cycles and afflicted by human interference, the Aral Sea in Turkestan (on the border of Kazakhstan and Uzbekistan) is dying. In a quarter of a century, it lost three-quarters of its surface area.

Water and Politics in the Middle East

When relations between countries and peoples are problematic, disputes over water can make them even worse. As populations grow and as demand for water rises, fears of future shortages intensify. Control by one state over sources of water needed by another may even lead to armed conflict. In recent years, for example, relations between Turkey and its neighbors to the south have worsened, largely because of Turkey's dam-building projects at the headwaters of two rivers that are crucial to Syria and Iraq: the Euphrates and the Tigris.

Water supply is a particularly difficult problem affecting relations among Israel and its neighbors. With under 6 million people, Israel annually consumes nearly three times as much water as Jordan, the West Bank Palestinian areas, and Gaza combined (total population: over 7 million). As much as half of Israel's water comes from sources outside the Israeli state.

The key sources of water for the entire area are the Jordan River and an aquifer beneath the West Bank. When Israel captured the Golan Heights from Syria and the West Bank from Jordan during the 1967 war, it gained control over both of these sources, including the Jordan River's important tributary, the Yarmuk (Fig. 34-4). As the map shows, the Sea of Galilee forms a large freshwater reservoir in the Jordan River Valley. This is the source of most of Israel's water. (Desalinization facilities do not yet contribute significantly.)

Figure 34-4 Key Water Resources in the Middle East.

The 1994 peace treaty with Jordan committed Israel to let Jordan have 200 million cubic meters (CMs) of water from surface sources under its control, chiefly the Yarmuk River. In the first year Israel would send Jordan 50 million CMs, and after 1995 the amount would double to 100 million. The 200-million level would be attained after the building of dams and facilities. Israel failed to deliver on the 1995 commitment, however, citing its own needs, the inadequacy of transfer systems, and Jordan's wasteful use of water. The Jordanians argued that this violated the terms of the peace treaty; the 50 million CMs that Israel did transfer amounted to only one-tenth of Jordan's annual needs. In 1997, when Israel announced that it would start construction of a dam on the Yarmuk that would yield water for Jordan as well as Israel, the Jordanians refused to cooperate. The unresolved water issue clouds the future of Israeli-Jordanian relations.

Water supply also complicates the relationships between Israel and its Palestinian neighbors in the West Bank and Gaza. The aquifer beneath the West Bank yields about 625 million CMs through hundreds of wells linked together by a system of pipelines. Of this, some 450 million CMs go directly to Israel; another 35 million are consumed by Israeli settlers on the West Bank, and only some 140 million are allotted to the West Bank's nearly 2 million Arabs.

This is unfair, say the Palestinian Arabs: if the West Bank is to become independent Palestinian territory, the water below the surface should belong to the Palestinians. But the Israeli cities of Tel Aviv and Jerusalem depend heavily on water from the West Bank, and Israel cannot survive without this source.

Why not? In part, the answer involves levels of economic development and habits of consumption. At the beginning of the twenty-first century, Israel was consuming over 2 billion CMs of water annually, or nearly 400 CMs per capita. Jordanians used only 150 CMs, Gaza residents 140, and West Bank Palestinians around 100. To many Arabs, these figures represent unfair allocations. To many Israelis, they are justified by contrasting economic requirements.

The water issue will complicate any hoped-for settlement of territorial disputes among Israel and its neighbors. Israel might contemplate the return of most of the Golan Heights to Syria, but about 30 percent of all water reaching the Sea of Galilee comes from the Golan Heights. Israel might consider yielding most of the West Bank to a Palestinian government, but approximately 30 percent of Israel's water supply comes from the West Bank aquifer. Governments may want to negotiate for lasting peace, but at a practical level they are constrained by water needs.

◆ ATMOSPHERE

The Earth, it is sometimes said, has six continents and seven seas—but it has only one ***atmosphere***, a thin layer of air lying directly above the lands and oceans. We depend on the atmosphere for our survival: we breathe its oxygen; it shields us from the destructive rays of the Sun; it moderates temperatures; and it carries moisture from the oceans over the land, sustaining crops and forests and replenishing soils and wells.

The atmosphere has a truly amazing capacity to cleanse itself. In 1883 the Indonesian volcano Krakatau erupted catastrophically, throwing 2.5 cubic miles (10 cubic kilometers) of rock and ash into the atmosphere. Total darkness prevailed in the area for nearly three days; dust from the explosion encircled the Earth and created vividly colored sunsets for years afterward. However, eventually the atmosphere cleared and all traces of the eruption disappeared. In 1980 the eruption of Mount St. Helens in the northwestern United States caused a similar, though much smaller, globe-encircling cloud of volcanic dust in the upper atmosphere. Again, the atmosphere soon cleansed itself.

Human pollution of the atmosphere, however, may result in longer lasting, possibly even permanent damage. True, the air disperses even the densest smoke and most acrid chemical gases. However, some of the waste pouring into the atmosphere may be producing irreversible change, not only in the ***troposphere*** (the lowest layer, up to about 10 miles, or 16 kilometers, high) but also in the upper-level ***stratosphere***. The nature of the change is still being debated, but two centuries of industrial expansion have caused an enormous increase in the pollution of the troposphere. While global concern and action to limit this pollution are much in evidence, the problem may be beyond control.

Global Warming

Most scientists argue that tropospheric pollution causes the Earth to retain more heat (hence the "greenhouse" theories referred to in Part One) and that its full effect will not be felt until well into the twenty-first century. Although estimates of global warming have been reduced, in the early 2000s computer models still predicted a global warming of 2°C to 3°C (about 3.5°F to 5.5°F) over the next 50 years. This might be enough to melt some glacial ice and raise sea levels as much as 6 inches (15 cm). Indeed, this may already be happening, as evidenced by the Rhode Island-sized chunk of ice that broke off from Antarctica in March 2002.

Moreover, changes in climate involve changes in the hydrologic cycle, affecting patterns of precipitation. These changes in turn can affect where certain types of vegetation can grow, which can alter everything from agricultural patterns to the location of animal habitats.

There is little consensus on the extent of greenhouse warming. Whatever the extent of global warming, there is no question that growing populations and increased human activity, ranging from the burning of tropical forests to pollution of the atmosphere by industry and automobiles, are having an unprecedented impact on the atmosphere. The amounts of key "greenhouse" gases, carbon dioxide (CO_2), methane, and nitrous oxides in the atmosphere have been increasing at a rate of about 2 percent per decade; automobiles, steel mills, refineries, and chemical plants account for a large part of this increase. Without doubt there will be consequences; all that remains uncertain is what those consequences will be.

Acid Rain

A byproduct of the enormous volume of pollutants spewed into the atmosphere is ***acid rain***. Acid rain forms when sulfur dioxide and nitrogen oxides are released into the atmosphere by the burning of fossil fuels (coal, oil, and natural gas). These pollutants combine with water vapor in the air to form dilute solutions of sulfuric and nitric acids, which then are washed out of the atmosphere by rain or other types of precipitation, such as fog and snow.

Although acid rain usually consists of relatively mild acids, it is caustic enough to do great harm over time to certain natural ecosystems (the mutual interactions between groups of plant and animal organisms and their environment). Already we know that acid rain is causing acidification of lakes and streams (with resultant fish kills), stunted growth of forests, and loss of crops in affected areas. In cities, corrosion of buildings and monuments has accelerated.

The geography of acid rain is most closely associated with patterns of industrial concentration and middle- to long-distance wind flows. The highest densities of coal and oil burning are associated with large concentrations of heavy manufacturing, such as those in Western and Eastern Europe and the United States. As these industrial areas began to experience increasingly severe air pollution problems in the second half of the twentieth century, many countries (including the United States in 1970) enacted legislation establishing minimal clean-air standards.

Recent studies reveal that countries of the former Soviet Union, especially Russia and Ukraine, suffer severely from acid rain. Antiquated factories in the industrial heartlands continue to emit the chemicals that create acid rain. The first research studies to report on acid rain in the Asian Pacific Rim countries suggest that the situation in East and Southeast Asia is worsening, with serious effects on natural vegetation.

In the United States and Western Europe, compliance with legislated emission reductions is having positive results. In Canada as well as in Scandinavia, where acid rain from neighboring industrial regions damaged forests and acidified lakes, recovery came faster than scientists had predicted. This evidence is now encouraging other countries to impose stricter controls over factory emissions.

◆ THE LAND

Over the centuries, human population growth has put increasing pressure on the land surface. More land is cleared and placed under cultivation, trees are cut down, and cities expand. The effects can be seen almost everywhere. So extensive are they that it is often difficult even to reconstruct what an area might be like in the absence of humans. The human impact on the Earth's land surface has several key aspects, of which the most significant are desertification, deforestation, soil erosion, and waste disposal.

Desertification

Climatologists have long known that the world's deserts expand and contract, growing especially in areas with substantial human populations (Fig. 4–1). This process has the same effect as glaciation because it increases the area of uninhabitable territory at the expense of habitable land. Marginal areas that supported some vegetation have been lost to the desert, and ***desertification*** threatens similar areas throughout the world.

Desert expansion is cyclic and results from natural causes. Some climatologists see the recent southward march of the Sahara as evidence of shifting climatic zones that may be related to an oncoming reglaciation. However, desertification is also the result of human activity. The southward expansion of the Sahara, which in the past 50 years has cost 270,000 square miles (700,000 square kilometers) of farming and grazing land, has been accelerated by overgrazing, woodcutting, soil exhaustion, and other environmental misuse.

Desertification became a matter of serious international concern during the great Sahel drought of the 1970s (which reappeared to the east in Ethiopia and Sudan in the mid-1980s). In 1977, it was the subject of the United Nations Conference on Desertification, held in Nairobi, Kenya. It became clear that desert expansion was occurring in many areas of the world. Reports from East Africa, India, Argentina, Australia, and North America all confirmed that fragile desert-margin ecosystems were being lost (Fig. 34-5). In China and Algeria, workers were mobilized to plant vegetation that would anchor the shifting sands, but without success. As our maps indicate, rates of natural population increase are especially high in much of the desert-dominated Muslim realm. Thus desertification is likely to increase in the future.

Deforestation

As habitable space is lost to expanding deserts, the world's forests also yield to human population pressure. From the tropical Amazon Basin to high-latitude North America and Eurasia, trees are cut down and woodlands shrink.

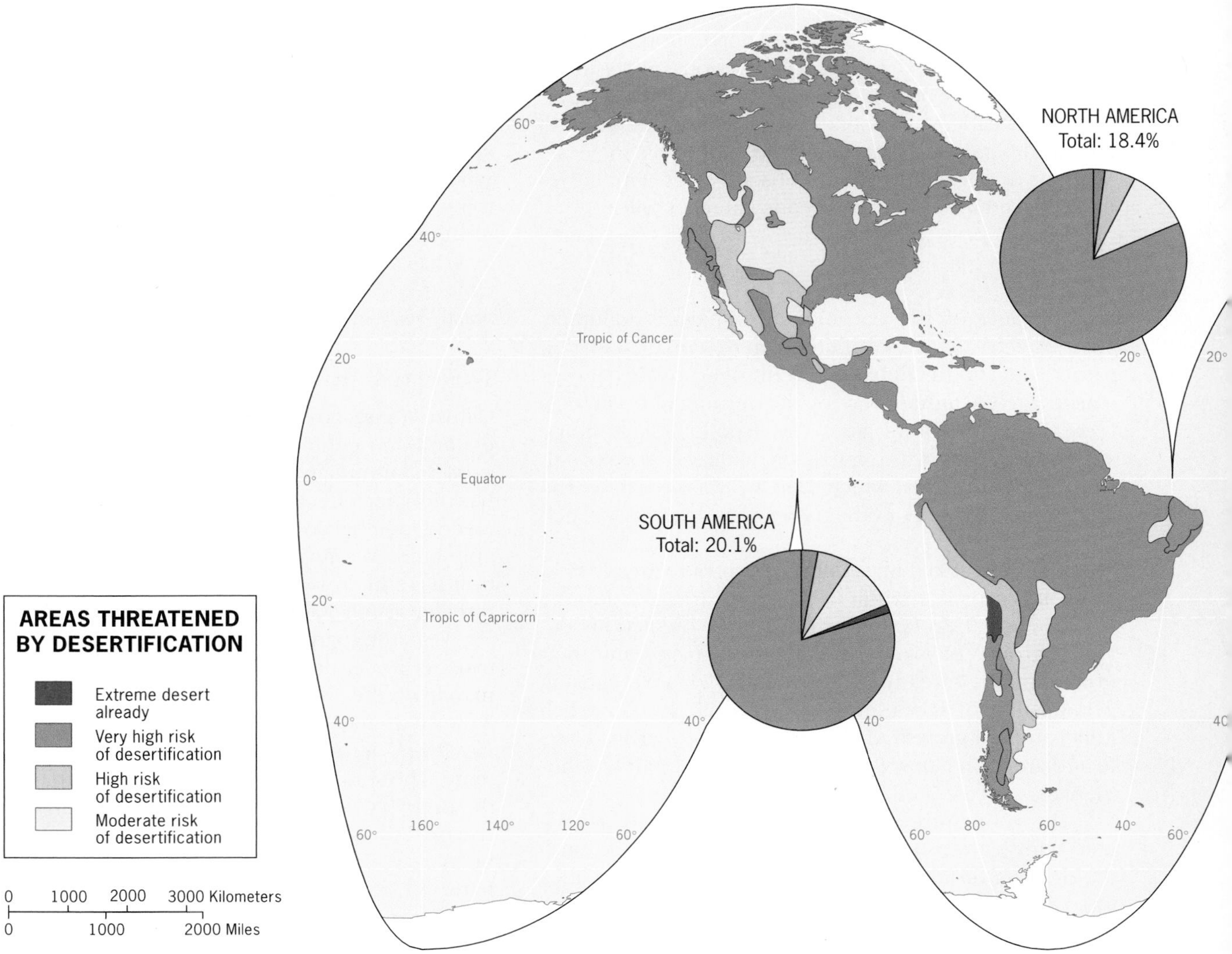

Figure 34-5 Areas Threatened by Desertification. Deserts expand and contract cyclically, but nature's cycles can be distorted by human intervention. This map shows areas threatened or affected. *Source*: From several sources, including J. Turk et al., Environmental Science (Philadelphia: Saunders, 1984), p. 305.

The world's forests, especially those of lower and middle latitudes, play a critical role in what biogeographers call the ***oxygen cycle***. Atmospheric oxygen is consumed by natural processes as well as by human activities. Forests counteract this loss through photosynthesis and related processes, which release oxygen into the atmosphere. The destruction of vast tracts of forest alarms ecologists and others, who warn of unforeseeable and incalculable effects—not only for the affected areas but for the planet as a whole.

In the early 1980s, the Food and Agriculture Organization (FAO) of the United Nations undertook a study of the rate at which forests were being depleted. This analysis showed that 44 percent of the tropical rainforest had already been affected by cutting and that more than 1 percent was being logged every year. If this rate of cutting were to continue, the entire equatorial rainforest would be gone in less than 90 years. The situation may be even more critical. Other studies have suggested that the FAO estimate was low and that at the present rate of logging and cutting these forests will be destroyed within just 45 years.

This is what is happening in the great forested areas that still survive in South America, Africa, and Southeast Asia. The smaller surviving stands—in such places as Central America and West Africa—will be gone even earlier. Yet, the effects of ***deforestation*** are not clearly understood. The reforestation (and harvesting) of deforested areas is not the whole answer, even if it could be done on a large scale. Forests in the United States, for example, consist mainly of second-growth trees, which replaced the original forest after it was logged. However,

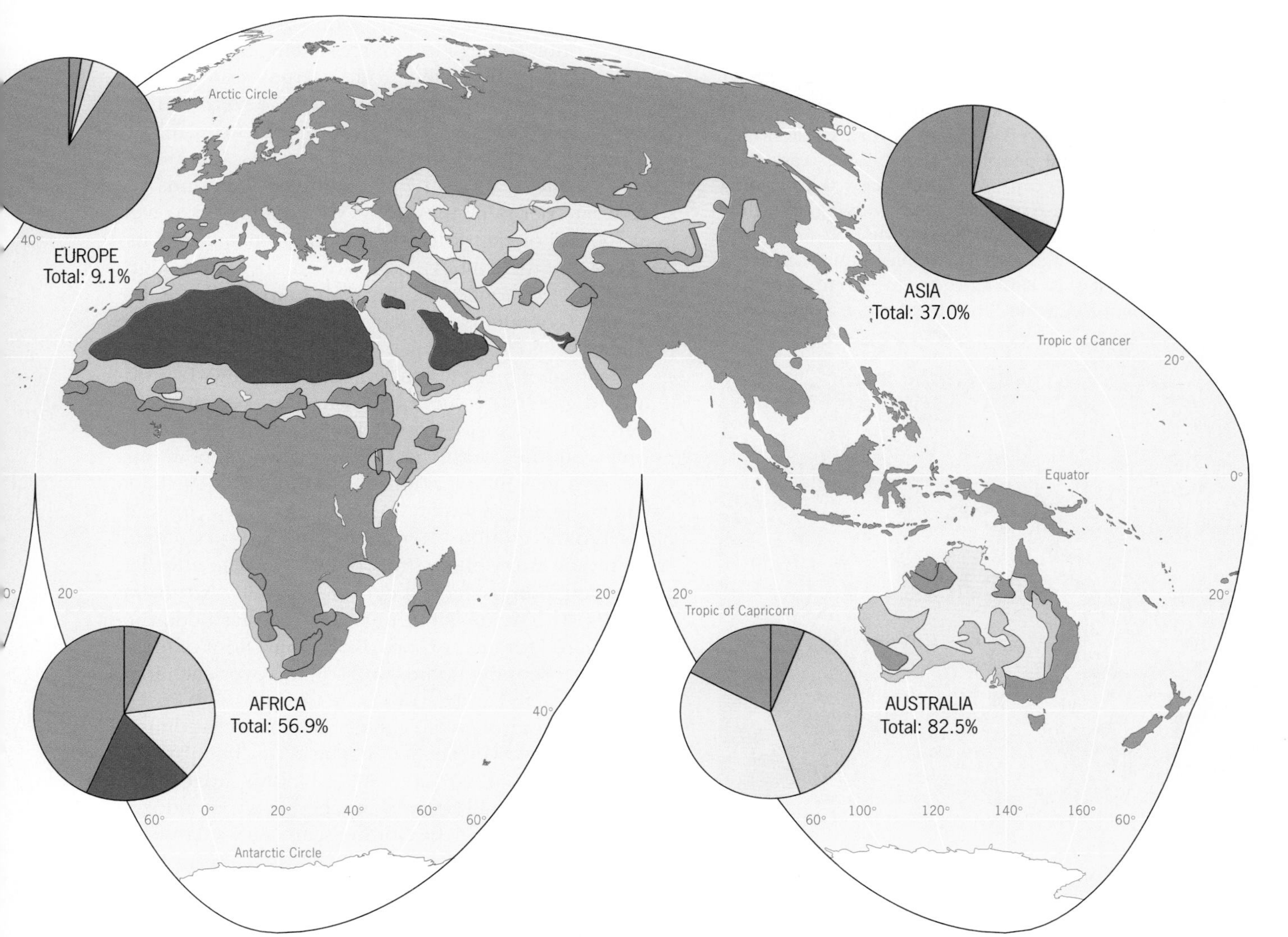

the controlled second-growth forest does not (as the natural forest did) have many trees dying of old age after their trunks and limbs become soft from rot. Thus many animal species that depend on holes in trunks and hollows in tree limbs cannot find places to nest. For them the forest has ceased to be a favorable habitat. Deforestation has many causes—expanding farmland, logging, roadbuilding, mining, and human settlement—and it has been going on for centuries. However, the threat to the last great undisturbed natural forests is recent and severe.

Soil Erosion

The loss of potentially productive soil to erosion has been described as a "quiet crisis" of global proportions. Ecologists Lester Brown and Edward Wolf (1984) point out that the increasing rate of this loss

> over the past generation is not the result of a decline in the skills of farmers but rather of the pressures on farmers to produce more. In an integrated world food economy the pressures on land resources are not confined to particular countries; they permeate the entire world. Many traditional agricultural systems that were ecologically stable as recently as midcentury, when there were 2.5 billion people in the world, are breaking down as world population moves toward 5 billion. (p. 9)

Why has ***soil erosion*** increased so much? Part of the answer lies in population pressure: the world population is moving toward 6.5 billion, having long since passed the 5 billion mark cited by Brown and Wolf. Associated with population growth is the cultivation of ever-steeper slopes, with hastily constructed terraces or without any terraces at all. As the pressure on land increases, farmers

From the field notes

"About 10 miles (16 km) from the Kenyan town of Meru the landscape showed signs of severe erosion. We stopped to talk with the people of these homesteads, and asked them about their crops. Yes, they knew that farming on slopes as steep as these would lead to 'gullying,' but they saw no alternative. You get a crop one or two years, and that's better than nothing, they said. Some neighbors whose village had lost most of its land had gone to the city, we were told, and now the place where they lived was like a desert."

are less able to leave part of their soil fallow (unused) to allow it to recover its nutrients. Shifting cultivators (see Part Six) must shorten their field rotation cycle, and as a result their soil, too, is less able to recover. As agricultural land use intensifies, water and wind erosion increases. Livestock are allowed to graze in areas where they destroy the natural vegetation; lands too dry for farming are nonetheless plowed, and wind erosion follows. It is estimated that the loss of soil to erosion amounts to more than 25 billion tons per year. According to Brown and Wolf, this is equal to 0.7 percent per year of all the soil now available, or 7 percent per decade. Soil is a renewable resource because it can recover with proper care. However, it is being "mined" as though it were a nonrenewable resource. International cooperation in food distribution, education of farmers and governments, and worldwide dissemination of soil-conservation methods are urgently needed to solve this "quiet crisis."

Waste Disposal

It is a sign of the times that the topic of waste disposal must be included in a discussion of environmental stress as it relates to population growth. If anything has grown faster than population itself, it is the waste generated by households, communities, and industries—much of it a matter of bulk, some of it a source of danger.

The United States, the world's largest consumer of resources, is also the largest producer of ***solid waste***, debris and garbage discarded by cities, industries, mines, and farms. According to current estimates, the United States produces about 1.7 kilograms (3.7 pounds) of solid waste per person per day, which adds up to well over 160 million metric tons (just under 180 million tons) per year. But the United States is not alone. Other high-technology economies with a high ratio of disposable materials (containers, packaging, etc.) face the same problems.

Disposal of these wastes is a major worldwide problem. The growing volume of waste must be put somewhere, but space for it is no longer easy to find. In poorer countries waste is thrown onto open dumps where vermin multiply, decomposition sends methane gas into the air, rain and waste liquids carry contaminants into the groundwater below, and fires pollute the surrounding atmosphere. In countries that can afford it, such open dumps have been replaced by ***sanitary landfills***. The waste is put in a hole that has been dug and prepared for the purpose, including a floor of materials to treat seeping liquids and soil to cover each load as it is compacted and deposited in the fill.

The number of suitable sites for sanitary landfills is decreasing, however, and it is increasingly difficult to design new sites. In the United States landfill capacity has been reached or will soon be reached in about a dozen States, most of them in the Northeast and Mid-Atlantic regions, and those States must now buy space from other States for this purpose. Trucking or sending garbage by rail to distant landfills is very expensive, but there are few alternatives.

Similar problems arise on a global scale. The United States, the European Union, and Japan export solid (including hazardous) wastes to countries in Africa, Middle and South America, and East Asia. While these countries are paid for accepting the waste, they do not have the capacity to treat it properly. So the waste often is dumped in open landfills, where it creates the very hazards that the exporters want to avoid. In the late 1980s the richer countries' practice of "managing" waste by exporting it became a controversial issue, and in 1989 a treaty was drawn up to control it. The treaty did not (as many poorer countries wished) prohibit the exporting of hazardous waste, although it did require the consent of the recipient country before the waste could be transported.

It is useful to differentiate between ***toxic wastes***, in which the danger is caused by chemicals, infectious materials, and the like, and ***radioactive wastes***, which are of two types: low-level radioactive wastes that give off small amounts of radiation and are produced by industry, hospitals, research facilities, and nuclear power plants, and high-level radioactive wastes, which emit strong radiation and are produced by nuclear power plants and nuclear weapons factories. In the United States, low-level radioactive wastes have for many years been disposed of in steel drums placed in six special government-run landfills, three of which are now closed.

High-level radioactive waste is extremely dangerous and difficult to get rid of. Fuel rods from nuclear reactors will remain radioactive for thousands of years and must be stored in remote places where there is no possibility that they will contaminate water, air, or any other part of the environment. In fact, no satisfactory means or place for the disposal of high-level radioactive waste has been found. Among many suggestions are deep shafts in the bedrock, chambers dug in salt deposits (salt effectively blocks radiation), ice chambers in Antarctica, burial beneath the ocean floor, and deposition in volcanically active mid-ocean trenches. Meanwhile, spent fuel rods (which last only about three years in the reactor) are put in specially designed drums and stored in one of about 100 sites, all of them potentially dangerous. In the early 2000s the U.S. government was developing two major disposal sites—one at Yucca Mountain in southern Nevada, for waste from commercial nuclear power plants, and the other near Carlsbad in southern New Mexico, for military waste.

There is a related problem: transportation of waste. Even if secure and safe storage can be found for high-level radioactive waste, the waste has to be transported from its source to the disposal site. Such transportation presents an additional hazard; a truck or train accident could have disastrous consequences.

The dimensions of the waste-disposal problem are growing and are becoming global. The threat to the planet's environment is not just over the short term but can exist for centuries, indeed millennia.

◆ BIODIVERSITY

A significant change that is related to all of the developments discussed so far is the accelerating loss of ***biodiversity***. An abbreviation of "biological diversity," biodiversity refers to the diversity of all aspects of life found on the Earth. Although the term is commonly used in referring to the diversity of species, it encompasses the entire range of biological diversity, from the genetic variability within individuals of a species to the diversity of ecosystems on the planet.

How many species are there? Estimates range from 10 million to 100 million, and no one is quite sure how many. So far only some 1.75 million species have been identified, and new species, particularly new species of insects, are being discovered regularly. Yet species are also becoming extinct at a rapid rate. It is difficult to say exactly how quickly extinctions are occurring, since we do not know how many species there are. What is clear, however, is that although extinction is a natural process, humans have dramatically increased rates of extinction, particularly over the last few hundred years. Estimates from the United Nations Environment Programme's Global Biodiversity Assessment indicate that 8 percent of plants, 5 percent of fish, 11 percent of birds, and 18 percent of the world's mammal species are currently threatened.

Human impacts on biodiversity have increased over time. The domestication of animals, followed by the agricultural domestication of plant life, caused significant changes in our relationship with other species. Large vertebrates have always been particularly hard hit by human activities. Many birds and mammals have been hunted not only for food but also for their skins, feathers, and so forth. During the eighteenth and nineteenth centuries, beaver populations in North America were drastically reduced as the beavers were trapped and skinned for their pelts; many bird species were hunted for their feathers, which were sold to decorate fashionable hats. Elephants and walruses continue to be hunted for their ivory tusks. From historical records we know that over 650 species of plants and over 480 animal species have become extinct in just the last 400 years. These represent only the documented extinctions. The actual number of extinctions that occurred during this period is almost certainly much higher.

In addition to hunting species, humans have also indirectly contributed to extinctions. Human travel, for instance, introduced new species to areas around the globe—rats are among the more destructive of these; they have had devastating effects on oceanic islands. Introduced species may cause extinctions by preying upon native species or competing with them for resources. A famous example is the dodo (*Raphus cuculatus*), which was hunted to extinction by humans, dogs, and rats on the island of Mauritius. Introduced species may also carry new diseases, leading to the decimation and extinction of local populations. On oceanic islands a combination of these forces led to large numbers of extinctions after the arrival of humans. It is estimated that 2000 species of birds on tropical Pacific islands were driven to extinction following human settlement.

The extinction of the passenger pigeon (*Ectopistes migratorius*) from the Western Hemisphere is a dramatic example of the devastating effects humans can have on other species. As recently as the early 1800s, there were many millions of passenger pigeons. The birds congregated in large flocks; early accounts described the sky being darkened as the birds flew overhead. Within less than 100 years, however, the passenger pigeon was gone. By 1900, the last known wild passenger pigeon had been shot. In 1914, the last captive passenger pigeon died in the Cincinnati Zoo. What caused the pigeon to die out so quickly? Part of its decline may have been due to natural factors, such as introduced diseases that may have spread through the large flocks, or, as some have suggested, storms that may have killed many birds at once. Regardless of these natural factors, human predation was ultimately responsible for the extinction of the passenger pigeon. Some of the human pressures on the birds were indirect, such as logging of forests, which reduced the amount of foraging habitat available to the pigeons. This was particularly damaging because beechnuts and acorns were an important food source for the birds. Other human effects were more direct. Passenger pigeons were valued for their meat, and millions were shot and then shipped by rail to urban centers like Chicago and New York. The birds' habit of congregating in large flocks made them easy targets for hunters—even when being shot at, the birds tended to remain together in large groups instead of dispersing. Thus it was a combination of human population pressures, technology, and economic forces that led to the demise of the passenger pigeon.

Identifying the nature and extent of environmental changes is only a first step toward understanding the extent of human alteration of the planet. A second, and more complicated, step is to consider the forces driving these changes. It is to this thorny issue that we turn in the next chapter.

◆ KEY TERMS ◆

acid rain
aquifer
Aral Sea
atmosphere
biodiversity
deforestation
desertification
ecosystem
environmental stress
hydrologic cycle
oxygen cycle
radioactive waste
renewable resources
sanitary landfill
soil erosion
solid waste
stratosphere
toxic waste
troposphere

◆ APPLYING GEOGRAPHIC KNOWLEDGE ◆

1. The Earth is warming, slightly and slowly as yet, but possibly more rapidly in the coming century. Such global warming will result in rising sea levels and, possibly, a higher frequency of severe storms. That can be a lethal combination for densely populated, low-lying coastal areas. Using population and terrain maps, identify coastal zones that are especially vulnerable to such environmental impact.
2. The building of dams and water diversion systems has altered natural water flows in many areas of the world. Such construction sometimes creates political problems even as it mitigates water shortages—not only between sovereign states but even among subnational units. Focus your attention on the waters of the Colorado River and report on the competition for this precious resource among interested parties in the U.S. Southwest and West.

Chapter 35

Confronting Human-Induced Environmental Change

From the field notes

"I watched as bulldozers attacked the tropical forest inland from the East Malaysian city of Kota Kinabalu on the northwestern coast of the island of Borneo, knocking down trees, hauling them to a clearing, and stacking them for burning. A supervisor explained that this would be the site of a new suburb of "KK," complete with shopping center, school, and medical clinic. 'Our population is growing fast,' he said, 'and soon we'll go even deeper in.' Borneo is not yet a densely peopled island, but its natural environments, habitats, and wildlife are under increasing threat. Population growth and reckless exploitation of the forest are destroying the biodiversity of this mini-continent."

KEY POINTS

◆ **Environmental change has natural as well as human causes. Current concerns over environmental change reflect humanity's role in accelerating the pace and extent of environmental change.**

◆ **While the populations of countries in the industrialized economic core are often smaller than those in the periphery, per capita consumption of resources in the rich countries is far greater.**

◆ **Modern transportation devices contribute to environmental change not just by consuming energy and producing pollution, but by facilitating global trade networks that fuel consumption in the wealthiest parts of the world.**

◆ **Environmental problems frequently cross political boundaries, complicating regulation and management efforts. Nonetheless, a number of international environmental accords have been adopted on issues ranging from biodiversity to protection of the ozone layer.**

◆ **Efforts to reduce global emissions of carbon dioxide in response to concerns over global climate change have been complicated by strong policy differences over feasible target levels and the extent to which the burden of emissions reduction should fall on the wealthiest, most industrialized countries.**

As we have seen, there is nothing new about human alteration of the environment. Deforestation, for example, has been going on since ancient times. The ancient Greeks and Romans cut down many of the trees of the Mediterranean region, leaving a profoundly altered environment in their wake. Much later and in a different place, Spanish invaders harvested the forests of Mexico for building materials and firewood. Yet in the modern era deforestation is taking place at a pace and scale heretofore unknown. The combined impact of expanded human populations, increased consumption, and technological advances has led to environmental changes that some experts view as irreversible.

In view of the magnitude of humanity's impact on the environment, efforts to understand and respond to global environmental change are of critical importance. In addressing this topic, we should remind ourselves that changes in the physical world are not always wrought by humans. Nature has its own cycles of change, and it is sometimes difficult to determine whether an observed change is attributable to nature or to humans. In southern Florida, for example, the struggle is on to save the Everglades—not just from human encroachment but from a drying trend. The causes of this trend are not entirely clear, but they may have natural as well as human causes. By channeling a certain amount of water into the Everglades in response to this trend, we may be counteracting natural forces.

Yet for all the power and mystery of nature, humans are now the dominant species on the planet, and the changes we observe in Earth's physical systems are being influenced, if not driven, by human activities. Geographers have long been interested in the nature and consequences of these changes, and throughout this book we have emphasized the ways in which humans shape the physical world. Geography, in fact, is one of the few academic disciplines in which the relationship between humans and the environment is a primary concern. One of the most influential nineteenth-century texts on this relationship, *Man and Nature*, (1865), was written by the geographer George Perkins Marsh. In 1955, geographers were centrally involved in an international interdisciplinary symposium on "Man's Role in Changing the Face of the Earth." This symposium, like Marsh's earlier book, focused primarily on local and regional changes. More recently, a symposium led by geographers on "The Earth as Transformed by Human Action" picked up where the 1955 discussion left off, addressing global environmental changes. The geographer's concern with how things are organized on the Earth and how they are connected in space provides a useful platform from which to consider human-induced environmental change.

As the study of environmental change has moved forward, one of the most important lessons we have learned is that global environmental systems are interconnected at numerous temporal and spatial scales. For example, the release of ***chlorofluorocarbons (CFCs)*** in Japan contributes to a growing hole in the Earth's ozone layer that is centered over Antarctica. Industrial production in the Netherlands and Germany contributes to acid rain in Scandinavia. The use of water from the Rio Grande for irrigation in northern New Mexico affects the amount and quality of the river's water that reaches southern New Mexico. Human actions—the activities we undertake individually and collectively—are increasingly important factors in all sorts of global environmental changes. To confront these changes we must consider the complex relationship between humans and the environment. ◆

◆ UNDERSTANDING ENVIRONMENTAL CHANGE

One of the challenges of understanding global environmental changes is simply comprehending the magnitude and rates of change involved in global processes. Geographers have always been interested in phenomena that occur at various scales and the ways in which they interact. In the past, many of the environmental problems that drew our attention occurred at local or regional scales. Recent global environmental changes have forced us to focus attention on the larger spatial scales at which many processes operate. Only recently, with the advent of air and space travel, have we been able to identify these changes with any precision. But global changes express themselves at all scales, from local to global. For example, deforestation can have a local effect by reducing the diversity of species in a particular area. It can have regional impacts by increasing sediment runoff into rivers. Finally, at a global scale, deforestation is associated with the release of carbon dioxide into the atmosphere and may affect global climate by altering processes that occur at the land surface. To fully understand deforestation we must keep all of these scales in mind.

Global changes have also forced us to think about rates of environmental change. Consider one of the issues discussed in the last chapter—the extinction of species. If we consider the entire history of the planet, approximately 95 percent of all the species that have ever existed have evolved and become extinct over the past 4 billion years. And as we saw in Chapter 33, there have been several periods of mass die-offs, such as the extinction of the dinosaurs at the end of the Cretaceous Period approximately 65 million years ago. During this time, 10 percent of terrestrial families and 15 percent of marine families became extinct. Thus extinction is a natural process that occurs regardless of human action. Why, then, are we concerned about loss of biodiversity today? It is because current rates of extinction may be 1000 to 10,000 times faster than natural extinction rates. Humans are accelerating the rate at which natural processes occur.

Several interrelated factors are responsible for the expanding impact of humans on the environment over the past two centuries. One of these is the dramatic growth of the human population. Even considering the minimal needs for human survival, there can be little doubt that the fourfold increase in the human population in the twentieth century has had significant environmental impacts. Another factor is consumption, which has increased dramatically in the modern world. Yet another is technology, which has both expanded the human capacity to alter the environment and brought with it increasing energy demands. Let us look at each of these factors in more detail.

Population

The human dimensions of global environmental changes are tied to increases in the size of the human population. Each individual requires a certain amount of resources to survive. By extension, the more people there are on the planet, the greater the demands on the Earth's environment. This relationship is so obvious that it is easy to see environmental change simply as a population issue. Although things are not that simple, population matters. A greater number of people translates into greater capacity for environmental change.

The impacts of population growth on the environment are all around us. In the United States, prime farmland is being gobbled up by expanding cities. In tropical areas, large tracts of forests are being cleared to meet the heating and cooking needs of growing populations. In China under Mao Zedong (1949–1976), when the government officially opposed population policies, deforestation was so extensive that Chairman Mao ordered every Chinese citizen to plant at least one tree. That campaign yielded an estimated 500 million trees, but today China's landscape is still marked by the scars of erosion. Whole countrysides have been laid waste, the topsoil gone soon after crops replaced natural vegetation. Now China is trying to undo the damage, but recovery is not always possible.

In light of the obvious link between population and environment, many see environmental change largely as a population issue. How helpful is this approach? It has the advantage of focusing attention on a factor whose importance is undeniable. Yet if environmental change is seen simply as a matter of numbers, some key dimensions of the issue will be overlooked. Do population

From the field notes

"It seems to me that governments of wealthy countries all too often assume that people in the global economic periphery are not really concerned about environmental issues: development there should proceed at all costs. But that is not true. Many leaders, teachers, and others in such countries as Brazil, Kenya, and India keep environmental problems in the public eye, and have attracted strong support in so doing. I ran into this demonstration in Mumbai, India in 1997: a local organization was drawing attention to the city's air pollution."

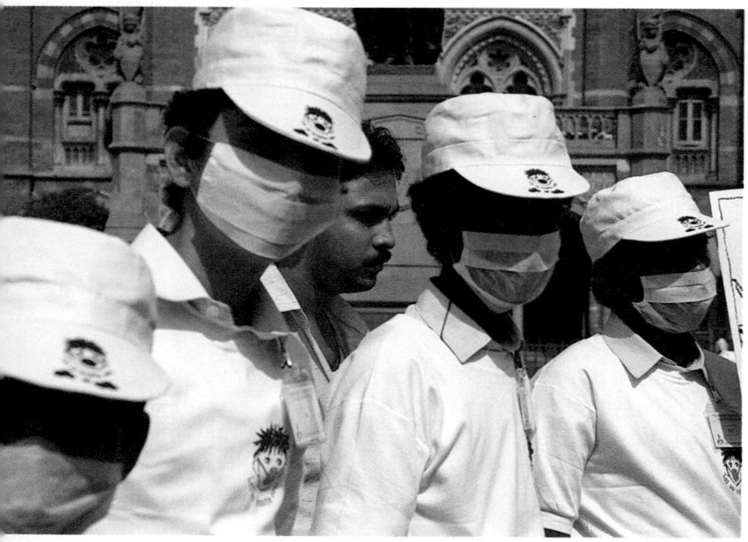

numbers have the same meaning in all places? What is the role of economic and social developments in the environmental area? Where should our concern with population be directed, since the practices of peoples in one part of the world can affect environments and peoples thousands of miles away? And how do we confront population growth without treading on deeply held cultural values? Addressing these questions requires that we look beyond mere numbers to questions of consumption and technology.

Patterns of Consumption

Maps of world population tend to underscore the magnitude of populations in some poorer countries, but they fail to convey another aspect of societies and their needs: the relative demands made by different peoples on the Earth's resources. Humans, like all species, are consumers. We rely on the Earth's resources for our very survival. At the most basic level, we consume water, oxygen, and organic and mineral materials. Over time we have developed increasingly complex ways of utilizing resources by such means as intensive agriculture and industrial production. Consequently, many societies now consume resources at a level and rate that far exceed basic subsistence needs. In a 1996 article on "Humanity's Resources" in *The Companion Encyclopedia of Geography: The Environment and Humankind*, I. G. Simmons notes that a hunter-gatherer could subsist on the resources found within an area of about 26 square kilometers, whereas today many people living in urban centers in the global economic core have access to resources from all over the planet.

The generally smaller number of people in the more affluent parts of the world make far greater demands on the Earth's resources than do the much larger numbers in the poorer countries. It has been estimated that a baby born in the United States during the first decade of the twenty-first century, at current rates, consumes about 250 times as much energy over a lifetime as a baby born in Bangladesh over the same lifetime. In terms of food, housing, and its components, metals, paper (and thus trees), and many other materials, the consumption of individuals in affluent countries far exceeds that of people in poorer countries. Thus rapid population growth in the poorer countries tends to be a local or regional matter, keeping rural areas mired in poverty. Population growth in the richer countries is also a matter of concern, one whose impact is not just local or regional but global.

All of this underscores the importance of thinking geographically about human impacts on the natural world. People living in the global economic periphery tend to affect their immediate environment, putting pressure on soil, natural vegetation, and water supplies, and polluting the local air with the smoke from their fires. The reach of affluent societies is much greater. The demand for low-cost meat for hamburgers in the United States has led to the cutting down of trees in Central and South America to make way for pastures and cattle herds. This, in turn, has greatly increased water demand in such areas (Table 35–1). Thus the American (and European, Japanese, and Australian) consumer has an impact on distant environments.

Table 35-1 Estimated Liters of Water Required to Produce 1 Kilogram of Food

Crop	Liters/Kg
Potatoes	500
Wheat	900
Corn	1400
Rice	1912
Chicken	3500
Beef	100,000

Source: D. Pimentel et al., *Bioscience*, Vol. 47, No. 2, February 1997, p. 98.

Globally, consumption is tied to technology, for (as we saw in Part Nine) the industrialized core has access to a vast array of transportation and communication technologies that allow advertisers to stimulate demand for particular goods around the world and allow manufacturers to bring those goods from distant places. Related technological developments also allow humans to manipulate atmospheric, land, oceanic, and biological systems in profound ways—as well as to expand the production of the material goods that consumers demand. Understanding the complex ties between technology and environmental change requires consideration of several different facets of the technology picture.

Technology

Technological advances have increased rapidly since the Industrial Revolution and today affect all aspects of our lives. We are continually developing technologies that we hope will improve our standard of living, protect us against disease, and allow us to work more efficiently. These technologies have not come without a cost. Resource extraction practices such as mining and logging, which provide the materials to produce technologies, have created severe environmental problems. Energy is required not only to develop new technologies but to use them as well; fossil fuel consumption has contributed to many types of pollution and may be a factor in climate change. Technological innovations have produced hazardous and toxic byproducts, creating pollution and health problems that we are only now beginning to recognize. Most significant for our discussion of global environmental change, however, is the fact that technology has enabled humans to alter large portions of the planet in a short space of time.

There are many dramatic examples of the role of technology in environmental change. Great open-pit mines exist where huge machines have carved away at the Earth's surface. The enormous clear-cuts of the Pacific Northwest forests are made possible by chainsaws, trucks, and even helicopters. The heavy blanket of smog that envelops cities such as Taipei is a product of the internal combustion engine and mechanized manufacturing. Key elements of the technologies that contribute to these examples of environmental change are developments in two critical sectors of the economy: transportation and energy. Let us look at these.

Transportation

Modes of transportation represent some of the most important technological advances in human history. Initially, transportation was limited to travel by foot or boat. Later, animals were domesticated and trained to carry

From the field notes

"This looming coal-burning power plant in southwestern Poland was built more than forty years ago. Yet as technology changed, the plant did not. Instead, it stands as a monument to the communist regime's single-minded devotion to production targets, irrespective of environmental costs or potential long-term efficiencies. Now the plant is being upgraded as part of a World Bank project, but work is proceeding slowly as project managers cope with aging infrastructure and a workforce little used to innovation."

From the field notes

"This was one of the most depressing days of this long South American field trip. We had been briefed and had seen the satellite pictures of the destruction of the rainforest, with ugly gashes of bare ground pointing like rows of arrows into the woods. But walking to the temporary endpoints of some of these new roads made a lot more impact. From the remaining forest around came the calls of monkeys and other wildlife, their habitat retreating under the human onslaught. Next week this road would push ahead another mile, the logs carted away and burned, the first steps in a process that would clear this land, ending billions of years of nature's dominance."

heavy loads. Within the last few millennia, humans learned how to capture wind power with sails, which allowed ships to travel long distances and eventually enabled humans to circle the globe. The invention of the steam engine created power for ocean vessels and railroad engines, whereas the internal combustion engine revolutionized travel and made possible the development of the automobile and the airplane. All of these innovations have required increased resource use, not only to make the vehicles that move people and goods, but also to build and maintain the related infrastructure—roads, railroad tracks, airports, parking structures, repair facilities, and the like. With each innovation the impacts seem to widen. As David Headrick points out in a study discussed in the *Companion Encyclopedia of Geography* (Douglas and Robinson, 1996), Chicago's O'Hare Airport covers a larger area (approximately 28 square kilometers) than Chicago's central business district (which covers approximately 8 square kilometers). Moreover, transportation innovations offer access to remote areas of the planet. There are vehicles that allow people to travel through extreme climates, to the bottoms of the ocean, and across the polar ice caps. These places, in turn, have been altered by human activity.

Transportation is also implicated in global environmental change—albeit sometimes indirectly. Advances in transportation have produced significant pollution, as seen, for example, in the extent of oil spills along major shipping lanes (Fig. 35-1). Modern modes of transport have also facilitated the introduction of new species to areas where they were not found previously. Over the last few centuries, as ships became more seaworthy and global voyages more frequent, the number of species spread from one part of the globe to another increased. Some organisms attached themselves to the bottom of ships, whereas others stowed away on board or were transported intentionally as a food source. In modern cargo ships, the taking on of seawater as ballast facilitates the transport of ***pelagic species*** (that is, species that live in the open sea) from one side of the globe to the other. One study estimates that between 1850 and 1970 San Francisco Bay received a new species every 36 weeks, and over the last decade this rate has increased to 1 species every 12 weeks. Diseases are also spread by transportation—rapid air travel has made it common for contagious disease outbreaks in one part of the world to spread quickly to other regions.

Finally, transportation facilitates the types of global networks that are necessary to the patterns of consumption outlined earlier. Many of the products available in stores—be they electronics or clothing or food—come from distant places. Resources are required to produce and ship them, and except those that meet basic subsistence needs, they all contribute to the greater strains placed on the environment by those living in the wealthier parts of the world. This realization has led some individuals to reduce their levels of consumption or to consume more environmentally friendly, locally produced products. These changes have had some effect, but so far their impact on the geography of global consumption has been marginal.

Figure 35-1 Location of Visible Oil Slicks. Oil slicks are a problem around the globe, as this map shows. *Source:* Organization for Economic Co-operation and Development, 1985. *The State of the Environment 1985*. (Paris: Organization for Economic Co-operation and Development), p. 76.

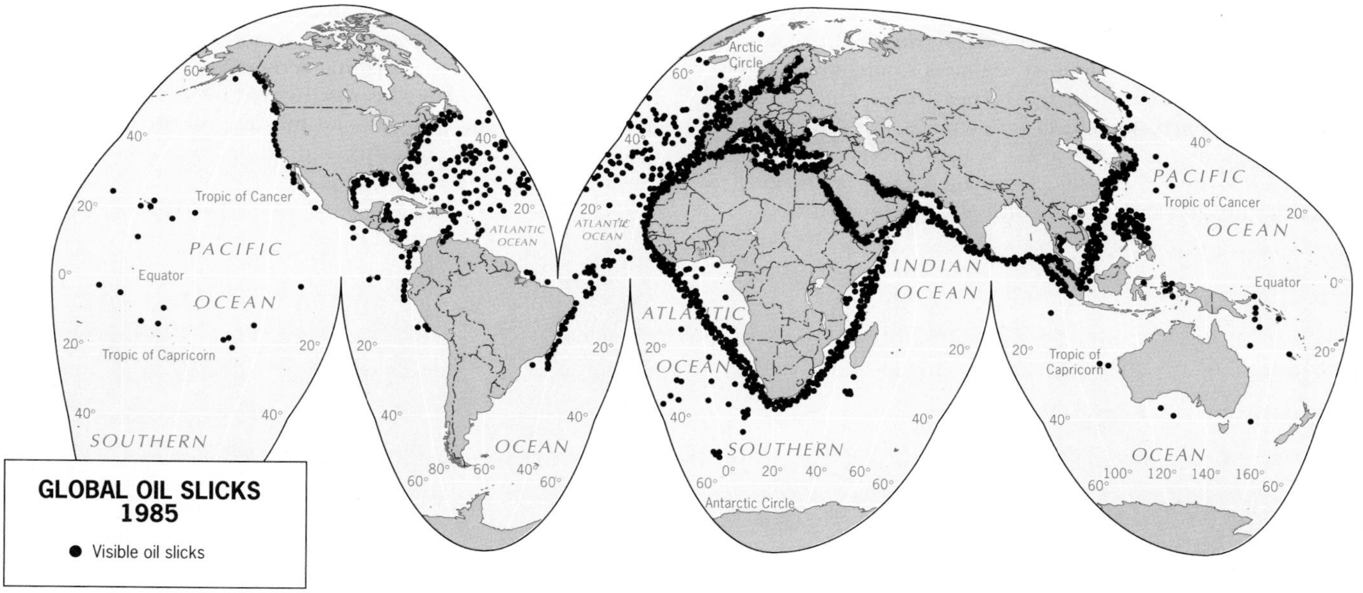

A SENSE OF SCALE

Wind Energy Parks in the European Union

The growing number of international environmental agreements signed in recent years reflects mounting international concern over the state of the global environment. The scope of these international agreements is primarily global in the sense that members of the international community agree to a global blueprint for action. How do these international agreements translate into regional or local action? What actual steps have signatory countries taken in their attempts to meet these global goals? Insights into these questions can be gained by looking at regional and local responses to a recent convention on climate change.

The UN-sponsored Framework Convention on Climate Change (FCCC) was signed by 154 countries (plus the European Union) at the June 1992 Rio de Janeiro Earth Summit. Although the stated goal of this treaty was to reduce carbon dioxide emissions globally, the agreement did not include specific emission targets or regulatory requirements.

Modern windmills that produce energy now function with increasing frequency in Europe, particularly in the Netherlands (shown here) and in Denmark.

Instead, the treaty allowed the signatory countries to develop their own national (and in the case of the European Union, regional) implementation plans. This has been happening in a number of cases, which implemention programs established that encourage both the development of "clean" renewable energy technologies and increased energy efficiency in buildings, transportation, and manufacturing.

In keeping with this approach, the European Union has mandated that a percentage of the funds it provides for regional development be used for renewable energy projects and increased energy efficiency. In 1994 alone, the EU provided ECU 175 million (US$159 million) for the development of renewable energy sources within the member states. Since 1994, the amount of EU money going toward renewable energy programs has increased even further. In one 1997 case, the EU provided ECU 43 million (US$39.1 million) for the construction of three wind energy parks in the State of Navarra in northern Spain. When completed, these wind energy parks will consist of a total of 115 wind turbines and will add 69 megawatts of "clean" electric energy to the region. And the regional government of Navarra, with the assistance of the EU, eventually hopes to add 44 additional turbines to the wind parks so that 95 megawatts of power can be generated. This amount of electricity can serve the needs of some 190,000 homes.

These wind energy parks not only help the EU meet its obligations under the FCCC; they also help Navarra achieve a goal of self-sufficiency in energy. Long-term plans call for the further expansion of Navarra's wind energy parks to provide close to 50 percent of the region's electric energy needs. As this expansion occurs, more will change than Navarra's energy situation. The wind energy parks, located in the Guerinda Mountains 30 km southeast of the city of Pamplona, will alter the local landscape and economy in ways that will shape the character of Navarra as a place in the twenty-first century.

Energy

Consumption of material goods is closely linked to consumption of energy. It takes energy to produce material goods, energy to deliver them to markets, and, for many products (refrigerators, automobiles, etc.), energy to keep them running. The resulting demands for energy are a factor in environmental change. Before the 1800s, human societies relied directly on solar energy in the form of plant and animal fuel sources, such as wood and animal fat. Today much of our energy supply comes from nonrenewable fossil fuels, such as coal, oil, and natural gas. Moreover, the evolution of tertiary, quaternary, and quinary economic activities has not reduced the consumption of nonrenewable resources. As populations

Figure 35-2 World Distribution of Fossil Fuel Sources. Geographical distribution of fossil fuel sources of carbon dioxide (CO_2) as of 1990 is depicted here. The basic pattern has remained the same. *Source*: *Science,* 25 July 1997.

grow, so does the demand for energy, and we can expect that over the coming decades energy production will expand to meet the increased demand. In developing countries in particular, demands for more energy are met by increasing the development of fossil-fuel sources. This helps explain why, according to the United States Department of Energy, global energy production was 75 percent greater in 1999 than it was in 1971.

If we look at the global distribution of fossil fuel sources of CO_2 (Fig. 35-2), we can see that production is concentrated in the highly industrialized part of the global economic core. Pollution associated with this energy production creates the acidic deposition discussed in Chapter 34. The damming of rivers for hydropower alters freshwater systems. Nuclear power is being experimented with throughout the world, but the highly volatile byproducts of this form of energy production and the potential for accidents have limited the expansion of nuclear energy.

Technology has played a key role in amplifying human-induced environmental change. At the same time, technologies are being developed to identify and solve environmental problems. Some of these offer alternative approaches to local energy production (see Sense of Scale Box: Wind Energy Parks in the European Union). In addition, remote sensing technologies help us under-

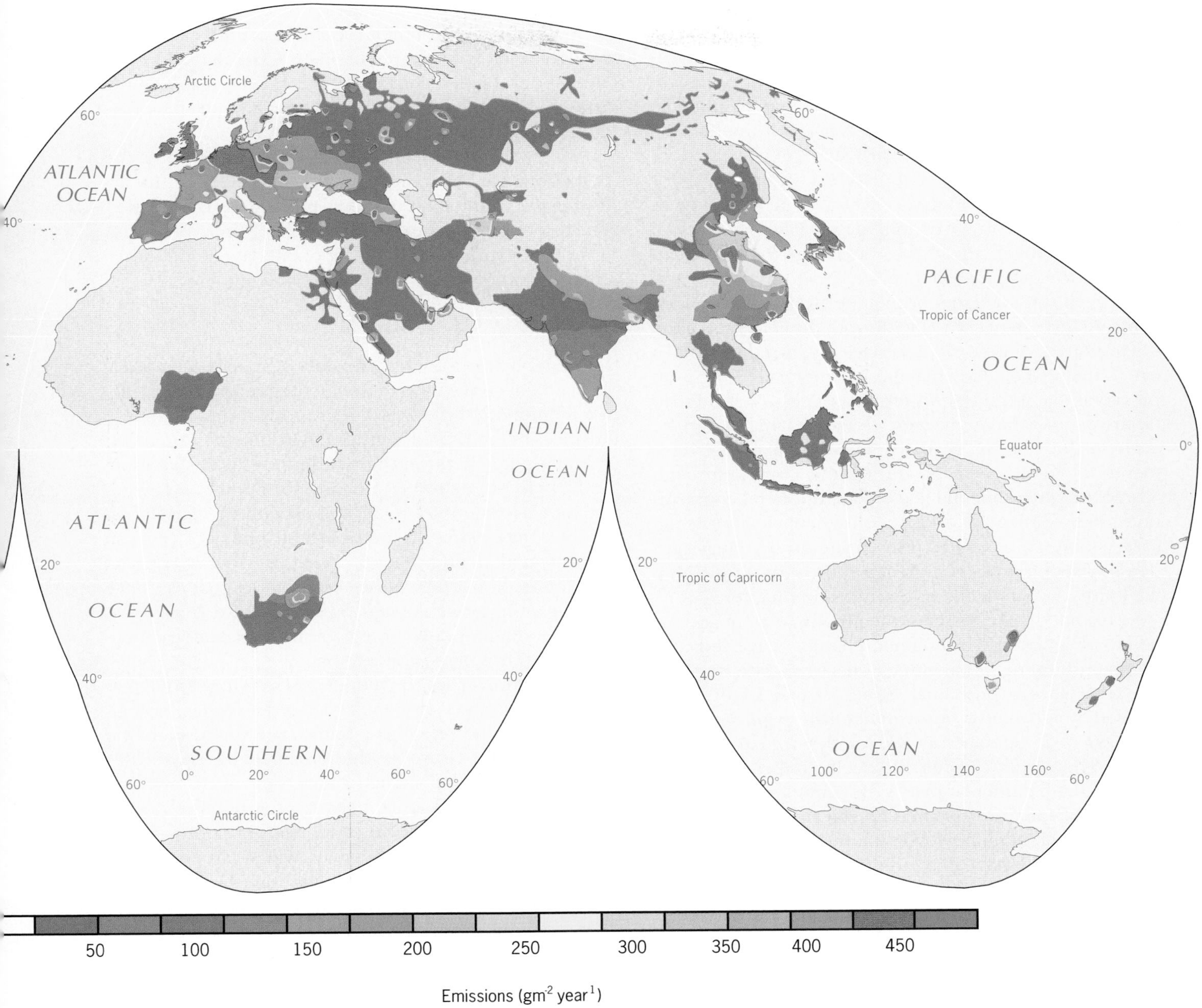

stand the rates and scales of global environmental changes. Only with the advent of satellite remote sensing systems in the 1970s, for example, were we able to gain reliable estimates of the global rate of deforestation. Geographic information systems (GIS) are being used by geographers and others to analyze data on global change in new and useful ways. One benefit of geographic information systems is that they enable us to visualize the relationships among different environmental systems. Finally, advances in communication technologies have allowed us to transmit technological information gained in one place to people in other parts of the world, creating a global dialogue on environmental change.

◆ POLICY RESPONSES TO ENVIRONMENTAL CHANGE

Technology is only one part of the picture of the human response to environmental change. The extent and rapidity of that change have led to numerous policies aimed at protecting the environment or reversing the negative impacts of pollution. These range from local ordinances that restrict urban development in environmentally sensitive areas to global accords on topics such as biodiversity and climate change.

A major challenge in confronting environmental problems is that many of those problems do not lie within a single jurisdiction. As we saw in Part Five, many environmental problems cross political boundaries, and people sometimes move across those boundaries in response to environmental pressures. Designing policy responses is thus complicated by the fact that the political map does not reflect the geography of environmental issues. The problem is particularly acute when environmental problems cross international boundaries, for there are few international policy-making bodies with significant authority over multinational environmental spaces. Moreover, those that do exist—the European Union, for example—often have limited authority and must heed the concerns of member states. Those concerns, in turn, may not coincide with the interests of the environment. Within democracies, politicians with an eye to the next election may hesitate to tackle long-term problems that require short-term sacrifices. Most authoritarian regimes have an even worse record, as can be seen in the policies of the Soviet-dominated governments of Eastern Europe during the communist era. Moreover, governmental leaders in peripheral countries find it very difficult to take action when, as is often the case, action requires reductions in already marginal standards of living and even greater difficulties in meeting the kinds of debt payments discussed in Chapter 27.

Despite these obstacles, the growing extent and urgency of global environmental changes have led to a number of international agreements to address some of the most severe problems. Some of these are spearheaded by so-called ***nongovernmental organizations (NGOs)*** that operate outside of the formal political arena. They tend to focus on specific issues and problems, often in particular places. Beginning with the 1972 ***United Nations Conference on the Human Environment*** in Stockholm, however, international governmental organizations have played a growing role as well.

The framework that currently guides international governmental activity in the environmental arena evolved out of the ***United Nations Conference on Environment and Development (UNCED)*** held in Rio de Janeiro in June 1992. The delegates to UNCED gave the ***Global Environment Facility (GEF)***—a joint project of the United Nations and the World Bank—significant authority over environmental action on a global scale. The GEF funds projects related to four issues: loss of biodiversity, climate change, protection of international waters, and depletion of the ozone layer. The delegates to UNCED believed that significant progress could be made through these funded projects, along with bilateral (that is, government-to-government) aid. They also made it easier for NGOs to participate in international environmental policy making.

These actions hold the promise of a more coherent approach to environmental problem solving than is possible when decisions are made on a state-by-state basis. Yet individual states continue to influence decision making in all sorts of ways. Take the case of the GEF. Even though the GEF is charged with protecting key elements of the global environment, it still functions in a state-based world, as suggested by Figure 35-3, a map from a 1994 World Bank technical report on the forest sector in Subsaharan Africa that divides the realm into "major regions" that cut across forest zones.

A few global environmental issues are so pressing that efforts are being made to draw up guidelines for action in the form of international conventions or treaties. The most prominent examples are in the areas of biological diversity, protection of the ozone layer, and global climate change. Let us take a brief look at these.

Biological Diversity

International concern over the loss of species led to calls for a global convention (agreement) as early as 1981. By the beginning of the 1990s, a group working under the auspices of the United Nations Environment Programme reached agreement on the wording of the convention, and it was submitted to UNCED for approval. It went into effect in late 1993; by 2001, 168 countries had signed it. The convention calls for the establishment of a system of protected areas and for a coordinated set of national and international regulations on activities that can have significant negative impacts on biodiversity. It also provides funding for developing countries that are trying to meet the terms of the convention.

The biodiversity convention is a step forward in that it both affirms the vital significance of preserving biological diversity and provides a framework for cooperation toward that end. However, the agreement has proved difficult to implement. In particular, there is an ongoing struggle to find a balance between the need of poorer countries to promote local economic development and the need to preserve biodiversity, which happens to be richest in the global economic periphery. Also, there has been controversy over the sharing of costs for conservation programs, which has led to heated debates over ratification of the convention in some countries. Nevertheless, this convention, along with a host of voluntary efforts, has helped both to focus attention on the biodiversity issue and to promote the expansion of protected areas. Whether those areas will succeed in providing long-term species protection is an open question that will occupy geographers and biologists for years to come.

Protection of the Ozone Layer

When found in the troposphere (0 to 16 kilometer altitude), ozone (O_3) gas is a harmful pollutant closely associated with the creation of smog. However, a naturally occurring ***ozone layer*** exists in the upper levels of the stratosphere (between 30 and 45 kilometer altitude). The ozone layer is of vital importance, since it protects the Earth's surface from the Sun's harmful ultraviolet rays. In 1985, a group of British scientists working in Antarctica

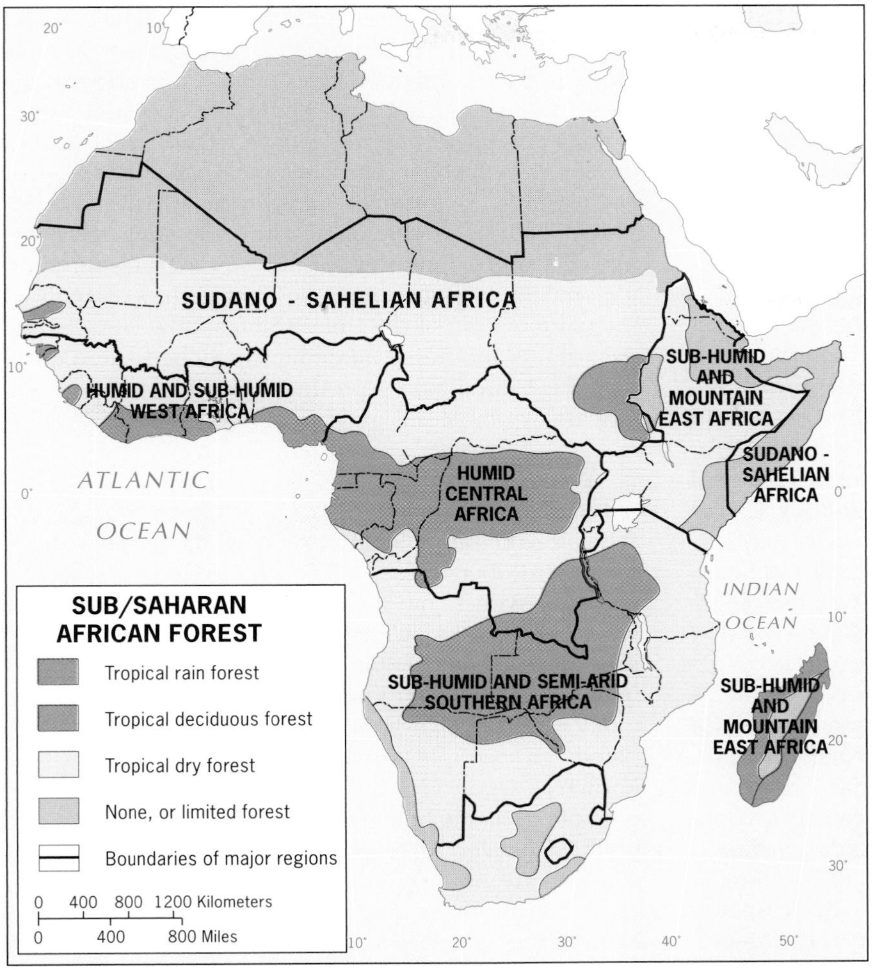

Figure 35-3 Major Regions and Forest Zones in Subsaharan Africa. This map is based on a figure in a World Bank technical paper on the forest sector in Subsaharan Africa. The map shows major regions of deforestation crossing state boundaries, but planning regions adhere to state boundaries. *Source:* N. P. Sharma, S. Rietbergen, C. R. Heimo, and J. Patel. *A Strategy for the Forest Sector in Sub-Saharan Africa,* World Bank Technical Paper No., 251, Africa Technical Department Series (Washington, D.C.: The World Bank, 1994).

discovered that the thickness of the ozone layer above the South Pole had been dramatically reduced, from 300 Dobson units (DUs) in the 1960s to close to 200 DUs by 1985. Studies revealed that the main culprits in ozone depletion were a group of human-made gases collectively known as CFCs (chlorofluorocarbons). These gases, used mainly as refrigerants, in fire extinguishers, and in aerosol cans, had only been in use since the 1950s and were thought to be completely harmless to humans. The strength of the scientific evidence pointing to a rapid reduction of the ozone layer led to an unusually rapid and united international response.

International cooperation began in 1985 with the negotiation of the ***Vienna Convention for the Protection of the Ozone Layer***. Specific targets and timetables for the phaseout of production and consumption of CFCs were defined and agreed upon as part of the international agreement known as the ***Montreal Protocol***, which was signed in September 1987 by 105 countries and the European Community. The original agreement called for a reduction in the production and consumption of CFCs of 50 percent by 1999. At a meeting in London in 1990, scientific data showing that ozone depletion would continue for many years after a phaseout of CFCs led the signators of the Montreal Protocol to agree to halt CFC production entirely by the year 2000. Finally, at a meeting in Copenhagen in 1992, the timetable for CFC phaseout was accelerated; participants agreed to eliminate CFC production by 1996 and to accelerate the phaseout of other ozone-depleting chemicals such as halons, hydrochlorofluorocarbons, carbon tetrachloride, methyl chloroform, and methyl bromide. This response is an encouraging example of international cooperation in the face of a significant, albeit clearly defined, problem. Unfortunately, the long residence time of CFCs in the atmosphere will mean that their effects will be felt for a long time to come.

Global Climate Change

Beginning in the late 1980s, growing concern about climate changes led to a series of intergovernmental conferences on the nature and extent of the human impact on the climate system. The second of these conferences, held in Geneva in 1990, was sponsored by the World

Meteorological Organization, the United Nations Environment Programme, and other international organizations. It brought together representatives from 137 states and the European Community. The delegates concluded that there was enough evidence of human impacts on climate to justify efforts to draw up a treaty on climate change. The final declaration, adopted after hard bargaining, did not specify any international targets for reducing emissions. Instead, it proclaimed climate change as a "common concern of humankind," while noting that "common but differentiated responsibilities" existed between the industrialized core and the less industrialized periphery.

In December 1990 the United Nations General Assembly approved the start of treaty negotiations. A draft convention was prepared and submitted to UNCED for consideration. The convention was presented in general terms, but it called on the developed countries to take measures aimed at reducing their emissions to 1990 levels by the year 2000 and to provide technical and financial support for emission-reduction efforts in the developing countries. The convention was signed by 154 States and the European Community in Rio de Janeiro.

For several years after UNCED, various committees met to discuss matters relating to the convention. By 1995, mounting concerns about the nature of long-term commitments under the convention led the participants in these discussions to call for a revised treaty that would cover the post–2000 period. They appointed a group to draft an agreement to be considered at a 1997 meeting in Kyoto, Japan. Different proposals were made in the months before this meeting, including one by the Association of Small Island States for a 20 percent cut in CO_2 by the year 2005 and one by the European Union for cuts of 7.5 percent by 2005 and 15 percent by 2010. The United States, however, was concerned about the economic effects of such cuts and the extent to which the burden of reducing emissions fell on the developed countries. It made a more modest proposal to return to 1990 CO_2 levels by 2012 and to reduce CO_2 levels below the 1990 benchmark thereafter.

After 10 days of tough negotiations, an agreement was reached that involved compromises for practically every participating country. The agreement set a target period of 2008–2012 for the United States, the European Union, and Japan to cut their greenhouse gas emissions by 7, 8, and 6 percent, respectively, below 1990 levels. In addition, the agreement reached in Kyoto did not obligate less developed countries to adhere to specific reduction goals; instead it called for voluntary emission reduction plans to be implemented individually by those countries with financial assistance from industrialized countries. These plans have been revisited in successive climate change summits in The Hague (November 2000), Bonn (July 2001), and Marrakech (November 2001). The Hague summit collapsed without any agreement, and a further setback occurred in March 2001 when a new presidential administration in the United States suddenly announced its intention to abandon unilaterally the Kyoto Protocol. The Bonn summit thus opened amidst serious differences among countries, but by the end of the summit countries other than the United States signed a statement calling for the Kyoto Protocol to be salvaged. This paved the way for the Marrakech summit, where most countries agreed to a set of general rules for international implementation of the Kyoto Protocol. Without the participation of the United States, however, the impact of this and future agreements will be limited given that the United States produces nearly 35 percent of global CO_2 emissions.

◆ THE FUTURE

What will the future be like? Many would agree with geographer Robert Kates (1994), who foresees a "warmer, more crowded, more connected but more diverse world" (p. 114). As we consider this prospect, we must acknowledge that global environmental changes illustrate the limits of our knowledge of the Earth. Many of today's global environmental changes were not anticipated. For example, one of the most widely used CFCs, known as Freon 12, was invented in 1931, but the thinning of the ozone hole over Antarctica was not reported until 1985, over 50 years later. Moreover, many global changes are nonlinear, and some are "chaotic" in the sense that future conditions cannot be reliably predicted. Nonlinearity means that small actions in certain situations may result in large impacts and may be more important than larger actions in causing change. Thresholds also exist in many systems which, once past, are irreversible. This occurs, for example, when the habitat for a species is diminished to the point where the species quickly dies off. Unfortunately, we may not be able to identify these thresholds until we pass them. This leaves open the possibility of "surprises," unanticipated responses by physical systems.

The complexity and urgency of the environmental challenge will tax the energies of the scientific and policy communities for some time to come (see Looking Ahead Box—The Social Challenges of Environmental Change). Geography must be an essential part of any serious effort to grapple with these challenges. The major changes that are taking place have different origins and spatial expressions, and each results from a unique combination of physical and social processes. We cannot simply focus on system dynamics and generalized causal relationships. We must also consider emerging patterns of environmental change and the impacts of differences from place to place on the operation of general processes. Geography is not the backdrop to the changes taking place; it is at the very heart of the changes themselves.

Looking Ahead

The Social Challenges of Environmental Change

In the late 1970s, a combination of political and economic circumstances yielded a sudden and unanticipated energy crunch. Americans, used to paying a fraction of the European cost of gasoline per gallon and accustomed to quick self-service fillups, found themselves paying higher prices and waiting in lines for hours to get fuel. Many gas stations limited their customers to 10 gallons per car or less; others restricted sales to long-time regular customers. As lines of cars snaked around city blocks and snarled traffic, disputes among drivers required added police and strained municipal budgets. Angry motorists, blaming OPEC member countries, called on the government to retaliate by limiting grain shipments to oil-exporting nations. "A bushel for a barrel" was a favorite bumper sticker.

But there was another sentiment, and it was this: "Why didn't our government see this coming?" Not only did the fuel shortage arise in short order; there was no preparation. The national distribution system faltered and many gas stations closed, some on certain days of the week, others permanently. Towns had no plans to deal with the gigantic backups. The federal government attempted to establish priorities (hospitals, schools first; commuters last), but enforcement was feeble. Speed limits on superhighways were reduced to 55 mph as a conservation (and safety) measure. The gas shortage dominated and clouded daily life for an entire nation. Sales of smaller, gas-efficient cars soared. Fuel-efficiency mandates on automobile manufacturers emanated from Congress.

Unfortunately, memories are short. The power of OPEC was broken, gasoline supplies recovered, and by the 1990s Americans were buying gas-guzzling SUVs and light trucks in unprecedented numbers, paying about one-third the price Europeans pay for a gallon of gas. In government, the debate over energy focused less on conservation than on the expansion of oil production from "safe" domestic sources such as northern Alaska.

Now consider what you have been reading in Part Eleven, and substitute "environment" for oil, and "population" for drivers. Just as our political leaders and economic planners should have foreseen the energy crunch of the 1970s, so we should now be preparing for a far greater challenge: a global change—or even reversal—of environmental fortunes, a disruption in the planet's productive capacity, and a food crisis. Certainly nature is trying to warn us. On the one hand, there is considerable evidence of global warming over the last few decades, which is being accompanied by a growing number of extreme climate events (within contemporary parameters). On the other hand, every centuries-long warming phase of the past 6000 years has ended suddenly and plunged comfortably warm and moist environs into bitter cold and scorching heat, drought, and desiccation. Ruined cities in present-day Southwest Asia bear silent witness to such events; ethnolinguistic maps reflect the desperate migrations induced by rapid climate change.

But that was before the Earth's human population exploded as it did during the latest warm phase. Not only numerically but also spatially, humanity pushed the limits of survival into the farthest frontiers. Nature's self-regulation is no more: each day the human population adds the equivalent of a city of 200,000 to our numbers. We did get an early warning in the middle of the twentieth century, when global climates cooled, farm production in "developing" areas stagnated, and social scientists warned of widespread famines ahead. But then warming resumed, the Green Revolution closed the food gap, and, like that gas crisis, memories of food shortages faded.

Now 6.3 billion people depend for their long-term survival on environmental conditions that are known to be short-term, and they are augmenting the uncertainties by altering the very atmosphere on which they rely. Either a continued warming or a relatively benign cooling of the kind the planet experienced between 1940 and 1970 would have massive impact on food supply (for example, by reducing triple-cropped paddies to double-cropped ones over a wide area of East Asia). But a very significant century-long warming or a Holocene-ending climatic reversal of the kind the Pleistocene has produced numerous times would be catastrophic, with unimaginable consequences.

What should be done to make our future more secure? Look back on what you have encountered in this book and count the ways: most urgent are controlling resource consumption in wealthier areas while reducing population growth in poorer areas through family planning; the education and empowerment of women, which invariably has major positive impact wherever it occurs; the expansion of research into crops modified to cope with cold, drought, and pests (genetically modified food is preferable to no food at all); a massive research program to create alternate energy sources, not only to substitute for oil but to prepare for the vast energy needs of a planet experiencing climate change; the large-scale dissemination of medicines from the producing countries to those in direst need, notably in Subsaharan Africa; the improvement of food-storage and distribution systems in the most vulnerable areas (famine is often a matter of local access, not global availability); and the strengthening of international organizations whose coordination will be needed when the challenge arises. As a reference to Part One will confirm, there are other, urgent needs. But a clash between the Earth's ability to sustain life and the character of its human occupance lies in our future, and we cannot claim not to have been warned.

KEY TERMS

chlorofluorocarbons (CFCs)
Global Environment Facility (GEF)
Montreal Protocol
nongovernmental organizations (NGOs)
ozone layer
pelagic species
United Nations Conference on Environment and Development (UNCED)
United Nations Conference on the Human Environment
Vienna Convention for the Protection of the Ozone Layer

APPLYING GEOGRAPHIC KNOWLEDGE

1. Suppose you were in charge of dividing up Africa into a series of regions that would become frameworks for planning and implementing policies to combat deforestation and soil erosion. What approach would you take in delimiting regions? What sources would you consult? What would your map of regions look like when it was completed?
2. Identify two areas of significant environmental degradation, one in a democratic country and one in a country with a recent or current authoritarian regime. Discuss what factors contributed to environmental degradation in each case. Specify which factors the cases have in common and which they do not.

Part Eleven
THE CHANGING ENVIRONMENTAL CONTEXT

At Issue: Revisited

Should all countries be subject to the same rules? Or should the poorer countries be exempt from some of the more costly regulations? And can an effective response be organized without undermining state sovereignty? The transnational character of many environmental problems poses a serious challenge to the modern state system. Organizing effective responses to global environmental problems requires international institutions with powers and authorities that have been traditionally reserved for states. As international institutions take on this critical role, they risk creating serious hardships if all places are treated alike. Instead, geographical variations in modes of livelihood, economic wealth, and social stability are unavoidable parts of the picture. In a world of increasingly globalized networks and problems, geography does not disappear. Instead, it become a profoundly important element of any effort to comprehend and confront changing international orders.

SELECTED BIBLIOGRAPHY

Part Eleven The Changing Environmental Context

Bennett, R., & Estall, R., eds. *Global Change and Challenge: Geography for the 1990s* (New York: Routledge, 1991).

Botkin, D. B. *Forces of Change: A New View of Nature* (Washington, D.C.: National Geographic Society, 2000).

Brown, L., & Wolf, E. *Soil Erosion: Quiet Crisis in the World Economy* (Washington, D.C., Paper No. 60, 1984).

Brown, L. R., et al. *State of the World* (New York: W. W. Norton, Annual).

Burroghs, W. J. *Does the Weather Really Matter?: The Social Implications of Climate Change* (New York: Cambridge University Press, 1997).

COHMAP members. "Climatic Changes of the Last 18,000 Years: Observations and Model Simulations." *Science* 241 (1988), pp. 1043–1052.

Davis, M. *Late Victorian Holocausts: El Niño Famines and the Making of the Third World* (London: Verso, 2001).

Diamond, J. *Guns, Germs and Steel: The Fates of Human Societies* (New York: W. W. Norton, 1997).

Douglas, I., Huggett, R., & Robinson, M., eds. *Companion Encyclopedia of Geography: The Environment and Humankind* (New York: Routledge, 1996).

Ehrlich, P., & Ehrlich, A. *Healing the Planet: Strategies for Resolving the Environmental Crisis* (Reading, Mass.: Addison-Wesley, 1991).

Energy Information Administration (EIA). *International Energy Annual 1999* (February 2001).

Fagan, B. *Floods, Famines and Emperors: El Niño and the Fate of Civilizations* (New York: Basic Books, 1999).

Fagan, B. *The Little Ice Age: How Climate Made History*, 1300–1850 (New York: Basic Books, 2000).

Grove, J. *The Little Ice Age* (London: Routledge, reprint, 1990).

Heywood, V. H., ed. *Global Biodiversity Assessment* (Cambridge: Cambridge University Press, 1995).

Intergovernmental Panel on Climate Change. *Climate Change 1995: The Science of Climate Change. Edited by J. T. Houghton et al. (Cambridge: Cambridge University Press, 1996).*

Intergovernmental Panel on Climate Change. *Climate Change 2001: Impacts, Adaptation, and Vulnerability; Contribution of Working GroUniversity Press II to the Third Assessment Report,* edited by J. J. McCarthy et al. (New York: Cambridge University Press, 2001).

Intergovernmental Panel on Climate Change. *Climate Change 2001: The Scientific Basis; Contribution of Working GroUniversity Press I to the Third Assessment Report,* edited by J. T. Houghton et al. (New York: Cambridge University Press, 2001).

Johnston, R. J. *Nature, State, and Economy: A Political Economy of the Environment. 2nd ed.*, (New York: John Wiley & Sons, 1996).

Johnston, R. J., Taylor, P. J., and Watts, M. J., eds. *Geographies of Global Change: Remapping the World in the Late Twentieth Century* (Oxford: Blackwell, 1995).

Jordan, A. "Paying the Incremental Costs of Global Environmental Protection: The Evolving Role of GEF." *Environment* 36 (1994): 12–20, 31–36.

Kates, R. W. "Sustaining Life on the Earth." *Scientific American* 271 (1994), pp. 114–122.

Krasnapolsky, V. A., & Feidman, P. D. "Detection of Molecular Hydrogen in the Atmosphere of Mars." *Science* 294, 30 November 2001, p. 1914.

Lamb, H. H. *Climate, History, and the Modern World.* 2nd ed. (London: Methuen, 1995).

Marsh, G. P. *Man and Nature* (Cambridge, Mass.: Belknap Press of Harvard University Press, 2000, originally publ. 1865).

McCoy, F., & Heiken, G., eds. *Volcanic Hazards and Disasters in Human Antiquity* (Boulder, Colo.: Geological Society of America, Special Paper, 2000).

Michaels, P. J., & Balling, R. C. *The Satanic Gases: Clearing the Air about Global Warming* (Washington, D.C.: Cato Institute, 2000).

Narendra, P. S., Rietbergen, S., Heimo, C. R., and Patel, J., eds. *A Strategy for the Forest Sector in Sub-Saharan Africa.* World Bank Technical Paper no. 251, Africa Technical Department Series (Washington, D.C.: The World Bank, 1994).

Park, C. C. *Tropical Rainforests* (New York: Routledge, 1992).

Philander, G. *Is the Temperature Rising?: The Uncertain Science of Global Warming* (Princeton, N.J.: Princeton University Press, 1998).

Rosendal, G. K. *The Convention on Biological Diversity and Developing Countries* (Boston: Kluwer Academic, 2000).

Rotberg, R. I., & Rabb, T. K. *Climate and History: Studies in Interdisciplinary History* (Princeton, N.J.: Princeton University Press, 1981).

Ryan, W., & Pitman, W. *Noah's Flood: New Scientific Discoveries about the Event That Changed History* 1st Touchstone ed. (New York: 2000).

Schrijver, N. *Sovereignty over Natural Resources: Balancing Rights and Duties* (Cambridge: Cambridge University Press, 1997).

Shafer, S., & Murphy, A. B. "The Territorial Strategies of International Governmental Organizations: Implications for Environment and Development." Global Governance 4 (1998): 257–274.

Simmons, I. G. "Humanity's Resources." In I. Douglas, R. Huggett, & M. Robinson, eds., *The Companion Encyclopedia of Geography: The Environment and Humankind* (New York: Routledge, 1996).

Stahle, D. W. et al. "The Jamestown and Lost Colony Droughts" *Science* 280 (1998): 564–567.

Stevens, W, K. *The Change in the Weather: People, Weather, and the Science of Climate* (New York: Dell Pub., 2001).

Thomas, W. L., Sauer, C. O., Bates, M. & Mumford, L., *Man's Role in Changing the Face of the Earth* (Chicago: University of Chicago Press, 1956).

Tuan, Y.-F. *Topophilia: A Study of Environmental Perception, Attitudes, and Values* (Englewood Cliffs, N.J.: Prentice-Hall, 1974).

Turekian, T. K. *Global Environmental Change: Past, Present, and Future* (Upper Saddle River, NJ: Prentice Hall, 1996).

Turner, B. L., II, Clarke, W. C., Kates, R. W., Richards, J. F., Mathews, J. T., & Meyer, W. B., eds. *The Earth as Transformed by Human Action: Global and Regional Changes in the Biosphere over the Past 300 Years* (Cambridge: Cambridge University Press with Clark University, 1990).

United Nations. *World Population Prospects: The 2000 Revisions* (New York: United Nations, 2001).

World Bank. *Natural Resource Management Strategy: Eastern Europe and Central Asia* (Washington, D.C.: World Bank, 2000).

World Bank. *World Development Report* (New York: Oxford University Press, Annual).

Young, O. R. *International Governance: Protecting the Environment in a Stateless Society* (Ithaca, N.Y.: Cornell University Press, 1994).

Young, O. R., ed. *Global Governance: Drawing Insights from the Environmental Experience* (Cambridge, Mass.: MIT Press, 1997).

Zebrowski, E. *Perils of a Restless Planet: Scientific Perspectives on Natural Disasters* (Cambridge; Cambridge University Press, 1997).

Resource A

Maps

The geographer's greatest ally is the map. Maps can present enormous amounts of information very effectively, and can be used to establish theories and solve problems. Furthermore, maps often are simply fascinating, revealing things no other medium can. It has been said that if a picture is worth a thousand words, then a map is worth a million.

Maps can be fascinating, but they often do not get the attention they deserve. You may spend 20 minutes carefully reading a page of text, but how often have you spent 20 minutes with a page-size map, studying what it reveals? No caption and no paragraph of text can begin to summarize what a map may show; it is up to the reader to make the best use of it. For example, in the chapters on population issues we study several maps that depict the human condition by country, in terms of birth and death rates, infant mortality, calorie intake, life expectancy, and so on. In the text, we can refer only to highlights (and low points) on those maps. But make a point of looking beyond the main issue to get a sense of the global distributions these maps represent. It is part of an intangible but important process: to enhance your mental map of this world.

While on the topic of maps, we should remind ourselves that a map—any map—is an incomplete representation of reality. In the first place, the map is smaller than the real world it represents. Second, it must depict the curved surface of our world on a flat plane, for example, a page of this book. And third, it must contain symbols to convey the information that must be transmitted to the reader. These are the three fundamental properties of all maps: scale, projection, and symbols.

Understanding these basics helps us interpret maps while avoiding their pitfalls. Some maps look so convincing that we may not question them as we would a paragraph of text. Yet maps, by their very nature, to some extent distort reality. Most of the time, such distortion is necessary and does not invalidate the map's message. But some maps are drawn deliberately to mislead. Propaganda maps, for example, may exaggerate or distort reality to promote political aims. We should be alert to cartographic mistakes when we read maps. The proper use of scale, projection, and symbolization ensures that a map is as accurate as it can be made.

◆ MAP SCALE

The *scale* of a map reveals how much the real world has been reduced to fit on the page or screen on which it appears. It is the ratio between an actual distance on the ground and the length given to that distance on the map, using the same units of measurement. This ratio is often represented as a fraction (e.g., 1:10,000 or 1/10,000). This means that one unit on the map represents 10,000 such units in the real world. If the unit is 1 inch, then an inch on the map represents 10,000 inches on the ground, or slightly more than 833 feet. (The metric system certainly makes things easier. One centimeter on the map would actually represent 10,000 cm or 100 meters.) Such a scale would be useful when mapping a city's downtown area, but it would be much too large for the map of an entire state. As the real-world area we want to map gets larger, we must make our map scale smaller. As small as the fraction 1/10,000 seems, it still is 10 times as large as 1/100,000, and 100 times as large as 1/1,000,000. If the world maps in this book had fractional scales, they would be even smaller. A large-scale map can contain much more detail and be far more representative of the real world than a small-scale map. Look at it this way: when we devote almost a full page of this book to a map of a major city (Fig. R-1), we are able to represent the layout of that city in considerable detail. But if the entire continental realm in which that city is located must be represented on a single page, the city becomes just a large dot on that small-scale map, and the detail is lost in favor of larger-area coverage (Fig. R-2). So the selection of scale depends on the objective of the map.

But when you examine the maps in this book, you will note that most, if not all, of them have scales that are not given as ratios or fractions, but in graphic form. This method of representing map scale is convenient from several viewpoints. Using the edge of a piece of paper and marking the scale bar's length, the map reader can quickly—without calculation—determine approximate distances. And if a map is enlarged or reduced in reproduction, the scale bar is enlarged or reduced with it and remains accurate. That, of course, is not true of a ratio or fractional scale. Graphic scales, therefore, are preferred in this book.

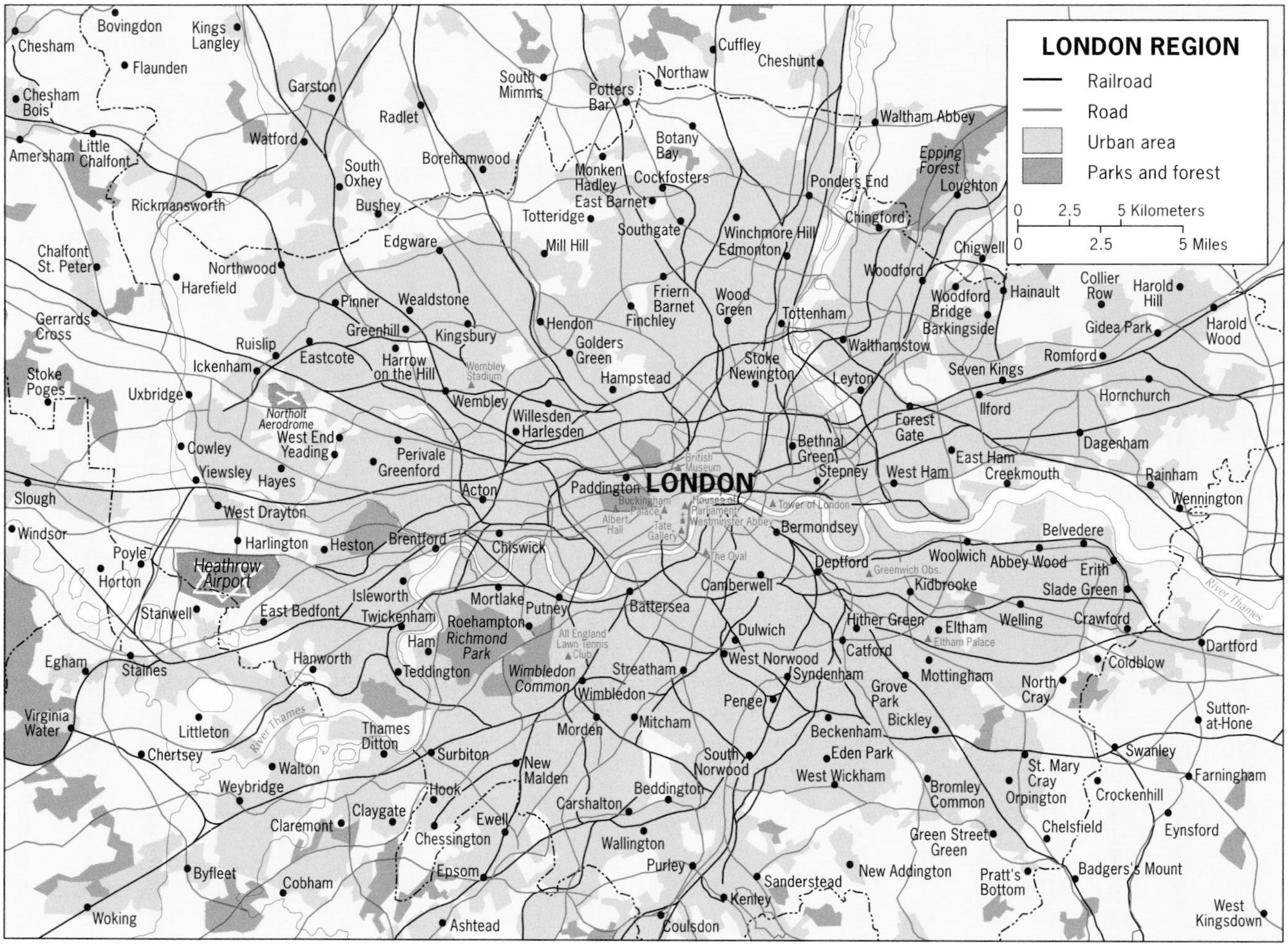

Figure R-1 The layout of a major city can be shown in considerable detail at this **large scale.**

◆ MAP PROJECTIONS

For centuries cartographers have faced the challenge of map projection—the representation of the spherical Earth, or part of it, on a flat surface. To get the job done, there had to be a frame of reference on the globe itself, a grid system that could be transferred to the flat page. Any modern globe shows that system: a set of horizontal lines, usually at 10-degree intervals north and south from the equator, called *parallels*, and another set of vertical lines, converging on the poles, often shown at 15-degree intervals and called *meridians* (see box, "Numbering the Grid Lines"). On the spherical globe, parallels and meridians intersect at right angles (Fig. R-3).

But what happens when these lines of latitude (parallels) and longitude (meridians) are drawn to intersect at right angles on a flat piece of paper? At the equator, the representation of the real world is relatively accurate. But go toward the poles, and distortion grows with every degree until, in the northern and southern higher latitudes, the continents appear not only stretched out but also misshaped (Fig. R-4). Because the meridians cannot be made to converge in the polar areas, this projection makes Antarctica look like a giant, globe-girdling landmass.

Looking at this representation of the world, you might believe that it could serve no useful purpose. But in fact, the *Mercator* projection, invented in 1569 by Gerardus Mercator, the Flemish cartographer, had (and has) a very particular function. Because parallels and meridians cross (as they do on the spherical globe's grid) at right angles, direction is true everywhere on this map. Thus the Mercator projection enabled navigators to maintain an accurate course at sea simply by adhering to compass directions and plotting straight lines. It is used for that purpose to this day.

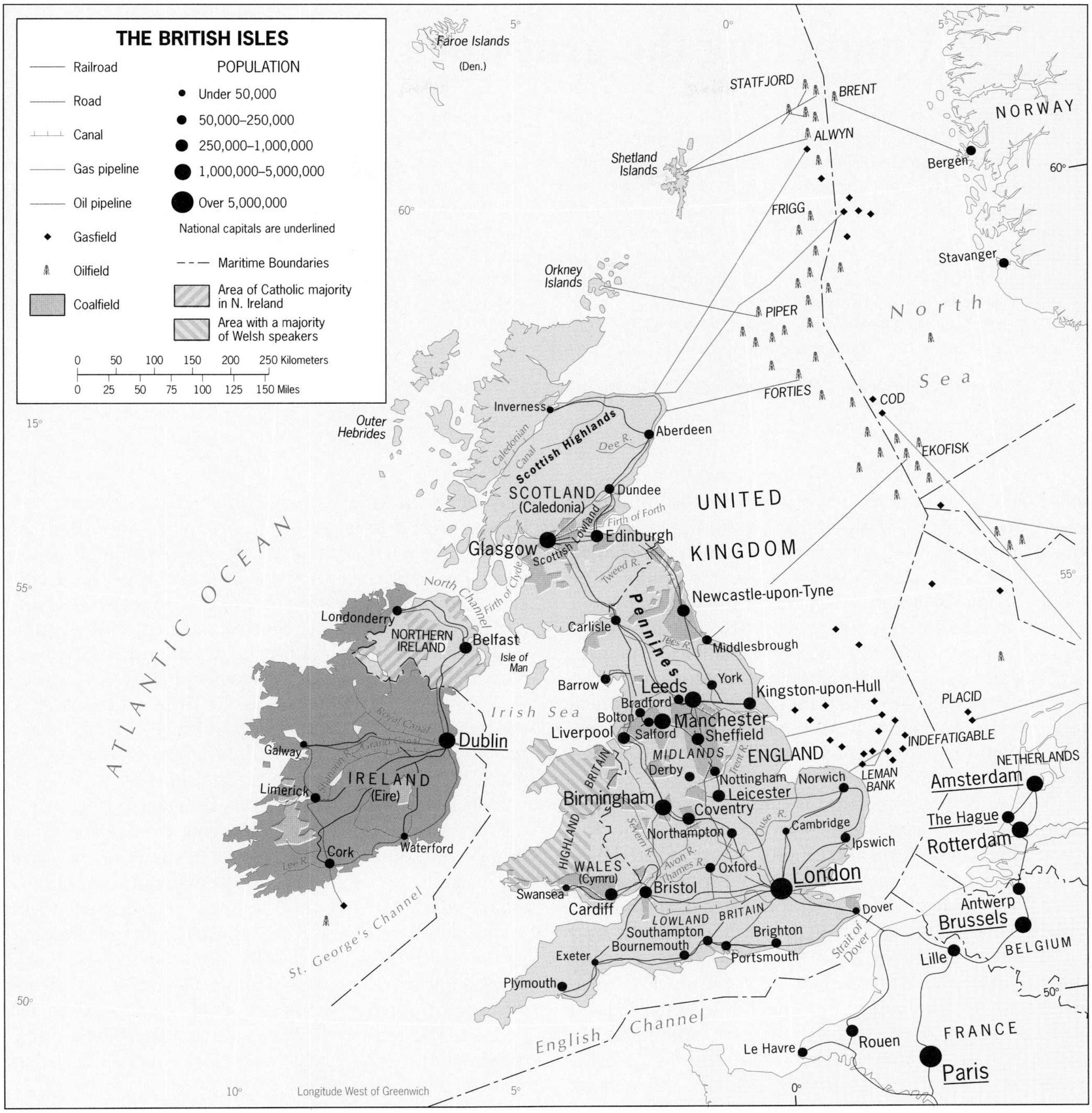

Figure R-2 Smaller scale allows display of larger area, but with less local detail.

The spatial distortion of the Mercator projection serves to remind us that scale and projection are interconnected. What scale fraction or graphic scale bar could be used here? A scale that would be accurate at the equator on a Mercator map would be quite inaccurate at higher latitudes. So the distortion that is an inevitable byproduct of any map projection also affects map scales.

One might imagine that the spatial (areal) distortion of the Mercator projection is so obvious that no one would use it to represent the world's countries. But in fact, many popular atlas maps (Mercator also introduced the term *atlas* to describe a collection of maps) and wall maps still use a Mercator for such purposes. The National Geographic Society published its world maps on a Mercator projection until 1988, when it finally

Numbering the grid lines

When cartographers girdled the globe with their imaginary grid lines, they had to identify each line by number, that is, by *degree.* For the (horizontal) latitude lines, that was easy: the equator, which bisects the Earth midway between the poles, was designated as 0° (zero degree) Latitude, and all parallels north and south of the equator were designated by their angular position (Fig. R-3). The parallel midway between the equator and the pole, thus, is 45° North Latitude in the Northern Hemisphere and 45° South Latitude in the Southern Hemisphere.

But the (vertical) longitude lines presented no such easy solution. Among the parallels, the equator is the only one to divide the Earth into equal halves, but *all* meridians do this. During the second half of the nineteenth century, maps with conflicting numbers multiplied, and it was clear that a solution was needed. The most powerful country at the time was Britain, and in 1884, international agreement was reached whereby the meridian drawn through the Royal Observatory in Greenwich, England, would be the *prime meridian,* 0° (zero degree) Longitude. All meridians east and west of the prime meridian could now be designated by number, from 0° to 180° East and West Longitude.

abandoned the practice in favor of a projection developed by the American cartographer Arthur Robinson (Fig. R-5). During the news conference at which the change was announced, a questioner rose to pursue a point: Why had the Society waited so long to make this change? Was it because the distortion inherent in the Mercator projection made American and European middle-latitude countries large, compared to tropical countries in Africa and elsewhere? Of course there was no such intent, but that questioner obviously understood the misleading subtleties inherent even in so apparently neutral a device as a map projection.

The Mercator projection is one of a group of projections called *cylindrical* projections. Imagine the globe's lines of latitude and longitude represented by a wire grid, at the center of which we place a bright light. Wrap a piece of photographic paper around the wire grid, extending it well beyond the north and south poles, flash the bulb, and the photographic image will be that of a Mercator projection (Fig. R-6). We could do the same after placing a cone-shaped piece of paper over each hemisphere, touching the grid, say, at the 40th parallel north and south; the result would be a *conic* projection (Fig. R-7). If we wanted a map of North America or Europe, a form of conic projection would be appropriate. Now the meridians do approach each other toward the poles (unlike the Mercator projection), and there is much less shape and size distortion. And if we needed a map of Arctic and Antarctic regions, we would place the photographic paper as a flat sheet against the North and South Poles. Now the photographic image would show a set of diverging lines, as the meridians do from each pole, and the parallels would appear as circles (Fig. R-8). Such a *planar* projection is a good choice for a map of the Arctic Ocean or the Antarctic continent.

Projections are chosen for various purposes. Just as the Mercator is appropriate for navigation because direction is true, other projections are designed to preserve areal size, keep distances real, or maintain the outlines (shapes) of landmasses and countries. Projections can be manipulated for many needs. In this book, we examine global distributions of various phenomena. The world map that forms the base for these displays is one that is designed to give prominence to land areas at the expense of the oceans. This is achieved by "interrupting" the projection where loss of territory (in this case water area) is not problematic.

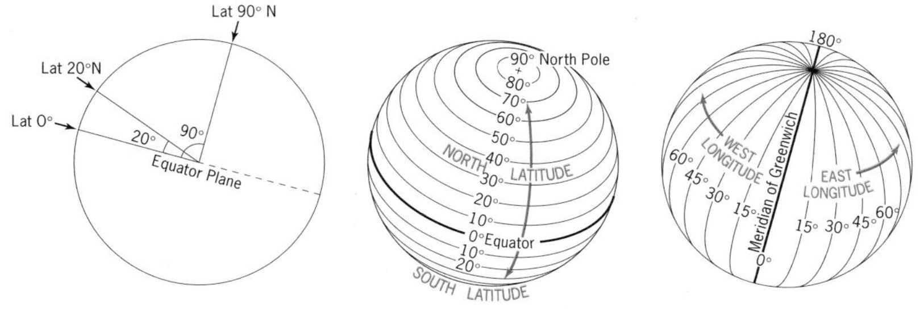

Figure R-3 Numbering of **grid lines.**

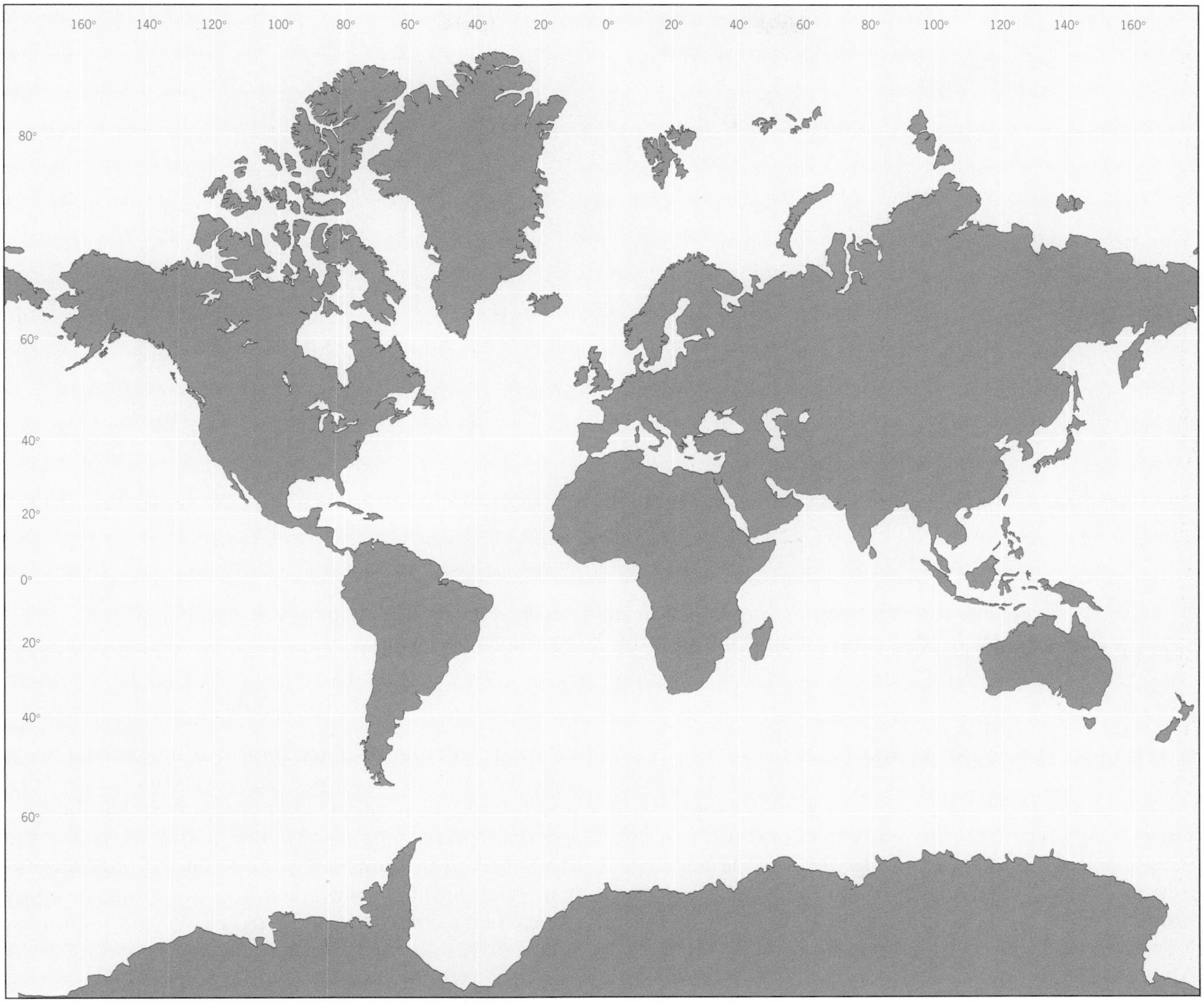

Figure R-4 Mercator's Projection greatly exaggerates the dimensions of higher-latitude landmasses, but direction is true everywhere on this map.

When a map is planned, therefore, the choice of projection is an important part of the process. Sometimes, an inappropriate selection weakens the effectiveness of a map and may even lead to erroneous interpretations. Of course, the problem diminishes when the area to be mapped is smaller and the scale larger. We may consider various alternatives when it comes to a map of all of North America, but a map of a single State presents far fewer potential problems of distortion. And for a city map—even of a large city such as Chicago—the projection problem virtually disappears.

The old problem of how to represent the round Earth on a flat surface has been attacked for centuries, and there is no single best solution. What has been learned in the process, however, will be useful in fields of endeavor other than Earthly geography. As the age of planetary exploration dawns, and our space probes send back images of the surfaces of the Moon, Mars, Jupiter, and other components of our solar system, we will have to agree once again on grids, equators, and prime meridians. What has been learned in our efforts to map and represent the Earth will be useful in depicting the universe beyond.

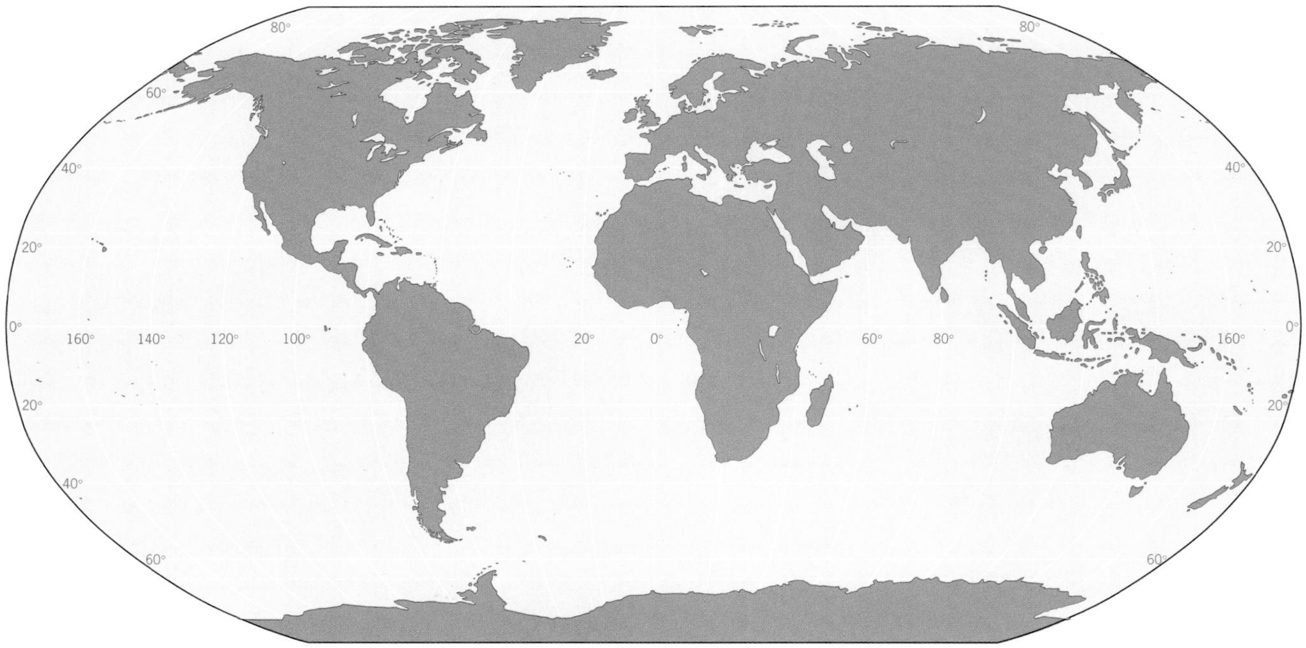

Figure R-5 The Robinson projection substantially reduces the latitudinal size magnification. It better approximates dimension, but it lacks directional utility.

◆ SYMBOLS ON MAPS

The third fundamental property of a map is its symbolization. Maps represent the real world, and this can be done only through the use of symbols. Anyone who has used an atlas map is familiar with some of these symbols: prominent dots (perhaps black or red) for cities; a large dot with a circle around it, or a star, for capitals; red lines for roads (double lines for four-lane highways), black lines for railroads; and patterns or colors for areas of water, forest, or farmland. Notice that these symbols respectively represent points, lines, and areas on the ground. For our purposes, we need not go further into map symbolization, which can become a very complex topic when it comes to highly specialized cartography in such fields as geology and meteorology. Nevertheless, it

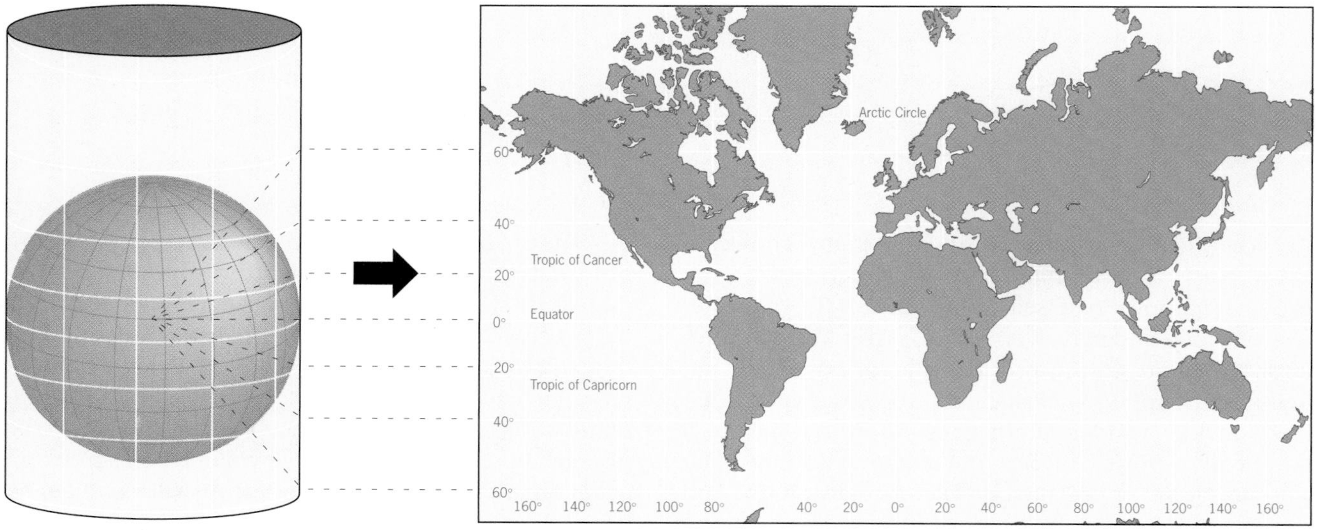

Figure R-6 Shadows of the globe's grid lines on wraparound paper: a **cylindrical projection** results.

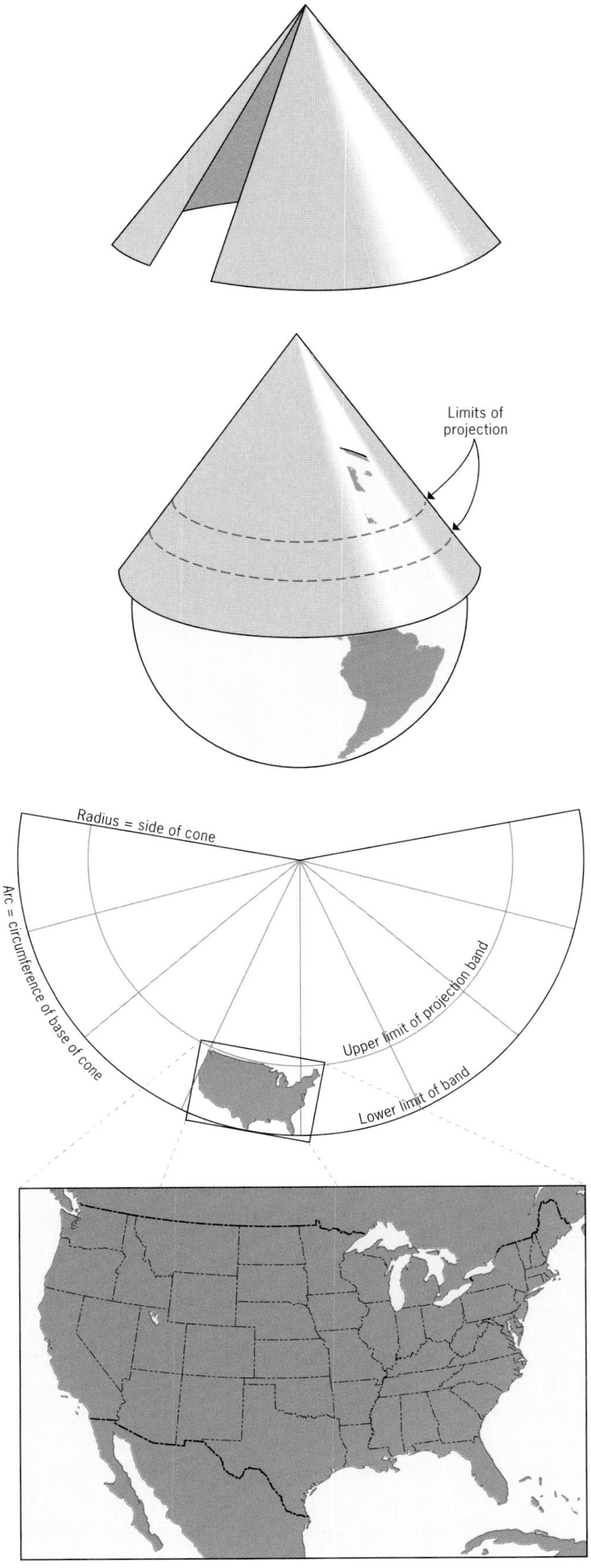

Figure R-7 Construction of a **conic projection.**

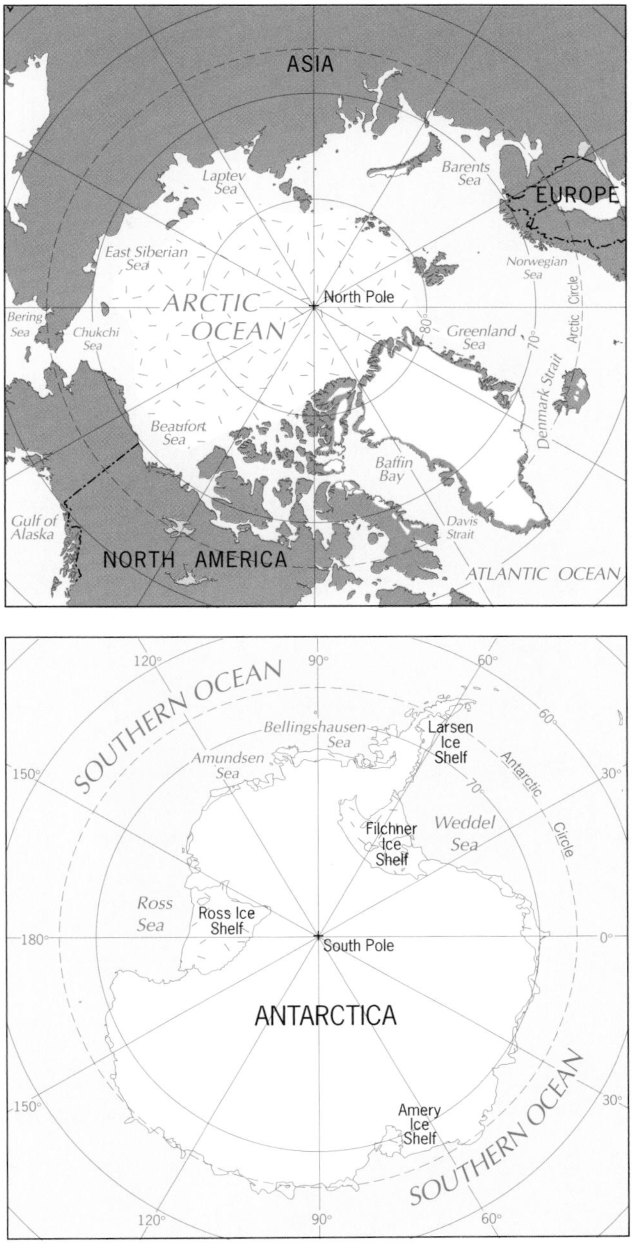

Figure R-8 Planar projection: now the light a the center of the globe projects diverging longitude lines on a flat sheet of paper placed over the North Pole (top) and the South Pole (bottom).

is useful to know why symbols such as those used on the maps in this book were chosen.

Point symbols, as we noted, are used to show individual features or places. On a large-scale map of a city block, dots can represent individual houses. But on a small-scale map, a dot has to represent an entire "city." Still, cities have various sizes, and those size differences can be put in categories and mapped accordingly (Fig. R-9). Thus New York, Chicago, and Los Angeles still

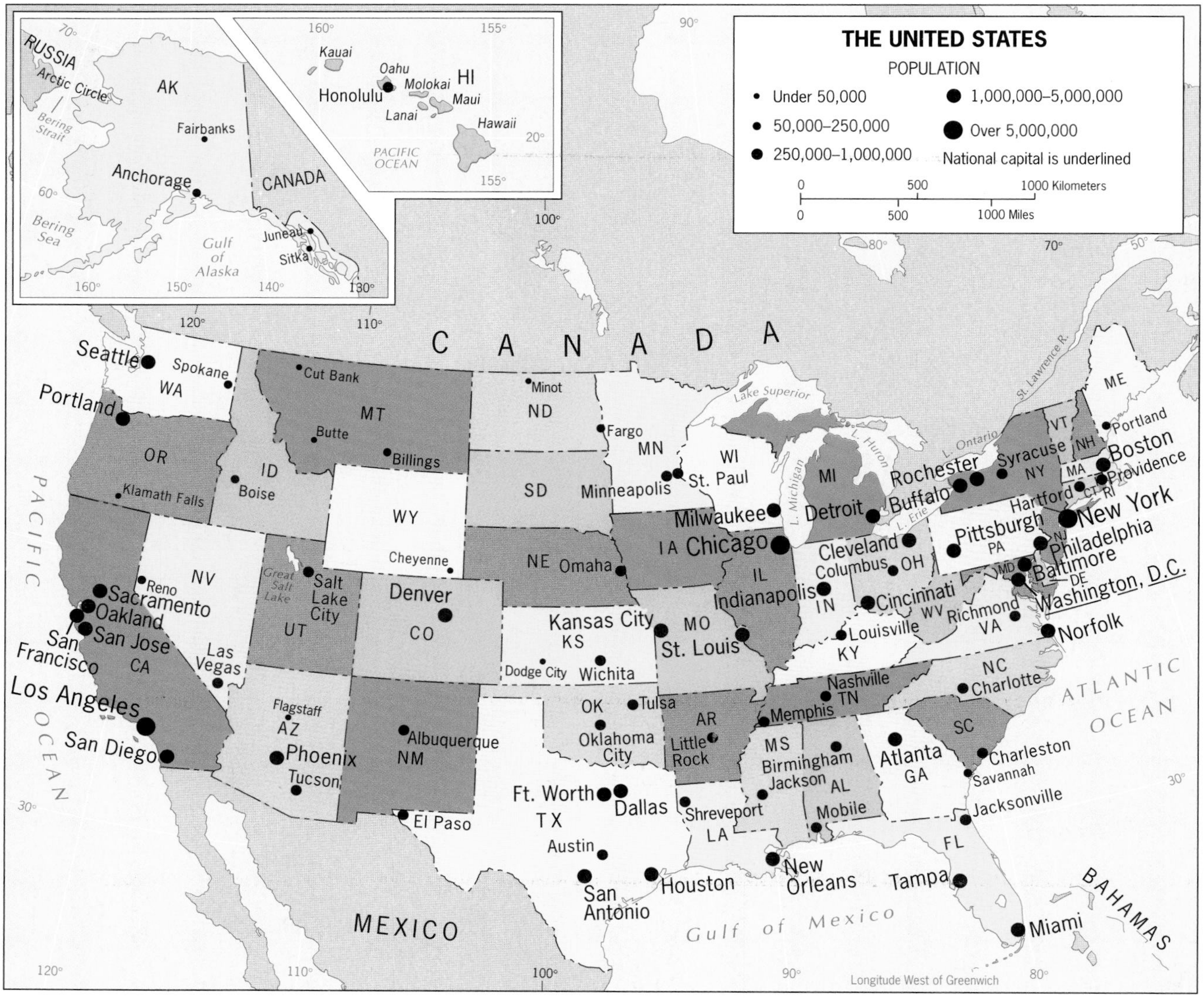

Figure R-9 This map uses **dot symbols** to indicate size categories of cities in the United States.

appear as dots on the map, but their dots are larger than those representing Tucson, Milwaukee, or Denver. A dimensional scale is added to the map's graphic scale, and at a glance we can see the relative sizes of major cities in the United States and Canada.

Line symbols include not only roads and railroads, but also political and administrative boundaries, rivers, and other linear features. Again scale plays its crucial role: on a large-scale map, it is possible to represent the fenced boundaries of a single farm, but on a small-scale map, such detail cannot be shown.

Some lines on maps do not actually exist on the ground. When physical geographers do their field work they use *contour* maps, lines that represent a certain consistent height above mean sea level (Fig. R-10). All points on such a contour line thus are at the same elevation. The spacing between contour lines immediately reveals the nature of the local topography (the natural land surface). When the contour lines at a given interval (e.g., 100 feet) are spaced closely together, the slope of the ground is steep. When they are widely separated, the land surface slopes gently. Of course contour lines cannot be found in the real world, and neither can the lines drawn on the weather maps in our daily newspaper. These lines connect points of equal pressure (isobars) and temperature (isotherms) and show the development of weather systems. Note that the letters iso (meaning "the same") appear in these terms. Invisible lines of this kind are collectively known as **isolines**, lines of equal or constant value. These are abstract con-

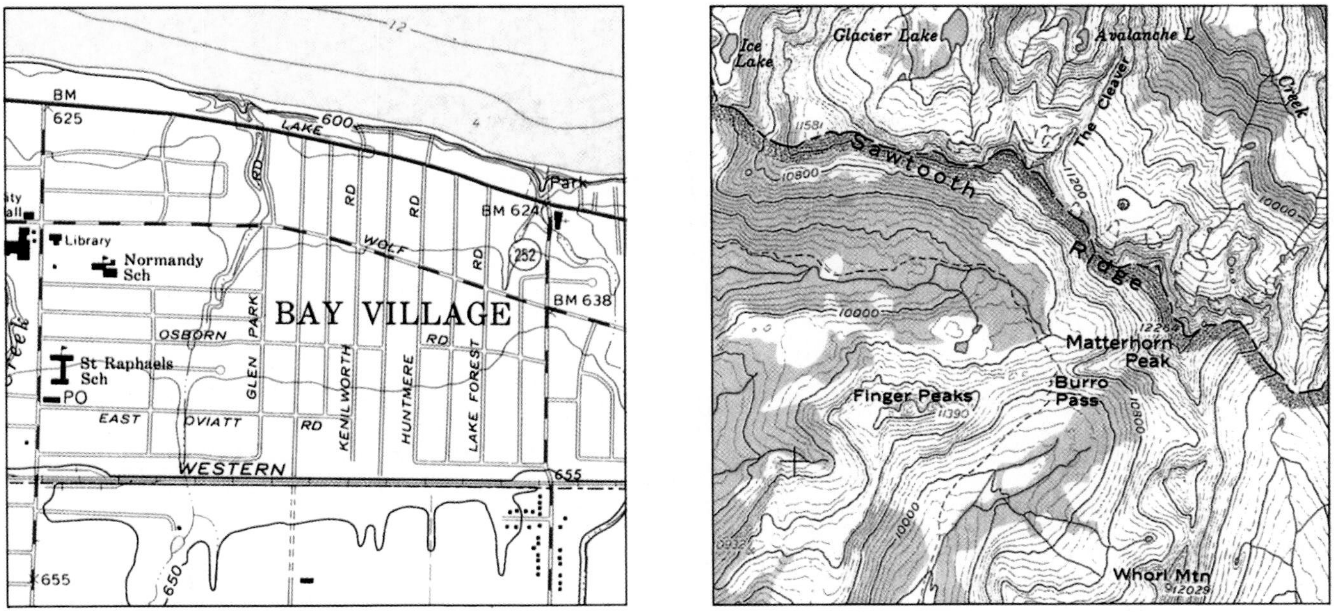

Figure R-10 Contour lines reflecting low relief (left) and high relief (right). The map at left is part of the U.S.G.S. North Olmstead Quadrangle, Ohio; the map at right is part of the U.S.G.S. Matterhorn Peak Quadrangle, California.

structions, but they can be of great value in geographic research and representation.

Area symbols take many forms, and we will see some of them on the maps in this book. Area symbols are used in various ways to represent distributions and magnitudes. Maps showing distributions (of such phenomena as regionally dominant languages or religions in human geography, and climates or soils in physical geography) show the world, or parts of it, divided into areas shaded or colored in contrasting hues. But be careful: those sharp dividing lines are likely to be transition zones in the real world, and a dominant language or religion does not imply the exclusion of all others. So distribution maps, and there are many in this book, tend to be small-scale generalizations of much more complex patterns than they can reveal. Again, maps showing magnitudes also must be read with care. Here the objective is to reveal *how much* of a phenomenon prevails in one unit (e.g., country) on the map, compared to others. The maps on population in Part Two are examples of such maps. The important cartographic decision has to do with color (or, in black and white, graytones). Darker should mean more, and lighter implies less. That is relatively easily done when the dominant color is the same. But on a multicolored map, the use of reds, greens, and yellows can be confusing, and first impressions may have to be revised upon examination of the key.

Some students who are first drawn to the discipline of geography go on to become professional cartographers, and their work is seen in atlases, foldout magazine maps, books, and many other venues. Although cartographic technology is changing, the world's great atlases and maps still are designed and produced by researchers, compilers, draughtspeople, and other specialists.

Area and Demographic Data for the World's States

	Land Area 1000 (sq mi)	Population 2002 (Millions)	Population 2010 (Millions)	Population Density Arithmetic	Physiologic	Birth Rate	Death Rate	Natural Increase	Doubling Time (years)	Infant Mortality per 1,000 (births)	Life Expectancy Males (years)	Females (years)	Percent Urban Pop	Per Capita GNP ($US)
WORLD	**51510.8**	**6238.1**	**6866.8**	**117.0**		**22**	**9**	**1.4%**	**51**	**57**	**64**	**68**	**45**	**$4,890**
Europe	**2197.2**	**582.6**	**580.4**	**265.2**		**10**	**11**	**0.0%**		**7**	**72**	**79**	**73**	**$16,518**
Albania	10.6	3.5	3.9	329.1	1,567.4	18	5	1.3%	55	22	69	74	46	$810
Austria	31.9	8.1	8.1	253.9	1,493.6	10	10	0.0%		5	75	81	65	$26,830
Belarus	80.1	9.9	9.7	123.6	426.2	9	14	−0.5%		11	63	74	70	$2,180
Belgium	11.8	10.2	10.3	866.1	3,608.9	11	10	0.1%	770	6	75	81	97	$25,380
Bosnia	19.7	3.8	4.0	194.8	1,391.6	13	8	0.5%	141	12	71	76	40	
Bulgaria	42.7	8.1	7.5	189.7	512.8	8	14	−0.6%		14	67	74	68	$1,220
Croatia	21.6	4.6	4.5	212.5	1,012.1	11	12	−0.1%		8	69	76	54	$4,620
Cyprus	3.6	0.9	0.9	253.0	2,108.4	14	8	0.6%	124	8	74	79	64	$11,920
Czech Rep.	29.8	10.3	10.2	344.3	839.6	9	11	−0.2%		5	71	78	77	$5,150
Denmark	16.4	5.3	5.5	323.8	539.7	12	11	0.1%	472	5	74	79	85	$33,040
Estonia	16.3	1.4	1.4	85.0	386.5	8	13	−0.5%		9	64	75	69	$3,360
Finland	117.6	5.2	5.2	44.3	553.8	11	10	0.1%	433	4	74	81	60	$24,280
France	212.4	59.9	61.6	281.9	854.3	13	9	0.4%	204	5	75	82	74	$24,210
Germany	134.9	81.9	81.2	607.4	1,840.6	9	10	−0.1%		5	74	80	86	$26,570
Greece	49.8	10.6	10.5	212.9	1,120.3	10	10	0.0%		7	75	81	59	$11,740
Hungary	35.7	9.9	9.6	277.3	543.8	9	14	−0.5%		9	66	75	64	$4,510
Iceland	38.7	0.3	0.3	7.9		15	7	0.8%	81	3	77	82	92	$27,830
Ireland	26.6	3.8	4.1	144.6	1,112.1	15	9	0.6%	116	6	73	79	58	$27,135
Italy	113.5	57.7	55.6	508.2	1,639.5	9	10	−0.1%		6	75	81	90	$20,090
Latvia	24.0	2.4	2.3	98.8	365.9	8	14	−0.6%		11	64	76	69	$2,420
Liechtenstein	0.1	0.1	0.1	507.0		14	7	0.7%	105	18	67	78		
Lithuania	25.0	3.7	3.6	147.7	301.4	10	11	−0.1%		9	67	77	68	$2,540
Luxembourg	1.0	0.4	0.5	403.2	1,680.0	13	9	0.4%	198	5	74	80	88	$45,100
Macedonia	9.8	2.0	2.1	206.9	4,139.0	15	8	0.7%	112	16	70	75	59	$1,290
Malta	0.1	0.4	0.4	3,360.1		12	8	0.4%	182	5	74	80	89	$10,100
Moldova	12.7	4.3	4.4	338.6	638.8	11	11	0.0%		18	63	70	46	$380
Netherlands	13.1	16.0	16.5	1,223.5	4,531.4	13	9	0.4%	193	5	75	81	61	$24,780
Norway	118.5	4.5	4.7	38.2	1,273.4	13	10	0.3%	217	4	76	81	74	$34,310
Poland	117.5	38.6	38.6	328.5	699.0	10	10	0.0%		9	69	78	62	$3,910
Portugal	35.5	10.0	9.7	281.7	1,083.4	11	11	0.0%		5	72	79	48	$10,670
Romania	88.9	22.4	21.7	251.5	613.3	11	12	−0.1%		21	66	73	55	$1,360

	Land Area 1000 (sq mi)	Population 2002 (Millions)	Population 2010 (Millions)	Population Density Arithmetic	Physiologic	Birth Rate	Death Rate	Natural Increase	Doubling Time (years)	Infant Mortality per 1,000 (births)	Males (years)	Females (years)	Percent Urban Pop	Per Capita GNP ($US)
Slovenia	7.8	2.0	2.0	255.9	2,132.5	9	10	−0.1%		5	71	79	50	$9,780
Spain	192.8	39.5	38.4	204.9	682.9	9	9	0.0%		6	74	82	64	$14,100
Sweden	158.9	8.9	9.0	55.9	798.5	10	11	−0.1%		4	77	82	84	$25,580
Switzerland	15.3	7.1	7.3	465.9	4,659.1	11	9	0.2%	315	5	77	83	68	$39,980
Ukraine	223.7	48.9	47.4	218.6	377.0	8	14	−0.6%		13	63	74	68	$980
United Kingdom	93.3	59.9	61.6	642.2	2,568.9	12	11	0.1%	546	6	74	80	89	$21,410
Yugoslavia	26.9	10.7	10.7	397.8	1,325.9	11	11	0.0%		10	70	75	52	
Russia	**6550.7**	**143.2**	**135.7**	**21.9**	**273.2**	**8**	**15**	**−0.7%**		**17**	**61**	**73**	**73**	**$2,260**
Armenia	10.9	3.8	3.9	351.4	2,067.2	10	6	0.4%	161	15	71	78	67	$460
Azerbaijan	33.4	7.8	8.6	234.7	1,303.9	15	6	0.9%	77	17	68	75	52	$480
Georgia	26.9	5.5	5.2	204.9	2,276.3	9	8	0.1%	462	15	69	76	56	$970
North America	**7567.5**	**316.4**	**342.6**	**41.8**		**14**	**9**	**0.5%**	**124**	**7**	**74**	**80**	**75**	**$28,230**
Canada	3849.7	31.0	33.0	8.1	174.4	11	7	0.4%	178	6	76	81	78	$19,170
United States	3717.8	285.4	309.6	76.8	415.1	15	9	0.6%	120	7	74	79	75	$29,240
Middle America	**1021.9**	**179.4**	**202.5**	**175.6**		**25.2**	**6**	**2.0%**	**35**	**37**	**72**	**73**	**66**	
Antigua and Barbuda	0.2	0.1	0.1	607.2	3,373.4	22	6	1.6%	45	17	69	74	37	$8,450
Bahamas	3.9	0.3	0.3	79.4	7,940.4	21	5	1.6%	45	18	70	77	84	
Barbados	0.2	0.3	0.3	1,782.4	4,817.3	14	9	0.5%	130	14	72	77	38	
Belize	8.8	0.3	0.3	36.0	1,797.8	32	5	2.7%	26	34	70	74	50	$2,660
Costa Rica	19.7	3.7	4.6	189.4	3,156.3	22	4	1.8%	39	13	75	79	45	$2,770
Cuba	42.8	11.3	11.4	265.5	1,106.1	14	7	0.7%	103	7	73	78	75	
Dominica	0.3	0.1	0.1	350.4	3,893.0	16	8	0.8%	83	15	75	80		$3,150
Dominican Rep.	18.7	8.8	10.1	469.2	2,234.2	28	6	2.2%	32	47	67	71	62	$1,770
El Salvador	8.0	6.6	7.9	824.1	3,052.4	30	7	2.3%	29	35	67	73	58	$1,850
Grenada	0.1	0.1	0.1	805.0	5,366.8	29	6	2.3%	30	14	68	73	34	$3,250
Guadeloupe	0.7	0.4	0.4	629.0	4,492.8	17	6	1.1%	61	10	73	80	48	
Guatemala	41.9	13.5	17.0	321.6	2,679.7	37	7	2.9%	24	45	61	67	39	$1,640
Haiti	10.6	6.6	7.8	624.5	3,122.4	33	16	1.7%	40	103	47	51	34	$410
Honduras	43.2	6.4	7.3	148.9	992.9	33	6	2.7%	25	42	66	71	45	$740
Jamaica	4.2	2.7	2.9	637.8	4,555.4	22	7	1.5%	45	24	70	73	50	$1,740
Martinique	0.4	0.4	0.4	993.2	12,415.6	15	6	0.9%	81	9	75	82	81	
Mexico	737.0	103.6	115.2	140.6	1,171.7	24	4	2.0%	36	32	69	75	74	$3,840
Netherlands Antilles	0.3	0.2	0.2	659.4	6,594.3	17	6	1.1%	62	14	72	78		
Nicaragua	46.9	5.4	6.7	115.4	1,281.8	36	6	3.0%	23	40	66	71	63	$370
Panama	28.7	3.0	3.3	104.5	1,493.0	22	5	1.7%	41	21	72	77	56	$2,990
Puerto Rico	3.4	4.0	4.1	1,167.8	29,195.0	17	8	0.9%	75	11	70	79	71	
Saint Lucia	0.2	0.2	0.3	855.1	10,689.3	19	6	1.3%	56	17	71	72	48	$3,660
St. Vincent and the Grenadines	0.2	0.1	0.1	682.8	1,796.7	19	7	1.2%	59	20	71	74	44	$2,560
Trinidad and Tobago	2.0	1.3	1.4	659.1	4,394.2	14	7	0.7%	103	16	68	73	72	$4,520

	Land Area 1000 (sq mi)	Population 2002 (Millions)	Population 2010 (Millions)	Population Density Arithmetic	Physiologic	Birth Rate	Death Rate	Natural Increase	Doubling Time (years)	Infant Mortality per 1,000 (births)	Males (years)	Females (years)	Percent Urban Pop	Per Capita GNP ($US)
South America	**6763.3**	**356.8**	**400.1**	**52.8**		**23**	**6**	**1.7%**	**41**	**34**	**66**	**73**	**78**	**$4,270**
Argentina	1056.6	37.8	41.6	35.8	397.7	19	8	1.1%	62	19	70	77	90	$8,030
Bolivia	418.7	8.6	10.0	20.6	1,031.2	30	10	2.0%	34	67	59	62	62	$1,010
Brazil	3265.1	175.2	193.6	53.7	1,073.4	21	6	1.5%	45	38	64	71	78	$4,630
Chile	289.1	15.6	17.2	54.0	1,079.1	18	5	1.3%	54	11	72	78	85	$4,990
Colombia	401.0	41.6	48.3	103.8	2,594.5	26	6	2.0%	34	28	65	73	71	$2,470
Ecuador	106.9	13.1	15.0	122.9	2,047.8	27	6	2.1%	33	40	67	72	63	$1,520
French Guiana	34.0	0.2	0.3	6.2	616.8	27	3	2.4%	29	18	71	77	79	
Guyana	76.0	0.7	0.8	9.5	476.3	24	7	1.7%	40	63	63	69	36	$780
Paraguay	153.4	5.8	7.2	37.7	629.0	32	6	2.6%	26	27	68	72	52	$1,760
Peru	494.2	28.3	32.6	57.2	1,905.4	27	6	2.1%	32	43	66	71	72	$2,440
Suriname	60.2	0.4	0.4	6.9	689.9	26	7	1.9%	37	29	68	73	69	$1,660
Uruguay	67.5	3.3	3.6	49.5	618.5	16	10	0.6%	107	15	70	78	92	$6,070
Venezuela	340.6	25.2	29.0	73.9	1,848.0	25	5	2.0%	34	21	70	76	86	$3,530
North Africa/ Southwest Asia	**7655.8**	**526.6**	**620.5**	**52.3**		**28**	**8**	**2.0%**	**35**	**52**	**63**	**69**	**54**	
Afghanistan	251.8	28.1	36.0	111.4	928.4	43	18	2.5%	28	150	46	45	20	
Algeria	919.6	33.0	38.4	35.8	1,194.9	29	6	2.3%	29	44	68	70	49	$1,550
Bahrain	0.3	0.7	1.1	2,692.0	269,204.7	22	3	1.9%	37	8	68	71	88	$7,640
Djibouti	9.0	0.6	0.8	69.8		39	16	2.3%	30	115	47	50	83	
Egypt	384.3	71.1	81.6	184.9	9,245.3	26	6	2.0%	35	52	64	67	44	$1,290
Eritrea	39.0	4.3	6.0	111.5	929.4	43	13	3.0%	23	82	52	57	16	$200
Iran	631.7	69.4	78.0	109.9	1,099.2	21	6	1.5%	48	31	68	71	63	$1,650
Iraq	168.9	24.4	31.0	144.5	1,204.4	38	10	2.8%	25	127	58	60	68	
Israel	8.0	6.4	7.2	800.0	4,705.9	22	6	1.6%	45	6	76	80	90	$16,180
Jordan	34.3	5.4	6.8	157.1	3,928.3	33	5	2.8%	24	34	68	70	78	$1,150
Kazakhstan	1031.2	15.0	14.9	14.6	121.4	14	10	0.4%	161	21	59	70	63	$1,650
Kuwait	6.9	2.3	2.9	333.0		24	2	2.2%	32	13	72	73	100	
Kyrgyzstan	74.1	5.0	5.3	68.1	973.2	22	7	1.5%	47	26	63	71	34	$380
Lebanon	4.0	4.3	4.8	1,083.9	5,161.3	23	7	1.6%	43	35	68	73	88	$3,560
Libya	679.4	5.4	6.5	7.9	788.7	28	3	2.5%	28	33	73	77	86	
Morocco	172.3	29.8	33.6	172.9	823.2	23	6	1.7%	41	37	67	71	54	$1,240
Oman	82.0	2.6	3.6	31.5		43	5	3.8%	18	25	69	73	72	
Palestinian Territ. (West Bank/Gaza)	2.4	3.3	5.0	1.4		41	5	3.6%	19	27	70	73		$1,560
Qatar	4.3	0.6	0.7	144.6	14,460.3	20	2	1.8%	38	20	70	75	91	
Saudi Arabia	830.0	22.9	29.7	27.6	1,380.4	35	5	3.0%	23	46	68	71	83	$6,910
Somalia	242.2	7.7	10.6	31.9	1,595.7	47	18	2.9%	24	126	45	48	24	
Sudan	917.4	30.8	37.0	33.5	670.4	33	12	2.1%	32	70	50	52	27	$290
Syria	71.0	17.4	21.2	245.1	875.4	33	6	2.7%	25	35	67	68	51	$1,020
Tajikistan	54.3	6.6	7.3	121.7	2,027.8	21	5	1.6%	43	28	66	71	27	$370
Tunisia	60.0	9.9	11.1	164.8	867.6	22	7	1.5%	44	35	67	70	61	$2,060

	Land Area 1000 (sq mi)	Population 2002 (Millions)	Population 2010 (Millions)	Population Density Arithmetic	Population Density Physiologic	Birth Rate	Death Rate	Natural Increase	Doubling Time (years)	Infant Mortality per 1,000 (births)	Males (years)	Females (years)	Percent Urban Pop	Per Capita GNP ($US)
Turkey	297.2	67.3	75.6	226.4	707.4	22	7	1.5%	46	38	67	71	66	$3,160
Turkmenistan	181.4	5.4	5.9	29.5	984.4	21	6	1.5%	48	33	62	69	44	
United Arab Emirates	32.3	2.9	3.3	90.5		24	2	2.2%	32	16	73	76	84	$17,870
Uzbekistan	159.9	25.7	28.0	160.4	1,782.4	23	6	1.7%	40	22	66	72	38	$950
Western Sahara	102.7	0.3	0.4	3.1		46	18	2.8%	24	150	46	48		
Yemen	203.9	18.0	26.2	88.1	2,937.0	39	11	2.8%	25	75	58	61	26	$280
Subsaharan Africa	**7916.3**	**646.8**	**781.0**	**81.7**		**41**	**16**	**2.6%**	**27**	**93**	**48**	**50**	**29**	**$522**
Angola	481.4	13.7	18.2	28.4	1,418.7	48	19	2.9%	23	125	45	48	32	$380
Benin	42.7	6.8	8.7	158.4	1,218.4	45	17	2.8%	24	94	49	51	38	$380
Botswana	218.8	1.6	1.5	7.5	753.4	32	17	1.5%	45	57	38	40	49	$3,070
Burkina Faso	105.6	12.6	16.2	119.3	917.8	47	18	2.9%	24	105	47	47	15	$240
Burundi	9.9	6.4	8.0	646.0	1,468.3	42	17	2.5%	28	75	46	47	8	$140
Cameroon	179.7	16.2	19.6	90.0	692.6	37	12	2.5%	27	77	55	56	44	$610
Cape Verde Is.	1.6	0.4	0.5	264.2	2,401.8	37	9	2.8%	25	77	65	72	44	$1,200
Central African Republic	240.5	3.6	4.1	15.1	504.7	38	18	2.0%	34	97	43	46	39	$300
Chad	486.1	8.5	12.0	17.6	585.4	50	17	3.3%	21	110	46	51	22	$230
Comoros Is.	0.9	0.6	0.8	737.3	2,106.5	38	10	2.8%	25	77	57	62	29	$370
Congo	131.9	2.9	3.6	22.3	1,113.0	40	16	2.4%	29	109	45	50	41	$680
Congo, The	875.3	55.4	75.3	63.3	2,109.0	48	16	3.2%	22	109	47	50	29	$110
Equatorial Guinea	10.8	0.5	0.6	48.6	972.8	41	16	2.5%	28	108	48	52	37	$1,110
Ethiopia	386.1	67.2	86.3	174.1	1,450.7	45	21	2.4%	29	116	45	47	15	$100
Gabon	99.5	1.3	1.6	12.6	1,259.7	38	16	2.2%	32	87	51	54	73	$4,170
Gambia	3.9	1.4	1.7	349.5	1,941.8	43	19	2.4%	29	130	43	47	37	$340
Ghana	87.9	20.4	22.9	232.6	1,938.5	34	10	2.4%	29	56	56	59	37	$390
Guinea	94.9	7.9	9.8	82.9	4,143.5	42	18	2.4%	29	98	43	47	26	$530
Guinea-Bissau	10.9	1.3	1.5	115.0	1,045.4	42	20	2.2%	31	130	47	44	22	$160
Ivory Coast	122.8	16.7	19.3	136.1	1,701.1	38	16	2.2%	32	112	45	48	46	$700
Kenya	219.8	31.6	32.7	143.7	2,052.9	35	14	2.1%	33	74	48	49	20	$350
Lesotho	11.7	2.2	2.3	186.7	1,697.6	33	13	2.0%	33	85	52	55	16	$570
Liberia	37.2	3.4	4.4	91.8	9,179.3	50	17	3.3%	21	139	49	52	45	
Madagascar	224.5	15.8	20.9	70.4	1,760.3	44	14	3.0%	24	96	51	53	22	$260
Malawi	36.3	10.8	11.5	297.5	1,652.7	41	22	1.9%	36	127	38	40	20	$210
Mali	471.1	11.9	15.7	25.3	1,263.5	47	16	3.1%	22	123	55	52	26	$250
Mauritania	395.8	2.9	3.6	7.2	720.9	41	13	2.8%	25	92	52	55	54	$410
Mauritius	0.8	1.2	1.3	1,569.4	3,202.8	17	7	1.0%	66	19	67	74	43	$3,730
Moçambique	302.7	19.9	20.2	65.9	1,647.6	41	19	2.2%	32	134	40	39	28	$210
Namibia	317.9	1.9	2.0	5.8	584.5	36	20	1.6%	42	68	47	45	27	$1,940
Niger	489.1	10.7	13.9	21.9	730.3	54	24	3.0%	23	123	41	41	17	$200
Nigeria	351.7	130.6	160.1	371.2	1,124.9	42	13	2.9%	24	77	52	53	36	$300
Réunion	1.0	0.7	0.8	743.5	4,373.3	20	5	1.5%	49	9	70	79	73	
Rwanda	9.5	7.5	7.7	793.2	2,266.2	43	20	2.3%	30	121	39	40	5	$230

	Land Area 1000 (sq mi)	Population 2002 (Millions)	Population 2010 (Millions)	Population Density		Birth Rate	Death Rate	Natural Increase	Doubling Time (years)	Infant Mortality per 1,000 (births)	Males (years)	Females (years)	Percent Urban Pop	Per Capita GNP ($US)
				Arithmetic	Physiologic									
São Tomé and Principe	0.3	0.2	0.2	737.3	36,867.4	43	9	3.4%	20	51	63	66	44	$270
Senegal	74.3	10.0	12.7	135.1	1,126.0	41	13	2.8%	25	68	51	54	41	$520
Seychelles	0.2	0.1	0.1	511.1	25,553.0	18	7	1.1%	65	9	67	73	59	$6,420
Sierra Leone	27.7	5.5	7.2	197.6	2,823.1	47	21	2.6%	26	157	42	47	37	$140
South Africa	471.4	44.5	40.8	94.5	944.8	25	12	1.3%	55	45	54	57	45	$3,310
Swaziland	6.6	1.0	1.3	157.3	1,430.2	41	22	1.9%	37	108	36	39	22	$1,400
Tanzania	341.1	37.4	46.3	109.6	3,652.6	42	13	2.9%	24	99	52	54	20	$220
Togo	21.0	5.3	6.2	253.1	666.0	42	11	3.1%	23	80	48	50	31	$330
Uganda	77.1	24.6	34.0	319.4	1,277.5	48	20	2.8%	24	81	42	43	15	$310
Zambia	287.0	10.0	11.7	34.7	496.2	42	23	1.9%	35	109	37	38	38	$330
Zimbabwe	149.4	11.5	10.7	77.2	1,102.2	30	20	1.0%	69	80	41	39	32	$620
South Asia	**1592.0**	**1376.7**	**1558.5**	**864.8**		**28**	**9**	**1.9%**	**36**	**74**	**60**	**61**	**30**	**$436**
Bangladesh	50.3	133.0	150.7	2,644.4	3,622.5	27	8	1.9%	38	82	59	58	20	$350
Bhutan	18.2	1.0	1.1	52.6	2,628.2	40	9	3.1%	22	71			15	$470
India	1148.0	1038.5	1168.3	904.6	1,615.4	27	9	1.8%	39	72	60	61	28	$440
Maldives	0.1	0.3	0.4	2,652.3	26,522.5	35	5	3.0%	23	27	71	72	25	$1,130
Nepal	52.8	25.1	30.3	475.6	2,797.5	36	11	2.5%	28	79	58	57	11	$210
Pakistan	297.6	159.2	186.3	534.8	1,980.7	39	11	2.8%	25	91	58	59	33	$470
Sri Lanka	25.0	19.7	21.4	786.5	5,618.2	18	6	1.2%	60	17	70	74	22	$810
East Asia	**4450.1**	**1517.2**	**1574.2**	**340.9**		**15**	**7**	**0.8%**	**87**	**29**	**70**	**74**	**38**	**$3,880**
China	3705.8	1294.4	1349.0	349.3	3,594.2	15	6	0.9%	79	31	69	73	31	$750
Japan	145.4	127.2	124.7	874.5	7,950.1	9	8	0.1%	462	4	77	84	78	$32,350
Korea, North	46.5	22.3	23.7	479.8	3,427.3	21	7	1.4%	48	26	67	73	59	
Korea, South	38.1	48.2	50.2	1,263.9	6,652.2	14	5	0.9%	82	11	71	78	79	$8,600
Mongolia	604.8	2.6	2.9	4.2	424.2	20	7	1.3%	50	34	60	66	52	$380
Taiwan	14.0	22.6	23.7	1,615.2	6,730.1	13	6	0.7%	97	7	72	78	77	
Southeast Asia	**1735.4**	**546.1**	**614.5**	**314.7**		**24**	**7**	**1.7%**	**41**	**46**	**63**	**67**	**36**	**$1,240**
Brunei	2.0	0.3	0.4	156.7	15,667.3	25	3	2.2%	32	24	70	73	67	
Cambodia	68.2	12.7	16.1	186.8	1,436.7	38	12	2.6%	27	80	54	58	16	$260
East Timor	5.7	0.8	1.0	145.4		34	16	1.8%	39	143	45	47		
Indonesia	705.2	219.0	240.8	310.6	3,106.1	24	8	1.6%	44	46	62	66	39	$640
Laos	89.1	5.5	6.6	61.4	2,047.9	41	15	2.6%	26	104	50	52	17	$320
Malaysia	126.9	24.2	29.3	191.0	6,367.6	25	5	2.0%	34	8	70	75	57	$3,670
Myanmar/Burma	253.9	50.9	57.8	200.4	1,335.8	30	10	2.0%	35	83	53	56	26	
Philippines	115.1	83.9	97.2	728.7	3,835.2	29	7	2.2%	31	35	66	69	47	$1,050
Singapore	0.2	4.1	5.6	16,934.4	846,720.0	13	5	0.8%	84	3	76	80	100	$30,170
Thailand	197.3	63.1	66.7	319.9	941.0	16	7	0.9%	70	22	70	75	31	$2,160
Vietnam	125.7	80.9	92.5	643.7	3,786.7	20	6	1.4%	48	37	63	69	24	$350
Austral Realm	**3067.9**	**23.3**	**24.9**	**7.6**		**13**	**7**	**0.6%**	**109**	**5**	**76**	**82**	**85**	**$19,639**
Australia	2966.2	19.4	20.8	6.6	109.7	13	7	0.6%	110	5	76	82	85	$20,640
New Zealand	103.5	3.9	4.1	37.3	414.5	15	7	0.8%	89	5	74	80	85	$14,600
Pacific Realm	**207.7**	**7.5**	**9.0**	**36.3**		**29**	**8**	**2.1%**	**34**	**6**	**54**	**56**	**21**	**$912**

	Land Area 1000 (sq mi)	Population 2002 (Millions)	Population 2010 (Millions)	Population Density Arithmetic	Population Density Physiologic	Birth Rate	Death Rate	Natural Increase	Doubling Time (years)	Infant Mortality per 1,000 (births)	Males (years)	Females (years)	Percent Urban Pop	Per Capita GNP ($US)
Federated States of Micronesia	0.3	0.1	0.1	389.9		33	7	2.6%	27	46	65	67	27	$1,800
Fiji	7.1	0.8	0.9	116.1	1,160.8	22	7	1.5%	46	13	65	69	46	$2,210
French Polynesia	1.4	0.2	0.2	147.5	14,746.5	21	5	1.6%	44	10	69	74	54	
Guam	0.2	0.2	0.2	998.6	9,078.6	28	4	2.4%	29	9	72	77	38	
Marshall Islands	0.1	0.1	0.1	1,492.1		26	4	2.2%	31	31	63	67	65	$1,540
New Caledonia	7.1	0.2	0.2	29.1		21	5	1.6%	42	7	69	77	59	
Papua New Guinea	174.9	5.0	6.1	28.8		34	10	2.4%	29	77	56	57	15	$890
Samoa	1.1	0.2	0.2	191.0	1,005.4	31	6	2.5%	28	25	65	72	21	$1,070
Solomon Is.	10.8	0.4	0.6	39.4	3,936.9	37	6	3.1%	23	25	69	74	13	$760
Vanuatu	4.7	0.2	0.2	45.0	2,248.5	35	7	2.8%	25	39	64	67	18	$1,260

Glossary

Absolute direction A compass direction such as north or south.

Absolute distance The physical distance between two points usually measured in miles or kilometers.

Absolute location The position or place of a certain item on the surface of the Earth as expressed in degrees, minutes, and seconds of latitude, 0° to 90° north or south of the equator, and **longitude**, 0° to 180° east or west of the **prime meridian** passing through Greenwich, England (a suburb of London).

Accessibility The degree of ease with which it is possible to reach a certain location from other locations. Accessibility varies from place to place and can be measured.

Acculturation Cultural modification resulting from intercultural borrowing. In cultural geography and anthropology, the term is often used to designate the change that occurs in the culture of a less technologically advanced people when contact is made with a society that is more technologically advanced.

Acid rain A growing environmental peril whereby acidified rainwater severely damages plant and animal life. Caused by the oxides of sulfur and nitrogen that are released into the atmosphere when coal, oil, and natural gas are burned, especially in major manufacturing zones.

Acropolis Literally "high point of the city." The upper fortified part of an ancient Greek city, usually devoted to religious purposes.

Activity (or **action**) **space** The space within which daily activity occurs.

Age-sex pyramid Graphic representation (profile) of a population showing the percentages of the total population by age and sex, normally in five-year groups.

Agglomerated (nucleated) settlement A compact, closely packed settlement (usually a hamlet or larger village) sharply demarcated from adjoining farmlands.

Agglomeration A process involving the clustering or concentrating of people or activities. The term often refers to manufacturing plants and businesses that benefit from close proximity because they share skilled-labor pools and technological and financial amenities.

Agrarian Relating to the use of land in rural communities or to agricultural societies in general.

Agribusiness A general term for large-scale, mechanized industrial agriculture that is controlled by corporate interests.

Agricultural density The number of inhabitants per unit of agricultural land. As used in population geography, agricultural density excludes urban residents so that it reflects the pressure of population in rural areas. **Physiologic density** measures the total population, urban and rural, against the agricultural land.

Agricultural Revolution The revolutionary transformation of agricultural practices, systems, and production. The First Agricultural Revolution, dating back 10,000 years, achieved plant and animal domestication. The Second Agricultural Revolution dovetailed with and benefited from the Industrial Revolution and witnessed improved methods of cultivation, harvesting, and storage of farm produce. The Third Agricultural Revolution, currently in progress, is based on new high-yielding strains of grains and other crops developed by genetic engineering.

Agriculture The purposeful tending of crops and livestock in order to produce food and fiber.

Angiosperms Plants whose seeds are encased in fruit.

Animism The belief that inanimate objects, such as hills, rocks, rivers, and other elements of the natural landscape (including trees), possess souls and can help as well as hinder human efforts on Earth.

Antecedent boundary A political boundary that existed before the **cultural landscape** emerged and stayed in place while people moved in to occupy the surrounding area. An example is the 49th parallel boundary, dividing the United States and Canada between the Pacific Ocean and Lake of the Woods in northernmost Minnesota.

Anthropogeographic boundaries Political boundaries that coincide substantially with cultural discontinuities in the human landscape, such as religious or linguistic transitions.

Apartheid Literally, "apartness." The Afrikaans term given to the policies of racial separation once practiced in South Africa and to the highly segregated sociogeographical patterns they produced—a system now being dismantled.

Aquaculture The use of a river segment or an artificial body of water such as a pond for the raising and harvesting of food products, including fish, shellfish, and even seaweed. Japan is among the world's leaders in aquaculture.

Arable Literally, cultivable. Land fit for cultivation by one farming method or another.

Area A term that refers to a part of the Earth's surface with less specificity than **region**. For example, urban area alludes very generally to a place where urban development has taken place, whereas urban region requires certain specific criteria on which a delimitation is based (e.g., the spatial extent of commuting or the built townscape).

Areal interdependence A term related to **functional specialization**. When one area produces certain goods or has certain raw materials or resources and another area has a different set of resources and produces different goods, their needs may be complementary; by exchanging raw materials and products, they can satisfy each other's requirements. The concepts of areal interdependence and complementarity are related: both have to do with exchange opportunities between regions.

Arithmetic population density The population of a country or region expressed as an average per unit area. The figure is derived by dividing the population of the areal unit by the number of square kilometers or miles that make up the unit.

Aryan From the Sanskrit Arya ("noble"), a name applied to an ancient people who spoke an Indo-European language and who moved into northern India from the northwest. Though properly a language-related term, Aryan has assumed additional meanings, especially racial ones.

Ashkenazim One of the two main ethnic groups within Jewish culture. This branch eventually settled in Central Europe after having been driven out of Jerusalem early in the first millennium A.D.

Assimilation The process through which people lose originally differentiating traits, such as dress, speech particularities or mannerisms, when they come into contact with another society or culture. Often used to describe immigrant adaptation to new places of residence.

Australopithecus Early hominid species dating to 4–5 million years ago; branches survived the Pliocene climate changes in Africa.

Autocratic A government that holds absolute power; rule is often by one person or a small group of persons who control the country by despotic means.

Balkanization The fragmentation of a region into smaller, often hostile political units.

Basic activities Economic activities whose products are exported beyond a region's limits. Nonbasic, or service, activities involve production and consumption within the region.

Bergmann's Rule A principle holding that the lower the mean annual temperature, the higher a population's mean body weight.

Biodiversity The total variety of plant and animal species in a particular place; biological diversity.

Biotechnology The use of genetically engineered crops in agriculture and DNA manipulation in livestock in order to increase production. Increasingly applied to more advanced stages of food production in the form of radiation of meats and vegetables to prolong their freshness.

Birth rate The crude birth rate is expressed as the annual number of live births per 1000 individuals within a given population.

Blockbusting Rapid change in the racial composition of residential blocks in American cities that occurs when real estate agents and others stir up fears of neighborhood decline after encouraging people of color to move to previously white neighborhoods. In the resulting outmigration, real estate agents profit through the turnover of properties.

Brahman A Hindu of the highest caste, most often a priest; a person believed to possess sacred knowledge and to be of the greatest purity. Brahmans (or Brahmins) alone are believed capable of carrying out particular religious rituals and tasks. In India, Brahmans have for many centuries been religious, intellectual, and even political leaders.

Break-of-bulk point A location along a transport route where goods must be transferred from one carrier to another. In a port, the cargoes of oceangoing ships are unloaded and put on trains, trucks, or perhaps smaller riverboats for inland distribution.

Brick A traditional building material made of hard, oven-baked or sun-baked blocks of mud shaped into standard sizes.

Buffer zone A country or zone separating ideological or political adversaries. In southern Asia, Afghanistan, Nepal, and Bhutan were parts of a buffer zone between British and Russian-Chinese imperial spheres. Thailand was a buffer state between British and French colonial domains in mainland Southeast Asia.

Cadastral map A large-scale map, usually created at the scale of 1:2500, depicting the value, extent, and ownership of land for purposes of taxation.

Cambrian Explosion First great success of complex life forms: burgeoning diversity of invertebrates between 500 and 600 million years ago.

Cartel An international syndicate formed to promote common interests in some economic sphere through the formulation of joint pricing policies and the limitation of market options for consumers. The Organization of Petroleum Exporting Countries (OPEC) is a classic example.

Cartography The art and science of making maps, including data compilation, layout, and design. Also concerned with the interpretation of mapped patterns.

Caste system The strict social segregation of people—specifically in India's Hindu society—on the basis of ancestry and occupation.

Cenozoic The era of recent life on the geologic time scale extending from 65 million years ago to the present; subdivided into the Tertiary and Quaternary periods.

Census A periodic and official count of a country's population.

Central business district (CBD) The downtown heart of a central city, the CBD is marked by high land values, a concentration of business and commerce, and the clustering of the tallest buildings.

Central place Any point or place in the urban hierarchy, such as a town or city, having a certain economic reach or **hinterland**.

Central place theory Theory proposed by Walter Christaller that explains how and where central places in the urban hierarchy would be functionally and spatially distributed with respect to one another.

Centrality The strength of an urban center in its capacity to attract producers and consumers to its facilities; a city's "reach" into the surrounding region.

Centrifugal forces A term employed to designate forces that tend to divide a country—such as internal religious, linguistic, ethnic, or ideological differences.

Centripetal forces Forces that unite and bind a country together—such as widespread commitment to a national culture, shared ideological objectives, and a common faith.

Child mortality rate A figure that describes the number of children that die between the first and fifth years of their lives in a given population.

Chlorofluorocarbons (CFCs) Synthetic organic compounds first created in the 1950s and used primarily as refrigerants and as propellants. The role of CFCs in the destruction of the ozone layer led to the signing of an international agreement (the **Montreal Protocol**).

Circulation In political geography, the system of integration and movement through language, education, transportation, and communications.

Cityscape The **landscape** of an urban area; the combined impression of a city's built and nonbuilt environments.

City-state An independent political entity consisting of a single city with (and sometimes without) an immediate **hinterland**. The ancient city-states of Greece have their modern equivalent in Singapore.

Civilization An advanced state of a society possessing historical and cultural unity whose attributes include plant and animal domestication, metallurgy, occupational specialization, writing, and **urbanization**.

Colonialism Rule by an autonomous power over a subordinate and alien people and place. Although often established and maintained through political structures, colonialism also creates unequal cultural and economic relations. Because of the magnitude and impact of the European colonial project of the last few centuries, the term is generally understood to refer to that particular colonial endeavor.

Commodification The process through which something is given monetary value. Commodification occurs when a good or idea that previously was not regarded as an object to be bought and sold is turned into something that has a particular price and that can be traded in a market economy.

Compact state A political-geographical term to describe a state that possesses a roughly circular, oval, or rectangular territory in which the distance from the geometric center to any point on the boundary exhibits little variance. Cambodia, Uruguay, and Poland are examples of this shape category.

Complementarity A condition that exists when two regions, through an exchange of raw materials and/or finished products, can specifically satisfy each other's demands.

Concentric zone model A structural model of the American central city that suggests the existence of five concentric land-use rings arranged around a common center.

Condominium In political geography, the shared administration of a territory by two governments.

Confucianism A philosophy of ethics, education, and public service based on the writings of Confucius and traditionally thought of as one of the core elements of Chinese culture.

Connectivity The degree of direct linkage between one particular location and other locations in a transport network.

Conservation The careful management and use of natural resources, the achievement of significant social benefits from them, and the preservation of the natural environment.

Contagious diffusion The distance-controlled spreading of an idea, innovation, or some other item through a local population by contact from person to person—analogous to the communication of a contagious illness.

Contagious disease A disease that can be transmitted among people, either through direct contact or through a vector.

Continental drift The notion hypothesized by Alfred Wegener concerning the fragmentation of Pangaea and the slow movement of the modern continents away from this core supercontinent.

Continental shelf The gently sloping, relatively shallow, submerged plain just off the coast of a continent, extending to a depth of around 180 meters (600 feet/1000 fathoms).

Conurbation General term used to identify large, multimetropolitan complexes formed by the coalescence of two or more major urban areas. The Boston-Washington **megalopolis** along the U.S. northeastern seaboard is an outstanding example.

Core area In geography, a term with several connotations. Core refers to the center, heart, or focus. The core area of a **nation-state** is constituted by the national heartland—the largest population cluster, the most productive region, the area with greatest **centrality** and **accessibility**, probably containing the capital city as well.

Core region In terms of the **core-periphery model**, the centers of economic, political, and/or cultural power within a given territorial entity.

Core-periphery model A model that describes how economic, political, and/or cultural power is spatially distributed between dominant **core regions**, and more marginal or dependent **semi-peripheral** and **peripheral regions**. The core-periphery model can be applied at a variety of spatial scales.

Core-periphery relationships The contrasting spatial characteristics of, and linkages between, the have (core) and have-not (periphery) components of a national or regional system.

Corridor In general, a spatial entity in which human activity is organized in a linear manner, as along a major transport route or in a valley confined by highlands. Specific meaning in politico-geographical context is a land extension that connects an otherwise **landlocked** state to the sea. History has seen several such corridors come and go. Poland once had a corridor (it now has a lengthy coastline); Bolivia lost a corridor to the Pacific Ocean between Peru and Chile.

Creole Ethnic term first applied in the Caribbean region to the native-born descendants of the Spanish conquerors and their local consorts.

Creole language A language that began as a pidgin but was later adopted as the mother tongue by a people in place of the mother tongue.

Creolization In a linguistic context, the process describing the convergence of two or more languages, forming a separate, new language. Primarily used to describe linguistic developments in the Caribbean region that resulted from the mixing of peoples during slavery and colonization. Increasingly creolization is used to denote wider, reciprocal processes of cultural intermixing and change.

Cultural diffusion The process of spreading and adoption of a cultural element, from its place of origin across a wider area.

Cultural ecology The multiple interactions and relationships between a culture and the natural environment.

Cultural landscape The forms and artifacts sequentially placed on the physical landscape by the activities of various human occupants. By this progressive imprinting of the human presence, the physical landscape is modified into the cultural landscape, forming an interacting unity between the two.

Cultural linkage A culturally shared trait that gives an ethnic or cultural group a strengthened sense of awareness and self-identity.

Cultural pluralism A society in which two or more population groups, each practicing its own **culture**, live adjacent to one another without mixing inside a single **state**.

Cultural revival The process of continuous reinvigoration of cultural traits and behavior in communities geographically separated from their original source area.

Cultural-political boundaries Political boundaries that coincide with cultural breaks in the landscape, such as language, religion, and ethnicity.

Culture The sum total of the knowledge, attitudes, and habitual behavior patterns shared and transmitted by the members of a society. This is anthropologist Ralph Linton's definition; hundreds of others exist.

Culture area A distinct, culturally discrete spatial unit; a region within which certain cultural norms prevail.

Culture complex A related set of culture traits, such as prevailing dress codes and cooking and eating utensils.

Culture hearth Heartland, source area, innovation center; place of origin of a major culture.

Culture realm A cluster of regions in which related culture systems prevail. In North America, the United States and Canada form a culture realm, but Mexico belongs to a different culture realm.

Culture region A region within which common cultural characteristics prevail.

Culture trait A single element of normal practice in a culture, such as the wearing of a turban.

Culture-environment tradition One of the four major areas of geographic research and teaching; the relationships between human societies and their natural environments.

Cyclical movement Movement—for example, nomadic migration—that has a closed route repeated annually or seasonally.

Death rate Expressed as the annual number of deaths per 1000 individuals within a given population.

Definition In political geography, the written legal description (in a treatylike document) of a boundary between two countries or territories. See also **delimitation**.

Deforestation The clearing and destruction of forests to harvest wood for consumption, clear land for agricultural uses, and make way for expanding settlement frontiers.

Deglaciation The withdrawal of an ice sheet from an area. Areas that have been deglaciated are characterized by certain features in the **landscape**, such as moraines, or low-profile rolling hills. Deglaciated areas are often agriculturally fertile.

Deglomeration The process of industrial deconcentration in response to technological advances and/or increasing costs due to congestion and competition.

Delimitation In political geography, the translation of the written terms of a boundary treaty (the **definition**) into an official cartographic representation.

Demarcation In political geography, the actual placing of a political boundary on the landscape by means of barriers, fences, walls, or other markers.

Demographic transition model Multistage model, based on Western Europe's experience, of changes in population growth exhibited by countries undergoing industrialization. High birth rates and death rates are followed by plunging death rates, producing a huge net population gain; this is followed by the convergence of birth rates and death rates at a low overall level.

Demographic variables Births (fertility), deaths (mortality), and migration. These are the three basic demographic variables.

Demography The study of patterns and rates of population change, including birth and death rates, migration trends, and evolving population distribution patterns.

Density A description of the quantity per unit area of a given object or living organism.

Density of population The number of people per unit area. Also see **arithmetic population density** and **physiologic density** measures.

Dependency theory A **structuralist model** that offers a critique of the **modernization model** of development. Based on the idea that certain types of political and economic relations (especially **colonialism**) between countries and regions of the world have created arrangements that both control and limit the extent to which regions can develop.

Desertification The encroachment of desert conditions on moister zones along the desert margins, where plant cover and soils are threatened by desiccation—through overuse, in part by humans and their domestic animals, and, possibly, in part because of inexorable shifts in the Earth's environmental zones.

Determinism See **environmental determinism**.

Development The economic, social, and institutional evolution of national states.

Devolution The process whereby regions within a **state** demand and gain political strength and growing autonomy at the expense of the central government.

Dialect Local or regional characterstics of a language. While **accent** refers to the pronounciation differences of a standard language, a dialect, in addition to pronounciation variation, has distinctive grammar and vocabulary.

Diaspora From the Greek "to disperse," a term describing forceful or voluntary dispersal of a people from their homeland to a new place. Originally denoting the dispersal of Jews, it is increasingly applied to other population dispersals, such as the involuntary relocation of Black peoples during the slave trade or Chinese peoples outside of Mainland China, Taiwan and Hong Kong.

Diffusion The spatial spreading or dissemination of a culture element (such as a technological innovation) or some other phenomenon (e.g., a disease outbreak). See also **contagious**, **expansion**, **hierarchical**, and **relocation diffusion**.

Diffusion routes The spatial trajectory through which cultural traits or other phenomena spread.

Disamenity sector The very poorest parts of cities that in extreme cases are not even connected to regular city services and are controlled by gangs or drug lords.

Dispersed settlement In contrast to **agglomerated** or **nucleated settlement**, characterized by a much lower density of population and the wide spacing of individual homesteads (especially in rural North America).

Distance decay The various degenerative effects of distance on human spatial structures and interactions.

Divided capital In political geography, a country whose administrative functions are carried out in more than one city is said to have divided capitals.

Domestication The transformation of a wild animal or wild plant into a domesticated animal or a cultivated crop to gain control over food production. A necessary evolutionary step in the development of humankind—the invention of **agriculture**.

Domino theory The belief that political destabilization in one country can result in the collapse of order in a neighboring state, starting a chain reaction of collapse.

Double cropping The planting, cultivation, and harvesting of two crops successively within a single year on the same plot of farmland.

Doubling time The time required for a population to double in size.

Dwyka Ice Age Global cooling beginning during the Carboniferous Period and extending into the Permian; the last ice age prior to the Late Cenozoic Ice Age now in progress.

Earth-science tradition One of the four major areas of geographic research and teaching; also known as **physical (natural) geography**.

Ecology Strictly speaking, the study of the many interrelationships between all forms of life and the natural environments in which they have evolved and continue to develop. The study of ecosystems focuses on the interactions between specific organisms and their environments. See also **cultural ecology**.

Economic reach The maximum distance people can be from a central place and still be attracted to it for business purposes. See also **hinterland**.

Economic tiger One of the burgeoning beehive countries of the Pacific Rim of Australasia. Using postwar Japan as a model, these countries have experienced significant modernization, industrialization, and Western-style economic growth since 1980. The four leading economic tigers are South Korea, Taiwan, Hong Kong, and Singapore.

Economies of scale The savings that accrue from large-scale production whereby the unit cost of manufacturing decreases as the level of operation enlarges. Supermarkets operate on this principle and are able to charge lower prices than small grocery stores.

Ecosystem A linkage of plants or animals to their environment in an open system as far as energy is concerned.

Ecumene The portion of the world's land surface that is permanently settled by human beings.

Edge cities A term introduced by American journalist Joel Garreau in order to describe the shifting focus of **urbanization** in the United States away from the **central business district (CBD)** toward new loci of economic activity at the urban fringe. These cities are characterized by extensive amounts of office and retail space, few residential areas, and modern buildings (less than 30 years old).

El Niño A periodic, large-scale, abnormal warming of the sea surface in the low latitudes of the eastern Pacific Ocean that produces a (temporary) reversal of surface ocean currents and airflows throughout the equatorial Pacific; these regional events have global implications, disturbing normal weather patterns in many parts of the world.

Electoral geography Subfield of geography that deals with various spatial aspects of voting systems, voting behavior, and voter representation.

Elongated state A state whose territory is decidedly long and narrow in that its length is at least six times greater than its average width. Chile and Vietnam are two classic examples on the world political map.

Emigrant A person migrating away from a country or area; an out-migrant.

Empirical Relating to the observable world, as opposed to theoretical abstraction.

Enclave A piece of territory that is surrounded by another political unit of which it is not a part.

Endemic A disease that is particular to a locality or region.

ENSO Acronym for El Niño Southern Oscillation; the reversal of the flow of ocean currents and prevailing winds in the equatorial Pacific Ocean that disturbs global weather patterns.

Entrepôt A place, usually a port city, where goods are imported, stored, and transshipped; a **break-of-bulk point**.

Environmental determinism The view that the natural environment has a controlling influence over various aspects of human life, including cultural development. Also referred to as environmentalism.

Environmental geography A subdivision of geography concerned with the relationships and interactions between humans and the environment.

Environmental perception The total impression individuals have of their surroundings which create a mental map.

Environmental stress The threat to environmental security by human action such as atmospheric and groundwater pollution, deforestation, oil spills, and ocean dumping.

Esperanto A made-up Latin-based language, which its European proponents in the early twentieth century hoped would become a global language.

Ethnic A basis for human identity based on a combination of people's **cultural traits** (traditions, customs, language, and religion) and ideas about their ancestry and **race**.

Ethnic cleansing The slaughter and/or forced removal of one ethnic group from its homes and lands by another ethnic group.

Ethnic islands Small, usually rural and ethnically homogeneous enclaves situated within a larger and more diverse cultural context.

Ethnic religion A religion that is particular to one, culturally distinct, group of people. Unlike **universalizing religions**, adherents of ethnic religions do not actively seek converts through evangelism or missionary work.

Ethnonationalism The identification and loyalty a person may feel for his or her **nation**.

Eugenic population policy Government policy designed to favor one racial sector over others.

Eugenic Protection Act Policy enacted by the Japanese government in 1948 that legalized abortion for social, medical, and economic reasons.

Euroregions Transboundary cooperation zones in Europe that conform to the rules of the Euregion Council. The first self-designed Euroregion was established along the Dutch-German border in the early 1960s, and the number of Euroregions has expanded significantly over the past two decades.

Exclave A bounded (nonisland) piece of territory that is part of a particular state but lies separated from it by the territory of another state.

Exclusive Economic Zone (EEZ) An oceanic zone extending up to 200 nautical miles from a shoreline, within which the coastal state can control fishing, mineral exploration, and additional activities by all other countries.

Expansion diffusion The spread of an innovation or an idea through a population in an area in such a way that the number of those influenced grows continuously larger, resulting in an expanding area of dissemination.

Expansive population policy Government policy that encourages large families and raises the rate of population growth.

Exponential growth Cumulative or compound growth (of a population) over a given time period.

External migration Migration across an international border.

Extractive sector See **primary economic activity**.

Extraterritoriality Politico-geographical concept suggesting that the property of one state lying within the boundaries of another actually forms an extension of the first state.

Favela Shantytown on the outskirts or even well within an urban area in Brazil.

Federal state A political-territorial system wherein a central government represents the various entities within a **nation-state** where they have common interests—defense, foreign affairs, and the like—yet allows these various entities to retain their own identities and to have their own laws, policies, and customs in certain spheres.

Federation See **federal state**.

Feng Shui Literally "wind-water." The Chinese art and science of placement and orientation of tombs, dwellings, buildings, and cities. Structures and objects are positioned in an effort to channel flows of *sheng-chi* ("life-breath") in favorable ways.

Fertile Crescent Crescent-shaped zone of productive lands extending from near the southeastern Mediterranean coast through Lebanon and Syria to the alluvial lowlands of Mesopotamia (in Iraq). Once more fertile than today, this is one of the world's great source areas of agricultural and other innovations.

Feudalism Prevailing political-geographical system in Europe during the Middle Ages when land was owned by the nobility and was worked by peasants and serfs. The nobility supported a king or lord, but much of the real power rested with the landowners. Feudalism also existed in other parts of the world, and the system persisted into this century in Ethiopia and Iran, among other places.

Folk culture Cultural traits such as dress modes, dwellings, traditions, and institutions of usually small, **traditional** communities.

Folk-housing region A region in which the housing stock predominantly reflects styles of building that are particular to the culture of the people who have long inhabited the area.

Food web (food chain) The notion that all plants and animals are in some way connected in an organic sequence in which each life-form consumes the form below and, at the same time, is consumed by the form above. Plant life constitutes the foundation of the food web; the meat-eating animals (carnivores) stand at the top.

Forced migration Human **migration** flows in which the movers have no choice but to relocate.

Fordist A highly organized and specialized system for organizing industrial production and labor. Named after automobile producer Henry Ford, Fordist production features assembly-line production of standardized components for mass consumption.

Foreign direct investment The investment of capital by a country or corporation in an area away from the home base of the investor—often in the form of actual factories and infrastructure.

Formal region A type of region marked by a certain degree of homogeneity in one or more phenomena; also called uniform region or homogeneous region.

Forward capital Capital city positioned in actually or potentially contested territory, usually near an international border; it confirms the state's determination to maintain its presence in the region in contention.

Fragmented state A state whose territory consists of several separated parts, not a contiguous whole. The individual parts may be isolated from each other by the land area of other states or by international waters.

Francophone A country or region where other languages are also spoken but where French is the **lingua franca**, or the language of the elite. Quebec is Francophone Canada.

Frontier Zone of advance penetration, usually of contention; an area not yet fully integrated into a politically organized area.

Functional differentiation A mode of distinguishing things or arrangements based on the purposes or activities to which they are devoted.

Functional region A region defined by the particular set of activities or interactions that occur within it.

Functional specialization The production of particular goods or services as a dominant activity in a particular location.

Gated communities Restricted neighborhoods or subdivisions, often literally fenced in, where entry is limited to residents and their guests. Although predominantly high-income based, in North America gated communities are increasingly a middle-class phenomenon.

Gateway state A state, by virtue of its border location between geopolitical power cores, that absorbs and assimilates cultures and traditions of its neighbors without being dominated by them.

Gender Social differences between men and women, rather than the anatomical, biological differences between the sexes. Notions of gender differences—that is, what is considered "feminine" or "masculine"—vary greatly over time and space.

Gender gap The differences in levels of health, education, income, opportunity, and participation in politics and public life that exist between males and females.

Gentrification The rehabilitation of deteriorated, often abandoned, housing of low-income inner-city residents.

Geographic information system (GIS) A collection of computer hardware and software that permits spatial data to be collected, recorded, stored, retrieved, manipulated, analyzed, and displayed to the user.

Geographic realm The basic **spatial** unit in our world regionalization scheme. Each realm is defined in terms of a synthesis of its total human geography—a composite of its leading cultural, economic, historical, political, and appropriate environmental features.

Geography From the Greek meaning "to write about the Earth." As a modern academic discipline, geography is concerned with the analysis of the physical and human characteristics of the Earth's surface from a **spatial** perspective. "Why are things located where they are?" and "What does it mean for things to be located in particular places" are central questions that geographical scholarship seeks to answer.

Geologic time scale The standard timetable or chronicle of Earth history used by scientists; the sequential organization of geologic time units, whose dates continue to be refined by ongoing research.

Geometric boundaries Political boundaries **defined** and **delimited** (and occasionally **demarcated**) as straight lines or arcs.

Geopolitics The study of the interplay between international political relations and the territorial/environmental context in which they occur.

Gerrymandering Redistricting for advantage, or the practice of dividing areas into electoral districts to give one political party an electoral majority in a large number of districts while concentrating the voting strength of the opposition in as few districts as possible.

Ghetto An urban region marked by particular ethnic, racial, religious, and economic properties, usually (but not always) a low-income area.

Glaciation A period of global cooling during which continental ice sheets and mountain glaciers expand.

Global Environment Facility (GEF) An organization created under the auspices of the United Nations and the World Bank in 1991, the GEF is an international funding clearinghouse for global environmental initiatives.

Globalization The expansion of economic, political, and cultural activities to the point that they become global in scale and impact. This process has been aided by technological advances in transportation, information management, and telecommunications.

Global-local continuum The notion that what happens at the global scale has a direct effect on what happens at the local scale, and vice versa. This idea posits that the world is comprised of an interconnected series of relationships that extend across space.

Gondwana The southern portion of the primeval supercontinent, Pangaea.

Gravity model A mathematical prediction of the interaction of places, the interaction being a function of population size of the respective places and the distance between them.

Green Revolution The successful recent development of higher-yield, fast-growing varieties of rice and other cereals in certain developing countries, which led to increased production per unit area and a dramatic narrowing of the gap between population growth and food needs.

Greenhouse effect The widely used analogy describing the blanket-like effect of the atmosphere in the heating of the Earth's surface; shortwave insolation passes through the "glass" of the atmospheric "greenhouse," heats the surface, is converted to long-wave radiation that cannot penetrate the "glass," and thereby results in trapping heat, which raises the temperature inside the "greenhouse."

Gross domestic product (GDP) The total value of all goods and services produced within a country during a given year.

Gross national product (GNP) The total value of all goods and services produced by a country's economy in a given year. It includes all goods and services produced by corporations and individuals of a country, whether or not they are located within the country.

Growing season The number of days between the last frost in the spring and the first frost of the fall.

Growth pole An urban center with certain attributes that, if augmented by a measure of investment support, will stimulate regional economic development in its **hinterland**.

Heartland theory A **geopolitical** hypothesis, proposed by British geographer Halford Mackinder during the first two decades of the twentieth century, that any political power based in the heart of Eurasia could gain sufficient strength to eventually dominate the world. Mackinder further proposed that since Eastern Europe controlled access to the Eurasian interior, its ruler would command the vast "heartland" to the east.

Hegemony The political dominance of a country (or even a region) by another country. The former Soviet Union's postwar grip on Eastern Europe, which lasted from 1945 to 1990, was a classic example.

Hierarchical diffusion A form of **diffusion** in which an idea or innovation spreads by trickling down from larger to smaller adoption units. An **urban hierarchy** is usually involved, encouraging the leapfrogging of innovations over wide areas, with geographic distance a less important influence.

Hierarchy An order or gradation of phenomena, with each level or rank subordinate to the one above it and superior to the one below. The levels in a national urban hierarchy are constituted by hamlets, villages, towns, cities, and (frequently) the **primate city**.

High seas Areas of the oceans away from land, beyond national jurisdiction, open and free for all to use.

High-technology corridors Areas along or near major transportation arteries that are devoted to the research, development, and sale of high-technology products. These areas develop because of the networking and synergistic advantages of concentrating high-technology enterprises in close proximity to one another. "Silicon Valley" is a prime example of a high-technology corridor in the United States.

Hinterland Literally, "country behind," a term that applies to a surrounding area served by an urban center. That center is the focus of goods and services produced for its hinterland and is its dominant urban influence as well. In the case of a port city, the hinterland also includes the inland area whose trade flows through that port.

Holocene The current **interglacial** period, extending from 10,000 years ago to the present on the geologic time scale.

Homo erectus Earliest species assigned to the genus *Homo*, evolved in Africa possibly more than 2 million years ago and dispersed into Eurasia. Body features similar to modern humans below the neck; brain size substantially larger than modern chimpanzees.

Homo sapiens The only living species of the genus *Homo*; modern humans.

Human geography One of the two major divisions of **geography**; the spatial analysis of human population, their cultures, activities, and landscapes.

Human territoriality A term associated with the work of Robert Sack that describes the efforts of human societies to influence events and achieve social goals by exerting, and attempting to enforce, control over specific geographical areas.

Hybridity The product of cultural mixing, especially new, transcultural forms that emerge between indigenous and colonial cultures in the contact zone brought about by colonization.

Hydrologic cycle The system of exchange involving water in its various forms as it continually circulates among the atmosphere, the oceans, and above and below the land surface.

Ice age A stretch of geologic time during which the Earth's average atmospheric temperature is lowered; causes the expansion of glacial ice in the high latitudes and the growth of mountain glaciers in lower latitudes.

Ice cap A regional mass of ice smaller than a continent-size ice sheet; while the Laurentide ice sheet covered much of North America east of the Rocky Mountains, an ice cap covered the Rockies themselves.

Ice sheet A large and thick layer of ice that flows outward in all directions from a central area where continuous accumulation of snow and thickening of ice occur. Also called continental ice sheet or continental glacier.

Iconography The identity of a region as expressed through its cherished symbols; its particular **cultural landscape** and personality.

Imam The political head of the Muslim community or the person who leads prayer services. In **Shiite** Islam the imam is immune from sin or error.

Immigrant A person migrating into a particular country or area; an in-migrant.

Imperialism The drive toward the creation and expansion of a colonial empire and, once established, its perpetuation.

Industrial Optimum Warming phase in Earth's climate commencing during the nineteenth century and coinciding with the Industrial Revolution.

Industrial Revolution The term applied to the social and economic changes in agriculture, commerce and manufacturing that resulted from technological innovations and specialization in late-eighteenth-century Europe.

Infant mortality rate (IMR) A figure that describes the number of babies that die within the first year of their lives in a given population.

Infrastructure The foundations of a society: urban centers, transport networks, communications, energy distribution systems, farms, factories, mines, and such facilities as schools, hospitals, postal services, and police and armed forces.

Insurgent state Territorial embodiment of a successful guerrilla movement. The establishment by antigovernment insurgents of a territorial base in which they exercise full control; thus, a state within a **state**.

Interactive mapping In geographic information systems (GIS) methodology, the constant dialogue via computer demands and feedback to queries between the map user and the map.

Interglacial Sustained warming phase between glacial advances during an ice age.

Internal migration Migration flow within a **nation-state**, such as ongoing westward and southward movements in the United States.

International migration **Migration** flow involving movement across international boundaries.

International refugees **Refugees** who have crossed one or more international boundaries during their dislocation and who now find themselves encamped in a different country.

Intervening opportunity The presence of a nearer opportunity that greatly diminishes the attractiveness of sites farther away.

Intranational refugees **Refugees** who have abandoned their town or village but not their country.

Irredentism A policy of cultural extension and potential political expansion aimed at a national group living in a neighboring country.

Irrigation The artificial watering of croplands. In Egypt's Nile Valley, basin irrigation is an ancient method that involved the use of floodwaters that were trapped in basins on the floodplain and released in stages to augment rainfall. Today's perennial irrigation requires the construction of dams and irrigation canals for year-round water supply.

Isogloss A geographic boundary within which a particular linguistic feature occurs.

Isolines Lines on a map depicting areas of same or like values. In meteorology, isobars depict areas with the same barometric pressure, and isotherms are used on weather maps to show areas with similar temperatures.

Jihad A doctrine within Islam. Commonly translated as "Holy War," Jihad represents either a personal or collective struggle on the part of Muslims to live up to the religious standards set by the Qu'ran.

K/T boundary Short for the geologic transition from the Cretaceous to the Tertiary Periods as well as the Mesozoic to the Cenozoic Eras, marked by the impact of a large comet and the demise of many animal species including most of the dinosaurs.

Karma In Hinduism and Buddhism, the force generated by a person's actions that affects transmigrations into a future existence, determining conditions and position in the next earthly stage of life.

Land bridge A narrow isthmian link between two large landmasses. They are temporary features—at least in terms of geologic time—subject to appearance and disappearance as the land or sea level rises and falls.

Landlocked An interior country or **state** that is surrounded by land. Without coasts, a landlocked state is at a disadvantage in a number of ways—in terms of **accessibility** to international trade routes and in the scramble for possession of areas of the **continental shelf** and control of the **Exclusive Economic Zone** beyond.

Landscape The overall appearance of an area. Most landscapes are comprised of a combination of natural and human-induced influences.

Late Cenozoic Ice Age The last great ice age that ended 10,000 years ago; spanned the entire Pleistocene epoch (2 million to 10,000 years ago), plus the latter portion of the preceding Pliocene epoch, possibly beginning as far back as 3.5 million years ago.

Latitude An imaginary line running parallel to the equator that is used to measure distance in degrees north or south from the equator.

Law of the Sea The United Nations Convention on the Law of the Sea (UNCLOS), signed by 157 states (but not including the United States) in 1982; established states' rights and responsibilities concerning the ownership and use of the Earth's seas and oceans and their resources.

League of Nations A global (supranational) organization established by the victors of World War I to preserve peace and security and to promote economic and social cooperation among its members.

Least cost theory Model developed by Alfred Weber according to which the location of manufacturing establishments is determined by the minimization of three critical expenses: labor, transportation, and agglomeration.

Liberal models A general term for economic development models which assume that (1) all countries are capable of developing economically in the same way and (2) economic disparities between countries and regions are the result of short-term inefficiencies in local or regional market forces. The **modernization model** of development is an example of a liberal model.

Life expectancy A figure indicating how long, on average, a person may be expected to live. Normally expressed in the context of a particular state.

Lingua franca A term deriving from "Frankish language" and applying to a tongue spoken in ancient Mediterranean ports that consisted of a mixture of Italian, French, Greek, Spanish, and even some Arabic. Today it refers to a "common language," a second language that can be spoken and understood by many peoples, although they speak other languages at home.

Little Ice Age Temporary but significant cooling between the fourteenth and the nineteenth century; accompanied by wide temperature fluctuations, droughts, and storms and causing famines and dislocation.

Location theory A logical attempt to explain the locational pattern of an economic activity and the manner in which its producing areas are interrelated. The agricultural location theory contained in the **von Thünen model** is a leading example.

Longevity gap The difference in the average length of life between males and females.

Longitude An imaginary line circling the Earth and running through the poles. Used to determine the location of things by measurement of the angular distance, in degrees east or west, from the **prime meridian**.

Main Street Canada's dominant **conurbation** that is home to more than 60 percent of the country's inhabitants; stretches southwestward from Quebec City in the middle St. Lawrence Valley to Windsor on the Detroit River.

Malnutrition Condition of ill health resulting from the deficiency or improper balance of essential foodstuffs in the diet, usually proteins, vitamins, and minerals. Two common forms of malnutrition among children in the world's poorer countries are kwashiorkor, a protein-deficient disorder, and marasmus, which results from insufficient protein and calories.

Malthusian Designating the early-nineteenth-century viewpoint of Thomas Malthus, who argued that population growth was outrunning the Earth's capacity to produce sufficient food. Neo-Malthusian refers to those who subscribe to such positions in modern contexts.

Manufacturing export zones A feature of economic development in peripheral countries whereby the host country establishes areas with favorable tax, regulatory, and trade arrangements in order to attract foreign manufacturing operations. The goods manufactured in these export zones are primarily destined for the global market.

Map projection An orderly arrangement of lines of **latitude** and **longitude**, produced by any systematic method, that can be used for drawing a map of the spherical Earth on a flat surface.

Maquiladora The term given to zones in northern Mexico with factories supplying manufactured goods to the U.S. market. The low-wage workers in the primarily foreign-owned factories assemble imported components and/or raw materials and then export finished manufactures.

Marasmus A disease that develops as a result of both a lack of protein and an insufficient caloric intake.

Median-line principle The system of drawing a political boundary midway between two states' coastlines when the territorial seas or EEZ are narrower than twice the standard or adopted limit.

Medical geography The study of health and disease within a geographic context and from a geographical perspective. Among other things, medical geography looks at sources, diffusion routes, and distributions of diseases.

Medieval Optimum A warm period in the Earth's environmental history that began around 2000 years ago and that witnessed the expansion of settlement into the northern latitudes of Eurasia, the peopling of Iceland, and the colonization of Greenland.

Megalopolis Term used to designate large coalescing supercities that are forming in diverse parts of the world; formerly used specifically with an uppercase M to refer to the Boston–Washington multi-metropolitan corridor on the northeastern seaboard of the United States, but now used generically with a lower-case m as a synonym for conurbation.

Mental map Image or picture of the way space (e.g., state or city) is organized as determined by an individual's perception, impression, and knowledge of that space.

Mercantilism In a general sense, associated with the promotion of commercialism and trade. More specifically, a protectionist policy of European **states** during the sixteenth to the eighteenth centuries that promoted a state's economic position in the contest with other countries. The acquisition of gold and silver and the maintenance of a favorable trade balance (more exports than imports) were central to the policy.

Mesolithic period The Middle Stone Age, starting in Europe at the end of the last glacial period over 10,000 years ago.

Mesozoic The era of life on the geologic time scale extending from 225 million years ago to 65 million years ago.

Metes and bounds survey A system of land surveying east of the Appalachian Mountains. It is a system that relies on descriptions of land ownership and natural features such as streams or trees. Because of the imprecise nature of metes and bounds surveying, the U.S. Land Office Survey abandoned the technique in favor of the **Rectangular Land Survey**.

Metropolitan area See **urban (metropolitan) area**.

Migration A change in residence intended to be permanent. See also **forced**, **internal**, **international**, and **voluntary migration**.

Migratory movement Human relocation movement from a source to a destination without a return journey, as opposed to **cyclical movement**.

Milpa agriculture Middle and South American subsistence agriculture in which forest patches are cleared for temporary cultivation of corn and other crops.

Miracle rice A high-yielding variety of rice developed in the Philippines in the 1960s and now widely planted in Asia.

Model An idealized representation of reality built to demonstrate certain of its properties. A spatial model focuses on a geographic dimension of the real world.

Modernization model A model of economic development most closely associated with the work of economist Walter Rostow. The modernization model (sometimes referred to as modernization theory) maintains that all countries go through five interrelated stages of development, which culminate in an economic state of self-sustained economic growth and high levels of mass consumption.

Monotheistic religion Belief system in which one supreme being is revered as creator and arbiter of all that exists in the universe.

Montreal Protocol An international agreement signed in 1987 by 105 countries and the European Community (now European Union). The protocol called for a reduction in the production and consumption of chlorofluorocarbons (CFCs) of 50 percent by 2000. Subsequent meetings in London (1990) and Copenhagen (1992) accelerated the timing of CFC phaseout, and a worldwide complete ban has been in effect since 1996.

Multicore state A state that possesses more than one core or dominant region, be it economic, political, or cultural.

Multinationals Internationally active corporations that can strongly influence the economic and political affairs of many countries they operate in.

Multiple nuclei model The Harris-Ullman model that showed the mid-twentieth-century American central city consisting of several land-use zones arranged around nuclear growth points.

Multiplier effect Expansion of economic activity caused by the growth or introduction of another economic activity. For example, a new basic industry will create jobs, directly or indirectly, in the non-basic sector.

NAFTA The North American Free Trade Agreement which took effect January 1, 1994, creating a free-trade area between the United States, Canada, and Mexico; provides for the tariff-free movement of goods and products, financial services, telecommunications, investment, and patent protection within and between the signatories.

Nation Legally, a term encompassing all the citizens of a state. Most definitions now tend to refer to a tightly knit group of people possessing bonds of language, ethnicity, religion, and other shared cultural attributes. Such homogeneity actually prevails within very few states.

Nationalism The desire on behalf of a group that sees itself as a **nation** to achieve self-government through the establishment or promotion of a **nation-state** with genuine **sovereignty**.

Nation-state Theoretically, a recognized member of the modern state system possessing formal **sovereignty** and occupied by a people who see themselves as a single, united **nation**. Most nations and states aspire to this form, but it is realized almost nowhere. Nonetheless, in common parlance nation-state is used as a synonym for country or state.

Natural increase rate Population growth measured as the excess of live births over deaths per 1000 individuals per year. Natural increase of a population does not reflect either **emigrant** or **immigrant** movements.

Natural resource Any valued element of (or means to an end using) the environment; includes minerals, water, vegetation, and soil.

Natural-political boundaries See **physical-political (natural-political) boundaries**.

Nautical mile By international agreement, the nautical mile—the standard measure at sea—is 6076.12 feet in length, equivalent to approximately 1.15 statute miles (1.85 kilometers).

Neanderthal Species of *Homo* that has been labeled a successor to *Homo erectus* and a forerunner of *Homo sapiens*; its place in the human sequence still is not clear. Marked by considerable refinement of tools and cultural progress during their 70,000-year heyday.

Neocolonialism The entrenchment of the colonial order, such as trade and investment, under a new guise. See also **postcolonialism**.

Neolithic period The New Stone Age marked by animal domestication, the beginnings of agriculture, the presence of crafts, and the diversification of tool-making industries.

Network (transport) The entire regional system of transportation connections and nodes through which movement can occur.

New industrial division of labor A late-twentieth-century set of global economic relationships characterized by a growing dominance of service industries in the global economic core and an associated shift of manufacturing to parts of the developing world.

New World Order A description of the international system resulting from the collapse of the Soviet Union in which the balance of nuclear terror theoretically no longer determined the destinies of states.

Nomadism Movement among a definite set of places—often **cyclical movement**. Nomadic peoples mostly are **pastoralists**.

Nongovernmental organizations (NGOs) International organizations that operate outside of the formal political arena but that are nevertheless influential in spearheading international initiatives on social, economic, and environmental issues.

Nonrenewable resource A resource that when used at a certain rate will ultimately be exhausted (metallic ores and petroleum are good examples).

Nucleated settlement See **agglomerated (nucleated) settlement**.

Official language In multilingual countries the language selected, often by the educated and politically powerful elite, to promote internal cohesion; usually the language of the courts and government.

One-child policy Official policy launched by China in 1979 to induce married couples to have only one child in an effort to control population growth.

Ozone layer The layer in the upper atmosphere located between 30 and 45 kilometers above the Earth's surface where stratospheric ozone is most densely concentrated. The ozone layer acts as a filter for the Sun's harmful ultraviolet rays.

Pacific Rim A far-flung group of countries and parts of countries (extending clockwise on the map from New Zealand to Chile) sharing the following criteria: they face the Pacific Ocean; they evince relatively high levels of economic development, industrialization, and urbanization; and their imports and exports mainly move across Pacific waters.

Paleolithic period The Old Stone Age, the earliest period of human development that is approximately coextensive with the Pleistocene epoch beginning over 2 million years ago and ending between 40,000 and 10,000 years ago, when communities subsisted on hunting and gathering and used tools of stone, bone, and ivory.

Pandemic An outbreak of a disease that spreads worldwide.

Pangaea The primeval supercontinent, hypothesized by Alfred Wegener, that broke apart and formed the continents and oceans as we know them today; consisted of two parts—a northern Laurasia and a southern **Gondwana**.

Parallel An east-west line of **latitude** that is intersected at right angles by meridians of **longitude**.

Pastoralism A form of agricultural activity that involves the raising of livestock. Many peoples described as herders actually pursue mixed agriculture, in that they may also fish, hunt, or even grow a few crops. But pastoral peoples' lives revolve around their animals.

Pelagic species Organisms that exist in open lake waters or open ocean waters.

Per capita Capita means *individual.* Income, production, or some other measure is often given per individual.

Perceptual region A region that only exists as a conceptualization or an idea and not as a physically demarcated entity. For example, in the United States, "the South" and "the Mid-Atlantic region" are perceptual regions.

Perforated state A **state** whose territory completely surrounds that of another state. South Africa, which encloses Lesotho and is perforated by it, is an example.

Periodic movement A form of migration that involves intermittent but recurrent movement, such as temporary relocation for college attendance or service in the armed forces.

Peripheral region In terms of the **core-periphery model**, peripheral regions are the least powerful regions and therefore are often marginalized or under the control of both **semi-peripheral regions** and **core regions**.

Permanent refugee **Refugees** who have been substantially integrated into the host country or host region and who are thus seen as long-term visitors.

Photosynthesis The formation of carbohydrates in living plants from water and carbon dioxide, through the action of sunlight on chlorophyll in those plants, including algae.

Physical (natural) geography One of the two major divisions of systematic geography; the spatial analysis of the structure, processes, and location of the Earth's natural phenomena such as climate, soil, plants, animals, and topography.

Physical-political (natural-political) boundaries Political boundaries that coincide with prominent physical features in the natural landscape—such as rivers or the crest ridges of mountain ranges.

Physiologic density The number of people per unit area of **arable** land.

Pidgin A **lingua franca** that has been simplified and modified through contact with other languages.

Plantation A large estate owned by an individual, family, or corporation and organized to produce a cash crop. Almost all plantations were established within the tropics; in recent decades, many have been divided into smaller holdings or reorganized as cooperatives.

Pleistocene The most recent epoch of the Late Cenozoic Ice Age, beginning about 1.8 million years ago and marked by as many as 20 glaciations and interglacials of which the current warm phase, the Holocene epoch, has witnessed the rise of human civilization.

Plural society A society composed of numerous ethnic groups.

Political ecology An approach to studying nature–society relations that is concerned with the ways in which environmental issues both reflect, and are the result of, the political and socioeconomic contexts in which they are situated.

Political geography A subdivision of **human geography** focused on the nature and implications of the evolving spatial organization of political governance and formal political practice on the Earth's surface. It is concerned with why political spaces emerge in the places that they do and with how the character of those spaces affects social, political, economic, and environmental understandings and practices.

Pollution The release of a substance, through human activity, that chemically, physically, or biologically alters the air or water into which it is discharged. Such a discharge negatively impacts the environment, with possible harmful effects on living organisms, including humans.

Polytheistic religion Belief system in which multiple deities are revered as creators and arbiters of all that exists in the universe.

Popular culture Cultural traits such as dress, diet, and music that identify and are part of today's changeable, urban-based, media-influenced society.

Popular region Same as **perceptual region**.

Population (age-sex) structure Graphic representation (profile) of a population according to age and sex.

Population density A measurement of the number of people per given unit of land.

Population explosion The rapid growth of the world's human population during the past century, attended by ever-shorter **doubling times** and accelerating rates of increase.

Population geography A subdivision of human geography that focuses on the spatial aspects of **demography** and the influences of demographic change on particular places.

Population policy Official (government) policy aimed at influencing the size, composition (structure), or growth of population.

Possibilism Geographic viewpoint—a response to determinism—that holds that human decision making is the crucial factor in cultural development, not the environment. Nonetheless, possibilists view the environment as providing a set of broad constraints that limit the possibilities of human choice.

Postcolonialism A recent intellectual movement concerned with examining the enduring impacts of **colonialism**, not just in economic and political relations (the focus of **neocolonialism**), but especially in cultural terms. Postcolonial studies examine the ways in which basic concepts of culture and forms of cultural interaction continue to be shaped by the hegemonic ideas and practices of colonialism.

Postindustrial economy Emerging economy, in the United States and a handful of other technologically advanced countries, as traditional industry is overshadowed by a higher-technology productive complex dominated by services and information-related and managerial activities.

Postmodernism A movement in art, philosophy, and the social sciences that argues that it is impossible to study reality objectively. It rejects the grand theoretical claims of the modern era and stresses the possibility of multiple interpretations in social inquiry, the arts, and politics. Applied to architecture, a postmodern style connotes a combination or mixture of historical and geographical references with cutting-edge aesthetics in the same complex.

Precambrian The era that precedes the Paleozoic era of ancient life on the geologic time scale, named after the oldest period of the Paleozoic, the Cambrian; extends backward from 570 million years ago to the origin of the Earth, now estimated to be about 4.6 billion years ago.

Primary economic activity Economic activity concerned with the direct extraction of **natural resources** from the environment—such as mining, fishing, lumbering, and especially **agriculture**.

Primate city A country's largest city—ranking atop the **urban hierarchy**—most expressive of the national culture and usually (but not always) the capital city as well.

Prime meridian An imaginary north-south line of **longitude** on the Earth grid, passing through the Royal Observatory at Greenwich in London, defined as having a longitude of 0°.

Primogeniture System where the eldest son in a family—or, in exceptional cases, daughter—inherits all of a dying parent's land.

Protectorate In Britain's system of colonial administration, a designation that involved the guarantee of certain rights (such as the restriction of European settlement and land alienation) to peoples who had been placed under the control of the Crown.

Prorupted state A type of **state** territorial shape that exhibits a narrow, elongated land extension leading away from the main body of territory. Thailand is an example.

Proxemics The individual and collective preferences for nearness or distance as displayed by different cultures.

Pull factor Positive conditions and perceptions that effectively attract people to new locales from other areas.

Push factor Negative conditions and perceptions that induce people to leave their abode and migrate to a new locale.

Push-pull concept The idea that **migration** flows are simultaneously stimulated by conditions in the source area, which tend to drive people away, and by the perceived attractiveness of the destination.

Quaternary The second of the two periods of the Cenozoic era of recent life on the geologic time scale extending from approximately 2 million years ago to the present.

Quaternary industries Service sector industries concerned with the collection, processing, and manipulation of information and capital. Examples include finance, administration, insurance, and legal services.

Quinary industries Service sector industries that require a high level of specialized knowledge or technical skill. Examples include scientific research and high-level management.

Race A categorization of humans based on skin color and other physical characteristics. Racial categories are social and political constructions because they are based on ideas that some biological differences (especially skin color) are more important than others (e.g., height, etc.), even though the latter might have more significance in terms of human activity. With its roots in sixteenth-century England, the term is closely associated with European **colonialism** because of the impact of that development on global understandings of racial differences.

Racism Frequently referred to as a system or attitude toward visible differences in individuals, racism is an ideology of difference that ascribes (predominantly negative) significance and meaning to culturally, socially, and politically constructed ideas based on phenotypical features.

Radioactive waste Hazardous-waste-emitting radiation from nuclear power plants, nuclear weapons factories, and nuclear equipment in hospitals and industry.

Rank-size rule In a model urban hierarchy, the idea that the population of a city or town will be inversely proportional to its rank in the hierarchy.

Realm See **geographic realm**.

Rectangular Land Survey Also called the Public Land Survey, the system was used by the US Land Office Survey to parcel land west of the Appalachian Mountains. The system divides land into a series of rectangular parcels.

Redlining A discriminatory real estate practice in North America in which members of minority groups are prevented from obtaining money to purchase homes or property in predominantly white neighborhoods. The practice derived its name from the red lines depicted on **cadastral maps** used by real estate agents and developers. Today, redlining is officially illegal.

Refugees People who have been dislocated involuntarily from their original place of settlement.

Region A commonly used term and a geographic concept of central importance. An **area** on the Earth's surface marked by a degree of formal, functional, or perceptual homogeneity of some phenomenon.

Regional science Discipline that emphasizes the application of modern spatial analytical techniques to the delimitation of regions and the analysis of regional problems and issues.

Regionalism The consciousness and loyalty to a **region** considered distinct and different from the state as a whole by those who occupy it.

Relative distance Distance measured, not in linear terms such as miles or kilometers, but in terms such as cost and time.

Relative location The regional position or **situation** of a place relative to the position of other places. Distance, **accessibility**, and connectivity affect relative location.

Relict boundary A political boundary that has ceased to function but the imprint of which can still be detected on the **cultural landscape**.

Religious fundamentalism Religious movement whose objectives are to return to the foundations of the faith and to influence state policy.

Relocation diffusion Sequential **diffusion** process in which the items being diffused are transmitted by their carrier agents as they evacuate the old areas and relocate to new ones. The most common form of relocation diffusion involves the spreading of innovations by a migrating population.

Remittances Money sent back by emigrants to those left behind, often in cash, forming an important part of the economy in impoverished megacity shantytowns.

Remote sensing A method of collecting data or information through the use of instruments (e.g., satellites) that are physically distant from the area or object of study.

Renewable resource A resource that can regenerate as it is exploited.

Restrictive population policy Government policy designed to reduce the rate of natural increase.

Rimland Term coined by Nicholas Spykman referring to the coastal rim of Eurasia, which Spykman maintained held the key to global power. A counterthesis to Mackinder's **heartland theory**.

Rural density A measure that indicates the number of persons per unit area living in the rural areas of a country, outside the urban concentrations.

Sahel Semiarid zone extending across most of Africa between the southern margins of the arid Sahara and the moister tropical savanna and forest zone to the south. Chronic drought, **desertification**, and overgrazing have contributed to severe famines in this area for decades.

Scale Representation of a real-world phenomenon at a certain level of reduction or generalization. In **cartography**, the ratio of map distance to ground distance; indicated on a map as a bar graph, representative fraction, and/or verbal statement.

Secondary economic activity Economic activity involving the processing of raw materials and their transformation into finished industrial products; the manufacturing sector.

Sector model A **spatial** model of the American central city that suggests that land-use areas conform to a wedge-shaped pattern focused on the downtown core.

Secularism The idea that ethical and moral standards should be formulated and adhered to for life on Earth, not to accommodate the prescriptions of a deity and promises of a comfortable afterlife. A secular state is the opposite of a **theocracy**.

Sedentary Permanently attached to a particular area; a population fixed in its location. The opposite of **nomadic**.

Semi-peripheral region In the context of the **core-periphery model**, intermediary regions in terms of the hierarchy of power between **core regions** and **peripheral regions**.

Sephardim One of the two main ethnic groups within Jewish culture. This branch settled in Northern Africa and later in the Iberian Peninsula after having been driven away from Jerusalem early in the first millennium A.D.

Sequent occupance The notion that successive societies leave their cultural imprints on a place, each contributing to the cumulative **cultural landscape**.

Service industry See **tertiary economic activity**.

Settlement density The amount of area in a country for each city with 100,000 people or more.

Shaman In traditional societies, a person is deemed to possess religious and mystical powers, acquired directly from supernatural sources. At times an especially strong shaman might attract a regional following; many shamans, however, remain local figures.

Shantytown Unplanned slum development on the margins of cities in the developing realms, dominated by crude dwellings and shelters made mostly of scrap wood, iron, and even pieces of cardboard.

Sharia religious law The system of Islamic law, sometimes called Qu'ranic law. Unlike most Western systems of law that are based on legal precedence, Sharia is based in varying degrees of interpretation of the Qu'ran.

Shatter belt Region caught between stronger, colliding external cultural-political forces, under persistent stress and often fragmented by aggressive rivals. Eastern Europe and Southeast Asia are classic examples.

Shifting cultivation Cultivation of crops in tropical forest clearings in which the forest vegetation has been removed by cutting and burning. These clearings are usually abandoned after a few years in favor of newly cleared forestland. Also known as slash-and-burn agriculture.

Shiites Adherents of one of the two main divisions of Islam. Also known as Shiahs, the Shiites represent the Persian (Iranian) variation of Islam and believe in the infallibility and divine right to authority of the **Imams**, descendants of Ali.

Site The internal physical attributes of a place, including its local spatial character and physical setting.

Situation The external locational attributes of a place; its **relative location** or regional position with reference to other nonlocal places.

Slash-and-burn agriculture See **shifting cultivation**.

Snowball Earth Theory A theory that suggests that the planet Earth went into a deep freeze in Precambrian times, an ice age so cold that it froze land and water from pole to pole. By implication, more recent ice ages have been milder.

Social stratification The differentiation of society into classes based on wealth, power, production, and prestige.

Southern Cone The southern, mid-latitude portion of South America constituted by the countries of Chile, Argentina, and Uruguay; often included as well is the southernmost part of Brazil, south of the Tropic of Capricorn (23½°S).

Sovereignty A principle of international relations that holds that final authority over social, economic, and political matters should rest with the legitimate rulers of independent states.

Spatial Pertaining to space on the Earth's surface; sometimes used as a synonym for geographic.

Spatial interaction See **complementarity** and **intervening opportunity**.

Special Economic Zone (SEZ) Specific **area** within a country in which tax incentives and less stringent environmental regulations are implemented to attract foreign business and investment.

Standard language The variant of a language that a country's political and intellectual elite seek to promote as the norm for use in schools, government, the media, and other aspects of public life.

State A politically organized territory that is administered by a sovereign government and is recognized by a significant portion of the international community. A state must also contain a permanent resident population, an organized economy, and a functioning internal circulation system.

State capitalism Government-controlled corporations competing under free-market conditions, usually in a tightly regimented society.

Stationary population level The level at which a national population ceases to grow.

Step migration Migration to a distant destination that occurs in stages, for example, from farm to nearby village and later to town and city.

Stratification (social) In a layered or stratified society, the population is divided into a **hierarchy** of social classes. In an industrialized society, the proletariat is at the lower end: elites that possess capital and control the means of production are at the upper level. In the traditional **caste system** of Hindu India, the "untouchables" form the lowest class or caste, whereas the still-wealthy remnants of the princely class are at the top.

Structuralist models A general term for models of economic development that treat economic disparities among countries or regions as the result of historically derived power relations within the global economic system.

Subsequent boundary A political boundary that developed contemporaneously with the evolution of the major elements of the cultural landscape through which it passes.

Subsistence The state of existing on the minimum necessities to sustain life; spending most of one's time in pursuit of survival.

Subsistence agriculture Self-sufficient agriculture that is small scale and low technology and emphasizes food production for local consumption, not for trade.

Suburb A subsidiary urban area surrounding and connected to the central city. Many are exclusively residential; others have their own commercial centers or shopping malls.

Suburban downtown Significant concentration of diversified economic activities around a highly **accessible** suburban location, including retailing, light industry, and a variety of major corporate and commercial operations. Late-twentieth-century coequal to the American central city's **central business district (CBD)**.

Suburbanization Movement of upper and middle-class people from urban **core areas** to the surrounding outskirts to escape pollution as well as deteriorating social conditions (perceived and actual). In North America, the process began in the early nineteenth century and became a mass phenomenon by the second half of the twentieth century.

Sunnis Adherents to the largest branch of Muslims, called the orthodox or traditionalist. They believe in the effectiveness of family and community in the solution of life's problems, and they differ from the **Shiites** in accepting as authoritative the traditions (sunna) of Muhammad.

Superimposed boundary A political boundary placed by powerful outsiders on a developed human landscape. Usually ignores preexisting cultural-spatial patterns, such as the border that now divides North and South Korea.

Supranational A venture involving three or more national states involving formal political, economic, and/or cultural cooperation to promote shared objectives. The European Union is one such organization.

Swidden agriculture See **shifting cultivation**.

System Any group of objects or institutions and their mutual interactions. Geography treats systems that are expressed **spatially** such as **regions**.

Systematic geography Topical geography: cultural, political, economic geography, and the like.

Takeoff Economic concept to identify a stage in a country's **development** when conditions are set for a domestic Industrial Revolution, which occurred in Britain in the late eighteenth century and in Japan in the late nineteenth century following the Meiji Restoration.

Technopole Centers or nodes of high-technology research and activity around which a **high-technology corridor** is sometimes established.

Temporary refugees **Refugees** encamped in a host country or host region while waiting for resettlement.

Territorial morphology A **state's** geographical shape, which can affect its spatial cohesion and political viability. A compact shape is generally easiest to govern; among the less efficient shapes are those exhibited by **elongated**, **fragmented**, **perforated**, and protruded ("prorupt") states.

Territorial sea Zone of seawater adjacent to a country's coast, held to be part of the national territory and treated as a segment of the **state** itself.

Territoriality In **political geography**, a country's or more local community's sense of property and attachment toward its territory, as expressed by its determination to keep it inviolable and strongly defended. See more generally **human territoriality**.

Tertiary economic activity Economic activity associated with the provision of services—such as transportation, banking, retailing, education, and routine office-based jobs.

Theocracy A **state** whose government is under the control of a ruler who is deemed to be divinely guided or under the control of a group of religious leaders, as in post-Khomeini Iran. The opposite of the theocratic state is the **secular** state.

Time-Distance decay The declining degree of acceptance of an idea or innovation with increasing time and distance from its point of origin or source.

Time-space compression A term associated with the work of David Harvey that refers to the social and psychological effects of living in a world in which **time-space convergence** has rapidly reached a high level of intensity.

Time-space convergence A term coined by Donald Janelle that refers to the greatly accelerated movement of goods, information, and ideas during the twentieth century made possible by technological innovations in transportation and communications.

Toponomy (or **Toponymy**) The study of the origins and meaning of place-names.

Total Fertility Rate (TFR) The average number of children born to a woman during her lifetime, as expressed for a total population.

Totalitarian A government whose leaders rule by absolute control, tolerating no differences of political opinion.

Township-and-Range System A rectangular land division scheme designed by Thomas Jefferson to disperse settlers evenly across farmlands of the U.S. interior. See also **Rectangular Land Survey**.

Toxic waste Hazardous waste causing danger from chemicals and infectious organisms.

Traditional Term used in various contexts (e.g., traditional religion) to indicate originality within a culture or long-term part of an indigenous society. It is the opposite of modernized, superimposed, or changed; it denotes continuity and historic association.

Transculturation Cultural borrowing that occurs when different cultures of approximately equal complexity and technological level come into close contact. In **acculturation**, by contrast, an indigenous society's culture is modified by contact with a technologically superior society.

Transhumance A seasonal periodic movement of **pastoralists** and their livestock between highland and lowland pastures.

Transition zone An area of spatial change where the peripheries of two adjacent realms or regions join; marked by a gradual shift (rather than sharp break) in the characteristics that distinguish these neighboring geographic entities from one another.

Tropical deforestation The clearing and destruction of tropical rainforests to make way for expanding settlement frontiers and the exploitation of new economic opportunities.

Truman Proclamation In September 1945, President Harry Truman proclaimed that the United States would regulate fisheries' activities in areas of the high seas adjacent to its coastline, and that U.S. jurisdiction over the continental shelf and its contents would be limited to the region within the 600-foot isobath.

Underdeveloped countries Countries that, by various measures, suffer seriously from negative economic and social conditions, including low per capita incomes, poor nutrition, inadequate health, and related disadvantaged circumstances.

Unitary state A **nation-state** that has a centralized government and administration that exercises power equally over all parts of the state.

United Nations A global (supranational) organization established at the end of World War II to foster international security and cooperation.

United Nations Conference on Environment and Development (UNCED) Also known as the Earth Summit, an international environmental conference held in Rio de Janeiro, Brazil, in 1992 that led to the signing of important international agreements on climate change and biodiversity.

United Nations Conference on the Human Environment The first internationally significant United Nations conference dealing with human impacts of the environment, held in 1972.

Universalizing religion A belief system that espouses the idea that there is one true religion that is universal in scope. Adherents of universalizing religious systems often believe that their religion represents universal truths, and in some cases great effort is undertaken in evangelism and missionary work.

Urban (metropolitan) area The entire built-up, nonrural area and its population, including the most recently constructed suburban appendages. Provides a better picture of the dimensions and population of such an area than the delimited municipality (central city) that forms its heart.

Urban geography A subfield of geography that focuses especially on urban places, their characteristics, processes of genesis and growth, their systems, relative location, and interrelationships.

Urban hierarchy A ranking of settlements (hamlet, village, town, city, metropolis) according to their size and economic functions.

Urban morphology The study of the physical form and structure of urban places.

Urban realms model A **spatial** generalization of the large, late-twentieth-century city in the United States. It is shown to be a widely dispersed, multicentered metropolis consisting of increasingly independent zones or realms, each focused on its own **suburban downtown**; the only exception is the shrunken central realm, which is focused on the **central business district**.

Urban system The functional and **spatial** organization of towns and cities.

Urbanization A term with several connotations. The proportion of a country's population living in urban places is its level of urbanization. The process of urbanization involves the movement of people to, and the clustering of people in, towns and cities—a major force in every geographic realm today. Another kind of urbanization occurs when an expanding city absorbs the rural countryside and transforms it into suburbs; in the case of cities in the developing world, this also generates peripheral **shantytowns**.

Vectored disease A disease carried from one host to another by an intermediate host.

Vernacular region(s) Same as **perceptual region** but at a larger spatial scale.

Vienna Convention for the Protection of the Ozone Layer The first international convention aimed at addressing the issue of ozone depletion. Held in 1985, the Vienna Convention was the predecessor to the **Montreal Protocol**.

Voluntary migration Population movement in which people relocate in response to perceived opportunity, not because they are forced to move.

Von Thünen model A model that explains the location of agricultural activities in a commercial, profit-making economy. A process of spatial competition allocates various farming activities into rings around a central market city, with profit-earning capability the determining force in how far a crop locates from the market. The original (1826) *Isolated State* model now applies to the continental scale and beyond.

Wattle Traditional dwelling built using poles and sticks that are woven tightly together and then plastered with mud.

Wisconsinan Glaciation The most recent glacial period of the Pleiostcene, enduring about 100,000 years and giving way, beginning about 18,000 years ago, to the current interglacial, the Holocene.

World cities Dominant cities in terms of their role in the global political economy. These are not the world's biggest cities in terms of population or industrial output. Rather, they are centers of strategic control of the world economy.

World-Systems Analysis Theory originated by Immanuel Wallerstein, who proposed that social change in the developing world is inextricably linked to the economic activities of the developed world. In this analysis, the world functions as a single entity, organized around a **new international division of labor** in which those living in poorer countries have little autonomy.

Younger Dryas A sudden return to glacial conditions about 12,000 years ago, probably resulting from the cooling of the North Atlantic Ocean when a large portion of the Laurentide Ice Sheet slid into the sea. Warming was interrupted for about 1000 years.

Ziggurat A lofty ancient Babylonian temple tower that symbolized power and authority.

Zionism The movement to unite the Jewish people of the **diaspora** and to establish a national homeland for them in Palestine.

Zoning Legal restrictions on land use that determine what types of building and economic activities are allowed to take place in certain areas. In the United States, areas are most commonly divided into separate zones of residential, retail, or industrial use.

Photo Credits

Chapter 1

Pages 1, 3, 7: H.J. de Blij. Page 10: Alexander B. Murphy.

Chapter 2

Pages 20 & 32: Alexander B. Murphy. Page 25: H.J. de Blij.

Chapter 3

Pages 35, 39, 42, & 48: Alexander B. Murphy.

Chapter 4

Pages 51, 53, & 59: H.J. de Blij.

Chapter 5

Pages 64 & 77: H.J. de Blij.

Chapter 6

Pages 79, 81, 83, & 93: H.J. de Blij.

Chapter 7

Pages 98, 100, & 104: H.J. de Blij.

Chapter 8

Pages 109 & 111: H.J. de Blij. Page 118: Alexander B. Murphy.

Chapter 9

Page 124: H.J. de Blij. Page 134: Alexander B. Murphy.

Chapter 10

Pages 136, 140, & 145: Alexander B. Murphy. Page 138: H.J. de Blij.

Chapter 11

Pages 153,155. & 162: H.J. de Blij. Page 161: Alexander B. Murphy.

Chapter 12

Pages 166, 168, 169, 173: H.J. de Blij. Page 175: Alexander B. Murphy.

Chapter 13

Page 180: Steve McCurry@/Magnum Photos, Inc. Pages 185, 190, 193: H.J. de Blij. Pages 188 & 192: Alexander B. Murphy.

Chapter 14

Pages 199, 203, & 214: Alexander B. Murphy. Page 201: H.J. de Blij.

Chapter 15

Pages 219, 224, & 228: H.J. de Blij. Page 221: Alexander B. Murphy.

Chapter 16

Pages 234 & 239: H.J. de Blij. Pages 238 & 248: Alexander B. Murphy.

Chapter 17

Pages 250, 253, 258: H.J. de Blij. Page 255 & 263: Alexander B. Murphy.

Chapter 18

Pages 269 & 284: Alexander B. Murphy. Pages 271, 274 & 276: H.J. de Blij.

Chapter 19

Pages 285 & 296: Alexander B. Murphy. Pages 288, 291–292: H.J. de Blij.

Chapter 20

Page 299: Alexander B. Murphy. Pages 301, 304, 309: H.J. de Blij.

Chapter 21

Pages 313, 315, 321 (top & bottom left), 325–325: H.J. de Blij. Page 321 (bottom right): Alexander B. Murphy.

Chapter 22

Pages 328 & 343: Alexander B. Murphy. Pages 330, 335, & 337: H.J. de Blij.

Chapter 23

Pages 347, 357, 359–360, 365: H.J. de Blij. Page 349: Alexander B. Murphy.

Chapter 24

Pages 367, 372, & 374: H.J. de Blij.

Chapter 25

Pages 377 & 386: H.J. de Blij. Page 380: Alexander B. Murphy.

Chapter 26

Pages 395 & 404: H.J. de Blij.

Chapter 27

Pages 407, 411, 414, & 415: Alexander B. Murphy. Pages 409 & 420: H.J. de Blij.

Chapter 28

Page 426: Alexander B. Murphy. Pages 428–431, 437: H.J. de Blij.

Chapter 29

Pages 439, 442, 446, 447, 448, 449: Alexander B. Murphy.

Chapter 30

Page 453: H.J. de Blij. Page 455: H.J. de Blij. Page 468: H.J. de Blij.

Chapter 31

Pages 479, 482, 484, 488: H.J. de Blij.

Chapter 32

Page 493: Richard Kalvar/Magnum Photos, Inc. Pages 495 & 504: H.J. de Blij.

Chapter 33

Page 511: Alexander B. Murphy. Pages 513, 519, 523, 526: H.J. de Blij.

Chapter 34

Pages 528, 530, 538: H.J. de Blij.

Chapter 35

Pages 541, 544, 547: H.J. de Blij. Page 545: Alexander B. Murphy.

Index